POLITICAL PARTIES
OF THE WORLD

POLITICAL PARTIES OF THE WORLD

2nd edition

A Keesing's Reference Publication

Compiled and edited by

Alan J. Day

and

Henry W. Degenhardt

Longman

POLITICAL PARTIES OF THE WORLD
2nd edition

Published by Longman Group Limited, Longman House,
Burnt Mill, Harlow, Essex CM20 2JE, United Kingdom

Distributed exclusively in the United States and possessions,
Canada and Mexico by Gale Research Company,
Book Tower, Detroit, Michigan 48226, USA

ISBN 0-582-90252-5 (Longman)

     0-8103-2034-7 (Gale)

Library of Congress Catalog Card Number: 80-83467

British Library Cataloguing in Publication Data
Day, Alan J.
   Political parties of the world. — 2nd ed.
   1. Political parties — Directories
   I. Title   II. Degenhardt, Henry W
   324.2'025   JF2051

   ISBN 0-582-90252-5

Printed in Great Britain by
The Eastern Press Limited, London and Reading

Contents

v

Introduction

In our introduction to the first edition of *Political Parties of the World* (published in 1980) we expressed the hope that the book would fill a perceived gap "by presenting within a single volume concise factual data on all of the world's active political parties, placed within the context of the prevailing constitutional situation in the particular country or territory". The intention was then, and is now with the second edition, "to contribute to a greater understanding of the phenomenon of political parties, which over recent decades has become virtually world-wide".

Between 1980 and mid-1984 (when the present volume went to press), many foreseeable and unforeseeable changes have taken place, not only in the addresses and leaderships of political parties but also, in some instances, in their orientation. Moreover, a substantial number of new parties have been formed, while quite a few listed in the 1980 volume have since become defunct. In countries with Western-type democracies many parties in power in 1980 are now in opposition, and vice versa. A number of countries—notably Ghana, Guinea, Liberia, Nigeria, Suriname and Upper Volta—have undergone coups involving the suspension or banning of all parties. On the other hand, some countries in which parties were outlawed in 1980 have since reverted to a pluralist system of government.

In the new edition we have attempted to chart all these various types of change as well as to update the continually shifting pattern of inter-party alliances which is such an important feature of the political life of many countries. We have also sought, in the introductory sections for each country or territory, to give greater precision to descriptions of electoral arrangements, in particular by indicating whether state financial support is available to political parties. Attention has also been given to descriptions of voting systems with a view to defining whether a particular country has a system of proportional representation or one based on the simple-majority principle.

As regards the problem of defining what is a political party (as opposed to a pressure group or a protest movement), we have continued to accept self-definition as a political party as the basic criterion for inclusion, finding in practice that this usually means that the particular organization is seeking to obtain direct political power over the process of government. As in the first edition, illegal parties have as a general rule not been included: for descriptions of these the reader is referred to the companion volume published in the Keesing's Reference Publications series in 1983 under the title *Political Dissent: An International Guide to Dissident, Extra-Parliamentary, Guerrilla and Illegal Political Movements*. As an exception to this rule, however, the present volume includes entries for officially unrecognized parties where the regime concerned has acknowledged the fact of their existence (e.g. in Bangladesh, Chile and Pakistan).

Information sources for the second edition have included data sent by the parties themselves, although as with the first edition the editors are themselves entirely responsible for the way and the extent to which such material has been used. Extensive use has again been made of the editorial resources of *Keesing's*

Contemporary Archives, to whose staff the editors are indebted for assistance of various kinds. Particular thanks are due to Ciarán Ó Maoláin for his major contribution to the Irish sections, as well as to those for the Caribbean and Pacific states; to Rasmus Jakobsen for his detailed guidance on Danish political parties; and to Carlos Parra for his help with the section on Chile.

Harlow/Bath   AJD
June 1984   HWD

Abbreviations used

ch.	chairman	l.	leader
comm.	committee	nat.	national
est.	estimated	parl.	parliamentary
exec.	executive	pres.	president
dir.	director	s.g.	secretary-general
fed.	federal	sec.	secretary
g.s.	general secretary		

Afghanistan

Capital: Kabul   Pop. 16,000,000

The Democratic Republic of Afghanistan was set up on April 27, 1978, by a Revolutionary Council which established a Government dominated by the (communist) People's Democratic Party of Afghanistan (PDPA) which effectively became the country's sole legal political party. Afghanistan has no parliament. Following massive Soviet intervention from December 1979 onwards, a provisional Constitution (known as the Basic Principles of the Democratic Republic of Afghanistan) was ratified by the PDPA on April 13, 1980, and by the Revolutionary Council on the following day. It laid down inter alia that Afghanistan would proceed "from backwardness to social, economic and cultural progress under the leadership of the PDPA"; that "the sacred and true religion of Islam" would be protected; and that the "traditional friendship and co-operation with the USSR" would be strengthened and broadened. It also provided that a Grand National Assembly or Supreme Council (*Loya Jirga*) would be the highest organ of state power but that pending its election by free and direct vote the Revolutionary Council would hold supreme power.

A National Fatherland Front, a broad alliance of political parties, mass organizations and tribal bodies, formed at a congress on June 15, 1981, with the object of promoting national unity, was to be under the guidance of the PDPA and to have a national congress meeting at least once every five years. This Front was, however, in late 1981 reported to have failed because of dissension between its two factions—the dominant *Parcham* (Flag) faction and the larger but less influential *Khalq* (People) faction.

People's Democratic Party of Afghanistan (PDPA, or Khalq)

Leadership. President Babrak Karmal (s.g.): Anahita Ratebzad, Soltan Ali Keshtmand, Dr Saleh Mohammed Ziray, Ghulam Dastagir Panjshiri, Nur Ahmed Nur, Maj.-Gen. Mohammed Rafi, Lt.-Col. Mohammed Aslam Watanyar, Mohammed Najibollah (other members of politburo)

Founded. 1965

History. The party was founded as an illegal organization by Nur Mohammed Taraki. In 1966 it was divided into two wings—the *Khalq* (People's) group led by Taraki and the *Parcham* (Flag) group led by Babrak Karmal. The *Khalq* group advocated the overthrow of the monarchy as a first step to socialism; after this overthrow had been carried out by left-wing officers in 1973 the group refused to abide by a Soviet directive to give whole-hearted support to the regime of President Daud (whereas the *Parcham* group co-operated with that regime). In July 1977 the two groups were reunited in the *Khalq* Party under Taraki's leadership with a view to building a Communist mass party.

The party came to power with the overthrow of President Daud by a Revolutionary Council in April 1978, when Taraki became Prime Minister and Babrak Karmal (known as a pro-Moscow hardliner) one of three Deputy Prime Ministers. The latter was, however, dismissed in July 1978 from his posts of Vice-President of the Revolutionary Council and of Deputy Prime Minister. In March 1979 Taraki surrendered the premiership to Hafizullah Amin (until then a Deputy Prime Minister and Minister of Foreign Affairs), and in September 1979 the latter replaced Taraki as President of the Republic and party leader. It was later revealed that Taraki had been killed in the takeover. It appeared that Hafizullah Amin did not enjoy Soviet

1

support (as Taraki had), and in late December 1979 a further change of regime occurred when Soviet troops entered the country and brought about the installation of Babrak Karmal as head of state and PDPA leader.

In subsequent years it was reported that disputes had continued between *Khalq* and *Parcham* supporters, and that the *Parcham* faction was dominating the National Fatherland Front.

Orientation. The PDPA is an orthodox Marxist-Leninist formation.

Structure. The party has a central committee, a politburo and a central committee secretariat.

Membership. 10,000 (est.)

Publications. Haqiqat Enqelab Saur

International affiliations. The PDPA is recognized by the Soviet-bloc Communist parties.

Albania

Capital: Tirana   Pop. 2,770,000

The Socialist People's Republic of Albania is, under its Constitution unanimously approved by the People's Assembly on Dec. 27, 1976, "the state of the dictatorship of the proletariat", exercised in effect by the Albanian Party of Labour, which is "the sole directing political power in state and society". The supreme legislative body is the (unicameral) People's Assembly of 250 members, elected once every four years, on a single list of candidates nominated by the Democratic Front (mass organization) and approved by universal suffrage of all citizens over the age of 18 years.

Elections to the Assembly held on Nov. 14, 1982, were officially stated to have resulted in an effective 100 per cent poll (with only one vote against and eight invalid).

Party of Labour of Albania (PLA)
Partia e Punës e Shyipërisë (PPS)

Address. Tirana, Albania

Leadership. Enver Hoxha (first sec. of central committee); Ramiz Alia, Muho Asllani, Adil Çarçani, Hajredin Celiku, Lenka Çuko, Hekuran Isai, Rita Marko, Pali Miska, Manush Myftiu, Simon Stefani (politburo members)

Founded. November 1941

History. During World War II the Albanian Communist Party took part in the resistance offered to the Italian occupiers by the National Liberation Front which in 1943, after certain anti-Communist elements had left it, became the Democratic Front under the leadership of Gen. Enver Hoxha, who proclaimed Albania's liberation from the Axis Powers on Nov. 29, 1944, and formed a provisional Government. In elections to a Constituent Assembly, held on Dec. 2, 1945, the Democratic Front obtained, according to official results, 93.18 per cent of the votes cast. The Assembly on Jan. 11, 1946,

proclaimed Albania a republic in which the Communist Party became the only authorized political organization. It changed its name to Albanian Party of Labour in November 1948.

The party, under Enver Hoxha's leadership, has maintained the Marxist concept of the class struggle as the basic criterion of the current international political situation and has opposed what it regarded as "revisionism", i.e. the 1948 Yugoslav break with the Soviet Union under Stalin and Khrushchev's alleged "abandonment of Marxism-Leninism", which Albania first attacked in 1961. As the country's ruling party, the PLA has embarked on a programme of "wiping out the economic base of feudalism and capitalism" in order "to build the economic base of socialism, to liquidate the economic and cultural backwardness left over from the past and to set up a developed multi-branch economy with modern industry and mechanized agriculture".

Orientation. As a Communist party based on Marxism-Leninism Mao Zedong

2

thought, the party opposes all "revisionism"—the Yugoslav model, Soviet "social-imperialism" and China's "three-world" theory—and it propagates reliance on its own strength in building a socialist and communist society.

Structure. The party has a central committee of 77 full and 38 alternate members, a politburo, a six-member secretariat and a 21-member control and audit commission. Party congresses are held once every five years, when office-bearers are elected.

Membership. 122,600 members and 24,363 candidate members (November 1981)

Publications. Zeri i Popullit (daily organ), 105,500; *Rruga e Partisë* (monthly theoretical organ) 17,750

International affiliations. The PLA has links with revolutionary Marxist-Leninist parties in other countries.

Algeria

Capital: Algiers (El Djezaïr)   Pop. 20,000,000

The Democratic and Popular Republic of Algeria is, under its 1976 Constitution, a one-party state in which the ruling party is the National Liberation Front (FLN). There are an executive President (nominated by the FLN and elected, and re-eligible, for a five-year term by universal adult suffrage), a Cabinet headed by a Prime Minister, and a 281-member National People's Assembly elected by universal adult suffrage, also for five years, on a sole list of the FLN. In elections held on March 5, 1982, when three candidates were nominated for each seat, 136 sitting deputies sought re-election but only 68 of them were successful.

National Liberation Front
Front de Libération Nationale (FLN)

Address. Place Emir Abdelkader, Algiers, Algeria

Leadership. President Benjedid Chadli (s.g.); Mohammed Cherif Messadia (head of secretariat); Rabah Bitat, Col. Abdallah Belhouchet, Boualem Ben Hamouda, Col. Mohammed Ben Ahmed Abdelghani, Dr Taleb Ibrahimi, Boualem Baki, Mohammed Hadj Yalla (other members of political bureau)

Founded. November 1954

History. The party was established in Cairo under the leadership of Mohammed Ben Bella to conduct the war of independence from French rule. After the achievement of independence by Algeria in 1962 the FLN suffered internal factional strife from which Ben Bella emerged victorious, becoming Prime Minister in September 1962 and President in April 1963; however, Ben Bella was himself deposed in June 1965 by Col. Houari Boumedienne, who held the party and government leadership until his death in December 1978. The FLN was reorganized and received a new statute at its 4th congress in January 1979, at which Benjedid Chadli was elected secretary-general of the party and selected as the sole candidate for the presidential election held the following month. In January 1984 President Benjedid Chadli was re-elected unopposed for a second five-year term.

Orientation. The FLN is a socialist party, advocating the maintenance of Islam as the country's religion, non-alignment and pan-Arabism. Under the 1976 Constitution the FLN constitutes "the vanguard, leadership and organization of the people with the aim of building socialism" and "the decisive responsibilities in the state are held by members of the party's leadership".

Structure. The party is based on the principles of democratic centralism and collective leadership. It has cells in town quarters and villages, divisions in municipalities, and federations in provinces. Its highest organ is the congress, which elects a central committee of 120-160 permanent members and 30-40 additional members elected for five years. The FLN congress also nominates the candidate for presidential elections. The central committee elects a political bureau of 17-20 members for a five-year term.

Publications. Al-Chaab, 50,000

Andorra

Capital: Andorra la Vella   Pop. 43,000

Joint suzerainty over the co-principality of Andorra (where loose party groupings operate within a parliamentary system) is held by the President of the French Republic and the Bishop of Urgel (in Spain), who both have local representatives in Andorra. The Andorran General Council (Parliament) has 28 members, the franchise being held by Andorran citizens over 21 (but over 28 for first-generation Andorrans). The total registered electorate in December 1981 was only 3,648.

It was not until 1981 that agreement was reached on the establishment of an Executive Council (Government), to be appointed by the elected General Council. Political parties are not officially admitted under Andorran law but the Democratic Party of Andorra (DPA) has nevertheless been formed. After elections held on Dec. 9, 1981, it was reported that the Conservatives had lost their majority on the General Council; about 74.5 per cent of the electorate took part in the vote, but of these 17.4 per cent cast blank votes. The country's first Executive Council was formed on Jan. 15, 1982, under the leadership of the First Syndic-General who described himself as a "liberal nationalist".

In a popular consultation held on May 28, 1982, 42.2 per cent of the voters opted for a new system of proportional representation at both national and parish level, 31.9 per cent voted in favour of maintaining the existing majority vote system and 23.4 per cent in favour of a mixed system of majority vote at national level and proportional representation at parish level. The abstention rate was 48.1 per cent. The two largest of the seven parishes, with 51 per cent of the electorate, voted for a fully proportional system.

Andorran Democratic Party
Partit Democràtic d'Andorra (PDA)

Address. Andorra la Vella, Andorra
Founded. October 1979
History. The PDA was constituted as a political party after the dissolution of the Andorran Democratic Association (*Agrupament Democràtic d'Andorra,* ADA) founded in 1976 as a merger of the "Democracy and Progress" group and moderates. The PDA did not participate as such in the elections of Dec. 9, 1981, and called on voters to cast blank ballot papers.

Orientation. The PDA is a democratic and nationalist party which has accepted Andorra's form of state as a co-principality but has called for a state structure in which the legislative, executive and judiciary powers are separate and where there is "a system of representative and pluralist parliamentary democracy", as well

as for the preservation of Andorra's historic traditions.

Conservative Group

Address. Andorra la Vella, Andorra
History. Conservatives, holding a majority of seats in the General Council and representing mainly the older generation of Andorran citizens, had until 1978 traditionally held the post of Syndic-General (chief executive of the Government). However, after retaining only half the seats in the Council as a result of partial elections held in 1977, a councillor for a newly-established parish was, as an independent, elected Syndic-General in December 1978.

Orientation. Most of the Conservatives have been opposed to constitutional reforms (including those proposed by the PDA).

4

Angola

Capital: Luanda   Pop. 7,200,000

The People's Democratic Republic of Angola is a one-party state, its sole legal party being the (Marxist-Leninist) Popular Movement for the Liberation of Angola—Party of Labour (MPLA-PT). This party is responsible for the political, economic and social leadership of the nation, and its chairman is also President of the Republic. The supreme state body is a National People's Assembly elected every three years by colleges composed of representatives chosen by all "loyal" citizens over 18 years old. There is a Government presided over by the head of state. The 206-member National People's Assembly was first elected in the latter half of 1980 and installed on Nov. 11 of that year.

Popular Movement for the Liberation of Angola-Party of Labour
Movimento Popular de Libertação de Angola, Partido do Trabalho (MPLA-PT)

Leadership. José Eduardo dos Santos (ch. and sec. for cadres); Lucio Lara (sec. for organization); Roberto António de Almeida (sec. for ideology, information and culture); Julio Mateus Paulo (Dino Matross) (sec. for defence and security); Henrique de Carvalho Santos Onambwe (sec. for state and judicial bodies); (Mrs) Maria Mambo Cafe (sec. for economic and social affairs); Santana André Pitra (sec. for production); Afonso van-Duném (Mbinda) (sec. for foreign relations); António Jacinto (director of secretariat)

Founded. Originally in 1956; December 1977 as MPLA-PT

History. The MPLA had been one of three national liberation movements fighting for Angola's independence from Portuguese rule. On Nov. 11, 1975, the People's Republic of Angola was proclaimed in Luanda under MPLA auspices, while the two other liberation movements—the National Union for the Total Independence of Angola (UNITA) and the National Front for the Liberation of Angola (FNLA)—jointly announced on Nov. 23, 1975, the formation of a rival Democratic People's Republic of Angola, based on Huambo (formerly Nova Lisboa); however, this "state" received no international recognition and the MPLA, with Cuban military support, subsequently gained control of most of Angola's territory.

At its first congress held in Luanda in December 1977 the MPLA restructured itself into a Marxist-Leninist party, the MPLA-PT, as a "vanguard of the proletariat" uniting workers, peasants and the "revolutionary intelligentsia" to be "guided by the principles of scientific socialism" with the aim of building "a new society free from the exploitation of man by man". On Sept. 20, 1979, the MPLA-PT central committee unanimously elected José Eduardo dos Santos as party chairman and President of Angola in succession to Dr António Agostinho Neto, who had died on Sept. 10 after having held the party leadership since 1962 and the presidency of the country since independence.

Orientation. The MPLA-PT is Marxist-Leninist, with the aim of the "consolidation of national unity" without "any tribal, regional or racial compromise"; the party is "non-aligned" in international relations.

Structure. Structured according to territorial and productive criteria at the base, the party has a 75-member central committee, a 14-member political bureau and a nine-member secretariat, as well as a central control commission.

Membership. 31,000

Antigua and Barbuda

Capital: St John's   Pop. 77,000

The islands of Antigua and Barbuda (and their uninhabited dependency of Redonda) are an independent state within the Commonwealth with the British sovereign as head of state (represented by a Governor-General). It has a bicameral Parliament consisting of a 17-member House of Representatives elected for up to five years by universal adult suffrage and a 17-member Senate, 11 members of which are appointed on the advice of the Prime Minister, four on that of the Leader of the Opposition, one at the discretion of the Governor-General and one on that of the Barbuda Council. A Cabinet, with a Prime Minister appointed by the Governor-General and ministers appointed on the recommendation of the Prime Minister, is responsible to the House of Representatives.

In elections to the House held on April 17, 1984, the Antigua Labour Party won all 16 Antigua seats, while the single Barbuda seat was retained by an independent candidate.

Antigua Caribbean Liberation Movement (ACLM)

Address. P.O. Box 493, St John's, Antigua and Barbuda
Leadership. Tim Hector (l.)
Founded. 1979
History. The ACLM, previously known as the Afro-Caribbean Liberation Movement, took part in the 1980 elections but gained less than 1 per cent of the vote.
Orientation. As a party of the "new left" the ACLM supported the attainment of independence by a united Antigua and Barbuda.

Antigua Labour Party (ALP)

Address. P.O. Box 424, St John's, Antigua and Barbuda
Leadership. Vere C. Bird Sr. (l.); Lester Bryant Bird (ch.)
Founded. 1968
History. The ALP was affiliated to the Antigua Trades and Labour Union (ATLU), of which Vere C. Bird Sr. had been a founder-member before becoming Antigua's first Chief Minister in 1960. The ALP was continuously in power from 1946 to 1971 but was in opposition in 1971-76. It was returned to power after gaining 11 (out of 17) seats in the House of Representatives in 1976. It won an additional two seats in the elections of April 1980, after it had campaigned for obtaining a mandate to proceed to full independence for Antigua and Barbuda (eventually achieved in November 1981).
Orientation. The ALP has favoured the economic and political integration of the Commonwealth Caribbean territories.
Publications. *The Workers' Voice* (twice weekly)

Barbuda People's Movement (BPM)

Leadership. Hilbourne Frank
History. Representatives of the BPM refused to sign the report of a constitutional conference held in London in December 1980, by which provision was made for independence for a united Antigua and Barbuda. In local elections held in March 1981 the BPM took all the seats on the Barbuda Council. In a "Barbuda Declaration" subsequently signed by a majority of Barbuda's 1,500 inhabitants a warning was issued that on attainment of independence of the two islands jointly they would establish a separate territory of Barbuda.
Orientation. In addition to its opposition to independence for Barbuda as part of Antigua, the BPM has campaigned for devolution of power to the Barbudan people and for Barbudan control of land (some of these demands being conceded in April 1981).

Organization for National Reconstruction

Leadership. Arthur Nibbs

History. This new party was created in Barbuda to challenge the dominant Barbuda People's Movement by co-operating with the central administration to promote the economic development of the island.

Progressive Labour Movement (PLM)

Leadership. Robert Hall (l.)
Founded. 1970
History. The PLM was formed as the political wing of the Antigua Workers' Union after a split in the Antigua Trades and Labour Union (to which the Antigua Labour Party was affiliated). In elections held in February 1971 the PLM gained 11 of the 17 seats in the then House of Assembly and thereupon formed a Government. In the 1976 elections, however, the PLM retained only five seats in the House of Representatives (also of 17 members) and the party therefore reverted to opposition. In 1981 it came into conflict with the Antigua Workers' Union, which unsuccessfully pressed for early elections to the PLM leadership.

Orientation. At the London constitutional conference of 1980 the PLM proposed the introduction of proportional representation and a unicameral legislature, and as these and other demands it made were rejected it refused to sign the conference report.

Publications. *The New Leader* (twice weekly)

United People's Movement (UPM)

Leadership. George Herbert Walter (l.)
Founded. 1982
History. G. H. Walter had been Premier of Antigua in 1971-76 as leader of the Progressive Labour Movement (PLM), from which he resigned in 1979 in connexion with charges of having mishandled state finances during his premiership. He was, however, acquitted of these charges on appeal in February 1980. He founded the UPM (in 1982) after failing to regain the leadership of the PLM.

Argentina

Capital: Buenos Aires   Pop. 28,300,000

The Republic of Argentina has an executive National President and a Vice-President, both elected for a six-year term by a 600-member electoral college which is itself elected by a system of proportional representation and by universal adult suffrage of all citizens over the age of 18 years. The country also has (i) a 252-member Chamber of Deputies elected for a four-year term by direct universal adult suffrage, one half of the deputies being elected every two years, and (ii) a 48-member Senate, of whose members one-third are elected every three years.

After six years of military rule, impetus for a return to democratic government was generated by the poor performance of the military leadership in the 1982 war with Britain over the Falkland Islands. Under a nine-point statute on political parties promulgated on Aug. 26, 1982, all parties were required to re-register within eight to 13 months; in order to be recognized as a national political party each was required to have at least 35,000 registered members and adequate representation in at least five provinces; party leaders were to be elected for not more than four years by direct secret ballot; parties which denied human rights or advocated "the replacement of the democratic system, the illegal and systematic use of force and the personal concentration of power" continued to be prohibited. On Jan. 20, 1983, all parties were required to register by March 30 and to submit party membership lists by May 30, 1983.

In the first elections held for seven years, held on Oct. 30, 1983, parties gained seats as follows: Radical Civic Union (UCR) 317, Justicialist Nationalist (Peronist)

Movement (JNM) 259, Intransigent Party (PI) 2, Movement for Integration and Development 2, others 20. The college thereupon elected the candidates of the UCR to the posts of National President and Vice-President. In elections to the Chamber of Deputies held on the same day the UCR gained 129 seats, the JNM 111 and the PI 3.

Christian Democratic Party
Partido Democrático Cristiano (PDC)

History. This party, which was one of the constituents of the *Multipartidaria* (see separate entry), nominated Francisco Cerro as its candidate in the 1983 presidential elections.
Membership. 68,000
International affiliations. Christian Democratic International; Christian Democratic Organization of America

Communist Party of Argentina
Partido Comunista de Argentina (PCA)

Leadership. Gerónimo Arnedo Alvarez (g.s.)
Founded. Jan. 6, 1918
History. The PCA was founded by the Marxist faction of the Socialist Party of Argentina. It was illegal from 1966 to May 1973, when it was legalized, but without being granted electoral rights. Two of its members had earlier in 1973 been elected to Parliament as candidates of an *Alianza Popular Revolucionaria*. It legally held a congress in August 1973 and a national conference in November 1975, when it claimed to have 145,000 members organized in 3,925 branches. With all other parties it was suspended, and its activities were banned, in 1976. In 1983, however, the PCA was again legalized and it presented Rubén Iscaro as its candidate in the presidential elections. The party's electoral slogan was "Communists and Peronists, we'll win together", but some rank-and-file resistance to this strategy contributed to the PCA's poor showing.
Structure. The PCA has a central committee elected at party congresses, an executive committee and a secretariat.
Membership. 76,000
International affiliations. The PCA is recognized by the Soviet-bloc Communist parties.

Democratic Integration Party
Partido de Integración Demócrata (PID)

Founded. Jan. 31, 1983
History. The military Government's Public

Information Secretariat, and the PID itself, denied on Feb. 23, 1983, that the Government was in any way involved in the establishment of this party, which had received heavy television coverage in Buenos Aires.

Democratic Leftist Front

Founded. June 1983
History. This electoral alliance between the Democratic Socialist and Progressive Democratic parties supported the candidacy of the latter party's leader, Rafael Martínez Raymonda, in the 1983 presidential elections.

Democratic Socialist Party
Partido Socialista Democrático (PSD)

Leadership. Américo Ghioldi (l.)
History. This party, which had formed part of the Union of the Democratic Centre (see separate entry), joined the Progressive Democratic Party (PDP) in a Democratic Leftist Front, with the PDP's leader as its candidate in the 1983 presidential elections.
Membership. 39,000

Federal Alliance
Alianza Federal

Founded. June 1983
History. This alliance was formed by four groups—the Federal Party, the Democratic Concentration (*Concentración Democrática*), the Popular Federalist Force (*Fuerza Federalista Popular*) and the Popular Line Movement (*Movimiento Linea Popular*)—and it supported Francisco Manrique, the Federal Party's leader, as candidate for the presidency in the 1983 elections.

Federal Party
Partido Federal

Leadership. Francisco Manrique (pres.)
History. Francisco Manrique was present at a meeting held on June 24, 1982, by

the newly-appointed President Reynaldo Bignone and some 30 politicians representing 14 political parties, at which President Bignone agreed to lift the ban on political activities and to hold general elections before March 1984. In the general elections held in October 1983 the Federal Party's president was the candidate of the Federal Alliance (see separate entry).

Orientation. The Federal Party subscribes to right-wing policy theses.

Independence Party
Partido de Independencia

Founded. Dec. 14, 1982
History. On its establishment this "nationalist" party proposed an emergency plan to avoid a civil war.
Structure. The party has a joint leadership of 11 members.

Intransigent Party
Partido Intransigente (PI)

Leadership. Oscar Alende (l.)
History. This left-wing party, originally a faction of the Radical Civic Union (UCR), refused in 1980 to take part in talks with the military Government on the normalization of political activities. The party's leader was a candidate in the presidential elections of October 1983, obtaining 2.5 per cent of the vote.
Membership. 90,000

Justicialist Nationalist Movement (JNM)
Movimiento Nacionalista Justicialista (MNJ)

Leadership. María Estela ("Isabel") Martínez de Perón (pres.); Deolindo Bittel (first vice-pres.); Dr Italo Lúder (1983 presidential candidate)
History. The party has its origins in the Peronist movement founded by Lt.-Gen. Juan Domingo Perón Sosa, who as President of Argentina in 1946-55 pursued policies based on extreme nationalism and aimed at social improvement (the latter policy being particularly associated with the President's then wife, Eva Perón). After his overthrow in 1955 Perón went into exile in Spain, from where he continued to direct the Peronist movement, although his party had been dissolved by decree and was divided into various factions.

In elections held in 1962 Peronists gained one-third of the votes, and the military

thereupon annulled the elections and dissolved Congress.

Elections held in March 1973 were won by the Peronist party, then known as the *Frente Justicialista de Liberación* (Frejuli), and its leader, Dr Héctor Cámpora, became President. However, he resigned three months later to make way for the election of Gen. Perón, who had returned from exile in November 1972. His wife, Maria Estela Martínez de Perón, became Vice-President and succeeded him as President on his death on July 1, 1974. She was overthrown in March 1976 by the military who installed a three-member junta as the country's rulers and suspended all political and trade union activities.

In August 1980 Peronist representatives were invited to take part in talks with the military Government on the normalization of political activities, and in July 1981 Peronists took part in the formation of the *Multipartidaria* (see separate entry) as an alliance calling for early general elections. Sanctions imposed on 25 Peronist leaders in 1976, preventing them from returning to Argentina from exile, were lifted on April 14, 1983, and those thus enabled to return included María Estela Martínez de Perón.

In the elections of Oct. 30, 1983, the JNM gained 39 per cent of the votes for members of the electoral college; it came second in the Chamber of Deputies, gained half the seats in the Senate and 11 of the 22 provincial governorships.

Structure. The JNM has had considerable support from its affiliated trade unions—the two wings of the General Confederation of Trade Unions and the "62 Organizations".
Membership. 3,005,355

Labour Party
Partido Laborista

Leadership. Juan Carlos Venturini (l.)
History. The party nominated Gregorio Flores as its candidate in the presidential elections of October 1983; he made little impact in the voting.
Orientation. Trotskyist formation.
Membership. 60,875

Movement for Integration and Development
Movimiento de Integración y Desarrollo (MID)

Leadership. Arturo Frondizi (l.); Rogelio Frigerio (vice-pres.)
Founded. 1963

History. The MID broke away from the Radical Civic Union (UCR) and later joined with Peronist and minor parties to support the (successful) Peronist candidate, Dr Hector Cámpora, in the 1973 presidential elections. In 1983 the candidate of the MID for the presidential elections was Rogelio Frigerio.

Orientation. The MID has aimed at integrating the Peronists in the nation's political life and has called for increased industrialization, the encouragement of domestic savings and foreign investment, and the opening of new markets abroad.

Membership. 143,759

Movement to Socialism
Movimiento al Socialismo (MAS)

Leadership. Rubén Visconti (l.)

History. In the October 1983 presidential elections the MAS candidate was Luis Zamora, who obtained some 55,000 votes.

Orientation. The MAS is a Trotskyist formation.

Membership. 55,173

International affiliations. The MAS has links with Trotskyist groups in other American countries, particularly in the United States.

Multipartidaria

Leadership. Dr Carlos Contín (spokesman)

Founded. July 14, 1981

History. This opposition alliance was formed by five parties—the (Peronist) Justicialist Nationalist Movement (JNM), the Christian Democratic Federation, the Movement for Integration and Development, the Intransigent Party and the Radical Civic Union (UCR)—and was thought to have the support of some 80 per cent of the electorate. On its foundation it called for the removal of all existing restrictions on political and trade union activities, the restoration of constitutional rule, full respect for human rights and a timetable for liberalization leading to free elections. On Dec. 16, 1981 the *Multipartidaria* called specifically for the lifting of the ban on political and trade union activities, for the holding of general elections without restrictions and for an official explanation of the fate of "thousands" of persons who had disappeared and were believed to have been murdered for political reasons; the alliance also proposed a plan which would allow for the reconstruction of the country's internal market.

On June 21, 1982, the *Multipartidaria* issued a "national reconstruction programme" in which it demanded the restoration of constitutional rights; the lifting of the state of siege (in force since 1974); the release of all political prisoners; the expansion of consumption, exports and investments by raising wages and reducing interest rates; a temporary ban on the import of products which could be locally manufactured; incentives for agriculture and industry; the rescheduling of Argentina's external debt (then said to amount to US $36,000 million); a reform of the financial system; and increased spending on health, education and housing.

On Dec. 16, 1982, the *Multipartidaria* convened in Buenos Aires a "march for democracy" which was attended by between 100,000 and 300,000 people. It also issued a document denouncing the military Government for its "ambiguity" on the timing and organization of elections, for "evasions" on the question of those who had disappeared, for "obscuring the truth" about the Falklands war, for upholding social and economic policies rejected by the people since 1976, and for continued violations of trade union rights. In February 1983 the *Multipartidaria* demanded (i) the lifting of restrictions barring certain Peronists (among them ex-President Maria Estela Martínez de Perón) from entering political life and (ii) an end to interference with the freedom of expression and the administration of justice. The *Multipartidaria* also supported a general strike called by the moderate section of the General Confederation of Labour for Dec. 6, 1982, and observed by some 90 per cent of the workforce.

Popular Socialist Party
Partido Popular Socialista (PPS)

Leadership. Guillermo Estévez Boero (l.)

Founded. Oct. 15, 1982

History. Tracing its origins from the historic Argentine Socialist Party founded in the 19th century Juan B. Justo, the PPS was formed with the co-operation of a Socialist Party of Chaco (*Partido Socialista del Chaco*) and an Argentine Socialist Confederation (CS). It supported the Peronist (JNM) candidate in the presidential elections of October 1983 and won 30,000 votes in the congressional contest. Susequently, moves were initiated to achieve a merger between the PPS, the Chaco Socialists, the CS and other small moderate socialist formations.

Orientation. The PPS has sought to create a constituency for European-style social democracy in Argentina.

Membership. 60,500

International affiliations. The PPS has been a member of the Socialist International, although Argentinian membership of that organization is currently suspended pending the further evolution of political forces in Argentina.

Progressive Democratic Party
Partido Democracia Progresista (PDP)

Leadership. Rafael Martínez Raymonda (l.)

History. Leaders of this party had, in March 1980, a first meeting with the Minister of the Interior as part of a dialogue on the normalization of political activities. For the 1983 presidential elections the PDP joined with the Democratic Socialist Party in a Democratic Leftist Front, with the PDP leader as its candidate.

Membership. 53,000

Radical Civic Union
Unión Cívica Radical (UCR)

Leadership. Dr Carlos Contín (pres.); Dr Raúl Alfonsín Foulkes (l.)

Founded. 1890

History. The UCR was in power from 1916 to 1930, when it was replaced by a military regime. The party strongly opposed the rule of President Juan Domingo Perón (1946-55). In 1956 a party congress nominated Arturo Frondizi as its presidential candidate, whereupon Dr Ricardo Balbín, who had unsuccessfully contested presidential elections in 1951, broke away from the UCR to found an *Unión Cívica Radical del Pueblo*. However, Frondizi, renaming his party the *Unión Cívica Radical Intransigente*, won the 1958 elections with the support of Peronists and left-wing groups.

In 1962 the armed forces deposed President Frondizi, and in 1963 Dr Arturo Umberto Illia, as candidate of Dr Balbín's party, was elected President. In 1966, however, he, too, was forced out of office by the military. In 1973 Dr Balbín, standing for a reunited UCR, twice unsuccessfully contested presidential elections; he died on Sept. 9, 1981.

In 1982 the UCR consisted of three factions—(i) a mainstream "national line" group led by Dr Contín, (ii) a "renovation and change" sector led by Dr Alfonsín and (iii) an Yrigoyenist Affirmation Movement led by Dr Luis León. A national committee meeting held on July 18-19, 1982, confirmed Dr Contín as president of the UCR but also adopted a document rejecting all collaboration with the military regime and calling for "a strong popular democracy" and the reorganization of the armed forces which were to play a purely defensive role.

In the 1983 elections the UCR candidate, Dr Alfonsín, won 51 per cent of the votes for the electoral college (charged with electing the President) and an absolute majority in the Chamber of Deputies, but only 16 of the 48 seats in the Senate and seven of the 24 provincial governorships.

Orientation. In his reform programme announced on July 31, 1983, Dr Alfonsín proposed the abolition of compulsory military service, the reduction of military expenditure from the existing level of about 10 per cent of gross national product to within 2 per cent, a reform of the code of military justice to make it conform to that of civil justice, and the creation of a body to make available "privileged information" to organizations dedicated to the defence of human rights.

Membership. 1,410,123

International affiliations. The Alfonsín majority wing of the UCR has links with European social democratic parties.

Social Democracy
Democracia Social

Leadership. Adml. (retd.) Emilio Massera (l.)

Founded. 1981

History. On Nov. 3, 1982, it was announced that Adml. Massera had been placed under a 20-day arrest by the Navy High Command after he had stated that Licio Gelli, the leader of the (Italian right-wing) Propaganda Due (P-2) masonic lodge, had rendered "unquestionably valuable services to the [Argentine] Republic, especially in the war against terrorism" and had helped to improve Argentina's image abroad since 1976. In a statement issued by Adml. Massera's press office later in November 1982 it was claimed that the party was "the only force capable of creating a new stage in the national movement".

Orientation. This party is a right-wing nationalist formation.

Union of the Democratic Centre
Union del Centro Democrático

Leadership. Américo Ghioldi (l.)

Founded. August 1980

History. This union was formed by eight minor political organizations, among them the *Unión Cristiana Demócrata* (led by Gerardo Ancarola), the *Partido Democracia*

Progresista (led by Rafael Martínez Raymonda) and the *Partido Socialista Democrático* (led by Américo Ghioldi) with the object of challenging the "domestic monopoly" of the populist movements.

Other Parties

Among some 300 minor political groupings in existence at the time of the October 1983 elections were the following:

Christian People's Party *(Partido Popular Cristiano,* PPC), a Christian democratic formation led by José Antonio Allende.

Marxist-Leninist Communist Workers' Party *(Partido Obrero Comunista Marxista-Leninista)*

National Party of the Centre *(Partido Nacional del Centro),* a conservative formation established in July 1980.

Popular Left Front *(Frente de Izquierda Popular,* FIP), led by Jorge Abelardo Ramos.

Revolutionary Communist Party *(Partido Comunista Revolucionario,* PCR), a pro-Peking offshoot of the Communist Party of Argentina.

Socialist Unification Party *(Partido Socialista Unificado,* PSU) led by Simón Lázara.

Workers' Political Party *(Partido Politico Obrero)*

Australia

Capital: Canberra (ACT)   Pop. 15,200,000

The Commonwealth of Australia, a member of the Commonwealth, is a parliamentary democracy with the British monarch as head of state and comprises six states, the Australian Capital Territory (ACT) and the Northern Territory. Legislative power is vested in a (federal) Parliament of the Commonwealth of Australia consisting of the Queen (represented by a Governor-General), a 64-seat Senate whose members serve six-year terms and a 125-seat House of Representatives elected for three years. The franchise for both Houses of Parliament is based on universal suffrage for all citizens above the age of 18 years with certain minimum residence qualifications; voting, which is compulsory, takes place under a preferential system, in single-member constituencies for the House of Representatives and in 10-member constituencies for the Senate.

The distribution of seats in the House of Representatives as a result of elections held on March 5, 1983, was as follows: Australian Labor Party (ALP) 75, Liberal Party 33, National Party 17. Elections held on the same date to renew half the Senate seats established the following distribution: ALP 30, Liberal Party 24, Australian Democrats Party 5, National Party 4, independent 1.

New South Wales. The state has a 99-member Legislative Assembly and a 60-member Legislative Council (Upper House of Parliament), both being elected by popular vote—the Assembly every three years and one-quarter of the Council also every three years. As a result of elections held on March 24, 1984, seats in the Legislative Assembly were distributed as follows: ALP 58, Liberal Party 22, National Party 15, independents 4.

Queensland. The Legislative Assembly (there is no Upper House) has 82 members elected in single-member constituencies. As a result of elections held on Oct. 22, 1983, seats were distributed as follows: National Party 41, ALP 32, Liberals 8, independent 1. (Two former Liberal state ministers joined the National Party on Oct. 25, giving that party a majority in the Assembly.)

South Australia. The House of Assembly has 47 members and the Legislative Council 21. Elections to the House of Assembly held on Nov. 6, 1982, resulted as follows: ALP 24, Liberal Party 21, National Party 1, Independent Labor 1.

Tasmania. The 35-member House of Assembly is elected every four years by proportional representation in five seven-member constituencies and by voters over the age of 18 with a six-month residential qualification. A 19-member Legislative Council, also elected directly by voters, has a six-year term with three members retiring annually and four every sixth year. Its members have no formal party allegiance. Elections to the House of Assembly held on May 15, 1982, resulted in the following distribution of seats: Liberal Party 19, ALP 14, Australian Democrat 1, independent 1.

Victoria. A Legislative Assembly of 81 members and a Legislative Council of 44 members are elected by voters over the age of 18, voting being compulsory. Following elections held on April 3, 1982, the Assembly was composed as follows: ALP 49, Liberal Party 24, National Party 8. The Legislative Assembly is elected for a maximum of three years and the Legislative Council for six, one-half of its members retiring every three years.

Western Australia. A 57-member House of Assembly is normally elected for three years and a 32-member Legislative Council for six years, half its members retiring every three years. Elections to the House of Assembly held on Feb. 18, 1983, resulted as follows: ALP 33, Liberal Party 19, National Country Party 3, National Party 2.

Northern Territory. There is a 25-member Legislative Assembly, fully elected by adult suffrage, and since July 1, 1978, a Ministry with increased self-government powers. In elections held on Dec. 3, 1983, seats in the Legislative Assembly were gained as follows: Country-Liberal Party 20, ALP 5.

Australian Democratic Labor Party (ADLP)

Address. 89 York St, Sydney, NSW, Australia

Leadership. P. J. Keogh (pres.); John Kane (g.s.)

Founded. April 1955

History. Founded as the Australian Labor Party (Anti-Communist) by right-wing members of the Australian Labor Party, chiefly from the latter's Roman Catholic section, the ADLP had between two and five representatives in the Senate during the years from 1956 to 1974. However, it has never gained any seats in the federal House of Representatives, even though in the elections of December 1977 it obtained about 10 per cent of the overall vote.

Orientation. The party is anti-communist and largely in support of the foreign policy of the Liberal-National Party coalition when the latter is in government.

Australian Democrats Party (ADP)

Address. 400 Flinders St., Melbourne, Victoria 3000, Australia

Leadership. Donald L. Chipp (l.)

Founded. May 1977

History. The party was founded by Donald Chipp, who had been Liberal Minister in federal Liberal-National (Country) Party Governments in 1966-68, 1969-72 and November-December 1975. The ADP obtained about 10 per cent of the votes but no seats in the Queensland state elections of November 1977, but it gained two seats in the Senate in partial elections to that House in December 1977, and another three in 1980, when it gained the balance of power which it has held in the Senate since then. It also holds a seat in the Tasmanian House of Assembly.

Orientation. The party's main aim has been to fight the erosion of living standards by inflation and rising labour costs; it has called for a shorter working week, the reduction of the pensionable age from 65 to 60 and increased planning for the effects of technology.

Australian Labor Party (ALP)

Address. P.O. Box 1, Canberra, ACT 2600, Australia

Leadership. Robert Hawke (l.); N. K. Wran, QC (nat. pres.); R. F. McMullan (nat. sec.)

13

Founded. 1901

History. Formed as a federal party from separate labour parties established in Australian states in the 1890s, the ALP is the oldest in Australia. In the first Commonwealth elections of 1901 it gained 16 seats in the House of Representatives and eight in the Senate. The first federal Labor Government held office for three months in 1904 under John Watson. Thereafter the party formed a minority Government from October 1908 to June 1909 (in which period it adopted the American way of spelling "Labor"), and after gaining a majority in both Houses of Parliament in April 1910 it was in office until May 1913, and again after elections in September 1914.

During World War I the party was practically destroyed as a result of the leadership's intransigence in the face of widespread anti-conscription views. The party did not return to power until after the elections of October 1929 but its Government was defeated in Parliament in November 1931 and the party lost the subsequent elections. After overcoming factional disputes the party's leader, John Curtin, was Prime Minister from October 1941 until his death in July 1945, when he was succeeded by J. B. Chifley, whose Government was defeated in December 1949.

During the 1940s and early 1950s the party was weakened by virulent anti-communist groups attempting to infiltrate the party, and it did not return to office until the elections of 1972. However, opposition to the Government of Gough Whitlam in the Senate (where it had lost its majority in May 1974) eventually led to the dismissal of the Government by the Governor-General in October 1975 and to the defeat of the party in the December 1975 elections.

In the elections of Oct. 18, 1980, the ALP made gains under the leadership of William Hayden but still remained in a minority with 51 seats in the House of Representatives. However, for the March 1983 elections the party changed its leader to Robert (Bob) Hawke and won an overwhelming majority with 75 of the 125 seats in the House.

Orientation. The ALP is democratic socialist, advocating "the democratic socialization of industry, production, distribution and exchange to the extent necessary to eliminate exploitation and other anti-social features". It seeks to secure social justice; economic security; freedom of speech, education, assembly, organization and religion; the right of the development of the human personality protected from arbitrary invasion by the state; free elections under universal and secret franchise, with government of the majority and respect for the rights of minorities; and the rule of law as a right of all.

Structure. The party has members within branches and affiliated trade unions, whose resolutions frame the party's policies. The party is organized on federal lines, and its supreme governing authority is the national conference which meets every two years and whose decisions are binding on every member and every section of the party. The party's chief administrative authority is the national executive, which is subject only to the authority of the national conference.

Membership. 50,000

Publications. Newsletter

International affiliations. Socialist International; Asia-Pacific Socialist Organization

---

Communist Party of Australia (CPA)

Address. 4 Dixon Street, Sydney, NSW 2000, Australia

Founded. October 1920

History. The party did not begin to grow until the depression of the 1930s. It was illegal during 1940-43. Defections from it led (i) in 1963 to the formation of the Communist Party of Australia (Marxist-Leninist) which followed the policies of the Communist Party of China and (ii) in 1971 to the creation of the Socialist Party of Australia, which followed the line of the Communist Party of the Soviet Union.

Orientation. The CPA is independent communist, with the aim of "a self-managed classless socialist society, liberation of women and other oppressed groups, self-determination for Australia's Aborigines, equality and co-operation among nations and ecological harmony". In its 1979 programme the CPA expressed its support for "national and social liberation movements throughout the world and especially in the ASEAN countries (Indonesia, Malaysia, the Philippines, Singapore and Thailand), East Timor, southern Africa, Latin America and the island nations of the South Pacific" and, in Australia, for creating "a broad alliance for social change in a socialist direction" with the ultimate aim of "a democratic, self-management socialism". At a congress held in June 1982 the CPA emphasized inter alia that it had "a role to play at all levels of building a mass disarmament movement".

Structure. The CPA is based on branches in factories, industries, institutions and localities, a committee being elected in each state by the state conference (and district committees being elected in certain populous districts). Every three years a federal congress elects about two-thirds of the members of a national committee, the remaining third being elected directly from the states and districts. The party no longer has titled officials. An eight-person national executive is responsible to the party's 30-member national committee.

Membership. 2,000

Publications. Tribune (weekly newspaper), 7,000; *Australian Left Review* (quarterly), 1,200

International affiliations. Aims to have relations with all communist and workers' parties, liberation movements, etc.

Communist Party of Australia (Marxist-Leninist)

Address. 168 Day St, Sydney, NSW 2,000, Australia

Leadership. Edward F. Hill (ch.)

Founded. 1967

History. The party was founded by former members of the Communist Party of Australia who supported the Chinese (against the Soviet) Communist view.

Publications. Vanguard

Liberal Party of Australia

Address. P.O. Box E13, Victoria Terrace, Canberra, ACT 2600, Australia

Leadership. Andrew Peacock (l.); Dr Jim Forces (fed. pres.); A. Eggleton (fed. director)

Founded. October 1944

History. The party was formed at a conference of representatives of several anti-Labor parties called by Robert Gordon Menzies in order to unify the anti-Labor forces throughout Australia. Liberal Governments were first formed in 1947 in Western Australia, South Australia and Victoria. The party first came to power at federal level in 1949 in coalition with the National Country Party and held office continuously until 1972. It again held office between 1975 and 1983.

Orientation. The Liberal Party is the major anti-socialist political party in Australia and is committed to the promotion of free enterprise and individual initiative. Its adherents cover a wide political spectrum from the centre to the right. Party objectives include support for the freedom and responsibility of the individual, commitment to social and economic progress, the minimization of insecurity and want, the encouragement of diversity and choice within a unified nation and the promotion of peace, justice and international cooperation throughout the world.

Structure. The party is a federal organization based on seven divisions (one in each of the six states and the Australian Capital Territory), which are autonomous and have their own constitutions. The party has a federal council consisting of delegates from the seven divisions and the federal office-bearers. Between meetings of the council, a federal executive comprising the organizational and parliamentary leaders is responsible for management and control of the party's affairs. There is a federal secretariat as headquarters of the federal party, to give professional support to the party's organizational and parliamentary wings. Each division has its own party headquarters to service the state organization and state parliamentary party.

Membership. 117,000

Publications. The Australian Liberal

International affiliations. International Democrat Union; Pacific Democrat Union

---

National Party of Australia

Address. Box E 265, Queen Victoria Terrace, ACT 2600, Australia

Leadership. Ian Sinclair (l.); Shirley McKerrow (fed. pres.); John England (fed. sec.)

Founded. 1916

History. The party, known as the Country Party until 1974, emerged as an independent Australian parliamentary force in the Parliament of Western Australia in 1914. By 1916 it had evolved a federal constitution and political platform and established federal representation, articulating a widespread feeling of injustice among primary producers and the country community at large. After going into a coalition with the predecessors of the Liberal Party, it was in government for more than 40 years. Although there has been a degree of merging of the identities of both parties the National Party still maintains many distinctive characteristics vis-à-vis the Australian political scene, even though it has been a minority party in the House of Representatives since its foundation. Between 1974 and 1982 the party was known as the National Country Party of Australia.

Orientation. Principal objectives are balanced national development based on free enterprise, with special emphasis on the needs of people outside the major metropolitan areas.

Membership. 100,000

Socialist Party of Australia

Address. 237 Sussex Street, Sydney 2000, Australia

Leadership. L. J. McPhillips (ch.); P. Symon (g.s.)

Founded. December 1971

History. The party was formed as a result of a breakaway from the Communist Party of Australia by pro-Moscow elements.

Orientation. The party seeks the establishment of a socialist republic in Australia, based on Marxism-Leninism.

Structure. The party's organizational principles are those of democratic centralism. The party has local and industrial branches, district committees, state committees and a central committee. The highest policy-making body of the party is its national congress.

Membership. 1,500 (est.)

Publications. *The Socialist* (fortnightly); *Australian Marxist Review* (quarterly)

International affiliations. The party is recognized by the Communist parties of the Soviet-bloc countries.

World Socialist Party of Australia

Addresses. P.O. Box 1440, Melbourne; P.O. Box 2291, Sydney, NSW; P.O. Box 1357, Brisbane, Queensland; P.O. Box 235, Northam 6401, Western Australia, Australia

History. This small formation of the Marxist left emerged as an Australian offshoot of the Socialist Party of Great Britain and has made some progress in the Australian trade union movement at shop-floor level.

Other Parties

The following parties operate at state level (with any state seats being shown in parentheses):

Independent Labor Party, in South Australia (one seat).

National Party, a breakaway group from the National Country Party which changed its name to National Party in 1982, present in Western Australia (two seats).

North Queensland Party, in Queensland.

In addition, the following minor parties have been reported to be active in recent years:

Australia Party

Call to Australia Party

Farm and Town Party

Progress Party, which took part (in New South Wales and Queensland) in the October 1980 general elections.

Austria

Capital: Vienna Pop. 7,600,000

Under the Austrian State Treaty signed on May 15, 1955, by the British, French, Soviet and US Governments and that of Austria, the Republic of Austria is a "sovereign, independent and democratic state" with a government "based on elections by secret ballot" and by "free, equal and universal suffrage". Austria has a bicameral parliament consisting of a 183-member National Council (*Nationalrat* or Lower House) and a 58-member Federal Council (*Bundesrat* or Upper House), both together forming the National Assembly (*Nationalversammlung*). The members of the *Nationalrat* are elected for a four-year term by equal, direct and secret ballot under a proportional representation system for 25 constituencies by all citizens over 19 years of age and resident in the constituency. The *Bundesrat* is elected for up to six years by the legislatures of the country's nine federal states (*Länder*), each of which has an elected assembly (*Landtag*). The President of the Republic is elected for a six-year term by general, equal and secret ballot of the registered voters. Each member of the Government must enjoy the confidence of a majority of the members of the *Nationalrat*.

Parties with at least five deputies in the *Nationalrat* are granted federal support (for publicity and campaigning) in the form of a lump sum and additional amounts in proportion to the number of votes received in previous elections. (In 1980 each of the three major parties received the equivalent of US$300,000.) In addition parties receive funds in proportion to the number of votes obtained, provided that they have received at least 1 per cent of the valid votes.

As a result of elections held on April 24, 1983, seats in the *Nationalrat* were distributed as follows: Socialist Party 90, Austrian People's Party 81, Liberal (Freedom) Party 12.

Austria Party
Österreich-Partei

Address. Webgasse 43, 1060 Vienna, Austria

Leadership. Franz Olah, Prof. Hans Klecatzky, Dr Karl Steinhauser

History. Franz Olah was a former Socialist Minister of the Interior and Prof. Klecatzky a former People's Party Minister of Justice. The party contested the 1983 general elections in Vienna, Styria and the Tirol.

Austrian Alternative List
Alternative Liste Österreich (ALÖ)

Address. Friedmanngasse 51/9, 1160 Vienna, Austria

Leadership. Martin Humer

Founded. October 1982

History. Modelled on the West German Green movement, the ALÖ stands for grass-roots democracy, non-violence, ecology and social concerns. The party has four seats in the Graz municipal council and in the 1983 general elections it obtained 1.3 per cent of the national vote.

International affiliations. The European Greens

Austrian People's Party
Österreichische Volkspartei (ÖVP)

Address. 1010 Vienna 1, Kärntnerstrasse 51, Austria

Leadership. Dr Alois Mock (ch.); Dr Michael Graff (s.g.)

Founded. 1945

History. The party was formed by representatives of the most important Christian Social groups of the 1918-38 era. In the first elections held to the *Nationalrat* of the second Republic of Austria in November 1945 the ÖVP gained 85 out of the 165 seats. It thereupon formed a coalition Government with the Socialists, and this coalition lasted until 1966 even though the ÖVP had lost its overall majority in the *Nationalrat* in 1949.

The party was in full control of the Government from 1966 (when it again gained 85 seats in the *Nationalrat*) to 1970, when it was narrowly defeated by the Socialists and went into opposition. It has remained there ever since, retaining 86 seats in the *Nationalrat* in the 1975 elections, 77 in those of 1979 and 81 (or 43.21 per cent of the vote) in those of April 1983.

Orientation. A Christian democratic and conservative party, the ÖVP stands for the juridical, political and cultural independence of Austria. It advocates the maintenance of private enterprise and in 1983 it opposed government proposals to close tax loopholes and to raise social security contributions.

Membership. About 500,000

Publications. *Südost Tagespost* (Graz, daily), 45,000

International affiliations. International Democrat Union; European Democrat Union; Christian Democratic International; European Christian Democratic Union

---

Christian Social Working Group
Christlich-Soziale Arbeitsgemeinschaft

Address. Kienzlstr. 30, 4730 Waizenkirchen, Austria

History. Based in the Tirol, this group gained only 0.66 per cent of the votes in that province in the 1979 elections.

Orientation. The group is committed to Roman Catholic family and moral values and has campaigned against pornography.

Communist League of Austria
Kommunistischer Bund Österreichs (KBÖ)

Address. Vienna, Austria

Leadership. Walter Lindner (ch.)

History. The KBÖ was originally a branch of the Communist League of West Germany (KDW). It is pro-Chinese.

Publications. *Klassenkampf*

Communist Party of Austria
Kommunistische Partei Österreichs (KPÖ)

Address. Höchstädtplatz 1, A-1206 Wien/ Vienna, Austria

Leadership. Franz Muhri (ch.); Erwin Scharf, Hans Kalt, Karl Reiter (secs.)

Founded. Nov. 3, 1918

History. The party was founded by left-wing Social Democrats and was a co-founder of the Comintern in 1919. Under Johann Koplenig (leader, 1924-65) it was forced into illegality by the Austrian Government in 1933 and from 1938 it organized national resistance against the Nazis after the German occupation.

The KPÖ was a co-founder, with the Socialists and Austrian People's Party, of the Second Republic of Austria in 1945; it was a member of the Government until 1947 and represented in Parliament until 1959. In 1974 it adopted a new "Marxist-Leninist programme" proposing democratic economic and political changes.

Orientation. The party's final aim is socialism, meaning "the establishment of a society under the leadership of the working class (dictatorship of the proletariat) to break the dictatorship of capital, to realize the broadest democracy for the working people".

Structure. District organizations send representatives to regional and national conferences and to the party congress (the party's highest political body, meeting every three years), which elects a 70-member central committee, a politburo and a secretariat.

Membership. 16,000

Publications. *Volksstimme* (daily), 41,000; *Weg und Ziel* (monthly), 3,000

International affiliations. The party is recognized by the Soviet-bloc Communist parties.

League of Democratic Socialists
Bund Demokratischer Sozialisten

Address. Gussriegelstr. 50, A 100-Vienna, Austria

History. This small Marxist grouping has close links with the Socialist Party of Great Britain.

Liberal Party of Austria or Austrian Freedom Party
Freiheitliche Partei Österreichs (FPÖ)

Address. Kärntnerstrasse 28/I, A-1010 Vienna, Austria

Leadership. Dr Norbert Steger (ch.); Walter Grabher-Meyer (g.s.)

Founded. April 1956

History. The party was formed by the merger of three right-wing groups, of which the strongest was the League of Independents (*Bund der Unabhängigen*), which in elections to the Lower House of Parliament in 1953 had gained 14 out of 165 seats. In the 1956 general elections the FPÖ gained only six seats, but from 1971 to 1973 it held 10 seats in the *Nationalrat* and 11 after the 1979 elections.

In 1983 it gained, for the first time, 12 seats and it thereupon joined with the Socialists in a coalition Government which took account of the liberal principles advocated by the FPÖ while it was in opposition (i.e. reform of economic ideas, democracy, community life and justice). In 1970-71 the FPÖ had already obtained the adoption of some of its demands, including the introduction of an exact system of proportional representation. It has also promoted the 1978 reform of family legislation and legislation in the field of environmental protection.

Orientation. The party seeks the maintenance and extension of fundamental freedoms and human rights, as well as increased justice in all spheres of social life.

Structure. Federal, with nine strongly independent *Länder* organizations. The party's supreme organ is its federal congress, which is held every two years and which elects the party's office-bearers.

Membership. 40,000

Publications. *Neue Freie Zeitung* (weekly), 30,000

International affiliations. Liberal International

Marxists-Leninists of Austria
Marxisten-Leninisten Österreichs

Leadership. Franz Strobel

Founded. 1965

History. The group contested one constituency in Vienna in 1966 and obtained 486 votes.

Orientation. The group is a Maoist offshoot of the Communist Party of Austria.

National Democratic Party
Nationaldemokratische Partei (NDP)

Address. Landstrassergürtel 19/3, 1030 Vienna, Austria

Leadership. Dr Norbert Burger (l.)

Founded. 1966

History. In the 1960s Dr Burger was the leader of a South Tirol liberation group, members of which (including himself) were convicted in Italy of terrorist activities. In the May 1980 presidential election Dr Burger won 3.2 per cent of the valid votes cast. The party did not contest the 1983 general elections.

Orientation. This right-wing party professes a "biological view of the world".

Structure. The NDP has a youth wing which is known as *Aktion Neue Rechte*.

Revolutionary Marxist Group
Gruppe Revolutionäre Marxisten (GRM)

Address. Anton Baumgartnerstr. 44/A6/5, 1232 Vienna, Austria

Leadership. Dr Hermann Dworczak

Founded. 1972

History. This formation contested the 1975 general elections in Vienna and gained 1,042 votes, but in 1979 it failed to obtain the required number of signatures to qualify for participation in the elections.

Publications. *Die Rotfront*

International affiliations. The movement is the Austrian section of the (Trotskyist) Fourth International.

Socialist Party of Austria
Sozialistische Partei Österreichs (SPÖ)

Address. Löwelstrasse 18, 1014 Vienna I, Austria

Leadership. Dr Fred Sinowatz (ch.); Fritz Marsch (g.s.)

Founded. 1889

History. The Social Democratic Workers' Party of Austria (*Sozialdemokratische Arbeiterpartei Österreichs*) was, in 1889, established as a Marxist party, reuniting the moderate and radical factions of a Social Democratic Workers' Party in Austria constituted in 1874 and agreeing to work for the establishment of universal franchise. After this objective had been achieved (though for men only) the party became the strongest in parliament, but was still excluded from all political decision-making. Before World War I the party advocated the transformation of the Austro-Hungarian Empire into a federal state of freely coexisting nations, but in fact the party was soon divided into national sections.

After the dissolution of the Empire the party emerged as the strongest in general elections held in February 1919 in the first Austrian Republic and was in power in coalition with the Christian Social Party until 1920, whereafter it went into opposition. As the party of Austrian Marxism it aimed at achieving complete power in the state and instituting socialism—as outlined in the party's Linz Programme of 1926, which did not exclude the use of extreme methods in case the bourgeoisie were to use force to prevent the social revolution. In 1934, however, the party was defeated and declared illegal by the Dollfus Government after the party's military wing had launched "armed resistance".

In the second Austrian Republic established in 1945 the party, assuming its present name, orientated itself towards the West with the object of preventing a Communist seizure of power. The party formed a coalition government with the Austrian People's Party and the Communists until November 1947, and thereafter various coalition governments with the People's Party until it went into opposition in 1966. It returned to power as the sole governing party in 1970 under the leadership of Dr Bruno Kreisky, forming a minority Government until 1971, when it gained an absolute majority in Parliament.

Thereafter it remained in power (increasing its absolute majority in the *Nationalrat* to 95 out of 183 seats in the elections of May 6, 1979) until 1983 when, in elections held on April 24, it lost five seats and therefore its absolute majority. The party thereupon formed a coalition Government with the Austrian Freedom Party, with Kreisky handing over both the government and the party leadership to Dr Fred Sinowatz.

Orientation. At a party congress held in May 1978 the SPÖ defined its objects as being the application of "the foundations and principal ideas of democracy in all spheres of social life", with labour being "conscious work in the service of the community" with a view to creating "a classless society" based on freedom, equality, justice and solidarity, and "true democracy" (not "uncontrolled domination" by functionaries, as in Communist

countries) with full freedom of religious belief and of thought. On economic matters the programme declared that a change of ownership would not by itself bring about a change towards democratic socialism and that it was in principle not necessary to enlarge the state and public sector of the economy, but that there should be democratic planning and co-determination by workers. The programme recognized the family as a lasting partnership charged with bringing up children. The programme also supported Austria's permanent neutrality and comprehensive measures for its defence.

Structure. The party has individual members and is organized at local, district and provincial level. There is a federal executive committee with representatives of all provinces, party sections for women, youth and old-age pensioners, and of the trade union movement.

Membership. 700,000

Publications. *Arbeiter-Zeitung* (Vienna, daily), 100,000; *Kärntner Tageszeitung* (Klagenfurt, daily), 51,000; *Die Neue Zeit* (Graz, daily), 79,000; *Oberösterreichisches Tagblatt* (Linz, daily), 24,000; *Salzburger Tagblatt* (daily), 14,000; *Die Zukunft* (fortnightly theoretical organ)

International affiliations. Socialist International

United Greens of Austria
Vereinigte Grüne Österreich (VGÖ)

Leadership. Alexander Tollmann, Herbert Fux

History. In the 1983 general elections this party obtained 1.89 per cent of the total vote.

Orientation. The VGÖ is a conservative-oriented ecologist formation, in contrast to the radical Austrian Alternative List (see separate entry).

Bahamas

Capital: Nassau (on New Providence Island)   Pop. 225,000

The Commonwealth of the Bahamas, a member of the Commonwealth, with the British monarch as head of state represented by a Governor-General, has a bicameral Parliament consisting of (i) a 43-member House of Assembly elected for five years by universal adult suffrage and (ii) a 16-member Senate to which nine members are appointed on the advice of the Prime Minister, four on that of the Leader of the Opposition and three at the Governor-General's discretion. The Prime Minister and his Cabinet are collectively responsible to Parliament.

In elections to the House of Assembly held on June 10, 1982, the ruling Progressive Liberal Party gained 32 seats and the Free National Movement the remaining 11.

Free National Movement (FNM)

Address. P.O.B. N-8181, Nassau, Bahamas

Leadership. John Henry Bostwick (ch.); Kendal G. L. Isaacs (l.)

Founded. 1972

History. In 1972–75 the FNM held eight seats in the House of Assembly on a platform of opposing early independence for the Bahamas. In the 1977 elections its parliamentary strength was reduced to three. In 1979 a Free National Democratic Movement (FNDM) was formed by John Bostwick, who had previously been leader of a Bahamian Democratic Party (BDP), together with two members of the House of Assembly elected for the FNM.

Following defections from the BDP and also from a Social Democratic Party (an offshoot of the BDP), the FNDM became the official Opposition in the House of Assembly late in 1981. At the dissolution of the House in 1982 the FNDM members decided to revert to the name of FNM for their party. (The Social Democratic Party had ceased to exist after its leader, Norman Solomon, had resigned from it in April 1982.) In the April 1982 elections the FNM gained 42.35 per cent of the vote (and 11 out of 43 seats in the House of Assembly).

Orientation. The FNM has accused the ruling Progressive Liberal Party of having harmed the country's economy by "excessive" state investment in hotel construction and management and of discouraging foreign investment.

Progressive Liberal Party (PLP)

Address. P.O.B. N-1107, Nassau, Bahamas

Leadership. Lynden O. Pindling (l.); Andrew Maynard (ch.); Arthur D. Hanna (parl. l.)

Founded. 1953

History. Founded as a predominantly Black-supported party, the PLP was a leading proponent of independence for the Bahamas. It has been in power since 1967, when it gained 18 seats in the 38-member House of Assembly and formed the islands' first all-Negro Government with the support of the sole representative of the (since defunct) Labour Party in the House. In general elections and a by-election held in 1972 the PLP won 30 of the 38 seats in the House, and it gained an additional two seats in 1982.

Orientation. The PLP conducted the 1977 elections on a platform of seeking "self-reliance as an economic way of life" with greater government involvement in a mixed economy, notably in tourism, banking, agriculture and fisheries.

Other Parties

Minor parties which unsuccessfully contested the general elections of June 10, 1982, were:

Commonwealth Democratic Party

Vanguard Nationalist and Socialist Party

Workers' Party

Bahrain

Capital: Manama   Pop. 350,000

In the Emirate of Bahrain the 30-member National Assembly was dissolved by the Emir on Aug. 26, 1975, and there are no legal political parties in the country.

Bangladesh

Capital: Dhaka (formerly Dacca)   Pop. 93,000,000

The People's Republic of Bangladesh, an independent state within the Commonwealth, has since March 24, 1982, been placed under martial law and ruled by a Chief Martial Law Administrator (Lt.-Gen. Hossain Mohammad Ershad, the Chief of Army Staff). On assuming power he suspended the Constitution, dismissed the President and Vice-President of the Republic, dissolved the Council of Ministers and Parliament, banned all "direct and indirect" political activities and demonstrations, imposed press censorship and forbade all criticism of the martial law regime (infringement of these regulations being punishable by imprisonment for up to seven years).

The Chief Martial Law Administrator also appointed a Council of Advisers (Cabinet) on March 25, 1982, and a new President of the Republic (Justice Abul Fazal Mohammad Assanuddin Choudhury, a retired Supreme Court judge) on March 26. Gen. Ershad said on March 24, 1982, that his main objectives were "to hold fair general elections in the country by making the situation suitable as soon as possible", and also to establish a new economic system for which he would have to "create a favourable climate for investment by private enterprise". The Council of Advisers was subsequently enlarged and redesignated Council of Ministers in May 1982. On Oct. 26, 1982, the Council extended Gen. Ershad's term of office as Chief of the Armed Forces by a further two years (from December 1982, when he would have been due to retire).

The ban on political activities in effect suspended (but did not dissolve) the country's political parties (numbering more than 20), of which the three major ones had gained seats (out of 300 elected seats) in the Parliament (*Jatiya Sangsad*) on Feb. 18, 1979, as follows: Bangladesh National Party (*Bangladesh Jatiyabadi Dal*) 207, Bangladesh Awami League 40, Bangladesh Moslem League 20, National Socialist Party (*Jatiya Samajtantrik Dal,* JSD) 9, other parties 8 and independents 16.

In November 1983 Lt.-Gen. Ershad announced that it had been decided to form a new national political party, the *Gana Dal* (People's Party), with a programme identical to recent policy objectives announced by the military regime.

Bangladesh Awami League

Address. 23 Bangabandhu Ave., Dhaka, Bangladesh

Leadership. Abdul Malek Ukil (l.); (Mrs) Sheikh Hasina Wazed (pres.); Abdur Rassaq (g.s.)

Founded. 1950

History. The party was formed as the Awami Moslem League and, as the Awami League, headed coalition governments in East Pakistan in 1956-58 and was represented in the Government of Pakistan in 1956-57 and in 1958. In elections held in 1970 it won 151 of the 153 East Pakistan seats in the Pakistan National Assembly and 268 of the 279 seats in the East Pakistan Assembly; subsequently it led (under the leadership of Sheikh Mujibur Rahman) the movement for independence from Pakistan and was the ruling party in Bangladesh in 1971-75. After the overthrow of Sheikh Mujibur it was temporarily banned and its leader, Abdul Malek Ukil, was imprisoned until April 1977.

In the 1978 presidential elections the Awami League was the strongest of the five parties supporting the Democratic United Front (*Ganatantrik Oikya Jote*) which unsuccessfully campaigned for the election of Gen. Mohammad Ataul Ghani Osmani. In the presidential elections of Nov. 15, 1981, the Awami League's candidate, Dr Kamal Hossain, received (according to the official results) 26.35 per cent of the vote, but he challenged this result on the grounds of alleged irregularities. The Awami League boycotted the swearing-in of the successful candidate, Abdus Sattar of the Bangladesh Nationalist Party, on Nov. 20.

Orientation. The Awami League has formed the main opposition party to the Bangladesh Nationalist Party. It advocates moderate socialism and is pro-Indian and pro-Soviet.

Bangladesh Awami League (Mizan Faction)

Address. 271/4 Elephant Rd, Dhaka, Bangladesh

Leadership. Mohammad Mizanur Rahman Choudhury (l.)

Founded. August 1978

History. This faction broke away from the Awami League led by Abdul Malek Ukil because of disagreements with the latter's policy.

Bangladesh Communist Party

Leadership. Moni Singh (l.); Mohammed Farhad (g.s.)

Founded. 1948

History. The party was founded in 1948 as the Communist Party of East Pakistan as an illegal organization, but it was later represented in the East Pakistan Provincial Assembly. By the promulgation of martial law in October 1958 it was driven underground again. After the breakaway of the pro-Chinese faction, which became the Communist Party of Bangladesh (ML—see separate entry), the party opposed the establishment of an independent East Pakistan (as Bangladesh). It was able to hold a congress in 1974 but in 1977 it was banned again.

The party was legalized in 1978 but was still constrained under a decree of Dec. 10, 1978, which prohibited all parties which were organized with foreign financial assistance, were affiliated to any foreign organization, propagated views detrimental to the sovereignty and security of Bangladesh or maintained an armed underground organization. In April 1980 the party's general secretary and 52 other leading party members were arrested for sedition, but Mohammed Farhad was released on bail on July 29, 1980.

Membership. 2,500 (est.)

International affiliations. The party is recognized by the Communist parties of the Soviet-bloc countries.

Bangladesh Ganatantrik Andolan

Leadership. Rashed Khan Memon (l.)

Founded. July 1978

History. The party was formed as a breakaway group from the Popular Unity Party, of which Rashed Khan Memon had been joint secretary.

Bangladesh Gono Azadi League

Address. 30 Banagran Lane, Dhaka, Bangladesh

Leadership. Maulana A. R. Tarkabagish (l.)

History. The League was one of five parties supporting the Democratic United Front (*Ganatantrik Oikya Jote*) which unsuccessfully campaigned in 1978 for the presidential candidature of Gen. Mohammad Ataul Ghani Osmani.

Bangladesh Labour Party

Address. 120 Motijheel C/A, Dhaka, Bangladesh

Leadership. Dr Mantaus Abdul Matin (l.)

History. The party supported the *Jatiyabadi* Front which successfully campaigned for the election of President Ziaur Rahman and it took part in the government formed by him in June 1978.

Orientation. The party is Islamic socialist in orientation.

Bangladesh Moslem League

Address. 281 Road No. 25, Dhanmondi R/A, Dhaka, Bangladesh

Founded. 1947

History. The Moslem League was the ruling party in East Pakistan in 1947-54, and during the war of independence for Bangladesh it supported Pakistan. Upon the achievement of independence by Bangladesh in 1971 the party was banned, but it returned to legality in 1977. In 1978 it supported the *Jatiyabadi* Front which successfully campaigned for the election of President Ziaur Rahman and it took part in the Government formed by him in June of that year.

Orientation. The League is a right-wing organization based on former religious parties.

Bangladesh National Awami Party (Bashani NAP)

Address. 226 Outer Circular Road, Dhaka, Bangladesh

Leadership. Abu Nasser Khan Bashani (pres.); Abdus Subhani (g.s.)

Founded. 1957

History. This party, formed under the leadership of Maulana Abdul Hamid Khan Bashani as a breakaway group (in East Pakistan) from the Awami League, was in 1967 split into two groups: a pro-Soviet wing led by Prof. Muzaffar Ahmed (see next entry) and a pro-Chinese wing led by Maulana Bashani. In 1974 the latter wing had fallen under the influence of right-wing Moslem elements and was openly anti-Indian and anti-Hindu. The Maulana dismissed the (left-wing) party secretary, Kazi Zakar Ahmed (who later formed the Popular Unity Party), and appointed Mashiur Rahman, a right-wing leader, as head of the party's organizing committee.

After being suppressed under martial law in August 1975, the party was officially authorized to operate again in September 1976. In 1978 it supported the *Jatiyabadi* Front, which successfully campaigned for the election of President Ziaur Rahman, and it took part in the Government formed by him in June of that year, with Mashiur Rahman becoming Senior Minister.

Orientation. The Bashani NAP is pro-Chinese.

Bangladesh National Awami Party (NAP-M)

Address. 21 Dhanmondi Hawkers' Market (1st floor), Dhaka 5, Bangladesh

Leadership. Prof. Muzaffar Ahmed (pres.); Pir Habibur Rahman (g.s.)

Founded. 1957 and again 1967

History. The party, formed as the National Awami Party of Pakistan, was split in 1967 over (i) the issue of provincial autonomy for the then East Pakistan and (ii) the party's attitude to the Ayub Khan Government. The majority formed the present party favouring regional autonomy and opposition to the "dictatorial anti-popular" Ayub Khan regime. The party took part in the 1971 "war of liberation" and its president became a member of the Consultative Committee of the provisional Government of Bangladesh in that year. After the establishment of an independent Bangladesh the party was in "constructive opposition", and in the 1973 general elections it gained 1,600,000 votes but no seats, and in 1979 it contested 89 seats and obtained nearly 500,000 votes but only one seat.

Orientation. The NAP-M is of the democratic left, anti-imperialist and non-communal, with the main object of establishing a society free from exploitation; it is pro-Soviet.

Structure. The party has a national conference meeting once every two years, a national council (which is its highest body between conference sessions) and a national working committee (including office-bearers), as well as district, local and trade committees.

Membership. 500,000

Bangladesh National League
Bangladesh Jatiya League

Address. 500 A Dhanmondi Residential Area, Road No. 7, Dhaka, Bangladesh

Leadership. Ataur Rahman Khan (l. and ch.); Abul Kalam (sec.)

Founded. 1970

History. Formed as the Pakistan National League in 1970, the party was renamed the Bangladesh Jatiya League in 1972, and it won one seat in Parliament in the 1973 general elections. It was banned in 1975 together with all other political parties, but the ban was lifted in 1976 and in the 1979 elections the party gained two seats in Parliament.

Orientation. The party's objective is "to achieve fully-fledged democracy wherein Parliament will be supreme and sovereign", this objective to be attained by constitutional means.

Structure. The party has a national council, a national working committee (of 15 office-bearers and 25 members nominated by the chairman), a parliamentary board and a parliamentary party.

Membership. 50,000

Bangladesh Nationalist Party (BNP)
Bangladesh Jatiyabadi Dal

Address. House No. 19A, Road No. 27 (Old) and 16 (New), Dhanmondi R/A, Dhaka, Bangladesh

Leadership. Abdus Sattar (pres.); Baddrudoza Choudhury (s.g.)

Founded. September 1978

History. The BNP was formed as an alliance by the bulk of the parties which had supported the President in his election in June 1978. They were the Moslem League, the National Awami Party led by Mashiur Rahman, the Popular Unity Party, the Labour Party and an organization representing the Hindu minority. These parties had been organized in the *Jatiyabadi* Front which had been formed by the Nationalist Democratic Party (*Jatiyabadi Ganatantrik Dal* or Jagodal, itself created in February 1978) as a political basis for the President's election campaign.

In September 1978 the BNP was formally constituted as a political party, but some sections of its constituent parties did not join the new organization. In the parliamentary elections of February 1979 the BNP gained 49 per cent of the votes cast (in a 40 per cent poll) and a two-thirds majority of seats in Parliament.

Abdus Sattar was Vice-President under President Ziaur Rahman, and after the latter's assassination on May 30, 1981, he acting President. In the presidential elections held on Nov. 15, 1981, and contested by over 30 candidates, he was elected as candidate of the BNP, gaining (according to the official result) 65.8 per cent of the votes.

Orientation. The BNP stands for parliamentary democracy. Its campaign for the election of President Ziaur Rahman in 1978 (which was largely conducted by the Moslem League) was strongly Islamic and anti-Indian.

Bangladesh Peasants' and Workers' Party
Bangladesh Krishak Sramik

Address. Sonargaon Bhavan, 99, South Kamalapur, Dhaka 17, Bangladesh

Leadership. A. S. M. Sulaiman (pres.); S. M. K. Zainal Abedin (s.g.)

Founded. October 1914

History. The party was founded, as the first political party of peasants in the then undivided Bengal under British rule, as the All-Bengal Praja Samity by Shere Bangla A. K. Fuzlul Huque, who was the first Chief Minister of the Krishak Praja-Moslem League coalition Government in Bengal in 1937. The party adopted its present name in December 1953 and formed, in 1954, a coalition Government with the United Front in the then East Pakistan, and a coalition Government with the Moslem League in 1955. From 1962 onwards the party was in opposition in the Parliament of Pakistan, where A. S. M. Sulaiman, then the party's general secretary, became chief whip of the opposition party in 1965. In Bangladesh the party is in opposition to the present regime.

Orientation. The party believes in the democratic political system, a society based on the principles of religion, with equal rights for all religions, and a welfare economy.

Structure. The party has a 500-member national council and a 35-member national executive committee. There are similar executive committees in the country's 21 districts and 61 sub-divisions, primary committees at village level and union committees in rural councils.

Membership. 650 full members and about 25,000 "primary" members (full party membership being allowed after three years of party service)

Publications. *Krishak Sramik Barta* (monthly), 5,000

Bangladesh People's League

Address. House No. 72, Dhanmondi Residential Area, Road No. 7/A, Dhaka, Bangladesh
Leadership. Dr Aleem-Al-Razee (ch.)
Founded. August 1976
History. Formed under the Political Parties Regulation 1976 and Martial Law Regulation No. XXII of 1976 (repealed in 1978), the party has been in opposition to the Government and boycotted the 1979 legislative elections.
Orientation. The party stands for "constitutional parliamentary democracy" and intends "to promote and develop socialistic consciousness among our people and ultimately to transform the society into one free from exploitation of man by man".
Structure. The party has a 41-member central committee with a chairman, a secretary-general and other office-bearers.
Membership. c.75,000

Bangladesh Scheduled Castes' Federation
Bangladesh Tafsili Jati Federation

Address. 4 Distillery Road, Gandaira, Dhaka-4, Bangladesh
Leadership. Rasaraj Mandal (l.); Jamini Kanta Mandal (convenor)
Founded. September 1976
History. An All-India Scheduled Castes' Federation was first organized in 1942, and after the partition of India in August 1947 the East Pakistan Scheduled Castes' Federation was set up and, on the establishment of an independent Bangladesh in December 1971, adopted its present name. It subsequently co-operated with the Government and its leaders served as cabinet ministers at different times. Its leader, with a mandate from the Federation, joined the Bangladesh Nationalist Party (BNP). The Federation did not contest the 1979 parliamentary elections. (In 1954, it had gained 26 seats out of 309 in the Assembly of East Pakistan, and in 1955 three in the Constituent Assembly of Pakistan.)
Orientation. The Federation seeks to remove the backwardness of the sub-castes of the Hindu community and to enable them to profit from social, economic, educational and political upliftment.
Structure. The party has a 45-member central committee as well as district and subdivisional committees.
Membership. 500,000

Bangladesh Socialist Party
Bangladesh Samajtantrik Dal (BSD)

Address. Dhaka, Bangladesh
Founded. December 1980
History. This small group broke away from the National Socialist party and laid claim to the leadership of that party.

Communist Party of Bangladesh (ML)
Bangladesher Samyabadi Dal (ML)

Address. 43/1 Juginagar, Dhaka-3, Bangladesh
Leadership. Mohammad Toha (ch.); Sukhendu Dastidar (g.s.)
Founded. 1966
History. Originally a branch of the Communist Party of India, the Communist Party of East Pakistan was formed in 1948 in conditions of illegality. It later had several members elected in the East Pakistan Provincial Assembly, partly through a four-party United Front, but was driven underground by the promulgation of martial law in October 1958, whereafter it was reorganized as a Marxist-Leninist party distinct from the pro-Moscow faction (which opposed an independent East Pakistan).
In 1966 it adopted a programme for the establishment of a "People's Democratic Republic of East Bengal". It later took part in the armed struggle for an independent Bangladesh but opposed the Government of Sheikh Mujibur Rahman and called for its overthrow (which took place in 1975). Thereafter the party worked as a legal party, and its chairman was a member of the National Parliament.
Orientation. The party seeks the establishment of a socialist government and attainment of social justice through a socialist pattern of the economy. The party is opposed to "Soviet social-imperialism".
Structure. The party is led by a 15-member central committee elected by a national congress, with its chairman being the leader of the party and its general secretary the chief executive. There are district committees and under them Thana committees composed of primary units. The central committee's day-to-day functions are discharged by a political bureau composed of five central committee members.
Membership. 1,400

Democratic League

Address. 68 Jigatola, Dhaka-9, Bangladesh
Leadership. Khandaker Moshtaque Ahmed (founder and l.)

Founded. 1976

History. The League's founder had been President of Bangladesh in August-November 1975, but was in February 1977 given a five-year prison sentence for alleged corruption and abuse of power. The League was banned in October 1977 for involvement in "terrorism, foreign infiltration and conspiracy", but this ban was lifted in November 1978.

Orientation. The League is a conservative formation.

Democratic United Front
Ganatantrik Oikya Jote

Leadership. Gen. Mohammad Ataul Ghani Osmani (l.)

Founded. 1978

History. This Front was supported by five parties, the strongest of which was the Awami League (the others being the *Gono Azadi* League, the *Jatiya Janata* Party, the pro-Moscow wing of the National Awami Party and the People's League). The aim of the Front was to campaign for the election of Gen. Osmani, who came second in the presidential election of 1978, polling 4,449,276 votes.

National People's Party
Jatiya Janata Party (JJP)

Address. 6 Folder Street, Wari, Dhaka-3, Bangladesh

Leadership. Ferdaus Ahmad Quarishi (ch.); A. K. Mujibur Rahman, Abdul Matin Chowdhury, Yusuf Ali (secs.)

Founded. September 1976

History. Formed while the major political parties were banned under martial law, the party called for the restoration of democratic order and was mainly responsible for the formation of a Democratic United Front (*Ganatantrik Oikya Jote*) which nominated Gen. (retd.) M. A. G. Osmani (the then JJP's convenor) as its candidate in the presidential elections of June 1978. Although his main opponent, President Ziaur Rahman, was confirmed in office (by over 15,000,000 votes), Gen. Osmani gained over 4,400,000 votes.

However, in the elections of Nov. 15, 1981, Gen. Osmani, standing again as the presidential candidate of the Democratic United Front, gained only 302,003 votes (out of a total of over 21,600,000) and forfeited his deposit.

Orientation. Progressive democratic with the objective of establishing an "egalitarian society on the basis of Bengali nationalism" and of "the emancipation of the whole Bengali nation all over the north-east of the sub-continent".

Structure. The party has a 51-member central committee, 65 district committees and numerous primary committees, and also separate wings for labour, students, women, youth and the peasantry

Membership. 25,000

Publications. *Deshbangla* (daily), 4,000

National Socialist Party
Jatiya Samajtantrik Dal (JSD)

Address. 23 D.I.T. Road, Malibagh (Choudhury para), Dhaka, Bangladesh

Leadership. Shajahan Siraj (l.)

Founded. 1972

History. The JSD was formed by a breakaway group of the Awami League. It created an armed wing whose leader had been commander of a "people's army" of peasant guerrillas in the Mymensingh sector in 1971, and the JSD itself was suppressed in 1974 after an alleged attempt to seize power. It was considered responsible for the November 1976 mutiny of the Dacca garrison which led to the formation of a new Government including, as Deputy Martial Law Administrator, Maj.-Gen. Ziaur Rahman, who later was appointed President. As such he disowned the JSD, and its leaders were arrested and subsequently tried and sentenced in July 1976 on charges of attempting to overthrow the Government, with their military leader being executed on July 21.

In October 1977 the JSD was officially dissolved, but in November 1978 it was again allowed to operate. Over 300 JSD members were released from prison in February 1979, but of those convicted in 1976 the former chairman and general secretary of the party remained in prison. The JSD nevertheless took part in the 1979 general elections. The JSD's military wing was accused of involvement in political murders in the first half of 1981. The party's candidate in the presidential elections of Nov. 18, 1981, was Maj. M. A. Jalil, who polled negligibly and forfeited his deposit.

Orientation. The JSD is a left-wing revolutionary party which has been engaged in armed struggle in the past.

Publications. *Gonokantha* (Voice of the People), 5,000

Popular Unity Party (PUP) or **United People's Party**

Address. 42/43 Purana Paltan, Dhaka, Bangladesh

Leadership. Kazi Zafar Ahmed

Founded. 1974

History. The PUP was formed by a breakaway group of the National Awami Party. In 1978 it supported the *Jatiyabadi* Front, which successfully campaigned for the election of President Ziaur Rahman, and it took part in the Government formed by him in June of that year. In October 1979, after the formal constitution as a political party of the Bangladesh Nationalist Party (which had superseded the *Jatiyabadi* Front), the PUP leader resigned as Minister of Education in October 1979.

Orientation. The PUP is pro-Chinese.

Barbados

Capital: Bridgetown   Pop. 250,000

Barbados, a member of the Commonwealth with the British monarch as head of state being represented by a Governor-General, has a 27-member House of Assembly elected for five years by universal adult suffrage and a 21-member Senate appointed by the Governor-General (12 senators on the advice of the Prime Minister, two on that of the Leader of the Opposition and seven at the Governor-General's discretion). The Prime Minister and his Cabinet are collectively responsible to Parliament.

In elections to the House of Assembly held on June 18, 1981, the Barbados Labour Party gained 17 seats and the Democratic Labour Party 10.

Barbados Labour Party (BLP)

Address. Grantley Adams House, 11 Roebuck Street, Bridgetown, Barbados

Leadership. John Michael Geoffrey (Tom) Adams (l. and ch.); Clyde Griffiths (g.s.)

Founded. 1938

History. The BLP held office in the pre-independence period from 1951 to 1961, the party's founder, Sir Grantley Adams (father of the present leader), becoming the first Prime Minister in a British West Indies territory when ministerial government was introduced in Barbados in 1954, and subsequently Prime Minister of the West Indies Federation during its brief existence from 1958 to 1962. In 1961 the BLP lost its majority in the Barbados House of Assembly to the Democratic Labour Party and remained in opposition until it obtained 17 of the 24 seats in the 1976 elections, which it won on a platform directed against alleged government corruption and waste and rises in the cost of living and unemployment. In the 1981 elections the BLP retained 17 seats in the House.

Orientation. The BLP is a social democratic party with a basic policy orientation owing much to the British Labour Party, on whose constitution that of the BLP is closely modelled. The party leader has expressed opposition to the policies of the Cuban and Guyana Governments and support for free enterprise within the context of a mixed economy.

Structure. The party has constituency branches and an annual delegate conference which elects a national executive committee of not more than 36 members.

Membership. 10,000

International affiliations. Socialist International

Democratic Labour Party (DLP)

Address. Kennington, George Street, St Michael, Barbados

Leadership. Errol W. Barrow (l.); Branford M. Taitt (pres.)

Founded. May 1955

History. The DLP was formed principally by dissident members of the Barbados Labour Party (BLP) who were disenchanted with the then BLP leadership. Having lost the 1956 elections to the BLP, the DLP came to power in 1961 (when it won 14 of the 24 seats in the House of Assembly); following its further election victory in 1966 the party leader, Errol Barrow, led Barbados to independence in

November of that year. After again being returned to power in 1971 the DLP remained in government until 1976, when it was defeated by the Barbados Labour Party in general elections. In the House of Assembly it won seven seats in 1976 and 10 in 1981.

Orientation. Claiming that the BLP had moved to the right, the DLP adopted left-wing policies in the 1970s and currently describes itself as a democratic socialist party. It lays emphasis on economic development, having during its 15 years of office introduced various measures to promote economic diversification and to improve social conditions.

Structure. The party has constituency branches, an annual delegate conference, a general council and an executive council.

Membership. 15,000

Other Parties

Political groups which have not contested recent elections include the following:

Movement for National Liberation (MNL), a party of the "new left".

People's Pressures Movement, a small grouping established in 1979 and led by Eric Sealy.

Belgium

Capital: Brussels   Pop. 9,810,000

The Kingdom of Belgium is a constitutional monarchy with a multi-party parliamentary democracy. It has a bicameral Parliament consisting of (i) a 212-member Chamber of Representatives elected for a four-year term by a system of proportional representation and by citizens over the age of 18 and (ii) a 181-member Senate (to which 106 senators are elected directly). As a result of elections held on Nov. 8, 1981, seats in the Chamber were distributed as follows: Christian People's Party (Flemish) 43, Freedom and Progress Party (Flemish liberal) 28, Socialist Party (Walloon) 35, Socialist Party (Flemish) 26, People's Union (Flemish nationalist) 20, Liberal Reform Party (Walloon) 24, Christian Social Party (Walloon) 18, Francophone Democratic Front—Walloon Association 8, others 10.

Devolution plans providing for Belgium to have, in addition to its central Government, separate governments for Brussels, Flanders and Wallonia have been debated for some years but are not yet fully implemented, having been the subject of continual dissension among the major and minor parties as to their application in specific local circumstances.

Belgian Labour Party
Partij van de Arbeid van België/Parti du Travail de Belgique (PvdA/PTA)

Leadership. Ludo Martens (l.)
Founded. November 1979
History. The party had its origin in an All Power to the Workers (*Alle Macht Aan De Arbeiders*, AMADA) movement, which had unsuccessfully contested the elections to the European Parliament in June 1979. The party took part in the 1981 elections but gained only 0.8 per cent of the vote and no seat in the Chamber of Representatives.

Orientation. A Marxist-Leninist party opposed to the "degeneration" of the Soviet Union and the Communist Party of Belgium, to state capitalism and "social fascism" and to the imperialism of the two super-powers, in particular of the Soviet Union. In internal politics the party stands for the defence of democratic rights, unity among workers and struggle against monopoly capitalism by both legal means, including elections, and "mass action", with the party opposing isolated acts of violence but not the use of force against any force used against the working class by the bourgeoisie.

Christian People's Party
Christelijke Volkspartij (CVP)

Address. 41 Twee Kerkenstraat, B-1040 Brussels, Belgium

Leadership. Frank Swaelen (pres.); Ludo Willems (s.g.)

Founded. 1945

History. Historically descended from the *Katholieke Vlaamse Volkspartij* (the Flemish wing of the *Parti Catholique Belge*), the CVP is the Flemish-speaking component of the Christian Social Party as formed in 1945—the Flemish and French-speaking wings having become effectively separate parties by the mid-1960s. The CVP is considerably larger than the PSC (normally receiving twice as many votes) and has provided the Prime Minister in recent governments in which both Christian Social parties have participated.

Orientation. Christian democratic, with emphasis on the human being's dignity, freedom, right to equality and readiness for responsibility. The party stands inter alia for "an economy in the service of man", with priority to be given to employment, stability of prices and avoidance of waste, social justice, a more important role for women in present-day society and full development of all through education and culture.

Structure. At its formation in 1945 the party's two wings, the PSC and the CVP, were given a measure of autonomy but remained under a single national committee responsible for policy decisions. However, since 1967 when the two wings disagreed over language and regional questions, they have held no joint congress and there has not been a national chairman. The two wings have developed their separate organizations and they contested the 1977 general elections on separate lists though with a common programme confined to national issues.

International affiliations. European People's Party; European Christian Democratic Union; Christian Democratic International

---

Christian Social Party
Parti Social Chrétien (PSC)

Address. Rue des Deux Eglises 41, B-1040 Brussels, Belgium

Leadership. Gérard Deprez (pres.); Jacques Lefèvre (s.g.)

Founded. 1945

History. The party has its historical origins in the *Union Catholique*, one of several Roman Catholic organizations set up in Belgium between 1846 and 1936, in which year it was superseded by the *Parti Catholique Belge*, which had French- and Flemish-speaking wings—the *Parti Catholique Social* and the *Katholieke Vlaamse Volkspartij*. This party, traditionally the strongest in Belgium, took part in coalition governments with various other parties before and during World War II, and its leader was Prime Minister during the war. At Christmas 1945 the party was replaced by the Christian Social Party which, in elections in February 1946, enhanced its position as the country's strongest party, gaining 92 out of the 212 seats in the Chamber of Deputies. However, it did not enter the Government until it formed a coalition with the Socialists in 1947, since when it has participated continuously in government, either alone or in coalition, except for the period 1954–58.

From the mid-1960s onwards the Belgian Christian Socials became effectively two separate parties—viz. the French-speaking PSC and the Flemish CVP (see preceding entry)—although Christian Social participation in government has so far always included both parties. Following further losses in the 1968 elections the PSC-CVP reverted to a coalition with the Socialists, which lasted until 1972. In January 1973 the Christian Socials entered a coalition with the Socialists and Liberals, and in 1974 formed a minority Government with the Liberals only, which was later in the year joined by the *Rassemblement Wallon*. The 1977 elections, in which the Christian Socials retained 80 seats in the Chamber, were followed by the establishment of a coalition Government under Christian Social premiership with the Socialists, the Francophone Democratic Front and the (Flemish) *Volksunie*. In April 1979 this Government was succeeded by a new Government formed by the above parties except the *Volksunie*.

In January 1980 the same parties, except the Francophone Democratic Front, took part in forming a coalition Government. In May 1980 the Liberals joined this Government but left it in October of that year. Thereafter a new Christian Social and Socialist coalition was formed; a new similarly-composed Government followed from April to September 1981. After the 1981 elections the pendulum swung to the centre-right, with the Christian Socials and Liberals entering into coalition.

International affiliations. European People's Party; European Christian Democratic Union; Christian Democratic International

Communist Party of Belgium
Kommunistische Partij van België/Parti
Communiste de Belgique

Address. Stalingradlaan 18/20 (18/20 Av. de Stalingrad), 1000 Brussels, Belgium

Leadership. Louis van Geyt (ch.); Jef Turf (Flanders vice-ch.); Claude Renard (Wallonia vice-ch.)

Founded. September 1921

History. The party was founded by Joseph Jacquemotte, a militant member of the (social democratic) union of employees, and some militant members of the (social democratic) Workers' Party. In the 1936 elections it gained nine seats in Parliament. During World War II the party formed, with other democratic forces, two underground anti-Nazi movements, and after the war it took part in a coalition Government from March 1946 until March 1947, when the party went into opposition. The number of seats gained by the party in elections to the Chamber of Representatives fell from 23 in 1946 to two in 1958, whereafter it rose to five in 1961 and six in 1965, and since then it has not exceeded five. Having changed its political orientation in 1954, the party has since 1961 "developed policies for democratic federalism and basic anti-capitalist structural reforms".

Orientation. The party's final aim is "the foundation of a socialist, pluralist and democratic society" and its present objectives are "the realization of a progressive alternative to monopolist policy", "gradual abrogation of the two antagonistic military blocs", an end to the arms race, the development of European security and co-operation, and "as soon as possible a democratic federalization of the Belgian institutions" with "direct and general elections of three regional councils".

Structure. The party has one national central committee, with a political bureau and a national secretariat, and also three regional councils with their own regional bureaux and chairmen. There are 23 district federations and many local and factory sections and cells.

Membership. 14,000

Publications. *Le Drapeau Rouge* (daily), 15,000; *De Rode Vaan* (weekly), 10,000

International affiliations. The party is recognized by the Soviet-bloc Communist parties.

Democratic Union for the Respect of Labour
Union Démocratique pour le Respect du
Travail/Respect voor Arbeid en Democratie
(UDRT/RAD)

Address. Chaussée de Boondael/Boondaelse Steenweg 548, 1050 Brussels, Belgium

Leadership. Robert Hendrick (pres.)

Founded. April 1978

History. First took part in elections in December 1978, gaining one seat in the Chamber of Representatives, where it increased the number of its seats to three in 1981.

Orientation. The party stands for defence of individual freedoms, parliamentary democracy, private property and free enterprise, with the priority objectives of tax reform and a harmonization of pensions.

Structure. The party has local sections, area committees and provincial offices as well as a political commission and a national council.

Membership. 4,000

Ecologist Party
Parti Écologiste (Ecolo)

Address. Rue Basse Marcelle 26, B-5000 Namur, Belgium

History. This party first contested general elections in 1978, but without gaining any seat. In the 1981 elections, however, in which it co-operated with the (Dutch-language) "Live Differently" (Agalev) movement (see separate entry), it gained two seats in the Chamber of Representatives and three in the Senate. Altogether the two formations gained 4.8 per cent of the national vote. By mid-1983 Ecolo had nine elected representatives at regional level and 79 in municipal councils.

International affiliations. The European Greens

Flemish Bloc
Vlaams Blok

Leadership. Karel Dillen (ch.)

Founded. May 1979

History. The party was first formed in November 1978 as an electoral alliance between two earlier parties founded in 1977—the *Vlaamse Volkspartij* (set up by Lode Claes, a former *Volksunie* senator) and a *Vlaams Nationale Partij* led by Karel Dillen—which formally merged in the new party in 1979. It was created by Flemish nationalists opposed to the constitutional concessions made by the *Volksunie* (as a member of the four-party coalition Government of 1977-79). Since 1978 it has held one seat in the Chamber of Representatives.

Orientation. Extreme Flemish nationalist, the party has rejected the devolution programme agreed to in principle in March 1978 by the country's major parties.

Francophone Democratic Front
Front Démocratique des Francophones (FDF)

Address. 127 Chaussée de Charleroi, B-1060 Brussels, Belgium

Leadership. Lucien Outers (pres.)

Founded. May 1964

History. The FDF was established as the *Front Démocratique des Bruxellois de Langue Française,* and its founders included former followers of a *Mouvement Populaire Wallon* and a (Christian) *Rénovation Wallonne.* In 1968 it absorbed the *Démocratie Bruxelloise* group (a federalist movement of Christian Social origin). The FDF contested general elections in the Brussels area only, gaining three seats in the Chamber of Deputies in 1965, five in 1968, 10 in 1971, nine in 1974, 10 in 1977, 11 in 1978 and six in 1981. In 1977 it joined the four-party coalition Government which agreed in principle in March 1978 on a constitutional devolution programme. It has not taken part in government since March 1980.

Orientation. The FDF's programme is concerned mainly with the development of the Brussels region, the maintenance of economic growth, the improvement of employment prospects and a halt to the depopulation of the Brussels region. The party stands for the establishment of a federal state and the preservation of the French character of Brussels.

Structure. The FDF has as its supreme organ a 59-member head committee which meets at least once a month and decides on programme and policy, taking into account the party's links with the *Rassemblement Wallon.* The committee's decisions are carried out by a 26-member permanent bureau, which also maintains party discipline.

Freedom and Progress Party
Partij voor Vrijheid en Vooruitgang (PVV)

Address. Regentlaan 47-48, 1000 Brussels, Belgium

Leadership. Guy Verhofstadt (ch.); P. Dewael (sec.)

Founded. 1970

History. The Flemish PVV is descended from the historic Belgian Liberal Party, the country's earliest political formation, which was founded in 1846 and was in power in 1857-70 and 1878-84 but which, with the emergence of the *Parti Ouvrier Belge* (subsequently the Socialist Party), declined to the status of Belgium's third strongest party after the Catholic and Socialist parties. Having participated in a succession of coalition governments after World War II, the Liberal Party was reconstituted as the *Parti de la Liberté et du Progrès* (PLP) in October 1961, but in 1970 the Flemish-speaking wing (PVV) became effectively a separate party as Belgium began to move towards a new constitutional structure based on federalism.

The PVV participated in a coalition with the Christian Socials, Socialists and PLP from 1973 to 1974 and in a coalition with the Christian Socials, Walloon Association (*Rassemblement Wallon*) and PLP from 1974 to 1977. Since December 1981 it has been in coalition with the Christian Socials and the Liberal Reform Party.

Orientation. Liberal and democratic.

Structure. The PVV has, in addition to its chairman, deputy chairman and administrative council, an executive committee, a political committee and a congress (as the party's supreme organ determining its doctrine).

Membership. 66,336

Publications. *PVV Magazine* (for members); *Libérale Telex*

International affiliations. Liberal International; Federation of Liberal and Democratic Parties of the European Community

---

Liberal Reform Party
Parti Réformateur Libéral (PRL)

Address. Centre International Rogier, 26e étage, Place Rogier, B.P. 570, 1000, Brussels, Belgium

Leadership. Louis Michel (ch.); M. E. Klein (s.g.)

Founded. June 1979

History. Descended from the historic Belgian Liberal Party (see separate entry for Freedom and Progress Party), the PRL was founded on June 23, 1979, as a merger of two French-speaking Liberal parties, the *Parti des Réformes et de la Liberté de Wallonie* (PRLW) and the Brussels Liberal Party. Of these the PRLW had been formed in November 1976 as the successor to the *Parti de la Liberté et du Progrès* (PLP). The latter had continued as the main French-speaking Liberal party following the establishment of the Flemish PVV as a separate formation in 1970, while the Brussels Liberals had adopted the traditional name of the party in June 1974 after having originally constituted a distinct formation called the *Parti Libéral Démocrate et Pluraliste* (PLDP) in January 1973. The PLP had participated in a minority coalition with the Christian Socials and PVV from 1974 to 1977, and the PRL took part in a similar coalition Government in May–September 1980. Following the November 1981 elections. the PRL entered a further coalition with the Christian Socials and the PVV.

Orientation. The party stands for political pluralism, liberalism, responsibility of the individual, a free-enterprise economy and federalism (with a single Parliament for the French-speaking community of Wallonia and Brussels).

Structure. The party has a presidency, a bureau, a standing committee and a congress.

Membership. 40,000

Publications. Questions pour Demain

International affiliations. Liberal International; Federation of Liberal and Democratic Parties of the European Community

---

Live Differently
Anders gaan leven (Agalev)

Address. Onderrichstraat 69, B-1000 Brussels, Belgium

History. This ecologist party of Dutch-speaking Belgians gained two seats in the Chamber of Representatives and one in the Senate in elections held in November 1981. Agalev members are active in the campaign against the deployment of US cruise missiles in Western Europe.

International affiliations. The European Greens

Marxist-Leninist Communist Party of Belgium
Parti Communiste Marxiste-Léniniste de Belgique

Leadership. Fernand Lefebvre (first sec.)
Orientation. Pro-Chinese
Publications. Clarté et L'Exploité

Party of German-speaking Belgians
Partei der deutschsprachigen Belgier (PDB)

Address. Hisselsgasse 59 A, 4700 Eupen, Belgium

Leadership. Clemens Drösch (ch.)
Founded. Dec. 12, 1971
History. As a result of the 1981 elections to the German Cultural Council the PDB held seven of the 25 seats on that Council. It has not been represented in the Chamber of Deputies or the Senate.

Orientation. The party stands for the rights of German-speaking Belgians to be equal to those of the Flemish and Walloon population groups within a federal Belgium.

People's Union
Volksunie

Address. Barrikadenplein 12, B-1000 Brussels, Belgium

Leadership. Vic Anciaux (ch.); Willy de Saeger (sec.)

Founded. December 1954

History. The party's representation in the Chamber of Representatives was insignificant until 1965, when it gained 12 seats, increasing them to 20 in 1969 and 22 in 1974, whereafter its strength fell back to 20 seats in 1977. In that year the party agreed to take part in a coalition Government (with Christian Socials, Socialists and the Brussels *Front Démocratique des Francophones*) and to approve inter alia a regional reform programme which was a compromise between demands by French- and Dutch-speaking Belgians. This compromise was not approved by a large section of the party and in the elections held in December 1978 it retained only 14 seats in the House. The party thereupon reverted to opposition, and in the 1981 elections it increased the number of its seats to 20.

Orientation. A Flemish nationalist party seeking autonomy for Flanders, the *Volksunie* describes itself as "socially progressive, tolerant, modern and forward-looking".

Structure. The party has a national council of 100 members representing its 18 regional branches (embracing 400 local branches) and a 15-member national committee.

Membership. 60,000

Publications. Wij (weekly), 15,000; *Vlaams-Nationale Standpunten* (quarterly)

International affiliations. Free European Alliance

Revolutionary Workers' League
Revolutionaire Arbeidersliga

History. This group took part in the 1978 and 1981 parliamentary elections but gained only 0.2 per cent of the total vote and no seats.

Socialist Party
Parti Socialiste (PS)

Address. Boulevard de l'Empereur 13, 1000 Brussels, Belgium

Leadership. Guy Spitaels (ch.); Roger Gailliez (nat. sec.)

Founded. 1885; re-est. October 1978

History. The PS was established as a separate party in October 1978 when the Belgian Socialist Party decided that its French-speaking and Dutch-speaking wings should operate separately because of differences which had arisen between them over the allocation of regional responsibilities under the proposed constitutional reform.

The PS is descended from the traditional socialist party, founded in April 1885 as the *Parti Ouvrier Belge,* with its base in the Walloon industrial areas and with support of the trade unions. After obtaining universal suffrage through a general strike, this party sent 28 members to the Chamber of Representatives in 1894, when it also drew up the Quaregnon Charter (the basic manifesto of Belgian socialism). The party remained in opposition until 1914 but was admitted to the Belgian Government-in-exile at Le Havre (France) in 1915 (during World War I, when most of Belgium was under German occupation). In 1938 Paul-Henri Spaak became Belgium's first socialist Prime Minister. Following the Nazi occupation of Belgium in 1940, the party went underground under the leadership of Achille van Acker.

It was reconstituted in 1944 as the Belgian Socialist Party, based on direct membership (instead of group affiliations). It took part in various coalition governments until 1949 and again (with the Liberals) from 1954 to 1958. Thereafter it was in power in coalition with the Christian Socials from 1961 to 1966 and from 1968 to 1972; with the Christian Socials and Liberals in 1973–74; and with Christian Socials, the (Brussels) Francophone Democratic Front and the *Volksunie* in 1977–78 and, from April 1979, with the same parties except the *Volksunie* (by which time the PS was operating separately from its Flemish counterpart).

A further coalition led by the Christian Socials and Socialists lasted from January 1980 until May 1980, when this coalition Government was reorganized and joined by members of the two Liberal parties. The PS also took part in the ensuing four-party Government (of Socialists and Christian Socials) in office from October 1980 to September 1981, whereafter the PS went into opposition.

Orientation. The party stands for democratic socialism which "in opposition to capitalist values based on the pursuit of private profit and of selfish interests" propagates "the moral, social and cultural values of a society freed of material needs and social iniquities". It holds that socialism, which is "internationalist by inspiration and methods", is inseparable from political, economic, social and cultural democracy. It therefore rejects private capitalism, state capitalism and totalitarian regimes as well as the denial of human rights, in particular the right to self-determination. The party's economic socialism is to be based on three principles—the nationalization of key sectors, planning and (in the long term) self-management.

Structure. The party's supreme organ is its congress, which determines its doctrine and programme and takes important decisions (including that on participation in government). There is a general council composed of delegates of the PS's 13 federations, members of its parliamentary group and the party's bureau. (The party co-ordinates its policies at national level with the Dutch-speaking Socialists by means of a co-ordinating committee.)

Membership. 135,000

International affiliations. Socialist International; Confederation of Socialist Parties of the European Communities (in both of which the PS and the Dutch-speaking Belgian Socialist Party constitute a single member party)

Socialist Party
Socialistische Partij (SP)

Address. Keizerslaan 13, 1000 Brussels, Belgium

Leadership. Karel van Miert (ch.); Gerrit Kreveld (nat. sec.)

Founded. 1885; re-est. October 1978

History. As the Flemish section of the Belgian Socialist Party (united until October 1978), this party had its origin in the *Belgische Werklieden Partij* founded in October 1885. As part of the united party it participated in all the coalition governments referred to under the French-speaking Socialist Party (see previous entry).

Orientation. The party aims at the establishment of a democratic socialist society in Belgium. It now lays emphasis on Flemish workers' interests and advocates the creation of only two regions—Flanders and Wallonia—in a federal Belgium (in which Brussels would have a special status, but not that of a region). At a congress held in March 1980 the party decided to

34

renounce the principles of Marxism and the class struggle. The party's chairman declared that a classless society was the party's ultimate aim but that it would take a long time to realize.

Structure. The party has 17 federations in Flanders. (For policies at national level there is a co-ordinating committee comprising representatives of both the SP and the PS.)

Membership. 130,000

International affiliations. Socialist International; Confederation of Socialist Parties of the European Community (in both of which the SP and the French-speaking Socialist Party constitute a single member party)

Unified Feminist Party
Parti Féministe Unifié

Address. 13, avenue du Pesage, 1050 Brussels, Belgium

Leadership. Non-hierarchical

Founded. March 19, 1972

History. Founded with the object of obtaining legal fulfilment of feminist demands (sexual, economic, social and cultural autonomy of women, and indirectly recognition of feminism as a distinct political creed independent of any other ideology), the party presented women only as candidates in the legislative elections of 1974, 1977, 1978 and 1981, and in the elections to the European Parliament in June 1979.

Orientation. The party advocates radical policies to secure autonomy for women, leading to autonomy for all individuals. The party calls for the establishment of a "self-managing democracy" and a ban on the production, use and stockpiling of nuclear, chemical and bacteriological weapons.

Structure. Complete regional autonomy, with a minimum of organs, allowing direct democracy to be exercised, and no multiple offices to be held. The party has no parliamentary or other public representation. It admits men as members and office-bearers.

Publications. *Libre* (bimonthly bulletin), 1,000

Walloon Association
Rassemblement Wallon (RW)

Address. 42 rue Rogier, 5000 Namur, Belgium

Leadership. Henri Mordant (pres.); Joseph Fievez (s.g.)

Founded. February 1968

History. A *Front Wallon* created in Charleroi in 1964 and a *Parti Wallon des Travailleurs* formed in Liège and Namur in 1965 merged in June 1965 to form a *Parti Wallon,* which was superseded by the RW. The latter decided in Liège on Feb. 28, 1968, to extend its activities to the whole of Wallonia. The RW took part in the coalition Government of Christian Socials and Liberals from June 1974 to March 1977 (after several leading RW members had left the party to join with the *Parti de la Liberté et du Progrès* to form the *Parti des Réformes et de la Liberté en Wallonie*).

Orientation. Towards a reorganization of the economy of Wallonia and for federalism.

Structure. The RW is organized at local, cantonal and district level and has an executive bureau, a federal bureau and a congress.

Membership. 9,500

Walloon Independence Party
Parti Indépendantiste Wallon

Leadership. Etienne Duvieusart (founder)

Founded. December 1980

History. This party was established as an offshoot of the Walloon Association (RW) after Etíenne Duvieusart had failed to be re-elected to the Senate as a member of the RW. The party sought the adherence of socialists, liberals and Christians standing for the independence of Wallonia, which was to have links with France.

Belize

Capital: Belmopan   Pop. 150,000

Belize became, on Sept. 21, 1981, a "sovereign democratic state" and an independent member of the Commonwealth as a constitutional monarchy with the British monarch being head of state and represented by a Governor-General, who acts on the advice of a Cabinet headed by a Prime Minister. There is a bicameral National Assembly consisting of (i) a House of Representatives of up to 29 members, elected by universal adult suffrage of citizens above the age of 18 years, and in single-member constituencies, and (ii) a Senate of eight members (five appointed by the Governor-General on the advice of the Prime Minister, two on the advice of the Leader of the Opposition and one on that of a Belize Advisory Council). Cabinet ministers are appointed similarly from among the members of the National Assembly.

In elections to the House of Representatives held on Nov. 21, 1979, the People's United Party gained 13 seats and the United Democratic Party (UDP) the remaining five. One of the UDP members resigned from the party in December 1982 to sit in the House as an independent.

People's United Party (PUP)

Address. Belize City, Belize
Leadership. George C. Price (l.)
Founded. 1950
History. The PUP was founded as a left-wing party with the support of the General Workers' Union and of the Roman Catholic Church. In 1951-54 it was said to have close connexions with the then left-wing Government of Guatemala. It has won substantial majorities in all elections held in the colony since the introduction of universal adult suffrage in 1954, and its leader became First Minister in 1961 and Premier in 1965. In winning the November 1979 elections, the PUP obtained 51.8 per cent of the votes.

Claiming to have received a mandate for early independence for Belize in two successive elections, the PUP Government obtained this independence by September 1981 without the holding of a referendum.

Orientation. The party has favoured a mixed economy and has sought to curb foreign investment in land.

United Democratic Party (UDP)

Address. 21 King Street, Belize City, Belize
Leadership. Manuel Esquivel (l.); Dean Lindo (ch.); Elodio Aragon (s.g.)
Founded. September 1973
History. The UDP was formed in a merger of the National Independence Party, the Liberal Party and the People's Development Movement. The party ratified its constitution in April 1974. The party has remained in opposition, winning 46.8 per cent of the votes in the November 1979 elections, in which it campaigned on a platform alleging that the Price Government was influenced by communism.

In 1981 the UDP unsuccessfully called for a referendum on the question of independence for Belize; it boycotted not only a parliamentary committee set up to study this question but also the independence celebrations held on Sept. 21, 1981. In July of that year extremist UDP members organized in a Belize Action Movement were involved in an anti-government demonstration.

Orientation. The UDP seeks the development of a true democratic society and the attainment of a viable economy by the encouragement of foreign investment.

Structure. The party has (i) a 30-member national executive committee elected at a biennial conference and (ii) a central committee consisting of members elected by the conference and of the members of the party's parliamentary group.

Membership. 5,000.

Benin

Capital: Porto Novo   Pop. 3,750,000

The People's Republic of Benin (formerly Dahomey) is ruled by a (military) National Council of the Revolution which takes decisions in conformity with those of the central committee of the left-wing Benin People's Revolutionary Party (*Parti de la Révolution Populaire du Bénin,* PRPB), the country's sole legal political organization. There is a National Revolutionary Assembly of 336 People's Commissioners elected by direct universal suffrage of citizens above the age of 18 years on Nov. 20, 1979, on a list of PRPB candidates which was, as officially announced, approved by 1,243,286 voters out of a total of 1,270,051 who had cast valid votes. The Assembly elects the head of state (President of the Republic) who is also head of the Executive Council (cabinet).

Benin People's Revolutionary Party
Parti de la Révolution Populaire du Bénin
(PRPB)

Leadership. President Mathieu Kérékou (l.)

Founded. December 1971

History. The party superseded a 67-member National Council of the Revolution, set up in October 1973 by the Revolutionary Military Government which had assumed power in October 1972. In November 1974 the National Council had been given a 14-member political bureau, and its aims had been defined as involving the establishment of a socialist society in the country.

Orientation. The party has Marxism-Leninism as "the revolutionary philosophy and the basis and guideline" of the country's "revolutionary movement", and its aim is "the scientific organization of the social and productive forces of the country for the defence of the revolution" by relying in the first instance on the country's own strength and economic and social resources.

Structure. The party has a 45-member central committee and a 13-member political bureau. Its supreme organ is its congress. Its organization is based on the principle of "democratic centralism" and there are "local revolutionary committees" at neighbourhood and village level.

Bhutan

Capital: Thimphu   Pop. 1,300,000

The Kingdom of Bhutan has a National Assembly (*Tsogdu*) elected by universal suffrage of all adults over the age of 17. The Assembly is required to pass a vote of confidence in the King by a two-thirds majority every three years and has powers of removal of the King and selection of a new one from members of the Royal Family. There are no political parties.

Bolivia

Capital: La Paz   Pop. 6,300,000

The Republic of Bolivia has an executive President elected for a four-year term by universal adult suffrage and a 157-member Congress consisting of a 130-member House of Representatives and a 27-member Senate similarly elected for four years. Elections are held under a system of proportional representation. Voters must be 21 years old or over, or at least 18 years if married. Voting is compulsory.

In elections held on June 29, 1980, parties provisionally gained aggregate seats in Congress as follows: Democratic Popular Unity (UDP) 57, National Revolutionary Movement—Historic Faction (MNR-H) 44, National Democratic Action (ADN) 30, Socialist Party—One (PS-1) 11. In presidential elections held on the same day the UDP candidate, Dr Hernán Siles Zuazo, obtained the highest number of votes, but not an absolute majority. As a result, there followed a military take-over on July 17, 1980, in response to which Dr Siles Zuazo the following month formed a clandestine government.

More than two years later, the armed forces announced on Sept. 17, 1982, a return to civilian rule, whereupon the electoral court decided on Sept. 23 that the June 1980 elections were valid. Accordingly, the Congress on Oct. 5 elected Dr Siles Zuazo as President of the Republic, and the latter proceeded to appoint a Cabinet of UDP ministers, including two Communists. The constituent parties of the UDP are the Leftist Revolutionary Nationalist Movement (MNRI), the Movement of the Revolutionary Left (MIR) and the (pro-Soviet) Bolivian Communist Party (PCB). Altogether 18 different parties were represented in Congress.

Authentic Revolutionary Party
Partido Revolucionario Auténtico (PRA)

Address. Calle Yanacocha 448, oficina 2, La Paz, Bolivia
Leadership. Dr Walter Guevara Arce (l.)
Founded. 1960
History. The party was established as a faction of the National Revolutionary Movement, the ruling party under the presidency of Dr Paz Estenssoro (in 1952-56 and 1960-64); Dr Guevara, the party's founder, unsuccessfully opposed Dr Estenssoro in the 1960 presidential elections. In 1974 Dr Guevara was sent into exile after he had criticized the Government of President Banzer.

In the 1968 and 1969 presidential elections the PRA supported Dr Estenssoro's candidacy for the presidency, and in August 1979 Dr Guevara was appointed interim President of the Republic, pending the holding of new elections in 1980. In the June 1980 elections, however, he obtained only 2.62 per cent of the vote.

Bolivian Socialist Falange—Gutiérrez Wing
Falange Socialista Boliviana (FSB)—Gutiérrez

Address. Av. Sánchez Lima 2278, La Paz, Bolivia
Leadership. Dr Mario Gutiérrez (l.)
Founded. August 1937
History. Originally formed on the model of the Spanish Falange under the Franco regime, the FSB first gained parliamentary representation in 1946 and by 1965 had 15 deputies and eight senators. Following the 1971 revolution which brought President Banzer to power the FSB co-operated with

the armed forces and the *Movimiento Nacionalista Revolucionario* within a Nationalist Popular Front but left the Government in 1974 and subsequently split into two wings.

The main Gutiérrez wing refused to support President Banzer's nominee in the July 1978 presidential elections, Gen. Pereda, and withdrew its own candidate, Col. José Patiño Ayaroa, shortly before the poll. Having expressed opposition to the military coup perpetrated by Gen. Padilla in November 1978, the Gutiérrez wing of the FSB participated in the Alliance for National Integration (APIN) coalition which backed the candidature of Gen. René Bernal Escalante in the inconclusive presidential elections of July 1979, Dr Gutiérrez being the vice-presidential running mate of the latter (who obtained 4.1 per cent of the vote).

Orientation. The FSB's 1937 programme included land reform and the nationalization of the country's tin mines (later carried out). Under principles agreed in May 1978 the Gutiérrez faction stands for a nationalist state serving the individual, an end to class struggle and a government of national unity, the rule of law and a social and political pact leading to the establishment of democracy in Bolivia.

Bolivian Socialist Falange—Moreira Wing
Falange Socialista Boliviana (FSB)—Moreira

Address. Calle Canoniga Ayllón esq. Boquerón 597 (Casilla 4937), La Paz, Bolivia

Leadership. Gastón Moreira Ostria (l.); Dr Augusto Mendizabal (s.g.)

History. Following the post-1974 split in the FSB, the smaller Moreira wing was given official recognition by the National Electoral Court in May 1978 following its decision to support President Banzer's nominee for the July 1978 presidential elections, Gen. Pereda. In the July 1979 presidential elections the Moreira wing of the FSB supported the candidature of Gen. Banzer within the Nationalist Democratic Action (ADN) coalition, the former President obtaining 14.9 per cent of the vote.

Orientation. The wing stands for "nationalism with social justice" in an enlarged and renewed Bolivia, with the peasants being given the same rights and duties as other citizens.

Structure. The party is headed by its leader and two sub-leaders, supported by regional secretaries and various party councils. The leader presides over a national executive, the party's supreme deliberative body.

Membership. 100,000

Publications. *Saber; Antorcha; La Prensa*—10,000 each

Bolivian Socialist Falange of the Left
Falange Socialista Boliviana de Izquierda (FSBI)

Address. Casilla No. 1649, La Paz, Bolivia

Leadership. Dr Enrique Riveros Aliaga (l.)

Founded. March 1970

History. The FSBI broke away from the Bolivian Socialist Falange for reasons of doctrine only, taking a leftist nationalist line. In December 1971 it formed the National Left-Wing Front (*Frente de Izquierda Nacional*) together with the *Movimiento Nacionalista de Izquierda* (MNI) and the *Movimiento Campesino Tupaj Catari* (MCTC). Under the Banzer dictatorship its leaders were persecuted, imprisoned and exiled, but in 1978 it nominated its leader as a candidate to the presidential elections, the result of which was annulled. The FSBI has since remained independent of all other parties.

Orientation. Towards a social, political and economic restructuring within the national revolution "equidistant from any outside orientation".

Structure. The party has a national central committee and, below it, departmental, provincial and cantonal committees.

Membership. 150,000

Bolivian Unity Party
Partido Unión Boliviana (PUB)

Address. Pichincha 729, esq. Indaburo, La Paz, Bolivia

Leadership. Walter Gonzales Valda (l.)

History. In the 1979 presidential elections the PUB presented its leader as its candidate; he obtained 1.29 per cent of the votes cast.

Christian Democratic Party
Partido Demócrata Cristiano (PDC)

Address. Casilla 4345, La Paz, Bolivia

Leadership. Dr Luis Ossio Sanjínes (pres.); Miguel Rochas (sec.)

Founded. February 1954

History. The PDC was founded as the *Partido Social Cristiano* and assumed its present name at a party congress in November 1964. Its intellectual foundations were study centres of the Church's social doctrine, the Bolivian Catholic Action and "Integral Humanism" (a centre for the study of the philosophy of Jacques Maritain), founded by Benjamin Miguel and Remo Di Natale. In partial elections to the Chamber of Deputies in 1962 the party gained one seat (for Benjamin Miguel).

In 1966 the party took part in the Government, being given responsibility for the Ministry of Labour and Social Security, but from 1969 onwards no political parties were allowed to participate in government. Under the dictatorship of President Banzer the PDC fought for human rights, fundamental freedoms and the holding of elections, but its president, Benjamin Miguel, was exiled in 1974 and its organizing secretary, Felix Vargas, forced to leave the country shortly afterwards.

For the elections held on July 1, 1979, the party joined the *Alianza del Movimiento Nacionalista Revolucionario* (A-MNR) with four other parties—the *Movimiento Nacionalista Revolucionario* (MNR), the *Partido Revolucionario Auténtico* (PRA), the *Frente Revolucionario de Izquierda* (FRI) and the *Movimiento Revolucionario Tupac Katari* (MRTK)—and gained nine seats in the Chamber and three in the Senate. On Jan. 31, 1983, a member of the party joined the coalition Government of the Democratic Popular Unity.

Orientation. Democratic centre-left, with the aim of promoting integral development with a human and democratic content.

Structure. Democratic—with, at national level: a national committee, a national consultative council, a national disciplinary tribunal; and at territorial level: departmental, provincial and regional committees.

Membership. 50,000

International affiliations. Christian Democratic International; Christian Democratic Organization of America

---

Communist Party of Bolivia
Partido Comunista de Bolivia (PCB)

Leadership. Jorge Kolle Cueto (first sec.)

Founded. January 1950

History. The party was founded by Marxist-Leninist members of a Revolutionary Left Party (established in 1940). In 1965 the party was split into two factions, one following the Moscow line (and currently led by Kolle Cueto) and one following the Chinese Communist Party's line. Both were declared illegal, but in the 1978 elections the pro-Moscow party supported the Democratic and Popular Unity Front whose presidential candidate was Dr Hernán Siles Zuazo, and it also supported his alliance, the Democratic Popular Unity (UDP), in 1979 and 1980. From 1982 onwards the party held two portfolios (Labour, and Mines and Metallurgy) in the UDP coalition Government.

Orientation. The party emphasizes the "need for democratic struggle" and rejects a coup d'état as a means of coming to power.

Structure. The party is based on cells of not less than three members; district committees elected at congresses appoint secretariats and working commissions; the party's supreme organ is its national congress, which elects a central committee, which in turn elects a political committee and a first secretary.

Membership. 300 (est.)

International affiliations. The PCB is recognized by the Soviet-bloc Communist parties.

Democratic Popular Unity
Unidad Democrática Popular (UDP)

Leadership. Dr Hernán Siles Zuazo (l.)

Founded. April 1978

History. The UDP was formed by its leader out of his own Leftist Revolutionary Nationalist Movement (or MNRI, a faction of the main Revolutionary Nationalist Movement, MNR), the Movement of the Revolutionary Left (MIR) and the pro-Moscow Communist Party. In the 1979 presidential elections the UDP's leader gained 35.98 per cent of the votes, narrowly defeating Dr Paz Estenssoro (leader of the MNR) but failing to obtain the required 50 per cent majority for election.

In the 1980 presidential elections Dr Siles Zuazo again came first, with 38.7 per cent of the vote. During the ensuing military regime he went into exile in Peru, from which he returned on Oct. 8, 1982, i.e. after the validation of the 1980 elections, and two days later he became President of the Republic. He formed a UDP coalition Government consisting mainly of MNRI members.

Orientation. As a democratic socialist movement, the UDP advocates an expansion of the public sector of the economy and trade union independence. Dr Siles Zuazo defined the UDP's aims on Oct. 8, 1982, as being to set up "an authentically representative government of a people who are mainly workers and peasants", to end "fratricidal struggles", to renegotiate the country's foreign debt "without accepting impositions which may affect our sovereignty" and to take joint action with Peru and Colombia to suppress drug trafficking.

Historic Revolutionary Nationalist Movement
Movimiento Nacionalista Revolucionario Historico (MNRH)

Address. Jenaro Sanjinés 541, Pasaje Kuljis, La Paz, Bolivia
Leadership. Dr Victor Paz Estenssoro (l.); Edwin Rodríguez Aguirre (exec. sec.)
Founded. June 1941
History. The MNR participated in the Government of President Gualberto Villarroel, which took power in December 1943 and was overthrown in July 1946. In the May 1951 presidential elections Dr Paz Estenssoro, the MNR leader living in exile in Argentina, received the largest number of votes (though not the required absolute majority). A military junta which had seized power after the 1951 elections was itself overthrown by the MNR in April 1952, whereupon Dr Paz Estenssoro returned from exile and assumed the presidency.

The MNR subsequently introduced land reform, universal franchise, the nationalization of mines and other measures favouring the workers. President Paz Estenssoro was overthrown by a military junta led by Vice-President (General) René Barrientos in November 1964.

In 1971 the MNR supported the coup by Col. Hugo Banzer Suárez and participated in his Government until November 1973, when it declared its opposition to President Banzer, whom it later accused of being an unpopular dictator fomenting corruption and self-enrichment. The MNR nominated Dr Paz Estenssoro as its candidate for the presidential elections on July 10, 1979, but he was unsuccessful.

Following the breakaway of its left wing—which became the Leftist Revolutionary Nationalist Movement (MNRI) in 1979—the MNR became known as the Historic Revolutionary Nationalist Movement (MNRH). In the 1980 presidential elections Dr Paz Estenssoro came second with 20.1 per cent of the vote. The MNRH was one of the parties which on June 26, 1982, called on the military Government to withdraw and to recall Congress as elected in 1980.
Orientation. Nationalist, for the formation of a strong and independent national state, and populist, for an alliance of classes.
Membership 700,000

Left Revolutionary Front
Frente Revolucionaria de Izquierda (FRI)

Address. Calle Mercado 996, 2° piso, of. 2, La Paz, Bolivia
Leadership. Dr Manuel Moráles Dávila (l.)
History. The party's unsuccessful candidate in the 1978 presidential elections (later cancelled) was supported by other left-wing groups, among them the Revolutionary Workers' Party (POR), the Marxist-Leninist Communist Party (PCB-ML) and the Revolutionary Party of the Nationalist Left (PRIN).

Leftist Revolutionary Nationalist Movement
Movimiento Nacionalista Revolucionario de Izquierda (MNRI)

Leadership. Dr Hernán Siles Zuazo (l.); Mario Velarde Dorado (sec.)
Founded. 1979
History. The MNRI broke away from the Nationalist Revolutionary Movement (MNR) of Dr Paz Estenssoro and became the leading force in the Democratic Popular Unity Alliance (UDP), as whose candidate in the 1979 and 1980 presidential elections Dr Siles Zuazo obtained the greatest number of votes. After the validation of the 1980 elections in 1982 he was elected President of the Republic on Oct. 5, 1982, by 113 votes (out of 153) in Congress, and he thereupon formed a UDP coalition Government. The Cabinet was predominantly composed of MNRI members, several of whom, however, resigned from the Government in May and July 1983 over disagreements with the President's austerity programme.

Mandate of Action and National Unity
Mandato de Acción y Unidad Nacional (MAN)

Address. Calle Comercio 1057, 3ᵉʳ piso, Casilla Postal 2169, La Paz, Bolivia
Leadership. Dr Gonzalo Romero Alvarez Garcia (l.); Dr Fernando Oblitas Mendoza (sec.)
Founded. January 1972
History. MAN was formed as a civilian response to the military Government in power since 1971; currently in opposition, some of its members had earlier held posts as ministers or under-secretaries or had been parliamentarians.
Orientation. MAN stands for the development of Bolivia's potential; national

unity; social justice; the defence of human rights and the family, women and children; self-determination and non-intervention; and the restoration of Bolivia's access to the sea.

Structure. The leadership rotates between two members who together constitute the national leadership council. There are also a national consultative council, secretaries at national level and regional structures throughout the country.

Membership. 2,000

Marxist-Leninist Communist Party of Bolivia
Partido Comunista Marxista-Leninista de Bolivia (PCB-ML)

Address. Palacio Legislativo, Vice-Presidencia del Hon. Senado, Plaza Murillo, La Paz, Bolivia

Leadership. Oscar Zamora Medinacelli (first sec.)

Founded. April 1965

History. The party arose out of a split in the Communist Party of Bolivia and supports the Chinese (Maoist) Communist line. From its inception the party waged an intensive struggle against the military regimes of Presidents Barrientos, Ovando and Banzer when it was an underground organization.

In the 1978 presidential elections it supported the candidate of the Left Revolutionary Front (FRI) but in the 1979 elections it was one of the left-wing groups which supported Dr Paz Estenssoro (leader of the National Revolutionary Movement—MNR). In the 1980 elections it was part of an alliance of the MNR and the FRI.

Orientation. For its guidance the PCB-ML has adopted Mao Zedong's thought as its ideology. Its aim is the national liberation of the Bolivian people and socialism according to the people's own characteristics and the particular and concrete reality. The party stands for the self-determination of nations, non-interference by other states and a new international economic order, and it is opposed to hegemonies of the superpowers.

Movement of the Revolutionary Left
Movimiento de Izquierda Revolucionaria (MIR)

Address. Av. América 119, 2° piso, La Paz, Bolivia

Leadership. Jaime Paz Zamora (l. and Vice-President of the Republic); Antonio Aranibar Quiroga (s.g.)

Founded. September 1971

History. The MIR arose out of "the people's struggle against the fascist coup" (overthrowing President Juan José Torres in 1971) in a merger of various left-wing groups. It claims to have taken part in almost all resistance activities against the regime of President Banzer, during which it repeatedly lost its leaders. In the 1978, 1979 and 1980 presidential elections it supported the candidature of Dr Hernán Siles Zuazo, standing for a Democratic Popular Unity (UDP) front.

The MIR strongly opposed the military regime in power in 1980–82 and Jaime Paz Zamora went into exile in Panama, from where he returned to La Paz on July 13, 1982. In October of that year he was elected Vice-President of the Republic and six MIR members joined the coalition Government with Dr. Siles Zuazo. In January 1983 the six MIR ministers withdrew from the Cabinet, but in April 1984 the party resumed ministerial participation on the basis of economic policy assurances.

Orientation. Established as a national (non-communist) Marxist party, the MIR seeks to organize the middle classes in a single "Social Revolutionary Bloc" around the working class and the worker-peasant axis with a view to "the national and social liberation of the Bolivian people".

National Leftist Revolutionary Party
Partido Revolucionario de la Izquierda Nacionalista (PRIN)

Address. Colón 693, La Paz, Bolivia

Leadership. Juan Lechín Oquendo (l.)

Founded. 1964

History. The party was established by its leader (head of the Mine Workers' Federation), then Vice-President of Bolivia, after he had been expelled from the ruling National Revolutionary Movement of Dr Paz Estenssoro owing to disagreement over tin miners' demands. Sr Lechín spent many years in exile between 1965 and February 1978. The PRIN took no part in the 1966 presidential elections. In the 1978 elections it supported the presidential candidate of the Left Revolutionary Front.

Orientation. A left-wing party without specific international affiliations.

National Left-Wing Movement
Movimiento de Izquierda Nacional (MIN)

Leadership. Dr Luis Sandoval Morón (l.)

History. The party supported the policies of the Revolutionary Nationalist Movement (MNR) which came to power in 1952, and also endorsed those of President Juan José Torres, whose left-wing regime was overthrown in 1971.

Orientation. The MIN aims at being a political mass organization conducting "the struggle for national liberation from the imperialist yoke and for the building of a free and just society". It is hostile to "US imperialism" and Brazil's "expansionist sub-imperialism".

Nationalist Centre
Centro Nacionalista (CEN)

Address. Héroes del Acre 1746, oficina *La Voz del Pueblo*, La Paz, Bolivia

Leadership. Dr Roberto Zapata de la Barra (l.)

Orientation. The party supports the armed forces in their attempt to reorganize the state; it rejects both "liberal democratic bourgeois capitalism" and "Marxist scientific socialism" as historically superseded; it stands for economic nationalism which will overcome the class struggle and create an integrated society with equality of opportunity.

Nationalist Democratic Alliance
Alianza Democrática Nacionalista (ADN)

Leadership. Gen. Hugo Banzer Suárez (l.)

Founded. 1979

History. The ADN was formed by its leader to contest the 1979 presidential and congressional elections; he had been President of Bolivia from 1971 to 1978. In the presidential elections of 1979 and 1980 he came third, polling respectively 14.88 and 16.9 per cent of the vote.

The ADN at first supported the military Government which came to power after the 1980 elections but withdrew its support from it on April 14, 1981, and in the following month Gen. Banzer was expelled from the country after being accused of plotting against the Government. The ADN was one of the parties which, on June 26, 1982, called on the military Government to withdraw and to recall Congress.

Orientation. The ADN is a right-wing nationalist movement.

Nationalist Revolutionary People's Movement
Movimiento Nacionalista Revolucionario del Pueblo (MNRP)

Address. Apartado de Correo No. 3030, La Paz, Bolivia

Leadership. Jaime Arellano Castañeda (l.)

Founded. April 1965

History. The MNRP was established by four members of the *Movimiento Nacionalista Revolucionario* (MNR) led by President Victor Paz Estenssoro, who was overthrown in the military coup of November 1964. The objective of the MNRP was to fight the right-wing military dictatorship. It took part in elections in 1966 and 1978 (the latter being subsequently annulled) but boycotted those of 1979.

Orientation. A nationalist party of the democratic left, the MNRP opposes both oligarchism and colonialism, and it advocates (i) the replacement of feudal structures by a progressive system under which natural resources would be exploited mainly by the state and the public sector would be complemented by a true national bourgeoisie; (ii) an alliance of classes (and not the Marxist idea of class struggle) because the formation of a national state "requires the consensus of all classes"; and (iii) relations with all countries according to the national need, and "militant solidarity" with the non-aligned countries of the third world.

Structure. The MNRP has base units at places of residence and work. Its organization embraces a national convention, a national leader, a national political committee, a secretary-general, a national executive committee, a national executive secretary and departmental and special commands.

Membership 50,000

International affiliations. The MNRP has links with Latin American parties of the democratic left.

Offensive of the Democratic Left
Ofensiva de Izquierda Democrática (OID)

Address. Plaza Venezuela 1440, Edificio Hermann, piso 11, La Paz, Bolivia

Leadership. Luis Adolfo Siles Salinas (l.)

Founded. 1979

History. The group's leader had, as leader of the Social Democratic Party, been President of Bolivia in April-September 1969. After supporting the

Democratic Popular Unity front led by Dr Siles Zuazo (who was his half-brother) he left it shortly before the 1979 presidential elections to set up the OID. He contested the 1980 presidential elections as the candidate of the OID but obtained only 2.64 per cent of the vote.

treaty under which Bolivia lost its access to the Pacific Ocean.
Structure. A national convention every two years elects the party's national leadership.
Membership. 30,000
Publications. Eco (weekly)

Organization of Revolutionary Unity
Organización de Unidad Revolucionaria (OUR)

Address. Comercio 979, Of. 14, 1er piso, La Paz, Bolivia
Leadership. Dr Mario Lanza Suárez (s.g.)
Founded. December 1977
History. Founded as a democratic and revolutionary political force with the object of promoting and co-operating in the Bolivian revolution "interrupted by various military governments for more than 20 years", the OUR intended to be a national liberation movement based on peasants and workers, but without any international ties. It formed part of the People's Democratic Unity front (*Unidad Popular y Democrática,* UDP).
Orientation. The party stands for industrial development, the rehabilitation of public and state enterprises and increased investment and production.
Structure. Based on committees in all departments of the country.
Membership. 5,000

Party of the National Revolution
Partido de la Revolución Nacional (PRN)

Address. Av. Saavedra No. 1026 (Casilla Correo No. 8466), La Paz, Bolivia
Leadership. Rubén Arias Alvis (l.), Luis Jiménez Espinoza (s.g.)
Founded. October 1966
History. In the absence of any parliament in Bolivia when the PRN was founded, the party concentrated on preparing for the elections scheduled for 1980. For the presidential elections it supported the candidate of the Gutiérrez faction of the *Falange Socialista Boliviana,* Col. José Patiño Ayaroa, who, however, refused to take part in the elections.
Orientation. The PRN is a party of the national left with the object of defending and pursuing the process of the national revolution of April 1952.
Structure. The PRN is led by a national executive committee, and its decisions are, by a national co-ordinating committee, conveyed to all departmental party groups throughout the country.
Membership. 50,000

Party of Socialist Republican Union
Partido de la Unión Socialista Republicana (PURS)

Address. Casilla Correo 3724, La Paz, Bolivia
Leadership. Dr Constantino Carrión V. (pres.); Pedro Montaño (s.g.)
Founded. January 1964
History. The PURS was formed by followers of the earlier *Partido Republicano Saavedrista,* the *Partido Republicano Genuino* and the *Partido Socialista* (which between them had provided six Presidents of the Republic). (Before 1952 the Socialist Republican Union had held 58 seats in the Chamber of Deputies and 17 in the Senate.) As an opposition party, the PURS has fought against all dictatorship and has opposed both fascism and communism.
Orientation. The party stands for constitutional government in Bolivia and opposes any US support for dictatorial government. It also supports the revision of the 1904

Revolutionary Movement of Bolivian Indian Peasants
Movimiento Agrario Revolucionario del Campesinado Boliviano (MARC)

Address. Calle Yanacocha No. 448, Oficína No. 17, La Paz, Bolivia
Leadership. Gen. (rtd.) René Bernal Escalante (pres.); Dr José Zegarra Cerruto (exec. sec.)
Founded. June 1978
History. The Movement was formed among peasants in Punata Province, in the Cochabamba District, with the object of their liberation through a revision of the land reform by which the land would belong to those who worked it with the most advanced technology. The Movement was part of the *Alianza Popular de Integración Nacional* (APIN), which also embraced the *Unión Democrática Cristiana* (UDC) and the *Falange Socialista Boliviana* (FSB), and contested the July 1979 general elections.

Orientation. Nationalist and Christian, with the main object of liberating the peasantry.

Structure. The movement has a national convention, a national council, a national executive committee, a departmental committee and departmental and other committees.

Revolutionary Nationalist Movement—Julio
Movimiento Nacionalista Revolucionario (MNR)—Julio

Address. Calle Claudio Pinilla 1648, La Paz, Bolivia

Leadership. Rubén Julio Castro (l.)

Orientation. The party is an off-shoot of the MNR which has fought since April 1952 for "an independent national state with truly democratic institutions", and with planning for some sectors of the economy (import control, public investments, foreign exchange and prices) and nationalization of strategic sectors (minerals, hydrocarbons, steel), with the state becoming "the principal agent of development".

Revolutionary Party of the National Left—Gueiler Wing
Partido Revolucionario de Izquierda Nacional Gueiler (PRING)

Address. Calle Mercado 996, 2° piso, La Paz, Bolivia

Leadership. Lidia Gueiler Tejada (1.)

History. This party's leader was, on Aug. 4, 1979, chosen as president of the newly-elected Chamber of Deputies (Lower House of Congress), and on Nov. 16, 1979, Congress appointed her interim head of state, pending new elections to be held in 1980. She formed a coalition Government composed mainly of members of the 1979 alliance of the National Revolutionary Movement (MNR). However, in July 1980 her Government was overthrown by the armed forces led by Gen. Luis García Meza, who denounced her regime as having allowed "communism, Castroism and anarchy".

Revolutionary Struggle Workers' Party
Partido Obrero Revolucionario-Combate (PORC)

Leadership. Hugo Gonzales Moscoso (l.)

Orientation. The PORC is a dissident Trotskyist Communist party.

Revolutionary Workers' Party
Partido Obrero Revolucionario (POR)

Leadership. Guillermo Lora (l.)

History. Although outlawed in 1967, the POR supported the candidate of the Left Revolutionary Front in the 1978 presidential elections (which were annulled).

Orientation. POR is an orthodox Trotskyist Communist party.

Social Democratic Party
Partido Social Demócrata (PSD)

Address. Edificio Barrosquira, 6° piso, La Paz, Bolivia

Leadership. Dr Antonio Chiquie Dipp (l.)

Founded. 1945

History. The PSD was established by middle-class intellectuals.

Socialist Party One
Partido Socialista Uno (PS-1)

Address. Cámara de Diputados, La Paz, Bolivia

History. The party's leader, Marcelo Quiroga Santa Cruz, unsuccessfully contested the 1978 and 1979 presidential elections, gaining 4.81 per cent of the votes in the latter. In the 1980 presidential elections he obtained 8 per cent of the vote. He was assassinated in July of that year. The PS-1 was one of the parties which, on June 26, 1982, called on the military Government to withdraw and to recall the Congress elected in 1980.

Tupaj Katari Indian Movement
Movimiento Indio Tupac Katari (MITKA)

Address. Av. Eduardo Avaroa 1091, La Paz, Bolivia

Leadership. Luciano Tapía Quisbert (l.)

History. The MITKA leader was an unsuccessful candidate in the 1978 presidential elections (subsequently annulled) and also in the 1979 presidential elections, when he gained 1.93 per cent of the vote.

Tupaj Katari Revolutionary Movement
Movimiento Revolucionario Tupaj Katari (MRTK)

Address. Calle Linares esq., Sagáruaga No. 901 (Casilla Postal No. 3636), La Paz, Bolivia

Leadership. Juan Condori Uruchi (pres.); Dr Clemente Ramos Flores (first nat. exec.); Daniel Calle M. (second nat. exec.)

Founded. May 1978

History. The MRTK has its origins in independence movements started under Spanish rule in 1781 (by Tupaj Katari in Bolivia and Tupaj Amaru in Peru) and continued as peasant movements in 1946-52, leading to land reform, universal suffrage and the nationalization of mines between 1952 and 1964, and to the creation of a Tupaj Katari Confederation in 1971.

The MRTK was one of the founders of the Democratic and Popular Unity Front in May 1978, and in the 1979 presidential election it was one of the component parts of the Alliance of the National Revolutionary Movement (MNR), whose leader and presidential candidate was Dr Victor Paz Estenssoro.

Orientation. A left-wing national democratic organization for all classes, based mainly on the peasants and other exploited strata, with the object of establishing a just society, majority rule and self-determination of the people.

Structure. The MRTK has a national executive committee (consisting of the three leaders named above) and executive committees at departmental, provincial and cantonal level.

Membership. 80,000

Publications. *Tupaj Katari* (monthly), 15,000

Workers' Vanguard Party
Partido de Vanguardia Obrera (VO)

Address. Plaza Venezuela 1452, La Paz, Bolivia

Leadership. Filemón Escobar (l.)

History. In the 1979 presidential elections the VO presented its own candidate, who came last in the poll, with 1.13 per cent of the votes cast.

Other Parties

The following parties have also been registered at the National Electoral Court:

Partido Revolucionario de los Trabajadores de Bolivia Romero (PRTBR). *Address.*

Calle Pisagua No. 385, La Paz. *Leader.* Rubén Romero Equino

Partido Socialista Aponte (PSA). *Leader.* Dr Orlando Capriles Villazon

Bloque de la Vanguardia Revolucionaria (BVR). *Leader.* Amadeo Vargas Arce

Partido de la Izquierda Revolucionaria (PIR). *Leader.* Dr Ricardo Anaya Arce

Partido Obrero Revolucionario Trotskista Posadista (PORTP). *Address.* Calle Goitia No. 13, La Paz. *Leader.* Carlos Flores Bedregal

Movimiento Popular de Liberación Nacional (MPLN). *Leader.* Ramiro Velasco Romero

Partido Liberal. *Address.* Venancio Burgoa 947, La Paz. *Leader.* Dr Eduardo Montes y Montes

Alianza Revolucionaria Barrientista (ARB). *Address.* Ed. Asbún nuevo, 2° piso, La Paz. *Leader.* Dr Jorge Burgoa Alarcon

Vanguardia Comunista del Partido Obrero Revolucionario (VCPOR). *Address.* Manuel Loza 2004, La Paz. *Leader.* Victor Sossa

Partido Revolucionario Auténtico Rios (PRAR). *Address.* Edificio Conavi, of. 3, piso 11, La Paz. *Leader.* Jorge Rios Gamarra

Partido Socialista Tito Atahuichi (PSTA). *Address.* Edificio Terrázas, calle Yanacocha No. 448, La Paz. *Leader.* Dr Sabino Tito Atahuichi

Partido Social Cristiano (PSC). *Address.* Casilla 8152, La Paz. *Leader.* Jaime Humérez Seleme

Alianza de Izquierda Nacional (ALIN) *Address.* Ed. Cosmos, of. 4, La Paz. *Leader.* Ruben Sánchez Valdivia

Partido Nacionalista del Pueblo (PNP). *Address.* Av. del Ejercito 1068, La Paz. *Leader.* Guillermo Mendoza Riglos

Partido Barrientista Auténtico (PBA). *Leader.* René Alvarez Puente

Organización Socialista de los Trabajadores (OST). *Address.* Gral. Lanza 1866, La Paz. *Leader.* Sonia Montaño

Unión Democrática Cristiana (UDC). *Address.* Calle Yanacocha 448, of. 20, La Paz. *Leader.* Freddy Vargas Méndez

Partido Revolucionario de la Izquierda Nacional Laboral (PRIN-L). *Address.* Casilla No. 1657, La Paz. *Leader.* Edwin Moller (g.s., representing collective leadership)

Movimiento Nacional Tupaj Katari (MNTK). *Address.* Calle Montaño 420, Figueroa 680. *Leader.* José Ticona

Movimiento Revolucionario Espartaco (MRE). *Address.* Villa Fatima, Calle 17 No. 1774, La Paz. *Leader.* Dulfredo Rúa

Bophuthatswana

Capital: Mmabatho   Pop. 1,500,000

The Republic of Bophuthatswana, whose independence is recognized only by the governments of South Africa, Ciskei, Transkei and Venda, has an executive President who is appointed by the country's Legislative Assembly and acts on the advice of an Executive Council (cabinet) appointed and headed by him. Of the unicameral Legislative Assembly's 105 members, 30 are nominated by regional authorities, 72 are elected by citizens over the age of 18 years (including those resident outside Bophuthatswana) and three are nominated by the President.

In elections held on Oct. 19, 1982, the ruling Bophuthatswana Democratic Party gained an overwhelming majority of seats.

Bophuthatswana Democratic Party (BDP)

Address. P.O. Box 10, Montshioa, 8681, Bophuthatswana

Leadership. President Lucas M. Mangope (l.); M. A. Kgomongwe (s.g.)

Founded. November 1974

History. The party was formed by members of the former ruling Bophuthatswana National Party (which was considered to have become ineffective) and immediately gained the adherence of a majority of the members of the then Legislative Council. The BDP leader, Chief Mangope (who has been the homeland's Chief Minister since 1972), led Bophuthatswana to independence from South Africa in December 1977, the BDP having in pre-independence elections in August 1977 won a large majority in the new Legislative Assembly.

Orientation. The party, in seeking to promote the interests and welfare of the people of Bophuthatswana, accepts the country's independence Constitution and advocates "an equitable distribution of wealth" and "the elimination of all forms of discrimination based on race, colour, culture, creed or sex".

In 1982 the party reaffirmed its belief in civil rights, including the right of Bophuthatswana citizens to work in South Africa and to renounce their Bophuthatswana citizenship. The party also recognized chieftainship as an integral part of the country's social order and discipline.

Structure. The party has local branches, regions, a head committee and a congress.

Membership. 600,000

National Seoposengwe Party (NSP)

Address. Mmabatho, Bophuthatswana

Leadership. Chief H. T. R. Maseloane (l.)

Founded. 1976

History. The NSP gained five of the 48 elective seats in the Legislative Assembly elected in August 1977 and thus became the official Opposition (holding also one out of 8 nominated seats).

Orientation. The NSP rejects the South African Government's "Black homelands" concept and advocates the retention of South African citizenship for inhabitants of these homelands. It accepts independence only on condition that Bophuthatswana's territory becomes one single unit.

Botswana

Capital: Gaborone   Pop. 1,020,000

In the Republic of Botswana the executive President is responsible to the National Assembly of 42 members, of whom 32 are elected by universal adult suffrage of citizens above the age of 21 years and in single-member constituencies. Of the other members, four are specially chosen by all members of the Assembly, four nominated by the President, and both the President and the Attorney-General are ex-officio members. There is also a House of Chiefs with advisory capacity, consisting of the chiefs of the eight principal tribes and four members elected by sub-chiefs.

Elections held for the National Assembly on Oct. 20, 1979, gave the Botswana Democratic Party 29 seats, the Botswana National Front two and the Botswana People's Party one in a 60 per cent poll.

Botswana Democratic Party (BDP)

Address. Tsholetsa House, P.O. Box 28, Gaborone, Botswana

Leadership. Dr Q. K. J. Masire (pres.); P. S. Mnusi (ch.); D. K. Kwelagobe (s.g.)

Founded. 1962

History. The party has been in power since March 1965, when it gained 27 out of 31 seats in the country's Parliament, and it took Botswana into independence in 1966.

Orientation. To follow "certain basic national principles of democracy, development, self-reliance and unity" which, "when applied in practice, are designed to achieve *Kagisano* social harmony".

Structure. The BDP is founded on sub-wards, branches (constituencies), regions and the national congress. There is a central committee drawing up party policies and co-ordinating party activities.

Publications. *Therisanyo* (Consultation), 3,000

Botswana Independence Party (BIP)

Address. P.O. Box 53, Serowe, Botswana

Leadership. Motsamai K. Mpho (pres.); Emmanuel R. Mokobi (s.g.)

Founded. August 1962

History. The BIP was formed by a breakaway movement from the then Bechuanaland People's Party, and it elected as its president Motsamai Mpho (who had in 1960 been deported to Bechuanaland from South Africa, where he had been an active member of the banned African National Congress of South Africa and had been among 156 persons arrested and tried for treason). The BIP was among the first three parties which contested the 1965 (pre-independence) elections but gained no seats; in 1969 its president gained a seat in Parliament, which he lost in 1979.

Orientation. "To awaken the political consciousness of the people of Botswana; to fight for immediate economic freedom of Botswana so as to be free from the economic pressure of the neighbouring White states; and to co-operate fully with other African independent countries so as to rid Africa of all forms of foreign domination."

Structure. The BIP's constitution provides for four national leaders, 10 national executive members, a youth league and a women's league.

Membership. 60,000

International affiliations. World Council of Peace; Afro-Asian People's Solidarity Organization

---

Botswana Liberal Party (BLP)

Leadership. Martin Chakaliso (l.)

Founded. 1983

Orientation. Speaking at the party's first rally following its registration, Martin

Chakaliso said in February 1984 that the BLP had been formed because Botswana had been stagnant socially and economically since independence. He pledged that the party would not seek alliance with other opposition parties because they had no base or financial standing.

Botswana National Front (BNF)

Address. P.O. Box 42, Mahalapye, Botswana

Leadership. Dr Kenneth Koma (l.); Mareledi Giddie (sec.)

Founded. October 1967

History. The party, in an attempt to form one strong opposition party, was founded by former members of the Botswana People's party, which had split into three factions. It first contested parliamentary elections in 1969, when it gained three seats on a platform of Africanization of government posts (but also of maintaining friendly relations with South Africa). Since 1974 the party has held two seats in the National Assembly, and in 1979 its leader unsuccessfully contested the presidential elections as the sole opposition candidate and the first ever nominated.

Orientation. The BNF is a social democratic party.

Structure. The BNF embraces three main elements—conservative/patriotic members, young people attracted to socialism, and petty bourgeois members. It has, as semi-autonomous organizations, a youth federation, a women's league and trade unions.

Membership. 10,000

Publications. *Puo-phaa* (Straight Talk), official organ; *Moagi* (vernacular paper)

Botswana People's Party (BPP)

Address. P.O. Francistown, Botswana

Leadership. P. K. Pudiephatshwa (sec.)

Founded. January 1960

History. The BPP was established with Philip G. Matante, a former member of the Pan Africanist Congress of South Africa (banned in that country), as its leader. In the first general elections held in the then Bechuanaland in March 1965 the BPP gained three seats in Parliament, whereupon its leader (who died in October 1979) became Leader of the Opposition. The party's representation in Parliament was reduced to two members in 1974 and to one in 1979.

Orientation. As a Pan Africanist party the BPP had as its first objective the early achievement of independence by Botswana.

Publications. *Masa* (monthly)

Botswana Progressive Union

Address. P.O. Box 50, Mahalapye, Botswana

Leadership. D. K. Kwele (pres.); G. G. Bagwasi (ch.); R. K. Monyatsiwa (s.g.)

Founded. 1982

History. This radical formation has been formed with the aim of challenging the political predominance of the Botswana Democratic Party.

Brazil

Capital: Brasília   Pop. 130,000,000

The Federative Republic of Brazil consists of 23 states, one Federal District and two territories. Legislative power is exercised by a National Congress consisting of (i) a Chamber of Deputies of 479 members elected for four years by universal adult suffrage and (ii) a Senate of 69 members elected for eight-year terms by direct secret ballot (each state being represented by three senators), one-third of its members being elected after four years and the other two-thirds after another four years. Executive power is exercised by the President, aided by ministers of state; he is elected for six years by an electoral college consisting of all members of the National Congress and delegates appointed by the state legislatures. A Vice-President is elected similarly.

Brazil has been under effective military rule since 1964 and until late 1979 had a limited party system under which, in addition to the government party, only one opposition formation was officially authorized. A reform bill approved by Congress on Nov. 22, 1979, provided for the dissolution of the two official parties and laid down rules for the introduction of a multi-party system under which new parties would be permitted provided that they guaranteed their allegiance to the "democratic system"; any party found guilty of "racial, religious or class bias" or having links with "foreign governments, bodies or parties" would not be recognized. In order to be formally constituted any new party has to win 5 per cent of the vote at the next elections spread over at least nine states, or have the support in Congress of 10 per cent of the members of each House.

Elections are held under a system of simple proportional representation, with each state being one multi-member electoral district and entitled to one federal deputy for every 300,000 inhabitants up to 25 deputies, and to one additional deputy for every 1,000,000 inhabitants thereafter. Voting is compulsory for citizens between the ages of 18 and 65 and optional for those over 65 years. In elections held in 1982 simultaneously for the posts of state governor, federal senator, federal deputy, state deputy, mayor and city councillor, members of the electorate were obliged to cast their vote for candidates of one party only by writing six names on a blank ballot paper provided. Ballot papers in favour of candidates for more than one party were void; and those listing fewer than six names of candidates of the same party were counted as votes for that party's candidates in the other posts. Parties were not allowed to form electoral alliances, and all parties were obliged to field candidates in all areas where they maintained a local branch.

In elections held on Nov. 15, 1982 (the first full multi-party contest to be held since 1962), parties gained seats in the Chamber of Deputies as follows: Social Democratic Party 234, Party of the Brazilian Democratic Movement 200, Democratic Labour Party 24, Brazilian Labour Party 13 and Workers' Party 8.

Brazilian Labour Party
Partido Trabalhista Brasileiro (PTB)

Leadership. (Sra) Ivete Vargas, Airton Soares (leaders)

Founded. 1980

History. A party of this name was first formed in 1945 by supporters of the late President Getulio Vargas (the uncle of Ivete Vargas), who was in office in 1930-45 and 1950-54. That party had supported his successor, President Juscelino Kubitschek (1955-60), and was the effective government party under President João Goulart (1961-64), whereafter it was banned in 1965, and its leaders went into exile. Among them was Leonel da Moura Brizola, who returned to Brazil after a partial amnesty of August 1979; however, in 1980 he founded the rival Democratic Labour party (see separate entry). By the end of 1980 the PTB had 334 branches.

Orientation. The party has called for a new constitution providing for a democratic multi-party system and political representation and rights for workers and students.

Democratic Labour Party
Partido Democratico Trabalhista (PDT)

Leadership. Leonel da Moura Brizola (l.); Carlos Augusto de Souza (pres. and s.g.)

Founded. June 26, 1980

History. This party was formed as an offshoot of the Brazilian Labour Party (see separate entry). Initially it was supported by 10 deputies. In the 1982 elections it gained 24 seats in the Chamber of Deputies, where it thus became the strongest of the three workers' parties. In the same elections the PDT leader obtained the governorship of Rio de Janeiro, the party's stronghold.

Orientation. The PDT regards itself as social democratic, has called for a programme for full employment and redistribution of income, has opposed internal colonialism and advocates land reform as well as industrial and agricultural production to meet the people's needs.

Party of the Brazilian Democratic Movement
Partido do Movimento Democrático Brasileiro (PMDB)

Leadership. Ulisses Guimarães, Teotonio Vilela, Miguel Arrões (leaders); Francisco Pinto (s.g.)

Founded. 1980

History. The PMDB was set up as the successor to the Brazilian Democratic Movement (MDB) which had been the opposition party under the two-party system in force from 1965 to the end of 1979. It was supported by about 100 members of the Chamber of Deputies and 20 senators (and also tacitly by Brazil's two illegal Communist parties). By the end of 1980 the PMDB had a total of 2,127 branches. In December 1981 it absorbed the Popular Party (see separate entry). In the 1982 elections it gained nine of the 23 state governorships.

Orientation. Said to represent the moderate elements of the former MDB, the party is Christian democratic and covers a wide spectrum from liberal conservatism to communism.

Popular Party
Partido Popular (PP)

Leadership. Tancredo Neves (l.)

Founded. January 1980

History. The PP was formed by dissident members of the National Renewal Alliance (Arena) which had been the government party from 1965 until 1979, when it was dissolved. By the end of 1980 the PP had a total of 869 branches, and by 1981 it had the support of 66 deputies and 10 senators. In February 1981 it decided to co-operate with the Party of the Brazilian Democratic Movement (PMDB) in opposing the official Social Democratic Party in the 1982 elections. In view of the ban on electoral alliances the PP and the PMDB agreed on Dec. 20, 1981, on the incorporation of the PP in the PMDB (although at a PP conference more than one-third of the delegates had voted against such incorporation). The two parties' merger was approved by the Supreme Electoral Tribunal on March 2, 1982.

Orientation. The PP was centrist in its policy aspirations.

Social Democratic Party
Partido Democrático Social (PDS)

Leadership. José Sarney (pres.); Prisco Vianna (s.g.)

Founded. 1980

History. The PDS is the direct successor to the Alliance for National Renewal (Arena) which was the government party from 1965 until 1979, when it was dissolved. It is built on Arena's organization, and by the end of 1980 it had a total of 3,066 branches. It was then reported to have the support of 213 of the then 420 deputies in the Chamber of Deputies and of 37 out of the 60 senators (whereas Arena had been supported by 231 deputies and 40 senators). After the 1982 elections, in which it did not gain an absolute majority in the Chamber of Deputies, it remained the strongest party and continued to be the instrument of the military-backed President to control the legislative process. In the 1982 elections the PDS also won 12 of the country's 24 governorships.

Orientation. The PDS is Christian demo-cratic and conservative, in favour of economic development and the attraction of foreign capital.

Workers' Party
Partido dos Trabalhadores (PT)

Leadership. Luis Inácio da Silva (Lula) (l.)

Founded. 1978
History. The party was established as an independent labour party with trade union support by da Silva, who had been a member of the original Brazilian Labour Party (formed in 1945 and the effective ruling party under President João Goulart in 1961–64). The PT also enjoys support from sectors of the Roman Catholic Church. Early in 1981 a group of 10 of its members were sentenced to imprisonment for from two to $3\frac{1}{2}$ years and disqualified from political activities for five years.

Orientation. The PT has called for a more equitable distribution of income, the creation of jobs, effective land reform and the establishment of real democratic freedoms. It claims to be neither socialist nor revolutionary but has called for "a society without exploiters and exploited".

Structure. The PT is organized in cells. By the end of 1980 it had branches in 625 (out of 3,959) municipalities and in 13 (out of 23) states.

Brunei

Capital: Bandar Seri Begawan   Pop. 215,000

The Sultanate of Brunei is an independent sovereign state within the Commonwealth. It has a Privy Council, a Council of Ministers and a Legislative Council of 20 members, all nominated by the Sultan. There has been a state of emergency in force since 1962, when the People's Party of Brunei (PRB—formed in 1959 and also known as the *Party Ra'ayet*) won all elective seats in the Legislative Council and thereafter staged a revolt which was suppressed.

Brunei People's Independence Front
Barisan Kemerdeka'an Ra'ayat Brunei (Bakar)

Leadership. Zainal Abidin Puteh (pres.)
Founded. 1966
History. Formed as an amalgamation of all former parties, Bakar has been the only party in Brunei since the rebellion of

1962, the Brunei People's Party having been banned in December of that year. As no legislative elections have been held since 1965 (when all but one of the 10 elected candidates were independents), there has been no opportunity for the party to test the extent of its political support in the country at large.

Bulgaria

Capital: Sofia   Pop. 8,900,000

The 1971 Constitution of the People's Republic of Bulgaria confirmed the Communist Party in the leading role which it had occupied since formally coming to power in 1947. Under the Constitution a single-chamber National Assembly (*Narodno Sobranie*) of 400 members is elected for five years from areas of equal population by direct, secret and universal suffrage (with all persons above the age of 18 years being entitled to vote or to be elected), with an absolute majority being required at a first ballot, failing which further ballots may be held until this requirement is met.

According to the official results of elections to the National Assembly held on June 7, 1981, 99.6 per cent of the voters had taken part in the poll and 99.93 per cent of them had cast their vote for the 400 candidates nominated by the Fatherland Front mass organization, of whom 271 were members of the Communist Party, 99 of the Agrarian People's Party and the remaining 30 without party affiliation.

Bulgarian Agrarian People's Party (BAPP)

Address. 1 Yank Zabunov St., Sofia 1000, Bulgaria

Leadership. Peter Tanchev (sec., First Deputy President of the State Council)

Founded. December 1899

History. One of the oldest agrarian parties in the world, the BAPP was created to express "the aspirations and desires of the peasant masses", which made up 80 per cent of the country's pre-1914 population. After parliamentary elections an independent BAPP Government ruled Bulgaria in 1920–23 but was overthrown by a right-wing military coup in June 1923.

The BAPP participated in the Fatherland Front which came to power in June 1944 (see entry below for Bulgarian Communist Party), but subsequently became split between those favouring continuance of the Front in the post-war period and the rightist Agrarians led by Nicola Petkov who refused to participate in the joint list of the Fatherland Front in the November 1946 elections. Later the greater part of his supporters joined the BAPP and the Fatherland Front. Official results of the 1946 elections gave the BAPP 86 per cent of the vote. Since 1946 the BAPP has been represented in the Government, and it currently has, in addition to 99 members in the 400-seat National Assembly, three members of the State Council and four ministers in the Council of Ministers.

Membership. 120,000

Publications. Zemedelsko Zname (daily); Zemya i progress (a journal)

International affiliations. The BAPP has "contacts with a total of 130 parties and organizations in more than 80 countries".

Bulgarian Communist Party
Bulgarska Komunisticheska Partia

Address. Deveto Septemvri Square, Sofia 1000, Bulgaria

Leadership. Todor Zhivkov (first sec. of central committee and politburo member); Grisha Filipov, Pencho Kubadinski, Stanko Todorov, Gen. Dobri Dzhurov, Petur Mladenov, Ognyan Doinov, Milko Balev, Todor Bozhinov, Chudomir Aleksandrov, Yordan Yotov (full politburo members)

Founded. July 1891

History. The party traces its descent from the Bulgarian Social Democratic Party founded in 1891, which as early as 1903 expelled "opportunists" from its ranks and which, as a revolutionary Marxist party, stood on the left wing of the pre-1914 Second International. The Bulgarian Communist Party (BCP) as such dates from 1919, in which year it was a founder member of the Third (Communist) International or Comintern—the non-Communist wing of the Bulgarian socialist movement continuing as the BSDP.

Having organized armed opposition to a succession of right-wing regimes in the inter-war period, the BCP played a leading role in the anti-Nazi resistance during World War II (for most of which Bulgaria was allied to Germany), its activities being directed from Moscow by Georgi Dimitrov (the Bulgarian secretary-general of the Comintern). The BCP initiated the formation of the Fatherland Front with left-wing Agrarians, Social Democrats and others which organized partisan resistance from 1943 and eventually seized power on Sept. 9, 1944, with the backing of the Red Army. In the following three years the Communists consolidated their position, Dimitrov becoming Prime Minister following the October 1946 elections and the rump of the BSDP being merged with the BCP in 1947. These events led in December 1947 to the formal establishment of a people's democracy enshrining the "dictatorship of the proletariat".

Following his death in 1949 Dimitrov was succeeded by the pro-Soviet Vlko Chervenkov, who became party leader in 1950. In 1954 Chervenkov was in turn succeeded as party leader by Todor Zhivkov (also pro-Soviet), who also assumed the premiership following the 8th BCP congress in 1962 and whose leadership since then has been unchallenged.

Orientation. The ultimate aim of the BCP is the construction of a communist society in Bulgaria.

Structure. The BCP is structured on the principle of democratic centralism and its supreme organs are the congress, and between congress sessions its central committee, which elects from among its members a politburo and a secretariat. National conferences and plenums are convened between congresses. The party's basic unit is the party branch and there are municipal, city, district and regional BCP organizations.

Membership. 825,876 (March 1981)

Publications. *Rabotnichesko Delo* (daily), 750,000–800,000; *Novo Vremé* (theoretical magazine)

Burma

Capital: Rangoon Pop. 34,200,000

The Socialist Republic of the Union of Burma is, under its Constitution approved in a referendum in December 1973, a one-party socialist state with a People's Assembly (*Pyithu Hluttaw*) whose 475 members have been approved by the ruling Burma Socialist Programme Party (Lanzin Party). The country has a President (who is chairman of a State Council) and a Cabinet (Council of Ministers) elected by the People's Assembly and headed by a Prime Minister.

The candidates nominated for the People's Assembly by the Burma Socialist Programme Party were most recently endorsed in elections held on Oct. 4-18, 1981, with the minimum age of voters being 18 years.

Burma Socialist Programme Party (BSPP)

Leadership. President Ne Win (ch. of central executive committee); U Aye Ko, Brig.-Gen. Sein Lwin (joint s.gs.)

Founded. July 1962

History. The party was formed by the Revolutionary Council (led by Gen. Ne Win), which had assumed power in March 1962, in order to implement its programme of "Burmese socialism", which was to modernize agricultural production and to develop appropriate industries in which private enterprise would be allowed to play a role. Under Burma's 1974 Constitution the BSPP is the country's "only political party leading the state", and under an order of the Council of State issued in August 1976 it was reaffirmed that "the Council of State and the central organs of power shall accept the leadership of the BSPP central committee and central executive committee", and that party leadership should be accepted by administrative councils at all other levels.

Structure. The party is organized at ward, village and district level; it has a central committee from which a 15-member central executive committee is elected; and a congress is its supreme body.

Publications. Lanzin Thadin (Party News, twice a month); *Party Affairs Journal* (monthly); *International Affairs Journal* (monthly)

Burundi

Capital: Bujumbura   Pop. 4,480,000

The Republic of Burundi has an executive President elected by universal adult suffrage for a five-year term, the sole candidate for this office being the president of the *Union pour le Progrès National* (UPRONA, the country's only legal political organization) and a 65-member National Assembly, to which 52 members are elected for a five-year term by universal adult suffrage and 13 are nominated by the President. In parliamentary elections held in October 1982 each elective seat was contested by two UPRONA candidates.

Union for National Progress
Union pour le Progrès National (UPRONA)

Address. B.P. 1810, Bujumbura, Burundi
Leadership. President J. B. Bagaza (ch.)
Founded. 1959
History. From its foundation by Prince Rwagasore, UPRONA fought against the Belgian colonial power for immediate independence; in 1961 it gained an over-whelming election victory, obtaining 58 out of 64 seats in the Legislative Assembly, whereupon it formed the first Government of an autonomous Burundi.

After the country had achieved full independence in July 1962, UPRONA again won a majority in elections to the National Assembly in 1965, and after the overthrow of the monarchy on Nov. 28, 1966, it was proclaimed the country's sole political party. However, it remained ineffectual until 1976 when it was reorganized as a party standing for "the sovereignty of the people expressed by a democratic process through democratic centralism".

Orientation. The party stands for "the creation of a just society in which all exploitation of man by man shall be prohibited" and seeks to apply socialist principles to African conditions.

Structure. The party is organized at five levels—cell, ward, commune, province and nation. There is a committee at each level, and also a national permanent secretariat which controls the committees as directed by the central committee of the party (which in December 1979 replaced a Supreme Council of the Revolution).

Membership. Over 1,200,000
International affiliations. UPRONA has "relations with the progressive parties of Africa, Asia and Eastern Europe and with the national liberation movements".

Cameroon

Capital: Yaoundé   Pop. 8,600,000

The United Republic of Cameroon is a one-party state which has, in addition to an executive President elected for a five-year term by popular vote and a Cabinet whose members must not be members of Parliament, a 120-member National Assembly (*Assemblée Nationale*) elected by proportional representation for a five-year term by universal suffrage; voters must be at least 21 years old and must have been resident in their constituency for at least six months.

In elections to the National Assembly, held on May 29, 1983, the list of candidates submitted by the Cameroon National Union (*Union Nationale Camerounaise,* UNC) was approved by 99.99 per cent of the voters in a turnout of 99.33 per cent, according to the official result.

Cameroon National Union
Union Nationale Camerounaise (UNC)

Address. B.P. 867, Yaoundé, Cameroon
Leadership. President Paul Biya (nat. pres.); Sengat Kuoh (pol. sec.)
Founded. Sept. 1966
History. The party was created in a merger of the country's leading parties—the *Union Camerounaise,* the Kamerun National Democratic Party, the Kamerun United Congress and the Kamerun People's National Convention—as sole legal party throughout both East and West Cameroon, which together became the United Republic of Cameroon in 1972.

Orientation. The party's aim is "to establish the union of all Cameroonians in peace, justice and solidarity". It stands for "planned liberalism", the balanced development of the nation and self-sufficiency; and for non-alignment, national independence and non-exclusive international co-operation.
Structure. The party is built up on cells, base committees, sub-sections and sections (corresponding to wards, villages, districts and departments), and its national organs are a congress, a national council, a central committee and a national political bureau.
Publications. L'Unité (monthly)

Canada

Capital: Ottawa   Pop. 25,000,000

The Dominion of Canada, a member of the Commonwealth with the British monarch as head of state, has a Governor-General representing the Queen and a Parliament consisting of (i) a Senate of 104 members appointed by the Governor-General (and serving until retirement) and (ii) a House of Commons (*Chambre de Communes*) of 282 members (since the 1979 elections) elected for five years by universal suffrage of citizens over the age of 18 years under a simple-majority system in single-member constituencies with an average of 52,000 voters each. Federally-registered political parties enjoy election expense privileges involving tax deductions and reimbursement from public funds for part of campaign expenses, which are limited by law.

The state gives indirect financial support to any party which meets certain fundamental requirements (by allowing individuals tax credits for gifts up to $500); to qualify, a party must either have one representative in Parliament or contest at least 50 electoral districts. The campaign expenditure of individual candidates is limited by law. The candidate has to make a deposit of $200 which is forfeited if he fails to win 15 per cent of the vote. Candidates who pass this barrier and meet certain other requirements are reimbursed by the state for a percentage of their electoral costs.

Following general elections held on Feb. 18, 1982, and several by-elections, seats in the federal House of Commons were at the end of August 1983 distributed as follows: Liberal Party (LP) 147, Progressive Conservative Party (PCP) 103, New Democratic Party (NDP) 31, independent 1, Social Credit Party (SCP) 0.

In Canada's 10 provinces seats in the legislatures were distributed as follows as a result of elections the dates of which are shown in parentheses: *Alberta* (Nov. 2, 1982)—PCP 75, NDP 1, independents (former SCP members) 2; *British Columbia* (May 5, 1983)—SCP 35, NDP 22; *Manitoba* (Nov. 17, 1981)—NDP 34, PCP 23; *New Brunswick* (Oct. 12, 1982)—PCP 39, LP 18, NDP 1; *Newfoundland* (April 6, 1982)—PCP 44, LP 8; *Nova Scotia* (Oct. 6, 1981)—PCP 37, LP 13, NDP 1, independent 1; *Ontario* (March 19, 1981)—PCP 70, LP 34, NDP 21; *Prince Edward Island* (Sept. 27, 1982)—PFP 21, LP 11; *Quebec* (April 13, 1981)—*Parti Québécois* 80, LP 42; *Saskatchewan* (April 6, 1982)—PCP 55, NDP 9.

In Yukon Territory elections to the Territorial Council held on June 7, 1982, resulted as follows: PCP 9, NDP 6, independent 1.

Communist Party of Canada

Address. 24 Cecil St., Toronto, M4K 3P3, Canada

Leadership. William Kashtan (l. and g.s.)

Founded. June 1921

History. Founded in illegality, the party became legal as the Workers' Party of Canada in 1922, reassumed the name of Communist Party in 1924, was illegal between 1931 and 1935, and again from 1940. It reconstituted itself in 1943 as the (legal) Labour-Progressive Party, which subsequently held seats in the House of Commons (one in 1943-47) and provincial Assemblies (two in Ontario until 1951 and one until 1955; one in Manitoba until 1958). It again became the Communist Party of Canada in 1959.

Orientation. The party advocates a constitution based on "equal voluntary partnership of two nations in an independent Canada", with public ownership of natural resources and energy, proclaiming Canada a nuclear-weapons-free zone, withdrawal of Canada from NATO and the North American Air Defence Command (NORAD), and eventually a socialist Canada. Short-term aims include the curbing of the powers of monopoly and of multinational corporations, the defence of vital interests of the working people and an end to US economic control.

Structure. The basic unit is the party club, and the highest organ is the convention, held every second year to elect a central committee which elects a central executive committee. Communists in Quebec are organized in the *Parti Communiste du Québec*, which follows the party's programme.

Membership. Under 5,000

Publications. *Canadian Tribune* (weekly); *Combat* (Quebec party organ); *Pacific Tribune* (British Columbia); *New Horizons* (Young Communist League); *Communist Viewpoint* (theoretical organ)

International affiliations. The party is recognized by the Communist parties of the Soviet-bloc countries.

Communist Party of Canada (Marxist-Leninist)

Address. Box 264, Adelaide Station, Toronto, Ontario, M5C 2J4, Canada

Leadership. Hardial Bains (g.s.)

Founded. March 1970

History. The party has sought to carry on educational, agitational and organizational work in major cities and regions. It is unrepresented in the Canadian Parliament.

Orientation. Advocating "the road of Marx, Engels, Lenin and Stalin", the party is "opposed to the revision of Marxism by present-day Soviet Union, China, Yugoslavia, Eurocommunism and the Soviet Union satellite bloc".

Structure. Democratic centralist.

Publications. The Marxist-Leninist (daily)

Green Party of Canada

Address. No. 214, 1956 West Broadway, Vancouver, BC, V6J 1Z2, Canada

Founded. November 1983

History. Established at a convention attended by 181 delegates from provincial green groups, the party aims to present at least 50 candidates in the next federal elections.

Orientation. The party's basic precepts are ecology, non-violence, grassroots democracy, human rights and equality.

Liberal Party of Canada
Parti Libéral du Canada

Address. 102 Bank Street, Ottawa, Ont. K1P 5N4, Canada

Leadership. John Turner (l.); Iona Campagnolo, PC (pres.); John Petryshyn (sec.)

Founded. 1867

History. The party was first in power under Alexander Mackenzie in 1873-78, thereafter in 1896-1911 under Sir Wilfried Laurier, in 1921-30 (except for a short period in 1926) under Mackenzie King, and in 1935-48 again under Mackenzie King and subsequently, until 1957, under Louis St Laurent. The party was returned to power under Lester Pearson in 1963; Pierre Trudeau became Prime Minister in 1968, held office until May 1979 and returned to power in February 1980. There are Liberal parties in each of Canada's 10 provinces, but none was in office in August 1983.

Orientation. A party of the centre which believes in the freedom of the individual, equality of access to opportunity, and social reform. It has expressed strong support for the UN campaign for world disarmament.

Structure. The party has a national executive consisting of elected office bearers and the presidents of the provincial parties as well as officers of the women's and youth commissions. The Liberal associations in the provinces are member organizations of the national party. For the purpose of reporting the raising and dispensing of party funds under the Election Expenses Act there is a Federal Liberal Agency.

Membership. 4,000,000 (est.)

Publications. Ad Lib; Policy Newsletter

International affiliations. Liberal International

Libertarian Party of Canada

Address. P.O.B. 190, Adelaide Station, Toronto, Ont. M5C 2J1, Canada

Leadership. Neil L. Reynolds (l.); Christian Sorensen (pres.)

Founded. 1933

National Movement of Quebeckers
Mouvement National des Québécois

Address. 82 ouest, rue Sherbrooke, Montreal, Quebec, H2X 1X3, Canada

---

National Union
L'Union Nationale

Address. 515 est Grande Allée, Quebec, G1R 2J5, Canada

Leadership. Jean-Marc Béliveau (l.)

Founded. 1936

History. The party was formed by Nationalists, Conservatives and dissident Liberals in the Province of Quebec, its first leader being Prof. Maurice Le Noblet Duplessis, who was Premier of Quebec in 1936-39 and from 1944 until his death in 1959. In the 1960 elections the party's strength in the National Assembly of Quebec was reduced from 72 (out of 93) seats to 43 (out of 95), the percentage of its votes falling from 52 in 1956 to 47 in 1960. In the 1962 elections its share fell further to 31 seats and 42.2 per cent of the vote. In 1966, however, it gained 55 (out of 107) seats in the Assembly and thereupon again formed a provincial Government. In 1970 the party was reduced to 17 (out of 108) seats in the Assembly (and 20 per cent of the vote).

In the 1973 provincial elections the party gained no seat, but it obtained one in a 1974 by-election. In the 1976 provincial elections the party returned to the Assembly with 11 (out of 110) members (having gained 18 per cent of the vote), but it lost all 11 seats in April 1981. (The party had not been represented in the federal House of Commons.)

Orientation. The party stands for Quebec's autonomy within the Canadian Confederation, based on the concept of a French-Canadian nation, and for close links with France. It is also strongly anticommunist.

New Democratic Party (NDP)

Address. 301 Metcalfe St., Ottawa, Ontario K2P 1R9, Canada

Leadership. J. Edward Broadbent (fed. l.); Tony Penikett (fed. pres.); Gerald Caplan (fed. sec.)

Founded. August 1961

History. Although individual representatives of the Canadian labour movement had served in the federal Parliament and in provincial legislatures since the early part of the century, not until the formation of the Co-operative Commonwealth Federation (CCF) in 1933 was there an organized party representing working people and small farmers.

In 1956 most of Canada's labour movement united in the Canadian Labour Congress, which in 1961 initiated the formation of the NDP as a broader-based social democratic party incorporating the CCF (which since 1944 had been in government in the province of Saskatchewan, where it retained the name CCF until 1967). The former CCF leader in Saskatchewan, T. C. (Tommy) Douglas, became the first federal leader of the NDP; in 1971 he was succeeded by David Lewis, who was in turn succeeded by Ed Broadbent in 1975.

In addition to Saskatchewan, the NDP has also formed governments in Manitoba and in British Columbia. At federal level the NDP has remained a relatively small third party behind the Liberals and Progressive Conservatives, although in the 1972-74 Parliament it held the balance of power between the two main parties.

Orientation. The NDP advocates the "application of democratic socialist principles to government and the administration of public affairs".

Structure. Federal, with the federal and each provincial NDP having its own programme. The party is based on constituency associations which are represented on provincial councils and the federal council, the main governing body between conventions which are held at least every two years to decide on party policies and to elect officers.

Membership. 116,000 individual and 275,000 affiliated (through trade unions, co-operatives etc.)

Publications. Ottawa Report (weekly during House of Commons sessions)

International affiliations. Socialist International

Progressive Conservative Party of Canada

Address. 161 Laurier Ave West, Suite 200, Ottawa, Ontario K1P 5J2, Canada

Leadership. Brian Mulroney (nat. l.); Peter Elzinga (pres.); Mrs Bobbie Millar (nat. sec.)

Founded. 1854

History. The party was founded as the Liberal-Conservative Party by Sir John A. Macdonald, the "father of Canadian Confederation". It held power, almost uninterrupted, from 1867 to 1896. Party policies during this period were characterized by great national economic programmes. A transcontinental railroad stretching for 3,000 miles was constructed to tie the fledgling nation together. Settlement programmes opened up the vast tracts of land on the Canadian prairies.

In 1911 the party was returned to power on a platform opposing reciprocity with the USA. In 1917, with the support of prominent Liberals, the party formed a Union Government. Defeated in 1921, the party remained out of office until the election of a Conservative Government under the leadership of R. B. Bennett, 1930-35.

Renamed the Progressive Conservative Party in 1942, the party next won a general election in 1957 with John Diefenbaker as its leader. In 1958 Diefenbaker secured re-election with the largest electoral victory ever recorded in Canada. Defeated in 1963, the party remained in opposition until May 1979, when Joe Clark led it to victory. Nine months later the Clark Government's first budget was defeated in the House of Commons and the Government fell.

Orientation. Enshrining an amalgam of British, French and American conservatism, the party stands for the preservation of the monarchy and parliamentary democracy; the multicultural composition of Canada and its bilingual nature; for private enterprise; a competitive market; individual initiative and personal liberties; and for measures taken for the common or collective good.

Structure. The national executive is the party's central governing body. Members are elected to the executive at "general meetings" held every two years. A steering committee exercises authority between meetings of the national executive.

Publications. PC Journal

International affiliations. International Democrat Union; Pacific Democrat Union

---

The Progressive Party

Address. c/o Sidney Green, 147 Westgate St. Winnipeg, Man. R3C 2E2, Canada

---

Quebec Party
Parti Québécois

Address. 7370 rue St-Hubert, Montreal, Quebec H3R 2N3, Canada
Leadership. René Levesque (pres.)
Founded. October 1968
· *History.* The party was formed in a merger of the *Mouvement Souveraineté-Association* (MSA, established in November 1967) and the *Rassemblement National* (RN). In Quebec provincial elections in April 1970 the party gained 24 per cent of the vote and seven of 108 seats; in October 1973 it obtained 30 per cent of the vote and six of 110 seats, whereupon it became the official opposition; and in November 1976 it won 41 per cent of the vote and 71 of 110 seats and came to power in Quebec, where it was re-elected in April 1981, gaining 80 of 122 seats.
Orientation. The party has a social democratic programme, the cornerstone of which is a commitment to achieve political sovereignty for Quebec and economic association with Canada ("*Souveraineté-Association*").
Structure. The party's supreme body is its congress, and, between congress sessions, its national council (consisting of some 250 local, regional and national representatives). A national executive council of 15 members elected by congress is responsible for day-to-day administration.
Membership. 160,000

Quebec Workers' Party
Parti des Travailleurs de Québec

Address. 4480 rue St-André, Montreal, Quebec H2J 2Z4, Canada
Leadership. G. Lachance (s.g.)

Social Credit Party of Canada
Parti Crédit Social du Canada

Address. P.O. Box 5851, Postal Station L, Edmonton, Alta. T6C 4G3, Canada
Leadership. Martin Hattersley (nat. sec.)

Founded. March 1935
History. The newly-established Social Credit League, led by William Aberhart, came to power in Alberta in August 1935, having won 56 of the 63 contested seats in the provincial Legislative Assembly, forming the first Social Credit government in the world and remaining in power in Alberta for 36 years (until 1971). The movement subsequently spread to other provinces, notably British Columbia and Quebec; in the former the Social Credit Party was in power from 1952 to 1972 and returned to government in that province in December 1975, when it won 35 out of 55 seats in the provincial Legislative Assembly.
The *Ralliement des Créditistes du Québec*, founded in August 1958 under the leadership of Réal Caouette, won 26 seats in the federal House of Commons in June 1962 (when Alberta and British Columbia each sent two Social Credit members to the House). After disagreements and electoral setbacks and defections the party was, at national level, established in 1971 as the Social Credit Party of Canada under the leadership of Réal Caouette, who was succeeded by André Fortin (1976-77), Lorne Reznowski (1978-79) and Fabien Roy (elected leader in March 1979). At federal level, a Social Credit Association of Canada was founded in Toronto in April 1944, but in the House of Commons the party has seen its representation (mostly gained in Quebec) decline from 15 seats in 1972 to six in 1979 and to none in 1980.
Orientation. The party's ideas are based on the theories developed in Britain by Maj. C. H. Douglas in 1919-23 advocating adjustment in monetary policy as a means of achieving general economic prosperity. The party stands for employee participation in the profits and shareholding of the business for which they work.
Structure. The party has a national executive, a national congress and a national convention which chooses the party's leader; there are provincial executives and congresses.

Socialist Party of Canada

Address. Box 4280, Station "A", Victoria, B.C. V8X 3X8, Canada
Leadership. L. G. Jenkins (g.s.)
Founded. 1931
History. The party has carried out "a programme of active education in the political-economic field". It has no parliamentary representation.
Orientation. The party advocates the establishment of a society based upon the

common ownership and democratic control of the means and instruments for producing and distributing wealth by and in the interests of the whole community throughout the world. It is opposed to all other parties ("left, right and centre") on the grounds that they "all support capitalism".

Structure. The party is opposed to having a leadership.

Membership. 20

Publications. Socialist Fulcrum (intermittent)

International affiliations. Links with Socialist Party of Great Britain

---

Unparty (of Canada)

Address. Box 6069, Station A, Toronto, Ont. M5W 1P5, Canada

Leadership. Mary Lou Gutscher (ch. of board); Lisa D. Butler (member of board); Robert Metz (pres. of Freedom Party of Ontario)

Founded. February 1980

History. The party has engaged in a range of activities aiming to promote the principles of liberty and individual responsibility.

Orientation. Libertarian

Structure. Similar to a private company, in that board members determine goals and principles and make executive appointments, without reference to majority rule.

Membership. 600

Publications. Freedom Flyer, 500

Western Canada Concept (WCC)

Address. 810 Courtney St, Victoria, B.C. V8W 1C4, Canada

Leadership. Douglas Christie (founder)

Founded. 1980

History. This party has advocated independence for the four western provinces of Canada—Alberta, Saskatchewan, Manitoba and British Columbia—covering about 30 per cent of Canada's total area and containing about 28 per cent of its population. The party gained its first parliamentary seat in a by-election to the Alberta legislature on Feb. 17, 1982, when its candidate (Gordon Kesler) obtained 42 per cent of the vote; however, he failed to be re-elected in the November 1982 provincial elections in Alberta (where the party secured 12 per cent of the popular vote in the 1983 general election).

Orientation. In addition to its "Western Canada" policy, the party advocates conservative economic policies, free trade, referenda and regional representation in an elected Senate.

Structure. There are four autonomous provincial branches.

Membership. 17,000 (Alberta 10,000, British Columbia 3,000, Saskatchewan 3,000, Manitoba 1,000)

Workers' Communist Party (Marxist-Leninist) of Canada

Leadership. Roger Rashi (ch.)

Founded. September 1979

History. The party was based on a Canadian Communist League (Marxist-Leninist) founded in 1975.

Orientation. Pro-Chinese

Structure. The party has a central committee which elects a political bureau.

Cape Verde

Capital: Praia Pop. 310,000

The Republic of Cape Verde is, under its Constitution approved on Sept. 7, 1980, a "sovereign, democratic, unitary, anti-colonialist and anti-imperialist republic". It has a National People's Assembly, an executive President and a Cabinet headed by a Prime Minister. The President is also the secretary-general of the country's sole legal political party, the African Party for the Independence of Cape Verde (PAICV). The 56-member National Assembly elected on Dec. 7, 1980, is composed exclusively of members elected on the ruling party's list, which was said to have obtained 93 per cent of the votes cast in a 75 per cent poll. However, not all members of the National Assembly are members of the PAICV, and parliamentary candidates can be chosen at mass meetings before the election.

African Party for the Independence of Cape Verde
Partido Africano da Independência de Cabo Verde (PAICV)

Address. C.P. 22, Praia, São Tiago, Cape Verde Islands
Leadership. President Aristides Maria Pereira (s.g.)
Founded. Jan. 20, 1981
History. The PAICV broke away from the African Party for the Independence of Guinea and Cape Verde (*Partido Africano da Independência da Guiné e do Cabo Verde*, PAIGC), whose rule in Guinea-Bissau was overthrown on Nov. 14, 1980.

Orientation. The PAICV defines itself as a liberation movement in power and the vanguard of the Cape Verdian people; it endeavours to "associate the popular masses with the decision-making process", and it stands for the principle of non-alignment, a new international economic order, peaceful coexistence, peace and complete disarmament, and African unity.
Structure. The party has, as its supreme body, a congress, a 42-member national council (the supreme body between sessions of the congress), a nine-member political commission and a secretariat.
Membership. 5,985 (June 1983)

Central African Republic

Capital: Bangui Pop. 3,200,000

The Central African Republic has been under military rule since Sept. 1, 1981, when President David Dacko was deposed and the Constitution and the country's political parties were suspended. Legislative and executive powers were assumed by a new Military Committee for National Recovery (CMRN) whose chairman, Gen. André Kolingba (Army Chief of Staff), became Chief of the General Staff of the Armed Forces, head of government and Minister of Defence.

The political parties legalized under the Constitution promulgated on Feb. 6, 1981, were subsequently banned in July 1981 and March 1982.

Chad

Capital: N'Djaména   Pop. 4,490,000

The Republic of Chad is ruled by a Council of State (consisting of 18 commissioners and 12 vice-commissioners) drawn from the members of the Armed Forces of the North (*Forces Armées du Nord*, FAN), which came to power (through civil war) in June 1982 and whose leader, Hissène Habré, became the official head of state in Chad on June 19, 1982. However, during the latter part of 1982, and also in 1983, this Government lost control of large areas of northern Chad to the rebel forces loyal to former President Goukouni Oueddei and backed by Libya. A rival "National Peace Government" had been set up by these forces in October 1982. In June 1984 the Chad regime created a new political organization designated the National Union for Independence and Revolution (UNIR), with Hissène Habré as chairman of its central committee.

Chile

Capital: Santiago   Pop. 11,500,000

The Republic of Chile has since the overthrow of its parliamentary Government on Sept. 11, 1973, been ruled (under emergency provisions) by a four-member junta of the commanders of the armed services and the para-military police, who dissolved the National Congress, banned the country's Marxist parties, placed all other parties into "indefinite recess" and prohibited all political activities. All remaining political parties were also banned on March 12, 1977. The head of the junta, Gen. Augusto Pinochet Ugarte, has since June 26, 1974, been Supreme Chief of State (or President) responsible for the administration of the country, while the agreement of the junta has been required for the appointment of ministers and other high-ranking officials and of generals.

Under a new Constitution which entered into force on March 11, 1981, President Pinochet was enabled to remain in office at least until 1989. In the latter year the junta would nominate a single presidential candidate who, if confirmed by plebiscite, would remain in power until 1997, when free presidential elections would take place; if the candidate was rejected President Pinochet would remain in office for another one year but would call for such elections within that year. The Constitution (which had been approved in a national plebiscite on Sept. 11, 1980, by 67.04 per cent of the votes cast, with 30.14 per cent against it) also provided for elections to a Chamber of Deputies and a Senate at the end of 1989.

Although the country's political parties were banned they continued their activities, even inside Chile, and from 1981 onwards members of the military Government acknowledged this fact. In January 1984 the Government published a draft political parties statute providing that they would be allowed to operate under certain defined conditions, notably that they accepted the existing constitutional order.

Chilean Socialist Bloc
Bloc Socialista Chileno

Founded. September 1983

History. Preceded by the *Convergencia Socialista*, this Bloc was created by majority sections of the Socialist Party (the predominant participant), the Movement for United Popular Action (MAPU), the MAPU Workers and Peasants (MAPU-OC) and the Christian Left, all of which had been part of Dr Allende's Popular Unity coalition. Together with other formations, the Bloc has been active within the broader-based Democratic Alliance (see separate entry) in the campaign for a restoration of democracy in Chile. Alliance parties not within the Bloc include the Radical Party (see separate entry), which has nevertheless indicated its intention of maintaining a special relationship with the Bloc.

Christian Democratic Party
Partido Democrático Cristiano (PDC)

Leadership. Gabriel Valdés Subercaseaux (pres.); José de Gregorio (s.g.)

Founded. 1957

History. The PDC was created as the successor to a National Falange founded in 1934; as a democratic reform party, it advocated a new social doctrine based on Christian humanism to overcome Chile's poverty and economic underdevelopment. The PDC's then leader, Dr Eduardo Frei Montalva, was President of the Republic from 1964 to 1970, when he was succeeded by the Socialist, Dr Salvador Allende Gossens, whose regime was strongly opposed by the PDC. The party at first gave tacit support to the military junta which had seized power in 1973 but by 1974 many PDC leaders increasingly opposed the regime. In effect, the PDC became divided, as members of its right wing began to co-operate with the junta whereas what appeared to be the party's main body opposed it and took part unofficially in initiatives outside Chile organized by the Popular Unity alliance of left-wing parties, although without ever being formally represented at meetings of the latter.

At a secret congress held in March 1975 the PDC issued a declaration describing the ruling military junta as a "right-wing dictatorship with fascist manifestations" and their policies as "erroneous, unjust and incompatible with our principles regarding human rights, economic orientation and the situation of the workers". On the other hand, the congress rejected any liaison with "clandestine organizations".

On March 28, 1975, the Christian Democratic broadcasting station, Radio Balmaceda, was closed for 10 days by order of the junta for having allegedly undermined the security of the state and endangered peace and national harmony. The radio had reported the resignation from administrative posts of three Christian Democrats and also the seizure of a book on European fascism written by Claudio Orrego, a former Christian Democratic deputy known as a firm opponent of Dr Allende.

Dr Frei declined to become a member of a consultative Council of State established on Dec. 31, 1975, on the grounds that the Council had no juridical basis and that the Government would in no way be bound by its advice. On the other hand, the authorities allowed "as an exception", on Jan. 23, 1976, the publication of a booklet by Dr Frei, criticizing various aspects of the military junta and pleading for a "democratic alternative" to its totalitarian rule.

The Christian Democratic weekly *Ercilla* was suspended on March 23, 1976 (the party's daily *La Prensa* having been forced to close in September 1973). Radio Balmaceda was closed indefinitely on Jan. 27, 1977, under a decree prohibiting political parties from operating radio stations.

On March 12, 1977, plans of two Christian Democrats—Andrés Zaldívar Larrain and Tomás Reyes—were published in the Santiago press, in which the co-operation of all political forces was called for in order to achieve a peaceful gradual transition to democracy. The Secretary-General to the Cabinet said that such plans would be "called subversive in any country", and on the same day the junta issued a decree banning all the remaining parties, i.e. the Christian Democrats, the National Party, the Radical Democrats and the Radical Left on the grounds that there was a Christian Democratic plot to overthrow the Government.

In a document released in Venezuela on Oct. 17, 1977, the PDC proposed that a "national movement of democratic restoration" should be created to replace Chile's military Government and demanded the convocation of a directly elected constituent assembly leading to an eventual full return to parliamentary democracy with an elected President; as an immediate step it proposed the lifting of the state of siege in force since September 1973 and renewed from time to time.

On Dec. 27, 1977, the PDC issued a statement urging the electorate to vote "no" in a plebiscite called for by President

Pinochet (for Jan. 4, 1978) to endorse a declaration of support for the President and for the "legitimacy" of the Government. The PDC condemned the holding of the plebiscite while the country was still under a state of siege and personal and press freedoms were still restricted; stated that the result would have no validity; and added that the plebiscite confused the concepts of fatherland and government and sought to divide Chileans between patriots and non-patriots. In the event, however, 75.3 per cent of the valid votes were reported to have been "yes" votes and only 20.39 per cent "no" votes.

Ex-President Frei, addressing an authorized meeting on Aug. 28, 1979, called for the formation of a civilian-military transitional government to restore full democracy within the next two or three years. The meeting, however, turned into an opposition demonstration which was broken up by police. Other such demonstrations took place that year.

On Oct. 16, 1980, the junta announced that Andrés Zaldívar, then PDC president touring Europe, would not be allowed to re-enter Chile unless he signed a document accepting the results of the plebiscite of Sept. 11, 1980, approving the new Constitution and the authority of the Government and the Constitution. He was inter alia accused of making denigratory statements about Chile to a Mexican newspaper and of thus threatening Chile's internal security. The PDC presidency was subseqently assumed by Gabriel Valdés.

Ex-President Frei died in Santiago on Jan. 22, 1982, when President Pinochet declared three days of official mourning; a government memorial service was held on Jan. 25 but later on the same day a main ceremony held by the family was addressed by Cardinal Raúl Silva Henríques (Archbishop of Santiago and Primate of Chile) and was heard by thousands of mourners.

Four exiled Christian Democrats who were not allowed to enter Chile for ex-President Frei's funeral included Jaime Castillo Velasco, president of the Chilean human rights commission, who had been expelled in August 1981 with three other prominent opposition figures after they had been accused of violating the ban on political activity and showing a "defiant attitude". In his capacity as a lawyer, Jaime Castillo Velasco had been acting for the family of Orlando Letelier, the former Chilean ambassador in Washington and minister in the Allende Government, who had been murdered in the US capital in 1976 by Chilean secret agents.

During 1983 the party joined with other left-of-centre democratic parties in the formation of alliances—in March the

Multipartidaria and in August the Democratic Alliance (see separate entries).

International affiliations. Christian Democratic International; Christian Democratic Organization of America

---

Communist Party of Chile
Partido Comunista Chileño (PCC)

Leadership. Luis Corvalán Lepe (s.g.)

History. A Socialist Workers' Party founded in 1912 decided at its fourth congress held in Rancagua in January 1922 to affiliate with the Third International and to change its name to Communist Party of Chile. By 1970 the PCC was the third largest among pro-Moscow Communist parties (after those of France and Italy) outside the Communist-ruled countries. In congressional elections held on March 2, 1969, the PCC gained 22 out of the 150 seats in the Chamber of Deputies; in the presidential elections of Nov. 4, 1970, it was part of the Popular Unity alliance, whose candidate, the Socialist Dr Salvador Allende, was elected President with 36.3 per cent of the votes cast. In the Popular Unity Cabinet formed subsequently, the PCC was given ministerial posts. On Dec. 3, 1971, the party (then claiming to have 150,000 members) set up a Revolutionary Workers' Front which established "antifascist brigades" in the factories.

On Jan. 16, 1972, the PCC criticized the "sectarian extremism" of the Revolutionary Movement of the Left (MIR) which had "alienated middle sectors" of the population and it emphasized that the "correct strategy" was to divide the opposition by attracting "progressive" sections of the Christian Democratic Party which supported economic and social change. In June 1972 Luis Corvalán, the PCC's secretary-general, publicly called for the consolidation of socialist gains and for slowing down further progress towards socialism in order to reassure public opinion and to win the congressional elections in 1973. In these elections the Popular Unity alliance gained 43.39 per cent of the votes cast for candidates for the Chamber of Deputies, against 54.70 per cent gained by the (opposition) Federation of Democratic Parties; in consequence, the Popular Unity alliance gained only 63 of the 150 seats in the Chamber (with the PCC gaining 25).

Following the banning of the PCC by the junta which took power on Sept. 11, 1973, the party went underground, carrying out secret activities despite serious losses resulting from the arrest or death of many of its members. The party claimed at the end of October 1973 (in *La Stampa* of Turin, Italy) that "a communal struggle" was being prepared "for the overthrow of the military regime". Thereafter the party co-ordinated its anti-junta activities in exile within the framework of the Popular Unity alliance (see separate entry). On Nov. 2, 1975, the Government alleged that Communists, of whom 15 had been arrested on Sept. 19, had planned to assassinate President Bordaberry of Uruguay during a state visit to Chile in September.

On Dec. 18, 1976, Luis Corvalán (held in detention in Chile since September 1973) was exchanged at Zurich airport against Vladimir Bukovsky (the Soviet dissident imprisoned in the Soviet Union since 1972). Corvalán was taken to the Soviet Union, where he made several statements on the policy of the PCC, notably one on Dec. 30, 1976, when he alleged that there were 3,300 political prisoners in Chile and that another 2,000 persons had disappeared. (On June 19, 1977, Jorge Montes—a PCC leader detained in Chile since July 1974—was released in exchange for the release of 11 German political prisoners held in the German Democratic Republic.)

On Jan. 4, 1977, Luis Corvalán called (in Moscow) for the formation of a united front of all democratic forces, including the Chilean Christian Democrats, against the "military dictatorship" in Chile; at the same time he declared that the PCC firmly adhered to the principles of "proletarian internationalism" and of the "dictatorship of the proletariat", claiming that the latter concept was more democratic than "any bourgeois form of government", although in Chile its implementation was a problem to be solved at a later stage. On Jan. 12, 1978, he appealed to the Chilean Christian Democrats for the setting-up of a "government of democratic union" which should speedily replace the military junta; he claimed that the majority of the military and the police in Chile wished to end repression and the existing situation.

In 1982 the PCC's political commission issued a renewed call for unity of all opposition strata seeking the overthrow of the military regime in Chile.

In October 1983 Gen. Fernando Matthei, the Air Force commander and a member of the military junta, stated that he would be willing to enter into negotiations with the banned PCC as "the Marxists" were "a reality in this country and I prefer to face the reality".

Democratic Alliance
Alianza Democrática (AD)

Founded. Aug. 6, 1983
History. This Alliance was formed by the principal non-communist progressive formations, namely the Christian Democrats, the Republicans, Social Democrats and Radicals (then engaged in a reunification process) and the Chilean Socialist Bloc (see separate entry). On its foundation it issued a 10-point plan covering the need for a solution to the economic situation, the human rights question, the restoration of civil liberties, the role of the armed forces, the nature of the democracy which it wished to establish, ethical conduct within the AD, the erosion of the general standard of living, the institution of a mixed economy, new labour legislation and autonomy for the universities. The AD also expressed its opposition to any form of one-party government which exercised control of the media and used violence against political opponents.

Following mass anti-government demonstrations early in August 1983, the AD called on President Pinochet to resign and demanded the holding of elections to a constituent assembly which would reform the Constitution and act as a legislature during a transitional period. Subsequently an AD delegation had talks with the Minister of the Interior (Sergio Onofre Jarpa) on Aug. 25 and Sept. 5, 1983, but these did not result in a timetable being laid down for the restoration of democracy.

Independent Democratic Union
Unión Democrática Independiente (UDI)

Leadership. Jaime Guzmán (pres.)
History. The UDI has given qualified support to the Pinochet regime and has in particular advocated the creation of a nominated parliament to deflect popular pressure for a restoration of democracy. It has sought to establish relations with right-wing elements in the Christian Democratic Party and the smaller centrist parties.

Multipartidaria

Founded. March 14, 1983
History. On its foundation this organizaton issued a "democratic manifesto" signed by Gabriel Valdés (president of the Christian Democratic Party), Hugo Zepeda and Julio Subercaseaux (of the Republican Party), Enrique Silva and Luis Fernando Luengo (of the Radical Party), Luis Bossay (of the Social Democrats) and Hernán Vodavonic, Julio Stuardo and Ramón Silva (representanting different factions of the Socialist Party).

Popular Democratic Movement
Movimiento Democrático Popular (MDP)

Leadership. Dr Manuel Almeyda (pres.); Jaime Insunza (g.s.)
Founded. Sept. 3, 1983
History. The MDP was set up as an opposition alliance of the Communist Party of Chile, the faction of the Socialist Party led by Clodomiro Almeyda, the Christian Left (*Izquierda Cristiana*), the Movement for United Popular Action (MAPU) and the Movement of the Revolutionary Left (MIR).

In early April 1984 the MDP general secretary, Jaime Insunza (a Communist), was expelled from Chile for engaging in "communist activities". This action followed the imprisonment within Chile of the MDP president, Dr Manuel Almeyda.

Popular Unity
Unidad Popular

Leadership. Dr Clodomiro Almeyda Medina (first sec. of executive committee)
Founded. 1969
History. Set up as an electoral alliance of left-wing parties, which led to the election of the Socialist Dr Salvador Allende Gossens as President on Nov. 4, 1970, the Popular Unity was deprived of all power through the military coup of Sept. 11, 1973 (on which day President Allende apparently committed suicide). A solidarity office of the Popular Unity was thereupon set up in Rome (Italy) and it disseminated news of persecution and repression of President Allende's supporters in Chile, claiming in November 1973 that more than 3,000 officers and men of the armed forces, loyal to Dr Allende, had been executed, and that others condemned to death had included leading Communists. Many of those sent to Dawson Island (off Tierra del Fuego) for detention had died, according to other sources. On May 1, 1974, all constituent parties of the Popular Unity issued a declaration calling for the formation of an "anti-fascist front" in order to end "illegal detention, tortures and summary executions" and to "regain democratic rights".

A meeting of leaders of the Popular Unity parties and the left wing of the Christian Democratic Party was held in July 1975 in Caracas (Venezuela), where they decided to work together for the restoration of "a just and socialist democracy in Chile"; at a further meeting in East Berlin in August 1975 they published a joint programme aimed at resisting the military regime and restoring democratic freedoms; and in October they met in London to discuss the establishment of unified headquarters. A further meeting of Popular Unity parties' leaders and left-wing Christian Democrats was held in New York in September 1976, whereafter Dr Almeyda (who had been expelled from Chile on Jan. 11, 1975) declared again that the aim of the Popular Unity was to establish an "anti-fascist" front with the participation of the Christian Democrats.

In a communiqué issued to the press in Santiago in mid-January 1981 it was announced that the parties constituting the Popular Unity alliance—the Communist Party, the Radical Party, two wings of the Socialist Party, the Christian Left, the Unified Popular Action Movement and the latter's Workers and Peasants offshoot—had joined with the Movement of the Revolutionary Left (MIR) to sign a declaration of unity providing for joint opposition to the Pinochet regime.

Anti-government demonstrators in Santiago in March 1983 used the Popular Unity slogan "bread, justice, work and liberty", although by then the alliance as a political factor had been largely transcended by other alliances of progressive forces such as the Chilean Socialist Bloc, the Democratic Alliance, the *Multipartidaria* and the Popular Democratic Alliance (see separate entries).

Project for National Development
Proyecto de Desarrollo Nacional (Proden)

Leadership. Jorge Lavandero (l.)
Founded. 1982
History. On Feb. 24, 1983, this group of centrist and right-wing political and trade union leaders called on President Pinochet to hand over power to the four-member military junta "as a preliminary step to democracy". A rally organized by Proden in Santiago on Oct. 11, 1983, attracted some 40,000 people. In late March 1984 Jorge Lavandero was attacked and beaten while returning home at night—a small right-wing group claiming responsibility.

Radical Party
Partido Radical

Leadership. Enrique Silva Cimma (pres.); Carlos González Márquez (g.s.)

Founded. 1863

History. The Radical Party became Chile's main progressive formation in the early 20th century and held the presidency in 1938-52. Strongly anti-communist in the post-war period, it later gravitated to the left and in 1969 joined the Popular Unity alliance (see separate entry) which secured the election of the Socialist leader, Dr Salvador Allende, to the presidency in November 1970. Radicals held ministerial posts throughout the period of Popular Unity rule, although the party was weakened by breakaways of elements opposed to its espousal of Marxism in 1971. Within Chile the Radical Party presently has its main strength among white-collar workers and teachers.

Together with the other Popular Unity formations, the Radical Party was banned by the military junta which seized power in September 1973. Thereafter it co-ordinated its efforts to overthrow the Pinochet regime within the Popular Unity alliance, with the particular role of ensuring liaison between the alliance and democratic socialist forces in other countries. More recently it has joined with other non-communist progressive forces within the Democratic Alliance and the *Multipartidaria* (see separate entries).

Since 1980 the Radical Party has experienced divisions between the external leadership in Mexico (which favoured armed struggle and closer relations with the Marxist-Leninist formations) and the internal party (which re-emphasized the social democratic character of the party). This led in 1983 to the election of a new leadership based within Chile, headed by Enrique Silva (a former president of the constitutional tribunal), who succeeded Anselmo Sule in the party presidency. The Radical Party is currently engaged in a reunification process with elements which broke away in the early 1970s with the aim of building a strong social democratic presence on the Chilean left.

As part of this process the Radicals in April 1984 formed the Socialist Democratic Federation together with the Social Democratic Party (see separate entry) and the small People's Socialist Union.

International affiliations. Socialist International

Republican Party
Partido Republicano

Leadership. Hugo Zepeda, Julio Subercaseaux
Founded. 1983

History. This party was formed by a majority faction of the (right-wing democratic) National Party—the democratic wing favouring a speedy return to genuine constitutional rule. The party has joined with anti-junta progressive formations in the *Multipartidaria* and the Democratic Alliance (see separate entries).

Social Democratic Party
Partido Social-Democrático

Leadership. Luis Bossay
History. This small centre-left formation has joined with other non-communist progressive formations in the *Multipartidaria* and the Democratic Alliance (see separate entries). It has entered into contact with the Radical Party (see separate entry) with a view to building a strong social democratic presence on the Chilean left. These contacts culminated in the formation in April 1984 of the Socialist Democratic Federation by the Social Democratic Party, the Radical Party and the small People's Socialist Union.

Socialist Democratic Federation—see under Radical Party and Social Democratic Party

---

Socialist Party
Partido Socialista

Leadership. Carlos Briones (s.g.)
History. The Socialist Party is one of the constituent parties of the Popular Unity alliance (see separate entry), which came to power when the Socialist leader, Dr Salvador Allende Gossens, was elected President of the Republic in November 1970. In his election programme Allende had made radical proposals, inter alia to replace the existing Parliament by an "assembly of the people", to nationalize all major foreign-owned companies and the banks and to develop close ties with Communist countries. After the overthrow of his regime on Sept. 11, 1973, the Socialist Party was banned (with all other member parties of the Popular Unity); of its members, many were sentenced to terms of imprisonment in 1974 and thereafter.

Party members were also involved in legal proceedings arising from an alleged conspiracy to infiltrate Socialists into the armed forces under President Allende's regime which a military court (which was trying them) deemed to have been illegal;

four defendants were sentenced to death for "treason and sedition" on July 30, 1974, but these sentences were, on Aug. 5, commuted to 30 years' imprisonment: 52 other defendants were given prison sentences of up to 20 years.

In 1977 a split occurred in the party in exile, when Pedro Vuskovic (who had been Minister of Economic Affairs under President Allende in 1970-72 and had gone into exile after the military coup of September 1973) was expelled from the Socialist Party in July 1977 for "activities tending to divide the party". He did not agree with the main body of exile opinion that the Chilean military regime could be overthrown with help from abroad, and in mid-October 1977 he claimed in London that the Popular Unity and the Christian Democrats aimed at "reconstituting the bourgeois democracy" which had previously existed in Chile, and that the increasing consumer capitalism in Chile and other Latin American countries was incompatible with democracy, which could only be achieved under a reconstructed Socialist Party.

Of Socialist leaders imprisoned ex-Senator Erich Schnake, given a 20-year sentence for conspiracy on July 30, 1974, was released on Dec. 23, 1977, on condition that he left the country. He said in Madrid early in January 1978 that he owed his release to Felipe González, secretary-general of the Spanish Workers' Party (PSOE), who had visited him in prison in August 1977.

At a meeting in Algeria in March 1978, delegates both from within Chile and from the party in exile elected a single party leadership and reaffirmed the unity of the party within the Popular Unity alliance and its increased co-operation with the Christian Democratic Party against the junta. Nevertheless, in the early 1980s the leadership of Carlos Altamirano came under challenge from two smaller Socialist Party factions, the most important led by Clodomiro Almeyda.

Whereas the Altamirano wing of the Socialist Party participated in the Chilean Socialist Bloc and thus in the Democratic Alliance, grouping a range of non-communist progressive forces, the Almeyda faction remained close to the Communists, with whom it is allied within the Popular Democratic Movement. All main factions of the Socialist Party were, however, represented in the *Multipartidaria* alliance of democratic formations launched in March 1983.

In April 1984 Altamirano was succeeded as secretary-general of the party by Carlos Briones, a former minister under the Allende presidency.

China

Capital: Beijing (Peking)　　　　　　Pop. 1,008,175,288 (July 1, 1982)

The People's Republic of China is, under its Constitution of 138 articles adopted by the Chinese National People's Congress on Dec. 4, 1982, "a socialist state under the people's democratic dictatorship led by the working class and based on the alliance of workers and peasants" in which "all power belongs to the people" and "the organs through which the people exercise state power are the National People's Congress (NPC) and the local people's congresses at different levels". The NPC consists of deputies elected for a five-year term "by the provinces, autonomous regions and municipalities directly under the central government and by the armed forces". All Chinese citizens above the age of 18 years have the right to elect and to be elected (except persons mentally ill or deprived of their political rights). The NPC and its permanent body, the Standing Committee, "exercise the legislative power of the state". The Standing Committee inter alia supervises the work of the State Council, i.e. "the central people's Government" and "the executive body of the highest organ of state power".

Contrary to the 1978 Constitution, the 1982 Constitution contained no references to the Communist Party of China (CPC), to Marxism-Leninism or to

Mao Zedong Thought in any of its articles, although in its preamble there were several references to "the Chinese people of all nationalities under the leadership of the CPC and the guidance of Marxism-Leninism and Mao Zedong Thought". The preamble also referred to the existence of "a broad patriotic united front" under the leadership of the CPC and "composed of democratic parties and people's organizations" and embracing "all socialist working people, all patriots who support socialism and all patriots who stand for reunification of the motherland" (i.e. for the incorporation of Taiwan in the Republic of China). Eight existing minor political parties date back to before the proclamation of the People's Republic on Oct. 1, 1949, and are composed mainly of intellectuals.

In elections to the NPC held between March 17 and the end of April 1983 only 700 of the 3,500 members of the NPC elected in 1978 were re-elected; the number of army representatives was reduced from 508 to 267; the number of representatives of national minorities was increased and 13 deputies were elected for Taiwan from among candidates nominated by citizens of Taiwan origin.

Communist Party of China (CPC)
Zhongguo Gongchan Dang

Leadership. Hu Yaobang (g.s.); Marshal Ye Jianying, Deng Xiaoping, Zhao Ziyang, Li Xiannian, Chen Yun (other members of the politburo's standing committee)

Founded. July 1921

History. Founded under the influence of the 1917 Russian revolution at a Shanghai conference attended by 12 delegates, the Communist Party of China (CPC) was instructed by the Soviet regime to co-operate with the then Nationalist Government (which received extensive Soviet aid from 1923) and to join the ruling Kuomintang as individual members while maintaining the CPC in being. In 1924 Mao Tse-tung (Mao Zedong)—one of 12 delegates at the party's founding conference—was elected to the CPC politburo. Appointed head of the party's peasant department in 1926, he put forward the view that the poor peasants formed a major revolutionary force in China—bringing him into conflict with Chen Tu-hsiu, the party's general secretary, who held to the orthodox Marxist view that a socialist revolution must be led by the industrial proletariat.

In April 1927 Chiang Kai-shek, the new leader of the Kuomintang, broke with his Communist allies, thousands of whom were massacred. Chen Tu-hsiu was removed from his post in August, and Mao was sent to Hunan to organize a peasant revolt. The "autumn harvest uprising" was a failure, however, and Mao was removed from the politburo; nevertheless, with about 1,000 followers he established his headquarters on Chingkanshan, a mountain on the Hunan-Kiangsi border, where in 1928 he was joined by Chu Teh (who became the outstanding Communist leader during the subsequent civil war). From this base the Communists gradually extended the area under their control until it covered a great part of Kiangsi and large areas of Hunan and Fukien. A "Chinese Soviet Republic" was established in 1931, with Mao as Chairman and Chu Teh as commander-in-chief, which after the Japanese invasion of Manchuria in 1931 declared war on Japan.

The party's central committee, which had been operating underground in Shanghai, joined Mao in Kiangsi in 1931. Differences arose over political and military policy, and Mao was removed from his military posts in 1932 and from his political posts in 1934. Four "extermination campaigns" by the Kuomintang forces were defeated during 1930-33, but a fifth, for which over 900,000 troops were mobilized, compelled the Communists in October 1934 to evacuate Kiangsi and to set out on the "Long March" to the north-west. During the march a conference was held in January 1935 at Tsun Yi, in Kweichow province, at which Mao was elected to the party chairmanship, which he retained until his death in 1976. After a 6,000-mile march through 12 provinces and over 18 mountain ranges and 24 rivers, and 15 major battles, fewer than 20,000 people out of 100,000 who had set out reached Shensi in October 1935, and established their new headquarters at Yenan.

In 1937 a revolt among his own followers forced Chiang Kai-shek to form an alliance with the Communists against Japanese aggression. Co-operation between the two parties broke down in 1941, when Kuomintang troops attacked a Communist unit, and for the next four years each side fought the Japanese in its own area.

When the Japanese surrendered in 1945 a Communist army of about 1,000,000 men controlled vast areas with a population of 90,000,000, but the 4,000,000 Kuomintang troops held all the major towns. Mao attempted to secure US support for the formation of a post-war coalition government, but his offers were rejected, and in 1946 civil war began. Despite their overwhelming numerical superiority, the Kuomintang forces' resistance collapsed in 1948-49, and on Oct. 1, 1949, Mao proclaimed the People's Republic of China in Peking, with himself as Chairman (President) of the Republic and Chou En-lai as Prime Minister.

The new regime was confronted by an economy ruined by years of war, and its economic problems were soon intensified by China's involvement in the Korean War. In consequence China was dependent for some years on the Soviet Union for economic and military aid, and the first five-year plan (1953-57) concentrated on the development of heavy industry on the Soviet model. From 1955 onwards, however, Mao set out to develop a distinctively Chinese form of socialism, and he secured his colleagues' reluctant consent to a more rapid socialization of agriculture. In a speech on "the correct handling of contradictions among the people" in 1957 he advocated the simultaneous development of agriculture and of heavy and light industry and the setting up of a large number of small and medium industrial enterprises together with a few large ones; at the same time he proposed a policy of "letting 100 flowers blossom and 100 schools of thought contend" and condemned bureaucratic methods which had led to strikes and other disturbances.

In 1958 the "Great Leap Forward" policy was adopted, whereby the agricultural cooperatives were transformed into communes combining agriculture with small-scale industry.

The new policy led to a political crisis. At a meeting of the Communist Party's central committee in December 1958 a resolution was adopted admitting that mistakes had been made in its application, and Mao announced his decision to resign the chairmanship of the Republic in order to concentrate on ideological questions. The Defence Minister, Marshal Peng Teh-huai, strongly criticized his policies in July 1959 and was subsequently replaced by Marshal Lin Biao. As a result of the increasingly strained relations between the Chinese and Soviet Communist parties the Soviet Union withdrew all technical aid to China in August 1960, and a succession of disastrous harvests added to the country's economic problems. Liu Shao-chi, who had succeeded Mao as Chairman of the Republic, and

Deng Xiaoping, the Communist Party general secretary, tried to solve the crisis by a policy whereby the peasants were allowed to cultivate private plots of land, a free market developed in the villages and increased use was made of bonuses and other material incentives in industry.

Regarding such policies as likely to lead to a return to capitalism, Mao in 1962 put forward the slogan: "Don't forget the class struggle." He was supported by Lin Biao, who launched a campaign in the Army for the study of Mao's thought and issued in 1964 the "Little Red Book" of quotations from his writings. Opposition in the party leadership remained strong, however, and in October 1965 Mao left Peking for Shanghai, which he made his base for his campaign against his colleagues. In May 1966 the Cultural Revolution was launched, and on May 16 the party's central committee issued a circular calling for a campaign against "those representatives of the bourgeoisie who have sneaked into the party, the Government, the Army and various spheres of culture". Demonstrations against the right wing of the party began in Peking University in the same month, and were followed by the appearance of the first of the big-character posters which were a major feature of the Cultural Revolution and by the formation of Red Guard units, composed of students and school-children. Mao returned to Peking on July 17, and presided over a meeting of the central committee on Aug. 1-12 which issued instructions for the conduct of the Cultural Revolution. While it was meeting he himself issued a poster headed "Bombard the Headquarters", which held up the students' action as an example, and on Aug. 18 he and Lin Biao reviewed a rally of 1,100,000 Red Guards.

The activities of the Red Guards soon aroused uneasiness, however, and from January 1967 "Revolutionary Rebels", consisting of adult workers, replaced them as the main agents of the Cultural Revolution. Pitched battles between rival factions followed in many cities and provinces, and China was reduced to a state of virtual anarchy. In these circumstances Mao was obliged to fall back on the support of the Army; the revolutionary committees which replaced the old local authorities in 1967-68 and the new provincial Communist Party committees formed in 1970-71 were largely under military leadership, and the Army took control of many ministries. The removal during the Cultural Revolution of many party and state officials, ministers and high-ranking officers, including Liu Shao-chi and Deng Xiaoping, left Lin Biao the most powerful figure in China after Mao; at the 1969 party congress he delivered the central committee's report, and the new party constitution in 1969 named him as Mao's successor.

The new party leadership soon split over questions of foreign policy. In view of the growing hostility between China and the Soviet Union, Mao and Chou En-lai favoured a détente with the United States, which was opposed by Lin Biao. Early in 1971 the latter's supporters, headed by his son Lin Li-kuo, began to plan a coup. After the announcement in July 1971 of President Nixon's forthcoming visit to Peking, Mao again withdrew to Shanghai to rally support against Lin and after his return to Peking Lin fled the country on Sept. 12, and was killed when his plane crashed in Mongolia. In his last years Mao's failing health forced him to live in seclusion. He presided over the 1973 party congress, but apparently took no part in its discussions. How far he was personally involved in the continued conflicts inside the party leadership, which led first to Deng Xiaoping's return to office in 1973 and then to his fall in April 1976, was unclear, since each faction accused the other of forging Mao's directives.

The death of Mao brought to a head the conflict between the radical and moderate factions within the CPC, from which the latter emerged victorious when the four radical members of the politburo—the "gang of four", including Mao's widow, Jiang Qing—were arrested in early October 1976 on a charge of plotting to seize power. At the same time Hua Guofeng (who had succeeded the late Chou En-lai as Premier in February 1976) was appointed chairman of the party, while in July 1977 Deng Xiaoping was rehabilitated to his former government and party posts, as a massive campaign was launched against the alleged misdeeds of the "gang of four". These four, and six alleged associates of Lin Biao, were sentenced on Jan. 25, 1981—Jiang Qing and Zhang Chinqiao to death with two years' reprieve, and the others to terms of imprisonment ranging from 16 years to life.

In 1977 the CPC propagated, as "a great strategic ideology laid down by Chairman Mao", the doctrine of the division of the world into three groups of states—super-powers, developed countries and developing third-world countries; under this "three worlds theory" the Soviet Union and the United States, as the two super-powers, were regarded as "the biggest oppressors and exploiters in today's world".

The party's 12th congress, held in September 1982, adopted a report by Hu Yaobang (the party's general secretary) on "creating a new situation in all fields of socialist modernization" which required the fulfilment of "great tasks". These were defined as "an all-round upsurge of the socialist economy", the building of "a high level of socialist spiritual civilization" and of "a high level of socialist democracy" (which had been, he said, "seriously undermined during the Cultural Revolution"), and "an independent foreign policy" directed against the "hegemonies" of the two super-powers (the USA and the USSR). China was to play its role as part of the Third World, with co-operation with "friendly socialist countries" (North Korea, Romania and Yugoslavia), with "common interests with Western countries in safeguarding peace and developing co-operation" and with the intention of "working together with the Japanese people and with far-sighted Japanese public figures".

In the new party constitution adopted by the congress it was explicitly stated that the class struggle was "no longer the principal contradiction" and that the party's general task was to "unite the people of all nationalities in working hard to achieve step by step the modernization of our industry, agriculture, national defence and science and technology".

Structure. Under a new party constitution adopted at the 12th party congress in September 1982, the party no longer has a chairman or a vice-chairman, and its general secretary has been given greater powers. The party has a central committee of 348 full and alternate members, of whom 211 are new members elected in 1982 (140 of them under 60 years old); a secretariat consisting of the general secretary and nine other members; a politburo of 19 full and three alternate members and its standing committee; a military commission with Deng Xiaoping as chairman; a central commission for inspecting discipline; and a central advisory commission, also chaired by Deng Xiaoping.

Membership. Over 40,000,000

Publications. *Renmin Ribao* (People's Daily, official organ of CPC central committee); *Beijing Ribao* (Peking Daily, organ of the Peking municipal committee of the party); *Hong Qi* (Red Flag, ideological journal, twice a month)

Other Parties

There are also eight "democratic parties", most of them founded in the 1940s. All were officially stated (in November 1979) to have co-operated with the Communist Party during the "war of resistance" against Japan and in the "war of liberation" against invasion and the Kuomintang; to have taken part in the Chinese People's Political Consultative Conference in

September 1949 and in other discussions; and to have been accepted in 1956 under Chairman Mao's principle of "long-term coexistence and mutual supervision" between the Communist Party and the democratic parties; but to have been suppressed during the Cultural Revolution and the rule of the "gang of four" in 1966-76.

On Oct. 11-22, 1979, these parties, as well as the All-China Federation of Industrialists and Businessmen, held their national congress in Beijing. Members of these parties constituted 6.9 per cent of the deputies of the Fifth National People's Congress in 1979.

The social bases of the eight parties were officially described as "the national bourgeoisie, the upper strata of the petty bourgeoisie in the cities and the intellectuals, and other patriotic people", and the parties themselves as "political alliances of socialist workers associated with them and patriots who support socialism".

The eight parties are as follows:

Revolutionary Committee of the Guomindang (Kuomintang)

Leadership. Wang Kunlun (acting ch.)
Founded. January 1948
History. The Committee was inaugurated in Hong Kong by elements of the Kuomintang who had opposed the policies of Chiang Kai-shek and had supported the Communist policy of continued resistance to the Japanese.

China Democratic League

Leadership. Shi Liang (ch.)
Founded. 1944
History. The League was formed from a League of Chinese Democratic Parties and Organizations founded in 1941. It was composed of intellectuals who opposed the Kuomintang's policies and, with Communist Party support, engaged in resistance to the Japanese and in the struggle for democracy, in which several of its leaders were assassinated. It was forced to dissolve in China in 1947 but some of its leaders continued its work in Hong Kong.

China Democratic National Construction Association

Leadership. Hu Juewen (ch.)
Founded. 1945
History. The Association is composed of "patriotic capitalists in industry and commerce and some intellectuals connected with business circles".

China Association for Promoting Democracy

Leadership. Zhou Jianren (ch.)
Founded. 1945
History. This Association was formed by intellectuals in Shanghai who worked in cultural and educational circles and in "patriotic democratic movements".

Chinese Peasants' and Workers' Democratic Party

Leadership. Ji Fang (ch.)
Founded. 1947
History. The party had its origins in the China Revolutionary Party, formed after Chiang Kai-shek's suppression of the Communists in 1927 and later renamed Provisional Action Committee of the Chinese Kuomintang and still later the Action Committee for the Liberation of the Chinese Nation, whose military and political activities, however, failed to overthrow Chiang Kai-shek's rule and whose founder was murdered in 1931. The party consists mainly of intellectuals working in medicine and public health.

Orientation. The party's predecessors propagated the establishment of a republic led by the national bourgeoisie, the petty-bourgeoisie and their intellectuals, but in 1935 the party turned towards the Communist Party and gradually abandoned its middle-of-the-road line and took an active part in the revolution led by the Communist Party.

Party for Public Interests
China Zhi Gong Dang

Leadership. Dr Huang Dingchen (ch.)
Founded. 1947
History. The party was preceded by groups founded by some overseas Chinese, which were reorganized in Hong Kong in 1947, when its members were re-registered. Most of them are "patriotic persons" from among Chinese who have returned from overseas.

Jiu San Society

Leadership. Xu Deheng (ch.)
History. *Jiu San* stands for Sept. 3 (the day in 1946 when the war against Japan

was ended). The party was set up by workers in cultural and educational circles.

Taiwan Democratic Self-Government League

Leadership. Cai Xiao (ch.)
Founded. 1947

History. The League was founded in Hong Kong by Chinese who had come from Taiwan and were engaged in "patriotic democratic activities". The League has called on people in Taiwan to unite, to fight against the "reactionary" Kuomintang, imperialist aggression and attempts to sever Taiwan from China.

Ciskei

Capital: Bisho   Pop. 2,100,000*

The Republic of Ciskei, which is recognized as an independent state by no governments except those of South Africa, Bophuthatswana, Transkei and Venda, has an executive President elected for a five-year term by a National Assembly which consists of 50 elected members and 37 hereditary chiefs. Elections to the National Assembly are held every five years with all citizens over 18 years (including those living outside Ciskei) being entitled to vote. To be officially recognized, political parties must have at least 10,000 members. The President of the Republic is responsible for appointing a Vice-President and a Cabinet.

Since the first elections held in 1978 the Assembly has been dominated by the Ciskei National Independence Party, and since 1980 the country has in effect been a one-party state.

* Only 700,000 are permanent residents.

Ciskei National Independence Party

Address. c/o National Assembly, Bisho, Ciskei
Leadership. President (Chief) Lennox Sebe (l.)
Founded. 1973
History. In elections to the then Legislative Assembly the party won all 22 elective seats, and 30 of the nominated seats also went to this party. The party's objective of achieving independence for Ciskei was approved in a referendum held on Dec. 4, 1980, and came into effect on Dec. 3, 1981.

Ciskei National Party

Leadership. Chief Justice Mbandla (l.)
History. In 1978 this party was given three nominated seats in the then Legislative Assembly. Although an opposition party, it supported independence for Ciskei as called for by the ruling Ciskei National Independence Party.

Colombia

Capital: Bogotá   Pop. 29,000,000

The Republic of Colombia has an executive President elected by direct popular vote for a four-year term and a bicameral Congress consisting of a 114-member Senate and a 199-member House of Representatives, both elected for four-year terms by universal adult suffrage of citizens over the age of 18 years (except members of the armed forces on active service, the police and persons deprived of their political rights). The President is elected by a simple majority and the legislatures are chosen by a list system of proportional representation. Competing lists may be presented by factions of any party but the votes gained by lists which do not obtain an electoral quota are credited to the most successful list of the same party.

In elections held on March 14, 1982, seats in the House of Representatives were gained in a 45 per cent poll as follows: Liberals 114, Conservatives 84, Democratic Unity of the Left 1. In presidential elections held on May 30, 1982, however, the Liberal vote was split by the emergence of a New Liberalism faction, with the result that the Conservative candidate was elected, gaining 46.8 per cent of the vote, against 41 per cent gained by the Liberal candidate and 10.9 by the New Liberalism candidate; only 1.2 per cent was obtained by the candidate of the Democratic Unity of the Left, this alliance consisting of the Communist Party of Colombia, the *Firmes* Movement, the Socialist Revolutionary Party and the Colombian Labour Party. The elections were also contested by the (Workers') Movement of the Revolutionary Left (MOIR), whose presidential candidate, however, withdrew from the contest.

Christian Democratic Party
Democracia Cristiana (DC)

Address. Ave. 42, 18-08, Apartado 25.867, Bogotá, Colombia

Leadership. José Agustín Linares (pres.); José Albendea (s.g.); Francisco de P. Jaramillo G. (hon. pres.)

Founded. August 1964

History. In a country where abstentions during elections have reached 60 or 70 per cent, the party has had little electoral impact, although it has had a notable intellectual influence in Colombian politics. The party took part in a United Front of Fr Camilo Torres Restrepo but withdrew from it when Marxists tried to dominate it (with Fr Torres joining the armed struggle of guerrillas in 1965).

In presidential elections in 1970 and 1978 the DC supported the (unsuccessful) moderate Conservative candidate, Dr Belisario Betancur, while in 1974 its own presidential candidate polled less than 7,000 votes and came fifth among the candidates. In the 1978 congressional elections, the DC supported the alliance of the National Opposition Union (UNO), the National Popular Alliance (ANAPO) and the Independent Liberal Movement (MIL). In the 1982 elections the DC supported, with other groups, a National Movement, as whose candidate Dr Betancur was elected President.

Orientation. Neither right nor left, opposed to the traditional Colombian constitutional system and seeking to establish a just society marked by solidarity and political democracy.

Structure. The party has a national assembly, a national council (of regional executive secretaries and former presidents), a national political committee, a general secretariat and regional and local committees.

Membership. 10,000

Publications. *Pensamiento Político,* 3,000; *Reto* (a bulletin), 5,000
International affiliations. Christian Democratic International; Christian Democratic Organization of America; Christian Democratic Youth of America

---

Communist Party of Colombia
Partido Comunista de Colombia (PCC)

Leadership. Gilberto Vieira (s.g.)
Founded. July 1930
History. The PCC was illegal for many years until it was given semi-legal status in 1957. In the 1974 presidential elections it was the leading force in the National Opposition Union (*Unión Nacional de Oposición,* UNO) whose candidate came fourth with over 130,000 votes (out of nearly 4,770,000). In the 1982 elections it formed part of the Democratic Unity of the Left (see separate entry).
Structure. The PCC is based on cells and has as its highest authority a congress convened every four years. The congress elects a central committee which in turn elects a secretariat and a central executive committee.
Publications. *Voz Proletaria* (weekly PCC organ); *Documentos Politicos* (PCC theoretical bi-monthly journal)
International affiliations. The PCC is recognized by the Communist parties of the Soviet-bloc countries.

Conservative Party of Colombia
Partido Conservador Colombiano (PCC)

Address. Calle 36, No. 16-56, Bogotá, Colombia
Leadership. Dr Belisario Betancur, Dr Misael Pastrana Borrero, Alvaro Gómez Hurtado (leaders); Elvira Cuervo de Jaramillo, Hernando Barjuch Martínez (secs.-gen.)
Founded. October 1849
History. The PCC is one of Colombia's two traditional parties (the other being the Liberal Party). From 1958 to 1978 there was, under a National Front agreement, an alternating four-year Conservative or Liberal administration.
After 1974 the Conservatives were divided into two factions, (i) the Conservatives led by Dr Pastrana Borrero (who had been President in 1970–74), who were known as Ospina-Pastranista Conservatives and who, in the 1978 general elections, won an overall total of 37 seats in the House of Representatives and 33 in

the Senate, and (ii) those led by Alvaro Gómez Hurtado (unsuccessful candidate in the 1974 presidential elections), who were known as the Alvaristas.
Under an agreement of Nov. 27, 1981, the party was reunited owing to the efforts of Dr Pastrana and Gómez Hurtado, and its candidate, Dr Betancur, was elected President in 1982
Orientation. The PCC is a democratic right-wing party advocating the rule of law, the maintenance of the three independent powers (legislative, executive and judicial), social justice on a Christian basis, and defence of the dignity of the human person.
Structure. The party has a national directorate of 18 members.
Membership. 2,500,000
Publications. *El Colombiano,* 100,000; *El País,* 60,000; *La República,* 50,000; *Occidente,* 30,000; *El Siglo,* 50,000

Democratic Unity of the Left
Unidad Democrática de la Izquierda

Leadership. Dr Gerardo Molina (presidential candidate)
Founded. 1982
History. This movement was an alliance of four left-wing organizations—the Communist Party of Colombia, the *Firmes* movement, the Socialist Revolutionary Party and the Colombian Labour Party—but in the presidential elections of May 30, 1982, its candidate obtained only 82,858 votes (or 1.2 per cent of the total valid poll).

Independent Revolutionary Workers' Movement
Movimiento Obrero Independiente Revolucionario (MOIR)

Leadership. Consuela de Montejo (presidential candidate)
History. This Maoist movement took part in the 1974 and 1978 presidential and congressional elections as part of a National Opposition Union (*Unión Nacional de Oposición,* UNO), which was led by the Communist Party of Colombia and was, in the 1978 elections, allied with the *Alianza Nacional Popular* (ANAPO) and an Independent Liberal Movement. The MOIR contested the 1982 congressional elections on its own, but as a result of its poor showing in these elections its presidential candidate, Consuela de Montejo, withdrew from the contest.

Liberal Party
Partido Liberal (PL)

Address. Avda. Jiménez 8-56, Bogotá, Colombia

Leadership. Dr Alfonso López Michelsen (l.)

Founded. 1815

History. As one of the country's two traditional parties (the other being the Conservative Party), the Liberal Party held the Presidency from 1930 to 1946, when it lost the presidential election because it had nominated two candidates of different Liberal factions. During much of this period the two parties collaborated in coalition Governments, even though the PL was the stronger of the two (gaining 73 seats in the House of Representatives in 1947, as against 58 won by the Conservative Party).

Early in 1948 the Liberal leader at the time broke off the coalition, and the two parties became involved in violent confrontation with each other. The PL leader was assassinated in April 1949, whereafter a serious insurrection devastated much of the country's capital. However, a new coalition Government was formed thereafter. The Liberals, who in congressional elections in June 1949 had remained the strongest party, boycotted the presidential elections of November 1949, but the Conservative President elected was deposed in 1953 by Gen. Gustavo Rojas Pinilla, the leader of the *Alianza Nacional Popular.*

After the latter's regime had ended in 1957, the Liberals and Conservatives concluded an agreement for alternate presidencies for the two parties during the 1958-74 period, with both parties having an equal number of seats in both Houses of Congress and an equal number of ministers in the Cabinet. This agreement was, largely owing to division in both parties, not applied to Congress from 1960 onwards, but the PL remained the strongest party in Congress. Nevertheless it formed a coalition Government with the Conservatives after the 1974 elections, in which it gained 113 out of 199 seats in the Lower House, and again after the 1978 elections— the Presidency having remained in PL hands.

In the March 1982 parliamentary elections the party retained its commanding position with 114 (out of 199) seats in the House of Representatives and 62 (out of 114) in the Senate. However, in the presidential elections of May 1982 the party was weakened by the formation of the New Liberalism faction (see separate entry) which fielded its own candidate, with the result that the official Liberal Party candidate, Dr López Michelsen, was defeated by the Conservative candidate.

Orientation. The PL stands for free enterprise and advocates moderate economic and social reforms.

Movement for National Renovation
Movimiento de Renovación Nacional (MRN)

Address. Apartado Aereo 91175, Bogotá, Colombia

Leadership. Gen. (rtd.) Alvaro Valencia Tovar (l.); Enrique Umaña (s.g.)

Founded. November 1977

History. The MRN was established in order to contest the presidential elections of June 4, 1978, in which its leader (who had been commander of the Army in 1974-75 but had been dismissed after reports of an intended army coup) obtained some 66,000 votes. It did not take part in later elections, as one of its principal aims was a reform of Congress in order to improve its quality.

Orientation. Democratic right-wing, advocating more active participation in political life by common citizens in order to restore real meaning to democracy.

Structure. Under its leader and national director, the MRN has a board of councillors and a secretary-general, as well as state boards.

Publications. *Renovación* (weekly)

National Popular Alliance
Alianza Nacional Popular (ANAPO)

Leadership. Joaquín Mejía (l.)

Founded. 1971

History. ANAPO was formed as a mass party to support ex-President Gustavo Rojas Pinilla (who had been dictator in 1953-57). Although not recognized as a political party, ANAPO took part in congressional elections in 1966 (as one of three groups constituting the "opposition"), gaining 36 (out of 180) seats in the Chamber of Representatives. In the Chamber elected in 1968, ANAPO obtained 42 seats (six out of 102 seats allotted to the Liberals and 36 out of 102 allotted to the Conservatives under the constitutional parity arrangement).

In 1970 ANAPO made further gains, obtaining 72 out of 210 seats in the Chamber as the strongest opposition party. In the 1974 general elections, however, ANAPO obtained only 15 out of 199 seats in the Chamber. In presidential elections held in the same year the party's then leader, María Eugenia Rojas de Moreno Díaz (ex-President Rojas Pinilla's daughter), as the first woman to stand for the Colombian presidency, obtained about 10 per cent of the total vote.

The 1978 presidential and congressional elections were contested by an alliance of the National Opposition Union, ANAPO and the Independent Liberal Movement and this alliance gained only four (out of 199) seats in the Chamber. ANAPO did not take part in the 1982 elections.

Orientation. ANAPO stands for "Colombian socialism" on a Christian social basis. Its programme involves the unification of all trade unions in one organization; discouragement of birth control; limitation of foreign investment; free education for all and free health services for the poor; and a hectare of land with a house for each homeless peasant.

Structure. ANAPO is organized on a hierarchical basis.

New Liberalism
Nuevo Liberalismo

Leadership. Dr Luis Carlos Galán Sarmiento (presidential candidate)

Founded. 1982

History. This faction of the Liberal Party was set up with the support of the prominent Liberal Dr Carlos Lleras Sarmiento (who had been President of the Republic in 1966-70), with the aim of opposing the official Liberal candidate in the 1982 presidential elections, Dr Alfonso López Michelsen. The latter was defeated by the Conservative candidate after Dr Galán had obtained 10.9 per cent of the valid votes.

Orientation. Dr Galán campaigned for the abolition of the existing two-party system and of the constitutional provision allowing former Presidents to seek re-election after a period out of office. His aim was to evolve the Liberal Party into a broad national movement of the centre-left.

Workers' Socialist Party
Partido Socialista de los Trabajadores (PST)

Leadership. María Socorro Ramírez (l.)

History. The PST leader unsuccessfully contested the 1978 presidential elections.

Comoros

Capital: Moroni (on Njazidja or Grand Comoro)   Pop. 370,000*

The Federal and Islamic Republic of the Comoros has, under its Constitution approved in a referendum on Oct. 1, 1981, a President elected for a six-year term by universal adult suffrage and a 38-member Federal Assembly elected similarly for a five-year term in single-member constituencies by citizens above the age of 18 years. There is a Cabinet headed by a Prime Minister appointed by the President, who shares with the Assembly the power to dismiss him. For the elections to the Federal Assembly held in December 1978 no political parties had been formed. However, following the Assembly's decision in January 1979 that a one-party system should be established for 12 years, the Union for Comorian Progress was formed as the country's sole political organization.

Within what it regards as its own borders, the Government of President Ahmed Abdallah has no authority over the island of Mayotte, whose population has opted by a substantial majority to remain under the sovereignty of France.

* Excluding Mayotte.

Union for Comorian Progress
Union pour le Progrès Comorien (UPC)

Founded. 1982

History. This party was officially set up to stimulate popular participation in the country's social and economic develop-

ment. It helped to organize the March 1982 elections to the Federal Assembly, although candidates stood in their individual capacity and not as party members, a procedure which highlighted the differences between the UPC and other African ruling parties.

Congo

Capital: Brazzaville   Pop. 1,600,000

The People's Republic of the Congo has been ruled by a Military Committee of the Congolese Party of Labour (*Parti Congolais du Travail*, PCT) since the assassination of President Marien Ngouabi on March 18, 1977, whereafter the Constitution was suspended and the National Assembly dissolved. Under a new Constitution approved in a referendum on July 8, 1979, provision was made for a popularly elected National People's Assembly consisting of members nominated by the PCT. The congress of the PCT appoints the country's President, who presides over a Council of Ministers headed by a Prime Minister. In elections to the People's National Assembly held on July 8, 1979, over 90 per cent of the voters were stated to have approved the PCT's official candidates.

Congolese Party of Labour
Parti Congolais du Travail (PCT)

Leadership. Col. Denis Sassou-Ngouesso (pres. of central committee)

Founded. December 1969

History. The party was created to supersede an earlier *Mouvement National de la Révolution* as the country's sole legal political organization.

Orientation. From the outset the party subscribed to Marxist-Leninist principles in order to realize "the proletarian ideals of the Congolese people in work, democracy and peace".

Structure. The party's highest organ is the national party congress, due to meet every five years. There is a central committee (of 60 members) meeting three times a year and directing party policies, and a politburo exercising the central committee's functions from day to day. There are also a military committee of 10 members and three specialized organizations (for trade unions, women and youth).

Publications. *Etumba* (weekly)

Costa Rica

Capital: San José   Pop. 2,300,000

The Republic of Costa Rica is a democratic multi-party state with an executive President elected for four years by universal adult suffrage. He appoints, and presides over, a Cabinet. Legislative power is held by a Legislative Assembly similarly elected by universal adult suffrage of all citizens above the age of 18 years and under a system of proportional representation. The Government subsidizes election campaign expenses per vote (in the following election) of any party which obtains a minimum of 5 per cent of the vote.

As a result of elections held on Feb. 7, 1982 (with the participation of 77 per cent of the electorate), seats in the Assembly were distributed as follows: National Liberation Party (PLN) 33, Unity Alliance 18, People United 4,

National Movement 1, Alajuela Democratic Party 1. The Unity Alliance consisted of the Democratic Renewal Party, the Christian Democratic Party, the Calderonist Republican Party and the Popular Union. The People United coalition included the (pro-Soviet communist) Popular Vanguard Party.

Calderonist Republican Party
Partido Republicano Calderonista (PRC)

Leadership. Alvaro Cubillo Aguilar (pres.); Gerardo Bolaños Alpízar (sec.)
Founded. August 1976
History. The party was founded by Rafael Angel Calderón after a split in the National Unification Party. In the 1978 elections it formed part of the successful conservative *Unidad Opositora* alliance and in the 1982 elections it was a member of the Unity (*Unidad*) alliance. In December 1983 it joined the Christian Social Party (see separate entry).

Cartago Agricultural Union
Unión Agricola Cartaginés

Leadership. Guillermo Brenes Castillo (pres.); Rodrigo Fallas Bonilla (sec.)
History. The party is one of several provincial movements and nominated its own candidates in the 1978 presidential and legislative elections, in which it gained one seat in the Legislative Assembly. In the 1982 elections it presented no presidential candidate and it lost its seat in the Assembly.

Christian Democratic Party
Partido Demócrata Cristiano (PDC)

Address. Apdo 4241, San José, Costa Rica
Leadership. Rafael Alberto Grillo-Rivera (pres.); Claudio Guevara Barahona (sec.).
Founded. 1962
History. The PDC has been a minor party in Costa Rica, unsuccessfully contesting presidential elections in 1970 and 1974, and gaining few seats in the Legislative Assembly. In 1978, however, it was one of the four parties forming the *Unidad Opositora*, whose candidate was elected President and which gained the largest number of seats, though not an absolute majority, in the Legislative Assembly. In the 1982 elections it was a member of the Unity (*Unidad*) alliance, and in December

1983 it became the leading partner in the Christian Social Party newly formed by the four member parties of the Unity alliance.
International affiliations. Christian Democratic International; Christian Democratic Organization of America.

Christian Social Party
Partido Social Cristiano

Address. c/o Aníbal Pérez Solís, P.O. Box 8075, San José. Costa Rica
Leadership. Rafael Angel Calderón Fournier (pres.); Roberto Tovar (sec.)
Founded. Dec. 17, 1983
History. This party was formed by the merger of the four parties previously allied in the Unity (*Unidad*) coalition (see separate entry), i.e. the Christian Democratic Party, the Democratic Renewal Party, the Calderonist Republican Party and the Popular Union. To the formation of this new unified party the Christian Democratic Party contributed the ideology and the human and material resources derived from an Institute of Political Studies (INDEP), set up to co-ordinate political education and organization throughout the country.

Costa Rican Socialist Party
Partido Socialista Costarricense

Leadership. Alvaro Montero Mejía (pres.); Alberto Salom Echeverría (sec.)
History. In the 1982 elections this party was part of the People United (*Pueblo Unido*) alliance.

Democratic Action for Alajuela
Acción Democrática Alajuelense

Leadership. Francisco Alfaro Fernández (pres.); Juan Bautista Chacón Soto (sec.)
History. In the 1982 elections this regional party gained one seat in the Legislative Assembly.

Democratic Party
Partido Demócrata (PD)

Leadership. Edwin Retana Chávez (pres.); Alvaro Gonzáles Espinoza (sec.)

History. The PD is a minor party whose candidate unsuccessfully contested the 1974 presidential elections. Its president was equally unsuccessful in contesting the 1982 presidential elections.

Democratic Renewal Party
Partido de Renovación Democrática (PRD)

Address. Avda. Central 3425, San José, Costa Rica
Leadership. Oscar Aguilar Bulgarelli (pres.); Miguel Angel Rodríguez Aguero (sec.)
Founded. 1947
History. The PRD was founded by Rodrigo Carazo Odio, who came fourth in that year's presidential election. As a conservative party, it joined the *Unidad Opositora* alliance for the 1978 elections, in which Carazo Odio was elected President and the alliance became the strongest party in the Legislative Assembly.

In the 1982 elections it was a member of the Unity (*Unidad*) alliance, and in December 1983 it joined the newly-formed Christian Social Party (see separate entry).

National Democratic Party
Partido Nacional Democrático (PND)

Leadership. Rodolfo Cerdas Cruz (pres.); Eladio Jara Jiménez (sec.)
History. This party's president had earlier been president of a Costa Rican Popular Front (*Frente Popular Costarricense*, FPC), which had contested the 1978 elections independently.

National Independent Party
Partido Nacional Independiente (PNI)

Address. Calle 18 y 20, Avda. Central, San José, Costa Rica
Leadership. Jorge González Martén (pres.); Alberto Pinto Gutiérrez (sec.)
History. The PNI, a strongly anti-communist party, was formed to contest the 1974 election (in which it gained six seats in the Legislative Assembly and its presidential candidate came third) but by 1978 it had declined, gaining no seats in the Assembly elections which took place in that year.

National Liberation Party
Partido Liberación Nacional (PLN)

Address. P.O. Box 2919, San José, Costa Rica
Leadership. José Figueres Ferrer (pres.); Oscar Arias Sánchez (s.g.)
Founded. October 1951
History. The founders of the PLN included members of the former Social Democratic Party. In the 1953 presidential elections the PLN leader was elected President of the Republic. Though losing the 1958 presidential elections, the party gained a majority in Congress in that year, while in 1962 the PLN won both the presidential elections and a majority in Congress. In 1966 it lost the presidency, but regained it in 1970 and retained it in 1974, while the party maintained its majority in Congress. In 1978, however, the PLN lost both the presidential and the congressional elections to the (conservative) *Unidad Opositora* alliance.

After the 1982 elections it returned to power, and Luis Alberto Monge (former secretary-general of the party) became President, having gained 53.7 per cent of the total vote.
Orientation. The PLN is "a social democratic party with the objective of a peaceful transformation of the social system into democratic socialism, eliminating the rift between social classes". During his election campaign Luis Alberto Monge called for "a return to the land", promised to stimulate agricultural production and to halt the rural exodus, and said that economic recovery was important to save Costa Rica from being "swept away in a whirlwind of violence". He supported proposals for a negotiated settlement of the conflict in El Salvador, and in this context he expressed regret that the Sandinista Government in that country was aligning itself with the Soviet Union and Cuba.
Structure. The PLN's supreme organ is a national assembly of 70 delegates. The party has a three-member national executive committee, a seven-member national political committee, seven provincial committees and seven provincial assemblies, 80 cantonal assemblies and 80 cantonal committees and 410 district assemblies.
Membership. 367,000
Publications. *Combate* (monthly), c. 15,000
International affiliations. Socialist International

National Movement
Movimiento Nacional

Leadership. Mario Echandé Jiménez (pres.); Rodrigo Sancho Roblés (sec.)
History. In the 1982 elections this conservative party gained one seat in the Legislative Assembly, and its president, who contested the presidential elections, obtained 3.7 per cent of the total valid votes.

People United
Pueblo Unido

Leadership. Rodrigo Roberto Gutiérrez
Founded. 1978
History. This alliance of left-wing parties gained three seats in the 1978 elections to the National Assembly. For the 1982 elections it consisted of the Costa Rican Socialist Party, the Workers' Party and the Popular Vanguard Party and gained four seats. Its presidential candidate, Rodrigo Roberto Gutiérrez, obtained 3.2 per cent of the total valid votes in the 1982 elections.

Popular Union
Unión Popular

Address. Calle Central, Avda. 2, San José, Costa Rica
Leadership. Manuel Jiménez de la Guardia (pres.); Carlos Alfredo Castro Charpentier (sec.)
History. The UP is a minor conservative party, which joined the successful *Unidad Opositora* alliance for the 1978 elections. In the 1982 elections this party was part of the Unity (*Unidad*) alliance, and in December 1983 it joined the newly-formed Christian Social Party (see separate entry).

Popular Vanguard Party
Partido Vanguardia Popular (PVP)

Address. Calle 10, No. 1037, San José, Costa Rica
Leadership. Manuel Mora Valverde (pres.); Humberto Elías Vargas Carbonell (sec.)
Founded. 1931
History. Founded as the Communist Party, the PVP adopted its present name in 1943, and was instrumental in forming the Costa Rican Confederation of Labour.

It was outlawed under the 1949 Constitution but regained legal status in May 1975. In the 1974 elections its members supported the Socialist Action Party, and in the 1978 and 1982 elections it formed part of the People United alliance.

In January 1984 the party was divided into two factions—one led by Manuel Mora Valverde and the other by Arnoldo Ferreto and Humberto Elías Vargas Carbonell. The former was reported to favour a peaceful solution of the conflicts in Central America, Mora Valverde having close ties with President Castro of Cuba; the latter faction was pro-Soviet and said to be willing to face a confrontation with the United States.

Orientation. In a programme adopted at a party congress in May 1971 the party called for "a democratic, popular, agrarian and anti-imperialist revolution followed by a socialist revolution as a single uninterrupted process", and at a 1976 congress the party's secretary-general advocated the transformation of Costa Rica into "Cuba's identical twin".

Structure. The PVP is organized in accordance with the principle of democratic centralism. Its supreme body is the congress, and between congress sessions its central committee plenum. The party is led by the central committee's political commission and secretariat.

Publications. *Libertad* (newspaper)
International affiliations. The PVP is recognized by the Communist parties of the Soviet-bloc countries.

Republican Union Party
Partido Unión Republicana

Address. Apartado Postal 5307, San José, Costa Rica
Leadership. Sigurd Koberg van Patten (pres.): Marino Donato Magurno (sec.)
Founded. July 1975
History. Formed by dissident members of the *Partido Unificación Nacional* (PUN, which was subsequently dissolved), the party was officially recognized in August 1975. In the national elections of 1978 it obtained only 8,700 votes or 1 per cent of the total, and no seats, but it had held one seat in Congress in 1974-78.
Orientation. The party advocates a "republican democratic type of government".

Socialist Action Party
Partido de Acción Socialista (PAS)

Leadership. Marcial Aguiluz Orellana (pres.); Arnaldo Ferreto Segura (sec.)

History. This party was formed after the Popular Vanguard Party—the pro-Moscow Communist Party—had been declared illegal in 1949. Largely supported by Communists, it unsuccessfully contested the 1970 presidential elections, won two seats in the 1974 legislative elections and was part of the People United alliance in the 1978 elections.

Socialist Workers' Organization
Organización Socialista de los Trabajadores (OST)

Address. Apdo. 949, San José, Costa Rica

Leadership. Marta Trejos Montero (pres.); Rosendo Fujol Mesalles (sec.)

Founded. May 1976

History. The OST was founded by a group of militant Marxists "in order to open up a workers' political perspective clearly distinguished from the opportunism of the Latin American Communist parties dependent on the leadership of the USSR, and also from the adventurism of guerrilla groups". It was legally recognized in May 1977 and took part in the general and presidential elections of February 1978, presenting "the first working-class presidential candidate in the country's history".

Orientation. The OST is a Marxist revolutionary party aiming at world revolution through "the seizure of power of workers' and peasants' councils as an integral part of the world's revolutionary process".

Publications. *Que Hacer* (official organ, fortnightly), 4,000

International affiliations. The OST is the Costa Rican section of the Fourth (Trotskyist) International.

Unity
Unidad

Leadership. Rafael Angel Calderón Fournier (presidential candidate)

Founded. 1982

History. This conservative alliance succeeded the earlier Opposition Union (*Unidad Opositora*), which was in power from 1978 to 1982. The new alliance comprised the following parties: the Christian Democratic Party, the Democratic Renewal Party, the Calderonist Republican Party and the Popular Union. In the 1982 elections it gained 18 seats in the Legislative Assembly and its presidential candidate, Rafael Angel Calderón

Fournier (who had been Foreign Minister until 1966), came second with 32.7 per cent of the total valid votes. In December 1983 the four Unity partners merged in a new party, the Christian Social Party (see separate entry).

Workers' Party
Partido de los Trabajadores

Leadership. Luis Fernando Astorga Gattgens (pres.); José Fabio Araya Monge (sec.)

History. In the 1978 and 1982 elections the party formed part of the People United alliance.

Orientation. This Maoist party originated as the political wing of a Revolutionary Movement of the People, a support group for the Sandinista National Liberation Front which came to power in Nicaragua in July 1979.

Other Parties

Costa Rica, being an open democracy with a long tradition of political participation, has a wide and ever-changing array of small political formations representing all parts of the ideological spectrum. However, none of these minor parties—some of which are listed below—has succeeded in mounting a serious challenge to the formations described above.

Costa Rican Concordia *(Concordia Costarricense),* led by Emilio Piedra Jiménez (pres.) and Roberto Francisco Salazar Madriz (sec.).

Independent Party *(Partido Independiente),* led by Eugenio Jiménez Sancho (pres.) and Gonzalo Jiménez Chaves (sec.).

National Christian Alliance *(Alianza Nacional Cristiana),* led by Victor Hugo González Montero (pres.) and Juan Rodríguez Venegas (sec.).

National Defence *(Defensa Nacional),* led by José Francisco Herrera Romero (pres.) and Emerita Córdoba Arrieta (sec.).

National Progress Party *(Partido Progreso Nacional,* PPN), led by Miguel Barzuna

Sauma (pres.) and Carlos Manuel Brenes Méndez (sec.).

National Unification Party *(Partido Unificación Nacional,* PUN), led by Guillermo Villalobos Arce (pres.) and Rogelio Ramos Valverde (sec.).

People's Action *(Acción del Pueblo),* led by Angel Ruíz Zúñiga (pres.) and Henry Mora Jiménez (sec.).

Radical Democratic Party *(Partido Radical Democrático),* a non-Marxist left-wing party founded in 1982.

Cuba

Capital: Havana   Pop. 10,000,000

The Republic of Cuba has a Government which since December 1961 has been designated as Communist. Under a Constitution approved in a referendum in February 1976 the Republic was defined as "a socialist state of work-people and other manual and intellectual workers"; the leading role of the Communist Party of Cuba was recognized; and the "fraternal friendship, aid and co-operation of the Soviet Union and other socialist countries" were acknowledged. Under this Constitution a 481-member National Assembly is elected indirectly for a five-year term by delegates elected to municipal assemblies (the basic organs of "people's power") by universal suffrage of citizens above the age of 16 years. Most of the candidates are Communist Party members; they need to obtain an overall majority in a first ballot, failing which a second (run-off) ballot is held. The head of state and government (currently Dr Fidel Castro Ruz, First Secretary of the Cuban Communist Party) is elected by the National Assembly as President of the Council of State, which is the country's highest representative body and which, in addition to its President, five Vice-Presidents and its secretary, has another 23 members. There is also a Council of Ministers headed by an Executive Committee, of which Dr Castro is Chairman. In elections to 169 municipal assemblies on Oct. 11 and 18, 1981, a total of 9,763 delegates were elected in a 97.2 per cent poll in the first ballot and another 10,725 delegates in a 93.6 per cent poll in the second ballot.

Communist Party of Cuba
Partido Comunista Cubano (PCC)

Address. Havana, Cuba
Leadership. Dr Fidel Castro Ruz (first sec.); Raúl Castro Ruz (second sec.); Juan Almeida Bosque, Ramiro Valdés Menéndez, Guillermo García Frías, Armando Hart Dávalos, Sergio del Valle Jiménez, Blas Roca Calderío, José R. Machado Ventura, Carlos Rafael Rodríguez Rodríguez, Pedro Miret Prieto, Arnaldo Milián Castro, Jorge Risquet

Valdés, Julio Camacho Aguilera, Osmany Cienfuegos Gorriarán (other members of politburo)
Founded. October 1965
History. The PCC traces its origins back to the anti-colonial Cuban Revolutionary Party founded in 1892 by José Marti and Carlos Balino, of whom the latter was among the founders of Cuba's first Marxist-Leninist party in August 1925 in conditions of clandestinity. This party became the Popular Socialist Party (PSP) under a change of name effected in 1943.

More directly, the present party derives from Fidel Castro's "26th of July Movement" named after the date of an early unsuccessful armed uprising against the Batista regime in 1953. Sentenced to a long prison term after the failure of the rising, Castro was subsequently amnestied and was able to leave Cuba for Mexico, where he gathered resources and supporters.

In early December 1956 Castro and a small group of fellow-revolutionaries (including Ernesto "Che" Guevara) landed in Cuba from the yacht *Granma* and established a guerrilla base in the Sierra Maestra mountains which became the centre of a growing popular movement for the restoration of democratic liberties and for social justice. Batista's position steadily crumbled and Castro's final offensive in mid-1958 met with little resistance, the victory of the Cuban revolution being proclaimed on Jan. 1, 1959.

The new regime, with Castro as Prime Minister, carried out a series of nationalization measures and a radical land reform, but many of his former supporters in the 26th of July Movement went into exile in the United States, with which diplomatic relations were broken off in January 1961. Isolated diplomatically and economically by the Organization of American States (OAS), Castro established close relations with the Soviet Union and other Communist states and internally initiated co-operation with the PSP, whose members had played little active part in the revolution. The abortive Bay of Pigs invasion by US-sponsored Cuban exiles in April 1961 accelerated this rapprochement and in mid-1961 Castro amalgamated the 26th of July Movement with the PSP and the Revolutionary Directorate to create the Integrated Revolutionary Organizations

(OCI). In December 1961 Castro for the first time avowed himself to be a Marxist-Leninist and shortly afterwards ousted the Communist "old guard" led by Anibal Escalante. In the course of 1962 a new United Party of the Cuban Socialist Revolution was established under Castro's leadership as the sole legal party and in October 1965 Castro announced that its name had been changed to the Communist Party of Cuba. The PCC held its first congress in December 1975 at which it adopted a party constitution and programme platform.

Orientation. The PCC is a Marxist-Leninist party committed to the establishment of a socialist economy and social structure. Closely aligned with the Communist Party of the Soviet Union, the PCC also regards itself as being in the vanguard of revolutionary struggle in Latin America and the Third World generally, particularly Africa, while the Cuban Government has participated actively in the Non-Aligned Movement notwithstanding its close Soviet ties and Comecon membership.

Structure. The PCC has, in its constitution, defined democratic centralism as the guiding principle of the party's organizational structure. It has some 20,000 branches, 169 municipal and 14 provincial committees, a central committee, a 13-member political bureau (politburo) and a nine-member secretariat.

Membership. 450,000

Publications. *Granma* (national daily organ), 600,000; party dailies in every province; *El Militante Comunista* (monthly of the Communist Party's central committee secretariat), 180,000

Cyprus

Capital: Nicosia   Pop. 835,000

Since February 1975 the Republic of Cyprus (a member of the Commonwealth) has been *de facto* divided into two states—the (Greek-Cypriot) Republic of Cyprus and the (Turkish-Cypriot) Turkish Republic of Northern Cyprus (not internationally recognized). The latter was declared on Nov. 15, 1983, by the Assembly of the Turkish Federated State of Cyprus, itself created after the occupation by Turkish troops of about 40 per cent of the island's area in July

1974. Both are multi-party states and have an executive President presiding over a Cabinet, as well as unicameral Parliaments elected by universal adult suffrage. In 1976 elections to the House of Representatives were held on the basis of a simple majority vote in single-member constituencies, but the 1981 elections took place under a complex system of proportional representation in six constituencies (in the Greek-Cypriot-controlled areas). The minimum voting age is 21 years, and voting is compulsory.

The Greek-Cypriot 35-member House of Representatives has, as a result of elections held on May 24, 1981, a distribution of seats as follows: the (communist) Progressive Party of the Working People (AKEL) 12, Democratic Rally 12, Democratic Party 8 and Socialist Party of Cyprus (EDEK) 3. In the Turkish-Cypriot Assembly the 40 seats are, as a result of elections held on June 28, 1981, distributed as follows: National Unity Party 18, the (Maoist) Socialist Salvation (Communal Liberation) Party 13, Republican Turkish Party (orthodox Communist) 6, Democratic People's Party 2 and Turkish Unity Party 1.

Centre Union
Enosi Kentrou

Address. c/o *O Kirykas*, Chanteclair Bldg., Nicosia, Cyprus
Leadership. Tassos Papadopoulos (pres.)
Founded. 1981
History. Tassos Papadopoulos, a former minister, was elected to the House of Representatives as an independent member in 1976. The Centre Union contested the parliamentary elections of May 24, 1981, but gained only 2.7 per cent of the vote and no seat.
Orientation. The party is right of centre.
Publications. *O Kirykas* (party organ, daily)

Democratic Party
Demokratiki Komma (DIKO)

Address. 13, Diagoras Street, Nicosia, Cyprus
Leadership. President Spyros Kyprianou (pres.)
Founded. 1976
History. This centre-right party was organized principally to continue the long-term struggle against the Turkish occupation of northern Cyprus (in 1974). In the 1976 elections it gained 21 of the 35 Greek Cypriot seats in the House of Representatives. Its president became President of the Republic of Cyprus in 1977 and was elected unopposed in January 1978; he was re-elected on Feb. 13, 1983, when he obtained 56.54 per cent of the vote as the candidate of the Democratic Alliance, consisting of his own party and

the Progressive Party of the Working People (AKEL).
DIKO won only eight seats in the House of Representatives on Feb. 13, 1983, but it remained in power (which it had held since its foundation) with the support of the (communist) AKEL.
Orientation. The party stands for the rights of the Greek Cypriot community and for the establishment of a bi-communal Federal Republic of Cyprus.
Publications. *I Eleftherotypia* (daily); *I Eleftherotypia Tis Defteras* (weekly)

Democratic Rally
Democraticos Synagermos (DISY)

Address. 4C Palama Street (P.O. Box 5305), Nicosia, Cyprus
Leadership. Glafcos Clerides (pres.)
Founded. June 1976
History. The Democratic Rally was formed by former members of the United Party, the Progressive Front and the Democratic National Party. In the 1976 general elections it polled 27.5 per cent of the vote but gained no seats as a result of the majority electoral system, being defeated by a three-party alliance of the Democratic Party, the Progressive Party of the Working People (AKEL) and the Unified Democratic Union of Cyprus (EDEK)—an alliance which it regarded as communist-inspired.
In the 1981 general elections, carried out on the basis of proportional representation, DISY polled 32 per cent of the votes and gained 12 of the 35 seats in the House of Representatives. In the 1983 presidential elections the party's president failed to be elected, gaining only about 34 per cent of

the votes, against 56.54 per cent for President Kyprianou of the Democratic Alliance (consisting of the Democratic Party and AKEL).

Orientation. This right-wing party believes in democracy, respect for human rights, private initiative and social justice.

Structure. The party has a president, two vice-presidents and a secretary-general (all elected by members), a central committee (as the party's supreme organ) and a political committee which, with the president, decides policies on most issues; current administration is carried out by a political bureau (the executive of the political committee). Under a new party constitution adopted on July 6, 1983, democratic rule within the party has been strengthened and all officials are elected by the elected representatives of party members.

Membership. 10,000

International affiliations. Christian Democratic International; European Christian Democratic Union; European Democrat Union; International Democrat Union

---

New Democratic Camp
Nea Demokratiki Parataxi (NEDIPA)

Address. c/o *To Vima*, Nicosia, Cyprus
Leadership. Alecos Michaelides (pres.)
Founded. 1980
History. The party was formed mainly by former members of the ruling Democratic Party (DIKO). In the elections to the House of Representatives on May 24, 1981, it gained no seat and only 1.9 per cent of the vote.

Orientation. The party has taken a stance to the right of centre.

Publications. *To Vima* (party organ, weekly)

Pan-Cyprian Renewal Front
Panglprion Ananeotikon Metopon (PAME)

Address. c/o *I Kypriaki*, Eiffel Bldg., 2 Chr. Sozou St., Nicosia, Cyprus
Leadership. Dr Chrysostomos Sofianos (pres.)
Founded. 1981
History. Dr Sofianos had been Minister of Education in 1976-80. In the 1981 elections to the House of Representatives his party gained 2.8 per cent of the votes and no seat.

Orientation. PAME is a left of centre formation.

Publications. *I Kypriaki* (party organ, weekly)

Progressive Party of the Working People
Anorthotikon Komma Ergazomenou Laou (AKEL)

Address. 10 Akamantos Street, Nicosia, Cyprus
Leadership. Ezekias Papaioannou (g.s., parl. l.)
Founded. 1926
History. AKEL is descended from the Communist Party of Cyprus, which held its first congress in 1926 but was declared illegal by British authorities in 1931. Constituted in 1941, AKEL absorbed the Communist Party but was itself illegal from 1955 to 1959, becoming legal again in December of that year, shortly before Cyprus attained independence. It claims to be the oldest and largest party in Cyprus and, although taking no part in the (Greek Cypriot) Government, it supports those government policies considered positive.

Orientation. As a communist party based on the principles of Marxism-Leninism, AKEL works for "the complete liberation of Cyprus and for socialism".

Structure. There are party groups, area and district committees; a central committee elects a political bureau and a secretariat.

Membership. 12,000

Publications. *Haravgi* (Dawn, daily); *Demokratia* (weekly)

International affiliations. AKEL is recognized by the Communist parties of the Soviet-bloc countries.

Unified Democratic Union of Cyprus
Eniea Demokratiki Enosi Kyprou (EDEK)

Address. 23 Constantinos Paleologous, Nicosia, Cyprus
Leadership. Dr Vassos Lyssarides (pres.); Takis Hadjidemetriou (s.g.)
Founded. February 1969
History. Under the name of Democratic Centre Union, the party gained two seats in elections held in July 1970 for the 35 Greek-Cypriot seats in the Cyprus House of Representatives. The party stood for the political independence of Cyprus, the nationalization of mines and the ending of British bases in Cyprus. It strongly opposed Greek interference in Cyprus and the Turkish invasion of Cyprus in 1974, and it supported the return to power of President Makarios (who had been temporarily deposed in 1974).

In elections held in September 1976 EDEK gained four seats in the House of Representatives (having contested the elections in an alliance with the ruling Democratic Party and the Progressive Party of the Working People). In the 1983 presidential elections Dr Lyssarides, as candidate of a National Salvation Front, polled 9.53 per cent of the total vote.

Orientation. EDEK is a socialist party, standing for radical socio-economic changes, the ending of the Turkish occupation of part of Cyprus and full implementation of UN resolutions on Cyprus.

Structure. EDEK has local groups, regional and district committees, a central committee, a politburo and a secretariat.

Publications. *Ta Nea* (daily), 6,250; *Anexartitos* (weekly), 7,000

International affiliations. Socialist International

Turkish Republic of Northern Cyprus

Communal Leap Party
Toplumscu Atilim Partisi

Leadership. Irsen Kucuk
Founded. July 1984.
Orientation. This new party regards the Turkish Cypriot community as an indivisible part of the Turkish nation.

Democratic People's Party
Demokratik Halk Partisi

Leadership. Ismet Kotak
Founded. February 1979
History. The party was established by Nejat Konuk, who was the first Prime Minister of the Turkish Federated State of Cyprus and who, with five other members of the Legislative Assembly, defected from the National Unity Party. However, on Dec. 10, 1981, he resigned as leader of the party, and in January 1982 he announced that he would sit in the Assembly as an independent.

In the 1981 presidential elections the party's candidate, Gen. Husamettin Tanyar, had received only 4.78 per cent of the total vote, while in the legislative elections held at the same time the party had won two seats. In March 1982 the party entered into a coalition Government with the National and the Turkish Unity parties. In December 1983 Nejak Konuk became Prime Minister of the newly-proclaimed Turkish Republic of Northern Cyprus.

Orientation. As a left-wing party based on social democratic principles and also loyal to the "principles of nationalism, revolutionism and secularism", it aims at

the achievement of an independent, non-aligned, bizonal, bicommunal, federal republic of Cyprus, which would tolerate no foreign bases. The party seeks to maintain good relations with all parties in Turkey without being formally attached to any of them.

National Unity Party
Ulusal Birlik Partisi (UBP)

Leadership. Mustafa Cagatay (parl. l.); Hakki Atun (g.s.)
Founded. 1975
History. Founded by Rauf Denktash, the UBP had its origins in an earlier National Solidarity (*Ulusal Dayanisma*) movement. After the party had won three-quarters of the 40 seats in the Turkish Cypriot Legislative Assembly in June 1976, its then secretary-general, Nejat Konuk, became Prime Minister of the Turkish Federated State of Cyprus, whose President, Rauf Denktash, was precluded by the state's Constitution from serving as the party's president or submitting to its discipline. Konuk, however, resigned as Prime Minister in March 1978, and subsequently, with other members of the party (including Osman Orek, his successor as Prime Minister), from the UBP, and formed the Democratic People's Party in February 1979. The UBP's strength in the Legislative Assembly was thus reduced from 30 to 24.

Denktash, who had become President of the Turkish Federated State of Cyprus in 1975 and had been formally elected in 1976, was re-elected President on June 28, 1981, when he obtained 51.77 per cent of the vote (in a contest with four other candidates). However, in legislative elections held on the same day his party's strength was further reduced to 18 members in the Legislative Assembly. As it remained the strongest party, it formed a new Government in August 1981; on Dec. 7, 1981, this Government fell after the adoption, by 21 votes to 17, of a motion of no confidence by the Socialist Salvation (Communal Liberation) Party, the Republican Turkish Party and the Democratic People's Party. The UBP thereupon formed a coalition Government with the Democratic People's Party and the Turkish Unity Party, which was sworn in on March 15, 1982.

Orientation. The party's programme and principles are based on those of Kemal Ataturk (the founder of the Turkish

Republic) and comprise social justice and peaceful coexistence in an independent, bizonal, federal state of Cyprus.

New Birth Party
Yeni Dogus Partisi

Founded. January 1984

History. The founding council of this new party, formed in the wake of the declaration of the Turkish Republic of Northern Cyprus in December 1983, consisted of four members of the Assembly, namely Aytac Besester, Baki Topaloglu, Ferhat Ulutas and Ismail Tezer.

Populist Party
Halkçi Parti (HP)

Leadership. Alper Y. Orhon (l.)

Founded. 1975

History. In the 1976 elections this party gained two seats in the Legislative Assembly but it has not been represented in Parliament since 1981.

Orientation. The HP is a social democratic party with the aim of achieving a bizonal federal republic of Cyprus.

Republican Turkish Party
Cumhuriyetçi Türk Partisi

Address. 99/A, Sht. Salahi Sevket Sokak, Lefkosa (Nicosia), Cyprus

Leadership. Özker Özgür (ch.); Naci Usar (g.s.)

Founded. December 1970

History. The party's founder, Ahmed Mithat Berberoghlou, unsuccessfully opposed Rauf Denktash in the February 1973 election of the Vice-President of Cyprus and also in the 1976 election for the presidency of the Turkish Federated State of Cyprus, but the party won two seats in the June 1976 elections to the 40-member Legislative Assembly of that state.

In the 1981 elections the party increased its number of seats in the Assembly to six (obtaining 15.1 per cent of the votes). In the presidential elections (in which Rauf Denktash was re-elected) it received 13 per cent of the vote.

Orientation. The party has declared itself to be "socialist, anti-imperialist, for the non-aligned movement and for priority to be given to the Cyprus problem on the basis of the top-level agreements reached between the leaders of the two communities".

Structure. The party's supreme body is its general congress, followed by the party council, which in turn is followed by the executive committee.

Membership. 2,500

Publications. *Yenidüzen* (New Order, weekly)

International affiliations. The party is recognized by the Communist parties of the Soviet-bloc countries.

Socialist Salvation (Communal Liberation) Party
Toplumcu Kurtulus Partisi

Leadership. Alpay Durduran (l.); Mehmet Altinay (s.g.)

Founded. 1976

History. In the 1976 general elections this party gained six seats in the Legislative Assembly, and in the 1981 elections it increased the number of its seats to 13. In the 1981 presidential elections its candidate, Ziya Rizki, came second with 30.46 per cent of the total vote.

Orientation. The party is a left-of-centre formation with a programme based on Ataturk's reforms, social democratic principles, social justice and peaceful coexistence in an independent, bizonal, federal state of Cyprus free of British bases.

Turkish Unity Party
Türkiye Birlik Partisi

Leadership. Ismail Tezer (l.)

Founded. 1978

History. This party was founded by settlers from Turkey. In the 1981 elections it gained one seat in the Legislative Assembly, and in March 1982 it entered into a coalition Government with the National Unity Party and the Democratic People's Party.

Orientation. The party is extreme right-wing, supporting the partition of Cyprus and the creation of an independent Turkish state on Cyprus closely allied with Turkey.

Czechoslovakia

Capital: Prague   Pop. 15,400,000

The Czechoslovak Socialist Republic has since Jan 1, 1969, been a federal socialist republic comprising the Czech Socialist Republic and the Slovak Socialist Republic, each of them with its own Government and National Council (unicameral Parliament, with 200 deputies in the Czech Council and 150 in the Slovak Council). There is a Federal Government and a bicameral Federal Assembly consisting of a directly elected House of the People (of 200 members—137 Czechs and 63 Slovaks) and a House of Nations (of 150 members—75 each elected by the Czech and the Slovak National Councils). The Federal Assembly elects the President of the Republic who appoints the Federal Government, the state's supreme executive organ (whose exclusive competence includes foreign affairs, defence, foreign trade, transport and posts and telecommunications). All representative bodies (except the House of Nations) are elected by universal, equal and secret ballot by citizens over the age of 18 years, and for a five-year term under an absolute majority system in single-member constituencies. Where no absolute majority is obtained on a first ballot, a simple majority obtained in a second ballot within 15 days is sufficient. Under the Constitution, however, the guiding force in society and the state is the Communist Party of Czechoslovakia. Votes are cast in favour of the list of candidates nominated by the National Front, a mass organization embracing not only the Communist Party of Czechoslovakia and the Communist Party of Slovakia (a constituent part of the Czechoslovak party) but also the Czechoslovak People's Party, the Czechoslovak Socialist Party, the Slovak Freedom Party, the Slovak Reconstruction Party, the trade unions and youth organizations.

Official results of elections held on June 5-6, 1981, to the Federal Assembly showed that 99.51 per cent of the registered electorate had cast valid votes and that 99.9 per cent of these votes has been for the candidates nominated by the National Front.The corresponding figures for elections held at the same time to the Czech National Council showed a 99.39 per cent poll and 99.95 per cent for the official list, and those for the Slovak National Council a 99.75 per cent turnout and 99.98 per cent cast for the official candidates.

Communist Party of Czechoslovakia
Komunistická Strana Ceskoslovenska (KSC)

Address. Nábr. Ludvíka Svobody 12, 125 II Prague I, Czechoslovakia
Leadership. Gustáv Husák (g.s.); Vasil Bilak, Peter Colotka, Karel Hoffmann, Alois Indra, Milos Jakes, Antonín Kapek, Josef Kempny, Josef Korcák, Jozef Lenárt and Lubomir Strougal (other full presidium members)
Founded. 1921

History. Before World War II the party was the only legal Communist party in Eastern Europe. In the Republic of Czechoslovakia reconstituted in 1945 it was one of four legal parties and it took part in the formation of a National Bloc of Working People, together with the Social Democratic and Social National parties. In elections held to a Constituent Assembly in May 1946, the party became the strongest in Bohemia-Moravia, gaining 93 seats out of 231, and the second strongest in Slovakia, with 21 out of 69 seats, whereupon a National Front coalition

Government was formed under a Communist Prime Minister (Klement Gottwald). Following dissension over a Communist-sponsored nationalization programme and the appointment of Communists to posts in the security policy in February 1948, when Communists took over 12 out of the 24 portfolios in a new Government, the party effectively seized power with the help of "action committees". In April 1948 the Social Democratic Party was formally merged with the KSC. Elections in May 1948 were (for the first time) held on a single National Front list, on which each member party was allotted a fixed number of seats.

Purges carried out in 1951 among the party's leaders were followed by trials resulting in sentences of imprisonment or death, the execution of 11 former party leaders in 1952 and further prison sentences in 1954; some of these trials were officially disowned in 1956 and most of those executed were posthumously rehabilitated in 1963. Early in 1968 a new central committee with Alexander Dubcek as first secretary embarked on a liberalization programme which, however, in the view of the Communist Party leaders of the Soviet Union (and also of those of Bulgaria, East Germany, Hungary and Poland) was liable to lead to the ultimate detachment of Czechoslovakia from the "socialist community". The subsequent Soviet-led intervention in August 1968 entailed the abandonment of the liberalization programme and the progressive removal of Dubcek from all positions of power and from party membership in 1969-70. Under the leadership of Gustáv Husák (since April 1969) the party has been guided by the need to maintain "friendly relations with the Soviet Union and other socialist countries", without whose "timely international aid" in August 1968 (as stated by Dr Husák on May 25, 1972) "the power of the working class in the country would have been overthrown".

Orientation. The KSC is a Communist party which is guided by the principle of "proletarian internationalism" and accepts the need for the "dictatorship of the proletariat" during the period of socialist construction.

Structure. The party is organized on the principle of democratic centralism, with basic industrial or residential units combined in district and regional organizations. The party's supreme organ is its congress, convened every five years; it elects a central committee and a central control and auditing commission. The central committee elects a presidium (to direct party work between central committee plenary sessions), a secretariat, a general secretary and secretaries.

Membership. 1,500,000

Publications. *Rudé Právo* (Prague, daily central organ), 950,000; *Tribuna* (central committee's weekly journal of ideology and politics), 78,000; *Tvorba* (central committee's weekly journal for politics, scientific and cultural matters), 81,000

Communist Party of Slovakia
Komunistická Strana Slovenska (KSS)

Address. 833 33 Bratislava, Hlboká 2, Czechoslovakia

Leadership. Jozef Lenárt (first sec.)

Structure. The party is the territorial organization in Slovakia of the Communist Party of Czechoslovakia (KSC); it has its own congress and central committee.

Publications. *Pravda* (Bratislava, daily), 330,000; *Uj Szó* (Bratislava, daily in Hungarian), 85,000

Czechoslovak People's Party

Address. Revolucni 5, 110 15 Prague I, Czechoslovakia

Leadership. M. Zalman (ch.); Josef Andrs (head of secretariat)

History. In the 1948 elections to the National Assembly, conducted on a single National Front list, this party was allotted 23 out of the 300 seats. It is still a member of the National Front.

Orientation. A Roman Catholic party.

Publications. *Lidova Demokracie* (Prague, daily official organ), 217,000

Czechoslovak Socialist Party

Address. nám Republiky 7, 111 49 Prague I, Czechoslovakia

Leadership. Bohuslav Kucera (l.); Jiri Fleyberk (central sec.)

History. Formerly the National Socialist Party, this party was, for the 1948 elections to the National Assembly, allotted 26 out of 300 seats on the sole list presented by the National Front, of which it continues to be a member.

Publications. *Svobodné Slovo* (Prague, daily official organ), 228,000

Slovak Freedom Party

Address. Stefánikova 6 c, 892 18 Bratislava, Czechoslovakia

Leadership. Michal Zakovic (pres.); Juraj Moravec (s.g.)

History. In the 1948 elections to the National Assembly, held on a single list presented by the National Front, this party was allotted three out of the 300 seats, and it has since continued as a member of the National Front.

Publications. *Sloboda*, 4,500

Slovak Reconstruction Party
Strana Slovenskej Obrody

Address. 897 16 Bratislava, Malinovského 70, Czechoslovakia

Leadership. Jozef Simuth (pres.)

Founded. 1948

History. This party, formerly known as the Slovak Democrats, was allotted 12 out of the 300 seats in the 1948 elections to the National Assembly, conducted on the basis of a single list presented by the National Front, of which it is still a member.

Orientation. The party, which functions in the territory of the Slovak Socialist Republic, has defined its mission as the strengthening and development of the socialist Constitution of the Czechoslovak Socialist Republic through the activities of its members in the representative organs at all levels, in the state organs as well as in the organs and organizations of the National Front, thus participating in the formation, implementation and control of the policies of the Czechoslovak Socialist Republic.

Publications. *L'ud* (People, Bratislava), 17,000

Denmark

Capital: Copenhagen   Pop. 5,200,000

In the Kingdom of Denmark, which is a democratic multi-party state, legislative power lies jointly with the monarch and the *Folketing* (Diet), while executive power is vested in the monarch who exercises it through a Cabinet headed by a Prime Minister. Of the 179 members of the (unicameral) *Folketing*, serving a four-year term, 135 are elected by proportional representation in 17 districts and 40 others are allotted in proportion to their total vote to parties which have not obtained sufficient returns in the districts. Under a 1964 electoral law no party qualifies for parliamentary representation unless it has obtained at least 2 per cent of the vote. For the Faroe Islands and Greenland two members each are elected to the *Folketing*. All citizens above the age of 18 years and permanently resident in Denmark are entitled to vote and are eligible to the *Folketing*. Parliamentary groups of parties receive from the state an annual grant (consisting of a basic amount and a sum related to the size of the group) to total the equivalent of $1,000,000.

As a result of elections held on Jan. 10, 1984, the 175 metropolitan seats in the *Folketing* were distributed as follows: Social Democrats 56, Conservative People's Party 42, *Venstre* Liberals 22, Socialist People's Party 21, Radical Liberals 10, Centre Democrats 8, Progress Party 6, Christian People's Party 5, Left Socialists 5. Of the two Faroes representatives one is a member of the *Venstre* Liberal Group and the other co-operates with the Conservative People's Party; the two Greenland representatives elected in January 1984 co-operate with the *Venstre* Liberals and the Social Democrats respectively.

Centre Democrats
Centrum-Demokraterne

Address. Laksegade 12, 1063 Copenhagen K, Denmark

Leadership. Erhard Jacobsen (l. and first ch.); Peter Duetoft (org. ch.); Yvonne Herløv Andersen (sec.)

Founded. November 1973

History. The party was established by its present leader who defected from the Social Democratic Party because of what he regarded as the latter's "increasingly leftist course". In elections held in December 1973 the new party of the centre gained 7.8 per cent of the votes and 14 seats in the *Folketing*; in the 1975 elections the party fell back to 2.2 per cent of the votes and four seats; in February 1977 it won 6.4 per cent of the vote and 11 seats and in October 1979 3.2 per cent and six seats.

In December 1981 the Centre Democrats won 8.3 per cent and 15 seats. However, in the January 1984 elections they retained only eight seats. In September 1982 the party joined a four-party coalition Government (with the Conservatives, the Liberals and the Christian People's Party).

Orientation. The party believes that "the private capitalist system evolved in Denmark through a 'mixed economy' interplay between Government and citizens" has been successful, and it "rejects any kind of experiments in socialism", but at the same time "advocates pragmatic co-operation between the Social Democrats and the non-socialist parties". The party stands for continued Danish membership of NATO and the European Community.

Membership. 2,500

Publications. *Centrum-Avisen* (10 times yearly), 5,000

Christian People's Party
Kristeligt Folkeparti

Address. Skindergade 24, 1159 Copenhagen K, Denmark

Leadership. Christian Christensen (l.); Flemming Kofod-Svendsen (ch.); Ebbe Jensen (s.g.)

Founded. April 1970

History. The party was founded as an interdenominational grouping to oppose free abortion, liberalization of pornography and other aspects of the "permissive" society. Taking part in general elections for the first time in 1971, the party gained 2 per cent of the votes and no seats in the *Folketing*, but in 1973 it obtained 4 per cent of the votes and seven seats (out of 179); after winning nine seats in the 1975

elections, it fell back to six seats (with 3.4 per cent of the vote) in 1977 and to five seats (2.6 per cent) in October 1979.

In the 1981 elections it obtained 2.3 per cent and four seats, which it increased to five in January 1984. In September 1982 it joined a coalition Government of Conservatives, Liberals and Centre Democrats and was given the portfolio of the Environment and Nordic Affairs. Closely modelled on the Norwegian Christian People's Party, the Danish party is not formally linked with any specific religious denomination.

Orientation. A social-liberal party following a broad middle-of-the-road policy on economic and foreign policy questions; but strongly committed to a responsible line in social policy.

Structure. There is an annual national convention, and an executive board meets five or six times a year.

Membership. 12,000

Publications. *Idé-Politik* (weekly), 7,000

Communist Party of Denmark
Danmarks Kommunistiske Parti (DKP)

Address. Dr Tvaergade 3, 1302 Copenhagen K, Denmark

Leadership. Jørgen Jensen (ch.); Poul Emanuel (sec.)

Founded. 1919

History. The DKP was founded in a merger of a majority of the Federation of Social Democratic Youth and other left-wing groups within the Danish socialist and labour movement under the influence of the 1917 Russian revolution. In 1920 the party joined the Communist International (Comintern).

The DKP first obtained seats in the *Folketing* in 1932. Under Nazi occupation it was illegal in 1941-45, but it took part in a coalition Government in 1945. In October of that year it gained 18 seats in the *Folketing*. Its parliamentary representation subsequently declined and after 1960 (following the formation of the Socialist People's Party) the party held no seats in the *Folketing* until 1973, when it returned with six members. In October 1979, however, it again failed to secure representation.

Orientation. The DKP is an orthodox communist party.

Structure. The DKP has basic branches subordinate to regional organizations. Its supreme organ is its congress, which is convened every three years and which elects a central committee, a control commission and auditors. The central committee elects an executive committee and a secretariat.

Membership. 10,000
Publications. *Land og Folk* (daily central organ), 13,000; *Tiden-Verden Rund* (theoretical journal), 3,200
International affiliations. The DKP is recognized by the Communist parties of the Soviet-bloc countries.

Communist Party of Denmark/Marxist-Leninists
Danmarks Kommunistiske Parti/Marxister-Leninister

Address. Griffenfeldsgade 26, 2200 Copenhagen N, Denmark
Leadership. Klaus Riis (1st sec.)
Founded. December 1978
History. This party contested the 1984 elections under the name Marxist-Leninist Party (*Marxistisk-Leninistisk Parti*) and obtained less than 0.1 per cent of the vote.
Orientation. This party evinces pro-Albanian sympathies.
Publications. *Arbejderen* (The Worker, daily); *Partiets Veg* (The Road of the Party, weekly)

Communist Workers' Party

Leadership. Svend Aage Madsen (ch.)
Founded. 1976
History. In the October 1979 elections this leftist formation obtained 0.4 per cent of the vote, a proportion which fell to 0.1 per cent in the December 1981 elections; on neither occasion did it secure representation. The party was unable to contest the January 1984 elections because it failed to collect the required number of voters' signatures (1/175th of the total valid vote in the previous elections).
Orientation. Originally Maoist in orientation, the party subsequently adopted a non-aligned leftist approach.
Publications. *Kommunistisk Tidsskrift*

Conservative People's Party
Det Konservative Folkeparti

Address. Tordenskjoldsgade 21, 1055 Copenhagen K, Denmark
Leadership. Poul Schlüter (l. & ch.); Torben Rechendorff (s.g.)
Founded. February 1916
History. The party is descended from the old Right (*Højre*) party, which had been represented in Parliament since 1849 but which had lost its traditional ruling position with the growth of Liberal and Social Democratic strength in the late 19th and early 20th centuries. As reconstituted in 1916, the new party abandoned the reactionary stance of the old Right and adopted a reform programme which included support for proportional representation (introduced in 1918). Since the rise to political predominance of the Social Democrats in the inter-war period, the Conservatives have sought to promote co-operation between non-socialist parties to provide an alternative to Social Democratic government.

Since the end of World War II, during which the party took part in national coalition governments, the Conservatives have been mainly in opposition—except for forming a coalition government (i) with the Liberal Party from 1950 to 1953 and (ii) with the Radical Liberals and Liberal Party in 1968-71. Their representation in Parliament fluctuated between 17 in 1947 and 37 in 1968, after which it fell to 31 in 1971, 16 in 1973 and 10 in 1975, but rose to 15 in 1977, to 22 in October 1979 and to 26 in 1981, when the party became the second largest (after the Social Democrats).

In September 1982 Poul Schlüter formed a coalition Government with three other non-socialist parties, and in the January 1984 elections the party increased its parliamentary representation to 42.
Orientation. The party seeks inter alia to "restore the balance between state and citizen, private and public industry, freedom and equality"; to "seek approval for easing the tax burden and abolish measures that . . . take away the citizen's incentive to work"; to "guarantee individual freedom and the right to own property in a socially secure society"; to promote "an active industrial policy which gives private industry a chance to develop on a basis of free and equal competition"; and to "guarantee justice and law and order and . . . the closest possible co-operation within NATO and the European Community".
Structure. The party is organized at local, district and provincial levels. A national council is the party's highest authority on political questions; in addition to delegates from various levels of the party organization it includes a party committee which is the highest authority on organizational questions.
Membership. 56,000
Publications. *Vor Tid* (Our Time, twice monthly), 3,650
International affiliations. European Democrat Union; International Democrat Union

Left Socialist Party
Venstresocialisterne

Address. Studiestraede 24, 1455 Copenhagen K, Denmark

Leadership. Collective

Founded. December 1967

History. The party was founded by six *Folketing* members who defected from the Socialist People's Party, and it gained 2 per cent of the vote and four seats in the 1968 *Folketing* elections; the party lost all these seats in 1971 but returned to the *Folketing* in 1975 (gaining 2.1 per cent of the vote and four seats), increasing its representation to five seats (2.7 per cent) in 1977 and to six seats (3.7 per cent) in October 1979. In December 1981, however, it obtained only five seats, which it retained in the January 1984 elections.

Orientation. An independent socialist formation opposed to Denmark's membership of the European Community, the party co-operates with socialist and revolutionary parties and groups in the West and the Third World.

Liberal Party
Venstre

Address. Søllerødvej 30, 2840 Holte, Denmark

Leadership. Henning Christophersen (ch.); Kurt Sørensen (g.s.)

Founded. 1870

History. The party was derived from the Friends of the Peasants (*Bondevennerne*) and first obtained its main support from small independent farmers (and later from sections of the urban middle class) opposed to the conservatism and political hegemony of the old Right party. In 1901 the *Venstre* formed a government backed by a parliamentary majority (successive Right administrations having previously ruled for periods on the strength of their support in the Upper House); but the party was weakened in 1905 by the breakaway of the Radical Liberals (who were in power in 1909-10 and 1913-20) and its influence reduced by the rise to political dominance of the Social Democrats in the late 1920s.

The party's recent representation in the *Folketing* has fluctuated considerably as follows: 28 (1943), 38 (1945), 49 (1947), 32 (1950), 42 (1953), 45 (1957), 38 (1960 and 1964), 34 (1968), 30 (1971), 22 (1973), 42 (1975), 21 (1977), 22 (1979), 20 (1981) and 22 (1984).

During World War II the party took part in a national coalition Government; in 1945-48 it was in power in a minority Government; in 1950-53 it was in a coalition Government with the Conservatives; thereafter it was again in a coalition Government with the Conservatives and Radical Liberals in 1968-71, formed a one-party minority administration from December 1973 to February 1975 and participated in a minority coalition with the Social Democrats from August 1978 to October 1979.

From September 1982 onwards the party held eight ministries in a four-party Conservative-Liberal coalition Government.

Orientation. Liberal, advocating decentralization of the administration and direct participation of the electorate in local affairs; worker participation in decision-making in large enterprises; tax reform towards consumer taxes; and continued support for NATO.

Membership. 90,000

Publications. *Liberal* (eight times yearly), 26,000

International affiliations. Liberal International; Federation of Liberal and Democratic Parties of the European Community

Progress Party
Fremskridtspartiet

Address. Christiansborg, 1218 Copenhagen K, Denmark

Leadership. V.A. Jakobsen (ch.); Helge Dohrmann (parl. l.)

Founded. August 1972

History. The party was founded by Mogens Glistrup on a platform advocating the gradual abolition of income tax, and thereby an increase in consumer demand and therefore also in the proceeds of value added tax, which would be sufficient to cover drastically reduced state expenditure (involving disbandment of most of the civil service, although the welfare state was to be preserved).

In the 1973 general elections the party gained 28 seats in the *Folketing*, thus becoming the second-largest party in Parliament, but by October 1979 it had fallen back to 20 seats (11 per cent) and to the status of fourth-largest party; in 1981 its parliamentary representation was reduced to 16, and in January 1984 to six.

Glistrup's parliamentary immunity was regularly suspended over several years in which charges of tax fraud were pending against him. After his final conviction by the High Court (the sentence being three years' imprisonment), he was expelled from the *Folketing* in July 1983. Five of the party's remaining members of the *Folketing* resigned from the party on Aug. 16, 1983 (after accusing Glistrup of manipulating the party for his own ends), but continued to sit in the House as independents with the intention of supporting the Government. After being re-elected in January 1984, Glistrup was again expelled from the *Folketing* the following month.

Orientation. In addition to the abolition of income tax and the highest degree of free enterprise without state interference, the party advocates the making of simple and understandable laws and a reduction of the public service sector; it stands for Denmark's continued membership of NATO.

Membership. 12,000

Publications. *Fremskridt* (Progress, weekly), 3,000

to unrestricted liberalism, in favour of spiritual, personal and political freedom and economic freedom within the limits imposed by a modern state, and strongly supporting Danish co-operation in the United Nations, the Council of Europe, the Nordic Council and other international bodies and contributions to international disarmament and the prosperity of developing countries.

Structure. The party is organized in the country's 103 constituencies and holds an annual national congress, which is the party's highest political and organizational authority.

Membership. Over 10,000

Publications. *Radikal Politik* (fortnightly), 10,000

International affiliations. Liberal International

Radical-Liberal Party
Det Radikale Venstre

Address. Christiansborg, 1218 Copenhagen K, Denmark

Leadership. Thorkild Møller (ch.); Niels Helveg Petersen (parl. l.); Jens Clausager (g.s.)

Founded. May 1905

History. Formed mainly by dissident left-wing elements of the Liberal (*Venstre*) Party, the *Radikale Venstre* party was inspired by the French Radical Party and at its foundation adopted the Odense Programme which inter alia called for Danish neutrality in war; constitutional reform, including votes for all at 21 (not totally achieved until 1961), a secret ballot, democratic local elections and provision for referendums; progressive taxation; and land reform.

The party was in office in two all-Radical cabinets in 1909–10 and 1913–20; in coalition with the Social Democrats in 1929–40; in a National Government in 1940–43; again with the Social Democrats in 1957–64 (the Single-Tax Party participating in 1957–60); and in 1968–71 with the Conservatives and the *Venstre* party under the premiership of the party's then leader, Hilmar Baunsgaard. Although the party has never been strong in postwar Parliaments, it doubled its number of seats held in the *Folketing* from 13 to 27 in the 1968 elections, while in the October 1979 elections it won 10 seats (5.4 per cent). It obtained nine seats in 1981 and 10 in January 1984.

Orientation. A social-liberal party equally opposed to state socialism and

Schleswig Party
Slesvigsk Parti/Schleswigsche Partei

Address. Vestergade 30, 6200 Aabenraa, Denmark

Leadership. Gerhard Schmidt (l.); Peter Iver Johannsen (s.g.)

Founded. August 1920

History. The party was established to represent the German minority in Denmark when, following the defeat of Germany in World War I, the northern part of Schleswig became part of Denmark as a result of a referendum held in February 1920. Since 1920 the party has been represented at local and district level in Northern Schleswig and also held one seat in the *Folketing* until 1964, when it fell below the required level of votes. In 1973 the seat was regained in an electoral alliance with the new Centre Democratic party, but on the eve of the October 1979 elections this arrangement was terminated, with the result that the new *Folketing* contained no representative of the Schleswig Party. Since then the party has not contested general elections.

Orientation. The party seeks to maintain intellectual and cultural relations with the German people and to take an active part in social functions within the Danish state.

Structure. The party is based on the *Bund Deutscher Nordschleswiger*, the leading organization of Germans in Denmark.

Membership. 4,500

Publications. *Der Nordschleswiger* (daily in German), 4,000

International affiliations. Federal Union of European Nationalities (FUEN)

Single-Tax Party or **Justice Party**
Danmarks Retsforbund

Address. Lyngbyvej 42, 2100 Copenhagen, Denmark
Leadership. Ib Christensen (ch.)
Founded. 1919
History. The party's representation in the *Folketing* fluctuated between two and six seats in the 1930s and 1940s, but rose to 12 seats in 1950, whereafter it declined to six in 1953. The party held nine seats from 1957 to 1960, none thereafter, five from 1973 to 1975, six from 1977 to October 1979, and five to 1981, since when the party has not been represented in the *Folketing*.

In its first and so far only experience of government, the party participated in a three-party coalition with the Social Democrats and Radical Liberals from May 1957 to November 1960, during which time a number of its policies were implemented, including a major trade liberalization and the introduction of a tax on unearned increments in land values; however, the latter legislation was later rescinded after the party left office.
Membership. 1,750
Orientation. The party professes the theories of the US economist Henry George (1839–97), who had advocated the imposition of a single tax (on land). It is opposed to Danish membership of the EEC.
Publications. *Ret og Frihed* (Justice and Freedom, monthly), 1,400

Social Democratic Party
Socialdemokratiet

Address. Nyropsgade 26, 5, 1602 Copenhagen V, Denmark
Leadership. Anker Jørgensen (ch.); Ejner Hovgaard Christiansen (g.s.)
Founded. 1871
History. The party first gained seats in the *Folketing* in 1884 and subsequently, supported by the trade union movement and labour co-operatives, became a popular movement with considerable influence. In 1913-20 it supported a minority Government formed by the Radical Liberals. In 1924 it became the strongest party (with 55 out of 148 seats) in the *Folketing*. It was first in government in 1924-26 under the premiership of Thorvald Stauning, who was subsequently Prime Minister from 1929 until his death in May 1942—at the head of a coalition with the Radical-Liberals until the German occupation of April 1940 and thereafter, for the following two years, of a national coalition administration. Having achieved its highest voting support to date in the 1931 elections (46.1 per cent), the Social Democratic Party was instrumental in introducing advanced welfare state legislation and other social reforms in the 1930s.

Since 1945 the Social Democrats have continued to be the predominant party in Denmark, participating either alone or in coalition in successive administrations interspersed with short periods of opposition. A Social Democrat (Vilhelm Buhl) headed the immediate post-war all-party coalition formed in May 1945, but after losing support in the October 1945 elections the Social Democrats were in opposition from November 1945 until November 1947, when a minority Social Democratic Cabinet took office under Hans Hedtoft. After a further period of opposition from October 1950, the party formed a minority administration in September 1953 under Hedtoft, which was continued (following the latter's death in January 1955) by Hans Christian Hansen. In May 1957 a majority coalition was formed between the Social Democrats, the Radical-Liberals and the Single-Tax Party, initially under the premiership of Hansen and later, following the latter's death in February 1960, under Viggo Kampmann. After gaining seats in the November 1960 elections the Social Democrats formed a two-party coalition with the Radical-Liberals under Kampmann, who was succeeded as Prime Minister by Jens-Otto Krag in September 1962.

Jens-Otto Krag reverted to a minority Social Democratic Cabinet in September 1964, but after losing seats in two successive elections the Social Democrats were in opposition from January 1968 until, after the party received increased support in the September 1971 elections, Krag was able to form a new minority Social Democratic Government in October 1971. Immediately after the October 1972 referendum decision in favour of Danish membership of the European Community, Krag (himself an ardent pro-European) resigned from the premiership and was succeeded by the trade union leader Anker Jørgensen. After a period of opposition from December 1973 (in which month the Social Democrats suffered a major election setback), in February 1975 the Social Democrats formed a new minority administration under Jørgensen, who in August 1978 entered into a coalition with the Liberal Party (the first-ever formal coalition between these two parties except for the 1940-43 national coalition). However, after a further Social Democratic advance in the October 1979 elections, Jørgensen formed a new minority Social Democratic Government later the same month.

Between 1953 and 1979 the party's share of the poll in general elections fluctuated between 42.1 per cent in 1960 and 25.6 per cent in 1973, but reached 38.3 per cent in 1979. The number of seats (out of 175) gained by it was 76 in 1960 and 1964, 46 in 1973, 53 in 1975, 65 in 1977 and 68 in 1979.

In the 1981 elections the party suffered a setback, gaining only 32.9 per cent of the votes and 59 seats. It remained in office until September 1982, when the Government resigned and the first Conservative Prime Minister since 1901 took office. In the January 1984 elections the party's strength in the *Folketing* was further reduced to 56 seats.

Orientation. Democratic socialist, advocating the maintenance and extension of human rights and civil liberties; the common ownership of the means of production; the strengthening of the United Nations; the maintenance of membership of NATO and the EEC; and Nordic co-operation.

Structure. Congress, meeting at least once every four years, is the party's highest organ; the party's executive committee meets every two months, and its bureau regularly. The party has 15 regional organizations, 103 constituency branches and 700 sections. The Danish Trade Union Confederation (LO) is represented in the party's organs, and vice-versa.

Membership. 110,000

Publications. *Vor Politik* (quarterly), 110,000; *Ny Politik* (ideological monthly), 3,500

International affiliations. Socialist International; Confederation of the Socialist Parties of the European Community

---

Socialist People's Party
Socialistisk Folkeparti

Address. Folketinget, Christiansborg, 1218 Copenhagen K, Denmark

Leadership. Gert Petersen (ch.); Lillian Ubbesen (sec.)

Founded. November 1958

History. The party was founded by followers of Aksel Larsen, who had been chairman of the Communist Party of Denmark (DKP), from which he was expelled in November 1958 after he had expressed his sympathy for President Tito and Yugoslav communism and had demanded "independence" for the DKP which, he said, should not "slavishly" follow the policy adopted by the Soviet Union; he had also criticized Soviet intervention in Hungary in 1956. The new party claimed after its foundation that it had 15,000 members, and it gained 11 seats in the *Folketing* in the 1960 elections. By 1966 its parliamentary representation had risen to 20, but by 1977 it had declined to seven, although in October 1979 it rose to 11 (5.9 per cent).

In 1981, however, it gained 21 seats (with 11.3 per cent of the votes) and it retained the same number of seats in the January 1984 elections.

Orientation. The party is an independent left-wing socialist formation, advocating unilateral disarmament and opposed to Danish membership of NATO and of the European Community. It supports Nordic co-operation and has given limited external support to Social Democratic Cabinets.

Socialist Workers' Party
Socialistisk Arbejderparti

Address. Blegdamsveg 28C, 2200 Copenhagen N, Denmark

Leadership. Collective

Founded. May 1980

History. This party took part in the 1981 elections to the *Folketing* but obtained less than 0.1 per cent of the total vote. It registered a similar performance in the January 1984 elections, which as in 1981 it contested under the designation The International, Socialist Workers' Party (*Internationalen, Socialistisk Arbejderparti*).

Publications. *Klassekampen* (Class Struggle, weekly)

International affiliations. Fourth (Trotskyist) International

Danish Dependencies

Faroe Islands

Capital: Tórshavn   Pop. 44,000

The Faroe Islands, though part of the Kingdom of Denmark (which retains responsibility for their foreign affairs, defence, judiciary and monetary system), have their own Government (*Landsstyret* or *Landsstyrid*), which deals with Faroese affairs, including fisheries (on which it has concluded several agreements with other Governments and with the EEC, of which it is not a member).The islands also have a 32-member Parliament (*Lagtinget* or *Løgtingid*), 27 of whose seats are filled by direct proportional election under universal adult suffrage and up to five by distribution to party lists under an equalization system. Two representatives from the Faroes sit in the Danish *Folketing*, the January 1984 elections resulting in the return of Union and People's Party candidates.

In elections held on Nov. 8, 1980, seats in the *Lagtinget* were obtained as follows: Union Party 8, Social Democrats 7, Republicans 6, People's Party 6, Self-Government Party 3, Progressive and Fisheries' Party 2.

People's Party
Fólkaflokkurin

Address. Løgtingid, Aarvegi, 3800 Tórshavn, Faroe Islands
Leadership. Jógvan Sundstein (ch.)
Founded. 1940
History. The party was founded in response to the depression of the 1930s but did not enter into any coalition government until 1950. From then on it was in power with the Union Party until 1954, and thereafter with the Self-Government Party until 1958. From 1963 to 1966 it was part of a coalition Government with the Republican, Self-Government and Progressive parties, its leader being Prime Minister.

The party was again in opposition from 1966 to 1974, when it formed a coalition with the Social Democrats and the Republicans, this Government being continued after the 1978 elections, in which the People's Party remained the fourth strongest party although its percentage share of the vote declined. In January 1981 it entered into a coalition Government with the Union and Self-Government parties.

Orientation. The People's Party favours free enterprise and wider political and economic autonomy for the Faroes within the Kingdom of Denmark. It is currently regarded as the most conservative party in the Faroes. Its representative in the metropolitan Parliament co-operates with the Conservative People's Party.

Publications. *Dagbladid* (twice weekly), 5,500

Progressive and Fisheries' Party
Framburds- og Fiskivinnuflokkurin

Address. Løgtingid, Aarvegi, 3800 Tórshavn, Faroe Islands
History. The party was established before the 1978 elections as a coalition between the Progressive Party (with one seat) and centre-oriented circles in the fishing industry. It obtained two seats in both the 1978 and 1980 elections. The Progressive Party itself had taken part in a coalition government between 1963 and 1966.

Orientation. The party has always had close links with the Fishermen's Association and has advocated increased internal self-government for the Faroes. In political orientation it is a "non-socialist, social, anti-communist" centre party.

Publications. *Sjon Fyri Søgn* (See For Yourself)

Republican Party
Tjódveldisflokkurin

Address. Løgtingid, Aarvegi, 3800 Tórshavn, Faroe Islands
Leadership. Erlendur Patursson (ch.)
Founded. 1948
History. Having secured two seats in 1950, the party (whose title means "Party for People's Government") came to prominence in 1954 when, as the *Lösrivelses* (secessionist) party, it gained six seats. It has since then maintained its strength and has, despite its differences with other parties over relations with Denmark, taken part in coalition governments (in 1963-66 and from 1974 to 1980).
Orientation. The party stands for secession of the islands from Denmark.
Publications. *14 September* (twice weekly), 3,600

Self-Government Party
Sjálvstýrisflokkurin

Address. Løgtingid, Aarvegi, 3800 Tórshavn, Faroe Islands
Leadership. Hilmar Kass (l.)
Founded. 1906
History. The party was founded with the aim of obtaining for the Faroese Parliament, which had only consultative functions, power to legislate on certain affairs. Having suffered the defection of its left wing in 1928 and of its right wing in 1940, the party became one of the centre.

From the granting of home rule to the Faroes in 1948, the party was a partner in successive coalition governments (1948–50, 1954–75); it was then in opposition until it entered, in January 1981, into a coalition Government with the Union and People's parties.
Orientation. A social-liberal party seeking, for the Faroes, political independence within the Kingdom of Denmark.
Membership. 1,700
Publications. *Tingakrossur* (weekly), 1,600

Social Democratic Party
Javnadarflokkurin

Address. Løgtingid, Aarvegi, 3800 Tórshavn, Faroe Islands
Leadership. Atli P. Dam (ch.)
Founded. 1928
History. The first local social democratic society was founded in 1925, and the party gained two seats in Parliament in January 1928. Although the party is usually referred to by its Danish name, its title actually means "Equality Party".

It took part in government in 1948–50, and in 1958 it became the strongest party in the local parliament (with eight out of 30 seats) and thereupon formed a coalition Government (with the Union and Self-Government parties). After being in opposition from 1963 to 1966, the party participated in successive coalitions and led a coalition with the People's Party and Republicans between 1974 and January 1981, since when it has been in opposition to a coalition of the Union, People's and Self-Government parties (see separate entries).
Membership. 1,000
Publications. *Sosialurin* (three times weekly), 6,000

Union Party
Sambandsflokkurin

Address. Løgtingid, Aarvegi, 3800 Tórshavn, Faroe Islands
Leadership. Pauli Ellefsen (ch.)
Founded. 1906
History. The Union Party was the first political party in the Faroes and, until 1958, often the strongest in the local parliament. It took part in successive coalition Governments until 1963 and again from 1966 to 1974 (with the Social Democrats and Self-Government Party). Thereafter it was in opposition until it formed, in January 1981, a coalition Government with the People's and Self-Government parties, with its leader as Prime Minister.
Orientation. The party stands for the maintenance of close relations between the islands and the Danish Crown and is conservative in internal affairs. In the metropolitan Parliament its representative is a member of the Liberal Group.
Publications. *Dimmalaetting* (Dawn, three times weekly), 11,600

Greenland

Capital: Nuuk (Godthaab)   Pop. 52,000

Greenland is an integral part of the Kingdom of Denmark (in the Parliament of which it has two representatives) with internal autonomy as introduced on May 1, 1979, and previously approved in a referendum on Jan. 17, 1979, by 70.1 per cent of participating voters. Greenland accordingly has its own Parliament (*Landsting*), to which 23 members are popularly elected by proportional representation in districts and up to a further three returned by parties which have failed to secure seats in the districts. It also has a Government (*Landsstyre*) with responsibility for internal affairs, trade and industry, education and cultural affairs and social affairs, while Denmark retains responsibility for foreign affairs, defence and monetary policy.

As a result of elections to the *Landsting* held on June 6, 1984, seats were distributed as follows: Forward (*Siumut*) 11, Feeling of Community (*Atassut*) 11, Eskimo Community (*Inuit Ataqatigiit*) 3.

Greenland entered the European Economic Community (EEC) on Jan. 1, 1973, as part of Denmark. On the basis of a referendum decision on Feb. 23, 1982, in favour of withdrawal, Greenland is scheduled to cease being a member of the EEC with effect from Jan. 1, 1985.

Eskimo Community
Inuit Ataqatigiit

Address. P.O.B. 321, 3900 Nuuk, Greenland
Leadership. Arqaluk Lynge (ch.); Jakob Lyberth (sec.)
Founded. 1978
History. In the referendum held on Jan. 17, 1979, on Greenland's proposed status as an autonomous region of Denmark, the Eskimo Community called unsuccessfully for a "no" vote. It obtained no seats in the 1979 elections, when its vote totalled 813, but in the 1983 elections it won 2,612 votes and two seats in the *Landsting*, whereafter it supported the *Siumut* Government. Following the June 1984 elections it joined a coalition administration with *Siumut*.
Orientation. As a Marxist-Leninist organization, the Federation called for Greenland's "total independence from the capitalist colonial power" and for Greenland citizenship to be restricted to those with an Eskimo mother or father. It is opposed to Greenland's continued membership of the European Community and has advocated the closure of US bases

in Greenland and the territory's eventual independence from Denmark.

Feeling of Community Party
Atassut

Address. P.O.B. 399, 3900 Nuuk, Greenland
Leadership. Otto Steenholdt (l.); Daniel Skifte (acting ch.)
Founded. 1978
History. *Atassut* was formed as a national organization in Greenland in 1978 and officially became a political party in September 1981. Its first leader, Lars Chemnitz, was Chairman of the pre-autonomy Council, but in the April 1979 Greenland elections *Atassut* (with 7,688 votes) was defeated by the *Siumut* party. In the April 1983 elections it became the largest party in terms of votes (11,443) but won the same number of seats as *Siumut* (12) and remained in opposition to the latter. Chemnitz resigned the party leadership in March 1984 and *Atassut* remained in opposition after the June 1984 elections.
Orientation. *Atassut* is a moderate, non-socialist party, favouring Greenland's

continued participation in the European Community. Its representative in the metropolitan Parliament co-operates with the Liberal Group.

Membership. 3,000
Publications. *Atassut*

Forward
Siumut

Address. P.O.B. 357, 3900 Nuuk, Greenland
Leadership. Jonathan Motzfeldt (ch.); Lars Emil Johansen (sec.)
Founded. July 1977
History. *Siumut* has its origins in political groups founded between 1971 and 1975, when a *Siumut* political movement was started with the publication of Greenland's first political review, *Siumut.* The party was formed by a congress of representatives of political groups (now numbering 46). The party obtained an absolute majority in the April 1979 elections (with 8,505 votes) and formed the first home-rule Government in Greenland on May 1, 1979, under the premiership of Jonathan Motzfeldt. It also returned Greenland's sole representative to the European Parliament in June 1979. The party continued to form the territory's Government even after the 1983 elections, in which it lost its absolute majority (winning 10,371 votes). After the June 1984 elections *Siumut* formed a coalition administration with the small Eskimo Community formation.

Orientation. The party's aims are to improve the status of hunters, fishermen and workers; to promote collective ownership and co-operation; and to further increased reliance on Greenland's own resources. The party has advocated Greenland's withdrawal from the European Community.

Structure. Local groups elect a general assembly which meets every other year to formulate party policy and to elect an 11-member steering committee and a chairman, who is leader of *Siumut*'s parliamentary group.

Membership. 5,000
Publications. *Siumut* (review), 1,500
International affiliations. Socialist International (consultative member)

Djibouti

Capital: Djibouti   Pop. 310,000

The Republic of Djibouti has a President (elected for a six-year term by universal adult suffrage), a Prime Minister who heads a Cabinet, and a 65-member Chamber of Deputies (also elected by universal adult suffrage). In elections held on May 21, 1982, all 65 candidates were elected to the Chamber on a list of the ruling Popular Rally for Progress (*Rassemblement Populaire pour le Progrès,* RPP), which had effectively become the sole legal party under legislation adopted in October 1981. The candidates comprised 26 Issas or other Somalis, 23 Afars and 16 Arabs. No candidates were presented by opposition groups and the list was officially stated to have received 78,031 votes out of a possible 95,995.

Djibouti People's Party
Parti Populaire Djiboutien (PPD)

Leadership. Moussa Ahmed Idriss (l.)
Founded. Aug. 15, 1981
History. Although most of this opposition party's members are Afars, there are also Issa recruits. Its executive committee includes two former Prime Ministers— Ahmed Dini Ahmed and Mohammed Abdallah Kamil, both Afars. It also includes Mohammed Ahmed Issa Cheiko, who had resigned as Minister of Public Health in June 1981, and Omar Osman Rabeh (an Issa who had been leader of the pre-independence *Front de Libération de la Côte des Somalis*). The PPD was also joined by 10 deputies, who were

thereupon not renominated as parliamentary candidates by the ruling Popular Rally for Progress (RPP).

The PPD's leader and members of its executive committee were temporarily detained after the President of the Republic had accused the new party of (inter alia) encouraging ethnic division, illegally distributing pamphlets and being in the pay of a foreign power. The PPD failed to be officially registered, and on Oct. 18, 1981, the Chamber of Deputies unanimously passed bills which in effect made Djibouti a one-party state ruled by the RPP. The PPD was therefore unable to nominate candidates for the 1982 elections.

Structure. The PPD has a 12-member executive committee.

Popular Rally for Progress
Rassemblement Populaire pour le Progrès (RPP)

Leadership. President Hassan Gouled Aptidon (ch.)
Founded. March 1979
History. The party was established to replace the *Ligue Populaire pour l'Indépendance* (LPAI), which had become the ruling party of the Republic of Djibouti after representing a majority of the Issa population in the territory before it achieved independence from France in June 1977. In March–April 1977 the LPAI had reached agreement on the formation of a *Rassemblement Populaire pour l'Indépendance* with (i) the militant pro-Somali Front for the Liberation of the Somali Coast, (ii) a parliamentary majority group led by Senator Barkat Gourad Hamadou (who had in 1976 broken away from the then ruling National Union for Independence, UNI), (iii) the left-wing Afar *Mouvement pour la Libération* and (iv) a faction of the UNI led by Omar Farah.

Following the approval by the Chamber of Deputies on Oct. 19, 1981, of a bill providing for the adoption of a one-party system, the RPP was accorded the status of the country's sole legal political party.

Structure. The party has a 12-member political bureau appointed by the President of the Republic.

International affiliations. Socialist Inter-African

Dominica

Capital: Roseau   Pop. 76,000

The Commonwealth of Dominica has been an independent republic within the Commonwealth since Nov. 3, 1978. It has a President elected by the House of Assembly, a Government headed by a Prime Minister, and a unicameral House of Assembly with 21 members elected by universal adult suffrage, with 11 Senators being elected or appointed to it in addition. The minimum voting age is 18 years, and candidates are elected by a simple majority in single-member districts.

In elections to the House of Assembly held on July 21, 1980, the (conservative) Dominica Freedom Party gained 17 seats, the newly-formed Dominica Democratic Labour Party two and independents two. Parties which contested the elections without gaining seats were the Dominica Labour Party and the ("new left") Dominica Liberation Movement Alliance. (The Dominica Democratic Labour Party was subsequently reunited with the Dominica Labour Party.)

Dominica Freedom Party (DFP)

Address. House of Assembly, Roseau, Dominica

Leadership. Mary Eugenia Charles (l.)

History. In the 1970 elections the DFP gained five out of the 14 seats in the legislature, but in 1975 its representation in the 21-member House of Assembly was reduced to three. A leading member of the DFP was appointed to the Cabinet formed in June 1979 by Oliver J. Seraphine (the Democratic Labour Party leader) but was dismissed in January 1980 after he had called for early general elections. The DFP had meanwhile remained in opposition to the Government.

For the elections of July 21, 1980, the DFP nominated 19 candidates, of whom 17 were successful, giving the party an overwhelming majority in the House of Assembly and enabling it to form a Government.

Orientation. According to Mary Eugenia Charles, the DFP is "liberal, democratic and anti-communist" and seeks to pursue a non-aligned foreign policy and to attract foreign investment to promote industrial development.

Dominica Labour Party (DLP)

Address. House of Assembly, Roseau, Dominica

Leadership. Oliver J. Seraphin (l.); Patrick R. John (dep. l.)

History. The DLP first came to power in 1959, when Dominica was given an enlarged Legislative Council. At the time of elections held in October 1970 (the first since Dominica had become an Associated State of Great Britain in 1967) the DLP was divided into two factions—the Le Blanc Labour Party, which obtained eight seats in the Legislative Assembly, and the DLP, which gained only one seat. The party was reunited in 1974 and continued in power until June 1979, when Patrick R. John, then leader of the DLP, was forced to resign with his Cabinet, following a general strike and unrest caused by disclosures of government negotiations with South African concerns.

In June 1979 a group comprising about half the DLP membership in the House of Assembly, under the leadership of Oliver J. Seraphine, broke away to form a Dominica Democratic Labour Party (DDLP) and a broadly-based Government. However, in elections held on July 21, 1980, the DDLP retained only two seats in the House of Assembly, and the DLP none. Both parties thereupon went into opposition, and in mid-1983 the DDLP was reunited with the DLP, with Seraphine as leader and John as deputy leader of the reunified party.

Orientation. The DLP advocates a "new socialism" based on a mixed economy, with the island's resources being locally owned and controlled, as well as a non-aligned foreign policy.

International affiliations. Socialist International

Dominica Liberation Movement Alliance (DLMA)

Leadership. Atherton Martin (l.)

Founded. 1979

History. The DLMA was set up by four left-wing groupings. Atherton Martin had been dismissed from his ministerial post in the Dominica Labour Party Government in October 1979 for his alleged left-wing opinions and for favouring closer ties with Cuba. For the July 1980 elections the DLMA fielded 16 candidates but the party obtained no seats in the House of Assembly and only 8.02 per cent of the votes. In September 1981 it accepted an offer from the Communist Party of Cuba for university scholarships in Cuba to be provided to students from Dominica.

Orientation. The DLMA regards itself as part of the Caribbean "new left" movement.

United Dominica Labour Party (UDLP)

Address. House of Assembly, Roseau, Dominica

Leadership. Michael A. Douglas (l.)

Founded. 1981

History. This party was established by Rosie Douglas and his brother, Michael A. Douglas, who had been elected to the House of Assembly in July 1980 as a member of the Dominica Democratic Labour Party (DDLP). Michael A. Douglas had left the DDLP after he had unsuccessfully tried to replace the leader of that party, Oliver J. Seraphine, who had failed to be re-elected to the House of Assembly in June 1980. Douglas then continued to sit in the House, but as the sole UDLP member. (The DDLP was in mid-1983 reunited with the Dominica Labour Party— see separate entry for the latter.)

Dominican Republic

Capital: Santo Domingo　　　　　　　　　　　　　　　　Pop. 6,200,000

The Dominican Republic has an executive President elected by universal adult suffrage for a four-year term and a Congress consisting of a 120-member House of Representatives and a 27-member Senate, both similarly elected at the same time as the President. The latter appoints, and presides over, a Cabinet. Voting is compulsory for all citizens above the age of 18 years, and elections to the Chamber of Deputies take place under a proportional representation system in each province in multi-member electoral districts, while voting for the Senate is by simple plurality.

In elections held on May 16, 1982, the presidential candidate of the ruling Dominican Revolutionary Party (PRD) defeated that of the Reformist Party (PR). In the Congress elected at the same time seats were gained as follows: (i) in the Senate PR 17, PRD 10, and (ii) in the Chamber of Deputies PRD 62, PR 50, Dominican Liberation Party 7, Constitutional Action Party 1.

Democratic Integration Movement
Movimiento de Integración Democrática (MID)

Address. Avda. Bolívar 154, Santo Domingo, D.N., Dominican Republic

Leadership. Francisco Augusto Lora (l.)

History. The party's leader contested the 1970 presidential elections for the MID, and also the 1978 presidential elections, in which he was supported by the Movement of National Conciliation and the Quisqueyan Democratic Party.

Orientation. The MID is a centre-right group.

Dominican Communist Party
Partido Comunista Dominicano (PCD)

Leadership. Narciso Isa Conde (s.g.)

Founded. 1944

History. The party was founded underground during the Trujillo dictatorship as the Dominican Revolutionary Democratic Party. It was known as the Dominican People's Socialist Party in 1946–65; in 1947 most party leaders were arrested and deported; in 1962 the party proclaimed as its short-term objective "a national liberation, anti-imperialist and anti-feudal revolution", and after operating as a semi-legal organization, the party was banned in October 1963. It took an active part in the 1965 civil war. The PCD was legalized in November 1977.

Orientation. The PCD is an orthodox communist party.

Structure. The PCD is based on the principles of democratic centralism; its highest authority is its congress, and between congresses its activities are directed by a central committee and a secretariat.

International affiliations. The PCD is recognized by the Communist parties of the Soviet-bloc countries.

Dominican Liberation Party
Partido de la Liberación Dominicana (PLD)

Address. Avda. Independencia 89, Santo Domingo, D.N., Dominican Republic

Leadership. Dr Juan Bosch Gaviño; Jesús Antonio Pichardo

Founded. 1973

History. The party was founded by Dr Bosch, the former leader of the Dominican Revolutionary Party (see separate entry). It unsuccessfully contested the presidential and congressional elections of May 1978.

Dominican Popular Movement
Movimiento Popular Dominicano (MPD)

Leadership. Julio de Peña Valdés
History. The party's founders included many former members of the Dominican Communist Party. Although considered illegal because of earlier terrorist activities, the MPD was one of the parties which constituted the 1974 electoral opposition alliance under the Santiago agreement.
Orientation. The MPD is an extreme left-wing formation.

Dominican Revolutionary Party
Partido Revolucionario Dominicano (PRD)

Address. Avda. Bolívar 107, Santo Domingo, D.N., Dominican Republic
Leadership. Jacobo Majluta (pres.); Dr José Francisco Peña Gómez (s.g.)
Founded. 1939
History. The PRD, founded in Havana (Cuba), was established inside the Dominican Republic on July 5, 1961, after the assassination of the dictator Rafael Leonidas Trujillo (who had ruled the country for over 30 years). In December 1962 the PRD took part in the first elections held since the overthrow of the dictatorship, and its presidential candidate (Dr Juan Bosch Gaviño) gained a majority of votes. His elected Government was, however, overthrown seven months later, when a triumvirate took power.

In April 1965 a civil and military insurrection inspired by the PRD broke out with the object of reinstating the constitutionally elected Government of 1963. With the avowed object of averting "communist danger", the US Government decided on military intervention in the Dominican Republic, and on April 28, 1965, some 42,000 US marines landed in the country. This action was legalized by the Organization of American States, and troops were also sent from other countries.

The conflict was ended with the installation of a provisional Government which in 1966 called for elections. These were won by Dr Joaquín Balaguer of the Reformist Party (with US support), whose Government lasted for 12 years, during which several hundred young insurrectionists lost their lives. In May 1978, however, the PRD overwhelmingly won the elections and Antonio Guzmán Fernández assumed the presidency. The PRD again triumphed in the May 1982 elections, with Dr Salvador Jorge Blanco being elected President and Dr José Francisco Peña Gómez mayor of Santo Domingo.
Orientation. The PRD is a left-of-centre, democratic socialist, party.
Membership. 400,000
International affiliations. Socialist International

National Civic Union
Unión Cívica Nacional (UCN)

Founded. 1961
History. The UCN emerged in 1961 as the largest and most influential opposition party (led by Dr Viriato Alberto Fiallo and Dr Rafael F. Bonnelly, who was President of the Republic in 1962-63). In the 1963 elections the UCN came second after the PRD. In 1974 the UCN was one of the opposition parties allied under the Santiago agreement and, like all the parties in the alliance except the People's Democratic Party, withdrew from the elections.

National Conciliation Movement
Movimiento de Conciliación Nacional (MCN)

Address. Calle Pina No. 207, Santo Domingo, Dominican Republic
Leadership. Dr Jaime Manuel Fernández G. (pres.); Victor Mena (org. sec.)
Founded. February 1969
History. The MCN was formed by Dr Héctor Garcia Godoy, who had been provisional President of the Republic in 1965-66, with the object of unifying the various Dominican groups divided by the 1965 civil war. After the death of Dr Garcia Godoy in April 1970 he was followed as leader of the party by Dr Fernández G.

The MCN supported the Reformist Party Governments elected in 1970 and 1974 but later withdrew its support. In the 1978 elections it was allied with the Democratic Integration Movement (MID), the (right-wing) Quisqueyan Democratic Party (PQD) and other groups.
Orientation. The MCN seeks to be a broad centre party unifying the progressive right and the moderate left in joint action for the benefit of the country.
Structure. The MCN has a national executive directory and directories in the capital, provinces and in municipalities.
Membership. 659,277

National Movement of Salvation
Movimiento Nacional de Salvación (MNS)

Leadership. Luis Julián Pérez (l.)
Founded. 1976
History. The party's leader had been a close collaborator of Dr Balaguer, the leader of the Reformist Party and President of the Republic from 1966 to 1978. However, shortly after the formation of the MNS the secretary-general of the then ruling Reformist Party announced that government officials who collaborated or sympathized with the new party would be dismissed as "traitors" on suspicion of seeking to oust President Balaguer.
Orientation. The MNS is a right-wing opposition group.

People's Democratic Party
Partido Demócrata Popular (PDP)

Address. Arz. Merino 259, Santo Domingo, D.N., Dominican Republic
Leadership. Adm. Luis Homero Lajara Burgos
History. Although a signatory to the 1974 Santiago agreement, establishing an alliance of opposition parties including five others which withdrew from the 1974 presidential elections, the PDP contested these elections as the only opposition party to do so and was unsuccessful.

Quisqueyan Democratic Party
Partido Quisqueyano Demócrata (PQD)

Address. Avda. 27 de Febrero No. 206 (Altos), Santo Domingo, D.N., Dominican Republic
Leadership. Gen. Elías Wessin y Wessin (l. and ch); Juan Manuel Taveras Rodríguez (g.s.)
Founded. June 1968
History. The party has been in opposition since its formation. In May 1970 Gen. Wessin unsuccessfully contested the presidential election. For the election of May 1974 the PQD joined an opposition coalition, but withdrew, with most of the other parties in this coalition, from the elections two days before they were held after a demand for a postponement of the elections had been refused by the Government.
In May 1978 the PQD supported the (unsuccessful) candidate of the Democratic Integration Movement but it did not take part in the congressional elections held at the same time because its leader, Gen. Wessin, had been deported in 1973 for alleged involvement in a right-wing plot against the Government in 1971. He did not return from exile until May 1978, shortly after the elections of that month.
Orientation. The PQD is a right-wing party standing for representative democracy, the rule of law and equality of justice and opportunity for all Dominicans.
Structure. The party has a central executive committee, a committee for the national district (of Santo Domingo), an action committee, provincial and municipal committees and sub-committees at lower levels.
Membership. 600,000
Publications. *Quisqueyano* (fortnightly official periodical), about 15,000

Reformist Party
Partido Reformista (PR)

Address. Apartado de Correos 1332 (Av. Tiradentes, Esq. San Cristobal), Santo Domingo, Dominican Republic
Leadership. Dr Joaquín Balaguer (pres.); Joaquín A. Ricardo (s.g.)
Founded. June 1964
History. The party was founded by followers of Dr Balaguer, who was President of the Republic for three consecutive terms from 1966 to 1978. Since 1978 it has been the largest opposition party opposing the ruling Dominican Revolutionary Party (see separate entry).
Orientation. The PR is a nationalist, land-based party which intends to reform the state through the creation of a large and powerful middle class and the upliftment of the peasant majority by land reform which will free it from "the decadent structure of neo-feudalism". The PR is opposed to the internationalism of Marxist and neo-Marxist groups.
Structure. The supreme body of the PR's cadres and active members is its national assembly consisting of delegates of all municipal and municipal district directories and members (100) of the central executive directory. There are also 28-member provincial directories. The party has basic units in both urban and rural areas. It has 20 secretariats which may set up organizations for various groups of members—women, young people, students, workers or peasants.
Publications. Official organ is the *Orientación Reformista* programme reproduced by 35 radio stations throughout the country.

Revolutionary Social Christian Party
Partido Revolucionario Social Cristiano
(PRSC)

Address. Las Mercedes 451, Apdo. postal 2571, Santo Domingo, D.N., Dominican Republic
Leadership. Dr Claudio Isidoro Acosta (pres.); Dr Alfonso Lockward (s.g.)
Founded. Nov. 29, 1961
History. Together with four of the five other opposition parties which had concluded the 1974 Santiago agreement (the UCN, PRD, PQD and MPD) the PRSC withdrew from the 1974 presidential elections.
Orientation. The PRSC is a party of the democratic left, rejecting both capitalism and communism.
International affiliations. Christian Democratic International; Christian Democratic Organization of America.

Other Parties

Christian Social Action Movement (*Movimiento de Acción Social Cristiana,* ASC)

Civilian Veterans' Party (*Partido de Veteranos Civiles,* PVC)

Constitutional Action Party (*Partido Acción Constitucional,* PAC), which in May 1982 gained one seat in the Chamber of Deputies.

Dominican Workers' Party (*El Partido de los Trabajadores Dominicanos*)

National Action Party (*Partido de Acción Nacional*), a right-wing formation.

Patriotic Union Party (*Partido Unión Patriótica,* PUP)

Social Democratic Alliance Party (*Partido Alianza Social Demócrata,* ASD), led by Dr José Rafael Abinader.

Ecuador

Capital: Quito   Pop. 8,800,000

The Republic of Ecuador has an executive President elected, together with a Vice-President, for a five-year term by universal adult suffrage. There is a unicameral Congress, to which 57 members are elected on a provincial basis and 12 on a national basis, all by universal adult suffrage for a five-year term. There is a Cabinet presided over by the President.

Voting is compulsory for citizens between the ages of 18 and 65 years. The President is elected by an absolute majority; if no candidate gains it in the first round, there follows a run-off election between the two best-placed candidates. The provincial members of the Congress (National Chamber of Representatives) comprise one from each province with less than 100,000 inhabitants and at least two from each other province. In order to qualify for participation in elections parties (other than alliances formed within six months prior to an election) must be recognized by the Supreme Electoral Tribunal, to which the party has to submit, inter alia, a certificate showing that at least 1.5 per cent of the registered electorate are members of the party in at least 10 provinces, including the principal cities. A party which does not obtain 5 per cent of the vote in two successive elections loses its official recognition.

In 1980 state assistance was given to two parties—the Concentration of Popular Forces (CFP), which received the equivalent of about $340,000, and the Democratic Left (ID), which was granted about $180,000.

By November 1981 seats in Congress were distributed as follows: Concentration of Popular Forces (Bucaram faction) 12, Democratic Left (ID) 12, Popular

Democracy (DP) 7, Conservative Party 6, Radical Liberal Party 4, Social Christian Party 2, Revolutionary Nationalist Party 2, Democratic Popular Movement (Maoist) 1, Democratic Party (PD) 1, non-aligned 22.

Christian Social Party
Partido Social Cristiano (PSC)

Leadership. León Febrés Cordero (l.)
Founded. 1951
History. This conservative party was founded to support Camilo Ponce Enríquez, who was President of Ecuador in 1956-60. In 1979 the PSC leader was elected to the Chamber of Representatives. In the second round of the 1984 presidential elections Léon Febrés Cordero was elected to the presidency on May 6 with some 52 per cent of the vote, having received the backing of other formations of the centre-right. He defeated Rodrigo Borja of the Democratic Left Party (see separate entry).

Communist Party of Ecuador
Partido Comunista Ecuatoriano (PCE)

Leadership. René Maugé Mosquera (s.g.)
Founded. 1926
History. The party was established as the Socialist Party of Ecuador, which decided in 1926 to join the Communist International. It assumed the name PCE in 1931. The party took part in a 1944 insurrection and in the Constituent Assembly which drew up the country's 1945 Constitution. The PCE was illegal in 1963-66, when many of its leaders were imprisoned.

At a congress in 1968 it adopted a programme for "national liberation in the framework of the anti-imperialist, anti-feudal, democratic revolution, with subsequent transition to socialist revolution". In the April 1979 congressional elections the PCE led an electoral front called the Popular Democratic Union (UDP), whose list was headed by the PCE leader but which failed to win any seats. In local and provincial elections held in December 1980 the UDP lost support.

Structure. The party is organized on the principles of democratic centralism. Its supreme authority is its congress, and between congress sessions party activities are directed by a central committee.

Publications. *El Pueblo* (daily central organ)

International affiliations. The party is recognized by the Communist parties of the Soviet-bloc countries.

Concentration of Popular Forces
Concentración de Fuerzas Populares (CFP)

Leadership. Averroes Bucaram (dir.); Galo Vayas, Rodolfo Baquerizo (leaders)
Founded. 1946
History. The CFP first contested presidential elections in 1956, when its candidate came third. Under the dictatorial powers of President Velasco Ibarra, the leader of the CFP (Assad Bucaram, who had twice been elected mayor of Guayaquil and later prefect of Guayas province) was in September 1970 deported to Panama, from where he did not return to Ecuador until January 1972.

Following the suspension of all political activities by President Rodríguez Lara in July 1974, a dialogue between the military Government and political parties was restored in 1976, and later that year the CFP called for immediate elections. In March 1978 it formed an alliance with the Christian Democrats. In the first round of presidential elections held on July 16, 1978, the CFP candidate (Jaime Roldós Aguilera) came first, gaining about 31 per cent of the votes, and he was elected President in the second round on April 29, 1979 (as the first civilian to hold that post since 1972).

The CFP, however, was by then effectively divided into two factions, following respectively Assad Bucaram and the President. Both these leaders died in 1981 (respectively in May and November). In the 1980 local and provincial elections the CFP had been relegated to third place. The Roldosist faction of the CFP decided in 1981 to join the Democratic Convergence alliance, and the Bucaram faction joined the Government of President Osvaldo Hurtado (of the Popular Democracy) in January 1982.

Orientation. The CFP is a centre-left party advocating the implementation of major social and economic changes.

Conservative Party
Partido Conservador (PC)

Leadership. José Terán Varea (dir.)
Founded. 1855
History. As the country's oldest party, the PC is based on a traditional alliance of church and state and has its roots in the Andean highlands. After participating in government from 1956 to 1960, the PC later formed part of the National Constitutional Front (FNC) established to contest the July 1978 presidential elections, but it withdrew in March of that year.

In local and provincial elections held in December 1980 the PC lost support.

Democratic Institutionalist Coalition
Coalición Institucionalista Democrática (CID)

Leadership. Gil Barragán Romero (l.)
History. This right-wing traditionalist party gained three seats in the congressional elections of April 1979. It subsequently co-operated with the Government of President Roldós.

Democratic Left Party
Partido Izquierda Democrática (ID)

Address. Juan León Mera 268 y Jorge Washington, Quito, Ecuador
Leadership. Rodrigo Borja Cevallos (l.); Raúl Baca Carbo (s.g.)
Founded. November 1977
History. The ID's candidate, Rodrigo Borja Cevallos, gained fourth place in the first round of presidential elections on July 16, 1978, with 11 per cent of the votes cast. The ID had earlier gained the post of mayor of Guayaquil from the Concentration of Popular Forces (CFP) but lost it on July 16, 1978. The ID supported the successful CFP candidate in the final round of the presidential elections in April 1979. In the congressional elections of the same month the party obtained 15 of the 69 seats (16.6 per cent of the national vote) and claimed to have become the country's second-strongest party after the CFP.

On Aug. 10, 1980, Raúl Baca Carbo was elected president of Congress and agreed to co-operate with the Government of President Roldós. In 1981 the ID supported, together with the Popular Democracy (DP), the faction of the CFP which was led by President Roldós, and from January 1982 onwards it supported a new majority alignment of parties embracing also the DP, the Democratic Party (PD), the Popular Democratic Union (UDP) and seven independents. At that time the ID held 12 seats in Congress and claimed to be the first political force in the country.

In the 1984 presidential elections the ID leader, Rodrigo Borja, lost in the run-off vote on May 6 after having led in the first round held on Jan. 29. In the second round Borja secured about 48 per cent of the vote and was defeated by the candidate of the Christian Social Party (see separate entry).

Orientation. The party's objectives include free parliamentary, political and economic democracy, a radical redistribution of wealth, a reduction of Ecuador's dependence on other countries, and economic and social democracy.
Membership. 250,000
International affiliations. Socialist International

Democratic Party
Partido Demócrata

Leadership. Dr Francisco Huerta Montalvo, Heinz Moeller (leaders)
History. Dr Huerta Montalvo had earlier been a member of the Liberal Party. In May 1982 the party had four members in the Chamber of Representatives.
Orientation. The party is social democratic in outlook.

Ecuadorean Popular Revolutionary Union
Unión Revolucionaria Popular Ecuatoriana (URPE)

Leadership. Jaime Galzara, Carlos Rodríguez (leaders).
Founded. 1980
History. The leaders of this alliance represented respectively a *Movimiento Segunda Independencia* and a *Comité del Pueblo*, both of which had formed part of the Left Broad Front (see separate entry).

Ecuadorean Roldosista Party
Partido Roldosista Ecuatoriano

Leadership. Abdalah Bucaram Ortiz (l.)

Founded. 1980
History. This party was set up in opposition to People, Change and Democracy—Popular Roldosista Party (see separate entry). Its leader claimed to be the true representative of the policies of his brother-in-law, the late President Jaime Roldós Aguilera, who had been killed in an aircrash in May 1981. The party was officially recognized in December 1982.

Ecuadorean Socialist Party
Partido Socialista Ecuatoriano (PSE)

Address. Edif. Bolívar, Apdo. 103, Quito, Ecuador
Leadership. Hector Soria (sec.)
Founded. 1933
Membership. 55,000

Left Broad Front
Frente Amplio de la Izquierda (FADI)

Leadership. René Maugé Mosquera (s.g.)
Founded. 1977
History. FADI was established as a left-wing alliance consisting of the Communist Party of Ecuador (PCE), the Committee of the People (a splinter-group from the Maoist Marxist-Leninist Communist Party), the Revolutionary Socialist Party (PSR), the Revolutionary Movement of the Christian Left (MRIC), the Movement for the Unity of the Left (MUI) and the Second Independence Movement (MSI). In the first round of presidential elections on July 16, 1978, FADI's leader came in sixth place with 5 per cent of the votes cast.

National Velasquista Party
Partido Nacional Velasquista (PNV)

Leadership. Alfonso Arroyo Robelly (l.)
Founded. 1952
History. This party was founded as a federation and a personal vehicle of President José Maria Velasco Ibarra, who was in power for five terms, most recently in 1968-72, and who died in 1977. (In July 1977 he had transferred his support to the presidential candidate of the Ecuadorean Democratic Action formed by his nephew, Jaime Acosta Velasco.) In the 1978-79 elections the major part of the PNV supported a National Constitutional Front,

an alliance of 11 centre-right parties. In the local and provincial elections of December 1980 it had little success.

People, Change and Democracy—Popular Roldosista Party
Pueblo, Cambio y Democracia—Partido Roldosista Popular (PCD-PRR)

Leadership. Ernesto Buenano Cabrera (s.g.)
Founded. 1980
History. The formation of this party under the name of *Pueblo, Cambio y Democracia* had been planned by President Jaime Roldos Aguilera (who died in May 1981) and was carried out by his brother, León Roldos Aguilera. The PCD-PRR was officially recognized in 1981. In January 1982 it withdrew its support from the Government of President Hurtado. In November 1982 it adopted its present name.

People's Democracy—Christian Democratic Union
Democracia Popular—Unión Demócrata Cristiana (DP-UDC)

Address. Calle Vargas 727 y Santa Prisca, Casilla Postal 2.300, Quito, Ecuador
Leadership. Dr Julio César Trujillo (nat. pres.); Dr Osvaldo Hurtado Larrea (s.g.)
Founded. April 1978
History. A Christian Democratic Party had first been established in November 1964 and had taken part in the 1970 constitutional Government. In December 1977 the Christian Democrats led by Osvaldo Hurtado formed the Popular Democratic Coalition (CPD) in alliance with the Progressive Conservatives led by Dr Trujillo (a non-traditionalist faction which had broken away from the Conservative Party in April 1977), and also with the *Frente Social Progresista* (FSP) led by José Corsino Cardenas and the *Unión Nacional Democrática* (UNADE) led by Luis Gómez Izquierdo. In April 1978, however, the supreme electoral tribunal barred the CPD from taking part in the forthcoming elections and the same month the Christian Democrats and the Progressive Conservatives formed the People's Democracy—Christian Democratic Union (DP-UDC).

In the presidential elections held in two ballots in July 1978 and April 1979 the DP-UDC supported the Concentration of

111

Popular Forces (CFP), whose candidates for the presidency and the vice-presidency (the latter being Osvaldo Hurtado) were successful. In congressional elections held on April 29, 1979, the DP-UDC gained five of the 31 seats obtained by the CFP.

Orientation. The DP-UDC supports Christian democratic doctrine and ideology and wishes to effect required changes in the country in freedom and democracy.

Structure. The party's supreme organ is its national congress, a gathering of national and provincial leaders. The party's national head council is its executive organ dealing with day-to-day tasks. There are provincial head councils and under them cantonal head committees.

Membership. 45,000

International affiliations. Christian Democratic International; Christian Democratic Organization of America

Popular Democratic Movement
Movimiento Popular Democrático (MPD)

Leadership. Dr Jaime Hurtado González (l.)

History. This electoral movement of the (Maoist) Marxist-Leninist Communist Party of Ecuador gained one national seat in the 1979 congressional elections. However, in local and provincial elections held in December 1980 it lost support.

Radical Alfarista Front
Frente Radical Alfarista (FRA)

Leadership. Cecilia Calderón de Castro (l.)

History. The FRA took part in the first round of presidential elections on July 16, 1978, its leader gaining fifth place with 9 per cent of the votes cast. In January 1979 the electoral tribunal withdrew its recognition of the FRA, and it thereupon supported the (successful) presidential candidate of the Concentration of Popular Forces (CFP) in the final round of presidential elections in April 1979.

Although the FRA had gained no seats in the 1979 congressional elections, it did well in local and provincial elections held on Dec. 7, 1980, when it obtained about 20 per cent of the total vote and over 50 per cent in Guayas department.

Radical Liberal Party
Partido Liberal Radical (PLR)

Leadership. Blasco Peña Herrera (l.)
Founded. 1895

History. The PLR is the principal heir of the traditional Liberal Party which was dominant in Ecuador for some 50 years and had its historical base in the coastal plain. Later it disintegrated into several factions. During the preparations for a return to civilian rule in 1976-77 the PLR withdrew from constitutional committees in protest against restrictions imposed by the Government on political freedoms.

In the first round of presidential elections on July 16, 1978, the PLR candidate (Raúl Clemente Huerta Rendón) won 21 per cent of the vote and took third place; at the same time the PLR gained the post of mayor of Quito.

In the congressional elections of April 1979 the PLR gained four seats. However, in local and provincial elections held in December 1980 this party lost support.

Revolutionary Nationalist Party
Partido Nacionalista Revolucionario (PNR)

Address. Calle Pazmiño 245, Ofc. 500, Quito, Ecuador

Leadership. Dr Carlos Julio Arosemena Monroy (nat. dir.); Jorge Acayturri (s.g.)

Founded. 1969

History. The PNR has its origins in a *Movimiento Nacional Arosemenista* (1961-63, when Dr Arosemena Monroy was President of Ecuador) and a *Movimiento Nacionalista Revolucionario* which was represented in the Constituent Assembly elected in October 1966. The PNR was officially recognized as a party in 1969. Apart from temporary support for President María Velasco Ibarra in 1970-71, the PNR has been in opposition.

The PNR opposed the holding of a referendum on a new Constitution in January 1978, advocating that voters should spoil their papers (which in fact was done by over 400,000 voters). It also abstained during the second ballot of presidential elections in April 1979, but took part in the parliamentary elections held at the same time, gaining one seat (for its leader).

Orientation. The PNR stands for a nationalist revolution and a free and sovereign Ecuador.

Structure. The PNR has a national convention, a co-ordinating committee and two regional and 20 provincial directors. It is organized at the levels of provinces, cantons, parishes and wards.

Membership. 50,000 active members; 20,000 registered sympathizers

Publications. *Ecuador Primero*

Socialist Revolutionary Party of Ecuador
Partido Socialista Revolucionario Ecuatoriano (PSRE)

Address. P. A. Diputado Jorge Chiriboga Guerrero, Palacio Legislativo, Of. 701, Quito, Ecuador
Leadership. Jorge Chiriboga Guerrero (s.g. of cent. comm.)
Founded. May 1961
History. A Socialist Party of Ecuador was first established in 1926. In 1944 the party assumed power, together with other revolutionary parties, and installed the nominee of an Ecuadorian Democratic Alliance as President. The party subsequently lost influence and in 1961 it assumed its present name by adding the word "revolutionary" in accordance with what it viewed as "the new political dynamics in Latin America". The party supported the Cuban revolution and national liberation movements in America and the rest of the world. Together with other revolutionary parties it opposed the military dictatorship in Ecuador and aspired to a new type of democracy. In 1979 its secretary-general was elected to the Chamber of Representatives.

Orientation. The PSRE is revolutionary and anti-imperialist, with the object of assuming power to enable the masses of Ecuador to build a free and sovereign people's democracy.
Structure. The party has basic units, committees at sectional, regional, and provincial levels, a central committee, a secretariat and a political bureau.
Membership. 20,000
Publications. *Tiempos de Lucha* (central organ)

Other Parties

Minor parties active in Ecuador include the following:

National Integration Movement (*Movimiento de Integración Nacional*, MIN), founded in January 1983 and led by Julio Ayala Serra.

Progressive Political Action (*Accion Politica Progresista*, APP), founded in December 1982 and led by Gen. Levoyer.

Egypt

Capital: Cairo Pop. 46,000,000

Under its 1971 Constitution as subsequently amended, the Arab Republic of Egypt is "a democratic and socialist state" with a limited system of party pluralism. There is a People's Assembly of whose 458 members 448 are directly elected by universal adult suffrage (and the remaining 10 are appointed by the President of the Republic). In elections to the Assembly held on May 27, 1984, the ruling National Democratic Party (NDP) obtained 390 seats and the New *Wafd* Party 58, while three other opposition parties failed to secure the minimum of 8 per cent of the valid votes required for representation. There is also a Consultative Council in which the NDP holds all 140 elective seats (another 70 being filled by the President). The franchise was restricted under a set of principles approved in a referendum in May 1978, providing that the right to belong to political parties and engage in political activities did not apply to those who had "participated in the corruption of political life" before the 1952 revolution or to those convicted of political offences or proved to have "carried out actions tending to corrupt political life or to subject the national unity or social peace to danger".

Under a code of ethics ("law of shame") approved by the People's Assembly on April 29, 1980, newly defined punishable offences included the inciting of opposition to the state's economic, political and social system and the dissemination of "false" or "extremist" statements deemed to have endangered national unity or social peace. Penalties proposed were imprisonment, fines, house arrest, suspension from political activity, dismissal from employment in the service of the state and restrictions on overseas travel.

Subject to the above restrictions, all citizens above the age of 18 years are entitled to vote, and voting is compulsory for men. Voting is carried out for lists, which must receive an absolute majority in the constituency, failing which a run-off election takes place between the two leading lists. Candidates must be resident in the district where they seek election.

Liberal Socialist Party (LSP)

Leadership. Mustapha Kamel Murad
Founded. 1976
History. Created from the right-wing component of the Arab Socialist Union, the LSP formed the right-wing parliamentary opposition to the regime of President Sadat. Its representation in the People's Assembly fell from the 12 seats won in 1976 to three following the June 1979 elections. However, in the May 1984 elections the party obtained no seats because it won only 0.6 per cent of the valid votes.
Orientation. The LSP believes that the state should control only heavy industry, with smaller enterprises being left in private hands, and has demanded more economic liberalization and increased foreign investment. It supports a judiciary independent of the President and has called for the latter to be chosen in a contested election rather than in a plebiscite.

Nasserite Party

Leadership. Dr Mohammed Hassanein Heikal, (Mrs) Hoda Nasser (leaders)
Founded. April 1979
History. Dr Heikal had been editor of the authoritative *Al Ahram* newspaper from 1956 to 1974, when he was dismissed over policy disputes with President Anwar Sadat. In 1978 he was banned from leaving the country, and in 1979 his newly-formed party did not receive official authorization to take part in the elections of that year. He was subsequently arrested but, following the assassination of President Sadat on Oct. 6, 1981, he was released on Nov. 25 of that year by President Hosni Mubarak, to whom he immediately gave his support.
Orientation. This party subscribes to the Arab socialist precepts enunciated by the late President Nasser.

National Democratic Party (NDP)

Address. People's Assembly, Cairo, Egypt
Leadership. President Mohammed Hosni Mubarak (pres.)
Founded. October 1978
History. The party's proposed formation was announced by President Sadat before the central committee of the Arab Socialist Union (ASU) on July 22, 1978. The ASU had been established in December 1962 as the country's sole political organization, but under a law of June 29, 1977, it was superseded by three political parties of which the Arab Socialist Party (ASP), a party of the centre supporting the Government, was the strongest in the People's Assembly.

Following the formation of the NDP, 306 of the 308 ASP's members in the People's Assembly joined the new party, which took over the assets and commitments of the ASP and which in the June 1979 elections won an overwhelming majority of the Assembly seats. On President Sadat's assassination in October 1981, Vice-President Mubarak succeeded to the presidency of both the country and the ruling party. In the May 1984 elections the NDP retained 390 of the 448 elective seats in the Assembly, with 72.99 per cent of the valid votes.
Orientation. The NDP's policies include "commitment to the principles of democratic socialism"; the achievement of "prosperity of the Egyptian individual"; the creation of "a modern state based on science and faith", with Islamic law being "a principal source of legislation". The press was to be added as a fourth power to "the three state powers" (legislative, executive and judiciary).

National Front Party

Leadership. Mahmoud al-Qadi, Mumtaz Nasser (leaders)
Founded. August 1978

History. The party's leaders had both previously been independent deputies in the People's Assembly. Their party, however, did not receive official authorization to take part in the 1979 elections.

National Progressive Unionist Party (NPUP)

Address. 1 Karim el Dawlah St., Cairo, Egypt
Leadership. Khaled Mohieddin (l); Dr Rifaat el-Said (sec.)
Founded. 1976
History. Created from the left-wing component of the Arab Socialist Union, the NPUP formed the left-wing parliamentary opposition to the regime of President Sadat, which it criticized vociferously. It claims to have suffered a degree of harassment and repression, particularly before the June 1979 elections, in which it failed to win a seat in the People's Assembly. The party also failed to obtain representation in the May 1984 elections, when it obtained 4.2 per cent of the valid votes (i.e. below the 8 per cent required minimum).
Orientation. The (atheistic) NPUP advocates state ownership of industry and the exclusion of foreign investment; it has also called for greater support for the Palestinian cause and was alone among the main parties in opposing the Egyptian Government for signing a peace treaty with Israel in March 1979.
Publications. Al Ahali (weekly)

New Wafd Party

Leadership. Fuad Serageddin, Ibrahin Farrag (leaders)
Founded. 1983
History. The original *Wafd* had been a popular liberal and nationalist movement in the 1920s but had been dissolved after the 1952 revolution. It was re-established in February 1978 but disbanded itself on June 2 of that year in protest against the passing of a bill giving legal effect to restriction of voting rights, as approved in a referendum; two days later the *Wafd's* two members of the People's Assembly declared themselves independents.

On Oct. 20, 1980, it was reported that a new *Wafd* party had been launched by a younger generation of *Wafd* supporters. On Oct. 29, 1983, a court ruled that the *Wafd* party had not voluntarily disbanded itself in 1978 and that the New *Wafd* Party had the legal right to contest forthcoming elections. The new party's ancestry in the pre-1952 *Wafd* was highlighted in February 1984 when the Council of State ruled that Fuad Serageddin and Ibrahin Farrag (both former ministers of the pre-Nasser era) could be readmitted to the leadership of the party. In the May 1984 Assembly elections the party obtained 58 seats (and 15.1 per cent of the valid votes), thus becoming the sole parliamentary opposition party.
Publications. Al-Masri al-Jadid

Socialist Labour Party (SLP)

Address. 12 Awalie el-Ahd St., Cairo, Egypt
Leadership. Ibrahim Mahmoud Shukri (l.)
Founded. November 1978
History. The party had its origins in the *Misr El Fatat* (Young Egypt), a socialist party of the 1930s, and was specifically exempted from the ban on pre-revolution parties contained in May 1978 referendum principles. Its leader had, before the provisional formation of the party in August 1978, been a cabinet minister since February 1977. In a document signed on Nov. 23, 1979, President Sadat and the People's Assembly representatives of the ruling National Democratic Party (NDP) backed the creation of the SLP as an "honest and constructive" opposition, following which Ibrahim Mahmoud Shukri announced on Nov. 30 that all the necessary formalities for the party's registration had been completed. In the June 1979 elections the SLP became the main opposition party to the NDP, but in the May 1984 Assembly elections it failed to obtain any seats, its 7.1 per cent share of the valid votes falling below the 8 per cent required minimum.
Orientation. The SLP stands for freedom to form political parties, freedom of the press, the independence of the judiciary, the election by universal suffrage, for a five-year term, of the President and the Vice-President of the Republic, an end to Egypt's "isolationism", the creation of the "United Arab States" and "balanced relations with the super-powers" with no involvement in their conflicts.

El Salvador

Capital: San Salvador   Pop. 4,800,000

Under a new Constitution enacted in December 1983, the Government of the Republic of El Salvador is headed by an executive President elected by universal adult suffrage (in two rounds if no candidate secures an absolute majority in the first round of voting). Also in December 1983 the Constituent Assembly elected on March 28, 1982, was redesignated as the country's legislative body, to remain in being until further elections in 1985.

In the Constituent Assembly the 60 seats were distributed as follows: Christian Democratic Party (PDC) 24, National Republican Alliance (Arena) 19, National Reconciliation Party (PCN) 14, Democratic Action (AD) 2, Salvadorean Popular Party (PPS) 1. (The Popular Orientation Party also took part in the elections but gained no seats.) In the "Government of national unity" set up on May 4, 1982, Arena and the PCN (both right-wing formations) each held four ministerial seats, the PDC held three, and the remaining seats were held by independents. For these elections voting was compulsory for citizens above the age of 18 years (except members of the armed forces and the security forces), who were issued with new identity cards (as there was no up-to-date electoral register). The ballot papers used showed the names and symbols of parties.

El Salvador, a densely populated country with the highest population growth rate (of 3.5 per cent per annum) in Central America, was for a long time under military rule following the suppression of a peasant rebellion in 1932 (at a cost of 30,000 lives including that of Farabundo Martí, the rebel peasants' leader). After elections held in 1972 and 1977 the opposition (of which the Christian Democrats then formed the major part) claimed that the ruling National Reconciliation Party had carried out massive electoral fraud, and many opposition candidates sought asylum abroad.

Following the overthrow of President Carlos Humberto Romero in October 1979, El Salvador's various left-wing groups became increasingly critical of the alleged right-wing tendencies of the new ruling junta and from 1980 mounted a concerted military and diplomatic campaign to overthrow the Government.

Broad National Front
Frente Amplio Nacional (FAN)

Leadership. Maj. Roberto d'Aubuisson Arrieta (l.)
Founded. 1980
History. Maj. d'Aubuisson, a former chief of intelligence, and several members of the newly formed FAN were temporarily arrested in May 1980 for the alleged planning of a right-wing coup. On March 3, 1981, he called for a seizure of power by the right-wing military, and in April of that year he was suspected, with followers of his party, to have been involved in the murder of the Archbishop of San Salvador

in March 1980. He later formed the Nationalist Republican Alliance (Arena—see separate entry), having returned from exile in Guatemala late 1981.
Orientation. FAN is extreme right-wing.

Christian Democratic Party
Partido Demócrata Cristiano (PDC)

Address. 3 A Calle Poniente 836, San Salvador, El Salvador
Leadership. José Napoleón Duarte (l.); Julio Adolfo Rey Prendes (s.g.)

116

Founded. 1960

History. The PDC contested the elections to a Constituent Assembly held in December 1961 as part of the United Democratic Party—an alliance with the (moderate) Revolutionary Action Party and the (right-wing) Social Democratic Party—but gained no seats. With other opposition parties, the PDC boycotted the 1962 presidential elections, but in those of 1967 its candidate obtained second place. It took part in the 1972 legislative and presidential elections and also in the 1979 presidential elections as the leading party in a National Opposition Union (UNO).

José Napoléon Duarte (who had returned from exile) was a member of the ruling junta set up after the overthrow of President Carlos Humberto Romero in October 1979, and on Dec. 13, 1980, he was appointed President of Ecuador, which he remained until after the election of the Constituent Assembly on March 28, 1982. In this election the PDC gained 40.7 per cent of the vote and 24 (out of 60) seats, and it was therefore faced with a majority of right-wing parties in the Assembly. It nevertheless took part in the new Government formed after the elections.

In the first round of presidential elections held on March 25, 1984, Duarte as the PDC candidate took 43.4 per cent of the vote, well ahead of the second-placed candidate. In the run-off contest in early May the PDC candidate easily defeated Maj. Roberto d'Aubuisson of the Nationalist Republican Alliance (Arena—see separate entry).

Orientation. The PDC is a left-of-centre party with mainly middle-class support. It has called for land reform, for the reduction of unemployment and for social justice. Its aim has been to form "a legitimate government from which both the left and the extreme right would be excluded".

Publications. Militante DC

International affiliations. Christian Democratic International; Christian Democratic Organization of America

Democratic Action Party
Partido Acción Democratica (PAD)

Leadership. René Fortín Magaña (l.)
Founded. 1981
History. The party's leader had briefly been a member of the military junta in 1960. In the March 1982 elections to the Constituent Assembly the PAD gained only 7.7 per cent of the vote and two seats.

Standing as the PAD candidate, René Fortín Magaña received 3.5 per cent of the vote in the first round of presidential elections held on March 25, 1984.

Orientation. The PAD is a centre-right party standing for private ownership of property and proclaiming its opposition to Communists, Socialists and Christian Democrats and to Soviet, Cuban and Venezuelan intervention in El Salvador.

National Reconciliation Party
Partido de Conciliación National (PCN)

Address. Calle Arce 1128, San Salvador, El Salvador
Leadership. Raúl Molina Martínez (s.g.)
Founded. 1961
History. The PCN was in power from December 1961, when it won all 54 seats in a Constituent Assembly; the latter transformed itself into a Legislative Assembly, which the PCN dominated until the coup of October 1979. It also won all presidential elections held in the 1960s and 1970s, although the official results of such elections were challenged by the opposition.

In the elections held on March 28, 1982, to the Constituent Assembly the PCN came third with 18.6 per cent of the vote and 14 seats. In the Government formed after the elections the PCN held four ministries. In October 1982, however, its strength in the Constituent Assembly was reduced to five members by the defection of its right wing, which formed the Salvadorean Authentic Institutional Party (see separate entry).

The party's candidate in the 1984 presidential elections was Dr Francisco José Guerrero, who registered third place in the first round (on March 25) with 19.3 per cent of the vote.

Orientation. As a right-of-centre and strongly anti-communist party supported by the Church and the military, with a following among peasants, the PCN has advocated substantial social and economic reforms.

Nationalist Republican Alliance
Alianza Republicana Nacionalista (Arena)

Leadership. Maj. Roberto d'Aubuisson Arrieta (l.); Mario Repdaelli (s.g.)
Founded. 1981
History. Maj. d'Aubuisson was, as the leader of the Broad National Front (FAN—see separate entry), temporarily arrested in May 1980 for alleged conspiracy against the ruling junta, which he had decried as "communist". In the March 1982 elections to the Constituent Assembly the party

117

came second with 29.1 per cent of the vote and 19 seats. With all parties represented in the Assembly except the Christian Democratic Party, Arena signed on March 30, 1982, an agreement to form a government of national unity which was to maintain parliamentary democracy and free enterprise, with human rights and social justice as the basis of harmonious coexistence.

In the interim Government formed subsequently Arena took four ministerial posts. With the other right-wing parties it decided on April 26, 1982, to consolidate previous reforms (concerning land distribution and the nationalization of banks) but not to proceed with further land reforms leading to the setting-up of peasant co-operatives.

Standing as the Arena candidate in the 1984 presidential elections, Maj. d'Aubuisson secured 29.8 per cent of the first-round vote (on March 25) and went into a run-off contest with José Napoleón Duarte of the Christian Democratic Party. The latter emerged as the comfortable victor on May 1.

Orientation. Arena stands for nationalism, individualism, the maintenance of law and order and the suppression of communism, i.e. uncompromising opposition to the left-wing guerrillas. It has accused the Christian Democrats of destroying the country's economic and social foundations and of aiding international communism.

Party for Renewal Action
Partido Acción Renovadora (PAR)

Leadership. Ernesto Oyarbide (l.)
Founded. 1944
History. The PAR was founded by Gen. José Asebcio Menéndez, a nationalist officer who won the presidential elections at that time. The party was suspended in 1968 but was re-registered in 1981; it was however, not represented in the Constituent Assembly elected on March 28, 1982. During the election campaign it claimed to represent the only true opposition.

Orientation. The party has advocated land reform, social justice, pluralism, the nationalization of banks and the transfer of private enterprise property to the workers.

Popular Orientation Party
Partido de Orientación Popular (POP)

Leadership. Gen. (retd.) José Alberto Medrano (l.)

Founded. 1981
History. Gen. Medrano was the founder of a paramilitary *Organización Democrática Nacional* (Orden), which co-operated with the security forces. He had also been the leader of an Independent United Democratic Front (*Frente Unido Democrático Independiente*, FUDI), as whose presidential candidate in the 1972 elections he had obtained about 10 per cent of the vote. (FUDI was represented in the Legislative Assembly in 1974-76.)

In the March 1982 elections to the Constituent Assembly the POP gained only 0.9 per cent of the vote and no seat. In the first round of the 1984 presidential elections on March 25 the POP candidate, Guillermo Trujillo, secured only 0.4 per cent of the votes.

Orientation. The POP is extreme right-wing, for "representative democracy" (not of parties), private property, no further land reform, the privatization of credit institutions and compensation for expropriated land-owners.

Salvadorean Authentic Institutional Party
Partido Auténtico Institucional Salvadoreño (PAIS)

Leadership. Col. Roberto Escobar García (s.g.)
Founded. October 1982
History. The party was formed by a right-wing majority faction of the National Reconciliation Party (PCN), of whose 14 members in the Constituent Assembly nine joined the PAIS, which subsequently aligned itself with the Nationalist Republican Alliance (Arena—see separate entry).

Col. Escobar was the PAIS candidate in the 1984 presidential elections, receiving 1.2 per cent of the vote in the first round on March 25.

Orientation. The PAIS is a right-wing party opposed to any accommodation with the country's left-wing guerrillas.

Salvadorean Popular Party
Partido Popular Salvadoreño (PPS)

Address. P.O.B. (01) 252, San Salvador, El Salvador
Leadership. Francisco Quiñónez Avila (s.g.)
Founded. 1965
History. The PPS was founded by defectors from the Party for Renewal

Action (PAR) who accused the latter party of being pro-communist; the PPS was also joined by certain leaders of the National Reconciliation Party (PCN). In the 1967 presidential elections the PPS candidate obtained third place, and in the 1972 presidential elections it won 3 per cent of the vote. In 1974 it gained four seats in the Legislative Assembly, and after 1978 it was the only opposition party to be represented in the Assembly.

In the March 1982 elections to the Constituent Assembly the PPS gained only 3 per cent of the vote and one seat. In the 1984 presidential elections, Francisco Quiñónez, as the party's candidate, secured 1.9 per cent of the vote in the first round held on March 25.

Orientation. The PPS is a minority conservative group representing business interests.

Stable Centrist Republican Movement
Movimiento Estable Republicano Centrista (Merecen)

Leadership. Juán Ramón Rosales y Rosales (presidential cand.)

History. In the first round of the 1984 presidential elections held on March 25 the Merecen candidate, Juan Ramón Rosales y Rosales, secured 0.5 per cent of the votes.

Equatorial Guinea

Capital: Malabo Pop. 320,000

The Republic of Equatorial Guinea is ruled by a Supreme Military Council headed by Lt.-Col. Teodoro Obiang Nguema Mbasago and in power since Aug. 3, 1979, when it overthrew the dictatorial regime of President Francisco Macias Nguema. A new Constitution approved by 95 per cent of the voters in a referendum on Aug. 15, 1982, provided for Lt.-Col. Obiang Nguema to remain head of state for a further seven years, after which there would be presidential elections by direct popular vote. The Constitution also provided for elections to a National Assembly with a five-year term and for the formation of a Council of State.

The first elections to the National Assembly were held on Aug. 28, 1983, when voters approved 41 representatives (one per constituency) selected by President Obiang Nguema to serve for a five-year term. There were no political parties, and the President retained control over the Assemby.

A provisional government-in-exile was formed in Paris on March 7, 1983, by a Democratic Movement for the Liberation of Equatorial Guinea, founded in 1981 and led by Manuel Rubén Ndongo.

Ethiopia

Capital: Addis Ababa Pop. 31,500,000

Ethiopia is a republic ruled by a Provisional Military Administrative Council (PMAC or *Derg*), whose Chairman (Lt.-Col. Mengistu Haile Mariam) is head of state and chairman of a Council of Ministers. A Commission for Organizing the

Party of the Working People of Ethiopia (COPWE) was set up in December 1979, but by the end of 1983 this Commission had not yet developed into a political mass party on the Soviet model, despite the country's close ties with the Soviet Union and the latter's allies, notably Cuba.

Commission for Organizing the Party of the Working People of Ethiopia (COPWE)

Address. P.O.B. 80001, Addis Ababa, Ethiopia

Leadership. Lt.-Col. Mengistu Haile Mariam (ch. of exec. committee)

Founded. 1979

History. COPWE's first congress was held in June 1980 and attended by some 800 members, and its second congress took place in January 1983, when about 1,600 members were present, including seven of the executive committee, 91 of the central committee and 26 alternate members of the central committee. At this congress the COPWE chairman stated that there were 6,500 COPWE cells but that more emphasis should be placed on recruitment, especially among the working class. The congress expelled 34 members, including six central committee members and two ministers, for "taking part in activities contrary to the organization's objectives".

In the final communiqué of the January 1983 congress it was stated that the third congress, to be held in September 1984, would see the establishment of the party and thus the completion of COPWE's work. Congress resolutions later implemented by the PMAC included one on nationwide military service based on a network of regional militias, and another on the establishment of an Institute for the Study of Ethiopian Nationalities, with a view to eventually offering limited autonomy to nine separate nationalities in Eritrea.

Orientation. The Commission subscribes to Marxist-Leninist principles and is pro-Soviet.

Structure. COPWE has cells and committees throughout the country and holds meetings at all levels. Its executive committee consists of the chairman and members of the standing committee of the PMAC.

Publications. *Serto Ader* (The Working People); *Meskerem* (September)

Fiji

Capital: Suva   Pop. 670,000

Fiji is an independent state within the Commonwealth, with the British monarch as head of state being represented by a Governor-General. It has a bicameral Parliament consisting of a 22-member Senate and a 52-member House of Representatives. While the senators are appointed for a six-year term, the House of Representatives is elected for five years by universal adult suffrage under a complex system embracing 12 Fijian communal seats, 12 Indian communal seats, three general communal seats, 10 Fijian national seats, 10 Indian national seats and five general national seats.

In elections to the House of Representatives held on July 11-17, 1982, seats were gained as follows: The Alliance 28, (the Indian) National Federation Party (NFP) 22 and (the Fijian) Western United Front (allied to the NFP) 2.

The Alliance

Address. 41 Gladstone Road (P.O. Box 688), Suva, Fiji

Leadership. Ratu Sir Kamisese Mara (pres.); Senator Jone Banuve (s.g.)

Founded. November 1965

. *History.* Following the holding of a London conference preparing for Fiji's independence, the Alliance was founded by Fijian, Indian, European and Chinese representatives. It won the first elections in 1966, gaining 22 out of the 36 elective seats in the Legislative Council. It participated in the pre-independence Government and formed the first independence Government in 1970. In 1972 elections the Alliance won 33 of the 52 seats in the House of Representatives.

In the April 1977 elections the Alliance retained only 24 of its seats but nevertheless continued in office as a minority Government. In fresh elections in September 1977 the Alliance gained 36 seats, giving its Government a majority of 20. In the July 1982 elections the party won 28 of the 52 seats in the House of Representatives.

Orientation. The Alliance's aims are "to promote goodwill, tolerance and harmony in multiracial Fiji, and to maintain and strengthen links with the Commonwealth and the Crown".

Structure. The constituent bodies of the Alliance are the Fijian Association, the Indian Alliance and the General Electors' Association (representing racial communities). The Alliance has branches (based on the constituent bodies), district councils, a management board (executive), a national council (which meets quarterly) and an annual delegate conference.

Fijian Nationalist Party (FNP)

Address. c/o P.O. Box 1336, Suva, Fiji

Leadership. Waisale Bakalevu (ch. and pres.); Sakeasi Butadroka (sec.)

Founded. January 1974

History. The party's founding member, Sakeasi Butadroka, who had been an assistant minister in the Government of the ruling Alliance party, broke away from the latter in November 1973. He considered that under the 1970 independence Constitution the interests of the indigenous Fijians had not been adequately provided for, seeing that Fijians had been given only 22 seats in Parliament, against 30 for non-Fijians (22 for Indians and eight for Europeans and Chinese). He also maintained that the Government was not paying enough attention to the development of Fijians in industry, commerce, education and other fields.

The FNP held one seat in Parliament from 1973 onwards and retained it in the elections of March-April 1977 (when it claimed to have received the support of 25 per cent of Fijian voters). However, it lost that seat in the following September elections and gained no seat in the 1982 elections.

Orientation. The FNP stands for "Fiji for the Fijians".

Structure. Only indigenous Fijians can become party members.

National Federation Party (NFP)

Address. c/o G.P.O. Box 228, Suva, Fiji

Leadership. Ram Sami Goundar (pres.); Siddiq M. Koya (l.)

Founded. July 1960

History. The party had its origins in a committee to aid sugar cane growers, set up in 1959. Founded as the Federation Party, it was the first political party to contest elections in Fiji in 1963, and in the 1966 elections to the Legislative Council it won all nine Indian communal seats (out of 36 elective seats) on a programme urging a common-roll system of elections. In April 1972 the party won 19 out of 52 seats in the House of Representatives.

In 1974 it was established as the National Federation Party (NFP) and in the election held in March-April 1977 it obtained 26 seats. Following the dissolution of the House shortly afterwards the NFP was divided into two factions of which, in new elections held in September 1977, the "flower" faction gained 12 seats and the "dove" faction three. The party therefore remained in its customary position of opposition.

By 1982 the party was reunited, however, and it fought the elections of that year in alliance with the newly-formed Western United Front (WUF). It increased the number of its seats in the House of Representatives to 22 (while the WUF gained only two).

On the resignation from Parliament of Jai Ram Reddy in April 1984, following a dispute with the Speaker and a four-month boycott of Parliament by the NFP, the leadership was assumed by Siddiq M. Koya on an interim basis. Koya had led the "dove" faction while Reddy had led the "flower" faction.

Orientation. Although the party had been founded as representing mainly Indians in Fiji, it has since 1974 campaigned for Fijian control of the Government. It claims to be a democratic socialist party.

National Labour and Farmers' Party

Leadership. Gurubux Singh (pres.)
Founded. 1982
History. The party was formed by ex-members of the National Federation Party (see separate entry) with the principal aim of representing rural workers of Indian stock, but made little impact in the July 1982 general elections.
Orientation. The party has sought links with labour parties in other countries.

Western United Front (WUF)

Address. P.O. Box 263, Sigatoka, Fiji
Leadership. Ratu Osea Gavidi (pres.); Isikeli Nadalo (sec.)
Founded. 1981
History. In 1977 Ratu Osea Gavidi had been elected to the House of Representatives as an independent and Isikeli Nadalo as a member of the National Federation Party (NFP). Other WUF members had defected from the Alliance. The WUF contested the 1982 elections under an electoral pact with the NFP and gained two seats in the House, while two of its members were subsequently nominated to the Senate. The WUF is supported mainly by Fijians in the west of Fiji and also by a large number of Indians.
Orientation. The WUF's object is to maintain Fijian participation in multiracial political parties.
Structure. The WUF has 50 branches with committees and officials.
Membership. 10,000

Finland

Capital: Helsinki   Pop. 4,850,000

The Republic of Finland, a democratic multi-party state, has a President elected for a six-year term by a college of 301 electors chosen by universal adult suffrage. He holds supreme executive power and appoints a Cabinet under a Prime Minister which must enjoy the confidence of the 200-member unicameral Parliament (*Eduskunta*) elected for a four-year term by universal adult suffrage. Parliamentary elections are held under a system of proportional representation in 15 electoral districts with the number of seats being allocated according to population census figures (and ranging from nine to 21 per district and one for the Aaland Islands). The state contributes to the financing of parties at the rate of the equivalent of about US $12,000 annually per member of Parliament.

In elections held on March 20-21, 1983, seats in Parliament were gained as follows: Social Democrats 57, Conservatives 44, Centre-Liberal Alliance 38, Finnish People's Democratic League (led by the Communist Party) 27, Rural Party 17, Swedish People's Party 11, Finnish Christian League 3, Ecologists 2, Constitutional Party 1.

Centre Party of Finland
Keskustapuolue (KP)

Address. Pursimiehenkatu 15, 00150 Helsinki 15, Finland
Leadership. Paavo Väyrynen (ch.); Seppo Kääriäinen (sec.)
Founded. 1906
History. The party was founded as the Agrarian Party, which stood for national independence, unification of the nation, improving the social status of the rural population and democratic procedures. In 1918 it resisted right-wing attempts to establish a monarchy in Finland.

Since World War II it has participated in government and the implementation of the Paasikivi-Kekkonen peace policy (involving good relations with the Soviet Union), and in 1965 it changed its name to Centre Party to express its support for the interests of all sections of the population.

Of the 61 governments formed in Finland since the country gained independence, 47 have involved participation by the Centre Party, which has supplied Prime Ministers on 19 occasions and also three Presidents of the Republic—Lauri Kristian Relander (1925-32), Kyosti Kallio (1937-40), and Urho Kaleva Kekkonen (1956-82). The party's parliamentary representation has varied from one-fifth to one-quarter of the seats in the Diet.

In June 1982 the party admitted as a member organization the Liberal People's Party, which had contested the 1979 elections under a pact with the Centre Party.

Orientation. The party supports representative democracy as defined in Finland's Constitution, improved living conditions, social equality and justice, a decentralized and balanced economy, and the promotion of peace and co-operation among nations, as well as "an active and peace-oriented policy of neutrality".

Structure. The party's supreme decision-making body is the congress, which meets every two years and elects office-bearers, including a party delegation (as the party's decision-making body between congresses) and a council (as the party's executive body, assisted by the party office headed by the secretary-general). The party has 21 district organizations, 304 communal (intermediate) organizations and about 3,000 branches, and also organizations for women, youth and students (represented on the central committee).

Membership. 304,000

Publications. Fourteen newspapers (total circulation about 460,000), including *Suomenmaa* (Helsinki), 33,000, and *Savon Sanomat* (Kuopio), 81,000

International affiliations. Liberal International (observer)

Communist Party of Finland
Suomen Kommunistinen Puolue (SKP)

Address. Sturenkatu 4, SF 00510, Helsinki 51, Finland

Leadership. Arvo Aalto (ch.); Aarne Aitamurto (s.g.)

Founded. August 1918

History. The party was illegal until 1944 whereafter it took part in government in 1944-48. Since 1945 the SKP has contested parliamentary elections as part of an alliance concluded with left-wing socialists and known as the Finnish People's Democratic League (SKDL). It took part in coalition governments in 1966-71, 1975-76 and 1977-82.

The departure of the SKDL (and thus of the Communist Party) from the centre-left coalition in December 1982 came after SKDL members of the Diet had voted against the Government's defence spending plans. The issue of government participation had been a source of continuing controversy within the SKP, with the minority "orthodox" (pro-Moscow) wing adopting a particularly critical attitude towards some coalition policies. Longstanding differences between this faction and the majority "revisionist" wing had dominated an extraordinary party congress held in May 1982, although subsequently a compromise was reached on the basis of the election of a new party chairman (Jouko Kajanoja) in succession to Aarne Saarinen (who had led the party since 1966).

However, after Kajanoja had joined forces with the "orthodox" minority, the 20th party congress held on May 25-27, 1984, elected "revisionist" office bearers, namely Arvo Aalto as chairman and Aarne Aitamurto as general secretary.

Orientation. As "a working-class party" based on "scientific socialism as developed by Marx, Engels and Lenin", the SKP aims at "realizing the socialist revolution in Finland by peaceful and democratic means—through reforms which will effect fundamental changes in power and ownership".

Structure. The SKP has a congress, a central committee, federations and sections (as basic units).

Membership. 35,000

Publications. *Kansan Uutiset* (daily), about 53,000; *Yhteistyö* (weekly)

International affiliations. The SKP is recognized by the Communist parties of the Soviet-bloc countries.

Constitutional Party of the Right
Perustuslaillinen Oikeistopuolue

Address. Unioninkatu 10 A 2, 00130 Helsinki 13, Finland

Leadership. Georg C. Ehrnrooth (ch.); Panu Toivonen (sec.)

Founded. October 1973

History. The party was established by dissident members of the National Coalition and Swedish People's parties to oppose what it called "a most serious slide to the left". Believing that "all established parties in Finland had ceased to defend the country's parliamentary democracy and allowed themselves to become political tools in the hands of President Urho Kekkonen", the party is not only in favour of direct presidential elections but is also opposed to the Government's "pro-Soviet" foreign policy. In the 1975 general elections the party gained one seat in the Diet, which it lost in 1979. However, it again gained one seat in 1983.

Orientation. Being centre-right, moderate reformist, the party seeks to defend parliamentary democracy and to oppose the presidential system which it regards as having grown stronger during President Kekkonen's period in power.

Membership. 3,000

Ecology Party
Vihrëa Eduskuntaryhmä

Address. 00102 Eduskunta, Helsinki, Finland

History. This formation embraces a number of local "green" groups. Having secured the return in 1980 of one member to the Helsinki City Council, the new party won two seats in the 200-member Diet in general elections held in March 1983.

Finnish Christian Union
Suomen Kristilliinen Liitto (SKL)

Address. Töölönkatu 50 D, 00250 Helsinki 25, Finland

Leadership. Esko Almgren (ch.); Jouko Jääskeläinen (sec.)

Founded. May 1958

History. Formed to propagate Christian ideals in public and political life, the SKL won its first seat in the Finnish Diet in 1970; it won four seats in 1972 and nine in both 1975 and 1979, but only three in 1983. It has close links with other Nordic Christian parties.

Orientation. The SKL is "a Christian party with a very strong fundamental basis"; it is part of the non-socialist bloc.

Structure. A party congress, held every year, elects a 60-member delegation, which in turn elects a party "government" which elects a six-member executive committee.

Membership. 20,000

Publications. *Kristityn Vastuu* (Responsibility of a Christian)

Finnish People's Democratic League
Suomen Kansan Demokraattinen Liitto (SKDL)

Address. Kotkankatu 11, 00510 Helsinki 51, Finland

Leadership. Kalevi Kivistö (ch.); Jorma Hentilä (s.g.)

Founded. 1944

History. The SKDL was established as an alliance of Communists and of other left-wing groups as a co-operative organization opposed to war and fascism and working for peace, friendly relations with the Soviet Union and social progress. Having obtained 49 seats (out of 200) in the 1945 elections, in 1948 the SKDL won 38 seats in the Diet (33 for Communists and five for left-wing Socialists). Its representation in the Diet eventually rose to 50 seats in 1958 (which made it the strongest party in the House). Since then the number of seats held by the SKDL has fluctuated between 47 (gained in 1962) and 27 (in 1983). The SKDL has been represented in centre-left coalition Governments in 1944-48, in 1966-71 and again from November 1976 to December 1982. (For the circumstances of its departure from the Government in December 1982, see separate entry for Communist Party of Finland.)

Membership. 172,000

Publications. *Kansan Tahto* (daily); *Hämeen Yhteistyö* (daily); *Folktidningen Ny Tid* (weekly)

Finnish Rural Party
Suomen Maaseudun Puolue (SMP)

Address. Pohjoinen Rautatienkatu 15 B (PL 519), 00100 Helsinki 10, Finland

Leadership. Pekka Vennamo (ch.); Urpo Leppänen (sec.)

Founded. February 1959

History. Formed by dissident members of the Agrarian (later Centre) Party to represent small farmers, the SMP had only one member in Parliament in 1959 and from 1966 to 1970, but in the latter year increased its representation to 18. Thereafter its parliamentary strength was reduced to two from 1975 to 1979, although it increased to seven seats in the latter year.

In the 1983 elections the party gained 288,000 votes or 9.7 per cent of the total and increased its representation in the Diet to 17. Thereafter it took part in a four-party coalition Government with the Social Democrats, the Centre Party and the Swedish People's Party.

Orientation. Non-socialist in basic philosophy, the party represents lower middle-class elements (small farmers and entrepreneurs) as well as war veterans.

Structure. An annual party meeting elects a council which in turn elects a party cabinet presided over by the party chairman.

Membership. 20,000

Publications. *Suomen Uutiset*, 40,000

Finnish Social Democratic Party
Suomen Sosialidemokraattinen Puolue (SDP)

Address. Saariniemenkatu 6, 00530 Helsinki 53, Finland

Leadership. Kalevi Sorsa (ch.); Erkki Liikanen (sec.)

Founded. 1899

History. Before World War II the SDP was the strongest party in Parliament (holding 85 out of the 200 seats in the Diet as a result of the 1939 elections). During the war, however, the party was split into a pro-German faction (led by Väinö Tanner) and a faction seeking accommodation with the Soviet Union. The latter faction, together with the Communist Party and other left-wing Socialists, in 1944 formed the Finnish People's Democratic League (SKDL) which in the 1945 elections to the Diet gained 49 seats (as against 50 obtained by the SDP).

In 1944-46 the SDP was a partner in a coalition Government, but three SDP ministers who had joined a new coalition Government formed in March 1946 were disowned by the party. The SDP took part in coalition Governments in January-March 1951, and from May 1954 to May 1957, at first with all parties except the Liberal-Finnish People's Party and the SKDL and from October 1954 with the Agrarian Party only.

In 1957 the party was divided into two wings—one which elected Väinö Tanner as party chairman and another led by Emil Skog and including the members who had taken part in the coalition Government with the Agrarians. In 1958 the party expelled two deputies, who in that year's elections stood as Independent Social Democrats and were after the elections joined by 10 other deputies. Later several left-wing Social Democrats, organized in a Social Democratic League (*Työväen ja Pientalonpoikain Sosialistinen Liitto*, TPSL), contested the 1966 elections in an electoral alliance with the SKDL and gained seven seats; but in 1970 and 1972 the TPSL, campaigning as the Social Democratic Union of Workers and Small Farmers, failed to win any seats. From August to November 1958 there was again a five-party coalition Government led by the Social Democrat K.-A. Fagerholm.

In May 1966 Rafael Paasio, elected SDP chairman in 1963, formed a coalition Government with the TPSL, the Centre (previously Agrarian) Party, and (for the first time since 1948) with the SKDL, and this Government was continued under Dr Mauno Koivisto as SDP Prime Minister, and with the addition of a minister from the Swedish People's Party, from March 1968 to May 1970. A further coalition Government, in power from July 1970 to October 1971, comprised representatives of the Centre, Swedish People's and Liberal parties as well as of the SDP and the SKDL (the last-named party leaving the coalition in March 1971). After the 1972 elections Paasio formed an SDP minority Government which was, in September 1972, succeeded by an SDP-led coalition Government with the Centre, Liberal and Swedish People's parties taking part.

From June 1975 the SDP took office in a non-political temporary Government including also representatives of the three above-mentioned parties, and from November 1975 to September 1976 the SDP participated in a five-party coalition Government led by the Centre Party and including also ministers from the Liberal Party, the Swedish People's Party and the SKDL.

From May 1977 onwards there was a similar five-party coalition Government, which was reduced to a four-party Government by the withdrawal of the Swedish People's Party in February 1978. In May 1979 the SDP formed a four-party centre-left coalition Government, with the Centre Party, the Swedish People's Party and the SKDL.

In January 1982 the SDP's candidate, Mauno Koivisto, was elected President of the Republic, and a new four-party centre-left coalition Government was formed, but in December 1982 the SKDL left the Government and its ministers were replaced by Social Democrats. In the March 1983 elections the SPD increased its representation in the Diet from 52 to 57 members, and it thereupon again formed a four-party coalition Government, this time with the Centre, Swedish People's and Rural parties.

Membership. 97,000

Publications. Suomen Sosialidemokraatti (Helsinki, daily), 45,000; *Kansan Lehti* (Tampere, daily), 22,000; *Eteenpäin* (daily); *Turun Paivälehti* (Turku, daily), 10,900; *Sosialistinen Aikakauslehti* (quarterly)

International affiliations. Socialist International

League of Civil Power
Kansalaisvallen Liitto (KL)

Address. Museokatu 24 A 4, 00100 Helsinki, Finland

Leadership. Kaarlo Pitsinki (ch.)

Founded. 1972

History. The present name of this organization was adopted in 1982 by the People's Union Party (*Suomen Kansan Yhtenaisyyden Puolue*, SKYP). It was formed by 12 former deputies of the Finnish Rural Party (which objected to the extension of President Urho Kekkonen's term of office) and was later joined by another deputy of the same party.

The SKYP agreed on Dec. 28, 1972, with all other parties—except the Rural Party and the Christian League—that extraordinary legislation was the simplest means of prolonging the term of office of President Kekkonen, and it supported a bill passed to that effect on Jan. 17-18, 1973. In the 1975 general elections, however, the SKYP retained only one seat, which it has since lost.

Orientation. The KL stands for reforms to improve the free social system and to create a more just, equal and democratic society.

Publications. *Yhtenäisyys* (weekly)

Liberal People's Party
Liberaalinen Kansanpuolue (LKP)

Address. Frederikinkatu 58A 6, Helsinki, Finland

Leadership. M. A. J. Itälä (ch.); Arne Berner (s.g.)

Founded. 1965

History. The LKP was formed by a merger of a former Finnish People's Party (founded in 1950 by the amalgamation of the Liberal Party with certain right-wing groups) and a Liberal Union. In the period since World War II Liberal representation in the Diet has varied from five seats to 13 (in 1954 and again in 1962), but in subsequent years it declined.

The LKP has repeatedly taken part in coalition governments, in particular in a five-party centre-left coalition in 1970-71 and in other coalitions between July 1972 and May 1977. In June 1982 the LKP entered the Centre Party as a member organization, but it remained a party in its own right within the framework of the Centre Party, being given two seats on that party's council and five in its delegation.

Orientation. The LKP is a moderate social-liberal formation.

Membership. 18,000

Publications. *Polttopiste* (weekly)

International affiliations. Liberal International

National Coalition Party
Kansallinen Kokoomus (Kok)

Address. Kansakoulukuja 3, Helsinki, Finland

Leadership. Ilkka Suominen (ch.); Jussi Isotalo (g.s.)

Founded. 1918

History. The Kok has been well represented in the Diet since Finland became independent in 1917, but it has never been the strongest party. Today it is the largest non-socialist party in Finland, embracing conservatives as well as liberal groups. The number of seats gained by the party in the Diet has fluctuated between 26 (in 1966) and 47 (in 1979).

With 44 seats gained in 1983, the Kok is the second largest party in the country. It has taken part in various coalition Governments, including the first purely non-socialist Government (since World War II) formed in 1963 by the Centre Party, the Kok, Liberals and the Swedish People's Party, and a similarly-based Government in 1964-66. Since May 1966 the Kok has been in opposition.

Orientation. The Kok is Finland's (centre-right) conservative party.

Membership. 80,000

Publications. *Aamulehti* (Tampere, daily), 137,000; *Karjalainen* (Joensuu, daily), 52,000; *Länsi-Suomi* (Rauma, daily), 18,000; *Satakunnan Kansa* (Pori, daily); *Nykypäiva* (weekly, for members)

International affiliations. European Democrat Union; International Democrat Union

---

Swedish People's Party of Finland
Svenska Folkpartiet i Finland

Address. Bulevarden 7 A, 00120 Helsinki 12, Finland

Leadership. Pär Stenbäck (ch.); Peter Stenlund (s.g.)

Founded. 1906

History. The party was established with the introduction of a single-chamber Parliament and of parties on a modern pattern in Finland in 1906; the party was created in the belief that the interests of Finland's Swedish-speaking minority would be best protected, and its "national and patriotic aims" best served, by a Swedish party organized on broad lines. Since World War II the party has repeatedly taken part in the formation of governments, most recently in the centre-left Cabinet formed in May 1983, in which it got two portfolios.

Orientation. Liberal, the party is an organization for "unified action" on behalf of the Swedish-speaking minority in Finland.

Structure. Organized locally in five (of 16) electoral districts.

Membership. 49,000

Publications. *Medborgarbladet* (monthly), 130,000

International affiliations. Liberal International; European Democrat Union (permanent observer)

France

Capital: Paris   Pop. 54,300,000

The French Republic has one of the most developed and at the same time most fluctuating multi-party systems in the world. Under its 1962 revised Constitution, an executive President is elected for a seven-year term by universal suffrage of citizens above the age of 18 years and by an absolute majority of the votes cast; there is a bicameral Parliament consisting of (i) a 295-member Senate, a third of whose seats are renewed every three years in indirect elections (apart from the seats of six senators representing French nationals living abroad) through departmental electoral colleges comprising deputies in the National Assembly, members of the departmental *conseils généraux* and representatives of local commune councils, and (ii) a 491-member National Assembly (*Assemblée Nationale*) elected for a five-year term by universal suffrage in single-member constituencies.

Deputies to the National Assembly are elected in single-member constituencies in two ballots with the provision that, to succeed in the first ballot, a candidate requires an absolute majority of the votes cast and at least one quarter of the number of votes of the registered electorate, whereas in the second ballot a relative majority is sufficient (and in the event of a tie the older of the candidates is elected). No candidate who has presented himself in the first ballot can be a candidate in the second ballot unless he has, in the first ballot, obtained a number of votes equal to at least 12½ per cent of the registered electorate; where only one candidate fulfils this condition, the candidate who obtained the second-largest number of votes in the first ballot may also stand for the second ballot; and where no candidate fulfils this condition the two candidates with the largest number of votes obtained in the first ballot may contest the second ballot. Each candidate has a designated substitute (*suppléant*) who takes the elected member's place if the latter accepts government office or dies. The *suppléant* may, however, resign in order that a by-election may be held.

A combination of majority voting and proportional representation was introduced for elections held in March 1983 in municipalities with populations of over 3,500 (but not in Paris, Lyons and Marseilles). Under this arrangement a party list obtaining more than 50 per cent of the valid votes in the first round takes half the seats plus one; the remaining seats are allocated, in proportion to share of votes, to all lists which obtain at least 5 per cent of the valid votes (including the victorious list itself). If no list secures an absolute majority in the first round, those which have secured at least 10 per cent of the valid votes are entitled to contest the second round, in which the list with most votes (not necessarily 50 per cent) is allocated half the seats plus one and the remaining seats are similarly shared on a proportional basis between all lists with more than 5 per cent of the votes. Any list which obtains between 5 and 10 per cent of the valid votes in the first round has the right to reach agreement with a stronger formation for the inclusion of its candidates in the latter's revised list for the second round.

General elections held on June 14 and 21, 1981, resulted in the Assembly seats being distributed as follows: Socialists and associates 285 (including 14 Left Radicals), the (Gaullist) Rally for the Republic (RPR) and associates 88, the (centrist) Union for French Democracy (UDF) and associates 63, Communists and associates 44, unattached 11. There is a multiplicity of other "orthodox" political parties without parliamentary representation, including several on both the extreme left and the extreme right.

Anarchist Combat Organization
Organisation Combat Anarchiste (OCA)

Founded. April 1976
History. The OCA has groups in Orleans, Paris, Grenoble and Albi and seeks to "transcend the traditional positions of anarchism" as advanced by the Anarchist Federation (see separate entry). It has rejected electoral participation and has sought to establish a presence in the universities, small businesses and among unemployed youth.

Anarchist Federation
Fédération Anarchiste

Leadership. Maurice Joyeux
Founded. 1954
History. As a loose umbrella organization for various local anarchist groups, the Federation has rejected electoral democracy as a "fraud" in the belief that "social justice cannot be achieved through the ballot box but only by daily struggle". However, there appeared to be no direct connexion between the Federation and the various militant anarchist groups which carried out violent acts in the late 1970s and early 1980s.
Orientation. Following from its anarchist philosophy, the Federation rejects the concepts of self-management (*autogestion*) advanced by the parliamentary left and calls for a more direct worker's control of industry.
Membership. 500

Centre of Social Democrats
Centre des Démocrates Sociaux (CDS)

Address. 205 boulevard Saint-Germain, 75007 Paris, France
Leadership. Pierre Méhaignerie (pres.); Jacques Barrot (s.g.)

Founded. May 23, 1976
History. The elements which comprise the present-day CDS have their roots in a 19th century movement which was aimed at reconciling Christians with the Third Republic and with democracy. After World War II these aims were represented by the *Mouvement Républicain Populaire* (MRP) of Georges Bidault and other resistance leaders, which was France's strongest party in the post-war period and took part in most Governments until 1955.

In March 1966 Jean Lecanuet (who had received 16 per cent of the votes in the first round of the 1965 presidential elections) formed the *Centre Démocrate* with MRP followers and others. In the 1969 presidential election the centrist candidate was Alain Poher (who received 23.3 per cent of the vote in the first round and 41.8 per cent in the second) but some centrists supported the successful Gaullist candidate, Georges Pompidou, thus abandoning previous centrist policy of acting as a balancing force between the "majority" parties and those of the left-wing opposition.

Following Pompidou's election as President, his centrist supporters, notably Jacques Duhamel, Joseph Fontanet and René Pleven, founded the *Centre Démocratie et Progrès* (CDP). In the March 1973 National Assembly elections the *Centre Démocrate* and the CDP separately maintained their parliamentary representation at about 24 seats each, the former as part of the *Mouvement Réformateur* (created in 1971 by various centrist elements then outside the "majority") and the latter in alliance with the Gaullists and Independent Republicans.

In the first round of the May 1974 presidential election the CDP supported the candidature of Jacques Chaban-Delmas (Gaullist) and the *Centre Démocrate* that of Valéry Giscard d'Estaing (Independent Republican), but both supported Giscard d'Estaing in the second round. Both formations participated in government

128

under President Giscard d'Estaing and were prominent in renewed attempts to establish greater cohesion of the French centre, notably the Federation of Reformers, created in June 1975 by six parties of the centre and centre-left as a successor to the old *Mouvement Réformateur*. The following year, at a constituent congress held in Rennes in May 1976, the *Centre Démocrate* and the CDP formally merged to form the Centre of Social Democrats (CDS) under the presidency of Jean Lecanuet.

For the March 1978 National Assembly elections the CDS joined with other non-Gaullist "majority" parties to form the Union for French Democracy (UDF, see separate entry), as part of which the CDS returned 35 deputies; it also contested the 1981 parliamentary elections, gaining 25 seats. The CDS has 72 representatives in the Senate.

Pierre Méhaignerie (a former Agriculture Minister), who succeeded Lecanuet as CDS president in March 1982, declared his intention to strengthen the autonomous identity of the party in the centre of the French political spectrum.

Orientation. The CDS is a Christian democratic formation whose aims include a strengthening of democracy, a "true presidential regime" restoring the powers of Parliament, with greater popular participation by means of a proportional vote, and autonomy for local authorities; the party also advocates a social market economy to encourage free enterprise, and democratic planning to create employment and to develop social justice and workers' responsibility. It also stands for the creation of a politically united Europe.

Structure. The CDS has local sections and departmental federations, a political council and a political bureau of 50 members; a national congress meets at least every two years.

Membership. 43,500

Publications. Démocratie Moderne (weekly), 25,000; *Action Démocrate; Action Rurale; France-Forum*

International affiliations. Christian Democratic International; European Christian Democratic Union; European People's Party

Christian Democracy
Démocratie Chrétienne

Address. 50 rue de Berri, 75008 Paris, France

Leadership. Alfred Coste-Floret

Founded. May 1977

History. This small centrist formation presented a limited number of candidates

in the May 1978 National Assembly elections under an electoral agreement with other non-Gaullist "majority" parties allied within the Union for French Democracy (see separate entry).

Communist Combat Organization
Organisation Combat Communiste (OCC)

Founded. December 1974

History. The OCC was formed by a dissident group of the Workers' Struggle (LO, see separate entry) which rejected the LO's "opportunist" line, particularly as regards the nature of the Soviet Union. It has emphasized the need to build revolutionary strength in factories and the trade unions and has rejected electoral participation.

Orientation. The OCC is a Leninist formation which maintains that there is as yet no truly socialist country in the world.

Communist Committees for Self-Management
Comités Communistes pour l'Autogestion (CCA)

Founded. December 1976

History. The CCA was formed as a merger of a dissident group of the Revolutionary Communist League and the *Courant B* faction of the Unified Socialist Party. The formation contested the March 1978 National Assembly elections in alliance with the Revolutionary Communist League and the Communist Organization of Workers (see separate entries).

For the 1981 general elections it nominated 83 candidates, of whom none were successful. The CCA had, however, declared its support for a left-wing majority.

Orientation. The movement is Trotskyist, with strong emphasis on workers' control.

Membership. 500

Communist Organization of France—Marxist-Leninist
Organisation Communiste de France—Marxiste-Léniniste (OCF-ML)

Leadership. Jacques Lucbert

History. Although it rejects electoral processes as "bourgeois trickery", the OCF-ML put up six candidates in the March 1978 National Assembly elections, none of whom were elected, and refused to enter into support agreements with other formations. It did not take part in the 1981 general elections.

Orientation. The OCF-ML is a Maoist formation which seeks to organize an avant-garde of the working class in opposition both to the right and to the "false left".

Membership. 500

Publications. *Drapeau Rouge* (monthly)

Communist Organization of Workers
Organisation Communiste des Travailleurs (OCT)

Founded. December 1976

History. The OCT was formed as a merger of (i) the *Gauche Ouvrière Populaire*, itself a predominantly Maoist alliance of the *Parti d'Unité Populaire* (a left-wing splinter group of the Unified Socialist Party) and the *Pour le Communisme* grouping, and (ii) the *Révolution* splinter group of the Revolutionary Communist League. The OCT contested the March 1978 National Assembly elections in alliance with the Revolutionary Communist League and the Communist Committees for Self-Management (see separate entries) under the slogan *Pour le Socialisme, le Pouvoir aux Travailleurs*, with which some 250 candidates (all unsuccessful) were associated. In July 1979 the *Révolution* element of the OCT announced its intention of rejoining the Revolutionary Communist League.

Orientation. The OCT seeks to build a mass revolutionary party embracing "new forms of struggle" such as the campaign for women's and soldiers' rights.

Membership. 1,800

Democratic Association of French Citizens Abroad
Association Démocratique des Français de l'Étranger (ADFE)

Address. 22 rue Drouot, 75009 Paris, France

History. This pro-socialist Association gained 40 of the 127 elective seats on the consultative *Conseil Supérieur des Français à l'Étranger* in elections held in May-June 1983. (Twenty consultative members were designated to this council by the Foreign Ministry.)

Democratic Socialist Party
Parti Socialiste Démocrate (PSD)

Address. 28 rue Davy, 75017 Paris, France

Founded. May 1975

History. The PSD was founded by Eric Hintermann, who was then a member of the executive of the Socialist Party and opposed to that party's alliance with the Communist Party. In the March 1978 National Assembly elections the party put up 73 candidates independently of other formations, one PSD deputy being elected.

A majority decision by the party's national council in May 1978 to seek affiliation with the Union for French Democracy (UDF)—formed by the non-Gaullist "majority" parties earlier in the year (see separate entry)—provoked the immediate breakaway of the left-wing minority, which subsequently formed the *Fédération des Socialistes Démocrates*, (FSD) under the presidency of Christian Chauvel. However, the PSD subsequently decided not to join the UDF.

In March 1982 Eric Hintermann formally rejoined the Socialist Party (having in the 1981 presidential elections withdrawn his own initial candidature in favour of François Mitterand) and became president of a new right-wing tendency (called *Amicale Social-Démocrate*) within the Socialist Party. The PSD continued to exist thereafter, although with greatly reduced influence; a proportion of its membership subsequently participated in the creation of the Social Democratic Party (see separate entry).

Orientation. The PSD candidates in the 1978 elections stood on a platform calling for the opening of "a third way towards French social democracy".

Structure. Federal (with 100 departmental federations), the party's supreme body being its national congress.

Publications. *Socialisme 2000* (20,000)

Ecologist Confederation and Ecologist Party
Confédération Ecologiste et Parti Ecologiste

Address. Cité Fleurie, 65 blvd. Arago, 75013 Paris, France

Leadership. Jean Brière, Guy Cambot, Solange Fernex, Jean Claude Jobert (spokespersons); Roger Fischer (sec.)

Founded. Nov. 1, 1982

History. The party has its origins in an ecologist movement which was founded in 1970 (in the wake of the 1968 student movement) and which presented, as its candidate in the 1974 presidential elections, René Dumont, who gained some 200,000 votes. It contested local elections in 1977, and in the 1978 general elections most of the 200 ecologist candidates stood under the banner of *Ecologie-78*.

In the 1979 elections to the European Parliament *Ecologie Europe* gained more than 900,000 votes or 4.4 per cent of the total French vote (failing to obtain the minimum 5 per cent required for representation). On Nov. 21, 1979, the followers of that movement and others set up a *Mouvement d'Ecologie Politique* (MEP), which was formally constituted on Feb. 16-17, 1980. Later in that year the MEP agreed with other groups, among them The Friends of the Earth (*Les Amis de la Terre*), to support the latter's leader, Brice Lalonde, in the 1981 presidential elections, in which he obtained over 1,126,000 votes (or 3.88 per cent of the total valid votes).

Constituting itself as a political party on Nov. 1, 1982, the MEP adopted the name of *Les Verts–Parti Ecologiste* (VPE), which was intended to embrace other ecologist movements into a unified party structure. In municipal elections held in 1983 the party obtained about 6 per cent of the votes and several dozen of its candidates were elected councillors. At a congress in Clichy in January 1984, the VPE formally merged with a Confederation of other "green" movements, to form the *Confédération Ecologiste et Parti Ecologiste*.

Orientation. The party's aim is to draw up a plan for an ecologist society and to work for its implementation. In its quest for peace between man and nature and among men the party rejects both capitalism and socialism and intends to create a balanced society. It stands for unilateral nuclear disarmament, non-alignment, France's withdrawal from NATO, election of the UN Security Council by the UN General Assembly and the abolition of the right of veto in the Security Council.

Publications. *Lettre-Contact* (monthly); *Journées d'Eté* (every summer)

International affiliations. The European Greens

Federation of Royalist Unions of France
Fédération des Unions Royalistes de France (FURF)

Leadership. Jean de Beauregard

History. The FURF did not participate in the March 1978 National Assembly elections, in which it effectively gave its backing to the "majority" parties, nor in those of June 1981.

Orientation. The FURF advocates the restoration of the monarchy and regards the left as "the most violent opponents of the monarchy, of society and of prosperity".

French Communist Party
Parti Communiste Français (PCF)

Address. 2 place du Colonel Fabien, 75019 Paris, France

Leadership. Georges Marchais (s.g.)

Founded. December 1920

History. The PCF came into being when a majority of the delegates at the December 1920 Tours congress of the Socialist Party (SFIO) voted in favour of membership of the Third (Communist) International (the Comintern). From 1921 to 1933 the party pursued a hard-line policy of class warfare and opposition to all "bourgeois" parties, including the SFIO. From 1934, however, it gave priority to the struggle against fascism and supported (without joining) the Popular Front Government formed in 1936 by Léon Blum (SFIO). Having approved the August 1939 German-Soviet non-aggression pact, following the German invasion of the Soviet Union in June 1941 it played an active part in the resistance and in November 1945 joined a government for the first and only time under Gen. de Gaulle despite the refusal of the latter to give the party any of the three portfolios which it wanted (Interior, Defence and Foreign Affairs). In May 1947, however, it was excluded from the Cabinet then headed by Paul Ramadier (SFIO) and was in opposition until 1981.

Having obtained about 26 per cent of the vote in the first two post-war general elections in October 1945 and June 1946 respectively, the PCF vote went up to 28.6 in November 1946 but then declined to 26.5 per cent in June 1951 and to 25.6 per cent in January 1956. In the first elections held under the Fifth Republic (in November 1958) the Communist vote fell to 18.9 per cent in the first round, but thereafter was maintained in successive elections at or slightly above the 20 per cent level, its first-round share in the 1973 and 1978 Assembly elections being 21.4 and 20.6 per cent respectively and 20.5 per cent in the June 1979 French elections to the European Parliament. In the 1969 presidential election the Communist candidate, Jacques Duclos, came in third place in the first round, with 21.3 per cent of the vote.

In December 1966 the then PCF secretary-general, Waldeck Rochet, signed an agreement with the non-Communist left-wing opposition parties allied within the Federation of the Democratic and Socialist Left (FGDS) providing for reciprocal voting support in the March 1967 National Assembly elections; on this basis Communist representation in the Assembly was increased to 73 seats, although this total was reduced to 34 in the June 1968 elections held in the aftermath of the May 1968 political and industrial crisis. Following the election in June 1971 of François Mitterrand to the leadership of the reconstituted Socialist Party (see separate entry), the PCF 12 months later signed a common programme with the Socialists (also endorsed by the Left Radicals), on which basis the left-wing alliance made major gains in the March 1973 Assembly elections, in which Communist representation was restored to 73 deputies.

From late 1974 serious strains developed within the union of the left, a steady growth of Socialist strength being viewed by the PCF as jeopardizing the equilibrium of the alliance and also encouraging the Socialists to revert to a centrist strategy. Principally because of resistance by the Socialists and Left Radicals to the extent of further Communist nationalization proposals, no agreement was reached on a revised common programme for the March 1978 National Assembly elections, in which the PCF presented its own manifesto. Although the operation of second-round support agreements enabled the left-wing parties (including the Communists) to make gains, they did not obtain the expected overall majority and relations between the PCF on the one hand and the Socialists and Left Radicals on the other remained strained.

The PCF's candidate in the 1981 presidential elections was Georges Marchais, who obtained 4,456,922 votes (or 15.35 per cent of the valid votes) in the first round; the party's central committee thereupon decided to urge voters to support François Mitterrand, the Socialist candidate, in the second round. In the 1981 parliamentary elections the PCF agreed with the Socialist Party on an arrangement for the second round under which the PCF would field sole candidates of the left in 37 (out of 320) constituencies (with the Socialist Party having a straight contest in 272 other constituencies). In the event the Communist representation in the National Assembly was reduced from 86 to 44 (including one associated member). In a new left-wing Government formed on June 23, 1981, the PCF was given the posts of two ministers, a delegate minister and a minister of state.

Orientation. The PCF is a Marxist-Leninist formation with the fundamental aim of transforming capitalist society into a "collectivist or communist society". Originally closely aligned with the Communist Party of the Soviet Union, the PCF refused to support the 1968 Soviet-led intervention in Czechoslovakia and in February 1976 the 22nd PCF congress repudiated the thesis of the dictatorship of the proletariat and came out in favour of a specifically French model for the transition to socialism. The PCF has, however, maintained its distance from the "Eurocommunist" strategies advanced by the Italian Communist Party in particular, and by 1980 was regarded as having reassumed many characteristics of an orthodox pro-Soviet party.

Structure. The PCF is structured according to the principles of "democratic centralism".

Membership. 700,000

Publications. *L'Humanité* (daily newspaper), 150,000; *Révolution* (weekly); *La Terre* (weekly for farmers), 180,000; *Les Cahiers du Communisme* (historical and political monthly); *Economie et Politique* (monthly economic review); *La Vie du Parti* (monthly propaganda and information bulletin); *Nouvelle Revue Internationale* (monthly international review); *Avant-Garde* (youth journal); *L'École et la Nation* (for educationalists)

International affiliations. The PCF is recognized by the Communist parties of the Soviet-bloc countries.

French Democratic Party
Parti Démocrate Français (PDF)

Leadership. Guy Gennesseaux (l.)
Founded. June 5, 1982
History. The PDF broke away from the Radical Party after the latter had refused Guy Gennesseaux's proposal that it should leave the Union for French Democracy (see separate entry).

Orientation. As an opposition left party, the PDF seeks "to construct a modern society of the third type—neither liberal (in the advanced sense) nor socialist (even in the democratic sense)".

French Nationalist Party
Parti Nationalise Français

Founded. December 1983
History. This extreme right-wing party was formed by "social and revolutionary" elements of the National Front (see separate entry) opposed to the leadership of Jean-Marie Le Pen.

Publications. *Militant.*

The Greens
Les Verts

Address. 52 rue Faubourg Poissonnière, F-75010, Paris, France

Founded. September 1983

History. *Les Verts* superseded a grouping called *Les Verts-Confédération Ecologiste* formed early in 1983 as an alliance of mainly regional groups established in the mid- and late 1970s. The organization has remained independent of the Ecologist Confederation and Ecologist Party (see separate entry).

International affiliations. The European Greens

Internationalist Communist Party
Parti Communiste Internationaliste (PCI)

Address. 87 rue du Faubourg St Denis, 75010 Paris, France

Leadership. Pierre Lambert (l.)

Founded. 1952

History. The PCI, known until December 1981 as the *Organisation Communiste Internationaliste* (OCI), was expelled in 1952 by the majority of the Fourth (Trotskyist) International leadership. That majority believed at the time (with the Belgian Ernest Mandel and others) that, confronted with the "cold war" situation, the Stalinist bureaucracy in the Soviet Union would be "forced to achieve socialism"—this belief being rejected by the majority of the French section. While the OCI had not fielded any candidates in the 1981 general elections, the PCI presented 185 lists in the municipal elections held in March 1983.

Orientation. The PCI is Trotskyist and stands for action by a united front of the Socialist and Communist parties.

Membership. 6,500

Publications. *Informations Ouvrières* (weekly)

International affiliations. Fourth (Trotskyist) International

---

Left Radical Movement
Mouvement des Radicaux de Gauche (MRG)

Address. 195 blvd. St Germain, 75007 Paris, France

Leadership. Jean-Michel Baylet (interim pres.)

Founded. July 1972

History. The MRG was formed by the left-wing members of the Radical-Socialist Party who in July 1972 endorsed the common programme issued the previous month by the Socialist and Communist parties (with which the Radical-Socialist majority then led by Jean-Jacques Servan-Schreiber refused to be associated). Initially organized as the Radical-Socialist Study and Action Group, the left-wing group was expelled from the Radical-Socialist Party in October 1972 and formally constituted itself as the MRG in December 1973 under the presidency of Robert Fabre.

Meanwhile, the Left Radicals had contested the March 1973 National Assembly elections on a joint list with the Socialist Party (called the *Union de la Gauche Socialiste et Démocrate*) which participated in a second-round reciprocal support arrangement with the Communists and returned 100 deputies, of whom 11 were Left Radicals.

In the contentious negotiations for a revision of the common programme for the March 1978 National Assembly elections, the MRG caused the first formal breakdown of talks in September 1977, when Fabre withdrew from the negotiations to signify that the MRG could not agree to the extent of the nationalization programme demanded by the Communists. For the elections the MRG drew up its own policy proposals which, although similar to the Socialists' programme, differed from those of both of the other left-wing parties in important respects. But the MRG's electoral alliance with the Socialists was maintained and (with a support arrangement with the Communists again coming into effect for the second round) the joint Socialist-Left Radical list obtained 113 seats, of which 10 went to the Left Radicals.

Immediately after the March 1978 elections Fabre repudiated the common programme of the left and resigned the presidency of the MRG, in which post he was succeeded in May 1978 by Michel Crépeau, who supported the continuation of the left-wing alliance. Thereafter the right wing of the MRG set up minority organizations within the party, notably the *Fédération pour une Démocratie Radicale* and the *Union Nouvelle pour une Europe de Progrès*, of which the former in October 1979 joined the Radical-Socialist Party.

Crépeau contested the first round of the 1981 presidential elections, gaining 642,777 votes (or 2.21 per cent of the total valid votes). In May 1981, however, he became a Minister in the left-wing Government. After concluding an electoral alliance with the Socialist Party on May 29, 1981, the MRG increased the number of its seats in the National Assembly to 14.

Orientation. Basing itself on the celebrated Radical-Socialist slogan "No enemy to the left", the MRG has participated in the union of the left strategy as a means of achieving a radical (but non-revolutionary) transformation of social and economic structures. Having played no

133

part in the drafting of the original 1972 common programme, the party has entered its own qualifications and interpretations, notably concerning the protection of liberties, recognition of the private sector and the need to strengthen parliamentary powers.

Publications. *Mouvement* (monthly)

Marxist-Leninist Communist Party
Parti Communiste Marxiste-Léniniste (PCML)

Address. 21 rue Pixéricourt, 75020 Paris, France

Leadership. Jacques Jurquet (s.g.)

Founded. August 1978

History. Ideologically and politically the PCML is the continuation of the *Parti Communiste Marxiste-Léniniste Français* (PCMLF) founded in December 1967 and banned by President de Gaulle in May 1968, but in semi-legal existence until August 1978. Marxist-Leninist groups had been formed in France from 1963 onwards by Communists who rejected the "revisionism" of the Soviet leadership and insisted on including "Mao Tse-tung thought" in their doctrine. In the March 1978 National Assembly elections the PCMLF participated in the (Maoist) *Union Ouvrière et Paysanne pour la Démocratie Prolétarienne* (UOPDP) with the Revolutionary Marxist-Leninist Communist Party (PCRML), which had been formed by other former PCMLF activists in 1974 (see separate entry). In the 1981 parliamentary elections the PCML unsuccessfully contested one seat. Meanwhile, moves to achieve a merger of the PCML and the PCRML had failed to come to fruition.

Orientation. The PCML is a Maoist formation whose strategic objective is proletarian revolution in France, i.e. "the defeat of the dictatorship of the bourgeoisie and the establishment of socialism guaranteed by the dictatorship of the proletariat in order to achieve a classless society and communism". This involves "struggle against the monopolist bourgeoisie as the principal enemy, rejection of revisionism and reformism, and struggle against the two super-powers preparing for war, and in particular against the more aggressive— Russian social-imperialism".

Structure. The party has cells, local and regional committees, a central committee and, as executive organs, a political bureau and a secretariat.

Membership. 3,000

Publications. *L'Humanité Rouge* (daily organ); *Prolétariat* (theoretical organ), 6,000; *La Faucille* (The Sickle, peasant journal) 3,000

Marxist-Leninist Union of Communists of France
Union des Communistes de France Marxiste-Léniniste (UCFML)

Leadership. Alain Badieu

Founded. 1971

History. The UCFML was formed by a small breakaway group of the Unified Socialist Party. It advocated abstention in the first round of the March 1978 National Assembly elections.

Orientation. The UCFML is a Maoist grouping which seeks to create a "broad workers' avant-garde". It has denounced the Communist Party as a "new bourgeoisie" and also the existing trade union movement as "the plague of the French working class movement".

Movement of Democrats
Mouvement des Démocrates

Address. 71 rue Ampère, 75017 Paris, France

Leadership. Michel Jobert (pres.)

Founded. March 1975

History. The Movement of Democrats was formally launched at a congress held in Paris on March 15-16, 1975, under the leadership of Michel Jobert, who had been Secretary-General of the Presidency from 1969 to 1973 under Georges Pompidou and then Minister of Foreign Affairs until the election of President Giscard d'Estaing in May 1974. Prior to the formation of the party, Jobert (who had professed no party allegiance hitherto) had undertaken a series of public meetings throughout France in an attempt to rally orthodox Gaullist opinion against what he regarded as Giscard d'Estaing's departures from the policies established under Presidents de Gaulle and Pompidou, especially in the field of foreign affairs.

In the March 1978 National Assembly elections the Movement put up 150 candidates (not including Jobert) independently of other groupings, none of whom were elected. Wishing to contest the 1981 presidential elections M. Jobert failed to obtain the required minimum of 500 sponsors. He was, however, Minister of External Trade from May 1981 until March 1983.

Orientation. The Movement propounds what it regards as orthodox Gaullist policies, including the need for detailed economic planning, workers' participation, national independence and the rejection of all political, military or economic hegemonies; it wishes to transcend the concepts of right and left in political life and to establish a "living democracy" based on greater individual responsibility.

Structure. The Movement has a 26-member council but has no party organization in the accepted sense, being based on local committees of supporters.

Publications. Lettre Mensuelle (monthly)

Movement of Social Liberals
Mouvement des Sociaux-Libéraux (MSL)

Address. 17 blvd. Raspail, 75007 Paris, France

Leadership. Olivier Stirn (l.)

Founded. February 1977

History. This Movement had broken away from the *Rassemblement pour la République* and merged with the Radical Party (see separate entry) in July 1977, but was relaunched in October 1981 by Olivier Stirn.

Orientation. The MSL was launched as a "movement of ideas" with "a French social democratic programme" which would appeal to "all Gaullists, Giscardians and Socialists of the centre-left".

National Centre of Independents and Peasants
Centre National des Indépendants et Paysans (CNIP)

Address. 106 rue de l'Université, 75007 Paris, France

Leadership. Philippe Malaud (pres.); François-Xavier Parent (s.g.)

Founded. January 1949

History. Originally formed in July 1948 as the *Centre National des Indépendants* (CNI) on the initiative of Roger Duchet and René Coty, the grouping quickly succeeded in federating most independent parliamentarians of the moderate right (although it did not enforce voting discipline on their part) and became the CNIP in January 1949 when it absorbed the *Parti Républicain de la Liberté*, a small peasant party. Between 1951 and 1962 it took part in various Governments, with its members Antoine Pinay being Prime Minister from March to December 1952 and René Coty serving as President from 1952 to 1959. In July 1954 the CNIP was joined by Gaullist dissidents of the *Action Républicaine et Sociale* who had supported the Pinay Government.

In 1958 it supported the advent to power of Gen. de Gaulle (whom President Coty asked to form a government in May 1958) and reached the peak of its voting strength (22 per cent) in that year's elections, following which it had 120 deputies in the National Assembly. Thereafter its influence declined. Deeply divided over De Gaulle's Algerian policy, it finally broke with him in October 1962 and in elections the following month lost practically the whole of its Assembly group when its outgoing deputies either were defeated or transferred to the "majority" as Independent Republicans (which under the leadership of Valéry Giscard d'Estaing later became the nucleus of the future Republican Party—see separate entry). In 1967-68 the CNIP formed an alliance with Jean Lecanuet's *Centre Démocrate* but proposals for a merger proved abortive. Although nominally an opposition leader during this period, Antoine Pinay (then the CNIP's honorary president) declined invitations to oppose De Gaulle and Georges Pompidou in the presidential elections of 1965 and 1969 respectively.

After 1969 the CNIP sought to rally to the "majority" via the Independent Republicans and in 1974 supported Giscard d'Estaing's successful presidential candidature. Thereafter it became one of the four main parties of the "presidential majority" and from 1976 was again represented in successive Governments formed by Raymond Barre. It contested the March 1978 National Assembly elections in electoral alliance with other non-Gaullist "majority" parties (although it did not join the Union for French Democracy formed in February 1978—see separate entry) and on the strength of a second-round electoral pact among all the "majority" parties secured the return of nine deputies. The CNIP also has 30 representatives in the Senate divided between two groups, namely the Independent Republicans of Social Action and the Union of Republicans and Independents.

Orientation. The party's aims are to defend "French moral and cultural values" and the family and to propagate economic liberalism, administrative decentralization and a stronger European Community.

Structure. The party's organization is decentralized, with decisions being made at departmental and at national level. The party's policy is directed by a 54-member executive committee in accordance with motions passed by a congress and national councils.

Membership. 25,000

Publications. *Le Journal des Indépendants* (weekly), 40,000

International affiliations. The CNIP's single representative in the European Parliament belongs to the Liberal and Democratic Group.

National Federation of Progressive Gaullists
Fédération Nationale des Gaullistes de Progrès (FNGP)

Leadership. Jacques Blache (nat. sec.)
Founded. April 1979
History. The FNGP was formed by a dissident group of the (Gaullist) Federation of Progressive Republicans after a dispute arising from the refusal of the leader of the latter formation, Jean Charbonnel, to support the Communist candidate in an election for the presidency of the Corrèze *conseil général*.
Orientation. The formation has proclaimed its "fidelity to the spirit of the union of the left and its total solidarity with the elected representatives and activists of the Socialist and Communist parties".

National Front
Front National (FN)

Address. 11 rue Bernouilli, 75008 Paris, France
Leadership. Jean-Marie Le Pen (pres.); Alain Renault (s.g.)
Founded. 1972
History. The FN was formed by Jean-Marie Le Pen (a Poujadist deputy from 1956 to 1962, during which period he was closely associated with the *Algérie française* campaign) as a grouping of various factions and personalities of the extreme right. Having put up about 100 unsuccessful candidates in the March 1973 National Assembly elections, the Front was joined by a large section of *Ordre Nouveau* after this movement had been banned in June 1973, but in November 1973 these elements broke away to form the *Faire Front* organization (which later evolved into the New Forces Party—see separate entry).

Le Pen contested the 1974 presidential election, obtaining 190,921 votes (0.74 per cent) in the first round on a "public safety" platform calling for drastic curbs on foreign immigration, vigilance against internal subversion, limitation of the right to strike, separation of the private and state sectors of the economy, abrogation of the 1962 Evian agreements under which Algeria became independent and strengthening of the Atlantic Alliance. The FN presented 160 candidates in the March 1978 Assembly elections, none of whom were elected.

Although wishing to contest the 1981 presidential elections, Le Pen failed to obtain the required minimum of 500 sponsors. However, following the victory of the left in the 1981 elections, the NF made efforts to establish itself as a legitimate organization on the right wing of the centre-right opposition and achieved some success in municipal elections held in March 1983, when it returned a representative to one of the new district councils in Paris and was allied with the (Gaullist) Rally for the Republic in at least one canton.
Orientation. The FN is an extreme right-wing nationalist formation.
Structure. The FN congress elects a 50-member central committee, which elects a political bureau, which in turn appoints the party president.
Membership. 7,000
Publications. *Le National* (monthly), 10,000

National Restoration
Restauration Nationale

Address. 10 rue Croix des Petits-Champs, 75001 Paris, France
Leadership. Guy Steinbach (s.g.)
Founded. 1947
History. This small formation has not taken part in any National Assembly elections. In 1971 it was weakened by a scission which led to the creation of the *Nouvelle Action Française* (NAF) which subsequently became the New Royalist Action (see separate entry).
Orientation. The formation seeks the restoration of the monarchy represented by the Count of Paris and is opposed both to the left majority and to "advanced liberalism" which, it claims, is the "precursor to the left".
Publications. *Aspects de la France*

National Union for Initiative and Responsibility
Union Nationale pour l'Initiative et la Responsabilité (UNIR)

Leadership. Jean-Maxime Lévêque (l.)
Founded. May 1982
History. Jean-Maxime Lévêque had been president of the Crédit Commercial de France, which was nationalized by the left-wing Government.
Orientation. The object of this group is to oppose the Government's nationalization programme.

New Forces Party
Parti des Forces Nouvelles (PFN)

Address. 7 blvd. de Sébastopol, 75001 Paris, France
Leadership. Jack Marchal, Roland Hélie, Roger Girard (s.g.)—collective leadership

Founded. November 1974

History. The PFN was formed principally by members of the *Faire Front* movement, itself created in November 1973 by former members of the extreme right-wing *Ordre Nouveau* who had briefly been part of the National Front (see separate entry) following the banning of *Ordre Nouveau* in June 1973.

The PFN presented 89 candidates in the March 1978 National Assembly elections, none of whom were elected. In the June 1979 French elections for the European Parliament the PFN presented a full list of 81 candidates (called *Union Française pour l'Eurodroite des Patries*) headed by Jean-Louis Tixier-Vignancour (who had contested the 1965 presidential election) and which obtained 265,911 votes (1.31 per cent) and no seats.

Seeking to contest the 1981 presidential elections, the party's candidate, Pascal Gauchon, failed to obtain the required minimum of 500 sponsors.

Orientation. Regarding itself as part of the French "new right", the PFN seeks to establish itself as the fourth wing of the "majority", to the right of the (Gaullist) Rally for the Republic (RPR).

Publications. *Minute*

New Royalist Action
Nouvelle Action Royaliste

Address. 17 rue Croix des Petits-Champs, 75001 Paris, France

Leadership. Bertrand Renouvin

Founded. 1971

History. Founded as the *Nouvelle Action Française* (NAF) by dissenters from the *Restauration Nationale*, the movement condemned those members of the former *Action Française* who had collaborated with the Nazis. The party propagated the restoration of a progressive monarchy in France under the Count of Paris as King.

Its leader was one of the unsuccessful candidates in the 1974 presidential elections, in which he stood in a "personal" capacity (so that his candidature could not be construed as an attempt to overthrow the Republic) and obtained 43,722 votes (0.2 per cent) in the first round. The party presented eight candidates in the March 1978 National Assembly elections, all of whom were eliminated from the running in the first round of voting.

Seeking to contest the 1981 presidential elections, Renouvin failed to obtain the required minimum of 500 sponsors.

Orientation. In addition to seeking the installation of a "popular monarchy", the party advocates freedom of the individual and opposes "liberal or state capitalism" as well as "industrial and financial feudalism" and "totalitarian systems—Marxist, fascist or racist".

Structure. The party has cells, sections and federations, a 10-member head committee and an elected national representative council.

Membership. 1,500

Publications. *Royaliste* (bimonthly), 10,000

Perspectives and Realities
Perspectives et Réalitiés

Leadership. Jean-François Deniau (pres.)

History. This federation of centrist clubs was launched in the mid-1960s by Jean-Pierre Fourcade—later a vice-president of the Union for French Democracy (UDF—see separate entry). Jean-François Deniau had been a European Commissioner and a Minister under President Giscard d'Estaing (as a leading member of the Republican Party, a constituent part of the UDF). Although politically non-partisan, the clubs have become a significant political force for the centre-right.

Orientation. The central aim of this federation is to promote Giscardian concepts of technocratic *dirigisme* at intellectual and official levels.

Structure. In November 1982 the federation claimed to have 280 active clubs throughout the country and some 30,000 members.

Popular Gaullist Movement
Mouvement Gaulliste Populaire (MGP)

Address. 103 rue Quincampois, 75003 Paris, France

Leadership. Jacques Debû-Bridel, Pierre Dabezies

Founded. April 1982

History. The MGP was formed by a merger of the *Union Démocratique du Travail* (UDT) led by Jacques Debû-Bridel and the *Fédération des Républicains de Progrès* (FRP) led by Pierre Dabezies.

The UDT had been set up in 1959 as a left-wing Gaullist formation and had rejoined the main Gaullist party (the Rally for the Republic, RPR) in December 1962. However, the UDT was reconstituted in January 1979, mainly by members of an *Union des Gaullistes de Progrès* (formed in May 1977), which had contested the

May 1978 National Assembly elections in alliance with the left-wing parties but had subsequently been split.

The FRP (also Gaullist) had been created in November 1976 by those who rejected the transformation, by Jacques Chirac, of the *Union Démocrate pour la République* (UDR) into the RPR. In March 1977 the FRP contested municipal elections in co-operation with the left-wing union and had about 500 candidates elected. In the March 1978 general elections the FRP presented some 40 candidates but, obtaining an average of only 2 per cent of the votes, gained no seats. In January 1978 the FRP absorbed the *Initiative Républicaine et Socialiste* (a smaller Gaullist group led by Léo Hamon).

In cantonal elections held in March 1979 FRP candidates received an average of 10 per cent of the votes. In the June 1981 general elections Pierre Dabezies, standing as the sole candidate of the left in a Paris constituency, narrowly gained the seat, but lost it in a by-election held in January 1982 on orders of the Constitutional Council.

Radical-Socialist Party
Parti Radical-Socialiste

Address. 1 place de Valois, 75001 Paris, France

Leadership. Didier Bariani (pres.); André Rossinot (g.s.)

Founded. June 1901

History. The oldest of the current French political movements (Radicals having been prominent in government even before the official establishment of the party in 1901), the Radical-Socialist Party played a dominant role in French politics under the Third Republic (to 1940) and also under the Fourth Republic (1945-58), despite a post-war decline in its parliamentary representation.

Traditionally a party without rigid structures, it suffered a series of splits in 1954-56, when Pierre Mendès-France moved the party to the left and sought to establish a disciplined structure. This caused two major right-wing breakaways leading to the creation of the *Rassemblement des Gauches Républicaines* in December 1955 by Bernard Lafay and Jean-Paul David and the Republican Centre in October 1956 by André Morice and Henri Queuille. At the end of 1958, however, Mendès-France and the left wing found themselves in a minority and subsequently broke away to participate in the formation of the Unified Socialist Party (see separate entry).

During the first decade of the Fifth Republic (1958-68) the Radical-Socialists,

under the leadership of René Billères, participated in moves towards a union of the non-Communist left and in 1965 joined the Federation of the Democratic and Socialist Left (FGDS), which made significant gains in the 1967 National Assembly elections. However, after the May 1968 crisis Maurice Faure moved the party back to a centrist orientation, which was consolidated following the election of Jean-Jacques Servan-Schreiber to the party presidency in 1971.

In June 1972 the party rejected the newly-revived strategy of a union of the left, as a result of which the left wing of the party broke away to form the Movement of Left Radicals (see separate entry). Thereafter the Radical-Socialist Party participated in various moves towards greater cohesion of the smaller centrist and centre-left formations and in the 1974 presidential election the party came out in support of Valéry Giscard d'Estaing (the decision to support whom was taken between the first and second rounds of voting, on the basis of a commitment by Giscard d'Estaing to introduce certain agreed reforms if elected).

After 1974 the party was represented in successive centre-right governments and pursued attempts to forge greater centrist and centre-left unity. In July 1977 it absorbed the small Movement of Social Liberals (see separate entry), which had been formed earlier in the year by Gaullist dissident Olivier Stirn. Shortly before the March 1978 general elections the Radical-Socialists joined the Union for French Democracy (UDF, see separate entry), an alliance of the non-Gaullist "majority" parties, and under the UDF banner returned seven deputies to the National Assembly. Shortly after its 79th annual conference in October 1979 the party was joined by a group of dissident Left Radicals who had rejected the latter formation's continued support for a union of the left.

In the 1981 general elections, which it again contested as part of the UDF, the party was left with only two seats in the National Assembly.

Orientation. The party advocates the separation of political power from economic power; its particular aims include reform of death duties and introduction of a wealth tax; decentralization and regionalization; and greater European unification. In 1983 it called for the exclusion of the Communists from the Government; the rejection of "socialism of the French kind"; and a centre-left coalition opposed to socialism.

Structure. The party's supreme body is its annual conference; it also has district committees and departmental and regional federations, as well as a national head committee and bureau.

Membership. 20,000

Publications. *Agence d'Information Radicale-Socialiste; Bulletin d'Information Radicale-Socialiste* (BIRS)

International affiliations. Federation of Liberal and Democratic Parties of the European Community

---

Rally for the Republic
Rassemblement pour la République (RPR)

Address. 123 rue de Lille, 75007 Paris, France

Leadership. Jacques Chirac (pres.); Bernard Pons (s.g.)

Founded. April 1947

History. Although reorganized under its present name in December 1976, the RPR is directly descended from the *Rassemblement du Peuple Français* (RPF) established in April 1947 by Gen. de Gaulle, who had previously been head of the Free French forces during World War II and then Prime Minister of the first post-liberation French Government (1944-46). Formed with the basic purpose of returning Gen. de Gaulle to power, in 1951 the RPF became briefly the strongest parliamentary party, but De Gaulle severed links with it in 1953 when some of its members accepted ministerial appointments.

Some months before the RPF's dissolution as a parliamentary party in April 1953, the *Action Républicaine et Sociale* (ARS) had been created by dissident Gaullists, while shortly after the dissolution former RPF deputies in the National Assembly formed the *Union des Républicains d'Action Sociale* (URAS), which became successively the *Centre National des Républicains Sociaux* (CNRS) in February 1954 and the *Groupe des Républicains Sociaux* in June 1954.

Following De Gaulle's return to power in mid-1958, the Gaullist movement was reconstituted for the November 1958 elections as the *Union pour la Nouvelle République* (UNR). In December 1962 the UNR was joined by left-wing Gaullists of the *Union Démocratique du Travail* (UDT)—itself formed in 1959—and the merged grouping became known as the UNR-UDT. In November 1967 the UNR-UDT was renamed the *Union des Démocrates pour la Cinquième République* (the title under which Gaullist candidates had contested the March 1967 National Assembly elections) and was at the same time strengthened by the inclusion of

former members of the (Christian democratic) *Mouvement Républicain Populaire* and other groups further to the left.

Shortly before the June 1968 elections, which were held in a climate of deep crisis after the events of the previous month, Gaullist candidates swept to a landslide victory under the title *Union pour la Défense de la République* (UDR). After those elections the Gaullist parliamentary group assumed the designation *Union des Démocrates pour la République* (UDR), which title was subsequently applied to the party as a whole until December 1976, when it was transformed into the RPR.

Having dominated the political life of the Fifth Republic under the presidencies of De Gaulle (1958-69) and Georges Pompidou (1969-74), the Gaullist party (then the UDR) lost the 1974 presidential election, in which its candidate, Jacques Chaban-Delmas, was eliminated after the first round. Although President Giscard d'Estaing governed through a Gaullist Prime Minister (Jacques Chirac) from 1974 to 1976, the resignation of Chirac in August of the latter year highlighted growing tensions between the Gaullist and Giscardian wings of the "majority" which were exacerbated by the transformation of the movement into the RPR at the end of 1976.

As president of the RPR, Chirac sought to lead the "majority" parties into the March 1978 National Assembly elections. However, after a dispute with the smaller "majority" parties over first-round electoral support arrangements—which contributed to the decision of the latter to create the Union for French Democracy (UDF—see separate entry)—RPR candidates contested the first round independently of other parties. The RPR narrowly remained the strongest "majority" formation (although the Socialists claimed to have displaced the Gaullists as the country's largest single party), a position which was consolidated in the second round when reciprocal support arrangements operated among the "majority" parties.

In French elections to the European Parliament held in June 1979 the RPR list (called *Défense des Intérêts de la France en Europe*) received only 16.3 per cent of the vote and came in fourth place behind the UDF, Socialist-Left Radical and Communist lists; but this poor performance was in part attributable to the coolness of Gaullist voters for the European idea.

In the first round of the 1981 presidential elections Jacques Chirac came third with 5,225,846 votes (or 17.99 per cent of the valid votes). He thereupon announced that in the second round he would vote for President Giscard d'Estaing who, backed by the UDF, had come first in the first round; Chirac added, however, that his supporters should vote "according to their conscience" in the second round, in which the Socialist candidate, François Mitterrand, was victorious.

For the ensuing parliamentary elections the leaders of the RPR and the UDF, respectively Chirac and Jean Lecanuet, concluded, on May 15, 1981, an agreement on the formation of an *Union pour la Majorité Nouvelle* (UMN). They subsequently agreed that jointly-backed UMN candidates would contest the first round in 385 of the 474 metropolitan constituencies and that in 88 others, where both parties would present candidates, the less well-placed candidate would be withdrawn from the second round. In the event the RPR representation in the National Assembly was reduced from 153 to 88 (including nine associated members).

Orientation. The RPR seeks to be the main political force supporting the institutions of the Fifth Republic and opposing the "tenets of collectivism"; it stands for national independence and a privilege-free society organized under the principles of liberty and responsibility. In its *Propositions pour la France* published in December 1977 it advocated a new economic policy (including expansion and measures to reduce unemployment), workers' participation in decision-making and new forms of social interdependence.

Structure. Although the RPR has a structure similar to other major French parties, considerable powers over the party's affairs are vested in the president, who inter alia appoints the RPR secretary-general.

Membership. 300,000

Publications. *La Lettre de la Nation* (daily); *Rassemblement-Actualité* (irregular)

International affiliations. International Democrat Union; European Democrat Union; European Progressive Democratic Group (in the European Parliament)

Republican Centre
Centre Républicain

Address. 13 boulevard Raspail, 75007 Paris, France

Leadership. André Morice (pres.)

Founded. October 1956

History. The small Republican Centre was formed by right-wing elements of the Radical-Socialist Party (see separate entry) who opposed that party's move to the left under Pierre Mendès-France. Following the establishment of the Fifth Republic in 1958, the formation sought to provide a

bridge between the "majority" parties and other centrist and centre-left groupings then nominally in the opposition, and in 1971 it joined the *Mouvement Réformateur*.

After the election to the presidency of Valéry Giscard d'Estaing in 1974 and the extension of the "majority" to the smaller centrist and centre-left parties, the Republican Centre was active in various alliances designed to bring greater cohesion to the centre left, notably the Federation of Reformers created in June 1975 and the Movement of the Reformist Left established in March 1975. In the March 1978 National Assembly elections Republican Centre candidates stood under the banner of the Union for French Democracy (UDF—see separate entry), although the party did not formally join this federation. Since 1974 several prominent Republican Centre members have rejoined the Radical-Socialist Party.

Republican Party
Parti Républicain (PR)

Address. 1 rue Villersexel, 75007 Paris, France

Leadership. Michel Poniatowski (hon. pres.); François Léotard (s.g.)

Founded. May 1977

History. The Republican Party was formed in May 1977 from the *Fédération Nationale des Républicains Indépendents* (FNRI), the *Génération Sociale et Libérale*, support committees for the election of Valéry Giscard d'Estaing as President of the Republic (in 1974) and *Agir pour l'Avenir*. The FNRI had been established by Giscard d'Estaing on June 1, 1966, from those members of the National Centre of Independents and Peasants (see separate entry) who had broken away in November 1962 and who subsequently formed part of the government "majority" while reserving a wide degree of freedom to criticize government policy.

Following the defeat of the Government in the 1969 referendum on regionalization and reform of the Senate and the consequent resignation of President de Gaulle, Giscard d'Estaing (who had refused to vote "yes" in the referendum) and the FNRI supported President Pompidou, after whose death Giscard d'Estaing was himself elected President in May 1974. Thereafter, although Giscard d'Estaing's first Prime Minister was the Gaullist Jacques Chirac (1974-76), the centre of gravity of the "majority" was moved to the left with the inclusion in the Government of Radical-Socialists and other centre-left formations—this and other factors giving rise to increasing tensions between the Gaullist and Giscardian wings of the "majority".

For the National Assembly elections of March 1978 the PR joined with other non-Gaullist "majority" parties to form the Union for French Democracy (UDF—see separate entry), as part of which the party returned 71 representatives to the National Assembly. In the 1981 elections to the Assembly, which it again contested as part of the UDF, the party's strength in the Assembly was reduced to 32 members.

Orientation. The PR regards itself as a centre movement with European and Liberal objectives "angled towards progress, enriched by radicalism and revitalized by the breath of Gaullism". Its current philosophy is closely based on the theses advanced by President Giscard d'Estaing in his book *Démocratie Française* published in 1977.

Structure. The PR's highest body is its annual congress, which elects a political bureau headed by the secretary-general, who is responsible for the party's national secretariat. The party also has a youth movement (*Autrement*), which was launched in October 1977.

Membership. 100,000

Publications. Arguments et Réponses (fortnightly); *L'Economie* (weekly); *L'Avant-Centre* (monthly)

International affiliations. Federation of Liberal and Democratic Parties of the European Community

---

Revolutionary Communist League
Ligue Communiste Révolutionnaire (LCR)

Address. p.a. Rouge, 2 rue Richard Lenoir, 93108 Montreuil, France

Leadership. Alain Krivine

Founded. 1973

History. The LCR succeeded the *Ligue Communiste*, which had been founded in April 1969 as the successor to the *Jeunesse Communiste Révolutionnaire* and the *Parti Communiste Internationaliste*. Both of these had been banned in June 1968 and the *Ligue Communiste* movement had itself been banned in June 1973 after organizing a violent counter-demonstration against the extreme right-wing *Ordre Nouveau* (which was banned at the same time).

The 1969 presidential election had been contested for the *Ligue Communiste* by Alain Krivine, who received 1.1 per cent of the votes cast in the first round, and in the March 1973 National Assembly elections the *Ligue* had put up 92 candidates jointly with the Workers' Struggle formation (see separate entry), who received 1.2 per cent in the first round.

In the 1974 presidential election (which was contested separately by a Workers' Struggle candidate) Krivine received only 0.4 per cent of the votes in the first round. The LCR contested the March 1978 National Assembly elections jointly with two other extreme left-wing formations (the Communist Organization of Workers and the Communist Committees for Self-Management—see separate entries) under the designation *Pour le Socialisme, le Pouvoir aux Travailleurs*, with which some 250 candidates were associated, none being elected.

Together with the Workers' Struggle the LCR obtained 3.5 per cent of the vote in the 1980 European elections. For the 1981 presidential election Krivine failed to secure the required minimum of 500 sponsors. For the ensuing parliamentary elections the party nominated 36 candidates (without success) and in municipal elections held in 1983 it gained 3 per cent of the vote.

Orientation. The LCR is Trotskyist, but in 1981 it declared its support for the left-wing Government.

Structure. The annual LCR congress elects a central committee, which in turn elects a political bureau.

Membership. 6,000

Publications. Rouge (weekly organ); *Critique Communiste* (monthly); *Cahiers du Féminisme* (monthly); *Inprécor* (fortnightly, under the auspices of the United Secretariat of the Fourth International)

International affiliations. Fourth (Trotskyist) International

---

Revolutionary Marxist-Leninist Communist Party
Parti Communiste Révolutionnaire Marxiste-Léniniste (PCRML)

Address. B.P. 68, 75019 Paris, Cédex 19, France

Leadership. Max Cluzot (s.g.)

Founded. 1974

History. The party was formed by a section of the former *Parti Communiste Marxiste-Léniniste Français* (PCMLF) founded in December 1967 and banned in May 1968, but subsequently in semi-legal existence. From early 1974 the PCRML took part in labour disputes and other activities, while in August 1978 other former PCMLF activists formed the Marxist-Leninist Communist Party (PCML—see separate entry). For the 1981 parliamentary elections the PCRML fielded 17 unsuccessful candidates, but it also declared support for the left-wing Government installed afterwards.

Orientation. The party is a Maoist formation which "fights for the socialist revolution in France" and is critical of the French Communist Party, whose plans it regards as leading to the establishment of state capitalism in France. It denounces the two super-powers' "threats of war" and supports all peoples opposed to them.

Structure. The party is based on cells (primarily in industrial enterprises) which are organized in federations covering several departments. There is a central committee elected by a congress composed of delegates elected by active members of the base organizations. Between sessions of the central committee the party is directed by its political bureau and political secretariat.

Membership. 2,500

Publications. *Le Quotidien du Peuple* (daily organ), 10,000; *Front Rouge* (theoretical and political review), 5,000

Social Democratic Party
Parti Social-Démocrate (PSD)

Address. 110 rue de Sèvres, 75015 Paris, France

Leadership. Max Lejeune (pres.)

Founded. December 1973

History. This party was established as the *Mouvement des Démocrates Socialistes de France* (MDSF) by former Socialists who were opposed to the common programme issued by the Socialist and Communist parties in June 1972 and who claimed to be following the authentic French Socialist tradition established by Jean Jaurès and Léon Blum. A consistent advocate of centrist unity, the Movement joined the *Mouvement Réformateur* in 1973 and the Federation of Reformers in 1975. The Movement's vice-president, Emile Muller, was a candidate in the May 1974 presidential election, in the first round of which he received 0.7 per cent of the vote. In early 1978 the Movement associated itself with the non-Gaullist "majority" parties in the Union for French Democracy (UDF—see separate entry), under which banner it returned four deputies in the March 1978 National Assembly elections.

As a result of the 1981 general elections the Movement retained no seat in the National Assembly. In October 1982 it adopted its present name of *Parti Social-Démocrate* and the meeting taking this decision was also attended by members of the Democratic Socialist Party (see separate entry).

Orientation. The PDS has propounded a humanist, reformist socialism rallying all socialist democrats, opposing any coalition with the Communists, improving the distribution of the national income and practising considered state intervention in the economy.

Structure. The party holds annual congresses and has a national bureau, a national council, federations and sections.

Membership. 4,000

Publications. *Le Démocrate Socialiste*, 8,000

Socialist Party
Parti Socialiste (PS)

Address. 10 rue de Solferino, 75333 Paris, France

Leadership. Lionel Jospin (first sec.)

Founded. April 1905

History. The party was formed as a merger between the Socialist Party of France (inspired by Jules Guesde) and the French Socialist Party (of Jean Jaurès) and henceforth formed the French Section of the Workers' International (SFIO), i.e. of the Second International. Although until 1914 the party had opposed war, it regarded World War I as a war of national defence for France. In 1920 the party was split, with a majority at a congress in Tours voting for membership of the Third (Communist) International (the Comintern) and founding the Communist Party, and the minority remaining in the Socialist Party (SFIO). After 1924 the Socialist Party supported Radical Governments, and in 1936, having become the strongest party in Parliament, it formed a Popular Front Government under Léon Blum with the Radicals (with the support, but not participation, of the Communist Party) until 1938. During World War II the (reconstituted) party took part in all resistance activities and participated in the Algiers Committee set up by Gen. de Gaulle.

After 1944 the party, with 142 seats in the National Assembly, took part in several Governments under the Fourth Republic and was responsible for large-scale nationalization. In 1947 a Socialist (Vincent Auriol) became President of the Republic and in 1956-57 the then SFIO leader, Guy Mollet, was Prime Minister of the Fourth Republic's longest-lived Government and played a major role in the creation of the European Economic Community. The party's parliamentary representation declined through the 1950s, however, and internal dissension and defections over the party's attitude to the Algerian war (1955-62) and the role of the Mollet Government in the 1956 Suez episode were exacerbated by the participation of Mollet and other

Socialists in the De Gaulle national coalition Government formed in mid-1958. Having supported the election of De Gaulle as President of the newly-established Fifth Republic in December 1958, the SFIO refused to participate in the Debré Government formed in January 1959, when the party went into opposition.

In a move to revive the electoral fortunes of the non-Communist left the SFIO in September 1965 joined with the Radical-Socialists and the Convention of Republican Institutions (CIR) to form the Federation of the Democratic and Socialist Left (FGDS) under the presidency of the CIR leader, François Mitterrand, who as leader of the former *Union Démocratique et Sociale de la Résistance* (UDSR) had participated in successive Fourth Republic Cabinets and had opposed Gen. de Gaulle's advent to power in 1958. As the candidate of the FGDS, and supported by the Communist Party and other left-wing formations, Mitterrand obtained 44.8 per cent of the votes against De Gaulle in the second round of the December 1965 presidential elections. Moreover, on the strength of a second-round electoral pact with the Communists the FGDS made significant gains in the 1967 National Assembly elections, winning 121 seats. However, in further Assembly elections held in June 1968 in the aftermath of the May 1968 political and industrial crisis the FGDS retained only 57 seats. During 1967-68 the SFIO majority had strongly supported moves to convert the FGDS into a united democratic socialist party, but the Federation's defeat in the June 1968 elections heightened political divergences between the constituent groupings and Mitterrand resigned from the presidency in November 1968, shortly before the Radical-Socialists decided against merging into the proposed new party.

Notwithstanding the collapse of the FGDS, the SFIO continued with plans for the creation of a broader "new" socialist party on the basis of a merger of the SFIO with Mitterrand's CIR and some smaller socialist clubs. On the eve of the May 1969 presidential elections what was intended as the constituent congress of the new party was held at Alfortville, but the CIR refused to back the presidential candidature of Gaston Defferre (leader of the SFIO right wing), who obtained only 5 per cent of the votes in the first round of the elections and was eliminated. Subsequently, the CIR did not participate when the new Socialist Party was formally established at the Issy-les-Moulineaux congress in July 1969 as a merger of the SFIO and the socialist clubs, with Alain Savary (formerly leader of the *Union des Clubs pour le Renouveau de la Gauche*) being elected first secretary. However, renewed efforts to bring the CIR into the new Socialist Party reached a successful conclusion with the holding of a "congress of socialist unity" at Epinay in June 1971 at which Mitterrand was elected first secretary of the party.

Thereafter the Socialist Party adopted a strategy of union of the left and in June 1972 signed a common programme with the Communists (also endorsed by the Left Radicals—see separate entry) on the basis of which the left made major gains in the March 1973 National Assembly elections, the Socialists and Left Radicals jointly returning 100 deputies, of whom 89 were Socialists. The following year Mitterrand opposed Valéry Giscard d'Estaing in the May 1974 presidential election as the agreed candidate of virtually the entire left in both rounds of voting; but he was narrowly defeated in the second round, in which he received 12,971,604 votes (49.19 per cent) against 13,396,203 (50.81 per cent) for Giscard d'Estaing.

The Socialist Party was further enlarged when in early 1975 it was joined by the minority wing of the Unified Socialist Party (see separate entry) led by Michel Rocard and also by a "third component" principally comprising affiliated members of the CFDT trade union federation. However, from late 1974 the steady growth of Socialist strength contributed to serious strains in the party's alliance with the Communists, these culminating in the failure of the left to agree on a revised common programme for the March 1978 National Assembly elections. While reciprocal support arrangements were operated by the left-wing parties in the second round, they failed to make the gains which had been widely expected, although the Socialists claimed to have become the country's largest single party with 23 per cent of the vote in the first round.

In the June 1979 French elections to the European Parliament the Socialist and Left Radicals presented a joint list of candidates which obtained 23.5 per cent of the vote compared with 20.5 per cent for a separate Communist list. While its relations with the Communists have continued to be acrimonious, the Socialist Party has repeatedly stressed its commitment to the union of the left as the strategy which social and economic realities dictate that it should follow but has blamed the Communists for the rupture of the union.

Standing as the Socialist Party's candidate in the 1981 presidential elections, François Mitterrand obtained 7,505,960 votes (or 25.85 per cent of the total valid votes) in the first round; in the second round, for which the Communist Party and other left-wing groups gave him support, he gained 15,708,262 votes (or 51.76 per cent of the valid votes—against 48.29 for the outgoing President Giscard d'Estaing). In the 1981 elections to the National Assembly the Socialists increased their seats from 107 to 265 and thus obtained an absolute majority. The left-wing Government formed by the Socialists after the presidential elections included two members of the Left Radical Movement, and in a government reorganization in June 1981 three Communists became ministers and another Communist a secretary of state.

Orientation. The party describes itself as a mass party intent on coming to power in order to initiate a transition to socialism by transforming France's economic structures, notably by means of a far-reaching nationalization programme.

Structure. The party's basic unit is the section (of at least five members over the age of 15 years); the party has a federation in each department and a national leadership consisting of a head committee, an executive bureau and a secretariat. An ordinary congress is held every two years, and between its sessions a national convention (comprising the head committee, the parliamentary party and one representative from each federation) meets to consider the action taken by the national leadership. A *Centre d'études, de recherches et d'éducation socialiste* (CERES) is a left-wing pressure group within the party.

Membership. 200,000

Publications. *L'Unité* (weekly); *Combat Socialiste* (monthly); *Le Poing et la Rose* (monthly internal organ); *La Nouvelle Revue Socialiste* (theoretical review)

International affiliations. Socialist Internaional; Confederation of Socialist Parties of the European Community

---

Solidarity and Liberty
Solidarité et Liberté

Address. 63 blvd. des Batignolles, 75017 Paris, France

Leadership. Charles Pasqua, Paul d'Ornano

Founded. December 1981

History. At the time of this movement's creation, Charles Pasqua was president of the (Gaullist) Rally for the Republic group in the Senate, and Paul d'Ornano a senator of the (centrist) Union for French Democracy.

Orientation. This association was intended to create "a centre of firm and resolute resistance" to the left (which had come to power after the 1981 elections) and to embrace "all who reject socialism and who want to act".

Unified Socialist Party
Parti Socialiste Unifié (PSU)

Address. 9 rue de Borromée, 75015 Paris, France

Leadership. Serge Depaquit (nat. sec.)

Founded. April 1960

History. The PSU was created as a merger of the *Parti Socialiste Autonome* (including former Radical-Socialist followers of Pierre Mendès-France) and two small factions of former Socialists and Communists respectively, the original aim of the party being to unite the left by drawing the Socialist Party (then the SFIO) further to the left and democratizing the Communist Party.

Having supported François Mitterrand as the joint left-wing candidate in the 1965 presidential election (although from outside the Federation of the Democratic and Socialist Left), the PSU participated in reciprocal support arrangements with the Socialists and Communists in the 1967 National Assembly elections. Thereafter it moved to the left under the leadership of Michel Rocard (who became national secretary in 1967) and was closely identified with the militant student and workers' movement of May 1968, during which it called for a common front of left-wing forces to "accentuate the paralysis of the Government" and wherever possible to set up "autonomous authorities expressing democracy in action". The 1969 presidential elections were contested for the PSU by Rocard, who received 816,471 votes (3.6 per cent) in the first round.

Although the PSU did not participate in the union of the left between the Socialists, Communists and Left Radicals created in 1972, it supported Mitterrand's further presidential candidature in May 1974 and thereafter Rocard sought to lead the PSU into the Socialist Party, resigning from the PSU leadership pending a merger. However, after the PSU national council had voted by a majority in October 1974 against union with the Socialists, Rocard took only a minority of the party into the Socialist Party in early 1975.

The PSU contested the March 1978 National Assembly elections within the *Front Autogestionnaire*, which had been launched in November 1977 as an electoral alliance at local level of the PSU, the Movement for a Non-Violent Alternative (MAN) led by Jean-Marie Muller and various ecological, feminist and regional groups and which put up 228 candidates (in some cases in alliance with the Communist Party) who were pledged to withdraw in the second round in favour of the best-placed candidate of the left. In

November 1979 the *Front Autogestionnaire* was transformed into the *Convergence pour l'Autogestion* under the leadership of Muller and Michel Mousel (the latter being succeeded as PSU national secretary in January 1980 by Mme Huguette Bouchardeau). Notwithstanding its continued participation in the broader *Autogestion* movement, the PSU continued to exist as a party in its own right.

Mme Bouchardeau contested the first round of the 1981 presidential elections but gained only 321,744 votes (or 1.11 per cent of the valid votes). In the ensuing parliamentary elections the PSU had an electoral alliance with *Alternative 81* (consisting of left-wing and ecologist groups) and it also agreed to withdraw its candidates in the second round of the elections in favour of the best-placed left-wing candidate. In December 1981 the party decided to seek closer alignment with the left-wing Government. In March 1983 Mme Bouchardeau became a secretary of state, and accordingly vacated the PSU leadership.

Orientation. The PSU seeks the widest possible alliance of popular forces to pave the way for genuine social and economic change and rules out any form of compromise with the right.

Structure. The PSU's supreme authority is its congress, which elects a national council and a national secretariat.

Membership. 7,000

Publications. *Tribune Socialiste* (weekly); *Critique Socialiste* (monthly)

Union for French Democracy
Union pour la Démocratie Française (UDF)

Address. 42 bis, blvd. de Latour-Maubourg, 75007 Paris, France

Leadership. Jean Lecanuet (pres.); G. Donnet, D. Bariani, F. Léotard, P. Méhaignerie (vice-presidents); Michel Pinton (s.g.)

Founded. February 1978

History. The UDF was formed on the eve of the March 1978 National Assembly elections as an electoral vehicle for the non-Gaullist "majority" formations, namely the Republican Party (PR), the Radical-Socialists and the Centre of Social Democrats (CDS)—for each of which see separate entries. Its creation was in part inspired by the decision of the (Gaullist) Rally for the Republic (RPR) to withdraw from first-round electoral pacts with the PR and the CDS on the grounds that these two parties' negotiation of separate first-round agreements with the Radical-Socialists (the most left-wing of the "majority" parties) had violated the terms of the RPR-PR-CDS agreement. (The UDF was not joined by the small National Centre of Independents and Peasants—see separate entry—even though this formation contested the elections in alliance with the UDF parties.)

The formation of the UDF was backed both by President Giscard d'Estaing (after whose 1977 book *Démocratie Française* the party was named) and by his Prime Minister, Raymond Barre; but its creation heightened acrimony between the Gaullist and the Giscardian wings of the "majority", the former viewing it as an attempt by the latter to engineer electoral superiority. In the actual elections the UDF candidates (who included representatives of other smaller centrist and centre-left groupings) trailed behind the RPR in terms of first-round voting support (21.5 to 22.6 per cent) but improved the aggregate representation of its constituent elements (assisted by a reciprocal support agreement with the RPR for the second round).

In a move to consolidate its increased parliamentary strength the UDF council on March 23, 1978, formally constituted the alliance into a federation of its constituent parties. Jean Lecanuet (leader of the CDS) became president of the new formation, which was opened to direct membership organized locally by the constituent parties. In the June 1979 French elections to the European Parliament the UDF list (*Union pour la France en Europe*) came top of the poll, with 27.6 per cent of the vote.

For the 1981 parliamentary elections the UDF concluded, on May 15, an agreement with the RPR on the formation of an *Union pour la Majorité Nouvelle* (UMN), an electoral alliance involving the presentation of jointly-backed UMN candidates in 385 of the 474 metropolitan constituencies and withdrawal from the second round of UDF candidates trailing behind RPR candidates in the other constituencies. Nevertheless the UDF's representation in the National Assembly was reduced from 116 to 63 (including 12 associated members). In local elections held in 1982 and 1983, however, the UDF emerged as the strongest party. While it had reaffirmed its co-operation with the RPR in November 1982, the formal alliance concluded by the formation of the UMN was allowed to lapse in 1983.

Orientation. The current object of the UDF is to give the French opposition the support required for regaining a political majority against the left-wing Government and its policies. With its liberal and European outlook the UDF aims at rallying a majority of the French people wishing to build a "just and pluralist society of free and responsible human beings".

Structure. UDF policy is defined by a 19-member national council, and carried out by a seven-member executive bureau; the UDF has sections in all metropolitan departments.

Membership. 300,000

Publications. *UDF 1* (daily information sheet), 3,000; *UDF-Scope* (information monthly for party workers), 30,000

International affiliations. European Democrat Union (permanent observer)

Union of French Citizens Abroad
Union des Français à l'Etranger (UFE)

History. This centre-right Union took part in elections held in May-June 1983 to the consultative *Conseil Supérieur des Français à l'Etranger* (CSFE) which consists of 127 members elected by proportional representation and 20 consultative members designated by the Foreign Ministry. The UFE was officially stated to have won about two-thirds of the seats on this council.

Union of Frenchmen of Good Sense
Union des Français de Bon Sens (UFBS)

Leadership. Gérard Furnon
Founded. September 1977
History. The UFBS was founded by Gérard Furnon after a protracted dispute with workers at his sweet factory who wished to establish a trade union organization. The party's founder and leader contested the March 1978 National Assembly elections but was not elected.

Orientation. The UFBS was established principally to oppose what its leader has described as "political trade unionism", which he regards as a threat to free enterprise.

Membership. 16,000

Union of Libertarian Communist Workers
Union des Travailleurs Communistes Libertaires (UTCL)

Founded. 1978
History. The UTCL was formed by a dissident group of the Anarchist Combat Organization (OCA—see separate entry) which rejected the latter formation's "anti-trade union" and "ultra-leftist" approach. It has not participated in elections.

Orientation. Part of the "libertarian current" in the extreme left, the UTCL seeks to build a "revolutionary alternative" both to the right and also to the "class collaboration" of the old left.

Workers' Struggle
Lutte Ouvrière (LO)

Address. B.P. 233, 75865 Paris, Cédex 18, France
Leadership. Arlette Laguiller
Founded. June 1968
History. Descended from a Trotskyist group which in 1940 rejected membership of the French Committees for the Fourth International, the LO is the successor to *Voix Ouvrière*, which was dissolved in June 1968. It contested the March 1973 National Assembly elections jointly with the *Ligue Communiste* (itself later succeeded by the Revolutionary Communist League—see separate entry), but in the May 1974 presidential election the two organizations put up separate candidates, that of the LO being Arlette Laguiller, who received 595,247 votes (2.3 per cent) in the first round.

In the March 1978 National Assembly election the LO presented 470 candidates independently of all other formations, but none were elected. For the June 1979 French elections to the European Parliament the LO reverted to a strategy of alliance with the Revolutionary Communist League, the two parties' joint list (*Pour les Etats-Unis Socialistes d'Europe*) obtaining 623,663 votes (3.1 per cent) but failing to secure representation.

In the 1981 presidential elections Arlette Laguiller obtained 668,057 votes, or 2.3 per cent of the total. In the ensuing parliamentary elections the LO fielded 158 candidates, all of them unsuccessful. From July 1982 onwards the LO co-operated with the Revolutionary Communist League in issuing a joint monthly supplement to their respective weekly newspapers.

Orientation. Of the major French Trotskyist parties, the LO has been the most hostile to the Socialist-Communist-Left Radical union of the left. In June 1979 Arlette Laguiller called for the creation of a broad "democratic revolutionary party". The LO regards the left-wing Government as "bourgeois" and its alleged anti-working-class policies as identical with those of the preceding right-wing Government.

Membership. 5,000
Publications. *Lutte Ouvrière* (weekly)

146

Regional Parties

BRITTANY

Breton Democratic Union
Union Démocratique Bretonne/Unvaniezh Demokratel Breizh (UDB)

Address. B.P. 304, 29200 Brest, Brittany, France
Leadership. Collective
Founded. January 1964
History. The UDB was founded during the aftermath of the Franco-Algerian war by young militants "aware of the colonial situation of their country" (i.e. Brittany) and regarding their struggle as one of decolonization or national liberation which according to the party "presupposes an alliance with the French working class and other left-wing forces to overthrow the existing political majority". Apart from contesting elections with its own candidates, the UDB has been represented, since 1977, within the union of the left on the city councils in most of Brittany's large cities (Nantes, Rennes, Brest and Lorient). It contested 17 seats in Brittany in the March 1978 National Assembly elections.

In January 1981 the UDB decided to launch a campaign of "resistance to the Giscardian regime", in particular to oppose the construction of a nuclear power station at Plogoff (south-western Brittany) and to demand job creation measures and increases in funds for promoting Breton culture. In the 1981 presidential elections it called for abstention in the first round but backed François Mitterrand in the second, while in the subsequent National Assembly elections it again fielded 17 candidates without success.

Orientation. The UDB seeks "a socialist Brittany as the only way of securing self-determination for the Breton people". The party has consistently condemned the violent methods of the Liberation Front of Brittany (both wings of which were banned in January 1974). Since the left took power in 1981, the UDB has criticized the slowness of the Government's regionalization project and also the "timidity" of its social policy.
Structure. The UDB has cells and sections organized in federations (in Brittany and also in Paris). The party's collective leadership is vested in a political bureau comprising 16 members elected by congress (every two years) and representatives of the federations.
Membership. 2,000
Publications. *Le Peuple Breton* (monthly), 10,000; *Pobl Vreizh* (in Breton), 1,700

Breton Fight
Argad Breizh

Leadership. Yves le Calvez (l.)
Founded. February 1979
History. Yves le Calvez had been the leader of *Strollad ar Vro*, the Country Party which was a member of the Breton Self-Rule Autonomous and Socialist Front (see separate entry). *Argad Breizh* was established as an autonomist but non-violent movement.

Breton Popular Aid
Skoazell Vreiz

History. This small movement was established as an independent autonomist group.

Breton Self-Rule Autonomist and Socialist Front
Front Autonomiste et Socialiste Autogestionnaire Breton (FASAB)

History. FASAB comprises the *Strollad ar Vro* (Country Party), the *Comité d'Action Breton* led by Dr Guy Caro and the *Sturm Breiz* movement. *Strollad ar Vro* (SAV) supported the presidential candidature of François Mitterrand (Socialist) in May 1974 on the basis of a commitment that the Socialist Party would advance the cause of ethnic minorities in France.
Orientation. FASAB claims to have no connexion with either wing of the militant Liberation Front of Brittany (banned in January 1974) but has neither approved nor condemned its violent activities. The SAV programme calls for home rule in Brittany to be exercised by an elected assembly of the Breton nation and by an executive or government elected by such an assembly, and for the right of the Breton people to be represented directly in European organizations; it also rejects capitalism (as economic centralism), state control (as political centralism) and the Marxist concept of the class struggle.

CORSICA

In addition to the local sections of the principal mainland parties, a number of specifically Corsican political formations have been active in recent years.

Union of the Corsican People
Unione di u Populu Corsu (UPC)

Leadership. Dr Edmond Siméoni (l.); Xavier Belgodère (s.g.)

Founded. July 1977

History. The UPC is Corsica's principal autonomist party and was formed as the successor to the *Associu di Patrioti Corsi* (APC). Although the island's political representation has largely remained in the hands of Corsican sections of the mainland parties, the APC and UPC have claimed credit for the economic, social and institutional reforms instituted in Corsica in recent years by the Paris Government in response to autonomist demands accompanied by a campaign of violence conducted by extremist groups.

In January 1980 an extreme wing of the UPC was involved in the temporary seizure of two hostages from among the members of a New Action Front against Independence and Autonomy (Francia). The regional council of Corsica subsequently accused the UPC of lending support, through its policies, to the banned Corsican National Liberation Front (FLNC).

In 1982 the UPC gave qualified approval to the left-wing Government's decentralization programme of March 1982, under which Corsica became a "territorial collectivity" with a direcly-elected Assembly (replacing the previous indirectly-constituted general council) with wider executive powers. However, in elections to this Assembly, held on Aug. 8, the UPC gained only 10.62 per cent of the total valid votes and seven (out of 61) seats.

Orientation. At a congress held in Ajaccio in August 1979 the UPC established three lines of action to bring about autonomy for Corsica without violence, namely (i) complete solidarity with all imprisoned activists (including those of the extremist FLNC), (ii) the holding of a referendum on internal autonomy for the island and (iii) internationalization of the Corsica question.

A UPC congress held on Aug. 9-10, 1980, reaffirmed the party's aim of self-government for Corsica in the social, economic and cultural fields (but with foreign affairs, defence and finance remaining the central Government's responsibility).

Structure. The highest body is the UPC congress which elects a 21-member political bureau.

Membership. 10,000

Publications. *Kyrn* (weekly)

1982 Electoral Lists

Elections to the new 61-member Corsican Assembly held on Aug. 19, 1982, were contested by the following groupings (many of them being lists presented by the Corsican federations of mainland parties):

Action for a New Corsica
Action pour une Corse Nouvelle
Led by Dominique Bucchini (a Communist member of the European Parliament), this official list of the Corsican Communist Party obtained 10.6 per cent and seven seats.

Control and Justice for All
Gestion et Justice pour Tous
Led by Camille Simonpieri (a former Communist), this list obtained 0.7 per cent of the vote and no seats.

Corsica New Voice
Corse Voix Nouvelle
This independent list led by Jean-Gaston Susini obtained 0.3 per cent and no seats.

Corsican People's Party
Partitu Populare Corsu (PPC)
Led by Dominique Alfonsi, this pro-autonomy formation secured 2.1 per cent and one seat.

Corsican Renaissance
Renaissance Corse
This list of independents led by Philippe Ceccaldi secured 2.1 per cent and one seat.

Defence of the Interests of Corsica
Défense des Intérêts de la Corse
Led by Jean Colonna of the (Gaullist) Rally for the Republic (RPR), this rightist list obtained 3.1 per cent and two seats.

Democratic Rally for the Future of Corsica
Rassemblement Démocratique pour l'Avenir de la Corse
Led by Denis de Rocca Serra (who subsequently joined the centre-left coalition administration of Corsica), this list secured 2.4 per cent and one seat.

Left Radical Movement for a Democratic Region
Mouvement des Radicaux de Gauche pour une Région Démocratique
Led by Prosper Alfonsi (the former Left Radical president of Corsica's regional council) and constituting the official Left Radical slate in the department of Haute-Corse, this list secured 10.4 per cent and seven seats. Prosper Alfonsi was subsequently elected President of the new Assembly and formed a centre-left coalition administration.

Rally for Corsica in National Unity
Rassemblement pour la Corse dans l'Unité Nationale
Led by Jean-Paul de Rocca Serra (an RPR deputy in the National Assembly), this list of Gaullist, Union for French Democracy (UDF) and "Bonapartist" candidates secured 28.1 per cent and 19 seats.

Regional Union for Progress
Union Régionale pour le Progrès
Led by José Rossi (of the Republican Party component of the UDF) and containing UDF dissidents opposed to formal alliance with the RPR, this list obtained 9.3 per cent and six seats.

Renewal of the Corsican Region
Renouveau de la Région Corse
Led by Jean-Louis Albertini (ex-RPR), this list obtained 2.7 per cent and one seat.

Republican Union for the Defence and Development of Corsica
Union Républicaine de Défense et de Promotion de la Corse
This list, led by Dom Philippe Semidei (a Left Radical dissident), obtained 1.7 per cent and one seat.

Socialist and Democratic List
Liste Socialiste et Démocratique
Led by Charles Santoni (former first secretary of the Socialist Party's Corse-du-Sud federation) and containing Socialist dissidents, this list secured 2.4 per cent and one seat.

Socialist Party (Corsican Federation)
Parti Socialiste (Fédération Corse)
This official Socialist list, led by Ange Pantaloni (first secretary of the party's Corse-du-Sud federation), secured 5.4 per cent and three seats.

Union for the Defence of the Corsican Economy
Union pour la Défense de l'Economie Corse
Led by Simon Cruciani, this list of independents obtained 1 per cent and no seats.

Union of the Corsican People (UPC)—see separate entry above for this party, which secured 10.6 per cent and seven seats.

Unity and Democracy
Unité et Démocratie
Led by Nicolas Alfonsi and containing official Left Radical candidates in the Corse-du-Sud department, this list secured 6.7 per cent and four seats.

OCCITANIA
(PROVENCE-LANGUEDOC)

Occitanian Nationalist Party
Parti Nationaliste Occitan (PNO)

Founded. 1959
Orientation. The PNO bases its campaign for an autonomous Occitania (i.e. Provence and Languedoc) on an anti-federalist and anti-European platform. It called on its followers to support "progressive forces" in the March 1978 National Assembly elections, particularly the Communist Party, left-wing Socialists and other candidates who came out clearly "against European and Atlantic integration".

Occitanian Socialist Movement
Mouvement Socialiste Occitan/Volem Viure al Pais (VVAP)

Founded. 1974
History. The VVAP is represented in some 30 departments in the Provence-Languedoc regions of Southern France. It presented several candidates in the March 1978 National Assembly elections in alliance with other regional and ecological movements.
Orientation. The VVAP seeks autonomy for Occitania on the basis of a "socialist alternative", on which its views converge with those of the Socialist Party (although the latter has not specifically endorsed the VVAP's autonomist objectives).

Occitanian Struggle
Lutte Occitane

Orientation. Closely associated with extreme left-wing formations, this organization campaigns for "the construction of a socialist Occitania" and places particular emphasis on cultural objectives in relation to the distinct traditions of the Occitanian region.

Poble d'Oc

Orientation. This small formation professes libertarian socialism based on workers' self-management and favours the creation of an Occitanian liberation front. However, such views have met with little popular response among the inhabitants of the region in question.

French Overseas Departments

Since February 1983 each of four of the five French overseas departments (i.e. French Guiana, Guadeloupe, Martinique and Réunion, but not Saint Pierre and Miquelon) has had, in addition to its (departmental) *conseil général* directly elected (by universal adult suffrage of citizens above the age of 18 years and by majority voting over two rounds in constituent cantons), an Assembly directly elected from party lists in proportion to the overall percentage of votes obtained by the lists in a single consultation. Political parties active in the overseas departments include not only local sections of metropolitan parties but also a number of formations specific to particular departments.

French Guiana

Capital: Cayenne   Pop. 73,000

French Guiana, as a French overseas department with the status of a region, has a 16-member *conseil général* and a 31-member Assembly, and is represented by one deputy in the French National Assembly and by one senator in the French Senate. In the first elections to the new departmental Assembly on Feb. 20, 1983, the Socialist-led list secured 14 of the 31 seats, a centre-right list 13, an extreme left-wing list of the (independent) *Union de Travailleurs de Guyane* 3 and an independent associated with the Socialists the remaining seat.

Guiana Decolonization Movement
Mouvement Guyanais de Décolonisation
(Moguyde)

Leadership. Roland Delannon (pres.)
Founded. October 1974
History. This nationalist Movement achieved no success in 1976 cantonal elections and has not taken part in further elections. It has claimed to be the first group openly to demand full independence for French Guiana.

Publications. *Pikan-Arè*; *Kromanti*, 1,000

Guiana Socialist Party
Parti Socialiste Guyanais (PSG)

Address. 34 rue Voltaire, Cayenne, French Guiana

Leadership. Elie Castor (l.)
Founded. 1956
History. The PSG has repeatedly held the presidency of the departmental *conseil général* and has become the strongest party in French Guiana. In 1981 Elie Castor was elected as the department's deputy in the French National Assembly. After the new departmental Assembly had been elected in February 1983 (in which the list backed by the PSG obtained 14 seats), the PSG and the other left-wing groups in the Assembly formed a six-member ruling bureau (administration).
Orientation. As a federation of the French Socialist Party, the PSG supports that party's devolution programme involving increased autonomy for French Guiana (as introduced by the left-wing metropolitan Government in 1982).

150

Pro-Independence Party of Guyanese Unity
Parti Indépendantiste de l'Unité Guyanaise
(PIUG)

Leadership. Albert Lecante
History. In January 1983 this party supported a minor strike action by public sector employees, and on Feb. 3 of that year it called on the Government to recognize "the right of the Guyanese people to self-determination" (whereas the French Prime Minister had claimed that no-one had posed the question of independence for French Guiana). The PIUG asserted that since May 1981 the "colonialism with the right" had merely been replaced by "colonialism with the Socialists".

Rally for the Republic
Rassemblement pour la République (RPR)

Address. 9-11 rue Franklin Roosevelt, Cayenne, French Guiana
Leadership. Paulin Bruné (pres.); Paul Rullier (s.g.)
Founded. 1946
History. The RPR, which has been consistently well represented in the department's *conseil général*, provided French Guiana's deputy in the French National Assembly until 1981. It contested the February 1983 election to the new French Guiana Assembly in an alliance with the Union for French Democracy (UDF) and other moderates, which won 13 (of the 31) seats. The alliance subsequently formed the opposition in the Assembly.
Orientation. The RPR is part of the (Gaullist) RPR in France and supports the retention of Guiana's departmental status.
Publications. *Objectifs Guyanes*

Union for French Democracy
Union pour la Démocratie Française (UDF)

Leadership. Serge Patient (l.)
Founded. 1979
History. Established as a branch of the metropolitan UDF, this party absorbed two earlier groups, the *Rassemblement pour la Défense de Guyane* and the *Mouvement pour le Progrès Guyanais* (MPG). The UDF contested the February 1983 elections as part of an alliance with the Rally for the Republic (RPR) and other centre-right moderates, which obtained 13 seats in the new departmental Assembly, and which subsequently formed the opposition in that House.
Orientation. The UDF stands for the retention of French Guiana's status as part of France, but with increased decentralization.

1983 Electoral Lists

For the elections to the new 31-member Assembly held on Feb. 20, 1983, the French Guiana parties presented lists as follows:

Guiana First, Union Yes
Guyane d'Abord, Union d'Accord
Led by Paulin Bruné, this list of the (Gaullist) Rally for the Republic (RPR), the (centrist) Union for French Democracy (UDF) and other "moderate" centre-right candidates obtained 40.1 per cent of the vote and 13 seats.

List for a Real and Democratic Decentralization in Guiana
Liste pour une Décentralisation Vraie et Démocratique en Guyane
This list of Socialist and other pro-autonomy leftists, led by Elie Castor, obtained 41.2 per cent and 14 seats. It subsequently became the leading component of a left-wing coalition administration.

List of Social-Professionals
Liste des Sociaux-Professionels
Led by Jean-Pierre Prévôt, this list of moderate independents obtained 4.4 per cent and no seats.

List of Workers of Guiana
Liste des Travailleurs de Guyane
Presented by the (independent) *Union des Travailleurs de Guyane* (UTG) and led by Guy Lamaze, this list obtained 8.9 per cent and three seats. The formation subsequently joined a left-wing coalition administration.

Union, Democracy, Promotion—Guiana
Union, Démocratie, Promotion—Guyane
This list of moderate leftists led by Jean-Serge Gérante secured 5.4 per cent and one seat. Its leader subsequently became a member of a left-wing coalition administration.

Guadeloupe

Capital: Pointe-à-Pitre   Pop. 328,400

Guadeloupe, one of the Windward Islands in the Caribbean, is a French overseas department with the status of a region. It has a 36-member *conseil général* and a 41-member Assembly. It has three representatives in the French National Assembly and two in the French Senate. In the first elections to the new departmental Assembly on Feb. 20, 1983, the centre-right list won 21 of the 41 seats, the Communist-led list 11 and the local Socialists 9.

Communist Party of Guadeloupe
Parti Communiste de Guadeloupe (PCG)

Address. 119 rue Vatable, 97110 Pointe-à-Pitre, Guadeloupe

Leadership. Guy Daninthe (s.g.)

Founded. 1944

History. Founded as a federation of the French Communist Party, the PCG was in 1955 reorganized as an autonomous party, independent of the metropolitan party. The PCG strongly supported departmental status for Guadeloupe and later advocated increased internal autonomy, but not full independence. It has become the strongest party of the left in Guadeloupe, securing generally about 45 per cent of the vote and holding the posts of mayor in the principal towns (Basse-Terre and Pointe-à-Pitre).

In the 1981 general elections the PCG gained one of the three Guadeloupe seats in the French National Assembly. It contested the February 1983 elections to the new Assembly for Guadeloupe as the leader of an alliance of left-wing forces, the *Union Démocratique et Anti-Colonialiste*, which gained 11 (out of 41) seats.

Orientation. The PCG's aim is to strive for the unity of all anti-colonialist forces and to contribute to the unity of the world communist movement on the basis of Marxist-Leninist principles and "proletarian internationalism". In May 1981 the PCG condemned the use of political violence and reaffirmed its rejection of "independence at any price".

Structure. The PCG has branches at places of work or residence; its supreme organ is a congress (convened every four years) which elects a central committee; the latter in turn elects a political commission, a secretariat and a secretary-general.

Membership. 1,500

Publications. *L'Etincelle* (The Spark)

International affiliations. The PCG is recognized by the Communist parties of the Soviet-bloc countries.

Departmentalist Socialist Movement of Guadeloupe
Mouvement Socialiste Départementaliste Guadeloupéen

Address. Mairie de Morne-à-l'Eau, 97111 Morne-à-l'Eau, Guadeloupe

Leadership. Abdon Saman (s.g.)

History. This formation, which favours the maintenance of full French status, has sought to mount a challenge to the departmental federation of the metropolitan Socialist Party.

Guadeloupe Federation of the Left Radical Movement
Fédération Guadeloupéenne du Mouvement des Radicaux de Gauche

Address. Grand Camp, 97110 Abymes, Guadeloupe

Leadership. Flavien Ferrand (pres.)

History. The Left Radicals have made little impression on the domination of the larger political formations in Guadeloupe.

Guadeloupe Federation of the Rally for the Republic
Fédération Guadeloupéenne du Rassemblement pour la République (RPR)

Address. Mairie d'Anse Bertrand, 97121 Bertrand, Guadeloupe

Leadership. José Moustache (sec.)

History. In the 1981 general elections this federation lost all three seats which it had previously held in the French National Assembly. It contested the February 1983 elections to Guadeloupe's new Assembly in an alliance with the Union for French Democracy and other centrist elements, which gained 21 (out of 41) seats and thereupon formed a ruling bureau (administration) presided over by José Moustache.

Guadeloupe Federation of the Socialist Party
Fédération Guadeloupéenne du Parti Socialiste

Address. Ave. du Général de Gaulle, Cité Jardin du Raizet, 97110 Abymes, Guadeloupe

Leadership. Claude Sully (s.g.)

History. In the 1981 general elections this federation gained one of the three Guadeloupe seats in the French National Assembly. In the 1983 elections to Guadeloupe's new Assembly it gained nine (out of 41) seats, and it thereupon became, after the Communists, the second opposition party in the House.

Guadeloupe Federation of the Union for French Democracy
Fédération Guadeloupéenne de l'Union pour la Démocratie Française (UDF)

History. In the 1981 general elections the departmental UDF gained one of the three Guadeloupe seats in the French National Assembly. It contested the February 1983 elections to the new Assembly for Guadeloupe in alliance with the (Gaullist) Rally for the Republic and other "moderate" elements (as the *Union pour le Développement et le Progrès de la Guadeloupe*), which gained an absolute majority (of 21 out of 41 seats) in the Assembly and which thereupon formed a ruling bureau (administration).

1983 Electoral Lists

Elections on Feb. 20, 1983, for a new 41-member Assembly in Guadeloupe were contested by the following party lists:

Democratic and Anti-Colonialist Union
Union Démocratique et Anti-Colonialiste

Led by Jérôme Cléry, this list of the Communist Party and other autonomist leftist groups secured 22.7 per cent of the vote and 11 seats.

Grouping of the Socialist Party of Guadeloupe
Groupement du Parti Socialiste de la Guadeloupe

This list of independent socialists of the Morne-à-l'Eau region, led by Benoît Chapiteau, obtained 0.8 per cent and no seats.

Guadeloupe Force for Progress
Force Guadeloupéenne du Progrès

Principally containing former Communists, this list led by Andy Léo obtained 2.7 per cent and no seats.

List for a Guadeloupe Rid of Exploitation and Oppression
Liste pour une Guadeloupe Débarrassée de l'Exploitation et de l'Oppression

Led by Gérard Séné, this Trotskyist list secured 1.7 per cent and no seats.

List of the Socialist Party Federation
Liste de la Fédération du Parti Socialiste

Led by Frédéric Jalton, this official Socialist Party list obtained 20.4 per cent and nine seats.

New Horizon for Guadeloupians
Nouvel Horizon pour les Guadeloupéens

This list of Socialist dissidents led by Harry Méry secured 2.7 per cent and no seats.

Union for the Promotion of Guadeloupians in the New Region
Union pour la Promotion des Guadeloupéens dans la Nouvelle Région

Led by Henri Beaujan, this list of independent centrists won 4.4 per cent and no seats.

Union for the Development and Progress of Guadeloupe
Union pour le Développement et le Progrès de la Guadeloupe

Containing Rally for the Republic, Union for French Democracy and other "moderates", this list led by Lucette Michaux-Chévry secured 44.8 per cent and an outright majority of 21 seats, enabling it to form an administration.

Martinique

Capital: Fort-de-France   Pop. 326,500

Martinique is a French overseas department with the status of a region. It has a 36-member *conseil général* and a 41-member Assembly. Martinique also has three representatives in the French National Assembly and two in the French Senate. In the first elections to the new departmental Assembly on Feb. 20, 1983, the left-wing pro-autonomy formations won a narrow aggregate majority of 21 of the 41 seats (Progressive Party of Martinique 12, Socialists 5 and Communists 4) against 20 for a list comprising local sections of the centre-right metropolitan parties.

Communist Party of Martinique
Parti Communiste Martiniquais (PCM)

Leadership. Armand Nicolas (l.)
Founded. 1957
History. The PCM has its origins in a communist movement dating back to 1920 but was not formed as the PCM until 1957. It has been strongly represented in local elected bodies and has dominated the Martinique *Confédération Générale du Travail* (CGT), the main trade union organization.

Although it had decided in 1974 to co-operate with the Progressive and Socialist parties in a permanent committee of the Martinique left, the PCM contested subsequent elections on its own, gaining only four seats in the February 1983 elections to the new departmental Assembly. Thereafter it took part in the formation of the left-wing ruling bureau (administration) of Martinique.

Orientation. The PCM had originally been committed to "popular and demo-cratic autonomy" for Martinique "within the framework of the French Republic", but in April 1980 it opted for a "struggle of national liberation" which would lead to autonomy as a first stage towards eventual independence.

Structure. The PCM has branches throughout the country, based on places of work or of residence. It has a congress, convened every four years, as the party's supreme authority which elects a central committee. The latter in turn elects a political commission, a secretariat and a general secretary.

Publications. *Justice* (national news-paper); *L'Action* (theoretical journal)

International affiliations. The PCM is recognized by the Communist parties of the Soviet-bloc countries.

Martinique Independence Movement
Mouvement Indépendantiste Martiniquais (MIM)/La Parole au Peuple

Leadership. Prof. Albert Marie-Jeanne (l.)
History. The MIM's leader declared in March 1980 that his organization would not take power through election but would use the *conseil général* and the mayors' offices to help the struggle for revolutionary unity in the Caribbean; that it was receiving help from other countries, including Cuba and the Soviet Union; and that its revolutionary means included armed struggle. For the 1981 general elections the MIM called for abstention, but it did take part in the February 1983 elections to the new departmental Assembly, though without gaining any seats.

Orientation. The MIM advocates com-plete independence for Martinique.

Progressive Party of Martinique
Parti Progressiste Martiniquais (PPM)

Leadership. Aimé Césaire (pres.)
Founded. 1936
History. The PPM has its origins in a communist movement dating from 1920. It was formed as a federation of the French

154

Communist Party but re-formed as an independent party in 1957. The party has been strongly represented in local elected bodies, and its leader has been elected mayor of the island's capital and a member of the French National Assembly. In 1974 the PPM joined the Communist and Socialist parties in forming a "permanent committee of the Martinique left".

In the February 1983 elections to the new departmental Assembly the PPM emerged as the strongest of the left-wing (pro-autonomy) parties, with 12 seats, and Aimé Césaire was subsequently elected to lead the new ruling bureau (administration). He called on the people to co-operate in the implementation of the Government's new measures, having earlier (at a February 1982 party congress) secured the exclusion from the PPM leadership of elements favouring a clear commitment to eventual independence for Martinique.

Orientation. On March 22, 1980, A. Césaire was quoted as having stated that "sooner of later" Martinique would be independent. At a congress held in July 1980 the party called for "autonomy for the Martinique nation as a stage in the struggle for independence and self-managing socialism".

Socialist Revolution Group
Groupe Révolution Socialiste (GRS)

Leadership. Gilbert Pago (l.)
History. This Trotskyist group took part in the formation of a permanent committee for struggle against repression by seven left-wing organizations of French Guiana, Guadeloupe and Martinique in December 1980. It contested the February 1983 elections to the new Assembly with its own list but gained no seats.

Other Parties

Departmental sections of metropolitan parties are present in Martinique, as follows:

Rally for the Republic (*Rassemblement pour la République*, RPR), led by Edmond Valcin.

Republican Party (*Parti Républicain*, PR), led by Jean Bally and Joé Sainte-Rose.

Socialist Federation of Martinique (*Fédération Socialiste de la Martinique* FSM), led by Simon Salpétrier.

Union for French Democracy (*Union pour la Démocratie Française*, UDR), led by Roger Lise.

1983 Electoral Lists

In the elections of Feb. 20, 1983, to the new 41-member Martinique Assembly the following party lists presented candidates:

Democratic Rally for the Renewal of Martinique
Rassemblement Démocratique pour le Renouveau de la Martinique
This list of the Progressive Party obtained 27.7 per cent of the vote and 12 seats, as a result of which its leader, Aimé Césaire, was able to form a left-wing coalition administration.

Departmentalist Union
Union Départmentaliste
Led by Michel Renard, this list of the Rally for the Republic, the Union for French Democracy and other "moderates" won 46 per cent and 20 seats.

List of the Communist Party of Martinique
Liste du Parti Communiste Martiniquais
Headed by George Gratiant, this list obtained 9 per cent and four seats, subsequently joining a left-wing coalition administration.

List of the Socialist Federation of Martinique
Liste de la Fédération Socialiste de la Martinique
Headed by Casimir Branglidor, this list obtained 12.3 per cent and five seats, subsequently joining a left-wing coalition administration.

Martinique Independence Movement
Mouvement Indépendantiste Martiniquais (MIM)
Headed by Albert Marie-Jeanne, this list secured 2.9 per cent and no seats.

Unitary List for a Free Martinique without Oppression or Exploitation
Liste Unitaire pour une Martinique Libre sans Oppression ni Exploitation
This pro-independence Trotskyist list led by Gilbert Pago secured 2 per cent and no seats.

Réunion

Capital: St Denis   Pop. 515,800

The island of Réunion is a French overseas department with the status of a region. As such it has a *conseil général* and a 45-member Assembly. It also has three representatives in the French National Assembly and two in the French Senate. In the first elections to the new Assembly on Feb. 20, 1983, the combined centre-right list obtained 18 of the 45 seats, the Réunion Communists 16, the Socialists 6 and "various right" candidates 5.

Association for Réunion as a French Department
Association Réunion Département Français (ARDF)

History. During 1982 this formation organized large demonstrations in protest against the French left-wing Government's proposals for decentralization as they affected Réunion. It was associated with unsuccessful attempts to secure the holding of a referendum on the proposed new Assembly. Members of the ARDF were included in the official list of the (Gaullist) Rally for the Republic and the (centrist) Union for French Democracy for the February 1983 elections to the new Assembly.

Communist Party of Réunion
Parti Communiste Réunionnais (PCR)

Leadership. Paul Vergès (s.g.)
Founded. 1959
History. The PCR was established on the basis of a branch of the French Communist Party. It has promoted united action with Socialists and left-wing Catholics. Paul Vergès was elected to the European Parliament on June 10, 1979. In the elections of Feb. 20, 1983, to the new Assembly for Réunion the PCR came second with 16 seats.
Orientation. The party stands for political autonomy for Réunion within the French Republic, and for the nationalization of the sugar industry, land reform and control over foreign trade. It is opposed to the militarization of the Indian Ocean and the establishment of US, British and other foreign military bases in the region.

In July 1980 the party called for "democratic and popular autonomy for Réunion through the right of self-determination of the people of Réunion".
Structure. The PCR has a congress, a central committee, a political bureau and a secretariat.
Publications. *Témoignages* (party newspaper), 6,000
International affiliations. The PCR is recognized by the Communist parties of the Soviet-bloc countries.

Left Radical Movement
Mouvement des Radicaux de Gauche (MRG)

Address. P.O.B. 991, 97479 Saint-Denis, Réunion
Leadership. Jean Marie Finck (pres.)
Founded. 1977
Orientation. The Réunion MRG stands for independence for the island, with its economy to be separate from, but assisted by, France.

Militant Departmentalist Front
Front Militant Départementaliste (FMD)

Leadership. Jean Fontaine (l.)
Founded. 1981
History. Jean Fontaine was in 1981 re-elected as an unattached (non-party) deputy in the French National Assembly. The FMD was associated with unsuccessful attempts to secure a referendum on the

left-wing Government's proposals for a new Assembly for Réunion. Members of the organization were included in the official centre-right list of the Rally for the Republic and the Union for French Democracy for the February 1983 elections to the new Assembly.

Orientation. The Front's aim is to rally "all the anti-Marxist family" to the cause of maintaining Réunion's French status.

Movement for the Independence of Réunion
Mouvement pour l'Indépendance de la Réunion (MIR)

Founded. November 1981

History. This Movement superseded an earlier *Mouvement pour la Libération de la Réunion* (MPLR) which had in turn its origins in the *Organisation Communiste Marxiste-Léniniste de la Réunion* (OCMLR), a Maoist group formed by defectors from the Communist Party of Réunion and led by Georges Sinamalé.

Orientation. The MIR has declared itself to be a Marxist formation seeking "total sovereignty" for the people of Réunion. It is opposed to the French left-wing Government which it has accused of perpetuating "the existing colonial situation".

Rally for the Republic
Rassemblement pour la République (RPR)

Leadership. Aristide Payet (s.g.)

History. The Gaullist RPR is represented by one of Réunion's three deputies in the French National Assembly (Michel Debré). It contested the February 1983 elections to Réunion's new Assembly on a joint list with the Union for French Democracy and other pro-French candidates, which came first with 18 seats.

Rally of Democrats for the Future of Réunion
Rassemblement des Démocrates pour l'Avenir de la Réunion (Radar)

Address. B.P. 866, 97477 Saint-Denis Cédex, Réunion

Formed. 1981

Orientation. Radar is a centrist formation.

Rally of Socialists and Democrats
Rassemblement des Socialistes et des Démocrates (RSD)

Leadership. Daniel Cadet (s.g.)

History. Daniel Cadet had, in June 1981 as the official candidate of the Socialist Party, unsuccessfully contested one of the three Réunion seats in the French National Assembly. In the February 1983 elections to the new Assembly of Réunion he headed a list styled Rally of Departmentalist Socialists, which gained no seats.

Réunion Federation of the Socialist Party
Parti Socialiste (PS)—Fédération de la Réunion

Leadership. Wilfride Bertile (1.); Jean-Claude Fruteau (s.g.)

History. In June 1981 Wilfride Bertile was elected to one of the three Réunion seats in the French National Assembly. In the February 1983 elections to Réunion's new Assembly the list headed by Bertile came third with six seats.

Orientation. The Réunion PS stands for the retention of the island's departmental status and supports the French left-wing Government.

Union for French Democracy
Union pour la Démocratie Française (UDF)

Leadership. Gilbert Gérard (s.g.)

Founded. 1978

History. The UDF was represented by a deputy in the French National Assembly until 1981, when it lost this seat to a Socialist. It contested the 1983 elections to Réunion's new Assembly on a joint list with the Rally for the Republic and other pro-French candidates, which came first with 18 seats (while a separate pro-UDF list gained five seats).

1983 Electoral Lists

The elections of Feb. 20, 1983, to the new 45-member Assembly for Réunion were contested by the following party lists:

Departmentalist Union for Renewal and Progress
Union Départementaliste pour le Renouveau et le Progrés

Headed by Auguste Legros and containing Rally for the Republic, Union for French Democracy and some militant pro-French candidates, this list obtained 38.8 per cent of the vote and 18 seats.

List for the Solidarity and Development of Réunion
Liste pour la Solidarité et le Développement de la Réunion
This list of the Communist Party headed by Paul Vergès secured 22.7 per cent and 11 seats.

New Union in the Interest of Réunion
Union Nouvelle dans l'Intérêt de la Réunion
Headed by Pierre Lagourgue, this list of centrists took 10.5 per cent and five seats.

Rally of Departmentalist Socialists
Rassemblement des Socialistes Départementalistes
Containing former members of the Réunion Socialist Party and other moderate leftists,

this list led by Daniel Cadet got 2.1 per cent and no seats.

Rally of Popular Forces for the Support of the Action of the President of the Republic and for the Development of Réunion
Rassemblement des Forces Populaires pour le Soutien à l'Action du Président de la République et pour le Développement de la Réunion
This list of Socialist dissidents headed by Jean-Max Nativel obtained 2.9 per cent and no seats.

Union for a Majority for Development
Union pour une Majorité de Développement
This list of the Réunion Socialist Party was headed by Wilfride Bertile and secured 13 per cent and six seats.

St Pierre and Miquelon

Capital: Saint-Pierre   Pop. 6,000

St. Pierre and Miquelon, two islands off the coast of Newfoundland (Canada), constitute a French overseas department, which has a *conseil général*, whose president is the department's representative in the French Senate. The islands also have a representative in the French National Assembly. The proposed transformation of the islands from an overseas territory into an overseas department, decided upon in 1976, was from August 1977 onwards strongly opposed by the population's elected representatives (in the *conseil général* as well as in the two municipal councils) and by the local trade union; these bodies demanded a special status for the islands, with fiscal and customs arrangements suited to their geographical position. There are no political parties specific to the islands.

In the second ballot of the elections to the French National Assembly held on June 21, 1981, the sitting Socialist-backed deputy, Albert Pen, was re-elected. In elections to the islands' *conseil général*, held in March 1982, a predominantly Socialist list headed by Albert Pen won all 14 seats unopposed on a platform of opposition to the islands' departmental status, and the councillors thereupon exerted pressure on the metropolitan Government to return the islands to territorial status.

French Overseas Territories

French Polynesia

Capital: Papeete, Tahiti   Pop. 149,000

French Polynesia is a French overseas territory whose Council of Government is presided over by a French High Commissioner and also comprises a Vice-President and six councillors elected by the 30-member territorial Assembly, itself elected every five years by French citizens above the age of 18 years on the basis of proportional representation in five electoral divisions. The territory is represented by two deputies in the French National Assembly and by one senator.

In the elections to the French National Assembly on June 21, 1981, one deputy of the (Gaullist) Rally for the Republic (RPR) and one affiliated to the (centrist) Union for French Democracy (UDR) were re-elected. In elections to the territorial Assembly held on May 23, 1982, parties gained seats as follows: RPR (*Tahoeraa Huiraatira*) 13, *Pupu Here Aia* 6, New Land (*Aia Api*) 3, *Ia Mana Te Nunaa* 3, *Taatira Polynesia* 1, United Front Party 1, others 3.

Ia Mana Te Nunaa

Address. B.P. 1223, Papeete, Tahiti, French Polynesia
Leadership. Jacques Drollet (s.g.)
Founded. 1976
History. The party has remained a minority group supporting the autonomist parties; it is recognised as a "fraternal party" by the French Socialist Party. In the May 1982 elections it won three seats in the Territorial Assembly.
Orientation. The party stands for "socialist independence" for French Polynesia, to be achieved by non-violent means.
Publications. *Te Ve'a Hepetoma* (weekly); *Ia Mana* (monthly)

Liberal Rally
Rassemblement des Libéraux/Pupu Taina

Address. B.P. 169, rue Cook, Papeete, Tahiti, French Polynesia
Leadership. Michel Law (l. and pres.)
Founded. October 1976
History. The party was established by moderate and liberal persons wishing to serve in public affairs. Its leader was elected to the territorial Assembly in May 1977.

Orientation. The party stands for the continued status of Polynesia as part of France, a free economic system directed towards economic and social progress, the development of local abilities, the building of a new society in Polynesia with the support of its different cultures, and the combating of all forms of oppression and discrimination. It is orientated towards the metropolitan Union for French Democracy (UDF).

New Land
Aia Api

Leadership. Emile Vernaudon (l.)
Founded. 1982
History. This party broke away from the United Front Party (*Te Eaa Pi*) and was briefly part of a coalition administration with the Rally for the Republic in June-September 1982, having won three seats in the May 1982 elections to the territorial Assembly.

Polynesian Socialist Party
Parti Socialiste Polynésien (PSP)

Leadership. Paul Koury (l.)
Founded. 1981

History. This party was established in order to support the newly-elected left-wing metropolitan Government. It failed to gain any seats in the May 1982 elections to the territorial Assembly.

Pupu Here Aia

Leadership. John Téariki (pres.)
Founded. 1965
History. In the 1967 elections to the 30-member territorial Assembly the party gained seven seats, thus giving the Assembly (in which the United Front Party had won 10 seats) an autonomist majority, which was, however, lost in 1972. In the 1977 elections the party was part of the United Front for Internal Autonomy (FUAI), of whose 14 seats it obtained nine—but it retained its separate identity. The territory was thereupon given increased autonomy.

In the 1981 general elections to the French National Assembly one of the party's leading members, Jean Juventin, was re-elected to one of the two French Polynesia seats. In the May 1982 elections the party gained six seats in the territorial Assembly, and in September 1982 it joined a coalition administration led by the Rally for the Republic.
Orientation. The party stands for an orderly transition to independence.
Membership. 7,000

Rally for the Republic
Rassemblement pour la République (RPR)/ Tahoeraa Huiraatira

Address. B.P. 471, Papeete, Tahiti, French Polynesia
Leadership. Gaston Flosse (pres.); Patrick Peaucellier (s.g.)
Founded. December 1977
History. The party was established as the Polynesian section of the metropolitan RPR and continued the policies of the parties opposed to increased autonomy for French Polynesia. From its foundation until 1982 it was a minority in the territorial Assembly, but in the June 1979 elections to the European Parliament the RPR obtained the largest share of the vote (44.7 per cent) in the territory.

In elections to the territorial Assembly held in May 1982 the party won about 30 per cent of the vote and 13 seats and, with the help of independent allies, it gained control of 18 of the Assembly's 30 seats. It thereupon formed a Government which

was led by Gaston Flosse and which took six of the seven portfolios. In the French National Assembly the party is represented by Tutaha Salmon.
Orientation. The party stands for the maintenance of French Polynesia's status as a French overseas territory but works actively for an internal autonomy statute due to enter into force during 1984.

Rally for Independence
Rassemblement pour l'Indépendance

Leadership. Oscar Temaru, Henri Hiro (leaders)
History. This pro-independence party took part in the May 1982 elections to the territorial Assembly but gained no seat.

Social Democratic Movement
Mouvement Social-Démocrate

Leadership. Frantz Vanizette, Maco Tevane (leaders)
History. This party, which had been part of the United Front for Internal Autonomy, contested the May 1982 elections to the territorial Assembly on its own but failed to secure representation.

Taatira Polynesia

Address. B.P. 283, Papeete, Tahiti, French Polynesia
Leadership. Arthur Chung (l.)
Founded. 1976
History. In the May 1982 elections to the territorial Assembly this party obtained one seat.

Te Taata Tahiti Tiama

Leadership. Charlie Ching
Founded. December 1975
History. The party obtained 5.6 per cent of the votes in the legislative elections of 1977. Its leader and founder had in 1972 been convicted of stealing ammunition but had been pardoned in 1975. In 1978–79 the party was accused of being linked to an anti-French terrorist group calling itself *Te Toto Tupana* (The Ancestors' Blood) which was responsible for murder, blackmail and attempted bomb attacks. In February 1979 Charlie Ching was sentenced

to five years in prison for having instigated acts of violence, especially against French military and nuclear installations, but on appeal this verdict was quashed on Dec. 9, 1979. No party activities have been reported since.

Orientation. The party has stood for complete independence for French Polynesia.

United Front Party
Te Eaa Pi

Leadership. Francis Sanford (l.)
History. In elections to the territorial Assembly in 1967 the party gained 10 out of 30 seats, thus emerging as the strongest single group in the Assembly. In the 1972 elections, however, it suffered a reverse, in that the two autonomist parties—the *Te Eaa Pi* and the *Pupu Here Aia*—won only 13 seats between them. Nevertheless, the autonomists remained in power with the help of independents. In the 1977 elections the *Te Eaa Pi* was part of the United Front for Internal Autonomy, but it retained its separate identity. In the 1982 elections it was reduced to one seat in the territorial Assembly.

Orientation. The *Te Eaa Pi* has campaigned for increased autonomy for French Polynesia, failing the achievement of which it would opt for complete independence.

New Caledonia

Capital: Nouméa   Pop. 144,200

New Caledonia is a French overseas territory administered by the French High Commissioner for the Pacific, appointed by the French Government, but with its own Council of Government and a 36-member territorial Assembly elected by universal adult suffrage under a system of proportional representation. In France the territory is represented by two deputies in the National Assembly and by one senator in the Senate.

In elections to the territorial Assembly held on July 1, 1979, only three parties obtained seats, as follows: the (Gaullist) Rally for Caledonia within the Republic (RPCR) 15, Independence Front 14 and Federation for a New Caledonian Society 7. In these elections the parties favouring the maintenance of the territory's French status (with varying degrees of internal autonomy) obtained 65.6 per cent of the total vote. However, of the Melanesians (or Kanaks) making up almost half the population of New Caledonia, some 60 per cent favoured independence for the territory.

In the French National Assembly elections of June 1981 the two sitting deputies were both re-elected—one for the RPCR and the other for a pro-independence opposition alliance.

Caledonian Fraternity
Fraternité Calédonienne

Leadership. Jeannine Bouteille (l.)
Orientation. This organisation is an association of pro-French Melanesians supporting the (anti-independence) Rally for Caledonia within the Republic (see separate entry). It has been active in various campaigns mounted by anti-independence movements to draw attention to the pro-French views of the majority.

Caledonian National Party
Parti National Calédonien (PNC)

Leadership. Georges Chatenet (l.)
Founded. 1981
Orientation. The PNC has called for reconciliation between the territory's ethnic groups and "mutual respect for the dignity of each" as the essential basis for progress towards a "pluri-ethnic" independence. As a pro-independence party the PNC

participates in the Independence Front (see separate entry).

Caledonian Union
Union Calédonienne (UC)

Address. 8 rue Gambetta, 1° Vallée du Tir, Nouméa, New Caledonia

Leadership. Roch Pidjot (pres.); Eloi Machoroi (s.g.)

Founded. 1952

History. The party was formed after Maurice Lenormand had become the first Melanesian to be elected to the French National Assembly. As the representative of the Melanesian people, supported by Whites, in particular from the trade union movement, the party propagated the idea of "two colours, one people".

Until 1972 the party was in a majority and in government; it later became the strongest opposition party, gaining nine seats in the territorial Assembly in 1977. Its leader (Roch Pidjot) has since 1964 repeatedly been elected to represent the territory in the French National Assembly and in 1979 became leader of the Independence Front (see separate entry).

The assassination of the then secretary-general of the UC, Pierre Declerq, on Sept. 19, 1981, was followed by serious clashes between Melanesians and Europeans. At a congress held on Nov. 12–14, 1981, the party developed plans for creating Melanesian regions as a basis for a unilateral declaration of independence. As a member of the Independence Front the UC was given a post in the pro-independence Government Council formed in June 1982. On Nov. 14 of that year the UC confirmed that it planned to declare the territory independent on Sept. 24, 1984.

Orientation. The party stands for progress for the Melanesians and has demanded internal self-government and, since 1977, independence for New Caledonia. The UC insists that only the indigenous Melanesians' claim to independence is legitimate and that only their views should be taken into account. It rejects the concept of "pluri-ethnic" independence advanced by the Caledonian National Party.

Structure. The party is organized at tribal and urban ward level and has regional committees and an annual congress (which determines the party's political line), a 30-member head committee and a seven-member executive committee.

Membership. 5,000

Publications. *L'Avenir Calédonien*, 3,000

Federation for a New Caledonian Society
Fédération pour une Nouvelle Société Calédonienne (FNSC)

Leadership. Jean-Pierre Aifa (l.)

Founded. 1979

History. The FNSC was formed as a merger of the following organizations: the *Mouvement Wallisien et Futunien* (established in 1979 by Wallis and Futuna islanders working in New Caledonia and led by Einau Melito as president); the *Parti Républicain Calédonien* (established in 1979 and led by Lionel Cherrier, then member of the French Senate); the *Union Démocratique* (founded in 1968 and led by Gaston Morlet); the *Union Jeunesse Calédonienne* (led by Jean-Paul Belhomme); and the *Union Nouvelle Calédonienne* (established in 1977 and led by Jean-Pierre Aifa).

After the July 1979 elections to the territorial Assembly, in which the FNSC had won 7 seats, it entered into a coalition Government Council with the Rally for Caledonia within the Republic (RPCR) in which it held two posts. In June 1982, however, this administration was succeeded by one led by the Independence Front, in which the same two FNSC members held office.

Orientation. The FNSC has advocated internal autonomy and a dialogue between the different population groups with a view to further reforms.

Independence Front
Front Indépendantiste (FI)

Leadership. Roch Pidjot (deputy in the French National Assembly); Jean-Marie Tchibaou (spokesman)

Founded. 1979

History. The FI was formed (in 1979) as an alliance of mainly Melanesian, pro-independence parties, notably the Caledonian Union, which had held nine seats in the territorial Assembly dissolved in May 1979. Later it was also joined by the Caledonian National Party and the Socialist Kanak Liberation.

In the 1979 elections the FI retained 14 seats in the territorial Assembly. It remained in opposition until June 1982 when it formed a Government Council with the (centrist) Federation for a New Caledonian Society (FNSC).

Draft proposals for a new autonomy statute presented by the French Government in March 1983 were strongly criticized by the FI as failing to meet the Melanesian people's aspirations to independence; the FI threatened to withdraw from the institutions of the Republic and to create a "provisional government" which would lead to the "unilateral proclamation of the independence of the Kanak people".

Progressive Melanesian Union
Union Progressiste Mélanésienne (UPM)

Address. p.a. M. André Gopea, Union Progressiste Mélanésienne, Assemblée territoriale, Nouméa, New Caledonia

Leadership. Louis Tamaï (pres.); Néoéré François (s.g.)

Founded. September 1974

History. The party was established as the *Union Progressiste Multiraciale*, which gained one seat in the territorial Assembly in September 1977. It subsequently adopted its present name and, in April 1979, joined (with other Melanesian pro-independence parties) the Independence Front, which in the July 1979 elections obtained 14 (out of the 36) seats in the Assembly, one of them for the UPM.

Orientation. The UPM is opposed to capitalism, neocolonialism and French imperialism. Its aim is the liberation of the Melanesians (Kanaks) and the creation of an independent socialist state, though with the restoration of the organization of Melanesian life under traditional chiefs.

Structure. The UPM has base units, regional committees, an executive bureau, an action committee, a central committee and a congress.

Membership. 2,300

Publications. *Avant Garde* (monthly), 1,000

Rally for Caledonia within the Republic
Rassemblement pour la Calédonie dans la République (RPCR)

Leadership. Jacques Lafleur

Founded. 1977

History. The RPCR was formed as the successor to earlier pro-French formations of conservative orientation. By 1979 it also embraced the following formations: the *Rassemblement pour la Calédonie* (established in 1977 and led by Jacques Lafleur and Roger Laroque); the *Rassemblement pour la République* (established in 1977 and led by Dick Ukeiwé); and the *Mouvement Libéral Calédonien* (founded in 1971 and led by Jean Leques).

After the 1979 elections to the territorial Assembly, in which the RPCR had gained 15 seats, it formed a Government Council with the participation of the (centrist) Federation for a New Caledonian Society (FNSC). However, in June 1982 this Council resigned and was succeeded by one formed under the leadership of the Independence Front.

Orientation. As a predominantly European party the RPCR has advocated departmental (rather than the existing territorial) status for New Caledonia.

Socialist Kanak Liberation
Libération Kanake Socialiste (LKS)

Leadership. Nidoish Naisseline (l.)

History. After the assassination in September 1981 of the then leader of the Caledonian Union (see separate entry), Nidoish Naisseline declared that his group would continue the struggle for independence until final victory, and he alleged that "fascist groups" were threatening the lives of elected pro-independence representatives. On Nov. 10, 1981, the LKS put demands to the French High Commissioner for initiating the process of decolonization, the dissolution of extreme right-wing movements and the requisition of all weapons.

The LKS subsequently supported the theses of the Caledonian National Party (see separate entry) and criticized the Caledonian Union's preparations for establishing Melanesian regions without knowing what was to be done with the land in these regions. As a member of the Independence Front, the LKS was given a post in the Government Council formed in June 1982.

Socialist Party of New Caledonia
Parti Socialiste de la Nouvelle Calédonie (PSNC)

Founded. 1981

History. The PSNC was launched as in effect an attempt to create a New Caledonian section of the metropolitan Socialist Party. However, at the inaugural congress of the party (on Oct. 21, 1981) delegates were divided over the independence issue. A minority favoured a clear commitment to independence and announced their intention to form a separate party, while the majority expressed preference for the structural reforms proposed by the new left-wing French Government.

Early in November 1981 the party condemned "all acts of violence no matter from which side". At a second congress held on Oct. 23, 1982, the PSNC, while expressing support for the Government's policy, criticized it for remaining silent on the future status of New Caledonia.

Union for French Democracy
Union pour la Démocratie Française (UDF)

History. The UDF in New Caledonia was formed in 1978 out of the *Entente Toutes Ethnies* (ETE), a group with Christian Democratic tendencies. In the 1979 elections it contested only the Loyauté Islands constituency.

Orientation. The UDF is part of the centre group of parties favouring internal self-government within the context of New Caledonia's continuation as a French overseas territory.

Wallis and Futuna Islands

Capital: Mata Utu   Pop. 10,900

These islands in the Pacific Ocean (north of Fiji and west of Samoa) are a French overseas territory with a Government under a French administrator and an elected territorial Assembly. The islands have one representative in the French National Assembly and one in the French Senate.

In the first ballot of the general elections held for the French National Assembly in June 1981, the islands' deputy—of the (Gaullist) Rally for the Republic (RPR)—was re-elected.

Elections to the 20-member territorial Assembly held on March 21, 1982, gave 11 seats to a list headed by the RPR's deputy in the French National Assembly (Benjamin Brial) and nine to candidates of the (centrist) Union for French Democracy (UDF) and associated lists.

Mayotte

Capital: Dzaoudzi   Pop. 52,000

Mayotte, one of the four main islands of the Comoros, has a special status equivalent to that of a French overseas territory, with a view to the later granting of the status of overseas department.

The island has one deputy in the French National Assembly and one member in the French Senate. In the elections of June 1981 a member of the Mayotte People's Movement (Jean-François Hory) was elected deputy under the designation of *Rassemblement Socialiste Mahorais*, but the French Socialist Party denied having given any support to him (or to any other candidate).

Mayotte Democratic Union
Union Démocratique Mahoraise

Leadership. Maoulida Ahmed (l.)
History. This centrist formation has sought, unsuccessfully so far, to challenge the political dominance of the Mayotte People's Movement (see separate entry).

Mayotte People's Movement
Mouvement Populaire Mahorais (MPM)

Leadership. Younoussa Bamana (l.)
History. Younoussa Bamana was the deputy for Mayotte in the French National Assembly until 1981. On Dec. 6, 1979, he voted against a five-year extension of Mayotte's special status and demanded instead full departmental status for the island.
Orientation. The MPM has been the principal party standing for Mayotte's continued exclusion from the Federal and Islamic Republic of the Comoros and aspiring to French departmental status for the island.

Mayotte Rally for the Republic
Rassemblement Mahorais pour la République (RMPR)

Leadership. Abdoul Anzizi (l.)
Orientation. The RMPR is the Mayotte branch of the metropolitan (Gaullist) RPR.

Party for the Democratic Rally of the People of Mayotte
Parti pour le Rassemblement Démocratique des Mahorais

Founded. 1978
Orientation. This party seeks Mayotte's unification with the Comoros.

Gabon

Capital: Libreville   Pop. 1,100,000

The Gabonese Republic has an executive President who is elected for a seven-year term by universal adult suffrage and who is head of state and of the Government, presiding over a Cabinet under a Prime Minister. There is a National Assembly, to which 84 members are elected also for a seven-year term by universal adult suffrage of Gabonese and foreign nationals over 21 years old, with all candidates being members of the Gabonese Democratic Party (*Parti Démocratique Gabonais*, PDG). President Omar Bongo was on Dec. 30, 1979, re-elected with 99.85 per cent of the votes cast (as officially announced), and in February 1980 a total of 84 PDG candidates were elected to the National Assembly and another nine were nominated by the President. The Government has resisted demands from some opposition quarters for the ending of Gabon's one-party system.

Gabonese Democratic Party
Parti Démocratique Gabonais (PDG)

Leadership. President Omar Bongo (s.g.): Léon Mebiame (dep. s.g.)
Founded. 1968
History. The party was set up by President Bongo, in succession to the *Bloc Démocratique Gabonais*, as the country's sole political organization in order to "guarantee national unity and the abolition of ethnic discrimination".

Through the years of PDG rule Gabon has remained one of the most stable Black African countries, although in the early 1980s opposition to President Bongo, particularly among students, coalesced around the Movement for National Renewal (Morena), which called for the creation of a second political party. The

President responded by insisting that Gabon was a one-party state.

Structure. The PDG has a congress, which is its supreme organ, a 211-member central committee, and a 27-member political bureau which has powers to issue decrees with the force of law. The secretary-general has powers to call on the Deputy Prime Ministers and other high-ranking officials as well as political commissioners to attend meetings of the political bureau in a consultative capacity.

Publications. *Dialogue* (monthly), 3,000

The Gambia

Capital: Banjul   Pop. 610,000

The Republic of The Gambia, a member of the Commonwealth, has a President who is elected by direct universal adult suffrage (of citizens above the age of 21 years) and is head of state as well as of government. There is a House of Representatives with 35 elective seats and eight other seats filled by four nominated members and four head chiefs (elected by the country's Chiefs in Assembly). Both the President and the House of Representatives are elected for five-year terms. As a result of elections held on May 4-5, 1982, the elective seats in the House of Representatives were distributed as follows: People's Progressive Party (PPP) 27, National Convention Party 3, independents 5 (who were former PPP adherents not nominated by that party).

On Feb. 1, 1982, The Gambia joined the Republic of Senegal in a Confederation of Senegambia, in which both states retained their independence and sovereignty, but agreed on the integration of their armed forces and security forces, economic and monetary union, and co-ordination in the fields of external relations, communications and other fields in which the confederal state might agree to exercise joint jurisdiction. The Confederation has a President (the President of Senegal), a Vice-President (the President of The Gambia), a Council of Ministers and a Confederal Assembly (one-third of its members chosen by the Gambian House of Representatives and two-thirds by Senegal's National Assembly).

National Convention Party (NCP)

Address. 4 Fitzgerald Street, Banjul, The Gambia

Leadership. Sherif Mustafa Dibba (l. and g.s.); Arfang Bakary Bojang (nat. ch.)

Founded. September 1975

History. In general elections held in April 1977 the party won five of the 35 elective seats in Parliament, and in a by-election necessitated by the death of one of its members the party held the seat concerned with an increased majority in June 1978. In local elections in April 1979 the party won 18 out of 54 contested seats, gaining 40 per cent of the votes cast.

Following an attempted coup in July 1981 Sherif Mustafa Dibba was accused of having been involved. He denied this in September 1981, stating that the plotters had tried to impose a Marxist-Leninist régime on the people of The Gambia which would "destroy our democratic institutions and liberty". He conducted his 1982 election campaign from prison but lost his seat in the House of Representatives, where his party's strength was reduced to three members.

Orientation. The party works for "a more just society where the resources of the nation shall be more equitably distributed among its citizens".

Structure. The party has branch committees at village, constituency and regional level, a national political bureau, a national executive committee and a national convention (which meets every two years).

Membership. 50,000

People's Progressive Party (PPP)

Leadership. President Sir Dawda K. Jawara

Founded. 1958

History. The PPP has governed The Gambia since 1962, when internal self-government was introduced (followed by full independence in 1965). It merged with the Congress Party in 1967, and it was instrumental in having the 1970 republican Constitution adopted.

The PPP régime has remained in the ascendancy in recent years, although a number of opposition groups, both legal and clandestine, have made their existence known. In July 1981 the Government survived an attempted coup by left-wing elements, who were put down with the assistance of Senegalese troops.

Orientation. As a moderate party, the PPP favours the maintenance of The Gambia's membership of the Commonwealth and has been instrumental in implementing its policy of entering into a confederation with Senegal, for which it sought, and claimed to have obtained, a mandate in the 1982 elections.

International affiliations. Socialist Interafrican

United Party (UP)

Address. P.O. Box 63, Banjul, The Gambia

Leadership. Pierre Sarr N'Jie (l.)

Founded. 1952

History. The UP was the government party until the introduction of internal self-government in 1962, when it gained only 13 of the 32 elective seats in the Legislative Council against 18 won by the People's Progressive Party (PPP). In the 1970 elections its strength was reduced to eight seats (against 24 won by the PPP), and it further declined to three seats in 1972, and one in 1977. The UP was opposed to the adoption of a republican Constitution which, it felt, would increase the power of the ruling PPP, and also to close association with Senegal (i.e. to the creation of the Confederation of Senegambia as agreed by the respective Governments in February 1982).

Although by 1982 the UP no longer existed as an organized party the general elections of that year were contested by three candidates who stood in its name in Banjul, where they were supported by the National Convention Party (which did not nominate candidates for these seats).

German Democratic Republic

Capital: East Berlin   Pop. 17,000,000

Under a Constitution adopted in 1968 the "supreme organ of state power" in the German Democratic Republic (GDR) is the unicameral Parliament (People's Chamber or *Volkskammer*) of 500 seats filled by members of the (Communist) Socialist Unity Party (SED), as well as by members of four other parties and of mass organizations. The *Volkskammer* elects a Council of State (whose Chairman is in effect the head of state) and a Council of Ministers (Cabinet). Real power, however, is held by the Politburo of the Central Committee of the SED.

The 500 members of the *Volkskammer*, who serve a five-year term, are elected by universal adult suffrage (of citizens over the age of 18 years) in the country's 14 districts and East Berlin under a simple majority system, where each elector votes for as many candidates as there are seats in the constituency, by crossing out from a single list the names of those candidates whom he does not favour. All candidates are nominated by the National Front of Democratic Germany, an organization under the leadership of the SED and embracing also four other parties as well as mass organizations.

The 500 seats in the *Volkskammer* are distributed as follows: SED 127, Christian Democratic Union 52, Liberal Democratic Party 52, National Democratic Party of Germany 52, Democratic Farmers' Party of Germany 52 and mass organizations 165 (including 60 for the Free German Trade Union

Federation). While the SED has been in overall control, the four other parties have since 1949 also been represented in successive Councils of Ministers.

In elections held on June 14, 1981, the percentage of valid votes cast for the National Front candidates was officially given as 99.86 (and the percentage poll as 99.21). An additional 179 candidates were elected to reserve lists.

Christian Democratic Union of Germany
Christlich-Demokratische Union Deutschlands (CDU)

Address. 108 Berlin, Otto-Nuschke-Strasse 59/60, GDR
Leadership. Gerald Götting (ch.)
Founded. 1945
History. The party was set up as the CDU of the Soviet zone of post-war Germany, and in the first elections held in that zone in September 1946 it came second (after the SED) in Brandenburg and Mecklenburg and third (after the SED and the LDP) in the two Saxonies and Thuringia. In the provisional *Volkskammer* of the German Democratic Republic (proclaimed in October 1949), elected as a German People's Council in May 1949, the CDU had been allotted 45 seats. It now holds 52 seats in the *Volkskammer*.
Orientation. The CDU describes itself as a party of Christian citizens of the GDR and a party of peace, democracy and socialism, and its characteristics as "loyalty to socialism, friendly co-operation with the working-class party (SED) and firm friendship with the Soviet Union".
Structure. The party has local committees, district and county executive committees and a national executive of 128 members. Delegates' conferences are held at district and county levels, and a party congress at national level every five years.
Membership. 125,000
Publications. *Neue Zeit* (Berlin, daily), 93,000; and five other daily newspapers

Democratic Farmers' Party of Germany
Demokratische Bauernpartei Deutschlands (DBD)

Address. 108 Berlin, Behrensstr. 47-48, GDR
Leadership. Ernst Goldenbaum (ch.)
Founded. June 1948
History. The DBD was established to protect the interests of (mainly small) farmers. In the German People's Council, which was elected in May 1949 and which, on the establishment of the GDR in October 1949, became the provisional *Volkskammer*, the DBD was given 15 seats. It now holds 52 seats.
Membership. 92,000
Publications. *Bauern-Echo* (Berlin, daily organ), 90,000

Liberal Democratic Party of Germany
Liberal-Demokratische Partei Deutschlands (LDPD)

Address. 108 Berlin, Johannes-Dieckmann-Strasse 48-49, GDR
Leadership. Dr Manfred Gerlach (ch.)
Founded. 1945
History. In the first election after World War II, held in the then Soviet zone in September 1946, the LDPD came second (after the SED) in both Saxonies and Thuringia and third (after the SED and the CDU) in Brandenburg and Mecklenburg. In the German People's Council elected in May 1949 and proclaimed the provisional *Volkskammer* of the newly established GDR in October 1949, the LDPD was given 45 seats. It now holds 52 seats in the *Volkskammer*.
Publications. *Der Morgen* (Berlin, daily organ), 52,000; *Liberal-Demokratische Zeitung* (Halle, daily), 56,000

National Democratic Party of Germany
National-Demokratische Partei Deutschlands (NDPD)

Address. 108 Berlin, Friedrichstr. 65, GDR
Leadership. Prof. Heinrich Homann (ch.)
Founded. June 1948
History. On its foundation the party appealed for the support of the lower middle class, including former followers of the Nazi Party. In the German People's Council elected in May 1949 and proclaimed the provisional *Volkskammer* of the newly established GDR, the NDPD

was in October 1949 given 15 seats. It now holds 52 seats in the *Volkskammer*

Orientation. Nationalist, in opposition to "monopolistic capital".

Publications. *National-Zeitung* (Berlin, daily), 55,000; and four other daily newspapers

---

Socialist Unity Party of Germany
Sozialistische Einheitspartei Deutschlands (SED)

Address. Am Marx-Engels-Platz 2, 1020 Berlin, German Democratic Republic

Leadership. Erich Honecker (g.s. of central committee); Hermann Axen, Horst Dohlus, Werner Felfe, Herbert Häber, Kurt Hager, Joachim Herrmann, Gen. Heinz Hoffmann, Werner Jarowinsky, Günter Kleiber, Werner Krolikowski, Erich Mielke, Günter Mittag, Erich Mückenberger, Konrad Naumann, Alfred Neumann, Günter Schabowsky, Horst Sindermann, Willi Stoph, Harry Tisch (other politburo members); Egon Krenz, Ingeburg Lange, Margarete Müller, Gerhard Schürer, Werner Walde (candidate members of politburo)

Founded. April 1946

History. The SED was formed after a congress of the Communist Party of Germany (KPD, founded in December 1918) and a congress of the Social Democratic Party (SPD) had decided in East Berlin (despite objections by a section of the SPD) to join forces in one party. In the first elections held in the then Soviet zone in September 1946 the SED obtained an overall majority. In elections for a "People's Congress" held in May 1949, a list drawn up by a "People's Council" (dominated by the SED) and comprising representatives of the SED and the four other parties of the zone obtained 66.1 per cent of the votes cast. In a German People's Council, elected by the People's Congress, the SED held 90 seats (out of 320). Since the establishment of the German Democratic Republic in 1949 the SED has, as the dominating partner in the National Front, held at least one-quarter of the seats in the *Volkskammer*.

Orientation. The SED is a "Marxist-Leninist" party and "the class-conscious and organized vanguard of the working class and all working people", and it is engaged in "shaping the developed socialist society".

Structure. Based on the principle of democratic centralism, the party is organized in primary organizations in enterprises and in urban and rural communities, with party meetings held at least once a month, and in town, city, district and territorial organizations. The party's supreme authority is its congress, convened every five years as a rule; it lays down the party's general line, defines its tactics and elects a central committee and a central auditing commission.

The central committee elects its general secretary, a politburo for political leadership and a secretariat for current affairs, as well as the party's general secretary.

Membership. 2,155,000

Publications. *Neues Deutschland* (central committee organ, daily), 1,090,000; *Berliner Zeitung* (daily), 328,000; and 14 daily district newspapers; *Einheit* (monthly journal on theory and practice), 245,000; *Neuer Weg* (journal for party life, twice a month), 205,000

Federal Republic of Germany

Capital: Bonn   Pop. 61,770,000

The Federal Republic of Germany is, under its Basic Law (or Constitution) of 1949, "a democratic and social federal state" whose organs are (i) the Federal Diet (*Bundestag*) elected for a four-year term in universal, direct, free, equal and secret elections by citizens over the age of 18 years; (ii) the Federal Council (*Bundesrat*) consisting of 45 members of the Governments of the Republic's 10 *Länder* (constituent states) and of West Berlin; (iii) the Federal President (*Bundespräsident*) elected for a five-year term by the Federal Assembly (*Bundesversammlung*), comprising the *Bundestag* members and an equal number of delegates nominated by the *Länder* parliaments; and (iv) the Federal Government consisting of the Federal Chancellor elected by the *Bundestag* on the proposal of the Federal President.

The *Bundestag* normally has 518 members, of whom 248 are elected by simple majority vote in single-member constituencies; another 248 are elected by proportional representation from party lists for each *Land*; and 22 are nominated by the House of Representatives of West Berlin (in proportion to the strengths of the parliamentary parties represented in it) but have no voting rights in the *Bundestag*. (Each elector has two votes—one for a direct vote for one of the 248 seats to be filled by direct vote in constituencies and another for the 248 seats to be filled from party lists, the candidates being chosen in the order in which their names appear on their party's list except for those already elected in a constituency.)

In order to qualify for representation in the *Bundestag* a party must gain at least 5 per cent of the total national votes cast or secure the election of at least three of its candidates by votes in the constituencies.

Under an Act of July 24, 1967, parties are defined as being a constitutionally necessary element of a free democratic order and as contributing to the formation of the national political will, inter alia by influencing public opinion, by encouraging public participation in political life and by training citizens for the assumption of public office. State subsidies are granted to all parties which obtain 0.5 per cent of the vote or more, in proportion to the number of votes which they obtain (recently at the rate of DM 3.50 or about US$1.20 per vote).

Elections to the *Bundestag* on March 6, 1983 (after which the number of elective seats was increased by two because of numerical anomalies in their distribution), resulted in the following party strengths: Social Democratic Party (SPD) 193, Christian Democratic Union (CDU) 191, Christian Social Union (CSU) 53, Free Democratic Party (FDP) 34, Green Party 27.

Each of the 10 *Länder* has its own *Landtag* (or *Bürgerschaft* in Hamburg and Bremen) normally elected for a four-year term and in which parties hold seats as follows (with the date of election shown in parentheses):

Baden-Württemberg. (March 25, 1984)—CDU 68, SPD 41, Green Party 9, FDP 8

Bavaria. (Oct. 10, 1982)—CSU 133, SPD 77

Bremen. (Sept. 25, 1983)—SPD 58, CDU 37, Green Party 5

Hamburg. (Dec. 19, 1982)—SPD 64, CDU 48, Green Alternative List 8

Hesse. (Sept. 25, 1983)—SPD 51, CDU 44, FDP 8, Green Party 7
Lower Saxony. (March 21, 1982)—CDU 87, SPD 63, Green Party 11, FDP 10
North Rhine-Westphalia. (May 11, 1980)—SPD 106, CDU 95
Rhineland-Palatinate. (March 6, 1983)—CDU 57, SPD 43
Saarland. (April 27, 1980)—SPD 24, CDU 23, FDP 4
Schleswig-Holstein. (March 13, 1983)—CDU 39, SPD 34, South Schleswig Electoral Union 1.

In *West Berlin*, which is not a constituent part of the Federal Republic, elections to the House of Representatives held on May 10, 1981, resulted in the following distribution of seats: CDU 65, SPD 51, Greens 9, FDP 7.

Bavaria Party
Bayernpartei (BP)

Address. Untere Weidenstr. 14, 8000 München 40, Federal Republic of Germany
Leadership. Max Zierl (ch.); Paul Herbert Schröeter (s.g.)
Founded. October 1946
History. The BP held 17 seats in the *Bundestag* in 1949–53 but has since failed to obtain the required 5 per cent minimum of the total vote. In the Bavarian *Landtag* the BP obtained 39 seats in 1950 and 28 in 1954, whereafter it took part in a four-party coalition *Land* Government, including Social Democrats, until October 1977. Following defections to the Christian Social Union, the BP's representation in the Bavarian *Landtag* was reduced to 14 in 1958 and to eight in 1962. Since 1966 the BP has not been represented in the *Landtag* because it has failed to obtain the required 10 per cent minimum of the vote in any one of Bavaria's seven electoral districts. It had some success in local elections in 1978, however, when it gained nine seats.
Orientation. The party's aim is to restore an independent Bavarian state (with the inclusion of the Palatinate, part of the *Land* of Rhineland-Palatinate) to form part of a German confederation within a United States of Europe based on equal rights for all European states. It stands for the preservation of the characteristics of the Bavarian people and their Christian faith.
Structure. The party is organized in eight districts as well as at sub-district and local level.
Membership. 3,200
Publications. *Bayernreport*

Bavarian State Party
Bayerische Staatspartei (BSP)

Address. 8400 Regensburg, Marschallstr. 4, Federal Republic of Germany

Leadership. Arthur Kreuzer (ch.); Gerhard Huber (g.s.)
Founded. September 1967
History. Since 1969 the BSP has taken part in local elections and also in elections to the *Landtag* of Bavaria (in that of 1970 in an alliance with the *Europapartei*), but has never gained more than 0.2 per cent of the vote. It has boycotted all *Bundestag* elections.
Orientation. The BSP stands for federalism, increased rights for Bavaria and a federal united Europe of regions (in which Bavaria, Catalonia, Wales and Scotland would be regions). The party has called for a referendum on the stationing in Germany of new US nuclear weapons, which it opposes.
Structure. The party is organized at local level and has seven district and three regional federations.
Membership. 3,000
Publications. *Föderalistische Alternative*, 3,000-4,000; *Bayerische Freiheit* (quarterly)
International affiliations. The BSP is the Bavaria Section of the European Federalist Party (as which it takes part in elections to the European Parliament).

Christian Bavarian People's Party—Movement of Bavarian Patriots
Christliche Bayerische Volkspartei—Bayerische Patriotenbewegung (CBV)

Address. c/o L. Volkholz, 8491 Grafenwiesen, Fessmannsdorf 36, Federal Republic of Germany
Leadership. Ludwig Volkholz (ch.)
Founded. October 1977
Orientation. The party advocates the establishment of a "free democratic European government" to be based on Christian brotherliness, the peaceful solution of conflicts and equal rights for all population groups and political opinions, as well as direct election of a Bavarian

state president and abolition of the 5 per cent barrier against parliamentary representation.

Christian Democratic Union
Christlich-Demokratische Union (CDU)

Address. Konrad-Adenauer-Haus, Friedrich-Ebert-Allee 73-75, D-5300, Bonn 1, Federal Republic of Germany
Leadership. Dr Helmut Kohl (ch.); Dr Heiner Geissler (s.g.); Dr K. G. Kiesinger (hon. ch.)
Founded. October 1950
History. The party was formed out of autonomous groups of Christian Democrats established in all parts of Germany in the autumn of 1945, partly by members of anti-Hitler resistance circles. In the first *Länder* elections held in West Germany in 1947 these groups emerged as the strongest or second strongest parties, and in the elections to the first *Bundestag* in August 1949, which the Christian Democrats contested as one party with the Christian Social Union (CSU) of Bavaria, the Christian Democrats became the strongest party.

Thereafter the Christian Democrats were in power until 1969—in coalition mainly with the Free Democratic Party (FDP) until 1957, when the Christian Democrats gained an absolute majority in the *Bundestag*, and again in coalition with the Free Democrats from 1961 to 1966, whereafter Christian Democrats and Social Democrats formed a grand coalition. The CDU leader, Dr Konrad Adenauer, was the first West German Federal Chancellor from 1949 to 1963. From 1969 the CDU was in opposition, although the CDU/CSU continued to form the largest contingent in the *Bundestag*.

In October 1982 the CDU returned to office (in coalition with the CSU and the FDP). At that time it also was in office in the *Land* Governments of Baden-Württemberg, Lower Saxony, North Rhine-Westphalia, Rhineland-Palatinate, Saarland (with the FDP) and Schleswig-Holstein, and also in West Berlin (with FDP support).
Orientation. The CDU regards itself as a "broadly-based classless party amalgamating traditions of Christian social thinking, liberalism and moderate conservatism". The party stand for "the solution of social conflicts within the framework of a free and social order based on the concept of a social market economy"; it is "dedicated to a policy of peace in a free world community"; and its main foreign policy objectives are "the preservation of peace in freedom; the reunification of Germany; political union of a free Europe; a joint Western security policy in the framework of NATO; close relations with the United States; and a constructive approach to the problems of developing countries in the framework of a world-wide free-market system". It has strongly supported the NATO decision on the deployment of new US nuclear missiles in Western Europe.
Structure. The CDU consists of the federal party and 13 *Länder* parties, with 269 district associations. There are a national party congress, a national committee and a national executive committee.
Membership. 680,000
International affiliations. Christian Democratic International; European Christian Democratic Union; European People's Party; European Democrat Union; International Democrat Union

Christian Social Union
Christlich-Soziale Union (CSU)

Address. Nymphenburger Strasse 64, 8000 München 2, Federal Republic of Germany
Leadership. Dr h.c. Franz Josef Strauss (ch.); Dr Otto Wiesheu (s.g.)
Founded. January 1946
History. The CSU was established in Bavaria by leaders of various Roman Catholic and Protestant groups with the object of the reconstruction of the economy on the basis of private initiative and property, the realization of Christian principles, the creation of a free democratic state, the restoration of the rule of law and a federal structure of Germany.

In elections to the first Bavarian *Landtag* in December 1946 the CSU gained 52.3 per cent of the votes cast and 104 out of 180 seats. Later, however, largely as a result of the emergence of the Bavaria Party (see separate entry), the CSU lost its absolute majority, gaining only 64 out of 204 seats in 1950. It formed a coalition Government with the Social Democrats until 1954, when it obtained 83 seats but was forced into opposition by a coalition of four other parties. In 1957 this coalition broke down and the CSU came to power in a three-party coalition government. In the 1958 elections it obtained 45.6 per cent of the vote and 101 seats in the *Landtag*, and since 1962, when it first gained an absolute majority in the *Landtag*, it has held power in Bavaria.

The party has co-operated closely with the Christian Democratic Union (CDU) which operates in the other *Länder* of the

172

Federal Republic, and has sent representatives to the *Bundestag*, among them Dr Strauss (a *Bundestag* member since 1949 and a federal minister for many years, in particular Federal Minister of Defence in 1956–62 and of Finance in 1966–69). He held leading posts in the CSU from 1949 onwards and was elected party chairman in March 1961.

The CSU joined the CDU and the Free Democrats in a federal coalition Government in October 1982.

Orientation. The CSU is Christian democratic, anti-socialist, for a free market economy "in the service of man's economic and intellectual freedom", and for combining national consciousness and support for a united Europe.

Structure. The party is organized at state, provincial, district and local level and has a presidency, an executive and a party congress, which is the party's supreme organ and determines its policy and programme.

Membership. 170,000

Publications. *Bayernkurier* (weekly official organ)

International affiliations. Christian Democratic International; European Christian Democratic Union; European People's Party; European Democrat Union; International Democrat Union

---

Christian Social Voters' Union in Saarland
Christlich-Soziale Wähler Union (CSWU) im Saarland

Address. Quierstrasse 11, D-6607 Quierschied, Federal Republic of Germany

Leadership. Josef Dörr (pres.)

Founded. Dec. 4, 1978

History. This group took part in Saarland local elections in 1979 and (unsuccessfully) in the Saarland *Landtag* elections in 1980.

Communist Party of Germany/Marxists-Leninists
Kommunistische Partei Deutschlands/ Marxisten-Leninisten (KPD-ML)

Address. Wellinghoferstrasse 103 (Postfach 30 05 26), 4600 Dortmund-Hörde (30), Federal Republic of Germany

Leadership. Ernst Aust (ch.)

Founded. December 1968

History. Founded in Hamburg mainly by members of the former Communist Party of Germany (KPD), the party opposed what it called "the treason of the

modern revisionists" (such as the East German leader Walter Ulbricht). This had led to "the capitalist degeneration of the German Democratic Republic (GDR) and its enslavement by Soviet social-imperialism and to the degeneration of the Socialist Unity Party (in the GDR and West Berlin) and the KPD (in West Germany) into bourgeois, revisionist, social-fascist parties".

The KPD-ML seeks to be a party for the whole of Germany and has a section in each of its three parts—the Federal Republic, West Berlin and the GDR, the last-named section being established in 1975–76 under conditions of illegality.

Orientation. On the basis of Marxism-Leninism and the doctrines of Marx, Engels, Lenin and Stalin, the KPD-ML continues the policies of the KPD founded by Karl Liebknecht and Rosa Luxemburg, aiming at violent socialist revolution, the establishment of the dictatorship of the proletariat and the creation of a unified, independent and socialist Germany.

Structure. Based on the organizational principle of democratic centralism.

Publications. *Roter Morgen* (weekly); *Der Weg der Partei* (bimonthly theoretical organ)

Democratic Green Lists
Demokratische Grüne Listen/Grüne Demokraten

Address. Königstr. 16, 2061 Rethwisch, Federal Republic of Germany

Leadership. Hermann Krog (ch.)

Founded. 1982

History. The group was founded to offer ecologists an alternative to the "extreme left-wing" Green Party (*Die Grünen*); it is confined to the *Land* of Schleswig-Holstein. At federal level it co-operates closely with the Ecologist Democratic Party (ÖDP). It is represented on some local councils but not in the *Landtag*.

Orientation. The formation is ecologist, neither right- nor left-wing.

Membership. 250

Democratic Socialists
Demokratische Sozialisten

Address. 3000 Hannover 1, Pablo-Neruda-Haus, Am Taubenfelde 30, Federal Republic of Germany

History. A Forum of Democratic Socialists was established on March 20, 1982, by two former deputies of the Social Democratic Party (SPD), Karl-Heinz Hansen and Manfred Coppik, who opposed the policy of Helmut Schmidt (then Federal Chancellor) of support for the NATO decision on the deployment of new nuclear missiles in Western Europe. The Forum subsequently decided to set up a new party which would stand to the left of the SPD and seek a union of left-wing and ecologist movements.

Ecological Democratic Party
Ökologisch-Demokratische Partei (ÖDP)

Address. Friedrich-Ebert-Allee 120, 5300 Bonn 1, Federal Republic of Germany
Leadership. Dr Herbert Gruhl (fed. ch.); A. Wittenburg (sec.)
Founded. March 6, 1982
History. The ÖDP is the successor to the *Grüne Aktion Zukunft* (GAZ) founded in July 1978 by Dr Gruhl, who had been elected to the *Bundestag* as a member of the Christian Democratic Union, from which he resigned on establishing the GAZ. The latter became a member of the *Sonstige Politische Vereinigung* (SPV), formed in March 1979 and embracing also the following groups: *Aktionsgemeinschaft Unabhängiger Deutscher, Grüne Liste Umweltschutz, Grüne Liste Schleswig-Holstein, Aktion Dritter Weg* and *Freie Internationale Universität.*

In January 1980 the SPV constituted itself as a political party, called the Green Party (see separate entry), which at a congress in March of that year adopted an essentially left-wing programme. Dr Gruhl and other members of the movement who disapproved of this development and wished to emphasize ecological aims founded on July 16, 1980, a *Grüne Föderation* which comprised the *Bremer Grüne Liste*, the GAZ, the *Grüne Liste Schleswig-Holstein*, the *Arbeitsgemeinschaft Ökologische Politik* (AÖP) and later also the *Grüne Liste Umweltschutz Hamburg* (GLUH). The ÖDP was subsequently formed by a merger of the GAZ, the GLUH and the AÖP.
Orientation. The ÖDP recognizes the Federal Constitution (Basic Law) and parliamentary democracy. However, it advocates the limitation of economic aspirations to what is possible within the bounds determined by nature. It regards the family as the ecological basis of society. It is opposed to the employment of foreign labour and to nuclear weapons as well as nuclear power, but advocates defence by efficient armed forces equipped with conventional weapons.
Publications. *Ökologische Briefe*

European Federalist Party, German Section
Europäische Föderalistische Partei, Sektion Deutschland

Address. Hopfensack 6, D-2000 Hamburg 11, Federal Republic of Germany
Leadership. Hans Joachim Krüger (ch.)
Founded. October 1971
Orientation. The party stands for the unification of Europe in a federal, democratic and social state, guaranteeing the rights and freedoms enshrined in the 1950 European Convention for the Protection of Human Rights and Fundamental Freedoms and preventing any expansion of communism in Europe.
International affiliations. Federalist International

European Labour Party
Europäische Arbeiterpartei (EAP)

Address. Adolfsallee 17, 6200 Wiesbaden, Federal Republic of Germany
Leadership. Helga Zepp-La Rouche (ch.)
Founded. December 1974
History. Since its foundation the EAP has operated on a European-wide basis, there being, in addition to the West German party, similar organizations in Denmark, Sweden, Italy, France and Belgium. The EAP first took part in West German federal elections in 1976 when it gained less than 0.1 per cent of the votes.
Orientation. The EAP works for the unification of Europe, the application of humanist principles to scientific, technological and economic progress (including the use of nuclear energy to industrialize the developing countries) and the establishment of an international order of lasting peace.

Fourth Party Action Group
Aktionsgemeinschaft Vierte Partei (AVP)

Address. c/o Günther Leyk, Friedrichstr. 29, 8000 München 40, Federal Republic of Germany
Leadership. Günther Leyk (ch.)
Founded. June 1978
Orientation. The AVP advocates the establishment of a fourth party to end the rule of the SPD-FDP federal coalition (which the CDU is deemed incapable of achieving); it also stands for responsible

democracy, maintenance of law and order, use of popular initiatives and referendums, a free enterprise economy, freedom of the press and reunification for all Germans.

Free Democratic Party
Freie Demokratische Partei (FDP)

Address. Thomas-Dehler-Haus, Baunscheidtstrasse 15, D 5300-Bonn, Federal Republic of Germany
Leadership. Gerhart Baum (pres.); Helmut Haussmann (s.g.)
Founded. December 1948
History. The FDP was formed at a conference held at Heppenheim (near Heidelberg) in December 1948 as a fusion of various independent Liberal and Democratic *Länder* organizations. The party was elected to the first *Bundestag* in 1949 with 11.9 per cent of the vote. Its then federal chairman, Dr Theodor Heuss, was the first Federal President (*Bundespräsident*).

The FDP was part of a coalition Government (with the Christian Democrats) until 1956, in opposition in 1956-61, and in power again with the Christian Democrats in 1961-66. From 1969 to 1982 it was part of a coalition Government with the Social Democrats (SPD). Its former chairman, Walter Scheel, was Federal President from 1974 to 1979.

On June 17, 1982, the party decided to ally itself with the Christian Democrats (CDU and CSU); its four ministers in the coalition Government with the SPD resigned on Sept. 17; and a new CDU-CSU-FDP coalition Government was formed on Oct. 4, 1982. This change was followed by the departure of leading members from the FDP and electoral setbacks (in Hesse on Sept. 26 and in Bavaria on Oct. 10, when the FDP lost all its seats in *Landtag* elections by failing to obtain the minimum 5 per cent of the vote).

In the general elections of March 6, 1983, the FDP lost 19 of its 53 seats in the *Bundestag* (gaining only 6.9 per cent of the total vote, against 10.6 per cent in 1980). However, on Sept. 25, 1983, the FDP returned to the Hesse *Landtag* with 8 seats.
Orientation. The FDP is a liberal party, taking a centre position in the political spectrum and seeking in particular to represent farming interests.
Publications. *Neue Bonner Depesche* (press service), 55,000
International affiliations. Liberal International; Federation of Liberal and Democratic Parties of the European Community

Free Social Union—Democratic Centre
Freisoziale Union—Demokratische Mitte
(FSU)

Address. Feldstr. 46, 2000 Hamburg 6, Federal Republic of Germany
Leadership. Dr Kurt Kessler (ch.)
Founded. 1976
Orientation. The party stands for the full rights of self-determination for the German people, conclusion of a peace treaty for the whole of Germany which is to have no military ties with East or West, true democracy with a system of purely proportional representation (without percentage barriers) and referendums, a social order with free competition and free trade, tax reduction and equal rights for women.

Free Union in Lower Saxony
Freie Union in Niedersachsen (FU)

Address. Unter den Linden 3, 3040 Soltau, Federal Republic of Germany
Leadership. Dr Jochen Rothardt (ch.)
Founded. June 1977
Orientation. The FU supports the maintenance of fundamental rights and freedoms, parliamentary control, the federal structure of the state and the rule of law, the decentralisation of the administration, a reduction of bureaucracy, simplification of the system of taxation and restoration of ecological equilibrium.

German Centre Party
Deutsche Zentrumspartei

Address. Straberger Weg 12, 4047 Dormagen 1—Nievenheim, Federal Republic of Germany
Leadership. Gerhard Woitzik (ch.)
Founded. 1969
History. This party has so far failed to make any progress in its self-appointed task of ending the dominance of the two main German political tendencies.
Orientation. As "the party of the Christian centre" it rejects both socialism and nationalism; calls for "a healthy plurality of parties" to replace the "two-party system" and for the further development of free and social democracy, peaceful reunification of Germany and a politically united Europe; and advocates harmonious co-operation between the state and the Christian churches which are "the foundation of our civilization".

German Communist Party
Deutsche Kommunistische Partei (DKP)

Address. Prinz-Georg-Str. 79, 4000 Düsseldorf, Federal Republic of Germany
Leadership. Herbert Mies (ch.); Karl Heinz Schroeder (sec.)
Founded. 1968
History. The party succeeded the original Communist Party of Germany (*Kommunistische Partei Deutschlands*, KPD) founded in Berlin in December 1918 by Karl Liebknecht, Rosa Luxemburg (both assassinated early in 1919), Wilhelm Pieck (later President of the German Democratic Republic) and others. This party grew to become the third strongest party in the Weimar Republic (between 1918 and 1933).

In elections to the *Reichstag* (the central Parliament) held in November 1932 the KPD obtained over 5,980,000 votes (or 17 per cent of the total) and 100 seats; even after Hitler had come to power in January 1933, the KPD still polled, in *Reichstag* elections held in March 1933, over 4,800,000 votes (or 12.1 per cent of the total) and obtained 81 seats. However, before the new *Reichstag* could meet on March 21, the KPD had been suppressed, with its leaders being sent to concentration camps or prison or going into exile or underground.

At the end of World War II the KPD was reconstituted. In January 1949 it separated itself organizationally from the Socialist Unity Party which had come to power in East Germany. The KPD was represented in most of the early *Landtage* (state parliaments) elected in West Germany, where its members rejected the new Basic Law (Constitution) of the Federal Republic in May 1949.

In the first federal elections, held in 1949, the KPD polled 1,360,000 votes and gained 15 seats, but in 1953 its vote fell to 611,000 and it won no seats. However, it still held four seats in the Bremen *Land* Parliament and two in the *Landtag* of Lower Saxony in 1956, when it was banned as being unconstitutional.

The DKP was formed (in 1968) on the basis of undertaking to observe the principles of the Basic Law. For the 1969 *Bundestag* elections it sought a common front with the Social Democratic Party but the latter rejected this approach out of hand. The DKP unsuccessfully contested the 1969 elections as part of an Action for Democratic Progress group, and in further *Bundestag* elections it obtained only 0.1 per cent of the vote in 1976 and 0.2 per cent in 1980 and 1983.

Orientation. In a statement of principles issued in April 1969 the DKP described itself as "the Marxist party of the working classes of the Federal Republic" and expressed its close connexion with the Socialist Unity Party of East Germany; it called for the recognition of the German Democratic Republic and of the existing frontiers in Europe and for a security system covering the whole of Europe, with the dissolution of NATO and of the Warsaw Pact. The DKP currently stands for disarmament and international détente. Its ultimate aim is socialism on the basis of the doctrines of Marx, Engels and Lenin and it rejects "right-wing and left-wing opportunism". In March 1976 the party's chairman emphasized its adherence to "true socialism" as represented by the Soviet Union and the German Democratic Republic and to "proletarian internationalism".

Structure. The party's highest authority is its congress, convened every four years; it elects party officials and a party board which in turn elects a presidium and a secretariat. The party has basic units at places of work or of residence and district as well as area organizations.
Membership. 49,000
Publications. *Unsere Zeit* (daily), 60,000; *Praxis* (theoretical journal)
International affiliations. The DKP is recognized by the Communist parties of the Soviet-bloc countries.

German Democratic Workers' Party
Deutsche Demokratische Arbeiterpartei (DDAP)

Address. c/o Josef Singer, 8491 Thenried 35, Federal Republic of Germany
Leadership. Josef Singer (ch.)
Founded. June 1978
Orientation. The party's object is to ensure social security for active and retired workers within the framework of a free democratic society.

German Peace Union
Deutsche Friedens-Union (DFU)

Address. Amsterdamer Str. 64, 5000 Köln 60, Federal Republic of Germany
Founded. Dec. 17, 1960
Orientation. In its programme of April 17, 1983, the DFU called for an active employment policy of the state, to be financed from reductions in the arms budget, an end to tax evasion, taxation of

foreign investments in low-wage countries and drastic reductions in subsidies. The DFU is opposed to the stationing of nuclear first-strike weapons in the Federal Republic and advocates a freeze in nuclear armaments, the renunciation of the use of force by both NATO and the Warsaw Pact member states, a nuclear test ban, a ban on chemical, biological and radiation weapons and other weapons of mass destruction, and a nuclear-weapons-free zone in Central Europe.

Structure. The DFU has a seven-member federal executive and a 59-member federal council.

Green Party
Die Grünen

Address. Colmantstr. 36, 5300 Bonn 1, Federal Republic of Germany

Leadership. Waltraud Schoppe, Antje Vollmer, Annemarie Borgmann (joint spokespersons)

Founded. March 16-17, 1979

History. The party was founded as the *Sonstige Politische Vereinigung* (SPV) *Die Grünen* in Frankfurt/Sindlingen by some 500 delegates representing various ecologist groups, namely the *Aktionsgemeinschaft Unabhängiger Deutscher* (AUD), the *Grüne Liste Umweltschutz* (GLU), the *Grüne Aktion Zukunft* (GAZ), the *Grüne Liste Schleswig-Holstein* (GLSH), the *Aktion Dritter Weg* (A3W) and the *Freie Internationale Universität*.

The establishment of *Die Grünen* as a a federal party took place in Karlsruhe on Jan. 12–13, 1980, at a conference attended by over 1,000 delegates. A congress held in Saarbrücken in March 1980 approved a federal programme and another congress held in Offenbach early in 1982 adopted a peace manifesto. Electoral successes were achieved in *Land* elections in Bremen (October 1979, four seats), Baden-Württemberg (March 1980, six seats), Lower Saxony (March 1982, 11 seats), Hamburg (October 1982, eight seats), Hesse (September 1983, seven seats), Baden-Württemberg again (March 1984, nine seats), and in the West Berlin election of May 1981 (nine seats).

In the *Bundestag* elections of March 6, 1983, the Greens obtained federal representation for the first time, winning 5.6 per cent of the vote and 27 seats. In February 1984 internal divisions surfaced when Gen. Gert Bastian, a leading member, resigned from the party in protest against what he regarded as its leftist tendencies (and thereafter sat in the *Bundestag* as an independent member).

Prominent in the rise of the Greens to political influence has been Petra Kelly, who was elected to the *Bundestag* in March 1983 and was widely regarded as the party's key leader. However, opposition within the party to "personality politics" contributed to her removal from the joint leadership (together with the other two members) in April 1984, when three relatively unknown women became joint spokespersons of the party. *Die Grünen* have also insisted on applying the principle of rotation under which elected representatives of the party stand down in mid-term in favour of others.

Orientation. In its programme adopted in March 1980 the party called for a world-wide ban on nuclear energy, prohibition of the use of chemical and biological weapons and of the deployment of nuclear missiles in Europe, unilateral disarmament, the creation of a demilitarized zone in Europe and the dismantling of NATO and the Warsaw Pact. The party also seeks the breaking down of large economic concerns into smaller units, a 35-hour week and the unlimited right to withdraw labour.

Structure. The party is organized at local, district and federal level. It has a congress (meeting at least twice a year) as the party's supreme organ; a federal committee (the supreme organ between congress sessions); and a federal executive.

Membership. 25,000

International affiliations. The European Greens

Independent Labour Party—German Socialists
Unabhängige Arbeiter-Partei—Deutsche Sozialisten (UAP)

Address. Postfach 10 38 13 (Bergmühle 5), 4300 Essen 1, Federal Republic of Germany

Leadership. Erhard Kliese (first ch.)

Founded. January 1962

Orientation. The party is "anti-communist, anti-fascist and anti-capitalist", and it proposes to achieve the reunification of Germany within a neutral European federation; to create "German socialism" and a national army on the basis of conscription; to set up an economic parliament (in addition to the political parliament); and to nationalize all large state and private enterprises with workers' control of management.

Structure. The party is organized at local and district levels and has a 16-member central bureau.

Membership. 2,700, plus 3,067 youth members (*Blaue Adler Jugend*)
Publications. *Reichs-Arbeiter-Zeitung* (monthly), 5,000

International World Peace Party
Internationale Weltfriedens Partei (IWP)

Address. 40 Leopoldstr. 109/IV, D 8000 München, Federal Republic of Germany
Leadership. Eugen Held (1st ch.)
Founded. Oct. 10, 1981
History. The IWP has participated in Bavarian and federal elections without success. It has also been represented at a series of international peace conferences, several of them in Eastern Europe.
Orientation. The IWP favours "stability and world peace" through the abolition of all weapons, which is to be achieved with democracy and freedom and steering a middle course between capitalism and communism.
Structure. Currently operational at Bavarian and federal level, the IWP aspires to a presence not only throughout the Federal Republic but also in other European countries, including those of the Soviet bloc.

Justice Party
Gerechtigkeitspartei Bundesrepublik Deutschland

Address. Wormserstr. 36 A, Postfach 410154, D-6800 Mannheim 31, Federal Republic of Germany
Leadership. Richard Herrmann (first ch.)
Founded. September 1971
History. The party has unsuccessfully contested *Landtag* elections in Baden-Württemberg and Hesse.
Orientation. The party stands for reduction of taxation and state interference, for a free market economy (though with controls over cartels and monopolies) and for education on the Summerhill model (of A. S. Neill).
Membership. Under 1,000
Publications. *Summerhill News* (pamphlets)

League of West German Communists
Bund Westdeutscher Kommunisten

Address. 5000 Köln 1, Kamekestr. 19, Federal Republic of Germany
History. This League superseded the Communist Party of Germany (*Kommunistische Partei Deutschlands,* KPD) founded in February 1970 under the leadership of Christian Semler. Carrying on the name of the original KPD established in 1918, this party was a Maoist formation which regarded "Soviet social-imperialism" as the main enemy of the German people and proclaimed as its aim an "independent, united and socialist Germany, the overthrow of capitalism in both German states, the dictatorship of the proletariat and a classless society". The KPD is pro-Chinese and anti-Albanian and has endorsed the Chinese "three worlds" theory.

Liberal Democrats
Liberale Demokraten

Address. Reuterstr. 44, 5300 Bonn, Federal Republic of Germany
Leadership. Ulrich Krüger (l.)
Founded. Nov. 27, 1982
History. This party was founded by former members of the Free Democratic Party (FDP) in protest against the latter party's decision to join the Christian Democratic and Christian Social parties in forming a coalition Government. Ulrich Krüger had been an FDP member of the *Landtag* of Hesse.

National Democratic Party of Germany
Nationaldemokratische Partei Deutschlands (NPD)

Address. Rötestr. 4, Postfach 2881, 7000 Stuttgart 1, Federal Republic of Germany
Leadership. Martin Mussgnug (ch.)
Founded. 1964
History. The NPD was founded as a national focus for a variety of extreme right-wing splinter groupings and was described in a government report as a "neo-Nazi party hiding beneath a democratic facade", although the party leadership strongly denied that the NPD had any Nazi connexions.

In *Bundestag* elections the NPD obtained about 2 per cent of the vote in 1965 and 4.3 per cent in 1969 and thus never achieved the minimum 5 per cent to qualify for seats. However, it was successful in several *Landtag* elections, gaining seats in 1966–67 (8 in Hesse, 15 in Bavaria, 4 in Schleswig-Holstein, 4 in Rhineland-Palatinate, 10 in Lower Saxony and 8 in Bremen) and in 1968 (12 in Baden-Württemberg), although it lost all these seats in the 1971–72 elections.

Since then it has had no parliamentary representation. In May 1967 it was split, its former chairman establishing a separate National People's Party. The NPD dissolved its West Berlin branch in October 1968 after the West Berlin Senate had asked the Western Allied Commandants to consider banning it, but the branch was restored soon afterwards.

In the *Bundestag* elections of 1980 and 1983 the NDP received only 0.2 per cent of the valid votes.

Orientation. While the party's founders included numerous former supporters of the Nazi regime, the NPD states its aims to be "to maintain Christian civilization on the basis of a free democratic order, with freedom of belief, conscience and religious and philosophical conviction", to orientate the country's defence policy towards the defence of Europe, to reject the "reality" of the Communist conquests of 1945, and to demand a revision of all relevant treaties.

Membership. 15,000

Party for Equitable Pensions, Taxation and Social Services
Partei für Renten-, Steuer- und Soziale Gerechtigkeit (PRS)

Address. c/o Willfred Wiechert, Staufenbergstr. 13, 3500 Kassel, Federal Republic of Germany
Leadership. W. Wiechert (ch.)
Founded. September 1978
Orientation. This small formation advocates protection of the environment, development of non-nuclear energy, import control for agricultural produce, transport reform involving increased use of railways and equal rights for all (including women).

Party for Germany and Europe
Partei für Deutschland und Europa (PDE)

Address. c/o Dr Loges, Schulstr. 4, D 7056 Weinstadt, Federal Republic of Germany
Leadership. Dr Rolf Loges and two other members of management committee
Founded. December 1982
History. This party was set up to contest the 1984 elections to the European Parliament.
Orientation. The PDE is a party of the centre with the aims of unification of the two German states, the creation of a united Europe on a federal basis, a strong reduction of income tax balanced by the

abolition of government subsidies, and a fundamental reform of the social security system.
Structure. The party has federal and provincial branches.
Membership. 1,000

Peace-loving Union of the German Peace Movement
Friedliebende Union der deutschen Friedensbewegung

Address. c/o Hartmut Neumann, Mühlweg 8, Postfach 1141, 7770 Überlingen, Federal Republic of Germany
Leadership. Hartmut Neumann (first ch.)
Founded. July 2, 1983
Orientation. The party claims to be the first alternative Christian party in Germany. It stands for the protection of the environment, the imposition of taxes on the consumption of raw materials and the utilization of the soil, the encouragement of technologies which save raw materials and energy, the rejection of all violence, the reunification of Germany within a generation, the prevention of war and opposition to all nuclear arms.
Structure. The party aspires to operate in the whole territory of the Federal Republic (and if possible also in the German Democratic Republic). It is organized at local district and *Land* level and has a congress, an executive and an arbitration committee.

Republican Party
Die Republikaner (REP)

Leadership. Franz Handlos (ch.); Ekkehard Voigt, Franz Schönhuber (deputy ch.)
Founded. Nov. 25, 1983
History. This party was launched by Franz Handlos and Ekkehard Voigt, who had both been elected to the *Bundestag* in March 1983 as members of the Christian Social Union (CSU), in protest against the involvement of Franz Josef Strauss, the CSU leader, in arranging a loan equivalent to US$375,000,000 to the German Democratic Republic. (Although both left the CSU they remained members of the *Bundestag*.) The leadership of the new party was also joined by two members of the former Citizens' Party (*Bürgerpartei*) led by Hermann Joseph Fredersdorf (of Baden-Württemberg).
Orientation. The party describes itself as "conservative, liberal and social", and

179

stands for the reunification of Germany, environmental protection, lower business taxes, restrictions on foreigners, referendums to be held on major questions and compulsory youth service.

Social Community Action (Party of Socially Insured Employees and Pensioners)
Aktion Soziale Gemeinschaft, die Partei der sozialversicherten Arbeitnehmer und Rentner (ASG)

Address. Seminarstr. 1, 5450 Neuwied, Federal Republic of Germany
Leadership. Hermann Krümpelmann (fed. ch.)
Founded. April 25, 1980
History. This party has been unable to submit the required 20,000 signatures which would allow it to participate in *Bundestag* elections. It has also failed to pass the 5 per cent minimum of votes barrier in other elections.
Orientation. The party stands for a liberal, democratic state with the rule of law, a uniform electoral system with proportional representation, a free market economy and, in particular, the rights of employees and pensioners in the private sector (who are disadvantaged by comparison with those in the public sector).
Structure. Branches in 10 *Länder*.
Membership. 3,000

Social Democratic Party of Germany
Sozialdemokratische Partei Deutschlands (SPD)

Address. 5300 Bonn 1, Ollenhauerstr. 1, Federal Republic of Germany
Leadership. Willy Brandt (ch.); Hans-Jochen Vogel (parl. l.), Peter Glotz (g.s.)
Founded. 1863
History. The origins of the party lie in the Association of German Workers founded by Ferdinand Lassalle in 1863 and the *Sozialdemokratische Arbeiterpartei* formed in 1869 by August Bebel and Wilhelm Liebknecht, both these parties merging in 1875. The party was outlawed from 1878 to 1890. However, before the outbreak of World War I it had become the strongest party in the *Reichstag* (the Parliament of the German Reich, but with limited powers only). After the establishment of the Republic in 1918, the party's then leader, Friedrich Ebert, became the new state's first Chancellor (Prime Minister) in 1918 and its first President (from 1919 to 1925). The party

was again banned (under Hitler) in 1933–45.

In the first elections to the *Bundestag* of the newly-established Federal Republic of Germany in 1949 the SPD emerged as the second strongest party with 131 out of 402 seats. However, it remained in opposition until 1966 (after gaining 151 out of 404 seats in general elections in 1953, 169 out of 497 in 1957, 190 out of 497 in 1961, and 202 out of 496 in 1965), when it entered into a grand coalition with the Christian Democrats which remained in office until 1969.

From that year until 1982 the SPD was in power in coalition with the Free Democratic Party. During this period the SPD carried out a new "Ostpolitik" involving the de facto recognition of the German Democratic Republic in its existing frontiers and improved relations with East European (Communist) states.

The party's traditionally strong representation in the *Bundestag*, which reached 218 members in 1980, fell to 193 in the elections of March 1983 (which still left it the strongest single party in the House if the Christian Democrats and Christian Socials are regarded as separate formations).

Orientation. The SPD is a social democratic party standing for social progress and democracy in political and economic life, involving co-determination by workers at enterprise level. The party's policy is based on its Programme of Principles adopted at Bad Godesberg on Nov. 15, 1959, which laid down that democratic socialism should be based on freedom and justice; that the state's armed forces should serve only for defence and be controlled by Parliament; that the production and use of nuclear arms and other weapons of mass destruction are forbidden; that the private ownership of the means of production should be protected and furthered within the limits set by an equitable social order; and that a just distribution of income and property should be achieved by appropriate incomes policies. In foreign affairs the SPD stands for European unification and continued membership of NATO as well as increased armaments control and effective disarmament efforts in Europe and elsewhere. In this context it opposed, in 1983, the NATO decision to deploy new US nuclear missiles in the Federal Republic.

Structure. The party has some 10,000 local branches, 22 regions and 250 districts. A party conference held every two years elects an executive committee which in turn elects a presidium.
Membership. 1,000,000

Publications. *Vorwärts* (weekly), 74,000; *Neue Gesellschaft* (monthly theoretical journal)

International affiliations. Socialist International; Confederation of Socialist Parties of the European Community

---

South Schleswig Voters' Union
Südschleswigscher Wählerverband—Sydslesvigsk Vaelgerforening (SSV)

Address. Norderstr. 74 1, D-2390 Flensburg, Federal Republic of Germany
Leadership. Gerhard Wehlitz (ch.); Paul O. Hertrampf (sec.)
Founded. August 1948
History. Approved by the British military authorities in 1948 as the successor to a (non-political) Association for South Schleswig, the party operates only in the part of the *Land* of Schleswig-Holstein north of the Kiel canal and represents the Danish and Friesian population in that area.

Under an agreement signed in Bonn on March 29, 1955, this national minority was exempted from the clause limiting parliamentary representation to parties obtaining at least 5 per cent of the vote in elections to the *Bundestag* and to the *Landtag* of Schleswig-Holstein (but this does not apply to local elections).

The SSV has one member in the *Landtag* and 120 members on municipal councils. However, its share of the *Landtag* votes has declined from 9.3 per cent in 1947 to 1.4 per cent in 1983. The party has not contested federal elections since 1965.
Orientation. A regional party representing the Danish and Friesian minority and promoting a democratic society on the Scandinavian model.
Membership. 5,000
Publications. *Kontakt*, about 20,000

Union for the Protection of the Environment and of Life (Free Green Union)
Union für Umwelt- und Lebensschutz (Freie Grüne Union)

Address. Guldenhagen 41, 3400 Göttingen, Federal Republic of Germany
Leadership. Dr Horst Göttig (ch.)
Founded. February 1978
Orientation. This party aims at the implementation of the multi-party principle as provided in the Basic Law (Constitution). It claims to be a "party of the centre" and proposes reforms aimed at the protection of future generations.

Women's Party
Frauenpartei

Address. Hasselkamp 26, 2300 Kiel 1, Federal Republic of Germany
Leadership. Hannelore Wohlers (ch.)
Founded. Sept. 30, 1979
History. This formation claims to have averted infiltration by communists, anarchists and right-wing extremists (including former and neo-Nazis). It has unsuccessfully contested *Landtag* elections (in Lower Saxony, Schleswig-Holstein and Bremen). It intends to participate in the formation of a European Feminist Party.
Orientation. The party is neither right- nor left-wing, but feminist (for a society without sex discrimination), pacifist and ecologist.
Structure. The party is organized in three *Länder.*
Membership. 335
Publications. *Argumente Notizen Nachrichten* (about six times a year); *Küche und Parlament* (a manifesto)

Other Parties

Other parties officially registered in the Federal Republic of Germany are as follows:

Action for New Politics *(Aktion Neue Politik),* c/o Albert Gotthold, 9800 Augsburg 21, Roseggerstr. 3, Federal Republic of Germany

Action for Repatriation of Foreigners—People's Movement against Foreign Domination and Environmental Destruction *(Aktion Ausländerrückführung—Volksbewegung gegen Überfremdung und Umweltzerstörung),* c/o A.-H. Marx, 54 Hanau 7 (Postfach 70 03 51), Federal Republic of Germany

Action Group for Ecological Politics *(Aktionsgemeinschaft Ökologische Politik),* c/o K.-G. Bringmann, 2863 Ritterhude, Fergerbergstr. 28, Federal Republic of Germany

Christian Party *(Christliche Partei),* 8000 München 44, Postfach 44 00 90, Federal Republic of Germany

Citizens' Party/Environment Union *(Bürgerpartei/Umweltunion),* c/o Dr med. H. Graunke, 8214 Bernau-Chiemsee, Alte Seestr. 21, Federal Republic of Germany

Citizens' Union *(Bürgerunion),* c/o W. Wiechert, 3500 Kassel, Staufenbergstr. 13, Federal Republic of Germany

Cosmopolitan Liberal Action *(Cosmopolitano-Liberale Aktion)*, c/o Kuenhold, 3578 Schwalmstadt 2, Paradeplatz 5, Federal Republic of Germany

Europe 2000 League for Free Peoples—Germany *(Europa 2000-Liga für Freie Völker—Deutschland)*, 8591 Pechbrunn, Postfach 53, Federal Republic of Germany

Federal Party for Labour and Social Welfare *(Bundespartei für Arbeit und Soziales)*, c/o Frau Hannelore Kappey, 3000 Hannover 1, Haltenhoffstr. 22, Federal Republic of Germany

German Democratic People's Movement *(Deutsch Demokratische Volksbewegung)*, c/o W. Symanek, 4235 Schermbeck 2, Kuhweg 110, Federal Republic of Germany

German Family Party *(Deutsche Familien-Partei)*, 8500 Nürnberg, Postfach 9435, Federal Republic of Germany

German People's Party *(Deutsche Volkspartei)*, 1000 Berlin 47, Postfach 471261, Federal Republic of Germany

German Republican Union *(Deutsche Republikanische Union)*, c/o Garre, 5204 Lohmar 21, Im Brögen 4, Federal Republic of Germany

German Social Union *(Deutsche Soziale Union, DSU)*, Possbergweg 61–63, D-4000 Düsseldorf 12, Federal Republic of Germany

German Tax and Environment Party *(Deutsche Steuer- und Umweltpartei)*, c/o Hans Willi Beyen, 4173 Kerken 2, Hülserstr. 16, Federal Republic of Germany

German Union *(Deutsche Union)*, c/o Hugo Trapp, 8900 Augsburg, Kreuzeckstr. 5, Federal Republic of Germany

Green List for Ecology, Lower Saxony *(Grüne Liste Ökologie Niedersachsen)*, c/o Bringmann, 2863 Ritterhude, Fergersbergstr. 28, Federal Republic of Germany

Green Party of Germany *(Grüne Partei Deutschlands)*, c/o Dr Huesgens, 5202 Hennef (Sieg) 4, Süchterscheid, Federal Republic of Germany

Haas-Eyb Party *(Haas-Eyb Partei)*, c/o Willy Haas, 7000 Stuttgart 50, Veitstr. 16, Federal Republic of Germany.

Hamburg List for a Halt to Foreigners *(Hamburger Liste für Ausländerstopp)*, 2000 Hamburg 52, Postfach 52 01 49, Federal Republic of Germany

Independent Social Democrats *(Unabhängige Soziale Demokraten)*, 5100 Aachen, Am Beverbach 2 a, Federal Republic of Germany

Independent German Peace Union *(Unabhängige Deutsche Friedens Union)*, 7516 Karlsbad, Danziger Str. 38, Federal Republic of Germany

Liberal Centre Party *(Liberales Zentrum)*, 4050 Mönchengladbach 2, Postfach 35 01 54, Federal Republic of Germany

Liberal German Labour Party *(Freiheitliche Deutsche Arbeiterpartei)*, c/o Martin Pape, 7000 Stuttgart 70, Allgäustr. 22, Federal Republic of Germany

Popular Front against Reaction, Fascism and War *(Volksfront gegen Reaktion, Faschismus und Krieg)*, 5100 Aachen, Mariahilfstr. 31, Federal Republic of Germany

Union for Concrete Protection of the Environment, Party of the Centre *(Union Konkreter Umweltschutz, Partei der Mitte)*, 4300 Essen 13, Gantenbergstr. 12 A, Federal Republic of Germany

Women for Parliament *(Frauen ins Parlament)*, c/o Frau A. Boldt, 4770 Soest, Osthofenstr. 50, Federal Republic of Germany

Working Group for Solidarity of Pensioners, Employees and Workers—Pensioners Party of Germany *(Arbeits-Solidargemeinschaft der Rentner, Angestellten und Arbeiter—Rentnerpartei Deutschlands)*, c/o Heinz Reichel, 5300 Bonn, Oberer Lindweg 29, Federal Republic of Germany

Zero Buck Party *(Null-Bock-Partei)*, c/o N. Kohlmüller, 6148 Heppenheim-Sonderbach, Kirchbergstr. 24, Federal Republic of Germany

West Berlin

The major parties of the Federal Republic of Germany also operate in West Berlin. Several smaller groups have unsuccessfully contested elections to the West Berlin House of Representatives, including the following party:

Socialist Unity Party of West Berlin
Sozialistische Einheitspartei Westberlins
(SEW)

History. The party was formed as the West Berlin section of the Socialist Unity Party of Germany (SED), the ruling party of the German Democratic Republic, and it first contested elections to the West Berlin House of Representatives in 1954, when it gained 2.7 per cent of the votes—this percentage being reduced to 1.9 in the 1958 elections. As the SED of West Berlin, the party obtained 1.4 per cent of the vote in 1963 and 2 per cent in 1967. Since 1971 it has campaigned as the SEW, gaining 2.3 per cent in 1971, 1.9 in 1975, 1.1 in 1979 and well below 1 per cent in 1981.

Orientation. The SEW is a Communist party following the political line of the SED in East Germany.

Publications. *Die Wahrheit*

Ghana

Capital: Accra   Pop. 12,200,000

In the Republic of Ghana (a member of the Commonwealth), a Provisional National Defence Council (PNDC) came to power on Dec. 31, 1981, by overthrowing the existing parliamentary regime, suspending the Constitution and proscribing all political parties. The country had previously been under military rule from June to September 1979. On Jan. 21, 1982, the PNDC appointed a civilian Government which included a number of established political figures, but effective power remained in the hands of the PNDC chairman, Flt.-Lt. Jerry Rawlings.

Under the PNDC's programme "people's defence committees" (PDCs) became the basic units of the state structure as "organizing centres for the revolution" which would enable the PNDC to remain aware of popular aspirations and needs throughout the country. Subsequently an Interim National Co-ordinating Committee (INCC) was set up to supervise and co-ordinate the work of the PDCs and also of recently established workers' defence committees (WDCs). In July 1982 the INCC was replaced by a 27-member National Defence Committee (NDC), which was, however, dissolved on Dec. 14, 1982, after accusations that it had been infiltrated by "counter-revolutionaries", and its functions were taken over by a standing committee of nine PNDC appointees. In February 1983 it was announced that a Community Defence Committee of between 40 and 100 PNDC appointees would be established, and in April 1983 the NDC was reconstituted.

In the absence of political parties, the undermentioned organizations have been active in support of the PNDC regime.

June 4 Movement

History. This Movement took its name from the date of the assumption of power on June 4, 1979, by a Revolutionary Armed Forces Council (RAFC) under the leadership of Flt.-Lt. Rawlings, which retained control until Sept. 24, 1979. As explained above, Flt.-Lt. Rawlings reassumed power at the end of 1981 at the head of a Provisional National Defence Council (PNDC).

National Democratic Movement

Orientation. This radical organization has as its central purpose the provision of political support for the PNDC regime.

Organizing Committee for the Defence of the Revolution

History. This Committee consists of representatives of the above two movements as well as of the Trades Union Congress, the people's defence committees and the workers' defence committees. It was responsible for organizing a pro-government demonstration on July 30, 1982, in support of the regime of Flt.-Lt. Rawlings as head of the Provisional National Defence Council.

People's Revolutionary League of Ghana (Prelog)

History. This formation was founded in 1979 to defend the aims of the military regime in power from June 4 to Sept. 24, 1979, in particular its anti-corruption campaign and the nationalization of major companies.

Greece

Capital: Athens   Pop. 9,700,000

Greece, or the Hellenic Republic, is a parliamentary democracy with a President as head of state who is elected by Parliament for a five-year term and who exercises legislative power jointly with Parliament and executive power jointly with the Government headed by a Prime Minister. The unicameral 300-member Parliament is elected for a five-year term by universal adult suffrage under a system of reinforced proportional representation.

Voting is compulsory for citizens above the age of 18 years (unless ill or incapacitated). Seats are allotted to each of 56 constituencies according to population, with seats per constituency ranging from one to 26. Voters have the right to indicate preferences. Parties must, under the 1975 Constitution, "serve the free functioning of democratic government". By-elections are held to fill any vacancies arising (except during the last year of Parliament). Although the Constitution provides for direct state financial support to parties, support has hitherto been indirect only (by publicity being given to party propaganda).

In parliamentary elections held on Oct. 18, 1981, the seats were contested by numerous parties but only three of them obtained more than 2 per cent of the valid votes cast and any seats—the Pan-Hellenic Socialist Movement (Pasok) 170, New Democracy 112 and the Greek Communist Party (KKE-Exterior) 13 (independents taking the other five seats).

Christian Democracy

Leadership. Nikolaos Psaroudakis
Founded. 1977
History. The group's founder and leader had been an outspoken critic of the military dictatorship in power in 1967-74. The group contested the 1977 elections as part of the Alliance of Progressive and Left-Wing Forces (APLF). In the October 1981 elections the party gained only 0.15 per cent of the votes and no seat.
Orientation. The party is a left-wing Christian democratic formation.
Publications. *Christianiki* (newspaper)

Communist Party of Greece—Exterior
Kommunistiko Komma Ellados (KKE—Exterior)

Address. 16 Odos Kapodistriou, Athens 147, Greece
Leadership. Harilaos Florakis (first sec.)
Founded. November 1918
History. The KKE-Exterior was illegal during most of the time until July 1974. During World War II it organized popular resistance to the Axis powers in the National Liberation Front (EAM) and the Greek People's Liberaton Army (ELAS) jointly with other parties. By the end of 1944 it claimed to have 400,000 members but in 1944-49 it was defeated in a civil war, the party being officially banned in July 1947. In 1951-67 it was part of the United Democratic Left (EDA), and from 1967 to 1974 it was prominent among the forces fighting against the dictatorship.

Upon being legalized the party contested the 1974 elections in a United Left Alliance, together with the KKE-Interior and the EDA, and in these elections the KKE-Exterior obtained five seats in Parliament. In the 1977 elections the party, which did not join any alliance, increased its share of the vote to 9.36 per cent, and this rose to 10.92 per cent in 1981. In the elections to the European Parliament held on Oct. 18, 1981, the party obtained three seats. The party has sought to establish co-operation with the Pan-Hellenic Socialist Movement (Pasok) since the latter's election victory in October 1981.
Orientation. An orthodox Marxist-Leninist party, the KKE-Exterior supports the Soviet Union as the vanguard of the world Communist movement. Its aim is to free Greece from "US domination" and to establish a popular government.
Membership. 73,000
Publications. *Nea Ellada* (daily); *Rizospastis* (daily); *Kommunistiki Epitheorisi* (monthly)

International affiliations. The KKE is recognized by the Communist parties of the Soviet-bloc countries.

Communist Party of Greece—Interior
Kommunistiko Komma Ellados Esoterikou (KKE es.)

Address. 19 Tritis Septemvriou Street, Athens, Greece
Leadership. Yiannis Banias (sec.)
Founded. 1968
History. The KKE es. was established by the interior bureau of the then united KKE, which was functioning underground inside the country while the party's political bureau had been in exile since the defeat of the left in the 1946-49 civil war. A split occurred at the 12th plenum of the KKE central committee held abroad in February 1968 without the participation of those central committee members who were working underground in Greece. Against a background of deep differences over the party line during the period leading up to the military coup of April 27, 1967, the plenum expelled some of the central committee's members, but its decisions were considered invalid by a majority of the members inside Greece.

Contesting the Greek elections of 1974 as part of a United Democratic Left, the KKE es. obtained two seats in Parliament; in the 1977 elections it obtained one of the two seats gained by an alliance of Progressive and Left-Wing Forces, of which it formed part. It lost this seat in the 1981 elections but gained one seat in the European Parliament in elections held in Greece on Oct. 18, 1981.
Orientation. At three congresses (held in 1976, 1979 and 1982) the party has reaffirmed its independence as a Eurocommunist party which does not accept the existence of an international centre of the Communist movement and which believes in "the democratic road to a socialism with freedom and self-management". It also stands for the participation of Greece in the European Community on more favourable terms.
Membership. 12,000
Publications. *Avghi* (Dawn, daily); *I Aristera Simera* (The Left Today, theoretical review)

Democratic Unity

History. This centrist alliance of the Party for Democratic Socialism (see separate entry) and the Agricultural Party

(KAE) obtained one seat in the elections to the European Parliament held on Oct. 18, 1981, but it gained no seat in the October 1981 elections to the Greek Parliament.

Greek National Political Society (EPEN)

Leadership. George Papadopoulos (l.)
Founded. January 1984
History. This new right-wing formation held its first assembly in Athens on Jan. 29, 1984, when 400 delegates decided to register the group as a political party. The assembly also adopted by acclamation as EPEN's leader ex-Col. George Papadopoulos, who had been dictator of Greece from 1967 to 1973, first as Prime Minister and then as President, and who was serving a sentence of life imprisonment for treason, commuted from the original death sentence passed in 1975. A taped message from Papadopoulos was played to 5,500 supporters at a rally marking the launching of the party.

A government spokesman said on Jan. 30, however, that Papadopoulos had been deprived of civil rights as part of his sentence and would accordingly not be eligible to stand in elections, either those for the European Parliament (due in June 1984) or those for the national Parliament (next due no later than autumn 1985).

Orientation. In his message to supporters, George Papadopoulos pledged to restore "Hellenic Christian ideals", including law and order in schools and universities, and to consolidate Greece's role in the Western camp.

Liberal Party

Address. 1 Vissarionos Street, Athens TT 135, Greece
Leadership. Nikitas Venizelos (l.)
Founded. 1981
History. Before founding this party Nikitas Venizelos had been a deputy of the Union of the Democratic Centre and briefly a member of the Unifying Centre Rally led by George Mavros. In the November 1981 general elections the Liberal Party obtained only 0.37 per cent of the votes and no seat.

Orientation. According to the leader of the party its aim is to revive the (liberal) political heritage of his grandfather, the former Prime Minister Eleftherios Venizelos (1864-1936).

Membership. 5,000
International affiliations. Liberal International (observer member)

National Front
Ethnikon Metapon

Address. 42 Panepistimiou St., Athens, Greece
Founded. October 1977
History. The party was organized by Stefanos Stefanopoulos, a former Prime Minister, as a conservative alternative to the New Democracy then led by Konstantinos Karamanlis. In the 1977 parliamentary elections it gained 6.82 per cent of the votes and four seats. It withdrew from the 1981 election campaign in order to avert the "dispersal of nationalist forces in the face of the Marxist threat", and several of its leading members were nominated as candidates of the New Democracy.

Orientation. This right-wing party advocates the restoration of Greek military participation in NATO, reprieve of the imprisoned leaders of the 1967-74 dictatorship, encouragement of business investment and a revision of the 1975 constitution; it also advocates restoration of the monarchy.

New Democracy
Nea Democratia (ND)

Address. 18 Rigilis Str., Athens 138, Greece
Leadership. Evangelos Averoff-Tossizza (ch.)
Founded. September 1974
History. In the December 1974 elections (the first to be held since 1964) the newly-established ND obtained 54.37 per cent of the votes cast and 220 out of the 300 seats in Parliament. In the 1977 general elections it retained 41.85 per cent of the votes, while in the October 1981 elections it received 35.87 per cent of the votes, which gave it 112 seats in Parliament. The ND was in power from the restoration of parliamentary democracy in 1974 until Oct. 18, 1981.

Following the election of Konstantinos Karamanlis, the party's founder, to the Presidency of the Republic in May 1980, George Rallis, until then Foreign Minister, became party leader and thus Prime Minister. Evangelos Averoff-Tossizza, who had been Minister of Defence in the ND administration, was elected leader on Dec. 9, 1981, following the party's heavy defeat in the October 1981 general elections.

Orientation. In April 1977 the ND adopted six "basic ideological principles", placing the party above the terms right, centre and left and defining its ideology as radical liberalism. ND voters cover a wide spectrum, excluding totalitarian groups on the right and parties with Marxist ideologies on the left.

International affiliations. International Democrat Union; European Democrat Union; Christian Democratic International; European Christian Democratic Union; European People's Party

---

Pan-Hellenic Socialist Movement
Panellinion Socialistikou Kinema (Pasok)

Address. Trikoupi 50, Athens, Greece

Leadership. Andreas G. Papandreou (pres.)

Founded. 1974

History. Pasok has its origins in the Pan-Hellenic Liberation Movement formed by Andreas Papandreou to oppose the military dictatorship which held power in Greece from 1967 to 1974. Andreas Papandreou had previously held ministerial office in a Centre Union administration headed by his father George Papandreou, but the experience of the colonels' coup (after which he had been briefly imprisoned before going into exile) had convinced him of the need for an unequivocally socialist party on the left.

Established in its present form after the collapse of the Greek military dictatorship, the party emerged as the third strongest in the 1974 parliamentary elections, when it gained 12 seats and 13.58 per cent of the vote, but in 1977 it gained 93 seats and 25.33 per cent of the vote and became the chief opposition party in Parliament. In the 1981 elections, however, Pasok gained an absolute majority in Parliament and it thereupon formed a Government.

Orientation. The party stands for national independence, the socialist transformation of society with a system of self-management, and a non-aligned policy in international affairs. Pasok's aims outlined in its government programme of November 1981 included a long-term policy towards the dissolution of NATO and the Warsaw Pact, renegotiation of the reintegration of Greece into NATO's military wing, the withdrawal of US military bases from Greece, the creation of a nuclear-free "zone of peace" in the Balkans, negotiation of a special relationship with the European Community and a referendum on Greece's continued membership of the Community. At a party congress in May 1984 Papandreou declared that in the absence of a socialist tradition in Greece, Pasok really had its roots in the National Liberation Front (EAM)—see under Communist Party of Greece—Exterior—of whose surviving civil war fighters some 30,000 had been repatriated from Eastern Europe to Greece by the Pasok Government.

Structure. The party has local organizations, district secretaries, a central committee with an executive bureau and a co-ordinating secretariat, as well as specialized commissions and branch organizations.

Membership. 40,000

Publications. *Exormisi* (weekly newspaper)

International affiliations. Pasok's European Parliament representatives are members of the Socialist Group (although the party has declined to join the Socialist International).

Party for Democratic Socialism (KDS)

Address. 9 Mavromichali Str., Athens, Greece

Leadership. Prof. Ioannis Pesmazoglou (pres.)

Founded. March 1979

History. The leader of the KDS (a former minister in the Government established in 1974) had participated in the formation of a (democratic socialist) Movement of New Political Forces in September 1974; in the 1974 elections he had been a successful candidate of the Centre Union-New Forces grouping.

In 1977 Prof. Pesmazoglou was re-elected as a candidate of the Union of the Democratic Centre (EDK), but was expelled from the EDK in March 1978 after he had advocated the adoption of democratic socialist policies which, he felt, might have prevented the replacement of the EDK by the Pan-Hellenic Socialist Movement (Pasok) as the main opposition party in the 1977 elections. The KDS was initially represented in Parliament by four members.

The party contested the October 1981 general elections in a centrist Democratic Unity (DE) alliance with the Agricultural Party (KAE) but without gaining any seats in Parliament.

Orientation. The KDS considers its policies to be related to those of social democratic and socialist parties of Western Europe. It stands for an extensive welfare state, increased workers' participation in decision-making and the maintenance of a multi-party parliamentary form of government; and also for Greece's entry into the

European Community, continued Greek political membership of NATO and the eventual abolition of US military bases in Greece.

Publications. *Agonas* (monthly)

Progressive Party

Leadership. Spyros Markezinis
Founded. 1955; revived November 1979
History. Having originally been formed in 1955, the revival of this party was announced in November 1979 by Spyros Markezinis (Prime Minister under the Papadopoulos regime in 1973), who accused the New Democracy Government of Konstantinos Karamanlis of betraying its conservative voters by adopting a quasi-socialist approach to economic problems and by keeping Greece outside the military wing of NATO.

In elections to the European Parliament held on Oct. 18, 1981, the party gained one seat, but in the simultaneous general elections the party obtained only 1.69 per cent of the votes and no seat.

Orientation. The party advocates a minimum of state interference in the economy and a "thoroughly pragmatic approach" to foreign affairs. Although a right-wing party, it is not committed to a restoration of the monarchy or to an amnesty for those convicted of offences connected with the period of military rule.

Revolutionary Communist Party of Greece
Epanastatiko Kommunistiko Komma Ellados (EKKE)

History. EKKE took part in the 1974 and 1977 parliamentary elections, obtaining respectively 0.02 and 0.23 per cent of the vote. EKKE contested the October 1981 general elections jointly with a Marxist-Leninist Communist Party, but this alliance gained only 0.08 per cent of the votes and no seat.

Orientation. The EKKE subscribes to Maoist precepts.

Revolutionary Left

History. A group of this name contested the October 1981 general elections but polled only 0.12 per cent of the votes and gained no seat in Parliament.

Unifying Centre Rally

Leadership. George Mavros (l.)
Founded. November 1980
History. George Mavros had in 1974 founded the Centre Union-New Forces, which later became the (liberal) Union of the Democratic Centre (see separate entry). From 1978 he had sat in Parliament as an independent member before forming the Centre Rally (later renamed Unifying Centre Rally) in an attempt to regain the leadership of the Greek liberals.

However, in September 1981 he abandoned this attempt and accepted nomination as a candidate of the Pan-Hellenic Socialist Movement (Pasok) in the 1981 general elections. Although he was elected he was not appointed to the Pasok Government. He thereupon sat in the House as an independent and announced in mid-November 1981 that his Unifying Centre Rally would resume its activities as a separate party.

Union of the Democratic Centre
Enose Demokratikou Kentrou (EDK)

Address. 12 Mavromichali Street, Athens 143, Greece
Leadership. Dr John G. Zighdis
Founded. 1974
History. The party is the political heir of the party established by Eleftherios Venizelos in 1910 and of the Centre Union under George Papandreou, which ruled Greece from November 1963 to March 1965, when its Government was dismissed by the King. During the dictatorship from 1967 to 1974 the party organized resistance against the regime and many of its leaders were persecuted and imprisoned.

Re-organized in 1974, the party received about 20 per cent of the votes in the 1974 elections and 12 per cent in 1977. In the general elections of October 1981, which revealed a polarization of votes between right and left, the party gained no seats, but it has since continued to function.

Orientation. The party professes democratic socialism and aims at the defence of popular sovereignty and the transformation of Greece into a modern welfare state with freedom of the individual and social justice. The party strongly supports Greece's participation as an equal partner in the European Community and believes in the political integration of Europe.

Structure. The party has local and regional committees, a secretary-general, a central committee, a political board and a parliamentary committee.

Publications. *Between Us* (for members), 3,000; *Anendotos* (weekly), 4,000

United Democratic Left
Eniaia Demokratike Aristerá (EDA)

Address. Academias St. 62, Athens, Greece

Leadership. Ilias Iliou (pres.); Manolis Glezos (sec.)

Founded. 1951

History. The party was created after the banning of the Communist Party and subsequently took part in all elections, continuing even after the Communist Party had been declared legal in 1974. In 1958 it gained 78 seats in Parliament; it contested the 1961 elections as part of a Pan-Democratic Agrarian Front of Greece (PAME), which obtained only 24 seats; in November 1963 the EDA gained 28 seats; but in February 1964 this number was reduced to 22.

Under the military dictatorship (1967-74) the EDA was banned, and in the 1974 elections it gained only one seat in Parliament (for its president), contesting the elections as part of the United Left. In the elections of November 1977 EDA obtained one of two seats won by an Alliance of Progressive and Left-Wing Forces (APLF).

For the October 1981 general elections the EDA recommended its supporters to vote for the candidates of the Pan-Hellenic Socialist Movement (Pasok) in all constituencies except one (where it campaigned for the Communist Party—Interior).

Orientation. The EDA is a formation of the left, standing for a plurality of political parties and rejecting the dictatorship of the proletariat.

Structure. The party has basic organizations in districts, regions, trade unions, places of work and universities.

Membership. 30,000

Publications. *The Greek Left*, 10,000; *EDA News*, 10,000

United Socialist Alliance of Greece (ESPE)

Leadership. Stathis Panagoulis (l.)

Founded. February 1984

History. The formation of the ESPE was announced on Feb. 22, 1984, by Stathis Panagoulis, who had resigned as Deputy Interior Minister in August 1982 and had subsequently been expelled from the ruling Pan-Hellenic Socialist Movement (Pasok) after accusing its leadership of reneging on election promises.

Orientation. This leftist formation declared that the working class was the "victim of the capitalist relations of production".

Grenada

Capital: St George's   Pop. 120,000

Grenada is an independent state within the Commonwealth with the British monarch as ceremonial head of state represented by a Governor-General. Having been Prime Minister since the New Jewel Movement (NJM) came to power in the 1979 revolution, Maurice Bishop was himself overthrown in a coup in mid-October 1983 by a rival faction of the NJM. Shortly after the formation of a new government US forces supported by small contingents from neighbouring Caribbean states landed on the island and quickly established control, after overcoming limited resistance by the Grenadan People's Revolutionary Army and a number of Cubans. Thereafter the Governor-General assumed full executive power, exercised with the support of an interim non-political Advisory Council, pending the holding of general elections in November 1984.

Political parties reported as being active in Grenada in the early months of 1984 are described below.

Christian Democratic Labour Party

Leadership. Winston Whyte
Founded. April 1984
History. A member of the Grenada Parliament before the 1979 revolution, Winston Whyte launched this party in the aftermath of the demise of the New Jewel regime with a view to contesting general elections due in November 1984.

Grenada Democratic Movement (GDM)

Leadership. Francis Alexis (l.)
History. This Movement's leader was a lawyer based in Barbados. In early April 1984 the party entered into a "togetherness pact" with the Grenada National Party and the National Democratic Party designed to present a centrist alternative between the New Jewel Movement on the left and the formerly ruling Grenada United Labour Party on the right.
Orientation. This party subscribes to social democratic precepts.

Grenada National Party (GNP)

Leadership. Hubert A. Blaize (l.)
Founded. 1956
History. The GNP held a majority of the elective seats in the Legislative Council between 1957 and 1961, and its leader was Chief Minister from September 1962 to August 1967, when the party held six out of the 10 elective seats in the Council. Between 1967 and 1979 it was the traditional opposition party. Following the demise of the New Jewel Movement (NJM) regime in late 1983, the GNP in April 1984 entered into a "togetherness pact" with the Grenada Democratic Movement and the National Democratic Party with the aim of presenting a centrist political alternative.
Orientation. The GNP is a moderate conservative party whose leader had in 1962 advocated a "unitary state" alliance of Grenada with Trinidad and Tobago.

Grenada United Labour Party (GULP)

Leadership. Sir Eric Gairy (l.)
Founded. 1950
History. The GULP was founded with the support of an associated trade union. From 1951 to 1957 it held a majority of elective seats in the Legislative Council. In elections held in March 1961 the GULP won eight out of 10 elective seats in the Council, and its leader (at first George Clyne and later Eric Gairy) was Chief Minister until June 1962 when the Constitution was suspended (because of unauthorized expenditure). In September

1962 the GULP was defeated in elections, retaining only four of the 10 elective seats.

However, the party won the 1967, 1972 and 1976 elections and was in power until being overthrown by the New Jewel Movement in March 1979. Thereafter Sir Eric Gairy went into exile, from which he returned to Grenada following the removal from office of the New Jewel Movement's "People's Revolutionary Government" in October 1983.

National Democratic Party (NDP)

Leadership. George Brizan (l.)

History. Following the demise of the New Jewel Movement (NJM) regime in October 1983, the NDP in April 1984 concluded a "togetherness pact" with the Grenada Democratic Movement and the Grenada National Party designed to present a centrist political alternative between the NJM on the left and the formerly ruling Grenada United Labour Party on the right.

Publications. Vision

New Jewel Movement (NJM)

Leadership. Kendrick Radix
Founded. 1972
History. The NJM had its origins in the Joint Endeavour for Welfare, Education and Liberation (JEWEL) movement, which merged in March 1973 with a "Master Assembly for the People" founded in mid-1972. The NJM contested the 1976 general elections as part of a People's

Alliance (embracing also the Grenada National Party and the United People's Party), which gained six out of the 15 seats in the House of Representatives (three of these six seats being held by NJM members).

The NJM came to power when it overthrew the Gairy Government in March 1979 and formed a "People's Revolutionary Government", which undertook to "restore democratic freedom" and to organize "free and fair elections". However, no elections were held by this regime, which was—after a conflict between rival factions, in which the party's leader, Maurice Bishop, was killed—removed from power by a US-led military operation (supported by contingents from Antigua, Barbados, Dominica, Jamaica, St Lucia and St Vincent and the Grenadines) in October 1983. After the arrest or death of most NJM leaders only remnants of the Movement were still active in early 1984, and in June 1984 Kendrick Radix announced the formation of a new socialist party called Maurice Bishop Patriotic Movement.

International affiliations. Socialist International

People's Action Group

Leadership. Winston Whyte (l.)
Founded. 1979
History. This Group was established as an alliance of small right-wing groups and included members of the United People's Party (which had, in 1976, contested elections in alliance with the New Jewel Movement).

Guatemala

Capital: Guatemala City

Pop. 7,900,000

The Republic of Guatemala has since March 23, 1982, been under the control of military officers who were close to the extreme right-wing anti-communist National Liberation Movement (MNL). On seizing power they suspended the 1966 Constitution and the existing political parties, and also declared null and void the results of presidential and congressional elections held on March 7, 1982 (in which voting had been compulsory for literate persons above the age of 18 years and optional for illiterates, but in which the turn-out was said to have been less than 50 per cent of the electorate). All political parties, however, declared themselves in favour of the new regime. On June 9, 1982, the President appointed by the officers, Gen. Efraín Ríos Montt, assumed sole executive and legislative functions as head of state and C.-in-C. of the Armed Forces.

On Sept. 15, 1982, the Government installed a 34-member advisory Council of State which in turn formed a 15-member commission to draft legislation on elections and political parties. However, the parties gradually turned against the Government of President Ríos Montt, and on Aug. 8, 1983, he was replaced by Brig.-Gen. Oscar Humberto Mejía Victores (until then Minister of Defence). As head of the High Command of the newly-formed Military Commanders' Council the latter declared that this Council would lead the Guatemalan people "along democratic and essentially nationalistic paths" and was committed "to fight by all means available to eradicate the Marxist-Leninist subversion which threatens our freedom and sovereignty" (i.e. to end the warfare or left-wing guerrillas which had intensified since July 1982). He also announced that a Constituent Assembly would be elected on July 1, 1984, and that civilian rule would be restored by 1985.

It was subsequently established that the Assembly would have 88 deputies (65 elected from districts and 23 from national lists), that voting would be compulsory and that parties would be required to obtain at least 4 per cent of the votes in order to retain their legality. By early 1984 over 30 new political groups were seeking official registration (in addition to several longer-standing parties), spanning the political spectrum. The (pro-Soviet Communist) Guatemalan Labour Party was specifically barred from electoral participation because of its involvement in anti-regime guerrilla warfare.

The official results of the 1982 congressional elections showed the distribution of seats in the 66-member unicameral Congress to be as follows: Popular Democratic Front (a conservative alliance of the Revolutionary Party, the Democratic Institutional Party and the Front of National Unity) 33, the (extreme right-wing) National Liberation Movement 21, the (right-wing) Nationalist Authentic Central 3, the (centrist) National Opposition Union (comprising the National Renewal Party and the Guatemalan Christian Democratic Party) 2, others 7.

Democratic Institutional Party
Partido Institucional Democrático (PID)

Address. 2A Calle 10-73, Zona 1, Guatemala City, Guatemala

Leadership. Jorge Lamport Rodil (l.); Donaldo Alvarez Ruíz (director)

Founded. 1965

History. In the presidential elections of March 1966 the PID candidate came second. In the 1970 and 1974 elections it was in alliance with the National Liberation Movement (MLN) but in the 1978 elections it co-operated with the Revolutionary Party.

The PID contested the March 1982 elections as part of a Popular Democratic Front, the other partners in which were the Revolutionary Party (PR) together with the Front of National Unity (FUN). The Front's candidate came first in the presidential elections and in the congressional elections it obtained 33 (out of 66) seats.

Orientation. The PID is a centre-right formation which has opposed the making of any concessions to the left-wing guerrilla movement.

Front of National Unity
Frente de Unidad Nacional (FUN)

Leadership. Col. Enrique Peralta Azurdia (l.)

Founded. 1977

History. Of the party's leaders Col. Peralta Azurdia unsuccessfully contested the 1978 presidential elections as the candidate of the National Liberation Movement (MNL), obtaining second place.

For the March 1982 elections the FUN was part of the Popular Democratic Front (with the Revolutionary Party and the Democratic Institutional Party) whose presidential candidate came first and which obtained 33 (out of 66) seats in Congress.

Orientation. FUN is a right-wing formation, standing for free enterprise.

Guatemalan Christian Democratic Party
Partido Democracía Cristiana Guatemalteca (PDCG)

Address. 8 Avda. 14-53, Zona 1, Guatemala City, Guatemala

Leadership. Mario Vinicio Cerezo (s.g.)

Founded. July 1968

History. In the presidential elections of 1970 the PDCG candidate came third; in the 1974 elections the PDCG took part in a National Opposition Front, whose candidate came second; in the 1978 elections it was part of the National Unity Front (Frenu), whose candidate came third; and in the presidential elections of March 7, 1982, it formed part of a centrist National Opposition Union (UNO), which also embraced the National Renewal Party (PNR) and whose candidate came third. At the same time the UNO gained three seats in Congress.

Later the PDCG broadly supported the Ríos Montt regime but expressed fears that its measures "might lead to polarization and the creation of a climate of fear" in the country. It was one of four parties which on Sept, 4, 1982, condemned the Council of State as a "mask" for the Government and called for "free and clean" elections. (A right-wing faction of this party has been led by the liberal, internationally known lawyer Dr Francisco Villagrán Kramer, who was Vice-President of Guatemala in 1978-80.)

Prior to the July 1984 Assembly elections the PDCG formed a Democratic Co-ordinating Board with 11 other centre-left parties in order to press for reform of the electoral law and impartiality on the part of the military.

Orientation. The PDCG is liberal and reformist.

Membership. 89,000

International affiliations. Christian Democratic International; Christian Democratic Organization of America

---

National Liberation Movement
Movimiento de Liberación Nacional (MLN)

Address. 5A Calle 1-20, Zona 1, Guatemala City, Guatemala

Leadership. Mario Sandóval Alarcón (l.)

Founded. 1960

History. The MLN had its origins in a "Liberation Movement" which overthrew the country's left-wing Government in 1954. The MLN came to power through a coup in 1963, but in the presidential elections of March 1966 its candidate came in third place. In 1970, however, its presidential candidate came first and was confirmed in office by a majority in Congress. For the 1974 elections the MLN concluded an alliance with the Democratic Institutional Party (PID), and their candidate was similarly proclaimed elected by a majority in Congress.

In 1978 the MLN presidential candidate obtained second place. In the March 1982 presidential elections the MLN candidate came second with 28.2 per cent of the votes, and in the congressional elections held at the same time the party obtained 21 seats.

In August 1982 several members of the MLN were suspected of involvement in preparations for a coup against President Ríos Montt. Of its leading members, Leonel Sisniega Otero went into exile and was in May 1983 reported to have left the MLN. (He later founded the Anti-Communist Unification Party.)

On Sept. 4, 1982, the MLN joined three other parties in issuing a statement condemning the proposed Council of State as a "mask" for the Ríos Montt Government and calling for "free and clean" elections. Early in 1983 the MLN called for a "holy war" against any attempt by President Ríos Montt to create a Protestant political party which would contest the elections promised by him. On Aug. 21, 1983, the MLN decided to give its support to the newly-installed President Mejía. For the July 1984 Assembly elections the MLN formed an alliance with the Nationalist Authentic Central (see separate entry).

Orientation. The MLN is an extreme right-wing anti-communist party said to have close links with the Roman Catholic Church.

Structure. The MLN has a private army of 5,000 men.

Membership. 95,000

National Unity Front
Frente Nacional de Unidad (Frenu)

History. Frenu was formed to contest the 1978 general elections as an alliance of the Christian Democratic Party, the Authentic Revolutionary Party and a Popular Participation Front, and its presidential candidate came third.

Orientation. Frenu is an alliance of centre-left parties.

Nationalist Authentic Central
Central Auténtica Nacionalista (CAN)

History. The CAN was earlier known as the Organized Arañista Central (CAO), which consisted of supporters of the former President Araña Osorio (elected in 1970 as the candidate of the National Liberation Movement). In the 1978 presidential elections the CAO was part of a centre-right alliance (with the Revolutionary Party and the Democratic Institutional Party), whose candidate was elected.

In the March 1982 elections the CAN's presidential candidate came fourth (and last) with only 10.2 per cent of the vote, but it gained three seats in Congress. The CAN was one of four parties which, on Sept. 4, 1982, condemned the proposed Council of State as a "mask" for the Ríos Montt Government and called for "free and clean elections". For the July 1984 Assembly elections the CAN formed an alliance with the National Liberation Movement (see separate entry).

Nationalist Renewal Party
Partido Nacionalista Renovador (PNR)

Leadership. Alejandro Maldonado Aguirre (l.); Mario Castrejón (s.g.)
History. This party was legalized in August 1979. It contested the March 1982 elections as part of the centrist National Opposition Union (UNO), i.e. in alliance with the Guatemalan Christian Democratic Party; the UNO presidential candidate came third (with 22.7 per cent of the vote) and UNO gained two seats in Congress. Although broadly supporting the Ríos Montt regime, the PNR was one of four parties which on Sept. 4, 1982, condemned the proposed Council of State as a "mask" for the Government and called for "free and clean" elections.
Membership. 72,000

Revolutionary Party
Partido Revolucionario (PR)

Leadership. Jorge García Granados
Founded. 1957
History. The PR came to power in March 1966, when it won 30 out of 55 seats in Congress. In the 1970 elections, however, its presidential candidate obtained second place. It contested the 1974 elections as part of a centrist alliance with a Guatemala Democratic Front, but the alliance's presidential candidate only obtained third place. For the 1978 elections the bulk of the PR supported the successful candidate of a centre-right alliance including also the Democratic Institutional Party and the Organized Arañista Central

(CAO), whereas a radical faction (the Authentic Revolutionary Party) supported the National Unity Front's Christian Democratic presidential candidate.

For the 1982 elections the PR was part of a Popular Democratic Front (whose other partners were the Democratic Institutional Party and the Front of National Unity). The presidential candidate of the Front came first (with 38.9 per cent of the vote) and it obtained 33 (of the 66) seats in Congress.
Orientation. The party has advocated land reform, administrative changes and increased national development.

United Revolutionary Front
Frente Unido de la Revolución (FUR)

Leadership. Andrino Diéguez (l.); César Augusto Toledo (s.g.)
Founded. 1977
History. The FUR succeeded a Revolutionary Democratic Union (*Unión Revolucionaria Democrática*, URD), which had been founded as a left-wing breakaway group of the Revolutionary Party and part of a National Opposition Front including also the Christian Democrats (in the 1974 elections). The former leader of the UDR, Alberto Fuentes Mohr (a former cabinet minister), was assassinated in January 1979 (reportedly by a secret Anti-Communist Army, ESA). Manuel Colom Argueta, the leader of the FUR, was similarly murdered in March 1979, after his party had obtained legal recognition.

The FUR took part in the formation, by over 72 parties and organizations in March 1979, of a Democratic Front against Repression (FDR) in order to denounce at national and international level all actions of repression committed in Guatemala against any popular and democratic sector and to provide aid to widows and orphans of the victims of such actions.

In 1982 the Front decided not to take part in the presidential and congressional elections because many of its leaders had been murdered during the previous two years. On the other hand, the FUR was the only opposition party prepared to participate in the Council of State installed by the Ríos Montt Government on Sept. 14, 1982.
Orientation. The FUR is democratic socialist in political aspiration.

Other Parties

Additional parties, some recently formed and others not formally legalized, include the following:

Anti-Communist Unification Party (*Partido de Unificación Anticomunista*, PUA), led by Leonel Sisniega and comprising elements which had broken away from the National Liberation Movement.

Civilian Democratic Front (*Frente Cívico Democrático*, FCD), led by Danilo Barillas

Democratic Revolutionary Unity (*Unidad Revolucionaria Demócrata*, URD)

Democratic Socialist Party (*Partido Socialista Democrático*, PSD), led by Carlos Gallardo Flores, currently based in Costa Rica and a member of the Socialist International.

Emerging Movement for Harmony (*Movimiento Emergente de Concordia*, MEC), led by Dario Chávez and Arturo Ramírez

Guatemalan Democratic Front (*Frente Demócrata Guatemalteca*), led by Clemente Marroquín Rojas

Humanist Movement for Democratic Integration (*Movimiento Humanista de Integración Democrática*)

New National Democratic Co-ordinating Board (*Nueva Coordinadora Nacional Democrática*, earlier known as the *Coordinadora Nacional Guevarista*)

Organized Popular Force (*Fuerza Popular Organizada*, FPO)

Pantinamit, led by Fernando Tezahuic Tohón and founded in 1977 to represent the interests of the Indian population.

Popular Democratic Force (*Fuerza Democrática Popular*)

Populist Party (*Partido Populista*)

Revolutionary Party of Central American Workers (*Partido Revolucionario de los Trabajadores Centroamericanos*, PRTC)

Social Christian Party (*Partido Social Cristiano*, PSC)

Socialist Party (*Partido Socialista*)

Union of the National Centre (*Unión del Centro Nacional*) led by Ramiro de Leon Carpio (s.g.)

Guinea

Capital: Conakry   Pop. 5,500,000

For 26 years after its declaration of independence from France 1958, Guinea was ruled by President Ahmed Sekou Touré and his *Parti Démocratique de Guinée* (PDG), in which was vested "sovereign and exclusive control of all sections of national life". However, a week after President Sekou Touré's death on March 26, 1984, the country's armed forces seized power in a bloodless coup and established a Military Committee of National Reform headed by Col. Lansana Conte (as President) and Col. Diara Traore (as Prime Minister). The new military regime suspended the Constitution and dissolved both the Popular National Assembly and the PDG.

Guinea-Bissau

Capital: Bissau   Pop. 840,000

The Republic of Guinea-Bissau is ruled by a predominantly military Revolutionary Council (composed almost exclusively of Guinean Blacks) which overthrew the Government of President Luis de Almeida Cabral, a Cape Verdian *mestiço* (half-caste), on Nov. 14, 1980, and dissolved the institutions of that Government. The leaders of the new regime (Maj. João Bernardo Vieira, previously Prime Minister, and Vítor Saúde Maria, previously Foreign Minister) declared after their assumption of power that they intended to pursue the political programmes of the (Marxist) *Partido Africano da Independência da Guiné e do Cabo Verde* (PAIGC), whose principles, they claimed, had been betrayed by President Cabral.

African Party for the Independence of Guinea and Cape Verde
Partido Africano da Independência da Guiné e do Cabo Verde (PAIGC)

Address. B.P. 106, Bissau, Guinea-Bissau

Leadership. Cdr. João Bernardo Vieira (s.g.); Dr Vasco Cabral (perm. sec. of central committee)

Founded. 1956

History. The party was founded by the late Amilcar Cabral and others to fight for the liberation of Portuguese Guinea and the Cape Verde Islands from Portuguese rule. It conducted an armed struggle in the then Portuguese Guinea from 1963 to 1974. In September 1973 the PAIGC organized a Government and declared Guinea-Bissau independent, and this independence was agreed to by Portugal in August 1974.

The PAIGC continued to be the sole ruling party after the military coup of November 1980, whose perpetrators declared themselves to be the true upholders of its political precepts. A PAIGC congress in November 1981 decided to retain the existing name of the party even though the Cape Verdian branch had broken away from the Guinea-Bissau branch in January 1981. At the same congress President Pereira of Cape Verde and other Cape Verdian founders, including ex-President Cabral, were expelled from the PAIGC, which thus became effectively a one-country party.

Orientation. The PAIGC is a pro-Soviet party which has co-operated with non-socialist countries in Africa and in the Western (developed) world.

Structure. The PAIGC has a 51-member high council (or central committee) and an executive committee (political bureau) of 24 members. It is committed to operating on the basis of the principle of democratic centralism.

Publications. *O Militante*

Guyana

Capital: Georgetown   Pop. 900,000

The Co-operative Republic of Guyana, a member of the Commonwealth, has under its Constitution, which came into effect on Oct. 6, 1980, a popularly elected executive President and a First Vice-President who is also Prime Minister. There is also a National Assembly to which 53 members are elected for a five-year term by universal adult suffrage, while another 12 members are elected by 10 regional democratic councils from among their own members and by a national congress of local democratic organs. The election of the above 53 members is carried out by citizens above the age of 18 years, with the whole country constituting one electoral district and seats allocated in proportion to votes for each party list.

According to the official results of elections held on Dec. 15, 1980, the 53 directly elected members of the National Assembly were distributed as follows: People's National Congress (PNC) 41, People's Progressive Party (PPP) 10, United Force (UF) 2. However, a team of observers led by (the British Liberal) Lord Avebury reported that "massive and blatant fraud" had been committed during the elections. The (co-operative socialist) PNC is supported mainly by the African section of the population, and the (pro-Soviet communist) PPP by the East Indian community. The elections were boycotted by two opposition parties—the Vanguard for Liberation and Democracy and the Working People's Alliance which, together with the PPP, condemned the official results as "fraudulent".

Democratic Labour Movement (DLM)

Leadership. Paul Tennassee (pres.)
Founded. April 1982
History. This small opposition grouping derives directly from the Right-to-Work Association/Front for Democratic Unionism (RWA/FDU). Its leader was detained in early 1984 after returning from a Caribbean tour during which he reportedly criticised the Forbes Burnham Government.

Liberator Party (LP)

Address. P.O. Box 730, Georgetown, Guyana
Leadership. Dr Gunraj Kumar (l.); Dr Makepeace Richmond (ch.); Kinsell France (sec.)
Founded. June 1973
History. The LP contested the 1973 elections and was stated to have won two out of 53 seats in the National Assembly but did not take them up because it considered that there had been "massive frauds" during the elections. The two seats were later taken up by the United Force which had contested the elections under the LP banner.

With the other opposition groups the LP boycotted a constitutional referendum held in July 1978, claiming afterwards that the turnout had been less than 15 per cent although the official percentage poll was 70 per cent and the official "yes" vote over 97 per cent of the votes cast. The LP now works in association with the (centre-left) Working People's Vanguard Party and the (centrist) People's Democratic Movement under the title "Vanguard for Liberation and Democracy" (VLD).

Orientation. The LP is a right-wing party which believes in providing opportunities so that "each can make his way in a meritocracy"; it is dedicated to freedom of conscience, speech, association and ownership of property, and to the protection of the aged and the infirm.

Structure. The party has a central executive, district committees and local groups.

Membership. 16,000

Publications. *The Liberator* (monthly), 5,000

People's National Congress (PNC)

Address. Congress Place, Sophia, P.O. Box 10330, Georgetown, Guyana

Leadership. Linden Forbes S. Burnham (l.); Dr Ptolemy A. Reid (dep. l. and g.s.); Bishwaishwar Ramsaroop (ch.)

Founded. October 1955

History. The party arose out of a faction of the People's Progressive Party (PPP) led by Forbes Burnham (who had been chairman of the PPP, with Dr Cheddi Jagan being the PPP leader). In the country's first general election after a new Constitution, held in 1957, and again in 1961, the PNC was left in a minority. In the 1964 elections, held on the basis of proportional representation, no party gained an absolute majority, although the PPP obtained the largest number of seats. The PNC, however, formed a coalition Government with the United Force party.

In the 1968 elections—the first held after Guyana achieved independence in 1966— the PNC obtained an absolute majority (of 30 seats, against 19 for the PPP and four for the United Force), and the coalition Government came to an end in September 1967, since when the PNC has had full control of the Government, more especially after gaining a two-thirds majority in Parliament in 1973.

Orientation. The PNC stands for "co-operative socialism", "national self-reliance" and "the closest possible association of Guyana with its Caribbean neighbours", while maintaining a link with international organizations and agencies with aims and objectives consistent with those of the PNC. In its 1974 "Declaration of Sophia" the PNC was described as "a socialist party committed to practising co-operative socialism" under which land and all foreign trade would be controlled in the interest of the nation, while of the domestic economy's three sectors—public, co-operative and private—the co-operative one would become dominant, though private investment from abroad was "welcome in specific fields" provided that the Government and/or co-operatives held "majority equity and real control"; the concept of PNC paramountcy over the Government was also enunciated. At its fifth biennial congress held in August 1983 the party declared its advocacy of "North-South dialogue, economic co-operation and collective self-reliance in the Third World".

Structure. The party's supreme authorities are its (biennial) congress and, between sessions of the latter, its general council. There are a central committee, an administrative committee (of party officers and co-opted members) and a secretariat. The party also has a women's arm and a youth arm—the Women's Revolutionary Socialist Movement (WRSM) and the Young Socialist Movement (YSM)—which not only play an important part in the party's organization but also make a major contribution to the social and economic life of the country as a whole. The party has 544 groups, organized in 53 districts and 10 regions.

Membership. 8,432

Publications. *The New Nation* (weekly), 23,400

People's Progressive Party (PPP)

Address. 41 Robb Street, Georgetown, Guyana

Leadership. Dr Cheddi Jagan (g.s.)

Founded. January 1950

History. The PPP arose out of a Political Affairs Committee formed in 1946 "to assist the growth and development of the labour and progressive movement to the end of establishing a strong, disciplined party equipped with the theory of scientific socialism". In its first manifesto the PPP pledged itself in 1950 to the "task of winning a free and independent Guyana [and] of building a just socialist society".- The PPP won the first elections under adult suffrage in 1953, but held office for only 4½ months, the British Government suspending the country's constitution in October 1953 "to prevent communist subversion".

Under a revised constitution the PPP gained, in August 1956, an absolute majority in the Legislative Assembly, and under a full internal self-government constitution the PPP gained 20 out of the 35 seats in the 1961 Legislative Assembly. However, in elections held on the basis of proportional representation in December 1964 the PPP failed to retain its absolute majority, and the PPP Government under Dr Jagan was deposed. The PPP thereupon boycotted Parliament until May 1965.

In the 1968 elections (the first held after Guyana had attained independence in May 1966) the PPP gained only 19 seats out of 53 (compared with 24 in 1964) in the Legislative Assembly, which was repeatedly boycotted by the (opposition) PPP. In elections held in 1973 the PPP gained 14 seats, but it called these elections "fraudulent" and boycotted the National Assembly until 1976. It also boycotted a referendum held in 1978 to change the Constitution.

Orientation. "Based on principles of Marxism-Leninism" with the "objective of achieving genuine political, economic and social liberation of the working people of Guyana through the attainment of socialism".

Structure. There are party groups, district and regional committees, and a central committee (which is elected by congress every three years and which elects a general secretary, an executive committee and a secretariat).

Publications. *Thunder* (theoretical journal, quarterly); *Mirror* (weekly); *Guyana Information Bulletin* (monthly, for overseas); *For Socialism in Guyana* (party programme)

International affiliations. The PPP is recognized by the Communist parties of the Soviet-bloc countries.

United Force of Guyana (UF)

Address. Unity House, 95 Robb & New Garden Sts., Georgetown, Guyana

Leadership. M. Fielden Singh (l.)

History. The UF first took part in elections when a 34-member Legislative Assembly was elected in 1961 under a new Constitution in the then British Guiana, and it gained four seats. In 1964 it gained seven seats in the 53-member legislature and entered into a coalition Government with the People's National Congress (PNC), under which the country became independent (as Guyana) in 1966.

The coalition was ended in 1968 after the UF had unsuccessfully opposed a bill enabling some 66,000 Guyanese abroad (most of them in Britain), constituting about 20 per cent of the total electorate, to vote for the Parliament of Guyana. In the 1968 elections the PNC obtained a majority of votes and seats while the parliamentary representation of the UF fell from seven to four members.

The UF was not represented in Parliament in 1973-80 but in the elections held on Dec. 15, 1980, it gained two seats.

Orientation. As a conservative party the UF has had support from Whites, Amerindians and other minority groups. It has called for rapid industrialization through a partnership between government and private enterprise.

Vanguard for Liberation and Democracy

Founded. 1979

History. This organization was set up as an alliance of the Liberator Party (see separate entry) and the Working People's Vanguard Party, which had previously been part of the Working People's Alliance (see separate entry).

Orientation. Strongly opposed to the People's National Congress regime, the formation is regarded as representative of business interests.

Working People's Alliance (WPA)

Address. 3A Queen & Holmes Streets, Georgetown, Guyana

Leadership. Collective, headed by Eusi Kwayana and Rupert Roopnaraine (co-chairmen)

Founded. July 27, 1979

History. From its formation as a pressure group in 1974, the WPA was an alliance of four independent political groupings—the African Society for Cultural Relations with Independent Africa (ASCRIA), Indian Political Revolutionary Associates (IPRA), Ratoon (a university-based left-wing group) and the Working People's Vanguard Party (WPVP). The WPVP left the alliance before it was constituted as a political party in 1979. On June 13, 1980, Dr Walter Rodney, the WPA's foremost leader, was assassinated (according to the WPA by an agent of the Burnham Government).

Orientation. The WPA is an independent Marxist party which has since 1979 worked for the replacement of the Burnham regime by a caretaker government of "all patriotic, anti-dictatorial and non-racial forces". After free and fair elections and the restoration of democracy, the party's long-term programme is the establishment of a multiracial working people's government. It has been widely regarded as the main focus of political opposition to the Burnham regime.

International affiliations. Socialist International (consultative member)

Haiti

Capital: Port-au-Prince   Pop. 5,800,000

The Republic of Haiti has an executive President (appointed for life), who presides over a Council of Ministers appointed by him. There is a unicameral National Assembly of 59 members elected for five years by universal adult suffrage of citizens over the age of 18 years. In an emergency the President is empowered to dismiss the Council of Ministers and the National Assembly and to govern by decree. In elections held on Feb. 12, 1984, the Party of National Unity, the country's sole legal party, was officially declared to have won all 59 seats (for most of which it had been opposed by independent candidates).

Party of National Unity
Parti de l'Unité Nationale (PUN)

Address. National Assembly, Port-au-Prince, Haiti
Leadership. President Jean-Claude Duvalier (l.)
Founded. 1963
History. The party was founded as the *Parti Unique de l'Action Révolutionnaire et Gouvernementale* by President François ("Papadoc") Duvalier, who was succeeded by his son in 1971. It is the sole authorized political party, its central object being to support the policies of the country's President.

While the PUN has remained the sole legal party, the regime of President Duvalier has come under increasing challenge from various internal and external opposition formations.Internally, a number of Christian democratic opposition parties have been formed, while the (pro-Soviet) United Party of Haitian Communists (founded in its present form in 1968) exists in clandestinity.

Honduras

Capital: Tegucigalpa   Pop. 4,000,000

The Republic of Honduras has an executive President who is elected for a four-year term by universal adult suffrage and who presides over a Cabinet. There is a unicameral Congress of 82 members, similarly elected for a four-year term. In elections held on Nov. 29, 1981 (marking the end of almost uninterrupted military rule since 1963), political parties gained seats as follows: Liberal Party 44, National Party 34, Innovation and Unity Party (PINU) 3, Christian Democratic Party (PDC) 1. About 80 per cent of the registered voters took part in the elections, which resulted in the assumption of power by Dr Roberto Suazo Córdova of the Liberal Party. Voting was compulsory for citizens above the age of 18 years and seats were allotted under a system of proportional representation according to an electoral quotient for each department.

Christian Democratic Party
Partido Demócrata Cristiano (PDC)

Leadership. Dr Hernán Corrales Padilla
History. The PDC was legally recognized on July 15, 1980, and in the 1981 elections it gained one seat in Congress, where it was in opposition to the Government. It accused the latter in September 1982 of planning a systematic extermination of opposition members.
International affiliations. Christian Democratic International; Christian Democratic Organization of America

Communist Party of Honduras
Partido Comunista de Honduras (PCH)

Leadership. Rigoberto Padilla Rush (g.s.)
Founded. 1954
History. This pro-Soviet party has been illegal for most of its life. In 1960 and in 1965–67 it suffered breakaways of factions opposed to its pro-Soviet line. In 1981 the party was given legal status.
Orientation. At a congress held in 1972 the party reaffirmed its loyalty to Marxism-Leninism and to "proletarian internationalism" and adopted a new programme and constitution defining its tasks as "struggle against the domination of US imperialism and the reactionary bourgeoisie and landowners and for an anti-imperialist, agrarian, popular and democratic revolution".
International affiliations. The PCH is recognized by the Communist parties of the Soviet-bloc countries.

Honduran Revolutionary Party
Partido Revolucionario Hondureño (PRH)

Address. Apartado Postal No. 1319, San Pedro Sula, Honduras
Leadership. Francisco Rodolfo Jiménez Caballero (s.g.)
Founded. Aug. 28, 1977
History. Preparations to establish the party were begun in December 1974 by a group of workers' and peasants' leaders allied with professional elements. Since its formal creation in August 1977, the PRH has not succeeded in winning representation in Congress.
Orientation. The PRH's outlook is social democratic, with the object of solving the problems facing the people of Honduras by exercising political power.
Structure. The party has a national assembly and other assemblies at departmental and local level. It also has executive committees at all levels.

Membership. 8,300
Publications. *Mensaje Revolucionario* (weekly)

Liberal Party of Honduras
Partido Liberal de Honduras (PLH)

Leadership. Dr Roberto Suazo Córdova
Founded. 1890
History. During the period following World War II the PLH first came to power in 1957, when it gained 37 seats in a 58-member Constituent Assembly and its candidate was elected President, which he remained until he was overthrown in 1963. A Constituent Assembly elected in 1965 was boycotted by the PLH, but its members later took their seats when the Assembly was converted into a Legislature.

The 1971 elections were contested under a "pact of national union" concluded by the PLH and the National Party (PN), with each of the two parties being given 32 seats in Congress and the presidency going to the party which had won the elections (in this case the PN, in a 60 per cent poll). The pact, however, broke down in 1973 when the PN disowned it over the division of government appointments between the two parties.

In elections to a Constituent Assembly held on April 20, 1980 (the first elections to take place since 1971), the PLH gained 35 (out of the 71) seats. The PLH thereupon joined a coalition Government (consisting of two military officers and six members each of the PLH and the National Party). The PLH also won the 1981 elections, in which its presidential candidate, Dr Suazo Córdova, gained 53.3 per cent of the votes and the party obtained 44 (out of the 82) seats in Congress, as a result of which a PLH Government was formed.

The party was, however, divided into several tendencies, namely (i) the popular left-of-centre *Alianza Liberal del Pueblo* (Alipo), founded in 1978 by a merger of the *Movimiento Villeda Morales* (based in San Pedro Sula) and the Democratic Left (*Izquierda Democrática*, based in Tegucigalpa), which was led by Jorge Arturo Reina and Carlos Roberto Reina, but which, at a party convention held in April 1981, remained in a minority; (ii) the conservative *rodista* tendency (named after the party's former leader, Modesto Rodas Alvarado, who had died in 1979), which was successfully led to the election victories of 1980 and 1981 by Dr Suazo Córdova; and (iii) the *Frente de Unidad Liberal* (FUL), which refused to attend the 1981 party convention after the executive had denied it registration as a tendency within the party.

In November 1982 six PLH members of Congress joined the Opposition. On Feb. 14, 1984, it was announced that the Reina brothers had constituted a separate faction under the name of *Movimiento Liberal Democrático Revolucionario* with J. A. Reina as president and Armando Aguilar Cruz as secretary-general.

Orientation. The PLH stands for democratic principles, social reform and Central American integration.

National Party
Partido Nacional (PN)

Leadership. Ricardo Zuñiga Augustinus
Founded. 1923
History. The PN was in power from 1932 to 1957, when it was defeated in elections to a 58-member Constituent Assembly, in which it won only 18 seats. In the 1965 Constituent Assembly it held a majority of seats and supported the military candidate for the presidency who had overthrown the Liberal Government in 1963.

In 1971 it concluded a "pact of national union" with the Liberal Party, providing for 32 seats in Congress for each of the two parties, while the presidency was obtained by the PN as the party with the largest number of votes. The pact was disavowed by the PN in 1973 over the distribution of government posts between the two parties.

In elections to a Constituent Assembly held on April 20, 1981, the PN obtained 33 (out of the 71) seats. It described these elections as "clean" and joined a coalition Government containing also two military officers and six members of the Liberal Party. In the November 1981 elections its presidential candidate, Ricardo Zuñiga Augustinus, came second with 40.9 per cent of the vote and the party obtained 34 of the 82 seats in Congress. It thus became the principal opposition party.

The PN contains several tendencies, among them (i) the *Movimiento Democratizador Nacionalista* (Modena) and (ii) the *Tendencia Nacionalista de Trabajo.*

Orientation. As a party of the right, the PN favours modest internal reform, economic and social development and Central American integration.

Socialist Party
Partido Socialista (Paso)

Leadership. Mario Virgilio Caras, Rogelio Martínez Reina
History. This party formed part of a *Frente Patriotico Hondureño* (FPH), which also embraced the Communist Party of Honduras and the Marxist-Leninist Communist Party, but did not present any candidates for the elections on Nov. 29, 1981. During 1981 the party's two leaders were temporarily detained, apparently by security forces. They stated later that they had been tortured and interrogated about alleged arms traffic to Salvadorean guerrillas.

Unity Innovation Party
Partido de Inovación y Unidad (PINU)

Address. Apdo. 105, Tegucigalpa, Honduras
Leadership. Dr Miguel Andonie Fernández
Founded. 1978
History. This party was legally recognized in 1978. It gained three seats both in the Constituent Assembly elected in April 1981 and in the Congress elected in November of that year.

Hungary

Capital: Budapest   Pop. 10,710,000

The People's Republic of Hungary, in which de facto power is held by the Politburo of the Central Committee of the Hungarian Socialist Workers' Party (HSWP), has a Presidential Council, whose Chairman is the head of state, a Council of Ministers under a Prime Minister, and a 352-member National Assembly (*Országgülés*) elected for five-year term, with all citizens above the age of 18 years being entitled to vote. These elections are held under an absolute majority system in single-member constituencies, and if necessary further ballots are held until an absolute majority is obtained. The National Assembly elects the Chairman of the Presidential Council. Candidates for the National Assembly must be supporters of the Patriotic People's Front (a mass organization dominated by the HSWP), though more than one candidate is permitted to stand in each constituency and candidates need to receive 30 per cent of the votes at nomination meetings.

In national elections held on June 8, 1980, only 15 seats were contested by more than one candidate, and the official candidates were stated to have obtained 99.3 per cent of the valid votes cast. By-elections were held for two seats on June 14, 1980.

Hungarian Socialist Workers' Party (HSWP)
Magyar Szocialista Munkáspárt

Address. Széchenyi rkp. 19, Budapest V, Hungary

Leadership. János Kádár (first sec.); György Aczél, Valéria Benke, Sándor Gáspár, Ferenc Havasi, Mihály Korom, György Lázár, Pál Losonczi, Laszlo Marothy, Lajos Mehes, Károly Németh, Miklós Ovári, István Sarlós (other members of politburo)

Founded. June 1948

History. The original Hungarian Communist Party was founded in November 1918 and took a leading role in the short-lived "Soviet Republic" declared in Hungary in 1919, its leading activists going underground during the succeeding "White Terror" and Horthy dictatorship. Many prominent Communists took refuge in Moscow and after World War II (during which Hungary was allied to the Axis powers) the entry into Hungary of Soviet forces was followed by the establishment of a provisional government in April 1945 comprising Communists, Smallholders, Social Democrats and the National Peasant Party. Although the Smallholders obtained an absolute majority (57 per cent) in elections held in November 1945, the coalition was continued, with a Communist as Interior Minister. Under the leadership of Matyas Rakosi, the Communists then effectively eliminated their coalition partners as independent political forces and in June 1948 the left wing of the Social Democratic Party merged with the Communist Party to form the United Workers' Party (UWP).

In elections held in May 1949 the UWP presented an unopposed joint list with four other parties called the People's Independence Front (PIF) and of the 395 seats in Parliament 270 were allotted to the UWP, which was subsequently renamed the Hungarian Workers' Party (HWP). In August 1949 a new Constitution was adopted similar to those of other East European "people's democracies" and in the elections of May 1951 the HWP was the only party to be mentioned in the manifesto of the PIF, which in October 1954 was replaced by the broader-based Patriotic People's Front (*Hazafias Nepfront*).

Meanwhile, former Social Democrats were gradually eliminated from the HWP leadership and purges conducted by the "Muscovites" against the "home Communists", notably Laszlo Rajk, who was executed in October 1949 after a show trial. Following Stalin's death in March 1953 Rakosi resigned from the premiership (although continuing as party leader) in which post he was succeeded in July 1953 by Imre Nagy, who embarked on a "new course" economic policy involving the halting of compulsory collectivization, greater emphasis on the production of consumer goods, the release of political prisoners and greater cultural freedom. However, in early 1955 the HWP central committee condemned the new policies as "rightist deviation", with the result that Nagy was removed from the premiership and dismissed from his party posts in April 1955.

Following Khrushchev's denunciation of Stalin at the 20th congress of the Soviet Communist Party in February 1956, Rakosi was obliged to resign from the Hungarian party leadership in July 1956. Thereafter, massive opposition built up to Rakosi's successor, Ernö Gerö (another "hard-liner"), culminating in the reappointment of Nagy to the premiership in October 1956 amid violent clashes between Hungarian demonstrators and Soviet forces (which were then withdrawn from the country). Nagy announced a new programme (including free elections, Hungary's withdrawal from the Warsaw Pact and a policy of permanent neutrality) and formed a national coalition administration including non-Communist representatives. Gerö was succeeded as party secretary by János Kádár, who initially supported Nagy's programme but in early November 1956 went over to the Soviet side. Soviet forces then returned in strength and crushed Hungarian resistance over several days of heavy fighting.

Nagy and his associates were executed as traitors and Kádár was confirmed as leader of the party, which was reconstituted as the Hungarian Socialist Workers' Party (HSWP). After a period of severe reprisals Kádár instituted a policy of reconciliation and limited liberalization—which, notwithstanding Hungary's participation in the Soviet-led intervention in Czechoslovakia in 1968, has been maintained to date.

Orientation. The HSWP continues to be a Soviet-aligned orthodox Communist party, although the Kádár regime's policy of cautious liberalization is regarded as having made Hungary the most liberal of the East European Communist states as regards economic, social and cultural policy.

Structure. Party congresses held every four years elect a central committee, which in turn elects a politburo and a secretariat.

Membership. 800,000

Publications. *Népszabadság* (People's Freedom, daily party organ) 727,000; *Esti Hirlap* (Evening Paper, daily organ of Budapest party committee), 239,000; *Tasardalmi Szemle* (Social Review, monthly theoretical and political journal) 45,000; *Partelet* (Party Life, monthly central committee journal) 95,000

Iceland

Capital: Reykjavik   Pop. 235,000

The Republic of Iceland is a multi-party parliamentary democracy with a President (elected by universal suffrage of citizens above the age of 20 years for a four-year term and re-eligible), under whom a Cabinet with a Prime Minister exercises executive power. There is a bicameral 60-member legislature, the *Althing* (elected also by universal adult suffrage and by proportional representation in eight multi-member constituencies for a four-year term), its Upper House consisting of one-third of the whole *Althing's* members elected at a joint sitting, and its Lower House comprising the remaining two-thirds of members.

As a result of elections held on April 24, 1983, the seats in the *Althing* were distributed as follows: Independence Party (conservative) 23, Progressive Party 14, People's Alliance (Communist-dominated) 10, Social Democrats 6, New Social Democrats 4, Feminists 3.

Feminist Party

History. Influenced by the growth of the women's movement in other Western countries in recent years, Iceland's feminists grouped together in a political organization which presented candidates in the April 1983 parliamentary elections. Possibly given credibility by the fact that Iceland's incumbent President was a woman, the feminists secured 5.5 per cent of the vote and three of the 60 *Althing* seats.

Independence Party
Sjálfstaedisflokkurinn

Address. Háaleitisbraut 1, Reykjavik, Iceland
Leadership. Geir Hallgrímsson (ch.)
Founded. 1929
History. The party was established by a merger of conservative and liberal groups. Having consistently been the strongest party in the *Althing* (usually with about 40 per cent of the votes, but not with an absolute majority), it briefly formed a minority administration in 1949-50. It has also taken part in numerous coalition governments—with Social Democrats and Communists in 1944–46, with the Progressive Party and Social Democrats in 1947–49, with the Progressive Party in 1950–56, with Social Democrats in 1959–71, with the Progressive Party in 1974–78 and again with that party from 1983. It briefly formed a minority Government in 1949–50.
Orientation. The Independence Party is a conservative liberal party, advocating Iceland's continued membership of NATO and the retention of the existing US base in Iceland.
Publications. *Morgunbladid* (Reykjavik, daily) 43,000; *Dagbladid & Visir* (Reykjavik, daily), 38,000; *Islendingur* (Akureyri, weekly); and about 10 local newspapers

People's Alliance
Althydubandalag

Address. Hvervisgata 105, Reykjavik, Iceland
Leadership. Svavar Gestsson (ch.)
Founded. 1956
History. The PA was formed by Communists and left-wing socialists of varying shades of opinion. The Communists were represented in the *Althing*, from the establishment of the Republic of Iceland in 1944, by between seven and 11 members until 1974 (having contested elections as part of a People's Front until 1956), and took part in a coalition Government in 1944–46. The PA also participated in coalition Governments (in 1956–58, 1971–74 and again after 1978). (Iceland's Communists have been independent of the Soviet Union since 1968 and did not take part in the 1969 Conference of World Communists parties.) Since the 1983 elections the People's Alliance has been in opposition.
Orientation. The PA advocates Iceland's withdrawal from NATO and closure of the US base.
Publications. *Thjódviljinn* (daily), 12,000

Progressive Party
Framsóknarflokkurinn

Address. Raudararstig 18, 105 Reykjavik, Iceland
Leadership. Steingrímur Hermannsson (ch.); Gudmundur Bjarnason (sec.); Haukur Ingibergsson (g.s.)
Founded. 1916
History. The party was established to represent farming and fisheries interests and the co-operative movement. Until 1978 it was consistently the second-strongest party in the *Althing*, and it took part in coalition Governments, with the Independence Party and Social Democrats in 1947–49, with the Independence Party in 1950–56, with Social Democrats and the People's Alliance in 1956–58, with the People's Alliance and the Union of Liberals and Leftists in 1971–74, with the Independence Party in 1974–78, with Social Democrats and the People's Alliance in 1978–79 and with the People's Alliance and dissident members of the Independence Party from February 1980.
In June 1983 it formed a coalition Government with the Independence Party, with Steingrímur Hermannsson as Prime Minister.
Orientation. The party's principal aim is to safeguard the Icelandic nation's economic and cultural independence on the basis of a democratic and parliamentary system, with emphasis on the freedom of the individual and his direct relations with the administration. The party also stands for basing the national economy on the initiative of financially independent persons who solve problems in unison and co-operation, with official operations remaining exceptional. The party has favoured Iceland's continued membership of NATO

but has called for the withdrawal of NATO's military forces from Iceland.

Publications. *Tíminn* (Reykjavik, daily), 18,000; *Dagur* (Akureyri, three times a week) 4,000; and several local weeklies and monthlies

International affiliations. Liberal International

Social Democratic Federation (SDF)

Leadership. Vilmundur Gylfason (l.)

Founded. 1982

History. This group broke away from the Social Democratic Party, with Vilmundur Gylfason presenting more radical policies than those which had, in his view, led to recent electoral setbacks for that party. In the 1983 general elections the SDF gained 7.3 per cent of the vote and four seats in the *Althing* (whereas the Social Democratic Party fell back from 10 to six seats and from 17.4 per cent to 11.7 per cent of the votes).

Social Democratic Party
Althyduflokkurinn

Address. Althyduhusid, Hvervisgötu 8-10, Reykjavik, Iceland

Leadership. Kjartan Johannsson (ch.); Karl Steinar Gudnason (sec.)

Founded. 1916

History. The SDP has always been a minority party with between six and nine seats in the *Althing* from 1944 to 1974 (when it retained only five seats), although it obtained 14 seats in 1978 and 10 in 1979. It has taken part in numerous coalition Governments—with the Independence Party and Communists in 1944-46, with the Independence and Progressive parties in 1947-49, with the Progressives

and the People's Alliance in 1956-58 (after which it briefly formed a minority Government) and with the Independence Party in 1959-71.

It was in coalition with the Progressive Party and the People's Alliance in 1978-79, formed a minority caretaker administration in October 1979 and went into opposition in February 1980. After the defection of left-wing dissidents, who formed a Social Democratic Federation, the party retained only six seats in the *Althing* elections of 1983.

Orientation. The SDP stands for state ownership of large enterprises, expanded welfare services and Iceland's continued membership of NATO.

Publications. *Althydubladid* (Reykjavik, daily), 5,000; *Althydumadurinn* (Akureyri, weekly), 3,500

International affiliations. Socialist International

Union of Liberals and Leftists
Samtök Frjálsyndra og Vinstri Manna

Leadership. Magnus T. Ólafsson

Founded. 1969

History. The party was formed mainly by former members of the People's Alliance and its first leader was the head of the Icelandic Confederation of Trade Unions. Having obtained five seats in the *Althing* in 1971, it took part in a coalition Government with the Progressive Party and the People's Alliance until 1974, when its parliamentary strength was reduced to two members. The party has not been represented in the *Althing* since 1978 and did not contest the 1979 and 1983 elections.

Orientation. The party is opposed to Iceland's membership of NATO and advocates the closure of the US base in Iceland.

India

Capital: Delhi   Pop. 730,000,000

The Union of India is, under its Constitution with amendments which came into force on Jan. 3, 1977, "a sovereign socialist secular democratic republic" (and a member of the Commonwealth) with a Parliament consisting of the President, the Council of States (*Rajya Sabha*) and the House of the People (*Lok Sabha*). The *Rajya Sabha* has up to 250 members, the majority of whom are elected by the elected members of the Legislative Assemblies of each state or union territory, while 12 members are appointed by the President of the Republic, and one-third of its members retire every second year. The *Lok Sabha* has 544 members elected for a five-year term by universal suffrage of citizens at least 21 years old under a simple majority system in single-member constituencies in the states and with up to 20 members representing union territories, while the President may nominate up to two additional members. The President is elected for a five-year term by the elected members of Parliament and of the Legislative Assemblies of the states; he appoints a Prime Minister and, on the latter's advice, other ministers, all of whom are responsible to Parliament.

Parties may be recognized, and be allocated a symbol, by the Election Commission provided that they received a minimum of 3 per cent of the vote at national or state level in the last preceding elections. Unrecognized parties are also registered with the Election Commission. Each candidate must pay a deposit of 500 rupees which is forfeited unless he obtains at least one-sixth of the votes cast in his constituency. Any vacancies arising are filled in by-elections.

There is in India a profusion of legal political parties both at national and at state level; divisions of existing parties, defections from these parties and formations of new parties have been frequent.

As a result of general elections held in January-February 1980 the principal parties held seats in the *Lok Sabha* as follows: Congress (I) 352, People's Party (*Lok Dal*) 41, Communist Party of India (Marxist) 36, Janata Party 31, *Dravida Munnetra Kazhagam* (of Tamil Nadu) 16, Congress 13, Communist Party of India 11. A total of 11 other parties gained from one to four seats each, and 17 seats went to independents.

Seats in the Legislative Assemblies of India's states (as resulting from elections held on the dates indicated in parentheses) were distributed as shown below. Abbreviations used are: BJP is the *Bharatiya* Janata Party; CPI is the Communist Party of India; CPI(M) is the Communist Party of India (Marxist).

Andhra Pradesh. (Jan. 5, 1983): *Telugu Desam* 202, Congress (I) 60, CPI(M) 5, *Majlis-Ittehad-ul-Mussalman* 5, CPI 4, BJP 3, Congress (J) 1, Janata 1, independents 12.

Assam. (February 1983): Congress (I) 90, Plains Tribal Council of Assam 3, independents 10. (Owing to widespread agitation and violence the poll was estimated at only about 10 per cent and voting was deferred in 18 constituencies.)

Bihar. (May 1980): Congress (I) 167, *Lok Dal* 42, Janata 13, *Jharkhand Mukti Morcha* 13, CPI(M) 6, Janata (S) 1, Forward Bloc 1, Marxist Co-ordination 1, independents 19.

207

Gujarat. (May 1980): Congress (I) 140, Janata 22, BJP 9, *Lok Dal* 1, independents 9.

Haryana. (May 19, 1982): Congress (I) 36, *Lok Dal* 31, BJP 6, Congress (J) 3, Janata 1, independents 12.

Himachal Pradesh. (May 19, 1982): Congress (I) 31, BJP 29, Janata 2, independents 6.

Jammu and Kashmir. (June 5, 1983): National Conference 46, Congress (I) 26, others 3.

Karnataka. (Jan. 5, 1983): Janata 95, Congress (I) 82, BJP 18, *Maharashtra Ekikaran Samiti* 5, CPI 3, CPI(M) 3, All-India *Anna Dravida Munnetram Kazhagam* 1, and independents.

Kerala. (May 19, 1982): *United Democratic Front*—Congress (I) 20, Congress (A) 15, Indian Union Moslem League 14, Kerala Congress (Joseph group) 8, Kerala Congress (Mani group) 6, National Democratic Party 4, Janata dissidents 4, Socialist Revolutionary Party 2, Praja Socialist Party 1, Revolutionary Socialist Party dissidents 1, independents 2; *Left Democratic Front*—CPI(M) 26, CPI 12, Congress (S) 7, Revolutionary Socialist Party 4, All-India Moslem League 4, Janata 4, Democratic Socialist Party 1, Kerala Congress (Socialist) 1, independents 4.

Madhya Pradesh. (May 1980): Congress (I) 246, BJP 60, Janata 2, CPI 2, *Lok Dal* 1, Republican Party 1, independents 8.

Maharashtra. (May 1980): Congress (I) 186, Congress 47, Janata 17, BJP 14, Peasants' and Workers' Party 8, CPI 2, CPI(M) 2.

Manipur. (January 1980): Congress (I) 13, Janata 10, CPI 5, Manipur People's Party 3, Kuki National Assembly 2, CPI(M) 1, independents 19, of whom 18 joined the Congress (I).

Meghalaya. (Feb. 17, 1983): Congress (I) 25, Hill State People's Democratic Party 15, All-Party Hill Leaders' Conference 15, Public Demands Implementation Convention 2, independents 3.

Nagaland. (Nov. 19, 1982): Congress (I) 24, Naga National Democratic Party 24, independents 12, of whom 8 later joined the Congress (I).

Orissa. (May 1980): Congress (I) 117, *Lok Dal* 13, CPI 4, Janata 3, Congress 2, independents 7.

Punjab. (May 1980): Congress (I) 63, *Akali Dal* 37, CPI 9, CPI(M) 5, BJP 1, independents 2.

Rajasthan. (May 1980): Congress (I) 133, BJP 32, Janata 8, *Lok Dal* 7, Congress 6, CPI 1, CPI(M) 1, independents 12.

Sikkim. (Oct. 12, 1979): Sikkim Janata Parishad 16, Sikkim Congress (Revolutionary) 11, Sikkim Prajatantra Congress 3, independent 1 (vacant 1).

Tamil Nadu. (May 1980): *Anna Dravida Munnetra Kazhagam* 129, *Dravida Munnetra Kazhagam* 38, Congress (I) 30, CPI(M) 11, CPI 10, Gandhi-Kamaraj National Congress 6, Tamil Nadu Congress (Kamaraj) 3, Forward Bloc 3, Janata 2, Moslem League 1, independent 1.

Tripura. (Jan. 5, 1983): CPI(M) 37, Congress (I) 12, *Tripura Upajatia Juba Samiti* 6, Congress (I) dissidents (independents) 3, Revolutionary Socialist Party 2.

Uttar Pradesh. (May 1980): Congress (I) 306, *Lok Dal* 59, Congress 13, BJP 11, CPI 7, Janata 4, Janata (S) 4, independents 17.

West Bengal. (May 1982): *Left Front*—CPI(M) 174, Forward Bloc 28, Revolutionary Socialist Party 19, CPI 7, Revolutionary Communist Party 2, Forward Bloc (Marxist) 2, Democratic Socialist Party 1, West Bengal Socialist Party 1, independents 4; *other parties*—Congress (I) 49, Congress (S) 4, Socialist Unity Centre 2, Gorkha League 1.

In three Union Territories seats were won as follows:

Arunachal Pradesh. (Jan. 13, 1980): Congress (I) 13, United People's Party of Arunachal 13, independents 4. (The Congress (I) group was subsequently increased to 21 by defections from other groups.)

Goa, Daman and Diu. (Jan. 3, 1980): Congress 20, *Maharashtrawadi Gomantak* 7, independents 3.

Pondicherry. (Jan. 3, 1980): *Dravida Munnetram Kazhagam* 14, Congress (I) 10, Janata 3, Moslem League 1, CPI(M) 1, independent 1.

National Parties

Akhil Bharat Hindu Mahasabha

Address. Hindu Mahasabha Bhawan, Mandir Marg, New Delhi 110001, India

Leadership. Vikram Narayan Savarkar (pres.); Gopal Godse (g.s.)

Founded. 1915

History. The Hindu Mahasabha, a minority party, sent four members to the *Lok Sabha* in 1952, two in 1957 and one in 1962, but has not been represented in that House since 1967. It also held seats in several state assemblies before 1967, notably in Madhya Pradesh (where it gained seven seats in 1957 and six in 1962).

Orientation. This right-wing party's aim is to establish a democratic Hindu state.

Membership. 100,000

All-India Communist Party

Leadership. Shripat Amrit Dange (g.s.)

Founded. April 13, 1980

History. The party was founded by Baburao Ranadive and (Mrs) Roza Deshpande, who was the daughter of S. A. Dange, the veteran leader of the Communist Party of India (CPI), who had left that party on Nov. 26, 1979, whereafter the CPI rejected his policy of support for the Congress (I). The new party expressed continued support for the Congress (I) on the grounds that the latter represented the "national bourgeoisie" and was striving to strengthen democratic socialism.

S. A. Dange was subsequently expelled from the CPI, joined the new party on May 1, 1981, and was elected its general secretary on May 29 of that year. His new party contested the West Bengal Legislative Assembly elections on May 19, 1982, in alliance with the Congress (I) and five other parties but gained no seat.

All-India Forward Bloc

Address. 128 North Avenue, New Delhi 110 001, India; also at 52/7 Bepin Behari Ganguli Street, 700 012 Calcutta, West Bengal, India

Leadership. Prem Dutta Paliwal (ch.); Chitta Basu, MP (g.s.)

Founded. 1939

History. Originally established as a left-wing group within the Indian National Congress, the Forward Bloc has had its principal support in West Bengal, where it held 13 seats in the State Assembly between 1962 and 1964. It gained 21 seats in that Assembly in 1969 and declined thereafter, winning no seats in 1972. In the 1977 elections, however, it obtained 26 seats in the Assembly, and 28 seats in 1982.

In other Legislative Assemblies it has four seats in Tamil Nadu and one in Bihar. In the *Lok Sabha* it has not held more than three seats (first gained in 1957 and again in 1977); it has two members in the *Rajya Sabha*. The party is a constituent of the Left Front in West Bengal and has four members in the State Cabinet.

Orientation. The party is socialist and advocates the nationalization of key industries and a redistribution of land.

All-India Jharkand Party

Address. 9 Pandit Pant Marg, New Delhi-1, India

Leadership. N. E. Horo (l.)

History. At national level this party has never held more than seven seats in the *Lok Sabha* (i.e. in 1957-62 and 1972-77). In the 1980 elections to the *Lok Sabha* it retained only one seat.

Orientation. The party represents the interests of the tribal peoples.

All-India Moslem League

Address. Sea-View, Kasargod, Kerala, India

History. The original Moslem League led by Mohammed Ali Jinnah had been the main representative of the Moslem people in India before partition (into India and Pakistan) in 1947 and had held 30 of the 102 elective seats in the Central Legislative Assembly of India constituted in 1946. While the Moslem League came to power in Pakistan in 1947, it obtained only one seat in the first *Lok Sabha* elected between October 1951 and February 1952, and it has never held more than four seats (between 1971 and 1977) in that house. Its stronghold has been in Kerala, where it gained 14 seats in the State Assembly in 1967 and 12 and 13 respectively in 1970 and 1977. It has also been represented in the State Assemblies of Tamil Nadu, where it gained seven seats in 1971 (but only one in 1977 and in 1980) and of West Bengal, where it won three seats in 1969, seven in 1971 and only one in 1972 and in 1977, and none in 1982.

Orientation. As the party of the Moslem minority, it has repeatedly contested elections in alliance with Communist and Socialist parties.

Bharatiya Janata Party (BJP)

Address. 11 Ashoka Road, New Delhi 110 001, India

Leadership. Atal Behari Vajpayee (pres.); Lalkrishna Advani, Sikander Bakht, Yagya Dutt Sharma, Jana Krishna Moorthy (gen. secs.)

Founded. April 1980

History. This party broke away from the Janata Party after the latter's executive had banned dual membership of Janata and the (Hindu paramilitary) *Rashtriya Swayam Sewak Sangh* (RSSS) based on the *Jan Sangh* party (see under entry for Indian People's Union). A. B. Vajpayee was a former Minister of External Affairs.

The BJP first gained representation in four state Legislative Assemblies in May 1980 (with nine seats in Gujarat, 60 in Madhya Pradesh, 14 in Maharashtra and 32 in Rajasthan). It gained further state Assembly seats on May 19, 1982 (six in Haryana and 29 in Himachal Pradesh). By November 1982 it held 16 seats in the *Lok Sabha* and 14 in the *Rajya Sabha* (mainly as a result of defections from other parties). On Jan. 5, 1983, it gained seats in two other Assemblies (three in Andhra Pradesh and 18 in Karnataka). However, it opposed the holding of legislative elections in Assam in February 1983 with the use of electoral registers including "foreigners" (i.e. immigrants from Bangladesh).

Having fought elections in alliance with the *Lok Dal*, the BJP formed, on Aug. 8, 1983, an opposition National Democratic Alliance with the People's Party (*Lok Dal*), with both parties retaining their separate identities.

Orientation. The BJP has strongly associated itself with the (Hindu communalist) *Rashtriya Swaram Sewak Sangh* (RSSS) paramilitary organization.

Communist Party of India (CPI)

Address. Ajoy Bhavan, Kotla Marg, New Delhi 110 002, India

Leadership. C. Rajeswara Rao (g.s.)

Founded. Dec. 26, 1925

History. The CPI was illegal until 1943. In the *Lok Sabha* it gained 23 seats in 1952, 29 in 1957 and 29 again in 1962. It was in government in the state of Kerala in 1957-59. Following the defection of a section which in 1964 formed the Communist Party of India (Marxist), the CPI retained 23 seats in the *Lok Sabha*. It took part in left-wing coalition Governments in Kerala in 1967-70.

Following the 1969 split in the Indian National Congress, the CPI gave its support to Indira Gandhi's party. In Kerala it formed a Government with Congress support in 1970 and with Congress participation in 1971. Contesting the 1971 *Lok Sabha* elections in alliance with the Congress, the CPI won 23 seats, and it subsequently supported the Congress Government's emergency measures in 1975-77.

Contesting the 1977 elections again in alliance with the Congress, the CPI retained only seven seats (all in Kerala or Tamil Nadu) in the *Lok Sabha*. In December 1977 the party's national council admitted that its support for the Congress's emergency rule had been a mistake. Shripat Amrit Dange, who had been a leading member of the CPI since India achieved independence, was subsequently expelled for anti-party activities, and became leader of the All-India Communist Party (see separate entry). In Maharashtra former CPI members advocating support for the Congress (I) established an All-India Communist Party in April 1980.

Orientation. The CPI's aim is the establishment of a socialist society led by

210

the working class and ultimately the achievement of a communist society. A CPI congress held in March-April 1978 denounced "anti-Sovietism", Maoism and Eurocommunism.

Structure. The party's basic organizations operate in enterprises and in residential areas, and they make up district organizations which are part of state party organizations. State party conferences elect the party's state councils, which in turn in each state elect the CPI's executive committee and secretariat. The party's supreme body is its congress which is convened every three years and elects a national council, which in turn elects the central executive committee, party chairman, general secretary and secretaries.

Membership. 466,429 (1983)

Publications. *New Age* (central organ of the CPI's national council); seven dailies and over 20 weeklies in various languages; *Party Life* (fortnightly in English)

International affiliations. The CPI is recognized by the Communist parties of the Soviet-bloc countries.

Communist Party of India (Marxist)—CPI(M)

Address. 4 Ashoka Road, New Delhi 110 001, India

Leadership. Samar Mukherjee, P. Ramamurti (leaders); E. M. S. Namboodiripad (g.s. of politburo)

Founded. 1964

History. The CPI (M) has its origins in the Communist Party of India (formed in Tashkent, USSR, by Indian Communists), whose activities were banned in India during British rule. After independence the party "faced government repression, especially in 1947-51, 1962-63 and 1975-77". The Communist Party of India was split in 1964 (over the attitude to the ruling Congress Party, India's border dispute with China and the Sino-Soviet ideological controversy), and for electoral purposes the Election Commission accepted the newly-formed CPI (M) as a separate party.

Initially pro-Chinese, the party declared its independence of China in 1968. The CPI (M) has participated in all general elections to Parliament and the state Assemblies. It formed the government in the state of Kerala in 1957-59 and led "united front" governments in Kerala in 1967-69 and in the state of West Bengal in 1967 and 1969. Since the 1977 election the CPI (M) has formed Left Front governments in West Bengal and Tripura, in both of which the CPI (M) had gained

absolute majorities of seats in the state Assemblies.

Orientation. "The immediate objective of the party is to complete the people's democratic revolution in the country, go over to the socialist revolution and ultimately build a communist society." At a congress held in April 1976 the party criticized both Soviet "revisionism" and the Maoist theory of "three worlds". In its election manifesto of Sept. 25, 1979, the party called for the defeat of the Congress (I), which it described as "the main authoritarian danger", and of the Janata Party which, it claimed, was dominated by "anti-democratic and casteist" forces; it advocated support for the *Lok Dal*-Congress alliance despite its "class limitations" but declared that only unity of the left-wing and democratic forces offered a long-term solution; and it proposed that the right to work should be a fundamental right and that there should be an expansion of the powers of the states, nationalization of monopolies, a just and equitable incomes and wages policy, abolition of landlordism, a minimum wage level based on need, safeguards for the rights of Moslems and equality for all India's languages.

Structure. The party has branches; local, town (or *taluga*), district and state committees; and a 44-member central committee, which elects the politburo and the general secretary.

Membership. 267,200

Publications. *People's Democracy* (weekly central English organ), 17,500; *Lok Lahar* (weekly central Hindu organ), 8,500; organs in the Malayalam, Tamil, Telugu, Kannada, Marathi, Gujerati, Punjabi, Bengali, Assamese and Oriya languages

---

Communist Party of India (Marxist-Leninist) (CPI-ML)

Leadership. Satya Narain Singh (g.s.)

Founded. 1969

History. The party was set up by an extreme faction of the Communist Party of India (Marxist). This faction supported urban terrorism and peasant revolts, in particular the Naxalite revolt of 1967. In November 1971 it was divided into two groupings—(i) one led by Satya Narain Singh, who supported the orthodox Maoist theory of establishing "liberated zones" by means of peasant revolts and (ii) another led by Charu Mazumdar (who had until then been the party's general secretary and who died in 1972), who advocated urban guerrilla warfare, whom the first group condemned for his "Trotskyite adventurist line" and whose policies were also criticised by the Chinese leadership.

The second group was by 1974 divided into two factions, one of which accepted the Chinese criticism and merged with the Satya Narain Singh group in December 1977, with the newly-merged party announcing that it would use parliamentary methods, while the other faction pursued guerrilla warfare as advocated by the late Lin Biao.

The CPI-ML, having been banned between July 1975 and March 1977, gained one seat in the West Bengal state Assembly in June 1977 and gained another in the Assam state Assembly in February 1978. In November 1979 the party announced that it would support the Janata candidates in the general elections in West Bengal, on the ground that the *Lok Dal*-Congress alliance, the CPI, the CPI (M) and the Congress (I) were all "pro-Soviet". When the CPI-ML contested the May 19, 1982, elections to the Legislative Assembly of West Bengal it obtained no seat.

Orientation. The party supports Maoist principles and the Chinese stand in the Sino-Soviet dispute.

Democratic Socialist Party (DSP)

Leadership. Hemavati Nardan Bahuguna (l.)

Founded. July 18, 1981

History. The DSP was established by a merger of three small parties—(i) the Democratic Socialist Front, founded on Jan. 25, 1981, by H. N. Bahuguna; (ii) the Socialist Party, which had assumed this name on March 7, 1981, and had previously been known as the Janata Party (Secular), led by Raj Narain, which had broken away from the People's Party (*Lok Dal*) in April 1980; and (iii) the Democratic (*Janwadi*) Party founded on April 5, 1981, by Chandrajit Yadav and Banarsi Das, who had also broken away from the *Lok Dal*. (Ch. Yadav, the only Democratic Party member of the *Lok Sabha*, dissociated himself from the merger, however.) The DSP subsequently had 11 members in the *Lok Sabha* (eight of the former Democratic Socialist Front and three of the former Socialist Party).

As part of a Left Front the DSP gained one seat in the West Bengal Legislative Assembly and as part of a Democratic Left Front one in the Kerala Legislative Assembly, both on May 19, 1982. On Sept. 4, 1983, the DSP joined an opposition United Front set up at national level by the Janata Party with the participation of the Congress (S) and the *Rashtriya* Congress.

Indian Congress (J)

Address. 6, Krishna Menon Marg, New Delhi 110 011, India

Leadership. Babu Jagjivan Ram (pres.); Shri Brij Mohan, Harbans Singh Bhalla (g. secs.)

Founded. Aug. 5, 1981

History. Jagjivan Ram, a former Deputy Prime Minister, had resigned from the Indian National Congress in February 1977 and had thereafter formed a Congress of Democracy which later merged with the Janata Party, which he left in March 1980 because he objected to that party's association with the Hindu communalist *Rashtriya Swayam Sewak Sangh* (RSSS). Jagjivan Ram had thereupon joined a Congress (U), from which the Congress (J) broke away in August 1981.

In elections to the Haryana state Assembly held on May 19, 1982, the Congress (J) gained three seats. It was then recognized by the election commission for Haryana and later became a registered party throughout India. The party has two members in the *Lok Sabha* and one in the *Rajya Sabha*, as well as one member in the Andhra Pradesh Legislative Assembly, elected on Jan. 3, 1983.

Structure. The party has state and district committees in every state of India.

Membership. Approx. 2,000,000

Indian National Congress (Congress)

Address. 3 Raisina Road, New Delhi 110 001, India

History. The existing Congress is the remnant of the original Congress from which the Congress (I)—see separate entry for Indian National Congress (I)—broke away in January 1978. In 1979 the Congress was joined by the Karnataka Congress (which had been set up in June 1979 and was led by Devaraj Urs, who had been expelled from the Congress-I in that month). From July 1978 to January 1980 the Congress was a partner in a coalition Government, first with the Janata Party and later with the People's Party (*Lok Dal*).

For the 1980 general elections Congress was allied with the *Lok Dal* in Andhra Pradesh, Gujarat, Madhya Pradesh, Rajasthan and West Bengal, whereas in Kerala it was allied with the two Communist parties and in Goa with the Congress (I). However, it gained only 13 seats in the *Lok Sabha*. In elections to Legislative Assemblies it obtained 20 seats in Goa (on Jan. 3, 1980), and two seats in Orissa, six in Rajasthan and 13 in Uttar Pradesh (all in May 1980). The only Congress Ministry (in Karnataka) resigned in January 1980.

Orientation. In its election manifesto of Dec. 7, 1979, the Congress reaffirmed its support for the late Jalaharwal Nehru's policies of democracy, socialism, secularism and non-alignment. It called for the promotion of public-sector industries ("against the unbridled growth of private capital"); scientific modernization and structural changes in agriculture, with a fair minimum wage for landless labourers; the encouragement of low-cost, labour-intensive and small-scale production based on domestic raw materials and designs; equal pay for women; and freedom of the press.

Indian National Congress (I)—Congress (I)

Address. 24 Akbar Road, New Delhi 110 001, India

Leadership. Indira Gandhi (pres. and parl. l.); G. Karuppiah Moodpanar, Chandulal Chandrakar, Dr Rajendra Kumari Rajpat, M. Satyanarayana Rao, Vasantdada Patil (gen. secs.)

Founded. January 1978

History. The original Congress Party (founded in 1885), whose leaders included the late Mahatma Gandhi and Jawaharlal Nehru, had been instrumental in leading India to independence in 1947, and it remained India's ruling party until 1977. It suffered its first division into an extremist and a moderate faction in 1907. In 1969 it was divided into two distinct parties, of which the Indian National Congress (Organization) became the country's first recognized opposition party, while the other party remained the ruling Congress led by Indira Gandhi. In 1975-77 the Congress ruled under emergency powers. Following the defeat of the Congress by the Janata Party in the *Lok Sabha* elections of March 1977 and also in 11 state elections in June 1977, a section of the party broke away from the Congress in January 1978 and elected as its president Indira Gandhi; this section decided on Feb. 1, 1978, to call itself the Indian National Congress (I).

In September 1979 the Congress (I) was joined by the Congress committees in Maharashtra and Punjab and by a number of prominent Congress members. During the last quarter of 1979 the Congress (I) was joined by the former Congress for Democracy (Secular) group led by H. N. Bahuguna and by various leading members of the Congress. For the January 1980 general elections the Congress (I) was allied with the *Dravida Munnetra Kazhagam* (DMK) in Tamil Nadu; with the Janata Party in Kerala; and with the Congress in Goa. (The last-named subsequently joined the Congress-I.) On July 23, 1981, the Election Commission ruled that, of the various existing Congress groups, the Congress (I) was the "real" Congress.

The Congress (I) has retained its dominant position in the *Lok Sabha* and the *Rajya Sabha*, and also in the Legislative Assemblies of Assam, Bihar, Gujarat, Haryana, Himachal Pradesh, Kerala, Madhya Pradesh, Maharashtra, Manipur, Meghalaya, Nagaland, Orissa, Punjab, Rajasthan and Uttar Pradesh. In Kerala the Congress (I) was, on Dec. 13, 1982, joined by a Congress (A) group which had, under the leadership of A. K. Anthony, broken away from the Congress (S) to take part in a United Democratic Front coalition government which had taken office in December 1981 under Congress (I) leadership.

Orientation. In its election manifesto of Dec. 1, 1979, the Congress (I), in addition to denouncing the Janata Party's alleged misrule, stated that it was opposed to press censorship and to coercion in the implementation of family planning; undertook to provide at least one adult in each family with employment; promised not to impose Hindi as an official language; pledged itself to attacking inflation, improving the investment climate in order to raise production, formulating a national incomes policy and restructuring of the tax system to reduce the burden on the middle classes.

Indian National Congress (Socialist)—Congress (S)

Leadership. Sharad Pawar (pres.)

Founded. August 1981

History. In June 1979 a group known as the Karnataka Congress and later the Congress (U) was set up by Devaraj Urs, who had been expelled from the Congress (I). This group, however, had its recognition withdrawn on July 23, 1981, by the Election Commission, which ruled that the true Indian National Congress was the Congress (I). A number of leading Congress (U) members resigned from it in May-September 1981, and on Aug. 5 of that year the group was split into the Congress (J)—see separate entry—and a faction which later became the Congress (S). D. Urs resigned from the latter group on Aug. 25, 1981, and Sharad Pawar (who had previously been leader of the Maharashtra Progressive Party) was elected president of the group.

On May 19, 1982, the Congress (S) gained four seats in the West Bengal Legislative Assembly (after being allied with the Congress (I) and five other parties) and three seats in the Haryana Assembly; on Jan. 5, 1983, it obtained one seat in the Andhra Pradesh Assembly. On Jan. 9, 1983, the Congress (S) in Orissa decided to merge with the Janata Party, and the Congress (S) in West Bengal did so in March 1983. In the *Rajya Sabha* the party has held three seats since 1982.

Indian People's Union
Bharatiya Jana Sangh or Jan Sangh

Leadership. Balraj Madhok (l.)
Founded. October 1951
History. The *Jan Sangh* was first represented in the *Lok Sabha* by three members elected in 1952 but its representation in the House gradually rose to 35 members elected in 1967. In 1971 it retained only 22 seats, but after it had become part of the newly-formed Janata Party in 1977 it had, in June 1978, a total of 90 of the 298 seats then controlled by the Janata Party. The *Jan Sangh* was said to have close links with the *Rashtriya Swayam Sewak Sangh* (RSSS), a para-military Hindu communal organization held responsible for widespread acts of violence, in particular against Moslems.

In August 1979 Balraj Madhok, who had been expelled from the original *Jan Sangh* in 1973 after being one of its founders, announced that the *Jan Sangh* had been revived as a separate party. However, this group remained insignificant and won no seats in the 1980 elections. The *Jan Sangh* members who had joined the Janata Party in 1977 formed a new party, the *Bharatiya* Janata Party, under the leadership of A. B. Vajpayee, in April 1980.

Orientation. The *Jan Sangh* is a right-wing Hindu nationalist party opposed to Moslem influence in Indian politics. In 1966 it called for decentralization of political power, free compulsory education, land reforms providing for peasant proprietorship, and "emancipation of the nation from the shackles of the English language"; it opposed nationalization of industry and any expansion of the public sector of the economy except in power, mineral oils and defence industries. On Aug. 9, 1981, B. Madhok demanded that India should be declared a Hindu state and that all conversions to other religions should be banned by law.

Janata Party

Address. 7 Jantar Mantar Rd, P.B. No 709, New Delhi 110 001, India
Leadership. Chandra Shekhar (pres.)
Founded. May 1977
History. The party was formed by an official merger of the Indian National Congress (Organization); of the *Bharatiya Lok Dal* (BLD) led by Charan Singh; of the *Bharatiya Jana Sangh* (or *Jan Sangh,* Indian People's Union) led by A. B. Vajpayee; of the Socialist Party led by George Fernandes; and of dissident members of the Congress. All of these had jointly fought the 1977 *Lok Sabha* elections which resulted in the defeat of Congress.

In May 1977 the Janata Party was joined by the Congress for Democracy, which had been formed in February 1977 by Jagjivan Ram. This finally gave the party 303 seats in the *Lok Sabha* (against 150 of the Congress). The party was subsequently beset by internal dissension, which led to the formation of the Janata Party (Secular) in July 1979.

In the January 1980 general elections the Janata Party retained only 31 seats in the *Lok Sabha*, and in subsequent elections to state Legislative Assemblies it was reduced to insignificance, gaining 10 seats in Manipur (in January 1980), 22 in Gujarat and eight in Rajasthan (both in May 1980). It has since continued to be internally divided.

On Sept. 4, 1983, the party announced that it was setting up a United Front with (i) the Congress (S) led by Sharad Pawar, (ii) the Democratic Socialist Party led by H. N. Bahuguna, and (iii) the *Rashtriya* Congress (in Gujarat) led by Ratubhai Adani (see also separate entries for these parties).

Orientation. In its election manifesto for 1980 the JP proposed constitutional amendments to prevent misuse of office by the President, the Prime Minister and caretaker governments; a ban on defections; state funding of elections and a public audit of election funds; and the lowering of the voting age to 18 years. It reaffirmed its commitment to socialism, with a commanding role for the public sector of the economy and decentralization. It further promised (i) constitutional amendments to guarantee the freedom of the press and to protect women's rights, (ii) rural development with all surplus land to be distributed to landless members of the scheduled castes and tribes within five years and ownership of land by tenants and sharecroppers cultivating it personally; and (iii) the retention of English as an additional official language until all states agreed to its replacement.

Membership. 3,000,000

Janata Party (Secular)
Janata (S)

Leadership. Raj Narain (l.)
Founded. July 1979
History. The party was formed by Janata members who objected to what they called the "authoritarianism" of Morarji Desai (then Janata Party leader) and his party's domination by the (Hindu communalist) *Jan Sangh*, and its main body consisted of the former *Bharatiya Lok Dal* (BLD). The Janata (S) formed a coalition Government (completed on Aug. 5, 1979) with the Congress, the Congress for Democracy (Secular), Socialist and independent members, which was supported by the *Anna Dravida Munnetra Kazhagam* (ADMK) and the Congress (I), but this Government was faced with defeat in the *Lok Sabha*, which was thereupon dissolved on Aug. 25, 1979. In September of that year the party was joined by Socialists led by George Fernandes and Madhu Limaye, as well as by an independent group, in the formation of the *Lok Dal*, to be led by Charan Singh as president. In April 1980, however, the Janata (S) was revived as a separate party under the leadership of Raj Narain. It gained one seat in the Bihar Legislative Assembly in May 1980 and four in the West Bengal Assembly in May 1982.

National Sanjay Organization
Rashtriya Sanjay Manch

Leadership. (Mrs) Maneka Gandhi (l.)
Founded. April 3, 1983
History. This organization, established by its leader (the widow of Indira Gandhi's son Sanjay, who had died in June 1980), has come out in opposition to Mrs Gandhi's Congress (I), in which Maneka Gandhi had previously led an opposition faction. The organization gained a seat in a by-election to the Uttar Pradesh Legislative Assembly on Dec. 23, 1983.
Orientation. The organization has campaigned against corruption and unemployment and for socialism and a secular and democratic state.
Structure. The organization has claimed to have established cells in all parts of India except Jammu and Kashmir and the north-east.
Membership. 800,000

People's Party
Lok Dal

Address. 15 Windsor Place, New Delhi 110001, India
Leadership. Charan Singh (pres.)
Founded. September 1979
History. The *Lok Dal* was established by the Janata Party (Secular), the Socialist group led by George Fernandes and Madhu Limaye, which had participated in the Janata (S) Government, and certain independent parliamentarians, among them Biju Patnaik (leader of the Orissa Janata Party, which had not recognized the split in the Janata Party). The *Lok Dal* entered into an alliance with the Congress led by Devaraj Urs, but this alliance broke down in the last quarter of 1979.

For the January 1980 general elections the *Lok Dal* was allied with the Congress in Andhra Pradesh, Gujarat, Madhya Pradesh, Rajasthan and West Bengal, and with the Communist Party of India (CPI) and the Communist Party of India (Marxist) (CPI-M) in Bihar and Uttar Pradesh. In these elections it gained 41 seats in the *Lok Sabha*.

In elections to state Legislative Assemblies held in May 1980 it won seats in Bihar (42), Gujarat (1), Madhya Pradesh (1), Orissa (13), Rajasthan (7) and West Bengal (59); in elections to the Haryana Legislative Assembly on May 19, 1982, it obtained 31 seats.

However, in August 1982 the *Lok Dal* was divided when a group calling itself *Lok Dal* (K), led by Karpoori Thakur as president and George Fernandes as general secretary, broke away to form a separate party until Jan. 27, 1983, when it merged with the Janata Party (which had earlier in January already been joined by the *Lok Dal* group in Orissa). What was known as the *Lok Dal* (C), with Swaran Singh as president and Shyam Nandan Mishra as general secretary, gained two seats in the Delhi Metropolitan Council in February 1983.

In August 1983 the party (which then held 25 seats in the *Lok Sabha* and six in the *Rajya Sabha*) allied itself with the *Bharatiya* Janata Party, but some *Lok Dal* leaders disagreed with this step and subsequently joined the Janata Party.
Orientation. In its election manifesto of Dec. 11, 1979, the *Lok Dal* advocated an economy based on small property (in which no individuals would have unrestricted freedom to exploit the needs of others and the state would not have unlimited power

to curb economic freedom), with priority for agriculture and cottage industries. Public enterprises which continued to show losses would be closed down except where they were part of the economy's basic structure, and public sector projects would be confined to those connected with national security or not attractive to private capital. All production or construction of "luxury items" (including refrigerators, television sets, skyscrapers, expensive cars, breweries, distilleries and casinos) would be prohibited. Peasant proprietorship was to replace farm tenancy, and householders would be made owners of the sites of their houses. Among other recommendations the party proposed the creation of a state fund to finance election expenses.

Publications. *Lok Dal Bulletin* (fortnightly)

People's Union for Civil Liberties and Democratic Rights

Founded. 1976

History. The Union was set up by members of all non-Communist parties in order to organize an effective opposition to the Government of the Indian National Congress led by Indira Gandhi. Its founder, Jaya Prakash Narayan, who also played a leading part in the formation of the Janata Party in 1977, died in October 1979. The Union was supported not only by the parties which later constituted the Janata Party but also by the Communist Party of India (Marxist).

Orientation. The Union's objectives were to restore civil liberties, freedom of the press and the independence of the judiciary; to establish a genuine egalitarian social order; and to formulate and implement economic policies designed to end unemployment and to raise production.

Republican Party of India (RPI)

Address. Azad Maidan, Fort, Bombay 400 001, India

Leadership. R. S. Gavai (pres.); N. H. Kumbhare (g.s.)

History. Originally known as the Scheduled Castes Federation, the party was represented in the *Lok Sabha* from 1952 to 1980, winning three seats in 1977 but retaining none in 1980.

Orientation. The party aims at the implementation of the objects stated in the preamble to India's Constitution. It represents the interests of the Harijans (untouchables) or Scheduled Castes.

Revolutionary Socialist Party (RSP)

Address. 780 Ballimaran, Delhi-110 006, India

Leadership. Tridib Chaudhuri (g.s.)

Founded. March 1940

History. Founded as a Marxist socialist party after the outbreak of World War II and during British rule, the RSP was "driven underground on account of anti-imperialist and anti-war activities". It began to function openly with a convention held in Delhi in 1946. It has participated in all parliamentary and state assembly elections in independent India since 1952, and it joined United Front coalition Governments in West Bengal and Kerala in 1967 and 1969 and again in 1977 and 1982, when it obtained 19 state Assembly seats in West Bengal and four in Kerala. It is currently a coalition partner in the Left Front state governments in West Bengal and Tripura. It has consistently been represented in the *Lok Sabha* since 1952.

Orientation. The RSP is a Marxist-Leninist left-wing party with the objective of establishing socialist rule and working people's power in India.

Structure. Democratic centralist, with the party's highest body being a central committee elected by delegates from district and state units to an all-India national party conference, which also elects a general secretary and a central executive council. The central committee appoints a seven-member central secretariat, which acts as the party's political bureau.

Membership. 17,500

Publications. *The Call* (in English), 5,000; *Ganavarta* (in Bengali), 17,000; *Pravaham* (in Malayalam), 3,500

State Parties

ANDHRA PRADESH

Janata Party (Andhra Pradesh)

History. The Andhra Pradesh Janata Party, which had gained 60 (out of 294) seats in the State Assembly in February 1978, decided in August 1979 to remain independent of the two central Janata parties. However, in the Jan. 5, 1983, elections its strength in the Assembly was reduced to one member.

Land of Telugu
Telugu Desam

Leadership. N. T. Rama Rao (l.)
Founded. March 29, 1982
History. Telugu is the language of Andhra Pradesh. At its foundation the party was joined by four Congress (I) members of the Andhra Pradesh Legislative Assembly and its leader (a popular film star) declared that it would support whichever party was in power in the Union Government but would pursue its own policy inside Andhra Pradesh, where it won one seat in the *Lok Sabha* in a by-election on Jan. 5, 1983, and another on June 19 of that year.

In the Legislative Assembly elections of Jan. 5, 1983, it gained an overwhelming majority of 202 (out of 294) Assembly seats; its leader thereupon formed a Ministry. On March 24, 1983, the Assembly approved (by 210 votes to one) a resolution to abolish the State Legislative Council (Upper House).

Orientation. The party has a radical economic programme, including provision of rice subsidies and free school lunches and a campaign against rural poverty and social prejudice (especially against women). It also stands for greater autonomy for the states (but within national unity and integration).

Majlis-Ittehad-ul-Mussalman

History. This Moslem group obtained five seats in the Andhra Pradesh Legislative Assembly elections on Jan. 5, 1983.

National Democratic Party

Leadership. Chenna Reddy
Founded. February 1984
History. The formation of this new party was announced (in February 1984) by Chenna Reddy, a former Chief Minister of Andhra Pradesh.

ASSAM

Assam Janata Dal

Leadership. Keshab Chandra Gogoi (l.)
Founded. September 1979
History. This party broke away from the ruling Janata Party in Assam and, under its then leader (Jogendra Nath Hazarika), formed a Government in Assam with the Janata Party (Secular) and the Progressive Democratic Front (and with the support of the Congress, the Congress-I and the Communist Party of India) but remained in power only until December 1979.

Plains Tribal Council of Assam (PTCA)

Address. P.O. and T.O. Kokrajhar, Dist. Goalpara, Assam, India
Leadership. Biruchon Doley (pres.); Charan Narzary (g.s.)
Founded. February 1967
History. The PTCA claims to be the only political party of some 2,000,000 people of the tribal population of the plains of Assam state. The PTCA boycotted parliamentary by-elections in the Kokrajhar (Scheduled Tribe) constituency in 1968 in protest against its delimitation. Its general secretary was in 1972 elected to the Assam Legislative Assembly and in 1977 to the *Lok Sabha*, the PTCA having been recognized as a state political party of Assam. In 1978 four members were elected to the Assam Legislative Assembly and joined a coalition government led by the Janata party. Taking part in the February 1983 elections it retained three seats in the Assembly.

Orientation. The PTCA stands for good relations with the central Government and for the creation of a separate Udayachal state to safeguard the interests of the plains tribal population.

Structure. The PTCA has a policy-making body, a central executive council, and subdivisional, district and local units.
Membership. 700,000
Publications. *RADAB* (weekly newspaper, in Bodo), 5,000

BIHAR

Jharkhand Mukti Morcha

Founded. 1980
History. This party broke away from the Jharkhand Party. It fought the May 1980 elections to the Legislative Assembly in Bihar in alliance with the Congress (I) and gained 13 seats for itself.

Orientation. The party claims to represent the tribal peoples of Bihar.

Shoshit Samaj Dal
Akhil Bharatiya

Address. Alok Bhawan, Murli Chak, Patna 14, Bihar, India
History. The *Shoshit Dal* (Group of the Exploited) broke away from the

Samyukta Socialist Party in Bihar in 1967 and gained 6 seats in the Bihar state Assembly in 1967 and two in 1972, but none thereafter.

GUJARAT

Rashtriya Congress

Leadership. Ratubhai Adani (pres.)
Founded. Dec. 26, 1982
History. This party was formed in Gujarat by dissident Congress (I) members who had unsuccessfully sought to overthrow Madhavsinh Solanki as leader of the Congress (I) and Chief Minister of Gujarat. The *Rashtriya* Congress became a member of the United Front led by the Janata Party, formed at national level on Sept. 4, 1983.

HARYANA

Vishal Haryana Party

Address. Rampur-Rewari, District Gurgaon, Haryana, India
Leadership. Rao Birender Singh (l.)
Founded. 1968
History. This party gained 13 seats in the Haryana state Assembly in 1968 but retained only three in 1971 and has held none since then. In the *Lok Sabha* it held one seat between 1971 and 1977. In the 1977 elections its leader was supported by Congress but was not elected.

JAMMU AND KASHMIR

Awami Action Committee (AAC)

History. In June 1979 the AAC, which was not represented in the state Assembly, joined (with the Janata Party, the Congress and the *Inqilabi* National Conference) a joint forum of opposition parties in the Kashmir state Assembly.

Inqilabi (Revolutionary) National Conference

Leadership. Mirza Mohammed Afzal Beg (l.)
Founded. November 1978
History. The party was formed by its leader after he had resigned as Deputy Chief Minister of Kashmir and been expelled from the ruling National Conference, of which he had been vice-president, on the grounds of allegedly conspiring to assume the Chief Ministership. In June 1979 the party formed a joint forum with the Janata Party, the Congress and the Awami Action Committee to oppose the state Government's "undemocratic policies". It is not represented in the Legislative Assembly.

Islamic Party
Jamaat-e-Islami Jammu & Kashmir

Address. Soura, Srinagar, Kashmir, India
Leadership. Sad-ud-Din (pres.); Sheikh Gulam Hassan (s.g.)
Founded. 1947
History. The party began its political activities in *panchayat* or village societies and first contested parliamentary elections in 1971 without gaining any seats, but it won five seats in the Kashmir State Assembly in March 1972. This representation was reduced to one seat in June-July 1977. No member of the party was returned in the 1983 general elections, during which it accused the contesting parties of "malpractices". However, the party is well represented in village *panchayats* and in two towns.
Orientation. The party propagates the following of the Islamic way of life.
Structure. The party has a president, a general secretary, provincial and district presidents and their secretaries, and a 34-member supreme consultative committee (*shoora*). It also has specialized departments, a women's wing and a students' wing.
Membership. 1,100 "basic" and 300,000 "associate" members
Publications. *Azan* (weekly), 3,000

Jammu and Kashmir National Conference (JKNC)

Address. Shaheedi Chowk, Jammu, Jammu and Kashmir, India
Leadership. Dr Farooq Abdullah (l. and Chief Minister)
Founded. 1938
History. The JKNC, which from its inception had close links with the Indian National Congress, was the ruling party in Jammu and Kashmir from 1947 to 1965 (gaining absolute majorities in elections to the Jammu and Kashmir Constituent Assembly in 1951 and to the State Assembly in 1957 and 1962). In January 1965 the JKNC's working committee decided to merge the party with the

Congress, and this decision was approved by the latter but not by a section of the JKNC which included 26 members of the State Assembly. In the 1967 elections this section retained only eight seats in the Assembly and none in the 1972 elections.

In 1975, however, the JKNC was revived under the leadership of Sheikh Mohammad Abdullah (who had been Chief Minister before 1955 and again since February 1975), and in the 1977 elections the JKNC returned to the State Assembly with 47 (out of 76) seats. In September 1978 the JKNC expelled Mirza Afzal Beg, who had been its vice-president and who, in November of that year, formed the *Inqilabi* (Revolutionary) National Conference. In the *Lok Sabha* the JKNC won two seats in 1977, when it was in alliance with the Congress, but it fought the 1980 general elections in alliance with the Congress (I) and gained three seats. In elections to the Legislative Assembly held on June 5, 1983, it retained 46 seats.

Orientation. As a socialist party opposed to Hindu communalism, the JKNC stands for the maintenance of Kashmir's status as an integral part of the Indian Union, but with special constitutional guarantees, in particular in respect of civil liberties.

KARNATAKA

Kannada Nadu

Leadership. A. K. Subbaiah (l.)
Founded. Aug. 28, 1983
History. This Karnataka party was established by former members of the *Bharatiya* Janata Party who disagreed with the latter party's decision to support the Janata Party Ministry in Karnataka.

Maharashtra Ekikaran Samiti (MES)

History. The MES has been a minority party in the state of Mysore (later Karnataka) since 1967, when it gained two seats in the state Assembly. By 1977 it had increased its representation to five seats, which it retained in the 1983 elections.
Orientation. The MES stands for the transfer of the Belgaum district (inhabited by Marathi-speaking people) from Karnataka to Maharashtra.

Revolutionary Front
Kranti Ranga

Leadership. S. Bangarappa (l.)
Founded. April 28, 1982

History. This party was formed in Karnataka by the state unit of the Congress (S) and merged, after the 1983 State Assembly elections, with the Janata Party (in alliance with which it had fought the elections in which it had won 11 seats). However, the merger decision was disputed by eight *Kranti Ranga* members of the Assembly, led by S. Bangarappa, who maintained the separate identity of the party and expelled from it three members who had accepted office in the Janata Party Ministry.

KERALA

Congress (A)

Leadership. A. K. Antony (l.)
History. The Congress (A) is a breakaway faction of the Indian National Congress (Socialist) or Congress (S)—see separate entry. It was one of eight groups which supported a United Democratic Front (UDF) Ministry formed in Kerala on Dec. 28 1981. In the state elections of May 19, 1982, which it contested as part of the UDF, it retained 15 seats in the Assembly and thereafter it continued to take part in government.

Indian Union Moslem League (IUML)

History. As part of the United Democratic Front of Kerala the IUML gained 14 seats in the Legislative Assembly elections of May 19, 1982. Its leader, C. H. Mohammad Koya (who died on Sept. 28, 1983), had held ministerial posts in several Kerala administrations since 1967.
Orientation. The IUML has called for increased Moslem representation in government service and for compensation for Moslems who were victims of communal riots.

Kerala Congress

Address. Kottayam, Kerala, India
Founded. November 1964
History. The Kerala Congress, which had broken away from the state Congress Party in 1964, took part in the Kerala Government in 1969 and in 1975-76. In the 1964 state elections the party gained 23 (out of 133) seats in the state Legislative Assembly, but in 1967 it won only five seats. In 1970 it increased its seats to 13. In 1975 it decided to support the Communist-Congress coalition Government. In the 1977 elections the main body

of the party, forming part of the ruling United Front, gained 20 seats, while dissidents known as the Pillai group, forming part of the Opposition Alliance, gained two (later increased to three). (This group had R. Balakrishna Pillai as chairman and leader and Eapen Jacob as secretary-general.)

By 1979 the Kerala Congress was divided into three groups. The strongest of these was the Mani group, which contested the Kerala state elections of January 1980 as part of a Left Democratic Front, embracing also the Communist Party of India (Marxist), the Congress, the Communist Party of India, the Revolutionary Socialist Party, the All-India Moslem League and the Pillai group of the Kerala Congress; this alliance won eight seats. The second strongest group was the Joseph group, which fought the same elections as part of a United Democratic Front, which also included the Congress (I), the Moslem League, the National Democratic party and the *Praja* Socialist Party, and which gained six seats. (The Pillai group obtained only one seat in these elections.) The Joseph group, allied with the Congress (I), and the Mani group (as part of a Left Front) each gained one seat in the *Lok Sabha* in January 1980.

In elections to the Kerala Legislative Assembly held on May 19, 1982, the Joseph group obtained eight and the Mani group six seats, both as part of the United Democratic Front (whereas the Pillai group gained no seat).

Kerala Congress (Socialist)

History. This group contested the May 19, 1982, elections to the Kerala Legislative Assembly as part of the Left Democratic Front and gained one seat.

Left Democratic Front

History. This Front was formed for the May 19, 1982, elections to the Kerala Legislative Assembly by the Communist Party of India (Marxist), the Communist Party of India, the Congress (S), the Revolutionary Socialist Party, the All India Moslem League, the Janata Party, the Democratic Socialist Party, the Kerala Congress (Socialist) and independents, and it gained 63 of the 140 seats in the Assembly.

National Democratic Party (NDP)

Address. NDP Central Office, Trivandrum, Kerala, India

Leadership. Kidangoor A. N. Gopalakrishna Pillai (pres.); Therambil Ramakrishnan (g.s.)

Founded. July 1973

History. The NDP was founded under the presidency of Kalathil Valayudhan Nair, a former Congress Minister in Kerala, who died in 1976. In the 1977 state Assembly elections the party, as an ally of the ruling front (of the Congress, the Communist Party of India, the Kerala Congress and the Moslem League) nominated six candidates, five of whom were elected. After the 1980 state elections the NDP held three seats in the Assembly and worked as part of the Congress-led opposition alliance. The latter was voted into power in 1982, when the NDP gained four seats, and one of its members (K.P. Ramachandran Nair) became Minister of Health and Tourism.

Orientation. The NDP stands for a democratic political system with the least possible inequalities of wealth and income and for special preference in the distribution of government benefits to economically weaker sections of the population.

Structure. The party's mass-membership is represented by elected committees at various levels from wards to the state; its activities are guided by a state executive council elected by the state committee. It has no units outside Kerala.

Praja Socialist Party (PSP)

Founded. 1952

History. The PSP was formed as a national party out of two smaller socialist parties—the Socialist Party and the Peasants', Workers' and People's Party (*Krisan Mazdoor Praja* Party or KMPP); in 1953 it was joined by the All-India Forward Bloc. The national PSP won 19 seats in the *Lok Sabha* in 1957, 12 in 1962, 13 in 1967 and two in 1971, after which it merged with the *Samyukta* Socialist Party to form the Socialist Party. The PSP, however, remained a separate party in Kerala.

In that state (known as Travancore-Cochin until 1956) the PSP had gained 12 seats in the state Assembly in 1952 and 19 in 1954; it formed a coalition Ministry with Congress support, which was in power in 1954-55; in the 1957 Kerala state elections it retained only nine seats in the

Assembly, but in 1960 it gained 20 Assembly seats and formed a coalition Ministry with the Congress until 1962; it retained no seats in the Assembly elected in 1965 and 1967; in 1970 it gained three seats as part of a Communist-led United Front and thereupon participated in a United Front Ministry until 1977.

Although it retained its three seats in the 1977 state elections it did not take part in the United Front Ministry formed subsequently. In the May 1982 elections (which it contested as part of the United Front), it retained only one seat in the Legislative Assembly.

Orientation. In internal affairs the PSP has called for land reform, the eradication of corruption, provision for the recall of elected representatives by their electors, and free education up to school-leaving age. In foreign affairs it has been opposed to military alliances and has advocated self-sufficiency in conventional and nuclear arms, close links with Asian countries against Chinese expansionism and friendly relations with both Arab states and Israel.

Socialist Revolutionary Party (SRP)

History. This party contested the May 19, 1982, elections to the Kerala Legislative Assembly as part of the Congress (I)-led United Democratic Front and gained two seats.

United Democratic Front

History. This alliance was formed for the May 19, 1982, elections to the Kerala Legislative Assembly by the Congress (I), the Congress (A), the Indian Union Moslem League, the Kerala Congress (Joseph group), the Kerala Congress (Mani group), the National Democratic Party, Janata dissenters, the Socialist Revolutionary Party, the *Praja* Socialist Party, Revolutionary Socialist Party dissidents and independents. It gained 77 of the 140 seats in the Assembly.

MAHARASHTRA

Peasants' and Workers' Party of India

Address. Mahatma Phule Road, Naigaum, Bombay 400 014, Maharashtra, India

Leadership. Dajiba Desai (g.s.)

Founded. 1949

History. The party gained two seats in the *Lok Sabha* in 1952 and four in 1957 but held none in 1967–77; it won five seats in 1977 but retained none in 1980. In Maharashtra, its stronghold, its strength declined from 31 seats gained in the State Assembly in 1957 to seven in 1972 but increased to 13 seats in 1978, whereupon it took part in a coalition Ministry within a Progressive Democratic Front (also including the Janata Party, the Maharashtra Progressive Congress and the Maharashtra Socialist Congress) until 1980, when it retained only eight seats in the Assembly.

Orientation. The party is a Marxist formation aiming to establish a people's democracy, nationalize all basic industries, promote industrialization and establish a unitary state with provincial boundaries to be drawn on a linguistic basis.

Membership. 10,000

Republican Party of India (Khobragade)

Address. Gandhi Road, Chandrapur, Maharashtra, India

Leadership. B. D. Khobragade (pres.); D. A. Kalti (g.s.)

History. In 1983 the party had one member in the *Rajya Sabha* and one member each in the state Assemblies of Maharashtra and of Madhya Pradesh.

Orientation. The party has striven for the improvement of the social and economic conditions of the scheduled castes, scheduled tribes, minorities and other weaker sections of the population. It has taken an interest in national problems, the improvement of social conditions of the masses, justice for poorer sections, the removal of economic disparities and the creation of a new social order based on social and economic equality.

Shiva Sena

Address. 771, Ranade Road, Bombay 23, Maharashtra, India

Leadership. Balasaheb Thackrey (l.)

Founded. 1966

History. The party was founded by its leader with the object of defending the economic interests of the native Maharashtrians against competition by immigrants from India's southern states, and some of its members took violent action against southerners and also against Communists. In March 1968 the *Shiva Sena* gained 40 (out of 140) seats in the Bombay municipal elections, but it has little influence elsewhere in Maharashtra. In 1969-71 the party extended its violent campaign to attacks on Moslems, and in September 1971 seven party members were sentenced to life imprisonment for murdering a Communist member of the Maharashtra state Assembly.

In a by-election in October 1970 the *Shiva Sena* had won its first seat in the state Assembly. In the Bombay municipal elections of March 1973 the *Shiva Sena* retained 39 seats, and one of its council members was elected Mayor of Bombay on April 2 of that year (with Moslem League, Socialist and opposition Congress support). In the 1978 and 1980 elections to the state Assembly the *Shiva Sena* obtained no seats, and in Bombay municipal elections held in November of that year it retained only 21 seats in the Council.

Orientation. *Shiva Sena* is a right-wing extremist Hindu party.

MANIPUR

Kuki National Assembly (KNA)

Address. K-pi No. 2, Kangpokpi Hill Town, P.O. Kangpokpi, Manipur, India

Leadership. J. F. Rothangliana (pres.); K. S. Seyboy (g.s.)

Founded. April 24, 1946

History. The KNA was originally formed as a social organization of the tribal people of Manipur. A constituent assembly of the KNA adopted, on Nov. 17, 1969, a constitution calling for equality of status among the different groups of Kukis and for their unity. The KNA first gained one seat in the state Assembly in 1967 and retained one in 1972.

In 1974 the KNA obtained two seats in the Assembly after contesting the elections in alliance with the Manipur People's Party (MPP) and the Manipur Hills Union, and it took part in a short-lived Ministry subsequently formed by the MPP and the Socialist Party. (The MPP was later merged with the Janata Party, which by mid-1977 held 55 of the 60 seats in the Manipur State Assembly.) In January 1980 the KNA retained its two seats in the state Assembly.

Orientation. The KNA stands for the political integration of the Kukis, the preservation of their culture and the bringing together of all Kukis and allied ethnic groups under one administration.

Structure. The party has a high command or "cabinet", an executive and a working committee. Its supreme organ is a general assembly meeting every five years. The party has eight district organizations.

Membership. 150,000 (above the age of 15 years from Manipur, Assam and Nagaland)

Manipur People's Party (MPP)

Address. People's Road, near Polo Ground, Imphal, Manipur, India

Leadership. Mohammed Alimuddin (l.)

History. The MPP was formed by dissident members of the Congress and first contested state Assembly elections in Manipur in 1972, when it gained 15 (out of 60) seats, whereafter its leader formed a coalition Government based on an alliance with the Socialists, the United Naga Integration Council, the Opposition Congress and 10 independents.

Following numerous defections and other changes, the MPP lost control of the state to the Congress in 1974, but after most Congress members of the Assembly and also the MPP had joined the newly-formed Janata Party in 1977 the latter formed the state's Ministry. In state elections held in January 1980 the MPP, once again an independent party, gained three seats in the Assembly, and it subsequently joined a coalition Ministry formed by the Congress (I) and the Congress.

MEGHALAYA

All-Party Hill Leaders' Conference (APHLC)

Address. Nongrim Hills, Laitumkhrah, Shillong-793003, Meghalaya, India

Leadership. Brington Buhai Lyngdoh (l.)

Founded. 1960

History. This party had been the ruling party since Meghalaya achieved autonomy within Assam in 1970 but in November 1976 the party officially decided to merge with the Congress, whereupon a Congress Ministry was set up in the state. However, four members of the previous Ministry decided to keep the party alive.

In elections held in February 1978 the APHLC retained 16 seats in the state Assembly (where it had gained 32 in 1972) and it thereupon formed a coalition Ministry with the Hill State People's Democratic Party and the Public Demands Implementation Convention, with B.B. Lyngdoh being Chief Minister until May 1981.

After the Feb. 17, 1983, elections to the Legislative Assembly (in which the APHLC retained 15 seats) B. B. Lyngdoh claimed majority support for a Ministry formed by him, but this was superseded by a Congress (I)-led Ministry which was sworn in on April 2, 1983, and in which one APHCL member took part. (Six defectors who supported this Ministry were, however, expelled from the APHCL on Aug. 1, 1983.)

Orientation. The APHLC had originally campaigned for the separation of hills districts from Assam, and this was achieved finally with Meghalaya becoming a state in 1972.

Hill State People's Democratic Party (HSPDP)

Address. Jaiaw, Shillong-793002, Meghalaya, India

Leadership. H.S. Lyngdoh (l.)

Founded. Oct. 10, 1968

History. The HSPDP was founded with the object of working for the establishment of a separate state from the parts of the state of Assam inhabited by the tribesmen of the Khasi, Jaintia and Garo Hills. The party first entered the Meghalaya Legislative Assembly in 1972 with nine (out of 60) members, whereupon it remained in opposition. In the 1977 *Lok Sabha* elections it gained one of the two Meghalaya seats, and in 1976 it increased its representation in the Legislative Assembly to 14 members.

In May 1979 the HSPDP joined a coalition Ministry with the Congress (I) and a faction of the All-Party Hill Leaders' Conference (APHLC). In October 1982 the latter decided to leave the Ministry and on Dec. 12 of that year two ministers defected from the APHCL to the Congress (I). Several HSPDP members were later reported to have supported the formation, on April 2, 1983, of a new coalition administration with the leader of the Congress (I) as Chief Minister.

Meghalaya Democratic Front

Leadership. Capt. Williamson Sangma (l.)

Founded. March 1983

History. This Front was formed by Capt. Sangma, the leader of the Congress (I) in Meghalaya, and embraced the Congress (I) members in the Legislative Assembly and also claimed support from four members of the Hill State People's Democratic Party (HSPDP), one of the All-Party Hill Leaders' Conference and two of the Public Demands Implementation Convention. The Front formed a state Government from which one of the HSPDP members withdrew on April 7, 1983.

Meghalaya United Parliamentary Party

Leadership. Brington Buhai Lyngdoh (l.)

Founded. February 1983

History. The party was set up by members of the All-Party Hill Leaders' Conference and the Hill State People's Democratic Party and formed a short-lived Ministry, superseded on April 2, 1983, by a Congress (I)-led Ministry.

Public Demands Implementation Convention (PDIC)

Address. Mission Compound, Shillong-793002, Meghalaya, India

History. The PDIC first gained representation in the Meghalaya state Assembly in February 1978, when it won two seats. It subsequently held a post in a coalition Ministry formed by the All-Party Hill Leaders' Conference with the participation of the Hill State People's Democratic Party. In the elections of Feb. 17, 1983, it retained its two seats in the Legislative Assembly, and it subsequently supported the Congress (I) Ministry.

NAGALAND

Naga National Democratic Party (NNDP)

Address. Burma Camp, Dimapur, Nagaland, India

Leadership. T. Aliba Imti (pres.); John Bosco Jasokie (l.)

Founded. 1969

History. The NNDP adopted its present name in December 1981, having previously been known as the United Democratic Front (UDF). (The Election Commission of India approved the change of name on Feb. 17, 1982.) The UDF was originally known as the United Front of Nagaland, as which it first contested state elections in 1969, when it gained 10 seats in the Nagaland state Assembly. After it had been joined by several defectors from the Naga Nationalist Organization (later known as the Congress), it adopted the name of United Democratic Front and increased its representation in the Assembly to 25 members in 1974 and to 35 in 1977.

The NNDP's leader at the time (Vizol) was Chief Minister of Nagaland in 1974-75 and again from November 1977 to April 1980 (the state having been under President's rule in 1975-77). An NNDP Ministry headed by J.B. Jasokie was in office from June 1980 until November 1982, when, in the elections held on Nov. 10, the NNDP retained only 24 seats (out of 60) in the Legislative Assembly; it subsequently did not take part in the Ministry formed by the Congress (I) with the support of independents. The UDF had gained one seat in the *Lok Sabha* in 1971 and had retained it in 1977, but in 1980 it failed to secure representation in that House.

Orientation. While in power the NNDP launched a programme of village development boards with a view to involving the people in organizing their economy according to their own resources and priority needs. In its 1982 election manifesto the party called inter alia for a peaceful settlement of the Naga political problem and for the "unification of all contiguous Naga areas in one administrative unit".

National Convention of Nagaland

Address. Kohima, Nagaland, India
History. The party gained only one seat in the 1977 elections to the Nagaland State Assembly, but none in 1982.

PUNJAB

All India Labour Party

Address. H. O. 23-Laxmi Market, Jalandhar-144001, Punjab, India
Leadership. Phuman Ram Chogitti (pres.); S. Kartar Singh Miglani (g.s.); Prof. H. R. Rai (sec.)
History. The party is registered with the Union Election Commission and has contested elections but without gaining any seats in legislatures.
Orientation. The party stands for non-violence, peaceful international co-operation and aid to the poor; it is opposed to all exploitation among men and between nations.

Shiromani Akali Dal

Address. Baradari Shri Dabar Sahib, Amritsar, Punjab, India
Leadership. Harchand Singh Longowal (pres.); Prakash Singh Majithia, Sukhinder Singh, Rajinder Singh (gen. secs.)
Founded. December 1920
History. As the supreme body of the Sikhs, the party took an active part in the struggle for Indian independence and for the formation of states on a linguistic basis. It was temporarily merged with Congress from October 1958 onwards but contested the 1962 Punjab state Assembly elections as an independent party. Although repeatedly affected by internal

differences leading to splits, the party became the strongest in Punjab in 1969, when it formed a Punjab coalition Ministry with the *Jan Sangh* until 1970, then ruling alone until 1971.

In the 1972 state elections it was defeated by Congress. In the state elections of June 1977, which the *Akali Dal* fought in alliance with the Janata Party and the Communist Party of India (Marxist), it won 58 out of 117 seats in the state Assembly and subsequently formed a coalition Government with the Janata Party. Following the victory of the latter party in the 1977 general elections the *Akali Dal* also took part in the Union Government formed by the Janata leader, the *Akali Dal* having won nine seats in the *Lok Sabha*. However, in the May 1980 elections to the Legislative Assembly the Akali Dal retained only 37 seats, and a Congress (I) Ministry subsequently took office.

Following serious communal riots in 1981, in which Sikh extremists were involved, the *Akali Dal* the following year launched a campaign (*Dharm-Yudha* or Holy Struggle) for an autonomous state of Punjab (similar in status to Jammu and Kashmir and to include adjacent Sikh-populated areas) and also in support of various religious demands. The widespread agitation and demonstrations resulted in the arrest of thousands of Sikh activists; in a serious clash in New Delhi on Oct. 11, 1982, four Sikhs were killed and 60 injured when police opened fire on armed protesters.

Negotiations resulted in no political concessions by the Government which, however, met some religious demands (declaring Amritsar a holy city where the sale of tobacco and liquor was banned). The *Akali Dal* claimed in January 1983 that about 105,000 *Akali Dal* members and sympathizers had been imprisoned and 155 Punjabis killed during the "struggle".

Violent incidents associated with Sikh demands continued to occur through 1983 and early 1984, leading the Government to declare the Punjab a "dangerously disturbed area" on April 3, 1984. In early June 1984 a fullscale crisis developed when government troops forcibly occupied the Sikhs' Golden Temple in Amritsar, where many Sikh extremists had taken refuge.

Orientation. The party stands for autonomy for all states in India, equal rights for all and safeguards for minorities. (It opposed the state of emergency imposed by Congress in 1975.)
Structure. The party is organized at village, circle, district and state level.
Membership. 1,000,000
Publications. *Akali Times* (daily, in Punjabi)

SIKKIM

Sikkim Congress for Democracy
Sikkim Prajatantra Congress

Address. Naya Bazar, P.O. Gangtok, 737101, Sikkim, India

Leadership. Nar Bahadur Khatiwada (pres.); Karma Gyampo Lama (sec.)

Founded. February 1977

History. The party was formed by former members of the Indian Congress. In the Sikkim Legislative Assembly it became the first recognized opposition party, with its president as Leader of the Opposition and holding five out of 32 seats. The party is in alliance with the Indian National Congress (I), having in the October 1979 state elections retained three seats.

Orientation. The party stands for "socialist democracy, secularism, fundamental rights of the individual and world peace".

Structure. The party's high command consists of the president, vice-presidents, general secretary, secretaries and the treasurer, as well as the presidents and secretaries of the district committees (as ex-officio members).

Membership. 67,000

Publications. *Bulletin* (in Nepali), 20,000

Sikkim Congress (Revolutionary)

Founded. 1979

History. The party, formed by dissident Janata Party members, gained 11 seats in the 1979 elections to the Sikkim state Assembly. It was the only opposition group in the Assembly. However, four of its elected members, led by B. B. Gurung, resigned from the party on April 30, 1983.

Sikkim Parishad (SP)

Leadership. Nar Bahadur Bhandari (l.)

Founded. 1977

History. Known then as the Sikkim Janata *Parishad*, the party first contested elections to the Sikkim state Assembly in October 1979 and gained 16 (out of 32) seats. Its leader thereupon formed an eight-member Ministry (with the support of an independent elected as a representative of the lamas). (The party's leader had earlier been secretary-general of a *Prajatantra* Party which had existed before Sikkim's accession to India in 1975—prior to the holding of any elections based on one man, one vote.)

The party adopted its present name after the 1980 *Lok Sabha* elections (in which it gained one seat), and in February 1980 it was recognized as the Sikkim unit of the Congress (I).

TAMIL NADU

All-India Anna Dravida Munnetra Kazhagam (ADMK)

Address. 156 Lloyds Road, Madras 600004, India

Leadership. M. G. Ramachandran (l.)

Founded. October 1972

History. The ADMK was established as a splinter group of the *Dravida Munnetra Kazagham* (DMK), the ruling party in Madras (later Tamil Nadu) which had gained 138 seats in the state Assembly in 1967 and 184 in 1971. By November 1973 the ADMK held 13 of these seats, and in 1977 it gained 130 seats in the Assembly and 18 in the *Lok Sabha*. It thereupon formed a Ministry in Tamil Nadu.

The ADMK, which had added the words "All-India" to its name in 1976, also operated in Pondicherry, where it gained 14 (out of 30) seats in the territorial Assembly in 1974 and thereupon formed a short-lived minority Ministry; in 1977 it retained its 14 seats and again formed a minority Ministry, which remained in office until November 1978.

While it had contested the 1977 *Lok Sabha* elections in alliance with the Congress, the ADMK stated in its manifesto issued for the 1980 general elections (in which it gained two seats) that it would support a government headed by the Janata Party leader, and this led to the exclusion of the ADMK from the Charan Singh government led by the Janata Party (Secular) formed in July 1979.

For the May 1980 elections to the Legislative Assembly the ADMK was allied with the two Communist parties, the Gandhi-Kamaraj National Congress, the Tamil Nadu Congress (Kamaraj) and the Forward Bloc. By obtaining 129 (out of 234) seats the ADMK gained an absolute majority in the Assembly and thereupon formed a Ministry under its leader.

Orientation. In a manifesto of September 1972 the ADMK called inter alia for transfer to the states of all powers not reserved for the central Government, abandonment of Hindi as India's national language and adoption of the regional language as the language of each state, with English as link language between states; total prohibition throughout India;

a ceiling on incomes; nationalisation of more banks, large-scale industries and the means of production and distribution of all essential commodities; confiscation of all "ill-gotten wealth"; and power for the electorate to recall elected representatives.

Dravida Munnetra Kazhagam (DMK)

Address. Arivagam, Royapuram, Madras 600013, India

Leadership. Dr Muthuvel Karunanidhi (pres.); K. Anbuzhan (g.s.)

Founded. 1949

History. The Dravidian Progress Movement (DMK) was originally founded by C. N. Annadurai, whose name was subsequently incorporated into the title of the All-India *Anna Dravida Munnetra Kazhagam* (ADMK) when the latter was formed as a result of a split in the DMK in 1972 (see separate entry above).

The DMK first obtained parliamentary representation in 1957, when it gained two seats in the *Lok Sabha* and 15 in the Madras (later Tamil Nadu) state Assembly. By 1967 it had become the strongest party in the state Assembly, with 138 seats (and the first non-Congress party to gain an absolute majority in a state Assembly). In 1971 it raised its representation in the Assembly to 184 members, but following the formation of the *Anna Dravida Munnetra Kazhagam* it retained only 48 seats in the 1977 state Assembly elections and lost control of the state.

In the *Lok Sabha*, where the party had gained 25 seats in 1967 and 23 in 1971, it was reduced to one seat in 1977. In Pondicherry, where it gained 15 (out of 30) seats in the 1969 elections, it formed a Ministry in coalition with the Communist Party of India until 1973, but it was reduced to two seats in the territorial Assembly in early 1974. In Mysore (renamed Karnataka in 1973) it gained a seat (for the first time) in the state Assembly in 1972 but lost it in 1978.

For the 1980 general elections the DMK entered into an alliance with the Congress (I), and it gained 16 *Lok Sabha* seats in these elections. In the same year it obtained 14 seats in the Pondicherry Legislative Assembly (in January) and 38 in the Tamil Nadu Assembly (in May).

Orientation. The DMK calls for full autonomy for the state of Tamil Nadu within the Indian Union and for the establishment of regional languages as state languages and of English as the official language.

Membership. 1,600,000

Ghandi-Kamaraj National Congress

History. This party broke away from the Congress and fought the May 1980 Legislative Assembly elections in Tamil Nadu in alliance with the All-India *Anna Dravida Munnetra Kazhagam*, the Communist Party of India, the Communist Party of India (Marxist) and two other parties; it gained six seats for itself.

Tamil Nadu Congress (Kamaraj)

Founded. October 1979

History. This party was formed by former members of the Congress (I) who were opposed to an electoral agreement made by the latter party with the *Dravida Munnetra Kazagham*. It fought the May 1980 elections to the Legislative Assembly in alliance with the All-India *Anna Dravida Munnetra Kazhagam*, the two Communist parties and another two parties, and it gained three seats for itself.

TRIPURA

Tripura State Congress for Democracy

Address. Old Colonel Bari, Hariganga Basah Road, Agartala, Tripura, India

Leadership. Prafulla Kumar Das (l.)

History. After being strengthened by the adherence of numerous defectors from the Congress, the party formed, in April 1977, a coalition Ministry with the Communisty Party of India (Marxist) until this Ministry was replaced by a Janata/CPI(M) coalition Ministry in July 1977. The party has not been represented in the state Assembly since 1978.

Tripura Tribal Youth Organization
Tripura Upajatia Juba Samiti

Address. Abhoynagar Agartala, 799005 Tripura, India

Leadership. Buddha Dev Burma (pres.); Shyamacharan Tripura (g.s.)

Founded. June 1967

History. This organization was founded by young Tripura tribesmen, after a setback for the (Communist) opposition in 1967 Tripura elections, to "fight democratically for constitutional rights of Tripura tribesmen". It gained six seats in the Tripura Legislative Assembly on Jan. 6, 1983.

Orientation. The movement is "a non-communist organization to develop the

Tripura tribes socially, economically and educationally", to campaign for an autonomous tribal district council, for the restoration of lands expropriated "in contravention of the 1960 Tripura Land Revenue Act", and for recognition of Kok Borok (the Tripuri language) as the state language and medium of instruction (in Roman script).

Structure. There is a 135-member central committee which lays down policies, and a central executive committee leading the party.

Membership. 12,000

Publications. *Chinikok* (in Bengali Kok Borok, weekly), 2,600

UTTAR PRADESH

Bharatiya Socialist Party

Address. Jalal Manzil, Gautam Badha Marg, Lucknow, 226001 Uttar Pradesh, India

Leadership. Shri Bhola Prasad Singh (ch.); Shri Mohammad Abdul Haleem (g.s.)

Founded. April 1977

History. The party (also known as *Bharatiya Samajwadi*) is an offshoot of the Socialist Party, most of whose leaders joined the Janata Party early in 1977. It had six members in the *Lok Sabha* dissolved in 1979 and 58 in state legislatures of various states, but has had no parliamentary representation in recent years.

Orientation. The party's aims are to create, "by democratic and peaceful revolution", a society "free from economic, social and political exploitation", to eliminate inequalities amongst nations and to set up a world parliament and a socialist society. The party's means include "extra-parliamentary and extra-legal individual and mass resistance".

Structure. The party has a 21-member executive committee, as well as state, district and city committees.

Publications. *ISP* (in English, Quilon, Kerala); *Shambook* (in Hindi, Patna, Bihar); *Quami Tarjuman* (in Urdu, Lucknow, Uttar Pradesh).

WEST BENGAL

Biplabi Bangla Congress (BBC)

Address. 73/C, Shyama Proad Mukherjee Road, Calcutta-26, West Bengal, India

Leadership. Ashish Bhattacharjee (g.s.)

Founded. July 1970

History. The BBC broke away from a formation called the Bangla Congress (which was part of the Congress before

1966 and again from 1971 onwards), and it gained three seats in the West Bengal Legislative Assembly in 1971, but it won none in elections held in March 1972. The party contested the elections of June 1977 as part of the Left Front and gained one seat, and as the result of the Left Front's election victory became a government party. It has held no seat since the May 1982 West Bengal Assembly elections.

Orientation. Towards "democratic socialism through mass revolution".

Structure. The party has an elected seven-member secretariat.

Membership. 25,000

Christian Democratic Party

History. This party contested the May 19, 1982, elections to the Legislative Assembly of West Bengal as part of an alliance with the Congress (I) and four other parties. It gained no seat for itself, however.

Forward Bloc (Marxist)

History. In 1952-57 this party held a total of 15 seats in various state assemblies but since then it has been confined to West Bengal, where it has held seats in the state Assembly—11 in 1956-57, two in 1957-62, one in 1967-71, two in 1971-72 and two since 1977.

Gorkha League

History. This party contested the West Bengal Legislative Assembly elections on May 19, 1982, in alliance with the Congress (I) and four other parties. It obtained one seat.

Left Front

History. This electoral alliance—formed in West Bengal by the Communist Party of India (Marxist), the Forward Bloc, the Forward Bloc (Marxist), the Revolutionary Socialist Party and the Revolutionary Communist Party—gained a majority in the 1977 elections to the West Bengal Legislative Assembly. After being joined also by the Communist Party of India, the West Bengal Socialist Party, the

Democratic Socialist Party and some independents, it obtained altogether 238 out of the 294 seats in the West Bengal Assembly in elections held on May 19, 1982.

Orientation. The Left Front stands for land reform, greater educational opportunities and measures against corruption.

Revolutionary Communist Party of India (RCPI)

Address. 5/1 Rammoy Road, Calcutta 700025, India

Leadership. Sudhin Kumar (sec.)

Founded. Aug. 1, 1934

History. The party was set up in Calcutta as an offshoot of the Communist Party of India and claims to be the only left-wing party in India to have remained outside and independent of the Indian National Congress even before India achieved independence. During the post-independence period the RCPI engaged in armed struggle which failed and seriously disrupted the party. Later, however, it was represented in the state legislatures of Assam, Maharashtra and West Bengal.

The RCPI contested the 1962 election to the West Bengal State Assembly in an alliance with the Communist Party of India (which gained 50 seats). In the 1969 election to that Assembly it won two seats as part of a United Front led by the Communist Party of India (Marxist)—CPI(M)—and it held a post in the United Front Ministry in 1969-70. In 1977 it obtained three seats as part of a Left Front also led by the CPI(M) and thereupon was also given a post in the Left Front Ministry. In the May 1982 elections, which it contested as part of the same Front, it retained two seats in the Assembly.

Socialist Unity Centre of India (SUCI)

Address. 48 Lenin Sarani, Calcutta 700 013, India

Leadership. Nihar Mukherjee (g.s.)

Founded. April 1948

History. The SUCI was founded as a Marxist-Leninist party by Sibhas Ghosh (who died in 1976) and was claimed to be "the only genuine Communist party in India". In West Bengal it formed part of a United Front which formed a state Government (led by the Bangla Congress) in 1967, in which the SUCI held the Ministry of Labour. In the West Bengal state elections in 1969 the SUCI increased its seats in the state Assembly from two to seven, and it was thereafter represented in the West Bengal United Front Government until 1970.

In the 1971 state elections the SUCI formed, together with the Forward Bloc, the Communist Party of India (CPI) and others, the United Left Front (ULDF), but the SUCI did not support a coalition Ministry formed by the Congress and supported by the CPI and the Forward Bloc. In the 1972 state elections the SUCI, as part of a Left Front, retained only one seat, but in 1977 it gained four seats in the state Assembly without taking part in any alliance. In Assam, the SUCI first gained two seats in the state Assembly in 1978.

In the May 1982 elections to the West Bengal Legislative Assembly it retained two seats. It also holds one seat in the Bihar Assembly.

Orientation. The SUCI regards all other Communist parties as "revisionists" and itself as "distinct from social democratic, modern revisionist and Trotskyist parties". It stands for "the establishment of socialism and ultimately communism as a means to achieve a world communist society".

Structure. The party is "democratically centralized" with a central committee and a political bureau headed by the general secretary, and operating through a number of different organizations (including trade unions).

Membership. 165,304

Publications. Organs in English, Bengali, Oriya, Assamese, Malayalam and Hindi (total circulation 200,000)

West Bengal Socialist Party

History. This party contested the May 19, 1982, elections to the Legislative Assembly as part of the Left Front (led by the Communist Party of India-Marxist). It obtained one seat.

Union Territory Parties

ARUNACHAL PRADESH

Arunachal People's Conference (APC)

Founded. September 1979

History. The APC was formed by dissident Janata Party members, who had withdrawn their support from the state Government. However, 12 of its foundation members almost immediately joined the United People's Party of Arunachal. The APC won no seats in the 1980 state elections.

United People's Party of Arunachal (UPPA)

Address. P.O. Itanagar, 791-111, Arunachal Pradesh, India
Leadership. Shri Tomo Riba (l.)
Founded. April 1977
History. The party was formed as the People's Party of Arunachal Pradesh (PPAP) by Shri Bakin Pertin and Shri Tomo Riba, who defected from the ruling Congress Party which later merged with the Janata Party. In the March 1977 general elections Shri Bakin Pertin had been elected to the *Lok Sabha* (defeating the Congress candidate). In the first Arunachal Pradesh Legislative Assembly elections held in February 1978 the PPAP gained eight out of 30 seats.

After being joined by 12 former Janata members of the Assembly in September 1979 the PPAP changed its name to the United People's Party of Arunachal (UPPA), under the leadership of Shri Tomo Riba who, claiming the support of 20 of the 30 Assembly members, formed a Ministry. However, this Ministry resigned on Oct. 13, 1979, after five UPPA members had joined the Congress (I). In the state elections held in January 1980 the UPPA obtained 13 seats.

Orientation. The party seeks "to ensure socio-cultural, socio-economic and socio-political stability" in Arunachal Pradesh.
Structure. The party has a Pradesh and district executive body, as well as sub-divisional, block and village committees.
Membership. 111,000

GOA

Maharashtrawadi Gomantak (MG)

Address. Altinho, Panaji, Goa, India
Leadership. (Mrs) Shashikala Kakodkar (pres.)
Founded. June 1963
History. The MG was the ruling party in the Union Territory of Goa from the first general election in that territory in December 1963, when the MG gained 14 (out of the 30) seats in the Legislative Assembly (and at the same time two seats in the *Lok Sabha*). It later gained 16 seats in the Assembly in February 1967, 18 in March 1972 and 15 in June 1977.

The party lost its seats in the *Lok Sabha* in 1971 but regained one in 1977 which it retained in the 1980 election. In the territorial elections of January 1980 it retained only seven seats in the Assembly, and it was thereafter succeeded in power by a Congress Ministry, while five of its elected members and its president decided to join the Congress (I). On July 3, 1983, however, three of them resigned from the Congress (I).

Orientation. The MG was predominantly supported by Hindus and advocated the merger of Goa with the State of Maharashtra (but such a merger was rejected in an official poll in January 1967).

MIZORAM

Mizo Janata Party

History. This party, which is independent of the national Janata Party, gained one seat in the Mizoram State Assembly in May 1978.

Mizoram Pradesh Congress

Address. Aizawl, Mizoram, India
Leadership. Lal Thanhawla (pres.); Lal Sainghaka (g.s.)
Founded. August 1961
History. The Mizoram Pradesh Congress was a district unit of the Assam Congress until January 1972, when Mizoram became a Union Territory. Since then it has been a state unit of the Indian National Congress. It was in power in the Mizoram District Council in 1970-72 and in the Mizoram Union Territory in 1974-77. Following the division of the Indian National Congress into Congress and Congress (I), the Mizoram Congress kept aloof and retained its own identity as a regional party, but more recently it has become one of the constituent units of the Congress (I) while retaining a certain functional autonomy. It has been the strongest opposition party in Mizoram, with eight (out of 30) seats in the Legislative Assembly.
Orientation. The party subscribes to the policies of Mrs Indira Gandhi's Indian National Congress.
Structure. The Mizoram Pradesh Congress has village, group, block and district committees, and a 35-member executive committee functioning on behalf of the party's general assembly.
Membership. 134,000
Publications. *Zoram Tlangau* (Herald of Zoram)

People's Conference (PC)

Address. G.H.Q., P.O. Aizawl, Mizoram, India
Leadership. Brig. Thenphunga Sailo (l.)
Founded. 1977
History. The PC came to power in Mizoram after the Assembly elections of May 1978, in which it gained 23 (of the 30) seats.

Indonesia

Capital: Jakarta   Pop. 157,000,000

The Republic of Indonesia is a unitary state with an executive President who governs with the assistance of a Cabinet appointed by him and who is elected (and is re-eligible) by a 920-member People's Consultative Assembly, the highest authority of the state. Of the Assembly's members, 460 are from the House of Representatives, the country's legislature, to which 364 members are elected for a five-year term by direct universal adult suffrage and the remaining 96 are appointed. The Assembly's other 460 members are government appointees, delegates of regional assemblies, and representatives of parties and groups (appointed in proportion to their elective seats in the House of Representatives).

All adults above the age of 17 years, or younger if married, are entitled to vote, except members of the armed forces and persons deprived of their civic rights (after release from detention as former members of the Indonesian Communist Party). Candidates are elected in multi-member provinces under a system of simple proportional representation.

As a result of elections held on May 4, 1982 (when 91.4 per cent of the registered electorate was officially stated to have voted), the elective seats in the House of Representatives were distributed as follows: Joint Secretariat of Functional Groups (Golkar) 246, (Moslem) United Development Party 94, Indonesian Democratic Party 24.

Indonesian Democratic Party
Partai Demokrasi Indonesia (PDI)

Leadership. Prof. Sunawar Suko-Wati (acting ch.)

Founded. 1973

History. The PDI was formed by a merger of five non-Islamic (nationalist and Christian) parties—the Indonesian Nationalist Party, the Movement for the Defence of Indonesian Independence, the Catholic Party, the Protestant Christian Party and the People's Party (*Partai Murba*, a left-wing group)—in implementation of a resolution by the People's Consultative Assembly.

In the 1977 elections to the House of Representatives the PDI gained 8.6 per cent of the total vote (in a 90 per cent poll). In the 1982 elections the party received less than 5 per cent in 14 provinces, less than 10 per cent in another eight and only 12 per cent in Jakarta (its main centre of support).

Joint Secretariat of Functional Groups
Sekber Golongan Karya (Golkar)

Leadership. Gen. Suharto (pres. & ch. of advisory board); Maj.-Gen. Amir Murtano (ch.); Sarwono Kusumaadja (sec.)

Founded. 1964

History. Golkar was formed as a loose alliance of various groups representing sectional interests (farmers, workers, veterans, women and youth), designed to counter-balance the influence of the Communist Party. The party was brought under government control in 1968 to provide a civilian basis for President Suharto's military regime.

In the 1971, 1977 and 1982 parliamentary elections Golkar obtained an absolute majority of the seats. In the 1982 elections it gained an overall majority of the votes in 25 (out of the 27) provinces, including Loro Sae (i.e. East Timor).

Structure. The party is financed by the state.

United Development Party
Partai Persatuan Pembangunan (PPP)

Leadership. Dr K.H. Idham Chalid (pres.); Dr H.J. Naro (ch.); Jahja Ubeid (s.g.)

Founded. 1973

History. The PPP was formed by a merger of four Islamic parties—the Muslim Scholars' Party, the Indonesian Islamic Party, the United Islamic Party of Indonesia and the *Perti* (Islamic) Party, in implementation of a resolution by the People's Consultative Assembly. In the 1977 election to the House of Representatives the PPP gained 29.3 per cent of the total vote (rather more than obtained in 1971 by the four parties from which it was formed).

The official results of the 1982 general elections, which gave the PPP 94 seats in the Assembly, were challenged by the party, which claimed in particular that it had overwhelming support in Jakarta, where it had won a majority in 1977 but only five seats in 1982 (against six for the ruling Golkar and two for the Indonesian Democratic Party). Overall it claimed to have received some 1,800,000 votes in the capital (against 1,200,000 for Golkar).

Orientation. The Islamic PPP has supported the Government in all matters other than religious ones.

Structure. Although the party has one national executive, the four constituent parties continue to exist as "non-political associations" and have their own affiliated organizations, e.g. for youth, women and farmers.

Iran

Capital: Tehran Pop. 40,000,000

The Islamic Republic of Iran is ruled by a Council of the Revolution consisting of (Shi'ite) Islamic spiritual leaders following the fundamentalist tenets of Ayatollah Ruhollah Khomeini, the "guardian of the state". There is a 270-member Parliament (*Majlis*) elected by direct universal suffrage, with the majority of seats being held by the Islamic Republican Party, a religious alliance. There are also a directly-elected President of the Republic (without real power) and a Cabinet. Political parties and other organizations enjoy freedom as long as they do not infringe "the principles of independence, freedom, national unity and the bases of the Islamic Republic".

All candidates in presidential and parliamentary elections must be approved by a (clerical) Council of Guardians. The minimum voting age is 16 years, but for the presidential elections of October 1981 it was lowered to 15 years. To be elected candidates must obtain an absolute majority, and if necessary several election rounds are held.

In parliamentary elections held on April 15 and May 17, 1984, the Islamic Republican Party won a further overwhelming victory, with the party's radical Marxist wing substantially increasing its presence in the *Majlis*.

Since 1980 parties other than the Islamic Republican Party have declined in influence, as many of their leaders have gone into exile. Moreover, the *Tudeh* (pro-Soviet Communist) party, which had supported the 1979 revolution but had subsequently opposed the Khomeini regime, was banned on May 4, 1983, and many of its leaders and activists were put on trial.

Communist Party of Iran
Hezb-e Komunist Iran

Leadership. Azaryun (s.g.)
Founded. 1979
Orientation. This party has taken an ideological and political line strongly opposed to the pro-Soviet People's (or *Tudeh*) Party, which was banned in May 1983.

Iranian Freedom Movement
Nelzat-Azadi

Leadership. Dr Mehdi Bazargan, Ahmed Haj Seyed Javadi, Dr Yadollah Sahabi
Founded. 1979
History. The movement's leaders had all held ministerial office in Governments set up under the Islamic revolutionary regime in 1979—Dr Bazargan as Prime Minister from February to November; Mr Javadi as Minister of the Interior from February to June and of Justice thereafter until November; and Dr Sahabi as Minister of Revolutionary Projects from February to September and of Research and Study thereafter until November 1979.

Dr Bazargan, who had a number of supporters in the *Majlis* elected in 1980, repeatedly criticized the Government, in particular in September 1981 when he accused the regime's leaders of being inaccessible to the average Iranian.
Orientation. The movement has advocated the establishment of an Islamic parliamentary democracy which would have the support of the ethnic minorities as well as of non-Shi'ite Moslems.

Islamic Republican Party (IRP)

Leadership. Hojatolislam Sayed Ali Khamenei (s.g.)
Founded. February 1978
History. The IRP was established as the political organization of Ayatollah Ruhollah Khomeini, the leader of the Islamic revolutionary movement which ended the rule of the Shah in February 1979. The Ayatollah himself did not expressly adopt the party as his own, but it was the principal organization to defend his theses in a referendum which led to the proclamation of the Islamic Republic of Iran in April 1979, and also in the election of a Constitutional Council of Experts in August 1979 and in the constitutional referendum of Dec. 2–3 of that year.

The IRP was successful, during 1979, in retaining majority support for the Ayatollah both against his political opponents on the left and in the liberal centre groups and against ethnic and religious minorities seeking a measure of autonomy. In the presidential election of January 1980 the IRP's candidate had to be withdrawn because he was found not to be of Iranian descent, and the party thereupon did not nominate an official candidate. After the election the IRP's then secretary-general declared that the party would support the elected President (Abolhassan Bani-Sadr) as long as he remained aligned on the Islamic revolutionary position but would oppose him if he deviated from it.

Following the deposition of President Bani-Sadr in June 1981, the IRP candidate, Mohammed Ali Radjai, was elected to the presidency by an overwhelming majority in July 1981. Following the assassination of President Radjai a month later, the IRP secretary-general, Hojatolislam Sayed Ali Khamenei, was elected President of the Republic on Oct.2, 1981

Meanwhile, Ayatollah Mohammed Hossein Beheshti, the party's first secretary-general, had been killed in an explosion on June 28, 1981, together with most other party leaders. However, in the course of 1981 the party was able to eliminate the influence of most of its opponents, in particular those with "moderate" or secular views and also the left-wing (Islamic) *Mujaheddin Khalq*, a movement which had taken to armed resistance. In this struggle the party made use of Revolutionary Guards (*pasdaran*), who carried out decisions made by revolutionary committees operating at local level, and also of the "Party of God" (*hezbollahi*) consisting of armed bands allied to the clergy and patrolling the major cities.
Orientation. The IRP's object is to maintain the Islamic Republic of Iran; one of its founder members, Dr Hassan Ayet, was instrumental in introducing into the Constitution Article 110 defining the functions of the Wali Faqih (the ruling theologian in accordance with the theories of Ayatollah Khomeini) as being to hold supreme authority over the country's President and Parliament.
Structure. The party has a central committee and a strong local organization based on the Moslem clergy.
Membership. 2,000,000
Publications. *Djoumhouri Islami*

Moslem People's Republican Party (MPRP)

Leadership. Hossein Farshi (s.g.)
Founded. 1979
History. The MPRP called for a "yes" vote in the March 1979 referendum on the

establishment of an Islamic republic in Iran, although it would have preferred a more democratic form of the question put to the voters (in order to show that there was freedom of opinion in Iran). In the August 1979 elections to a Constituent Council of Experts the MPRP called for abstention on the ground that there could be no free elections during "the current disturbances and civil war". It also called for a boycott of the referendum held on Dec. 2–3, 1979, to obtain approval of the Constitution of the Islamic Republic of Iran.

Immediately after the December 1979 referendum MPRP activists were reported to have taken part in a rebellion in Tabriz (north-western Iran) by Turkish-speaking followers of Ayatollah Kazem Shariatmadari (originally the party's spiritual leader), but the revolt collapsed after the latter withdrew his support from the party and its offices were stormed by Revolutionary Guards. In May 1980 two MPRP leaders, including the party's then secretary-general (Abolhassan Rostamkhani), were executed for their part in the rebellion and other offences.

Orientation. The MPRP is "firmly anti-imperialist and religious, but not clerical".

It is opposed to a theocratic dictatorship as envisaged under the country's Constitution.

Pan-Iranist Party (PIP)

Leadership. Mohsen Pezeshkpour (l.)
Founded. 1967
History. The party first contested general elections in August 1967, when it gained five (out of 219) seats in the *Majlis* (Chamber of Deputies) and five (out of 279) in a Constituent Assembly. It retained one seat in the *Majlis* until Iran was proclaimed a one-party state in March 1975 and all parties other than the newly-established *Rastakhiz* (National Resurrection) party were officially dissolved. The PIP was reconstituted in June 1978 and was joined by several parliamentarians who defected from the *Rastakhiz* party.

Orientation. As a nationalist party with a record of opposing the Shah's regime the PIP supported the establishment of an Islamic republic in Iran.

Iraq

Capital: Baghdad   Pop. 15,000,000

The Republic of Iraq is, under its 1968 Constitution, a popular democratic and sovereign state with Islam as its state religion and its economy "based on socialism". It is ruled by a Revolutionary Command Council (RCC) headed by a President (Saddam Hussein Takriti), who is also secretary of the *Baath* Arab Socialist Party of Iraq, and a Vice-President. In 1973 a National Progressive Front was formed by the *Baath* party with the participation of a faction of the Democratic Party of Kurdistan and the Iraqi Communist Party (ICP); the latter, however, was suppressed in mid-1979 (when it had about 2,000 members).

The President is elected by a two-thirds majority vote of the RCC (the "supreme organ of the state") from among its members (whose number was, in June 1982, reduced from 15 to nine). A 250-member (legislative) National Assembly is elected for a four-year term by civilians (communists or property owners being disqualified) under a system of proportional representation (one member for every 50,000 citizens).

Of the 250 members elected to the National Assembly on June 20, 1980, 175 were *Baath* party members, and all candidates had to express their belief in the principles of the 1968 revolution (which had brought the party to power).

A Kurdish Legislative Council of 50 members was elected on Sept. 19, 1980, with limited powers (to pass legislation for the Kurdish region on social, cultural and economic development as well as on health, education and labour matters), but this Council was not supported by a majority of Kurds, whose ultimate aim was full autonomy or even complete independence for Kurdistan.

Apart from the Kurds and the ICP, the predominantly Sunni Moslem regime in Baghdad has encountered strong opposition from militant elements of the Shi'ite Moslem community (constituting more than half of Iraq's population), the latter being in sympathy with and supported by the regime of the Islamic Republic of Iran (with which Iraq has been at war since September 1980). The Iraqi *Baath* party has also been actively opposed by dissident Baathists supported by the Government of Syria.

Baath Arab Socialist Party
Hizb al-Baath al-Arabi al-Ishtiraki

Address. P.O. Box 6012, Al Mansour, Baghdad, Iraq
Leadership. Michel Aflaq (s.g. of pan-Arab command); Saddam Hussein Takriti (s.g. of regional command)
Founded. April 1947
History. Theoretical preparations for the formation of the *Baath* (Renaissance) party were made by its founder, Michel Aflaq, and others in the late 1940s, and party cells were established, spreading from Syria to Lebanon, Jordan and Iraq (see also *Baath* Arab Socialist Party of Syria). In Iraq the party was a member of the National Front which organized the overthrow of the monarchy in 1958, and from 1959 to 1963 it fought against the dictatorship of President Kassem, which it overthrew in February 1973.

The *Baath* was again suppressed under the dictatorship of the Aref brothers from November 1963 to July 1968, when the regime was overthrown by a Revolutionary Command Council led by the party, which has been the leading ruling party in Iraq since then. In July 1973 it set up the National Progressive Front (see separate entry) in which all political parties in Iraq (including the Communist Party and the Democratic Party of Kurdistan) were to co-operate. In 1974 it implemented autonomous rule for the Kurdish minority in Iraq (under a law announced in March 1970). The party also nationalized all shares of foreign oil companies in Iraq in June 1972.

Orientation. The party's three main aims are unity, freedom and socialism for the Arab nation. The party is opposed to imperialism, Zionism and reaction; it supports all liberation movements, as well as socialist and progressive forces; and it has taken a leading part in the struggle for freedom for Palestine and in opposing the US-Egyptian-Israeli agreements.

Structure. As a pan-Arab party, the *Baath* party is subject to the national leadership elected by a congress attended by representatives of the party's regions and districts in the Arab world, and this leadership is the supreme authority and formulates the party's long-term strategy. Under it there are regional leaderships (e.g. in Lebanon and Syria) responsible for the handling of regional affairs under the guidance of the national leadership. All members of the Revolutionary Command Council of Iraq are party members, and so are more than half the leadership of the National Progressive Front.

Membership. 1,500,000
Publications. *Ath-Thawra* (daily official organ), 200,000; *Al-Jumhuriyeh* (semi-official), 180,000
International affiliations. Afro-Asian People's Solidarity Organization

---

Kurdistan Revolutionary Party (KRP)

Leadership. Sattar Taher Sharef (s.g.)
Founded. 1972
History. The KRP was formed by a group of former members of the Democratic Party of Kurdistan (DPK), who disagreed with the DPK leader (Mullah Mustafa Barzani) and established a "provisional leadership", which in 1978 regarded itself as the legitimate successor to Mullah Barzani's DPK.

A faction of the KRP was admitted to the National Progressive Front in 1974, and on Aug. 16, 1981, Baghdad radio broadcast a statement by the KRP renewing its pledge to support the party and revolution headed by Saddam Hussein. The statement denounced the regime of Ayatollah Khomeini in Iran, declaring that while Kurds in Iran were subjected to persecution the Kurds in Iraq were developing their autonomous rule as "a precious fruit of the 1968 revolution under the *Baath* party".

National Progressive Front (NPF)

Leadership. Haim Haddad (s.g.)
Founded. July 1973

History. The NPF was formed under a joint manifesto of the *Baath* Arab Socialist Party and the Iraqi Communist Party (ICP) and it was joined in 1975 by representatives of Kurdish parties and organizations and other national and independent forces. At the formation of the NPF the ICP recognized the privileged role of the *Baath* party, which was to have a majority in the NPF and in the National Assembly. However, the ICP was suppressed in mid-1979.

Patriotic Union of Kurdistan (PUK)

Leadership. Jalal Talabani (l.)
Founded. July 1975
History. The PUK was set up by a merger of the Kurdistan National Party, the Socialist Movement of Kurdistan and the Association of Marxists-Leninists of Kurdistan. It has been in conflict with the Democratic Party of Kurdistan (founded in 1946, originally led by Mullah Mustapha Barzani and later by his son Masoud Barzani, and supporting the Islamic revolution in Iran). PUK guerrillas (*Pesh Merga*) were involved in a resumed armed struggle against Iraqi government forces from 1976 onwards. However, in January 1984 it was reported that an agreement had been reached between the Government of Iraq and the PUK, providing for a ceasefire between their respective forces, for the extension of the Kurdish autonomous region southwards to include areas around Kirkuk and Khanuqah as well as increased Kurdish autonomy, and for the formation of a 40,000-strong Kurdish army "to protect Kurdistan against foreign enemies" (i.e. in particular Iran).

Ireland

Capital: Dublin   Pop. 3,675,000

The Republic of Ireland is, under its 1937 Constitution, "a sovereign, independent democratic state" with a President elected for a seven-year term by universal adult suffrage; he holds specific constitutional powers and is advised by a Council of State. Legislative power is vested in the National Parliament (*Oireachtas*) consisting of the President and two Houses—(i) a House of Representatives (*Dáil Éireann*) of 166 members elected for a five-year term by adult suffrage of citizens above the age of 18 years, and (ii) a Senate (*Seanad Éireann*) of 60 members, of whom 11 are nominated by the Prime Minister, six elected by the universities and 43 chosen by representatives of vocational and administrative bodies. Executive power is held by a Government headed by a Prime Minister (*Taoiseach*) and responsible to the *Dáil*.

Elections to the *Dáil* are held by the single transferable vote method of proportional representation, i.e. each voter can indicate a second choice, which is taken into account when the first choice has obtained more than sufficient votes, or too few votes, to be selected. To be successful a candidate must gain a certain quota (the total district vote divided by the number of district seats, plus one vote). Electoral districts have from three to five seats each, but by-elections are held in a whole district, which is regarded as a single-seat area for the purpose.

Under an electoral act of 1963 parties are entitled to receive a subsidy from public funds in proportion to the number of seats which they gained in the last previous election. (Thus *Fianna Fáil* received the equivalent of about US $150,000 in 1980, and *Fine Gael* about US $93,000 in 1981.) Decisions about the registration of parties are made by the clerk of the *Dáil*. (Provisional *Sinn Féin*, regarded as the political wing of the Irish Republican Army, has been refused registration.) Parties receiving at least 1 per cent of the vote are entitled to representation in Parliament.

As a result of elections held on Nov. 24, 1982, seats in the *Dáil* were distributed as follows: *Fianna Fáil* 75, *Fine Gael* 70, Labour Party 16, Workers' Party 2, Independent *Fianna Fáil* 1, independents 2. Parties not represented in Parliament include the Communist Party of Ireland, the Democratic Socialist Party (which took part in the elections but failed to gain any seats) and Provisional *Sinn Féin*.

British & Irish Communist Organization (B&ICO)

Address. Dublin, Ireland

Orientation. This small neo-Stalinist group is alone among the Irish Marxist parties in subscribing to the "two nations theory" according to which the North should be recognized as forming a separate state.

Publications. *Political Bulletin*

Communist Party of Ireland (CPI)

Address. James Connolly House, 43 East Essex Street, Dublin 2, Ireland

Leadership. Andrew Barr (ch.); Michael O'Riordan (g.s.)

Founded. June 1933

History. The CPI had its origins in a Communist organization formed in Ireland in 1921, which lapsed in 1922-23, and in later Irish Revolutionary Workers' Groups set up to constitute a party. The CPI was a single organization for both parts of Ireland until 1940, whereafter the southern part of the organization temporarily suspended its activities and the northern part adopted the name of CPI. In 1948 it was decided to reconstitute a (Marxist-Leninist) party, which functioned in 1949–62 at first as the Irish Workers' League and later as the Irish Workers' Party (IWP). In 1970 the IWP and the CPI were reunited under a national executive committee which was given overall authority between congresses to be held both in the Republic of Ireland and in Northern Ireland, where there are two separate area committees. The party has not been represented in Parliament.

Publications. *Irish Workers' Voice* (weekly, Dublin); *Irish Socialist* (monthly, Dublin); *Irish Socialist Review* (quarterly, Dublin); *Unity* (weekly, Belfast)

International affiliations. The CPI is recognized by the Communist parties of the Soviet-bloc countries.

Communist Party of Ireland (Marxist-Leninist) (CPI M-L)

Leadership. David Vipond

History. This small group is organized on both sides of the border. It follows a pro-Albania line in the ideological debate among different Irish communist movements and is particularly critical of the alleged deviations of Communist China.

Publications. *Red Patriot*

Democratic Socialist Party (DSP)

Address. P.O. Box 806, Dublin 8, Ireland

Leadership. Jim Kemmy (pres.); Martin McGarry (sec.)

Founded. March 31, 1982

History. Jim Kemmy had been elected to the *Dáil* as an independent socialist in June 1981. In January 1982 he withdrew his support from the minority *Fine Gael*-Labour Party coalition Government on the issue of budget proposals which he considered inequitable; in the ensuing elections held on Feb. 18 he was re-elected with a greatly increased majority. He subsequently also opposed the budget measures of the new *Fianna Fáil* Government. His Limerick socialist organization and the existing Socialist Party dissolved on the creation of the DSP. The latter unsuccessfully contested seven seats in the November 1982 general elections, Kemmy losing his seat to the Labour Party (which had campaigned against him on the abortion issue).

Orientation. The DSP is socialist, democratic, secular (i.e. opposed to what it calls "the undemocratic power of the Roman Catholic Church in the areas of education, health and family law") and post-nationalist.

Structure. The party's annual conference decides on policy and elects a president and a 15-member executive committee which chooses other national officers from among its members. The party is organized in local branches.

Membership. 350

Publications. Local newsletters; *Free Press* (in Limerick, Cork and Dublin); *The 'Core* (Dublin); *Dun Laoghaire Tribune*; *The Democratic Socialist* (national discussion journal)

Federalism and Peace Movement

Leadership. Michael O'Flanigan, Michael O'Mahoney (founders)

Founded. June 15, 1983

History. The founders of this Movement are both former members of Provisional *Sinn Féin*

Orientation. The Movement's founders called for a return to the policy of federalism (*Eire Nua*) abandoned by *Sinn Féin* in 1981, and they expressed the hope that this policy would be supported by a majority of Provisional *Sinn Féin* members. The Movement is opposed to the use of violence as a means of achieving Irish unity.

Fianna Fáil (FF)

Address. 13 Upper Mount Street, Dublin 2, Ireland

Leadership. Charles J. Haughey (pres.); Frank A. Wall (g.s.).

Founded. 1926

History. *Fianna Fáil* (lit. "Soldiers of Destiny") was founded by Eamonn de Valera, first Prime Minister and later President (until 1973). It has consistently been the largest party in Parliament and it was in power in 1932–48, 1951–54, 1957–73, 1977–81 and 1982. In the early 1980s there have been a series of challenges to the leadership of Charles Haughey, but as at early 1984 he had successfully repulsed them all.

Orientation. The party stands for the peaceful ending of partition; the restoration of Irish as a spoken language; social justice; and national self-sufficiency. It favours Ireland's continued membership of the European Community, accepts the latter's common agricultural policy, but opposes any extension of the powers of the European Parliament. It favours nuclear disarmament and wants the whole of Ireland to be a nuclear-weapon-free zone. In its November 1982 election manifesto the party called for a reduction in the size of the civil service, a five-per cent limit on public sector pay increases and tax reductions, and for decisions on Northern Ireland and external policy to be made on the basis of Irish requirements.

Membership. 55,000

Fine Gael (FG)

Address. 51 Upper Mount Street, Dublin 2, Ireland

Leadership. Dr Garret FitzGerald (l. and pres.); Finnbar Fitzpatrick (g.s.)

Founded. 1933

History. The party was formed out of the *Cumann na nGaedheal* party, which had established the first Irish Government following the 1921 treaty under which Ireland (of the 26 counties) accepted dominion status. *Fine Gael* was the second strongest party in the *Dáil* from its foundation onwards and took part in coalition Governments (with the Labour and other parties) in 1948–51 and 1954–57 and (with the Labour Party only) in 1973–77 and from June 1981 to February 1982. In December 1982 *Fine Gael* returned to office as the major party in a coalition Government with the Labour Party.

Orientation. Christian democratic, and in favour of a political solution to the Northern Ireland problem through the establishment of a power-sharing Government in that province. In October 1982 it published a Policy of Economic Recovery programme involving inter alia measures to reduce inflation, a revision of the taxation system, reforms of the government structure and the state's basic law, and the establishment of an all-Ireland security council, an all-Ireland court and prisons system and a new police force which could operate on both sides of the border.

Structure. *Fine Gael* is a national party with some 2,000 branches organized in constituencies and co-ordinated by a national executive and a national council. It has a youth organization (Young *Fine Gael*) of approximately 150 branches and a trade union group.

Membership. 40,000

Publications. *National Democrat*

International affiliations. European People's Party; European Christian Democratic Union; Christian Democratic International

The Green Alliance
Comhaontas Glas

Address. 15 Upper Stephen St., Dublin 2, Ireland

Leadership. Raymond Crotty (spokesman)

Founded. 1981

History. This party was established as the Ecology Party of Ireland, partly under the influence of the Ecology Party of the United Kingdom and partly from anti-nuclear and environmental protection groups in Ireland. It was unsuccessful in the November 1982 general elections, for which it presented seven candidates.

Orientation. The party stands inter alia for "self-reliance" for Northern Ireland which would lead to political independence from Britain, for reducing dependence on energy and investment in renewable sources from sun, wind and wave power, use of recycled materials, production of lasting goods, legislation to control pollution and banning lead in petrol, encouraging self-help organizations and reducing dependence on the state.

Structure. The party consists of a network of semi-autonomous groups with a national framework for policy formulation where necessary.

International affiliations. The European Greens

Independent Fianna Fáil

Leadership. Neil Blaney (l.)
Founded. 1971
History. The party's leader had been *Fianna Fáil* Minister of Agriculture in 1966–70 and was dismissed from his post after he had argued that in pursuing the aim of ending Ireland's partition the use of force should not be excluded (whereas the *Fianna Fáil* leadership had indicated that force should not and could not be used). At the dissolution of the *Dáil* in 1973 there were three Independent *Fianna Fáil* members, but only one (Neil Blaney) was re-elected in that year; another party member was elected in a by-election in 1976; but in 1977 only Blaney was re-elected. In June 1979 Blaney was elected to the European Parliament.

After being re-elected to the *Dáil* in June 1981 as well as in February and November 1982 Blaney remained the party's sole representative in the House.

Orientation. Seeks the reunification of Ireland in accordance with the wishes of the majority of all Ireland's population.

Irish Republican Socialist Party (IRSP)
Pairti Poblachtach Sóisialach na h-Éireann

Address. 34 Upper Gardiner Street, Dublin 1, Ireland
Leadership. Jim Lane (ch. of nat. executive); Antony Doran (g.s.)
Founded. December 1974
History. The IRSP was founded in 1974 as the result of a split in the "Official" Republican Movement ("Official" *Sinn Féin* and the Official IRA) between a majority favouring participation in elections and a minority which sought the resumption of the military campaign against the British presence in the North. The IRSP is regarded as the political wing of the Irish

National Liberation Army (INLA), which was organized at the same time and began operations in 1975, mainly in the North and in Britain. Several IRSP members (and the INLA leader, Seamus Costello) were killed in feuding in 1975 and 1977 between INLA and the "Official" IRA. The IRSP and the "Official" *Sinn Féin* (now the Workers' Party—see separate entry) came to regard each other as Trotskyist and Stalinist respectively.

The IRSP presented one candidate in the 1977 general elections, and he was unsuccessful. In the June 1981 general elections three IRSP members imprisoned in Northern Ireland stood as candidates of an H-Block/Armagh Committee, which gained two seats in the *Dáil*. Two IRSP members were elected councillors in Belfast (Northern Ireland) in 1981 and three died as a result of their hunger strike in the Long Kesh prison (Belfast) in that year, while four others were assassinated.

Orientation. The IRSP advocates "the ending of British rule in Ireland and the establishment of a united democratic socialist republic".

Membership. 2,457 in Ireland; 410 in Europe and the USA
Publications. *Starry Plough* (monthly)

Labour Party

Address. 16 Gardiner Place, Dublin 1, Ireland
Leadership. Richard (Dick) Spring (l.); Michael D. Higgins (ch.); Colm Ó Briáin (g.s.)
Founded. 1912
History. The Labour Party was the first opposition party in the *Dáil Éireann* of the Irish Free State in 1922–26; it supported the *Fianna Fáil* minority Government under Eamonn de Valera in 1937–38 but opposed the 1937 Constitution of Eire (providing inter alia for a directly-elected President, superseding the Governor-General of the Irish Free State); it participated in a five-party coalition Government in 1948–51, in a coalition Government with *Fine Gael* and *Clann na Talmhan* in 1954–57 and in a coalition Government with *Fine Gael* in 1973–77, from June 1981 to February 1982, and again from December 1982—providing the Deputy Prime Minister in all these governments. In recent years the Labour strategy of participating in coalitions with *Fine Gael* has been opposed by a substantial minority within the party.

Orientation. The party's aim is the peaceful transformation of Ireland's present society by democratic means into a socialist republic. In its November 1982 election campaign it called for increased taxation of capital wealth, a strong independent national development programme and greater economic democracy (through worker participation and the democratic ownership of the banking system); with regard to Northern Ireland it expressed opposition to all violence and emphasized the importance of dialogue between the Irish and British Governments. It also advocates strict and principled neutrality for Ireland.

Structure. The party has branches in towns and sections of cities, and the branches are directly represented at the party's annual conference, the supreme policy-making body, which elects a 20-member national executive augmented by eight members co-opted from the parliamentary party and eight others with specialist qualifications.

Membership. 6,000

International affiliations. Socialist International; Confederation of Socialist Parties of the European Community

---

People's Democracy

Address. Dublin, Ireland
Leadership. Eamonn McCann
Founded. 1968
History. This Trotskyist group is mainly present in the North but also operates in the Republic. It has had cordial relations with the Provisional IRA.
International affiliations. This formation is the Irish section of the Fourth (Trotskyist) International.

Sinn Féin or Provisional Sinn Féin

Address. 44 Parnell Square, Dublin 1, Ireland
Leadership. Gerry Adams (pres.); Brendan Swords, Denise Cregan (g.secs.)
Founded. 1905
History. The original *Sinn Féin* ("We Ourselves") claimed to be the oldest political party in Ireland and became the main Republican organization following the destruction of the Irish Citizen Army and the Irish Republican Brotherhood in the Easter 1916 rising in Dublin. In the general elections held to the British House of Commons in 1918, *Sinn Féin* gained 73 (out of 105 Irish) seats and subsequently declared the setting-up of an independent Constituent Assembly (*Dáil Éireann*) in Dublin which, however, functioned only briefly as most of its members were imprisoned. There ensued three years of

guerrilla war against British forces, after which *Sinn Féin*, under the leadership of Eamonn de Valera, concluded, in 1921, a treaty with Britain which led to the division of Ireland and the creation of the Irish Free State. The treaty also divided *Sinn Féin*, one part of which accepted it as a first step towards independence for Ireland, while the other, led by de Valera, rejected it. The anti-treaty wing of *Sinn Féin*, organized as the Irish Republican Army (IRA), fought the pro-treaty Government until 1923, whereas de Valera abandoned the radical republican policies and founded a new party, *Fianna Fáil*, in 1926.

Sinn Féin first took part in elections to the *Dáil* in 1957, when it gained four seats on a programme of "breaking the connexion with England, ending the British imperial system" and setting up "a national government having complete jurisdiction over the entire territory of the nation" (i.e. including Northern Ireland). However, the party had previously declared that any of its candidates elected would not take their seats in the *Dáil* until *Sinn Féin* had gained a majority in the 26 counties and had established an All-Ireland Parliament. *Sinn Féin* lost all its four seats in the 1961 elections.

In 1969 "Provisional" *Sinn Féin* broke away from "Official" *Sinn Féin* to become the political arm of the Provisional Irish Republican Army ("Provos"), which broke away from the Official IRA as a direct-action organization with the object of launching a guerrilla campaign to make Northern Ireland ungovernable and to force the British to withdraw their armed forces and also to relinquish all responsibility for the province. While the Provisional IRA has been declared illegal, Provisional *Sinn Féin* has remained a legal political party (under the name of *Sinn Féin*) in the Republic of Ireland and, since the mid-1970s, in Northern Ireland. Its members have, however, been banned from appearing on the government-controlled radio and television service in the Republic.

In the June 1981 elections to the *Dáil* the party supported the list of the National H-Block/Armagh Committee containing nine prisoners held in Northern Ireland (six from the Provisional IRA and three from the Irish Republican Socialist Party), of whom two were elected. Contesting the February 1982 elections as a separate party, it gained no seat in the *Dáil*, and in November 1982 it decided to take no part in the *Dáil* elections of that month. However, in elections held on Oct. 20, 1982, to a Northern Ireland Assembly, five Provisional *Sinn Féin* members (out of 78) were elected. Moreover, in elections to the British House of Commons on June

9, 1983, Gerry Adams was elected in Belfast West (where in the seat previously held by the moderate socialist Gerry Fitt he gained over 16,000 votes). Adams was elected president of the party in November 1983 in what was widely regarded as a victory for younger, Northern-based radical elements against a more nationalist old guard.

Orientation. The party has undertaken to "oppose censorship and agitate against the suppression of free speech" and to "rally the nationalist people of Ireland behind the republican banner for a democratic socialist republic, developing radical alternative policies to replace British colonial rule in the six counties [of Northern Ireland] and neo-colonial rule in the 26 counties of the Republic of Ireland".

Structure. The party is organized on both sides of the border in branches (*cumainn*) and district committees (*cómhairlí ceanntaire*) usually based on electoral boundaries; it has an annual conference (*Árd Fhéis*) and a national executive (*Árd Cómhairle*) of 25 elected members.

Publications. An Phoblacht/Republican News (weekly), 42,000; *Iris* (quarterly), 3,000; *Saoirse* (Irish-language, occasional), 2,000

The Workers' Party
Pairtí na nOibrí

Address. 30 Gardiner Place, Dublin 1, Ireland

Leadership. Tomás Mac Giolla (pres.); Seamus Lynch (vice-pres. and Northern ch.); Séan Garland (g.s.)

Founded. 1905

History. The Workers' Party was known as "Official" *Sinn Féin* until 1977 and as *Sinn Féin* The Workers' Party until 1982. It was the socialist tendency of *Sinn Féin*, from which Provisional *Sinn Féin* broke away in 1969 (see entry under *Sinn Féin*), and it continued to develop in a socialist direction during the 1970s. The military wing of the party was the "Official" Irish Republican Army (IRA), sometimes referred to as the People's Liberation Army, which together with the party and various associated organizations was known as the "Official Republican Movement". The Official IRA in 1972 announced the cessation of its military activities except for "defensive and retaliatory actions"; following feuds with the Irish National Liberation Army in 1975 and 1977 and with the Provisional IRA in 1977, it is now thought to have disbanded in line with the party's decision to pursue its aims by constitutional means.

In 1977 the party changed its name to *Sinn Féin* The Workers' Party and presented candidates in 16 constituencies, none of whom was successful. It was, however, represented at local government level. In April 1982 it dropped the prefix *Sinn Féin* from its name. In the *Dáil* it has been represented by one member elected in June 1981, three elected in June 1982, but only two since November 1982 (although it increased its overall vote in that election).

Orientation. The party seeks a united democratic socialist republic in which the working classes will own and control the wealth and resources of the country. It opposed the Labour Party's 1983 decision to join a coalition Government with *Fine Gael*, and it has called for the creation of full employment and an increase in national income by an annual average of 5 per cent for the rest of the 1980s. The party also stands for Ireland's neutrality, disarmament and control of nuclear weapons.

Structure. The party is organized both in the Republic of Ireland and in Northern Ireland (where it unsuccessfully took part in the October 1982 elections to the Assembly).

Publications. Irish People (weekly), 30,000; *Workers' Life* (monthly), 12,000; *Northern People* (weekly, Belfast); *Ireland* (monthly); *Women's View* (quarterly); *Class Politics* (quarterly)

Israel

Capital: Jerusalem (not recognized as such by the United Nations)

Pop. 4,000,000*

The state of Israel is a parliamentary democracy with a President elected by Parliament by a simple majority for a five-year term, a Government under a Prime Minister and a unicameral 120-member Parliament (*Knesset*) elected for a four-year term by secret, universal, direct suffrage of all citizens above the age of 18 years under a system of proportional resrepresentation, with the whole country forming a single constituency. To qualify for representation in the *Knesset* a party must obtain at least 1 per cent of the valid votes cast.

Elections to the *Knesset* held on June 30, 1981, and contested by 31 lists resulted in the following distribution of seats: Consolidation (*Likud*) 48, Alignment (consisting of the Israel Labour Party and the United Workers' Party, *Mapam*) 47, National Religious Party 6, Union of Israel (*Agudat Israel*) 4, Democratic Front for Peace and Equality (mainly the pro-Soviet New Communist Party) 4, Zionist Revival Movement (*Tehiya*) 3, Israeli Tradition Movement (*Tami*) 3, State Renewal Movement (*Telem*) 2, Change (*Shinui*) 2, Civil Rights Movement 1.

The 21 lists which failed to obtain the necessary 1 per cent of the valid votes included five which had obtained seats in 1977, namely the Union of Israel Workers (*Poalei Agudat Israel*), the Independent Liberal Party, the United Arab List, Peace and Development (Samuel Flatto-Sharon's list) and the *Shelli* Peace and Equality Movement.

* Excluding the population of the "administered territories".

Alternative Party

Founded. Oct. 20, 1983
History. This party was set up by some 100 activists from various protest movements, including *Yesh Gvul* ("There is a limit"), the Committee against the War in Lebanon and the *Shelli* party (but not from the Peace Now Movement).

Bloc of the Faithful
Gush Emunim

Leadership. Rabbi Moshe Levinger
History. This organization has been engaged in the unauthorized establishment of Jewish settlements in territory occupied by Israel since the 1967 war. It also organized a "Stop the Sinai Withdrawal" movement which tried in Spring 1982 to resist the Israeli evacuation of Sinai (in terms of the 1979 Israeli-Egyptian peace treaty).

Change
Shinui

Leadership. Prof. Amnon Rubinstein (l.)
Founded. 1973
History. This group was created as a protest movement against "mismanagement" which had led to setbacks in the early part of the 1973 war. Late in 1976 it merged with the Democratic Party (founded by Prof. Yigael Yadin) under the name Democratic Movement for Change (DMC), which described itself as a party of the centre. In 1977 the DMC was joined by some members of the Free Centre who had left *Likud* and also by several Labour

Party members. The DMC joined the *Likud*-led Government in October 1977 (although its demands for electoral reforms had not been met). In August 1978 seven DMC deputies broke away from the DMC to form a Movement for Change and Initiative.

The rump DMC, led by Prof. Yadin and with seven deputies in the *Knesset*, remained in the Government as the Democratic Movement. In November 1979 one of its deputies broke away to form the *Oded* party (see separate entry). The deputies of the Movement for Change and Initiative (*Shinui ve Yozme* or *Shai*) included five members of the original *Shinui* group, who had opposed the DMC's decision to join the Government in 1977. On Feb. 18, 1981, Prof. Yadin announced the dissolution of his Democratic Movement. The *Shinui* group subsequently reconstituted itself as an independent party to contest the 1981 *Knesset* elections, in which it gained two seats. The *Shai* group, on the other hand, has not been represented in the *Knesset* since then.

Civil Rights Movement
Tenua le-Zechouot ha-Ezrakh

Leadership. Mrs Shulamit Aloni
Founded. 1973
History. Founded as a breakaway movement from the Israel Labour Party, the Civil Rights list won three seats in the December 1973 elections. Mrs Aloni subsequently joined the Labour-led coalition Government formed in May 1974 but resigned in October 1974 in protest against the allocation of portfolios to the National Religious Party. In the 1977 elections the Civil Rights Movement retained only one seat and in February 1980 participated with other left-wing and feminist groupings in the formation of the "Movement for Sane Zionism". In the 1981 elections the Civil Rights Movement retained its seat in the *Knesset*.

Orientation. The movement campaigns for women's rights and greater freedom for the individual from the religious establishment, as well as for electoral reform; it is moderate on foreign policy issues.

Consolidation
Likud

Leadership. Itzhak Shamir (l.)
Founded. September 1973

History. The *Likud* was formed as a party bloc consisting of the following component parties:

(1) *Gahal*, an electoral alliance formed in 1965 by (i) *Herut*, a movement originating in the Revisionist Zionists of the 1920s and 1930s (led by Zeev Jabotinsky) and founded by Menahem Begin after achievement of statehood in 1948 as a merger of his own *Irgun Zvai Leumi* (which fought the British Mandate authorities by violent means) and the *Hagana* with the object of unifying the "Land of Israel" on both sides of the Jordan river and of enabling a free-enterprise economy to function in the new state; and (ii) the Liberal Party of Israel (see separate entry). *Gahal* joined the National Unity Government led by Levi Eshkol (of the then Israel Labour Party—*Mapai*) prior to the 1967 war but left that Government in opposition to a decision to accept a US peace initiative. The two parts of *Gahal* (*Herut* and the Liberal Party) have continued to function as separate factions.

(2) *La'am* ("For the Nation"), formed in March 1976 by a merger of (i) the Independent Centre (an extreme right-wing party which had split from the Free Centre in 1974); (ii) the State List, founded in 1968 by David Ben-Gurion when he refused to follow *Rafi* in its merger with the Labour Party; and (iii) the Land of Israel Movement, formed after the 1967 war by Labour dissidents to advocate the retention by Israel of the entire Land of Israel. The *La'am* was divided into two groups in November 1978—one of them being led by Yigal Horowitz who resigned from the Cabinet in September 1978 in protest against the Camp David agreement with Egypt but who returned as Minister of Finance in October 1979

(3) *Ahdut* (a one-man faction constituted by Hillel Seidel).

In May 1977 *Likud* was joined by the Realization of Zion (*Shlomzion*), headed by ex-Gen. Ariel Sharon, who had played an active part in the formation of *Likud*.

Two *Likud* deputies defected to the opposition Labour Party on May 18, 1982, but the following month *Likud's* parliamentary strength was increased when the formation was joined by the two deputies of the State Renewal (*Telem*) Movement (see separate entry). Menahem Begin, the *Likud* leader who had been Prime Minister since 1977, resigned on Aug. 28, 1983, to be succeeded by Itzhak Shamir as party leader and Prime Minister.

Orientation. *Likud* has contested elections on a platform of indivisible Israeli sovereignty over the Land of Israel (i.e. including the West Bank and Gaza) and government non-interference in the economy.

Structure. *Likud* has no organization outside the *Knesset*, as its components maintain their independent structures. The chairmanship of the parliamentary *Likud* rotates annually between *Herut* and the Liberal Party. *Herut* has an 800-member central committee and a 45-member executive. The Liberal Party has a national convention, a central committee and an executive.

Democratic Front for Peace and Equality
Hazit Democratit le-Shalom ve-Shivayon
(Hadash)

Leadership. Meir Vilner, Tawfiq Toubi (*Rakah*); Charlie Biton (Black Panthers)
Founded. 1977
History. *Hadash* was established as an electoral alliance comprising principally the *Rakah* New Communists (see separate entry) and a section of the Black Panther movement of oriental Jews. The *Hadash* list obtained five seats in the May 1977 elections, but only four in the June 1981 elections, when its support came principally from Israel's Arab population.

Independence
Atzmaut

Leadership. Prof. Ezra Zohar
History. This movement, advocating the promotion of free enterprise and the abolition of income tax, declared its intention in March 1984 to present candidates in the forthcoming general elections.

Independent Liberal Party
Mifleget Liberalit Atzmait

Address. 48 King George Street, P.O.B. 23076, Tel-Aviv, Israel
Leadership. Moshe Kol (ch.); Jehuda Shaari (ch. of executive); Nissim Elied (g.s.)
Founded. July 1965
History. The party has its origins in the Progressive Party which was founded in 1949 and merged with the General Zionists to form the Liberal Party in 1961. When the Liberal Party formed an electoral alliance with the *Herut* in 1965, a small faction seceded under the leadership of Pinhas Rosen to form the Independent Liberal Party, which obtained five seats in 1965, four in 1969 and in 1973, but only one in 1977 and none in 1981. The

party took part in coalition Governments between 1966 and 1977.
Orientation. The Infdependent Liberal Party stands for a "moderate foreign policy" and supports "all constructive peace negotiations"; it advocates "a controlled economy with free initiatives for free enterprises".
Membership. 20,000
Publications. *Tmoroth* (monthly); *Die Liberale Rundschau* (monthly); *Igeret* (quarterly)
International affiliations. Liberal International

Israel Labour Party
Mifleget Avoda Hayisraelit

Address. P.O. Box 3263, Tel-Aviv, Israel
Founded. January 1968
Leadership. Shimon Peres (ch.); Haim Bar-Lev (s.g.)
History. Although it traces its origins back to the earliest socialist Zionist organizations, the present Israel Labour Party dates from the reunification in January 1968 of *Mapai* (the traditional Labour Party) with *Ahdut Avoda* and *Rafi*. The former had been a separate faction since 1954 and the latter since 1965, when David Ben-Gurion (the former *Mapai* Prime Minister who had led Israel to statehood) had broken away with followers such as Moshe Dayan to form a separate party. Ben-Gurion and a minority faction of *Rafi* remained outside the merger (which was supported by Dayan) and later formed the State List, which became part of *La'am* (see entry for Consolidation).
The Labour Party, as consistently the largest party in the *Knesset*, led coalition Governments from 1948 to 1977 and in that period was the predominant influence in the country's political life. The 1969, 1973, 1977 and 1981 elections were contested by the Labour Party on a joint "Labour Alignment" list with the small left-wing United Workers' (*Mapam*) Party (see separate entry). The Labour Party has been in opposition since 1977.
Orientation. The Labour Party is a Zionist democratic socialist party, placing emphasis on the value of pioneering in a collective or co-operative framework (in kibbutz or moshav); it stands for centralized control of the economy and has organic links with the *Histadrut* (trade union federation) and its enterprises and co-operative ventures. It believes in territorial compromise as a means of achieving peace with the Arabs (most of its members in the *Knesset* having voted in favour of the September 1978 Camp David agreements).

Structure. The Labour Party has a 3,000-member convention which normally meets every four years and elects an 830-member central committee which in turn elects a 157-member secretariat and a 51-member leadership bureau. A United Arab List is affiliated to the Labour Party for electoral purposes.

Membership. 250,000

Publications. *Davar* (daily, *Histadrut*-sponsored) 45,000; *Migvan*, 5,000; *Spectrum* (monthly)

International affiliations. Socialist International

Israeli Tradition Movement (Tami)

Leadership. Aharon Uzan (l.)

Founded. May 1981

History. This party was founded by Aharon Abu-Hatzeira, who had been a member of the National Religious Party and was Minister of Religious Affairs until June 1981. As a member of *Tami* he was appointed Minister of Labour, Social Welfare and Integration of Immigrants in August 1981, but he resigned on April 23, 1982 (after being convicted of embezzlement of funds and given a suspended prison sentence), when he was succeeded by Aharon Uzan. Another *Tami* member, Pessach Grupper, was appointed Minister of Agriculture on Aug. 28, 1983

Orientation. The central object of *Tami* is to represent the interests of the oriental Jews (Sephardim).

Liberal Party of Israel

Address. 68 Ibn Gvirol St., P.O. Box 16273, Tel-Aviv, Israel

Leadership. Itzhak Moda'i (ch. of presidium); Abraham Sharir (ch. of executive); Meir Huberman (s.g.)

Founded. 1961

History. The party was formed from a merger of the General Zionist Party (which had played a central role in Israel from 1948 to 1961) and the (smaller) Progressive Party. For the 1965 *Knesset* elections the party formed an electoral alliance with the *Herut* party (while a small group of Liberals left the party to form the Independent Liberal Party—see separate entry). For the 1973 *Knesset* elections the Liberal Party and the *Herut* party formed, together with several smaller opposition parties, an electoral alliance known as the *Likud*. Although each of these parties retained its separate identity and institutions, their representatives formed a single faction in the *Knesset*, in local councils and in the *Histadrut*. Except for a

period in the early 1950s and its participation in the Government of National Unity in 1967-70, the Liberal Party was in opposition until May 1977, when it gained 15 of the 45 *Likud* seats and subsequently took part in the *Likud* Government. Simha Ehrlich, the party's veteran leader, died on June 19, 1983

Orientation. The party's "four broad principles" are Zionism, private initiative, democratic reform and the defence of human rights. It advocates retention of the non-Egyptian territories occupied after the 1967 war.

Structure. The party has a national convention, a central committee and an executive.

International affiliations. Liberal International

Kach Movement

Leadership. Rabbi Meir Kahane

History. As a candidate of this movement Rabbi Kahane unsuccessfully contested the 1977 general elections. After he had, in April 1977, announced that he would establish a Jewish settlement in Nablus (on the occupied West Bank of the river Jordan) he was banned from entering the West Bank. However, he continued his illegal activities and was repeatedly imprisoned, inter alia for provoking disturbances. In April 1982 adherents of the Jewish Defence League (to which the *Kach* movement was affiliated and which was based in the United States) tried to resist the evacuation of Jewish settlers from the Sinai peninsula (under the terms of the 1979 peace treaty between Israel and Egypt).

On March 10, 1983, a number of *Kach* members were arrested while attempting to establish a Jewish settlement on the Temple Mount in Jerusalem (which was under the jurisdiction of an Islamic council). On Jan. 5, 1984, Rabbi Kahane was arrested for supporting a terrorist group which had claimed responsibility for attacks on Christian and Moslem religious sites.

Orientation. The *Kach* movement seeks the forcible expulsion of all Arabs from territories occupied by Israel since the 1967 war and a legal ban on sexual relations between Moslems and Jews.

National Religious Party (NRP)
Hamiflaga Hadatit Leumit

Address. 166 Ibn Gvirol Street, Tel-Aviv, Israel

Leadership. Dr Joseph Burg (ch.); Danny Vermus (s.g. of NRP); Raphael Ben Natan (s.g. of *Hapoel Hamizrachi*)

Founded. July 1956

History. The establishment of the NRP was preceded by the founding of the *Mizrachi* trade union organization for National Religious Zionist Jews in 1902 and of the *Hapoel Hamizrachi* trade union (with socialistic aims) by religious pioneers in 1922. With the establishment of the state of Israel in 1948 both these organizations became political movements and took part in all *Knesset* elections. In 1956 they merged in the NRP, which participated in the government coalition led by the *Mapai* Labour Party until 1958, when the NRP ministers resigned in protest against government support for a definition of who was to be officially regarded as a Jew.

The NRP re-entered a coalition Government in December 1959 and in 1967 (on the eve of the Six-Day War) successfully pressed for the formation of a Government of National Unity. The party took no part in government for three months in 1974 (owing to a renewed controversy over "Who is a Jew"). In December 1976 the NRP ministers were dismissed from the Cabinet after nine of its 10 members of the *Knesset* had abstained from supporting the Government in a vote of confidence, but following the 1977 general election the NRP joined the victorious *Likud* in forming a new coalition Government under Menahem Begin, which was continued after the 1981 elections.

Orientation. The NRP seeks "the renewal of the life of the Jewish people in the Land of Israel according to the *Torah*" and recognizes the unity of the Jewish people both in Israel and abroad as an essential principle. It also seeks "to further co-operation between different segments of the population, to expand settlements and to encourage Jewish immigration".

Structure. The NRP's supreme body is its assembly, below which there are a central council and a joint executive committee of the NRP and the *Hapoel Hamizrachi*. The former has its own executive committee and the latter a central committee, which together have a joint secretariat.

Membership. 135,000

Publications. *Hatsofe* (daily), 35,000

New Communist Party
Reshima Kommunistit Hadasha (Rakah)

Address. P.O. Box 26205, Tel-Aviv, Israel

Leadership. Meir Vilner (g.s.); Tawfiq Toubi (Arab deputy)

Founded. 1965

History. The party is descended from the Socialist Workers' Party of Palestine founded in 1919, which was renamed the Communist Party of Palestine in 1921 and the Communist Party of Israel (*Maki*) in 1948, the latter holding between three and six parliamentary seats from 1949 to 1961. *Rakah* was formed on the eve of the 1965 elections when the Soviet-orientated, anti-Zionist wing split from the largely pro-Zionist rump, the New Communists winning three seats in both 1965 and 1969 elections whereas the *Maki* Communists took only one on each occasion.

Strongly based in Israel's Arab population, *Rakah* increased its representation to four seats in 1973 and contested the 1977 elections as part of the Democratic Front for Peace and Equality (see separate entry), which won five seats, whereas the *Maki* Communists joined *Shelli* (the Peace and Equality Movement, see separate entry). In the 1981 elections *Rakah* again took part as the leading component of the Democratic Front for Peace and Equality. The Israeli Communists have taken no part in government coalitions.

Orientation. Guided by Marxist-Leninist ideology, the party has as its long-term aim the establishment of a socialist system in Israel; in the shorter term it seeks "to achieve a just and stable peace between Israel and the Arab countries, a just solution for the Palestinian problem based on the right of Palestinian Arab people to self-determination", as well as "democracy, social progress and peace".

Structure. The party's highest institution is its national congress held every four years, which elects a central committee (the party's highest organ between congresses) and a central control commission. The party has districts, branches and basic cells.

Publications. *Zo-Haderekh* (This Way, weekly, in Hebrew); *Al-Ittihad* (Alliance, biweekly, in Arabic); *Der Weg* (in Yiddish)

International affiliations. The party is recognized by the Communist parties of the Soviet-bloc countries.

Oded Party

Leadership. Mordechai Elgrabli, Eli Dayan

Founded. November 1979

History. The party had first been formed as a faction within the Democratic Movement (of which Mordechai Elgrabli had been one out of seven deputies in the *Knesset*). The faction represented mainly Israeli intellectuals of North African extraction seeking to bridge the socio-economic gap between Jews of European extraction and those from oriental countries. It decided to form itself into a separate party after expressing opposition to an austerity programme announced by the Government in November 1979.

Orientation. Independent in orientation, *Oded* has foresworn any automatic alignment with either the Government or the opposition.

Peace and Development
Pituah ve Shalom

Founded. May 1977
Leadership. Samuel Flatto-Sharon (l.).
History. The party was founded by its leader with the objective of implementing its "neo-liberal" philosophy in the *Knesset*. In the 1977 elections it gained 35,000 votes, or 1.8 per cent of the total, entitling it to two seats in the *Knesset*, although only one was taken up (by Flatto-Sharon, who generally supported the Begin Government after its formation in June 1977)

Flatto-Sharon's election to the *Knesset* gave him immunity from extradition to France (his country of origin), where in September 1979 he was sentenced in absentia to five years' imprisonment for fraud, forgery and tax evasion committed before he emigrated to Israel. In the 1981 elections, however, he failed to retain his seat in the *Knesset*.

Orientation. Flatto-Sharon has advocated equitable solutions of social and economic problems with emphasis on relations with the Jewish people all over the world.

Political Zionist Opposition (Ometz)

Founded. January 1982
History. This organization was formed with the stated intention of acting as an umbrella group for opponents of the *Likud* Government. Its founders included a group of *Knesset* deputies from the Labour, *Mapam* and Civil Rights parties and also Dedi Zucker, a former leader of the Peace Now Movement (committed to Israeli withdrawal from Lebanon), as well as several leading academics. Many of its members took the view that the Labour Party had ceased to act as an effective opposition to the Government and had moved significantly to the right.

Progressive List for Peace

Leadership. Mohammed Miari
Founded. 1983

History. Formed by Arab and Jewish elements advocating concessions by Israel to bring about a general Middle East peace agreement, this movement declared its intention to contest the 1984 general elections on that platform. Its leader, an Arab lawyer from Haifa, was briefly detained by the Israeli police in October 1983 after allegedly having secret talks with representatives of the Palestine Liberation Organization (PLO) in Geneva.

Orientation. The movement advocates the establishment of a Palestinian state and dialogue between the Israeli Government and the PLO.

Rally of Religious Zionism
Mahane Zioni Dati (Matzad)

Leadership. Rabbi Haim Druckman (l.)
Founded. March 1983
History. This party broke away from the National Religious Party, as a member of which Rabbi Druckman had been elected to the *Knesset* in 1981. In March 1982 he had voted against the Government's decision to withdraw from Sinai and also against its budget proposals.

Orientation. This religious party is explicitly "maximalist" on issues of Israel's territorial claims while continuing generally to support the *Likud* Government coalition.

Renewed Zionism Party (Tzomet)

Leadership. Rafael Eitan
Founded. October 1983
History. A former Israeli Chief of Staff, Lt.-Gen. Eitan stated on the formation of this party that its principal object would be to secure Israeli sovereignty over all of the biblical "land of Israel", including the West Bank, the Gaza Strip and the Golan Heights.

Orientation. Lt.-Gen. Eitan stated that *Tzomet* had an "ideological affinity" with the right-wing Zionist Revival Movement (see separate entry) but would maintain a separate identity.

Sephardic Torah Guardians (Shas)

Leadership. Itzhak Peretz
History. This ultra-orthodox Jewish party was formed by scissionist elements of the Union of Israel to contest the July 1984 general elections.

Shelli Peace and Equality Movement
Shalom-Shivyon le-Israel (Shelli)

Address. P.O. Box 46109, Tel Aviv, Israel

Leadership. Ran Cohen (ch.)

Founded. March 1977

History. Shelli was formed before the 1977 elections by Arieh Eliav (a former secretary-general of the Labour Party who had sat in the *Knesset* as an independent since late 1975) and Uri Avneri (who had been a member of the *Knesset* from 1969 to 1973, when his *Meri* list failed to secure representation)—both of whom were associated with the "Israeli Council for Peace with the Palestinians". The *Shelli* list for the 1977 elections also embraced the *Moked* grouping (an earlier alliance of the *Maki* pro-Zionist Communists, the *Siah* New Leftists and other leftist elements) and a section of the Black Panther movement of oriental Jews. In the May 1977 elections *Shelli* obtained two seats. In the 1981 elections, however, *Shelli* failed to obtain representation.

Orientation. Shelli stands for peace and equality for Israel. Its members are Israeli citizens irrespective of nationality and religion. The movement advocates a democratic, human socialism and seeks a peace settlement with the Arab peoples and with the Palestinian people, based on mutual recognition of the right of all peoples to self-determination and to a sovereign state. *Shelli* is opposed to any discrimination on national, communal, class-linked, religious or sexual grounds. *Shelli* considers itself part of the labour movement and is represented on the executive committee of the Israel Federation of Labour (*Histadrut*) and in a number of trade unions and labour councils.

Structure. The party's supreme organ is its congress which meets every four years. There are an 85-member council and a 13-member leadership committee.

Membership. 1,600

Publications. Acheret ("Another Path"), 2,000; a bi-monthly on workers' questions, 41,500

State Renewal Movement (Telem)

Founded. April 4, 1981

History. This organization was founded by Gen. (retd.) Moshe Dayan as an independent centrist group comprising mainly elements from the Democratic Movement (which had been dissolved on Feb. 18, 1981) and from the *Rafi* faction (of the *La'am* component of the *Likud* front) led by Yigal Horowitz, who had resigned as Minister of Finance on Jan.

12, 1981, whereupon the three *Rafi* members of the *Knesset* had withdrawn their support from the Government. In the June 1981 elections the *Telem* gained two seats in the *Knesset*. M. Dayan died on Oct. 16, 1981. The *Telem* was subsequently dissolved and its two deputies joined the *Likud* on June, 16, 1982.

Orientation. Telem made proposals for the occupied territories, including a plan for unilateral establishment of Palestinian autonomy on the West Bank.

Together
Yahad

Leadership. Ezer Weizman

History. This centrist party was formed in the run-up to the July 1984 elections by Ezer Weizman, a former leading member of the right-wing *Herut* formation who had been Defence Minister under Menahem Begin from 1977 until his resignation in May 1980.

Union of Israel
Agudat Israel

Address. P.O.B. 326, Jerusalem 91002, Israel

Leadership. Abraham Hirsch (s.g.)

Founded. 1912

History. As a movement of extreme orthodox Jews, *Agudat Israel* was, before the establishment of the state of Israel, opposed to political Zionism on religious grounds. It contested the 1973 elections jointly with the Union of Israel Workers (see separate entry) within the Torah Front, which won five seats and which in December 1976 introduced the no-confidence motion against the then Labour Prime Minister (for alleged violation of the Jewish sabbath) which led indirectly to the resignation of the Government.

Agudat Israel contested the May 1977 elections separately, winning four seats and subsequently agreeing to give parliamentary support to the Begin Government on the basis of a number of legislative undertakings by the latter in the religious and social fields. In December 1979 *Agudat Israel* was instrumental in securing the passage of an amendment to the abortion law cancelling the existing clause permitting abortions on social and economic grounds. In the 1981 elections it retained its four seats in the *Knesset*.

Orientation. Agudat Israel stands for strict observance of Jewish religious law backed by appropriate legislation. It is generally moderate on foreign policy.

Structure. All decisions of *Agudat Israel* are subject to the Council of Sages (a body of leading rabbis).
Publications. *Hamodia* (daily)
International affiliations. Agudat Israel World Organization

Union of Israel Workers
Poalei Agudat Israel

Leadership. Dr Kalman Kahane
Founded. 1924
History. The party is a working-class off-shoot of the Union of Israel (*Agudat Israel*—see separate entry), with which it jointly contested the 1973 elections within the Torah Front. Standing separately in the 1977 elections, it won one seat in the *Knesset* but it did not regain it in 1981.
Publications. *Shearim* (daily)

United Workers' Party
Mifleget Hapoalim Hameuchedet (Mapam)

Address. P.O. Box 1777, Tel-Aviv 61016, Israel
Leadership. Victor Shemtov (s.g.)
Founded. 1948
History. Originating from left-wing socialist Zionist groups active before Israel's independence, *Mapam* was formed by a large Kibbutz movement (*Kibbutz Arsi*), workers, members of the intelligentsia, young persons, people from development towns and Arabs (*Mapam* being the only Zionist party to include Arabs). *Mapam* has been the driving force behind the peace movement in Israel, and it plays a leading role in the struggle for social and economic equality. In 1969 it joined the Labour Alignment and has since then contested elections with the Israel Labour Party while maintaining its autonomous institutions and a separate platform.
Orientation. *Mapam* is a left-wing socialist Zionist party independent in ideology and organization. Its ideology has Marxist roots but has changed in the direction of humanist democratic socialism, and its outlook is secular. It believes in a just peace solution based on the principle of self-determination and mutual recognition between Israel and the Palestinians within a Jordanian-Israeli framework (without closing other options). *Mapam* is categorically opposed to annexation and to the settlements in occupied territories. It believes in the gradual realization of socialism by the utilization of means already available in Israel, such as the Kibbutz movement, the Federation of Labour and workers' co-operatives.
Structure. The party has a congress which elects a national council. The latter elects a central committee, which in turn elects a secretariat, a leadership bureau and the secretary-general.
Publications. *Al Hamishmar* (daily), 30,000
International affiliations. Socialist International

Zionist Revival Movement
Tenuat Hathiya (Tehiya)

Leadership. Prof. Yuval Ne'eman, Geula Cohen, Chanan Porat (leaders)
Founded. October 1979
History. At its founding convention *Tehiya* drew individual members from existing right-wing organizations such as the *Gush Emunim* (Bloc of the Faithful) of militant Jewish settlers, the Land of Israel Movement and the *En Vered* Circle (each of which continued to exist outside the new party framework). The *Tehiya* leadership includes Mrs Geula Cohen and Moshe Shamir, who had been members of the *Herut* wing of the *Likud* front and who had defected from the *Likud* parliamentary group in July 1979 to form a Radical National Party (*Banai*). In the 1981 elections *Tehiya* won two seats in the *Knesset* and in July 1982 it joined the *Likud*-led government coalition, with Prof. Ne'eman becoming Minister of Science and Technology.
Orientation. *Tehiya* advocates the declaration of Israeli sovereignty over the occupied West Bank, Gaza Strip and Golan Heights (without the local Arab inhabitants becoming Israeli citizens) and the intensification of Jewish settlement of these areas.

Addendum. In elections to the *Knesset* held on July 23, 1984, parties obtained seats as follows: Labour Alignment 44, Consolidation (*Likud*) 41, Zionist Revival Movement (including the Renewed Zionist Party) 5, Democratic Front for Peace and Equality (*Hadash*) 4, National Religious Party 4, Sephardic Torah Guardian (*Shas*) 4, Civil Rights Movement 3, Change (*Shinui*) 3, Together (*Yahad*) 3, Union of Isreal 2, Rally of Religious Zionists (*Matzad* or *Morasha*) 2, Progressive List for Peace 2, Kach Movement 1, Political Zionist Opposition (*Ometz*) 1, Israeli Tradition Movement (*Tami*) 1.

Italy

Capital: Rome   **Pop. 57,000,000**

The Italian Republic is, under its 1948 Constitution, "a democratic republic founded on work". It has a bicameral Parliament consisting of (i) a Senate (*Senato della Repubblica*), to which 315 senators àre elected for five years on a regional basis and five more senators may be nominated for life by the President of the Republic who himself becomes a senator for life upon expiry of his term of office (unless he declines), and (ii) a 630-member Chamber of Deputies (*Camara dei Deputati*) elected for five years by universal and direct suffrage of citizens above the age of 18 years under a list system with proportional representation (except for a simple-majority system in the single-member constituency of Aosta Valley).

Chamber elections are held in 32 constituencies having from one to 47 seats each; each party presents a list of names up to the number of seats in the constituency; voters may indicate preferences by striking out names on the list; the candidate with most preferences goes to the top of the list; and any vacancy arising is filled by the candidate next on the list (i.e. there are no by-elections). The President of the Republic is elected for seven years at a joint session of both Houses of Parliament and of three delegates from each of 19 regional councils and one from Aosta Valley and requires a two-thirds majority in the first, second or third ballot, but an absolute majority is sufficient in any ballot held thereafter. In the 1978 presidential elections the candidate of the Socialist Party (Sandro Pertini) was on July 8 elected on the 16th ballot by 832 out of 995 votes cast.

The reorganization of the Fascist Party, through which Benito Mussolini had ruled the country from 1922 to 1943, is forbidden by the Constitution. Under an act of 1974 parties are entitled to receive public financing in proportion to their share of the national vote. (About 40 per cent of such funds have been received by the Christian Democrats.) Elections held to the Chamber of Deputies in June 1983 resulted in the following distribution of seats: Christian Democrats 225, Communist Party 198, Socialist Party 73, Italian Social Movement (neo-fascist) 42, Republican Party 29, Democratic Socialist Party 23, Liberal Party 16, Radical Party 11, Proletarian Democracy 7, others (regional parties) 6.

Christian Democratic Party
Partito Democrazia Cristiana (DC)

Address. Piazza del Gesù 46, I-00186 Rome, Italy

Leadership. Ciriaco De Mita (s.g.); Flaminio Piccoli (pres.)

Founded. 1943

History. The DC, the heir to the *Partido Popolare* founded before World War I, took part in the first congress of (six) Italian democratic parties to be held for over 20 years (in Bari in January 1944), in coalition governments formed from April 1944 onwards, and in the formation of a National Consultative Council in 1945. Its leader at the time, Alcide de Gasperi, was Prime Minister from December 1945 until August 1953.

In general elections to a Constituent Assembly in June 1946 the DC emerged as the strongest party with 35.2 per cent of the votes and 207 (out of 556) seats. In elections to the Chamber of Deputies held in April 1948 it gained 48.7 per cent of the votes and 307 (out of 574) seats, but in June 1953 the DC's strength in the Chamber was reduced to 262 seats (based on 40.1 per cènt of the votes). From August 1953 onwards the DC continued in office either as the sole government party or in coalition, at first with Liberals and Democratic Socialists, and later also with Republicans. In the 1958 elections it obtained 42.2 per cent of the votes and 273 seats in the Chamber. In elections held since 1963 the DC has maintained its position as the strongest party.

At a congress in Naples early in 1962 the DC had approved a policy of "opening to the left" (*apertura a sinistra*) involving the formation of administrations relying on Socialist support. The DC formed coalition governments including Socialists from July 1964 to June 1968 and from December 1968 to July 1969; it accepted other coalition partners between March 1970 and February 1971 and from June 1972 to July 1973. Thereafter it again included Socialists in its Government from July 1973 to November 1974, when it formed a coalition with Republicans only. From July 1976 onwards it was in power as a minority Government.

However, in March 1977 the DC concluded an agreement with five other parties, including the Communist Party (CPI), which undertook to give external support to the DC Government. In March 1978 the DC entered into a limited policy agreement with the CPI, but the latter withdrew from both agreements in January 1979, whereupon the DC formed a coalition Government with the Democratic Socialists and Republicans. This administration fell at the end of March 1979 after losing a confidence vote, whereupon premature elections in June 1979 resulted in the DC retaining its position as the largest parliamentary party (although its percentage declined slightly). In August 1979 the DC formed a coalition with the Democratic Socialists and Liberals under the premiership of Francesco Cossiga.

There followed further DC-led coalition Governments until June 1981, when the DC joined a coalition Government headed by Giovanni Spadolini of the Republican Party, the first non-Christian Democrat to head a post-war Italian administration. In December 1982 the DC resumed the leadership of a coalition Government, but after the June 1983 general elections in which the DC's representation in the Chamber of Deputies was reduced from 262 to 225 members, it agreed to join the first coalition Government to be led by a Socialist (Bettino Craxi).

Orientation. As a Christian Democratic party of the centre, the DC has been both under clerical influence and intent on social reform. It has strongly maintained Italy's adherence to the European and Atlantic communities.

Structure. The DC has allowed the existence of several tendencies within the party, reflecting differences on policy questions, in particular the attitude towards the Communist Party, the country's second political force.

Membership. 1,500,000

Publications. Il Popolo (daily), 111,000; *La Discussione* (weekly), 50,000

International affiliations. Christian Democratic International; European Christian Democratic Union; European People's Party

---

Communist Party of Italy (Marxist-Leninist)
Partito Comunista (Marxista-Leninista) de Italia (PC(ML)I)

Founded. April 1972

History. This party was formed by followers of the *Unione dei Comunisti Italiani (Marxisti-Leninisti)* founded in October 1968. It has no parliamentary representation.

Continuous Struggle
Lotta Continua

Leadership. Guido Vale

History. This group was involved in terrorist attacks and clashes with right-wing extremists from 1972 onwards. In the 1979 general elections the group formed part, with the Proletarian Democrats (who had in 1976 gained six seats in the Chamber of Deputies), of a *Nuova Sinistra Unita* (NSU, New United Left) which, however, won no seats.

Orientation. *Lotta Continua* is regarded as being inspired by Maoist precepts.

Democratic Socialist Party of Italy
Partito Socialista Democratico Italiano (PSDI)

Address. Via di S. Maria in Via 12, 00187 Rome, Italy

Leadership. Giuseppe Saragat (ch.); Pietro Longo (sec.)

Founded. January 1947

History. The party dates from a split in the Italian Socialist Party at the January 1947 Rome congress, when an important section led by Giuseppe Saragat opposed the Pietro Nenni Socialists' popular front policy (involving an alliance with the Communists). Originally formed as the Workers' Socialist Party (PSLI), it merged with other factions in 1952 to become the PSDI.

During 1947–62 the Democratic Socialists took part in coalition Governments of the centre (with Christian Democrats, Liberals and Republicans) and in 1963–74 in centre-left Governments (with Christian Democrats, Socialists and Republicans). During this period there was an ultimately abortive attempt at reunification between the Democratic Socialists and the Socialists.

In 1974–76 the PSDI supported Christian Democratic governments sustained from outside by centre-left parties and in 1976–79 Christian Democratic Governments supported by the Republicans, Communists and Socialists. In August 1979 the PSDI joined a coalition with the Christian Democrats and Liberals. Since October 1980 the PSDI has taken part in all coalition Governments which have included the Socialist Party.

Orientation. The PSDI is a reformist party aiming at the realization of the ideals of democratic socialism.

Structure. The PSDI has a 101-member central committee elected by a congress, a 31-member executive board elected from the central committee, and a secretary elected by the congress. There are 3,000 local committees and clubs, organized in 100 provincial federations and 20 regional committees.

Membership. 200,000

Publications. *L'Umanità* (daily), 80,000; *Ragionamenti* (monthly review); *Donna Oggi* (bi-monthly); *Tempo Presente* (weekly)

International affiliations. Socialist International; Confederation of Socialist Parties of the European Community

---

Italian Communist Party
Partito Comunista Italiano (PCI)

Address. Via delle Botteghe Oscure 4, 00186 Rome, Italy

Founded. 1921

Leadership. Alessandro Natta (sec.)

History. Formed as a result of the split in the Italian Socialist Party at the 1921 Leghorn congress, the PCI went underground during the Mussolini period, its then leader, Palmiro Togliatti, escaping to Moscow, where he worked for the Comintern until his return to Italy in 1944. In the early 1940s the PCI played a leading role in the struggle against the fascist regime and the German Nazi occupation forces.

Under Togliatti's leadership the PCI participated in the post-war coalition Government until being excluded in May 1947, after which it mounted a violent campaign of political and industrial opposition. Following the decisive election victory of the Christian Democrats in April 1948 the PCI took the road of democratic opposition and subsequently developed into the largest and most influential non-ruling Communist party in Europe. Throughout the post-war period the PCI has consistently been the second strongest party (after the Christian Democrats) in terms of both votes and seats in Parliament.

Since 1975 the PCI has governed a large number of regions, provinces and municipalities, together with other left-wing formations, in particular in four (out of 20) regions (Piedmont, Emilia Romagna, Tuscany and Umbria), in 34 out of 94 provinces and in 35 out of 95 principal cities (including Turin, Genoa, Milan, Venice, Bologna, Ancona, Perugia, Rome, Naples and Bari). Municipalities in which the PCI takes part in government contain approximately 50 per cent of Italy's population.

At national level, the PCI's claims for admission to government responsibility have so far been resisted, although following the sharp increase in the party's vote in the June 1976 elections (to over 34 per cent) successive Christian Democratic-led Governments accepted parliamentary support from the PCI, initially through abstention and subsequently, from March 1978, on the basis of the PCI being included in the official parliamentary majority. The PCI withdrew from this arrangement in January 1979 and reverted to a position of full opposition.

Orientation. On the basis of Togliatti's thesis of "polycentrism" within the world communist movement, the PCI has shown considerable independence from the Soviet Union and has become the foremost advocate of "Euro-communism", upholding the right of full national autonomy for each party and also criticizing survivals of Stalinism within the Communist-ruled countries. In the Italian political framework the PCI calls for the achievement of socialism by peaceful, democratic means and has also for many years advocated an "historic compromise" between communism and catholicism as the basis for the government of the country. In May 1983 the CPI committed itself to a "democratic alternative" left-wing government and to an immediate halt to the proposed deployment of US cruise missiles in Comiso (Sicily).

Structure. The CPI is based on cells of at least five party members at places of work, cultural or social centres or on a territorial basis. Cells and sections in any area are combined in federations and there are local, city, zonal and regional committees. The party's highest authority is its national congress, held once in four years; it elects a central committee and a control and an auditing commission. The central committee (179 members) jointly with the central control commission (57 members) elects the party's leadership, i.e. a directing board of 34 members and a secretariat of nine members.

Membership. 1,700,000

Publications. *L'Unità* (daily), 150,000; *Rinascità* (weekly); *Critica Marxista* (every two months); *Politica ed Economia* (every two months)

International affiliations. The PCI is recognized by the Communist parties of the Soviet-bloc countries.

Italian Liberal Party
Partito Liberale Italiano (PLI)

Address. Via Frattina 89, I-00187 Rome, Italy

Leadership. Giovanni Malagodi (hon. pres.); Aldo Bozzi (pres.); Valerio Zanone (sec.)

Founded. 1848

History. The PLI has its roots in the 19th-century liberal movement. Founded by Count Camillo di Cavour (the diplomatic architect of Italian unification), it was a strong proponent of Italian unity. In the period following World War II it increased its representation in the Chamber of Deputies from 13 members in 1953 to 39 in 1963; thereafter it declined to five seats in 1976, although it won nine seats in June 1979 and 16 in June 1983. The party has participated in several post-war coalition governments, most recently with the Christian Democrats and Democratic Socialists in the Cossiga Cabinet formed in August 1979 and in the Socialist-led Craxi Cabinet formed in 1983.

Orientation. The PLI is a democratic party standing for free enterprise (though with worker participation), as well as liaison with and continued Italian support for NATO.

Membership. 43,417

Publications. *L'Opinione; Libro Aperto*

International affiliations. Liberal International; Federation of Liberal and Democratic Parties of the European Community

Italian Republican Party
Partito Répubblicano Italiano (PRI)

Address. Piazza dei Caprettari 70, 00186 Rome, Italy

Leadership. Giovanni Spadolini (pol. sec.); Adolfo Battaglia (1. in Chamber) Bruno Visentini (pres.)

Founded. 1894

History. The party has its origins in the *Giovine Italia* of 1831, who as republicans fought, under the leadership of Giuseppe Mazzini, for national unity and independence. The PRI was dissolved by the Facist regime and reconstituted in 1943, taking part in the Resistance. Under the republican constitution introduced in January 1948 the PRI has been a partner in numerous coalition Governments led by Christian Democrats under Alcide de Gasperi between 1948 and 1953, under Amintore Fanfani in 1962–63, under Aldo Moro between 1963 and 1968, under Mariano Rumor in 1968–69, under Rumor and Emilio Colombo from 1970 to 1972, under Rumor and Moro from 1973 to 1976, under Giulio Andreotti in March–August 1979, under Francesco Cossiga in April–September 1980 and under Arnaldo Forlani from October 1980 to May 1981.

From June 1981 to November 1982 Giovanni Spadolini headed a coalition Government including Christian Democrats, Socialists, Democratic Socialists and a Liberal, and in August 1983 the PRI joined a similar broadly-based but Socialist-led coalition Government.

Orientation. The PRI stands for the defence of representative institutions, the expansion of local autonomy and civil rights, economic planning and a social pact, and for a European and Atlantic foreign policy.

Structure. The party's national organs are a national congress, a national council, a national leadership, a secretarial committee and the political secretary. The party is organized at local, sub-provincial and provincial level and in regional federations.

Membership. 110,000

Publications. *La Voce Repubblicana* (daily official organ), 25,000

International affiliations. Federation of Liberal and Democratic Parties of the European Community

Italian Social Movement—National Right
Movimento Sociale Italiano—Destra Nazionale (MSI-DN)

Address. Via Quattro Fontane 22, I-00184 Rome, Italy

Leadership. Giorgio Almirante (sec.)

Founded. 1946

History. The MSI first contested parliamentary elections in 1948, winning six seats in the Chamber of Deputies. Between 1953 and 1972 its representation in the Chamber fluctuated between 29 and 24 members. It contested the 1972 general elections in an alliance (known as the

National Right—DN) with the Italian Democratic Party of Monarchical Unity, and this alliance gained 56 seats in the Chamber. The two parties formally merged as the MSI-DN in January 1973, but in the 1976 elections the new party obtained only 35 seats in the Chamber.

The MSI-DN did not rule out the use of violence in its activities, and its extremist members were involved in numerous clashes and other acts of violence, which were not approved by the party as a whole. In December 1976 a total of 26 MSI-DN parliamentarians (17 deputies and nine senators) broke away from the party to form a right-wing group known as *Democrazia Nazionale* (DN), which was led by Ernesto De Marzio; it repudiated all fascist tendencies and announced that it would support the Christian Democrats. However, in the 1979 elections this group won no seats, while the rump MSI retained 30 seats in the Chamber of Deputies.

In the 1983 elections the party made significant gains both at national and at regional and provincial level, gaining 42 seats in the Chamber of Deputies (with 6.8 per cent of the vote).

Orientation. An extreme right-wing, strongly anti-Communist party, some of whose members have been prosecuted for "neo-fascist" activities and whose leader has called for a "second republic" with a popularly elected President and a Parliament of a corporate structure.

Membership. 400,000

Publications. *Il Secolo d'Italia* (daily), 80,000

Italian Socialist Party
Partito Socialista Italiano (PSI)

Address. Via del Corso 476, 00186 Rome, Italy

Leadership. Bettino Craxi (s.g.)

Founded. 1892

History. The PSI has suffered three major splits since 1921; in that year a group broke away to found the Italian Communist Party; in 1947 the Saragat Democratic Socialists opposed to an alliance with the Communists broke away from the Pietro Nenni wing and eventually formed the Italian Democratic Socialist Party (PSDI); and a merger in 1966 of the PSI and the PSDI was followed in 1969 by the latter breaking away again.

The PSI has been strongly represented in the Chamber of Deputies since 1953, with the number of seats held by it rising to 87 in 1963 (while in 1968 the combined PSI and PSDI, known as the *Partito Socialista Unificato*, gained 91 seats in the

Chamber). Since the 1963 "opening to the left", the PSI has repeatedly co-operated with the Christian Democrats either by joining in coalition governments or through external support.

After it had for many years been a member of coalition governments led mainly by the Christian Democrats, the PSI resigned from the Fanfani Government in April 1983. In the ensuing general elections of June 1983 it increased its representation in the Chamber of Deputies from 62 to 73 members, and in June 1983 it formed the first Socialist-led Government based on a coalition of Christian Democrats, Democratic Socialists, Republicans and Liberals. (The PSI had, on Oct. 7, 1980, agreed with the PSDI on long-term co-operation with the ultimate aim of constituting a "third force" as an alternative to the Christian Democrats and the Communists.)

Orientation. The PSI believes that the achievement of socialism is inseparable from democracy and individual freedom. Its aims include increased prosperity, freedom and social justice. A five-point programme outlined by Craxi on Aug. 9, 1983, provided inter alia for measures to achieve economic recovery, social reforms and the modernization of state institutions, as well as for a foreign policy rejecting unilateral disarmament and reaffirming the Government's determination to deploy cruise missiles at Comiso (Sicily) in accordance with a 1979 NATO decision.

Membership. 500,000

Publications. *Avanti* (daily), 130,000; *Mondo Operaio* (monthly)

International affiliations. Socialist International; Confederation of Socialist Parties of the European Community

---

Party of Proletarian Unity for Communism
Partito di Unità Proletaria per il Comunismo (PdUP)

Address. Via Tomacelli 146, Rome, Italy

Leadership. Lucio Magri (sec.)

Founded. 1974

History. The party, which succeeded an earlier Party of Proletarian Unity formed in December 1972, is in its present composition mainly constituted by followers of the former *Manifesto* movement, which had seceded from the Communist Party of Italy (CPI) because it opposed the latter's proposal for an "historic compromise" with the Christian Democrats.

In the 1976 elections the PdUP participated as part of the *Democrazia Proletaria*, which gained six seats in the Chamber of Deputies. In the June 1979 elections the PdUP nominated its own candidates (of whom six were elected). It also returned one member to the European Parliament in June 1979. In the 1983 general elections, however, votes cast for the PdUP were counted with those for the Italian Communist Party (PCI).

Orientation. The PdUP works for achieving unity of the left and a renewed discussion of the strategy of the workers' movement with old and new communist and socialist organizations (with the aim of ending Christian Democratic dominance in Italy).

Structure. The PdUP has a secretariat, a political bureau, a national committee and federations in all provinces.

Membership. 8,000

Publications. *Compagne e Compagni* (weekly), 20,000; *Il Manifesto* (daily)

Proletarian Democracy
Democrazia Proletaria (DP)

Founded. 1968

History. In 1976, when the DP included the Party of Proletarian Unity for Communism (PdUP—see separate entry), it gained six seats in the Chamber of Deputies. In the 1979 general elections the DP was part of a New United Left (*Nuova Sinistra Unita*), which also comprised the Continuous Struggle (*Lotta Continua*) group and which gained no seats in the Chamber of Deputies. Contesting the 1983 elections as an independent party, the DP obtained seven seats in the Chamber.

Radical Party
Partito Radicale (PR)

Address. Via di Torre Argentina 18, 00186 Roma, Italy

Leadership. Marco Pannella (l.); Francesco Rutelli (sec.)

Founded. December 1955

History. Originally formed by a left-wing faction of the Liberal Party, the Radical Party became concerned with civil rights from 1962 and in 1970 sponsored the divorce law and subsequently campaigned against the use of the referendum to change the law. It successfully supported legislation on conscientious objection, the lowering of the age of majority to 18 years, more liberal laws on drug offences and family relations and the partial legalization of abortion.

Having obtained four Chamber seats in 1976, the Radicals achieved a significant success in the 1979 elections in which they won 18 Chamber seats (3.4 per cent of the vote) and two in the Senate. In 1983 the party announced at first that it would not take part in the general elections and later that it would campaign for the casting of blank or invalid ballot papers. In the event 11 members of the party were elected to the Chamber by 2.2 per cent of the voters. The Radicals were the first Italian party to have a woman secretary (in 1977–78).

Orientation. The party stands for non-violence, anti-militarism, human and civil rights and advocates the construction of a "socialist and democratic society". It has also campaigned for women's and homosexual rights, against nuclear energy and against extermination by famine in the Third World.

Structure. Under the party's "federative" structure regional Radical parties associate at national level only to decide on annual issues and to elect the leadership at a yearly congress; non-Radical movements can associate with the party, and party members can be associated with other parties.

Membership. 5,000

Publications. *Notizie radicali* (fortnightly), 50,000

International affiliations. War Resisters' International; Technical Co-ordination Group of European Parliament

---

Unified Communist Party of Italy
Partito Comunista Unificado de Italia

Leadership. Osvaldo Pesce (g.s.)

Orientation. At its third congress held in July 1978 the party affirmed its adherence to the principles of Marxism-Leninism and Mao Zedong thought, its support for the Chinese Communist Party and its opposition to terrorism. It has no parliamentary representation.

Workers' Power
Potere Operaio

History. This movement, led by extreme left-wing intellectuals, arose out of the 1968 student unrest, and in 1979 some of its members were arrested for alleged involvement in terrorist acts. It has no parliamentary representation.

Regional Parties

FRIULI-VENEZIA GIULIA

Friuli Movement
Movimento de Friuli

History. As a regional party advocating increased autonomy for Friuli (part of the Friuli-Venezia Giulia special statute region), the party has gained only a few seats in the Regional Council (three in 1968 and two in 1973), and in 1978 its share of the vote was only 4.5 per cent. In the 1983 elections it retained its two seats on the Council.

Movement for Trieste
Movimento Per Trieste

Leadership. Manlio Cecovini (l.)
History. This movement was founded in protest against certain provisions of the 1975 Treaty of Osimo (ratified in 1977), envisaging inter alia the establishment of an industrial free zone on both sides of the border with Yugoslavia near Trieste. The movement's candidates for the 1979 parliamentary elections (one of whom was successful) included members of the Radical Party and of the (right-wing) Italian Social Movement (MSI). In the city of Trieste the movement emerged, in these elections, as the strongest party, with 27.4 per cent of the vote. In the 1983 general elections it lost its seat in the Chamber of Deputies, but it retained the four seats gained in the Friuli-Venezia Giulia Regional Council in 1979.
Orientation. The Movement has called for the development of Trieste as a city port with a statute within the region.

SARDINIA

Sardinian Action Party
Partito Sardo d'Azione

History. The party had between four and five members in the Regional Council of the (special statute) region of Sardinia until 1969 and took part in regional coalition governments with the Christian Democrats and Democratic Socialists until 1967, when it went into opposition. Its representation in the Regional Council declined to three in 1969 and one in 1974, but rose to three in 1979. The party gained one seat in the Chamber of Deputies in 1983.
Orientation. The party stands for full regional autonomy for Sardinia.

TRENTINO-ALTO ADIGE

Social Democratic Party of South Tirol
Sozialdemokratische Partei Südtirols (SPS)

Address. I-39100 Bozen (Bolzano), Eisackstr. 6, Italy
Leadership. Willi Erschbaumer (ch.)
Founded. November 1972
History. The party has its origins in the *Tiroler Sozialdemokratische Partei* (founded in 1892) and the *Sozialistischer Wählerverein Vorwärts* (set up in 1908). By 1919 this social democratic movement had 11,000 members, but it was suppressed by the Fascist regime in 1924. In 1973–78 the newly established SPS held two seats in both the *Landtag* (Provincial Assembly) of South Tirol and the Regional Assembly of Trentino-Alto Adige, but in 1978 this representation was reduced to one seat in each Assembly, the party gaining only 2.22 per cent of the votes in South Tirol.
Orientation. A democratic socialist formation, the SPS seeks to defend the interests of the German-speaking working people in South Tirol and to achieve autonomy for the province.
Structure. The party has 116 local groups and seven district organizations, as well as young generation, women's and factory working groups.
Membership. 1,400
Publications. *Südtiroler Zeitung* (monthly), 7,000

Social Progress Party
Soziale Fortschrittspartei

Orientation. The Social Progress Party is a small liberal formation of the German-speaking population in Alto Adige (Bolzano) province of the Trentino-Alto Adige special statute region.

South Tirol People's Party
Südtiroler Volkspartei (SVP)

Address. Passagio Vintler/Durchgang 16, 39100 Bolzano/Bozen, Italy
Leadership. Dr Silvius Magnago (ch.); Dr Bruno Hosp (s.g.)
History. The SVP has held three seats in the Italian Chamber of Deputies since 1948. The party's struggle for equal rights for the German-speaking population of South Tirol (the province of Bolzano) led to Austro-Italian agreements on the status of the province in 1969–71 and a new statute for the Trentino-Alto Adige region

in 1971. The SVP has been the strongest in the South Tirol *Landtag* and the second-strongest (after the Christian Democrats) in the Regional Council of Trentino-Alto Adige.

Orientation. The SVP is a Christian democratic party of the German-speaking population of Bolzano province (South Tirol).

Membership. 71,000

Publications. *Volksbote*

International affiliations. European Democrat Union (permanent observer); European Christian Democratic Union (observer); European People's Party

---

Trentino Tirol People's Party
Trentiner Tiroler Volkspartei (TTVP)

Address. Rosministrasse 122, I-38100 Trento, Italy

Leadership. Dr Heinrich Pruner (g.s.)

History. The TTVP is the counterpart, in the Trentino province, of the South Tirol People's Party in the Bolzano (or Alto Adige) province of the Trentino-Alto Adige region. It has been represented by two or three members in the provincial council of Trentino and thereby in the Regional Council (comprising the two provincial councils).

International affiliations. European Democrat Union (permanent observer)

VAL D'AOSTA

Val d'Aosta Progressive Union
Union Valdôtaine Progressiste

History. This group was formed by dissidents from the Val d'Aosta Union (see separate entry). It joined the latter

party and the Christian Democrats (who altogether held 18 out of 35 seats in the Val d'Aosta Regional Council) in forming a regional Government (*giunta*) in 1978. In the June 1983 elections, in which it was allied with the *Democratici Popolare* group, it retained four seats in the Council (whereas it had previously held five).

Val d'Aosta Rally
Rassemblement Valdôtain

History. This group was an alliance of the autonomist groups in the special statute region of Val d'Aosta. It won one seat in the Chamber of Deputies in 1979, and it retained this seat in 1983.

Val d'Aosta Union
Union Valdôtaine

History. This regional party, seeking increased autonomy for the Val d'Aosta special statute region, was not represented in the Regional Council until 1959. It then gained 15 (out of 35) seats as a result of an electoral alliance with three left-wing parties (whereas in 1954 it had contested the elections outside any alliance and had gained no seats although obtaining 29 per cent of the votes). The number of its seats subsequently declined to seven in 1963 and four in 1968. However, by 1978 its share of the vote had risen to 24.7 per cent, and it thereupon entered a regional coalition Government.

As a result of elections held in June 1983 the party remained the strongest party with nine seats in the Regional Council.

Ivory Coast

Capital: Yamoussoukrou   Pop. 9,100,000

The Republic of the Ivory Coast has an executive President elected for a five-year term, and re-eligible, by universal adult suffrage. A 1980 constitutional amendment provided for a Vice-President to be elected at the same time as the President. The latter appoints, and presides over, a Cabinet, while legislative power is held by a 147-member National Assembly also elected for five years by universal adult suffrage from a list submitted by the Democratic Party of the Ivory Coast (*Parti Démocratique de la Côte d'Ivoire*, PDCI), the country's sole legal political party. Voters must be at least 21 years old, and to be elected candidates must obtain an absolute majority of valid votes cast in the first ballot, failing which a second ballot is held to choose between the two best-placed candidates.

In elections to the National Assembly held in two rounds on Nov. 9 and 23, 1980, the 147 seats were contested by 649 PDCI candidates, of whom 121 were elected to the Assembly for the first time. The turn-out was, however, only about 30 per cent.

Democratic Party of the Ivory Coast
Parti Démocratique de la Côte d'Ivoire (PDCI)

Address. Maison du Parti, Abidjan, Ivory Coast

Leadership. President Félix Houphouët-Boigny (l.)

Founded. 1946

History. The party was originally the Ivory Coast section of the *Rassemblement Démocratique Africain* (RDA), the independence movement in French West Africa. Since the country achieved independence in 1960 the party has been firmly in power, with its leader being four times re-elected as President of the Republic.

Orientation. The party's aim has been to consolidate the country's independence on the basis of a free-enterprise economy in co-operation with other West African states and the maintenance of good relations with France.

Structure. The party has a 32-member political bureau, and this bureau and the cabinet together are, under the President's direction, the country's decision-making bodies. There is also a 100-member central guiding committee.

Publications. *Fraternité-Matin* (daily party organ), 25,000; *Fraternité-Hebdo* (weekly party organ)

Jamaica

Capital: Kingston   Pop. 2,100,000

Jamaica, a member of the Commonwealth with the British monarch as head of state being represented by a Governor-General, has a bicameral Parliament consisting of (i) a 60-member House of Representatives elected for five years by universal adult suffrage and (ii) a 21-member Senate to which 13 senators are appointed by the Governor-General on the advice of the Prime Minister and the remaining eight on the advice of the Leader of the Opposition. The Prime Minister and his Cabinet are responsible to Parliament. Voters must be at least 18 years old. Candidates are elected by simple majority in single-member constituencies and forfeit their deposit unless they obtain at least 12.5 per cent of the valid constituency votes.

In elections to the House of Representatives held on Oct 30, 1980, the Jamaica Labour Party gained 51 seats and the People's National Party (PNP) only nine after having been in power since 1972. New elections held on Dec. 15, 1983, were boycotted by the two major opposition parties, and the Jamaican Labour Party therefore gained all 60 seats, 54 of them uncontested.

Christian Conscience Party

Founded. 1983
History. This party contested only one seat in the December 1983 elections to the House of Representatives but was unsuccessful.

Jamaica Labour Party (JLP)

Address. 20 Belmont Road, Kingston 5, Jamaica
Leadership. Edward Seaga (l.); Dr Ronald Irvine (ch.); Bruce Golding (sec.)
Founded. 1943
History. The party was established by Sir Alexander Bustamante as the political arm of his trade union. In the first elections held under a self-government Constitution in 1944, the JLP gained 23 of the 32 seats in the House of Representatives. In the 1949 elections it held its majority, retaining 17 seats (mainly with support from rural areas), but from 1955 to 1962 it was in a minority and thus in opposition. It was returned to power in 1962, when it gained 26 out of 45 seats in the House, and in 1967 it obtained 33 out of 53 seats. The

JLP was in opposition to the People's National Party from 1972 to 1980. In the latter year it increased its parliamentary representation from 13 to 51 seats in the House, and formed a Government. In early elections held in December 1983 and boycotted by the two main opposition parties it gained control of all 60 seats.

Orientation. The JLP supports free enterprise and social justice, the privatization of state enterprises, economic expansion, harmony between capital and labour, and a non-aligned foreign policy without being "tied to any super-power". In 1978 it expressed opposition to the introduction of republican status for Jamaica, but later it favoured such status, although with a President with purely ceremonial functions.

Jamaica United Front

Leadership. H. Charles Johnson (l.)
Founded. 1983
History. The leader of this party was arrested in June 1980, together with two other civilians and 26 members of the Jamaica Defence Force, for alleged involvement in an attempted coup to overthrow

the (People's National Party) Government but was acquitted in October 1981. His Front contested one seat in the December 1983 elections to the House of Representatives but was unsuccessful.

Orientation. The Front is a right-wing formation.

People's National Party (PNP)

Address. 89 Old Hope Road, Kingston 6, Jamaica

Leadership. Michael N. Manley (pres.); Dr Paul Robertson (g.s.)

Founded. 1938

History. Founded by Norman Manley (the father of the present leader) and affiliated with the Jamaican Trade Union Council since 1943, the PNP gained 18 out of 32 seats in the House of Representatives in elections held in 1955 and came to power for seven years with Norman Manley as Chief Minister, increasing its parliamentary majority to 29 out of 35 seats in 1959. It was, however, defeated in the 1962 elections, when it retained only 19 seats, and it did not return to power until 1972, when it obtained 37 out of 53 seats in the House.

Following a severe economic crisis the PNP was heavily defeated in the October 1980 elections, being reduced from 47 to nine seats in the House. It later abandoned some of its left-wing tenets but boycotted the December 1983 elections and was as a result no longer represented in the House.

Orientation. The PNP is a democratic socialist formation, originally modelled on the British Labour Party; it advocates the nationalization of public utilities and follows a foreign policy of non-alignment and co-operation with left-wing third-world governments. It favours republican status with an executive President for Jamaica.

International affiliations. Socialist International

Republican Party

Founded. 1983

History. This party unsuccessfully contested two seats in the December 1983 elections to the House of Representatives.

Workers' Party of Jamaica (WPJ)

Leadership. Dr Trevor Munroe (g.s.)

Founded. December 1978

History. The WPJ was formally constituted by the Workers' Liberation League, which had been established by Dr Munroe by 1974 with the aim of creating a Marxist-Leninist party. Affiliated to the University and Allied Workers' Union, the WPJ in 1980 gave "critical support" to the People's National Party and was de facto in alliance with it in the elections of that year. Later, however, it moved away from that party although it also boycotted the 1983 elections.

Orientation. The WPJ is an urban-based pro-Soviet Communist party.

Publications. Struggle

International affiliations. The WPJ is recognized by the Communist parties of the Soviet-bloc countries.

Japan

Capital: Tokyo   Pop. 120,000,000

The Empire of Japan is a constitutional monarchy with a parliamentary system in which the Emperor, as head of state, has (under the 1946 Constitution) no governing power. Executive power is vested in a Cabinet and legislative power in a bicameral Diet (*Kokkai*) consisting of (i) a 252-member House of Councillors (*Sangi-in*) of whose members one-half are popularly elected for a six-year term every three years, and (ii) a 511-member House of Representatives (*Shugi-in*) elected for a four-year term.

Of the 126 councillors elected to the Upper House once every three years, 76 are elected in single-member constituencies and 50 in a national constituency of the whole electorate. The members of the House of Representatives are elected in 130 electoral districts of greatly varying sizes. Except for one single-member district, each district has from three to five members. Voters must be at least 20 years old and have a residence established for three months. Each candidate must pay in a deposit of 100,000 yen (about US$400), and in each district the (three to five) candidates with the most votes are elected. Candidates forfeit their deposits if they gain less than 20 per cent of the valid votes divided by the number of seats in the district. As from 1983 the 50 national list seats in the House of Councillors are allocated on the basis of proportional representation and the 76 constituency seats are won by simple majority—the results being moderated by the d'Hondt system.

As a result of partial elections to the House of Councillors held on June 26, 1983, parties held seats in the Upper House as follows: Liberal-Democratic Party (LDP) 137, Socialist Party of Japan (SPJ) 44, Clean Government Party (*Komeito*) 26, Japan Communist Party (JCP) 14, Democratic Socialist Party (DSP) 11, New Liberal Club (NLC)—*Shaminren* alliance 2, Salaried Workers' Party (*Salaryman Shinto*) 2, Welfare Party (*Fukushi-to*) 1, Tax Party (*Zeikinto*) 1, independents 11 (three seats being then vacant).

Elections to the House of Representatives held on Dec. 18, 1983, resulted in the following distribution of seats: LDP 250, SPJ 112, *Komeito* 58, DSP 38, JCP 26, NLC 8, *Shaminren* 3, independents 16.

Clean Government Party
Komeito

Address. 17 Minamimoto-machi, Shinjuku-ku, Tokyo 160, Japan

Leadership. Yoshikatsu Takeiri (ch.); Junya Yano (s.g.)

Founded. November 1964

History. Formed as the political wing of the Buddhist *Soki Gakkai* lay movement, the party secured representation in the Upper House from July 1965 and won 25 seats in its first Lower House elections in 1967, subsequently increasing this total to 47 in 1969. Having fallen back to 29 seats in the Lower House in 1972, it rose to 56 in 1976 and to 57 in 1979. In 1980 it retained only 33 seats but in 1983 its representation increased again to 58 and its share of the vote to 10.1 per cent.

The party has consistently advocated the formation of a centre-left reformist coalition (excluding the Communists) to challenge the ruling Liberal-Democratic Party. Since 1968 *Komeito* has campaigned for the gradual abolition of the Japan-US Security Treaty.

Orientation. Based on a new concept of "humanitarian socialism" which values "the dignity of human life above all else", the party seeks to establish "an economic system which will guarantee free and responsible economic activity with fair distribution of the fruits thereof"; to "construct a welfare society" with "both social prosperity and individual happiness"; to "bring about permanent peace and prosperity for all people through independent and peaceful diplomacy formulated on the principles of equality, reciprocity and non-interference in the affairs of other peoples or nations"; to uphold the constitution of Japan, "protect the fundamental rights of freedom of religion, assembly and expression" and "create a firmer foundation for parliamentary democracy, eliminating all forms of violence". *Komeito* has also called for greater awareness of the environmental effects of nuclear power plants.

Structure. The party's highest decision-making body is the national convention, which meets annually and elects a central executive committee.

Membership. 140,000

Publications. *Komei Shimbun* (daily), 850,000

Communist Party (Marxist-Leninist)

Leadership. Chaji Harada (ch.); Takaharu Sumioka (g.s.)

Founded. January 1980

History. The party was formed as a merger of the Communist Party (Left) and the Japanese Communist Party (Marxist-Leninist).

Publications. *Jinmin Shinpo*

Democratic Socialist Party (DSP)
Minshushakaito

Address. 19-12 Shiba Sakuragawa-cho 1, Minatoku, Tokyo, Japan

Leadership. Ryosaku Sasaki (ch.); Saburo Tsukamoto (g.s.)

Founded. January 1960

History. Following an earlier split between the right-wing and left-wing factions of the Socialist Party of Japan (SPJ) in 1951–55 the DSP was formally constituted by right-wing former SPJ members who broke away in October 1959 in opposition to the SPJ's Marxist tendencies and definition of itself as a class party. In the House of Representatives the DSP's representation rose from 17 members in 1960 to 31 in 1969, declined to 19 in 1972

but increased to 29 in 1976 and to 35 in 1979; since then it has fallen back to 32 seats in 1980 and only 11 in 1983 (when it secured 7.3 per cent of the vote). In recent elections it has promoted the concept of an alliance of centre-left parties (excluding the Communists) to challenge the ruling Liberal-Democratic Party.

Orientation. Democratic socialist in orientation, the DSP stands for the preservation of fundamental human rights, the maintenance of a democratic society, the creation of a socialist economy with limitation of nationalization to key industries, and the gradual abolition of the US-Japanese security treaty. In 1980 the DSP called for a stronger and self-reliant national defence network under civilian control.

Structure. The party is organized in communities, constituencies and prefectures, with conventions at all levels, and holds an annual convention which elects a central executive committee. The DSP's main base is *Domei*, the Japanese Confederation of Labour (of 2,100,000 members).

Membership. 40,000

Publications. *Renovation* (monthly magazine), 30,000; *Shukan Minsha* (daily party organ), 100,000

International affiliations. Socialist International; Asia-Pacific Socialist Organization

---

Japan Communist Party (JCP)
Nikon Kyosanto

Address. Sendagaya 4-26-7, Shibuya-ku, Tokyo, Japan

Leadership. Tetsuzo Fuwa (ch.)

Founded. July 1922

History. The JCP was founded as an illegal party and did not become legal until 1945. In the 1949 general elections it gained 22 seats in the House of Representatives, but in later elections it obtained few seats until it won 14 in 1969, 38 in 1972, 17 in 1976, 39 in 1979, 29 in 1980 and 26 in 1983 (when it secured 9.3 per cent of the vote).

Orientation. For many years the JCP presented itself as a democratic party independent of external influences. It was not recognised by the Chinese Communist Party and it practically broke off relations with the Soviet Communist Party (CPSU) in 1964, when it rejected a Soviet invitation to join in preparation for a world Communist conference. In July 1976 it abandoned the theory of the dictatorship of the proletariat and replaced the term "Marxist-Leninism" by that of "scientific socialism" in its programme. In 1979 it condemned

Chinese "aggression against socialist Vietnam" and at the same time it reached a rapprochement with the CPSU. It has called for the immediate abrogation of the US-Japanese Security Treaty, military non-alignment and reduced defence spending.

Structure. The JCP has branches on a residential and occupational basis; it is organized at district and prefectural level; and its supreme organ is a congress, which elects a central committee which in turn elects a chairman and a presidium. The latter appoints a permanent bureau and a secretariat.

Membership. 470,000

Publications. *Akahata* (daily organ), over 3,250,000; *Zen-ei* (monthly theoretical review of central committee)

International affiliations. The JCP is recognized by the Communist parties of the Soviet-bloc countries.

Liberal-Democratic Party of Japan (LDP)
Jiyu-Minshuto

Address. 7, 2-chome, Hirakawacho, Chiyoda-ku, Tokyo, Japan

Leadership. Yasuhiro Nakasone (pres.); Susumu Nikaido (s.g.); Tatsuo Tanaka (ch. of exec. council)

Founded. November 1955

History. The party was formed by a merger of the Liberal Party (led by Taketora Ogata) and the Democratic Party (led by Ichiro Hatoyama, then Prime Minister). The latter had been created in 1954 by the defection from the Liberal Party of 33 members of the House of Representatives and two of the House of Councillors, and had been joined by the parliamentarians of the Progressive and Japan Liberal parties (both of which were dissolved).

The LDP has consistently been the largest in Parliament, but retained its absolute majority only narrowly after the 1976 elections. In November 1978 the party, for the first time, elected its president by means of a "primary election" in which about 1,500,000 members and "friends" of the LDP had the right to vote, and which was followed by a "run-off" election by the party's Diet members to decide the result between the two front-runners from the primary election. ("Friends" of the LDP were members of a free national congress—*Jiyu Kokumin Kaigi*, a fund-raising organization.)

In elections held in October 1979 the party gained only 248 seats in the Diet, and the minority Government which it formed thereafter survived only until May 1980. In new elections held in June 1980 the DLP regained its absolute majority

with 284 seats. In the December 1983 elections, however, it retained only 250 seats (and 45.8 per cent of the vote) in the 511-member Diet, thereby losing its absolute majority. However, eight independent deputies subsequently joined the LDP, which then proceeded to form a coalition Government with the small New Liberal Club (see separate entry).

Orientation. The LDP adheres to the principles of parliamentary democracy and at its formation described itself as a party "for the people, for pacifism, with progressive ideas" and "seeking the realization of a welfare state". It stands for private enterprise, a continuation of the alliance with the United States, and the expansion of Japanese interests in Asia.

Structure. A feature of the LDP has been its division into a number of factions which have operated separate organizations during election campaigns. During 1977 the factions were officially dissolved, but separate groupings of parliamentary party members remained in existence.

Membership. 1,500,000

Publications. *Jiyu Shimpo* (weekly)

International affiliations. International Democrat Union; Pacific Democrat Union

---

New Liberal Club (NLC)
Shin Jiyu Club

Address. Nagato-cho 1-7-1, Chiyoda-ku, Tokyo, Japan

Leadership. Seiichi Tagawa (rep.); Yohei Kono (dep. rep.); Toshio Yamaguchi (s.g.)

Founded. June 1976

History. The Club was founded by several former parliamentary members of the Liberal-Democratic Party (LDP) who accused the latter party of "political and spiritual corruption" and intended to work towards "new conservative politics".

The Club has successfully contested elections to the Diet, gaining 17 seats in 1976, four in 1979, 12 in 1980 and eight in December 1983 (when its share of the vote was 2.4 per cent). Following these last elections the NLC entered into a coalition Government led by the Liberal-Democratic Party.

The NLC has also been represented in the House of Councillors; it contested the June 1983 elections to that House in an alliance with the Social Democratic Federation (*Shaminren*), which retained two seats.

Salaried Workers' Party
Salaryman Shinto

Address. House of Councillors, Nagato-cho 1-7-1, Chiyoda-ku, Tokyo, Japan

Leadership. Prof. Shigeru Aoki (l.)

History. Benefiting from the new system of proportional representation for the national seats in the House of Councillors, this party gained two seats in that House in the June 1983 partial elections.

Orientation. The party has campaigned for a reform of the tax system, which it has deemed to be unfair to salaried workers.

Second Chamber Club
Ni-in Club

Address. House of Councillors, Nagato-cho 1-7-1, Chiyoda-ku, Tokyo, Japan

Leadership. Isamu Yamada (sec.)

History. This Club is a remnant of the Green Wind Club (*Ryukufukai*), created in the House of Councillors in 1946-47. Members of this Club were elected to that House as independents on June 26, 1983.

Social Democratic Federation (SDF)
Shaminren

Address. Yotsuya Bldg., Yotsuya 2-1, Tokyo, Japan

Leadership. Hideo Den

Founded. March 1977

History. The party was founded (orginally as the Socialist Citizens' League) by Saburo Eda, who had been the leader of a right-wing faction of the Socialist Party of Japan (SPJ), but it won only one seat in elections for half the seats in the House of Councillors in July 1977. It was later joined by three other SPJ parliamentarians. In the 1980 elections it won three seats in the House of Representatives, which it retained in 1983 (when its share of the vote was 0.7 per cent). For the June 1983 elections to the House of Councillors it was allied with the New Liberal Club, and this alliance gained two seats in that House.

Orientation. The SDF was to be "a new party distinctly different from the existing Socialist and Communist parties".

Socialist Party of Japan (SPJ)
Nikon Shakaito

Address. 1-8-1 Nagatacho, Chiyoda-ku, Tokyo, Japan

Leadership. Masashi Ishibashi (ch.); Makoto Tanebe (s.g.)

Founded. November 1946

History. The SPJ was in power from May 1947 to March 1948 as part of a post-war coalition Government. In 1951 it was divided into a right-wing and a left-wing party, the latter opposing the conclusion of the peace treaty between Japan and the USA. In 1955, however, the two wings were reunited on a joint programme "to change the country's structure into one of socialistic form through democratic and peaceful means" and "to recover complete independence for Japan" (involving the replacement of the US-Japanese security pact by a broader agreement including also the Soviet Union and China).

In October 1959, however, a number of right-wing SPJ members broke away to form (in January 1960) the Democratic Socialist Party (see separate entry). The SPJ's representation in the House of Representatives declined from 145 in 1960–63 to 90 in 1969–72; having increased to 123 in 1976, it fell back to 107 in 1979, but rose to 112 in 1983 (when the party secured 19.5 per cent of the vote).

Having consistently opposed the formation of a centre-left alliance which excluded the Communists, following the October 1979 elections the SPJ reversed this policy and now envisages participating in a "progressive" coalition with other non-Communist formations.

Orientation. The party's basic programme commits it to non-alignment, a non-aggression pact among the great powers and transition from capitalism to socialism by parliamentary means. In 1980 it called for a halt to nuclear power development and reduced defence spending. It also favours a complete ban on the financing of political parties by the private business sector.

Structure. The party comprised several factions until they disbanded themselves late in 1977. The SPJ's policies are determined by its annual convention and directed by its central executive committee. The SPJ is strongly based in the *Sohyo* General Council of Trade Unions.

Membership. 55,000

Publications. *Shakai Shimpo* (twice weekly)

International affiliations. Socialist International; Asia-Pacific Socialist Organization

Tax Party
Zeikinto

Address. House of Councillors, Nagato-cho 1-7-1, Chiyoda-ku, Tokyo, Japan
History. This party obtained one seat in the House of Councillors in partial elections held on June 22, 1980.

Welfare Party
Fukushi-to

Address. House of Councillors, Nagato-cho 1-7-1, Chiyoda-ku, Tokyo, Japan
Leadership. Eita Yashiro (l.)
History. As a result of the new system of proportional representation for the national seats in the House of Councillors this party gained one seat in that House in June 1983.
Orientation. The party has called for improved facilities for the disabled.

Other Parties

The following parties were among those which unsuccessfully contested the June 1983 partial elections to the House of Councillors.

Education Party

Japan Reform Party (*Nihon Yonaoshi*), standing for the abolition of nuclear weapons and a more prominent international position for Japan.

Liberal Party for the Expulsion of Kakuei Tanaka from Political Circles, a right-wing party opposed to former Prime Minister Tanaka (of the Liberal-Democratic Party), who was accused of having accepted bribes from the (US) Lockheed Aircraft Corporation.

Liberal Supra-Partisan Club, demanding a revised system of insurance.

Movement for Peace and Democracy, opposed to nuclear weapons and for the withdrawal of revised history textbooks which minimized the nature of Japanese aggression in China and Korea between 1910 and 1945.

Non-Partisan Citizens' Federation, campaigning for the protection of the Constitution and for political reform.

Plebeian Party, calling for "sexual liberation".

Political Federation of Japanese People, which is strongly anti-communist.

World Jorei-Kai, standing for the use of homoeopathic medicines.

Jordan

Capital: Amman　　　　　　　　　　　　　　　　　Pop. 3,500,000

In the Hashemite Kingdom of Jordan there have been no legal political parties since the abolition of the semi-official Arab National Union in 1976. After nearly a decade without any parliamentary tier to government, King Hussein issued a decree on Jan. 5, 1984, recalling the National Assembly (*Majlis Al-Umma*), which he had dissolved in 1974. Under the 1952 Constitution the Assembly consisted of a 60-member House of Representatives, composed of 30 deputies elected every four years from the East and West Banks of the River Jordan respectively, and a Senate of 30 members appointed by the King. As a result of the Israeli capture of the West Bank in 1967 there had been no elections to the Assembly since April of that year. The Assembly had been dissolved in November 1974 in accordance with constitutional amendments passed earlier the same month after King Hussein, acting on the basis of decisions reached by the Rabat Arab League summit of October 1974, had declared that the Palestine Liberation Organization (PLO) should henceforth have sole responsibility for the West Bank. Reconvened briefly in extraordinary session in February 1976, the Assembly had approved constitutional amendments postponing elections indefinitely and empowering the King to recall the existing Assembly when required.

Kampuchea

Capital: Phnom-Penh   Pop. 6,000,000

Under its 1981 Constitution the People's Republic of Kampuchea (PRK), formerly Cambodia, is an independent sovereign state "gradually advancing towards socialism". It has a Council of State whose Chairman is supreme commander of the armed forces and chairman of a National Defence Council, and a Council of Ministers headed by a Prime Minister. All power is defined as belonging to the people and is exercised through a National Assembly and other elected bodies. The Assembly is elected by voters who must be at least 18 years old and voting takes place in multi-member constituencies where the number of candidates exceeds the number of seats. All candidates are nominated by the Kampuchean United Front for National Construction and Defence (KUFNCD), of which the (communist) Kampuchean People's Revolutionary Party (KPRP), the country's sole legal political party, is the main force.

Elections to the 117-member National Assembly, held on May 1, 1981, were contested by 148 candidates and were officially stated to have shown that 99.17 per cent of the 3,417,339 electors had taken part in the vote.

Although the Government of the PRK is in control of by far the greater part of Kampuchea's territory, it is not recognized by a majority of the member states of the United Nations on the grounds that the KRP Government was installed after "foreign intervention", i.e. by Soviet-backed forces of Vietnam. The UN majority therefore continues to recognize the Government of "Democratic Kampuchea" as legitimate.

Under an agreement signed in Kuala Lumpur (Malaysia) on June 22, 1982, a coalition Government of "Democratic Kampuchea" was established in July of that year by three organizations opposed to the PRK—the *Khmer Rouge* Government of Democratic Kampuchea (led by Khieu Samphan and recognized by the United Nations as the country's legitimate Government), the Moulinaka movement (of Prince Norodom Sihanouk, who had been head of state until 1976) and the Khmer People's National Liberation Front (KPNLF, led by Son Sann, a former Prime Minister under Prince Norodom Sihanouk).

Kampuchean People's Revolutionary Party (KPRP)

Address. Phnom-Penh, Kampuchea

Leadership. Heng Samrin (g.s.); Pen Sovan, Sai Phutang, Chea Sim, Bou Thang, Hun Sen, Chea Soth and Chan Si (other members of Political Bureau)

Founded. 1951

History. The KPRP was founded at the time when the Indo-Chinese Communist Party formed in 1930 by Ho Chi Minh was divided into separate Communist parties for Cambodia, Laos and Vietnam. The KPRP changed its name to Communist Party of Kampuchea at a secret congress held in Phnom-Penh in 1960. It was subsequently divided into supporters of North Vietnam and a Maoist (pro-Chinese) faction led by Pol Pot (then known as Saloth Sar) which began in 1973 to purge the supporters of North Vietnam; most of the latter fled to Vietnam and later, together with defectors from the Communist Party of Kampuchea of Pol Pot, held a reorganization congress in January 1979 (after the overthrow of the Pol Pot regime). The party then reverted to the name of Kampuchean People's Revolutionary Party. (Pol Pot's party dissolved itself in

September 1981, following the creation of a "Patriotic and Democratic Front of the Great National Union of Kampuchea"—in opposition to the Heng Samrin regime—in September 1979.) Since then the KRRP has sought to consolidate its authority as the country's sole ruling party in the face of substantial internal resistance by followers of the former regime and by other forces.

Orientation. At the party's fourth congress held in May 1981 emphasis was laid on close solidarity with Vietnam and Laos as well as "with the Soviet Union and other fraternal socialist countries and with the international communist and workers' movement on the basis of Marxism-Leninism and proletarian internationalism". On the country's economy it was agreed that its three components—the state, collective and private sectors—had each to play a significant role "at the current stage" and that the operation of a free market would be permitted.

Structure. The party has a Central Committee of 19 full and two alternative members and a Political Bureau of eight members, as well as a secretariat.

Kampuchean United Front for National Construction and Defence (KUFNCD)

Address. Phnom-Penh, Kampuchea
Founded. December 1978
Leadership. Heng Samrin (ch. of Presidium); Chea Sim (ch. of Nat. Council); Yos Por (s.g.)
History. This Front was originally set up as the Kampuchean National United Front for National Salvation (KNUFNS) in a "liberated zone" of Kampuchea to oppose the then ruling *Khmer Rouge* Government of Pol Pot in "Democratic Kampuchea". The founding congress was reported to have been attended by over 200 "representatives of all sections of the Kampuchean people", including some of Buddhist clergy and of ethnic minorities. It adopted its present name at its third congress held in December 1981.
Orientation. At its third congress the Front reaffirmed its strong support for the political line of the Kampuchean People's Revolutionary Party, which was confirmed as "the leading nucleus" of the Front.
Structure. The Front has an 80-member National Council and a seven-member honorary Presidium.

Kenya

Capital: Nairobi　　　　　　　　　　　　　　　　　　　　Pop. 16,000,000

The Republic of Kenya, an independent state within the Commonwealth, has an executive President who serves a (renewable) five-year term and is nominated by the Kenya African National Union (KANU), the country's sole legal political party; unless he is the sole candidate he is elected by popular vote. He appoints, and presides over, a Cabinet, and there is also a Vice-President. The President must be an elected member of the National Assembly, which consists of 158 members elected for five years by universal adult suffrage of voters who must be at least 18 years old, and by a simple majority in multi-member constituencies, and of 12 further members nominated by the President. All candidates must be members of KANU and are nominated in primary elections (which in 1983 were also open to other political groups). Any vacancy arising is filled by a by-election.

In elections to the 158 elective seats of the Assembly, held on Sept. 26, 1983, only five members of the outgoing Assembly were returned unopposed, and five cabinet ministers, 12 assistant ministers and about 40 per cent of the members of the previous Assembly were defeated, while the turn-out was estimated at only about 40 per cent.

Kenya African National Union (KANU)

Address. P.O. Box 72394, Nairobi, Kenya

Leadership. President Daniel T. Arap Moi (l.); Isaac Omolo Okero (ch.); Robert S. Matano (s.g.)

Founded. March 1960

History. KANU was preceded by the Kenya African Union (KAU), of which Jomo Kenyatta became president in 1947; in April 1953 he was convicted of managing the Mau Mau terrorist organization and thereupon served six years in prison; thereafter he was placed under restriction. However, after his release in August 1961 he assumed the presidency of the newly-formed KANU in October of that year and entered a coalition Government with the Kenya African Democratic Union (KADU) in April 1962.

In May 1963 KANU won an absolute majority in pre-independence general elections and Kenyatta became Prime Minister and, in December 1964, executive President of the Republic of Kenya. With the voluntary dissolution of KADU in November 1964 KANU became in effect the country's sole political party. (The Kenya People's Union formed in 1966 by Oginga Odinga was banned in 1969.)

In April 1981 the President ordered the banning of parliamentary groups within KANU because they "encouraged tribal and ethnic divisions". During 1982 a number of alleged dissidents were expelled from KANU, among them Oginga Odinga, who was expelled in May 1982 as he was "about to launch a socialist opposition party" and held under house arrest from November 1982 until October 1983.

Orientation. KANU stands for centralized government, racial harmony, Kenyanization of the economy, development (including industrialization) on a free-enterprise basis, and "positive non-alignment" in foreign affairs.

Structure. The party's office-bearers are elected by a delegate conference, including all members of Parliament, with a tacit agreement that each of the eight seats on the national executive of KANU should go to one of the country's eight provinces.

Publications. *Kenya Times* (daily, in English); *Kenya Leo* (daily, in Swahili)

Kiribati

Capital: Tarawa   Pop. 60,000 (1979)

The Republic of Kiribati, formerly the Gilbert Islands, became an independent state within the Commonwealth on July 12, 1979, with an executive President presiding over a Cabinet. There is a unicameral House of Assembly to which 35 members are elected in 23 electoral districts by universal suffrage of persons above the age of 18 years (with a second ballot being held in any multi-member constituency where no candidate obtains more than half the votes cast in a first ballot).(The Constitution also provides for an appointed member representing the community from the island of Banaba resident in Rabi, which is part of Fiji, and the Attorney General is an ex-officio member of the House.)

Candidates contest elections as independents, as there are no political parties. There exists, however, an informal opposition group, called "Mouth of the People" (*Wiia I-Kiribati*), which was responsible for the resignation of the Government on Dec. 10, 1982, after the House of Assembly had voted against a bill involving increases in certain civil service salaries.

In elections held on Jan. 12 and 19, 1983, two cabinet ministers and eight other members lost their seats in the House, but all other members of the Government were re-elected.

Democratic People's Republic of Korea

Capital: Pyongyang   Pop. 19,000,000

The Democratic People's Republic of Korea (or North Korea) is, under its Constitution adopted on Dec. 27, 1972, "an independent socialist state" in which the working people exercise power through the Supreme People's Assembly, elected by universal adult suffrage, and also through people's assemblies at lower level. The Supreme People's Assembly elects the country's President, and he convenes and presides over an Administrative Council (Cabinet). For elections to the Assembly a single official list of candidates is submitted by the Democratic Front for the Reunification of the Fatherland (i.e. theoretically of both North and South Korea), which consists of the country's leading party, the Korean Workers' Party (KWP), and also two small parties—the (religious) Chondoist Chongu (officially stated to comprise former Buddhist believers) and the Korean Social-Democratic Party (known until January 1981 as the Korean Democratic Party), both formed in 1945. The General Secretary of the KWP's Central Committee is also head of state and supreme commander of the armed forces.

In general elections to the Supreme People's Assembly held on Feb. 28, 1982, it was officially claimed that all votes had been cast for the 615 candidates on the sole official list.

Workers' Party of Korea
Chosun No-Dong Dang

Address. The Central District, Pyongyang, Democratic People's Republic of Korea

Leadership. President Kim Il Sung (g.s.), Kim Il, Gen. Oh Jin Wu, Kim Chong Il, Li (Yi) Jong Ok (other members of Presidium); President Kim Il Sung, Kim Il, Gen. Oh Jin Wu, Kim Chong Il, Li (Yi) Jong Ok, Park Sung Chul, Choe Hyon, Yim Chun Chu, So Chol, O Baek Yong, Kim Chung Nin, Kim Yong Nam, Chon Mun Sop, Kim Hwan, Yon Hyung Muk, O Kuk Yol, Kye Ung Tae, Kang Song San, Park Hak Im, Choe Yong Nim, So Yun Sok (full members of Political Bureau)

Founded. October 1945

History. The party was set up at the end of World War II in the part of Korea (north of the 38th parallel) occupied by Soviet forces; with the establishment of the Democratic People's Republic of Korea in that part of the country in February 1948 it became the ruling party of the new Republic. It merged with the National Party in 1949, when the Democratic Front for the Unification of the Fatherland was formed, embracing "patriotic" parties and mass organizations, with the object of Korean reunification. In 1961 the party recognized the Communist Party of the Soviet Union as "the vanguard of the world Communist movement" but in 1963 it took up a pro-Chinese attitude.

In 1966 the party issued a strongly-worded declaration affirming the right of all Communist parties to decide their own policies, and since then it has endeavoured to maintain friendly relations with both the Soviet and the Chinese Communist parties. From 1975 onwards the party has laid increasing emphasis on the concept of national independence and self-reliance (*Juche*), which has been defined as involving political independence, economic self-reliance and national self-defence.

In addition to the Workers' Party of Korea, the Democratic Front for the Reunification of the Fatherland (which is headed by a central committee and has as its press organ *Chokuk Tongil*) also embraces the (religious) Chondoist Chongu party (founded in February 1946) and the

Korean Social-Democratic Party (formed in 1945), which has a quarterly organ called *Choson Sahoeminjudang*.

Orientation. The party's "immediate objective" is "to achieve the complete victory of socialism" in the northern half of the Republic (i.e. in North Korea as distinct from South Korea), "establish national sovereignty on a nationwide scale and accomplish the independent, peaceful reunification of the country". Its ultimate goal is "to build an ideal society of mankind where the *Chasujong* (independence) of the popular masses has been fully realized".

Structure. The party has cells, primary party committees and party committees in cities (or districts), counties and provinces (or municipalities directly under the country's central authority), and there is a Central Committee.

Membership. 3,000,000

Publications. *Rodong Sinmun* (official organ), 1,000,000; *Kulloza* (Working People, a magazine), 100,000

Republic of Korea

Capital: Seoul   Pop. 39,500,000

The Republic of Korea (South Korea) has under its Constitution (which was overwhelmingly approved in a referendum on Oct. 22, 1980, and came into effect on Oct. 27 of that year) a President elected for a single seven-year term by an electoral college itself elected by universal adult suffrage and a National Assembly (also elected by universal adult suffrage, but for four years). The President is empowered to take emergency measures only in time of armed conflict or a similar emergency, and such measures must be approved by the National Assembly; he can also dissolve the Assembly, with the Cabinet's approval, but not within the first year after the Assembly's election, and not twice for the same reason.

Following the promulgation of the October 1980 Constitution the previous National Assembly and all political parties were dissolved. In addition, a total of 109 of the 231 members of the previous Assembly (among them two prominent party leaders) were excluded from political life. There followed the registration of 17 new parties, among them the Democratic Justice Party (DJP), the Democratic Korea Party (DKP), the Korean National Party (KNP) and the Civil Rights Party (CRP).

Under a presidential election law adopted on Dec. 26, 1980, by the then Legislative Council the electoral college was to elect the President of the Republic from candidates nominated by political parties or by 300 to 500 members of the electoral college. In elections to the 5,278 seats of this electoral college, held on Feb. 11, 1981, seats were gained as follows: DJP 3,676, DKP 411, KNP 48, CRP 20, independents 1,123. In the presidential elections held on Feb. 25, 1981, incumbent President Chun Doo Hwan received 4,755 votes, Yoo Chi-Song 404, Kim Chong Chul 85 and Kim Eui Taek 26.

Under the electoral law there are 92 electoral districts, each returning two members to the National Assembly, with no party being allowed to nominate more than one candidate in each district. The party winning the largest number of seats obtains a further 61 seats, and 31 other seats are distributed, in proportion to the number of seats won, among other parties which win more than five seats. No party can therefore win more than 153 of the 276 seats in the Assembly. Constitutional amendments require a two-thirds majority, i.e. approval by at least two parties. Under a Political Parties' Law parties which fail to win a seat or at least 2 per cent of the valid votes cast are dissolved. The minimum voting age is 20 years.

As a result of elections held on March 25, 1981, seats in the National Assembly were distributed as follows: DJP 151, DKP 81, KNP 25, Democratic Socialist Party 2, CRP 2, New Political Party 2, Democratic Farmers' Party 1, *Anmin* Party 1, independents 11.

Four parties which had failed to win a seat or to secure 2 per cent of the valid votes and which were therefore dissolved under the electoral law were the Christian Democratic Party, the Socialist Party of Korea, the Unification People's Party and the *Wonilminlip* Party.

Civil Rights Party (CRP)

Address. 170 Insa-dong, Chongno-ku, Seoul, Republic of Korea
Leadership. Kim Eui-Taek (pres.)
Founded. November 1980
History. This party had only 20 members elected to the electoral college (which was to elect the President of the Republic) and its president, as candidate for the country's Presidency, gained only 26 (out of 5,270 valid) votes in February 1981. In the March 1981 elections to the National Assembly it gained only one seat.

Democratic Farmers' Party

History. This party seeks to represent those engaged in agriculture but gained only one seat in the National Assembly elected in March 1981.

Democratic Justice Party (DJP)

Address. 155-2 Kwanhoon-dong, Chongno-ku, Seoul, Republic of Korea
Leadership. President Chun Doo Hwan (pres.); Chong Nae-hiuk (ch.); Kwon Ik-Hyun (s.g.)
Founded. November 1980
History. The formation of the DJP was sponsored by members of the former ruling Democratic Republican Party (DRP) and the (opposition) New Democratic Party. In the March 1981 National Assembly elections it gained elective seats in all but two of the electoral districts and the highest vote in 77 of the 92 districts. It was more successful in the urban areas than its main predecessor, the DRP, had been.
Orientation. The party is the political instrument of President Chun Doo Hwan.

Democratic Korea Party (DKP)

Address. 1-643 Yoido-dong, Yong-deungpo-ku, Seoul, Republic of Korea
Leadership. Yoo Chi-Song (pres.); You Han-Yul (s.g.)
Founded. November 1980
History. The formation of this party was sponsored by some members of the former New Democratic Party. In the March 1981 National Assembly elections it emerged as the largest opposition party, with 81 seats in the National Assembly.
Orientation. The party has called for a two-party rather than a multi-party democratic system. At a convention held in January 1983 the DKP declared that it would seek democratic reforms and was willing to admit former politicians after they had been released from banning orders.

Democratic Socialist Party (DSP)

Address. 340, 2-ka Taepyong-ro, Seoul, Republic of Korea
Leadership. Ko Ching-hun (pres.); Kim Kap-su (ch.)
Founded. November 1980
History. The formation of this party was sponsored by former members of the dissolved United Socialist Party. The latter formation had been founded in 1961, was banned in 1961-63 and 1973-74 and had proclaimed its aim as being "the realization of democratic socialist ideals in Korean society and of national reunification on the basis of non-aligned neutrality". The DSP gained two seats in the National Assembly elected in March 1981, and on March 24, 1982, it absorbed the New Political Party (of which Kim Kap-su had been president and which also held two seats in the Assembly). The DSP thus became the fourth largest parliamentary group.

270

Human Welfare (Anmin) Party

History. This party gained only one seat in the National Assembly elected in March 1981.

Korea National Party (KNP)

Address. 1-28, Chung-Dong, Chung-Ku, Seoul, Republic of Korea
Leadership. Kim Chong Chul (pres.); Cho Jung Koo (ch. of nat. convention); Cho Byung Kyu (ch., central committee); Shin Chul Kyun (s.g.)
Founded. Jan. 23, 1981
History. Preparations for the formation of this party were made from Nov. 28, 1980, onwards. On Jan. 26, 1981, the party nominated its president as a candidate for the election of the President of the Republic by an electoral college, but in the election itself, held on Feb. 25, 1981,

he obtained only 85 votes (out of a total of 5,270 valid votes). In National Assembly elections held on March 25, 1981, the KNP obtained 2,150,000 votes, or 13.3 per cent of the valid votes, and 25 seats, becoming the third strongest political party in the country.
Orientation. The KNP stands for parliamentary government, an expansion of the rights of the people, prosperity in a free economy, national self-reliance and equitable distribution of the products of the economy among all Koreans. It seeks a harmonization of reform and conservation on the basis of order and tradition.
Structure. The KNP has a national convention, a party council, a central committee, a policy committee, and a central secretariat. It is organized at city, district and provincial level.
Membership. 500,000
Publications. *Kuk Min Dang Bo* (newspaper), 200,000

Kuwait

Capital: Kuwait   Pop. 1,500,000

Kuwait is an hereditary monarchy in which the Amir exercises executive power through a Council of Ministers under a Prime Minister. It has a National Assembly *(Majlis)* directly elected by some 43,000 registered voters (who must be above the age of 21 years), or about 3 per cent of the country's total population. (Some 41 per cent of the population are Kuwaiti citizens, and among those excluded from the franchise are not only immigrants, but also all women, members of the armed forces and all those who cannot trace their ancestry in the state back to 1920.) At the elections of February 1981 there were 450 candidates for 50 seats in 25 constituencies, with their political aims ranging from Islamic fundamentalism to the collectivist left, while political parties remained banned. The elections resulted in the defeat of all left-wing and most right-wing candidates in a moderate poll, and most of the successful candidates were middle-class professional men.

Laos

Capital: Vientiane   Pop. 4,000,000

The People's Democratic Republic of Laos was established in December 1975 by the *Neo Lao Haksat* (Lao Patriotic Front), whose chairman became President of the Republic, while the General Secretary of the Lao People's Revolutionary Party (LPRP, the Laotian Communist Party, which is the country's sole legal political organization) became Prime Minister. The name of the Lao Patriotic Front was in February 1979 changed to Lao Front for National Construction. A People's Congress of 264 representatives elected by local authorities met in December 1975 and appointed a 45-member Supreme People's Council, which was inter alia to draft a new Constitution. There have been no general elections since the establishment of the LPRP's regime.

Lao People's Revolutionary Party (LPRP)
Phak Pasason Pativat Lao

Leadership. Kaysone Phomvihane (g.s.); Gen. Khamtay Siphandone, Nouhak Phoumsavan, Phoumi Vongvichit, Gen. Phoune Sipraseuth, Sisomphone Lovansay, Prince Souphanouvong (other members of the Political Bureau)

Founded. March 1955

History. The LPRP was founded as the People's Party, on the declaration of Laos as an independent country, to continue the work of the Communist Party of Indochina. The party was the leading force in the Laotian Patriotic Front (*Neo Lao Haksat*), whose military arm was the *Pathet Lao*. The latter had fought a civil war against the Laotian Government of Prince Souvanna Phouma from 1963 to 1973, when a coalition Government was formed by the two sides.

However, in December 1975 the *Neo Lao Haksat* set up a People's Democratic Republic with the secretary-general of the LPRP—which had adopted its present name in 1972—as Prime Minister. On Feb. 16, 1979, the *Neo Lao Haksat* was replaced by a Lao Front for National Reconstruction which, under the leadership of the LPRP, was to strengthen national solidarity and to promote socialism and the development of the country's economy; it has a 76-member central committee.

Orientation. On assuming full power the LPRP declared that, while relying on the dictatorship of the proletariat, its task was to carry out socialist changes and to build socialism. The party has a special and close relationship with the Communist Party of Vietnam, and it has expelled a number of pro-Chinese members.

Structure. The party has a Central Committee of 49 full and six alternate members, headed by a Political Bureau of seven members.

Membership. 35,000

Publications. *Siang Pasason* (Voice of the People), 10,000

International affiliations. The LPRP is recognized by the Communist parties of the Soviet-bloc countries.

Lebanon

Capital: Beirut   Pop. 3,000,000

The Republic of Lebanon has an executive President (customarily a Maronite Christian) elected by a 99-member Chamber of Deputies which is itself elected for a four-year term by universal adult suffrage. The President appoints a Cabinet, which is traditionally headed by a Sunni Moslem Prime Minister. The allocation of top political, administrative and military posts has been subject to the unwritten "National Covenant" of 1943, which also provides that there must be six Christians to every five Moslems in the Chamber; a strict grouping according to party affiliation is therefore not possible. In view of the internal security situation there have been no general elections since April 1972 and the life of the Chamber elected then has been repeatedly extended since the expiry of its term in 1976.

Since independence was achieved in 1943, tensions between Lebanon's various ethnic and religious communities have regularly erupted into open hostilities between the assorted militia groups maintained by the contending factions. From the early 1970s the situation became additionally complex as a result of Lebanese Christian hostility to the presence in the country of large numbers of Palestine Liberation Organization (PLO) guerrillas, who were accused of having established a "state within a state" threatening Lebanon's political integrity as well as its national security vis-à-vis Israel. Serious clashes in April 1975 steadily escalated into a full-scale civil war by September of that year, with predominantly right-wing Christian forces ranged against a leftist alliance of Lebanese Moslems and Palestinian guerrillas.

Despite numerous peace efforts and the deployment in Lebanon in late 1976 of an Arab Deterrent Force (ADF), consisting mainly of Syrian troops, followed by the deployment of a UN Interim Force in Lebanon (UNIFIL) in 1978 and of a four-nation international peace-keeping force in 1982, armed conflicts have persisted in Lebanon. By July 1981 there were more than 40 different private armies operating in the country. The principal conflicts arose out of antagonisms between (i) the ADF and the (right-wing Maronite-Christian) Phalangists led by the Gemayel family; (ii) the Phalangists (with Israeli backing) and the Palestinians; (iii) the Phalangists and left-wing groups forming the National Movement led by Walid Jumblatt, the Druse leader; (iv) the Maronite supporters of the Gemayel family and those of ex-President Soleiman Frangié; (v) pro-Iraqi and pro-Iranian groups; (vi) supporters of the Iraqi *Baath* party and those of the Syrian *Baath* party; (vii) Sunni Moslems and Alawite Moslems in Tripoli; (viii) the predominantly Shi'ite communist parties and the (also Shi'ite) Moslem fundamentalist *Amal* movement; and (ix) Palestinians in southern Lebanon and the forces of the autonomous Christian régime established there with Israeli backing. By early 1984 the main conflict was between the Lebanese Army on the one hand and Druse and *Amal* forces (with Syrian support) on the other, with the latter gaining control of Beirut. The offical PLO guerrillas were defeated and expelled from Lebanon during 1983 by a Syrian-backed PLO faction.

Israeli forces have remained in occupation of parts of southern Lebanon following the invasion of June 1982.

Baath Arab Socialist Party
Hizb al-Baath al-Arabi al-Ishtiraki

Leadership. Assem Kanzo (pro-Syrian faction); Abdel Magid al Rafei (pro-Iraqi faction)

History. Originally established as the Lebanese regional command of the pan-Arab *Baath* (see entries for *Baath* Arab Socialist Party under Iraq and Syria), the Lebanese *Baath* became divided into pro-Iraqi and pro-Syrian factions and has not attained the degree of influence exercised by the party in Iraq and Syria. In the 1975-76 civil war and its aftermath both Lebanese *Baath* factions formed part of the left-wing National Movement which sought basic changes in the country's constitutional and social structure in favour of the Moslem community.

Constitutional Party
Ad-Destour

Address. Rue Michel Chiha Kantari, Beirut, Lebanon

Leadership. Michel Bechara al-Khouri

Founded. 1943

History. The party played a leading role in the struggle against the French mandate and in drafting Lebanon's 1943 Constitution. It was subsequently in power until 1953, when it was defeated in general elections.

Orientation. The party is an Arab nationalist formation of the political and business élite; it has formed part of the "Chehabist" group of parties.

Democratic Party
Parti Démocrate

Leadership. Joseph Mughaizel (s.g.)

Founded. 1969

History. The party has remained a minority group with little influence amid the polarization of attitudes which has characterized the Lebanese political scene since the 1975-76 civil war.

Orientation. The party stands for a secular, democratic policy, for private enterprise and for social justice.

The Helpers
An-Najjade

Address. P.O. Box 3537, Beirut, Lebanon

Leadership. Adnane Moustapha al-Hakim (pres.)

Founded. 1936

Orientation. This formation has proclaimed itself as a pan-Arabic party standing for Arab socialism.

Membership. 3,000

Publications. *Sawt al-Uruba* (daily)

Kurdish Democratic Party of Lebanon
Parti A Demoqrat A Kurdi e Lubnan

Address. Hutit Bldg., 4th & 6th floor, Boustany Street, Wat-Wat, Beirut, Lebanon

Leadership. Riad Jamil Meho (s.g.)

Founded. 1960

History. Established as a secret organization in support of the Kurdish revolutionaries in Iraq and Iran led by (the late) Mullah Mustafa Barzani, the party campaigned for the rights of Kurds in Lebanon (including the right to have Lebanese nationality and to serve in Lebanon's armed forces); the party was not legalized until September 1970. After the party's founder and leader, Jamil Ali Meho, had gone to Iraq he was held captive by Kurds hostile to him until March 1974, when he returned to Lebanon.

Arrested by Syrian forces during the civil war in Lebanon in January 1978, Jamil Ali Meho was held in a Syrian prison until early 1980. He died on Dec. 16, 1982, and 40 days later Riad Jamil Meho was elected as the party's secretary-general. He and other party leaders were temporarily arrested in March 1983 when the Lebanese Army took action against the party, closing its office and suppressing its publication, *Denge Kurd* (Voice of the Kurds).

Orientation. The party seeks the creation of a "Greater Kurdistan" for the Kurdish people in Turkey, Iran, Iraq and Syria.

Structure. The party has a central committee and a political bureau.

Lebanese Christian Democratic Union
Union Chrétienne Démocrate Libanaise (UCDL)

Address. P.O. Box 11-5512, Beirut, Lebanon

International affiliations. This small party has observer status at the European Christian Democratic Union

Lebanese Communist Party
Parti Communiste Libanais (PCL)

Leadership. George Hawi (s.g.)

Founded. October 1924

History. The PCL began its activities by fighting against the French occupation of Lebanon (under a League of Nations mandate) and for national independence, democratic freedoms and social and economic demands of the working people. In 1925 it became affiliated to the Communist International (Comintern). The party did not achieve any measure of legality until 1936 and was first recognized by law in 1970.

In 1965 the PCL formed part of the National Progressive Front, and in the civil war which broke out in April 1975 it joined the Lebanese National Movement and strengthened its alliance with the Palestine liberation movement. Its forces have, however, been involved in clashes with the militia of the Moslem fundamentalist *Amal* movement. In fighting between the two sides in April 1982 a total of 79 persons were killed and 194 injured.

Orientation. The PCL has adopted the aims of the Lebanese National Movement. Its final aim is to establish a national democratic régime to open the road to transition to socialism.

Structure. The supreme organ of the PCL is its national congress, convened every four years. It elects a central committee, which in turn elects a political bureau, a secretariat and the secretary-general. The party is organized in base, sectional, regional and departmental committees, all elected at party conferences, and its organization is based on democratic centralism.

Publications. *An-Nida* (The Appeal, daily); *At-Tarik* (The Road, a cultural, political and theoretical monthly review); *Gantch* (a weekly in Armenian)

International affiliations. The CPL is recognized by the Communist parties of the Soviet-bloc countries.

Lebanese Front

Founded. March 1976
History. This right-wing Christian Front was formed by the Phalangist Party (*Al-Kata'eb*). the National Liberal Party (led by Camille Chamoun) and the forces of ex-President Soleiman Frangié, as well as several other Christian leaders. In February 1977 the Front proposed the creation of a confederacy in Lebanon, with each religious community being free to establish its own military, financial and other institutions. It also called on the Arab states to help relocate the Palestininans who had entered Lebanon since 1970. Forces of this Front, and in particular the Phalangist militia, were held responsible for the killing of some 460 civilian Palestinian refugees in the Sabra and Shatila camps near Beirut in September 1982. (In a June 1983 report by Lebanon's military prosecutor-general the Phalangist Party was completely exonerated of any blame for the massacre.)

Lebanese National Movement (LNM)

Leadership. Walid Jumblatt (l.)
Founded. 1969
History. This alliance of left-wing parties was the successor to a Front of Patriotic and Progressive Parties and Personalities, formed in 1964 on an initiative of Kamal Jumblatt, then leader of the Progressive Socialist Party (PSP—see separate entry), and including the Arab Nationalist Movement and the Lebanese Communist Party (LCP). By 1975 the LNM included the following major parties: the PSP, the LCP, the Organization for Communist Action in Lebanon (OCAL), the Movement of Independent Nasserists (*al-Mourabitoun*), the Syrian National Social Party and the pro-Syrian branch of the *Baath* party; among minor groups adhering to the LNM were the pro-Iraq branch of the *Baath* party and the Kurdish Democratic Party Organization.

Orientation. In 1975 the LNM called for a revision of Lebanon's government structure, in particular the replacement of denominational representation by a system of proportional representation, and for a strong secular Lebanese Army to defend the country and to promote the Palestinian cause. The general aims of the LNM are to safeguard the unity of the people, the territorial integrity of Lebanon and its Arab character, to defend its independence and sovereignty, to liberate southern Lebanon from Israeli occupation, and to strengthen co-operation with Arab countries, in particular Syria, and with the Soviet Union, the socialist countries and the non-aligned and third-world countries.

Structure. The LNM has no armed forces but a joint military command to co-ordinate the military units of its constituent parts. It has a central political council and an executive committee which formulates the Movement's policies.

National Bloc
Bloc National

Leadership. Raymond Eddé (l.); Antoine Abu-Zaid (s.g.)

Founded. 1943

History. The National Bloc has been one of the Chamounist (Christian) parties and a member of a triple alliance (with the National Liberal and the Phalangist parties) which withdrew from a "National Coalition" Government in January 1969. The party gained five seats in the 1972 elections to the National Assembly.

Orientation. The Bloc is a right-wing Maronite formation standing for the traditional power-sharing between Christians and Moslems and opposed to military participation in government.

National Liberal Party
Parti National Libéral (PNL)/Hizb al-Wataniyeen al-Ahrar

Address. Rue du Liban, Beirut, Lebanon

Leadership. Camille Chamoun (pres.); Dory Chamoun (s.g.)

Founded. September 1958

History. The party was founded by supporters of Camille Chamoun, who was President of the Republic in 1952-58 and thereafter assumed the party's presidency. It was part of the "Chamounist" group of parties and of a triple alliance embracing also the National Bloc and the Phalangist Party, a right-of-centre group opposed to Arab nationalism. The party gained five seats in the 1972 elections to the National Assembly. On Nov. 7, 1982, the party rejected a proposal by an Arab League committee to set up a body to prevent the illegal import of arms into Lebanon.

Orientation. The PNL is a Maronite Christian formation of conservative tendencies.

Structure. The party has a leadership council and a (consultative) general committee.

National Salvation Front

Founded. July 23, 1983

History. This Front was established as a democratic opposition alliance by Walid Jumblatt, leader of the (Druse) Progressive Socialist Party, the (Christian) ex-President Soleiman Frangié and the former Prime Minister Rashid Karami, leader of the Parliamentary Democratic Front. The formation of this Front followed an agreement between Lebanon and Israel on the withdrawal of Israeli troops from Lebanon concluded in May 1983.

Structure. The Front has a presidential council headed by Soleiman Frangié and a 12-member national council.

Organization for Communist Action in Lebanon (OCAL)

Leadership. Mohsen Ibrahim (s.g.)

Founded. 1970

History. The OCAL was formed by a merger of two groups—the Movement of Lebanese Socialists and Socialist Lebanon. Its militia has been involved in clashes with the forces of the Moslem fundamentalist *Amal* and has fought against Israeli troops in Lebanon.

Orientation. The Organization is reformist rather than revolutionary. It has strongly supported the Palestinian movement but has suggested that the creation of a Palestinian state on the West Bank and the Gaza Strip might be acceptable.

Structure. The OCAL is based on small cells and has regional committees, a central committee and a political bureau.

Parliamentary Democratic Front
Al-Jabha al-Damukratiya al-Barlamaniya

Leadership. Rashid Abdul Hamid Karami

History. As the leading party in the "Chehabist" group of parties (named after President Fuad Chehab, in office from 1958 to 1964), mainly Moslem, left-of-centre and inclined towards pan-Arabism, this party has played a leading role in government. Its leader, a Sunni Moslem, was a cabinet minister for many years between 1954 and 1976, and Prime Minister in 1955-56, 1958-60, 1961-64, 1965-66, 1966-68, 1969-70 and 1975-76, when he made efforts to achieve reconciliation between Christians and Moslems.

At the end of 1982 Rashid Karami headed a committee of faction leaders which approved an agreement reached between the Lebanese and Syrian Governments on the deployment of a Lebanese internal security force to keep the peace in Tripoli. In April 1984 Karami was again invited (this time by President Gemayel) to form a government with the aim of bringing the warring factions together.

Orientation. The Front is a mainly Sunni Moslem formation advocating the maintenance of the traditional power-sharing between Christians and Moslems.

Phalangist Party
Phalanges Libanaises/Al-Kata'eb

Address. P.O. Box 992, Beirut, Lebanon

Leadership. Pierre Gemayel (l.); Joseph Saade (g.s.)

Founded. 1936

History. This party has played a major role in Lebanese politics since the country became independent in 1943. In the 1958 civil war it backed the legal Government. As part of a triple alliance (with the National Liberal Party and the National Bloc) it withdrew from a "National Coalition" Government in January 1969. In the last elections to the Chamber of Deputies held in 1972 the party gained seven (out of 99) seats. During the civil war which began in 1975 the party co-operated to some extent with the National Liberal Party of Camille Chamoun. Two successive Presidents of Lebanon, the late Bachir Gemayel and Amin Gemayel (the present incumbent), were both the sons of the party's leader.

Orientation. As the largest of the Christian (Maronite) parties, the Phalangists are a nationalist, democratic, reformist, militant party deeply involved in the civil war against left-wing Moslems and Palestinians.

Membership. 100,000

Publications. *Al-Amal* (daily, in Arabic), 29,000; the party also has two radio stations, the (private) Voice of Lebanon and the Free Voice of Lebanon

---

Progressive Socialist Party
Parti Socialiste Progressiste/Al-Hizb al-Takadumi al-Ishteraki

Address. P.O. Box 2893, Beirut, Lebanon

Leaderhsip. Walid Jumblatt (pres.); Fouad Salman (g.s.)

Founded. 1948

History. The party was a leading one in the "Chehabist" group of parties and took part in many of the Governments formed by Rashid Karami (the leader of the Parliamentary Democratic Front). The party's founder, Kamal Jumblatt (a Druse), led a coalition of Moslem groups during the 1975-76 civil war but was assassinated in March 1977, the party leadership devolving on his son. The party gained 10 seats in the 1972 elections to the National Assembly. During the civil war and subsequently the party became the Druse community's political organ with its own militia and Walid Jumblatt has emerged as the principal leader of left-wing Moslem groups forming the National Movement.

Orientation. The PSP advocates socialism to be attained by constitutional means.

International affiliations. Socialist International

Socialist Revolutionary Party
Parti Socialiste Révolutionnaire (PSR)

Founded. 1964

Leadership. Youssef Moubarak

History. The PSR arose out of a pro-Chinese faction of the Lebanese Communist Party.

Syrian National Social Party

Leadership. Ina'am Ra'ad

Founded. 1932

History. The party's founder, Antoine Saadé, was repeatedly arrested under the French mandate régime, spent the years of World War II abroad and returned to Lebanon in 1947. His party was subsequently involved in raids on Lebanese frontier posts from Syria, and after being handed over to Lebanon by the Syrian authorities he was condemned to death and executed in July 1949, with his party being outlawed in Lebanon.

The party was again active in the 1958 civil war in Lebanon, supporting President Camille Chamoun against the forces led by Rashid Abdul Hamid Karami (later leader of the Parliamentary Democratic Front). Following the reconciliation between the warring parties it was allowed to resume legal existence as the National Social Party which unsuccessfully contested the 1960 general elections.

At the end of 1961 it was involved in an unsuccessful coup, and the party was thereupon dissolved on Jan. 1, 1962. The party became legal again in 1969 and contested the 1972 general elections, as a result of which it is represented by one supporter in the National Assembly.

Orientation. The party advocates the creation of a greater Syria comprising Cyprus, Iraq, Jordan, Lebanon, Palestine and Syria. It is non-sectarian.

Structure. The party has a supreme council which elects the party leader and is itself elected by life members of the party. It also has an administrative council.

Publications. *Sabah al-Khair* (weekly); *Fikr* (monthly)

Tashnag Party
Parti Tachnag

Leadership. Collective

Founded. 1890

History. The *Tashnag* existed as the dominant nationalist party in the independent Armenian Republic of Erevan of 1917-21, in opposition to the pro-Soviet *Hanchag* (*Hundak*) party, established as a socialist party in 1887. In 1921 this republic became part of the Soviet Union which agreed that Turkey should retain the provinces of Kars and Ardahan. In Lebanon the *Tashnag* Party has generally been represented in the National Assembly, but not in the Government. It gained three seats in the 1972 elections to the National Assembly.

Orientation. The *Tashnag* is the principal Armenian party in Lebanon.

Lesotho

Capital: Maseru   Pop. 1,400,000

The Kingdom of Lesotho, an independent member of the Commonwealth, is a constitutional hereditary monarchy in which the monarch has no political power. Its bicameral Parliament consisting of a nominated 33-member Senate and an elected 60-member National Assembly was prorogued in 1970 after the discovery of alleged electoral irregularities, and the Constitution was suspended. An interim National Assembly nominated in April 1973 contained 34 members of the Basotho National Party, 19 members of three opposition parties, 11 persons nominated for distinguished service to the country and 22 chiefs, and this Assembly was to draft a new Constitution. In a bill introduced in the Assembly on May 18, 1983, provision was made for a new National Assembly of 60 elected and not more than 20 nominated members.

Basotho Congress Party (BCP)

Address. P.O. Box 111, Maseru, Lesotho

Leadership. Gerard Ramoreboli (parl. l.); Geoffrey Kolisang (s.g.)

Founded. 1952

History. The BCP was founded as the National Basutoland Congress (NBC) by Ntsu Mokhehle. In January 1960 it obtained 29 out of the 40 seats in a National Council (indirectly elected by the country's nine district councils, of whose 162 seats the NBC had won 73—but only 35,000 of the total electorate of 191,000 had taken part in the district council elections). In the first general elections held in the then Basutoland in 1965 (under the country's self-government Constitution), the party gained only 25 seats (against 31 obtained by the Basutoland National Party and four by the Marema-Tlou Freedom Party).

Following the suspension of the Constitution in 1970 after elections in which the BCP claimed to have gained a majority of votes and seats, the BCP refused to cooperate with the Government. An interim National Assembly, appointed by the Prime Minister in 1973, however, contained several members of the BCP, and in 1975 the BCP's parliamentary leader was appointed to the Cabinet.

A section of the BCP, on the other hand, had in January 1974 made an unsuccessful attempt to overthrow the Government, and its leader, Ntsu Mokhehle, had left the country to organize resistance to the Lesotho Government through the armed wing of his faction of the BCP, the "Lesotho Liberation Army" (LLA). The latter was responsible for killing, on July 5, 1982, Koenyama Chakela, who had returned to Lesotho from exile under an amnesty of September 1980 and had become secretary-general of the internal BCP.

Orientation. The BCP is a left-wing African nationalist formation.

Basotho National Party (BNP)

Address. P.O. Box MS 124, Maseru 100, Lesotho

Leadership. Dr Leabua Jonathan (pres.); Evaristus R. Sekhonyana (ch.); Vincent M. Makhele (s.g.)

Founded. April 1959

History. The party won the first election held under the Basutoland self-government Constitution in 1965 with a narrow margin of votes over the Basutoland (later Basotho) Congress Party, gaining 31 out of the 60 seats in the Legislative Assembly. The BNP pioneered the country's independence, which was achieved on Oct. 4, 1966.

The result of new elections held in January 1970 was declared null and void by the four main political leaders, the Constitution was suspended and a state of emergency was declared, during which the BNP remained in power. The country's four parties agreed on April 30, 1970, that the January elections should be disregarded.

The state of emergency was lifted in July 1973, and in 1975 three members of other parties—the Basutoland Congress Party and the Marema-Tlou Freedom Party—were appointed to the Cabinet headed by the BNP's president.

Orientation. The BNP is a progressive traditionalist party which recognizes the role played by chiefs in Lesotho in a system under which the land belongs to the nation and not to individuals. In relations with South Africa the BNP stands for pragmatism and the maintenance of good neighbourliness despite opposition to South Africa's internal policies.

Structure. The BNP has a general conference, a council, an executive committee, and committees of youth and women at district, constituency, polling station and village levels.

Membership. 280,000

Marema-Tlou Freedom Party

Leadership. Edwin Lenaya (vice-pres.); B. M. Khakhetla (s.g.)

Founded. 1962

History. This minor party opposed the suspension of the Constitution in 1970, but in November 1975 one of its members accepted appointment as Minister to the Prime Minister and Minister without Portfolio. In September 1983 the party protested against government measures taken against electioneering by opposition parties.

Orientation. This party is of royalist and moderate conservative persuasions.

United Democratic Party (UDP)

Address. P.O. Box 776, Maseru 100, Lesotho

Leadership. Charles D. Mofeli (l.); B.L. Shea (nat. ch.); M. J. Lephoma (s.g.)

Founded. February 1967

History. The UDP was formed by defectors from the former (opposition) Basutoland Congress Party. It has been in opposition to the ruling Basotho National Party. In the National Assembly, nominated in 1973 as a political reconciliation measure, the UDP obtained two seats. With two other opposition parties, the UDP has been represented in the Cabinet by one minister.

In August 1983 the UDP called for the establishment of diplomatic relations between Lesotho and South Africa and also for the restoration of Lesotho's diplomatic relations with Taiwan (broken off when relations were established with China on May 14, 1983); at the same time it accused the ruling Basotho National Party of maintaining strong links with communists in order to obtain their support for a one-party dictatorship in Lesotho. The UDP also called for the release of all political detainees and a general amnesty for exiles. Charles Mofeli was thereupon expelled from the National Assembly on July 12. On Sept. 27, 1983, he called for the resignation of Chief Leabua Jonathan, the Prime Minister, for the appointment of a caretaker Government by the King and for the early holding of general elections, and in October 1983 he protested against government measures taken to prevent electioneering by his party.

Orientation. The UDP stands for "national unity, a multi-party system, a combination of public and private enterprise, a bill of rights and foreign investment". The party states that as the basis of its policies it "places the supremacy of God above all other considerations".

Structure. The UDP is organized at village, district and national level.

Membership. 26,000

Liberia

Capital: Monrovia   Pop. 2,000,000

The Republic of Liberia is ruled by a Military People's Redemption Council (PRC) which, under the leadership of Master Sergeant (later C.-in-C.) Samuel K. Doe, assumed power on April 12, 1980, and holds all legislative and executive power. There is no Parliament and there are no legal political parties.

Of the leaders of political parties which had been in opposition to the previous regime of President William Tolbert but who had rallied to the PRC Government, (i) Dr Togba-Nah Tipoteh, former leader of the Movement for Justice in Africa (Moja), resigned as Minister of Planning and Economic Affairs on Aug. 27, 1981, after being accused of being implicated in an attempted counter-coup earlier that month, and (ii) Gabriel Bacchus Matthews, former leader of the (socialist) Progressive People's Party, was dismissed as Minister of Foreign Affairs on Nov. 20, 1981, for anti-government remarks and actions. Matthews was thought to have reservations about the Government's gravitation towards the United States, the closure of the Libyan embassy in Liberia in May 1981, and the expulsion of a number of Soviet diplomats on May 12; on March 26, 1982, however, he was appointed Director-General of the Cabinet. He resigned from that office in April 1983 in order to be able to stand as a candidate in general elections scheduled for 1985.

A draft constitution presented by a constitutional commission on April 11, 1983, provided for an executive consisting of a President (elected for four years by universal adult suffrage of registered voters) and his Cabinet, a Senate (similarly elected for eight years) and a House of Representatives (elected for four years), both Houses having equal powers to legislate.

Libya

Capital: Tripoli   Pop. 3,300,000

The Popular Socialist Libyan Arab *Jamahiriyah* ("State of the Masses"), under the Constitution of March 1977, has a General People's Congress (GPC) "assisted by" a General Secretariat as its executive, while a General People's Committee acts as Cabinet. According to Col. Moamer al Gaddafi (Kadhafi)—who remained effective head of state and leader of the country despite surrendering the general secretaryship of the GPC in March 1979—"direct people's democracy" constitutes the foundation of Libya's political system and the basic people's power consists of basic people's congresses, people's committees, trade unions and the GPC, which appoints the General People's Committee. There are no political parties.

Liechtenstein

Capital: Vaduz   Pop. 26,000

The Principality of Liechtenstein is a constitutional and hereditary monarchy which, under its 1921 Constitution, has a Government appointed by the Prince on the proposal of the unicameral Diet (*Landtag*) of 15 members, who are elected for a four-year term on the basis of universal suffrage of male citizens above the age of 20 years and under a system of proportional representation in two constituencies (with parties obtaining less than 8 per cent of the votes cast failing to qualify for the distribution of seats). (Female suffrage was introduced at local level in 1976, and on April 17, 1977, women took part in communal elections for the first time. Female suffrage at national level had been rejected in a referendum in 1973 although it had previously been approved unanimously by the *Landtag*.)

Landtag elections held on Feb. 4 and 7, 1982, resulted in the Patriotic Union (*Vaterländische Union*) gaining 8 seats and the Progressive Citizens' Party (*Fortschrittliche Bürgerpartei*) the remaining 7.

A proposed constitutional amendment to the effect that a party which gained more than half the votes in a national election should automatically receive a majority of seats in the *Landtag* was rejected in a referendum (of male citizens above the age of 20) held on May 10, 1981, by 2,387 votes (52.9 per cent) to 2,127 (47.1 per cent).

Christian Social Party
Christlich Soziale Partei (CSP)

Address. 9493 Schaanwald, Liechtenstein

Leadership. Fritz Kaiser (ch.); Rupert Walser (sec.)

Founded. 1962

History. The party has never won any seats in the *Landtag* (Diet) and did not contest the 1978 and 1982 general elections.

Patriotic Union
Vaterländische Union

Address. Austrasse 52, FL-9490 Vaduz, Liechtenstein

Leadership. Dr Otto Hasler (pres.); René Ritter (sec.)

Founded. 1918

History. On its foundation as the People's Party, the party gained a majority in the 1918 general elections on its programme of economic union with Switzerland and a new constitution giving the people increased rights. The party's first members were recruited mainly among workers who had worked abroad as seasonal labour and had seen democratic and trade union institutions functioning.

The party retained its majority and formed the Government until 1928. In 1938 it merged with the *Heimatdienst* movement to form the Patriotic Union, which since that date has governed the country jointly with the Progressive Citizens' Party, as the junior coalition partner until 1970 and in 1974–78 and as the senior partner in 1970–74 and from 1978. In the February 1982 elections the party's share of the vote was 53.5 per cent.

Orientation. The party favours the constitutional monarchy and the reigning dynasty; it defends democracy and social progress and has remained a people's party with supporters among all sections of society.

Structure. The party has an eight-member presidency and a head committee of about 50 members, as well as local groups in municipalities. The party has no registered members.

Publications. *Liechtensteiner Vaterland* (five times a week), about 7,000.

International affiliations. European Democrat Union; International Democrat Union

---

Progressive Citizens' Party
Fortschrittliche Bürgerpartei (FBP)

Address. Feldkircherstr. 5, 9494 Schaan, Liechtenstein

Leadership. Herbert Batliner (ch.); Edgar Nipp (sec.)

History. Having formed the Government from 1928 to 1938, the FBP has been in coalition with the Patriotic Union since 1938, as senior partner until 1970 and in 1974–78 and as junior partner in 1970–74 and from 1978. In the 1978 *Landtag* elections the FBP won one seat fewer than the Patriotic Union notwithstanding its higher share of the popular vote (51.1 per cent). In the 1982 elections the party's share of the vote fell to 46.5 per cent.

Orientation. A conservative party.

Publications. *Liechtensteiner Volksblatt* (Schaan, five times a week), 7,000

International affiliations. European Democrat Union; International Democrat Union

Luxembourg

Capital: Luxembourg-Ville   Pop. 365,000

The Grand Duchy of Luxembourg is a constitutional hereditary monarchy in which the head of state exercises executive power through a Government and takes part in the legislative process. There is a unicameral Parliament—a 64-member Chamber of Deputies elected (in four electoral districts) by universal suffrage of citizens above the age of 18 years for a five-year term (voting being compulsory). Proportionality is determined in each district, and each voter has the same number of votes as there are seats for the district; voters may cast their votes for a single party list or choose candidates from several parties. There is also an advisory Council of State of 21 members chosen for life by the sovereign.

In parliamentary elections held on June 17, 1984, seats in the Chamber of Deputies were obtained as follows: Christian Social Party 25, Socialist Workers' Party 21, Democratic Party 14, Communist Party 2, The Green Alternative 2.

Christian Social Party
Chreschtlech-Sozial Vollekspartei (CSV)/
Parti Chrétien-Social (PCS)

Address. 38 rue du Curé, Luxembourg-Ville, Luxembourg

Leadership. Pierre Werner (l.); Jean Spautz (pres.); Jean-Pierre Kraemer (s.g.)

Founded. 1914

History. Founded as the *Parti de la Droite*, the party adopted its present name in 1945. Since 1919 the party has taken part in coalition government with various other parties and has supplied Prime Ministers as follows: Emile Reuter (1919–25), Joseph Bech (1926–37), Pierre Dupong (1937–53), Joseph Bech (1953–58), Pierre Frieden (1958–59) and Pierre Werner (1959–74, and again from 1979). The party formed a coalition with the Democratic Party following the June 1979 elections (in which it obtained 34.5 per cent of the vote), prior to which it had been in opposition since 1974.

Orientation. The party sees its objective as the "promotion of a policy of solidarity and social progress under the guidance of Christian and humanist principles".

Membership. 8,800

Publications. *CSV-Profil* (weekly), 75,000

International affiliations. Christian Democratic International; European Christian Democratic Union; European People's Party

Communist Party of Luxembourg
Parti Communiste Luxembourgeois (PCL)/
Kommunistisch Partei vu Lëtzebuerg (KPL)

Address. 14 rue Christophe Plantin, Luxembourg Gasperich, B.P. 1463, L-1014 Luxembourg

Leadership. René Urbany (ch.)

Founded. January 1921

History. Formed as a result of a split in the Socialist Workers' Party (LSAP), the PCL has been represented in the Chamber of Deputies since 1945, the number of seats held by it fluctuating between three in 1954–64 and six in 1968–74, and declining to two in 1979. The PCL took part in the national unity Government of 1945–47. It has since then been in opposition but has co-operated with the LSAP at local level. In the June 1979 elections the PCL obtained 5.8 per cent of the vote, compared with 10.4 per cent in 1974.

Orientation. The PCL is a Marxist-Leninist party. It pursues its own road to socialism according to the country's conditions but it is in solidarity with all progressive forces in the world and in particular with the existing socialist countries. At present the PCL fights for disarmament, peace and peaceful coexistence, for an independent economic policy (comprising the nationalization of the steel industry), for national sovereignty and for social and democratic progress. Although the party regards NATO as "an aggressive alliance of the imperialist powers" it considers it unrealistic for the time being to demand Luxembourg's withdrawal from NATO.

Structure. The party consists of groups whose highest authority is the annual general meeting, which elects group committees and delegates to the party congress, convened every three years as the party's supreme authority. The congress elects a central committee which in turn elects an executive and a secretariat.

Publications. *Zeitung vum Letzeburger Vollek* (daily), 8,000

International affiliations. The party is recognized by the Communist parties of the Soviet-bloc countries.

Democratic Party
Parti Démocratique (PD)

Address. 46, Grand'rue, Luxembourg-Ville, Luxembourg

Leadership. Colette Flesch (ch.); Henri Guthen (s.g.)

History. The party has been, since 1979, the second strongest in the Chamber of Deputies, where from 1964 it increased the number of seats held from six to 11 in 1968, 14 in 1974 and 15 in 1979 (when its share of the vote was 21.3 per cent). The PD has taken part in coalition governments: in the national unity administration of 1945–47, in coalition with the Christian Socials in 1947–51 (when the PD was known as the *Groupement Patriotique et Démocratique*), in 1959–64 and in 1968–74, and with the Socialists in 1974–79. Since July 1979 it has again been in power with the Christian Socials.

Orientation. A liberal party, the PD stands for free enterprise, a strong European Community and NATO.

Membership. 6,000

Publications. *Letzeburger Journal* (daily), 8,000

International affiliations. Liberal International; Federation of Liberal and Democratic Parties of the European Community

---

Enrolés de Force

History. This organization is a pressure group claiming compensation from the Government of the Federal Republic of Germany for the forcible recruitment of some 12,000 Luxembourg citizens into the German Army during World War II, when Luxembourg was formally incorporated in the "Reich" in August 1942.

The Green Alternative
Dei Grëng Alternativ

Address. Boîte Postale 2711, Luxembourg

Founded. June 1983

History. This organization was founded by a number of individuals and groups, including free radio and youth groups, environmentalists and former socialists, with the intention of contesting national and European elections in 1984.

Orientation. Similar to that of the Greens in the Federal Republic of Germany, the Luxembourg formation is in favour of freedom from force, grassroots democracy, solidarity among peoples everywhere, ecology and social concern.

International affiliations. The European Greens

Socialist Workers' Party
Letzeburger Sozialistesch Arbechterpartei
(LSAP)/Parti Ouvrier Socialiste Luxembourgeois (POSL)

Address. Casino Syndical, 2, rue de la Boucherie, Luxembourg-Ville
Leadership. Robert Krieps (pres.); Robert Goebbels (g.s.)
Founded. 1902
History. Formed as the Luxembourg Social Democratic Party, the party made little earlier progress because of the qualified franchise. After a minority had broken away in 1921 to form the Communist Party, the party first took part in the Government from the end of 1937, after which the Socialist ministers laid the basis for modern social legislation.

During the Nazi occupation the party was dismembered, but after World War II it re-emerged under its present name and took part in a Government of National Union until 1947, when it returned into opposition. Following renewed government participation in 1951–59 and 1964–68, the party was defeated in the 1968 legislative elections, whereafter its right wing formed the Social Democratic Party (which has since become defunct).

The party was later reconstructed and made gains in the elections of 1974, after which it joined a coalition Government with the Democratic Party; it returned to opposition after losing three seats in the June 1979 elections (in which it secured 24.3 per cent of the vote).

Orientation. The LSAP declares itself to be "a socialist party fighting for greater justice and democracy at all levels of society".

Structure. The party has local and regional organizations, a head committee, a general council and a national congress.

Membership. 6,000

Publications. *Tageblatt* (daily), 25,000; *LSAP-Militant*, 10,000

International affiliations. Socialist International; Confederation of Socialist Parties of the European Community

Madagascar

Capital: Antananarivo Pop. 9,200,000

The Democratic Republic of Madagascar has an executive President elected for seven years by universal adult suffrage of citizens above the age of 18 years. He is also Chairman of a Supreme Revolutionary Council which is "the guardian of the Malagasy Socialist Revolution" and the members of which are, as to two-thirds, nominated by the President and, as to the other third, chosen by him from a list presented by the National People's Assembly which is elected by universal adult suffrage, normally for five years. The Government headed by a Prime Minister appointed by the President is responsible to the National People's Assembly.

In elections to the 137-member National Assembly held on Aug. 28, 1983, when only the seven parties belonging to the National Front for the Defence of the Revolution (*Front National pour la Défense de la Révolution*, FNRD) were allowed to take part and over 500 candidates were presented, seats were gained (in a 74 per cent poll) as follows: President Didier Ratsiraka's Vanguard of the Malagasy Revolution (Arema) 117, Congress Party for Malagasy Independence (AKFM) 9, Popular Impulse for National Unity (Vonjy) 6, Movement for Proletarian Power (MFM) 3, National Movement for the Independence of Madagascar (Monima) 2; the remaining two parties—the Vondrona Sosialista Monima (VSM) and the Malagasy Christian Democratic Party (Udecma–KMTP)—together obtained less than 1 per cent of the vote and no seat.

Congress Party for Malagasy Independence
Parti du Congrès de l'Indépendance de Madagascar (AKFM)

Address. 43 Lalana Rakotomalala Ratsimba, Andravoahangy, Antananarivo, Madagascar

Leadership. Pastor Richard Andriamanjato (l.)

Founded. 1958

History. The AKFM, established in the same year that Madagascar became an autonomous state within the French community, campaigned for full independence (which was attained in June 1960). It was the main opposition party, based mainly on the capital, to the ruling Social Democratic Party of President Philibert Tsiranana. In municipal elections held in 1969 it obtained 43 out of 60 seats in Antananarivo and a slight majority in the port of Tamatave.

After the deposition of President Tsiranana in 1972, the AKFM supported the new military Government. The AKFM leader, who had for many years been Mayor of Antananarivo, became a member of the ruling Supreme Revolutionary Council established in June 1975 after a period of considerable internal instability.

Orientation. The AKFM is a left-wing alliance of radicals and middle-class nationalists with pro-Soviet Communist influence, supporting the Government within the National Front.

Malagasy Christian Democratic Union
Union Démocratique Chrétien Malgache (Udecma–KMPT)

Leadership. Solo Norbert Andriamorasata (l.)

Founded. 1976

History. The party was formerly known as the *Rassemblement National Malgache* and, as the Union of Christian Democrats of Madagascar (Udecma), tried to oppose President Tsiranana in presidential elections in January 1972, but its leader was disqualified as presidential candidate as being under the minimum age of 40 years. Its leader became a member of the ruling Supreme Revolutionary Council set up in 1975.

Orientation. Progressive Christian democratic, supporting the Government.

International affiliations. Christian Democratic International

Movement for Proletarian Power
Mouvement pour le Pouvoir Prolétarien (MFN) or "Pouvoir aux Petits"

Leadership. Manandafy Rakotonirina

Founded. December 1972

History. The MFM opposed the military Government of Gen. Gabriel Ramanantsoa set up in 1972, and its leader was temporarily arrested in 1973. However, the party supported the Government of President Didier Ratsiraka established in 1975, and its leader became a member of the ruling Supreme Revolutionary Council.

Orientation. The Movement for Proletarian Power espouses extreme left-wing precepts, which it regards as being the ideological key to the emancipation of the country's under-privileged classes.

National Movement for the Independence of Madagascar
Mouvement National pour l'Indépendance de Madagascar (Monima)

Leadership. Monja Jaona

Founded. 1960

History. Monima traditionally has its stronghold in Toliary (Tuléar) and the island's extreme south, where it was involved in an insurrection in 1970, whereafter Monima was temporaily banned and its leader imprisoned as a "Maoist plotter". However, he was released under an amnesty in 1972 and the ban on the party was lifted.

Monima subsequently supported the socialist military Government until 1977, when it withdrew from the National Front, with the result that it was allotted no seats in the National People's Assembly elected in that year.

Having unsuccessfully opposed President Didier Ratsiraka in presidential elections held on Nov. 7, 1982, Monja Jaona called for a general strike. He was thereupon dismissed from the Supreme Revolutionary Council (to which he had been appointed in 1981), and on Dec. 15, 1982, he was placed under house arrest. He was released in August 1983, however, and allowed to contest the general elections, in which he gained one of the two seats obtained by his party in the National Assembly.

Orientation. Monima is a radical socialist party, standing for the nationalization of large land-holdings and the industrialization of the island's southern areas, and opposed to co-operation agreements with France and to "military or other bases of foreign imperialists".

Popular Impulse for National Unity
Elan Populaire pour l'Unité Nationale
(VONJY)

Leadership. Dr Jérôme Marojama Razanabahimy
Founded. 1973
History. The party's leader became a member of the ruling Supreme Revolutionary Council set up in 1975.
Orientation. VONJY is a moderate nationalist party "for socialist revolution in national unity", supporting the Government within the National Front.

Vanguard of the Malagasy Revolution
Antoky Ny Revolosiona Malagasy/
Avantgarde de la Révolution Malgache
(Arema)

Address. B.P. 865, Antananarivo, Madagascar
Leadership. President Didier Ratsiraka (s.g.)
Founded. March 1976
History. Established by President Ratsiraka as the revolutionary nucleus of the National Front for the Defence of the Malagasy Socialist Revolution, Arema won about 95 per cent of all seats in indirect provincial elections held in May 1977. Of the list of 137 candidates, nominated for subsequent elections to a National People's Assembly by the National Front, 112 were

allotted to Arema in 1977, this number rising to 117 in the August 1983 elections.
Orientation. Arema is socialist in acccordance with the charter of the Malagasy socialist revolution published in October 1975 and calling for the nationalization of the country's mineral resources and for rapid economic, social and cultural development.
Structure. The party, based on cells and federations, has a congress, a central committee and an executive bureau of 77 members.

Vondrona Sosialista Monima

Address. B.P. 367, Antananarivo, Madagascar.
Leadership. Remanindry Jaona, Gabriel Rabearimanana
Founded. 1978
History. This Marxist-Leninist group broke away from the National Movement for the Independence of Madagascar (Monima—see separate entry) in order to support the National Front. Remanindry Jaona was subsequenly appointed to the Supreme Revolutionary Council but was dismissed from it in January 1983, apparently because he had supported Monja Jaona, the Monima leader, in the November 1982 presidential elections.
Publications. Tolona Sosialista (monthly)

Malawi

Capital: Lilongwe   Pop. 6,200,000

The Republic of Malawi, a member of the Commonwealth, has an executive President appointed for life. He is also the head of the Government. Of the members of the National Assembly, 101 are elected for a five-year term by universal adult suffrage under a simple majority system in multi-member constituencies from candidates nominated by district committees of the Malawi Congress Party (MCP)—the country's sole legal political organization—and approved by the President, who may appoint up to 15 additional members to the Assembly. The leader of the MCP is Dr Hastings Kamuzu Banda, who has led Malawi since independence in 1964 and who was made Life President in 1971.

In elections held on June 29-30, 1983, some 225 candidates contested 75 seats (while in 21 constituencies the sitting MCP candidates were returned unopposed); more than two-thirds of the sitting members of Parliament were defeated (as officially stated on July 3). In addition the President appointed eight men and three women to the National Assembly. Five seats remained vacant (according to an official statement because no candidates in the constituencies concerned had passed the required test of proficiency in the English language).

Malawi Congress Party (MCP)

Address. Lilongwe, Malawi

Leadership. President H. Kamuzu Banda (pres.); Robson Watayachanga (admin. sec.)

Founded. 1959

History. The MCP was founded as the Nyasaland African Congress, which campaigned for the independence of Nyasaland (then part of the Federation of Rhodesia and Nyasaland, from 1953 to December 1963), attained as Malawi in July 1964. The MCP first obtained a majority in the Nyasaland Legislative Council in 1961; its leader became Prime Minister in February 1963; and in 1966 he became President of the Republic of Malawi, being made Life President in 1971. The MCP has remained virtually unchallenged within Malawi over the last two decades.

Orientation. The party stands for multi-racialism and for economic development with foreign aid, including that of South Africa, with which Malawi has developed close relations under the MCP.

Structure. All adults are required to join the MCP, which is strictly disciplined; its executive committee has been repeatedly re-organized to exclude offenders against the party's code of conduct.

Malaysia

Capital: Kuala Lumpur   Pop. 14,300,000

The federation of Malaysia, consisting of Peninsular Malaysia, Sabah and Sarawak (the two latter being geographically parts of the island of Borneo), is an independent member of the Commonwealth. It has a Supreme Head of State who is elected every five years, from among themselves, by the nine rulers of Malay states (i.e. not including the governors of Malacca, Penang and Sarawak and the ruler of Sabah) and who appoints a Cabinet headed by a Prime Minister. Malaysia has a bicameral Parliament (*Parlimen*) consisting of (i) a 58-member Senate (*Dewan Negara*), 26 of whose members are elected by simple majority for six-year terms, two by each of the 13 state Legislative Assemblies, and 32 appointed by the head of state; and (ii) a 154-member House of Representatives (*Dewan Ra'ayat*), elected by universal adult suffrage for a five-year term and by simple majority in single-member constituencies. Each of the 11 federative states of Peninsular Malaysia and also Sabah and Sarawak have Legislative Assemblies (called *Dewan Negri* except in Sarawak where it is known as the Council *Negri*) with both directly elected members and members appointed by the head of state. The minimum voting age is 21 years.

In federal general elections held in April 1982 parties obtained seats in the House of Representatives as follows: National Front 132, Democratic Action Party 9, Islamic Party of Malaysia (Pan Malayan Islamic Party) 5, independents 8. The National Front embraces 10 political formations (the leading party being the United Malay National Organization) representing all the main ethnic communities. The principal illegal political formations are the old Communist Party of Malaya (CPM), founded in 1930, and the Communist Party of Malaysia, formed in December 1983 by two radical splinter groups of the CPM.

As a result of elections held in Peninsular Malaysia on April 22, 1982, seats in State Legislative Assemblies were distributed as follows (NF=National Front, DAP=Democratic Action Party, PMIP=Pan Malayan Islamic Party): *Johore*—NF 32; *Kedah*—NF 24, PMIP 2; *Kelantan*—NF 26, PMIP 10; *Malacca*—NF 18, DAP 2; *Negri Sembilan*—NF 22, DAP 2; *Pahang*—NF 31, DAP 1; *Penang*—NF 25, DAP 2; *Perak*—NF 38, DAP 4; *Perlis*—NF 11, PMIP 1; *Selangor*—NF 31, DAP 1, independent 1; *Trengganu*—NF 23, PMIP 5.

In *Sabah* elections to the Legislative Assembly held on March 23–28, 1981, resulted as follows: Sabah People's Party (Berjaya) 43, United Sabah National Organization 3, Sabah Chinese Consolidated Party 1 (vacant 1). In *Sarawak* elections held on Sept. 15–22, 1979, gave the NF 45 and independents 3 seats.

National Parties

Democratic Action Party (DAP)

Address. 77 Road 20/9, Paramount Garden, Petaling Jaya, Selangor, Malaysia

Leadership. Dr Chen Man Hin (ch.); Lim Kit Siang (g.s.)

Founded. 1966

History. Formed as the Malaysian offshoot of the Singapore People's Action Party, the DAP participated in general elections for the first time in 1969, when it won 13 parliamentary and 31 state Assembly seats; in 1974 it gained nine parliamentary and 21 state Assembly seats;

and in 1978 16 parliamentary and 24 state Assembly seats. In 1982, however it retained only nine parliamentary (and 12 state Assembly seats), winning 19.6 per cent of the valid vote.

Strongly based in the Chinese community, the DAP has been the main opposition party in the Malaysian Parliament since 1969, although its activities have been somewhat circumscribed by prosecutions of prominent members on various charges.

Orientation. The DAP seeks the establishment by constitutional means of a democratic, socialist pattern of society in Malaysia.

Structure. The party is based on branches and has standing state subcommittees and a central executive committee.

Membership. 12,000

Publications. *The Rocket* (official organ), 30,000

International affiliations. Socialist International; Asia-Pacific Socialist Organization

---

Front Malaysian Islamic Council
Barisan Jama'ah Islamiah Se Malaysia (Berjasa)

Address. 4960 Jalan Bayam (Dusun Muda), Kota Bharu, Kelantan, Malaysia

Leadership. Haji Wan Hashim b. Hj. Ahmad (ch.); Mahmood Zuhdi b. Hj. Ab. Majid (s.g.)

Founded. September 1977

History. The party was formed by Dato Muhamad Nasir, who became its chairman and who had been expelled from the Islamic Party of Malaysia, which was itself expelled from the federal National Front coalition in December 1977. In the March 1978 state Assembly elections in Kelantan, Berjasa supported the National Front, with which it subsequently formed a coalition Government.

Berjasa did not take part in the federal general elections of July 1978, but in 1980 it joined the National Front and in the April 1982 general elections it contested two federal seats unsuccessfully, winning only 0.7 per cent of the valid vote. It has one seat in the federal Cabinet.

Orientation. Berjasa is a pro-Islamic formation.

Structure. The party has a central committee presided over by its chairman.

Membership. 50,000

Publications. *Voice of Jama'ah*

Islamic Party of Malaysia
Parti Islam Se Malaysia (PAS or PMIP)

Address. 28-A, Jalan Pahang Barat, off Jalan Pahang, Kuala Lumpur, Malaysia

Leadership. Haji Yusuf bin Abdullah Rawa (pres.); Haji Hassan Haji Shukri (sec.)

Founded. 1951

History. The PAS arose out of the Muslim Ummah movement led by Ulema (Muslim scholars) to fight against "Western imperialism and colonialism". Early Ulema organizations in Malaysia included a Higher Islamic Council (formed in 1947), and the *Hizbul Muslimin* (an Islamic political party established in 1948). The PAS (also known as the Pan Malayan Islamic Party, PMIP) was founded (in 1951) to seek independence based on Islamic principles.

In the first elections of the independent Federation of Malaya held in August 1959 the party gained 13 out of 104 seats in the Federal House of Representatives. In April 1964 it won nine out of 159 seats in the Malaysian Federal Parliament, where it increased its representation to 12 members in 1969. As from Jan. 1, 1973, it joined the ruling Alliance to form a National Front and its leader subsequently entered the Government.

In December 1977, however, the PAS was expelled from the National Front. In elections held in March 1974 to the state Assembly of Kelantan, which the party had controlled since 1959, it won only two seats (out of 36), and in the federal elections of July 1978 its representation in the Federal House of Representatives was reduced to five members. The party has since been in opposition. Its five federal seats won in the May 1982 general elections were secured with 14.5 per cent of the valid vote.

Orientation. The party seeks the establishment of the Islamic system in society and the nation, including maintenance of the nation's independence and sovereignty, preservation of Malay as the country's national language and Arabic as the second language, and rejection of all "man-made" ideologies (such as communism, socialism and pragmatism). Extremist PAS members were said to have close relations with the Moro National Liberation Front in the Philippines and with Moslem separatists in southern Thailand.

Structure. The supreme council of the PAS is its annual general meeting, which elects members of the party's executive committee every two years. There is a state liaison committee responsible for co-ordinating party activities in the states and for implementing party policies at state level. The party is organized in administrative districts or in parliamentary constituencies.

Membership. 250,000

Malay Nationalist Revolutionary Party of Malaya (MNRPM)
Partai Kebangsaan Melayu Revolusioner Malaya

Leadership. Abdullah C.D. (ch.)
Founded. May 24, 1981
History. The MNRPM replaced an earlier Malay National Party (MNP), an extreme left-wing formation founded in 1945, banned in 1948 and later engaged in guerrilla warfare against the Government. The MNRPM's chairman was a member of the central committee of the banned Communist Party of Malaya, founded in 1930.
Orientation. The policy of MNRPM, as defined in a manifesto broadcast on June 11, 1981, is "to unite with communists, socialists, nationalists and religious groups" in "an anti-imperialist, national united front", to set up a "national democratic coalition government" and to carry out "an independent and non-aligned foreign policy". The party is regarded as pro-Chinese.
Structure. The party is led by a central committee.

Malaysia Indian Moslem Congress
Kongres Indian Muslim Malaysia (Kimma)

Address. 47, Lorong Tuanku Abdulrahman, Kuala Lumpur, Malaysia
Leadership. Dato A. S. Dawood (pres.); Lebbai Gani bin Naina Pillai Naricar (sec.)
Founded. Oct. 4, 1977
Orientation. The party's aim is to unite the Malaysian Indian Moslems, with emphasis on their loyalty to Malaysia, and to improve their harmony and peace with other communities in the country as well as their economic and educational opportunities.
Structure. The party has a 29-member central council and 115 branches throughout Malaysia.
Membership. 20,000

Malaysian Chinese Association (MCA)

Address. P.O. Box 10626, 163 Jalan Ampang, Kuala Lumpur, Malaysia
Leadership. Datuk Dr Neo Yee Pan (pres.); Tan Sri Chong Hon Nyan (s.g.)
Founded. 1949
History. The MCA is a component party of the National Front (which has ruled Malaysia since 1974). Earlier the MCA was an original partner in the tripartite Alliance which ruled Malaysia in 1957–74. In the 1982 general elections the MCA was returned with 24 seats (out of 28 seats contested) and 16.3 per cent of the valid votes. In the National Front Government formed thereafter the MCA was given four ministerial posts, six posts of deputy minister and one of parliamentary secretary.
Orientation. The MCA is a purely Chinese-based party representing the interests of the Chinese community while preserving inter-racial goodwill and harmony in a multiracial country.

Malaysian Indian Congress (MIC)

Address. Tingkat 7, Menara Manickavasagam 1, Jalan Rahmat, Kuala Lumpur, Malaysia
Leadership. Y.B. Dato S. Samy Vellu (pres.); Y.B. Encik M. Mahalingam (s.g.)
Founded. 1946
History. The MIC was founded to represent the interests of the Indian community in Malaysia. It formed part of the Alliance Party and after 1973 of the National Front, gaining four seats in the Lower House of the Federal Parliament in 1974, three in 1978 and again four in 1982 (when it obtained 1.9 per cent of the valid votes). Thereafter it was given three posts in the National Front Government (one at ministerial and two at deputy ministerial level).

Malaysian People's Movement Party
Parti Gerakan Rakyat Malaysia (PGRM or Gerakan)

Address. c/o Chief Minister's Office, Bungunan Tunku Syed Putra, Penang, Malaysia
Leadership. Dr Lim Keng Yaik (pres.); Leong Khee Seong (s.g.)
Founded. March 1968
History. The party was formed by United Democratic Party members, leaders of the moderate wing of the Labour Party and a group of academics, and was strengthened by the accession of a group of former Malaysian Chinese Association reformists. The PGRM captured the Penang state Government in 1969 and, having entered into a coalition with the Alliance

Party in 1972, it is still the major party in that Government, with its national chairman being the Chief Minister.

As a member of the ruling National Front, the PGRM is represented in the federal Government by one minister and one deputy minister and currently has five members in the federal House of Representatives and one in the Senate. In the May 1982 general elections it obtained 3.5 per cent of the valid votes.

Orientation. The PGRM upholds the Constitution of Malaysia and advocates "an egalitarian Malaysian society based on humanitarian and democratic principles". The party seeks "to ensure social and economic justice", with "public ownership of the vital means of production and distribution", the "individual ownership of economic lots of land by the peasants and workers and the efficient utilization of land by co-operative and joint management"; it also seeks "equal pay and privileges" for women, and to "eliminate the causes which have made the Malays and other indigenous people economically weak".

Structure. The party has branches, divisions, state liaison committees, a central committee and a central working committee.

Membership. 14,000
Publications. *Gerakan Rakyat* (People's Movement)

Malaysian People's Socialist Party
Partai Sosialis Rakyat Malaysia (PSRM)

Address. 94c, Jalan Bangsar, Kuala Lumpur, Malaysia
Leadership. Encik Kassim Ahmad (ch.); Abdul Razal Ahmad (s.g.)
Founded. 1955
History. In the 1959 general elections the party, then known as the People's Party, won two seats as part of the Malayan People's Socialist Front (an alliance with the now defunct Labour Party of Malaya). The party also won four State Assembly seats (in Pahang, Selangor and Penang). It adopted its present name in 1968.

Between 1976 and 1981 the party's leaders were detained for alleged pro-communist activities, and it was banned from holding public rallies. In the 1978 general elections it obtained only 0.7 per cent of the votes cast. In 1982 it contested the elections in alliance with the Democratic Action Party but gained no seat.

Orientation. This left-wing socialistic party has demanded better political, social and economic treatment of the people, in particular the poor, and a more equitable multiracial society in Malaysia.

Publications. *Mimbar Sosialis* (monthly, in Malay)

Moslem Front
Ilizbul Muslimin

Leadership. Datuk Haji Mohamed Asri bin Haji Muda (l.)
Founded. March 24, 1983
History. This party broke away from the Islamic Party of Malaysia (PAS), of which its leader had been president. It was joined by four of the five PAS members elected to the federal House of Representatives in April 1982 and thus became the second largest opposition party in the House after the Democratic Action Party.

Orientation. The party's leaders had opposed the ascendancy of the "theocratic" element in the Islamic Party of Malaysia (see separate entry).

National Consciousness Party
Kesatuan Insaf Tanah Air (KITA)

Address. 7c, Jalan Murai Dua, Baru Kompleks, Jalan Ipoh, Kuala Lumpur, Malaysia
Leadership. Tuan Asri bin Yussof (ch.); Tuan Haji Shamsuri bin Misu (s.g.)
Founded. April 1974
History. After failing to gain any seats in parliamentary elections in 1974 and 1978, KITA joined the (opposition) *Barisan Rakyat* (People's Front), a new political movement which was itself unsuccessful in the 1982 elections.

Membership. 5,000

National Front
Barisan Nasional

Address. c/o Dewan Ra'ayat, Kuala Lumpur, Malaysia
Leadership. Encik Abdul Ghafar Baba (sec.)
Founded. 1973
History. The National Front superseded the earlier (Malaysian) Alliance Party, which had been founded in 1952 and held power in Malaysia from the country's attainment of independence in 1957. The Alliance Party had consisted of the United Malay National Organization (UMNO), the Malaysian Chinese Association (MCA), the Malaysian Indian

Congress (MIC) and the Sabah and Sarawak Alliances.

In the April 1982 general elections the Front embraced 11 parties: *in Peninsular Malaysia*—UMNO, the MCA, the MIC, the Malaysian People's Movement (*Gerakan*), the Front Malaysian Islamic Council (*Berjasa*) and the People's Progressive Party (PPP) of Perak; *in Sabah*—the Sabah People's Party (*Berjaya*) and the United Sabah National Organization (USNO); *in Sarawak*—the United Traditional Bumiputra Party (PPBB), the Sarawak United People's Party (SUPP) and the Sarawak National Party (SNAP).

In April 1984, however, the USNO was expelled from the Front by unanimous decision of the other members, taken because the USNO leadership had opposed Front policy at federal level, notably by declaring a 1983 constitutional amendment bill illegal.

The Front contests elections as a single political body, with candidates of the constituent parties undertaking not to stand against each other.

Orientation. The National Front is essentially a conservative alliance of parties accepting that Malays should be predominant politically and receive positive discrimination at the economic level.

Pan Malayan Islamic Party (PMIP)—see Islamic Party of Malaysia

---

People's Front
Barisan Rakyat (BARA)

History. This Front contested the April 1982 federal elections as an opposition party but gained no seats, despite having been joined by the National Consciousness Party (KITA—see separate entry).

Social Justice Party
Parti Keadilan Mayharakat (Pekemas)

Leadership. Shaharyddin Dahalan (ch.)
Founded. 1971
History. Formed by dissident left-wing members of the Malaysian People's Movement Party (*Gerakan*), the party gained one seat in the federal parliamentary elections of 1974; in the 1978 elections it won only 0.86 per cent of the vote and no seat. In 1982 it also failed to secure representation.

Socialist Democratic Party
Partai Sosialis Demokratik

Address. 205, Jalan Bukit Bintang, Kuala Lumpur, Malaysia
Leadership. Ismail Hashim (ch.); Fan Yew Teng (s.g.)
Founded. January 1978
History. The party was founded by former members of the Democratic Action Party who had been expelled or had resigned from that party. The party was registered one week before the federal and state elections of July 1978, in which it failed to secure representation.
Orientation. The party is leftist, democratic and non-racial.
Membership. 4,500

United Malay National Organization (UMNO)

Address. 399 Jalan Tuanku Abdul Rahman, Kuala Lumpur, Malaysia
Leadership. Datuk Seri Dr Mahathir bin Mohamed (pres.); Abdul Ghafar Baba (s.g.)
Founded. May 1946
History. The party was "formed to fight for national independence and safeguard the interests of the indigenous people", later including "the interests of all the resident communities". Since the attainment of independence in 1957, UMNO has been the dominant party in Malaysia as the leading partner in successive electoral alliances, namely the Alliance Party, which won a majority of seats in elections in 1959, 1964 and 1969, and the National Front, which similarly won the elections of August–September 1974, of February 1978 and of April 1982.

UMNO has in recent years been the guiding force in the introduction of measures to give special rights to Malays in the economic and social fields, on the grounds that Malays are unacceptably disadvantaged in these areas.

Orientation. UMNO seeks "to safeguard Malay interests and work for national unity" and to "practise a neutral foreign policy".

Structure. Power lies with the party's general assembly, which meets annually. The main policy-making body is the party's supreme council consisting of elected and nominated members. Below it there are a state liaison committee, divisional committees and branch committees.

Membership. 600,000
Publications. *Suara Bersatu* (monthly), 10,000

Workers' Party of Malaysia
Parti Pekerja-Pekerja Malaysia (PPM)

History. The PPM unsuccessfully contested the 1978 federal elections as an opposition party, gaining only 0.05 per cent of the total votes cast.

Regional Parties

PERAK

People's Progressive Party (PPP)

Address. 23 Jalan Bandar Raya, Ipoh, Perak, Malaysia
Leadership. Sen. S.I. Rajah (pres.)
Founded. 1955
History. The PPP joined the National Front before the 1974 federal elections. It had gained four seats in the federal House of Representatives in 1969 but retained only one in 1974 which it lost in 1978.
Orientation. The PPP is a regional party based on the Ipoh area of Perak.

SABAH

Sabah Chinese Consolidated Party
Persatuan China Sabeh

Address. P.O. Box 704, Kota Kinabalu, Sabah, Malaysia
Leadership. Chan Tet On (s.g.)
Founded. 1964
History. Before 1963 there had been two Chinese political parties in Sabah—the United Party and the Democratic Party—which merged to form the National Party. This party merged with the North Borneo Chinese Association to form the Sabah Chinese Association (SCA), which as from July 1979 changed its name to Sabah Chinese Consolidated Party (in order to absorb members of the Sabah Chinese United Party, which was dissolved). In 1965 the SCA joined the Sabah Alliance Party, which was the ruling party until 1976, when the SCA withdrew from the Alliance Party.
Orientation. The party's aim is "to safeguard and uphold the interests of the Chinese and to work with other political organizations with similar aims".
Structure. The party has a 39-member central executive committee (including 10 officials and four members appointed by the president, the remainder being elected by delegates). Each constituency may form a division provided there are three branches with 100 members each.
Membership. 14,000

Sabah Democratic Rakyat Party

Address. No. 11 Jalan Sentosa, Kampong Air, c/o P.O. Box No. 1232, Kota Kinabalu, Sabah, Malaysia
Leadership. Datuk Hj. Taulani Bin Haji Jalaluddin (founder); Musa Bin Datuk Taulani (pres.); Abdul Hamid Bin Haji Bulat (s.g.)
Founded. 1975
History. The party was formed by defectors from the United Sabah National Organization (USNO) shortly after the latter had been asked to join the National Front. The party's activities are confined to the state of Sabah, where it is in opposition and "third among the eight parties in the state".
Orientation. Among the party's eight principles is that of uniting the indigenous peoples of Sabah. It also intends to practise the five principles (*Rukunegara*) of Malaysia (for details see under Sabah People's Party).
Structure. The party's leadership includes a committee of 12 elected and five appointed members; the party's founder (see above) is chairman of the committee's advisory board.
Membership. 68,000

Sabah Front
Barisan Sabah

Founded. 1981
History. This Front was an electoral alliance between the United Sabah National Organization (USNO), the Sabah Chinese Consolidated Party and the *Pasok* Party (based on the indigenous Kadazan population). The two first-named parties gained three and one seats respectively in the March 1981 elections to the Sabah Legislative Assembly, while *Pasok* gained none. The *Pasok* party also contested the April 1982 federal elections without gaining any seat.

Sabah People's Party
Bersatu Rakyat Jelata Sabah (Berjaya)

Address. P.O. Box 2170, Karamunsing, Kota Kinabalu, Sabah, Malaysia
Leadership. Datuk Harris Mohammad Salleh (pres.); Haji Mohammad Noor bin Haji Mansoor (s.g.)
Founded. July 15, 1975

History. The *Berjaya* came into power in Sabah after the 1976 general elections which it fought on a platform pledging an end to corruption, nepotism and discrimination at all levels. *Berjaya* is a component part of the National Front, the ruling formation of Malaysia's federal Government.

In the April 1982 federal elections it increased its seat total in the House of Representatives from eight to 10, obtaining 2 per cent of the overall vote. It is represented in the federal Cabinet by one minister.

In April 1984 five independent members of the House from Sabah were accepted as members of the *Berjaya*.

Orientation. The party's aims are to preserve the integrity, independence and democratic status of the nation and to uphold the principles of the *Rukunegara*, i.e. faith in God, loyalty to king and country and maintenance of the Constitution, the rule of law, good behaviour and morality; to protect the rights and interests of Sabah within the Federation of Malaysia; to safeguard and promote the special position of the natives and the constitutional rights of every citizen in Sabah; to promote national unity, self-respect, self-reliance and a sense of commitment to creating a prosperous, stable and just society; and to respect the freedom of religion.

Structure. The *Berjaya* has 48 divisions in Sabah and a congress which meets annually. Party officials elected every three years include the president, the deputy president, seven vice-presidents, the secretary-general and 20 committee members.

Membership. 400,000

United Sabah National Organization (USNO)

Leadership. Tan Sri Mohamed Said bin Keruak (pres.)

History. Following the 1978 general elections, which it contested as part of the National Front, USNO was not represented in the federal Government. Of the USNO members elected to the Sabah Legislative Assembly in April 1976, nine later transferred their allegiance to the ruling Sabah People's Party (*Berjaya*), and in the March 1981 elections USNO retained only three seats in that Assembly. While still a member of the National Front at federal level, in Sabah USNO was in opposition to the ruling *Berjaya* (also a member of the National Front).

In the April 1982 federal elections USNO lost all its five seats in the House of Representatives, securing only 0.7 per cent of the valid overall vote. Subsequently, in April 1984, the USNO was expelled from the National Front on the grounds that its leadership had opposed Front policies, notably by declaring a 1983 constitutional amendment bill illegal.

United Sabah People's Organization (USPO)
Pertubuhan Rakyat Sabah Bersatu

Address. Tingkat 3, 9 Jalan Bendahara, Berjaya, Kg. Air, P.O.B. 993, Kota Kinabalu, Sabah, Malaysia

History. This party has no parliamentary representation.

SARAWAK

Sarawak National Party (SNAP)

Address. 304/5 Mei Jun Building, Rubber Road, P.O. Box 2960, Kuching, Sarawak, Malaysia

Leadership. Datuk James Wong Kim (pres.); Encik Joseph Balan Seling (s.g.)

Founded. April 10, 1961

History. The SNAP was a member of the Alliance Party until 1966, and it joined the National Front in 1976, having won 18 out of the 48 seats in the state Assembly in 1974 and nine seats in the Federal House of Representatives in the same year. The SNAP has been in power in Sarawak with its two National Front partners—the United Traditional Bumiputra Party and the Sarawak United People's Party (SUPP). In the April 1982 federal elections it retained six of the nine seats won in 1978.

On July 18, 1983, three of the party's federal members of Parliament and nine state Assembly members resigned from the party on the grounds that it had not sufficiently advanced the cause of the Dayaks (the largest and longest-established population group in the state), and they expressed their intention to form a new party, which would also co-operate with the SNAP's two partners in the National Front.

Orientation. The SNAP is a multiracial but predominantly rural-based party.

Sarawak Native People's Party
Parti Rakyat Jati Sarawak (Pajar)

Leadership. Ali Kaw
Founded. 1978

History. Pajar was established to cater for the needs of Sarawak's native people. It contested the 1978 federal election and the 1979 Sarawak state elections as an opposition party but gained no seats.

Sarawak People's Organization (SAPO)

Address. Miri, Sarawak, Malaysia
Leadership. Raymond Seztu (s.g.)
History. SAPO won the only seat which it contested in the 1978 federal parliamentary elections, but gained no seat in the 1979 Sarawak state elections.
Orientation. SAPO is a mainly Chinese-supported opposition party.

Sarawak United People's Party (SUPP)

Address. P.O. Box 454, Kuching, Sarawak, Malaysia
Leadership. Datuk Amar Stephen Yong Kuet Tze (pres.); Datuk Dr Wong Soon Kai (s.g.)
Founded. 1959
History. The SUPP joined the National Front before the 1974 elections. It is represented by one minister in the federal Government and it has been in power in

Sarawak with its two National Front partners—the United Traditional Bumiputra Party and the Sarawak National Party (SNAP). In the April 1982 federal elections the SUPP fielded seven candidates in Sarawak, of whom five were elected (a decline of one as compared with the 1978 result).

United Traditional Bumiputra Party
Partai Pesaka Bumiputra Bersatu (PPBB)

Address. Jalan Satok, Kuching, Sarawak, Malaysia
Leadership. Datuk Patinggi Tan Sri Haji Abdul Rahman Yaakub (pres.)
History. This party arose out of a merger between *Bumiputra* (a mixed ethnic party), *Pesaka* (a Dayak and Malay Party) and the Sarawak Chinese Association, and it became part of the National Front. Following the 1978 and 1982 federal elections it was represented in the Federal Cabinet by one minister. It has been in power in Sarawak with its two National Front partners—the Sarawak United People's Party (SUPP) and the Sarawak National Party (SNAP).

In the April 1982 federal elections eight PPBB candidates stood in Sarawak and all were elected.

Maldives

Capital: Malé   Pop. 160,000

The Republic of the Maldives has an executive President elected for a five-year term by universal adult suffrage, a Cabinet presided over by the President and a 54-member People's Council (*Majlis*) with 46 of its members similarly elected for five years and the remaining eight appointed by the President. Of the elected members, eight are from the capital and the remaining 38 are two from each of 19 electoral districts (groups of atolls). Women have the right to vote but may not hold office. The members of the Cabinet, appointed by the President, are individually responsible to the *Majlis*. There are no political parties.

In a presidential "referendum" held on July 28, 1978, the sole candidate nominated by the *Majlis* (Maumoun Abdul Gayoom) was, as officially announced, elected with almost 90 per cent of the votes cast.

Mali

Capital: Bamako   Pop. 7,200,000

Since 1968 the Republic of Mali has been ruled by a Military Committee of National Liberation (MCNL) with an executive President (Brig.-Gen. Moussa Traoré), who is head of state and government, as well as secretary-general of the *Union Démocratique du Peuple Malien* (UDPM), the country's sole legal political party. There is an 82-member National Assembly elected for a three-year term by universal adult suffrage on a list of the UDPM. In elections held on June 13, 1982, the list was, as officially stated, approved by 99.92 per cent of the valid votes in a turn-out of 95.89 per cent.

Mali People's Democratic Union
Union Démocratique du Peuple Malien (UDPM)

Leadership. President Moussa Traoré (g.s.)

Founded. March 1979

History. The UDPM was established by the Military Committee of National Liberation (which had seized power in November 1968) as the country's sole legal party. Its tasks were to include the nomination of candidates for presidential and parliamentary elections, as provided for in the country's 1974 Constitution. The decision to establish the UDPM was announced by President Moussa Traoré on Sept. 22, 1976 (the 16th anniversary of the proclamation of independence), as a means of mobilizing all active cadres for the task of strengthening the unity of the nation and building an independent national economy.

President Moussa Traoré has repeatedly promised a return to civilian government but so far this objective has taken the form of the appointment of civilians to the Government. Various opposition groups, both internal and external, have challenged the ascendancy of the UDPM (notably in two attempted coups in October 1978 and December 1980), but the regime has weathered these local difficulties without apparent difficulty.

Structure. The UDPM functions on the principle of democratic centralism. Its supreme organs are a congress and, between congress sessions, its national council of 137 members and a 19-member central executive bureau.

Publications. *La Voix du Peuple* (daily)

Malta

Capital: Valletta   Pop. 330,000

The Republic of Malta is an independent member of the Commonwealth and has a 65-member House of Representatives (*Il-kamra tad-Deputadi*) elected for a five-year term by direct universal suffrage of citizens above the age of 18 years under a single transferable vote system of proportional representation in 13 electoral divisions. The House elects the President of the Republic, also for a five-year term, and he appoints a Prime Minister and, on the latter's advice, other ministers and the judges.

In general elections held on Dec. 12, 1981, the Labour Party gained 34 seats and the Nationalist Party 31 in the House of Representatives.

Communist Party

Address. 205 Old Bakery St., Valletta, Malta

Leadership. Antony Vassallo (s.g.)

Founded. 1968

History. This party has made very little impression on the dominance of the Malta Labour Party as the major left-wing party both in electoral terms and within the Maltese trade union movement.

Orientation. The party was not represented at the 1976 East Berlin conference of European Communist parties and is not associated with any specific tendency within the international Communist movement.

Membership. 150

Publications. *Zminijietna* (Our Times, monthly)

Malta Labour Party (MLP)

Address. Il-Macina, Senglea, Malta

Leadership. Dominic Mintoff (l.); Carmel (Karmenu) Mifsud Bonnici (designate l.); Renald Dalli (pres.); Marie-Louise Coleiro (g.s.)

Founded. 1920

History. In the first elections to a Maltese Legislative Assembly held in October 1947 under a new Constitution (restoring to Malta responsible internal self-government such as it had had in 1921–30) the MLP, then led by Dr Paul Boffa, gained 24 out of the Assembly's 40 seats. A Government formed by Dr Boffa was in office until September 1950. In

October 1949, however, the MLP was split, with Dr Boffa founding a (moderate) Independent Labour Party, which gained 11 seats in the 1950 Assembly elections, seven (as the Malta Workers' Party) in 1951 and three in 1953, whereafter it contested no further elections.

The MLP first gained a majority of seats (23 out of 40) in the Assembly in 1955 and was thereafter in power under Dom Mintoff until 1958, when his Government resigned over a dispute with Britain on Malta's constitutional future. In the 1962 general election the MLP was defeated, gaining only 16 out of 42 seats in Parliament, after the Roman Catholic Church hierarchy had called on the electorate not to vote for the MLP. It was not returned to power until 1971, when it won 28 out of the 55 seats in Parliament, and it has been in government since then. In May 1978 it was officially amalgamated with the (26,000-strong) General Workers' Union.

Returned to power in the December 1981 elections, the MLP came under severe criticism from the opposition Nationalist Party for achieving a parliamentary majority on the strength of fewer popular votes than the Nationalists. After a lengthy constitutional crisis, during which the Nationalists boycotted the House of Representatives, an accommodation was reached in mid-1983 under which the Nationalists resumed parliamentary participation in return for an undertaking from the Labour Government to enter into formal discussions on a revision of electoral arrangements before the next general elections.

Orientation. A democratic and socialist party standing for non-alignment and peaceful co-operation among all states bordering the Mediterranean.

Structure. The party has a 17-member national executive elected by an annual conference

Membership. 20,000

International affiliations. Socialist International

Nationalist Party
Partit Nazzjonalista

Address. 28 Our Lady of Sorrows Street, Pietà, Malta

Leadership. Dr Eduard Fenech Adami (l.); Dr Louis Galea (s.g.)

Founded. 1880

History. The party has its origins in the wave of nationalism which swept Europe in the 19th century and it fought successfully for self-government and later independence. Between 1887 and 1903, when Malta had representative government, the party held all elective seats in the Council of Government. After a period of colonial rule representative government was reintroduced in 1921 and the party held a majority of seats until 1927 (when the Constitutional and Labour parties formed an alliance). When the party regained a majority in 1933, the self-government constitution was revoked.

During World War II several leaders of the party were detained or exiled, but from 1950 to 1955 the party was in government in coalition with the Workers' Party. It later held office from 1962 to 1971 (during which period Malta became independent in 1964).

The party was narrowly defeated by the Labour Party in 1971 and again in 1976. In the elections of Dec. 12, 1981, the party gained 50.9 per cent of the vote but only a minority of seats in the House of Representatives. The party subsequently started a civil disobedience campaign and boycotted sessions of the House until March 29, 1983. A government ban enforced in January 1983 on all contacts between the party and foreign diplomats was condemned by the European Parliament in March 1983.

Orientation. The party "upholds the Christian democratic ideology".

Structure. Sectional committees in towns and villages send representatives to district committees, which in turn send representatives to the general council (the party's highest body, with about 600 members). There is a policy-making executive committee.

Membership. 28,000

Publications. *In-Nazzjon Taghna* (daily), 16,000; *Il-Mument* (weekly), 20,000; *The Democrat* (weekly), 6,000

International affiliations. Christian Democratic International; European Christian Democratic Union; International Democrat Union (associate member); European Democrat Union (permanent observer)

Progressive Constitutional Party (PCP)

Address. 4 Naxxar Road, Birkirkara, Malta

Leadership. Mabel Strickland (l.)

Founded. October 1953

History. The PCP has its origins in the Constitutional Party (CP) founded by Lord Strickland (father of Miss Strickland) in 1921, dissolved in 1941 and re-formed in 1950. This party held four seats in the then Legislative Assembly from 1950 to 1953. The PCP was formed by CP members opposing that party's policy of favouring co-operation with the Malta Labour Party. However, it did not gain representation in Parliament except in 1962–66, when it held one seat.

Orientation. The PCP stands for a viable Maltese economy based on tourism, light industry and ship-repairing, for association with the European Community, and for continued membership of the Commonwealth, a defence treaty with Britain and an agreement with NATO.

Publications. *Forward/Il Quddiem* (fortnightly)

Mauritania

Capital: Nouakchott   Pop. 1,650,000

The Republic of Mauritania (a member of the Arab League) is ruled by a Military Committee of National Salvation (CMSN) of 27 members, headed by a chairman who is President of the Republic (posts held by Lt.-Col. Khouna Ould Haidalla since January 1980). There is also a civilian Council of Ministers headed by a Prime Minister, but there is neither a parliament nor a legal political party. Under a Constitutional Charter published on July 28, 1978, executive power was given to the Chairman of the Military Committee of National Recovery (which was superseded by the CMSN on April 6, 1979); the Charter was to remain effective "until new democratic institutions are established".

On Dec. 19, 1980, the CMSN published a draft Constitution providing inter alia that Mauritania should be "an Islamic, parliamentary, indivisible and democratic republic" with a President elected for a (non-renewable) six-year term and a National Assembly which would be elected for a four-year term. Political parties were to be permitted (although not the Mauritanian People's Party, which had been the country's sole legal party until July 1978). By mid-1984, however, no substantive steps had been taken towards finalizing this draft or implementing its provisions.

Mauritius

Capital: Port Louis   Pop. 1,000,000

Mauritius is an independent state within the Commonwealth, with the British monarch as head of state being represented by a Governor-General. It has a Cabinet under a Prime Minister and a Legislative Assembly of 70 members, 62 of whom are elected in 21 constituencies for a five-year term by universal suffrage of citizens above the age of 18 years, while up to eight are appointed by the Supreme Court from among the unsuccessful candidates with the greatest number of votes.

As a result of elections held on Aug. 21, 1983, the 62 elective seats in the Legislative Assembly were distributed as follows: Mauritian Socialist Movement—Labour Party 37, Mauritian Militant Movement 19, Mauritian Social Democratic Party 4, Organization of the People of Rodrigues 2.

Independence Party—see entries for Independent Forward Bloc, Mauritius Labour Party and Muslim Committee of Action

Independent Forward Bloc

Address. 14 Sookdeo Bissoondoyal St., Port Louis, Mauritius

Leadership. Ramnath Jeetah (l.); G. Gangaram (ch.); W. A. Foondon (sec.)

Founded. April 1958

History. Among the party's founder members was the late Sookdeo Bissoondoyal. who was a member of the Legislative Council and later the Legislative Assembly from 1948 to 1976 and who campaigned for the introduction of universal adult suffrage, which was granted by Britain in 1956. The party, together with the Mauritius Labour Party, advocated full independence for Mauritius, which was attained in March 1968.

From 1964 to 1969 the party was a partner in a coalition Government with the Labour Party and the Muslim Committee of Action, and these three parties together contested the pre-independence 1967 general elections as the Independence Party, gaining 43 of the 70 seats in the Legislative Assembly. The party left the coalition in March 1969 after disagreements with the Labour Party, and it gained no seats in the 1976 general elections nor subsequently.

Sookdeo Bissoondoyal, who was inspired by his elder brother, Prof. B. Bissoondoyal, had led the country to independence step by step. On the eve of the 15th anniversary of independence it was acknowledged that Prof. Bissoondoyal had been the first Mauritian to pronounce the word "Independence".

Structure. The party has an executive guided by representatives of the party's nine districts.

Membership. 60,000

Mauritian Militant Movement
Mouvement Militant Mauricien (MMM)

Leadership. Paul Bérenger (l.); D. Fokeer (pres.); Ponapar Naiker (s.g.)

Founded. 1970

History. The MMM was officially held responsible for serious labour unrest in 1971, which led to the proclamation of a state of emergency in December of that year, and to government action against MMM members and trade unions controlled by the MMM. In the 1976 general elections, however, the MMM emerged as the strongest party with 34 out of 70 seats in Parliament (though its strength was later reduced to 32 by two defections to the Labour Party). The MMM nevertheless remained in opposition to a coalition Government formed by the Labour-led Independence Party and the Mauritian Social Democratic Party. In municipal elections in April 1977 the MMM gained control of three (out of five) towns, including Port Louis. In 1978 and 1979 the MMM was again involved in serious labour unrest.

In general elections held on June 11, 1982, the MMM, then in alliance with the *Parti Socialiste Mauricien* (PSM), gained 42 of the elective seats in the Legislative Assembly. It subsequently formed a coalition Government with the PSM (which had won 18 seats). In March 1983, however, Paul Bérenger (the founder of the MMM and then its secretary-general, and also Minister of Finance) and eight other MMM ministers (as well as two from the PSM) resigned from the Government over a dispute concerning the status of the Creole language (which Bérenger and his supporters wanted to make the official language of Mauritius, in place of English).

A new Government formed by Aneerood Jugnauth (then president of the MMM and Prime Minister), however, did not command a majority in the Assembly. The MMM expelled Jugnauth and his colleagues from the party, and he thereupon founded the Mauritian Socialist Movement (see separate entry). In the ensuing general elections of Aug. 21, 1983, the MMM was reduced to 19 of the 62 elective seats.

Orientation. This Marxist party has declared its ultimate object as being the introduction of self-managing socialism in stages. In 1982 it proposed selective nationalization, an expanded welfare state, a job creation scheme, a wealth tax, a drive against tax and customs duty evasion, and in foreign affairs strict non-alignment and the restoration to Mauritian sovereignty of Diego Garcia (currently part of the British Indian Ocean Territory), as well as republican status for Mauritius. In September 1982, however, Paul Bérenger stated that the country would first of all have to meet the conditions of the International Monetary Fund to achieve a revival of the economy.

Mauritian Social Democratic Party
Parti Mauricien Social Démocrate (PMSD)

Address. P.O. Box 599, Port Louis, Mauritius

Leadership. Sir Gaëtan Duval (l.); Deoraj Ram (pres.); J.C. Philibert (s.g.)

History. The PMSD held three seats in the Legislative Assembly elected in 1959, eight in that elected in 1963, and 23 in the Parliament elected in 1967. It took part in a Government of national unity in 1969-73 when its leader was Minister of External Affairs, Tourism and Emigration. Its departure from the coalition in December 1973 followed reports of serious disagreement between Gaëtan Duval and the Prime Minister over the former's desire to pursue a policy of dialogue with South Africa. Duval was also Mayor of Port Louis until 1977.

The PMSD was a coalition partner of the Independence Party alliance led by the Mauritius Labour Party from December 1976 to June 1982. In the elections held in the latter month it gained no elective seats but was given two filled by appointees. In the 1983 elections, in which it supported the Mauritian Socialist Movement—Labour Party alliance, it gained four seats and was given a ministerial post in the Government which was subsequently formed by the alliance partners.

Orientation. The PMSD is an anti-communist, pro-Western party, representing mainly the Franco-Mauritian and Creole middle class.

International affiliations. Socialist Inter-African

Mauritian Socialist Movement
Mouvement Socialiste Mauricien (MSM)

Leadership. Aneerood Jugnauth (l.)
Founded. April 8, 1983
History. This party broke away from the Mauritian Militant Movement (MMM), of which Aneerood Jugnauth had been president. He had also been the head of a coalition Government formed after the MMM's victory in the general elections of 1982. The other partner in this coalition had been the *Parti Socialiste Mauricien* (PSM), which had, under the leadership of Harish Boodhoo, broken away from the Labour Party in 1979. The coalition Government, however, lost its majority in the Legislative Assembly in March 1983 over the issue of making Creole the country's official language (as proposed by a section of the MMM). After the PSM had joined the newly-formed MSM, the ensuing elections of Aug. 21, 1983, were contested by the MSM in alliance with the Mauritius Labour Party; this alliance gained 37 of the 62 elective seats in the Assembly, and it thereupon formed a Government led by Jugnauth.

Orientation. The MSM's orientation is socialist, with a similar ideology as that of

the MMM. On becoming Prime Minister again in 1983 Jugnauth called for a constitutional amendment to make Mauritius a republic within the Commonwealth.

Mauritius Democratic Union
Union Démocratique Mauricienne (UDM)

Address. 10 Barracks St., Port Louis, Mauritius
Leadership. Guy Ollivry (l.) Germain Comarmond (s.g.)
Founded. November 1970
History. The party was founded by former members of the Mauritian Social Democratic Party (PMSD) who opposed what they regarded as the movement to the right of the coalition Government formed in 1969 by the PMSD and the Independence Party. The party failed to win any seats in subsequent elections.

Orientation. The aims of the party include a system of parliamentary democracy based on proportional representation and an economic system based on workers' co-ownership of the capital of all enterprises and the development of the co-operative movement in sectors where co-ownership of capital is inapplicable.

Structure. The party has a leader, a 12-member executive committee and branches throughout the country, with a national convention being held every year.

Mauritius Labour Party (MLP)

Address. 7 Guy Rozemont Square, Port Louis, Mauritius
Leadership. Sir Seewoosagur Ramgoolam (l.); Harry Boolack (ch.); James Burty David (g.s.)
History. The MLP was in power (partly in coalition with smaller parties) throughout the process leading Mauritius in stages to internal self-government and eventual independence. In the Legislative Assembly set up under the 1947 Constitution it held 14 out of the 19 elective seats; in elections held in 1959 it gained 23 (out of 40) seats; and in 1963 it retained 19 of these seats. Its leader, who had become the island's first Chief Minister in 1961, formed an all-party Government in November 1963. In the 1967 pre-independence elections the MLP, together with the Muslim Committee of Action and the Independent Forward Bloc, formed an alliance known as the Independence Party, which obtained 43 of the 70 seats in a new Legislative Assembly elected in August 1967 under a new

Constitution. The alliance lost its majority in the 1976 elections but remained in power in coalition with the Mauritian Social Democratic Party (PMSD), with which it had earlier been in coalition in 1969-73. In the June 1982 elections it gained none of the elective seats but was given two of those filled by appointees. It was thereafter in opposition until August 1983, when it contested the elections in alliance with the Mauritian Socialist Movement (MSM—see separate entry). This alliance gained 37 of the elective seats in the Assembly; it was also supported by the PMSD (which obtained four seats) and was given five additional seats filled by appointees. It thereupon joined a new coalition Government led by the leader of the MSM, incumbent Prime Minister Aneerood Jugnauth.

Orientation. The MLP has been dominated by Hindu Indians (making up 52 per cent of the population, against 17 per cent Moslem Indians or Pakistanis, 3 per cent Chinese and 28 per cent Whites, Blacks and Creoles). It has claimed to represent all shades of opinion, although its basic orientation is democratic socialist. It has generally been pro-Western.

International affiliations. Socialist International; Socialist Inter-African

---

Mauritius People's Progressive Party

Address. 38 Sir William Newton St., Port Louis, Mauritius

Leadership. T. Sibsurun (s.g.)

Orientation. This party is a left-wing formation standing for the demilitarization of the Indian Ocean region.

International affiliations. Afro-Asian People's Solidarity Organization

---

Muslim Committee of Action
Comité d'Action Musulman (CAM)

Address. c/o Secretary General, P.O. Box 882, Port Louis, Mauritius

Leadership. Razack Peeroo (ch.); Raouf Bundhun (s.g.)

Founded. 1958

History. Founded with a view to fighting for constitutional safeguards and parliamentary representation for minorities, especially the Muslim community, the Committee was in electoral alliance with the ruling Labour Party in 1958-82 (this alliance being known as the Independence Party since 1967) and was represented in Parliament and in the Government from 1959 to 1982.

Orientation. This formation seeks to fight for the rights of the Muslim community (constituting about 17 per cent of the population of Mauritius).

Structure. There is a central executive committee, with the secretary being the chief executive. There are also regional committees throughout the country.

Membership. 4,000

Organization of the People of Rodrigues
Organisation du Peuple Rodriguais (OPR)

History. The OPR won the two elective seats of the island of Rodrigues in both the June 1982 and the August 1983 elections to the Legislative Assembly. Before the 1982 elections the OPR had declared that it would support the alliance of the Mauritian Militant Movement (MMM) and the *Parti Socialiste Mauricien* (PSM). In the Government formed after the 1983 elections the OPR was given the portfolio of Rodrigues and the Outer Islands.

Republican Centre Party
Parti du Centre Républicain

Address. 17 Jules Koenig Street, Port Louis, Mauritius

Leadership. France Vallet (pres. & l.); Jean Claude Nourainsing (sec.)

Founded. September 1971

History. The party was formed out of opposition to the formation of a coalition Government and the postponement, in November 1969, of general elections (last held in 1967) until 1976. It charged the Governor-General, the Prime Minister and the Speaker of the Legislative Assembly with "flouting the letter and spirit of the Constitution of Mauritius". This charge was allowed on appeal to the Privy Council, but it remained ineffectual as the Government subsequently amended the Constitution.

Orientation. This party is "democratic, moderate, anti-communist and opposed to pressure groups from both capitalist and third-world countries".

Structure. The party has a supreme national congress (meeting periodically); a national committee of up to 35 members which elects a leaders' committee of five to seven members; and 21 area committees to which each party branch elects nine members.

302

Mexico

Capital: Mexico City   Pop. 77,000,000

The United Mexican States are a federal republic consisting of 31 states and a federal district (around the capital), with an executive President who is elected by universal adult suffrage for a six-year term and who heads a Cabinet. There is a bicameral National Congress consisting of (i) a Federal Chamber of Deputies of 400 members elected by universal adult suffrage for three years, 300 of them by majority vote in single-member districts and the other 100 by proportional representation, and (ii) a 64-member Senate (comprising two senators for each state and for the federal district), also elected by universal adult suffrage for three years. Each state has a governor elected for six years and a Chamber of Deputies elected for three years. For each deputy and senator a substitute is also elected.

To qualify for taking part in elections a party must have been active for four years and must have at least 65,000 members, of whom at least 3,000 must be resident in each of half the states. A new party may gain temporary recognition but must obtain at least 1.5 per cent of the total national vote to retain its recognition. No candidate can stand for office unless he has a party affiliation. Parties receive some official assistance for congressional elections (including free postage and telegraph services in proportion to their total previous vote, and also equal television and radio time).

In the elections to the Federal Chamber of Deputies held on July 4, 1982, the ruling Institutional Revolutionary Party (PRI) gained 299 of the 300 seats filled by majority vote, the remaining seat going to the National Action Party (PAN); the 100 seats filled by proportional representation were distributed as follows; PAN 54, United Socialist Party of Mexico (PSUM) 17, Popular Socialist Party (PPS) 11, Socialist Workers' Party (PST) 10, Mexican Democratic Party (PDM) 8. Presidential elections held on the same day were won by the PRI candidate, Miguel de la Madrid Hurtado, who received the support of the PPS and the Authentic Party of the Mexican Revolution (PARM).

Authentic Party of the Mexican Revolution
Partido Auténtico de la Revolución Mexicana (PARM)

Address. Rio Nazas 168, Mexico D.F., Mexico

Leadership. Jesús Guzmán Rubio (pres.); Prof. Rubén Rodríguez Lozano (s.g.)

Founded. March 1954

History. The party was formed by a dissident faction of the Institutional Revolutionary Party claiming to represent the political and social demands of the 1910 revolution. Since 1954 it has contested all federal, state and municipal elections, campaigning against "exploitation and injustice, for the citizen's rights and freedoms, for economic development and social justice against misery and ignorance, for the sovereignty and self-determination of all nations and against all forms of dictatorship". The party gained only one seat in the Federal Chamber of Deputies in elections held for 162 seats in 1958 and five seats (out of 210) in 1964. By 1979 it held 10 seats in the Federal Chamber.

In the July 1982 elections PARM supported the presidential candidate of the ruling Institutional Revolutionary Party but gained only 1.1 per cent of the vote and no seat in the Chamber of Deputies;

it consequently lost its registration as a party.

Orientation. The PARM is a right-wing party standing for "the implementation of the social, economic and cultural principles and postulates of the Mexican revolution."

Structure. The PARM has an eight-member supreme presidium, a national executive committee of 21 members and 21 secretaries, and committees at state, district and municipal level.

Membership. 191,500
Publications. *El Auténtico*

Community Action
Acción Comunitaria (Acomac)

History. Acomac was officially registered as a national political association in December 1978.

Orientation. Its aim is "to promote progressive social change" to allow "better application of collective justice".

Institutional Revolutionary Party
Partido Revolucionario Institucional (PRI)

Address. Insurgente Norte 61, C.P. 06350, Mexico D.F., Mexico
Leadership. Adolfo Lugo (pres.); Mario Vargas (s.g.)
Founded. March 4, 1929
History. The PRI was founded as the *Partido Revolucionario Nacional*, which was renamed the *Partido de la Revolución Mexicano* in 1938; the party assumed its present name in 1946. It began as a coalition of local and state groups, which had their roots in the revolutionary period from 1910 to 1917, and it developed a broad base in the labour, agrarian and "popular" sectors.

The PRI has dominated Mexico's political life from its foundation, consistently winning overwhelming majorities in the National Congress and automatically securing the election of its candidate to the presidency (e.g. with 74.4 per cent of the vote in July 1982). Competition within the PRI for congressional and presidential nominations ensures that the Mexican system remains pluralist, despite the dominance of the party in actual elections.

Orientation. As a moderate left-wing party the PRI has covered a wide spectrum of opinion from conservative to moderate socialist policies, with its successive leaders, as Presidents of the Republic, representing varying factions. The PRI has notably

conducted an independent foreign policy, playing a leading role in the Third World and among non-aligned nations.

Publications. *La República; Linea*

Mexican Democratic Party
Partido Demócrata Mexicano (PDM)

Address. Edison 89, Colonia Tabacalera México 1, D.F., Mexico
Leadership. Gumersindo Magaña Negrete (pres.); Roberto Picón Robledo (organization sec.)
Founded. May 1971
History. Between May 1971 and May 1975 the party held 22 constituent assemblies in the country's states and by 1979 it had committees in all 28 states. In May 1978 the PDM was allowed to register as a political party on condition that it gained at least 1.5 per cent of the vote in the July 1979 congressional elections, which it did (obtaining 10 seats in the Chamber of Deputies under the proportional representation arrangement).

In the July 1982 elections the PDM's presidential candidate obtained 1.9 per cent of the vote and the party retained eight seats in the Chamber.

Orientation. Opposed to both fascism and communism, the PDM stands for "integral and humanist democracy", a pluralist government, the rejection of both capitalism and Marxism, reforms under which workers would become owners or joint owners of the enterprises in which they worked, and protection of the family.

Structure. The party has a national congress, a 20-member national consultative body, an elective college consisting of a national committee and state party presidents, and a national executive committee. It is organized at local, district and state level.

Membership. 450,000
Publications. *El Demócrata* (official organ), 30,000

Mexican Workers' Party
Partido Mexicano de los Trabajadores (PMT)

Address. Bucareli 20, sexto y octavo piso, Mexico 1, D.F., Mexico
Leadership. Heberto Castillo (pres.); José Alvarez Icaza (sec.)
Founded. September 1977
History. The party has taken no part in government, alliances or coalitions. It regards political power in Mexico as being

"monopolized by the party of the national oligarchy" (i.e. the Institutional Revolutionary Party) and the electoral law as "anti-democratic and anti-constitutional". The PMT has concentrated on "defending the nation's human and material resources, especially those of energy"; it has worked among the "exploited and oppressed" workers and peasants of Mexico. The PMT is not registered, since it failed to obtain the minimum 1.5 per cent of the total vote in the 1979 congressional elections.

Orientation. The PMT is a leftist (but not pro-Cuban) formation whose aim is to replace Mexico's economic, political and social structure by one in which the means of production are owned by society; it seeks a "people's democracy" and a society based on equality and justice without discrimination or privilege. The PMT is committed to fighting to attain power by all means at its disposal.

Structure. The party's highest organ is the national assembly (ordinarily convened every three years and composed of delegates from all state, municipal or base committees). There is a national plenum consisting of a nine-member national committee and the chairmen of the state (or federal district) committees. There are assemblies and committees at state, municipal and base level (with base committees having at least three members at places of work, in residential areas or in schools).

Membership. 20,000
Publications. *Insurgencia Popular* (monthly official organ), 10,000

National Action Party
Partido Acción Nacional (PAN)

Address. Angel Urraza No. 812, Col. del Valle, México D.F. 03109, Mexico
Leadership. Abel Vicencio Tovar (pres.); Bernardo Rátiz Vázquez (sec.)
Founded. September 1939
History. Founded as "the only independent opposition party in Mexico", the PAN has taken part in elections for Congress since 1943, for local government since 1946 and for the presidency since 1952, although it did not officially contest the 1976 presidential elections. In the July 1982 presidential elections the PAN candidate, Pablo Emilio Madero, obtained some 3,700,000 votes or 16.4 per cent of the total. Since 1958 the PAN has, in national elections, maintained its position as the strongest of the opposition parties.

Orientation. The PAN is a social Christian formation, standing for democratic principles, human rights, common welfare and "the establishment of a democratic and solidaristic government".

Structure. The PAN has committees and assemblies at district level, committees and councils at state level, and a national committee, a national council, a national assembly and a national convention.

Membership. 500,000
Publications. *La Nación,* 100,000

Popular Socialist Party
Partido Popular Socialista (PPS)

Address. Avda. Alvaro Obregón No. 185, Col. Roma, Cuauhtémoc 06977, D.F., Mexico
Leadership. Jorge Cruickshank García (s.g.)
Founded. June 1948
History. A call for the formation of a Popular Party was first made at an anti-Franco meeting in Mexico City on July 18, 1946, by Vicente Lombardo Toledano (vice-president of the World Federation of Trade Unions and president of the Workers' Federation of Latin America), and this led to the holding of a constitutional assembly of the party on June 20, 1948.

After unsuccessfully contesting the 1952 presidential elections, the party decided in October 1960 to become a party of the proletariat with a Leninist structure; it thereupon assumed the name of PPS. In 1964 it gained 10 seats in the Federal Chamber of Deputies. In the 1976 presidential elections it supported the successful candidate, José López Portillo, of the ruling Institutional Revolutionary Party (PRI). In congressional elections held at the same time the PPS gained about 1,000,000 votes, its leader becoming the first opposition candidate to win a Senate seat since 1929.

In the 1979 congressional elections the PPS gained 11 seats in the Chamber. In the 1982 elections the PPS supported the (successful) presidential candidate of the PRI, who agreed to an accord of 13 essential points with the PPS. As no Mexican parliamentarian may hold his seat for two successive terms, Jorge Cruickshank (elected to the Senate in 1976) left that House but won a seat in the Chamber of Deputies in 1982, when the party retained its 11 seats.

Orientation. The PPS proclaims itself a "working-class party based on Marxism-Leninism with the object of building socialism in Mexico, developing the Mexican revolution through the unity of the patriotic and democratic forces to confront North American imperialism and the country's oligarchic bourgeoisie".

Structure. The PPS is based on demo-
.:ratic centralism, with base units of three
or more members at places of work
or residence, which elect delegates to
municipal, state and national assemblies.
The national assembly is the party's highest
organ; it meets every three years and
elects a central committee, which meets
every six months and which elects a
national leadership and its secretary-general, and which is the party's permanent
organ. Prospective members have to be
candidate members for at least six months.

Publications. *Nueva Democracía*
(quarterly theoretical review), 5,000; *El
Combatiente* (weekly political and theoretical information organ), 25,000

Revolutionary Party of Workers
Partido Revolucionario de Trabajadores
(PRT)

Leadership. (Sra) Rosario Ibarra de la
Piedra

History. The PRT contested the general
elections in 1982, when its presidential
candidate (Sra Ibarra de la Piedra) gained
1.9 per cent of the total vote, but the
party obtained no seat in Congress.

Orientation. The PRT is a Trotskyist
formation.

Social Democratic Party
Partido Social Democrata (PSD)

Leadership. Manuel Moreno Sánchez
(l.)

History. The PSD contested the 1982
elections but its presidential candidate
(Manuel Moreno Sánchez) obtained only
0.2 per cent of the total vote and the
party gained no seat in Congress. It
consequently lost its official registration.

Socialist Workers' Party
Partido Socialista de los Trabajadores (PST)

Address. Avda. Mexico 199, Col.
Hipódromo-Condesa, 06170 Mexico D.F.,
Mexico

Leadership. Rafael Aguilar Talamantes
(pres.); Graco Ramírez Abreu (s.g.)

Founded. July 1973

History. The PST was founded as a
break-away group of a "1968 Movement",
which had been led by the present leaders
of the Mexican Workers' Party (see

separate entry) and had been involved in
the 1968 student unrest. It late. accepted
a number of former left-wing guerrillas as
members, and in June 1977 it was reported
to have formed a National Assembly of
Forces of the Left as a loose alliance with
the Movement of Socialist Action and
Unity (MAUS) and a Communist splinter
group, with the object of obtaining government recognition as a legal political party.

The PST obtained temporary official
registration in May 1978, and full registration after it had been given 10 seats in
the Chamber of Deputies (under the
proportional representation arrangement)
as a result of the 1979 elections. In the
1982 elections its presidential candidate
(Candido Diaz Cerecedo) obtained 1.5 per
cent of the vote and the party 11 seats in
the Chamber.

Orientation. The PST, a Marxist-Leninist formation, stands for "the union
of scientific socialism with the workers'
movement and the people themselves";
free unions; the nationalization of all
foreign companies and banks; government
control of basic industries and natural
resources, and government monopoly in
foreign trade; collectivization of land;
democratization of teaching; and a general
amnesty for political prisoners.

Structure. The PST has a national
assembly, national council of leaders,
central committee, political commission
and executive commission.

Membership. 132,000

Publications. *El Insurgente Socialista*
(central committee organ); *El Eslabon*
(internal bulletin)

Unification and Progress
Unificación y Progreso (UPAC)

History. UPAC was officially registered
as a national political association in
December 1978.

Orientation. UPAC's aim is "to recover
the true ideals of Mexican social liberalism".

Unified Socialist Party of Mexico
Partido Socialista Unificado de México
(PSUM)

Address. Monterrey 159, Colonia
Roma, 06 700 México D.F., Mexico

Leadership. Pablo Gómez Alvarez (s.g.)

Founded. November 1981

History. The PSUM was formed by a
merger of five left-wing revolutionary
organizations—the Mexican Communist
Party (founded in November 1919); the
Mexican People's Party (which arose out

306

of a breakaway, in 1976, of left-wing elements from the pro-government Popular Socialist Party); the Revolutionary Socialist Party (which had replaced the earlier Movement of Socialist Organization formed in 1974); the Movement of Socialist Action and Unity (founded in 1969); and the Popular Action Movement (formed in January 1981 by intellectuals and trade unionists).

The PSUM seeks to link the ideas of past Mexican revolutions with the theory of scientific socialism and describes itself as the product of a merger of various currents of the workers' and revolutionary movement in Mexico. In the 1979 federal elections the PSUM partners (except the Popular Action Movement) had obtained 703,000 votes and 18 seats in the Chamber of Deputies. For the 1982 elections the PSUM was allied with the small (Trotskyist) Socialist Workers' Party (see separate entry) and the leftist Socialist Current, obtaining 17 seats in the Chamber and 3.7 per cent of the votes for its presidential candidate, Arnaldo Martínez Verdugo.

Orientation. The aim of the PSUM is socialist revolution defined as "a new political, economic and cultural revolution" which would bring the working class and its allies to power and would be the start of "a new society based on the labour of its partners and in which wealth would be the property of society". The party's programme accordingly calls for the nationalization of basic industries, banks, land, the media, transport and the public services essential for the country's economic development.

Structure. The PSUM accepts the principle of democratic centralism. Its highest authority is the national congress (held every three years), which elects a central committee which leads the party between congress sessions and in turn nominates a 17-member political commission.

Membership. 600,000 (August 1983)

Publications. *Así Es* (weekly); *Boletín del Grupo Parlamentario* (bimonthly); *Memoria* (bimonthly)

International affiliations. The PSUM describes itself as both patriotic and internationalist; it forms part of the international Communist movement but seeks to maintain close relations with all democratic and revolutionary movements in the world. The party is recognized by the Soviet-bloc Communist parties.

Unity of the Communist Left
Unidad de Izquierda Comunista (UIC)

Founded. 1973

History. The UIC is a breakaway group of the Mexican Communist Party (PCM). It was officially registered as a national political association in December 1978.

Orientation. The UIC supports Soviet communism and, in the short run, "the fight for political power for the workers and the people of Mexico and participation of the working classes and democratic forces in government at all levels".

Monaco

Capital: Monaco-Ville   Pop. 30,000

The Principality of Monaco is an hereditary monarchy in which legislative power is exercised jointly by the Prince and an 18-member National Council. The National Council is elected for a five-year term by universal suffrage of citizens by birth above the age of 25 years under a system of proportional representation, with the whole country being one constituency, and with an absolute majority— not less than a quarter of the registered voters—being required on a first ballot and a simple majority in a second ballot. Executive power is held jointly by the Prince and a Council of Government.

In elections held in January 1983 all 18 seats on the National Council were won by the National and Democratic Union.

Democratic Union Movement
Mouvement Union Démocratique (MUD)

History. The MUD first contested elections in 1973, when it won one seat in the National Council. It was unsuccessful in the 1978 and 1983 elections.
Orientation. The MUD is a communist formation with a trade union base.

Monaco Action
Action Monégasque

History. The party first contested elections in 1973, when it gained one seat in the National Council. It did not contest the 1978 elections.
Orientation. Liberal.

Monaco Socialist Party
Parti Socialiste Monégasque (PSM)

History. The PSM unsuccessfully contested the 1978 and 1983 elections to the National Council.

National and Democratic Union
Union Nationale et Démocratique (UND)

Leadership. Jean-Charles Rey (l.)
Founded. 1962
History. The UND was formed by a merger of the previous *Union Nationale des Indépendants* and the *Entente Nationale Démocratique*, and it has held all 18 seats in the National Council except between 1973 and 1978, when two seats were held by two opposition parties. Jean-Charles Rey (the UND leader) is President of the National Council.
Orientation. The UND supports the policies of the reigning Prince.

Mongolia

Capital: Ulan Bator   Pop. 1,773,000

The Mongolian People's Republic is "a sovereign democratic state of working people" in which "supreme state power" is vested in the People's Great *Hural* (Assembly) elected for a four-year term by universal adult suffrage of citizens above the age of 18 years (on single-candidate lists for each district). Effective political power is held by the (Communist) Mongolian People's Revolutionary Party (MPRP), the First Secretary of whose Central Committee is head of state and Chairman of the Assembly's Presidium. There is also a Council of Ministers as the country's highest executive power.

In elections held in June 1981 the Assembly's 370 seats were filled by candidates elected unopposed from lists of the MPRP and of a "non-party bloc" which, as officially stated, obtained 99.9 per cent of the votes.

Mongolian People's Revolutionary Party (MPRP)
Mongol Ardyn Khuv'sgalt Nam

Address. Ulan Bator, Mongolia
Leadership. Yumjaagiyn Tsedenbal (first sec.); Bat-ochiryn Altangerel, Jambyn Batmönh, Bugyn Dejid, Damdiny Gombojav, Sampilyn Jalan-Aajav, Damdinjavyn Maydar, Demchigiyn Molomjamts, Tümenbayaryn Ragchaa (other full members of Politburo)
Founded. March 1921
History. The MPRP was originally a broad front of forces opposed to the restoration of Chinese suzerainty over Outer Mongolia in 1919, these forces succeeding, with Soviet assistance, in establishing independence in 1921. It was not until 1934 that the Communist-dominated faction in the MPRP gained the ascendancy, and until 1952 the party was led by Marshal Choybalsan, who had fought against the Chinese for Mongolia's independence. Since 1952 the MPRP has been led by Marshal Tsedenbal, while MPRP leaders attempting to replace him were expelled from the party in 1962–63.
Orientation. The party has close links with the Soviet Communist Party and has

taken Moscow's side in the Sino-Soviet dispute.

Structure. The MPRP has general meetings for branch organizations (at least once a month); conferences for regional, city or district organizations (not less than every two or three years); and a congress for the whole party (held at least every five years). The congress elects a central committee and, between the latter's plenary meetings, party activities are guided by a political bureau and a secretariat.

Membership. 76,000
Publications. *Ünen* (Truth, daily organ of central committee), 113,000; *Namyn Amyidral* (Party Life, central committee's political and theoretical monthly), 25,000; *Ediin Zasgiin Asuudal* (Economic Problems, political and economic journal of central committee, every two months), 25,000; *Ukhunlagch* (Agitator, central committee journal), 40,000

Morocco

Capital: Rabat   Pop. 23,000,000

The Kingdom of Morocco is "a sovereign Moslem state" and "a constitutional democratic and social (hereditary) monarchy", with the King appointing, and presiding over, a Cabinet. There is a unicameral Chamber of Representatives, whose 267 members (including three from the Moroccan-occupied Western Sahara) are elected for a six-year term—178 of them by direct universal adult suffrage of citizens of 21 years or older and in single-member constituencies, and 89 by an electoral college consisting of communal and municipal councillors and representatives of professional bodies and employees' organizations.

Following elections held on June 3 and 21, 1977, seats in the then 264-member Chamber were distributed as follows: Independents (Royalists) 141 (who were organized in the National Rally of Independents in October 1978), Independence Party *(Istiqlal)* 49, Popular Movement 44, Socialist Union of Popular Forces (USFP) 16, *Union Marocaine du Travail* (UMT) 6, Constitutional and Democratic Popular Movement (MPCD) 3, Party of Action (PA) 2, the (Communist) Party of Progress and Socialism (PPS) 1, *Union Générale des Travailleurs Marocains* (UGTM) 1, non-party member 1.

New parliamentary elections due on Sept. 2, 1983, were in July 1983 postponed until after the holding of a proposed referendum on the future of Western Sahara (of which Morocco had taken control between 1975 and 1979).

Constitutional and Democratic Popular Movement
Mouvement Populaire Constitutionnel et Démocratique (MPCD)

Leadership. Abdelkrim Khatib (l.)
Founded. 1966
History. The MPCD broke away from the Popular Movement in 1966, claiming to have a broader base in urban areas. It gained 452 seats (out of some 13,500) in the 1976 communal elections and three seats in the Chamber of Representatives in the 1977 general elections (in which its share of the vote was 2.03 per cent). Although it has taken no part in government, the MPCD in March 1979 accepted representation, through its leader, in a 10-member Defence Council established by King Hassan to act with the Government on questions of national security and territorial integrity, with particular reference to the Western Sahara question (on which there has been very little policy difference between the Moroccan parties notwithstanding their clashes on other issues).

Orientation. The MPCD is conservative and royalist.
Publications. *Al Maghreb Al Arabi*

Constitutional Union
Union Constitutionelle (UC)

Leadership. Maati Bouabid (l.)
Founded. March 1983
History. This Union was formed by Maati Bouabid, who had been a leading member of the (moderate socialist) National Union of Popular Forces (UNFP). However, after he had in October 1977 been appointed Minister of Justice in a Government of National Unity (although his party was not represented in Parliament) the UNFP disowned him for having accepted government office. In March 1979 he became Prime Minister (while retaining the Justice portfolio until November 1981, when he surrendered it but remained Prime Minister). As such he launched the UC as a constitutionalist party. In municipal elections held on June 10, 1983, the UC took second place with 17.59 per cent of the total vote. In a new national coalition Government formed on Nov. 30, 1983, Maati Bouabid became Minister of State without portfolio.

Independence Party
Istiqlal

Leadership. Mohammed Boucetta (g.s.)
Founded. 1943
History. *Istiqlal* was the leading political force in Morocco before independence (achieved in 1956). The party took part in government, together with independents and others, from 1956 to 1963. In 1959 it was divided into two factions with its left-wing faction subsequently forming the National Union of Popular Forces (UNPF). In the 1963 elections to the 144-member House of Representatives *Istiqlal* gained 41 seats, becoming the second strongest party in the House; the result was, however, contested by *Istiqlal*, which boycotted subsequent local elections.

In July 1970 *Istiqlal* and the UNFP, while retaining their separate identities, formed a National Front with the object of achieving political, economic and social democracy based on land reform and the nationalization of the key sectors of the economy. Like the UNFP, *Istiqlal* officially boycotted the 1970 parliamentary elections, but nine of the 240 members of the Chamber of Representatives were later described as *Istiqlal* followers. In the 1976 communal elections *Istiqlal* gained 2,184 seats out of some 13,500.

Following the 1977 parliamentary elections *Istiqlal*, as the second strongest party in the Chamber of Representatives, joined a Government of National Unity with five

ministers and three secretaries of state. It also provided two representatives on a 10-member Defence Council set up by King Hassan in March 1979. It has remained in the Government since then. In municipal elections held on June 10, 1983, it came third with 16.77 per cent of the total vote.
Orientation. Originally a conservative nationalist movement, *Istiqlal* later adopted a reformist attitude.
Publications. *Al Alam* (daily); *L'Opinion* (daily)
International affiliations. Socialist Inter-African

Liberal Progressive Party
Parti Libéral Progressiste (PLP)

Leadership. Aknoush Ahmadou Belhaj
Founded. 1974
History. The PLP was established as an association of wealthy landowners and merchants. In the 1976 communal elections it gained only five seats and it is currently unrepresented in Parliament.
Orientation. The PLP stands for the freedom of the individual, free enterprise and the protection of land ownership.
Publications. *Al Adala* (sporadic)

National Democratic Party (NDP)
Parti National Démocratique

Leadership. Mohammed Arsalane Al-Jadidi (s.g.)
Founded. April 1981
History. This party was founded as the Democratic Independents, a group which, under the leadership of Abdelhamid Kacemi, broke away from the National Rally of Independents (RNI). By November 1981 this group commanded 61 seats in the Chamber of Representatives (leaving the RNI with 79 seats). Constituted as the NDP, the party held its first congress on June 11–13, 1982, when Mohammed Arsalane Al-Jadidi (who was Minister of Labour and National Revival) called on the 6,000 members present to make the NDP an effective counterweight to the traditional parties, which (he claimed) the RNI had failed to be. In municipal elections held on June 10, 1983, the NDP gained 11.72 per cent of the total vote (taking sixth place). In the national coalition Government formed on Nov. 30, 1983, the NDP leader was appointed a Minister of State without portfolio.
Orientation. The party has undertaken to work within the framework of the

constitutional monarchy, to support the democratic process, to defend Morocco's territorial integrity and to reduce social and economic disparities between people and regions.

National Rally of Independents
Rassemblement National des Indépendants (RNI)

Leadership. Ahmed Osman
Founded. October 1978
History. The RNI was set up by its leader (then Prime Minister) in order to give cohesion to the independents, who were the King's supporters and by far the largest group in Parliament and in the country, where they had in 1976 gained 8,607 out of some 13,500 seats in communal elections. The RNI provided two representatives on a 10-member Defence Council set up by King Hassan in March 1979.

While 141 RNI members were sitting in the Chamber of Representatives after the party's formation in 1978, their number was reduced by the creation of the National Democratic Party (see separate entry) in April 1981. In the June 1983 municipal elections the RNI took fourth place with 14.12 per cent of the total vote. In the national coalition Government formed on Nov. 30, 1983, its leader became a Minister of State without portfolio.

Orientation. Royalist, the RNI is essentially a political vehicle for King Hassan.

Publications. *Al Maghrib; Al Mithaq Al Watani*

National Union of Popular Forces
Union Nationale des Forces Populaires (UNFP)

Address. B.P. 747, Casablanca, Morocco
Leadership. Moulay Abdullah Ibrahim
Founded. September 1959
History. As a continuation of the liberation movement which led to Morocco's attainment of independence in 1956, the UNFP was set up in 1959 as the progressive wing of the nationalist movement which had until then been organized in the *Istiqlal*. In December 1962 the UNFP boycotted the referendum on a new Constitution on the grounds that the latter was being "imposed from above". In the 1963 parliamentary elections the UNFP gained 28 out of 144 seats (or 22.28 per cent of the votes).

The party boycotted local elections held the same year and most of its leaders were, shortly before these elections, arrested for allegedly plotting against the state. Of these leaders 11 were subsequently sentenced to death and others to imprisonment, but all were amnestied in April 1965 except those sentenced in absentia. These included the party's leader, Mehdi Ben Barka, who disappeared in Paris in October 1965 and was presumed to have been murdered.

In the same year (1965) a state of emergency was declared and Parliament was dissolved. When the state of emergency was lifted in 1970 and a new Constitution was announced, the UNFP formed a National Front with *Istiqlal* and boycotted the referendum on the Constitution. The National Front also boycotted a referendum on a further new Constitution in March 1972.

In communal elections held in 1976 UNFP candidates obtained 113 seats (out of some 13,500) although the party did not officially take part in these elections. It also boycotted the 1977 parliamentary elections, but the *Union Marocaine du Travail*, with which the UNFP has strong ties, gained six seats in the elections. Maati Bouabid, a leading member of the UNFP, was in October 1977 appointed Minister of Justice in the Government of National Unity (although the UNFP was not represented in Parliament), and in March 1979 he was appointed Prime Minister (while retaining the Justice portfolio). The UNFP subsequently disowned him and also refused to participate in a 10-member Defence Council set up by King Hassan in March 1979. Maati Bouabid later formed a new party called the Constitutional Union (see separate entry).

Having remained outside Parliament, the UNFP also boycotted the June 1983 municipal elections.

Orientation. The UNFP is a moderate socialist formation.

Publications. *Al Ittihad Al Wattani* (sporadic)

Party of Action
Parti de l'Action (PA)

Leadership. Dr Abdullah Senhaji (g.s.)
Founded. December 1974
History. The PA was founded by a group of Berber intellectuals with a view to the "construction of a new society through a new élite". In the 1976 communal elections it gained only 58 seats (out of some 13,500). In the 1977 parliamentary elections it gained only two seats, and in municipal elections of June 1983 it obtained less than 1 per cent of the total vote.

Orientation. The PA is a middle-class non-revolutionary party, standing for democracy and progress.

Publications. *Al Amal* (sporadic)

Party of Progress and Socialism
Parti du Progrès et du Socialisme (PPS)

Address. 32 rue Ledru Rollin, B.P. 152, Casablanca, Morocco

Leadership. Ali Yata (s.g.)

Founded. August 1974

History. The PPS is the continuation of the Moroccan Communist Party which was founded in 1943 and banned in 1952, and of the *Parti de la Libération et du Socialisme*, formed in 1968 and prohibited in 1969. In the parliamentary elections of June 1977 the PPS obtained 2.31 per cent of the valid votes and one seat (out of 176 directly elected seats).

The PPS participated through its leader in the 10-member Defence Council set up by King Hassan in March 1979. In the 1977 parliamentary elections it gained one seat, and in municipal elections held in June 1983 it obtained less than one per cent of the total vote.

Orientation. Founded on the basis of scientific socialism, the PPS aims at building a socialist society in an independent and united Morocco.

Structure. The PPS operates on the principle of "democratic centralism", with cells, sections and regions, and with a central committee, a political bureau and a secretariat.

Membership. 35,000

Publications. *Al Bayane* (daily, in Arabic); French language daily; monthly reviews

International affiliations. The PPS is recognized by the Communist parties of the Soviet-bloc countries.

Popular Movement
Mouvement Populaire (MP)

Leadership. Mahjoubi Aherdane (s.g.)

Founded. 1957

History. The Movement was founded to oppose the *Istiqlal's* endeavours to form a national union as the basis for a one-party system. It was banned in 1957–58, but joined the Government in 1961 and has altogether taken part in eight different cabinets (including the national coalition Government formed in November 1983).

The party supported the country's new Constitution approved in a referendum in 1972 and accepted two seats on the 10-member Defence Council set up by King Hassan in March 1979. In the general elections of 1977 the MP gained 44 seats in the Chamber of Representatives. In the June 1983 municipal elections it came fifth with 12.19 per cent of the total vote. In the national coalition Government formed on Nov. 30, 1983, the MP leader was appointed a Minister of State without portfolio.

Orientation. As an agrarian party, the Movement fights for the "disinherited masses" in the countryside, for "Moroccan authenticity" and for social justice.

Structure. The MP's base consists of local cells and offices as well as regional offices and assemblies. It has a secretariat-general, a political bureau, an executive committee, an administrative commission, a national council and a general assembly or congress.

Publications. *Al Haraka* (weekly), 150,000

Socialist Union of Popular Forces
Union Socialiste des Forces Populaires (USFP)

Address. 17 rue Oued Souss Agdal, Rabat, Morocco

Leadership. Abderrahim Bouabid (first sec.)

Founded. September 1959

History. The party was originally the Rabat branch of the National Union of Popular Forces (UNFP). This branch was temporarily suspended by the Government in April 1973, and in September 1974 it changed its name to USFP. After the party had given strong support to the Government's policy on the Western Sahara, several of its members imprisoned in 1973 were released and others were acquitted in further trials during 1975–76. (However, the editor of the party's newspaper in Casablanca was assassinated in December 1975.)

In local elections held in November 1976 the USFP gained 6.53 per cent of the seats, and in the parliamentary elections of June 1977 it obtained 16 out of the 176 directly elective seats and 14.64 per cent of the valid votes. The party had two representatives on the 10-member Defence Council set up by King Hassan in March 1979.

In June 1981 the *Confédération Démocratique du Travail* (CDT), to which the USFP is linked, called a general strike in protest against price increases decreed by the Government. Anti-government demonstrations led to clashes with security forces in Casablanca which resulted in a death toll officially given as 66, but as 637 by the USFP. In ensuing trials 186 members of the USFP or the CDT were sentenced to imprisonment, among them Abderrahim Bouabid and two other members of the USFP's political bureau (sentenced on Sept. 24, 1981, for disturbing public order); however, they were granted a royal pardon on Feb. 28, 1982. After the June events the USFP's publications were temporarily banned.

In October 1981 the deputies of the USFP withdrew from the Chamber of Representatives in protest against a constitutional amendment (approved in a referendum on May 30, 1980) to extend the life of the Chamber from four to six years. However, the USFP took part in the municipal elections of June 1983, in which it gained 3.46 per cent of the vote (whereafter it complained, with other opposition parties, that the elections had not been conducted fairly). In the national

coalition Government formed on Nov. 30, 1983, to organize a referendum on the future of Western Sahara and also general elections, the USFP leader was appointed a Minister of State without portfolio.

Orientation. The USFP is progressive, with the objective of creating a socialist society.

Structure. Based on cells, the party has regional organs in every province, a national administrative commission of 62 members elected by the national congress, and a central committee comprising the above commission and representatives of the provinces, the women's and the youth organizations and a political bureau.

Membership. 100,000

Publications. *Al Ittihad al Ichtiraki* (daily, in Arabic); *Al Machrou* (The Project, quarterly, in Arabic)

International affiliations. Socialist Inter-African; Afro-Asian People's Solidarity Organization

Mozambique

Capital: Maputo   Pop. 13,000,000

The People's Republic of Mozambique is, under its 1975 Constitution, "a sovereign, independent and democratic state" in which "power belongs to the workers and peasants united and led by Frelimo (the Front for the Liberation of Mozambique)", which is "the leading force of the state and society". The president of Frelimo is the head of state and directs and presides over a Council of Ministers. The People's Assembly, the state's "supreme organ" and "the highest legislative organ of the state", is elected by universal suffrage of citizens above the age of 18 years.

In elections to the first People's Assembly, held in December 1977, voters in 894 local communities elected, by a show of hands, an electoral college for each community, and these colleges elected community councils of a total membership of 22,230 chosen from a list of candidates drawn up by Frelimo. The community councils in turn elected 3,390 members to 112 district councils and 460 members to 10 urban councils. Out of these council members 734 were appointed to 10 provincial councils, and the latter in turn elected, from among themselves, the 226 members of the People's Assembly by secret ballot.

Front for the Liberation of Mozambique
Frente da Libertação de Moçambique
(Frelimo)

Address. C.P. 4030, Av. 24 de Julho 1921, Maputo, Mozambique

Leadership. Samora Moisés Machel (pres.)

Founded. 1962

History. Frelimo was formed by a merger of three nationalist movements—the *União Democrática Nacional de Moçambique* (founded in 1960), the Mozambique African Nationalist Union (established in 1961) and the *União Africana de Moçambique Independente.* Led by Eduardo Mondlane until his assassination in Tanzania in 1969, Frelimo conducted an armed struggle against Portuguese colonial rule from 1964 to 1974. In the latter year it concluded an agreement with the post-revolutionary Portuguese Government providing for full independence by June 1975, which was duly achieved with the Front assuming power.

At the third Frelimo congress in February 1977 the Front was restructured into a political party. On the strength of the experience of the war of liberation the Frelimo Party officially adopted Marxism-Leninism as its ideological and theoretical foundation. Declaring itself to be the leading force of the state and Mozambican society, Frelimo identified itself as a vanguard party seeking to create a voluntary and militant alliance of workers, peasants, soldiers, revolutionary intellectuals and other workers.

While the Frelimo Party thus established itself in power on the classic model of the one-party African state, the Government President Samora Machel has experienced difficulties in recent years arising not only from economic failures but also from a serious internal security threat posed by the Mozambique National Resistance Movement, allegedly with South African backing.

Orientation. In the process of building socialism Frelimo's economic policy seeks to create "an independent, planned and advanced economy able to satisfy the growing needs of the people". The party applies an independent foreign policy based on the struggle for peace, democracy and progress. Frelimo's fourth congress (April 26–30, 1983) reaffirmed the general guidelines laid down in 1977 in the economic and social directives of the third congress.

Structure. The party has as its central organs a congress, a 130-member central committee, an 11-member political bureau, a secretariat of the central committee and a control committee.

Namibia (South West Africa)

Capital: Windhoek   Pop. 1,080,000

The territory of Namibia (South West Africa), a former League of Nations mandate administered as an integral part of South Africa, was in October 1966 declared to be under United Nations responsibility. In fact it continued to be under the control of South Africa, which on July 6, 1977, appointed an Administrator-General for a transitional period intended to lead to the territory's independence. By early 1984, however, no final agreement had been reached between South Africa and the United Nations on the modalities of achieving independence. Without the consent of the United Nations, South Africa held, in December 1978, elections to a Constituent Assembly on the basis of one man, one vote for all persons over the age of 18 years born or resident for the previous four years in the territory. In May 1979 it was decided to convert the Constituent Assembly into a National Assembly with legislative powers and with the addition of 15 nominated members to the 50 Assembly members elected in 1978.

The territory's 18-member (White) Legislative Assembly, in which the National Party had on April 24, 1974, won all seats, continued in existence, although a number of its members changed their allegiance to the Republican Party.

The 50 elected members of the Constituent Assembly were distributed as follows: Democratic Turnhalle Alliance (DTA) 41, Action Front for the Preservation of Turnhalle Principles (Aktur) 6, Namibia Christian Democratic Party 1, Reconstituted National Party (HNP) 1, Rehoboth Liberation Front 1. Among parties which boycotted the elections were the South West Africa People's Organization (SWAPO, which is recognized by the UN General

Assembly as the "sole representative of the Namibian people"), and the Namibian National Front.

On July 1, 1980, the South African Government created a 12-member Council of Ministers with executive powers in internal matters (subject to the veto of the Administrator-General, and with the South African Government retaining responsibility for constitutional matters, foreign affairs and overall security), while with effect from Aug. 1, 1980, the Council of Ministers also controlled a defence force, the "South West African Territorial Forces", and from Sept. 1, 1980, the police (except the security police). Elections were also held for Administrative Authorities in eight of the territory's ethnic areas in November 1980.

However, on Jan. 18, 1983, the National Assembly was dissolved after the Council of Ministers had resigned following the failure of the president of the DTA (Peter Kalangula) to convert the Alliance into a unitary party, as well as serious disputes between the DTA and the Administrator-General. The latter thereupon took over the government of the territory until an independence plan could be agreed.

Action Front for the Preservation of Turnhalle Principles (Aktur)

Leadership. Kosie Pretorius (l.)
Founded. December 1977
History. Aktur was formed by leaders of the National Party to represent that party's Turnhalle constitutional proposals. It has been joined by the South West African Action Group led by Jacques Pierre (Percy) de Mowbray Niehaus, former leader of the (defunct) United Party, and it is supported by more than half the White population of South West Africa.

Additional groups which joined Aktur were the Damara Action Group led by G. Conteb, the Kavango Action Group led by Alex Kudumo and the Rehoboth Action Group led by Pieter Diergaardt.
Orientation. While basically supporting the Democratic Turnhalle Alliance proposals for a future government, Aktur opposes desegregation of most public institutions and in areas of the territory which are residential.

Caprivi Alliance Party

Leadership. Richard Mamili (l.)
History. This party, affiliated to the Democratic Turnhalle Alliance, was the only one to nominate candidates for the Caprivian Representative Authority, which was therefore established without a poll in November 1980.

Christian Democratic Action for Social Justice

Leadership. Peter Kalangula (l.)
Founded. May 1982
History. This movement was founded by Peter Kalangula, who had resigned on Feb. 15, 1982, as president of the Democratic Turnhalle Alliance (DTA) because he had failed to convince the DTA's executive committee that the DTA should fight the next elections not as an alliance but as a single united (and not ethnically divided) party. He also complained that the DTA had failed to persuade the South African Government to abolish apartheid completely in Namibia.

Christian Democratic Party (CDP)

Leadership. Andrew J. F. Kloppers (l.)
Founded. 1983
History. A. J. F. Kloppers was a former member of the Labour Party and subsequently (for the Liberal Party) a member of the Constituent (later National) Assembly. The Liberal Party was then a member of the Action Front for the Preservation of Turnhalle Principles (Aktur, which was led by the National Party), from which Kloppers withdrew on June 12, 1979, after he had supported an Abolition of Racial Discrimination Bill passed by the Assembly but opposed by Aktur. The newly-established CDP became a member of the Democratic Turnhalle Alliance (DTA).

Damara Council

Leadership. Justus Garoeb (l.)

History. In elections to the Damara Representative Authority, held in November 1980, this group obtained 23 of the 40 seats, with 28.3 per cent of the registered electorate voting for it. The group is a constituent party of the Namibia National Front.

Structure. Justus Garoeb stated in March 1984 that his group had an "external wing" in Botswana.

Orientation. As a left-wing group the Damara Council has been described as a "sleeping partner" of SWAPO.

Damara Executive Committee

Leadership. Oscar Kharuchab (l.)

History. In elections to the Damara Representative Authority, held in November 1980, this Committee obtained the votes of 1.1 per cent of the registered electorate and one seat in the Authority. The Committee is a member of the Namibia People's Liberation Front.

Democratic Turnhalle Alliance (DTA)

Address. P.O. Box 173, Windhoek, SWA/Namibia

Leadership. Chief Kuaimo Isaac Riruako (pres.); Dr Ben Africa (vice-pres.); Dirk Mudge (ch.); Johan de Waal (chief sec.); Billy Marais (sec.)

Founded. November 1977

History. The DTA is an alliance of 11 groups, comprising the (White) Republican Party, the Namibia United Democratic Organization, the Rehoboth Baster Association, the South West African People's Democratic United Front, the Namibian Democratic Turnhalle Party, the Bushmen Alliance, the Caprivi Alliance, the Kavango Alliance, the Christian Democratic Party, the National Democratic Party and the Seoposengwe Party. It has also been supported by the Organization of German-Speaking Southwesters.

In September 1981 the DTA expressed acceptance of a plan devised by five Western powers (Canada, France, West Germany, the United Kingdom and the United States) for a constitution for an independent Namibia providing that it should be "a unitary, sovereign and democratic state" under a constitution approved by two-thirds of the proposed constituent assembly.

During 1982 the Council of Ministers, appointed on July 1, 1980, with Dirk Mudge as Chairman, came increasingly into conflict with the South African-appointed Administrator-General, in particular over the slow pace of change towards self-government and the phasing-out of apartheid legislation, which had led to an apparent decline in support for the DTA. The latter had already been weakened by the defection, in February 1982, of its former president, Peter Kalangula, after he had been overruled by the DTA's executive committee on the question of making the DTA a unitary party, as he had wished.

In September 1982 Mudge objected to South African plans to install an ethnically-based interim government, and on Oct. 7 he said that the DTA would, as a "liberation movement", take up the struggle against any such government. He resigned, with the entire Council of Ministers, on Jan. 18, 1983, whereupon the Administrator-General dissolved the National Assembly and the territory reverted to direct rule by the South African Government.

Orientation. The DTA was the driving force towards the unilaterally organized elections of December 1978 to a Constituent Assembly and towards the conversion of this Assembly into a National Assembly. Its principal aim is to achieve independence for Namibia on the basis of equal rights, personal freedom, democracy and free enterprise. The DTA regards itself as the only political organization strong enough to defeat at the polls the South West Africa People's Organization (SWAPO) which is supported by the United Nations and the Soviet Union.

Federal Party (FP)

History. The FP had its origins in the United National South West Party, counterpart to the (White) United Party in South Africa. The FP constituted itself as a non-racial party in 1978 but lost much White support while gaining some from other population groups. It was a member of the Namibia National Front (NNF) until July 1979, when it reverted to the status of an independent party after refusing to be merged in a unitary NNF.

Orientation. The FP supports the efforts of Western powers to achieve an internationally acceptable solution of the problem of Namibia's independence.

316

Kavango Alliance

Leadership. G. Shakadaya (l.)

History. This member of the Democratic Turnhalle Alliance gained all four seats in the Kavango Legislative Assembly in elections held in November 1980, when it received 87.5 per cent of the total registered votes.

Labour Party of South West Africa

Leadership. Barney Barnes (l.)

History. The party was founded as the Federal Coloured People's Party which subsequently, as the Labour Party, became a non-racial organization. It held half the seats in the South West Africa Coloured Council (an advisory body for the Coloured, i.e. mixed-race, population group) until the elections of November 1980, when it increased the number of its seats to 11 (out of the total of 15). It was then led by Joey Julius and was a member of the Democratic Turnhalle Alliance (DTA). In 1982, however, it was expelled from the DTA.

Liberal Party

Leadership. Andrew J. F. Kloppers (l.)

History. In 1977-79 the Liberal Party was part of the National Party-led Action Front for the Preservation of Turnhalle Principles (Aktur). As an independent party, the Liberal Party opposed the Labour Party (then a member of the Democratic Turnhalle Alliance) in elections to the Coloured Council in November 1980 but gained only four of the 15 seats on that Council.

Liberator Democratic Party
Bevryder Demokratiese Party

Leadership. L. J. G. Diergaardt (l.)

History. This party is a coalition of the Rehoboth Liberation Front and the Rehoboth Democratic Party, led by K. G. Freigang.

Multi-Party Conference (MPC)

Founded. November 1983

History. The first session of this Conference, held in Windhoek on Nov. 12, 1983, was attended by 104 delegates representing seven parties—the Damara Council, the Democratic Turnhalle Alliance (DTA), the Namibian Christian Democratic Party (NCDP), the (White) National Party, the Rehoboth Liberation Front (RLF), the South West Africa National Union (SWANU) and the SWAPO-Democrats. However, the NCPD withdrew from the MPC in December 1983 and the Damara Council did so in March 1984, whereas the (Coloured) Labour Party had earlier joined the Conference.

On Feb. 24, 1984, leaders of the then six MPC member parties—Hans Diergaardt of the RLF, Justus Garoeb of the Damara Council, Moses Katjiuongua of SWANU, Dirk Mudge of the DTA, Andreas Shipanga of the SWAPO-Democrats and Jannie de Wet of the National Party—agreed on a declaration of basic principles in which it was stated that the right of the Namibian people to self-determination and independence was paramount; the declaration added that "the only concrete plan on independence" was the UN Security Council's Resolution 435 (of Sept. 29, 1978, providing for the election of a constituent assembly and the presence of a UN Transition Assistance Group with a military section), to the implementation of which they committed themselves. In order to prepare the territory for independence under MPC leadership the declaration also called for the drafting of a permanent constitution. In April 1984 the MPC members agreed on a Namibian Bill of Rights to be enshrined in the proposed constitution of an independent Namibia.

Namibia Democratic Coalition

Leadership. L. J. G. Diergaardt (l.)

History. This party alliance comprises the Rehoboth Liberation Front (of Rehoboth Basters), the NUDO Progressive Party (of Hereros) and the Liberal Party (of Coloureds), led by Andrew J. F. Kloppers.

Namibia Independence Party (NIP)

Leadership. Charlie Hartung

History. This party has held half the elected seats in the South West Africa Coloured Council but claims to be non-racial. Its leaders took part in the Turnhalle constitutional conference but dissociated themselves from its proposals for government based on ethnic representation.

The party proposed in October 1981 that all parties should agree on constitutional principles before proceeding to elections to a Constituent Assembly, and that the Constitution should be unamendable for 10 years after independence.

Namibia National Front (NNF)

Address. P.O. Box 20031, Windhoek, SWA/Namibia

Leadership. Justus Garoeb (pres.)

History. The NNF is an alliance of various parties and organizations opposed to the Democratic Turnhalle Alliance (DTA) and includes the Damara Council led by Justus Garoeb, the Mbanderu Council (of Hereros) led by Chief Nguvauha Munjuku, the Namibia Progressive Party (of Namas) led by A. Vries and the South West African National Union (SWANU) led by Moses Katjiuongua.

Two other groups which have disaffiliated from the NNF are the Federal Party (of Rehoboth Basters) led by Hendrik Buys and the Namibia Independence Party (of Coloureds) led by Charlie Hartung. The NNF did not take part in the 1978 elections to a Constituent Assembly. It was constituted as a unitary party in July 1979.

Orientation. The NNF stands for the establishment of an independent republic with universal adult franchise, a democratic system of government with a unicameral Parliament to which one-third of the members would be elected in single-member constituencies, another third of the seats would be divided among political parties and the last third among minority groups. The executive would consist of a (figure-head) President, a Prime Minister and a Cabinet. Namibia would be a unitary state but might have from two to five provincial councils. The NNF supports the principle of a mixed economy, with public and private participation but excluding "unhealthy monopolies and other forms of abuse".

Namibia People's Liberation Front (NPLF)

Leadership. Kefas Conradie (pres.)

History. The NPLF embraces three groups—the (Nama) Bondelswarts Group led by Anna Christiaans, the Damara Executive Council led by Oscar Kharuchab and the (Nama) Voice of the People group led by Kefas Conradie.

Namibia United Democratic Organization (NUDO)

Leadership. Chief Kuaimo Isaac Riruako (l.)

History. NUDO was formed as the political arm of the traditional Herero Chiefs' Council supporting the aims of the Democratic Turnhalle Alliance, of which it became a constituent part. NUDO's first leader, Chief Clemens Kapuuo, was assassinated in March 1978. In elections held in November 1980 to a Herero Representative Authority, NUDO received 50.9 per cent of the total votes and 34 of the 35 seats on the Authority (in a 53.1 per cent poll).

Namibian Christian Democratic Party
Namibië Christelike Demokratiese Party (NCDP)

Address. P.O. Box 690, Tsumeb, SWA/Namibia

Leadership. J. K. N. Röhr (l.); Ludwig Katjipu (sec./treas.); W. Adam, S. Amushila, J. Kandjimi, Th. Mukoya, W. Webster, S. Shifafura

Founded. October 1978

History. The party was founded to contest the 1978 elections of a Constituent Assembly as an alternative to the left-wing SWAPO and a "true opposition" to the South African Government's apartheid policy. In November 1980 it contested elections to the four-member Kavango Legislative Assembly, its Kavango leader being Faustinus Sikongo, but it gained only 12.4 per cent of the vote and no seat.

Orientation. The NCDP stands for the creation of an independent and indivisible Namibia (including Walvis Bay) with a democratic party system based on Christian principles and with an independent judiciary and a general charter of democratic and fundamental human rights enforceable by law. It also advocates a free market economy based on private property, with a strong social responsibility, with the encouragement of co-operatives in agriculture and with freedom to form trade unions. The party envisages a legislature of 60 seats, 40 of which are to be filled by the parties according to their proportion of votes gained, and the remaining 20 by members nominated by provincial councils on the basis of party strengths in the provinces, with no party gaining less than 3 per cent of the vote being entitled to directly elective seats.

Namibian Democratic Turnhalle Party

Leadership. Daniel Luipert
History. The party consists mainly of supporters of the Nama Council, an appointed body for the Nama (Hottentot) community. It is a constituent part of the Democratic Turnhalle Alliance.

National Democratic Party (NDP)

Leadership. Tara Imbili (l.)
Founded. 1977
History. Based on the Democratic Ovamboland Independence Party, the ruling party in the Ovambo Black homeland, the party was in 1977 proclaimed to be open to all races. It was one of the original members of the Democratic Turnhalle Alliance (DTA), of which Peter Kalangula (then NDP leader) became president in succession to Pastor Cornelius Ndjoba, the founder of the NDP, on Nov. 1, 1980. (Pastor Ndjoba was killed by an anti-tank mine on Nov. 25, 1982.)

In February 1982, Kalangula withdrew from the DTA after policy differences with Dirk Mudge (Chairman of the Council of Ministers). He also resigned the presidency of the NDP and in May 1982 founded the Christian Democratic Action for Social Justice (see separate entry), taking the bulk of NDP members with him into the new party.

Orientation. The NDP sought to unite the people of Namibia against "Russian expansionism" from the north. It aimed at establishing five provinces in an independent Namibia and escaping from the framework of ethnic representation.

National Party of South West Africa
Nasionale Party van Suidwesafrika (NP)

Leadership. Kosie Pretorius (l.)
History. From 1945 to September 1977 the party was federated with the ruling National Party in South Africa. The NP of South West Africa held all 18 seats in the Territory's (White) Legislative Assembly from March 1966 to September 1977. For the elections to the Constituent Assembly in December 1978 the NP set up the Action Group for the Preservation of Turnhalle Principles (Aktur). It objected to the conversion of the Constituent Assembly into a National Assembly with legislative powers and the NP members of

Aktur withdrew from the Assembly in July 1979. In elections held in November 1980 to the 18-member (White) Legislative Assembly the NP retained 11 seats.

Orientation. A White party originally formed to uphold White supremacy but later in favour of an independent Namibia provided it was based on separate institutions for the territory's various ethnic groups.

NUDO Progressive Party of Namibia (NPPN)

Leadership. Johannes Karuaihe (l.)
Founded. February 1980
History. This party arose out of the suspension of two executive members of the Namibia United Democratic Organization (NUDO) on Feb. 5, 1980. However, in elections to the Herero Representative Authority held in November 1980 the NPPN obtained only 1.1 per cent of the votes and one seat.

Organization of German-Speaking Southwesters
Interessengemeinschaft Deutschsprachiger Südwester

Address. P.O.Box 1208, 9000 Windhoek, SWA/Namibia
Leadership. Dr H. Halenke (hon. pres.); Dr W. Weitzel (pres.); K. Becker (ch.); W.T. Behnsen (sec.)
Founded. August 1977
Orientation. The organization describes itself as "the political mouthpiece of the German-speaking community in Namibia" and has identified itself unconditionally with the endeavour of the democratic political parties in the territory to attain freedom and independence. It stands for a free and democratic legal and social order and for a free economy; it opposes the claims to power of all totalitarian organizations; and it condemns the use of violence as a means of settling political controversies. It has welcomed the efforts of five Western nations towards a solution of the independence question but has described the United Nations as "hardly an honest mediator in the service of arriving at a fair and balanced solution".
Structure. The organization has a 12-member board and a 10-member executive committee.
Membership. 3,000
Publications. *IG-Kurier* (quarterly), 3,000

Reconstituted National Party
Herstigte Nasionale Party (HNP)

Leadership. Sarel Becker (l.)
History. The HNP in Namibia is part of the HNP in South Africa. In elections to the (White) Legislative Assembly held in November 1980 the HNP obtained only 10.4 per cent of the vote and no seat.
Orientation. The HNP stands for the maintenance of White supremacy and has called for the incorporation of South West Africa in the Republic of South Africa.

Rehoboth Baster Association (RBA)

Leadership. Dr Benjamin Africa
History. The RBA has held half the seats in the Rehoboth Legislative Council (for the "homeland" of the Rehoboth Basters). It is part of the Democratic Turnhalle Alliance.

Rehoboth Liberation Front
Baster Bevrydingsfront

Leadership. L.J.G. Diergaardt (l.)
History. This party, which has held half the seats in the Rehoboth Legislative Council, was temporarily a partner, with the Namibia Young Pioneers, in a Namibia Patriotic Coalition led by Dr Mburumba Kerina but later dissolved.

Republican Party of South West Africa
Republikeinse Party van Suidwesafrika (RP)

Leadership. Dirk Mudge (l.)
Founded. September 1977
History. The RP was founded as a break-away group from the (White) National Party (NP) and gained the support of eight of the 18 NP members of the (all-White) Legislative Assembly of South West Africa. It has been the driving force in organizing the Democratic Turnhalle Alliance. In elections to the Legislative Assembly, held in November 1980, the party gained 41.5 per cent of the vote but only seven seats.
Orientation. The RP stands for co-operation between all race groups in the territory with the object of achieving independence for South West Africa on the basis of the Turnhalle proposals, while continuing to oppose "evil powers" such as SWAPO.
Publications. *Die Republikein* (five times a week), 10,000

Seoposengwe Party

Leadership. Chief Constance Kgosiemang (l.)
Founded. Jan. 23, 1980
History. This party was formed by the Tswana Alliance within the Democratic Turnhalle Alliance. It was the only party to nominate candidates for the Tswana Representative Authority, which was therefore constituted without a poll in November 1980.

South West Africa National Union (SWANU)

Leadership. Moses Katjiuongua (pres.)
Founded. 1959
History. The party, mainly supported by Hereros in urban areas, has declined in influence and is a member of the Namibia National Front. With reference to Western proposals for transition to independence for Namibia SWANU argued in October 1981 that the choice between a one-party and a multi-party system should be left to the Namibian people and that a proposed guarantee of private property rights would perpetuate the wealth of the White minority.

South West Africa People's Organization (SWAPO)

Address. P.O. Box 1071, Windhoek, SWA/Namibia
Leadership. Sam Nujoma (pres., based in Lusaka, Zambia); Daniel Tjongarero (vice-pres., based in Windhoek)
Founded. 1960
History. Founded by Herman Toivo ja Toivo (who was sentenced to 20 years' imprisonment in 1968 by a South African court and was released in March 1984 after serving 16 years), SWAPO evolved from the Ovamboland People's Organization (founded in 1957) with the object of gaining support from ethnic groups other than the Ovambos, and it gradually absorbed a number of smaller parties from various parts of the territory.

Since 1966 SWAPO's external wing, operating from Zambia and, after 1974, also from Angola, has been conducting warfare against targets in Namibia through its military arm, currently known as the People's Liberation Army of Namibia (PLAN). SWAPO has opposed any participation in South African-organized elections. SWAPO has been recognized by the Organization of African Unity and the UN General Assembly as "the sole legitimate representative of the people of Namibia". Inside Namibia SWAPO has taken no part in any elections but it has enjoyed widespread support, in particular in the north of the country.

Speaking on behalf of SWAPO, Tjongarero said in October 1981 (with reference to Western proposals for transition to independence) that a constitution should be decided upon by a constituent assembly elected after the implementation of UN Security Council Resolution 435 (of Sept. 29, 1978), which provided for the establishment of a UN Transition Assistance Group (UNTAG) with a military section.

Orientation. SWAPO stands for the achievement of Namibia's independence as a result of an international conference and the complete withdrawal of South African armed forces, and for the creation of a neutral and non-aligned state in Namibia. In 1976 SWAPO's central committee defined its objective as the establishment of "a popular democratic people's government . . . founded upon the will and participation of all the Namibian people" with SWAPO being "the vanguard party of the working class, peasantry and progressive intellectuals" which would build "a classless, non-exploitative society based on scientific socialist ideals and principles" and opposed to "all reactionary tendencies of individualism, tribalism, racism, sexism and regionalism". Although the people's government was to exercise effective control over the means of production and distribution, the party's leaders have stated that wholesale nationalization would not be carried out and that there would in practice be a mixed economy.

Structure. SWAPO has a central committee based in Lusaka. (A national executive inside Namibia was dissolved in June 1979 after its offices had been demolished by a "White Resistance Movement".)

South West African People's Democratic United Front (SWAPDUF)

Leadership. Engelhardt Christy
History. Formerly the Damara United Front, SWAPDUF became part of the Democratic Turnhalle Alliance and claimed to be a non-racial party. It controlled the (appointed) Damara Representative Authority until the elections of November 1980, as a result of which it retained only 16 of the 40 seats in the Authority (having gained 20.1 per cent of the votes of the registered electorate of Damaras).

SWAPO-Democrats

Leadership. Andreas Shipanga (l.)
Founded. June 1978
History. The SWAPO-Democrats are based on former SWAPO members expelled from that organization in 1976 and subsequently detained in Tanzania but released in May 1978. The party did not take part in the 1978 elections to a Constituent Assembly. Mrs Ottilie Abrahams, who had been secretary-general of the SWAPO-Democrats, and her husband, Dr Kenneth Abrahams, were expelled from the organization in July 1980 and joined the Namibia Independence Party.

United Namibian People's Party

Founded. August 1980
History. This party was set up by four former executive members of the SWAPO-Democrats group.

Nauru

Capital: Domaneab   Pop. 7,500

The Republic of Nauru, an independent state with a special relationship with the Commonwealth, has a unicameral Parliament of 18 members elected for up to three years by universal adult suffrage (compulsory for those over 20 years old) in eight electoral districts, a President elected by Parliament for its duration from among its members, and a five-member Cabinet composed of members of Parliament.

The country's first recognizable political formation, the Nauru Party, came to power in December 1976 when its leader, Bernard Dowiyogo, was elected President. Despite the party's victory in the December 1977 elections the Government's legitimacy was constantly challenged by former President Hammer DeRoburt, who was re-elected to the presidency in May 1978. In December 1978 Nauru Party members, including Dowiyogo, accepted ministerial posts in DeRoburt's administration and the party thus effectively ceased to exist as a distinct political organization. DeRoburt was re-elected to the presidency after the December 1981 and December 1983 elections, on the first occasion unopposed and on the latter occasion by 10 votes to six of members of the new Parliament.

Nepal

Capital: Katmandu   Pop. 17,000,000

The Kingdom of Nepal is, under its 1962 Constitution, a "constitutional monarchical Hindu state". Political parties have been banned since Jan. 5, 1961; the "basic units of democracy" are elected village and provincial councils (*panchayats*). Under amendments to the Constitution approved in a referendum (which rejected the restoration of political parties) on April 2, 1980, 112 members of the country's National Assembly are elected by direct adult suffrage of citizens 21 or more years old and by simple majority in multi-member districts, and another 28 members are nominated by the King. The Prime Minister is appointed by the King on the recommendation of the National Assembly to which the Council of Ministers (Cabinet) is responsible.

Nepali Congress Party (NCP)

Leadership. Krishna Prasad Bhattarai (working pres.)

Founded. 1946

History. The NCP has been the country's leading political party and was in office from 1959 until December 1960, when it was dissolved by the King. Many of its leaders were subsequently detained or placed under house arrest for varying periods. Bisheshwar Prasad Koirala, then the NCP's leader, called on party workers in 1978 to cease all political activity in order to achieve national conciliation, but his call was rejected by the party's central working committee.

Although officially banned since Jan. 5, 1961, the NCP was able to hold, on Dec. 1–3, 1982, a national conference in Katmandu, attended by some 500 delegates. The conference decided that, despite the lack of tangible results, the NCP should follow the "national reconciliation" policy of B.P. Koirala (who had died on July 21, 1982). The party's political resolution called for an understanding between the King and the people to "avert the crisis of the country's existence".

K.P. Bhattarai defined the NCP's ultimate aim as to establish complete democracy through peaceful means. An 11-point economic programme adopted by the conference included land reform, incentives to increase small-farm output, price stabilization, and measures to tackle unemployment.

Orientation. In a manifesto issued in January 1956 the NCP defined its aim as the achievement of socialism by peaceful and democratic methods and of a government which would be a constitutional monarchy on the British model, with a cabinet responsible to the people's representatives and a unicameral legislature elected by universal adult suffrage, a foreign policy based on neutrality and coexistence, industrialization and state planning of the national economy.

The Netherlands

Capital: The Hague   Pop. 14,300,000

The Kingdom of the Netherlands (which comprises the Netherlands in Europe and the Netherlands Antilles) is a constitutional and hereditary monarchy whose two parts enjoy full autonomy. The Netherlands in Europe has a multi-party system reflecting the country's religious and social composition and reinforced by proportional representation. The bicameral Parliament (*Staten-Generaal*) consists of (i) a 75-member First Chamber (*Eerste Kamer*) elected by the country's 11 provincial councils for a six-year term (one-half of its members retiring every three years but being immediately re-eligible) and (ii) a 150-member Second Chamber (*Tweede Kamer*) elected for a four-year term by direct universal suffrage of resident citizens above the age of 18 years (although voting is not compulsory but may be carried out by proxy) and by proportional representation with the whole country forming one constituency. Seats are allotted on a quota basis to each party which obtains this quota (equal to the total of votes cast divided by 150—the number of seats), with the remainder of seats going to those parties which have obtained most votes per seat. The Crown (advised by a Council of State) and the Second Chamber may propose bills, while the First Chamber can approve or reject, but not amend, such bills. The executive power rests with the Crown and a Council of Ministers, whose members may not be members of the *Staten-Generaal*.

As a result of elections held on Sept. 8, 1982, seats in the Second Chamber were distributed as follows: Labour Party 47, Christian Democratic Appeal 45, People's Party of Freedom and Democracy 36, Democrats '66 6, Pacifist Socialist Party 3, Communist Party 3, State Reform Party 3, Radical Political Party 2, Reformational Political Federation 2, Centre Party 1, Reformed Political Association 1, Evangelical Progressive People's Party 1.

Centre Party
Centrumpartij

History. In the 1981 general elections this (neo-fascist) party gained only some 12,000 votes, but in the 1982 elections it obtained over 68,000 votes and one seat in the Second Chamber.

Christian Democratic Appeal
Christen Democratisch Appèl (CDA)

Address. dr. Kuyperstraat 5, 2514 BA 's-Gravenhage, Netherlands

Leadership. R.F.M. (Ruud) Lubbers (l.); P. Bukman (ch.); M. Smits (s.g.)

Founded. April 1975

History. The CDA was founded as a federation of the Anti-Revolutionary Party (*Anti-Revolutionaire Partij*), the Christian Historic Union (*Christelijk-Historische Unie*) and the Catholic People's Party (*Katholieke Volkspartij*) in an attempt by these confessional parties to reverse the steady decline in their vote since 1945. The CDA was constituted as a unified party on Oct. 11, 1980, after a five-year preparatory phase. It gained 49 seats in the Second Chamber in 1977, 47 in 1981 and 45 in 1982.

Since 1977 the CDA has been leading coalition governments—with the Liberals until September 1981, with the Labour Party and the Democrats '66 until May 1982, with the Democrats '66 only until November 1982, and with the Liberals since then.

Orientation. As a right-of-centre Christian democratic party, the CDA accepts the biblical evidence of God's promises, acts and commandments as being of decisive significance for mankind, society and government. Regarding itself as representing the entire Dutch population it attaches great importance to the pronouncement of the Christian Churches and also takes account of the ideas of the various social groups. The party's programme of basic principles is inspired by the CDA's Christian political conviction.

Membership. 145,000

Publications. *CDActueel* (weekly); *CDVerkenningen* (monthly); *Bestuursforum* (monthly)

International affiliations. Christian Democratic International; European Christian Democratic Union; European People's Party

Communist Party of the Netherlands
Communistische Partij van Nederland (CPN)

Address. Hoogte Kadijk 145, 1018 BH Amsterdam; or Postbus 20.165, HD Amsterdam, Netherlands

Leadership. (Mrs) Elli Izeboud

Founded. 1918

History. Formed by the left of the Social Democratic Workers' Party, the Communist Party saw its representation in the Second Chamber fall during the post-war period from 10 in 1946 to three in 1959; thereafter it rose to seven in 1972, but was reduced to two in 1977. Since 1981 the party has had three representatives in the Second Chamber. It has never participated in government although it was offered (and refused) a seat in the first post-war administration formed in 1945.

In mid-January 1984 a congress of the CPN, the Pacifist Socialist Party and the Radical Political Party (see separate entries) was held to investigate the possibilities for political co-operation between the three formations. A contact group was formed called "Left Breakthrough", although the majority in each party remained in favour of preserving an independent identity.

Orientation. The party's draft programme of 1983 maintained that socialism could be achieved in the Netherlands only by the united activities of all forces aspiring to socialism; that socialism would have to be democratic, humane, progressive and peace- and freedom-loving; and that the transition to a socialist society would be a process of more or less prolonged phases. The CPN stands for a democratic parliamentary form of state with a multi-party system, i.e. the right to form parties and the right to opposition. In November 1982 the party expressed solidarity with "democratic opposition groups" in Czechoslovakia and Poland.

Structure. The party has a 55-member head committee elected at a congress (held every two years), but the number of members can change after any congress.

Membership. 25,000

Publications. *De Waarheid* (daily); *Politiek en Cultuur* (monthly theoretical magazine); *CPN-Ledenkrant* (monthly journal for members and supporters)

Co-operation on the Right
Binding Rechts

Address. Krijgsmansveld 309, Apeldoorn, Netherlands

Leadership. E. J. Harmsen (l.)

Founded. October 1968

History. This group is an offshoot of the Farmers' Party (*Boerenpartij*, BP).

Democrats '66
Democraten '66 (D'66)

Address. Bezuidenhoutseweg 195, Den Haag, Netherlands

Leadership. Laurens Brinkhorst (ch.); J. Michiel ten Brink (sec.)

Founded. 1966

History. Founded with "a commitment to change inspired by a sense of responsibility for the future" and its first aim being "the democratization of certain constitutional laws", the party obtained representation in the Second Chamber with seven seats in 1967 and 11 seats in 1971, but only six seats in 1973 and eight in 1977. After that year the D'66 increased their electoral support significantly, gaining over 11 per cent of the vote and 17 seats in the Second Chamber in 1981.

However, a downward trend reappeared in 1982, since when the party has represented only about 5 per cent of the electorate and has held six seats in the Second Chamber. It regards the Labour Party as its most obvious partner for any participation in government and with that party (and three others) took part in a coalition Government in 1973–77 and (with one other party) in 1981–82. The D'66 has called for the abolition of proportional representation based on party lists and also for the direct election of the Prime Minister.

Orientation. The party stands for respect for the human being and acceptance of responsibilities for the oppressed and the underdeveloped countries, and also for the lowest-paid and those most likely to succumb to social pressures. It stresses the need to deal with the "very disturbing side-effects" of the industrial era, to protect the environment and to improve the quality of life.

Membership. 10,000

Publications. *De Democraat* (15 times a year), 11,000

Dutch People's Union
Nederlandse Volks-Unie

Address. Postbus 10366, 1001 EJ Amsterdam, Netherlands

Leadership. Joop Glimmerveen (l. and ch.); F. Zoetmulder (sec.)

Founded. March 1971

History. The party first took part in elections in May 1974, and in the 1977 elections to the Second Chamber of Parliament it gained 33,268 votes or 0.4 per cent of the total vote. Although a ban on the party had been advocated by a majority of members of Parliament it was in April 1979 officially declared to be a legal party.

Orientation. This formation subscribes to nationalist precepts.

Publications. *Wij Nederland* (quarterly)

Evangelical Progressive People's Party
Evangelische Progressieve Volkspartij (EPV)

Leadership. Dr K. van der Sluis

Founded. January 1978

History. The EPV was formed to promote a "consciously progressive policy" as prescribed by the gospel. It is opposed to the coalition Government led by the Christian Democratic Appeal. In the 1982 parliamentary elections it obtained one seat in the Second Chamber.

Farmers' Party
Boerenpartij (BP)

Address. 18 Bovenweg, Bennekom, Netherlands

Founded. 1958

History. This party first obtained parliamentary representation in 1963. It gained one seat in the Second Chamber in 1977 but none in 1981 or 1982.

Orientation. The BP has opposed bureaucracy, centralized government, big business, personal taxes and socialism.

The Greens
De Groenen

Address. c/o Groen Platform, Gerckenshaag 13, 6228 EL Maastricht, Netherlands

Founded. 1984

History. This group was formed by various green lists and other environmental and ecologist groups. Early in 1983 an opinion poll found that in general elections a green party might obtain up to 12 per cent of the vote.

International affiliations. The European Greens

Independent Party
Onafhankelijke Partij (OPA)

Address. Nederlandlaan 1, 6414 HA Heerlen, Netherlands

Leadership. M. A. van der Wijst (l.); A. van Hout (sec.)

Founded. January 1966

History. The party has no representation at national level, and prefers co-operation with other parties, notwithstanding its name.

Orientation. Progressive, democratic and non-doctrinal, the party seeks "practical improvements and co-operation".

Labour Party
Partij van de Arbeid (PvdA)

Address. Nicolaas Witsenkade 30, 1017 ZT Amsterdam, Netherlands

Leadership. Joop den Uyl (l.); Max van den Berg (ch.); Wim van Velsen (g.s.)

Founded. 1946

History. The PvdA was formed after World War II, in succession to the Social Democratic Workers' Party, and was from 1946 engaged in the reconstruction of the Netherlands after the German occupation. Its leader, Willem Drees, was Prime Minister of a Socialist-Catholic coalition Government from 1948 to 1958, whereafter the PvdA was in opposition—except briefly in 1965-66, when it took part in a coalition Government with the Catholic People's Party (KVP) and the Anti-Revolutionary Party (ARP). The PvdA was weakened in 1970 by a right-wing breakaway by followers of Dr Willem Drees (son of the post-war Prime Minister of the same name), who formed the "Democratic Socialists 1970" (DS-70) party. Although DS-70 gained eight seats in the 1971 elections, thereafter its representation declined. (Having failed to win any seats in the 1981 or 1982 elections, the party was dissolved in January 1983.)

In 1971 and 1972 the PvdA contested elections on a joint programme with the Democrats '66 and the Radical Political Party, and in 1973 it formed a coalition Government with these parties and also the KVP and the ARP, with the PvdA leader becoming Prime Minister. This was the first Dutch Government with a left-wing majority of ministers. After the 1977 elections, in which the PvdA increased its seats in the Second Chamber from 43 to 53, it went into opposition to a centre-right Government led by the Christian Democratic Appeal. From September 1981 to May 1982 the party took part in a coalition Government with the Christian Democratic Appeal and the Democrats '66. Since then the PvdA has been in opposition.

Orientation. The PvdA is a democratic socialist party with the aim of building a new type of socialist society through democratic means.

Structure. The party's highest organ is its congress, at which over 800 party sections are represented and which decides on policy guidelines and election platforms; there is a 21-member executive presided over by the party chairman.

Membership. 125,000

Publications. *Socialisme en Democratie* (monthly), 3,500; *Voorwarts* (every two weeks)

International affiliations. Socialist International; Confederation of Socialist Parties of the European Community.

Netherlands Roman Catholic Party
Rooms Katholieke Partij Nederland (RKPN)

Address. Postbus 100, 2270 AC Voorburg, Netherlands

Leadership. Kl. Beuker (pres.); J. A. A. Leechburch Auwers (s.g.)

Founded. January 1972

History. The party was founded because of what it regarded as the failure of the Catholic People's Party (later part of the Christian Democratic Appeal) to maintain Catholic principles in questions such as abortion, sexuality and euthanasia. The party held one seat in the Second Chamber of Parliament from 1972 to 1977, after which it continued to campaign as an "action group".

Orientation. The party seeks to maintain Christian principles (as propagated by the Roman Catholic Church) in political and social life.

Membership. 5,000

Publications. *Nieuwsbrief van de RKPN,* 3,000

Pacifist Socialist Party
Pacifistisch Socialistische Partij (PSP)

Address. Postbus 700, 1000 AS Amsterdam, Netherlands

Leadership. Marko Mazeland (ch.); John Hontelez (g.s.)

Founded. January 1957

History. The party, set up with about 300 members, soon gained seats in the Second Chamber of Parliament—two in 1959, four in 1963 and 1967, two in 1971 and 1972, only one in 1977 and three in May 1981 and again in September 1982. It has not taken part in government. (For moves towards political co-operation between the PSP and two other left-wing parties in early 1984, see separate entry for Communist Party of the Netherlands.)

Orientation. The PSP is left-wing, combining pacifism and socialism.

Membership. 10,000
Publications. Bevrijding (Liberation), 11,000; *International Bulletin* (occasional)

People's Party for Freedom and Democracy
Volkspartij voor Vrijheid en Democratie (VVD)

Address. Koninginnegracht 57, 2514 AE 's-Gravenhage, Netherlands
Leadership. J. Kamminga (ch.); E.H.T.M. Nijpels (pol. l.); J.W.A. van den Berg (g.s.)
Founded. 1948
History. This undenominational party succeeded the pre-war Liberal State Party and the Liberal Democratic Union. It holds 36 seats in the Second Chamber of Parliament. In 1982 it joined in a coalition with the Christian Democratic Appeal and was given the posts of Deputy Prime Minister (as which G.M.V. van Aardenne was appointed) and of five other ministers.
Orientation. The VVD is a liberal party, strongly advocating free enterprise but also supporting social security and recommending workers' participation in profits and management.
Membership. 100,000
Publications. Vrijheid en Democratie
International affiliations. Liberal International; Federation of Liberal and Democratic Parties in the European Community

---

Radical Political Party
Politieke Partij Radikalen (PPR)

Address. Singel 277, 1012 WG Amsterdam, Netherlands.
Leadership. Mrs Ria Beckers (l.); Wim de Boer (ch.)
Founded. 1968
History. Formed as a break-away group by left-wing members of the Catholic People's Party, including anarchist and strongly socialist elements, the party gained two seats in the Second Chamber of Parliament in general elections held in 1971 (which it contested on a joint programme with the Labour Party and the Democrats '66) and seven seats in the 1972 elections.

From 1973 to 1977 the PPR took part in centre-left coalition governments (including the Labour Party and the Catholic People's Party). In 1977, however, the party's share in the total vote dropped to 1.69 per cent (from 4.8 per cent in 1972) and it retained only three seats in the Second Chamber; it has been in opposition since then. In the 1982 elections it retained two seats. (For moves towards political co-operation between the PPR and two other left-wing parties in early 1984, see separate entry for Communist Party of the Netherlands.)

Orientation. The PPR advocates a democratization of power; democratization and nationalization of production; protection of the environment; and the banning of nuclear weapons and energy.
Structure. The party's supreme organ is its congress (held twice a year); between congress sessions it is the 100-member party council. There is a 15-member party board, and the party has provincial, regional and local action centres.
Membership. 7,500
Publications. Radikalenkrant (official organ, 15 times a year)

Reformational Political Federation
Reformatorische Politieke Federatie (RPF)

Address. Laan 88, P.O.B. 302, 8070 AH Nunspeet, Netherlands
Leadership. P. Langeler (ch.); drs. H. Visser (sec.)
Founded. March 1975
History. The Federation was formed by the National Evangelical Association, dissenters from the Anti-Revolutionary Party (ARP) and associations of reformed (Calvinist) voters. In 1981, and again in 1982, it gained two seats in the Second Chamber (with 108,000 votes in 1981 and 125,000 in 1982). In 1982 it also obtained 10 seats in provincial elections and about 100 in municipal elections.
Orientation. The RPF seeks a reformation of political and social life in accordance with the Bible and the Calvinistic tradition and creed.
Structure. The party is headed by a 15-member board, and it has 11 provincial contact councils and 175 local electoral associations.
Membership. 10,000
Publications. Nieuw Nederland (monthly), 12,000

Reformed Political Association
Gereformeerd Politiek Verbond

Address. Berkenweg 46, Postbus 439, 3800 AK Amersfoort, Netherlands
Leadership. J. van der Jagt (ch.); L. Hordijk (sec.)
Founded. April 1948
History. The founders of the Association claimed to represent the continuation

of the ideas of the Dutch national Calvinists of the 16th and 17th centuries, but on the basis of recognition of the separation of Church and State and of spiritual and fundamental freedoms. Before World War II the Anti-Revolutionary Party had claimed to represent these ideas, but the founders of the Association objected to the "partly liberal and partly socialistic" tendencies which they believed to be developing in that party.

Structure. The party's highest political organ is its national assembly of local representatives, and its executive committee is a central union council of nine members.

Membership. 13,000

Publications. *Ons Burgerschap*

Socialist Workers' Party
Socialistische Arbeiderspartij (SAP)

Address. Sint Jacobstraat 10-20, 1012 NC Amsterdam, Netherlands

Leadership. Rene Visser (nat. sec.)

Founded. December 1974

History. This party was formed as the International Communist League (*Internationale Kommunistenbond*, IKB) by a merger of (i) the Revolutionary Communist Group (RCB) founded in 1972 and consisting of most of the sympathizers of the Fourth International, and (ii) the Communist League Proletarian Left (KBPL), expelled as a left-wing group from the Pacifist Socialist Party (PSP) in

1972. It adopted its present name on June 4, 1983.

Orientation. The SAP is a Trotskyist revolutionary Marxist group intent on establishing a socialist society based on organs of the working class.

Structure. On the basis of democratic centralism, cells elect regional committees; every two years a national congress is held to determine the political line and to choose a central committee, which is the party's highest organ between congresses and which elects a political bureau.

Membership. 600

Publications. *Klassenstrijd* (biweekly), approx. 2,000; *De Internationale* (bi-monthly theoretical organ), approx. 900

International affiliations. Dutch section of Fourth (Trotskyist) International

State Reform Party
Staatkundig Gereformeerde Partij (SGP)

Address. Laan van Meerdervoort 165, Den Haag, Netherlands

Leadership. Rev. H. G. Abma (ch.); C. G. Boender (sec.)

Founded. 1918

History. This small Protestant party has attracted consistent electoral support over the years, sufficient to give it three Second Chamber seats in each of the three general elections held in May 1977, May 1981 and September 1982 respectively.

Orientation. The SGP is Calvinist in basic ethos.

Publications. *De Banier* (fortnightly)

Netherlands Antilles

Capital: Willemstad (Curaçao)   Pop. 265,000

The Netherlands Antilles are, under the 1954 Charter of the Kingdom of the Netherlands, part of that kingdom together with the metropolitan Netherlands—with both partners enjoying full autonomy in internal affairs and united on a footing of equality for the protection of their common interests. The Dutch Crown is represented by a Governor who has executive powers in external affairs which he exercises in co-operation with the Council of Ministers responsible to the legislature (*Staten*). The latter has 22 members elected by universal adult suffrage for the various islands—Curaçao 12, Aruba 8, Bonaire 1, and Saba, St Maarten and St Eustatius together 1. The island of Aruba is scheduled to achieve separate independence by 1996.

In elections to the *Staten* held in June 1982 seats were gained as follows: New Antilles Movement (MAN) 6, People's Electoral Movement (MEP) 5, Democratic Party 4, National United People's Party (NVP-U) 3, Aruban People's Party (AUP) 2, Aruban Patriotic Party (PPA) 1, Bonaire Progressive Union 1.

Aruban Patriotic Party
Partido Patriotico Arubano (PPA)

Address. Oranjestad, Aruba, Netherlands Antilles

Leadership. Benny Nisbet (l.)

History. The PPA held four seats in the Legislative Assembly in 1969–73 (when it participated in a four-party coalition) and three thereafter. It took part in a coalition Government formed in 1977 by the Democratic Party and the National United People's Party. In the 1979 elections to the Legislative Assembly the PPA's representation was reduced from three members to one.

Orientation. The PPA is opposed to complete independence for Aruba and is largely supported by non-Aruban inhabitants of the island.

Aruban People's Party
Arubaanse Volkspartij (AVP)

Leadership. Henny Eman (l.)

History. The AVP held four seats in the *Staten* between 1969 and 1973, when it was a partner in a coalition Government (with the Democratic Party, the National United People's Party and the Aruban Patriotic Party), but it lost all its seats in 1973 and did not return to the *Staten* until 1979.

The AVP boycotted a referendum held on March 25, 1977, when 83 per cent of the valid votes cast by Aruba's voters were in favour of independence (in a 70 per cent poll). In elections to the Island Council of Aruba held on April 25, 1979, the AVP gained four out of the nine seats.

Orientation. The AVP stands for Aruba's independence from Curaçao, its leader having been a charismatic figure in the separatist movement since World War II.

Bonaire Progressive Union
Unión Progresista Bonairiana (UPB)

Address. P.O.B. 55, Kralendijk, Bonaire, Netherlands Antilles

Leadership. Rudi Ellis (l.); C.V. Winklaar (s.g.)

History. The UPB first gained the Bonaire seat in the Legislative Assembly in 1977; it lost it in the 1979 elections but regained it in 1982.

Orientation. The UPB has supported the National United People's Party.

Membership. 2,134

Democratic Party
Democratische Partij van Curaçao (DP)

Address. Neptunusweg 28, Willemstad, Curaçao, Netherlands Antilles

Leadership. Agustín M. Díaz (l.)

Founded. Dec. 8, 1944

History. From 1958 onwards the DP was in power, at first with the support of parties from islands other than Curaçao, and from 1969 until 1973 with the National United People's Party (NVP-U). Thereafter it was in opposition. In the 1977 elections to the Legislative Assembly the DP again emerged as the strongest party, and its leader thereupon formed a coalition Government with the NVP-U and the Aruban Patriotic Party, but this Government resigned in April 1979 and in elections held in July 1979 the DP lost half its seats. Since June 1982 it has held four seats.

Orientation. The DP stands for independence for the Netherlands Antilles as one entity, but with internal self-government for each of the six islands. It has liberal socialist objectives.

Democratic Party (DP)—Windward Islands

History. This branch of the Democratic Party has traditionally held the Windward Islands seat (for the islands of Saba and St Eustatius and the southern part of St Maarten) in the Legislative Assembly.

National United People's Party
Nationale Volkspartij-Unie (NVP-U)

Address. Willemstad, Curaçao, Netherlands Antilles

History. The NVP-U was in opposition until 1969 and thereafter partner in a coalition Government with the Democratic Party. After gaining five seats in the Legislative Assembly in August 1973 it formed a coalition Government with the People's Electoral Movement and the Workers' Liberation Front. However, after losing two of its five seats in the Legislative Assembly in 1977 the NVP-U joined a coalition Government led by the Democratic Party. This Government resigned in April 1979 and in subsequent elections the NVP-U was reduced to two seats in the Legislative Assembly. Earlier the NVP-U had undergone a split with its leader, Juancho Evertsz, forming a separate

Akshon Social Kristian party (which gained no seats). In June 1982 the party increased the number of its seats in the Assembly to three.

Orientation. The NVP-U is a Christian social party favouring independence for the Netherlands Antilles as one entity, but with a federative system.

International affiliations. Christian Democratic International

---

New Antilles Movement
Movementu Antiyas Nobo (MAN)

Address. La Plataweg 2a, Willemstad, Curaçao, Netherlands Antilles

Leadership. Dominico F. Martina (l.); Angel Salsbach (g.s.)

Founded. April 1979

History. The party was established by its leader, who had seceded from the Workers' Liberation Front. In elections to the Council of the island of Curaçao in April 1979 it gained six out of 21 seats, while in elections to the islands' *Staten* in June 1982 it obtained six of the 22 seats.

Orientation. The MAN stands for the continued cohesion of the Netherlands Antilles in an independent state.

` *International affiliations.* Socialist International (consultative member)

People's Electoral Movement
Movimiento Electoral di Pueblo (MEP)

Address. Cumana 84, Oranjestad, Aruba, Netherlands Antilles

Leadership. Gilberto François (Betico) Croes (l. and pres.)

Founded. February 1971

History. The MEP first gained representation in the *Staten* of the Netherlands Antilles in August 1973 and subsequently joined the central Government, and since April 1975 it has held a majority of seats in the Council of the island of Aruba. In September 1975 the *Staten* adopted an MEP motion recognizing the principle of self-determination for Aruba, and in a referendum held in March 1977 some 83 per cent of those voting (in a 70 per cent poll) approved the MEP's objective of independence for Aruba. The MEP was not, however, admitted to the central Government after elections held in June 1977, but it returned to the Government after elections held in July 1979. In elections to the 21 seats of the Aruba Island Council in April 1979, the MEP gained 12 seats and it thereupon formed the Aruba Government.

The MEP subsequently led the Aruba delegation to a Round Table Conference in the Netherlands, where it was agreed that Aruba would become a full partner in the Kingdom of the Netherlands in 1986 and achieve independence in 1996.

In September 1981 the MEP left the Government of the Netherlands Antilles after that Government had rejected the MEP's claim that Aruba should retain sole rights to all oil exploitation off its coast (whereas the Government held that they should be held jointly by all six islands).

Orientation. The MEP is a social democratic party without distinction of race, religion or social origins. Its aim is an independent Aruba with co-operation with the other islands of the Netherlands Antilles and in a commonwealth relationship with the Kingdom of the Netherlands. The MEP supports the 1945 UN Declaration of Human Rights.

Structure. The MEP has as its highest organ a party congress which nominates the party's leader, who is president of the MEP's congress, council, board and general meeting. The MEP's council elects the members of the board (other than the president), which is charged with executing resolutions of the congress and the council.

Membership. 9,000

Publications. *Progreso,* 25,000

International affiliations. Socialist International (consultative member)

Workers' Liberation Front
Frente Obrero de Liberación (FOL)

Address. Willemstad, Curaçao, Netherlands Antilles

Leadership. Wilson Godett (l.)

Founded. 1973

History. The FOL arose out of labour disputes and held three seats in the Legislative Assembly until 1979, when it failed to win representation. It was a member of a coalition Government with the National United People's Party until 1977.

Orientation. FOL is socialist, in favour of a federative system based on voluntary participation by the different islands and on prior exact determination of the constitutional structure.

New Zealand

Capital: Wellington

Pop. 3,200,000

The Dominion of New Zealand, a member of the Commonwealth, is a parliamentary democracy with the British monarch as head of state represented by a Governor-General. It has a unicameral 92-member House of Representatives elected for a three-year term by residents above the age of 18 years and by a simple majority in 88 single-member constituencies and four Maori constituencies. It has a Cabinet headed by a Prime Minister appointed by the Governor-General.

As a result of elections held on Nov. 28, 1981, seats in the House of Representatives were distributed as follows: National Party 47, Labour Party 43, Social Credit Political League 2.

Communist Party of New Zealand

Address. Box 1785, Auckland, New Zealand
Leadership. Central committee.
Orientation. The party declares itself to be "Marxist-Leninist".
Membership. Undisclosed
Publications. *People's Voice* (fortnightly)

New Democratic Party

Leadership. J. B. O'Brien
Founded. May 1972
Orientation. The party supports free enterprise and is opposed to nationalization and centralization of government.

New Zealand Labour Party (NZLP)

Address. P.O. Box 6146, Te Aro, Wellington, New Zealand
Leadership. David R. Lange (l.); J. P. Anderton (pres.); John T. Wybrow (s.g.)
Founded. July 1916
History. The party had its roots in the Political Labour League (1905–08), the first New Zealand Labour Party (1910–12), the United Labour Party (1912–13) and the Social Democratic Party (1913–16). The party formed in 1916 was committed to "the socialization of the means of production, distribution and exchange" and during World War I its six members of Parliament refused to enter into any coalition government. The party grew from 11,000 members (including 72 affiliated trade unions) in 1918 to almost 46,000 members in 1925.

The NZLP did not come to power until 1935, when it obtained a majority of 30 in the House of Representatives and subsequently laid the basis of the country's welfare state system. By 1946 its majority was reduced to four and in 1949 it lost power. It returned to Government in 1957 with a majority of only two seats but was again defeated in 1960 (losing seven seats). The party thereafter was again in office from 1972 to 1975, initially under Norman Kirk and subsequently, following Kirk's death in 1974, under the leadership of W. E. (Bill) Rowling. From 1975 to 1984 it was in opposition.

Orientation. The NZLP is a democratic socialist party.
Structure. The party is based on branch membership and affiliated trade unions; the party's controlling body is the New Zealand council which operates between annual conferences.
Membership. 240,000
International affiliations. Socialist International; Asia-Pacific Socialist Organization

New Zealand National Party

Address. National Centre, 35–37 Victoria St., Wellington, New Zealand
Leadership. (Mrs) Sue Wood (pres.); Robert D. Muldoon (l.); P. B. Leay (sec.)

Founded. 1936

History. After the Labour Party had been in power from 1935 to 1949, the National Party gained a majority in general elections in the latter year and subsequently was in office until 1956, when it was narrowly defeated by the Labour Party. It was returned to power, with narrow majorities in at least seven constituencies, in 1960 and thereafter was in office until 1972.

Following a Labour Government which was in power in 1972–75, the National Party was returned to office after gaining 55 seats as against 32 retained by Labour. In the 1978 election its share of the vote fell from 47.2 per cent in 1975 to 39.5 per cent, but it nevertheless retained a majority of seats. Its share of the vote was 39.8 per cent in 1978 and 39.2 per cent in 1982, but it remained in power until 1984.

Orientation. The National Party is a conservative formation standing for private enterprise, a property-owning democracy and personal freedom; it nevertheless accepts the principle of the welfare state system created by the Labour Party in the period 1935 to 1949.

International affiliations. International Democrat Union; Pacific Democrat Union

---

New Zealand Party

Leadership. Robert (Bob) Jones (founder)

Founded. Aug. 22, 1983

Orientation. This right-wing party has campaigned for an immediate tax reform by lowering direct taxes and substituting a flat income tax of 30 per cent on incomes of over NZ$10,000 per annum. Its founder has expressed his intention as being to force the National Party to abandon its "socialist" tendencies and to revert to the principles on which it was founded.

International affiliations. Christian Democratic International

---

New Zealand Social Credit Political League

Address. P.O. Box 11-174, Manners Street Post Office, Wellington, New Zealand

Leadership. Bruce Craig Beetham (l.); J. S. Lipa (pres.)

Founded. 1954

History. This party first secured representation in Parliament in 1966, when it obtained 14.4 per cent of the vote and its then leader, Vernon Cracknell, was elected

(this being the first time that a third party was, in addition to the two major parties, represented in Parliament). However, the party lost this seat in 1969 and was unrepresented until a by-election in February 1978 was won by its current leader, who retained it in the November 1978 general elections. A by-election in 1981 was won by the party's deputy leader. In the 1981 elections the party obtained 20.7 per cent of the vote and retained its two seats in the House of Representatives.

Orientation. The Social Credit philosophy is directed towards a fairer distribution of ownership in a "property-owning democracy, a nation of self-employed, owner-operators, co-operative ventures and worker shareholders", with "decentralization of power and government responsibility". In 1982 the party adopted a policy of "armed neutrality".

Structure. In addition to its leader and president, the League has a deputy leader, four vice-presidents, some 20 dominion councillors and a dominion secretary.

Membership. 33,000

Publications. *Social Credit Guardian* (monthly)

New Zealand Socialist Unity Party

Address. 64 Symonds St., P.O. Box 1987, Auckland 1, New Zealand

Leadership. G. H. Andersen (pres.); G. E. Jackson (g.s.)

Founded. 1966

History. The party was formed as a result of an ideological split in the Communist Party, as a result of which the pro-Soviet wing broke away to form this separate party.

Orientation. The party is a Marxist formation basing itself on the working class and seeks to build a socialist New Zealand.

Structure. The party is based on democratic centralism.

Publications. *New Zealand Tribune* (monthly), 3,000; *Socialist Politics*, 350; *Information Bulletin*, 200

International affiliations. The party is recognized by the Communist parties of the Soviet-bloc countries.

New Zealand Values Party

Address. P.O. Box 137, Wellington, New Zealand

Leadership. Janet Robough, Alan Wilkinson (leaders); Barry Creswell (pres.); Cathy Corbett (sec.)

Founded. May 1972

History. The party contested general elections in about half the constituencies in 1972 and in all in 1975, when it polled 5.2 per cent of the vote, and in 1978, when its vote dropped to 2.5 per cent of the total.

Orientation. The party's concerns are ecological, for decentralization and a community-based co-operative economy and society.

Structure. A party conference decides on policy and directions, and a national council (elected by office-holders and delegates from each of 18 regions) oversees the party's administration. Branches, grouped into regions, have control at local level.

Membership. 2,500

Publications. *Linkletter* (monthly newsletter)

International affiliations. The party has links with the West European Green movement.

New Zealand Women's Political Party

Founded. April 1982

History. This party announced its intention to nominate at least one woman candidate for elections in 1984.

Orientation. The party stands for "full representation of women by women" in Parliament.

Self-Government Party
Manu Motuhake

Leadership. Matiu Rata

Founded. 1979

History. This Maori party was founded after Matiu Rata, who had been Minister of Maori Affairs in 1972-75, had resigned from the Labour Party. It nominated candidates for the four Maori constituencies but gained no seats in the November 1981 elections to the House of Representatives.

Socialist Party of New Zealand (SPNZ)

Address. P.O. Box 1929, Auckland, New Zealand

Founded. 1931

History. The party has been inspired by the Socialist Party of Great Britain. It has campaigned, inter alia, against mass unemployment, the waging of war, the Labour Party (for never having been socialist) and the Communist Party (for abandoning the class struggle and true socialism). It has never had any parliamentary representation.

Membership. 30–40

Publications. *The Socialist Viewpoint*

Addendum. In general elections held on July 14, 1984, to a House of Representatives expanded to 95 members, the Labour Party was returned to power with 56 seats against 37 for the National Party and two for the Social Credit Political League.

New Zealand Associated Territories

Cook Islands

Capital: Avarua, Rarotonga   Pop. 18,000

Under a Constitution proclaimed on Aug. 8, 1965, the Cook Islands—associated with New Zealand—have complete control over their own affairs except for external policy and defence, for which the Government of New Zealand retains responsibility, and they may unilaterally declare their independence if they so wish. There is a Cabinet headed by a Premier and responsible to a 24-member Legislative Assembly elected by universal adult suffrage.

In elections held on March 30, 1978, the Cook Islands Party (which had been in power for 13 years) obtained 15 seats and the Democratic Party the remaining seven in the then 22-member Assembly. However, this result was overturned on July 25, 1978, by the Chief Justice who ruled that there had been "unlawful conduct" and that eight seats awarded to the Cook Islands Party had in fact been lawfully won by the (opposition) Democratic Party, which thus obtained 15 of the Assembly's 22 seats and formed a Government.

In elections held on Nov. 2, 1983, to a 24-member Assembly the Democratic Party won 13 seats and the Cook Islands Party the remaining 11.

Cook Islands Party (CIP)

Address. Rarotonga, Cook Islands
Leadership. Geoffrey Henry (l.)
Founded. 1965
History. Until 1978 the party won all elections held under the 1965 Constitution which made the islands an internally self-governing state in free association with New Zealand. However, upon a ruling by the Chief Justice (see introduction above), the party's representation in the Legislative Assembly was in July 1978 reduced to seven out of 22 seats. The party's then leader, Sir Albert R. Henry, who had been Premier of the Cook Islands from 1965 to 1977, was, after admitting responsibility for electoral irregularities, on Aug. 21, 1979, barred by the Rarotonga High Court from taking part in politics for three years; however, this order was overturned in October 1979 by three judges of the New Zealand Supreme Court sitting as the Cook Islands Appeal Court.

Sir Albert died in January 1981 and was succeeded as party leader by his son Geoffrey. The CIP was briefly in office again from April to August 1983, after it had, in elections held on March 30, 1983, gained 13 of the 24 seats in the Legislative Assembly. Geoffrey Henry, however, resigned as Premier on Aug. 2 after an appeal court ruling that he had breached a constitutional provision by not resigning before the end of the seventh day of the Legislative Assembly's new session. In the new elections held on Nov. 2, 1983, the CIP lost its majority in the Assembly and thereupon went into opposition.

Democratic Party (DP)

Address. P.O. Box 202, Rarotonga, Cook Islands
Leadership. Sir Thomas Davis (l.)
Founded. 1972
History. The DP was in opposition until July 1978, when it obtained a majority in the Legislative Assembly as a result of a decision by the Chief Justice (see introduction above) and thereupon formed a Government. It remained in office until March 1983 when it was defeated in general elections held at the end of that month, but was returned to power as a result of the November 1983 elections, in which it gained 13 seats (against 11 retained by the Cook Islands Party). The DP thereupon formed a Government under Sir Thomas Davis.

Unity Movement

Founded. 1978
History. This movement is opposed to party politics but contested the general elections of 1979 and 1983 without, however, gaining any seat.

Niue

Capital: Alofi   Pop. 3,300

The island of Niue has since October 1974 had self-government in free association with New Zealand, which retains responsibility for Niue's defence and external affairs. There is a Premier assisted by three ministers. Legislative power is held by an elected Assembly, which may call upon New Zealand to legislate for the island. There are no organized political parties.

Nicaragua

Capital: Managua   Pop. 3,000,000

The Republic of Nicaragua is ruled by a junta of national reconstruction which heads a provisional Government installed in July 1979 following the defeat of President Anastasio Somoza Debayle by the forces of the Sandinista National Liberation Front (FSLN) after 18 months of civil war. (Ex-President Somoza was assassinated in Asunción, Paraguay, on Sept. 17, 1980, but the Government of Nicaragua denied any involvement in this murder despite suggestions to the contrary by the Government of Paraguay.) The FSLN announced on Aug. 23, 1980, that preparations for general elections would not begin until 1984, and under a decree issued on Aug. 27, 1980, all electoral activity was banned until 1984. A Council of State, appointed as an auxiliary legislative body, first met on May 4, 1980; its 51 members included representatives of 32 of the country's political, labour, social and popular organizations and also of the private sector of the economy.

On March 23, 1981, five opposition parties—the Nicaraguan Social Christian Party, the Social Democratic Party, the Nicaraguan Democratic Movement, the Democratic Conservative Party and the Constitutionalist Liberal Party—issued a joint statement declaring that the Government was trying to impose a Marxist-Leninist dictatorship on the country and was violating the freedom of political and trade union organizations.

Despite such criticism the Sandinista regime continued to take further restrictive measures. On Sept. 9, 1981, the Government introduced a state of "economic and social emergency", establishing severe penalties for staging strikes, for occupying land outside the agrarian reform programme, for taking over factories, for obstructing production, and also for "inciting foreign governments to inflict damage on the national economy".

Under a bill drafted by the FSLN in 1981 the right to establish political parties was made subject to the following conditions: the party's fundamental principles must be "popular, pluralistic, anti-imperialist and anti-racist"; details of the party's membership, leaders and electoral platform must be submitted to the Council of State; and the party must be represented on the Council of State and abstain from "activities against public order and the stability of the institutions of the national reconstruction Government". The bill was approved by the Council of State on Aug. 17, 1982, and was promulgated three months later. General elections were subsequently scheduled to be held in 1985, provided there was "normality".

Communist Party of Nicaragua
Partido Comunista de Nicaragua (PCN)

Leadership. Elías Altamirano (s.g.)
Founded. 1967
History. This party was banned under the Somoza regime. Legalized after the Sandinista revolution, it soon began to criticize the new regime as not being sufficiently revolutionary. On Oct. 6, 1981, PCN members published a document on the "serious economic crisis and the deviation of the Sandinista revolution". The Government, however, accused the PCN of having conducted "organized and systematic sabotage against the national

economy". Four PCN members, arrested on Oct. 20, 1981, were sentenced to seven months in prison on Oct. 29 of that year.

Orientation. The PCN is a pro-Chinese formation.

Structure. The PCN has a radical trade union wing, the Council for Union Action and Unity (*Consejo de Acción y Unidad Sindical*, CAUS).

Constitutionalist Liberal Party
Partido Liberal Constitucionalista (PLC)

Leadership. Ramiro Sacasa Guerrero (l.)

History. Derived from the centrist wing of elements within the pre-revolutionary National Liberal Party opposed to President Somoza, the PLC joined the Democratic Co-ordinating Board set up in July 1981. It is one of 32 organizations represented on the Council of State, although it is opposed to the Sandinista regime.

Democratic Conservative Party of Nicaragua
Partido Conservador Demócrata de Nicaragua (PCDN)

Leadership. Emilio Alvarez Montalbán (l.); José Castillo Osejo (nat. co-ordinator)
Founded. 1979
History. The representative of this "moderate" party (which had been the largest opposition party under President Somoza) resigned from the Council of State in November 1980. In July 1981 the party joined other opposition groups in forming the Democratic Co-ordinating Board. However, its then leader, Adolfo Calero Portocarrero, left the country early in 1983 and joined the Nicaraguan Democratic Forces (FDN), founded in November 1981 as a political-military organization which would "liberate our people from Marxist totalitarianism" and which was then based in Honduras and Florida.

Democratic Co-ordinating Board
Coordinadora Democrática (CD)

Founded. July 1981
History. The CD was set up as an alliance of opposition parties comprising the Nicaraguan Social Christian Party (PSCN) led by Adán Fletes Valle, the

Democratic Conservative Party of Nicaragua (PCDN) then led by Adolfo Calero Portocarrero, the Constitutionalist Liberal Party (PLC), the Social Democratic Party (PSD) led by Wilfredo Montalván, the Higher Council for Private Enterprise (Cosep) and two opposition trade union federations—the Trade Union Confederation for Unity (CUS) and the Nicaraguan Workers' Central (CTN).

Independent Liberal Party
Partido Liberal Independiente (PLI)

Address. Ciudad Jardin F29, Managua, Nicaragua
Leadership. Virgilio Godoy Reyes (l.)
Founded. 1946
History. This party was formed to rally Liberals disagreeing with the National Liberal Party, which was the vehicle of the ruling Somoza family. Like other opposition parties it boycotted most elections held under the Somoza regime. The party joined the pro-Sandinista Patriotic Front for the Revolution on the latter's formation in 1980.
Orientation. The PLI had advocated the restoration of civil and political freedoms.
International affiliations. Liberal International

Nicaraguan Democratic Movement
Movimiento Democrático Nicaragüense (MDN)

Leadership. Alfonso Robelo Callejas (pres.)
Founded. April 1978
History. The MDN was founded by a group of businessmen to oppose President Somoza's regime. It became a component of the Broad Opposition Front formed in July 1978 and also participated in the Sandinista regime which came to power in July 1979. However, as a Christian democratic party the MDN was soon in disagreement with the Sandinista Government. Although represented on the Council of State, the MDN withdrew its representative from the Council after the Government had banned an MDN-inspired political rally on Nov. 9, 1980.

In November 1981 the MDN stated that it would not co-operate with the Nicaraguan Social Christian and Social Democratic parties in seeking a dialogue with the Government. Robelo Callejas, who had on Oct. 21, 1981, been prevented from leaving the country, succeeded in departing from Nicaragua in June 1982 after the Government had declared his property forfeit because of his "aggressive activities" against the authorities.

On Aug. 15, 1982, the MDN called on students at Catholic schools to strike in protest against government hostility to the Church, and this led to clashes with members of pro-Sandinista youth organizations in which two people were killed, up to 20 injured and 80 arrested. In December 1982 the MDN joined the Democratic Revolutionary Alliance (*Alianza Revolucionaria Democrática*, ARDE), which was founded in Costa Rica and called on the Sandinista Government to hold elections before June 1983, but stated at the same time that it would not abandon its "military option".

Nicaraguan Social Christian Party
Partido Socialcristiano Nicaragüense (PSCN)

Address. Apdo. 4774, Managua, D.N., Nicaragua

Leadership. Agustín Jarquín Anaya (pres.); Luís Vega Miranda (s.g.)

Founded. 1957

History. In the 1967 elections the PSCN supported the National Opposition Union. Following the Sandinista revolution in 1979 the PSCN had a representative on the Council of State, but he resigned from the Council in November 1980. In October 1980 Adán Fletes Valle, then leader of the PSCN, was prevented from leaving the country. In July 1981 the party joined the Democratic Co-ordinating Board. In November 1981 the party called for a "national reflection dialogue" and all-party meetings with the Government.

In July 1983 the PSCN demanded an end to an allegedly government-supported campaign against the Roman Catholic Church (adhered to by the majority of Nicaragua's people), and also the release of five party members arrested between May 1982 and April 1983 and sentenced or awaiting trial for alleged subversive activities, as well as of other political prisoners.

Orientation. The PSCN is Christian democratic, for the protection of the family, workers' participation and free trade unions.

Structure. The PSCN has a seven-member national executive (which includes the party's president and its secretary-general), seven national councillors and a national disciplinary tribunal.

Membership. 42,000

Publications. *El Socialcristiano*

International affiliations. Christian Democratic International

Nicaraguan Socialist Party
Partido Socialista Nicaragüense (PSN)

Leadership. Luís Sánchez Sancho (s.g.)

Founded. 1939

History. The party, which was illegal until July 1979, took an active part in the political struggle against the Somoza regime and it organized and led the trade union movement. The party's representative on the Council of State is vice-president of that Council. The PSN forms part of the pro-Sandinista Patriotic Front of the Revolution set up in 1980.

Orientation. The PSN is a pro-Soviet communist party. During its period of illegality the party proclaimed as its immediate aim to free Nicaragua from US domination and the local oligarchy and to transform it into a genuine independent state, to which end it called for the unity of "all patriots in a democratic opposition". Pursuing democratic, pluralistic and non-aligned policies, the party plans to convert the Sandinist revolution into a socialist one.

International affiliations. The PSN is recognized by the Communist parties of the Soviet-bloc countries.

Patriotic Front for the Revolution
Frente Patriótico para la Revolución (FPR)

Founded. July 23, 1980

History. This Front was set up by the Sandinista National Liberation Front (SNLF) with the object of supporting the "patriotic and democratic" policy of the Government while acknowledging the FSLN's supreme position in the defence and promotion of the Nicaraguan revolution along democratic lines. The other parties in the FPR are the Independent Liberal Party, the Popular Social Christian Party and the Nicaraguan Socialist Party.

Popular Social Christian Party
Partido Popular Social Cristiano (PPSC)

Leadership. César Delgadillo Machado (l.)

Founded. 1976

History. This party joined the pro-Sandinista Patriotic Front for the Revolution set up in 1980.

Sandinista National Liberation Front
Frente Sandinista de Liberación Nacional
(FSLN)

Leadership. A nine-member national directorate

Founded. 1960

History. Named after Augusto César Sandino, a revolutionary leader killed by Nicaragua's National Guard in 1934, the FSLN was set up to conduct guerrilla warfare with the eventual object of overthrowing the dictatorial regime of President Anastasio Somoza Debayle, and in the 1970s its activities expanded into widespread civil war. It had, however, at the same time gained growing support not only among workers but also among business and professional people and the clergy.

On March 8, 1979, three factions of the FSLN—the *Terceristas* (or Insurrectionists), the (Marxist-Leninist) Prolonged Popular War (GPP) and the Proletarian Tendency—agreed on a programme of concerted action to overthrow President Somoza. On June 16 the FSLN formed (in Costa Rica) a "provisional junta of national reconstruction" including representatives of other anti-Somoza groupings, which on July 16 formed a provisional government council. On July 19 this junta and a Government set up by it took control in Managua. In September 1979 the new Government prohibited the use of the description "Sandinista" by any party other than the FSLN, which was described as "the legal vanguard of the Nicaraguan revolutionary process" and the sole "defender and loyal interpreter of the principles and objectives of the Sandinista ideology".

Increasing radicalization of the FSLN during its first years in power led to the defection of a number of prominent figures among its members. These included Edén Pastora Gómez, who had played a leading role in the revolution but who resigned as Deputy Minister of Defence and head of the Sandinista People's Army (EPS) on July 7, 1981, and left the country to form a Sandinista Revolutionary Front. This organization later joined a Democratic Revolutionary Alliance (*Alianza Revolucionaria Democrática*, ARDE) formed in Costa Rica in December 1982. In May 1983 the ARDE began military operations against the EPS after the Sandinista Government had not responded to an ultimatum of April 15, 1983, demanding the withdrawal from Nicaragua of Cuban forces sent there to assist the EPS.

Orientation. Under a programme issued on April 5, 1979, the FSLN called for the creation of a provisional Government of national unity, national reconstruction, a new national army, a non-aligned foreign policy and the expropriation of the assets of the Somoza family to provide a fund for national reconstruction. Its aims include improved standards of living, increased participation of the working people in decision-making and progressive nationalization of the economy.

Structure. The SNLF has organized neighbourhood defence committees to mobilize mass support and to assist the Government in public health, educational and security programmes.

Membership. 60,000

Social Democratic Party
Partido Social Democrático (PSD)

Leadership. Wilfredo Montalván (s.g.)

Founded. September 1979

History. The PSD, which had broken away from the Nicaraguan Social Christian Party, was at first officially accused of not having taken part in the struggle of the Sandinista National Liberation Front and of not sharing the latter's political principles and aspirations. The PSD joined the anti-Sandinista Democratic Co-ordinating Board set up in July 1981, although Wilfredo Montalván stated in November 1981 that his party was willing to co-operate in a proposed "national reflection dialogue". On Nov. 28, 1981, he and another PSD member were appointed to the Council of State.

Niger

Capital: Niamey   Pop. 5,800,000

The Republic of Niger is ruled by a Supreme Military Council which, on assuming power in April 1974, suspended the Constitution and dissolved the National Assembly and the *Parti Progressiste Nigérien*, until then the country's sole legal political organization. The President of the Supreme Military Council, Lt.-Col. Seyni Kountché, heads a (largely civilian) Council of Ministers, to which a Prime Minister was first appointed on Jan. 24, 1983.

A National Council for Development, orginally an advisory body, was in 1983 reconstituted as part of an elective system, with youth groups, village councils and producers' co-operatives at local level and subregional and regional councils above them, culminating in the National Development Council as the highest tier of a "development society".

Nigeria

Capital: Lagos (new capital, Abuja, under construction)   Pop. 84,700,000

The Federal Republic of Nigeria, an independent state within the Commonwealth, consists of 19 federative states and a federal capital territory. The 1979 Constitution under which Nigeria returned to civilian government after nearly 14 years of military rule specified that the country's governmental structure should be "based on the principles of democracy and social justice". Under that Constitution there was a President elected by universal adult suffrage for a four-year term; he was Chairman of the Council of State, presided over the federal Cabinet and had powers to appoint federal ministers.

Under the 1979 Constitution there was a federal National Assembly consisting of (i) a Senate of five members from each state, and (ii) a House of Representatives of 450 members—each House being elected for a four-year term by universal adult suffrage. Each state had its own similarly elected House of Assembly. The Constitution provided for freedom of assembly and association, including the right to form or belong to a political party; but with a view to overcoming ethnic and regional divisions parties were required to avoid the use of any names, emblems or mottos with religious or ethnic connotations; moreover, their activities could not be confined to one part of Nigeria.

Nigeria's first general elections since before the 1966 military coup were held in August-September 1983, with President Shehu Shagari of the National Party of Nigeria (NPN) being returned to the federal presidency with 46 per cent of the popular vote against 30.1 per cent for Chief Obafemi Awolowo of the United Party of Nigeria (UPN), 13.5 per cent for Dr Nnamdi Azikiwe of the Nigerian People's Party, 6.8 per cent for Alhaji Hassan Yusuf of the People's Redemption Party (PRP), 2.5 per cent for Alhaji Waziri Ibrahim of the Great

Nigeria People's Party (GNPP) and 1.1 per cent for Tunji Braithwaite of the Nigeria Advance Party (NAP). The elections to the House of Representatives resulted in the following distribution of seats: NPN 306, UPN 51, NPP 48, PRP 41 (with neither the GNPP nor the NAP securing representation).

Only three months after being sworn in for his second term of office, President Shagari was overthrown on Dec. 31, 1983, in an almost bloodless coup led by Maj.-Gen. Mohammed Buhari, who formed a Supreme Military Council with himself as its chairman. The new military regime suspended the 1979 Constitution and banned all political parties.

Norway

Capital: Oslo   Pop. 4,600,000

In the Kingdom of Norway, a constitutional and hereditary monarchy, the King exercises his authority through a Council of State (Cabinet) led by a Prime Minister and responsible to Parliament (the *Storting*) of 155 members elected for a four-year term by universal suffrage of citizens above the age of 18 years on the basis of proportional representation, the country being divided into 19 electoral districts each represented by between four and 15 members of Parliament. The *Storting* divides itself by election into an Upper House (*Lagting*) of 39 of the *Storting*'s members and a Lower House (*Odelsting*) of the remaining 116 members, these two Houses having to consider separately any questions relating to legislation. In the event of disagreement any bill can be approved only by a majority of two-thirds of the *Storting* as a whole.

Parties receive public funds in proportion to their electoral support and partly to subsidize their educational activities.

As a result of elections held in September and December 1981, seats in the *Storting* were distributed as follows: Labour Party 66, Conservatives 53, Christian People's Party 15, Centre Party 11, Left Socialists 4, Progressive Party 4, Liberal Party 2.

Centre Party
Senterpartiet

Address. Peder Claussønsgt. 2, Postbox 6890 St. Olavspl., Oslo, Norway
Leadership. Johan J. Jakobsen (ch.); Svein Sundsboe (s.g.)
Founded. 1920
History. Originating from the agrarian trade union, the party was founded as the Agrarian Party with the object of gaining greater political and parliamentary influence for those working in rural occupations and of raising them to the level of other occupations. Since 1946, when co-operation with the agrarian trade union was ended, the party has been independent and has worked for society in general, changing its name to Centre Party

in 1959, thus emphasizing its position between the right-wing and left-wing parties.

In 1931-33 the party formed a minority Government, and after unsuccessful efforts to work with the Conservatives and the Liberals the party, in 1935, entered into a "crisis compromise" with the Labour Party, which then came to power. In 1963 the party entered into a minority Government coalition with other non-socialist parties; from 1965 to 1971 it took part in a majority non-socialist Government; and in 1972-73 again in a minority Government with the Liberals and the Christian People's Party.

The party was in opposition to Labour Governments from 1973 to September 1981, when it gave its general support to a minority Conservative administration. In

340

June 1983 it entered a majority three-party centre-right Government headed by the Conservatives.

Orientation. The party is non-socialist and stands for occupational, regional and social equalization, a mixed (private and public ownership) economy and the development of the welfare state.

Structure. Under a central organization there are local organizations in counties and municipalities (the party being strongest in rural areas); the party also has a youth and a women's section.

Membership. 60,000

Publications. *Sentrum* (10 times a year), 50,000

Christian Democratic (or People's) Party
Kristelig Folkeparti

Address. Rosenkrantzgt. 13, Box 1477, Vika, Oslo 1, Norway

Leadership. Kjell Magne Bondevik (ch.); Harald Synnes (parl. l.)

Founded. 1933

History. Founded in the Hordaland constituency, the party had one member elected to the *Storting* in 1933 and two in 1936. Established at national level by 1945, it gained eight seats and later steadily increased its parliamentary representation, winning 22 seats in 1977 and thus becoming the country's third strongest party (although in 1981 it retained only 15 seats). It has taken part in majority coalition Governments in 1965-71 (with the Conservatives, Liberals and the Centre Party) and in a minority coalition Government with the Centre Party in 1972-73 under the premiership of Lars Korvald. In June 1983 it entered a centre-right Government with the Conservatives and the Centre Party.

Orientation. The party's basis is the Christian faith (guiding its view of man and his rights and duties in society as well as the use of resources); the party is democratic, non-socialist (though with strong social involvement) and centrist (i.e. for state control and guidance but not, as a rule, state involvement in economic affairs).

Structure. A general assembly (of delegates elected by regional assemblies and meeting every second year) elects a national central board; the latter, together with the chairmen of 19 regional boards (elected annually by delegates of regional assemblies of local groups) and the members of the parliamentary group, forms a national committee; there are also a women's and a youth organization.

Membership. 60,000

Publications. *Folkets Framtid* (political organ, twice weekly), 16,000; *Idé* (periodical, four times a year), 2,500; *Valo Forlag* (publishing house); several local monthly newspapers

International affiliations. Christian Democratic International

---

Communist Party of Norway
Norges Kommunistiske Parti

Address. Grønlandsleiret 39, Postboks 3634, GB, Oslo 1, Norway

Leadership. Hans I. Kleven (ch.); Odd S. Karlsen (sec.)

Founded. November 1923

History. The party was founded by left-wing members of the Labour Party after the latter had withdrawn from the Comintern, which it had joined in 1919. During the Nazi occupation (1940-45) the party continued to work underground, and in the 1945 general elections it won 11 seats. However, in the 1949 elections the party lost all these seats and its central committee thereupon "purged" the party of "Trotskyist, bourgeois-nationalist and Titoist" elements. In 1953 the party gained three seats in the *Storting*, and in 1957 only one, which it lost in 1961.

Having not been represented in Parliament since 1961, the party in 1973 joined a Socialist Election Alliance (comprising also the Socialist People's Party and other left-wing groups), which won 16 seats in the 1973 elections to the *Storting*. In November 1975, however, the party decided not to dissolve itself in order to merge in a new Socialist Left Party but to continue as a Communist Party—thus conforming to a message from the Communist Party of the Soviet Union stating that "a homogeneous Marxist-Leninist party" was "necessary" and that "all manifestations of opportunism of the right and left" should be rejected.

In the 1977 general elections the party gained only 0.4 per cent of the votes and no seats, and in 1981 it retained only 0.3 per cent.

Structure. The party has a 35-member central committee, a 15-member political bureau and a secretariat of six members; its congress meets every third year.

Membership. 4,000

Publications. *Friheten* (Freedom, weekly), 8,000

International affiliations. The party is recognized by the Communist parties of the Soviet-bloc countries.

Conservative Party
Høyre

Address. Høyres Hovedorganisasjon, Stortingsgt. 20, Oslo 1, Norway

Leadership. Kaare Willoch (l.); Fridtjov Clemet (s.g.)

Founded. 1884

History. Since its foundation the Conservative Party has participated in 13 governments—two of them being one-party governments and the others coalitions with non-socialist parties. Since the war the party has been in coalition with the Liberal, Christian Democratic and Centre parties (briefly in 1963 and from 1965 to 1971). The party's electoral support has varied from about 50 per cent in 1894 to around 20 per cent in the years after 1933 and to 31.8 per cent in the 1981 general elections.

On the basis of the substantial gains made by the party in the September 1981 elections, the Conservative leader, Kaare Willoch, formed a one-party minority administration. In June 1983 this was transformed into a majority three-party Government when both the Centre Party and the Christian Democrats accepted cabinet membership.

Orientation. The party believes in a "conservative progressive" policy, founded on the Christian cultural heritage, the rule of law and democracy, to ensure "freedom and social responsibility, partnership in society, the right to private property, and mutually binding national and international co-operation".

Structure. The party has local groups in every municipal district, and they are organized in 19 county organizations. Its annual convention elects the leadership for a two-year period. A central board (of about 45 members) holds bimonthly meetings, while an executive council (of chairmen, two elected members, the leader of the parliamentary group, and representatives of the women's association and Young Conservatives) meets weekly.

Membership. 175,000

International affiliations. European Democrat Union; International Democrat Union

Liberal Party
Venstre

Address. Moellergt. 16, Oslo 1, Norway

Leadership. Odd E. Dørum (l.); Kjell Strømme (s.g.)

Founded. 1884

History. Whereas in 1936 the party held 23 seats in the *Storting*, its parliamentary representation after World War II was consistently lower than that figure (its 21 seats gained in 1949 being reduced to 14 by 1961, though rising to 18 in 1965). Of its 13 members elected in 1973, a majority supported the projected entry of Norway into the European Community; after such entry had been rejected in the referendum of September 1972, the anti-EEC minority participated in a coalition Government with the Christian People's and Centre parties, while the pro-EEC Liberals subsequently formed the Liberal People's Party. The Liberal Party was thus left with only four seats in the *Storting*, and this number was reduced to two in the elections held in September 1973. It retained two seats in 1977 and 1981.

Orientation. The *Venstre* is a radical liberal party also concerned with ecological and environmental ("green") policies.

Membership. 12,000

Publications. Var Framtid (weekly)

International affiliations. Liberal International

Liberal People's Party
Det Liberale Folkepartiet

Address. Prinsensgt. 7, P.O.B. 510 Sentrum, Oslo 1, Norway

Leadership. Magne Lerheim (ch.); Odd Baarnes (sec.)

Founded. 1972

History. The party was founded by members of the Liberal Party who favoured Norway's entry into the European Community (which was rejected in a referendum held in September 1972) and of the 13 Liberal members elected to the *Storting* in 1969 nine joined the new party. In the 1973 elections, however, the party gained only one seat (while the Liberal Party retained only two); since 1977 (when it gained only 1.7 per cent of the vote) it has held no seat in the *Storting*. In the 1981 elections it obtained only 0.6 per cent of the vote.

International affiliations. Liberal International

Norwegian Labour Party
Det Norske Arbeiderparti (DNA)

Address. Youngstorget 2 A, Oslo 1, Norway

Leadership. (Mrs) Gro Harlem Brundtland (ch.); Ivar Leveraas (s.g.)

Founded. 1887

History. By the end of the 19th century the party had 17,000 members and commanded 24,000 votes. In 1904 it won four seats in Parliament, and by 1915 the party had 62,000 members and gained 198,000 votes (32 per cent of the total electorate). In 1918 the party's leadership was taken over by its left wing, largely under the influence of the Russian revolution, but disagreements ensued over membership of the Third International (Comintern). In 1921 dissenters formed the Social Democratic Party and in 1923 the Communist Party was formed, but in 1927 a basis was found for the reunification of the Norwegian Labour Party and the Social Democratic Party, with some Communists also joining the reunified party, which in that year obtained 368,000 votes (or 36.8 per cent of the total vote), and formed its first (short-lived) Government. In 1933 the party gained 40 per cent of the vote, and in 1935 it formed its second Government.

Under Nazi occupation during World War II the party was illegal and its leaders went into exile or were sent to German concentration camps. At the end of the war, the party's chairman formed a broad coalition Government, and in October 1945 it obtained a majority in Parliament, whereupon a Labour Government was formed, and the party remained in office until 1965. The party was again in power from 1971 to 1972, when the Government resigned on being defeated in a referendum rejecting Norway's membership of the European Community. During the 1973-81 period the party formed a (minority) Government, but went into opposition following its setback in the September 1981 elections.

Orientation. The DNA stands for democratic socialism, the "abolition of class distinctions and all social, economic and cultural inequalities in society".

Membership. 180,000

Publications. 42 daily newspapers (with a total circulation of 500,000)

International affiliations. Socialist International

Progressive Party
Fremskrittspartiet

Address. Box 815 Sentrum, Oslo 1, Norway

Leadership. Carl I. Hagen (ch.)

Founded. April 1973

History. The party was established as Anders Lange's Party for a Strong Reduction in Taxation and Public Intervention, its founder being a well-known dog-kennel owner who had become a national celebrity as a result of his political comments in a dog-breeding magazine which he edited. Following Lange's death in 1974, the party took its present name in January 1977. In the 1973 general elections it gained four seats in the *Storting* but lost all these in the 1977 elections. However, in the 1981 elections it gained four seats and 4.5 per cent of the vote.

Orientation. The party propagates Adam Smith's economic theories and the rights of the individual.

Structure. The party has local groups, 19 county sections, a national assembly, a council and an executive committee.

Membership. 10,000

Publications. *Fremskritt* (weekly newspaper), 3,600

Socialist Left Party
Sosialistisk Venstreparti

Address. St Olavsgt. 27, Oslo 1, Norway

Leadership. Prof. Theo Koritzinsky (ch.); Erik Solheim (sec.)

Founded. March 1975

History. The formation of the party was preceded by the establishment in 1973 of the Socialist Electoral Alliance by three groups—the Communist Party, the Socialist People's Party and the Left Social Democratic Organization; in the 1973 elections the Alliance gained 16 seats in the *Storting* (and 11.2 per cent of the votes cast) on an anti-EEC, anti-NATO and strongly socialist platform. Following the conversion of the Alliance into the Socialist Left Party in March 1975, the Communist Party decided in November 1975 not to dissolve itself in order to join the new party, and in the general election of September 1977 the Socialist Left Party gained only 4.1 per cent of the votes and two seats. However, in 1981 it gained four seats in the *Storting* (with 5 per cent of the votes).

Orientation. The party stands for "national independence, socialism and full employment on a Marxist basis".

Structure. The party has a national congress meeting every two years, a 27-member national committee meeting four times a year, a 15-member central committee meeting fortnightly and a five-member executive committee, which meets once a week.

Membership. 10,000

Publications. *Ny Tid* (weekly newspaper)

Workers' Communist Party
Arbeidernes Kommunistparti Marxist-Leninistene (AKP-ML)

Leadership. Paal Steigan (ch.); Sigurd Allern (sec.)
Founded. 1975
History. This group arose out of the youth organization of the Socialist People's Party, which was in 1975 absorbed in the Socialist Left Party (see separate entry). The AKP-ML has contested elections as part of a Red Electoral Alliance (*Röd Valgallianse*, RV), but has failed to secure representation in the *Storting*. In the 1981 elections the Alliance gained 0.7 per cent of the vote.

Other Parties

Other registered parties not represented in the *Storting* are the following:

Lappish People's List (*Samefolkets Liste*)

Norwegian Democratic Party (*Norges Demokratiske Parti*)

Single Persons Party (*Ensliges Parti*)

Women's Free Popularly-elected Representatives (*Kvinnenes Frie Folkevalgte*)

Oman

Capital: Muscat   Pop. 1,500,000

The Sultanate of Oman is ruled by decree, with the advice of an appointed Cabinet and a 45-member State Consultative Assembly consisting of members of the Government and appointed citizen's representatives. There are no recognized political parties.

Pakistan

Capital: Islamabad   Pop. 87,000,000

The Islamic Republic of Pakistan is ruled by a martial law administration set up in July 1977 and headed by President (Gen.) Zia ul-Haq. Under martial law imposed by the latter, Parliament was dissolved and some provisions of the 1973 Constitution were suspended. Political parties were declared dissolved on Oct. 16, 1979, but remained active. An interim Constitution promulgated on March 24, 1981, provided inter alia that, when political activity was permitted by the President, only those parties which were registered with the Election Commission on Sept. 30, 1979, would be entitled to function. All other parties were dissolved and their property was confiscated; new parties could be formed only with the Chief Election Commissioner's permission, and the President was empowered to dissolve any party "operating in a manner prejudicial to the Islamic ideology or the sovereignty, integrity or security of Pakistan".

As at Sept. 30, 1979, there existed about 80 political parties; 56 of these had registered with the Election Commission, and 44 had submitted their accounts (as required under the amended Political Parties Act); but the Commission announced on Oct. 2, 1979, that only 16 had been granted registration, and that unregistered parties would not be allowed to contest elections. The country's two most influential parties had refused to register, viz. the (democratic socialist) Pakistan People's Party (of the late Zulfiqar Ali Bhutto) and the (Islamic) Pakistan National Alliance (with the exception of the *Jamaat-i-Islami*, one of its six constituent parties). (The official result of the last general elections held in Pakistan, on March 7, 1977—to a National Assembly which never met, owing to the imposition of martial law on July 5—was widely regarded as "rigged"; it showed the distribution of seats as being: Pakistan People's Party 155, Pakistan National Alliance 36, Qayyum Moslem League 1, independents 8.)

On Dec. 24, 1981, President Zia announced the formation of a Federal Advisory Council (of not more than 350 members, who would be appointed by the President) to act as a bridge between the present martial law administration and a future Islamic democratic government, advising on the form which the latter should take. In an inaugural address to the Council on Jan. 11, 1982, the President said that it was not a substitute for Parliament and would cease to exist when an elected National Assembly came into being, although he added that elections could not be held under present circumstances without endangering the country's security and integrity. The country's main political parties, however, regarded the formation of the Council as an unacceptable measure and continued to call for an end to martial law and for the holding of democratic elections under the 1973 Constitution.

Conference of Ulema of Islam
Jamiat-i-Ulema-i-Islam

Leadership. Maulana Fazlur Rahman (pres.); Maulana Mufti Mahmud (l.)

History. Formerly allied with the National Awami Party (which was banned in 1975), the *Jamiat-i-Ulema-i-Islam* was a founder member in January 1977 of the Pakistan National Alliance (see separate entry) formed to contest the March 1977 general elections against the then ruling Pakistan People's Party led by Zulfiqar Ali Bhutto, its leader becoming president of the Alliance. Following the military takeover of July 1977, the party accepted representation in President Zia's Government in 1979 but continued to press for an early end to martial law and the holding of democratic elections.

Orientation. This fundamentalist party advocates a constitution based on Islamic teachings.

Conference of Ulema of Pakistan
Jamaat-i-Ulema-i-Pakistan (JUP)

Leadership. Maulana Shah Ahmad Noorani (pres.); Maulana Abdus Sattar Niazi (s.g.)

Founded. 1968

History. Established by left-wing mullahs, this fundamentalist party gained seven seats in the 1970 National Assembly elections (in the North-West Frontier Province and Baluchistan). In 1977 it became one of the original members of the Pakistan National Alliance (see separate entry) opposed to the then ruling Pakistan People's Party led by Z. A. Bhutto, but broke away from it in July 1978. It was one of the three major parties which registered with the Election Commission by Sept. 30, 1979. Originally a member of the Movement for the Restoration of Democracy (see separate entry) founded in February 1981, it withdrew from this alliance in the following months.

On March 2, 1982, Maulana Shah Ahmad Noorani claimed that 10,000 people had recently been arrested, the majority of them political activists, and that many had been tortured at camps in Lahore and Karachi. A government spokesman responded that there was no basis for the allegation of torture and that the number of people detained had been grossly exaggerated.

Orientation. The JUP subscribes to a progressive version of Islamic fundamentalism.

Islamic Assembly
Jamaat-i-Islami

Leadership. Mian Tufail Mohammad (pres.); Qazi Hussain Ahmad (s.g.)

Founded. 1941

History. This extreme Islamic party advocates the establishment of an Islamic state in Pakistan. It won four seats in the 1970 general election (in Punjab, Sind and the North-West Frontier Province) and contested the 1977 election as part of the Pakistan National Alliance (PNA—see separate entry) opposed to the then ruling Pakistan People's Party led by Z. A. Bhutto. Following the military takeover of July 1977 it supported the police under President Zia's regime in their repression of anti-Bhutto demonstrators. Expelled from the PNA in 1979 (when it accepted representation in President Zia's Government), the *Jamaat-i-Islami* was one of three major parties which registered with the Election Commission by Sept. 30, 1979, as required under an amended Political Parties Act announced a month earlier.

Following President Zia's decision of Oct. 16, 1979, to postpone elections and to ban party political activity, *Jamaat-i-Islami* pressed for early elections and the ending of martial law while continuing to give broad support to the regime's objectives. In April 1982 a party spokesman said that co-operation with the Zia regime hitherto had been based on the expectation that democracy would eventually be restored.

Orientation. The *Jamaat-i-Islami* is a right-wing ultra-orthodox Islamic fundamentalist party based in the lower middle class.

Structure. The party has a militant student organization, *Jamiat-i-Talaba* (JIT), members of which have been involved in clashes with rival groups at universities.

Labourers' and Farmers' Party

Leadership. Fatheyab Ali Khan
History. This rurally-based party was a signatory of the declaration issued on Feb. 6, 1981, at the establishment of the Movement for the Restoration of Democracy (see separate entry), in whose subsequent campaign for a return to parliamentary government it played a full part. Fatheyab Ali Khan was one of several opposition leaders arrested on March 22, 1982, and temporarily detained in a move by the authorities to forestall demonstrations on Pakistan's national day (March 23).

Moslem League

Leadership. The Pir of Pagaro (pres.)
History. This party, earlier referred to as the "Conventionist" Moslem League,

was one of three groups into which the original Moslem League (which achieved independence for Pakistan in 1947) was divided in 1962. It continued to hold a dominant position under the regime of President Ayub Khan, who joined it in May 1963 and became its leader. However, in the 1970 elections, the League gained only two seats (in Punjab) out of the 291 contested seats in the National Assembly. Following the July 1977 military takeover, the Moslem League took a restrained line in calling for a return to parliamentary government and in July 1978 accepted representation in President Zia's Government.

In 1979 a faction known as the Chatta group, led by Khwaja Khairuddin, seceded from the Moslem League and joined, in 1981, the Movement for the Restoration of Democracy (MRD—see separate entry). Khwaja Khairuddin had, as senior vice-president of the League, publicly criticized the Government of Z. A. Bhutto and had thereupon been expelled from Pakistan, being regarded as a citizen of Bangladesh, where he had his origin, although he had opposed the creation of Bangladesh. While the Khairuddin group subsequently participated in the MRD's campaign for a return to parliamentary democracy, the Pir of Pagaro's followers expressed opposition to the holding of early elections on the grounds that circumstances were not propitious.

Movement for the Restoration of Democracy (MRD)

Founded. Feb. 5, 1981
History. This Movement was formed as an alliance of seven political parties—the Pakistan People's Party (PPP), the Solidarity Party, the National Democratic Party, the Pakistan Republican Party, the Conference of Ulema of Pakistan, a faction of the Moslem League led by Khwaja Khairuddin, and the Kashmir Moslem Conference—whose leaders signed a declaration calling for the immediate lifting of martial law, President Zia's resignation, fair and free elections to the National and Provincial Assemblies within three months and restoration of the 1973 Constitution. On Feb. 6, 1981, the declaration was also signed by leaders of the National Liberation Front and the Labourers' and Farmers' Party.

Following student unrest and the arrest during February 1981 of numerous opposition leaders—Maulana Fazlur Rahman of the Conference of Ulema of Islam, Nasrullah Khan of the Pakistan Democratic

Party, Mian Mahmud Ali Kasuri of the Solidarity Party, Lt.-Gen. Tikka Khan, Aftaab Sherpao and Maj.-Gen. Nasirullah Babar (all three of the PPP)—the action committee of the Movement for the Restoration of Democracy met in Lahore on Feb. 23-24 and issued a call for a civil disobedience movement to remove the Government, beginning with a day of protest on March 2 and culminating in a general strike on March 23. The Conference of Ulema of Pakistan, however, was not represented at the Lahore meeting and subsequently withdrew from the alliance.

Seven of those who took part in the meeting were afterwards arrested, among them Begum Bhutto (the widow of Zulfiqar Ali Bhutto, the former Prime Minister hanged in 1979 for "conspiracy to murder"). The planned day of protest, however, received only limited support, partly as a result of the arrests of political leaders in the wake of the hijacking of a Pakistani aircraft by members of the militant movement *Al Zulfiqar*.

Following President Zia's creation at the end of 1981 of an appointed Federal Advisory Council to act as a bridge between the present martial law administration and a future Islamic democratic government, the MRD leaders described the Council as an undemocratic attempt to "hoodwink the nation and the outside world" and maintained that it had been created only because of international concern about the military regime. In the course of 1982 the MRD also condemned President Zia's proposal of May 6 for the creation of a "Higher Command Council" to give a permanent role to the armed forces in decision-making and also the idea of holding elections on a non-party basis. At the same time it pressed for the release of political detainees, claiming in a statement issued in early June 1982 that 5,000 political workers were in detention and that 300 had been tortured.

National Awami Party (NAP)

Leadership. Khan Abdul Wali Khan (pres.)

History. In the 1970 general elections the pro-Soviet faction of the NAP (led by Khan Abdul Wali Khan) won six seats (out of the 291 contested) in the National Assembly (three each in Baluchistan and the North-West Frontier Province, NWFP). A pro-Chinese faction of the NAP, led by Maulana Bhashani, did not contest the elections. On the accession of Z. A. Bhutto to the presidency of Pakistan in December 1971 (i.e. after the secession of

East Pakistan as Bangladesh) the NAP promised support to the new Government but in January 1972 the NAP (and its ally, the Conference of Ulema of Pakistan—see separate entry) criticized President Bhutto's refusal to end martial law and declined his invitation to join the Government. The NAP also demanded that new governors for Baluchistan and the NWFP should be chosen from the NAP (as the largest party in both provinces).

Following a rebellion in Baluchistan in 1973-74 (when the NAP had its own militia) and the assassination of Hayat Mohammed Khan Sherpao, Home Minister of the NWFP, on Feb. 8, 1975, the Pakistan Government declared the NAP illegal on Feb. 10, 1975. This order was unanimously upheld by the Supreme Court on Oct. 30, 1975, on the grounds that the NAP had never reconciled itself to the existence and ideology of Pakistan; had attempted to bring about the secession of the NWFP and Baluchistan through insurrection, terrorism and sabotage; had, to destroy the idea of a single Moslem nation, promoted the concept that Punjabis, Pathans, Baluchis and Sindhis constituted separate nations, each of which had the right of self-determination; and had attempted to propagate hatred of Punjab in the other provinces.

However, Khan Abdul Wali Khan, who had been arrested when the party was banned, was released on Dec. 9, 1977 (i.e. after the July 1977 military takeover), and Gen. Zia, the Martial Law Administrator, said on Jan. 1, 1978, that all charges of conspiracy against him and 15 other former NAP members had been withdrawn. Meanwhile, elements of the banned NAP had in 1976 formed the National Democratic Party (see separate entry).

On April 16, 1982, Khan Abdul Wali Khan had talks with President Babrak Karmal of Afghanistan in Kabul, after which he expressed his support for the (communist) regime in Afghanistan and his "concern over the war of fratricide among Pashtuns in their own territory which has been instigated by imperialism and the regional reaction".

Orientation. The NAP is a left-wing party seeking to represent the interests of workers and peasants. It is a remnant of the Bangladesh National Awami Party, which also had a pro-Soviet and a pro-Chinese wing.

National Democratic Party (NDP)

Leadership. Sherbaz Khan Mazari (pres.); Zahorul Heque (s.g.)

347

History. The NDP was formed in 1976 as a successor to the banned National Awami Party (NAP—see separate entry), which represented peasant and worker interests and had taken a pro-Chinese line. The banning of the NAP was due to its alleged involvement in terrorist activities in favour of the secession of Baluchistan and the North-West Frontier Province. Having been a member of the Pakistan National Alliance formed in January 1977 (see separate entry), in February 1981 the NDP joined with other parties to form the Movement for the Restoration of Democracy (see separate entry) and has been active since in campaigning for early elections.

Pakistan Democratic Party (PDP)

Leadership. Nawabzada Nasrullah Khan (l.); Sheikh Nasim Hasan (s.g.)
Founded. June 24, 1969
History. The PDP was formed by a merger of four previous right-wing parties, as announced by these parties' then leaders—Air Marshal Asghar Khan of the Justice Party, Nurul Amin of the National Democratic Front (and Leader of the Opposition in the previous National Assembly), Chaudri Mohammad Ali of the *Nizan-i-Islam* party (and Prime Minister from August 1955 to August 1956), and Nawabzada Nasrullah Khan of the West Pakistan Awami League (and convenor of a Democratic Action Committee earlier in 1969). In the 1970 elections it gained only one seat in the National Assembly (in East Pakistan). In 1977 it joined the Pakistan National Alliance (see separate entry). Nawabzada Nasrullah Khan, the PDP leader, was one of three opposition leaders arrested on Feb. 16, 1981, in a move by the authorities to prevent exploitation of student riots then in progress throughout Pakistan.

Pakistan Musawat Party

Leadership. Mohammad Haneef Ramay (ch.)
Founded. 1978
History. This left-wing party was established to advance the cause of the "rule of the people". The party's chairman was a former left-wing member of the Pakistan People's Party (PPP) who had in 1975 gone into opposition and joined the Moslem League in November 1975; on Sept. 21, 1976, he was given a prison sentence for creating disaffection against the Bhutto Government and making a speech calculated to damage Pakistan's relations with other countries and to cause disaffection among the armed forces.

Pakistan Khaksar Party

Leadership. Mohammad Ashraf Khan (l.)
Founded. 1947
History. This party became a member of the Pakistan National Alliance (see separate entry) formed in January 1977. Unlike some other Alliance parties, it did not become represented in government following the military takeover of July 1977. One of the features of the programme of this Islamic party is its advocacy of military training for everyone.

Pakistan National Alliance (PNA)

Leadership. Maulana Mufti Mahmud (pres.); Prof. Ghafoor Mufti Ahmad (g.s.)
Founded. Jan. 11, 1977
History. This Alliance was formed by nine opposition parties for the purpose of jointly contesting the general elections of March 7, 1977, on the basis of a democratic and Islamic platform. The parties were the Solidarity Party (a liberal party led by Air Marshal Mohammed Asghar Khan), the National Democratic Party (formed in 1976 by Sherbaz Khan Mazari and regarded as the successor to the left-wing National Awami Party banned in 1975), the Moslem League, the Pakistan Democratic Party, the Moslem Conference, the Islamic Assembly, the Conference of Ulema of Pakistan, the Conference of Ulema of Islam (whose leader, Maulana Mufti Mahmud, was elected president of the PNA) and the Pakistan Khaksar Party.

The PNA stood for lifting the state of emergency, restoration of the freedom of the press, a reduction in public expenditure, a land reform policy more radical than that of Z. A. Bhutto's Government, some denationalization measures, the abolition of income tax, strict neutrality in foreign policy as well as "the purification of society according to Islamic tenets".

However, the PNA gained only 36 out of the 200 general seats in the National Assembly elected on March 7, 1977, mainly in the North-Western Frontier Province and in Karachi, where its election campaign had been received with great enthusiasm. The PNA thereupon denounced the elections as "rigged", and there followed protest demonstrations and strikes leading to rioting in many localities until May 20, with about 350 people being killed. The PNA boycotted the provincial elections held on March 10, when almost all seats in the Provincial Assemblies were taken by the ruling Pakistan People's Party. Z. A. Bhutto rejected the PNA's charges and maintained on March 8 that it had been defeated because the "medieval views" of some of its leaders had "alienated all classes".

The elected PNA members refused to take their seats in the National Assembly and between March 31 and April 20, 1977, the Election Commission declared void elections in six Punjab constituencies because of grave irregularities and ordered fresh elections to be held. In the opposition press it was claimed that the Chief Election Commissioner had said that he was convinced that the elections had been massively rigged in more than half the constituencies. During the continuing unrest martial law was imposed on April 21 in Karachi, Hyderabad and Lahore. A general strike called by the PNA was observed in all the major towns on April 22, and many persons were killed in clashes with police and troops. As most of the PNA leaders were arrested on April 24, 1977, the PNA general council elected the Pir of Pagaro (a religious leader and president of the Moslem League) as its acting president.

On April 23, 1977, Z. A. Bhutto was reported to have agreed to new parliamentary and provincial elections under the control of the judiciary and the Army. The Pir of Pagaro was allowed to have talks with the imprisoned PNA leaders and stated on April 27, 1977, that the PNA would agree to Z. A. Bhutto's remaining in office as head of a government of national unity pending new elections, provided that the PNA was given two-thirds of the portfolios. On the other hand Air Marshal Asghar Khan said (in a statement smuggled out of prison on May 1, 1977) that the PNA would not compromise on its demand for Z. A. Bhutto's resignation and for new elections, and he appealed to the Army to refuse to obey orders from the "illegal" Government. There followed inconclusive negotiations between Z. A. Bhutto and the PNA leaders, among whom the Pir of Pagaro was placed under house arrest on May 14, but was released on May 19, as were other arrested PNA leaders during the next few weeks.

The negotiations having failed to lead to an agreement, the Army carried out a bloodless coup in Rawalpindi on July 5, 1977 (arresting Z. A. Bhutto and several members of his Government, as well as the most prominent members of the PNA except Begum Wali Khan).

Of the PNA's leaders, the Pir of Pagaro and Mian Tufail Mohammed (of the Islamic Assembly) were soon released. The new military regime of Gen. Mohammed Zia ul-Haq introduced inter alia some of the traditional Koranic punishments advocated by the religious wing of the PNA (such as whipping or amputation of the left hand for certain offences).

In the election campaign which led to the indefinite postponement of the general elections by Gen. Zia on Oct. 1, 1977, the PNA leaders were said to have pleaded for the postponement because their alliance had failed "to bring out the crowds" (whereas the Pakistan People's Party appeared to have mass support). However, Maulana Mufti Mahmud, the restored president of the PNA, denied on Nov. 4 that the PNA had requested the postponement and said that, unless elections were held in March 1978, Pakistan would be plunged into chaos. Requests from the PNA that the elections should be held in March and normal political activities, which had been banned on Oct. 1, should be permitted, were rejected by Gen. Zia on Dec. 1, 1977. Air Marshal Asghar Khan, the leader of the Solidarity Party, announced on Nov. 11, 1977, that his party had withdrawn from the PNA.

A new development took place in 1978, when Prof. Ghafoor Mufti Ahmad, the PNA's general secretary, announced on Aug. 6 that the PNA had decided to join the Government, whereupon the National Democratic Party, opposing this decision, broke away from the PNA. The all-civilian Government formed by President Zia on Aug. 23, 1978, accordingly included representatives of four of the original PNA member parties—the Moslem League (which had already been represented in a Cabinet formed on July 5, 1978), the Conference of Ulema of Islam, the Islamic Assembly and the Pakistan Democratic Party (but not of the Moslem Conference or the Khaksar). The Conference of Ulema of Pakistan had by then also withdrawn from the PNA. However, on April 15, 1979, the PNA ministers resigned from the Government, although the Alliance undertook to give qualified support to the Government from outside.

At a demonstration at Mirpur (Azad Kashmir) on April 27, 1980, PNA leaders (together with leaders of the Moslem League and the Kashmir Moslem Conference) called for President Zia's resignation and for free elections, and on Oct. 7 of that year Nasrullah Khan (the PNA's vice-president) announced that a 10-party declaration was to be issued calling for civilian rule and general elections; however, the publication of the declaration was delayed owing to dissension between the parties on the method of transition to democracy.

Pakistan National Party (PNP)

Leadership. Mir Ghaus Bakhsh Bizenjo (ch.); Syed Qaswar Gardezi (s.g.)

Founded. June 1979

History. This party was formed by elements which broke away from the National Democratic Party (see separate entry). Its chairman had been a leading member of the National Awami Party (see separate entry) and had been Governor of Baluchistan under Z. A. Bhutto's regime in 1972-73. The PNP refused to register with the Election Commission by Sept. 30, 1979, as required by an amended Political Parties Act announced by President Zia on Aug. 30, 1979. The PNP later joined the Movement for the Restoration of Democracy (see separate entry).

Orientation. The PNP stands for increased decentralization, with complete autonomy for Pakistan's four provinces and the federal Government retaining responsibility only for defence, foreign affairs and communications.

Pakistan People's Movement
Pakistan Awami Tehrik

Leadership. Rasool Bux Palejo (pres.); Imtiaz Alam (s.g.)

Structure. This formation consists of the *Naujawan Mahaz* youth organization, the Sind Peasants' Committee, the *Sind Shagird Tehrik* student movement, the *Mehnat Kash Majaz* workers' association, the Punjab *Jamhoori* (Republican) Front, a national students' organization, the Workers' and Peasants' (*Mazdoor Kissan*) Party group led by Ali Bacha (resident in Moscow) and the Punjab *Lok* (People's) Party.

Orientation. The formation is of extreme left-wing orientation.

Pakistan People's Party (PPP)

Leadership. Begum Nusrat Bhutto (ch.); Dr Ghulam Hussain; Gen. (retd.) Tikka Khan (secs.-g.)

Founded. Dec. 1, 1967

History. The PPP was founded by Zulfiqar Ali Bhutto, who had held various ministerial appointments since 1958. In June 1966 he resigned from the Government of President Ayub Khan and denounced it as "a dictatorship with the label of democracy". The East Pakistan branch of the PPP was dissolved on March 3, 1969, after Bhutto had failed to support East Pakistan's demand for full autonomy. In the first general elections held in Pakistan on a "one man, one vote" basis (under the martial law regime of President Yahya Khan) on Dec. 17, 1970, the PPP gained 81 of the 291 contested seats in the National Assembly (all but one in the Punjab and Sind provinces) and became the strongest party in West Pakistan.

Following the secession of East Pakistan (as Bangladesh) in December 1971, Bhutto succeeded Gen. Yahya Khan as President of (West) Pakistan and, in a Cabinet of civilians formed on Dec. 24, took responsibility for Foreign Affairs, Defence, the Interior and Interprovincial Co-ordination, with most other portfolios being held by PPP members. While martial law was maintained, the PPP Government introduced numerous reforms in the social, educational and economic fields and also a new interim Constitution (approved by the National Assembly on April 17, 1972), under which Bhutto was sworn in as President on April 21—martial law having ended on the previous day when it had been declared illegal by the Supreme Court. In October 1972 the PPP reached agreement with the other political parties on a new Constitution providing for a federal and parliamentary form of government, and such a Constitution was adopted by the National Assembly on April 10, 1973 (with all-party support). Under this Constitution Bhutto relinquished the office of President on Aug. 13, 1973, having been elected Prime Minister by the National Assembly on the previous day. In the Senate, newly elected in July, the PPP held 35 of the 45 seats.

In a Cabinet reorganized on Oct. 22, 1974, Bhutto remained Prime Minister and Minister of Foreign Affairs and Defence. During 1975, however, the PPP was weakened by the defection of a number of its leading members; among them, Ghulam Mustafa Khar, former Governor and Chief Minister of the Punjab, resigned from the PPP on Sept. 24, accusing Bhutto of imposing a dictatorship on the country. Altogether two members of the National Assembly and 15 of the Punjab Assembly resigned from the PPP in September 1975. Others who resigned from the PPP were Mohammad Haneef Ramay (former Chief Minister of Punjab) on Oct. 15, 1975, and Rasul Bakhsh Talpur (former Governor of Sind) on Oct. 17; like G. M. Khar they had been founder members of the PPP.

Nevertheless, in the general elections held on March 7, 1977, the PPP gained 155 of the 200 general seats in the National Assembly. G. M. Khar later rejoined the PPP and was, in June 1977, appointed political adviser to Bhutto, then Prime Minister.

The rule of Bhutto and the PPP came to an end in July 1977 when, after his conflict with the Pakistan National Alliance (PNA—see separate entry), his Government was overthrown by a bloodless coup by the Army under the leadership of its Chief of Staff, Gen. Mohammed Zia ul-Haq. The PPP's central committee then decided on Aug. 3, 1977, to participate in the general elections which were planned for Oct. 18, 1977 (but in fact never took place). Also during August 1977, several leading PPP members withdrew their support from Bhutto, among them Mir Taj Mohammad Khan Jamali (former Minister of Health), who announced on Aug. 13 that he was forming an independent group which would contest the elections in Baluchistan in co-operation with the PNA, and also Rana Mohammad Hanif Khan (former Minister of Local Government) and Syed Nasir Ali Rizvi (deputy general secretary of the PPP), who resigned from the PPP on Aug. 17, 1977.

On Sept. 3, 1977, Bhutto was arrested on a charge of conspiracy to murder; he was found guilty and sentenced to death, with four other men, on March 18, 1978. Gen. Zia stated on Sept. 6 that Bhutto was "an evil genius" who had been "running this country on more or less Gestapo lines, misusing funds, blackmailing people, detaining them illegally and even perhaps ordering people to be killed". On Sept. 17, 1978, ten other leading members of the PPP were arrested, among them four members of Bhutto's last Cabinet. The arrest of Bhutto was followed by demonstrations in his favour, in particular in Punjab and Sind. On Oct. 1, 1978, Gen. Zia postponed the proposed elections indefinitely mainly on the grounds that the election campaign had resulted in "a state of confrontation . . . between the political parties". Foreign observers, however, took the view that the real reason for the postponement was Gen. Zia's fear that the PPP would win the elections.

Despite widespread international criticism, especially by other Islamic governments, of the death sentence imposed on Bhutto, an appeal by him against his conviction and sentence was dismissed by the Supreme Court on Feb. 6, 1979 (with four of the seven judges rejecting his appeal and three upholding it). On March 24, 1979, the court implicitly recommended that the death sentence should not be carried out; nevertheless, and despite numerous international appeals for clemency, President Zia refused to commute the sentence and Bhutto was hanged on April 4, 1979.

Following Bhutto's execution, the Government then temporarily adopted a conciliatory attitude to the PPP, releasing some of its leaders from detention and lifting the censorship on its newspaper, *Musawat*. However, Miss Benazir Bhutto (Bhutto's daughter) and Lt.-Gen. Tikka Khan immediately launched an anti-government campaign, and pictures and tape recordings of speeches of Bhutto were sold freely. Leadership of the PPP thereafter passed to Bhutto's widow, Begum Nusrat Bhutto.

In elections to municipal and district councils held in Punjab, Sind, the North-West Frontier Province (NWFP) and Baluchistan between Sept. 20 and 27, 1979, candidates were forbidden to identify themselves with political parties, but those supported by the PPP were reported to have won between 60 and 80 per cent of the seats in Punjab and the NWFP, and to have been returned unopposed to many seats in Sind. In Rawalpindi, 31 of the 50 seats were won by PPP-supported candidates, most of whom had been imprisoned or flogged under President Zia's regime.

The PPP was one of Pakistan's four major parties (the others being the Pakistan National Alliance, the National Democratic Party and the Pakistan National Party) which refused to register by Sept. 30, 1979. On Oct. 16, 1979, the President finally announced that the proposed general elections had been postponed indefinitely, and all political parties were dissolved. The announcement was followed by the arrest of numerous political leaders (officially stated on Oct. 21 to number 372) and the banning of the PPP newspapers *Musawat* and *Sadaqat*. In November 1982 Begum Bhutto was allowed to leave Pakistan for health reasons.

Orientation. At its foundation the PPP described its policy as one of Islamic socialism, democracy and independence in foreign affairs.

People's Republican Union
Awami Jamhoori Ittehad

Leadership. Afzal Bangash (pres.); Abid Hassan Manto (sec.)

History. This alliance embraces four parties—the Pakistan Socialist Party, the *Awami Jamhoori* Party, the Bangash group of the Workers' and Peasants' (*Mazdoori*

Kissan) Party and the First United Workers' Assembly (*Mutahida Mazdoor Majlise-Awal*).

Orientation. The Union is of extreme left-wing orientation.

Progressive People's Party

Leadership. Maulana Kausar Niazi (ch.)
Founded. 1978
History. This party broke away from the Pakistan People's Party (PPP). Its chairman had held ministerial office in PPP administrations in 1972-77, when he was regarded as being conservative.

Qayyum Moslem League (QML)

Leadership. Khan Abdul Qayyum Khan (l.)
History. This party was one of the three factions into which the original Moslem League (which achieved independence for Pakistan in 1947) was divided in 1962. In the 1970 general elections the QML obtained nine of the 291 contested seats in the National Assembly (seven of them in the North-West Frontier Province, NWFP). Under the regime of Z. A. Bhutto, leading members of the QML held high office; after being Chief Minister of the NWFP, the QML leader was a minister in various cabinets from March 6, 1972, to Jan. 12, 1977; Aslam Khattak, who had been Speaker in the NWFP Assembly, was appointed Governor of the NWFP on Feb. 13, 1973; and Jam Ghulam Qadir became Chief Minister of Baluchistan on April 27, 1973. In the elections of March 9, 1977, however, the QML retained only one seat in the National Assembly (which was subsequently dissolved under the martial law regime of Gen. Zia ul-Haq on July 5, 1977). On Nov. 15, 1977, the QML's leader declared that it had decided to co-operate with the Solidarity Party (see separate entry).

At the outbreak of the 1971 civil war, which led to the breakaway of East Pakistan (as Bangladesh), the QML had supported "maximum provincial autonomy consistent with a viable centre" but rejected any arrangement which jeopardized the country's integrity.

Solidarity Party
Tehrik-i-Istiqlal

Leadership. Air Marshal Asghar Khan (pres.); Ashaf Vardag (acting pres.); Musheer Ahmad Pesh Imam (s.g.)
Founded. 1978
History. Founded on a platform of maintaining both Islamic and democratic values, the *Tehrik-i-Istiqlal* was one of the three major parties which registered with the Election Commission by Sept. 30, 1979. Previously it had been a constituent party of the Pakistan National Alliance (see separate entry) formed in January 1977 but had withdrawn in November of that year.

Although the *Tehrik-i-Istiqlal* was banned, like all other parties, in October 1979, its central working committee met in Lahore on April 5-6, 1980, and demanded the immediate ending of martial law, elections to the National and Provincial Assemblies and the release of political prisoners. Air Marshal Asghar Khan was released from house arrest on April 18, 1980, but was again placed under house arrest on May 29 after making speeches denouncing the martial law regime. On Aug. 8, 1980, Ashaf Vardag called for a *jihad* (holy war) against the Government and said that the only way to end the martial law regime was by co-operation between all parties opposed to it, including the Pakistan People's Party.

In February 1981 the *Tehrik-i-Istiqlal* joined with eight other parties in the Movement for the Restoration of Democracy (see separate entry) to campaign for an end to martial law and a return to parliamentary democracy. Following President Zia's creation at the end of 1981 of an appointed Federal Advisory Council to act as a bridge between the martial law administration and a future Islamic democratic government, Mian Manzoor Ahmed Watoo (a leading member of the party) said that the formation of the Council was "a bogus stunt devoid of all meaning and content" and that only an elected assembly could have a mandate for constitutional change.

Panama

Capital: Panama City Pop. 2,000,000

The Republic of Panama is in effect ruled by its National Guard under the command of (the pro-Western and anti-communist) Gen. Rubén Darío Paredes, on whose recommendation the President of the Republic is appointed and forms a Cabinet. A 505-member National Assembly of Community Representatives was elected for a six-year term in August 1978, when no candidate was allowed to represent a political party. A National Legislative Council, to act as an upper chamber, was formed in 1980 of 19 elected members and 37 members appointed from among the members of the National Assembly. Of the 505 members of the Assembly, 398 subsequently joined the newly-established Democratic Revolutionary Party.

Voting is compulsory for citizens aged 18 years or more and is carried out by secret ballot in single-member districts where one representative and one alternative are elected by simple majority. A candidate for the presidency must obtain over 50 per cent of the vote, failing which the National Assembly decides on the winner by simple majority.

In constitutional reforms approved in a referendum on April 24, 1983, it was specified, inter alia, that the President's term of office should be reduced from six to five years, that serving members of the National Guard should be barred from voting, and that all members of the National Legislative Council should be nominated by political parties. Parties officially registered since July 1982 include those listed below.

Broad Popular Front
Frente Amplio Popular (Frampo)

Leadership. Renato Pereira (l.)
Founded. 1979
History. The Frampo was formed with the object of providing a broader base for the Democratic Revolutionary Party (the political base of the military regime). It was supported by left-wing groups including an Independent Lawyers' Movement.
Membership. 35,000

Christian Democratic Party
Partido Demócrata Cristiano (PDC)

Address. Apdo. 6322, Panama City 5, Panama
Leadership. Ricardo Arías Calderón (dir.); Guillermo Cóchez Jr. (s.g.)
Founded. 1960
History. In the 1968 presidential elections this party's candidate came third.

In elections to the Legislative Council held in 1980 it won two seats.
Membership. 36,000
International affiliations. Christian Democratic International

Democratic Revolutionary Party
Partido Revolucionario Democrático (PRD)

Address. Apartado 2650, Panama 9-A, Panama
Leadership. Prof. Berta Torrijos de Arosemena (pres.)
Founded. Sept. 22, 1979
History. The PRD arose out of the national liberation movement led by Gen. Omar Torrijos Herrera, who headed a revolutionary Government installed on Oct. 11, 1968, but who retired from it later. He continued to lead the social and political movement out of which the PRD arose, and he was its leader until his death

353

in an air crash on July 29, 1981. The PRD is the country's predominant political formation, its candidate, Nicolas Ardito Barletta, emerging the victor in the May 1984 presidential elections over Arnulfo Arias Madrid (who was backed by a coalition of opposition parties).

Orientation. The PRD stands for social reform and claims to have affinities with social democratic parties in Europe and nationalist ones in Latin America, describing itself as "democratic, revolutionary, popular, pluralist and principled". It aims to make all sections of the people participate in the task of creating a politically, culturally and socially more just country for the benefit of all its citizens and especially its neediest.

Structure. The PRD has basic units of from 25 to 100 members who elect municipal and provincial leaders and also delegates to the national congress, which is the party's supreme authority and meets every three years to determine party policy and to elect a 300-member directorate and a five-member executive committee. The directorate meets every three months, lays down the political line and elects a 30-member political commission and a secretariat.

Membership. 206,000

Labour Party
Partido Laborista (Pala)

Leadership. Carlos Eleta Almarán; Azael Vargas

Founded. Sept. 8, 1982

History. This right-wing party supported the candidature of Gen. Rubén Dario Paredes (C.-in-C. of the National Guard) for the 1984 presidential elections, but on the latter's withdrawal transferred its support to Nicolas Ardito Barletta (also of the ruling Democratic Revolutionary Party).

Liberal Party
Partido Liberal (PL)

Address. Apartado 8420, Panama City 7, Panama

Leadership. Arnulfo Escalona Ríos (l.)

History. The party's candidate was defeated in presidential elections in 1968. The PL was not represented at a Miami (Florida) meeting of traditional opposition parties in February 1978, and it was the only party whose leader took part in sessions of a commission convened later in 1978 to consider the legalization of parties, the implementation of an electoral law and constitutional changes. Since August 1982 the PL has been represented in the Cabinet led by the Democratic Revolutionary Party.

Membership. 47,000

International affiliations. Liberal International

National Opposition Front
Frente Nacional Opositora (Freno)

Founded. March 1979

History. On its formation the Freno called for direct parliamentary elections and full freedom of expression. The Front embraced several unregistered opposition parties of varying political persuasions, namely the right-wing Agrarian Labour Party (*Partido Laborista Agrario*, PLA) founded in 1940; the left-of-centre Democratic Socialist Party (*Partido Demócrata Socialista*, PDS), Independent Democratic Movement (*Movimiento Independiente Democrático,* MID) and Panamanian Social Democratic Party (*Partido Social-democrático Panameño*) led by Winston Roblés; and the Socialist Workers' Party (*Partido Socialista de los Trabajadores*), a Trotskyist formation.

Nationalist Liberal Republican Movement
Movimiento Liberal Republicano Nacional-ista (Molirena)

Leadership. César Arrocha Graell (l.)

History. This party was officially registered on Oct 21, 1981, and authorized to recruit members from January 1982. It held its first congress on Aug. 1, 1982.

Membership. 50,779 (1982)

Panamanian Party
Partido Panameñista (PP)

Leadership. Dr Arnulfo Arias Madrid

Founded. 1938

History. The party's leader was President of Panama in 1940-41 and 1949-51 and (for 11 days) in 1968, being deposed at the end of each of these periods. He was successful in the 1968 presidential elections as the candidate of a National Union, which comprised also four other parties. The party was represented at the Miami (Florida) meeting of traditional opposition parties held in February 1978.

In October 1979 members of the PP were accused of involvement in an anti-government plot.

Orientation. The PP is a nationalist, anti-communist party.

Membership. 70,000

Panamanian People's Party
Partido del Pueblo de Panama (PPP)

Leadership. Rubén Darío Sousa (g.s.)
Founded. 1943
History. The PPP succeeded the Communist Party of Panama, founded in April 1930 and dissolved in 1943. Following a period during which the PPP was a reformist party, it adopted Marxist-Leninist principles in 1951. In September 1968 the PPP decided to transform itself into "a mass party of the working class and other working people" and to support "the progressive socio-economic reforms" of the Government and the restoration of national sovereignty over the Panama Canal Zone.
Structure. The PPP is organized at local level (in enterprises and at places of residence) and has local, zonal and regional committees. Its supreme authority is a national congress (meeting every four years), which elects a central committee.

The latter in turn elects from among its members a political bureau, a national executive committee and a general secretary.

Membership. 36,000
Publications. *Unidad* (monthly)
International affiliations. The PPP is recognized by the Communist parties of the Soviet-bloc countries.

Popular Action Party
Partido de Acción Popular (Papo)

Leadership. Carlos Iván Zúñiga (l.)
History. Papo was the only party to oppose the constitutional reform approved in a referendum on April 24, 1983.
Orientation. Papo is social democratic and centrist.
Membership. 34,000

Popular Nationalist Party
Partido Nacionalista Popular (PNP)

Leadership. Olimpio Sáez (1.)
Membership. 31,000 (1982)

Papua New Guinea

Capital: Port Moresby   Pop. 3,200,000

Papua New Guinea, a multi-party parliamentary democracy, is an independent state within the Commonwealth with the British monarch as head of state being represented by a Governor-General who is elected by the country's House of Assembly. Executive power is held by a Cabinet headed by a Prime Minister, and legislative powers are vested in the 109-member House of Assembly elected for five years by voters above the age of 18 years and by simple majority in 89 single-member local districts and (one each) in the country's 19 provinces and the national capital district—with each voter casting two votes (one for the local and one for the provincial candidate).

As a result of elections to the House of Assembly held on June 5-26, 1982 (in 108 constituencies), the provisional distribution of 104 seats was as follows: *Pangu Pati* 47, National Party 14, People's Progress Party 10, Melanesian Alliance 8, United Party 6, *Papua Besena* 3, Diro independents 11, other independents 5. (The Diro independents were a group of prominent businessmen, senior administrators and others formed in 1981 by Ted Diro, who had resigned as commander, with the rank of brigadier-general, of the Papua New Guinea Defence Force; however, Diro and his group later joined the National Party.)

Melanesian Alliance

Address. P.O.B. 6516, Boroko, Papua New Guinea
Leadership. Fr John Momis (ch.); Fabian Wau Kawo (g.s.)
Founded. February 1980
History. The founders of this Alliance were (i) Fr Momis, who had been leader of a movement which had, in 1975, declared the island of Bougainville to be the "Independent Republic of the North Solomons" but had in August 1976 recognized the island as a province of Papua New Guinea with increased autonomy, and who had held ministerial office between August 1977 and February 1980; and (ii) John Kaputin, who had been a member of the *Pangu Pati* Government between October 1978 and February 1980. They set up the Alliance as a party opposed to the *Pangu Pati* Government, which was defeated by a vote of no confidence on March 11, 1980. In the Government formed by an alliance of opposition parties on March 13 of that year the Melanesian Alliance held three posts, of which Fr Momis held the Decentralization portfolio and Kaputin the Ministry of Finance. After the 1982 elections the Melanesian Alliance again went into opposition.
Orientation. The Alliance is a socialist formation.
Membership. 300

National Party (NP)

Leadership. Iambakey Okuk (l.)
History. The National Party gained 10 seats in the House of Assembly in 1972 but retained only three in 1977. It took part in the coalition Government led by the *Pangu Pati* between 1972 and 1977, when two of its former leaders joined the new (*Pangu Pati*-led) coalition Government as independents (one of them being replaced as minister in November 1978).

A new National Party was constituted early in 1980 under the leadership of Iambakey Okuk, who had until then been leader of a People's United Front, which had been the principal opposition party in the House of Assembly. The new NP formed a broad opposition alliance with the People's Progress Party, a large section of the United Party, the Melanesian Alliance and the *Papua Besena* movement.

The formation of this alliance led to a vote of no confidence being passed against the Government headed by Michael T. Somare (the leader of the *Pangu Pati*) on March 11, 1980, and to the formation of a coalition Government by the alliance two days later, with the leader of the People's Progress Party becoming Prime Minister.

After the *Pangu Pati* had remained substantially the largest single party in the June 1982 general elections, in July 1982 Okuk resigned from the leadership of the NP and was succeeded by Ted Diro. The latter's bloc of independents associated themselves with the NP which thereupon, commanding 25 seats, became the second strongest group in the House of Assembly. However, after winning a by-election Okuk re-entered Parliament on Aug. 1, 1982, and resumed the party leadership. The following day Somare returned to power at the head of a *Pangu Pati*-United Party coalition.

Pangu Pati (PP)

Address. P.O.B. 623, Port Moresby, Papua New Guinea
Leadership. Michael T. Somare (l.)
Founded. June 1967
History. Founded as a party advocating internal self-government leading to independence for Papua New Guinea, the PP gained 11 out of 84 elective seats in the 1968 elections to the House of Assembly. In 1972 it became the second strongest party in the House, with 31 out of 100 elective seats, and its leader became the first Chief Minister of Papua New Guinea, leading a coalition Government (including the New Guinea and People's Progress parties). Following the 1977 elections, in which the PP became the strongest party in the House, it continued to lead a coalition Government, including mainly independents and the People's Progress Party (PPP). (In November 1978 the latter was replaced as a coalition partner by the rump of the United Party.)

However, in March 1980 the party lost the confidence of the House and went into opposition to a five-party coalition led by the leader of the People's Progress Party. Following the 1982 elections the PP returned to power on Aug. 2, 1982, in coalition with the United Party.

Orientation. Based mainly on urban areas, the PP was the leading pro-independence party.

Papua Besena

Leadership. Gerega Pepena (l.)
History. This movement's original leader, Josephine Abaijah, was the first woman to be elected (as an independent) to the House of Assembly (in 1972). Contesting its first elections in 1977 the *Papua Besena* gained five seats in the House, and it subsequently remained in opposition until it participated, in March 1980, in the formation of a coalition Government led by the People's Progress Party. In the 1982 elections it retained only three seats, and Josephine Abaijah was not re-elected.
Orientation. *Papua Besena* is a Papuan nationalist party committed to a republican form of government for Papua New Guinea.

Papuan Action Party

Leadership. Dr Reuben Taureka, Gavera Rea (founders); Sere Petri (l.)
Founded. 1982
History. The party's two founders were both former *Pangu Pati* cabinet ministers. The party took part in the 1982 general elections but gained no seats.

Papuan National Alliance (Panal)

Leadership. (Mrs) Waliyato Clowes (l.)
Founded. 1980
History. This party was formed by Waliyato Clowes and about eight "moderate" members of Parliament supporting the 1980-82 Government of Sir Julius Chan (the leader of the People's Progress Party).
Orientation. The Panal dissociated itself from the "radical separatist" aims of the *Papua Besena* (with which Mrs Clowes had previously been associated).

People's Progress Party (PPP)

Leadership. Sir Julius Chan (l.); Hudson Arek (ch.)

Founded. 1970
History. In the 1972 elections the PPP gained 10 out of the 100 elective seats in the House of Assembly, and it took part in later coalition Governments headed by the *Pangu Pati*. However, after increasing its parliamentary representation to 18 seats in the 1977 elections, the PPP withdrew from the governing coalition in November 1978, charging the *Pangu Pati* with failure to consult on important decisions.

From March 1980 until the 1982 elections the PPP led a coalition Government with the participation of the Melanesian Alliance, the National Party, the *Papua Besena* movement and a section of the United Party. After the elections the PPP-led alliance broke up during July 1982, and the party again went into opposition.
Orientation. Represented in all areas except the highlands, the party has taken a conservative attitude.

United Party (UP)

Leadership. Raphael Doa (l.)
Founded. 1969
History. At its formation as a highlands-based party, the UP was opposed to early independence. Following the February–March 1972 elections the UP became the strongest party in the House of Assembly, with 40 out of 100 elective seats. The party nevertheless remained in opposition, before and after the 1977 elections, in which it lost its leading position in the House. A split in the UP in March 1978 led to the formation of the People's United Front in May 1978, and in November 1978 the rump of the UP entered a coalition Government led by the *Pangu Pati*.

However, in February 1981 the rump UP transferred its allegiance to the coalition Government formed in March 1982, led by the People's Progress Party and already including the other section of the UP. The UP was thus reunited. After the 1982 elections, in which the UP obtained six seats, it withdrew from the coalition late in July 1982 and joined a Government led by the *Pangu Pati* and supported by independents.
Orientation. The UP is conservative, favouring the retention of links with Australia.

Paraguay

Capital: Asunción   Pop. 3,470,000

The Republic of Paraguay is, under its 1967 Constitution, a "representative democracy" with an executive President elected (and re-eligible) for a five-year term by universal adult suffrage. Since coming to power in a military coup in 1954, President (Gen.) Alfredo Stroessner has been elected for seven successive terms as the candidate of the National Republican Association—Colorado Party, which has been the country's dominant party since 1940. Legislative power is held by a bicameral Congress consisting of a Senate of at least 30 members and a Chamber of Deputies of at least 60 members, both elected for five-year terms by direct adult suffrage. However, the party which gains a majority in parliamentary elections obtains two-thirds of the seats in both Houses of Congress, the remainder of the seats being divided among the minority parties in proportion to their electoral strength. Voting is compulsory for citizens between the ages of 18 and 60 years.

Under legislation introduced in 1981, parties were prohibited from urging voters to return blank ballot papers or to abstain as a form of protest; in order to be registered, a party was required to have 10,000 members distributed among at least one-third of the country's electoral districts; the Communist Party and any party with "similar aims" remained banned; and other prohibited parties were those with international links and those which preached "racial, religious or class struggle" or "hatred among Paraguayans".

In elections held on Feb. 6, 1983, some 90 per cent of the votes were, according to official results, cast in favour of President Stroessner and his National Republican Association—Colorado Party, while the remaining votes went to the Radical Liberal Party and the Liberal Party (in a 90 per cent poll), all other parties having called for abstention.

Authentic Liberal Radical Party
Partido Liberal Radical Auténtico (PLRA)

Leadership. Dr Domingo Laíno (l.); Miguel Angel Martínez (pres.)
Founded. 1978
History. The PLRA broke away from the Unified Liberal Party (see separate entry) and became the largest of the various factions which have arisen from the original Liberal Party. Dr Laíno had in 1974 been elected leader of the legal Radical Liberal Party. As the vice-president of the PLRA he visited the United States in June 1978, when he testified on the human rights situation in Paraguay before the General Assembly of the Organization of American States and recommended that sanctions should be taken against his country.

After his return Dr Laíno was arrested in Asunción on July 7, 1978, and charged with subversion and associating with left-wing extremists, but he was released on Aug. 9, 1978. He was temporarily detained in 1979 and 1980, but in March 1981 he visited Brazil where he was in touch with Brazilian opposition groups and also with exiled members of the Popular Colorado Movement (see separate entry). On Dec. 17, 1982, he was expelled from Argentina after the Paraguayan authorities had accused him of having slandered the late Nicaraguan President Anastasio Somoza Debayle, assassinated in Asunción in 1980.

As an unregistered opposition party the PLRA was the principal partner in the National Agreement of 1978 and as such called for a boycott of all elections.

358

Orientation. The PLRA is a left-of-centre liberal party.

Febrerista Revolutionary Party
Partido Revolucionario Febrerista (PRF)

Address. Casa del Pueblo, Manduvira 552, Asunción, Paraguay

Leadership. Euclides Acevedo (pres.); Ricardo Lugo Rodríguez (g.s.)

Founded. 1936

History. The party took its name from the month of February 1936 when its leader at the time, Col. Rafael Franco, seized power. He remained President until he was deposed by an army coup in 1937. The party was subsequently banned until 1946, when it was given representation in the Government. However, after the suppression of a revolt led by Col. Franco in 1947 it was again banned (together with the Liberal Party). In 1959 its leaders signed an agreement with the Liberal Party (both parties' leaders being in exile in Buenos Aires) to set up a National Union to co-ordinate the activities of all opposition forces and to boycott the 1960 congressional elections.

Having been allowed to operate again, the PRF subsequently boycotted elections until 1967, when it gained three seats in a constitutional convention. In 1968 it obtained one seat in the Chamber of Deputies but it boycotted the 1973 congressional elections. For the 1977 elections to a constitutional convention and the 1978 presidential and congressional elections it asked its supporters to cast blank ballot papers.

The PRF is the only officially registered party which is a partner in the 1978 National Agreement of opposition parties—the other partners being the Christian Democratic Party, the Authentic Liberal Radical Party and the Popular Colorado Movement (Mopoco); all of them called for a boycott of the 1983 elections. During this period the PRF became divided between a conservative wing led by Alarico Quiñones and the majority radical wing led by Euclides Acevedo.

Orientation. The PRF subscribes to democratic socialist precepts.

Publications. *El Pueblo; El Progreso*

International affiliations. Socialist International

Christian Democratic Party
Partido Demócrata Cristiano (PDC)

Address. Colón 871, casi Piribebuy (Casilla de Correo N. 1318), Asunción, Paraguay.

Leadership. Luis Alfonso Resck (pres.); Jorge Dario Cristaldo (sec.)

Founded. May 1960

History. As a party opposed to the Government of President Stroessner, the PDC has refused to take part in any elections and is not officially recognized. In 1978 it entered into a National Agreement with three other opposition parties— the Authentic Liberal Radical Party, the Febrerista Revolutionary Party and the Popular Colorado Movement (Mopoco)— which had also boycotted elections. In July 1981 the party's president was expelled from Paraguay after he had been arrested for alleged subversive activities and had begun a hunger strike.

Orientation. The PDC seeks the "transformation of the country's existing political structure into a true democracy" and transition from a state of underdevelopment to economic development, on the basis of private ownership and free enterprise.

Structure. The party is organized in districts and regions and has separate sections for youth, labour, farmers and women; it has a national committee and a national convention.

Membership. 38,000

Publications. *DE-CE* (party organ), 10,000; *Revolución* (for CD Youth), 5,000

International affiliations. Christian Democratic International; Christian Democratic Organization of America

---

Liberal Party
Partido Liberal (PL)

Leadership. Dr Hugo Fulvio Celauro (l.)

Founded. 1961

History. The present PL is a remnant of the original Liberal Party which was in power in Paraguay for 30 years until 1940 and was officially dissolved for "subversive activities" in April 1942. The restored PL was split in 1961, when the majority of members seceded to form the Radical Liberal Party (PLR). The (rump) PL was officially recognized as a political party and unsuccessfully opposed President Stroessner in presidential elections in 1963 (as the *Movimiento Renovación*, the only opposition party to take part in the election), in 1968, in 1973 and in 1978 (though it had boycotted 1977 elections to a constitutional convention). In 1977 a majority of its members seceded from the PL to form a new Unified Liberal Party (see separate entry). As the PL's candidate in the 1983 presidential elections Dr

Celauro obtained only 3.2 per cent of the vote.

Orientation. The PL stands for free enterprise and the democratization of Paraguay's regime; it is strongly anti-communist.

National Republican Association—Colorado Party
Asosiación Nacional Republicana—Partido Colorado

Leadership. President (Gen.) Alfredo Stroessner (l.); Dr Juan Ramón Chávez (ch.); Mario Abdo Benítez (sec.)

History. Dating back to the 19th century, the Colorado Party has been the ruling party in Paraguay since 1940, from which year until 1968 it was the only party to be represented in the Chamber of Deputies. The party has experienced some disunity, notably in 1959, when dissidents formed a separate Colorado Popular Movement in exile after President Stroessner had dissolved the Chamber of Deputies which had condemned police methods used to suppress student demonstrations. The party has become the political base of President Stroessner (in power since 1954).

Orientation. Conservative in its political approach, the Colorado Party has emphasized the need for stability and vigilance against left-wing "extremism".

Structure. The organization of the party is highly centralized, and it has over 200 local branches. Affiliation is required for all members of the military and public service.

Membership. 1,300,000

Publications. *Patria* (daily)

Popular Colorado Movement
Movimiento Popular Colorado (Mopoco)

Leadership. Mario Mallorquín, Juan Chávez (leaders in exile)

Founded. 1959

History. Mopoco broke away from the ruling Colorado Party over disagreements with President Stroessner's policies. In 1974 the Mopoco was officially held responsible for an alleged plot to kill the President, and over 1,000 persons were arrested in this connexion, while some Mopoco members fled the country. As an unregistered party the Mopoco was one of the partners in the opposition National Agreement concluded in 1978.

Radical Liberal Party
Partido Liberal Radical (PLR)

Address. Yegros y Manuel Domínguez, Asunción, Paraguay

Leadership. Justo Pastor Benítez (l.)

Founded. 1961

History. The PLR was established by a majority of the members of the original Liberal Party. In 1967, as the principal opposition party, it gained 28 (out of 109) seats in a National Constitutional Convention, and in 1968 it obtained 16 (out of 60) seats in the Chamber of Deputies, which it retained in the 1973 elections. In 1977 it suffered the defection of a majority of its members who with a majority of the remaining Liberal Party formed a Unified Liberal Party. The PLR boycotted the 1977 elections to a constitutional convention and unsuccessfully opposed President Stroessner in the 1978 presidential elections. In the 1983 presidential elections its candidate, Enzo Doldán, received only 5.7 per cent of the vote.

Orientation. The PLR is moderate conservative.

Publications. *El Radical* (weekly)

Teeté Liberal Party
Partido Liberal Teeté (PLT)

Leadership. Prof. Carlos A. Levi Ruffinelli (pres.); Fernando Levi Ruffinelli

Founded. 1977

History. This small branch of the Liberal movement in Paraguay took part in the 1978 general elections, when it was given four seats both in the Senate and in the Chamber of Deputies. It did not contest the 1983 elections.

Orientation. The PLT is a right-wing liberal formation for free enterprise and the principle of *laissez-faire*.

Unified Liberal Party
Partido Liberal Unificado (PLU)

Founded. 1977

History. The PLU was formed by majorities of the earlier Liberal and Radical Liberal parties. It refused to take part in elections to a constitutional convention in 1977 and has been denied legal recognition. A breakaway group subsequently formed the Authentic Liberal Radical Party (see separate entry).

Peru

Capital: Lima   **Pop. 18,000,000**

The Republic of Peru has an executive President elected for a four-year term by universal adult suffrage, a Cabinet presided over by a Prime Minister and a bicameral Congress consisting of a 60-member Senate and a 180-member Chamber of Deputies elected similarly and at the same time as the President. Voting is mandatory for citizens above the age of 18 years. The Congress is elected by proportional representation, with each department having at least one deputy (while Lima, the capital, has 40). Each party nominates 180 candidates for the Chamber and 60 for the Senate.

As a result of general elections held on May 18, 1980 (ending 12 years of military rule), seats in the Chamber of Deputies were distributed as follows: Popular Action (AP, centre-right) 98, American Revolutionary Popular Alliance (APRA, centre-left) 58, Christian Popular Party (PPC) 10, National Workers' and Peasants' Front (FNTC or Frenatraca) 4, Workers' Revolutionary Party (PRT, Trotskyist) 3, Popular Democratic Unity (UDP, Maoist) 3, Union of the Revolutionary Left (UNIR, also Maoist) 2, United Left (UI) 2. In the Senate parties gained seats as follows: AP 26, APRA 18, PPC 6, UNIR 2, UI 2, PRT 2, UDP 2, FNTC 1, Popular Front of Workers, Peasants and Students (FOCEP) 1.

Registered Parties

American Revolutionary Popular Alliance
Alianza Popular Revolucionaria Americana
(APRA)

Address. Av. Alfonso Ugarte 1016, Lima 5 (P.O. Box 1815, Lima 100), Peru

Leadership. Armando Villanueva del Campo (pres.); Luís Alberto Sánchez (pres. of pol. commission); Alán García Pérez (g.s.)

Founded. 1930

History. Claiming to be the first truly revolutionary movement in Latin America, APRA was founded in Mexico in 1924 and spread to several South American countries, although it became a significant party only in Peru, where it was banned in 1931–45 and again in 1948–56. Its founder, Dr Victor Raúl Haya de la Torre, was in exile in Mexico in 1923–30; imprisoned in 1932–33; a refugee at the Colombian embassy in Lima in 1948–53; and in exile again in 1954–56 and 1968–69.

In presidential elections held in June 1962 he obtained the highest number of votes but not one-third of the total as required for election to the presidency, so that it was for Congress to decide on the winner; however, Dr Haya de la Torre's withdrawal in favour of Gen. Manuel Odría (the candidate of the Odriista National Union, who had obtained third place) failed to prevent a military take-over. In new elections held in June 1963 Dr Haya de la Torre came second with 34.3 per cent of the vote in the contest for the presidency, while APRA emerged as the strongest party with 58 out of 140 seats in the Chamber of Deputies. APRA nevertheless remained in opposition.

The new military Government installed in 1968 received qualified support from APRA following the return to the country of Dr Haya de la Torre in 1969, but the party was nevertheless held responsible for "illegal actions" in connexion with its trade union activities in 1970–76. It remained the country's strongest party in the 1978 elections to a Constituent Assembly (with 35 per cent of the vote). Dr Haya de la Torre died in August 1979 at the age of 84.

Thereafter the party became divided into a right and a left wing, and in the

1980 general elections it was relegated to second place. However, in municipal elections held on Nov. 13, 1983, APRA regained its first place with 35 per cent of the national vote. The APRA general secretary, Alán García, has been selected as the party's candidate for the 1985 presidential elections.

Orientation. APRA is a popular democratic left-wing party, founded as a nationalist revolutionary movement to fight imperialism, to attain political unity in Latin America, to achieve international control of the Panama Canal and progressively to nationalize land and industry.

Membership. 700,000

International affiliations. Socialist International (consultative member)

Christian Democratic Party
Partido Demócrata Cristiano (PDC)

Address. Avenida España No. 321 (Apartado 4682), Lima 1, Peru

Leadership. Carlos Blancas (ch.)

Founded. January 1956

History. One of Peru's many Christian democratic groupings, the party was in power in coalition with the Popular Action in 1963–66. The party's 12 members of the Chamber of Deputies and five senators elected in 1963 retained their seats until Oct. 3, 1968, when the armed forces established a revolutionary Government. In late 1966 a conservative splinter group of the PDC broke away to form the Christian Popular Party (see separate entry). The PDC is not represented in Congress.

Orientation. The PDC is Christian democratic, regarding the state as existing for the development of the human being; it advocates a society in which work will prevail over capital and the social interest over that of the individual.

Structure. The supreme organ of the party is the national executive committee, which is part of a national secretariat embracing also four departments (for organization, ideology, propaganda and administration). There are also women's, youth and labour sections. The party is organized at departmental, provincial and district level.

Membership. 95,000

International affiliations. Christian Democratic International; Christian Democratic Organization of America

---

Christian Popular Party
Partido Popular Cristiano (PPC)

Address. Av. Alfonso Ugarte No. 1406, Lima, Peru

Leadership. Dr Luis Bedoya Reyes (l. and nat. political sec.)

Founded. December 1966

History. The party was formed by a conservative faction which split away from the Christian Democratic Party (see separate entry). In the 1978 elections to a constituent assembly the PPC came second, winning 25 (out of 100) seats. However, in the 1980 general elections it retained only 10 seats (out of 200) in the Chamber of Deputies. Thereafter it co-operated in government with the Popular Action party until April 1984, when it relinquished its two ministerial portfolios, while indicating that it would continue to give voting support to the Government. In the municipal elections of Nov. 13, 1983, it gained 20 per cent of the vote in Lima.

Orientation. The PPC is a conservative Christian social formation.

Structure. The PPC has a 15-member national committee, a 21-member national executive committee, and, in addition to eight national secretariats, 24 departmental, 152 provincial, 1,630 district, and 514 zonal secretariats.

Membership. 120,000

Marxist Revolutionary Workers' Party/ Socialist Workers' Party
Partido Obrero Marxista Revolucionario/ Partido Socialista de los Trabajadores (POMR/PST)

Address. Jr. Apurimac 465, Lima 1, Peru

Leadership. Senator Ricardo Napurí, Enrique Fernández Chacón (leaders)

Founded. 1982

History. This unified party was formed by a merger of the POMR founded in 1971 and the PST founded in 1974. The POMR had broken away from the Popular Front of Workers, Peasants and Students (FOCEP).

Orientation. The POMR/PST is a Trotskyist formation.

Movement of Hayista Bases
Movimiento de Bases Hayistas (MBH)

Address. Pasaje Velarde 180, Lima 1, Peru

Leadership. Dr Andrés Townsend Ezcurra (l.)

Founded. 1981

History. Dr Townsend had been a leading member of the American Revolutionary Popular Alliance (APRA—see separate entry), in which he was the head of a faction which rejected the proposal (made by the APRA leader Armando Villanueva del Campo) that APRA should form an alliance with "the responsible left" and had instead insisted that APRA itself was "the only responsible left". At an APRA congress held in August 1980 Dr Townsend declared himself "in rebellion" and six months later he was expelled from APRA, whereupon he founded the MBH as a movement adhering to the "fundamental principles" of APRA, as established by the late Dr Victor Raúl Haya de la Torre.

National Integration Party
Partido de Integración Nacional (Padin)

Address. Av. Arequipa 331, Lima 1, Peru
Leadership. Miguel Angel Mufarech (g.s.)
Founded. January 1982
History. This party was established by former members of the Christian Popular Party (PPC) who were opposed to that party's continued support for the Popular Action party (AP).
Orientation. The party is a centre-right formation.

National Workers' and Peasants' Front
Frente Nacional de Trabajadores y Campesinos (FNTC or Frenatraca)

Address. Av. Colonial No. 105, Lima 1, Peru
Leadership. Senator Dr Róger Cáceres Velásquez (pres.); Dr Edmundo Huanqui Medina (s.g.)
Founded. May 12, 1968
History. The party has its origins in the *Frente Departamental de Trabajadores i Campesinos* which, as a regional party in Puno, was successful in municipal elections in 1963 and 1966 and which in 1963 sent three members to Congress. After 10 years during which there was no democracy in Peru the FNTC re-emerged at the end of 1977 and was again successful in municipal elections in Puno. In elections to a constituent assembly in June 1978 it gained four seats, and it again won four seats in the Chamber of Deputies elected in May 1980 (and one in the Senate).
Orientation. The Front is left-wing nationalist, based on the tenets of ancient Peru (*Tahuantisuyo*).
Structure. Supreme authority is held by a national congress which meets every two or three years. There is a 17-member national executive committee, constituting a political bureau.

Odriista National Union
Unión Nacional Odriísta (UNO)

Leadership. Fernando Noriega (l.)
History. The UNO's founder, Gen. Manuel A. Odría, was head of the ruling junta in 1948–50 and the President of Peru in 1948–56, during which period he banned the American Revolutionary Popular Alliance (APRA). In presidential elections held in June 1962 he came third. Following the military coup in July 1962 he went underground. However, in June 1963 the party was allowed to take part in presidential elections, and its leader gained 25.6 per cent of the vote (obtaining third place). Following Odría's death in 1974, the party's influence declined, and it gained only two seats in the constituent assembly elected in 1978 and none in the 1983 congressional elections.
Orientation. The UNO is a right-wing formation.

Peruvian Communist Party—Unity
Partido Comunista Peruano (PCP-Unidad)

Address. Jr. Lampa 774, Lima 1, Peru
Leadership. Senator Jorge del Prado (g.s.)
Founded. October 1928
History. The original PCP was founded by José Carlos Mariátegui under the name of Socialist Party of Peru (which was changed to Communist Party in 1930); under the 1933 Constitution, it was excluded from taking part in elections and had no legal status. In January 1964 pro-Chinese elements broke away from the PCP to form a Communist Party (Marxist-Leninist). From October 1968 onwards the PCP supported the "anti-imperialist and anti-oligarchic transformations" begun by the revolutionary Government of the armed forces. The party played a role in the restoration of the General Confederation of Labour which was officially recognised in 1971. It contested the 1978 elections to a Constituent Assembly as the PCP-*Unidad*, which emerged as the country's fifth strongest party. For the 1980 congressional elections the PCP-*Unidad* was part of the United Left (see separate entry).
Orientation. Originally pro-Soviet, the party has more recently been independent.
Structure. The party's organization is based on the principles of democratic centralism. Its supreme organ is a national

congress and, between congress sessions, its central committee.

Publications. *Unidad* (weekly)

Popular Action
Acción Popular (AP)

Address. Paseo Colón 218, Lima, Peru
Leadership. Fernando Belaúnde Terry (l.); Dr Javier Alva Orlandini (s.g.)
Founded. June 1956
History. In presidential elections held in 1956 the party's leader came second, and in the 1962 elections he was again defeated, although only by a narrow margin. After the annulment of these elections he was, in elections held in June 1963, elected President as the joint candidate of the AP and the Christian Democratic Party, but he was overthrown in a military coup in October 1968. The AP then split into a Belaúnde faction opposed to co-operation with the military junta and a pro-junta faction led by ex-Vice-President Edgardo Seoane Corrales, the former being banned in 1974. Although this ban was lifted in January 1976 when ex-President Belaúnde was allowed to return from exile, the AP refused to take part in the 1978 elections of a Constituent Assembly on the grounds that the Government had not fully guaranteed the sovereignty of this Assembly. (As a result of the congressional elections of 1963, the AP had had 56 deputies and 19 senators.)

In the 1980 elections, however, ex-President Belaúnde was elected President by winning 45.4 per cent of the votes cast (i.e. more than 36 per cent as required for a candidate to win outright), and in the Chamber of Deputies the AP gained an absolute majority (of 98 seats out of 180). It thereupon formed a Government with the participation of the (conservative) Christian Popular Party (PPC). The party suffered a setback in municipal elections held on Nov. 13, 1983, when it obtained only 12 per cent of the vote in Lima (against 35 per cent in 1980). In April 1984 President Belaúnde appointed a new Cabinet (under the premiership of Sandro Mariátegui) in which the PPC ceased to be represented.

Orientation. AP is democratic, nationalist and revolutionary, seeking to defend the interests of the working class.
Structure. The party has a 70-member national plenum as well as departmental, provincial and district committees.
Membership. 900,000
Publications. *Adelante*, 50,000

Popular Democratic Unity
Unidad Democrática Popular (UDP)

Address. Plaza 2 de Mayo 46, Lima 1, Peru
Leadership. Alfonso Barrantes Lingán (l.)
Founded. 1978
History. The UDP was formed by two extreme left-wing groups—the Revolutionary Vanguard (VR) and the Movement of the Revolutionary Left (MIR) led by Carlos Tapia (see separate entries for these groups). The UDP gained four seats in the Constituent Assembly elected in 1978, and in 1980 three in the Chamber of Deputies and two in the Senate. It subsequently joined the United Left (see separate entry).

Popular Front of Workers, Peasants and Students
Frente Obrero, Campesino, Estudiantil y Popular (FOCEP)

Address. Jr. de la Unión 706, Of. 220, Lima 1, Peru
Leadership. Senator Dr Genaro Ledesma Izquieta (ch.)
Founded. 1962
History. The FOCEP was not legalized as a party until 1978. In the elections of that year to a Constituent Assembly it came third, gaining 12 (out of 100) seats. As a result of the 1980 general elections, however, it was reduced to one seat in the Senate. It contested the 1983 municipal elections as part of the United Left.
Orientation. The Front is a Trotskyist formation.

Revolutionary Communist Party
Partido Comunista Revolucionario (PCR)

Address. Plaza 2 de Mayo, Lima 1, Peru
Leadership. Manuel Dammert (g.s.)
Founded. 1974
History. The PCR has contested elections in 1980 and 1983 as part of the United Left (see separate entry).

Revolutionary Socialist Party
Partido Socialista Revolucionario (PSR)

Address. Plaza Bolognesi 123, Lima, Peru
Leadership. Gen. Leónidas Rodríguez Figueroa (ch.); Senator Enrique Bernales (g.s.)

Founded. November 1976

History. The PSR was formed by a majority of an earlier *Movimiento de la Revolución Peruano*, and its leader had been one of the leaders of the 1968 military revolution. In January 1977 the PSR leader and three other prominent supporters of the party were deported from Peru but they returned under an amnesty of March 1978. In the 1978 elections to a constituent assembly the PSR emerged as the country's fourth strongest party (with six out of 100 seats). It contested the 1980 general elections as part of the United Left (see separate entry).

Orientation. The PSR called, at its foundation, for "the defence, deepening and consolidation of the reforms already begun and those still needed to take the country out of the capitalist system and build Peruvian socialism".

Socialist Party of Peru
Partido Socialista del Perú (PSP)

Address. J. Azángaro 105, Lima 1, Peru

Leadership. Dr María Cabredo de Castillo (l.)

Founded. 1930

History. This small left-wing formation has made little political impact despite having existed for over half a century.

Union of the Revolutionary Left
Unión de Izquierda Revolucionaria (UNIR)

Address. P.O. Box 1165, Lima 100, Peru

Leadership. Senator Rolando Breña Pantoja (ch.); Jorge Hurtado (g.s.)

Founded. 1979

History. The UNIR comprises three left-wing groups, namely the Communist Party of Peru—Red Fatherland (PC del P-*Patria Roja*), the National Liberation Front (FLN) and the Fernández Gasco faction of the Movement of the Revolutionary Left (MIR-Perú) (see separate entries). In the 1980 general elections the UNIR gained two seats in the Chamber of Deputies and two in the Senate. The UNIR subsequently joined the United Left (which obtained 33 per cent of the national vote in municipal elections held in November 1983). The UNIR held its first national congress on Nov. 25-27, 1983.

Membership. 50,000

Publications. *El Unirista*, 10,000

United Left
Izquierda Unida (IU)

Address. Av. Grau 184, Lima 23, Peru

Leadership. Dr Alfonso Barrantes Lingán (ch.)

Founded. 1980

History. This alliance comprises six left-wing parties, namely the Popular Front of Workers, Peasants and Students (FOCEP), the Revolutionary Communist Party (PCR), the Peruvian Communist Party-Unity (PCP-*Unidad*), the Popular Democratic Unity (UDP), the Union of the Revolutionary Left (UNIR) and the Revolutionary Socialist Party (PSR). In 1980, when it did not yet include FOCEP and UNIR, it gained two seats in the Chamber of Deputies and two in the Senate. In municipal elections held in the same year the IU obtained 27 per cent of the national vote, and the six-party IU gained 33 per cent of the vote in Lima in the 1983 municipal elections, when it also obtained the mayorship of Lima for its chairman.

Workers' Revolutionary Party
Partido Revolucionario de los Trabajadores (PRT)

Address. Apartado Postal 2449, Lima 100, Peru

Leadership. Hugo Blanco (rep. of collective leadership)

Founded. Oct. 8, 1978

History. This party had its origins in small groups which had left the Popular Democratic Unity (UDP) and the Popular Front of Workers, Peasants and Students (FOCEP), and it was part of the FOCEP until 1979. It was legalized in 1980 when it produced signatures of 90,000 supporters. In the 1980 general elections it obtained 5 per cent of the vote and three seats in the Chamber of Deputies and two in the Senate. In municipal elections held in November 1980 it gave critical support to the United Left. A number of PRT activists were subsequently imprisoned and Hugo Blanco was suspended from the Chamber of Deputies. After it had obtained less than 1 per cent of the national vote in the November 1983 municipal elections the PRT decided to apply for membership of the United Left.

Orientation. The PRT is a revolutionary Marxist formation.

Structure. Leninist, based on democratic centralism.

Membership. 5,000 in August 1980, later unknown

Publications. *Combate Socialista*, 2,500
International affiliations. The PRT is the Peruvian section of the Fourth (Trotskyist) International.

Unregistered Parties

Communist Party of Peru—Red Fatherland
Partido Comunista del Perú (PC del P-Patria Roja)

Address. P.O. Box 51, Lima 100, Peru
Leadership. Alberto Moreno (g.s.); Senator Rolando Breña Pantoja (spokesman)
Founded. 1969
History. This party originates from a split in the original Peruvian Communist Party (founded in 1928) in 1963, when a Maoist faction formed the Communist Party of Peru—Red Flag (see separate entry). When a majority of the latter became pro-Albanian in 1969, the pro-Chinese faction formed the Red Fatherland PC. As a member of the Union of the Revolutionary Left (UNIR, formed in 1979), it gained parliamentary representation.

Communist Party of Peru—Red Flag
Partido Comunista del Perú—Bandera Roja

Founded. 1963
Orientation. Formed by Maoist elements of the main Peruvian Communist Party, the Red Flag party was weakened in 1969 when pro-Chinese elements opposed to the party's adoption of a pro-Albanian stance formed the Communist Party of Peru—Red Fatherland (see separate entry).

Majority Peruvian Communist Party
Partido Comunista Peruano Mayoría

History. This group broke away from the CPC-*Unidad* as a pro-Soviet offshoot.

Movement of the Revolutionary Left
Movimiento de Izquierda Revolucionaria (MIR)

Leadership. Carlos Tapia (g.s.)
Founded. 1959
History. The MIR was formed as a left-wing offshoot of the American Revolutionary Popular Alliance (APRA)

by Luis de la Puente, who in 1965 conducted guerrilla warfare against the military regime in Peru. In 1978 this faction of the MIR joined the Popular Democratic Unity (see separate entry).

Movement of the Revolutionary Left of Peru
Movimiento de Izquierda Revolucionaria (MIR-Perú)

Leadership. Dr Gonzalo Fernández Gasco (l.)
Founded. 1959
History. This faction of the MIR (for other faction see above) formed part of the Union of the Revolutionary Left established in 1979. In 1965 Dr Fernández Gasco had been a guerrilla leader in the armed struggle of the left against the military regime.

National Liberation Front
Frente de Liberación Nacional (FLN)

Address. Emancipación 412, Of. 203, Lima 1, Peru
Leadership. Senator Dr Angel Castro Lavarello (ch.)
History. This group gained parliamentary representation as a member of the Union of the Revolutionary Left (see separate entry).

Peruvian Democratic Movement
Movimiento Democrático Peruano (MDP)

History. This right-wing movement took part in the 1978 elections to a Constituent Assembly but gained only about 20,000 votes and no seat.

Revolutionary Socialist Party (Marxist-Leninist)/Militant Movement of the Revolutionary Left
Partido Socialista Revolucionario (Marxista-Leninista)/Movimiento de Izquierda Revolucionaria—El Militante (PSR-ML/MIR-El Militante)

Orientation. This unified organization stands politically near to the Popular Democratic Unity (UDP).

366

Revolutionary Vanguard
Vanguardia Revolucionaria (VR)

Leadership. Javier Díez Canseco (g.s.)
Founded. 1965
History. In 1971-72 VR members were held responsible for numerous acts of violence, including bank robberies and the killing of policemen. In 1976 the VR controlled the Peruvian Peasants' Confederation, which had organized land seizures in protest against slow progress in land reform. In 1978 it joined with a faction of the Movement of the Revolutionary Left (MIR) to form the Popular Democratic Unity (see separate entry).

Revolutionary Vanguard—Proletarian Communist
Vanguardia Revolucionaria—Proletario Comunista (VR-PC)

Leadership. Eduardo Figari (l.)
History. This group is an unofficial member of the United Left (see separate entry).

Socialist Political Action
Acción Politica Socialista (APS)

Leadership. Gustavo Mohme (l.)
History. This small leftist formation has remained insignificant as compared with other groupings of the Peruvian left.

Philippines

Capital: Quezon City (Manila)　　　　　　　Pop. 50,000,000

The Republic of the Philippines is ruled by a President who holds wide-ranging executive powers and is elected (under constitutional amendments approved in a referendum on April 7, 1981) for a six-year term by universal adult suffrage of all citizens above the age of 16 years. Legislative power is held by a National Assembly, in which 183 elective seats were, as a result of general elections held on May 14, 1984, officially declared to have been won as follows: New Society Movement (KBL) 110, opposition alliance parties 62, others 11.

Voting is compulsory for citizens of the required age (except those convicted of crimes). Candidates are elected by simple majority in two-member districts. Political parties are admitted provided they have been certified not to be subversive.

President Ferdinand Edralin Marcos, who had been in power since 1965, was on June 18, 1981, re-elected by popular vote for six years as the candidate of the KBL, obtaining, according to the official result, 88 per cent of the vote (against 12 other candidates).

Christian Community Movement

History. This Movement has opposed the seizure of peasant land for conversion into sugar plantations. Several of its members were found murdered in a village on Negros island in January 1981. The Movement is one of a number of anti-Marcos formations based in the Roman Catholic population.

Christian Social Movement

History. This small formation has participated in the opposition to the Marcos regime, which it seeks to move towards greater democratic participation and more socially-conscious policies.
International affiliations. Christian Democratic International

Coalition against the Marcos Dictatorship

Leadership. Geline Avila (nat. co-ordinator)
Founded. 1982
History. This formation has sought to rally the various movements opposed to the regime of President Marcos.

Compact

Founded. January 1984
History. An alliance called "Compact" was formed early in 1984 under an agreement signed by representatives of opposition parties and groups, namely the Liberal Party, *Kaakbay*, the Philippine Democratic Party, the People's Power Movement—Fight, the Nationalist Alliance, Justice for Aquino Justice for All (JAJA) and the Interim National Association. Compact announced that it would launch a nationwide campaign against the Marcos Government and would discuss forthcoming elections with the United (Nationalist) Democratic Organization (Unido).

Liberal Party
Partido Liberal

Leadership. Senator Gerardo Roxas (pres.)
Founded. 1946
History. The party was formed by the centre-liberal wing of the original Nationalist Party, and it was in power until 1952. In 1961 its then leader, Diosdado Macapagal, was elected President (having been Vice-President since 1957). It has been in opposition since 1965 and its secretary-general until his arrest under martial law in 1972 was Benigno Aquino Jr., who later became associated with the People's Power Movement—Fight (see separate entry) and who was assassinated on Aug. 21, 1983, on his return to Manila from self-imposed exile in the United States.

The party boycotted the 1980 provincial and local elections in protest against the continuation of martial law. As part of the United Democratic Opposition it also boycotted the 1981 presidential elections. In 1982 it became part of the United (Nationalist) Democratic Organization (Unido).
Orientation. Like the Nationalist Party, the Liberal Party has favoured private enterprise but with a more open attitude to foreign investment.

Mindanao Alliance

Address. Cagayan de Oro, Mindanao, Philippines
Leadership. Governor Homobono Adaza (l.)
Founded. February 1978
History. This Alliance was established by Ruben R. Canoy, Aquilino Pimentel and Homobono Adaza. It gained one seat in the interim National Assembly elected in April 1978, and it later contested regional elections in Mindanao. It was a member of the United Democratic Opposition set up in February 1980. In 1981 Canoy and Pimentel joined the Social Democratic Party.
Orientation. The Alliance stands for the economic development of Mindanao and for the protection of civil and human rights.

Moslem Democratic Party (MDP)

History. This party, confined to the island of Mindanao, presented only six candidates in elections to regional assemblies held in Southern and Western Mindanao in May 1979, when all elective seats in these assemblies were gained by the government New Society Movement, and after a boycott of these elections had been called for by the Moro National Liberation Front (which had since 1971 waged armed struggle against government forces).

Movement for Independence, Nationalism and Democracy

History. Two officials of this Movement—J. Antonio Carpio and Grace Vinzons Magana—were arrested in July 1981 after they had advocated an election boycott.

National Union for Liberation (NUL)

Leadership. Diosdado Macapagal (l.)
Founded. 1979
History. The NUL's leader had, as a member of the Liberal Party, been President of the Philippines in 1961–65 and had

(in a book published in the United States in 1976) called on the armed forces to "free the people from dictatorship". In the provincial, municipal and local elections of January 1980 the NUL presented some 900 candidates and, after most of them had been unsuccessful, formally complained of alleged irregularities in the counting of votes. In 1982 the NUL joined the United (Nationalist) Democratic Organization (Unido).

Nationalist Party (NP)
Partido Nacionalista

Leadership. José Laurel (pres. of majority faction); José Roy (pres. of minority faction)
Founded. 1907
History. Since 1946 this party has consisted of the right wing of the original Nationalist Party. It came to power in November 1952, when Ramón Magsaysay (who had been a member of the Liberal Party until March of that year) was elected President, and it retained the presidency until 1961. In 1965 the party was joined by Ferdinand Marcos (who had until then been a member of the Liberal Party), and in November 1965 he was, as the Nationalist Party's candidate, elected President. He has been in power since then. After the establishment of the New Society Movement the party went into opposition but had some limited success in the provincial, municipal and local elections held in January 1980.

Prior to the 1981 presidential elections the party was split, with a majority of delegates electing José Laurel as party president in place of José Roy. The latter's faction, however, nominated Alejo S. Santos as the party's presidential candidate (who came second with 1,716,429 votes or about 8 per cent of the total). President Marcos had allowed the NP to take part in the elections but had stated on Jan. 18, 1981, that he would challenge any NP victory as the party had been dismantled on the establishment of his New Society Movement in 1978—a claim which was rejected by José Roy. In 1982 the NP joined the United (Nationalist) Democratic Organization (Unido).
Orientation. The NP has traditionally been opposed to foreign investment in the Philippines.

New Society Movement
Kilusan Bagong Lipunan (KBL)

Leadership. Imelda Marcos (l.)
Founded. 1978

History. This Movement was formed by former supporters of the Nationalist Party and of President Ferdinand Marcos (husband of the Movement's leader). The Movement gained overwhelming majorities in elections held in April 1978 to the interim National Assembly and in provincial, municipal and local elections held in January 1980. In municipal elections held on May 17, 1982, and which were marked by violent incidents in which some 400 people were killed, the KBL was officially stated to have gained 85 per cent of the votes.
Orientation. The party has set itself the task of implementing the creation of a "new society" in the Philippines in accordance with the President's ideas.

People's Power Movement—Fight
Lakas ng Bayan (Laban)

Leadership. Lorenzo Tañada (ch.)
Founded. 1978
History. In the elections held on April 7, 1978, to an interim National Assembly this party contested 21 elective seats but failed to gain any of them after Benigno Aquino (then its leader) had conducted the election campaign from prison, where he had been held since 1972 under martial law. In protest against the continuation of martial law, the party boycotted the provincial, municipal and local elections of January 1980.

In 1982 the *Laban* party joined the United (Nationalist) Democratic Organization (Unido), and it was one of the opposition parties which established the Compact alliance in January 1984.

Philippine Communist Party
Partido Komunista ng Pilipinas (PKP)

Leadership. Felicismo Macapagal (s.g.)
Founded. Nov. 7, 1930
History. The PKP was illegal in 1932–38, 1942–45 and 1947–74. During World War II it had organized the *Hukbalahap* (Anti-Japanese People's Army), groups of which continued guerrilla warfare even after the war until subdued by government forces in the 1970s. In 1968 the party was divided into a pro-Chinese faction (whose military wing, the New People's Army, subsequently intensified the guerrilla war) and a pro-Soviet faction, which was recognized as the legal PKP in October 1974.
Structure. The PKP's basic unit is the nucleus, organized at places of work or in

neighbourhoods. The party's highest organ is its congress, which elects a central committee; the latter in turn elects a political bureau and a secretariat.

Publications. *Ang Komunista* (for mass circulation); *Organisador*

International affiliations. The PKP is recognized by the Communist parties of the Soviet-bloc countries.

Philippine Democratic Party (PDP)
Pilipino Lakas Ng Bayan

Leadership. Lorenzo Tañada (ch.)
Founded. Feb. 7, 1982
History. The PDP was established at a meeting of some 400 delegates in Cebu City (including members of the Liberal and Nationalist parties, the People's Power Movement and the Mindanao Alliance). It claimed to represent about 80 per cent of the country's opposition forces and to consist of peasants, agricultural workers and some intellectuals. One of its leaders, Aquilino Pimentel (who was mayor of Cagayan de Oro, on Mindanao), was on April 17, 1983, reported to have been imprisoned for alleged revolutionary activities. In 1982 the PDP joined the United (Nationalist) Democratic Organization (Unido).

Orientation. The PDP has proclaimed as its aim the fight against all forms of imperialist domination.

Social Democratic Party (SDP)

Leadership. Francisco S. Tatad, Ruben R. Canoy (leaders)
Founded. December 1981
History. This party was set up by 14 members of various opposition groups, among them (i) Francisco Tatad (who had been dismissed as Secretary for Information in 1980 after he had protested against President Marcos's martial law policies, and had thereafter founded the Visayan Faction party, and (ii) Ruben Canoy, who had been a co-founder of the Mindanao Alliance, from which he had been expelled and which denounced the SDP as "a counterfeit opposition" loyal to President Marcos.

Orientation. The SDP is both anti-Marcos and anti-Marxist.

Union for Democracy and Liberty

Leadership. Jovito Salonga (l.)
Founded. 1979

History. The party's founder was a former Liberal senator, who on Oct. 17, 1979, called on President Marcos to lift martial law (in force since 1972), to form a caretaker Government and to hold fresh elections in order to forestall "a major upheaval". He was temporarily detained from Oct. 20 to Nov. 27, 1980, whereafter he was kept under house arrest.

United (Nationalist) Democratic Organization (Unido)

Leadership. Salvador H. Laurel (pres.); Abraham Sarmiento (s.g.)
Founded. February 1982
History. Unido was formally launched on April 23, 1982, as an alliance of anti-Marcos groups, including the United Democratic Opposition set up in February 1980, the Nationalist Party, the Philippine Democratic Party, the People's Power Movement—Fight and the Liberal Party. Its leaders also included Raul S. Manglapus, the founder of a Movement for a Free Philippines in exile in the United States.

The United Democratic Opposition had been established under the leadership of Salvador Laurel and Gerardo Roxas (leader of the Liberal Party) as an alliance of eight opposition groups, including the Liberal Party, the Visayan Faction, the Mindanao Alliance, the National Union for Liberation and the Concerned Citizens' Group of Zamboanga City (on Mindanao). On Feb. 5, 1981, it had announced that it would boycott the coming presidential elections and called for the convening of a constituent assembly to draft a new constitution before the holding of presidential elections. It also joined in a civil disobedience campaign.

Visayan Faction
Pusyon Bisaya

Leadership. Francisco S. Tatad (l.)
Founded. January 1978
History. The 13 elective seats in the interim National Assembly gained by this party in the April 1978 elections were all in the Visayas region of the central Philippines. The party was part of the United (Nationalist) Democratic Opposition formed in 1981, and later in that year it was superseded by the Social Democratic Party (see separate entry).

Poland

Capital: Warsaw   Pop. 36,000,000

The Polish People's Republic is, under its Constitution as amended in February 1976, "a socialist state" in which the role of "leading political force in the building of socialism" is vested in the Polish United Workers' Party (PUWP). Until further constitutional changes in July 1983, the PUWP dominated a National Unity Front (NUF), of which the other members were the United Peasants' Party, the Democratic Party, the "social organizations of the working people" and "the patriotic associations of all citizens" (including the Roman Catholic *Znak* and *Pax* groups). The 1976 constitutional amendments also contained the provision that the state would "strengthen friendship and co-operation with the USSR and other socialist states". While supreme power is exercised by the Politburo of the Central Committee of the PUWP, the authority of the Republic is vested in the 460-member Diet *(Sejm)*, which is elected for a four-year term by all citizens above the age of 18 years on a single list in 460 constituencies (and under an absolute majority system in a first ballot and, if necessary, a simple majority in a second ballot). The *Sejm* in turn elects a Council of Ministers with a Chairman (Prime Minister).

According to the official results of elections held on March 23, 1980, there had been a percentage poll of 98.87, and 99.52 per cent of the valid votes had been cast for the list of the NUF. Seats in the *Sejm* were distributed as follows: PUWP 261, United Peasants' Party 113, Democratic Party 37 and independents 49.

Following the emergence in 1980–81 of the "Solidarity" free trade union movement, which the Government and the PUWP eventually regarded as a threat to the regime, a state of martial law was imposed from Dec. 13, 1981, until July 22, 1983. During this period power was exercised by a Military Council of National Salvation headed by Gen. Wojciech Jaruzelski, who was Chairman of the Council of Ministers and also First Secretary of the Central Committee of the PUWP. The "Solidarity" movement was formally abolished on Oct. 8, 1982. Under constitutional amendments approved by the *Sejm* on July 20, 1983, the NUF was replaced by a Patriotic Movement of National Rebirth (PRON), formed in the autumn of 1982 as a government-sponsored organization to initiate political reforms "on the basis of the alliance and co-operation of the country's three parties in the building of socialism".

Democratic Party
Stronnictwo Demokratyczne

Address. Ul. Rutkowskiego 9, Skr. Poczt. 381, Warsaw-00-021, Poland

Leadership. Prof. Edward Kowalczyk (pres. and Vice-President of the Council of State)

Founded. April 1939

History. The party was founded from democratic clubs first established in the 1930s by intellectuals, professional people and white-collar workers as a democratic and liberal movement to oppose successive right-wing dictatorial regimes. During World War II the party took part in the resistance movement, and after the war in the establishment of the people's republic under Communist rule. As a non-Marxist party it has taken part in all spheres of public life, mainly in the services sector; more than 60 per cent of its members are intellectuals, and about 30 per cent are artisans and small traders.

Structure. The party has a congress (convened every five years) which elects a central committee (with a presidium and a secretariat). There are also voivodship (provincial) conferences of delegates (meeting every five years to elect voivodship committees with presidiums), and similar conferences (meeting every 2½ years) at town and district level. There is an elaborate system of control and judiciary commissions.

Membership. 100,000

Publications. *Kurier Polski* (daily), 170,000; *Ilustrowany Kurier Polski* (daily), 100,000; *Tygodnik Demokratyczny* (weekly), 40,000; *Biuletyn Stronnictwa Demokratycznego* (monthly), 4,500; *Zeszyty Historyczno-Polityczne SD* (quarterly), 1,500

Polish United Workers' Party (PUWP)
Polska Zjednoczona Partia Robotnicza (PZPR)

Address. 00920 Warsaw, Nowy Swiat 6, Poland

Leadership. Gen. Wojciech Jaruzelski (first sec.); Kazimierz Barcikowski, Tadeusz Czechowicz, Jozef Czyrek, Zofia Grzyb, Stanislaw Kalkus, Hieronim Kubiak, Zbigniew Messner, Miroslaw Milewski, Stefan Olszowski, Stanislaw Opalko, Tadeusz Porebski, Jerzy Romanik, Albin Siwak, Marian Wozniak (other full members of Politburo)

Founded. December 1948

History. The PUWP was formed by a merger of the (Communist) Polish Workers' Party—which had superseded the Communist Party of Poland established in 1918—and the Polish Socialist Party (after "deviationists" had been expelled from both these parties). The PWP had formed part of the Soviet-backed "Lublin Committee", which had declared itself the provisional government of Poland towards the end of 1944 and had later been the dominant force in the post-war coalition regime.

In 1956 the party's central committee removed from its political bureau all "Stalinist" elements and appointed as the party's first secretary Wladyslaw Gomulka (who had served five years in prison for "Titoism" and "nationalist deviationism"); he thereupon advocated the theory of "different roads to socialism" (i.e. not necessarily adherence to the Soviet model) and reversed a number of earlier repressive measures. In 1959, however, Gomulka emphasized the need to oppose "revisionism" which led to questioning the fundamentals of Marxism-Leninism, and in 1964

the PUWP firmly supported the USSR in the Sino-Soviet dispute. The party also supported the Soviet intervention in Czechoslovakia in 1968.

Following riots caused by major increases in food and fuel prices Gomulka was in December 1970 replaced by Edward Gierek, who thereupon announced a price freeze, wage increases and other reforms. The PUWP leadership has since then laid emphasis on the need to maintain close relations with the Soviet Union.

In September 1980 Gierek was replaced by Stanislaw Kania, who was faced with the fact that something like a quarter of the PUWP members had joined the "Solidarity" free trade union movement led by Lech Walesa. A party congress held in July 1981 was attended by many first-time participants and also by Solidarity members. However, in October 1981 Kania was replaced by Gen. Jaruzelski, who was already Chairman of the Council of Ministers. Upon the imposition of martial law on Dec. 13, 1981, and the effective banning of Solidarity many leading party members were relieved of their posts and a number were detained for trial on various charges (among them Gierek). Serious industrial and social disturbances ensued in many parts of the country, but gradually the Government was able to re-establish full control. In February 1983 Gen. Jaruzelski found it necessary to call on the PUWP to launch a campaign to eliminate "apathy" within the party.

Structure. The party is organized on the principle of democratic centralism. It has base units at places of work or residence, subordinated to city or rural committees which in turn are below voivodship (provincial) committees directly subordinated to the party's central committee. The supreme organ of the party's organization is the general meeting, and the party's supreme authority is its congress which is convened every five years and elects the central committee and a central auditing commission. The central committee elects a political bureau and a secretariat, and it also sets up a central party control commission.

Membership. 2,650,000 (over 3,000,000 in July 1980)

Publications. *Trybuna Ludu* (daily), 1,000,000; *Nowe Drogi* (theoretical and political monthly), 85,000

United Peasants' Party
Zjednoczone Stronnictwo Ludowe (ZSL)

Address. ul. Grzybowska 4, 00-131 Warsaw, Poland

Leadership. Roman Malinowski (ch.)

Founded. 1948

History. The ZSL is the successor to traditional Polish peasant movements (which first emerged in Galicia, the Austrian sector of a partitioned Poland) whose principal objectives up to 1918 included the recovery of national independence. In 1918–26 some peasant parties took part in coalition Governments and others were in opposition; between 1926 and 1939 the movement opposed the regime established after the coup by Jozef Pilsudski, and in 1931 the movement was consolidated into one peasant party, which played a conspicuous part in resistance to the Pilsudski regime in 1932–37.

Under Nazi occupation the peasant movement formed its own resistance battalions (which grew to some 160,000 men), and its representatives were members of underground political authorities and of the Polish Government in exile in London. After 1944 the movement was divided into (i) the Peasant Party, which in December 1944 entered a Soviet-backed provisional government in Lublin, and (ii) the Polish Peasants' Party, which opposed the government.

In 1949 the two parties were reunited under the party's present name and accepted a common programme for the transformation of Poland into a socialist country. Since then the ZSL has taken part in the Government; there are four ZSL members in the Council of State (one as deputy chairman and one as a secretary); and in the Government it has a deputy premier, two ministers and 10 deputy ministers.

In March 1983 the party criticized the Government's freeze on food prices and its failure to provide for economic measures strong enough to produce sufficient machinery and equipment for farming in 1983–85.

Orientation. The ZSL seeks to organize the peasants for the construction of socialism (private peasant ownership of land having been guaranteed by the Government since 1956 and by a constitutional guarantee of 1983).

Structure. The central authority of the ZSL is its congress (held every five years). Its supreme executive elects a presidium, and there are party committees, with their presidiums, at voivodship (provincial) and commune level.

Membership. 465,000 (1983)

Publications. *Zielony Sztandar* (twice weekly central organ), 150,000; *Dziennik Ludowy* (daily), 200,000; *Wies Wspolczesna* (theoretical monthly), 12,500; *Tygodnik Kulturalny* (weekly), 50,000; *Gazeta Ludowa* (Poznan), 40,000; *Wiesci* (Cracow), 120,000

Portugal

Capital: Lisbon   Pop. 10,300,000

The Republic of Portugal is, under its 1976 Constitution reflecting the aims of the 1974 revolution, "a democratic state based . . . on pluralism . . . with the objective of ensuring the transition to socialism". It has a President elected by universal adult suffrage for a five-year term; an Assembly of the Republic of 250 members elected by universal adult suffrage of citizens above the age of 18 years for a four-year term under a system of proportional representation in 18 multi-member electoral districts (in which party lists may contain as many names as there are seats, and also those of several alternates); and a Government under a Prime Minister appointed by the President.

As a result of elections held on April 25, 1983, seats in the Assembly were distributed as follows: Socialists 101, Social Democrats 75, Communists 44, Democratic Social Centre 30.

**Christian Democratic Party
Partido da Democracia Cristão (PDC)**

Address. Rua Passadiço 28-2°, Lisbon, Portugal
Leadership. Santos Ferreira (s.g.)
History. During the 1975 election campaign the PDC was exposed to left-wing attacks and was prohibited from engaging in political activities. In the 1976 elections it gained only 0.52 per cent of the vote. It contested the general elections of Oct. 5, 1980, in alliance with the (neo-fascist) National Front and the Independent Movement for National Reconstruction—Party of the Portuguese Right; however, this alliance obtained only about 20,000 votes. The PDC has played no significant role since then.
Orientation. The PDC is on the right of the political spectrum.

**Democratic Social Centre Party
Partido do Centro Democrático Social (CDS)**

Address. Largo do Caldas 5, 1100 Lisbon 2, Portugal
Leadership. Dr Francisco Lucas Pires (pres.); Dr Vieira de Carvalho (s.g.)
Founded. 1974
History. The party's first president, Prof. Diogo Freitas do Amaral, who had been a member of the Council of State under the Salazar regime, was associated with a political study group (*Assosiação Programa*) formed in 1974. As a centrist party with its stronghold in the country's northern area, the CDS was in late 1974 and early 1975 exposed to violent attacks by left-wing groups and was prevented from holding its first congress in Oporto in January 1975. In the April 1975 elections, for which it had formed an alliance with the Christian Democratic Party (whose activities were banned), the CDS obtained 16 (out of 250) seats in the Constituent Assembly. In the 1976 parliamentary elections it emerged as the third strongest party with 15.9 per cent of the vote and 42 (out of 263) seats.

The CDS contested the 1979 and 1980 elections as part of the Democratic Alliance, gaining 46 seats in the Assembly of the Republic in 1980. However, contesting the 1983 elections on its own, the CDS was reduced to 30 seats in the Assembly. The CDS was in government in coalition with the Socialist Party (PSP) in January-July 1978 and with the Social Democratic Party (PSD) from June 1980 until April 1983.

Orientation. The CDS stands for a social market economy with consumer participation in production planning.
Publications. *Folha CDS* (weekly); *Democracia 76* (fortnightly)
International affiliations. European Christian Democratic Union; European People's Party (observer); Christian Democratic International; International Democrat Union; European Democrat Union

**Independent Movement for National Reconstruction—Party of the Portuguese Right
Movimento Independente de Reconstrução Nacional—Partido da Derecha Portuguesa (MIRN-PDP)**

Leadership. Gen. Kaulza Oliveira de Arriaga (l.)
Founded. October 1978
History. The MIRN was founded in June 1977 by Gen. Kaulza de Arriaga (who had been commander of the Portuguese forces in Mozambique from September 1974 to January 1976). On Oct. 22, 1978, it constituted itself as the *Partido da Derecha Portuguesa*, which polled negligibly in the 1980 parliamentary elections (in which it was allied with the Christian Democrats) and has played no significant role since then.
Orientation. As a militant extreme right-wing and anti-Marxist party, the MIRN-PDP has called in particular for a revision of Portugal's Constitution.

**Independent Social Democratic Party
Partido Social-Democrata Independente (PSDI)**

Address. Travessa do Fala-Só 9-10, 1200 Lisbon, Portugal
Leadership. Joaquim Magalhães Mota (g.s.)
Founded. June 27, 1980
History. The party has its origins in the Independent Social Democratic Association formed on June 8, 1979, by deputies who had broken away from the Social Democratic Party (PSD). After the Association had been constituted as a political party it entered the Republican and Socialist Front set up by the Socialist Party (PSP) and the Union of the Socialist and Democratic Left (UESD), and as part of this Front it gained four seats in the Assembly of the Republic elected on Oct. 5, 1980. The party took part in the revision of the Constitution in 1981–82 and

presented a first draft. It also gained seats in local elections in 1982. For the 1983 general elections the PSDI agreed with the PSP on a common list, and it gained three seats in the Assembly.

Orientation. The PSDI stands for social democracy.

Structure. The PSDI has a seven-member (permanent) political committee, a council (meeting bimonthly) and a congress (held bi-annually). It has an autonomous youth movement, and its parliamentary group is also autonomous.

Publications. Acção Social Democrata—ASD (bimonthly), 4,500

National Front
Frente Nacional

Founded. March 27, 1980

History. The National Front was launched by the *A Rua* newspaper with the aim of rallying all right-wing forces for the forthcoming presidential and parliamentary elections. It contested the 1980 general elections in alliance with the Christian Democratic Party and the Independent Movement for National Reconstruction—Party of the Portuguese Right, but this alliance gained only some 20,000 votes, and the National Front has played no role since then.

Orientation. An extreme right-wing formation, the Front established links with similar movements in Italy and Spain.

People's Democratic Union
União Democrática Popular (UDP)

Address. Alexandro Herculano 55, Lisbon, Portugal

Founded. 1974

History. In the presidential elections of June 1976 the UDP supported, with two other left-wing groups, the unsuccessful candidature of Maj. Otelo Saraiva de Carvalho. The UDP held one seat in the 1975 Constituent Assembly and one Assembly seat from 1976 to 1983.

Orientation. The UDP is an extreme left-wing formation.

People's Monarchist Party
Partido Popular Monárquico (PPM)

Address. Rua do Alecrim 72-2° A, Lisbon, Portugal

Leadership. Gonçalo Ribeiro Telles (l.)

History. The PPM is the continuation of a monarchist (anti-republican) party dating back to before World War I. The party contested the 1979 and 1980 parliamentary elections as part of the Democratic Alliance gaining five and six seats respectively in the Assembly of the Republic. However, in the 1983 general elections, which it contested on its own, it obtained only 0.5 per cent of the vote and no seat.

Popular Unity Force
Força de Unidade Popular

Leadership. Maj. Otelo Saraiva de Carvalho (l.)

Founded. Jan. 30, 1980

History. This group succeeded the United Workers' Organization (OUT). Its leader was an unsuccessful candidate in the 1976 presidential elections, the December 1979 general elections and the presidential elections of Dec. 7, 1980, which he contested as the candidate of the United Popular Front (*Frente Unida Popular,* FUP).

Orientation. The Force is an independent left-wing formation.

Portuguese Communist Party
Partido Comunista Português (PCP)

Address. Rua Soeiro Pereira Gomes 1, 1699 Lisbon, Portugal

Leadership. Collective; Alvaro Cunhal (s.g.)

Founded. March 1921

History. The party was illegal between May 1926 and April 1974. Thereafter the party took part in provisional Governments between May 1974 and July 1976. In elections to a 250-member Constituent Assembly in April 1975 the PCP gained 30 seats and 12.5 per cent of the votes; in elections to the Legislative Assembly held a year later it obtained 40 seats and 14.6 per cent of the votes; in presidential elections held in June 1976 the PCP's candidate won only 7.6 per cent of the votes. In municipal elections held in December 1982 it obtained 21 per cent of the votes, and in Assembly elections held in April 1983 the party (within the United People's Alliance) gained 18.2 per cent of the vote and 44 seats.

Orientation. Guided by the principles of Marxism-Leninism, the PCP defines as its supreme goals the "building in Portugal of socialism and communism". The party is currently "fighting for the defence of nationalization, land reform, workers' control and freedoms and rights achieved by the revolution and for the consolidation of the democratic régime embodied in the Constitution". The PCP has strongly opposed Eurocommunism.

Structure. The PCP's organic structure is based on the principles of "democratic centralism". The party's supreme organ is the congress, meeting as a rule every three years. There is a 133-member central committee, and the party has a territorial and workshop basis.

Membership. 200,000

Publications. *Avante* (Forward, the party's weekly central organ), 76,500; other newspapers and magazines (the party owning two publishing houses and a chain of bookstores)

International affiliations. The PCP is recognized by the Communist parties of the Soviet-bloc countries.

Portuguese Democratic Movement
Movimento Democrático Português (MDP)

Address. Rua Artilharia Um 105, Lisbon, Portugal

Leadership. José Manuel Tengarrinha (l.)

Founded. 1969

History. The party has its origins in Democratic Electoral Committees (*Comissões Democráticas Eleitorais*, CDE) which opposed the Caetano Government (in power in 1968–74). These Committees unsuccessfully contested parliamentary elections in 1969 and withdrew their candidates from the 1973 elections in protest against government repression during the election campaign. After the revolution of April 25, 1974, the CDE became the MDP and took part in several coalition Governments. In the 1975 elections to a Constituent Assembly the party gained five (out of 250) seats and 4.12 per cent of the vote. It took no part in the 1976 parliamentary elections, and in the presidential elections of that year it supported the unsuccessful candidate of the Communist Party.

For the 1979 and 1980 parliamentary elections the MDP was allied with the Communist Party in a United People's Alliance, gaining for itself three seats in 1979 and two in 1980. In the 1980 presidential elections it supported the successful candidature of Gen. Ramalho Eanes. For the 1983 elections the alliance with the Communist Party was abandoned, and the party has since then held no seats in Parliament.

Orientation. Since 1981 the party has advocated "a socialist democracy for Portugal", a policy of negotiations and dialogue in international affairs, the abolition of all military blocs, a new economic and social order and support for the non-aligned movement. It has also opposed the use of nuclear weapons in the Iberian peninsula.

Portuguese Socialist Party
Partido Socialista Portuguesa (PSP)

Address. Rua da Emenda 46, 1200 Lisbon, Portugal

Leadership. António Macedo (ch.); Dr Mario Alberto Nobre Lopes Soares (g.s.)

Founded. 1875

History. A first Socialist Party of Portugal was founded in 1875. It was a member of the Second International and played a minor role in Portugal's first period of democratic government in 1910–26. During the period of the fascist "New State" (1928–74) socialists were engaged in clandestine work in various democratic movements, and in 1964 they formed the Portuguese Socialist Action (*Acção Socialista Portuguesa*, ASP), which led to the clandestine reconstruction of the Socialist Party of Portugal in West Germany. Among the leaders of the ASP was Dr Soares, who was repeatedly arrested and banished from metropolitan Portugal.

Having last been exiled in 1970, Dr Soares returned to Portugal after the military coup in April 1974, whereafter the PSP took part in Portugal's first coalition government (for almost 50 years) formed in May 1974. In elections to a Constituent Assembly held in April 1975 the PSP emerged as the strongest party with 116 (out of 250) seats. Between July and September 1975 the PSP was (together with all other parties except the Communist Party) outside the Government. In the April 1976 parliamentary elections the PSP won 34.97 per cent of the (metropolitan) vote and 107 (out of 263) seats.

In the presidential electons of June 1976 the PSP supported the successful candidature of Gen. António dos Santos Ramalho Eanes, and in July 1976 Dr Soares became Prime Minister of a (minority PSP) Cabinet which also contained independents and members of the armed forces. This Government was followed, in January–July 1978, by a second Soares Cabinet including members of the Democratic Social Centre Party. The PSP subsequently supported a Cabinet of independents appointed in October 1978.

After the party had suffered numerous defections it was decisively defeated in the parliamentary elections of December 1979, when it lost its position as the strongest party in Parliament and went into opposition. However, in the elections held in April 1983 the party gained 36.2 per cent of the valid votes and 101 (out of 250) seats in the Assembly. It thereupon formed a coalition Government with the Social Democratic Party.

Orientation. The party advocates a society with greater social justice and co-operation between the public, private and co-operative sectors, while respecting public liberties and the will of the majority expressed through free elections.

Structure. The party, based on local sections and district federations, has a bi-annual conference, a national committee (of 181 members), a political committee (of 40 members) and a permanent commission (of seven members).

Membership. 120,000

Publications. *Acção Socialista* (weekly), 10,000

International affiliations. Socialist International; Confederation of Socialist Parties of the European Community

Portuguese Workers' Communist Party
Partido Comunista dos Trabalhadores Portugueses (PCTP/MRPP)

Address. Trav. André Valente No. 7, 1200 Lisbon, Portugal

Leadership. Arnaldo Matos (g.s.)

Founded. December 1976

History. The PCTP arose out of the *Movimento Reorganizativo do Partido do Proletariado* (MRPP) formed in September 1970 with the object of "founding a real communist party in Portugal". Following clandestine political work under the Salazar-Caetano dictatorship, the MRPP was prevented from taking part in the Constituent Assembly elections of April 1975 and many of its militants, opposing the Vasco Gonçalves Government (which it regarded as "social-fascist"), were temporarily imprisoned. The MRPP contested the April 1976 parliamentary elections but gained no seats. In the June 1976 presidential elections it supported the (successful) candidature of General Ramalho Eanes.

The party also contested general elections in 1979, 1980 and 1983, regional elections in the Azores and Madeira in 1980 and local elections in 1979 and 1983, winning several seats in the latter year. In the 1980 presidential elections it again supported the candidature of Gen. Ramalho Eanes.

Orientation. The party is "guided by the application of the principles of Marxism, Leninism and Maoism to the Portuguese Revolution". The PCTP stands for the short-term objective of establishing a People's Democratic Republic through a United People's Democratic Front and for "the final and supreme objective" of "realizing communism in Portugal". The party has condemned the "counter-revolutionary coup d'état which took place in China after the death of Mao Zedong" and the "social-fascist clique restoring capitalism in that country"; it has also denounced "treacherous attacks" on Mao Zedong and his legacy by the "Albanian opportunists led by Enver Hoxha", whose regime it regards as "a new social-fascist bourgeois dictatorship".

Structure. The party's supreme organ is its national congress. The party has a central committee, a permanent committee and committees at local level, all elected annually, while the party's basic organization is the cell.

Membership. Several thousand

Publications. *Luta Popular* (central organ), 15,000

Proletarian Revolutionary Party
Partido Proletariano Revolucionario (PPR)

Leadership. Dr Isabel do Carmo, Carlos Melo Antunes (co-founders)

History. Six members of this party, among them the above co-founders, unsuccessfully contested the 1980 general elections from prison, where they were held after being convicted of responsibility for, or involvement in, acts of violence committed by the party's military wing, the Revolutionary Brigades, since 1974.

Orientation. The PPR is a Maoist formation.

Republican and Socialist Front
Frente Republicana e Socialista (FRS)

Founded. June 1980

History. This Front was formed as an electoral alliance for the general elections of Oct. 5, 1980, by the Socialist Party (PSP) with the participation of the Union of the Democratic and Socialist Left (UESD) and the Independent Social Democratic Party (PSDI); it gained 74 seats in the Assembly of the Republic. The FRS was, however, not revived for the general elections of April 1983, in which the PSDI nominated candidates on a common ticket with the PSP (and gained three seats in the Assembly of the Republic).

Revolutionary Socialist Party
Partido Socialista Revolucionario (PSR)

Address. Rua Palma 268, Lisbon, Portugal
Founded. October 1978
History. The PSR was formed by a merger of two Trotskyist groups—the International Communist League and the Revolutionary Workers' Party. It unsuccessfully contested the 1979 and 1980 general elections.
Orientation. The PSR seeks to provide "a specific alternative to today's social democracy, Eurocommunism and Maoism".

Social Democratic Party
Partido Social Democrata (PSD)

Address. 39 Rua de Buenos Aires, 1296 Lisbon, Portugal
Leadership. Carlos Alberto Mota Pinto, Eurico de Melo, Henriques Nascimento Rodrigues (leaders)
Founded. May 1974
History. The PSD—known as the Popular Democratic Party (PDP) until Oct. 4, 1976—took part in the first four and the sixth provisional Governments set up after the revolution of April 25, 1974 (overthrowing the Salazarist regime of President Caetano), between May 1974 and June 1975 and from September 1975 to June 1976, when it went into opposition. It supported the election of President António dos Santos Ramalho Eanes in 1976. It was the second strongest party in the April 1975 Constituent Assembly (with 27 per cent of the votes) and in the Parliament elected in April 1976 (with 24 per cent of the votes).

The PSD contested the 1979 and 1980 parliamentary elections as part of the Democratic Alliance and gained 79 and 82 seats for itself respectively, and it retained 75 seats in the 1983 elections (which it fought on its own). The PSD supported a non-party Government from November 1978 to June 1979 and took part in coalition Governments (i) with the Democratic Social Centre Party (CDS) from January 1980 to August 1981, (ii) with the CDS and the People's Monarchist Party from September 1981 to April 1983 and (iii) with the Socialist Party from June 1983 onwards.
Orientation. The PSD stands for a reformist approach to social democracy within the Western tradition of humanism and individuality. Its main support is that of the working classes but it also defends the interests of "an important private sector of the economy".
Structure. The party has a congress of 800 members meeting annually, a national council of 70 members meeting eight times a year, a 17-member political committee, a nine-member jurisdictional council, regional political committees (in the Azores and Madeira), district political committees and occupational and residential branches.
Membership. 85,000
Publications. *Povo Livre* (weekly newspaper, official organ), 15,000

Union of the Socialist and Democratic Left
União da Esquerda Socialista Democrática (UESD)

Leadership. António Lopes Cardoso (pres.)
Founded. 1978
History. The party unsuccessfully contested the December 1979 general elections. Its leader is a former (Socialist) Minister of Agriculture.

United People's Alliance
Aliança Popular Unida/Aliança Povo Unido (APU)

Founded. 1979
History. This electoral coalition was formed by the Portuguese Communist Party (CPC) and the Portuguese Democratic Movement (MDP) to contest the 1979 and 1980 general elections, in which the APU obtained respectively 47 seats (44 for the PCP and three for the MDP) and 41 seats (39 for the PCP and two for the MDP) in the Assembly of the Republic. The Alliance was, however, not renewed for the 1983 general elections.

Workers' Party for Socialist Unity
Partido Operario de Unidade Socialista (POUS)

History. This party has polled minimally in general elections held since 1979. Its candidate in presidential elections held on Dec. 7, 1980, António Aire Rodrigues (who had been a deputy of the Socialist Party), polled only 12,612 votes (or 0.22 per cent of the total).
Orientation. The POUS is a Trotskyist formation.

Portuguese Dependent Territory

Macao

Capital: Nome de Deus de Macau   Pop. 262,000

The Portuguese territory of Macao is administered as a "special territory" under the Portuguese legislature by a governor appointed by the President of Portugal after consultation with the local population. It has far-reaching internal autonomy and a Legislative Assembly to which five members are appointed by the governor and 12 are elected—six by universal adult suffrage and six indirectly by business associations—for a three-year term.

There are no political parties as such, but three civic associations are represented in the Legislative Assembly.

Association for the Defence of the Interests of Macao
Associação para a Defesa dos Interesses de Macau

Founded. 1974

History. This Association was formed by Portuguese businessmen to defend their interests. In the elections to the Portuguese Constituent Assembly held in April 1975 this group obtained the seat for Macao. It is also supported by the Roman Catholic Church and is conservative in outlook.

Independent Group of Macao
Grupo Independente de Macau (Gima)

History. This association based on independent members of the Legislative Assembly has remained in a small minority as compared with the two groupings detailed here.

Macao Democratic Centre
Centro Democrático de Macau (CDM)

Leadership. Francisco Brito (l.)

Founded. May 1974

History. The CDM was formed by officials and intellectuals who had recently arrived from Portugal. Following its candidate's failure to secure election to the Portuguese Constituent Assembly the CDM decided in July 1975 to reduce its activities.

Orientation. The CDM is of democratic socialist orientation.

Qatar

Capital: Doha   Pop. 270,000

The state of Qatar has a Council of Ministers appointed and presided over by the head of state (the Amir) and assisted by a 30-member Advisory Council appointed for a three-year term. There is no parliament and there are no official political parties.

Romania

Capital: Bucharest   Pop. 22,600,000

The Socialist Republic of Romania, in which the Communist Party has the leading role (as reaffirmed in the 1965 Constitution), has a 369-member Grand National Assembly (*Marea Adunare Nationala*) which is elected for a five-year term by all citizens above the age of 18 years and from "one or more" candidates in single-member constituencies. Where no absolute majority is obtained in a first ballot, further ballots may be held until such a majority is achieved. When not in session the Assembly has its legislative powers delegated to the State Council, whose President is the head of state. Communist authority is exercised in part through a Socialist Democracy and Unity Front (SDUF), which is led by the Romanian Communist Party and the National Council of which acts as a consultative body to the Council of Ministers.

In elections held on March 9, 1980, for the 369 seats of the Assembly many of the constituencies were contested by two or three candidates, all candidates having been nominated by the SDUF. According to the official results the turn-out was 99.99 per cent, and of those who voted 98.52 per cent voted in favour of SDUF candidates and 1.48 per cent voted against. Of the elected deputies, 47 represented ethnic minorities (mainly Hungarians and Germans). For these minorities there are two consultative National Councils—one Hungarian and one German.

Romanian Communist Party
Partidul Comunist Român (PCR)

Address. Str. Acadamiei 34, Bucharest, Romania

Leadership. President Nicolae Ceausescu (g.s.); Stefan Andrei, Iosif Banc, Emil Bobu, Elena Ceausescu, Nicolae Constantin, Constantin Dascalescu, Petru Enache, Gheorghe Oprea, Ion Patan, Gheorghe Radulescu and Ilie Verdet (other members of permanent bureau)

Founded. May 1921

History. The PCR was created when the left-wing section of the Social Democratic Workers' Party (founded in March 1893) decided to transform itself into a Communist party and to affiliate to the Communist International. As a legal party it sought to represent the interests of the workers and worked to consolidate the unitary national state created in 1918. It was banned in April 1924 and thereafter it operated underground, with party congresses being held abroad (in Vienna in September 1924, in Kharkov in June 1928 and in Moscow in December 1931). It played an important role in organizing an antifascist and anti-war demonstration in Bucharest in December 1931, and in 1941–44 it built a broad national front on the basis of which it led the antifascist resistance of the Romanian people.

state created in 1918. It was banned in April 1924 and thereafter it operated underground, with party congresses being held abroad (in Vienna in September 1924, in Kharkov in June 1928 and in Moscow in December 1931). It played an important role in organizing an antifascist and anti-war demonstration in Bucharest in December 1931, and in 1941–44 it built a broad national front on the basis of which it led the antifascist resistance of the Romanian people.

Following Romania's decision in August 1944 to switch from the Axis to the Allied side in World War II, the Communist Party was part of successive electoral alliances, initially in a National Democratic bloc (with the Liberal, Peasants' and Social Democratic parties) and later in a People's Democratic Front (PDF) with the Social Democrats and two smaller left-wing groups. In elections to a National Assembly held in November 1946 the PCR obtained 73 out of the 348 seats gained by the PDF (out of a total of 414 seats).

In early 1948 the PCR merged with the Social Democratic Party to form the Romanian Workers' Party (RWP), the opposition Social Democrats and other non-communist parties being progressively outlawed thereafter. In elections held in March 1948 the PDF obtained 405 seats in the National Assembly and in the Government formed thereafter the RWP held 15 of the 21 ministerial posts. In elections held in November 1950 the PDF presented, for the first time, a single list of candidates for the National Assembly, and this was officially stated to have obtained 98 per cent of the valid votes cast in a 97 per cent poll.

Gheorghe Gheorghiu-Dej, the RWP's leader, was Prime Minister from 1952 to 1955, whereafter he was first secretary of the RWP. In March 1956, after the Communist Party of the Soviet Union had condemned the "cult of personality" (i.e. of Stalin), the RWP decided to correct its "failure to observe the Leninist principle of party democracy" and from then onwards the party increasingly asserted its political independence. In June 1956 it restored its relations with the League of Communists of Yugoslavia (broken off in 1948); in October 1956 it stated that there were "differing forms and methods for the construction of socialism"; and in February-March 1964 it attempted to act as a mediator in the Sino-Soviet dispute and appealed for unity among all Communist parties.

Following the death of Gheorge Gheorghiu-Dej in March 1965, Nicolae Ceausescu was elected first secretary of the party, and at a party congress held in July 1965 he emphasized Romania's political and economic independence and its determination to proceed with industrialization (in defiance of the "international socialist division of labour" policy of Comecon). The congress decided to change the RWP's name to Romanian Communist Party (RCP). In December 1967 Nicolae

Ceausescu (whose title had been changed to general secretary at the 1965 party congress) was elected President of the Council of State and in March 1974 the Grand National Assembly elected him to the newly-created post of President of the Republic. Earlier, in April 1968, the party had denounced the Gheorghiu-Dej regime as having "violated the most elementary standards of legality and justice", and had rehabilitated a number of "deviationists" dismissed from their posts and sentenced (some of them to death) under that regime.

At a party congress held in November 1974 President Ceausescu appealed for "a genuine historic reconciliation between the Communist and Socialist parties of the world" and said that the RCP should "continue to avoid in the future involvement in actions condemning other parties".

At a congress held in November 1979 and a national conference of December 1982 the party endorsed programmes of action designed to update the country's economic structures and to intensify economic development to enable Romania to join the ranks of medium-developed countries and to develop "worker socialist democracy".

Structure. The PCR has primary organizations in enterprises and residential areas, and it is organized at communal, municipal and regional level. Its supreme organ is the congress, convened every five years; in 1974 the congress elected a central committee of 251 full members and 174 alternate members. Between congresses the central committee may convene a national conference. There is an executive political committee (of 23 full and 19 alternate members) and a permanent bureau (consisting of the central committee's general secretary and 13 other members).

Membership. 3,341,248 (November 1983)

Publications. Scinteia (The Spark, daily organ), over 1,400,000; *Era Socialista* (bimonthly theoretical and political journal), 67,000

Rwanda

Capital: Kigali   Pop. 5,200,000

The Rwandese Republic is, under its Constitution approved in a referendum on Dec. 17, 1978, "a democratic, social and sovereign republic based on government of the people, by the people and for the people". It has an executive President, elected for a five-year term by the people and re-eligible, and a (legislative) National Development Council. The latter body has 70 seats filled (also for five years) by direct elections by universal adult suffrage from a list of 91 candidates who are members of the *Mouvement Révolutionnaire National pour le Développement* (MRND), the country's sole legal political organization.

In presidential elections held on Dec. 19, 1983, President Juvénal Habyarimana was re-elected President as the sole candidate of the MRND. In legislative elections held on Dec. 26, 1983, to the 70 seats of the National Decelopment Council 17 former members lost their seats and 23 new ones were elected.

National Revolutionary Movement for Development
Mouvement Révolutionnaire National pour le Développement (MRND)

Address. Boîte postale 1055, Kigali, Rwanda

Leadership. President Juvénal Habyarimana (pres. and founder); Bonaventure Habimana (s.g.)

Founded. July 1975

History. The establishment of the MRND as the sole ruling party was announced by President Habyarimana on the second anniversary of the July 1973 military coup, following which political organizations had been banned. The new party embraced both military and civilian elements and its central purpose was avowedly to strengthen the position of the military regime, in particular by overcoming the tribal divisions from which the country had suffered in the recent past.

Orientation. The party advocates "peace, national unity and democratic and revolutionary developments by the people for the people".

Structure. The MRND has organs at local, prefectural and national level, and there is a central committee, a national congress and a presidency. Every citizen is by right a member of the MRND.

Publications. *Agence Rwandaise de Presse; La Relève* (bimonthly); *Imvaho*

St Kitts and Nevis

Capital: Basseterre (St Kitts)   Pop. 45,000

The federation of St Kitts and Nevis—consisting of the islands of St Kitts (St Christopher) and Nevis in the eastern Caribbean—is an independent member of the Commonwealth with the British monarch as head of state being represented by a Governor-General. It has a unicameral National Assembly normally elected for a five-year term by universal adult suffrage of citizens above the age of 18 years. It also has a Cabinet headed by a Prime Minister and collectively responsible to the National Assembly. (St Kitts and Nevis had formerly been linked with Anguilla—currently still a British dependency—within the UK Associated State of St Kitts-Nevis-Anguilla.)

The National Assembly, however, does not have powers to pass laws having effect in the island of Nevis in matters specifically reserved to a Nevis Island Assembly consisting of one elected member for each of five constituencies and three or more nominated members (their number not exceeding the number of elected members). From among the members of the Nevis Island Assembly the Governor-General appoints a Premier and two other members to form a Nevis Island Administration. The Governor-General also appoints a Deputy Governor-General for Nevis Island. (The Nevis Island Assembly has power to provide for the separation of Nevis from St Kitts under certain conditions, including approval by a two-thirds majority of the votes cast in a referendum held in Nevis.)

As a result of the first post-independence elections held on June 21, 1984, the People's Action Movement won six of the eight St Kitts seats and the Labour Party two, while all three Nevis seats were won by the Nevis Reformation Party (NRP). The NRP had earlier won all five seats in the Nevis Assembly in elections held in August 1983.

Labour Party

Address. Church Street (P.O. Box 239), Basseterre, St Kitts-Nevis

Leadership. Lee L. Moore (l.); Joseph N. France (sec.)

Founded. 1932

History. The party won all elections held between 1936 and 1975. It was in power until 1980, when in elections held in February of that year it won 58 per cent of the valid votes in St Kitts (and 16 per cent in Nevis) but its parliamentary strength was reduced from five to four elective seats. It subsequently went into opposition to a coalition Government formed by the People's Action Movement and the Nevis Reformation Party, and its position has further weakened in the general elections of June 1984..

Orientation. The party declares itself to be of socialist orientation.

Structure. The party has a national executive, nine branches and a youth section.

Publications. *Labour Spokesman* (twice a week), 1,500

Nevis Reformation Party (NRP)

Address. P.O. Box 480, Charlestown, Nevis, St Kitts-Nevis

Leadership. Simeon Daniel (l.); Levi Morton (sec.)

Founded. December 1970

History. In elections to the St Kitts-Nevis-Anguilla Assembly the party won one of the two Nevis seats in 1971 and both seats in 1975 and 1980. In local council elections it won six of the nine seats in 1971 and all nine seats in 1975. In an unofficial referendum held in 1977 the party's policy of secession of Nevis from St Kitts was supported by 4,393 votes (against 14).

After the 1980 elections the NRP formed a St Kitts-Nevis coalition Government with the People's Action Movement. After gaining all five seats in the newly-established Nevis Island Assembly in 1983, its leader, Simeon Daniel, became the first Premier of Nevis on Sept 19, 1983.

Orientation. The NRP seeks "political independence for the people of Nevis".

Structure. In addition to five party office-bearers there is an executive committee.

Membership. 10,000

People's Action Movement (PAM)

Leadership. Dr Kennedy A. Simmonds (l.)

History. The PAM first entered the pre-independence Assembly in May 1971, when it gained one of the two seats for Nevis. It failed to gain any seats in the 1975 general elections, but its leader was elected to the House of Assembly in a by-election in St Kitts in January 1979. In the February 1980 general elections it obtained three of the nine elective seats in the Assembly and it thereupon formed a coalition Government with the Nevis Reformation Party. This Government concluded with the British Government an agreement which led to independence for St Kitts-Nevis on Sept. 19, 1983. In the June 1984 general elections the PAM secured an overall majority.

Orientation. While in opposition to the Labour Party, the PAM advocated independence on a basis of greater economic strength for the islands and development pledges from foreign donors.

United National Movement

Address. Charlestown, Nevis, St Kitts-Nevis

Leadership. Eugene Walwyn (l.)

History. This small formation has sought to challenge the position of the longer-established parties but has as yet made little political impact.

St Lucia

Capital: Castries   Pop. 130,000

St Lucia, one of the Windward Islands, is an independent state within the Commonwealth with the British monarch as head of state being represented by a Governor-General. It has a bicameral Parliament consisting of (i) a 17-member House of Assembly elected for five years by universal adult suffrage of citizens above the age of 18 years and by simple majority in single-member constituencies and (ii) an 11-member Senate appointed by the Governor-General (six senators on the advice of the Prime Minister, three on the advice of the Leader of the Opposition and two by consultation with religious, economic and social bodies). The Prime Minister and his Cabinet are responsible to Parliament.

In elections to the House of Assembly held on May 3, 1982, the (conservative) United Workers' Party gained 14 seats, the St Lucia Labour Party two and the Progressive Labour Party one seat.

Progressive Labour Party (PLP)

Address. No. 19, St Louis Street, Castries, St Lucia

Leadership. George Odlum (l.); Peter Josie (pol. l.); Frances Michel (g.s.)

Founded. May 1981

History. The PLP was created after a progressive faction broke away from the (more moderate) St Lucia Labour Party (SLP). George Odlum had been associated with the "new left" movement in Commonwealth Caribbean politics and had held ministerial office in the SLP Government in power until April 1981. He was an adviser to an interim Government of national unity headed by the deputy leader of the PLP, Michael Pilgrim, in January–May 1982. However, in the general elections of May 3, 1982, the PLP gained only 27.1 per cent of the vote and one seat in the House of Assembly, both Odlum and Pilgrim losing their seats.

Orientation. The PLP has described itself as "mildly socialist".

Structure. The PLP has succeeded in establishing a significant presence in the trade union movement.

International affiliations. Socialist International (consultative member)

St Lucia Labour Party (SLP)

Address. Castries, St Lucia

Leadership. Neville Cenac (l.); Charles Agustin (ch.); Evans Calderon (sec.)

Founded. 1946

History. The party had been in opposition since St Lucia became one of the West Indian Associated States (i.e. with the United Kingdom) in 1967 until July 1979, when it formed a Government after gaining 12 out of the 17 seats in the St Lucia House of Assembly. It had earlier campaigned unsuccessfully for the holding of a referendum before the achievement of the island's independence.

From 1980 onwards the SLP was increasingly divided by disagreements between Allan F. L. Louisy (then party leader and Prime Minister) and George Odlum (deputy leader and Foreign Minister). On April 14, 1981, Odlum and three other SLP members voted against the Government's budget proposals and on April 30 they brought about the resignation of Louisy as Prime Minister (although he had been re-elected party leader on March 28).

A new SLP Government led by Winston Cenac gained the support of one of Odlum's followers, but it resigned on Jan. 16, 1982, because it had lost the support of the Chamber of Commerce, the public sector trade unions and even the police. George Odlum and his followers had earlier seceded from the SLP and formed the Progressive Labour Party (see separate entry). In the May 1982 general elections the SLP retained only 16.5 per cent of the valid votes and two seats in the House of Assembly. A prolonged leadership struggle ensued, from which Neville Cenac (younger brother of the former Premier) and a group on the right of the party eventually emerged victorious.

Orientation. The SLP has campaigned for measures to reduce unemployment and for a wider distribution of the benefits of economic development. The SLP Government favoured St Lucia's membership of the non-aligned nations and established diplomatic relations with Cuba and North Korea.

Structure. The SLP has traditional links with the trade union movement, but this backing has been eroded in recent years.

Publications. Etoile

United Workers' Party (UWP)

Address. Castries, St Lucia

Leadership. John G. M. Compton (l.)

Founded. 1964

History. The UWP was in power from before 1967, when the island became one of the Associated States of the British West Indian islands, until July 1979. In 1974 it had been returned to power on a programme of seeking full independence for St Lucia, but in the post-independence elections of July 1979 it was defeated and it subsequently went into opposition.

From January to May 1982 the UWP took part in a coalition Government of national unity supported by all three parties. However, in the general elections of May 3, 1982, the UWP won an overwhelming victory, gaining 56.4 per cent of the valid vote and 14 seats in the House of Assembly (12 of them by absolute majorities), and it thereupon formed a Government.

Orientation. Pro-Western, the UWP conducted its 1982 election campaign under the slogan "Christians ever, communists never". It called for encouragement of private enterprise in agriculture, an agricultural development corporation, expansion of tourism, and new investment in export-oriented manufacturing industries based on local raw materials.

St Vincent and the Grenadines

Capital: Kingstown   Pop. 130,000

St Vincent and the Grenadines is an independent state with the status of a "special member" of the Commonwealth (similar to the status of Nauru and Tuvalu), with the British monarch as head of state being represented by a Governor-General. The country has a House of Assembly consisting of 13 representatives elected for a five-year term by universal adult suffrage of citizens above the age of 18 years and by simple majority in single-member constituencies, and six senators appointed by the Governor-General (four on the advice of the Prime Minister and two on that of the Leader of the Opposition). There is a Cabinet which is "to advise the Governor-General in the government of St Vincent" and which is collectively responsible to the House of Assembly.

In elections to the House held on Dec. 5, 1979, the ruling St Vincent Labour Party gained 11 of the 13 elective seats and the New Democratic Party the remaining two.

Movement for National Unity (MNU)

Leadership. Dr Ralph Gonsalves, Caspar London (leaders)
Founded. 1982
History. Dr Gonsalves had previously been the leader of the left-wing United People's Movement (see separate entry).

New Democratic Party (NDP)

Address. P.O. Box 619, St Vincent and the Grenadines
Leadership. James F. Mitchell (pres.); George Owen Walker (s.g.)
Founded. December 1975
History. The party's president had been elected to the St Vincent legislature as a member of the St Vincent Labour Party (SVLP) in 1966 and re-elected as an independent in 1972. As such he held the balance of power in the 13-member House of Assembly between the SVLP and the People's Political Party (PPP), and he became Premier of a PPP Government. After the leader of the PPP and his wife, who were both members of the Government, had withdrawn their support from him, the House was dissolved in 1974. In the ensuing elections (in which the PPP was defeated) James Mitchell retained his seat as an independent, and

he subsequently, with George Walker, formed the NDP, whose constitution was approved at a convention held in 1976.

The NDP boycotted a constitutional conference held in London in 1978 and also the vote on the draft independence Constitution in the House of Assembly on Feb. 9, 1979. In the 1979 general elections the NDP gained 30 per cent of the vote, and it thereupon became the official opposition, although Mitchell was not re-elected in that poll. He was, however, re-elected in a by-election on June 23, 1980.

Orientation. The NDP is a democratic party supporting political union in the Caribbean, social development and free enterprise.
Structure. The party has a central committee and holds an annual convention.
Membership. 7,000

People's Democratic Movement (PDM)

Leadership. Dr Kenneth John (l.)
History. The PDM joined the United People's Movement (see separate entry) upon the latter's formation in 1979, but withdrew from it in July 1981.

People's Political Party (PPP)

Leadership. Clive Tannis (l.)

Founded. 1952

History. The PPP, holding five of the nine seats in the then Legislature, was in power until 1967, when its representation was reduced to three members. In the 1972 elections the PPP won six of the 13 seats in the House of Assembly, and it thereupon joined a Government led by an independent. This Government lost the confidence of the House in 1974. The PPP leader (and his wife) thereupon concluded a unity agreement with the St Vincent Labour Party (SVLP) for the ensuing elections, in which the PPP retained only two seats (both uncontested by the SVLP). The PPP leader thereafter held office in an SVLP Government until April 1978. In the 1979 elections the PPP gained only 2.4 per cent of the votes cast and no seat in the House of Assembly.

Orientation. The PPP had in 1967–69 been opposed to the granting of the status of an Associated State to St Vincent before the holding of new elections. It boycotted a constitutional conference held in London in September 1978 and called for new elections or a referendum to be held before the granting of independence.

Progressive Democratic Party (PDP)

Leadership. Randolph Russell (l.)

Founded. 1981

History. Randolph Russell had been elected to the House of Assembly in 1979 as a member of the St Vincent Labour Party and had become a cabinet minister, but he resigned as such in May 1981 and thereafter sat in the House as an independent member. He became Leader of the Opposition in July 1981.

St Vincent Labour Party (SVLP)

Leadership. R. Milton Cato (l.)

Founded. 1955

History. The SVLP came to power after elections to the nine-member legislature in May 1967, when it gained six seats (against three obtained by the People's Political Party). The party's leader became Chief Minister and subsequently, from October 1969 (when St Vincent became an Associated State), Premier. In the 1972 elections the SVLP gained only six of the 13 seats in the House of Assembly, and it thereupon went into opposition until 1974, when the House was dissolved. In the subsequent elections the SVLP gained over 69 per cent of the vote and 10 seats. It has been

in power ever since, although in the 1979 elections the percentage of votes cast for it declined to 53.5.

Orientation. The party called for full independence without the prior holding of a referendum or of general elections. It is a moderate socialist party advocating a mixed economy, and it follows a conservative foreign policy.

Publications. *The Star*

St Vincent National Movement (SVNM)

Leadership. Dr Gideon Cordice (l.)

History. This small formation has sought to transcend existing political divisions in St Vincent, but has failed as yet to make any substantial impact.

United People's Movement (UPM)

Address. P.O. Box 519, Kingstown, St. Vincent

Leadership. Renwick Rose (l.)

Founded. August 1979

History. The UPM was formed as an alliance of the Youlou United Liberation Movement (Yulimo), the People's Democratic Movement (see separate entry) and a rural group known as *Arwee*. In the 1979 elections the UPM gained 14.4 per cent of the vote but no seats in the House of Assembly.

Orientation. The UPM is a party of the "new left" (denounced as "communist" by the leader of the ruling St Vincent Labour Party).

Working People's Party (WPP)

Leadership. Calder Williams (l.)

Founded. March 1980

History. Calder Williams had been elected to the House of Assembly in 1979 as a member of the New Democratic Party (see separate entry) and had been appointed Leader of the Opposition. However, he resigned from this post in July 1981 in favour of Randolph Russell, who had left the St Vincent Labour Party to sit in the House as an independent member and later founded the Progressive Democratic Party (see separate entry). Williams established the WPP together with two NDP-appointed senators as an opposition party.

San Marino

Capital: San Marino   Pop. 22,000

In the Republic of San Marino legislative power is vested in a 60-member Grand and General Council elected every five years by universal adult suffrage of citizens above the age of 18 years and by a system of proportional representation. Two of its members are appointed every six months to act as Captains-Regent who, with a Congress of State (Government), exercise executive power. Since 1978 the country has been governed by a coalition of the Communist, Socialist and Socialist Unity parties.

As a result of elections to the Grand and General Council held on May 29, 1983, seats were distributed as follows: Christian Democrats 26, Communists 15, Socialists 9, Socialist Unity Party 8, Socialist Democracy Party 1, Committee for the Defence of the Republic 1. In municipal elections held in May 1980 the left-wing coalition had gained control in eight out of nine wards.

Christian Democratic Party of San Marino
Partito Democratico Cristiano Sammarinese

Address. Piazzetta Bramante Lazzari 1, Città-47031, San Marino
Leadership. Clara Boscaglia (s.g.); Federico Bigi (pres. of central council); Fernando Bindi (pres. of council group)
Founded. April 1948
History. From 1948 to 1957 the party was in opposition to the Government of San Marino's Communist and Socialist parties, but after the latter had lost their majority in 1957 the party joined a coalition Government together with the Independent Democratic Socialists, and from 1973 to 1978 it was in power in coalition with the Socialist Party of San Marino. After the elections of May 1978, in which the party increased its parliamentary representation from 25 to 26 seats and remained the Republic's strongest party, it went into opposition to a newly-formed three-party left-wing coalition Government.
Orientation. The party stands for freedom, democracy, pluralism and social justice and for a humane and just society offering free development to the individual. The party has always sought an alliance with other democratic forces in the country, as well as closer relations with the United Nations, the Council of Europe and the European Communities.
Structure. The party's supreme organ is the congress, which meets every three years and elects a 40-member central council as the party's deliberative organ. The central council nominates a nine-member central committee as the party's executive organ.
Membership. 3,000
Publications. San Marino (official party organ), 3,500
International affiliations. Christian Democratic International; European Christian Democratic Union

Committee for the Defence of the Republic
Comitato per la Difesa della Repubblica (CDR)

Address. Città, via Capannaccia, San Marino
Leadership. Bonelli Menetto, Cardinali Marino, Suzzi Valli Pietro
Founded. March 1974
History. Founded as a movement with liberal ideas and in order to defend the values of the country's historical tradition and its sovereignty, the CDR is pragmatic in its political activities and has declared itself to be anti-communist and anti-Marxist. It fights against the established parties and their organizations and for freedom of the citizen and the person. The CDR is in opposition.
Orientation. The CDR regards itself as "liberal-conservative, Roman Catholic and democratic and for a social market economy".

Structure. The CDR is a movement of opinion open to all citizens. It has a collective and democratic leadership without an hierarchical structure.

Publications. *Il Sammarinese* (periodical), 2,000

Marxist-Leninist Communist Party of San Marino
Partido Comunista Marxista-Leninista di San Marino (PCML)

Founded. March 1968

History. The PCML was formed as a pro-Chinese party by defectors from the San Marino Communist Party. It contested the 1974 general elections but obtained only 0.8 per cent of the votes cast. It has played no significant political role since then.

San Marino Communist Party
Partito Comunista Sammarinese

Address. Via Sentier Rosso, 1, San Marino 47031, San Marino

Leadership. Ermenegildo Gasperoni (pres.); Umberto Barulli (sec.)

Founded. July 1941

History. From 1945 to 1957 the party was in government with the Socialist Party, the two Captains-Regent of San Marino being then a Communist and a Socialist. A left-wing coalition with the Socialist and Socialist Unity parties was established after the elections of May 1978, with the Communist Party holding four ministries.

In municipal elections held in May 1980 the party won four out of eight mayors' posts. The general elections of May 1983 were again won by the left-wing coalition, and the two Captains-Regent have been a Communist and a Socialist.

Orientation. The party favours collaboration with democratic and socialist parties in its efforts to achieve a socialist society, as well as peace throughout the world and co-operation with all nations and people "for a better world".

Structure. The party has a 35-member central committee, a seven-member control committee, a 15-member head office and a five-member secretariat. It has 17 cells and five territorial departments.

Membership. 1,000

Publications. *La Scintilla* (monthly), 1,500

International affiliations. The party is recognized by the Communist parties of the Soviet-bloc countries.

San Marino Socialist Party
Partito Socialista Sammarinese (PSS)

Leadership. Adriano Reffi (l.)

History. Between 1945 and 1957 the PSS was in power in a coalition Government with the Communists. The party was thereafter in opposition until May 1973, when it formed a coalition Government with the Christian Democrats, from which it withdrew in 1977. A new Government was not formed until after the 1978 elections (in which the PSS retained its eight seats in the Grand and General Council). As a result the PSS returned to power in a coalition Government including also the Communists and the Socialist Unity Party. In the 1983 elections the PSS gained a ninth seat in the Grand and General Council, and it has remained in power in the left-wing three-party coalition.

Orientation. Left-wing socialist.

Socialist Democracy Party
Partito di Democrazia Socialista (PDS)

Founded. December 1975

History. The PDS was formed as the right wing of the former Independent Democratic Socialist Party, which was split in 1975. It is the most moderate of San Marino's three socialist parties. It held three seats in the Grand and General Council until the May 1978 elections, when its representation was reduced to two members. It did not join the left-wing coalition Government formed subsequently. In the 1983 elections it retained only one seat in the Council.

Socialist Unity Party
Partito Socialista Unitario (PSU)

Address. Via della Tana 117, San Marino 47031, San Marino

Leadership. Emilio Della Balda (pres.); Pio Galassi (hon. pres.); Patrizia Busignani (s.g.)

Founded. December 1975

History. The PSU originated from the left wing of the former Independent Democratic Socialist Party, which was split in 1975. It subsequently held five seats in the Grand and General Council, and in the May 1978 elections it gained seven seats. It thereupon joined a coalition Government formed in July 1978 with the participation of the Communists and the Socialists. In the 1983 elections it gained eight seats in the Council, and the coalition Government has since remained in power, with the PSU being responsible for Finance and the Budget, Social Security and Health, Tourism, Sport, Agriculture and Commerce.

Orientation. The PSU is a democratic socialist party.

International affiliations. Socialist International

São Tomé and Príncipe

Capital: São Tomé Pop. 105,000

The Democratic Republic of São Tomé and Príncipe is an "independent, unitary and democratic state" in which "the leading force" is the Movement for the Liberation of São Tomé and Príncipe (MLSTP). The Supreme organ of the state is a 40-member People's Assembly consisting of the Political Bureau of the MLSTP, the Government and other members chosen by the MLSTP. The Assembly, appointed for four years, elects the President of the Republic for the same term of office. In fact, however, by May 1984 there had been no elections since the People's Assembly was formed in 1979.

Movement for the Liberation of São Tomé and Príncipe
Movimento de Libertação de São Tomé e Príncipe (MLSTP)

Leadership. President Manuel Pinto da Costa (s.g.)

Founded. 1960

History. The party was originally established (in 1960) as the Committee for the Liberation of São Tomé and Príncipe, based in Libreville (Gabon). Having taken its present name in 1972, the MLSTP was recognized by the Organization of African Unity in 1973. Following the overthrow of the Caetano regime in Portugal in April 1974 the new Portuguese Government later in that year recognized the MLSTP as the sole representative of the people of São Tomé and Príncipe and an independence agreement was signed in November 1974.

A transitional government formed in December 1974 contained four MLSTP ministers (and a fifth appointed by the Portuguese Government). In April 1975 two of the MLSTP ministers were dismissed for inciting hatred against Whites in contravention of MLSTP orders. An all-MLSTP Government was formed on the achievement of independence in July 1975. In September 1979 one of the MLSTP's foremost leaders, Miguel dos Anjos da Cunha Lisboa Trouvoada (who had been the country's first Prime Minister until April 1979), was relieved of his remaining ministerial posts and arrested on charges of plotting against the regime—this occurrence revealing serious divisions in the MLSTP. He was, however, released in July 1981. The MLSTP has effectively remained the country's sole ruling party.

Structure. The party has a co-ordinating council as its highest organ.

Saudi Arabia

Capitals: Riyadh (royal capital),
Jeddah (administrative capital) Pop. 10,200,000

The Kingdom of Saudi Arabia is under the direct rule of the King, who is also the Prime Minister and who presides over a Council of Ministers. There is no Parliament nor are there any legal political parties.

Senegal

Capital: Dakar   Pop. 6,050,000

The Republic of Senegal has an executive President elected by universal adult suffrage for a five-year term and re-eligible. He chooses and appoints a Cabinet headed by a Prime Minister responsible to a 120-member National Assembly elected at the same time as the President. The minimum voting age is 21 years. Of the Assembly's 120 members 60 are elected by simple majority in 30 electoral districts and the other 60 by proportional representation from national lists presented by each party. (For the creation of the Confederation of Senegambia see under The Gambia, page 166.)

Under constitutional amendments made in 1976, 1978 and 1981, a total of 15 political parties (including several extreme left-wing groups) have been registered, although no party is allowed to be identified with a race, a religion, a sect, an ethnic group, a sex, a language or a region). Under the electoral code parties are not allowed to form alliances.

In elections to the National Assembly held on Feb. 27, 1983, and contested by eight parties, the ruling Socialist Party obtained 111 seats, the Democratic Party eight and the National Democratic Rally one (in a 56 per cent poll).

African Independence Party
Parti Africain de l'Indépendance (PAI)

Address. B.P. 820, Dakar, Senegal
Leadership. Majhemout Diop (pres.); Bara Goudiaby (s.g.)
Founded. September 1957
History. Originally founded as a (pro-Soviet) Marxist-Leninist party, the PAI campaigned for the independence of Senegal and other French colonies but decided in 1962 to confine its activities to Senegal. It did not contest the 1959 (pre-independence) elections in Senegal. It was illegal from 1960 onwards and its president went into exile, returning to Senegal in 1976, when the party was legalized as one of three officially recognized parties. In elections to the National Assembly in February 1978, the PAI obtained only 0.32 per cent of the votes and no seat. In the 1983 elections it increased its share of the vote to 0.47 per cent but still gained no seat.
Orientation. The party is regarded as representing the Marxist-Leninist political current to the left of the ruling Socialist Party.
Structure. There are a party congress, a central committee and an executive secretariat.

Publications. *Lutte* (Struggle, monthly), 1,000; *Momsareew* (Independence), 1,000
International affiliations. The PAI is recognized by the Communist parties of the Soviet-bloc countries.

African Party for the Independence of the Masses
Parti Africain pour l'Indépendance des Masses (PAIM)

Leadership. Aly Niane (s.g.)
Founded. 1982
History. Although recently legalized, the PAIM boycotted the 1983 general elections in protest against the ban on the formation of electoral alliances.

Communist Workers' League
Ligue Communiste des Travailleurs (LCT)

Leadership. Mahmoud Saleh (founder)
Founded. 1982
History. Although officially registered, the LCT boycotted the 1983 general

elections in protest against the ban on the creation of electoral alliances.

Democratic League—Movement for the Workers' Party
Ligue Démocratique—Mouvement pour le Parti des Travailleurs (LD-MFT)

Leadership. Babacar Sané, Mamadou Ndoye, Abdoulaye Bathily (leaders)
History. This party was officially registered in 1981. It took part in the 1983 general elections and obtained 1.12 per cent of the votes but no seat in the National Assembly.
Orientation. The LD-MFT is an independent Marxist formation opposed to French and International Monetary Fund influence.
Publications. *Vérité*

National Democratic Rally
Rassemblement National Démocratique (RND)

Leadership. Cheikh Anta Diop (s.g.)
Founded. February 1976
History. The RND did not initially secure official recognition (for which it applied in September 1977) because under the three-party system introduced in 1976 its political ground to the left of the ruling Socialist Party was officially regarded as already occupied by the African Independence Party (see separate entry). The RND disputed this view and called for a boycott of the February 1978 presidential and congressional elections, in which the abstention rate of over 37 per cent was regarded as reflecting, at least in part, the party's boycott call.
The RND was legalized in 1981. Taking part in the 1983 elections, it gained 2.62 per cent of the vote and one seat in the National Assembly. However, it contested this result and refused to sit in the new Assembly.
Orientation. The RND is a non-Marxist left-wing opposition group.
Publications. *Taxaw!* (Stand up!)

Party of Independence and Labour
Parti de l'Indépendance et du Travail (PIT)

Leadership. Seydou Cissokho, Amath Dansoko

History. This pro-Soviet Marxist-Leninist party was officially registered in 1981. It took part in the 1983 general elections but obtained only 0.55 per cent of the vote and no seat in the National Assembly.

People's Liberation Party
Parti pour la Libération du Peuple (PLP)

Leadership. Babacar Niang (s.g.)
Founded. July 1983
History. The PLP was formed by dissidents of the National Democratic Rally, of which Babacar Niang was deputy secretary-general until his expulsion in June 1983 for "divisive activities". The PLP achieved legal recognition in September 1983.
Orientation. The PLP believes in "the principles of anti-imperialist solidarity and non-alignment". It favours the use of national Senegalese languages (rather than French) in assemblies, schools and public administration.

Popular Democratic Movement
Mouvement Démocratique et Populaire (MDP)

Leadership. Mamadou Dia (l.)
History. Mamadou Dia was Prime Minister of Senegal until December 1962, when the office of Prime Minister was abolished and he was accused of having attempted to overthrow the Government. He was held in prison from 1963 to 1974. The MDP, which he founded, was not registered until 1981. He objected to the fact that the Confederation of Senegambia had been created on Feb. 1. 1982, without consultation of the two countries' population. In that year he attempted to unite the various opposition groups in a *Coordination de l'Opposition Sénégalaise Unie*. In the 1983 general elections the MDP obtained 1.14 per cent of the vote and no seat in the National Assembly.
Orientation. The MDP has advocated socialist self-management for the economy.

Rally for National Salvation
Rassemblement pour le Salut National

Leadership. Sidi Lamine Niasse (l.)
History. This organization has propagated Islamic fundamentalism, and its leader has maintained close relations with Libya.

Revolutionary Movement for New Democracy
Mouvement Révolutionnaire pour la Démocratie Nouvelle/And-Jëf (MRDN)

Leadership. Landing Savane (1.)
History. This Maoist party was officially registered in 1981. It boycotted the 1983 general elections in protest against the ban on the creation of electoral alliances.
Publications. *Jaay Doole Bi*

Senegalese Democratic Party
Parti Démocratique Sénégalais (PDS)

Address. 7 Rue de Thiong, B.P. 5, Dakar, Senegal
Leadership. Abdoulaye Wade (s.g.); Fara N'Diaye (nat. co-ordinator)
Founded. July 1974
History. The PDS became officially recognized in August 1974 (becoming at that time the country's only legal opposition party) and under the three-party system introduced in March 1976 adopted a "liberal democratic" political stance, to the right of the country's ruling Socialist Party. The PDS first took part in elections in May 1977, when it gained over 15 per cent of the votes in partial local elections. In February 1978 the party contested presidential elections in which its secretary-general obtained 17.38 per cent of the votes cast, and parliamentary elections in which it gained 17 out of 100 seats and 17.12 per cent of the votes cast.

In the 1983 general elections the PDS obtained 13.98 per cent of the vote and eight seats, but it disputed this result and refused to sit in the new Assembly. In July 1983 it called for a round-table conference of all parties to discuss Senegal's economic difficulties.
Orientation. The party's aim is to set up in Senegal, by democratic means, a democratic and socialist society which will eventually enable every citizen fully to develop his personality.
Structure. Based on "democratic centralism", the party has cells of 25 members, sectors of eight to 10 cells, sections, federations, and regional conventions, and also a national convention, a congress, a political bureau and an executive secretariat.
Membership. 600,000
Publications. *Le Démocrate* (monthly); *Takku* (a bimonthly youth journal); *La Vérité* (bimonthly, in Arabic)
International affiliations. Liberal International (observer)

Senegalese People's Party
Parti Populaire Sénégalais (PPS)

Leadership. Dr Oumar Wone (1.)
History. The PPS was officially registered in 1981. In the 1983 general elections it obtained 0.2 per cent of the vote and no seat in the National Assembly.
Orientation. The PPS takes an independent Marxist line.

Senegalese Republican Movement
Mouvement Républicain Sénégalais (MRS)

Leadership. Boubacar Guèye (s.g.)
Founded. 1977
History. The MRS was legalized under a constitutional amendment approved in December 1978 which provided for the existence of a third opposition formation to the ruling Socialist Party in addition to the "Marxist-Leninist" African Independence Party and the "liberal democratic" Senegalese Democratic Party (see separate entries). However, the party boycotted the 1983 general elections.
Orientation. The MRS is a right-wing conservative party, standing for private property and traditional values in family life and religion.

Socialist Party of Senegal
Parti Socialiste du Sénégal

Address. B.P. 12010, Dakar, Senegal
Leadership. President Abdou Diouf (g.s.); Moustapha Niasse (pol. sec.); Mamadou Faye (perm. sec.)
Founded. 1958
History. The present Socialist Party is descended from the *Parti Socialiste Sénégalais* formed in the 1920s under the leadership of Lamine Guèye, who in 1937 became political director of the Senegal section of the metropolitan French Socialist Party (SFIO). Originally based in the urban municipalities, after World War II the Senegal SFIO spread its influence to the rural bush areas, the main architect of this change of emphasis being Léopold Sédar Senghor (who was elected to the French National Assembly in 1945 together with Lamine Guèye).

After the party leadership had rejected his proposals for a basic reform of the policies and structure of the Senegal SFIO, Senghor broke away in September 1948 to form the *Bloc Démocratique Sénégalais* (BDS), which heavily defeated the Senegal SFIO in the 1951 and the 1955 National

Assembly elections. In the mid-1950s the BDS attracted many of the new generation of nationalist intelligentsia into its ranks and also increased its support among the country's majority Moslem population, notwithstanding Senghor himself being a Catholic. In 1957 the BDS became the *Bloc Populaire Sénégalais* (BPS), with which Lamine Guèye's grouping (now called the *Parti Sénégalais d'Action Socialiste*) merged in February 1958 to form the *Union Progressiste Sénégalaise* (UPS).

The UPS led Senegal to full independence in 1960 and has been the country's ruling party ever since. Although it was in effect the country's only legal party between 1964 and 1974, the Constitution continued to guarantee a plurality of political parties and in 1974 the Senegalese Democratic Party was officially recognized as an opposition party (see separate entry). Following the introduction of a three-party system in March 1976 (later expanded to cover further parties), the UPS changed its name to Socialist Party at an extraordinary congress in December 1976.

In the National Assembly the party gained 83 out of 100 seats in the 1978 elections and 111 out of 120 seats in 1983. Abdou Diouf succeeded Senghor as President of the Republic in January 1981 and was in February 1983 elected for a five-year term, having obtained 83 per cent of the vote cast in a contest against four other candidates on a 56.7 per cent turnout.

Orientation. The party subscribes to democratic socialism, aiming at the creation of a "healthy and popular democracy in liberty and equality". Ex-President Senghor himself, a noted writer and poet as well as political leader, is a foremost theorist of African socialism and has developed the concept of *négritude* as the complex of spiritual and essentially socialist values inherent in traditional African culture.

Structure. The party has local sections, affiliated or integrated organizations, regional unions, a central committee and a political bureau.

Membership. 1,300,000

Publications. *L'Unité Africaine* (monthly), 4,000

International affiliations. Socialist International; Socialist Interafrican

---

Socialist Workers' Organization
Organisation Socialiste des Travailleurs (OST)

Leadership. Mbaye Bathily (founder)

Founded. 1982

History. Although officially registered, the OST boycotted the 1983 general elections in protest against the ban on the creation of electoral alliances.

Orientation. The OST is an independent Marxist-Leninist formation.

Union for People's Democracy
Union pour la Démocratie Populaire (UDP)

Leadership. Hamédine Racine Guisse (l.)

Founded. 1981

History. This pro-Albanian party, comprising former supporters of the Revolutionary Movement for New Democracy (*And-Jëf*), was officially registered in 1981. However, it boycotted the 1983 general elections in protest against the ban on the creation of electoral alliances.

Seychelles

Capital: Victoria (on Mahé)   Pop. 66,000

The Republic of Seychelles, a member of the Commonwealth, has an executive President elected by universal adult suffrage (of citizens above the age of 17 years) and a National Assembly, to which 23 members are elected by simple majority in single-member constituencies and another two members are appointed to represent small islands with no fixed population (all candidates having to be members of the Seychelles People's Progressive Front, the country's sole legal political organization). The President is head of the Cabinet and also holds portfolios, while there are six other ministers.

In parliamentary elections held on Aug. 7, 1983, the 23 elective seats were contested by 30 candidates, 17 of whom were returned unopposed.

Seychelles People's Progressive Front (SPPF)

Address. P.O. Box 154, Victoria, Mahé, Seychelles

Leadership. France Albert René (pres.); Guy Sinon (s.g.)

Founded. June 1964

History. The party was founded as the Seychelles People's United Party (*Parti Uni du Peuple Seychellois,* SPUP) by Albert René, who was first elected to the Legislature in a by-election in 1965. The party campaigned for the introduction of universal suffrage and a status of association with Britain. In 1970 it gained five of the 15 elective seats in the National Assembly. It subsequently campaigned for complete independence for Seychelles and was in January 1973 recognized as a national liberation movement by the Organization of African Unity (OAU), whereupon the then ruling Seychelles Democratic Party (SDP) reversed its previous position (which had been in favour of continued association with Britain) to a request for independence.

In elections held in April 1974 the SDP gained about 21,000 votes and 13 seats in the Legislative Assembly while the SPUP, with 19,000 votes, obtained only two of the seats. René, however, entered a coalition government in 1975, and upon the achievement of independence by the Republic of Seychelles in June 1976 he became Prime Minister. In June 1977, however, militant SPUP supporters overthrew the Government of President James Mancham, the SDP leader, and installed René as President of the Republic. In May 1978 the SPUP, under a new constitution proclaimed in March 1979, adopted its present name and became the country's sole political party (the SDP having dissolved itself), as subsequently confirmed under the March 1979 Constitution.

Orientation. The SPPF is socialist, for the political and economic independence of Seychelles and a foreign policy of "positive non-alignment".

Structure. The party's supreme organ is its congress, which meets once a year; between its sessions the central executive committee (elected for three years) meets regularly to carry out congress decisions. The party is based on 23 branches organized at district level and with their own district committees. Four mass organizations integrated in the SPPF are the National Workers' Union, the Seychelles Women's Organization, the Youth League and the People's Defence Forces.

Publications. *The People,* 1,000

Sierra Leone

Capital: Freetown   Pop. 3,740,000

The Republic of Sierra Leone is an independent state within the Commonwealth. Under the 1978 Constitution approved in a referendum in June of that year it is a one-party state, with the All-People's Congress (APC) as the country's sole legal party. It has an elected executive President serving a seven-year term, a First and a Second Vice-President and a Cabinet appointed by the President and presided over by him. There is a House of Representatives of 85 elective constituency seats, 12 seats held by elected paramount chiefs and up to seven seats filled by persons appointed by the President. The minimum voting age is 21 years. The selection of up to three candidates for each of the 85 elective constituency seats (to be won by simple majority) is carried out at primary elections by secret ballot of the elected members of the local party constituency executive, but is subject to a veto by the APC's central committee.

In elections to the House of Representatives held on May 1 and June 26, 1982, a total of 66 of the 85 elective seats were contested by 173 candidates and 19 were declared to have been filled by unopposed candidates (all of them having declared themselves to be members of the APC). The 12 seats allocated to paramount chiefs were also filled by unopposed candidates.

All-People's Congress (APC)

Address. 39 Siaka Stevens St., Freetown, Sierra Leone

Leadership. President (Dr) Siaka Probyn Stevens (l. and s.g.)

Founded. 1960

History. Before Sierra Leone achieved independence in April 1961, the APC had demanded that elections should be held before the independence date and had mobilized workers in support of its demand, with the result that a temporary state of emergency was declared 10 days before independence day. In elections held in April 1962 the APC won 20 out of the 62 directly-elected seats in the House of Representatives. The result of elections to the 66-member House, held on March 17, 1967, appeared to be inconclusive, and the appointment of the APC leader as Prime Minister was followed by a military coup, as a result of which the Constitution was suspended and the House of Representatives dissolved. In a report issued in December 1967 by a commission of inquiry it was concluded that the March 1967 elections had been won by the APC and that its leader had been duly elected Prime Minister.

After the military regime had been overthrown by army NCOs and Dr Stevens had returned from exile he formed, in April 1968, a coalition Government led by the APC but containing also Sierre Leone People's Party (SLPP) members. By November 1968 the APC had, through by-elections, raised its representation in the House of Representatives to 42 (out of 66) seats. In subsequent years the APC continued to increase its parliamentary representation, partly as a result of measures taken under a state of emergency and of the SLPP deciding in September 1972 to boycott all by-elections. In elections held in May 1973 the APC won 84 of the 85 elective seats in the House. Following further elections held in 1977 the distribution of the 85 elective seats in the House was, by October 1977, APC 70, SLPP 15. The establishment of a one-party state was approved in a referendum in June 1978, with all SLPP members of the House eventually joining the APC.

Orientation. A left-wing party originally supported by wage-earners and part of the lower middle class, the APC has campaigned successfully for the establishment of a republican form of government.

Singapore

Capital: Singapore   Pop. 2,500,000

The Republic of Singapore, an independent member of the Commonwealth, has a (largely ceremonial) President elected by Parliament for a four-year term and a unicameral Parliament elected for five years by universal adult suffrage of citizens above the age of 21 years and by simple majority in 75 single-member constituencies. The President appoints a Cabinet headed by a Prime Minister and responsible to Parliament.

In parliamentary elections held on Dec. 23, 1980, all 75 seats were retained by the ruling People's Action Party (PAP), with 37 candidates (including 11 ministers and three ministers of state) being returned unopposed and the PAP gaining 77.6 per cent of the valid votes in the remaining 38 constituencies. However, in a by-election held in one constituency on Oct. 31, 1981, the secretary of the Workers' Party was elected to Parliament.

People's Action Party (PAP)
Partai Tindakan Rakyat

Address. 11 Napier Road, Singapore 1025, Singapore

Leadership. Lee Kuan Yew (s.g.); Ong Teng Cheong (ch.)

Founded. November 1954

History. The PAP was formed by a group of trade unionists and intellectuals around Lee Kuan Yew, who in May 1955 defined the party's aim as "immediate independence for a free, democratic and non-communist Malaya" and "the destruction of the colonial system by methods of non-violence". Having won only three out of 30 seats in its first election in 1955, in elections held in May 1959 to the 51-member Legislative Assembly (under the 1957 Constitution conferring home rule on Singapore) the PAP gained an absolute majority of 43 seats and thereupon formed a Government. In 1961, however, the party's effective majority was reduced to 26 out of 51 members of the Assembly as a result of defections and the formation of the Socialist Front (*Barisan Sosialis*). In elections held to the Singapore Legislative Assembly shortly after the incorporation of Singapore in the newly-established Federation of Malaysia in September 1963, the PAP gained 37 seats, the *Barisan* 13 (principally on an anti-federation platform) and an independent candidate one.

In August 1965 Singapore seceded from the Federation of Malaysia, and since December 1965 the PAP has been in government as the ruling party of the independent Republic of Singapore, a member of the Commonwealth and a non-aligned state. In the 1968 elections the PAP took all 58 seats in the Legislative Assembly (51 of its candidates being returned unopposed). In elections in September 1972 the PAP gained 69.9 per cent of the votes cast and all 65 parliamentary seats, and in December 1976 it similarly obtained all seats in Parliament (then increased to a total of 69). Following criticism of the alleged repressive nature of the Singapore Government expressed by member parties of the Socialist International (of which the PAP had been a member since 1966), the PAP withdrew from that organization in 1976.

In parliamentary elections held in December 1980 the PAP obtained all seats (then increased to 75), but in a by-election held in October 1981 it lost one seat to the Workers' Party.

Orientation. Originally a democratic socialist party, the PAP has in recent years combined strong anti-communism with pragmatism, promoting the development of Singapore on the basis of a strongly free-market economy and at the same time continuing to place emphasis on social welfare. In December 1982 the PAP redefined its objectives as being to defend the independence and territorial integrity of Singapore, to safeguard freedom and well-being through representative and democratic government, to build a multiracial society tolerant to all and with commitment to Singapore, to create a disciplined and self-reliant society with compassion for the aged, sick and handicapped as well as the less fortunate, and to achieve optimum economic development, social and cultural fulfilment in harmonious and co-operative social relationships.

Structure. Since the mid-1950s, when Communists made an attempt to take over the party from within, the PAP has operated a cadre system under which only selected members can elect or be elected to higher party bodies; ordinary membership is open to all Singapore citizens.

Membership. 8,000–10,000

Publications. *Petir* (official organ)

Singapore Democratic Party (SDP)

Leadership. Chiam See Tong (s.g.)

Founded. 1981

History. This party has opposed the Government's labour legislation outlawing strikes and other industrial action. In the December 1980 elections it contested three seats but gained only 1.77 per cent of the national vote and no seats. In a by-election of Oct. 31, 1981, it supported the successful candidate for the Workers' Party.

Orientation. The SDP stands for freedom of speech and a free press.

Singapore Justice Party (SJP)

History. This party presented two candidates in the December 1980 general elections but obtained only 0.83 per cent of the national vote and no seat.

Singapore Malays National Organization (SMNO)
Pertubohan Kebangsaan Melayu Singapura (Pekemas)

Address. 218-F, Changi Road, Singapore 1441, Singapore

Leadership. Rahman Zin (pres.); Sahid Sahooman (sec.)

History. The SMNO was founded as an affiliate of the United Malays National Organization (UMNO) in Malaysia. It was reorganized in 1967, and in the December 1976 parliamentary elections it fielded two candidates as part of a Joint Opposition Council. In the 1980 elections it fielded three candidates, but it has gained no seats. It has been in opposition to the Government since its inception.

Orientation. The SMNO stands for the advancement of the Malay language and culture and of Islam (without interfering in the affairs of other religions).

Structure. The SMNO is open to all Singapore citizens who are of Malay origin or Moslems who have adopted Malay customs.

Socialist Front
Barisan Sosialis

Address. 436-C Victoria Street, Singapore 0719, Singapore

Leadership. Dr Lee Siew Choh (ch.)

Founded. 1961

History. The party was established by former members of the ruling People's Action Party after disagreement over the proposed merger of Singapore with Malaya and formation of the federation of Malaysia. Most of the party's leaders were arrested in February 1963 and detained without trial. In the elections to Singapore's Legislative Assembly in September 1963 the party gained 13 out of the 51 seats. However, 11 of the party's members subsequently resigned from the Legislative Assembly. The party boycotted later by-elections; two members elected to the Assembly disappeared (avoiding arrest) and three others were arrested soon after their election.

The party refused to accept Singapore's secession from the federation of Malaysia in 1965, and it boycotted the sessions of the Singapore Parliament and also the 1968 elections. In the elections of 1972 and 1976 the party failed to gain any of the seats which it contested, having in the latter contest fielded six candidates as part of the Joint Opposition Council. In the 1980 elections it unsuccessfully contested four seats.

Among those arrested in 1963 (for alleged "pro-communist agitation") was Dr Lim Hock Siew, a co-founder of the party and then its secretary-general, who was in November 1978 confined to an island, from which he was released on Sept. 6, 1982, on condition that he refrained from political activity.

Orientation. The *Barisan* is left-wing, with the final object of achieving a unified democratic Malaya, including Singapore.

United Front

Leadership. Chan Yoke Kwong, Mohamad Mansor bin Rahman

Founded. 1973

History. The party was set up by a group of former members of the Workers' Party led by Ng Ho. The party nominated 15 candidates in the December 1976 general election which it unsuccessfully contested as part of a Joint Opposition Council. In the 1980 election it unsuccessfully contested eight seats.

Orientation. The party's declared aim is to set up a "liberal democratic society".

United People's Front (UPF)

Address. 715, 7th Floor, Colombo Court, Singapore 0617, Singapore

Leadership. Harbans Singh (s.g.)

Founded. 1974

History. The UPF was founded as an alliance of five opposition groups—the United National Front, the Singapore Malays National Organization (SMNO), the Singapore Chinese Party, the Justice Party, and the United Malays National Organization of Singapore—together with some former members of the Socialist Front (*Barisan Sosialis*) and the United Front. However, the SMNO dissociated itself from the UPF in 1975. Six UPF candidates unsuccessfully contested the December 1976 general elections, and 14 the December 1980 elections, equally unsuccessfully.

Orientation. The UPF opposes the Government of the People's Action Party as "authoritarian and repressive".

Workers' Party of Singapore

Address. Suite 602, Colombo Court, Singapore 0617, Singapore

Leadership. Wong Hong Toy (ch.); Joshua Benjamin Jeyaretnam (s.g.)

Founded. 1971

History. The party was originally founded in 1957 by David Marshall (who had been Singapore's first Chief Minister in 1955–56), and it was revived in 1971 by its present secretary-general. Its 22 candidates contesting the December 1976 general elections were all unsuccessful, and so were its eight candidates in the December 1980 elections. However, in a by-election held on Oct. 31, 1981, J. B. Jeyaretnam was elected and thus became the sole opposition member in Parliament.

Orientation. The party calls for a more democratic constitution, closer relations with Malaysia and the establishment of diplomatic relations with China, as well as for the creation of a welfare state.

Solomon Islands

Capital: Honiara (Guadalcanal)   Pop. 247,000

The Solomon Islands are an independent state within the Commonwealth, with the British monarch as head of state being represented by a Governor-General. Legislative power is vested in a unicameral 38-member National Parliament elected by universal adult suffrage by simple majority in single-member constituencies for up to four years. There is a Cabinet composed of a Prime Minister and 14 other ministers and responsible to Parliament.

In a general election held on Aug. 6, 1980, the majority of seats in the National Parliament was won by independents. A Cabinet was thereupon formed by a coalition of independents and the Solomon Islands United Party, but this Cabinet was in September 1981 replaced by a new one composed of independents and members of the People's Alliance Party and the National Democratic Party.

The new Government has issued a programme of action which provides inter alia for constitutional reforms to create a federated republic and (in response to demands for regional autonomy) the transfer to the provinces of responsibilities currently held by the Ministry of Home Affairs.

National Democratic Party (Nadepa)

Leadership. Bartholomew Ulafa'alu (l.)
Founded. 1976
History. This party was formed as the political wing of the Solomon Islands trade union movement and was the only grouping to contest the 1976 general elections on a party basis, winning five (out of 38) seats in the Legislative Assembly. It was in opposition until September 1981, when it joined a coalition Government led by the People's Alliance Party and was given two ministerial posts.

People's Alliance Party (PAP)

Address. P.O.B. 722, Honiara, Guadalcanal, Solomon Islands
Leadership. Solomon Mamaloni (l.); E. Kingmele (sec.)
Founded. 1979
History. The PAP was formed by a merger of (i) the People's Progressive Party (PPP), which was founded in 1973, was led by Solomon Mamaloni and was in coalition governments with the Solomon Islands United Party (SIUPA), with Mamaloni as Chief Minister in 1974-76, and (ii) the Rural Alliance Party, which was founded in November 1977, was led by David N. Kausimae, had two members elected to the then Legislative Assembly in 1976 and rejected coalition with other parties.

At the dissolution of Parliament in 1980 the PAP had only one member (Kausimae) in Parliament, in which most members sat as independents. On Aug. 31, 1981, Mamaloni was elected Prime Minister, whereupon he formed a coalition Government with the National Democratic Party and independents (to which seven PAP ministers were appointed).

Orientation. The stated aims of the PAP-led Government included constitutional reforms to create a federated republic, the setting-up of a "Melanesian alliance" with Papua New Guinea and Vanuatu and the establishment of diplomatic relations with China in 1983-84.

People's Progressive Party—see under People's Alliance Party (PAP)

Rural Alliance Party—see under People's Alliance Party (PAP)

Solomon Islands United Party (SIUPA)

Leadership. Peter Kenilorea (1.)
Founded. 1973
History. Some members of the SIUPA took part in a Government led by the then leader of the People's Progressive Party (PPP) from August 1974 onwards, but the party itself, which held nine of the 24 seats in the Legislative Assembly, was not admitted to coalition with the PPP until December 1975. It obtained five portfolios in a Cabinet exercising self-government, which came into force on Jan. 2, 1976. After most of the candidates for the general elections of June 1976 had stood as independents, Peter Kenilorea was elected Chief Minister, and he appointed a Government containing also members of the PPP. He became the country's first Prime Minister at its declaration of independence on July 7, 1978.

Following the 1980 general elections he formed a new Government with the participation of independents. However, in September 1981 this Government was replaced by one led by the leader of the People's Alliance Party, and the SIUPA went into opposition.

Somalia

Capital: Mogadishu   Pop. 5,500,000

The Somali Democratic Republic (a member of the Arab League) is ruled by the leadership of the Somali Revolutionary Socialist Party (SRSP), whose secretary-general, Gen. Mohammed Siyad Barreh, is head of state and directs the Government with the assistance of an appointed Council of Ministers. A People's Assembly of 171 members is elected by citizens above the age of 18 years for a five-year term on a list of the SRSP.

In elections to the Assembly held on Dec. 30, 1979, the SRSP candidates were endorsed, according to the official result, by 99.91 per cent of the voters. There were a small number of "no" votes and spoiled ballot papers.

Somali Revolutionary Socialist Party (SRSP)

Leadership. President Mohammed Siyad Barreh (s.g.)

Founded. July 1976

History. The SRSP was set up by President Siyad Barreh as the country's sole political organization to achieve "progress and prosperity under the aegis of scientific socialism". The newly-formed party was given the powers of the Supreme Revolutionary Council which had been formed when army commanders seized power in 1969; all members of the Council became members of the party's central committee.

Orientation. The SRSP is a socialist formation. At its inaugural congress in 1976 Siyad Barreh said that of the two economic systems in the world he was convinced of "the historical inevitability of the eventual victory of the socialist system".

Structure. The SRSP's central committee has 57 members and has formed 16 bureaux. It is headed by a political bureau consisting of the President, three Vice-Presidents of the Republic and the head of the National Security Service.

International affiliations. Socialist Inter-African

South Africa

Capitals: **Pretoria** (administrative)
          Cape Town (legislative)
          Bloemfontein (judicial)   Pop. 24,000,000

The Republic of South Africa is a unitary independent state in which the right to vote for and to be elected to Parliament and any of the four Provincial Councils is reserved for White citizens above the age of 18 years. There is a unicameral Parliament, the House of Assembly, consisting of (i) 166 members elected by simple majority in single-member constituencies for a five-year term by direct popular votes of Whites above the age of 18 years, and (ii) 20 members appointed by the State President, who is himself elected for a seven-year term by an electoral college consisting of the members of Parliament. The State President is assisted by a Vice State-President and by an advisory 60-member President's Council comprising White, Coloured (i.e. mixed-race), Indian and Chinese (but not African) representatives.

At the end of 1983 political parties held elective seats in the House of Assembly as follows: National Party 115, Progressive Federal Party 26, Conservative Party of South Africa 17, New Republic Party 8. Of parties not represented in the House, the strongest is the Reconstituted National Party (*Herstigte Nasionale Party*), which in the 1981 elections obtained 13.8 per cent of the valid votes but no seats.

A Republic of South Africa Constitution Bill, finally approved by the House of Assembly on Sept. 9, 1983, by 119 votes (of the National and New Republic parties) to 35 (of the Progressive Federal and Conservative parties) and enacted on Sept. 22, 1983, provided inter alia for (i) a single Parliament with three separate chambers for White, Coloured (mixed-race) and Indian representatives; (ii) an executive President combining the functions of the current State President and Prime Minister and to be chosen by an electoral college of 50 Whites, 25 Coloureds and 13 Indians drawn from the three chambers; (iii) a Cabinet which might include Coloureds and Indians; (iv) maximum devolution and decentralization of central government powers, with local authorities wherever possible for each population group; and (v) standing committees of the three chambers to promote consensus. The (White) House of Assembly would have 166 directly elected members (as hitherto), eight members elected by the 166 members on the basis of proportional representation, and four (one for each province) appointed by the President; the (Coloured) House of Representatives would have 80 directly elected, three indirectly elected and two appointed members; and the (Indian) House of Delegates would have 40 directly elected, three indirectly elected and two nominated members.

The Act was approved by White voters in a referendum held on Nov. 2, 1983, when 65.95 per cent of the votes were cast in favour and 33.53 per cent against, while 0.52 per cent of the voters had spoilt their ballot papers in a 76.02 per cent turnout. The Act was to be implemented in the second half of 1984.

White Parties

Action for Our Own Future—see under Conservative Party of South Africa (CPSA)

Conservative Party of South Africa (CPSA)
Konserwatiewe Party van Suid-Afrika

Leadership. Dr Andries Treurnicht (l.); A.C. van Wyk (g.s.)
Founded. March 20, 1982
History. This party was formed by former members of the ruling National Party (NP) who had been expelled from the NP on March 3, 1982, after refusing to support the NP leadership's proposals for power-sharing with Coloureds (people of mixed race) and Indians, and who had on March 4 elected Dr Treurnicht as their leader. On its formation the CPSA was joined by three right-wing groups not represented in the House of Assembly—the National Conservative Party founded in 1979 by Dr Cornelius P. Mulder (until then leader of the Transvaal NP and a cabinet minister), the *Aksie Eie Toekoms* (Action for Our Own Future) founded in February 1981 and led by Prof. Alkmaar Swart, and a South Africa First Campaign (an English-language group) led by Brendan Wilmer.

In February 1983 Dr Treurnicht and two other members of the House of Assembly resigned their seats in response to a challenge by the NP; in the ensuing by-elections on May 10, 1983, two of them were defeated by NP candidates but Dr Treurnicht was re-elected, this being the first time that the CPSA had won a seat in a parliamentary election.

In early June 1984 Dr. Treurnicht resigned from the *Broederbond* (the semi-secret society of the Afrikaner elite, of which he was a former chairman) in protest against the organization's support for the 1983 constitutional changes. The previous month he had attended the inaugural rally of a new right-wing movement called the *Afrikaner Volkwag.*
Orientation. The CPSA is for the maintenance of White supremacy and is against power-sharing with any other race group.
Publications. *Die Patriot* (weekly)

National Party of South Africa
Nasionale Party van Suid-Afrika (NP)

Address. P.O. Box 1698, Cape Town 8000, South Africa
Leadership. P. W. Botha (nat. l.)

Founded. July 1914
History. The NP was founded by General J. B. M. Hertzog and his followers who left the ruling South African Party (SAP) because they insisted that in the Government's building of a "united White nation" Afrikaans- and English-speaking people should retain their separate identities. In the House of Assembly the NP gained 27 seats in October 1915, 44 in March 1920, 45 in February 1921 and 63 in June 1924, whereupon it formed, with the Labour Party, a coalition Government under which Afrikaans replaced Dutch as the country's second official language, bilingualism was fostered in the civil service and important legislation was passed to strengthen the colour bar in industry.

In the 1929 general election the NP won 78 seats (against 61 for the SAP led by General J. C. Smuts and eight for the Labour Party). In 1933 the NP and the SAP formed an alliance which led to their fusion as the United Party (UP) in December 1934, when they together commanded 144 seats in the National Assembly. The fusion was, however, not approved by a minority of the NP which constituted itself as the Purified National Party under Dr D. F. Malan and gained 27 seats in the 1938 elections to the House of Assembly.

On the outbreak of World War II, a minority of the UP, advocating South Africa's neutrality, rejoined Dr Malan's party in a Reunited NP, which came to power in 1948, when it gained 70 seats, against 65 won by the UP (and nine by a short-lived Afrikaner Party and six by the—White—Labour Party). The NP's policies were subsequently supported by an increasingly greater part of the White electorate, and since 1953 the party has held an absolute majority of seats in the House of Assembly.

In March 1982 the NP expelled 16 of its members from the House of Assembly, and a further two resigned from it later, because of their opposition to the party's decisions on constitutional reform which involved a degree of power-sharing with Coloureds and Indians.
Orientation. Having achieved its objective of establishing an independent Republic of South Africa, the NP has increasingly won support even among the English-speaking section of White South Africans for its policies—the maintenance of a united White South Africa; the promotion of immigration by those who "can be readily assimilated by the nation"; equal rights for Afrikaans- and English-speaking population groups; acceptance of the existence of disparate race groups—Whites, Coloureds, Indians and Blacks, with the last-named being given self-determination

and offered the option of independence in their respective homelands; and the principle of "South Africa first in foreign affairs", based on non-intervention in the affairs of other countries and peaceful coexistence with other states. Since 1969 the party leadership has followed an open-minded, or enlightened (*verligte*), policy designed to bring about changes in the application of the official line of "separate development" of the various race groups.

Structure. The party has four separate organizations (one in each province), based on branches in every polling district, represented in a constituency council, each of which is in turn represented in a provincial head committee—the supreme body in the province, its authority being superseded once a year when a provincial congress meets. A national council meets once a year but its decisions must be approved by each provincial party.

Membership. 1,000,000

Publications. The principal daily newspapers supporting the NP are *Die Burger* (Cape Town), 74,000; *Beeld* (Johannesburg); *Die Vaderland* (Johannesburg), 60,000; *Die Transvaler* (Pretoria)

National Conservative Party —see under Conservative Party of South Africa (CPSA)

New Republic Party (NRP)

Address. P.O.B. 1539, Cape Town 8000, and P.O.B. 974, Johannesburg 2000, South Africa

Leadership. Vause Raw (l.)

Founded. June 1977

History. The New Republic Party was officially launched with the support of the majority of MPs of the United Party, which had disbanded itself after failing to find a common basis with other groups for the formation of a single opposition party. While the NRP retained 23 (originally United Party) seats in the existing House of Assembly, the 1977 general elections saw its representation in the House reduced to 10 members (nine from Natal and one from the Cape Province, with none from the other two provinces). In the 1980 general elections it lost two of its Natal seats. It has since supported the Government's constitutional reform, though with reservations.

Orientation. In a programme published in June 1977, the party expressed its wish that (i) White, Coloured and Indian people should "participate fully and equitably in decision-making at all levels of power";

(ii) "existing and future autonomous and independent units" (e.g. Black homelands) should preferably be linked "on a confederal basis . . . while retaining full jurisdiction in their own areas"; (iii) the existing Black homelands should be developed urgently into viable economic and political units; and (iv) non-homeland Blacks should be given self-government "to the maximum extent economically and geographically possible, with machinery for necessary co-ordination". The party also advocated "the prohibition of Marxist-socialist and communist organizations".

Progressive Federal Party
Progressiewe Federale Party (PFP)

Address. P.O. Box 1475, Cape Town 8000, South Africa

Leadership. Dr Frederik van Zyl Slabbert (l.); Colin Eglin (nat. ch.); Alex Boraine (ch. of fed. exec.)

Founded. 1977

History. The PFP has its origins in the Progressive Party established in November 1959 by defectors from the United Party and holding one seat in the House of Assembly between 1961 and 1974, when it gained seven seats. In 1975 this party was joined by the Reform Party (set up by further defectors from the United Party) to form the Progressive Federal Party with 11 seats in the House of Assembly. In September 1977 it was joined by six further former members of the United Party (which was then being dissolved) and became the Progressive Reform Party (and also the official opposition in Parliament). (The party is also the official opposition in the Provincial Councils of the Cape Province and the Transvaal.)

In the 1981 general elections it increased its representation in the House of Assembly to 26 members. It has opposed the Government's 1983 constitutional reform on the ground that it excluded "70 per cent of the population, namely the Blacks", and has called for referendums for the Coloured and Indian communities and new elections for the Whites.

Orientation. The PFP stands for "a new constitution" for South Africa, with "full and equal citizen rights for all South Africans without discrimination on the grounds of race, colour, religion or sex; the sharing of political rights by all citizens without the domination of one group by another; an open society free from statutory apartheid . . .; equality of opportunity for all citizens in the economy; [and] the right of every individual to the protection of his life, liberty and property and access to the judiciary in defence of these rights". To this end the party advocates inter alia "federation with decentralization of powers" and "proportional representation without majority domination".

Structure. The party has nine regional formations (Cape Province 3, Transvaal 3, Natal 2, Orange Free State 1).

Publications. *Deurbraak* (Breakthrough, including *Progress,* bilingual newspaper)

Reconstituted National Party
Herstigte Nasionale Party (HNP)

Address. P.O. Box 1888, Pretoria, South Africa

Leadership. J. A. Marais (l.); W. T. Marais (ch.); L. F. Stofberg (sec.)

Founded. October 1969

History. The formation of the party followed the expulsion from the ruling National Party (NP) of four NP members of the House of Assembly who had opposed the *verligte* (enlightened) policies of the NP which they regarded as left-wing because they did not maintain a rigid (*verkrampte*) separation of the races (e.g. in sport). The party has failed to gain any parliamentary representation but won one seat in the (multiracial) Assembly elected in South West Africa in December 1978. It claims to represent "the basic views" of the Afrikaner population—views to which "a very large portion of the ruling NP subscribe or are attracted". It has, however, so far rejected approaches by the newly established Conservative Party of South Africa (see separate entry) to achieve electoral co-operation between the two parties against the ruling National Party.

Orientation. The HNP is a conservative, right-wing party advocating the "maintenance of White supremacy in southern Africa, with a homelands policy for non-White racial and ethnic groups".

Structure. The party's structure is democratic, with all leaders being elected, except an appointed full-time secretary.

Publications. *Die Afrikaner* (Pretoria, weekly), 15,000

South Africa First Campaign —see under Conservative Party of South Africa (CPSA)

Non-White Parties

Azanian People's Organization (Azapo)

Leadership. Lybon Mabasa (pres.); Muntu Myeza (g.s.)

Founded. September 1979

History. Azapo was established by Blacks as part of the "Black Consciousness" movement which had earlier been represented by various organizations banned by the authorities in October 1977, the most prominent of these organizations having been the Black People's Convention (BPC), which had been set up in 1972 and had then declared its object to be "to unite and liberate Blacks from psychological and physical oppression . . . in one political organization", to "popularize the philosophy of Black Consciousness and Black solidarity" and to "create and maintain an egalitarian society".

Orientation. Azapo is opposed to all racial discrimination and has refused to negotiate with the existing authorities. It rejects co-operation with the Government by the Black "homelands" leaders as based on acceptance of the Government's separate development policies. ("Azania" is the Black Africans' name for South Africa.)

Black United Front

Leadership. Chief Gatsha Buthelezi (l.)

Founded. November 1977

History. The Black United Front was launched by Chief Gatsha Buthelezi, Chief Minister of the KwaZulu (Black) homeland, who had on Nov. 8, 1977, agreed on its formation with two other homelands Chief Ministers—Prof. Hudson Ntsanwisi of Gazankulu and Dr Cedric Phatudi of Lebowa.

Orientation. Chief Buthelezi stated on the day of the party's foundation that it would not be anti-White but "pro-South Africa Black and White" and in favour of a non-racial system, which meant an end to the pass laws, to influx control (to keep Blacks out of White areas), to "Bantu education" (imposed on Blacks by the Government) and to the homelands policy leading to "independent mini-states".

Congress of the People (Cope)

Leadership. Peter Marais (l.); E.M.S. le Fleur (nat. ch.)

History. This Coloured group is represented on the President's Council and favours complete non-racialism in the determination of political and social policies.

Democratic Party of South Africa

Leadership. J. B. Patel (l.)

Founded. September 1979

405

History. Following elections held on Nov. 4, 1981, to the (official advisory) South African Indian Council (SAIC), this party held four of the 45 seats on this Council. However, only 10.5 per cent of the voters took part in these elections.

Orientation. The Democratic Party is an Indian political formation standing for political and economic stability, and opposed to alliance with any race group as it wishes to be on friendly terms with all groups in working for "a truly democratic form of government through discussion and negotiation with all racial groups" and for the protection of minorities without domination by any one racial group.

Indian Reform Party

Leadership. Y. M. Chinsamy (l.)

History. The party's leader, then a member of the (official) South African Indian Council, supported (in November 1976) a call for the formation of "an alliance of the Black and Brown peoples of South Africa". In 1978 the party adhered to the South African Black Alliance led by the (Zulu) *Inkatha* movement.

Orientation. The party is a left-wing (minority) group of South Africa's Indians, supporting co-operation with other non-White parties.

Labour Party of South Africa (LP)
Arbeidersparty van Suid-Afrika

Address. P.O. Box 87, Athlone 7760, South Africa

Leadership. Rev. Allan Hendrickse (l. and ch.)

Founded. 1966

History. In the 1969 elections to the Coloured Person's Representative Council (CPRC) the LP gained 26 of the 40 elective seats, but the 20 nominated candidates were all opposed to the LP's policies, so that the party did not obtain control of the CPRC. In 1975, however, the LP gained 31 of the 40 elective seats and formed the CPRC's Executive. (Under a bill passed in 1975, however, the Government was empowered to exercise the functions of the CPRC if deemed necessary in order to prevent the destruction of the CPRC by the LP's policy of boycotting its work.)

While in control of the CPRC, the LP refused to approve its budget and even adjourned it. In 1980 the Government proposed to replace the prorogued CPRC by a nominated 30-member Coloured Persons' Council, but the LP refused to participate in such a Council, and the Government abandoned the idea in 1981. The LP also boycotted the nominated advisory President's Council established in February 1981.

However, at an annual congress held at Eshowe (Natal) on Jan. 3, 1983, the LP decided—while rejecting the Government's constitutional proposals, mainly because they made no provision for the participation of Blacks, and reiterating its demand for a one-man one-vote system—to take part in the proposed three-chamber Parliament. After this decision had been attacked by Chief Gatsha Buthelezi, chairman of the South African Black Alliance (SABA), the LP resigned from the alliance in April 1983, having joined it in 1978.

Orientation. The LP has opposed the Government's separate development policies and has since 1974 increasingly expressed its solidarity with Black movements demanding equal rights for all.

National Forum

Founded. 1983

History. At a conference held on June 11–12, 1983, at Hammanskraal (near Pretoria) delegates from some 200 organizations unanimously adopted a National Forum manifesto proclaiming their "struggle for national liberation directed against the system of racial and capitalism" which, they claimed, held "the people of Azania (i.e. South Africa) in bondage for the benefit of a small minority of White capitalists and their allies, the White workers and the reactionary sections of the Black middle-class".

National People's Party

Leadership. Amichand Rajbansi (l.)

History. This party's leader is executive chairman of the (official advisory) South African Indian Council (SAIC), on which the party holds 34 of the 45 seats as a result of elections held on Nov. 4, 1981 (when the turnout was, however, only 10.5 per cent). The SAIC decided on Jan. 12, 1983, to give the Government's constitutional reform proposals a reasonable chance provided they were approved by the Indian community in a referendum.

New Freedom Party

Address. Eendragstr. 15, Bellville 7530, South Africa

History. This party superseded an earlier Freedom Party of South Africa which had until January 1978 been known as the Federal Party of South Africa. The latter party had, in elections to the Coloured Persons' Representative Council (CPRC) held in 1969, obtained 11 of the 40 elective seats and had, with the support of the CPRC's 20 nominated members, formed that Council's Executive until 1975, when it gained only eight of the elective seats and went into opposition. The party has remained a minority Coloured movement.

Orientation. The Freedom Party has called for the repeal of all racially discriminatory legislation in South Africa; for a government based on power-sharing; for a free-enterprise capitalistic system leading to the sharing of wealth; for making industrial land available without legal restrictions; and for equality before the law, work opportunities for all and open educational institutions. It is opposed to Marxism and communism and advocates the defence of South Africa by all its people against its enemies.

People's Congress Party

Founded. January 1983
History. This party was established by Coloured people opposed to the Government's constitutional reform proposals and thus dissenting from the Labour Party of South Africa (which had hitherto represented the majority of Coloured opinion).

South African Alliance (SAA)

Founded. September 1979
History. The SAA was formed by a group of members of the Coloured Persons' Representative Council, among them Dr W. J. Bergins (former leader of the Freedom Party), all of whom broke away from the latter party.

South African Black Alliance (SABA)

Leadership. Chief Gatsha Buthelezi (ch.)
Founded. March 1978
History. SABA was formed by *Inkatha* (the Zulu movement), the (Coloured) Labour Party and the Indian Reform Party with the objective of working out a programme for a national convention for the drafting of a non-racial Constitution

for South Africa. It was later joined by the Basotho National Party (*Dikwankwetla*), the ruling party for the Qwaqwa homeland, and the *Inyandza* national movement of the KaNgwane homeland. The Labour Party, however, withdrew from the SABA in April 1983 after it had been criticized for agreeing to co-operate with the Government in the proposed three-chamber Parliament.

Orientation. At a conference held on Oct. 16–17, 1982, the SABA rejected the Government's constitutional proposals and in a resolution (which was not to be binding on the Coloured and Indian parties) reaffirmed its "commitment to a constitution of South Africa which allows all its citizens, irrespective of race or colour or culture or creed, to participate directly in the government of the country".

Transvaal Indian Congress (TIC)

History. The original TIC had its origins in the Transvaal British Indian Association founded by Mahatma Gandhi in 1902. In the 1940s the TIC was taken over by radical members who participated in a defiance campaign against "unjust laws" in 1952. The TIC was a signatory of the 1955 Freedom Charter sponsored by the African National Congress, but in 1960 its leaders were banned or went into exile.

On Jan. 23, 1983, the TIC was revived by a committee opposed to the (official) South African Indian Council, with the object of mobilizing resistance by Indians and Coloureds to participation in the new constitutional institutions proposed by the Government.

Orientation. In 1983 the TIC reaffirmed its commitment to the 1955 Freedom Charter and to the Congress Alliance in which the (banned) African National Congress was the senior partner.

United Democratic Front (UDF)

Leadership. (Mrs) Alberthina Sisulu, Oscar Mpetha, Archie Gumede (leaders)
Founded. May 21, 1983
History. The decision to form the UDF was taken by delegates of 32 organizations, among them the Transvaal Indian Congress, the Council of Unions of South Africa and the South African Allied Workers' Union. It was formally launched on Aug. 20, 1983, to oppose the Government's constitutional proposals. The UDF's leaders were linked to the anti-apartheid

movement, including the African National Congress (ANC). Oscar Mpetha was on June 28, 1983, sentenced to five years in prison for inciting a crowd to demonstrations and singing protest songs in August 1980. Following the approval of the constitutional changes by the White electorate in a referendum on Nov. 2, 1983, the UDF declared that it would concentrate on persuading Coloureds and Indians to boycott the new constitutional institutions.

Structure. The UDF is open to "democrats" of all races but not to persons or organizations working within officially sanctioned government structures.

Black Homelands Parties

In South Africa's Black homelands there are legislative assemblies and a number of organized political parties, details of which are given below.

GANZANKULU

The Ganzankulu Legislative Assembly has 26 elective and 42 nominated seats; there are no parties as such.

KANGWANE

The KaNgwane Legislative Assembly has 42 seats. There are no political parties, but there is an *Inyandza* national movement, which is a member of the South African Black Alliance (SABA).

In 1982 the KaNgwane Executive Council headed by Enos Mabuza, its Chief Minister, successfully resisted an attempt mounted by the South African Government to dissolve the Legislative Assembly and to cede the KaNgwane homeland to the neighbouring Kingdom of Swaziland.

KWANDEBELE

A Legislative Authority established on Oct. 1, 1979, was subsequently converted into a Legislative Assembly, which in May 1982 instructed the homeland's Executive Council to begin negotiations with the South African Government on the granting of full independence to KwaNdebele. There are no political parties in the homeland.

KWAZULU

The KwaZulu Legislative Assembly has 55 elective and 76 nominated seats. All candidates in the 1978 elections had to be members of *Inkatha ya KwaZulu*, described as a cultural movement. Led by Chief

Gatsha Buthelezi, the Chief Minister of KwaZulu, it is opposed to the South African Government's homelands policy and rejects independence of a KwaZulu consisting of "separate pieces of inadequate territory", and it stands for sharing by Blacks in South Africa's economy which they have helped to develop. *Inkatha* was said to have 750,000 members (in 1983). The chairman of its national council is Dr F. T. Mdlalose and its secretary-general is Dr Oscar Dhlomo.

LEBOWA

The Lebowa Legislative Assembly has 40 members elected by universal adult suffrage in 12 constituencies, and 60 nominated members. In elections to the 40 elective seats, which were contested by 139 candidates, more than three-quarters of the seats were gained by the ruling Lebowa People's Party, with two of its candidates being returned unopposed.

Black People's Party (BPP)

Leadership. Chief A. S. Molefe
Founded. 1977
History. The BPP was formed in 1977 as a party open to all citizens of South Africa and has remained a minority formation in the Legislative Assembly.
Orientation. The BPP claims the whole of the Transvaal Province as Lebowa territory and regards Lebowa as an integral part of South Africa, in which it demands direct representation in the central Government.

Lebowa People's Party (LPP)

Leadership. Dr Cedric N. M. Phatudi (l.)
Founded. June 1973
History. Following its formation the LPP absorbed the Lebowa National Party led by Chief Maurice M. Matlala (also established in June 1973). It is the ruling party in Lebowa, of which Dr Phatudi is Chief Minister.
Orientation. The LPP has no clear programme but its leader has repeatedly stated that he will not accept independence for Lebowa and that this issue should be decided by the people of Lebowa.

QWAQWA

The Qwaqwa Legislative Assembly has 20

elected and 40 nominated members. In elections held on April 19-21, 1980, the Basotho National Party (*Dikwankwetla*) obtained all 20 elective seats.

Basotho National Party
Dikwankwetla

Address. c/o Private Bag 817, Witsiesh-oek, 9870, Qwaqwa, South Africa

Leadership. T. Kenneth Mopeli (l.); L. P. Tau (nat. ch.); S. K. Marumo (sec.)

Founded. 1975

History. In the first elections held in the Qwaqwa homeland in 1975 the party won 19 of the 20 elective seats in the Legislative Assembly, and it has been the homeland's ruling party since then. In the March 1980 Assembly elections the party won all 20 seats.

Orientation. The party stands for an ultimate Black federation in South Africa.

Structure. The party has a national conference composed of delegates of several regional conferences.

Membership. 500,000

Basotho Unity Party (BUP)

Address. P.O. Box 5173, Phuthad-itjhaba 9866, South Africa

Leadership. M. H. Mota (l.); L. M. Mapogoshe (ch.); F. H. Moloi (sec.)

Founded. November 1974

History. The BUP first contested elections to the Qwaqwa Legislative Assembly in March 1975, when it gained one seat (for its leader who became Leader of the Opposition). In January 1979 the BUP was joined by five members of the ruling Basotho National Party, and it subsequently became the official Opposition. However, in the April 1980 elections the BUP retained no seats in the Assembly.

Orientation. The BUP stands for democratic government "of the people, by the people and for the people". When in power it intends to negotiate with the South African Government for more land to be given to the Basotho (expected to number 2,000,000).

Spain

Capital: Madrid   Pop. 38,000,000

The Kingdom of Spain is, under its 1978 Constitution, a "democratic state" and a "parliamentary monarchy" which guarantees the right to autonomy of all "nationalities and regions" of Spain. The country has a Cabinet headed by a Prime Minister and responsible to a bicameral Parliament consisting of a Congress of Deputies of 350 members elected by direct adult suffrage and a 208-member Senate also elected by adult universal suffrage, both for four-year terms. The Senate also contains 49 regional representatives appointed on the basis of the distribution of population.

The minimum voting age is 18 years. Candidates are elected by proportional representation with a minimum of deputies for each province, and the remainder in proportion to the province's population. In elections to the Congress of Deputies voters indicate a preference for a list only but not for particular candidates. Parties must obtain at least 3 per cent of the vote in any province in order to qualify for a seat in that province. The state partially subsidizes parties in proportion to the number of votes which they obtain in parliamentary elections.

Regional parliaments exist in Andalusia, Aragon, Asturias, the Balearics, the Basque region, the Canaries, Cantabria, Castile-La Mancha, Castile-León,

Catalonia, Extremadura, Galicia, La Rioja, Madrid, Murcia, Navarra and Valencia.

As a result of elections held on Oct. 28, 1982, parties were represented in the Congress of Deputies as follows: Socialists 202, Popular Alliance 106, Union of the Democratic Centre 12, Convergence and Union (Catalonia) 12, Basque Nationalist Party (PNV) 8, Communist Party/Unified Socialist Party of Catalonia 4, Democratic and Social Centre 2, the (Basque extremist) *Herri Batasuna* 2, Catalan Republican Left 1, Basque Left 1.

Of the above parties the Union of the Democratic Centre, which had previously been the government party, dissolved itself on Feb. 18, 1983.

National Parties

Carlist Party
Partido Carlista

Leadership. Mariano Zufia (s.g.)
Founded. 1934
History. The Carlist Party has its origins in the Carlist movement, formed to pursue the claim to the Spanish throne by the Carlist line of the Spanish royal house. (The Carlists had opposed the succession of King Ferdinand VII, on his death in 1833, by his daughter Isabella instead of by his brother, Don Carlos, after whom the movement was named and whose descendants it subsequently supported.) The movement's principles were defined in 1936 by Don Alfonso Carlos, then its head, as including the Roman Catholic unity of Spain, the natural and organic constitution of its regions, a legitimate monarchy and a modern adaptation of the principles and spirit of Spain's secular traditions. Although the Carlists supplied General Franco with some of his best troops in 1936, they opposed his dictatorial regime, and in 1968 the movement's leaders, in particular Don Carlos Hugo de Borbón (the party's former president), were expelled from Spain by the Franco regime.

The Carlist movement has had its strongest support in Navarra and the Basque provinces. In Galicia the party supported the draft autonomy statute (similar to the statutes of Catalonia and the Basque region) approved in a referendum on Dec. 21, 1980, by 71 per cent of the voters (in a 26 per cent poll). The party has, however, played no electoral role.

Orientation. The Carlists are a monarchist and Roman Catholic party propounding a federal state and also advocating workers' self-management.

Structure. The party is organized at local and provincial level. It has a federal council comprising representatives of the Carlist parties of the country's nationalities and regions, a federal executive committee and secretaries-general of nationalities.

Publications. *I.M.* (*Información Mensual*), 25,000

Coalition of Popular Struggle
Coalición de Lucha Popular

History. This alliance, consisting of the Communist Party of Spain—Marxist-Leninist and the Republican Convention of the Peoples of Spain, contested regional elections in five regions on May 8, 1983.

Communist Party
Partido Comunista (PC)

Leadership. Ignacio Gallego (s.g.)
Founded. Jan. 15, 1984
History. Ignacio Gallego had resigned from the central committee of the Communist Party of Spain (PCE) on Oct. 11, 1983, on the grounds that the party's current policies would lead to its destruction. The PC's constituent congress was attended by a strong delegation from the Communist Party of the Soviet Union.

Orientation. Explicitly pro-Soviet, the PC intends to adhere to constitutional legality and to avoid actions which would lead to its falling into illegality. It opposes Spain's proposed entry into the European Communities and Spain's integration in the Western defence system, as well as the Eurocommunism of the PCE, which it regards as having abandoned communism. It advocates class struggle as a method of political action.

Communist Party of Spain
Partido Comunista de España (PCE)

Address. Calle Santísima Trinidad 5, Madrid 10, Spain
Leadership. Gerardo Iglesias (s.g.)

Founded. April 1920

History. The PCE was illegal from 1939 until April 1977. During this period it was actively engaged in resistance to the Franco regime. In the 1960s it developed close links with the Italian Communist Party and supported the latter's independence of Moscow and policy of co-operation with non-Communist parties in democratically-elected governments. The PCE condemned the Soviet intervention in Czechoslovakia in 1968, whereupon the Communist Party of the Soviet Union temporarily supported a minority faction in the PCE led by Enrique Lister until a reconciliation between the two factions took place in October 1974. In July of that year the PCE had joined the Democratic Junta which was formed in Paris by Spanish opposition parties to work for the establishment of "a pluralist democracy based on popular sovereignty". In March 1976 the Junta joined with the (socialist) Democratic Platform to form the Democratic Co-ordination Front.

Upon its legalization in 1977 the PCE decided to "support the democratic course of the monarchy" and reiterated its earlier decision to take part in elections jointly with the Unified Socialist Party of Catalonia (PSUC), an autonomous part of the PCE. The Communists gained 20 seats in the Congress of Deputies elected in June 1977, and 23 in that elected in March 1979, but only four in that elected in October 1982. By 1981 the PCE was divided into four factions—(i) the Eurocommunists, who rejected any leading role of the Soviet Union in the international communist movement, opposed the Soviet intervention in Afghanistan and were led by Santiago Carrillo, then the PCE's secretary-general; (ii) the "renovators" (about one-quarter of the delegates at the party's 10th congress held on July 28–Aug. 1, 1981), standing for greater internal democracy and a more forthright endorsement of Eurocommunism; (iii) an uncompromising pro-Soviet section, referred to as "Afghans"; and (iv) the Leninists who supported the dictatorship of the proletariat.

On Jan. 11, 1982, the PCE's central committee criticized the declaration of martial law in Poland and the role of the Soviet Union in recent events in that country; it was also reported to have proposed the creation of "a new International to supersede the existing models, especially those which, after the Polish events, could clearly be seen to have failed". Following the party's losses in the October 1982 elections Carrillo resigned on Nov. 6, 1982, to be succeeded as secretary-general by Gerardo Iglesias, who maintained the PCE's Eurocommunist line. In local elections held on May 8, 1983, the PCE increased its share of the vote to 7.9 per cent (against only 3.9 per cent in the October 1982 general elections).

Orientation. At its congress of April 1978 the PCE defined itself as being "Marxist, democratic and revolutionary" and dropped the word "Leninist" from its official title. The party supports the democratic road to socialism. It is opposed to Spain's accession to NATO and stands for a non-aligned foreign policy.

Structure. The party's supreme organ is its congress, which elects a central committee. The latter in turn elects an executive committee and a secretariat. The PCE includes the autonomous Unified Socialist Party of Catalonia, the Communist Party of Galicia and the Basque Communist Party.

Membership. 200,000

Publications. *Mundo Obrero* (daily party organ); *Nuestra Bandera* (journal)

Communist Party of Spain—Marxist-Leninist
Partido Comunista de España—Marxista-Leninista (PCE-ML)

History. This party was legalized by the Constitutional Court on Feb. 10, 1981. It contested regional elections in five regions on May 8, 1983, in an alliance (Coalition of Popular Struggle) with the Republican Convention of the Peoples of Spain.

Communist Unification of Spain
Unificación Comunista de España

History. In elections to the Andalusian Parliament held on May 23, 1982, this movement presented candidates in all eight provinces but gained no seats.

Communist Workers' Party of Spain
Partido Comunista Obrero de España (PCOE)

Founded. January 1978

History. This party, formed by Stalinist defectors from the Communist Party of Spain (PCE), was legalized in June 1979. It contested regional elections held in 11 regions on May 8, 1983, in alliance with the Unified Communist Party of Spain (PCEU).

Orientation. The PCOE has rejected the policies of the PCE as "opportunist and revisionist deviation" and regarded that party as "practically social-democratic". The PCOE stands for the nationalization of banks and key industries, for land reform and for the rejection of Spain's entry into NATO and the European Community.

Structure. The PCOE has an 81-member central committee and an 11-member executive committee.

Democratic Action Party
Partido de Acción Demócrata (PAD)

Leadership. Francisco Fernández Ordóñez (s.g.)
Founded. March 1982
History. This party was formed by social democratic defectors from the Union of the Democratic Centre (UCD). Francisco Fernández Ordóñez, a former Minister of Justice, left the UCD late in 1981. On Jan. 23, 1983, the PAD integrated itself with the Spanish Socialist Workers' Party (PSOE). Its candidates were included in the PSOE list for the October 1982 general elections and one of the PAD's founders, Javier Moscoso, was given a ministerial post in the Socialist Government, which resulted from the elections.

Democratic and Social Centre
Centro Democrático y Social (CDS)

Leadership. Adolfo Suárez González, Agustín Rodríguez Sahagún (leaders)
Founded. July 29, 1982
History. Adolfo Suárez González had become Prime Minister in July 1976 and had founded the Union of the Democratic Centre (UCD) in 1977. In the June 1977 elections the UCD had become the strongest party, with 165 out of the 350 seats in the Congress of Deputies. However, Suárez resigned on July 28, 1982, both as Prime Minister and as leader of the UCD because of both right-wing and left-wing dissent in his party (in response to which he stressed that in his view the UCD should remain a centrist party). The newly-formed CDS was registered as a political party on Aug. 23, 1982, but in the October 1982 elections it obtained only two seats in the Congress of Deputies. In local elections held on May 8, 1983, the party obtained only 1.7 per cent of the vote.
Orientation. The CDS stands for the defence of democracy, the strengthening of civil power and the consolidation of

regional autonomy with the full co-operation of the nationalist minority parties.

Democratic Reformist Party
Partido Reformista Democrático (PRD)

Leadership. Antonio Garrigues Walker, Miquel Roca Junyent (leaders)
Founded. 1983
History. Antonio Garrigues Walker had been president of the Liberal Democratic Party (LDP), which had been formed in July 1982 by some 200 members of 60 liberal clubs (combined in a Liberal Federation early in 1982) and had included former members of the Union of the Democratic Centre (UCD); the LDP had not taken part in the 1982 general elections. On Feb. 21, 1984, Garrigues Walker signed a political agreement with Ignacio Camuñas Solis, the leader of the Liberal Action Party (PAL), in order to strengthen progressive liberalism.
Orientation. The PRD is a progressive liberal formation, seeking to provide an alternative to both socialism and the conservatism of the Popular Alliance.
International affiliations. Liberal International

Feminist Party of Spain
Partido Feminista de España (PFE)

Leadership. (Srta) Lidia Falcón (l.)
Founded. July 1983
History. At its first congress, held in Barcelona, the party elected a nine-member executive, and set itself the task of advancing the social, legal and political status of women in a society regarded as retaining extreme forms of male domination.

Liberal Union
Unión Liberal (UL)

Leadership. Fernando Chueca-Goytia (ch.); Pedro Schwartz (s.g.)
Founded. Jan. 14, 1983
History. The UL contested regional and local elections on May 8, 1983, in alliance with the Popular Alliance and the Popular Democratic Party.

Party of Socialist Action
Partido de Acción Socialista (Pasoc)

Address. Espoz y Mina 5-1°, Madrid, Spain
Leadership. Miguel Peydro (pres.); Modesto Seara (s.g.)
Founded. Jan. 23, 1983
History. This party superseded the earlier *Partido Socialista Obrero Español-Historico.*
Orientation. Pasoc is placed to the left of the ruling Spanish Socialist Workers' Party (PSOE).

Popular Alliance
Alianza Popular (AP)

Address. Genova 13, Madrid 4, Spain
Leadership. Manuel Fraga Iribarne (pres.); Jorge Verstrynge Rojas (s.g.)
Founded. 1976
History. Formed as a centre-right party after the death of Franco, the AP won 16 seats (out of 350) in the Congress of Deputies and two (out of 207) in the Senate in the June 1977 general elections. The party was divided over the question of whether to approve Spain's new Constitution in October 1978, and for the March 1979 general elections it formed, with other right-wing groups, the Democratic Coalition, which won only nine seats in Congress, and three in the Senate.

The AP contested the general elections of Oct. 28, 1982, in alliance with the Popular Democratic Party, and this alliance gained 106 seats in the Congress and 54 in the Senate, thus becoming the principal opposition party. It contested regional and local elections on May 8, 1983, in alliance with the Popular Democratic Union and the Liberal Union.
Orientation. The AP declares itself to be Liberal, conservative and reformist, for the defence of public order, the family and its values and the unity of Spain, for support of the middle classes and for increased free enterprise.
Structure. The party is organized throughout the country and is led by its president, secretary-general and parliamentary group.
Membership. 150,000
International affiliations. International Democrat Union; European Democrat Union

Popular Democratic Party
Partido Demócrata Popular (PDP)

Address. Calle Alcala 30, Madrid, Spain
Leadership. Oscar Alzaga (l.); Julien Guimón (s.g.)
Founded. July 24, 1982
History. This party was established by a right-wing faction of the Union of the Democratic Centre (UCD) consisting of 12 deputies and eight senators. It was registered as a political party on July 28, 1982. It undertook to support the then UCD Government until new elections were held. Following the dissolution of the UCD on Feb. 18, 1983, the PDP was joined by further former UCD members who were allocated senior posts in the party. For the October 1982 general elections and the May 1983 regional and local elections the PDP allied itself with the Popular Alliance (see separate entry).
International affiliations. International Democrat Union; European Democrat Union; Christian Democratic International; European Christian Democratic Union; European People's Party (observer)

Revolutionary Communist League
Liga Comunista Revolucionaria (LCR)

History. This party's sixth congress held in Barcelona in January 1981 was attended by some 300 delegates.
Orientation. The LCR stands for unity of the left in a Leninist party which would constitute an alternative to the Spanish Socialist Workers' and Communist parties and be based on democratic centralism. It has also advocated a federal structure for Spain.
International affiliations. The LCR is the Spanish section of the Fourth (Trotskyist) International.

Spanish Falange
Falange Española de las JONS (Juntas de Ofensiva Nacional-Sindicalista)

Leadership. Diego Márquez Jorillo (l.)
History. This organization, dating from the Franco era, contested the March 1979 general elections as part of the National Union, which obtained one seat in the Congress of Deputies. The National Union also included the New Force (*Fuerza Nueva*), which had been formed in 1976 under the leadership of Blas Piñar but

which dissolved itself on November 20, 1982. The Spanish Falange unsuccessfully presented candidates in Barcelona and Lérida in the 1980 elections to the Catalan Parliament. However, it did not contest the 1982 general elections in order to minimize divisions within the "forces opposing Marxism".

Orientation. Standing for the restoration of traditionalist authoritarian government, the Falange has proclaimed itself opposed to all separatism and to both Marxism and capitalism.

Spanish Socialist Workers' Party
Partido Socialista Obrero Español (PSOE)

Address. Ferraz 70, Madrid 8, Spain
Leadership. Felipe González Márquez (s.g.); Prof. Ramón Rubial (pres.)
Founded. 1879
History. The party, which had played a prominent role in the history of the Spanish Republic, especially between 1931 and the victory in 1938 of Franco's forces in the Civil War, was illegal from that time until 1977. In the later years of the Franco era serious differences between the party's internal wing and its exiled leadership based in Toulouse (France) culminated in the former gaining control of the party at a congress held in Paris in 1972, at which Felipe González was elected secretary-general. Although not yet legalized, in June 1975 it took part, with various other opposition parties (but not the Communist Party), in the formation of the Democratic Platform, which in March 1976 joined with the Democratic Junta—itself formed in July 1974 by the Communist Party, the Popular Socialist Party (PSP) and several other left-wing opposition organizations—to create the Democratic Co-ordination Front, which called for the restoration of civic and political rights, autonomy for Spain's regions and consultation of the people on the future form of government for Spain.

The broad-based Democratic Co-ordination Front subsequently embarked on negotiations with the Government on political reforms, which led, early in 1977, to the legalization of political parties including the PSOE and the PSP, after the PSOE had in December 1976 been allowed to hold its first legal congress in 44 years. The PSOE contested the 1977 elections together with the Catalan Socialist Party (PSC/PSOE). In April 1978 the PSOE and the PSP were merged and as a result the unified party held 124 seats in the Congress of Deputies (PSOE 118, PSP 6).

In the March 1979 general elections the PSOE, together with its Basque and Catalan wings, obtained 121 seats in the Congress of Deputies and 68 in the Senate. In the October 1982 elections it gained absolute majorities in both Houses—202 out of the 350 seats in the Congress of Deputies and 134 out of the 208 elective seats in the Senate. It thereupon formed a Government in which two posts were given to its Catalan wing and one to the Democratic Action Party.

Orientation. The PSOE is a democratic socialist party. Its longstanding definition of itself as Marxist was, principally on the initiative of Felipe González, effectively dropped at an extraordinary congress in September 1979, which decided that Marxism should be viewed as a "critical but not dogmatic instrument for the analysis and transformation of social reality" and that the party's goals should be a classless society based on democracy, self-management and decentralization. The party also stands for liberalization of laws on abortion and divorce and for a reduction of state grants to church schools. It has been opposed to Spain's integration in NATO but has worked for the full accession of Spain to the European Communities.

Structure. The PSOE has a 152-member federal committee which exercises authority between party congresses.
Membership. 135,000
International affiliations. Socialist International; Confederation of Socialist Parties of the European Community

---

Spanish Solidarity
Solidaridad Española (SE)

Founded. 1982
History. The SE was formed by Lt.-Col. Antonio Tejero Molina, who had been sentenced to 30 years' imprisonment for his involvement, with other army officers, in an attempt to overthrow the Government on Feb. 23, 1981. At the party's foundation his sentence was still subject to appeal, but it was subsequently confirmed on April 28, 1983. The SE contested the October 1983 general elections but obtained only 28,451 votes and no seats.
Orientation. The SE is an extreme right-wing formation.

Unified Communist Party of Spain
Partido Comunista de España Unificado (PCEU)

Founded. May 2, 1980
History. The PCEU was formed by a group of defectors from the Communist

Party of Spain (PCE). It contested regional elections in 11 regions on May 8, 1983, in alliance with the Communist Workers' Party of Spain (PCOE).

Orientation. The PCEU's aims (as stated in August 1983) are to remain independent (and not to be subordinate to any bloc) and to confront the ruling Spanish Socialist Workers' Party (PSOE) with a proper alternative which would lead to unity of the left.

Workers' Party of Spain
Partido de Trabajadores de España (PTE)

Founded. July 1979

History. The PTE was formed by a merger of the Spanish Labour Party led by Eladio García Castro and the Workers' Revolutionary Organization (ORT) led by José Sanromo Aldeo, neither of which was represented in the *Cortes.*

The Labour Party had been established in 1968 and formally constituted in March 1973, following which it had participated in various anti-Franco alliances. In the 1977 legislative elections the party won 140,000 votes and in Catalonia formed an electoral alliance called the Catalan Left which obtained one seat. In the 1979 general elections the party won 200,000 votes (1 per cent) but not enough in any electoral district to give the party a seat.

The ORT had been formed in October 1969 and had engaged both in clandestine activities against the Franco regime and in various political alliances of left-wing and other opposition parties. It had not taken part in the 1977 or the 1979 elections.

The PTE was unsuccessful in the 1982 elections.

Orientation. In its constitution the party defined its ideological basis as "Marxism-Leninism enriched by the contributions of universal significance as made by Mao Zedong" and the party's aim as being to "lead the working classes and the masses . . . to the building of socialism through the dictatorship of the proletariat till the abolition of all classes and the establishment of a communist society". The constitution also stated that the party would "follow the theory of the three worlds" (as propounded by the Chinese Communist Party).

Regional Parties

ANDALUSIA

Andalusian Communist Movement
Movimiento Comunista Andaluz

History. In elections to the Andalusian Parliament held on May 23, 1982, this Movement presented candidates in all eight provinces but gained no seats.

Andalusian Party
Partido Andalucista

Address. Ramón y Cajal 1-9a-2, Edificio Sevilla 1, Seville, Spain

Leadership. Luis Uruñuela (s.g.)

Founded. 1976

History. This regional formation was founded in 1976 as the Andalusian Socialist Party (PSA) and legalized the following year. Campaigning on a regionalist rather than a socialist platform in the 1979 parliamentary elections, the PSA won five seats in the Congress of Deputies, making inroads into support for the Spanish Socialist Workers' Party (PSOE) in Andalusia. In the March 1980 elections to the Catalan Parliament the PSA won two seats on the strength of the immigrant vote in that region.

The PSA opposed the Andalusian autonomy statute (approved by a large majority in a referendum of October 1981) on the grounds that it did not go far enough. In the May 1982 elections to the Andalusian regional parliament (won by the PSOE), the PSA took three seats and 5.4 per cent of the vote. In the October 1982 general election it supported the PSOE. At the party's fifth congress in February 1984 the PSA changed its name to Andalusian Party and elected a new leadership.

Orientation. The party is a progressive nationalist formation seeking the maximum level of self-government for Andalusia.

Structure. The party's congress elects a 32-member national committee, to which the secretary-general is responsible.

Membership. 10,000

Publications. *Andalucía Libre; Boletín Andalucista*

Andalusian Unity
Unidad Andaluza

Leadership. Manuel Clavero Arévalo (founder)

Founded. January 1981

History. The founder of this group was a former Minister of Culture who had defected from the Union of the Democratic Centre (which was dissolved on Feb. 18, 1983).

Orientation. Humanist, non-Marxist, democratic and autonomist, "but not separatist".

ARAGON

Aragonese Regional Party
Partido Aragonés Regionalista (PAR)

Address. Paseo de Sagasta 20, Zaragoza 6, Spain

Leadership. Hipólito Gómez de las Roces (pres.)

History. In the 1982 general elections the PAR was allied with the (right-wing) Popular Alliance.

Orientation. The PAR is a party representing a minority favouring autonomy for Aragon (i.e. separate from the Basque region).

BALEARICS

Majorcan Union
Unió Mallorquina (UM)

Leadership. Jeronimo Albertí (l.)

History. As a result of elections held on May 8, 1983, the liberal UM obtained six seats in the Majorcan regional council and held the balance of power between 21 Popular Alliance, 21 Socialist and four Nationalist deputies.

BASQUE REGION

Basque Communist Party
Partido Comunista de Euzkadi/Euzkadiko Partidu Komunista (EPK)

Address. c/o Astarlao, No. 2, 3° drcha., Bilbao 1, Vizcaya, Spain

Founded. May 1935

History. While Communist cells had existed in the Basque region since 1921 (their first leaders including Facundo Perezagua and Dolores Ibarruri), the party was not formed until 1935. It became part of the Basque Popular Front (with socialists, left-wing nationalists and republicans), which won the 1936 elections, with Leandro Carro becoming the first Communist deputy for Vizcaya province. From July 1936 the Basque Communists fought on the Republican side in the Civil War and participated in the first Basque autonomous government formed on Oct. 7, 1936.

Throughout the Franco period the party fought underground for its aims of "democracy, socialism and Basque national freedom" and in 1947 was expelled from the Basque Government in exile. In 1974 it became one of the initiators of the Basque Democratic Assembly, which was constituted in December 1975, and it was legalized on Jan. 11, 1978.

In elections to the new Basque regional Parliament held in March 1980 the Communists won one of the 60 seats and 3.9 per cent of the votes cast. In the February 1984 elections, however, the EPK retained no seat in the Basque Parliament.

Since 1981 the Basque Communist Party has suffered serious divisions. In October of that year one-quarter of its central committee (including Ramón Ormazábal Tife, until then its president) were expelled, and shortly afterwards the Spanish Communist Party (PCE) dissolved the EPK's central committee after the latter had rejected PCE demands, inter alia to condemn terrorism unequivocally, to maintain respect for the Spanish Constitution and the Basque autonomy statute, and also unity of action with the PCE; the central committee was replaced by a special committee. Early in 1982 a faction led by Roberto Lertxundi Barañano (former EPK secretary-general) broke away to join the Basque Left—Left for Socialism group (see separate entry).

Structure. The EPK is the Basque wing of the Communist Party of Spain, but has had its own congress, central committee and secretariat.

Publications. *Euzkadi Obrera* (fortnightly official organ); *Hemen eta Orain* (Here and Now, bimonthly theoretical, political and cultural review)

Basque Left
Euzkadiko Ezkerra (EE)

Address. Avda. de España 7-3°, San Sebastián, Spain

Leadership. Juan María Bandrés Molet (l.); Mario Onaindía Machiondo (s.g.)

History. The EE has held one seat in the Congress of Deputies and one in the Senate since the elections of June 1977; both these members voted with the small minority rejecting the Constitution on Oct. 31, 1978, on the grounds that it did not provide for adequate autonomy for the Basque region. In elections to the new Basque regional Parliament held in March 1980 the EE won six of the 60 seats and 9.7 per cent of the votes cast. It retained its six seats in the February 1984 elections.

Orientation. The EE is an extreme left-wing Basque autonomist movement.

Basque Left—Left for Socialism (EE-IS)

Leadership. Juan María Bandrés Molet (pres.); Mario Onaindía Machiondo (s.g.)

Founded. March 1982

History. This formation arose out of a merger of a faction of the Basque

416

Communist Party (EPK) led by Roberto Lertxundi Barañano and the Basque Revolutionary Party (EIA), which had been the chief component of the Basque Left (see separate entry).

Orientation. The EE-IS is opposed to armed violence in the Basque region.

Basque Nationalist Party
Partido Nacionalista Vasco (PNV)

Address. Gran Via 38-7°, Bilbao 1, Spain

Leadership. Roman Sodure (pres.); Carlos Garaicoetxea (Premier of Basque Government)

Founded. 1893

History. In the 1977 elections the PNV gained eight seats in the Congress of Deputies. On Oct. 31, 1978, its representative in the *Cortes* abstained from voting on Spain's Constitution and the party also called for abstention in the referendum on the Constitution on Dec. 6, 1978, when the abstention rate exceeded 56 per cent in the provinces of Guipuzcoa and Vizcaya. In the 1979 elections to general juntas, the PNV became the strongest party (with 33 out of 81 seats in Guipuzcoa and 40 out of 90 seats in Vizcaya). In elections to the new Basque regional Parliament held in March 1980 the PNV emerged as substantially the strongest party, with 25 of the 60 seats and 37.6 per cent of the votes cast. In elections to the Basque Parliament held on Feb. 26, 1984, the PNV increased its share of the vote to 42 per cent and gained 32 out of 75 seats.

The PNV has also been represented in the Congress of Deputies, gaining eight seats in 1977, seven in 1979 and eight again in 1982. The PNV has agreed to leave its leader ample freedom of decision as Premier of the Basque Government (since April 1980).

Orientation. The PNV stands for an autonomous Basque region, with its own administration and police force, within the Kingdom of Spain. It is opposed to the use of violence as practised by the illegal Basque Nation and Liberty (ETA) movement.

International affiliations. Christian Democratic International; European Christian Democratic Union; European People's Party (observer)

Basque Revolutionary Party
Euskal Iraultzako Alderdia (EIA)

Leadership. Mario Onaindía Machiondo (s.g.)

Founded. April 1977

History. The EIA was formed as a non-violent group seceding from the politico-military branch of the (illegal) Basque Nation and Liberty (ETA) movement. It contested the 1977 elections as part of the Basque Left (EE). Having been refused legalization in 1977, the EIA altered its statutes and subsequently obtained legal recognition in January 1978. (The party's secretary-general was condemned to death in Burgos in 1970 for involvement in the killing of the political police chief in Guipúzcoa Province, had his sentence commuted to 30 years' imprisonment and was released in May 1977.) In March 1982 it joined in the formation of the Basque Left—Left for Socialism movement (see separate entry).

Orientation. The EIA is a Marxist party advocating the creation of a Basque state (including Basque provinces in France).

Popular Coalition
Coalición Popular (CP)

History. The CP was created as an alliance of Popular Alliance supporters and former members of the Union of the Democratic Centre (which had dissolved itself in February 1983) to contest the Feb. 26, 1984, elections to the Basque Parliament, in which it gained seven seats.

United People
Herri Batasuna (HB)

Address. Ribera 15-1°, Guecho, Vizcaya, Spain

Leadership. Juan Domínguez Lázaro (l.)

Founded. 1979

History. The HB was set up as an alliance of various extremist Basque nationalist groups—the Basque Nationalist Action (ANV), the Basque Nationalists (ESB) and two illegal organizations, *Hasi* and *Laia*. It has close links with the illegal terrorist *Euzkadi ta Azkatasuna* (ETA) movement. In addition to the three seats gained in 1979 in the Congress of Deputies, the HB also won seats on general juntas—19 (out of 81) in Guipuzcoa and 19 (out of 90) in Vizcaya—as well as 10 (out of 77) in the Navarra Provincial Parliament.

The HB called for abstention from voting in the referendum held in the Basque region in October 1979, when in a 59 per cent poll 90.3 per cent of those voting approved an autonomy statute for the region. In elections to the new Basque regional Parliament held in March 1980 the HB won 11 of the 60 seats and 16.3 per cent of the votes cast.

It retained its 11 seats in that Parliament in elections held on Feb. 24, 1984, but in the October 1982 elections to the Congress of Deputies its strength was reduced from three to two seats. However, the party has boycotted all sessions of the Congress since 1979 and of the Basque Parliament since 1980. In April 1984 the Spanish High Court overturned an earlier decision by the Interior Ministry that the HB could not be permitted to operate as a political party because of its links with the ETA.

Orientation. The Marxist-orientated HB stands for the establishment of an independent Basque state.

CANARY ISLANDS

Union of the Canary People
Union del Pueblo Canario (UPC)

Address. Perojo 29 piso alto, Las Palmas, Gran Canaria, Spain

Leadership. Isabel Sánchez Martín (l.)

History. The UPC gained one of the 13 Canary Islands seats in the Congress of Deputies elected in 1979, and it also won seats in island councils (five out of 27 in Gran Canaria and three out of 27 in Tenerife).

Orientation. The UPC is a party advocating independence for the Canary Islands and is said to be linked to the separatist Movement for the Self-Determination and Independence of the Canary Archipelago (MPAIAC) based in Algiers.

CATALONIA

Catalan Republican Left
Esquerra Republicana de Catalunya (ERC)

Address. Carrer Villarroel 45 ent., Barcelona 11, Spain

Leadership. Heribert Barrera i Costa (s.g.)

Founded. 1931

History. The ERC was the majority party in the Catalan Parliament of 1932. Between 1952 and 1976 it was part of a *Reagrupamento Socialista i Democràtic de Catalunya.* Before being legalized in August 1977 the ERC contested legislative elections in June 1977 with independent candidates in an alliance called *Esquerra de Catalunya (Front Electoral Democràtic),* together with the *Partido del Trabajo de España* and other organizations.

In the 1979 elections, which it contested in alliance with a National Front, the ERC gained one seat each in the Congress of Deputies and in the Senate. In elections for the new Catalan regional Parliament held in March 1980 the ERC obtained 14 of the 135 seats and 9 per cent of the vote. In the October 1982 general elections it obtained one seat in the Chamber of Deputies.

In elections to the Catalan Parliament held on April 29, 1984, the ERC's strength was reduced to five members.

Orientation. The ERC's economic programme has included proposals for preferential credits for small and medium-sized enterprises, the promotion of Catalan products abroad, and fiscal measures to aid the creation of jobs.

Structure. The organs of the ERC, which has a federal structure, are a general secretariat, an eight-member secretariat, an executive council, a national congress and militant base groups.

Catalan Solidarity (SC)

History. This group took part in the elections to the Catalan Parliament held on March 20, 1980, but gained no seat.

Catalonia in the Senate
Catalunya al Senat

History. This alliance was formed by the Convergence and Union (*Convergencia i Unió,* CiU) and the Catalan Republican Left (*Esquerra Republicana de Catalunya,* ERC) for the 1982 elections to the Spanish Senate, in which it gained seven seats for its two partners.

Centrist Party of Catalonia
Partido Centrista de Catalunya

Leadership. Antoni Canyellas Balcels (pres.); Carlos Sentis Anfruns (hon. pres.)

Founded. Dec. 22, 1979

History. This party was created by the merger of the *Unió Democrática de Centre Ampli* and the Catalan branch of the Union of the Democratic Centre (UCD), then the Spanish government party but dissolved in 1982. In the 1980 elections the party obtained 18 (out of the 135) seats in the Catalan Parliament. It thereupon took part in the Catalan Executive Council formed in May 1980.

Orientation. The party has declared itself a protagonist of Catalan nationalist aspirations.

Structure. The party has a national executive committee, executive committees in every district and a national political council consisting of 20 members from each of the districts and the members of the national executive committee. Its supreme authority is a national congress which meets every two years.

Communist Workers' Party of Catalonia
Partit Comunista Obrero de Catalunya (PCOC)

History. The PCOC contested the 1980 elections to the Catalan Parliament but gained no seats.

Orientation. The PCOC presented itself (in 1980) as "a revolutionary party defending the interests of the working class, peasants and other working people of Catalonia" and striving for the establishment of a "democratic and federative people's republic" with communism as its ultimate goal, for which it regarded as essential bases "the dictatorship of the proletariat and international solidarity of workers' and progressive forces in proletarian internationalism".

Publications. *Endavant* (party organ)

Convergence and Union
Convergència i Unió (CiU)

Address. Provença 273 bajo, Barcelona, Spain

Leadership. Jordi Pujol Soley (l. and premier of Catalan Government)

Founded. 1979

History. The CiU was formed as an alliance of two parties—the *Convergència Democràtica de Catalunya*, founded in 1974 as a centre-left Catalan nationalist party under the leadership of Jordi Pujol, and the *Unió Democrática de Catalunya*. The CiU contested the 1977 general elections as part of a Democratic Pact for Catalonia, which obtained 11 seats in the Congress of Deputies. In the 1979 general elections the CiU retained eight seats in the Congress.

In elections to the new regional Catalan Parliament held in March 1980 the CiU displaced the Catalan Socialists as the region's strongest political force, winning 43 of the 135 seats and 28 per cent of the votes cast. Subsequently the CiU leader, Jordi Pujol, was elected Premier of the *Generalitat* (Catalan Government) and proceeded to form a coalition administration with the Catalan branch of the Union of the Democratic Centre (the ruling party at national level) and a number of independents. In the October 1982 general elections it increased its representation in the Congress to 12 members. In elections to the Catalan Parliament held on April 29, 1984, the CiU obtained 46.8 per cent of the vote and 72 (out of 135) seats, so that it was able to form a majority administration.

Democratic Union of Catalonia
Unió Democrática de Catalunya (UDC)

Address. C/ Valéncia 246 pral., Barcelona 7, Spain

Leadership. Miquel Coll i Alentorn (pres. of nat. council); Josep Antoni Duran i Lleida (pres. of gov. committee)

Founded. Nov. 7, 1931

History. The UDC was founded to promote recognition of Catalonia's national character and social progress in a real democracy and in accordance with Christian humanism. In 1932 it had one member in the Spanish Parliament and one in the Parliament of Catalonia. During the civil war several UDC members were assassinated and General Franco ordered the execution of its then leader, Carrasco i Formiguera.

In 1976, however, it held its fifth congress, and it subsequently joined the (nationalist) *Convergència Democrática de Catalunya* in the alliance named *Convergència i Unió* (CiU). The UDC held three posts in the Catalan Government (*Generalitat*), having gained eight seats in the Catalan Parliament on March 20, 1980. In the general elections of Oct. 28, 1982, the UDC gained three seats in the Spanish Congress of Deputies and one in the Senate. In municipal elections held on May 8, 1983, a total of 384 UDC councillors were elected. The party has remained a partner in the CiU.

Orientation. The UDC is a Christian democratic formation.

Structure. An ordinary national congress held every year determines policy and elects a 15-member governing committee. A national council of about 115 members meets every month to lay down the strategy to be carried out by the governing committee. The party has territorial sections which are represented on the party's organs.

Publications. *Nova Veu* (twice a month, for members)

International affiliations. Christian Democratic International; European Christian Democratic Union; European People's Party (observer)

Left Bloc for National Liberation
Bloc d'Esquerra d'Alliberament Nacional (BEAN)

History. This Bloc contested the 1980 elections to the Catalan Parliament without gaining any seat. It was composed of representatives of the *Bloc Català de Treballadors* (BCT) and the *Partido Obrero de Unificación Marxista* (POUM).

Orientation. The Bloc stands for self-government for Catalonia and for a radical and pluralist socialism.

Left Nationalists (NE)

History. This group took part in the elections to the Catalan Parliament held on March 20, 1980, but gained no seat.

Liberal Democratic Party of Catalonia
Partido Liberal de Cataluña (PDLC)

Leadership. José María García Perrote (s.g.)

Founded. 1983

History. This party did not contest the municipal elections of May 8, 1983, stating that it was not ready for them.

Party of Catalan Communists (PCC)

Leadership. Pere Ardiaca (pres.); Juan Ramos (s.g.)

Founded. April 1982

History. At the constituent congress of this party 30 former (pro-Soviet) members of the Unified Socialist Party of Catalonia (PSUC)—the Catalan branch of the Communist Party of Spain (PCE), led by Fr Francisco Garcia Salve—rejected all formal links with the PCE and dissociated themselves from all social and economic pacts which the Workers' Commissions (the Communist trade unions) had concluded with employers since 1977. The PCC was estimated to represent about 7,500 of the PSUC's original 18,000 members.

Party of Socialists of Catalonia
Partit dels Socialistes de Catalunya (PSC-PSOE)

Leadership. Raimon Obiols (first sec.)

Founded. July 16, 1978

History. The PSC-PSOE was established by a merger of the *Partit Socialista de Catalunya (Congrès 1976)*, the Catalan federation of the Spanish Socialist Workers' Party (PSOE) and the *Partit Socialista de Catalunya (Reagrupament)*. In the 1979 elections to the Spanish Parliament it came first in all provinces of Catalonia except Lérida (where it came second). In the 1980 elections to the Catalan Parliament it obtained 33 (out of the 135) seats. It contested the 1982 general elections in alliance with the PSOE.

Orientation. This Catalan formation is of democratic socialist persuasions.

Unified Socialist Party of Catalonia
Partit Socialista Unificat de Catalunya (PSUC)

Address. Ciutat 7, Barcelona 2, Spain

Leadership. Gregorio López Raimundo (pres.); Antonio Gutiérrez Díaz (s.g.)

Founded. July 1936

History. The PSUC was formed by a merger of four groups—the *Unió Socialista de Catalunya*, a section of the Catalan federation of the Spanish Socialist Workers' Party (PSOE), the Communist Party of Catalonia and the Proletarian Catalan Party (*Partit Català Proletari*). The PSUC was legal in 1936-39 when it took part in the Government of Catalonia and in the civil war against General Franco's forces. From 1939 to 1976 it waged underground warfare against the Franco dictatorship.

After returning to legality in 1976 the PSUC took part in the provisional government of Catalonia. In elections to the new Catalan regional Parliament held in March 1980 it obtained 19 per cent of the vote and 25 of the 135 seats. It contested Spanish general elections in 1977, 1979 and 1982 as part of the Spanish Communist Party (PCE). In elections to the Catalan Parliament held on April 29, 1984, the party's strength was drastically reduced to six members.

Orientation. As the Catalan branch of the PCE the PSUC has declared its immediate aims as being the consolidation of democracy, advance towards socialism, and the maintenance of autonomy and self-government in Catalonia.

Structure. The party has an executive committee, a central committee with a secretariat, committees at various levels, and commissions of the central committee.

Publications. *Treball* (weekly), 10,000; *Nous Horitzons* (bimonthly review), 1,500

Unity for Socialism
Unitat pel Socialisme

Founded. 1980

History. This electoral alliance was formed for the March 1980 elections to the Catalan Parliament (in which it gained no seat) by four left-wing groups—the *Liga Comunista Revolucionaria* (LCR), the *Moviment Comunista de Catalunya* (MCC), the *Organización Comunista-Bandera Roja* (OCE-BR) and the *Partit del Treball de Catalunya* (PTC).

Orientation. This Marxist alliance has proposed to achieve political unity of the left in opposing the national unity presented by the Catalan provisional Government; it is republican, in favour of Catalonia's right to self-determination, including independence; and it is opposed to any social contract, to the building of nuclear reactors and to Spain's entry into NATO.

GALICIA

Galician Left
Esquerra Gallega (EG)

History. This party gained one seat in the Galician regional parliament elected on Oct. 20, 1981 (in a 44 per cent poll).

Galician Party
Partido Gallego

History. This party supported a "yes" vote in the referendum held on Dec. 21, 1980, on the draft regional statute for Galicia.

Popular National Bloc of Galicia—Galician Socialist Party
Bloque Nacional Popular de Galicia—Partido Socialista Gallego (BNPG-PSG)

History. This Marxist-Leninist party was opposed to the draft autonomy statute for Galicia approved in a referendum on Dec. 21, 1980. It obtained three seats in the regional Parliament elected on Oct. 20, 1981.

Union of the Galician People
Unión del Pueblo Gallego

History. This Union opposed the draft regional statute for Galicia approved in a referendum on Dec. 21, 1980.

NAVARRA

Union of the Navarrese People
Unión del Pueblo Navarro (UPN)

Address. Paseo de Viana 1-4°, Pamplona, Spain

Leadership. Javier Gomara (pres.)
Founded. 1979
History. This party contested the 1982 general elections in alliance with the (right-wing) Popular Alliance. In regional elections held in Navarra on May 8, 1983, the UPN obtained 13 (out of 50) seats. It declared its support for the coalition of the Popular Alliance, Popular Democratic Party and Liberal Union.
Orientation. The UPN subscribes to Christian social precepts.

VALENCIA

Unity of the People of Valencia
Unitat del Poble Valencià

History. This alliance of two parties—the *Agrupamento del País Valencià* and the *Partit Nacionalista del País Valencià*—contested regional elections in Valencia on May 8, 1983.

Valencian Union
Unión Valenciana

History. For the general election of October 1982 this regional party allied itself with the (right-wing) Popular Alliance. For regional elections held on May 8, 1983, the party was also allied with the Popular Democratic Party and the Liberal Union.

Ceuta and Melilla

Ceuta National Party
Partido Nacional Ceuti (PNC)

History. Local council elections held on May 8, 1983, this party gained only two (out of 25) seats.

Spanish Nationalist Party of Melilla
Partido Nacionalista Español de Melilla

History. The statutes of this party were approved by the Ministry of the Interior in November 1980.
Orientation. The party stands for the defence of the interests of Melilla and of its Spanish character.

Sri Lanka

Capital: Colombo   Pop. 15,200,000

The Democratic Socialist Republic of Sri Lanka (formerly Ceylon) is an independent state within the Commonwealth with a multi-party system and parliamentary democracy. It has an executive President elected for a six-year term by universal adult suffrage. He is head of state and President of the Government and appoints (or dismisses) the Prime Minister and members of the Cabinet. He is also empowered to dissolve Parliament—which is a 168-member Assembly similarly elected for a six-year term by citizens above the age of 18 years under a system of proportional representation in multi-member districts and determined at district (not national) level.

Following the re-election of President Junius R. Jayawardene on Oct. 20, 1982, for a further six-year term, the current term of Parliament, due to expire in August 1983, was extended for another six years under a constitutional amendment unanimously approved by the Government on Oct. 27, 1982, and also approved by Parliament on Nov. 5 and in a referendum held on Dec. 22 of that year, when 54.7 per cent of the valid votes were cast in favour of the amendment in a 71 per cent poll. Under a further constitutional amendment approved by Parliament on Feb. 20, 1983, vacant seats in the Assembly were to be filled by by-election rather than by party appointment.

By early 1983 the distribution of seats in Parliament was as follows: United National Party 143, Tamil United Liberation Front 15, Sri Lanka Freedom Party 6, Communist Party 1, Ceylon Workers' Congress 1, vacant 2.

All Ceylon Tamil Congress

Address. Congress House, 120 Main Street, Jaffna, Sri Lanka

Leadership. S. R. Kanaganayagam (pres.); G. G. Ponnambalam (g.s.)

Founded. Oct. 29, 1944

History. As a spokesman for the Tamil nation in Sri Lanka, the party has contested parliamentary seats in the northern and eastern parts of the country and has agitated for balanced representation of minorities in the Legislature. It coalesced with the United National Party governments of the day in 1948, 1952 and 1953 on the basis of responsive co-operation.

Orientation. The party seeks "equality of status and freedom for the Tamil nation" on the basis of their inalienable right of self-determination.

Structure. There is an annual convention and the party has a general council and a working committee.

Ceylon Workers' Congress

Address. 72 Ananda Coomaraswamy Mawatha, Colombo 7, Sri Lanka

Leadership. Savumyamoorthy Thondaman (pres.); Muthu Sangaralingam Sellasamy (sec.)

Founded. 1940

History. The Ceylon Workers' Congress has been part of the United Tamil Liberation Front (TULF) since 1976 and within this alliance won a seat in the 1977 parliamentary elections. It was one of the parties which took part in a preliminary conference called by the Government to discuss the Tamil issue on Dec. 21, 1983.

Orientation. The Congress has sought to represent the interests of Tamil workers on tea plantations in Sri Lanka (many of them still British-owned).

Publications. *Congress News* (fortnightly, in English); *Congress* (fortnightly, in Tamil)

Communist Party of Sri Lanka

Address. 91 Cotta Road, Colombo 8, Sri Lanka

Leadership. K. P. de Silva (s.g.)

Founded. July 1943

History. The party was established as the Communist Party of Ceylon on the basis of a United Socialist Party and various Communist groups existing in the country. While the party had gained four parliamentary seats in 1965 and six in 1970, it retained nonc in the 1977 elections, which it contested after withdrawing from a United Left Front embracing also the Sri Lanka Equal Society Party and the People's Democratic Party. The party returned to Parliament when it won a seat in a by-election on Jan. 12, 1981. In the October 1982 presidential elections it supported the candidature of Hector Kobbekaduwa of the Sri Lanka Freedom Party.

Under a state of emergency imposed in May 1983 in connexion with intercommunal violence, which subsequently led to great loss of life and property among Tamils, the party was banned from July 30 to mid-October 1983. Although it at first declined to attend round-table conferences on the Tamil issue proposed by the Government, it was one of the parties represented at an interim conference on this question on Dec. 21, 1983.

Orientation. Now essentially pro-Soviet, the party has called for the nationalization of banks, estates and factories, and for the use of national languages (rather than English).

Structure. The party's primary organizations are based on places of work or residence, and there are area and district committees. The party's supreme authority is its national congress (to be convened every two years), which elects a central committee, a central control commission and a central auditing commission. The central committee elects a political bureau, a secretariat, and other bureaux and officc-bearers, as well as editors of party organs.

Publications. *Aththa* (Truth, daily, in Sinhala); *Shakthi* (weekly, in Tamil); *Forward* (weekly, in English)

International affiliations. The party is recognized by the Communist parties of the Soviet-bloc countries.

Democratic Workers' Congress (Political Wing)

Address. 98A Mohideen Masjid Road, P.O. Box 1009, Colombo 10, Sri Lanka

Leadership. Abdul Aziz (pres.); Vythilingam Palanisamy Ganesan (sec.)

Founded. December 1978

History. Although politically active since 1939, this trade union was not registered as a political party until 1978. Its president was returned to Parliament in 1952, representing people of Indian (Tamil) origin settled on plantations. In 1970–77 he was a nominated member under Mrs Bandaranaike's coalition Government, with the aim of representing these Indian people's interests. The party was one of those which participated in a preliminary conference called by the Government to discuss the Tamil issue on Dec. 21, 1983.

Orientation. The party's aim is to eliminate social and economic exploitation and inequality, the profit motive and all forms of anti-social concentration of power. It stands for the all-round development of the human personality.

Membership. 250,000

Publications. *Jananayaga Thozhilali* (Democratic Worker, fortnightly, in Tamil)

International affiliations. World Federation of Trade Unions

New Equal Society Party
Nava Sama Samaja Party (NSSP)

Leadership. Vasudeva Nanayakkara (l.)

Founded. September 1982

History. The NSSP nominated its leader as a candidate in the Oct. 20, 1982, presidential elections, but he obtained only 0.26 per cent of the vote. During the intercommunal violence of mid-1983 the NSSP was banned on July 30, but it was officially indicated in December of that year that the ban might be lifted if it was established that the party did not pose a security risk.

Orientation. The NSSP is a Trotskyist formation.

People's Liberation Front
Janatha Vimukhti Peramuna (JVP)

Address. 73 Dharmarama Road, Colombo 9, Sri Lanka

Leadership. Rohana Wijeweere (l.)

History. As a Maoist organization the JVP was responsible for an attempt to overthrow the Government in April 1971. After being outlawed it regained legal status in February 1977. In district council elections held on June 4, 1981, it won 18 seats in six councils, including four of the 16 seats in Colombo. For the presidential elections of Oct. 20, 1982, it nominated its leader who, however, obtained only 4.2

per cent of the vote. During the period of severe intercommunal violence in mid-1983 the JVP was banned on July 30, 1983, but it was officially indicated in December 1983 that the ban would be lifted if it was established that the party did not pose a security risk.

People's United Front
Mahajana Eksath Peramuna (MEP)

Address. 195 Kew Road, Colombo 2, Sri Lanka
Leadership. Dinesh P.R. Gunawardene (g.s.)
Founded. 1956
History. The MEP was established by Philip Gunawardene, regarded as the architect of the Sri Lanka socialist movement. It was formed as a result of a merger of part of the Sri Lanka Equal Society Party, the Sri Lanka Freedom Party and the *Bhasha Peramuna;* it was in government in 1956–59, when far-reaching economic, political and cultural reforms were carried out. It was later in partnership with a (Tamil) National Liberation Front (*Jatika Vimukhti Peramuna*). In a by-election held on May 18, 1983, it gained a seat in Parliament, and it was one of the parties which took part in a preliminary conference held on Dec. 21, 1983, to discuss the Tamil issue.
Orientation. The MEP is a strongly Sinhalese and Buddhist left-wing party advocating a self-reliant national economy and scientific socialism.

Sri Lanka Communist Party (Left)

Founded. September 1982
History. This independent party was reported to have formed a preparatory committee with a secretary.

Sri Lanka Equal Society Party
Lanka Sama Samaja Party (LSSP)

Address. 457 Union Place, Colombo 2, Sri Lanka
Leadership. Bernard Soysa (g.s.); Dr N. M. Perera (l.)
Founded. December 1935
History. At its foundation the party announced as its objects freedom from British rule and the achievement of socialism. Through its deputies and outside the Legislature it endeavoured "to secure

measures of benefit to the working class and the broad masses". The party was banned during World War II but was active as an underground organization and sought to build organizational links with other Trotskyist groups in India and co-operate with them, particularly in the struggle for Indian freedom launched in August 1942.

In 1945 the LSSP formally affiliated to the Fourth International but it was expelled from this body in 1964 for participating in a coalition Government with the Sri Lanka Freedom Party (SLFP) with three ministers on a 14-point programme approved in Parliament in December 1964. In June 1970 the party (with three ministers) entered a coalition with the SLFP and the Communist Party, but it left the Government in September 1975.

Since 1977 the party has not been represented in parliament, but members had previously been elected as follows: two in 1936, 15 in 1947, nine in 1952, 14 in 1956, 10 in March 1960, 12 in July 1960, 10 in 1965 and 19 in 1970.

For the presidential elections of Oct. 20, 1982, the LSSP nominated Dr Colvin de Silva as its candidate but he obtained only 0.9 per cent of the vote. It was one of the parties which took part in a provisional conference held on Dec. 21, 1983, to discuss the Tamil issue.
Orientation. The Trotskyist LSSP seeks "the building of a socialist society with a multiparty political system, where the fullest democracy is enjoyed by the people both in the political and the economic fields". The LSSP also stands for the implementation of the principle of self-management.
Structure. The party's highest authority is vested in a congress of delegates and, between congress sessions, in a central committee elected by the congress. The central committee elects officers, among them a general secretary, and appoints a political and an organizational bureau.
Membership. 20,000
Publications. *Samasamajaya, Samadharmam* and *Samasamajist* (weeklies, in Sinhala, Tamil and English respectively)

Sri Lanka Freedom Party (SLFP)

Address. 301 T.B. Jayah Road (Darley Road), Colombo 10, Sri Lanka
Leadership. Anura Bandaranaike (l.); Ratnasiri Wickremanayake (sec.)
Founded. 1951
History. The SLFP first came to power as a partner in a People's United Front (MEP) in 1956. Following a split in the

MEP in June 1959, it held office as the sole goverment party until March 1960. It underwent a split late in 1959, with its right wing subsequently forming the Ceylon Democratic Party (which gained only four seats in the March 1960 general elections and two in the July 1960 elections). The SLFP was again in power from July 1960 to 1965 and in 1970–77, in coalition with the (Trotskyist) Sri Lanka Equal Society Party in 1964–68 and 1970–75.

On Oct.16, 1980, the party's former leader, (Mrs) Sirimavo Bandaranaike, was deprived of her civil rights for seven years on the grounds of abuse of power while she had been Prime Minister (in 1970–77), a government resolution to this effect being opposed only by the SLFP and Tamil United Liberation Front (TULF) members of Parliament. For the Oct. 20, 1982, presidential elections the SLFP presented as its candidate Hector Kobbek-aduwa (who had been a cabinet minister in 1970–77), and he obtained 39.1 per cent of the vote (against 52.9 per cent for President Jayawardene) in an 81 per cent poll.

In November 1982 the SLFP appeared divided, as only two of its members (one of them being Maithripala Senanayake, the party's president) voted in favour of the extension of the current Parliament's term by another six years. In by-elections held on May 18, 1983, the party increased its parliamentary representation from six to nine members, and after the exclusion of the TULF members from the House in October 1983 it became the official opposition. Having at first declined to take part in talks with the Government on the Tamil issue, the SLFP was represented at a preliminary conference on this subject on Dec. 21, 1983.

Orientation. The SLFP campaigned vigorously for Sri Lanka's attainment of republican status (achieved in 1972); it stands for a non-aligned foreign policy, for the progressive nationalization of industry and for Sinhalese as the official language (with certain safeguards for ethnic minorities).

Publications. *Dinaya* (daily); *Sathiya* (weekly)

Sri Lanka Liberal Group

Address. 368B Galle Road, Colombo 3, Sri Lanka
Leadership. M. M. Mohideen (pres.); K. B. Wijesinghe (s.g.)
International affiliations. Liberal International

Sri Lanka People's Party (SLPP)

Leadership. Chandrike Kumaran-atunge, Vijaya Kumaranatunge, T. B. Ilangaratne
Founded. January 1984
History. The SLPP was founded by a left-wing splinter group of the Sri Lanka Freedom Party (SLFP). One of the party's leaders, Chandrike Kumaranatunge, is a daughter of the former SLFP leader, Mrs Bandaranaike.

Tamil Congress

History. This party was one of the components of the Tamil United Liberation Front (TULF), but for the presidential elections of Oct. 20, 1982, it nominated its own candidate, Kumar Ponnambalam, who obtained 2.7 per cent of the vote and came first in Jaffna (northern Sri Lanka). On May 11, 1983, however, it decided to withdraw its candidates from local elections in response to a boycott call issued by separatist guerrillas. On the other hand, in contrast to the TULF, the Tamil Congress was one of the parties which took part in a premilinary conference called by the Government to discuss the Tamil issue on Dec. 21, 1983.

Orientation. The Tamil Congress seeks the establishment of *Eelam* as a separate state for the Tamil population of Sri Lanka.

Tamil Eelam Liberation Front (TELF)

Leadership. Dr S. Dharmalingam (pres.)
History. In connexion with violent incidents in which Tamil property was attacked, Dr Dharmalingam called, in June 1983, for a United Nations peacekeeping force to be sent to Trincomalee (north-eastern Sri Lanka). He was thereupon detained on July 2, while the TELF's weekly *Sutantiran* was banned. Another leading member of the TELF, Selva Rajah Yogachandran ("Kutimani"), who had been convicted of murdering a policeman, was himself killed by other prisoners in a massacre of 35 Tamil prison inmates on July 25, 1983.

Tamil United Liberation Front (TULF)

Address. 238 Main Street, Jaffna, Sri Lanka
Leadership. M. Sivasithamparam (pres.); Appapillai Amirthalingam (s.g.)

Founded. May 1976

History. The TULF was initially organized as the Tamil Liberation Front (*Tamil Vimukthi Peramuna*, TVP) which included the Federal Party (*Illankai Tamil Arasu Kadchi*, ITAK), the National Liberation Front (*Jatika Vimukthi Peramuna*, JVP), the Tamil Congress, the Moslem United Front and the Ceylon Workers' Congress. It succeeded an earlier Tamil Liberation Front formed before the 1970 elections by the Federal Party and the Tamil Congress.

The TULF contested the 1977 general elections in 24 constituencies in the predominantly Tamil northern and eastern provinces, and as a result of the elections it became the largest opposition group in Parliament. However, the TULF consistently refused to take part in parliamentary action in so far as it took no account of Tamil aspirations. The TULF did not take part in the 1982 presidential elections (although the Tamil Congress, one of its components, did).

After the extension of the current Parliament for another six years the TULF announced on Nov. 5, 1982, that its members would resign their seats in August 1983. Participating in local elections on May 18, 1983 (despite a boycott call issued by separatist guerrillas), the TULF gained majorities on several councils in the predominantly Tamil areas. However, on July 23, 1983, a TULF convention decided to renounce the parliamentary path towards the establishment of *Eelam* (i.e. a separate Tamil state) and to boycott a round-table conference called by President Jayawardene (to the first session of which the TULF had not been invited).

In the wake of widespread intercommunal violence, which led to great loss of life and property among Tamils, Parliament passed, by 150 votes to none, on Aug. 5, 1983, constitutional amendments under which parties advocating separatism were to be banned and members of Parliament were obliged to take an oath forswearing separatist aspirations. The TULF members thereupon refused to take this oath and absented themselves from Parliament, with the result that on Oct. 23 they were declared to have forfeited their seats.

In connexion with the Tamil crisis A. Amirthalingam met (Mrs) Indira Gandhi, the Indian Prime Minister, in New Delhi in August 1983, and he afterwards expressed the hope that Indian mediation might lead to meaningful discussion between the TULF and the Sri Lanka Government; he nevertheless reaffirmed that Tamils would never renounce their aspirations of creating a separate state in Sri Lanka. On Sept. 3, 1983, he also met President Jayawardene, who, however, insisted that the TULF must renounce

separatism before it could be invited to a round-table conference. The TULF, on the other hand, reiterated in October that it continued to be opposed to all forms of violence.

Orientation. The TULF stands for the creation of Tamil *Eelam* as an independent state (to consist of the predominantly Tamil areas of Sri Lanka).

United National Party (UNP)

Address. 532 Galle Road, Colombo 3, Sri Lanka

Leadership. Junius Richard Jayawardene (pres.); Harsha Abeywardene (sec.)

Founded. 1947

History. The UNP was in power from the achievement of independence in 1947 until 1956, from March to July 1960 and in 1965-70. In opposition in 1970–77, the party supported the 1972 Constitution (under which Sri Lanka became a republic) introduced by the Government led by the Sri Lanka Freedom Party (SLFP) and headed by (Mrs) Sirimavo Bandaranaike.

The UNP returned to power as a result of its landslide victory in the July 1977 general elections, thus maintaining the post-independence pattern of ruling parties always being defeated at the next available election. The UNP administration moved the following year to introduce a presidential form of government, with Junius R. Jayawardene vacating the premiership to become President. On the basis of the popular mandate given to President Jayawardene in the presidential election of October 1982 (when he was confirmed in power by 52.9 per cent of the votes cast), the UNP Government subsequently introduced a constitutional amendment extending the life of the 1977 Parliament for a further six years.

Orientation. The UNP claims to be a democratic socialist party. It advocates a neutralist, non-aligned foreign policy and supports the status of Sinhala as the country's official language.

Publications. *The Journal* (weekly, in Sinhala and English)

Working People's Party of Sri Lanka

Founded. September 1982

History. This small left-wing formation has set itself the task of challenging the dominance of the longer-established left-wing parties as regards support from among working people.

Sudan

Capital: Khartoum   Pop. 19,028,000

The Democratic Republic of the Sudan has an executive President, who is nominated by the Sudanese Socialist Union (SSU), the country's sole legal political organization, and who is also Prime Minister (although he may appoint another person to this post). There is a National People's Assembly of 151 members elected by universal adult suffrage of citizens above the age of 18 years, all candidates having to be approved by the SSU. Elections to the Assembly held in December 1981 gave 52 seats to candidates from the northern Sudan, 16 to candidates from the Southern Region and 70 to the Alliance of Working Forces (or professional bodies), while 13 members were directly appointed by the President.

The Sudan has eight regions, each with a governor, a People's Assembly and a regional government. Of these eight regions. Bahr el Ghazal, Equatoria and Upper Nile were between 1972 and June 1983 combined in a Southern Region with a 115-member People's Assembly. Elections to this Assembly held in April 1982 were contested by SSU-approved candidates representing three groups—(i) a unity group led by Abel Alier (then a Vice-President of Sudan), (ii) a "divisionist" group led by Lt.-Gen. Joseph Lagu and favouring a return to the division of the Southern Region into the three provinces which had existed until 1972, and (iii) a "compromise" group led by Samuel Aru Bol and advocating a solution described as "Change Two" (C-2). On June 23, 1982, the new Assembly elected, by 62 votes to 49 with four abstentions, Joseph James Tombura (a divisionist allied with the C-2 group) as President of the High Executive Council (the Southern Region's Government), his coalition being referred to as "Change Three" (C-3). On the establishment of the three separate regions in the south in June 1983, the members of the Southern Region's Assembly were divided among the assemblies of the three new southern regions.

A Charter of Integration between Sudan and Egypt, signed on Oct. 12, 1982, for a 10-year period of political and economic integration of the two countries provided for (i) a High Council of Integration under the chairmanship of the two countries' Presidents and (ii) a Nile Valley Parliament consisting of 20 members from each of the two legislatures and 10 other members appointed by each President. This 60-member Parliament held its first session in Khartoum on Oct. 25-31, 1983.

Sudanese Socialist Union (SSU)

Address. P.O.B. 1850, Khartoum, Sudan

Leadership. President Jaafer Mohammed al Nemery (pres.)

Founded. October 1971

History. The SSU was created by President Nemery, on the model of the Arab Socialist Union of Egypt, as a mass party to supersede the Communist Party and Arab nationalist groups. From 1972 to 1978 the SSU was mainly a support organization for government policies aimed at bringing about development changes within the existing socio-economic structure. Since 1978 the SSU has tended to take part in initiatives and in decision-making. Thus the SSU endorsed, in February 1981, a decision by President

Nemery to open an office in Khartoum for the (anti-Soviet) Afghan *mujaheddin* and recommended that they should be granted financial and moral support.

Orientation. Under the SSU's national charter, approved by a constituent assembly in January 1972, the party's principle is that of "national unity", admitting neither "class struggle" nor liberal democracy, and functioning under the protection of the armed forces. The SSU's tasks include the elimination of all forms of exploitation,

improved social security and equal rights for women.

Structure. Hierarchical in structure, the SSU has as its leading organs a national conference, a central committee and a political bureau of 17 members.

Publications. The country's entire press was placed under the control of the SSU in May 1976.

International affiliations. Socialist Inter-African

Suriname

Capital: Paramaribo   Pop. 350,000

The Republic of Suriname has since February 1980 been ruled by a National Military Council (NMC) led by Sgt.-Maj. (later Lt.-Col.) Desi Bouterse, who successively dismissed the country's President and suspended its Constitution (on Aug. 15, 1980); he later announced (in March 1981) that Suriname would strengthen its relations with Cuba and follow "a clear socialist course". The NMC succeeded in foiling several attempts by army officers to overthrow it, and on Nov. 27, 1981, it set up a "Revolutionary Front" including "political parties, progressive organizations and other sectors". On March 31, 1982, a mainly civilian Government was set up. However, as a result of a confrontation between the Government and the country's trade unions in October-December 1982 the NMC on Dec. 8 declared a state of martial law, dismissed the Government and destroyed the headquarters of the opposition media and of the largest right-wing trade union, the *Moederbond*. Lt.-Col. Bouterse stated on Dec. 20 that he intended to form a "truly revolutionary government", and he added on Dec. 30 that there would "never again" be a parliamentary democracy in Suriname of the type in existence until February 1980. A new civilian Government was appointed on Feb. 26, 1983.

Feb. 25 United Movement

Founded. 1983

History. The planned formation of this Movement as a new political party was announced by Lt.-Col. Bouterse on June

30, 1983. His apparent intention was to create a front-type political organization as a channel for support for the military regime which seized power in February 1980.

Swaziland

Capital: Mbabane   Pop. 650,000

The Kingdom of Swaziland is normally ruled by a Paramount Chief (*Ngwenyama*) as King, who exercises authority through a Cabinet headed by a Prime Minister. There is a Parliament of 40 members elected by an electoral college from among its 80 members, this college being itself elected by public ballot and the majority of its members being members of the *Imbokodvo* National Movement. A Senate consists of 10 members elected by the electoral college and another 10 nominated by the King. Both Houses have purely advisory functions. All political parties were banned under a new Constitution proclaimed on Oct. 13, 1978.

Following the death of King Sobhuza II on Aug. 21, 1982, his senior widow Dzeliwe became Queen Mother and Regent for an indefinite period. She appointed a Supreme Council of State (Liqoqo) under the chairmanship of Prince Sozisa who was also the "Authorized Person" to assist the Queen Mother. However, on Aug. 9, 1983, the Queen Mother was deposed in controversial circumstances and replaced as Regent by Royal Wife Ntombi.

A new Parliament and Senate were elected by the normal procedure during October 1983.

Imbokodvo National Movement (INM)

Founded. 1964

History. The *Imbokodvo* ("Grindstone") National Movement was established on an initiative by King Sobhuza II, who personally selected as its first leader Prince Makhosini Jameson Dlamini (who also became Prime Minister, retiring from this office in 1975). The INM was supported by Whites (organized at first in a European Advisory Committee and later the United Swaziland Association, or USA). In elections held in 1964 the INM won 68.6 per cent of the votes and the USA 16 per cent; in 1967 elections the INM raised its share of the vote to 79.4 per cent, but in 1972 this share dropped to 78.03 per cent. In elections held after the introduction of a new system based on the traditional *tinkhundla* (local councils) in October 1978 all candidates were recruited from, and presented by, the INM.

Orientation. The INM is a traditionalist movement, but with a policy of modernization, development and the elimination of illiteracy.

Structure. The INM is in fact the political wing of the traditional National Council (*libandla*), a consultative body of chiefs, councillors, headmen and adult males.

Sweden

Capital: Stockholm   Pop. 8,380,000

The Kingdom of Sweden is a parliamentary democracy in which the monarch has purely ceremonial functions as head of state. There is a Cabinet headed by a Prime Minister and responsible to a unicameral Parliament (*Riksdag*) of 349 members elected for a three-year term by universal adult suffrage of citizens above the age of 18 years under a system of proportional representation, with 310 seats being filled in 28 multi-member constituencies and the remaining 39 allocated to parties according to a complex formula. A party must obtain 4 per cent of the national vote to qualify for a seat. State subsidies have been paid to parties represented in Parliament, partly as a party support grant equivalent to about $36,300 per seat per annum, and partly as a secretarial grant (at a higher rate to opposition parties than to parties in government).

As a result of elections held on Sept. 19, 1982, seats in the *Riksdag* were distributed as follows: Social Democratic Labour Party 166, Moderate Party 86, Centre Party 56, Liberal Party 21, Communist Left Party 20.

Centre Party
Centerpartiet

Address. Box 22107, 104 22 Stockholm, Sweden

Leadership. Thorbjörn Fälldin (ch.); Allan Pettersson (s.g.)

Founded. 1910

History. Formed for the purpose of representing the population in the country's rural areas, the party has developed into one of the centre with supporters in both rural and urban districts. It first gained parliamentary representation in 1917 and formed its first Government in June 1936. From October 1936 it co-operated in government with the Social Democrats, and in 1939–45 in a national coalition Government. In 1951–57 the Centre Party was again a partner with the Social Democrats in a coalition Government; and in 1976–78 it headed a three-party Government including also the Liberals and the Moderate (Conservative) Party, this coalition being re-established after the September 1979 elections. In elections to the *Riksdag* in September 1982 it gained 15.5 per cent of the valid votes and 56 (out of 349) seats. Thereafter it went into opposition.

Orientation. The party works for a decentralized society with a social market economy, with all parts of the country having an equal chance to develop; for the protection of the environment; and for the use of technology not only for man's material welfare but also for his mental well-being. The party is strongly opposed to the development of nuclear energy capacity.

Structure. The party has 4,963 sections, organized in 29 districts (as at the end of 1981).

Membership. 235,000

Publications. Svensk Politik, 137,000; Politisk Tidskrift, 7,000; Ung Center, 35,000

International affiliations. Nordic Union of Centre Parties

Christian Democratic Party
Kristen Demokratisk Samling (KDS)

Address. Box 451, 101 26 S-Stockholm, Sweden

Leadership. Alf Svensson (ch.); Per-Egon Johansson (sec.)

Founded. 1964

History. The party gained some 78,000 votes in its first general election in 1964 and by 1982 this total had increased to 103,820 (1.9 per cent). The party has failed to pass the 4 per cent bar to representation in the *Riksdag*, although it has won over 300 seats in local councils, in elections for which its aggregate vote has exceeded 100,000.

Orientation. The KDS describes itself as "the third alternative in Sweden, where all parties are socialistic or non-socialistic". It propagates "a new way of life" and concentrates on social problems, calling inter alia for a review of the abortion law. It also calls for a halt to the building of nuclear power stations.

Structure. The KDS has a youth organization (Christian Democratic Youth), with 6,000 members in 130 local groups, and a women's organization (KDS-K) with 2,000 members.

Membership. 24,000.

Publications. *Samhällsgemenskap* (Social Community, weekly), 12,000

International affiliations. Christian Democratic International (observer)

Communist Left Party
Vänsterpartiet Kommunisterna (VPK)

Address. Kungsgatan 84, 112 27 Stockholm, Sweden

Leadership. Lars Werner (ch.); Bo Hammar (sec.)

Founded. May 1917

History. One of the oldest Communist parties in the world, the party was formed as the Social-Democratic Left Party as a result of a split in the Social Democratic Party of Sweden. It changed its name to Communist Party in 1919, when it joined the Communist International (Comintern), to which it belonged until that organization's dissolution in 1943. In 1967 the party adopted its present name, to signify its aim of becoming "a forum for the whole socialist left". Throughout its history the party has been represented in Parliament, and for long periods Social Democratic Governments have relied on Communist support. In both the 1979 and the 1982 general elections the VPK obtained 5.6 per cent of the valid votes.

Orientation. Regarded as "Eurocommunist" in outlook, the party seeks "to fight for the interests of the working people in Sweden with the perspective of transforming Sweden into a socialist society". It has generally supported the ruling Social Democratic Labour Party and has publicly condemned incursions into Swedish waters by Soviet submarines.

Structure. The party has 320 base organizations and 22 party districts. Its congress, meeting every third year, elects a 35-member central committee (comprising also 15 candidate members), which elects the party chairman and a nine-member executive.

Membership. 18,000

Publications. *Arbetartidningen Ny Dag* (weekly), 20,000; *Socialistisk Debatt* (six times a year, theoretical organ)

Communist Party of Sweden
Sveriges Kommunistiska Parti (SKP)

Address. Box 5088, 10424 Stockholm, Sweden

Leadership. Roland Pettersson (ch.); Jan-Olof Norell (sec.)

Founded. June 1967

History. The party was formed by pro-Chinese elements of the old Communist Party (renamed the Communist Left Party in 1967) and other groupings, notably the Clarté League (named after the Clarté movement of Henri Barbusse in 1916). The party claimed to have influenced Sweden's foreign policy to shift from "informally US-allied to heavily pro-Vietnamese" during the Vietnam conflict of the late 1960s and early 1970s. Since 1974 the SKP has campaigned strongly against the Soviet Union and what it regards as the latter's growing influence on Sweden's public opinion.

Orientation. An independent Communist party, basing itself on the Swedish people's "tradition of rebellion", the European democratic tradition and the international Marxist/Maoist tradition, the SKP emphasizes that national independence and democratic freedom are essential for the working people to prevent decline into "a new brutal system of exploitation and oppression".

Structure. Democratic centralist, the SKP has some 120 local branches.

Publications. *Gnistan* (Spark, weekly), 5,000; *Marxistisk Forum* (quarterly), 1,000

Ecology Party of Sweden
Miljöpartiet

Address. Box 22096, S-104 Stockholm, Sweden

Leadership. Political board with rotating chairmanship; Christer-v. Malmborg (s.g.)

Founded. Sept. 20, 1981

History. In the general elections of Sept. 19, 1982, the party obtained 91,787 votes (1.7 per cent) and thus failed to gain any seats. On the other hand, it has succeeded in obtaining representation in over 30 per cent of local councils.

Orientation. The party stands for nature conservation, agricultural production to achieve national self-sufficiency in basic foodstuffs, the phasing-out of nuclear energy, support for the peace movement, the creation of nuclear-weapons-free zones in Scandinavia and Europe, a flexible retirement age and the ending of discrimination against immigrants. It has also called for a six-hour day, lower interest rates and reduced economic growth.

Structure. An annual congress elects a political, an administrative, a constitutional and a newspaper board. There are 20 regional and about 200 local branches.

Membership. 3,500-5,000

Publications. *Alternativet i Svensk Politik*, 10,000

International affiliations. The European Greens

Liberal Party
Folkpartiet

Address. Luntmakargatan 66, Box 6508, S-113-83 Stockholm, Sweden

Leadership. Bengt Westerberg (l.); Gunnar Bäckström (s.g.)

Founded. 1934

History. Organized liberalism began in Sweden at the end of the 19th century with the objectives of social justice, universal suffrage and equality. After World War I a Liberal-Social Democratic Party coalition Government led by a Liberal Prime Minister completed the process of democratization, but the introduction of universal suffrage reduced the party's influence, and between 1923 and 1934 the party was split over the issue of alcohol prohibition. Nevertheless it formed governments in 1926–28 and 1930–32, and it took part in the National Government during World War II.

In 1948 the party became the second strongest in the Second Chamber of the *Riksdag* with 57 seats, but by 1968 the seats it held in that Chamber had declined to 34. In the unicameral *Riksdag* (in existence since January 1971) it gained 58 seats in 1970, but only 34 in 1973 and 39 in 1976, whereafter it took part in the first non-socialist Government to be formed in Sweden for 44 years in coalition with the Centre and Moderate (Conservative) parties.

The collapse of this coalition in October 1978 over the nuclear issue was followed by a year of minority Liberal rule under Ola Ullsten; but as a result of the September 1979 elections the three-party non-socialist coalition was re-established. The Conservative Party, however, left this Government in 1981 after disagreements on taxation, and the Liberal and Centre parties formed a minority Government

until the September 1982 elections brought the Social Democrats back to power. In those elections the Liberal vote dropped to 5.9 per cent.

Orientation. The Liberal Party advocates a free and decentralized economy, respect for individual freedom and basic human rights, and a system of parliamentary democracy.

Structure. The party's members are organized in 700 local associations which form 26 regional associations. There is a 28-member national executive, 23 of the members being elected by the national convention normally held every two years.

Membership. 50,000

Publications. *Utsikt* (official organ), 60,000

International affiliations. Liberal International

Moderate Party
Moderata Samlingspartiet

Address. Box 1243, S-111 82, Stockholm, Sweden

Leadership. Ulf Adelsohn (ch.); Georg Danell (s.g.)

Founded. 1904

History. The party participated in coalitions or formed minority governments several times before 1932, after which the Social Democrats were in almost uninterrupted power for 44 years (though during World War II all democratic parties took part in the government). The party increased its support during the 1950s, gaining more than 20 per cent of the vote in the 1958 general elections, but subsequently it declined, gaining only 11.6 per cent of the vote in the 1970 elections, prior to which it changed its name from Conservative to Moderate Party.

Later the party advanced again, gaining 15.6 per cent of the vote in the 1976 elections, whereupon it entered a coalition government (with the Centre and Liberal parties), which was dissolved in October 1978 but re-established after the September 1979 elections, in which the party made a significant advance. The Moderate Party left the coalition in May 1981 amid disagreements over fiscal policy. In the elections of September 1982 the party gained further support (23.6 per cent of the vote) and thus became the dominant non-socialist party in Sweden, although the Social Democrats were returned to power.

Orientation. The party combines a conservative heritage with liberal ideas into a moderate, anti-socialist policy in favour of a free-market economy and individual freedom of choice.

Structure. The party has around 1,000 local and 31 regional associations, a party congress of 219 delegates and a party executive of 19 members.

Membership. 180,000.

Publications. *Medborgaren* (members' monthly), 100,000

International affiliations. International Democrat Union; European Democrat Union

---

Socialist Party (Swedish Group)

Address. Ake Spross, Bergsbrunna, Villawag 58, 75 256 Uppsala, Sweden

Orientation. This small leftist formation has links with the Socialist Party of Great Britain.

Swedish Social Democratic Labour Party
Sveriges Socialdemokratiska Arbetareparti (SAP)

Address. Socialdemokraterna, Svea-vägen 68, 105 60 Stockholm, Sweden

Leadership. Olof Palme (ch.); Bo Toresson (sec.)

Founded. April 1889

History. The party sent its first member to the *Riksdag* in 1896, namely Hjalmar Branting, who, after being Minister of Finance in 1917–18, became Prime Minister in Sweden's first Social Democratic Government in 1920; he was Prime Minister again in 1921–23 and in 1924–25. The percentage of votes gained by the party rose from 28.5 in 1911 to 53.8 in 1940, whereafter it declined to 46.7 in 1944 and remained more or less stable until 1968, when it rose to 50.1; in the three succeeding elections its percentage fell to 42.9 in 1976, but rose slightly to 43.3 in September 1979 and to 45.6 per cent in September 1982.

Except for a short interval in 1936, the party was in office from 1932 to 1976—in coalition with the Centre Party between 1936 and 1939 and between 1951 and 1957, in a four-party coalition during World War II, and at other times as a minority party requiring the support of one or more other parties on important issues. The party's 44 years of virtually uninterrupted power established the record for continuous governmental power by a social democratic party, and also resulted in Sweden becoming what is widely regarded as a model social democracy. During its 90 years of existence the party has had only four leaders, namely Hjalmar Branting, Per-Albin Hansson, Tage Erlander and Olof Palme (since 1969).

Having gained 166 seats in the *Riksdag* in the elections of Sept. 19, 1982, the party returned to power (after six years in opposition) and formed a minority Government supported by the Communist Left Party (with 20 seats in the House).

Orientation. The party seeks "to transform society in such a way that the right of decision over production and its distribution is placed in the hands of the entire nation"; to replace "a social order based on classes" by "a community of people in partnership on a basis of liberty and equality"; and to work for "Sweden's non-alignment and neutrality in war" and for "world peace on the basis of self-determination for every nation, of social and economic justice, of détente and disarmament and of international co-operation".

Structure. The party is based on local Social Democratic clubs and has "labour communes" in every municipality (to which local trade union branches are affiliated), forming party districts in which an annual district congress is the highest policy-making body. Every party district is divided into constituencies for the election of delegates to the party congress, held every three years. There is an executive with executive committees, constituting the supreme policy-making body between congresses.

Membership. 1,060,000

Publications. *Aftonbladet* (trade union daily), 400,000; *Stockholms Tidningen*, 44,500; *Aktuelt*, 140,000; *Tiden* (ideological monthly)

International affiliations. Socialist International

Swedish Workers' Communist Party
Sveriges Arbetarepartiet Kommunisterna (SAK)

Leadership. Rolf Hagel (ch.)

Founded. February 1977

History. The party was formed by three local sections of the Communist Left Party (VPK), and was joined by two of the 17 VPK members elected to the *Riksdag* in 1976, although neither was re-elected in September 1979, when the party obtained only 10,797 votes and failed to secure representation (as it did also in the September 1982 elections).

Orientation. The SAK, a party "based on the principles of Marxism-Leninism and proletarian internationalism", rejects the "Eurocommunist" orientation of the VPK leadership and has close relations with the Communist Party of the Soviet Union.

Switzerland

Capital: Berne   Pop. 6,500,000

The Swiss Confederation is a republic in which power is held by the electorate (consisting of all citizens above the age of 20 years). The latter not only elects members of the Federal Assembly (*Bundesversammlung* or *Assemblée Fédérale*) and of cantonal and local councils but also has powers to vote on constitutional amendments or on other matters, including international treaties, in a referendum if requested by a minimum of voters (50,000 for constitutional amendments and 30,000—or eight cantons—for other matters).

The bicameral Federal Assembly comprises (i) a Council of States (*Ständerat* or *Conseil des États*) consisting of two members for each of 20 cantons and one for each of six half-cantons, the electoral process being left to be decided upon by each of the cantons or half-cantons, and (ii) a 200-member National Council (*Nationalrat* or *Conseil National*) elected for a four-year term in proportion to the population of the cantons (each of the 20 cantons and six half-cantons being represented by at least one member). In most cantons and half-cantons the elections are conducted under a list system with proportional representation, with voters being able to cast preferential votes; in a minority of cantons and half-cantons a simple majority system applies in single-member constituencies.

The President of the Confederation, who is also President of the *Bundesrat* or *Conseil Fédéral* (seven-member Government), is elected, together with a Vice-President, for a one-year term by the two Houses of Parliament, which also elect the members of the Government.

In elections to the National Council held on Oct. 23, 1983, seats were gained as follows: Radical Democratic Party 54, Social Democratic Party 47, Christian Democratic Party 42, Swiss People's Party 23, Independents' Party 8, Swiss Liberal Party 8, National Action/Republican Movement 5, Progressive Organizations of Switzerland/Autonomous Socialist Party 4, Evangelical People's Party 3, Federation of Green Parties in Switzerland 3, Party of Labour (Communist) 1, Free List (independent ecologist) 1, independent 1. The turnout in these elections was 48.9 per cent, as against 48 per cent in 1979.

Autonomous Socialist Party
Partito Socialista Autonomo (PSA)

Address. Case postale 319, 6501 Bellinzona, Ticino, Switzerland

Leadership. Werner Carobbio (sec.)

Founded. April 1969

History. The PSA was formed by left-wing elements of the Social Democratic Party centred in Ticino, who broke away to form a "Marxist, revolutionary, anti-capitalist and internationalist" party. It contested the October 1979 elections on a joint list with the Progressive Organizations of Switzerland (POCH) which won three seats in the *Nationalrat* (Lower House), one of which went to the PSA. The PSA has eight representatives in the Ticino cantonal parliament. In the 1983 general elections, which it again contested on the POCH list, the PSA retained its seat in the *Nationalrat*.

Orientation. The PSA seeks "to struggle for socialism and the overthrow of capitalism".

Structure. The party has 65 local groups, five regional sections, a 39-member cantonal committee, a seven-member political bureau and a three-member secretariat.

Membership. 1,200
Publications. *Politica Nuova* (weekly),
3,500

Christian Democratic Party of Switzerland
Christlichdemokratische Volkspartei der
Schweiz/Parti Démocrate-Chrétien Suisse,
(PDC)

Address. Klaraweg 6, Case postale
1759, CH-3001 Berne, Switzerland
Leadership. Flavio Corri (pres.); Dr
Hans Peter Fagagnini (s.g.)
Founded. April 1912
History. The party was founded as the
Swiss Conservative Party (*Parti Conservateur Suisse*), following the establishment of
national (i.e. not cantonal) parties by
Socialists in 1882 and Radicals in 1894 and
a call for a Swiss (Roman) Catholic Party.
By adopting the name Conservative Party
the founders emphasized the political
rather than the religious (denominational)
character of the new party, which was
joined by representatives of Christian trade
unions, which had set up Christian Social
parties in denominationally mixed cantons.
In 1957 the party adopted the name *Parti
Conservateur Chrétien-Social Suisse*, and in
1970 took its present name as that of a
party organized at federal level (and no
longer a union of cantonal parties).
Since 1919 the PDC has been represented
in the Government (Federal Council) by
two of its members and since the 1975
elections it has been the strongest party in
the Upper House and the third-largest in
the *Nationalrat* (Lower House); it also
has the strongest contingent of women. Its
share of the vote in the October 1983
elections was 20.2 per cent.
Orientation. A party congress of delegates held in Berne on March 26,
1983, approved a programme for 1983–87
advocating the encouragement of family
life, protection of the individual, preservation of the economy and of a healthy
environment, freedom and responsibility
of the media, an efficient administration,
"peace in independence and solidarity"
(i.e. maintenance of the country's armed
forces), increased aid for the Third World,
support for genuine disarmament efforts
and détente, and entry into the United
Nations (with a declaration of neutrality),
the International Monetary Fund and the
World Bank.
Structure. The party's supreme organ is
an assembly of delegates to which each
canton sends a delegation the size of which
is proportional to its political strength. The
assembly prepares an action programme for
each new Parliament and determines the

party's attitude to federal bills; it elects
the party president, the members of the
party committee (the PDC's steering and
executive organ) and the party's presidency
(the committee's executive organ), a control commission and an arbitration tribunal.
Membership. 60,000
Publications. *Inside* (a party workers'
journal), 2,400
International affiliations. Christian
Democratic International; European Christian Democratic Union; European Democrat Union (permanent observer)

Evangelical People's Party
Evangelische Volkspartei der Schweiz
(EVP)/Parti Évangélique Suisse

Address. Josefstr. 32, Postfach 7334,
CH-Zurich, Switzerland
Leadership. Paul Gysel (pres.); Hans
Schoch (sec.)
Founded. 1919
History. The party first became represented in the *Nationalrat* in 1919; it held
two seats in that House in 1959–67 and
has held three ever since. The EVP's share
of the vote in the October 1983 general
elections was 2.1 per cent.
Orientation. The EVP is a progressive
party with principles based on Protestant
precepts.

Federation of Green Parties of Switzerland
Grüne Parteienföderation der Schweiz/
Fédération Suisse des Partis Ecologistes

Founded. May 1983
History. This moderate ecologist Federation was formed as an alliance of the
Groupement pour l'Environnement in the
canton of Vaud (which had gained one
seat in the National Council in 1979),
the *Parti Ecologique* of Geneva, the
Mouvement pour l'Environnement of Neuf-
chatel, the *Grüne Partei* of Zurich and the
Green Party of North-West Switzerland. In
the 1983 general elections this Federation
obtained 2.9 per cent. of the vote and
three seats in the National Council. In
these elections an independent ecologist (a
former member of the Radical Democratic
Party) gained one seat on a Free List
(*Freie Liste*) in Berne.
The 1983 elections were also contested
by a group known as *Alternativ Grüne*,
which had broken away from the Federation, but it gained no seat.

International affiliations. The Federation has links with other Green movements within the European Greens but has
not formally joined the latter organization.

Green Federation
Grüne Föderation/Fédération Verte

Formed. June 1983
History. This left-wing Federation was
formed by 12 different ecologist groups.
Orientation. The Federation has called
for a "change in our way of living", an
"active peace policy" and the eventual
abolition of the Swiss Army.

Independents' Party
Landesring der Unabhängigen (LdU)/
Alliance des Indépendants

Address. Laupenstrasse 3, CH-3008
Berne, Switzerland
Leadership. Dr Walter Biel (pres.); Dr
Jürg Schultheiss (sec.)
Founded. 1936
History. The party has, since World
War II, been well represented in the
Nationalrat, where it held 10 seats between
1951 and 1967, when its representation
rose to 16. Since then it has declined (to
13 in 1971, 11 in 1975 and eight in 1979
and 1983). It has not taken part in
government. In the October 1983 general
elections the LdU obtained 4 per cent of
the vote.
Orientation. Liberal and social, the
LdU aspires to defend middle-class and
consumers' interests.

Jura Entente
Entente Jurassienne

Leadership. Jean-Claude Crevoisier
History. This movement for autonomy
for the Jura canton won one seat in the
Nationalrat in October 1979 (in the Berne
canton), the candidate elected being Jean-
Claude Crevoisier, a former Social Democratic deputy and left-wing advocate of
separatism for the Jura canton; it did not
retain this seat in the 1983 elections,
however.

Jura Popular Unity
Unité Jurassienne et Populaire

Leadership. Jean-Marie Mauron (pres.)
History. This party gained one seat in
the *Nationalrat* in the October 1979

elections, but did not retain it in the 1983
elections.
Orientation. Based at Tavannes (in the
canton of Berne), this right-wing movement
stands for the incorporation of the southern
Jura in the canton of the Jura established
on Jan. 1, 1979.

Jura Rally
Rassemblement Jurassien

Orientation. Constituted by members
of various Swiss parties, this group stands
for the creation of "one canton of all six
francophone districts" of Jura and for the
"liberation" of francophone territory which
is not yet part of the canton.

National Action for People and Homeland (NA)
Nationale Aktion für Volk und Heimat/
Action Nationale/Azione Nazionale

Address. Postfach 59, CH-8956 Killwan-
gen, Switzerland
Leadership. Hans Zwicky (ch.); Anita
Wilhelm (sec.)
Founded. 1961
History. In 1968 the NA launched a
campaign for setting a ceiling on the
proportion of foreigners resident in Switzerland and initiated a national referendum
to that end, which was defeated by a slight
majority in June 1970. Although the
Government subsequently issued certain
restrictive regulations on foreign residents
the NA continued its campaign and
launched another initiative, which was also
rejected by a majority of citizens in 1974.

Following an increase in the number of
naturalizations the NA undertook a further
initiative together with one demanding the
submission of all future treaties with
foreign countries to a referendum. The
Federal Council and Parliament thereupon
drafted a counter-proposal which was
approved in a referendum in March 1977.
In 1981 the NA asked for a referendum
on a proposed bill relaxing some of the
existing restrictions on foreign workers,
and this bill was subsequently, on June 6,
1982, rejected by a large majority of those
citizens who took part in the vote.

In the 1967 elections to the *Nationalrat*
the NA gained one seat for its founder,
Dr James Schwarzenbach who, however,
left the NA in 1970 and later founded the
Swiss Republican Movement (see separate
entry). In the 1971 *Nationalrat* elections
the NA gained four seats (while the

Republican Movement obtained seven); by October 1979 the NA's representation had fallen to two; but in 1983 it rose again to four seats, after the party had contested the elections on a joint list with the Republican Movement which obtained 3.5 per cent of the vote.

Orientation. In addition to its central aim, the party calls for "the protection of the natural environment, full employment of the Swiss population, political independence, and security, law and order in liberty".

Structure. The party is directed by a 35-member central committee; its executive organ is a nine-member directorate headed by the central president; and its supreme authority is a national conference of delegates.

Membership. 6,000

Publications. *Volk und Heimat*, 7,000 subscribers; *Peuple et Patrie*, about 1,000 subscribers

---

**Political and Social Action Movement
Mouvement d'Action Politique et Sociale**

Leadership. Luc de Meuron (pres.)

Founded. October 1977

History. This Movement replaced a previous *Mouvement National d'Action Républicaine et Sociale*, which had a programme similar to that of the (right-wing, anti-immigrant) Swiss Republican Movement (see separate entry). Luc de Meuron had been president of the Republican Movement for Western Switzerland.

Orientation. In its charter the Movement lists as its objectives the defence of the family, of private enterprise and of local communities.

**Progressive Organizations of Switzerland
Progressive Organisationen der Schweiz/
Organisations Progressistes Suisses (POCH)**

Address. Postfach 725, Aarauerstr. 7, CH-4600 Olten, Basel, Switzerland

Leadership. Georg Degen (cent. sec.)

Founded. 1971

History. The POCH first contested elections in 1975 by presenting joint lists with the Autonomous Socialist Party (PSA) in Ticino, but only one candidate (of the PSA) was elected to the *Nationalrat*. In the 1979 elections the POCH/PSA alliance gained three seats (one of them for the PSA). In the October 1983 elections the POCH took three of the four seats obtained by the alliance, which secured

2.2 per cent of the vote. In cantonal elections held in April 1983 the POCH increased its seats from one to three in Zurich and from five to 10 in Lucerne.

Orientation. The POCH are an independent left-wing formation based on "scientific socialism" and ecological standpoints, campaigning for "a classless society without exploitation and repression". In international politics the party's guideline is anti-imperialism.

Membership. 1,000

**Radical Democratic Party of Switzerland
Parti Radical-Démocratique Suisse/Freisinnig-Demokratische Partei der Schweiz (FDP)**

Address. Place de la Gare 10, CH-3001 Berne, Case postale 2642, Switzerland

Leadership. Dr Bruno Hunziker (pres.); Hans-Rudolf Leuenberger (sec.)

Founded. 1894

History. The FDP claims to be "the founder of modern Switzerland" in that "after a confrontation with conservative forces in 1848 it laid the foundations for the Swiss federal state as it exists today". An FDP group was established in the Federal Assembly in 1878, i.e. 16 years before the establishment of the party as such.

The introduction of proportional representation in 1919 diminished the party's influence in the *Nationalrat* but it held a dominant position in the federal Government until 1959 when it formed a coalition Government with the Social Democrats, Christian Democrats and Agrarians; this coalition has been maintained ever since (the Agrarians becoming the Swiss People's Party in 1971). In the October 1983 general elections the FDP became the country's strongest party with 23.4 per cent of the vote and 54 of the 200 *Nationalrat* seats.

Orientation. Regarding itself as the heir to 19th-century liberal ideas, the FDP seeks "to develop rights, to ensure prosperity on the basis of a free economy, to defend Swiss independence by armed neutrality, to protect the autonomy of the cantons and to develop social security".

Structure. The cantonal party groups elect a 300-member assembly which in turn elects a 50-member council of delegates, which has permanent committees. There are a head committee of 9–11 members elected by the assembly and a secretariat-general.

Membership. 140,000

Publications. *Information*, 5,000; *Revue Politique*, 1,200; *Der Freisinn*, 70,000

International affiliations. Liberal International

437

Socialist Workers' Party
Parti Ouvrier Socialiste/Sozialistiche Arbeiterpartei

Founded. 1968
History. This party derives from the Revolutionary Marxist League (LMR) which was set up (in 1968) by some 100 French-speaking intellectuals who defected from the Swiss (Communist) Party of Labour. It has been particularly active in trade unions and also in the anti-nuclear movement. The party's new name was adopted in 1980.
Orientation. The party aims at being the vanguard of the New Left in Switzerland and in the class struggle for a new social order.
Structure. The party has a 34-member central committee which is elected by delegates to a national congress and which in turn elects a political bureau. It applies the principle of democratic centralism, and it was in 1978 estimated to have some 500 militant members.
Publications. La Brèche (periodical)
International affiliations. The party is the Swiss section of the Fourth (Trotskyist) International.

Swiss Liberal Party
Parti Libéral Suisse/Liberale Partei der Schweiz (LPS)

Address. Case postale 625, CH-3018 Berne, Switzerland
Leadership. Dr Rudolf Th. Sarasin (ch.); J.-S. Eggly (cent. sec.)
History. Descended from the Liberal movement of the 19th and early 20th century, and following the absorption of the Liberals in many Swiss cantons into the Radical Democratic and Christian Democratic parties, the party maintained itself as a Liberal Party with its own identity in the four cantons of Geneva, Vaud, Neuchâtel and Basle City. These four cantonal parties together form, at national level, the current Swiss Liberal Party (which took its present name in 1977, having previously been the Liberal Democratic Union of Switzerland).

The Liberals have established close co-operation in the *Nationalrat* with the Evangelical People's Party (see separate entry). In the October 1983 general elections the LPS retained eight seats on the basis of 2.8 per cent of the vote.
Orientation. The party stands for "the maintenance of federalism and of the market economy and the guaranteeing of individual freedom and responsibility, without ignoring the need for solidarity and the necessity of the functions of the state". It also calls for protection of the individual, the maintenance of an efficient defence force and of "armed neutrality", co-operation with the Third World, improvement of the quality of life, the use of natural gas and nuclear power as an alternative to oil, and freedom of information (but with state control over radio and television frequencies).
Structure. The party's organs are an assembly of delegates and a central committee (with a central bureau), their membership being based on quotas for the different cantonal parties.
Publications. Bulletin d'Information du PLS (quarterly)
International affiliations. Liberal International

Swiss Party of Labour
Parti Suisse du Travail/Partei der Arbeit der Schweiz

Address. Vieux-Billard 25, Case postale 232, 1211 Geneva 8, Switzerland
Leadership. Armand Magnin (s.g.); Jean Vincent (hon. pres.)
Founded. October 1944
History. The party was founded mainly by Communists (whose party had been banned shortly before World War II) and left-wing socialists who had been expelled or had resigned from the Swiss Social Democratic Party. It is organized in about 12 cantons, in particular in Geneva, Vaud, Neuchâtel and Basle, and has members on about 10 local councils, among them those of Geneva, Chiasso and Le Locle.

In the October 1979 general elections the party obtained 2.1 per cent of the vote but in the 1983 elections its representation in the *Nationalrat* fell from three members to one on the basis of a share of 0.9 per cent of the vote.
Orientation. The party has defined its aims as being "to defend and promote the material and ideal interests of the Swiss population, to put into practice the equality of men and women and to free them of any kind of exploitation and subjugation, to defend and broaden democratic rights, to work for a large majority for the overcoming of capitalism, for the development of Swiss society towards socialism and later communism, to contribute to the protection and consolidation of world peace, and to aim at a balanced relationship between men, production and nature". In its principles the party bases itself on "scientific socialism, founded by Marx and

Engels, developed by Lenin and other scientists of the revolutionary movement"; it claims to define its policies in full independence, taking into account historical and national conditions.

Structure. The party's supreme organ is its congress. There are also a party conference, a central committee which directs the party's policy between sessions of the two higher organs, a political bureau, a secretariat and a central control commission. Decisions are taken on the basis of democratic centralism.

Membership. 5,000

Publications. *Voix Ouvrière* (weekly, in French); *Vorwärts* (weekly, in German); *Lavoratore* (weekly, in Italian)

International affiliations. The party is recognized by the Communist parties of the Soviet-bloc countries.

Swiss Party of the Handicapped and Socially Disadvantaged
Schweizerische Partei der Behinderten und Sozialbenachteiligten (SPBS)

Leadership. Fritz Bütikofer (pres.)
Founded. March 1984
History. This new party was formed in Berne with the aim of launching a popular initiative to secure for handicapped people the right to work.
Membership. 100

Swiss People's Party
Schweizerische Volkspartei (SVP)/Parti Suisse de l'Union Démocratique du Centre (UDC)

Address. Ahornweg 2, CH-3000 Berne 9, Switzerland
Leadership. Dr Fritz Hofmann (pres.); Dr Max Friedli (s.g.)
Founded. 1971
History. The party arose out of (i) the Farmers', Traders' and Citizens' (i.e. Agrarian) Party formed in Zurich in 1917 and in Berne in 1918, and joined by the artisans and former Conservative Liberals of the canton of Berne in 1921, becoming a government party in 1929, and (ii) the former Swiss Democratic Party (founded in 1942), which had its origins in the Democratic Party established in the canton of Zurich in 1867, the Democratic and Workers' Party set up in the canton of Glarus in 1890 and the Democratic Party founded in Grisons in 1942.

Since the union of the two parties as the Swiss People's Party in 1971 the latter has continued to hold the one seat in the Federal Council (*Bundesrat* or Government) which the Agrarian party had held since 1959 in coalition with the Radical Democrats, Social Democrats and Christian Democrats. In the October 1983 general elections the SVP retained its 23 seats in the *Nationalrat* on the basis of 11.1 per cent of the vote.

Orientation. The SVP is a liberal democratic formation.

Structure. The party is organized at local, district and cantonal level, has an assembly of about 600 delegates, a central committee of about 70 members and a head committee of some 20 members.

Membership. 83,000

Swiss Republican Movement
Schweizerische Republikanische Bewegung/ Mouvement Républicain Suisse

Address. Busenhardstr. 9, CH-8704 Herrliberg, Switzerland
Leadership. Franz Baumgartner (l.)
Founded. 1971
History. The movement was founded by Dr James Schwarzenbach, the former leader of the National Campaign against Foreign Domination, which had unsuccessfully campaigned for legislation to reduce the foreign population in Switzerland. In the 1971 general elections the Republican Movement gained seven seats in the *Nationalrat*, while the National Campaign won four. After January 1973 the two organizations co-operated in one parliamentary group, but Dr Schwarzenbach and three other Republican Movement members of the *Nationalrat* left the parliamentary group in May 1974.

In the 1975 elections the movement gained only four seats in the *Nationalrat*, and its decline (to one seat only, in Geneva, in 1979) was largely attributed to the rejection of its radical proposals by the parliamentary majority and to legislation restricting immigration and permanent settlement of foreigners. The movement's strongholds are mainly in German-speaking Switzerland. It contested the 1983 general elections in alliance with the National Action (see separate entry) and this alliance gained five seats in the *Nationalrat* (and 3.5 per cent of the vote), including one for the Republican Movement.

Orientation. A right-wing formation aiming at protecting Switzerland from foreign influence, the Swiss Republican Movement has also campaigned since 1979 for the protection of small businesses.

Swiss Social Democratic Party
Sozialdemokratische Partei der Schweiz
(SPS)/Parti Socialiste Suisse/Partito Social-
ista Svizzero

Address. Postfach 4084, CH-3001, Berne, Switzerland

Leadership. Helmut Hubacher (ch.); Christoph Berger (g.s.)

Founded. 1870

History. Following its initial foundation the party was organized into a federal body in 1882 and quickly became a powerful political force in the country, particularly after the introduction of proportional representation in 1919. In the post-1945 period it has regularly obtained about 25 per cent of the total vote and since 1959 has held two of the seven seats in a four-party coalition Government also including the Radical Democrats, Christian Democrats and People's Party.

During the 1970s "new left" elements were in the ascendancy within the party, which accordingly adopted more radical policies (although with little effect on governmental action). However, at a congress held in Lugano in November 1982 a new programme of basic principles was adopted by a large majority, confirming the reformist, social democratic character of the party and thus representing a clear defeat for the left wing, which had argued for a socialist programme based on the concept of self-management.

In the October 1982 general elections the SPS was outpolled by the Radical Democratic Party for the first time for 58 years, being reduced to 22.8 per cent of the vote and 47 of the 200 *Nationalrat* seats as against 24.4 per cent and 51 seats in 1979. Thereafter opposition within the SPS to continued participation in the federal coalition Government came to a head when the party's nomination of female left-winger Lillian Uchtenhagen for a ministerial post failed to secure the support of the other coalition parties. However, a recommendation from the executive in favour of withdrawal from the Government was effectively rejected by an emergency party congress in Berne in February 1984 by 773 votes to 511.

Orientation. The 1982 Lugano programme of basic principles commits the SPS to a social democratic, reformist approach to politics, seeking to relate basic socialist concepts to the new characteristics of a modern industrial society. The programme also called for a nuclear-weapons-free Europe.

Structure. The party's highest authority is the congress, which elects an executive and other top office-holders.

International affiliations. Socialist International.

Vaud League
Ligue Vaudoise

History. This small formation has sought to promote what it regards as the "historically founded" legitimacy of the canton of Vaud (Waadtland).

Vigilance

History. This movement, allied to the Swiss Republican Movement (see separate entry), has been represented in the Geneva City Council since 1967. It increased the number of seats held in the Council from seven gained in 1979 to 13 in March 1983, and those held in the Geneva Cantonal Council from 10 to 21 in the same period.

Orientation. The group has campaigned against foreign influences and in particular against the admission to Switzerland of refugees and of non-Whites.

Syria

Capital: Damascus   Pop. 10,420,000

The Syrian Arab Republic is, under its 1973 Constitution, a "socialist popular democracy" with an executive President, who is secretary-general of the *Baath* Arab Socialist Party and also president of the National Progressive Front (NPF) embracing the country's five legal parties—the *Baath* Arab Socialist Party, the (Nasserite) Socialist Unionist Movement, the (also Nasserite) Arab Socialist Union, the (anti-Egyptian) Arab Socialist Party and the Syrian Communist Party. There is a legislative People's Council (*Majlis al Shaab*) elected for a four-year term by universal adult suffrage of citizens above the age of 18 years and under a simple-majority system in single-member constituencies. The President appoints a Vice-President, a Prime Minister and other ministers.

In elections to the People's Council held on Nov. 9–10, 1981, the NPF took all 195 seats (whereas in 1977 it had obtained 159 seats and the remaining 36 had gone to independents). Of the 1,558 candidates 45 were returned unopposed. The *Baath* Arab Socialist Party won 60 per cent of the seats, and the Communist Party (which, although a member of the NPF, contested the elections independently) lost all six seats which it had held previously. Two Communists were nevertheless appointed to the new Cabinet formed on Dec. 3, 1982.

Arab Socialist Party (ASP)
Al-Hizb al-Ishtiraki al-Arabi

Leadership. Abdul Ghani Kannout
History. The ASP has taken part in government since 1970. In the 1973 elections to the People's Council it obtained three seats and has continued to be represented therein as part of the National Progressive Front.
Orientation. The ASP is anti-Egyptian and seeks a return to free competition among political parties.

Arab Socialist Union (ASU)
Al-Ittihad al-Ishtiraki al-Arabi

Leadership. Dr Jamal Atasi (l.); Fawzi Kayyali (s.g.)
History. The ASU dates back to Syria's union with Egypt (under President Nasser) in the United Arab Republic (1958–61). In the 1973 elections it obtained six seats in the People's Council and has continued to be represented therein as part of the National Progressive Front.

Orientation. The ASU subscribes to "Nasserist" socialist ideals, although its original pro-Egyptian attitude has been moderated in the light of recent Syrian-Egyptian estrangement over the general Middle East situation.

Baath Arab Socialist Party
Hizb al-Baath al-Arabi al-Ishtiraki

Address. National Leadership, P.O.B. 849, Damascus, Syria
Leadership. President Hafez al-Assad (s.g.)
Founded. April 1947
History. The foundation of an Arab *Baath* Party was officially announced at its first congress in Damascus, where a four-member leadership consisting of Michel Aflaq, Salah Bitar, Jalal al-Sayyed and Wahin al-Ghanem was elected by 200 delegates, most of them from Syria but others being Jordanians, Lebanese, Palestinians or nationals of other Arab countries. The party arose out of a merger of (i) the Arab Revival Movement, which was founded in Damascus early in 1940 by

441

Michel Aflaq and Salah Bitar and which changed its name to the Arab *Baath* in 1943, and (ii) the Arab *Baath* Party, founded in Damascus in 1940 by Zaki al-Arsouzi, this group being more inclined to socialism than the Arab Revival Movement.

In the early 1950s the party began to establish branches in most other Arab countries, in particular in Iraq, Jordan and Lebanon. In December 1953 it absorbed the (Syrian) Socialist Arab Party and assumed the name of *Baath* Arab Socialist Party. In 1958 Michel Aflaq announced the dissolution of the *Baath* in Syria and Egypt, but this dissolution was denounced late in August 1960 by a party congress convened in Beirut (Lebanon), which decided to continue the party's organization and activities in Syria and Egypt. In February 1963 it led a successful revolution in Iraq, and in March 1963 a similar one in Syria.

After the party's rule in Iraq had been overthrown at the end of 1963, the party's main power base was in Syria, where it has implemented important political, social and economic changes on the constitutional basis that the party leads the state. Following a crisis in its ranks in 1966, the party expelled its rightist wing, in which Michel Aflaq and Salah Bitar were prominent.

Orientation. The *Baath* stands for Arab unity, freedom and socialism (although the party is not Marxist) and in general for the unification of all Arab countries in one independent Arab state with a socialist regime. The party has therefore given support to the Algerian revolution and opposed all military pacts in the region. In 1955 it adopted a non-aligned position. It expressed solidarity with Egypt in the 1956 Suez war, contributed to the establishment of the unity of Egypt and Syria in 1958, opposed Syria's separation from Egypt in 1961, and demanded the liberation of all Arab lands occupied by Israel in 1967 and the restoration of the rights of the Palestinian people, including their right to self-determination and the establishment of their own independent state on their land. Following Syria's participation with Egypt in the October 1973 war, the *Baath* opposed President Sadat's policy after that war, in particular the Camp David agreements and the Egypt-Israel peace treaty. The *Baath*-dominated Syrian Government thereafter initiated a plan for unity between Iraq and Syria in 1978, participated in the "Confrontation and Steadfastness Front" in 1978, concluded a friendship treaty with the Soviet Union in 1980, confronted Israel on its invasion of Lebanon in 1982, and rejected the Israel-Lebanon agreement of 1983.

Structure. A plenary national congress held every four years elects a 21-member regional command and a 75-member central committee, which in turn elects a secretary-general. Each Arab country in which there is a party organization has its own regional leadership with its own regional secretary.

Membership. Over 800,000 in Syria

Publications. *Baath* (daily newspaper and official organ), 40,000; *Al-Munadel* (monthly magazine on ideological, organizational and political issues), 10,000

Socialist Unionist Movement (SUM)
Al-Haraka at-Tawhidiyya al-Ishtirakiyya

Leadership. Sami Soufan (l.); Dr Abdul Fayiz Ismail (s.g.)

History. The SUM has been represented in the Government since 1967 and is also represented in the People's Assembly through its membership of the National Progressive Front.

Orientation. Like the Arab Socialist Union (see separate entry), the SUM proclaims "Nasserist" socialist ideals but has tended to moderate its pro-Egyptian stance in the light of the serious tension between the Syrian and Egyptian Governments.

Syrian Communist Party (SCP)

Leadership. Khalid Bakdash (s.g.)

Founded. 1924

History. Until 1958 the party was part of a joint Communist Party of Syria and Lebanon, and it was forced underground when all political parties were abolished in Syria by decree in March 1958. Following the revolution of March 1963 and the assumption of power by the nationalist Baathists in 1966, co-operation was established between them and the SCP at government level. The SCP's secretary-general had been the first Communist to be elected to Parliament (in 1954), and the SCP was represented in the Government in 1966–68 and after 1970. In the 1973 elections to the People's Council it obtained seven seats.

Following an attempt made in 1971 by a majority of the SCP's leadership to make the party less dependent on Soviet influence, and a reconciliation among most of its leaders upon Soviet advice, a minority was expelled from the SCP in December 1973 and formed a separate (pro-Palestinian) organization, led by Riad Turk, in January 1974.

442

As part of the National Progressive Front the SCP gained six seats in the People's Council in 1977, but it contested the 1981 elections on its own and retained no seat in the Council.

Orientation. The SCP, regarded as the largest Communist party in the Arab world, supports the "progressive" trends in the ruling *Baath* party and the strengthening of friendly relations with the Soviet Union.

Publications. Nidal al Shaab (People's Struggle)

International affiliations. The SCP is recognized by the Communist parties of the Soviet-bloc countries.

Taiwan

Capital: Taipei

Pop. 19,000,000

Taiwan, officially the Republic of China, has a President elected (and re-eligible) by the National Assembly for a six-year term. The National Assembly, the vast majority of whose members are life members elected in mainland China in 1948, has limited powers. The country's highest administrative organ is the Executive *Yuan*, whose Council (the Cabinet) is responsible to the Legislative *Yuan* composed of elected members, the overwhelming majority of whom also hold "life-term" seats, with nearly 300 surviving from among those elected in 1947–48 to represent constituencies on the Chinese mainland. Elections to fill Taiwan seats have been held from time to time, and in 1980 a total of 27 members were appointed from among overseas Chinese communities. The minimum voting age is 20 years, and candidates may not stand for parties other than the Kuomintang and are subject to other restrictions, such as attending joint rallies with other candidates.

In elections to 71 seats in the Legislative *Yuan*, held on Dec. 3, 1983, the Kuomintang gained 62 seats and the remaining nine were won by independents. Among independent candidates a loose *tangwai* group had been formed under the leadership of Kang Ning-hsiang to work for democratic freedoms and a multi-party system, but it had no electoral success. The Minister of the Interior reaffirmed on Jan. 18, 1984, that the Government would not authorize the formation of new parties.

China Democratic Socialist Party

Address. No. 6, Lane 357, Ho-ping East Road, Section 2, Taipei, Taiwan

Leadership. Yang Yu-tse (ch. of presidium); Chang Yun-ching (s.g.)

Founded. 1932

History. The party arose out of a merger between the National Socialists (a political association of scholars and professors organized in 1932) and the Democratic Constitutionalists (organized in San Francisco, USA, to promote constitutional government in China), which both supported the Kuomintang Government in the war of resistance against Japan and later united in the present party. The party sent delegates to the Chinese Constituent Assembly in November 1946 and, after the promulgation of the Constitution in January 1947, participated in the Legislative *Yuan*. On April 13, 1947, it signed a common political platform with the Kuomintang, the Young China Party and non-party members. In 1948 it had 212 members in the (Taiwan) National Assembly and 29 in the Legislative *Yuan*. By May 1979 its respective representation in these bodies was 35 and six.

Orientation. The party is concerned with promoting democracy in keeping with Chinese national characteristics, traditions and culture; making China a democratic socialist country by democratic means; raising living standards through industrialization in co-ordination with agricultural development; and assuring freedom from want and narrowing the gap between rich and poor.

Structure. In addition to a five-member presidium, the party has a central standing committee, a central control committee, a secretariat and various specialized departments and committees.

Membership. 30,000

Publications. *Renaissance* (Taipei, monthly); *Universe* (Taipei, monthly); *Liberty* (Hong Kong, monthly)

Nationalist Party of China
Chung-kuo Kuo-min-tang or Kuomintang

Address. 11 Chungshan South Road, Taipei, Taiwan

Leadership. Chiang Ching-kuo (ch.); Tsiang Yien-si (s.g.)

Founded. November 1894

History. The party was founded as the *Hsing Chung Hui* by Dr Sun Yat-sen, the father of the Republic of China, and played a major role in the overthrow of the Manchu regime in 1911; it was renamed the Kuomintang in October 1919. Upon Dr Sun's death in 1925 the leadership passed to the late President Chiang Kai-shek who by 1927 had unified most of China and who in that year purged the Kuomintang of Communists (accepted as individual members of the party under Sun Yat-sen) and thus initiated over two decades of civil war.

Chiang Kai-shek's attempts to reconstruct the nation by consolidation under the Nationalist Party (Kuomintang) were interrupted by the Japanese invasion of Manchuria in 1931 and the consequent war with Japan, for part of which the Kuomintang co-operated with the Communists against the invaders. Although recognised by the Allies as the government of China during and after World War II, the Kuomintang and Chiang Kai-shek were faced with increasing opposition from 1945 and were eventually defeated by the Communists in a renewed civil war.

With the Communist victory in 1949, the Kuomintang Government withdrew to Taiwan, from where it subsequently continued to strive for the recovery of mainland China and where the party has remained the predominant political force notwithstanding the death of Chiang Kai-shek in April 1975.

Orientation. Guided by Dr Sun's ideology of San Min Chu I, the party aims at implementing the "three principles of the people"—(i) to recover the Chinese mainland from communism to establish a democratic, prosperous and peaceful China, (ii) to rejuvenate the national culture and (iii) to remain in the camp of democracy.

Structure. Organized on democratic lines, the Kuomintang enforces majority rule within its quadrennial (party) congress, which is the party's supreme organ, while during its recess that role is taken by the central committee, which is headed by a chairman assisted by party councillors, a secretary-general and three deputy secretaries-general. Party policies and activities are carried out by 12 departments under the central committee.

Membership. 2,070,000

Publications. *Chung-yang Jih-pao* (Central Daily News); *Chung-hwa Jih-pao* (China Daily News); *Chung-yang Yueh-kan* (Central Monthly)

Young China Party
Ching-nien Tang

Founded. 1923

Orientation. This is a small anticommunist party which has generally supported the Kuomintang.

Tanzania

Capital: Dar es Salaam (to be replaced by Dodoma) Pop. 20,000,000

The United Republic of Tanzania is a one-party state in which, under the 1977 Constitution, the Revolutionary Party (*Chama Cha Mapinduzi*) is the dominant organization both at central and at regional level. An executive President is elected for a four-year term by universal adult suffrage, is re-eligible and is the head of state and of the Government; there is also a Vice-President who is the head of the Executive of the islands of Zanzibar and Pemba. (Under the 1977 Constitution the President and Vice-President have to be natives respectively of mainland Tanzania and of Zanzibar, or vice versa.) There is a Cabinet headed by a Prime Minister, while a separate Executive in Zanzibar deals with internal Zanzibari affairs under the control of the Revolutionary Council of Zanzibar.

Legislative power is vested in a National Assembly partly elected for a five-year term by universal adult suffrage of citizens in single-member constituencies and partly appointed. The minimum voting age is 18 years. Nominees for elective seats in the National Assembly must be named by at least 25 voters registered in the electoral district for selection by the district conference of the Revolutionary Party, the national executive committee of which finally chooses two or more candidates who will compete for the seat.

In elections held on Oct. 26, 1980, for the 111 elective seats in the National Assembly (including 10 seats for the islands of Zanzibar and Pemba), each single-member constituency was contested by two candidates; some 40 members of the previous Assembly were defeated. The elected members selected another 40 from among candidates nominated to represent the regions and mass organizations.

Revolutionary Party
Chama Cha Mapinduzi (CCM)

Address. P.O. Box 50, Dodoma, Tanzania

Leadership. Mwalimu (Dr) Julius Kambarage Nyerere (ch.); Ali Hassan Mwinyi (vice-ch.); Rashidi Mfaume Kawawa (s.g.)

Founded. February 1977

History. The CCM was formed by the amalgamation of (i) the Tanganyika African National Union (TANU) which, established in July 1954 under Dr Nyerere's leadership, led Tanganyika to independence on Dec. 9, 1961, and the status of a republic a year later, and (ii) the Afro-Shirazi Party (ASP) which was founded in February 1957 under the leadership of the late Sheikh Abeid Amani Karume, overthrew the Arab rulers of Zanzibar in January 1964 and established the People's Republic of Zanzibar, with the ASP as its sole party.

Following the establishment of the United Republic of Tanganyika and Zanzibar (in April 1964)—named Tanzania from Oct. 1, 1964—and the adoption of a one-party Constitution in July 1965, TANU became the sole party of mainland Tanzania. In February 1967 the party issued the Arusha Declaration outlining its policy of socialism and self-reliance—this policy being endorsed by the ASP. At a joint conference held in Dar es Salaam on Jan. 21, 1977, TANU and the ASP decided on the dissolution of both parties and the creation of the CCM, the day designated for the formal establishment of the new party being Feb. 5, 1977—i.e. the 10th anniversary of the Arusha Declaration.

Shortly before the 20th anniversary of the Union of Tanganyika and Zanzibar, Aboud Jumbe on Jan. 29, 1984, resigned as President of Zanzibar, Vice-President of Tanzania and vice-chairman of the CCM, apparently because of dissatisfaction among Zanzibaris over his resistance to demands of greater autonomy for Zanzibar (and Pemba). He was succeeded by Ali Hassan Mwinyi, who was formally elected President of Zanzibar on April 19, 1984, as the sole (CCM) candidate.

Orientation. On the basis of its creed—that all human beings are equal, that every individual has a right to dignity and respect as a human being, and that socialism and self-reliance are the only way of building a society of free and equal citizens—the CCM is committed to building socialism and self-reliance as defined in the Arusha Declaration, with traditional African values of living and working together for the good of all being taken into consideration.

Structure. The party's supreme organ is the national conference, which meets every five years and elects (by secret ballot) the national chairman and vice-chairman of the party, and also a 40-member national executive committee, which is the party's most powerful body. This committee nominates the candidate for the presidency of the Republic of Tanzania (its choice to be approved by the national conference in a secret ballot); it also elects a 15-member central committee from among its own members and including the party's secretary-general.

The party is organized at regional, district and branch level (having branches in over 8,000 villages and also in urban areas and at places of work), the party's primary organ being the cell (in residential areas and at places of work). The CCM has five designated mass organizations, namely the Youth Organization, the Union of Tanzania Women, the Union of Tanzania Workers, the Union of Co-operative Societies and the Tanzania Parents Association.

Membership. 1,500,000

Publications. *Uhuru* (daily official organ, in Kiswaheli), 100,000; *Mzalendo* (Sunday newspaper, in Kiswaheli), 100,000; *Ujamaa*

Thailand

Capital: Bangkok   Pop. 49,500,000

The Kingdom of Thailand is a constitutional monarchy with a bicameral Parliament consisting of (i) a 244-member Senate appointed by the King on the recommendation of the Prime Minister and (ii) a 324-member House of Representatives elected by adult suffrage of persons 21 or more years old (but excluding persons with alien, i.e. mainly Chinese, fathers), usually in single-member constituencies. A Cabinet headed by a Prime Minister is appointed by both Houses of Parliament meeting jointly. Since 1976 the post of Prime Minister and other key posts in the Cabinet have been held by officers of the armed forces.

Elections to the 324 seats in the House of Representatives held on April 18, 1983, resulted in the following distribution of seats: Social Action Party 92, Thai Nation Party (*Chat Thai*) 73, Democratic Party 56, Thai People's or Citizens' Party (*Prachakorn Thai*) 36, Siam Democratic Party 18, National Democracy Party 15, other parties 10, independents 24. The turnout in these elections was 53 per cent (as against 44 per cent in the 1979 elections).

Democratic Party (DP)
Prachatipat

Leadership. Pichai Rattakul (l.); Marut Bunnag (dep. l. & g.s.)

Founded. 1946

History. The party was founded by Seni Pramoj, who had during World War II formed the Free Thai Movement to fight against Japan and who was Prime Minister briefly in 1945–46 and again in 1975 and 1976. In National Assembly elections the party gained 72 seats in 1975 and 114 in 1976, being in each case the largest party in the Assembly.

In the 1979 elections to the House of Representatives it retained only 32 seats, (out of 301), but in 1983 it increased its representation to 56 (out of 324) members in the House. It has taken part in coalition governments since 1976.

Orientation. The DP is moderate liberal, conservative and monarchist.

Mass Line Party

Leadership. Maj.-Gen. Sudsai Hasdin (l.)

History. The leader of this party was also the leader of the militant right-wing Red Gaurs organization, which was involved in numerous acts of violence against left-wing forces, and was held responsible for a massacre of students and an attack on the headquarters of the New Force Party in 1976. In March 1981 Maj.-Gen. Hasdin was appointed minister attached to the office of the Prime Minister, Gen. Prem Tinsulanond.

Orientation. This party is extreme right-wing and anti-communist.

National Democracy Party (NDP)
Chat Prachathippatai

Leadership. Gen. Kriangsak Chamanan (l.)

Founded. 1981

History. Gen. Kriangsak Chamanan had earlier headed the *Seritham* party, which had held 21 seats in the House of Representatives elected in April 1979. He had become Supreme Commander of the Armed Forces and Prime Minister (and Minister of the Interior) in 1977. The NDP was presented for formal registration on Sept. 9, 1981, when it was said to be supported by 49 members of the House of Representatives. After the 1983 elections, in which it obtained 15 seats in the House of Representatives, it joined the four-party coalition Government formed by Gen. Prem Tinsulanond.

Orientation. The NDP is a right-wing formation.

New Force Party
Palang Mai

Founded. 1974

History. This party was established by a group of intellectuals opposed to the military regime.

Orientation. The party is left of centre, advocating reforms on social democratic lines.

Social Action Party
Kit Sangkhom

Leadership. M. R. Kukrit Pramoj (l.); Kasem Sirisamphan (s.g.)

History. The party was formed as an offshoot of the Democratic Party. In National Assembly elections the party gained 28 seats in 1975 and 56 in 1976, when it became the third largest party in the Assembly. Its leader (brother of the Democratic Party's then leader) was Prime Minister in 1975–76. It was in opposition until March 1980 when, having won 82 seats in the April 1979 elections to the House of Representatives, it became the strongest party in a coalition Government including also the Thai Nation Party and the Democratic Party. It did not take part in government between March 1981 and May 1983, when it commanded 92 seats in the 324-member House. Since then it has been a partner in a four-party coalition Government (with the Democratic, Thai Citizens' and National Democracy parties).

Orientation. Moderate conservative, the party has opposed dictatorial tendencies in government.

Social Agrarian Party
Kaset Sangkhom

Leadership. Sawat Khamprakorb (l.)

Founded. 1974

Orientation. The Social Agrarian Party is a military-supported right-wing formation.

Social Democratic Party (SDP)
Sangkhom Prachatipatai

Leadership. Klaew Norpati (l.)

History. The SDP was founded by former members of the Socialist Party and the United Socialist Front (USF), both of which had gone underground after a military coup in October 1976. (The Socialist Party had obtained 15 seats in 1975 general elections and two in 1976, and the USF 10 in 1975 and one in 1976.) It has won no seats in Parliament.

Thai Citizens' Party or Thai People's Party
Prachakorn Thai

Founded. 1979

Leadership. Samak Sundaravej (l.)

History. In the House of Representatives this party gained 32 seats in 1979 and 36 in 1983. It did not take part in government until the formation of a four-party coalition Government in May 1983.

Orientation. Right-wing, the party has ties with extremist militant groups and also the military.

Thai Nation Party
Chat Thai

Leadership. Maj.-Gen. Pramarn Adireksan (l.); Banharn Silapa-archa (s.g.)

History. In National Assembly elections the party gained 18 seats in 1975 and 45 in 1976, when it became the second largest party in Parliament, and it has remained so. It took part in coalition Governments between March 1980 and May 1983, but did not join the four-party Government formed after the 1983 elections. In July 1982 it was joined by the nine members of Parliament of the Social Justice Party, and in April 1983 it absorbed the Siam Democratic Party, led by Col. Pol Rerngprasertwit, and also the Progressive Party, led by Uthai Phimchaichon (who was elected Speaker of the House of Representatives on April 26, 1983).

Orientation. This party is a right-wing formation.

Togo

Capital: Lomé   Pop. 2,900,000

The Togolese Republic is ruled by an executive President who is head of the state and of the Government (which has no Prime Minister). The President is also chairman of the Rally of the Togolese People (*Rassemblement du Peuple Togolais,* RPT), the country's sole legal political organization, under a Constitution approved in a referendum on Dec. 30, 1979. The Constitution also provided (i) for a 67-member National Assembly to be elected on a sole list proposed by the RPT and by universal adult suffrage (of all citizens above the age of 18 years, as announced on Dec. 16, 1979), and (ii) for the popular election of the President for a seven-year term.

In elections also held on Dec. 30, 1979, President Gnassingbé Eyadéma was overwhelmingly confirmed in office and the National Assembly candidates listed by the RPT were officially declared to have received 99.9 per cent of the votes cast.

Rally of the Togolese People
Rassemblement du Peuple Togolais (RPT)

Leadership. President Gnassingbé Eyadéma (ch.)

Founded. November 1969

History. Following the 1967 military coup, the constituent congress of the RPT unanimously elected President Eyadéma as its chairman on Nov. 29, 1969. At a further congress held in November 1971, the party re-elected the President as chairman and nominated him as candidate for the country's presidency, but he insisted that this should be confirmed in a referendum, which was done on Jan. 9,

1972. At his wish, the RPT also abolished the post of party secretary-general to "avoid all dualism". Since then the RPT has ruled on the model of the one-party African state, without encountering any serious challenge to its authority.

Structure. The party's congress meets every three years, and its 22-member central commitee at least every three months. A nine-member political bureau is appointed by the President. The RPT is financed by compulsory contributions (of half a month's wage per annum from workers and the equivalent of 2 French francs per month from farmers).

Tonga

Capital: Nuku'alofa (Tongatapu) Pop. 100,000

The Kingdom of Tonga (of 169 islands in the south-west Pacific Ocean) is a member of the Commonwealth and has a Cabinet headed by a Prime Minister and a Legislative Assembly which, in addition to a Speaker and the members of the Cabinet, comprises seven representatives of the nobles and seven representatives of the people; the latter representatives are elected every three years by male literate and tax-paying Tongans and all female literate Tongans (all having to be over the age of 21 years). There are no political parties.

Transkei

Capital: Umtata Pop. 2,400,000

The Republic of Transkei is a country whose independence is not internationally recognized except by South Africa and the other three independent Black homelands, namely Bophuthatswana, Ciskei and Venda. It has a President elected for a seven-year term by the country's National Assembly; he appoints, and acts on the advice of, an Executive Council (Cabinet) headed by a Prime Minister. The National Assembly is a unicameral Parliament composed of 75 chiefs and paramount chiefs co-opted by their peers and 75 members elected for a five-year term by Transkei citizens over 25 years old (including those resident in the Republic of South Africa).

In elections held on Sept. 24, 1981, the Transkei National Independence Party gained 74 of the elective seats, and the Democratic Progressive Party the remaining one.

Democratic Progressive Party (DPP)

Leadership. Caledon Mda (l.)
Founded. March 1979
History. The DPP was formed by a merger of three opposition parties—the Transkei National Progressive Party led by Caledon Mda, the Democratic Party led by Chief Sabata Dalindyebo and the New Democratic Party represented by N. G. Jafta; at the time of its creation, the party commanded 18 out of 150 seats in the National Assembly. The party's first leader, Chief Sabata Dalindyebo, was deposed as a paramount chief and fled the country in 1980 (after he had been convicted of

violating the dignity or injuring the reputation of the President of Transkei). In 1981 he was reported to have joined the (South African banned) African National Congress (ANC). In the 1981 elections the DPP presented only six candidates, of whom Mda was the only one to be elected to the National Assembly.

Orientation. The DPP has opposed the South African policy of setting up Black homelands and granting them "independent" statehood.

Transkei National Independence Party (TNIP)

Leadership. Paramount Chief Kaiser Matanzima (l.)

Founded. 1964

History. In the first elections to a Transkei Legislative Assembly, held in November 1963, when there were no political parties, followers of Chief Matanzima gained no more than 15 of the 45 elective seats, but he was nevertheless elected Chief Minister with the support of most of the 64 nominated members of the Assembly. In the 1968 elections the TNIP won 28 of the 45 elective seats, and with the support of 57 nominated chiefs it subsequently gained control of more than three-quarters of the Assembly.

In the 1973 elections the TNIP retained 25 elective seats and remained in power with the support of nominated chiefs. In elections held in September 1976 to the National Assembly of the Republic of Transkei (declared independent on Oct. 26, 1976) the TNIP gained 69 of the 75 elective seats, while of the 75 nominated members of the new Assembly 72 gave their support to the TNIP. In the 1981 elections it gained 74 of the 75 elective seats in the Assembly.

Orientation. The TNIP has been the chief advocate of independence for Transkei. In its 1973 election manifesto it accepted the South African policy of "separate development" leading to full independence for "Black homelands", but it also stated that South Africa should belong to Black and White equally and its wealth should be shared by all inhabitants, and that there should be freedom of the individual, including the freedom to seek work anywhere in South Africa without pass laws.

Transkei People's Freedom Party (TPFP)

Leadership. Cromwell Diko (l.)

Founded. 1976

History. This party was formed by its leader, a former member of the ruling Transkei National Independence Party, with the support of former adherents of the Democratic Party, and it thereupon became the official opposition in the National Assembly. However, since the 1981 elections the TPFP has not been represented in the National Assembly.

Trinidad and Tobago

Capital: Port of Spain   Pop. 1,100,000

The Republic of Trinidad and Tobago, a member of the Commonwealth, has a President elected for a five-year term by an electoral college constituted by the members of the country's bicameral Parliament which consists of (i) a 36-member House of Representatives elected for five years by universal adult suffrage of citizens above the age of 18 years and by simple majority in single-member constituencies, and (ii) a 31-member Senate appointed by the President (16 senators on the advice of the Prime Minister, six on the advice of the Leader of the Opposition and nine at his own discretion). The Prime Minister and his Cabinet are collectively responsible to Parliament.

In elections to the House of Representatives held on Nov. 9, 1981, the People's National Movement (PNM) was returned for a sixth consecutive term of office by gaining 26 seats; the United Labour Front (ULF) gained eight seats; and the Democratic Action Congress (DAC) gained the two seats allotted to the island of Tobago.

In response to demands by the DAC the island of Tobago was in September 1980 given internal self-government with a 15-member Tobago House of Assembly, to which 12 members were to be elected for four years by universal adult suffrage (of Tobago residents) and the remaining three to be chosen by the elected members. In the first elections to this House, held on Nov. 24, 1980, the DAC won eight of the popularly-elective seats and the PNM the remaining four. The three members elected by the new House were all of the DAC.

Democratic Action Congress (DAC)

Address. 44, 10th Street, Barajaria, Trinidad and Tobago
Leadership. A. N. R. Robinson (ch.); Euadue Gordon (sec.)
Founded. April 1971
History. The party was formed by a merger of two opposition groupings—the Action Committee of Dedicated Citizens and part of the Democratic Labour Party, which was then the official Opposition. The party's founder was A. N. R. Robinson, who in 1970 had resigned as deputy leader of the ruling People's National Movement.

The DAC campaigned for electoral reform in 1971–74, demanding the abolition of voting machines and a complete registration of voters. In the September 1976 elections the DAC won only the two seats for the island of Tobago which it retained in the 1981 elections.

Orientation. The DAC stands for a democratic political and economic transformation and in particular national independence, regional unity, public ownership of natural resources, and an equitable distribution of wealth.
Structure. The DAC has a national congress, to which a national committee and a strategy committee are responsible; there are also action groups and constituency committees.
Membership. 18,500
Publications. *Guide to Change for Trinidad and Tobago*

Fargo House Movement (FHM)

Leadership. Dr Winston Murray (l.)
Founded. 1980
History. The FHM was established in Tobago by Dr Murray, who had been one of the two members of the Democratic

Action Congress (DAC) elected to the (national) House of Assembly but had in 1978 repudiated the DAC leadership and been suspended from that party. He supported the bill granting self-government to Tobago (which the DAC opposed as "inadequate"). The FHM contested the November 1980 elections to the new Tobago House of Assembly but obtained only 2.3 per cent of the vote and no seat.

National Joint Action Committee (NJAC)

Address. 48 Hermitage Rd., Gonzales, Belmont, Trinidad and Tobago
Leadership. Makandal Daaga (l.); Winston Leonard (ch.)
Founded. February 1969
History. The NJAC was established as a federation of various organizations in Trinidad, and in 1970 also in Tobago. It played a leading role in the "Black Power" action in 1970, when Makandal Daaga (then known as Geddes Granger) and other NJAC leaders were arrested and detained under emergency regulations in force from October 1971 to June 1972. The NJAC continued to work outside the established political system until the general elections of Nov. 9, 1981, for which it nominated 28 candidates but in which it received (as officialy announced) only 3.3 per cent of the vote and no seat. The NJAC claimed afterwards that the elections had not been free and fair and that there had been a low turnout.
Orientation. The NJAC has proclaimed as its aims the creation of "a society built on the psychological basis of man" and an end to the "oppressive society" by the people obtaining "control over the machinery of state" and over the economy.
Publications. *Liberation*; *Free Caribbean.*

Organization for National Reconstruction (ONR)

Leadership. Karl Hudson-Phillips (l.)
Founded. April 1980
History. Karl Hudson-Phillips, the founder of the ONR, had been a prominent member of the ruling People's National Movement (PNM), but had resigned as Attorney General in 1973 and had, in 1979, announced his intention of succeeding the Prime Minister (Dr Eric Williams, the leader of the PNM). In March 1980 he was suspended from the PNM after criticizing a speech by the Prime Minister.

At the inaugural convention of the ONR in January 1981 he again attacked Dr Williams's premiership and accused the Government of corruption and inefficiency. In the 1981 general elections the ONR gained 22 per cent of the vote (mainly at the expense of the United Labour Front) but no seat.

People's National Movement (PNM)

Address. 1 Tranquillity St., Port of Spain, Trinidad and Tobago
Leadership. George M. Chambers (l.); F. C. Prevatt (ch.); Alvan Quamina (g.s.)
Founded. 1956
History. The PNM was created by Dr Eric Williams (who died in March 1981) as the first modern political party in Trinidad and Tobago, and it has been in power ever since 1956. In general elections to a 24-member Legislative Council, held in September 1956, the PNM gained 13 seats; in a 30-member House of Representatives (under full internal self-government) elected in 1961 the PNM won 20 seats.

Following the achievement of full independence within the Commonwealth in 1962, the PNM held its majority in the 36-member House of Representatives, gaining 24 seats in 1966 and all 36 in 1971, and, with 53 per cent of the vote, retaining a two-thirds majority in the House in 1976. In the 1981 elections it increased its representation in the House from 24 to 26 members. In the Tobago House of Assembly elected on Nov. 24, 1980, it holds four of the 15 seats.
Orientation. The PNM is a moderate, nationalistic party standing for fundamental rights and freedoms, support for local enterprise and also planned distribution of shares in state-held factories and companies. Although predominantly African, the PNM stands for national unity of all population groups.

People's Popular Movement

Leadership. Michael Als (l.)
Founded. 1981
History. A pro-Soviet Communist party, the People's Popular Movement has so far remained a marginal force in the politics of Trinidad and Tobago.
Membership. 100 (est.)
International affiliations. The PPM is recognized as a Communist party by the parties of the Soviet bloc.

Tapia House Movement (THM)

Address. Tapia House, 112-114 Duke St., Port of Spain, Trinidad and Tobago

Leadership. Lloyd Best (l.); Arnold Best (sec.)

Founded. May 1976

History. Following a split in the New World Group, a Tapia ("Mud Wall") House Group was formed in November 1968 as a "Fabian, Gandhian, Owenite" wing, as against the more activist "Moko" wing (which later became the United National Independence Party led by Dr James Millette). In its early period the Group served as a forum for opposition to the Government among younger radical intellectuals in Trinidad, and its political significance was enhanced when four Tapia members were in 1974 nominated to the Senate, where they constituted the Opposition.

In the 1976 general elections Tapia put up 29 candidates but received only 3.8 per cent of the total vote and no seats. In 1981 it likewise obtained no seat, although it was a partner in the Trinidad and Tobago National Alliance of moderate left-wing parties.

Orientation. The Movement seeks "to establish for the Caribbean and the West Indian people a democratic, humane and participatory republic composed of island city-states; to eliminate racial discrimination and prejudice, repudiate social class and social snobbery and to reject religious bigotry and intolerance".

Structure. A council of representatives of local constituency parties meets monthly, the national executive meets weekly, and a general assembly of members is held at least once a year; there is a three-member full-time central office.

Membership. 10,000

Publications. *Tapia* (party organ); *Trinidad and Tobago Review* (monthly)

Trinidad and Tobago National Alliance (TTNA)

Founded. 1981

History. The TTNA constituted an electoral agreement intended to create a united moderate-left opposition. The agreement was concluded by the Democratic Action Congress (DAC), the Tapia House Movement (THM) and the United Labour Front (ULF). In the November 1981 elections, however, the TTNA partners gained only 10 of the 36 seats in the House of Representatives (ULF 8, DAC 2, and THM none).

United Labour Front (ULF)

Address. 12 Hobson St., San Fernando, Trinidad and Tobago

Leadership. Basdeo Panday (l.); Nizam Mohammed (ch.); Kelvin Ramnath (g.s.)

Founded. March 1976

History. The party arose out of an industrial organization of oil and sugar workers' unions formed in February 1975, which was transformed into a political party to contest the general elections of September 1976. Allied with some smaller left-wing groups, the ULF won 10 of the 36 seats in the House of Representatives, where it subsequently formed the opposition. In August 1977 the Marxist wing of the party led by Raffique Shah attempted to take over the leadership, but the moderates led by Basdeo Panday eventually succeeded in retaining control.

The ULF gained 10 seats in the National Assembly in 1976 but retained only eight in 1981, when it contested the elections under an electoral agreement known as the Trinidad and Tobago National Alliance, led by Basdeo Panday and including the Democratic Action Congress and the Tapia House Movement (see separate entries).

Orientation. In the 1976 elections the ULF used the slogan "Let those who labour hold the reins" and campaigned for greater local control of the "commanding heights" of the economy; for a national land policy to ensure that all land reverted to the ownership of local citizens; for the nationalization of foreign trade and the local operations of multinational corporations; for the setting up of state distribution centres for a wide variety of goods; and for the introduction of workers' participation in the management of enterprises.

Structure. The party is based on local groups; the party congress, the party's highest authority, meets annually and elects a central committee (which meets quarterly) and a central executive (responsible for day-to-day affairs).

Membership. 10,000

Publications. *Battlefront* (fortnightly), 10,000

Tunisia

Capital: Tunis Pop. 6,700,000

The Republic of Tunisia has an executive President who, under the 1959 Constitution, is elected for a five-year term by universal adult suffrage of citizens above the age of 20 years. However, the present incumbent, President Habib Bourguiba, who is also president of the Destour Socialist Party, was on Nov. 3, 1974, appointed President for life. He appoints a Government headed by a Prime Minister. The country's 136-member National Assembly is similarly elected for a five-year term under a simple-majority system in 23 multi-member constituencies.

Elections held on Nov. 1, 1981, were contested by a National Front embracing the Destour Socialist Party and the country's trade union federation (*Union Générale des Travailleurs Tunisiens*, UGTT) as well as by three opposition parties, but all 136 seats were obtained by the National Front. None of the opposition formations obtained the minimum 5 per cent of the valid vote which had been laid down by the Government as the basic requirement for official recognition as a legal political party.

Destour Socialist Party
Parti Socialiste Destourien (PSD)

Address. Blvd. 9 Avril 1938, Tunis, Tunisia

Leadership. President Habib Bourguiba (life ch.); Mohamed M'Zali (s.g.); Mongi Kooli (head of pol. bureau)

Founded. 1934

History. Though there was a nationalist party in Tunisia from 1920—i.e. the *Destour* ("Constitution") movement—a popular independence movement only emerged in 1934 when Habib Bourguiba broke away to form the Neo-Destour party. The failure of the 1936 Popular Front Government in Paris to introduce reforms encouraged the Neo-Destour's growth, but a successful general strike in 1938 and associated unrest led to Bourguiba's arrest and the dissolution of the party.

Despite the forced exile of Bourguiba in 1945, the party was reorganized by Salah Ben Youssef and led the demand for Tunisian independence. On the return of Bourguiba in 1949 internal autonomy was promised and a new Ministry formed in August 1950 included several Neo-Destour representatives. However, a resumption of violence led to the arrest of most of the party leadership in 1952 and full civil war was only averted by the proposals of Pierre Mendès-France in July 1954 leading to the granting of internal autonomy in 1955 and full independence the following year, soon after which the monarchy was abolished and Bourguiba installed as President.

The Neo-Destour was renamed the Destour Socialist Party in October 1964 and has, throughout the post-independence period, dominated the Tunisian political scene.

Attempts made in 1970–71 by "liberal" members of the PSD to liberalize both the party and the country's Constitution were successfully resisted by the President, whom the ninth PSD congress in September 1974 (by acclamation) elected party chairman for life. The congress similarly recommended his appointment as President of the Republic for life, and the required constitutional amendment was unanimously approved by the National Assembly on March 18, 1975.

In what was described as an "opening" of the ruling party, the 121 National Assembly seats at issue in the November 1979 elections were each contested by two candidates; however, in the absence of any nominations from opposition parties all 242 names on the ballot papers were nominees of the PSD. It contested the 1981 general elections as the leading force in a National Front which also incorporated the trade union federation and which gained all 136 seats in the National Assembly. These elections were also contested by three opposition parties, as part of a move to a genuine multi-party system.

Orientation. The party stands for a pragmatic "Tunisian socialism" based on economic planning.

Structure. The PSD has a congress which elects an 80-member central committee, and it also has a 20-member political bureau.

Membership. 800,000

International affiliations. Socialist Interafrican.

Movement of Popular Unity
Mouvement de l'Unité Populaire (MUP)

Founded. 1973

History. The MUP originally comprised supporters of Ahmed Ben Salah, the former Economy and Planning Minister who, after having been a leading theorist of the ruling Destour Socialist Party's approach to socialism, was dismissed and sentenced to 10 years' imprisonment in 1970 but who escaped in 1973 and subsequently reappeared in exile. The MUP refused to seek participation in the November 1979 elections.

On Feb. 13, 1981, President Bourguiba granted an amnesty to all MUP members still subject to restrictions or in exile, except to Ahmed Ben Salah. This amnesty followed a meeting between the President and an MUP group led by Mohamed Bel Hadj Amor and opposed to Ben Salah. This group thereupon participated in the November 1981 elections but obtained only 0.8 per cent of the vote and thus failed to gain the 5 per cent share which the Government had earlier specified as a minimum requirement for eventual legal registration. (Nevertheless, the group obtained legalization in 1983.) The Ben Salah faction of the MUP continued its established policy of boycotting elections.

Orientation. The MUP seeks a basic democratization of the Tunisian political system as a means of proceeding to the construction of a genuinely socialist economy and society.

Movement of Socialist Democrats
Mouvement des Démocrates Socialistes (MDS)

Leadership. Ahmed Mestiri (s.g.)
Founded. June 1978

History. Before constituting itself into a political party in June 1978, the Movement had come into being in 1971 when "liberals" within the ruling Destour Socialist Party (PSD) had called on the Government to liberalize and modernize the country's political life and institutions. Ahmed Mestiri was expelled from the PSD in January 1972, as were seven other "liberals" in 1974. In 1977 the movement began to establish itself as a significant opposition group and created a national council for the protection of public liberties. However, both President Bourguiba and his Prime Minister strongly condemned the movement in 1977–78, and the party was not legally recognized. It refused to seek participation in the November 1979 elections notwithstanding the Government's decision that each seat would be contested by two candidates. In March 1980 the PSD political bureau rescinded the expulsions of Mestiri and the other seven liberals in an apparent attempt to bring those associated with the MDS back into the ambit of the ruling party.

In July 1980 the Mestiri faction was authorized to publish two new journals. It continued to oppose the Government and was one of the three opposition parties which unsuccessfully contested the 1981 general elections, failing to gain 5 per cent of the vote as required for eventual legal recognition. By then an anti-Mestiri "moderate" faction had emerged within the MDS, inclined to an accommodation with the ruling PSD.

On March 22, 1982, the MDS called, together with the Communist Party, the Movement of Popular Unity and the (unauthorized) Islamic Trend Movement, for the repeal of unconstitutional laws, the restoration of political freedoms, the release of political detainees and the return of Tunisians from exile (in particular of Ahmed Ben Salah—see under Movement of Popular Unity). At that time the MDS was estimated to enjoy the support of some 30 per cent of the voters in Tunis and suburbs. Despite its poor performance in the 1981 elections the MDS was legalized in 1983.

Orientation. The party's aims are "the safeguarding of the dignity of citizens", public liberty, the establishment of a socialist régime without exploitation and with economic development being placed "at the service of sound justice", and the building of "the great Maghreb as a step on the road to Arab unity and the consolidation of solidarity with Islamic and African countries".

Structure. The party has eight assistant secretaries-general.

Publications. *Errai* (Arabic weekly); *Démocratie* (French-language monthly)—

both of moderate faction; *Al Moustaqbal* (weekly); *l'Avenir* (weekly)—both of Mestiri faction

---

Tunisian Communist Party
Parti Communiste Tunisien (PCT)

Leadership. Mohamed Harmel (s.g.)
Founded. 1937
History. During World War II the PCT contributed to the resistance to the Italian and German occupation of Tunisia. Later it supported Habib Bourguiba's Neo-Destour Party in its "nationalist" struggle against colonialism. It took part, without gaining any seats, in various elections between 1956 and 1959, when it supported Bourguiba as the sole candidate for the presidency. In January 1962 it was ordered to cease its activities. Thereafter it gave conditional support to the Government's "progressive" economic policies until 1969, when it began to oppose the Government and was formally banned.

With the introduction of party pluralism the PCT was legally recognized on July 18, 1981, and it contested the general elections of Nov. 1 of that year, but unsuccessfully. Since then it has supported new trends which it discerned in Tunisia's economic and social policies and its process of democratization. It called, on Sept. 9, 1981, for the withdrawal of Soviet forces from Afghanistan, and it has also demanded the release of imprisoned supporters of the unrecognized (Moslem fundamentalist) Islamic Trend movement.

Orientation. The PCT is generaly pro-Soviet, for a policy of non-alignment and support for all liberation movements.

Publications. *Al-Tariq Al-Jahid* (New Road)

International affiliations. The PCT is recognized by the Communist parties of the Soviet-bloc countries.

Turkey

Capital: Ankara   Pop. 47,000,000

Since Sept, 12, 1980, the Republic of Turkey has been under military rule, which was installed with the object of ending what was seen by the military as a slide to anarchy through the activities of terrorist groups of both the right and the left. On assuming power the Chief of the General Staff (Gen. Kenan Evren) and the commanders of the four armed services (Army, Navy, Air Force and Gendarmerie) abolished Parliament, suspended all political activities and set up a National Security Council, which formed a mainly civilian Government and, under a constitutional amendment of Oct. 28, 1980, assumed the functions of Parliament. On Oct. 16, 1981, the military rulers ordered the dissolution of all political parties and the confiscation of their property, while declaring their aim to be the development of a new democratic system based on solid foundations.

A new Constitution overwhelmingly approved in a referendum held on Nov. 7, 1982, specified that Turkey was a democratic, secular and social state in which legislative power belonged to the Grand National Assembly (Parliament) and in which the President and a Council of Ministers exercised executive power. In addition to nearly 200 main articles, the new Constitution contained a number of "temporary articles", the first of which stated that Gen. Evren was to become President of the Republic for a period of seven years, while the other four members of the National Security Council were assured leading positions in a Presidential Council as the chief advisory body to the President. The process of a gradual return to civilian rule subsequently began on April 24, 1983, when a presidential decree lifted the general ban on political activity, although certain restrictions remained, notably in that about 100 former party leaders continued to be barred from political activity for 10 years.

In order to be considered for official registration parties had to obtain the signatures of 30 approved founding members, but the National Security Council could refuse recognition without giving any reasons. To win seats in the Grand National Assembly parties had to obtain at least 10 per cent of the national vote. Under a political parties law which came into force on April 24, 1983, it was illegal (i) to form or join any communist-orientated party or any party which sought to impose the rule of one social class over another, (ii) to create a religious basis for the state, and (iii) to establish a dictatorship. Parties were banned from any trade union affiliation and were required to deposit their funds with the state banks.

Elections to the 400-member Grand National Assembly, held on Nov. 6, 1983, were contested by only three authorized parties, and the resultant distribution of seats was as follows: Motherland Party 212, People's Party 117, Nationalist Democracy Party 71. One of the elected Motherland Party members was subsequently disqualified.

Of 483 independents wishing to take part in the general elections, only 55 were given permission to stand, and all were unsuccessful. Voting was obligatory for all persons aged 21 years or more, except those who had not voted in the November 1982 constitutional referendum. Three additional parties—the Right Way Party, the Social Democratic Party and the Welfare Party—were allowed to participate in local elections on March 25, 1984.

Parliamentary Parties

Motherland Party (MP)
Anatavan Partisi

Leadership. Turgut Özal (l.)
Founded. May 20, 1983
History. Turgut Özal held key ministerial positions between 1978 and 1982 and was regarded as being committed to encouraging the growth of private industry, favouring intensified relations with Islamic countries of the Middle East, but opposed to the declaration of full independence by the Turkish Federated State of Cyprus. The National Security Council announced on June 8, 1983, that seven members of the MP would have to resign from the party, failing which the MP would be closed down. However, the MP was allowed to contest the general elections of Nov. 6, 1983, when it won an absolute majority in the Grand National Assembly. It was also successful in local elections held on March 25, 1984, when it gained about 41.5 per cent of the votes and control of 54 of the municipal councils of the 67 provincial capitals.
Orientation. The MP's general election programme called for a free market economy, clear estimates for future spending and economic measures which would eliminate political terrorism.

Nationalist Democracy Party (NDP)
Milliyetci Demokrasi Partisi

Leadership. Turgut Sünalp (l.); Ulka Soylemezoglu (s.g.)
Founded. May 16, 1983
History. The party's leader is a retired general, and he and his policies are said to be backed by the military rulers. In the November 1983 general elections one of its candidates was the Prime Minister, Adml. Bülent Ülüsü. In these elections it came in third place with 23.27 per cent of the votes, while in municipal elections held on March 25, 1984, its share of the vote fell back to 6.4 per cent. Thereafter evidence of internal strains surfaced when the entire central executive and administrative council of the party as well as five of its deputy leaders submitted their resignations during April 1984, pending a reassessment of the NDP's future role.
Orientation. The NDP is a right-wing party.

People's Party (PP)
Halkci Partisi

Leadership. Necdet Calp
Founded. May 20, 1983
History. On June 9, 1983, the National Security Council called on seven PP members to resign from the party, failing which the latter would be closed down. In

the 1983 elections the PP was said to have benefited from the exclusion of the former socialist parties. In these elections it came second with over 30 per cent of the vote, but in local elections held on March 25, 1984, it obtained only about 8 per cent of the total vote.

Orientation. The PP places itself on the centre-left of the political spectrum.

Other Parties

Grand Turkey Party
Buyuk Türkiye Partisi

Leadership. Gen. Ali Fethi Esener
Founded. May 20, 1983
History. The party was banned on May 31, 1983, after it had been alleged that it was a continuation of the former Justice Party led by Süleyman Demirel (who was Prime Minister in 1965–71, 1975–77 and 1979-80). At the same time seven of its members were arrested and sent for detention at an army base (among them Demirel himself, who was detained until Sept. 30, 1983).

Orientation. This party subscribes to conservative principles similar to those embraced by the former Justice Party.

Rebirth Party

History. This party remained unregistered as all of its 38 founders were rejected by the National Security Council on July 8, 1983.

Reformist Democracy Party

Founded. March 21, 1984
History. Founded on the eve of the local elections of March 25, 1984, this party was intended to occupy a "progressive centrist" position in the political spectrum.

Republican Conservative Party

Founded. July 7, 1983
History. Although established in good time to do so, this moderate right-wing party was not authorized to contest the elections to the Grand National Assembly held in November 1983.

Right Way Party

Leadership. Ahmet Nusret Tuna, Yildirim Avci (leaders)
Founded. May 1983
History. This party was said to be backed by Süleyman Demirel, the former leader of the (banned) Justice Party. By December 1983 the party had recruited more than 100 former members of Parliament of the defunct Justice Party and also the whole leadership of the Grand Turkey Party (see separate entry), which had been banned on May 31, 1983. Although excluded from the November 1983 general elections, it was allowed to contest local elections in March 1984, in which it came third with about 13.5 per cent of the vote. On April 6, 1984, however, the prosecutor's office applied to the Constitutional Court for the closing-down of the party on the ground that it was an illegal continuation of banned former parties.

Orientation. The party is of conservative orientation.

Social Democratic Party (Sodep)

Leadership. Prof. Erdal Inönü (l.)
Founded. June 6, 1983
History. Prof. Inönü declared on Aug. 20, 1983, that "a return to sound democracy" would not be realized by the date of the general elections (which took place on Nov. 6, 1983, and in which the Sodep was not allowed to take part). However, it did contest local elections held in March 1984 when it obtained 23.3 per cent of the vote and emerged as the second strongest party (after the Motherland Party).

Supreme Duty Party

Leadership. Baha Vefa Karatay (l.)
Founded. May 1983
Orientation. This formation (which did not contest the November 1983 general elections) subscribes to right-wing principles and policies.

Welfare Party

History. This party was allowed to contest the local elections held on March 25, 1984, when it obtained about 7 per cent of the votes.

Orientation. The Welfare Party is an Islamic fundamentalist formation.

Tuvalu

Capital: Fongafale (Funafuti)   Pop. 8,000

Tuvalu (formerly part of the Gilbert and Ellice Islands colony) is an independent state with special statute within the Commonwealth and with the British monarch as head of state being represented by a Governor-General. It has a five-member Cabinet headed by a Prime Minister and a 12-member House of Assembly elected by universal adult suffrage. There are no political parties, but an "opposition group" has been formed in the House of Assembly. No other political organizations have been reported to exist.

In elections held on Sept. 8, 1981, eight of the 12 sitting members of the House of Assembly were re-elected but the four others were defeated. A member of the opposition group was thereafter elected Prime Minister.

Uganda

Capital: Kampala   Pop. 13,000,000

The Republic of Uganda, a member of the Commonwealth, has an executive President elected by the members of a National Assembly to which 126 members are elected by universal adult suffrage of citizens above the age of 18 years and by simple majority in single-member constituencies (with separate ballot boxes for each party) and to which up to 10 additional members may be appointed by the President. The latter is head of state and of Government, which also has a Vice-President.

In elections to the National Assembly—the first since 1972—held in December 1980 elective seats were gained as follows: Uganda People's Congress 74 (with 17 members being returned unopposed), Democratic Party 51, Uganda Democratic Movement 1. The Conservative Party also contested the elections but gained no seat.

As a result of defections by Democratic Party members to the Uganda People's Congress, by January 1983, the latter held a total of 91 seats (including 10 filled by nominated members from the Uganda National Liberation Army, the country's armed forces) while the Democratic Party retained 40 seats and several other seats had been declared vacant.

Conservative Party (CP)

Leadership. J. Mayanjankangi (l.)
Founded. March 1979
History. The party's leader was Prime Minister of the Kingdom of Buganda in 1964-66. (Buganda was an autonomous part of Uganda until September 1967, when it was brought under the control of the central Government in a unitary republic.) The CP gained no seats in the 1980 general elections.
Orientation. The CP stands for Buganda traditionalism.

Democratic Party (DP)

Address. P.O. Box 1658, Kampala, Uganda
Leadership. Paul Ssemogerere (l.)
Founded. 1953
History. The DP was banned in 1969 when the Uganda People's Congress Government of President Milton Obote created a one-party state. It nevertheless maintained widespread support, especially in southern Uganda. It was revived for the 1980 general elections but some of its candidates were disqualified by the Electoral Commission on Dec. 9. After the 1980 elections, the official result of which gave the DP 51 of the 126 elective seats in the National Assembly, some DP members alleged that certain results had been falsified. However, those candidates who had been declared elected took their seats in the Assembly on Dec. 23, 1980, with Paul Ssemogerere becoming Leader of the Opposition. In March 1981 he complained of arbitrary arrests of certain DP members of the Assembly, and on May 7 of that year he was quoted as saying that there had been assassinations of DP supporters since the day after the elections; that the President had, despite his call for national reconciliation, made many political appointments; and that the DP could therefore no longer play its role as the political opposition.

Some DP followers later supported the so-called Uganda Freedom Movement (UFM), which had in February 1981 begun anti-government guerrilla operations. Francis Bwengye, then secretary-general of the DP, declared himself, in May 1981, in favour of the guerrilla warfare of the UFM, which he called the military wing of the DP; he claimed to be leading a group which represented a majority of the DP, and called on DP members of the National Assembly to cease their parliamentary activities. However, Ssemogerere denied Bwengye's claims and dismissed him from his post as DP secretary-general.

In November 1981 a number of DP members and office bearers were arrested (and some of them beaten up) after they had officially been accused of being anti-government guerrillas. On the other hand, in response to President Obote's call for unity and reconciliation, a number of DP members of the National Assembly joined the Uganda People's Congress. They included John Magezi (opposition chief whip) and five others, who declared their defection from the DP on Jan. 2–3 1982. By January 1983 the DP still held 40 seats in the National Assembly.
Orientation. The DP stands for a mixed economy and a national Government.

Uganda Patriotic Movement (UPM)

Leadership. Yoweri Museveni (pres.); Jabeli Bidandi Sali (s.g.)
Founded. June 5, 1980
History. Yoweri Museveni was Minister of Defence and acting President under the interim regime of President Godfrey L. Binaisa (from June 1979 to May 1980) and founded the UPM as a party opposed to the Uganda People's Congress of Dr Obote. The UPM held its first delegate conference on Nov. 17–20, 1980, when its constitution and party manifesto were approved. For the 1980 elections it nominated, among other candidates, ex-President Binaisa, who was, however, not elected. (He had been under house arrest but was released in December 1980 and shortly afterwards left the country.)

Museveni was the only UPM candidate to be elected to the National Assembly, but immediately afterwards he went into hiding and founded a People's Revolutionary Army, later known as the National Resistance Army, which embarked on anti-government guerrilla warfare. Numerous UPM followers, including staff members and students at Makerere University (Kampala), were arrested in February and March 1980 (among them Jabeli Bidandi Sali, who was, however, unconditionally released on Oct. 30, 1981), while some were killed and others left the country. Under an agreement signed by Museveni in London on Jan. 7, 1982, the National Resistance Army joined the Uganda Popular Front formed by a total of four Ugandan exile groups opposed to the Obote regime.

Uganda People's Congress (UPC)

Address. P.O. Box 1951, Kampala, Uganda

Leadership. President (Dr) Apollo Milton Obote (l.); Dr John M. M. Luwuliza-Kirunda (s.g.)

Founded. 1960

History. Dr Obote became Prime Minister in April 1960 and his party, pursuing socialist policies, making Uganda a unitary republic in September 1967 and banning all opposition parties in December 1969, remained in power until January 1971 when its regime was overthrown by the Army led by Maj.-Gen. (later Field Marshal) Idi Amin Dada. The latter became President of Uganda and had full executive powers until he was overthrown in 1979 by a force of Tanzanian troops and Ugandan exiles, including UPC supporters,

whereupon Dr Obote returned from exile in Tanzania.

There followed two successive provisional Governments, the second of which was superseded in May 1980 by a Military Commission headed by Paulo Muwanga, a prominent UPC member. He organized the 1980 general elections which gave the UPC an absolute majority in the National Assembly and thus restored the party to power, with Dr Obote being elected President.

Orientation. The UPC's election manifesto, approved by a party congress in Kampala on Nov. 4–6, 1980, advocated a mixed economy with favourable conditions for attracting foreign investment and co-operation with Kenya and Tanzania in a revived East African Community. At the same time Dr Obote called for the united support of all Ugandans regardless of ethnic divisions.

Union of Soviet Socialist Republics

Capital: Moscow   Pop. 271,200,000 (Jan. 1, 1983)

Under its 1977 Constitution the Union of Soviet Socialist Republics (USSR) is "a socialist state of the whole people", in which "the Communist Party of the Soviet Union (CPSU) is the leading and guiding force of Soviet society and the nucleus of its political system, of all state and public organizations". The USSR comprises 15 Union Republics, of which by far the largest is the Russian Soviet Federative Socialist Republic (RSFSR). There are also Autonomous Republics (16 within the RSFSR and four in three other Union Republics) and Autonomous Regions (five within the RSFSR and three in three other Union Republics). There are Supreme Soviets (Parliaments) for the USSR and for each of the Union Republics, the Autonomous Republics and the Autonomous Regions, all elected for five-year terms in constituencies on the basis of universal suffrage by secret ballot of citizens over the age of 18 years, with the right to nominate candidates being exercised by the CPSU, the trade unions, the All-Union Leninist Young Communist League, co-operatives and other organizations, labour collectives and meetings of military servicemen. The USSR Supreme Soviet (*Verchovnyi Sovet SSSR*) consists of two chambers with an equal number (750) of deputies—(i) the Soviet of the Union (*Sovet Soyuza*) elected in single-member constituencies with approximately equal populations under an absolute majority system (with a second and further ballots being held until an absolute majority is obtained), and (ii) the Soviet of Nationalities (*Sovet Nationalnostey*) consisting of 32 deputies from each Union Republic, 11 from each Autonomous Republic, five from each Autonomous Region and one from each Autonomous Area. There is a USSR Council of Ministers headed by a Chairman (Prime Minister) and there are Councils of Ministers in each Union Republic.

In elections to the USSR Supreme Soviet on March 4, 1984, 99.99 per cent of the electorate was officially stated to have voted. In the elections to the Soviet of the Union 183,897,278 persons voted for the sole CPSU-approved candidates and 109,072 against, while in the elections to the Soviet of Nationalities those voting for the sole candidates totalled 183,592,183 and those against 96,763.

Communist Party of the Soviet Union (CPSU)
Kommunisticheskaya Partiya Sovetskogo Soyuza

Address. Moscow-132, Staraya Pl. 4, CC CPSU, USSR

Leadership. (February 1984): Konstantin Chernenko (s.g. of Central Committee); Geidar Aliyev, Mikhail Gorbachov, Viktor Grishin, Andrei Gromyko, Dinmukhamed Kunayev, Grigory Romanov, Vladimir Shcherbitsky, Mikhail Solomentsev, Nikolai Tikhonov, Dmitry Ustinov, Vitaly Vorotnikov (other full members of Politburo); Gen. Viktor Chebrikov, Pyotr Demichev, Vladimir Dolgikh, Vasily Kuznetsov, Boris Ponomaryov, Eduard Shevardnadze (candidate members of Politburo)

Founded. 1903

History. The present CPSU is directly descended from Vladimir Ilyich Ulyanov Lenin's majority (Bolshevik) wing of the Russian Social Democratic Labour Party (itself established in 1898) which at the party's second congress held in London in July-August 1903 out-voted the minority (Menshevik) wing led by Yuliy Martov on Lenin's proposal that in existing Russian conditions the party must become a tightly-disciplined vanguard of professional revolutionaries. In 1912 the Bolshevik wing established itself as a separate formation which became a legal party in Russia following the overthrow of the Tsar in February 1917 and which in October 1917 seized power from the Mensheviks. Thereafter the party changed its name to Russian Communist Party (Bolsheviks) in 1918, to All-Union Communist Party (Bolsheviks) in 1925, and to its present name in 1952.

Following Lenin's death in January 1924, Joseph Stalin (who had become general secretary of the Central Committee in April 1922) took full control over the party and government. He then proceeded to eliminate all actual and potential rivals on the right and left of the party, notably Leon Trotsky (the architect of the Communist victory in the post-revolution civil war), who was expelled from the party in November 1927, exiled in January 1929 and finally murdered by Stalin's agent in his Mexican home in August 1940.

From October 1925 Stalin adopted the programme of the eliminated leftist opposition by launching the first five-year plan of rapid industrialization and the forcible collectivization of agriculture (the latter involving the virtual elimination of the land-owning peasants, or kulaks, as a class). Between 1928 and 1938 total industrial output almost quadrupled, although agricultural output declined. The assassination of politburo member Sergei Kirov in December 1934 led to the great purges of the late 1930s in which almost the entire generation of party activists formerly associated with Lenin disappeared. In December 1936 a new Constitution was promulgated under which the Communist Party was enshrined as the leading force in the state.

After the interval provided by the August 1939 Stalin-Hitler pact, the German invasion of the Soviet Union in June 1941 coincided with Stalin's assumption for the first time of formal government responsibilities as Chairman of the Council of People's Commissars (i.e. Council of Ministers) and as Chairman of the State Defence Committee and supreme commander. The eventual victory of the Soviet forces and their penetration into Eastern Europe led to the establishment of Soviet-aligned Communist regimes in a number of states, causing post-war tensions in relations with the Western powers which eventually deteriorated into the Cold War. During the post-war period Stalin remained in absolute control of the party and state apparatus and mounted further purges of suspected opponents.

Immediately after Stalin's death in March 1953 moves were initiated to reverse the Stalinist system and the cult of his personality. Stalin's secret police chief, Lavrenti Beria, was executed and Stalin's designated successor, Georgi Malenkov, was immediately ousted from the party leadership by Nikita Khrushchev and was replaced as Prime Minister by Nikolai Bulganin in February 1955. Under Khrushchev's leadership the CPSU in 1955 re-established relations with the Yugoslav Communists (hitherto regarded as right-wing deviationists) and in his celebrated "secret" speech to the 20th party congress in February 1956 Khrushchev denounced the Stalinist terror.

Khrushchev's denunciation of Stalin triggered off serious challenges to the Communist regimes in Poland and also in Hungary, where orthodox Communist rule was re-established by Soviet military intervention in November 1956. In March 1958 Khrushchev added the chairmanship of the Council of Ministers to his party leadership, but growing doubts within the CPSU leadership about his internal and external policies culminated in his removal from the party and government leadership in October 1964, in which posts he was succeeded by Leonid Brezhnev and Alexei Kosygin respectively.

Under Brezhnev's leadership the cautious liberalization policy of the Khrushchev era was largely halted or reversed. Although the Soviet Government pursued a policy of détente with the West, its refusal to countenance deviation from Communist orthodoxy was demonstrated by the Soviet-led intervention in Czechoslovakia in 1968, following which Brezhnev enunciated his doctrine that Communist countries are entitled to intervene in other Communist countries if the preservation of socialism is deemed to be threatened (i.e. the implementation of "proletarian internationalism"). This principle also underlies the attitude of the CPSU to sister parties in other countries, notably in Afghanistan, Vietnam and Poland.

Having established a position of complete authority as party leader, Brezhnev was elected President of the Presidium of the Supreme Soviet of the USSR (i.e. head of state) in June 1977. On that occasion he said that the decision to combine the party leadership and the USSR presidency demonstrated "the constant growth of the leading role of the Communist Party", which had—and would continue to have—the function of determining the political line on "all key questions of state life".

Meanwhile CPSU congresses marked important developments in the party's policies and work. The 21st congress of the CPSU (1959) affirmed the "final and complete victory of socialism" in the USSR, where the state based on the dictatorship of the proletariat had grown into a "state of the whole people". The party's 22nd congress (1961) adopted its third programme charting routes in "building communism". The 24th congress (1971) emphasized that "a developed socialist society" had been built in the USSR. The 24th congress also adopted a peace programme which was further developed by the 25th (1976) and 26th (1981) congresses. The party thus steered the USSR towards developing further its status as a great power.

The Brezhnev policies have been largely continued by his successors—Yury Andropov (in office from Nov. 12, 1982, to Feb. 9, 1984) and Konstantin Chernenko (since Feb. 13, 1984).

Orientation. The party's internal policy is aimed at raising the people's material and cultural living standards and at building communism. Foreign policy objectives are the protection of peace and consolidation of all progressive forces in their struggle against the danger of a thermonuclear world war.

Structure. The guiding principle of the CPSU's organizational structure is democratic centralism. Primary party organizations at the work-places of Communists are united into district, urban, regional and republic organizations. The highest body is the general meeting (for primary organizations), the conference (for higher organizations), or the congress (for republic organizations). Executive bodies are bureaus or committees, and central committees in the Union Republics. The party's supreme body is the congress, convened at least once every five years, which elects the Central Committee; the latter directs the party's activities between congresses. The Central Committee elects a Politburo to direct the work of the party between plenums of the Central Committee and a secretariat (the effective centre of political power) to direct day-to-day work.

Membership. (Jan. 1, 1983) 18,117,903 full members and candidate members

Publications. Pravda (daily organ), 10,100,000; *Kommunist* (theoretical and political journal, 18 issues per year), over 950,000

United Arab Emirates

Capital: Abu Dhabi   Pop. 1,100,000

The United Arab Emirates are a federal union of seven sheikhdoms whose rulers constitute a Supreme Council—the highest federal authority—which elects from among its members a President and a Vice-President. The President appoints a Prime Minister and a Cabinet. Legislative power is held by a 40-member consultative Federal National Council appointed for two years by the seven partners in the federation. There are no political parties.

United Kingdom

Capital: London   Pop. 55,850,000

The United Kingdom of Great Britain and Northern Ireland is a hereditary constitutional monarchy in which the monarch, as head of state, has numerous specific responsibilities. The supreme legislative authority is Parliament, consisting of (i) a 650-member House of Commons, with a life of not more than five years, directly elected under a simple-majority system in single-member constituencies, with the right to vote being held by British subjects (and citizens of any Commonwealth member country or the Republic of Ireland resident in the United Kingdom) above the age of 18 years, and (ii) a House of Lords, in which more than 1,000 peers and peeresses have the right to a seat for life. The latter include hereditary peers and peeresses, life peers and peeresses appointed by the monarch, 16 law peers and 26 bishops of the Church of England. The Government is headed by a Prime Minister who is leader of the party which commands a majority in the House of Commons. Each candidate standing for election to the House of Commons has to pay a deposit (until recently £150) which is forfeited if he obtains less than one-quarter of the valid votes in his constituency. Any vacancies arising are filled through by-elections.

As a result of general elections held on June 9, 1983, seats in the House of Commons were distributed as follows: Conservatives 397, Labour 209, Alliance 23 (i.e. Liberal Party 17 and Social Democratic Party 6), Official Unionist Party (Northern Ireland) 11, Democratic Unionist Party 3, Scottish National Party 2, *Plaid Cymru* (Welsh Nationalists) 2, Ulster Popular Unity Party 1, Social Democratic and Labour Party (Northern Ireland) 1, Provisional *Sinn Féin* (Northern Ireland) 1.

British National Party (BNP)

Founded. 1960

History. The BNP was established as an alliance of the League of Empire Loyalists, the White Defence League and the National Labour Party. A split in the BNP was caused by the formation of a paramilitary élite corps (named "Spearhead") under the leadership of Colin Jordan and John Tyndall, who broke away from the BNP. Although the National Front claimed that the BNP was one of its founder members in 1967, the BNP later emerged as an independent party contesting 53 constituencies in the June 1983 general elections, in which, however, all its candidates lost their deposits.

Orientation. The BNP is an extreme right-wing, racial nationalist formation.

Communist Party of Great Britain (CPGB)

Address. 16 St John Street, London EC1M 4AL, United Kingdom

Leadership. Michael McGahey (ch.); Gordon McLennan (g.s.)

Founded. 1920

History. The party was formed as a result of a merger between the British Socialist Party, the majority section of the Socialist Labour Party, the South Wales Socialist Society and members of other groupings. Its application for affiliation to the Labour Party was rejected and individual members were later expelled from that party. The party has, however, consistently sought co-operation with Labour Party members and other socialists in campaigns on specific issues, e.g. the post-war peace and anti-nuclear weapons movement, cam-

465

paigns against the Vietnam war and against the 1971 Industrial Relations Act.

In the 1983 general elections the party fielded 34 candidates, all of whom lost their deposits, with none of them winning more than 2.8 per cent of the votes in his constituency.

Orientation. The party seeks to achieve "a socialist Britain in which the means of production, distribution and exchange will be socially owned and utilized in a planned way for the benefit of all". The party's general secretary has insisted that "the road to socialism in Britain will be different from that taken in the Soviet Union" and that in Britain "the transfer of power will take place according to the history and traditions of the British people". The party has repeatedly been critical of Soviet policies. Its annual congress of Nov. 15, 1981, supported the executive committee's view that the USSR should not have intervened in Afghanistan (in December 1979); however, an amendment to this resolution, supporting the Soviet intervention but calling for the complete withdrawal of Soviet troops, was defeated by 157 votes to 115. The congress overwhelmingly called for the return to power of a Labour Party government (although of "a new type").

Structure. The party has about 1,000 area and workplace branches, 15 district committees in England, a Scottish and a Welsh committee, and an executive committee.

Membership. 15,691

Publications. *Morning Star* (daily); *Comment* (fortnightly), 5,000; *Marxism Today* (monthly), 5,000

International affiliations. The CPGB is recognized by the Communist parties of the Soviet-bloc countries.

Conservative and Unionist Party

Address. Conservative Central Office, 32 Smith Square, London SW1P 3HH, United Kingdom

Leadership. Margaret Thatcher (l.); John S. Gummer (ch.)

Founded. About 1830

History. The Conservatives trace their history back to the 17th and 18th century, and the modern party was formed by Sir Robert Peel, who established the first Conservative Government in 1834, shortly before which the term "Conservative" was first used as opposed to "Tory" (a term of Irish origins applied to members of the political grouping which from 1679 opposed Whig attempts to exclude the future James II from the succession to the throne).

The party assumed its present name in 1912 when it was formally joined by the Liberal Unionists (former Liberals who opposed home rule for Ireland and had supported the Conservative Party since 1886). During World War I the party took part in a coalition Government. It was returned to power in 1922 and remained so for most of the inter-war years (from 1931 as the dominant party in a National Government) and during the World War II all-party coalition (under Winston Churchill from May 1940 to July 1945).

After heavily losing the 1945 elections, the Conservatives were in opposition until 1951 and thereafter in power until 1964. The next Conservative Government under Edward Heath in 1970–74 successfully negotiated Britain's entry into the European Community. After being in opposition from 1974, the party was returned to power in May 1979 under the leadership of Margaret Thatcher (the first woman leader of a major British political party).

In the post-war period the Conservative Party has been led by Winston Churchill (1940–55), Anthony Eden (1955–57), Harold Macmillan (1957–63), Sir Alec Douglas-Home (1963–65), Edward Heath, the first leader elected by the parliamentary party (1965–75), and Margaret Thatcher (since February 1975).

Orientation. The Conservative Party has traditionally espoused empirical and pragmatic policies, on the basis that "the state exists for the benefit of the individual and not vice versa". The party stands for "decentralization and diffusion of power, free enterprise, lower taxes on earnings", and it believes that "the free market to regulate supply and demand" is "the best means of achieving economic progress".

Structure. The party has three elements—(i) the National Union representing its mass membership; (ii) the parliamentary party; and (iii) the party headquarters with a central office (and area offices throughout the country) and a research department serving the parliamentary party. The party's basic unit is the constituency association which chooses its parliamentary candidate, and the associations are affiliated to the National Union. There are a separate Scottish Conservative and Unionist Association and a Scottish central office.

Membership. 2,000,000

Publications. *Conservative Newsline* (monthly), 150,000; *Politics Today* (fortnightly), 4,000

International affiliations. International Democrat Union; European Democrat Union

Co-operative Party

Address. 158 Buckingham Palace Road, London SW1W 9UB, United Kingdom

Leadership. B. Hellowell (ch.); D. J. Wise (sec.); Alf Morris (ch., parl. group)

Founded. 1917

History. Established by a decision of the British Co-operative Union (the central body representing British consumer and other co-operatives) in order to secure for the co-operative movement direct representation in Parliament and on local authorities, the party first contested a parliamentary election in 1918, when it gained its first seat. It has been represented in Parliament ever since, in alliance with the Labour Party whereby its candidates stand as "Labour and Co-op" candidates. In June 1983 there were eight members in the House of Commons and eight in the House of Lords. There have been Co-operative members in all Labour Governments since 1924.

Orientation. The party is closely allied with the Labour Party by national agreement.

Structure. The party is controlled by the Co-operative Union through a national executive committee elected by Co-operative societies which subscribe to the Co-op Party fund. Additionally there are individual members of the party and local party branches.

Membership. 15,000 (individual); 10,000,000 (affiliated)

Publications. *Platform* (bimonthly journal), 35,000

International affiliations. International Co-operative Alliance

---

Ecology Party

Address. 36/38 Clapham Road, London SW9 0JQ, United Kingdom

Leadership. Jonathon Porritt, Jean Lambert, Paul Ekins (co-chairs of elected council)

Founded. 1973

History. The party nominated 54 candidates for the 1979 general elections, but all of them lost their deposits and gained an average of only 1.2 per cent of the vote in the contested constituencies, its best results being 2.8 per cent in two. In the 1983 general elections Ecologists contested 108 seats, the highest vote for any candidate being 2.9 per cent.

Orientation. The party is a democratic political party whose policies are based on the principle that people must live in harmony with nature within the limitations of the earth's finite supply of resources. Its aims include unilateral disarmament, a ban on all nuclear as well as chemical and biological weapons, an end to Britain's involvement in NATO, basic material security through a national income scheme, community-based self-reliance, land reform, decentralization, proportional representation and increased aid for third-world countries.

Structure. The party is organized on decentralist and non-hierarchical principles. A conference held twice a year is supreme in all policy-making. Between conferences party business is conducted by an elected council.

International affiliations. The European Greens

Fellowship Party

Address. Woolacombe House, 141 Woolacombe Road, Blackheath, London SE3 8QP, United Kingdom

Leadership. Rowland Hilder (pres.); Ronald Mallone (g.s.); Sidney Hinkes (ch.)

Founded. June 11, 1955

History. The party claims to have been the first to present petitions against all governments' nuclear weapons tests, and this action led to the establishment of the Campaign for Nuclear Disarmament (CND). It has opposed military conscription, the rearming of Germany, Italy and Japan, the invasions of Hungary, Czechoslovakia, Vietnam, Afghanistan and Grenada, and the wars over Vietnam, Suez and the Falklands. It fielded the first anti-H bomb candidates in London, and it has contested numerous elections without, however, gaining any parliamentary seats.

Orientation. Policy aims of this pacifist party include total world disarmament; common ownership of the means of production and distribution; conservation; the pooling of world resources for use of all; support for international law and the United Nations; opposition to all pollution, nuclear power, the European Community, the Warsaw Pact and NATO. It advocates proportional representation, industrial democracy and decentralization.

Structure. The party has a national executive consisting of 16 full members and six office-bearers elected by full members at annual conferences. Policy is decided by conferences and, between them, by the executive. The party's objects and principles can be altered only by a two-thirds majority of full members.

Publications. *Day by Day*, 3,000

International affiliations. Standing Joint Pacifist Committee; links with the Pacifist Socialist Party of the Netherlands

Labour Party

Address. 144-152 Walworth Road, London SE17, United Kingdom

Leadership. Neil Kinnock (l.); Jim Mortimer (g.s.)

Founded. 1900

History. The party was formed as the Labour Representation Committee at a conference held in London attended by representatives of the trade unions, the Independent Labour Party, the Fabian Society and other socialist societies and convened as a result of a decision by the Trades Union Congress to seek improved representation of the labour movement in Parliament. Later in 1900 two Labour members were elected to Parliament. The name of the Committee was changed to the Labour Party in 1906, when there were 29 Labour members in the House of Commons. The first Labour Government was in office from January to November 1924, and the second from June 1929 to August 1931, both under the premiership of Ramsay MacDonald.

The party joined a coalition during World War II and won an overwhelming victory in the 1945 general elections under the leadership of Clement Attlee (party leader from 1933 to 1955). That Government carried out many social and economic reforms, among them the National Insurance and National Health Acts, remaining in office until 1951. After 13 years in opposition (for part of which the party was led by Hugh Gaitskell), Labour was narrowly returned to power in 1964 and consolidated its majority in the 1966 elections, on both occasions under the leadership of Harold Wilson, who remained in office until losing the 1970 elections to the Conservatives.

Labour returned to office as a minority administration in March 1974 after becoming the largest single parliamentary party in the elections of the previous month, and subsequently achieved a narrow overall majority in the October 1974 elections. Wilson vacated the leadership in 1976 to be replaced by James Callaghan, who was obliged to enter into a parliamentary pact with the small Liberal Party after Labour's majority had been eroded by by-election defeats. In the May 1979 general elections the Labour Party suffered a decisive defeat and has been in opposition since then.

After the 1979 election defeat Labour's left wing gained the ascendancy within the party, this development contributing to the defection of some right-wing elements and the eventual formation of the Social Democratic Party in March 1981 (see separate entry). Personifying Labour's "old left", Michael Foot (who succeeded Callaghan in 1980) sought to unify the party on the basis of radical policy commitments, while at the same time moving to expel alleged Trotskyist infiltrators of the "Militant Tendency". Nevertheless, in the June 1983 elections Labour went down to a further heavy defeat, its 27.6 per cent share of the votes being the party's lowest since 1918. In a move to repair the party's public image, the party conference in October 1983 elected Neil Kinnock (then 41) as the party's youngest ever leader.

Orientation. Clause IV (4) of its constitution states that the Labour Party seeks "to secure for the workers by hand or by brain the full fruits of their industry and the most equitable distribution thereof that may be possible upon the basis of the common ownership of the means of production, distribution and exchange, and the best obtainable system of popular administration and control of each industry or service". In its policy documents of the early 1980s the party has stressed the need for a positive state role in the regeneration of the British economy and the creation of jobs. Recent party conferences have voted in favour of unilateral nuclear disarmament while at the same time rejecting motions for a British withdrawal from **NATO**.

Structure. The party is organized in members' branches, a number of which together form a constituency party, affiliating to the party nationally. Trade unions and socialist societies affiliate to the party at national, regional and local level. There are 11 regional councils. The annual conference, the party's supreme policy-making body, elects a national executive committee responsible for policy-making between conferences and for the administration of party business. There are also separate sections for women and for young members (Labour Party Young Socialists). The Labour Party leader is elected at the party conference by an electoral college in which votes are held by trade unions (40 per cent), constituency parties (30 per cent) and the parliamentary party (30 per cent).

Membership. 6,881,000 (individual as well as trade union affiliated)

Publications. *Labour Weekly*; *New Socialist* (monthly); *Focus* (quarterly, on women's issues)

International affiliations. Socialist International; Confederation of Socialist Parties of the European Community

---

Liberal Party

Address. 1 Whitehall Place, London SW1A 2HE, United Kingdom

Leadership. David Steel (l.); John Griffiths (pres.); Roger Pincham (ch.); W. N. Hugh-Jones (s.g.)

History. English liberalism had its origins in the 17th-century struggle by Whigs in favour of freedom of conscience and civil rights which led ultimately to Parliament being accepted as the country's supreme authority rather than the Crown (the term Whig, which is of Scottish origin, being applied to those who opposed the succession of James II in 1685 on account of his Catholic sympathies). The term Liberal Party was formally used by Lord John Russell in 1839 in letters to Queen Victoria. Liberal Governments held office for $52\frac{1}{2}$ out of the $83\frac{1}{2}$ years up to 1914. The National Liberal Federation, set up in 1877, was the national political organization and Liberals were the first to produce manifestos; they introduced a national system of education, the secret ballot, the foundations of the welfare state and a reform of the House of Lords. During World War I, when the party led a coalition Government under David Lloyd-George, it became divided and began to decline, a process accelerated by the rise of the Labour Party on the strength of universal adult suffrage.

During World War II some Liberals held office, and Sir William Beveridge, a Liberal MP in 1944-45, was the architect of the post-war National Health Service and welfare state. While the number of seats gained by the party in elections to the House of Commons had varied from six (in 1951, 1955 and 1959) to nine in 1964 and 12 in 1966, it fell back to six in 1970. In February 1974, however, the party gained over 6,000,000 votes (or 19.3 per cent of the total) and 14 seats, whereas in October 1974 it fell back to 13 seats (for 5,348,193 votes or 18.3 per cent of the total).

In 1976 the party leader was for the first time elected directly by party members. Between March 1977 and July 1978 the party supported the Labour Party Government in pursuit of economic recovery. In the post-war period the Liberal Party has been led by Clement Davies (1945-56), Jo Grimond (1956-67), Jeremy Thorpe (1967-76) and David Steel (since July 1976).

Since 1981 the party has contested elections, both at local and at national level, as part of the Liberal/SDP Alliance (see separate entry).

Orientation. Its 1969 constitution states that the Liberal Party "exists to build a liberal society in which every citizen shall possess liberty, property and security, and none shall be enslaved by poverty, ignorance or conformity" and that its chief care is for the rights and opportunities of the individual, and in all spheres it sets "freedom first".

Structure. With the object of electing Liberals to local, national and European parliaments, there are national parties in Scotland, Wales and Northern Ireland and regional parties in England, with each party having its own organization (in England directed by a national executive committee and administered by a finance and administration board). An annual joint assembly amends the constitution, makes party policy and elects the president and other officers to the party council which, like the standing committee and the parliamentary party, makes policy decisions. There are constituency organizations and bodies representing specific interests.

Membership. 100,000

Publications. *Liberal News* (weekly), 8,000

International affiliations. Liberal International; Federation of Liberal and Democratic Parties of the European Community

---

Liberal/SDP Alliance

Founded. 1981

History. The proposed formation of this Alliance was first set out in a joint statement issued by the Liberal and Social Democratic parties on June 16, 1981, under the title *A Fresh Start for Britain*, in which the two parties agreed not to oppose each other in elections. After winning a number of by-elections to the House of Commons on the basis of this agreement, the Alliance contested the 1983 general elections with an agreed distribution of candidates between the two parties. However, although the Alliance gained 7,793,778 votes or 25.4 per cent of the total (i.e. 4,222,784 votes for 322 Liberal candidates and 3,570,994 for the Social Democratic Party's 311 candidates), it obtained only 23 of the 650 seats, 17 of them for Liberals.

Orientation. The Alliance manifesto for the 1983 general elections included the following aims: an end to the two-party system in Britain, a reduction of unemployment by sustained policies for growth based on "carefully selected increases in public spending and reductions in taxation" and direct action to provide jobs, an incomes policy, protection of the environment on "the polluter pays" principle, the introduction of a system of proportional representation (with preferential voting by single transferable vote), adherence to the principle of collective security and commitment to NATO (including its nuclear component), continued membership of the European Community and an increase in Britain's contribution to aid for the poorest countries.

Structure. The Alliance established a Joint Leaders' Advisory Committee, and seeks to ensure that the two constituent parties do not oppose each other in elections.

National Front (NF)

Address. 50 Pawsons Road, Croydon CR0 2QF, Surrey, United Kingdom

Leadership. Andrew Brons (ch.); Martin Webster (nat. activities organizer)

Founded. February 1967

History. The NF was founded as a result of a merger of the British National Party, the League of Empire Loyalists and the Racial Preservation Society. It has nominated candidates in all general elections since its formation, i.e. 10 in 1970, 54 in February 1974, 92 in October 1974, 303 in 1979 and 60 in 1983. It has also frequently contested parliamentary by-elections in which it received its best result in West Bromwich in 1973 with 16.02 per cent of the vote.

NF meetings and demonstrations have frequently been attacked, leading to riots in Red Lion Square (London) in 1974, Lewisham (south-east London) in 1977 and Southall (a centre of heavy Asian population to the west of the capital) in 1979. The right of NF candidates to hire halls for election meetings was upheld in a High Court ruling in November 1982, but NF marches have been banned under a Public Order Act; moreover, NF leaders have been sentenced for "incitement to racial hatred" under the Race Relations Act for articles in NF publications. Although the NF has undergone regular splits, it has remained the largest and best-known British racial-nationalist party.

Orientation. The fundamental policy of the NF is "the restoration and preservation of British national sovereignty". Hence the NF is a racial-nationalist movement which opposes multi-racialism and seeks to restore Britain as an ethnically homogeneous population state. It seeks to liberate Britain from all internationalist ties such as the United Nations, the Common Market, NATO, the International Monetary Fund, the World Bank, etc. It opposes the international financial system and "bankers' usury" and other systems whereby the economies of the nations of the world are integrated, leading to political integration and the development of a "world government". The NF opposes "big business capitalism" and monopoly and favours small privately-owned enterprises and workers' co-operatives. The NF opposes communism and international Zionism. It seeks to establish a special relationship between Britain and the former "White Dominion" countries.

Structure. The governing body of the NF is the national directorate, of whose 18 seats six become vacant each year and are filled by postal ballot of the entire membership. Each year the directorate elects four of its members to join the chairman and deputy chairman in an executive council which is empowered to act for and on behalf of the directorate between monthly directorate meetings. Members in defined areas are formed into branches. The functioning of the national directorate and all sub-units of the party is regulated by the NF constitution which can be amended only by vote of the membership attending annual general meetings, which all members are entitled to attend.

Publications. *Let Britain Live!* (manifesto of NF); *National Front News* (monthly), 10,000; *Nationalism Today* (six-weekly news review/comment magazine); *Bulldog* (bi-monthly paper for young people); *New Nation* (quarterly ideological magazine)

National Party

Address. 6 Pawsons Road, Croydon, Surrey, United Kingdom

Leadership. John Kingsley Read (ch.)

Founded. 1974

History. This right-wing party broke away from the National Front (NF), seeking to promote more moderate policies than those of the NF.

Publications. *Britain First*

Revolutionary Communist Party of Britain (Marxist-Leninist)

Leadership. David Williams (s.g.)

Orientation. This party takes a pro-Albanian line and is ideologically hostile to all other communist parties, including both Soviet and Chinese "revisionism".

Publications. *Workers' Weekly*

Scottish National Party (SNP)

Address. 6 North Charlotte St., Edinburgh EH2 4JH, Scotland, United Kingdom

Leadership. Donald Stewart (pres.); Gordon Wilson (ch.); Neil R. MacCallum (nat. sec.)

Founded. 1934

History. The SNP was founded as a merger of the National Party of Scotland and the Scottish Party. It won a by-election in Motherwell in April 1945 but lost this House of Commons seat in the general elections three months later. Thereafter the SNP held only single seats in the House of Commons—Hamilton from 1967 to 1970, Western Isles from 1970 to 1974 and Govan from 1973 to February 1974; but in the February 1974 general elections the SNP won seven seats with 21.9 per cent of the vote in Scotland.

In the October 1974 elections the SNP gained 11 seats with 30.4 per cent of the Scottish vote, whereupon the then Labour Government produced an Act to set up a devolved Scottish Assembly. While the SNP had already lost three by-elections in Scotland in 1978, the March 1979 referendum on the Assembly resulted in about 52 per cent of those taking part in the referendum voting in favour of a Scottish Assembly (but only 32.85 per cent of those entitled to vote—the turnout having been only 63.72 per cent).

The UK Parliament thereupon refused to set up the Assembly and in the 1979 general elections the SNP lost all but two of its seats (although it still polled 17.2 per cent of the Scottish vote). Both these seats in the House of Commons were retained in the 1983 elections but the SNP's share of the Scottish vote contracted to 11.8 per cent (331,975 votes), which was only slightly more than in 1970. Since 1979 the SNP has held one seat in the European Parliament.

Orientation. The SNP identifies itself as "moderate, left-of-centre" on economic and social questions; its basic aim is Scottish independence, i.e. the establishment of a democratic Scottish Parliament within the Commonwealth.

Structure. The SNP is based on autonomous branches and constituency associations, which send delegates to the party's supreme governing body, the annual national conference. The party's national council, which meets four times a year, acts as the party's governing body between conferences. An elected national executive committee runs the party between meetings of council. A commission of inquiry has been appointed to examine reforms of the party structure.

Membership. 40,000 (est.)

Scottish Socialist Party

Leadership. Stephen Maxwell (convenor)

Founded. Jan. 29, 1983

History. This group has its origin in a left-wing and republican "1979 group" within the Scottish National Party (SNP), whose "traditionalist" policy of regarding Scotland's independence as its sole aim the group opposed. In June 1982 the group was barred from the SNP, and later that year it became an interim committee of the new Scottish Socialist Society which was eventually formally launched in January 1983.

Social Democratic Party (SDP)

Address. 4 Cowley St., London SW1P 3NB, United Kingdom

Leadership. Dr David Owen (l.); Shirley Williams (pres.); Richard Newby (nat. sec.)

Founded. March 26, 1981

History. The SDP was formally launched with the support of 14 members of the House of Commons and about 20 members of the House of Lords, following the formation, in January 1981, of a Council for Social Democracy under the joint leadership of four former Labour cabinet ministers—Roy Jenkins, Dr David Owen, William Rodgers and Shirley Williams. The three last-named had on Aug. 1, 1980, claimed that the Labour Party could regain electoral support for progressive policies only if it remained firmly committed to parliamentary democracy, rejected the class war, accepted the mixed economy and attached importance to the ideals of freedom, equality and social justice. In the House of Commons 12 Labour members decided on March 2, 1981, to sit in the House as Social Democrats; by October 1981 their example had been followed by eight others, while the SDP was also joined by a former Conservative member of the House (Christopher Brocklebank-Fowler).

On June 16, 1981, the SDP entered in principle into an electoral alliance with the Liberal Party. In a by-election at Crosby on Nov. 21, 1981, Shirley Williams was elected to the House of Commons as the Alliance's candidate. By Dec. 2, 1981, the total strength of the SDP in the House had risen, through further defections from the Labour Party, to 25. In the general elections of June 1983, however, which the SDP contested as part of the Alliance, it retained only six seats in the House. The party is supported by 41 peers in the House of Lords.

Orientation. The SDP is a left-of-centre party advocating a change in the political system by the introduction of proportional representation; a consistent economic strategy involving investments in new industries and a flexible incomes policy; the reduction of unemployment through the creation of new jobs and other measures; support for a mixed economy; a fair distribution of wealth; decentralization; and co-operation with other countries, in particular in the European Community and in NATO, pursuing multilateral but not unilateral disarmament.

Structure. A council of some 400 members elected from "area parties" (the basic or constituency units of the party) is the SDP's policy-making organ. A national committee, consisting of the party's members of Parliament, elected members and one peer, is the party's executive steering committee.

Membership. 50,000

Publications. *The Social Democrat*; *Open Forum* (discussion papers)

Socialist League

Leadership. Collective

Founded. 1956

History. The Socialist League derives from the International Marxist Group (IMG), which was formed as a breakaway group of the Communist Party after the Hungarian crisis of 1956. It worked as a secret Trotskyist group inside the Labour Party but came out into the open in 1968. It did not contest any parliamentary elections under its own name, but a Socialist Unity group, with Tariq Ali (a leading IMG member) as one of nine candidates, unsuccessfully took part in those of 1979. (Tariq Ali subsequently applied for membership of the Labour Party.) The IMG changed its name to Socialist League in 1982.

Orientation. The League's declared aim is the overthrow of the capitalist system, and it is intent on unifying the extreme left-wing groups in Britain in one revolutionary party (in particular with the inclusion of the Socialist Workers' Party).

Publications. *Red Weekly*, 10,000; *Imprecor* (monthly)

International affiliations. The League is the British section of the Fourth (Trotskyist) International.

Socialist Party of Great Britain (SPGB)

Address. 52 Clapham High St., London SW4 7UN, United Kingdom

Founded. 1904

History. In the course of its history, the SPGB has opposed both world wars and has advocated "the need for a majority of the population democratically to take control of the state and establish a system of common ownership". In contesting parliamentary and local elections (with regular lack of success) it has remained "consistently opposed to the political parties right or left". The SPGB has links with similarly named and orientated parties in a number of other developed countries.

Orientation. The SPGB is a Marxist party seeking "the establishment of a world-wide community based on the common ownership and democratic control of the means of wealth distribution and production".

Structure. The local branch is the organization's unit. Annual conferences attended by instructed delegates take binding decisions. An executive committee elected annually by postal ballot of the whole membership is answerable to the annual conference. The party is opposed to any form of leadership and its general secretary, who is an administrative officer only, is also elected annually by postal ballot.

Membership. 700

Publications. *Socialist Standard* (monthly), 3,000-4,000

Socialist Workers' Party (SWP)

Address. P.O. Box 82, London E2, United Kingdom

Leadership. Duncan Hallas (ch.)

Founded. 1950

History. Founded as the International Socialists and known under that name until 1977, this party is opposed to what it regards as the authoritarian socialism of the Soviet bloc. Under its new name the SWP has worked towards "the building of a nucleus of a serious revolutionary party", not by infiltrating the labour movement but in influencing it in a leftward direction from outside. It is not averse to the use of force in support of socialist legislation opposed by forces of the right. It has not taken part in recent general elections, but it has led militant campaigns through the Anti-Nazi League and the Right to Work movement.

Orientation. The SWP subscribes to Trotskyist precepts.

Structure. The party has an SWP Student Association claiming to have 2,000 sympathizers.

Membership. 3,600

Publications. *Socialist Worker* (weekly), 34,000; *Socialist Review* (monthly); *International Socialism* (quarterly theoretical organ)

Sons of Cornwall—Cornish National Movement
Mebyon Kernow

Address. Trewolsta, Trewirgie, Redruth, Cornwall, United Kingdom
Leadership. R. G. Jenkin (ch.); Len Truran (nat. sec.)
Founded. 1951
History. The Movement developed from an organization dedicated to the furtherance of the Cornish language and culture and by 1960 claimed to have the active support of three Cornish members of Parliament belonging to other parties. In 1974 *Mebyon Kernow* decided to campaign in parliamentary elections, and MPs of other parties have since then no longer been eligible for membership. It has "independent" representatives on the county council and official representatives on various local councils. In the 1983 general elections it unsuccessfully contested two seats.
Orientation. The Movement embraces "all political viewpoints" but its "primary aim is Cornish self-government".
Structure. The Movement has individual members, groups, branches, constituency committees and an executive council.
Membership. 5,000-6,000
Publications. *Cornish Nation* (quarterly), 1,000; *An Forth* (The Way)
International affiliations. Federal Union of European Nationalities; Bureau of Unrepresented Nationalities in Europe; Celtic League

---

Welsh Nationalist Party-Party of Wales
Plaid Cymru

Address. 51 Heol yr Eglwys Gadeiriol/Cathedral Road, Caerdydd/Cardiff CF1 9HD, Wales, United Kingdom
Leadership. Dafydd Wigley (pres.); Dafydd Iwaw (ch.); Dafydd Williams (g.s.)
Founded. August 1925
History. The party has contested all elections to the Westminster Parliament since 1945 but remained a comparatively small movement until in July 1966 its president gained a seat in the House of Commons in a by-election at Carmarthen. Although the party lost that seat in 1970, it gained two other seats in February 1974, and in addition regained the Carmarthen seat in October of that year. The party is also represented in local government and (in 1978) controlled two Welsh district councils. In the May 1979 general elections in obtained 132,544 votes (0.4 per cent of the national total), holding the Caernarvon and Merioneth seats but losing Carmarthen to Labour. In 1983 it held its two seats and obtained altogether 125,309 votes.
Orientation. The party seeks full self-government for Wales, representation at the United Nations and restoration of the Welsh language and culture.
Structure. The party has branches which elect representatives to constituency committees represented on the national council, which meets four times a year. The party's supreme body is the annual conference, which elects leading officials and a national executive committee.
Membership. 30,000
Publications. *Y Ddraig Goch* (monthly); *Welsh Nation* (monthly)

Workers' Revolutionary Party (WRP)

Address. 21b Old Town, London SW4 0JT, United Kingdom
Leadership. Mike Banda (g.s.)
Founded. 1973
History. The WRP succeeded the Socialist Labour League (founded in 1959) and at first worked inside the Labour Party. Since 1974 it has unsuccessfully contested general elections. In 1979 it nominated 60 parliamentary candidates who gained a total of 12,631 votes (and no seats). In the 1983 general elections it unsuccessfully contested 22 seats. The party's best known members are the actress Vanessa Redgrave and her brother Corin Redgrave.
Orientation. Generally regarded as Trotskyist, the WRP stated in its 1979 election manifesto that it sought "to carry out revolutionary socialist change peacefully and democratically", including the nationalization without compensation of financial institutions and major industries. The WRP is not only in favour of a "revolutionary alternative" in internal British left-wing politics but also of the Republican movement in Ireland and of the Palestine Liberation Organization (and is therefore anti-Zionist).
Structure. The WRP has formed a Trade Union Alliance movement, and it has a Young Socialists movement, mainly among students.
Publications. *Newsline* (daily)

Other Parties

Other parties or groups which unsuccessfully contested the June 1983 general elections included the following (with each party contesting only one constituency unless otherwise stated in parentheses):

Common Market Party
Council for United Ireland
Freedom Party
Independent Communist
Independent Conservative (6)
Independent Democratic Unionist Party
Independent Labour (4)

Independent Liberal (4)
Irish National Party
Isle of Wight Residents' Party
Labour Independent
Modern Democratic Party
Multiracial Political Party
National Labour Party
Progressive Liberal
Revolutionary Communist (4)
Scottish Ecologists
Spare the Earth Ecology
United Country Party
Wessex Regionalists (10)
Women for Life on Earth (2)
Workers' Party for a Workers' State

Northern Ireland

Capital: Belfast   Pop. 1,560,000

Northern Ireland is a province of the United Kingdom of Great Britain and Northern Ireland, comprising six of the nine counties in the historic Irish province of Ulster. Under the Northern Ireland Act of July 1974 the Secretary of State for Northern Ireland and his ministers are responsible to the United Kingdom Parliament at Westminster for the government of Northern Ireland. Under a Northern Ireland Act 1982 elections were held on Oct. 20, 1982, to a Northern Ireland Assembly, the main task of which was to make recommendations for a full or partial devolution of powers from Westminster to Northern Ireland. The 78-member Assembly was elected for a four-year term under the single transferable vote system of proportional representation (as used in the Republic of Ireland) on the basis of the then existing 12 constituencies for elections to the United Kingdom House of Commons. The resultant distribution of seats in the Assembly was as follows: Official Unionist Party (OUP) 26, Democratic Unionist Party (DUP) 21, Social Democratic and Labour Party (SDLP) 14, Alliance Party 10, Provisional *Sinn Féin* 5, Independent Unionist 1, Ulster Popular Unionist Party (UPU) 1.

As a result of the June 9, 1983, general elections the 17 Northern Ireland seats in the United Kingdom House of Commons (filled by simple majority in single-member constituencies) were distributed as follows: OUP 11, DUP 3, UPUP 1, SDLP 1, Provisional *Sinn Féin* 1.

Alliance Party of Northern Ireland

Address. 88 University St., Belfast BT7 1HE, Northern Ireland
Leadership. Oliver Napier (l.); Jane Copeland (ch.); Susan Edgar (sec.)
Founded. April 1970
History. Formed with the intention "to cross the sectarian divide in Northern Ireland" the party first contested elections in 1973, when it obtained 9.2 per cent of the

vote for the Northern Ireland Assembly. It subsequently entered into a coalition with the Social Democratic and Labour Party (SDLP) and a section of the Unionist Party to form the Northern Ireland power-sharing Executive in January-May 1974. In the May 1975 Constitutional Convention elections the party obtained 9.8 per cent of the vote, and in the 1977 local government elections 14.3 per cent of the vote, thus becoming the third largest political party in Northern Ireland. In the province's Assembly elected in October 1982 the party gained 10 (out of 78) seats (obtaining 9.3 per cent of the vote).

Orientation. The Alliance claims to be a "pragmatic, non-doctrinaire and non-sectarian party of the centre"; it favours the maintenance of Northern Ireland's union with Great Britain.

Structure. The party's basic units are 33 associations which send delegates (approximately six each) to the party council which is the party's governing body and meets quarterly; there is also an annual conference.

Membership. 12,000

Publications. *Alliance* (monthly.), 7,000

Communist Party of Ireland (CPI)

Address. Unity Press, 4 Exchange Place, Belfast 1, Northern Ireland

History. The CPI has operated in Northern Ireland as an integral part of the all-Ireland party (see entry under Ireland), although there is a Northern Committee based in Belfast.

Publications. *Unity* (fortnightly)

Democratic Unionist Party (DUP)

Address. 296 Albertbridge Road, Belfast BT5 4GX, Northern Ireland

Leadership. The Rev. Dr Ian R. K. Paisley (l.); Peter Robinson (dep. l.); James McClure (ch.)

Founded. 1969

History. The party was formed from two "loyalist" groups (Ulster Protestant Action and the Ulster Constitution Defence Committee) as the Protestant Unionist Party (PUP) to oppose the politics of the then Unionist Government under Terence O'Neill, whose conciliatory attitude towards the Republic of Ireland it regarded as likely to lead to "the destruction of Ulster". The PUP gained its first two parliamentary seats in by-elections to the Northern Ireland Parliament in April 1970, and Dr Paisley won a seat in the Westminster Parliament in June 1970. In 1971 the PUP was transformed into the Democratic Unionist Party (DUP).

Dr Paisley retained his seat in Westminster, being elected as a member of the United Ulster Unionist Council (UUUC) in February and October 1974 and re-elected as the DUP candidate in 1979 when the party gained two further seats at Westminster. It retained its three

seats in 1983. In Northern Ireland, the DUP gained eight (out of 78) seats in the Northern Ireland Assembly on June 28, 1973; 12 seats (out of 46 UUUC seats) in elections held on May 1, 1975, to the Constitutional Convention (which, after inconclusive sessions, was dissolved in March 1976); and 71 out of 526 seats in 26 district council elections held on May 8, 1977. In June 1979 Dr Paisley was elected to the European Parliament.

In the Northern Ireland Assembly elected in October 1982 it is the second strongest party with 21 seats (out of 78).

Orientation. The DUP stands for the maintenance of Northern Ireland as an integral part of the United Kingdom; the imposition and maintenance of the rule of law in Northern Ireland; and a policy of social betterment and equal opportunity for all sections of the community. It opposes any constitutional arrangement involving the sharing of power between Unionist and National parties.

Structure. Based on Westminster constituencies, with local branches electing delegates to a central delegates' assembly.

Irish Independence Party (IIP)

Address. 24 Northland Road, Derry, Northern Ireland

Founded. October 1977

Leadership. Jim Murphy (l.); Frank MacManus (dep.l.); Fergus McAteer (ch. central exec.)

History. On its foundation the party attracted the remaining support of the now-defunct Nationalist Party and some members of the dominant constitutional nationalist party, the SDLP. It has always condemned political violence but has on occasion shared platforms with Provisional *Sinn Féin* on matters such as the rights of Republican prisoners. In recent years it has tended to concentrate on local government, having 21 councillors across Northern Ireland, and has withdrawn candidacies in Northern Ireland and Westminster elections in favour of the SDLP in order to avoid splitting the nationalist vote.

Orientation. The party seeks to dissolve the link with Britain in a phased and orderly manner, to secure political and economic independence for Ireland with national reunification through a constitutional conference. It opposes Republican violence but sees this as a consequence of the British presence.

Structure. The party has a number of branches co-ordinated by a central executive.

Irish Republican Socialist Party (IRSP)

History. The IRSP is organized both north and south of the border, so that the party in Northern Ireland is the same as that based in Dublin (see entry under Ireland).

Labour and Trade Union Groups

Founded. 1975
History. With the gradual demise of the Northern Ireland Labour Party (NILP), which still formally exists but has effectively ceased to function as a party, a number of small apparently autonomous groups have been formed in urban centres including Derry and Newtownabbey. They advocate the re-formation of a labour party based on the Northern Ireland trade union movement, and occasionally contest elections.
Orientation. The policies advocated by the Labour and Trade Union Groups are broadly similar to those advanced by the British Labour Party, i.e. democratic socialist. The groups are non-sectarian in the religious sense.

Labour Movement in Local Government

Leadership. Paddy Devlin, Robert Clarke
Founded. May 1984
History. This Movement was launched with the immediate aim of contesting local government elections in 1985 and presenting candidates representing the labour and trade union movement. It has appealed to the British Labour Party for political support.
Orientation. The Movement seeks to build a "real majority" by representing the "common human needs of all people in Northern Ireland", in preference to becoming "embroiled in the fruitless and circular debate about constitutional changes 'by consent' ".

Labour Representation Committee (LRC)

Founded. 1984
History. The LRC is the successor to the Campaign for Labour Representation in Northern Ireland (CLRNI), which was founded in the mid-1970s.
Orientation. The Committee campaigns for the extension of the British Labour Party to Northern Ireland, where the Labour Party at present permits individual membership but does not allow the formation of branches or active participation in politics in its name.

Northern Ireland Labour Party (NILP)

Address. 100 University Street, Belfast 7, Northern Ireland
Leadership. Robert Clarke (ch.); Cecil Allen (g.s.)
History. The NILP was originally strongly based in the Northern Ireland trade union movement and has traditional (but not institutional) links with the British Labour Party. It became the first non-Unionist party to participate in a Northern Ireland Government, when David Bleakley held the Community Relations portfolio from March to September 1971. In the May 1975 Constitutional Convention elections it obtained only 1.4 per cent of the vote and returned one member (David Bleakley), the party's strength and influence suffering erosion in the growing polarization of Northern Ireland politics. It took no part in the 1982 Assembly or the 1983 general elections and has a continued existence that is more formal than real.
Orientation. The NILP is democratic socialist, non-sectarian (but drawing most of its original strength from the Protestant working class).
International affiliations. Socialist International; Confederation of Socialist Parties of the European Community (consultative member)

Official Unionist Party (OUP)

Address. 3 Glengall Street, Belfast BT12 5AE, Northern Ireland
Leadership. James Molyneaux (l.)
Founded. 1905
History. The party dominated the Northern Ireland Parliament from the latter's establishment under the 1920 Government of Ireland Act (which came into force in 1921) until the introduction of direct British rule in March 1972. During the period it was known as the Ulster Unionist Council (which remains its official name despite the adoption of the OUP form in 1974). In the Westminster Parliament the party became an independent group in February 1972, when its members ceased to take the whip of the (British) Conservative and Unionist Party—but it nevertheless remained organizationally linked with that party. The

OUP retained the majority of members of the party on the split in 1974 which led to the formation of the more liberal Unionist Party of Northern Ireland.

In June 1979 John Taylor was elected to the European Parliament for the OUP as one of Northern Ireland's three representatives in that body. The OUP has remained the dominant Ulster Unionist party in the Northern Ireland Assembly, in the House of Commons and in the district councils.

Orientation. The party stands for Northern Ireland's continued link with the British Crown; the application of the British parliamentary system in Northern Ireland, with the latter's Government being responsible for internal security; parity of representation of Northern Ireland in the British Parliament; and the rejection of any imposed institutionalized association with the Republic of Ireland.

Progressive Unionist Party (PUP)

Leadership. Hugh Smyth
Founded. 1980
History. The party is widely regarded as the successor to the Volunteer Political Party (VPP), the acknowledged political wing of the illegal "loyalist" paramilitary Ulster Volunteer Force (UVF), though no such connexion is advertised by the present PUP leadership. Its sole elected representative is Hugh Smyth, deputy mayor of Belfast; it has stood without success in other elections.
Orientation. PUP is a populist loyalist organization based in Protestant working-class areas of Belfast.

Provisional Sinn Féin (SF)

Address. 51/53 Falls Road, Belfast 12, Northern Ireland
Leadership. Gerry Adams (pres.)
Founded. 1905
History. Sinn Féin, as the party prefers to call itself, operates as a single organization in Northern Ireland and the Republic of Ireland. It broke away from the "Official" republican movement (now represented by the Workers' Party) in 1969. It is the political wing of the Provisional Irish Republican Army (IRA), which is engaged in violent struggle against the British régime in Northern Ireland. *Sinn Féin* has increasingly been gaining support among the Roman Catholic population of Northern Ireland, largely at the expense of the Social Democratic and Labour Party (SDLP). A member of *Sinn Féin*, Owen Carron, was elected to the House of Commons in a by-election on Aug. 20, 1981, in succession to a convicted member of the IRA, Robert (Bobby) Sands (who had been elected on April 9, 1981, but had died on May 5 as a result of his hunger strike in prison). Contesting the October 1982 elections to the Northern Ireland Assembly SF gained five seats (with 10.15 per cent of the vote). However, the member of Parliament and the five elected Assemblymen refused to take up their seats, contending that neither body had any legitimate authority. (*Sinn Féin* has consistently maintained that the last valid elections in Ireland were those for the national parliament or *Dáil* in 1917, when *Sinn Féin* won a majority of the seats.) It was officially announced on Nov. 5, 1982, that the Assemblymen would have access to junior ministers on constituency matters but not to the Secretary of State for Northern Ireland until the party had dissociated itelf from violence.

Sinn Féin first won a seat on a district council in a by-election in Omagh on March 22, 1983, when its candidate obtained 55 per cent of the vote. In the June 1983 general elections SF gained one seat in the House of Commons (for Adams in Belfast West) and came second in two other constituencies (having contested altogether 14 of the 17 Northern Ireland seats).

Orientation. SF has defended the IRA's campaign of violence as "legitimate". In its 1983 election manifesto the party declared its opposition to the SDLP and its commitment to a "democratic socialist" Republic of Ireland, and concluded: "We see the six-county state (i.e. Northern Ireland) as irreformable and believe that full civic rights, an end to discrimination, unemployment, social deprivation and sectarianism can only be achieved when we achieve our national rights—that is independence and unity."

Structure. The party's branches are co-ordinated by county or district committees; there are four provincial executives, one of which includes Northern Ireland; the party's national executive is based in Dublin and the highest authority in the party is the annual conference, or *Ard Fhéis.*

Social Democratic and Labour Party (SDLP)

Address. 38 University Street, Belfast BT7 1FZ, Northern Ireland
Leadership. John Hume (l.); Seán Farren (ch.); Eamonn Hanna (g.s.)

Founded. August 1970
History. The party was formed by members of the then Northern Ireland Parliament, comprising two of the former Republican Labour Party, one of the Northern Ireland Labour Party, one Nationalist and three independents. It participated in the short-lived power-sharing Executive in 1974, when its leader was Gerry Fitt (who later left the party).

The SDLP, contesting the Northern Ireland Assembly elections in October 1982, gained 14 seats but did not take them up because of continued Unionist opposition to power-sharing. In June 1979 John Hume was elected to the European Parliament, and in June 1983 he was elected to the United Kingdom House of Commons. The party had previously been represented at Westminster by Gerry Fitt from 1966 until November 1979, whereafter he sat as an "independent socialist" until he was defeated (in Belfast West) in the 1983 general elections.

Orientation. As the principal representative of the Roman Catholic population in Northern Ireland, the SDLP, a left-of-centre party, stands for partnership between Protestants and Catholics in Northern Ireland and between both parts of Ireland, with a view to eventual reunification by consent. The SDLP is anti-sectarian and strongly repudiates violence. It has also declared its solidarity with the European peace movement and all efforts to rid the world of nuclear weapons, and it has committed itself to the maintenance of Ireland as a nuclear-weapon-free zone.

Publications. *The Social Democrat* (monthly)

International affiliations. Socialist International; Confederation of Socialist Parties of the European Community

---

Ulster Liberal Party

Address. 24 Landseer St., Belfast BT9 6AL, Northern Ireland
Leadership. Michael Warden (ch.); Tony Coghlan (vice-ch.); P. Mateer (sec.)
History. The party was represented in the pre-1972 Parliament of Northern Ireland but has not contested any elections in recent years. Many of its members joined the Alliance Party on the latter's formation in 1970.
Orientation. The party is associated with the British Liberal Party and supports the latter's policy on Northern Ireland.
Membership. 30–40
Publications. *Focus* (occasional)

Ulster Loyalist Democratic Party (ULDP)

Leadership. John McMichael (l.)
Founded. c. 1981
History. The party is an offshoot of the (working-class loyalist) Ulster Defence Association (UDA), founded in 1972. It has stood unsuccessfully in elections to the Northern Ireland Assembly.
Orientation. The UDA, to which the UDLP is generally regarded as subordinate, was founded as a reaction to Republican violence, with the aim of preserving the union between Northern Ireland and Great Britain. In later years, although the UDA as such remained a paramilitary organization with no direct participation in constitutional politics, the UDA leadership, first in the New Ulster Study Group and then in the ULDP, showed a willingness to consider other constitutional options, principally that of an independent Northern Ireland state.

Ulster Popular Unionist Party (UPUP)

Leadership. James Kilfedder (l.)
Founded. January 1980
History. This party was first known as the Ulster Progressive Unionist Party, and its founder and leader has represented the Down, North, constituency in the House of Commons since 1970 (having earlier sat for Belfast, West, in 1964–66). Shortly after the October 1974 general elections he left the former United Ulster Unionist Coalition at Westminster and sat as an independent until the May 1979 elections, in which he was re-elected as an Ulster Unionist. In October 1982 he was elected to the Northern Ireland Assembly (of which he became the Speaker), and in June 1983 he was re-elected to the House of Commons.
Orientation. The UPUP stands for devolved government in Northern Ireland and for proportional representation in Westminster elections; it also supports the desegregation of Northern Ireland's schools. It is generally regarded as the most liberal of the Unionist parties.

**The Workers' Party
Pairtí na nOibrí**

Address. 6 Springfield Road, Belfast, Northern Ireland
Leadership. Tomás Mac Giolla (pres.); Séamus Lynch (Northern ch.)
Founded. 1905.
History. This party operates both in

Northern Ireland and in the Republic of Ireland (see entry under Ireland); it was originally the political wing of the Official Irish Republican Army. In Northern Ireland it operated as *Sinn Féin* until 1966; as the Republican Clubs until 1977; as the Workers' Party—Republican Clubs until 1982; and thereafter as the Workers' Party. It contested the October 1982 elections to the Northern Ireland Assembly but obtained only 2.72 per cent of the vote and no seat. For the general elections of June 1983 to the United Kingdom House of Commons it nominated candidates in 14 of the 17 Northern Ireland constituencies but gained no seats.

Orientation. The Workers' Party is a Marxist party aiming at unity between Protestant and Catholic workers in order to achieve an all-Ireland socialist republic.

Structure. The party has branches, district committees and a six-county executive; the highest authority in the party is the annual conference, or *Ard Fhéis*, which appoints a national executive based in Dublin.

World Socialist Party of Ireland

Address. 147 Gilnakirk Road, Belfast 5, Northern Ireland

International affiliations. This party is linked with the Socialist Party of Great Britain.

United Kingdom Crown Dependencies

Channel Islands

Capital: St Helier (Jersey)   Pop. 130,500

The Channel Islands, attached to the Crown of England since 1066, consist of Jersey and Guernsey with dependencies. Each of the two islands has a lieutenant-governor representing the British monarch and a bailiff appointed by the Crown as President of each of the States (legislatures) and of the Royal Courts. The States of Jersey consist of 12 senators elected for six years (six of them retiring every three years), 12 constables elected for three years and 28 deputies elected also for three years—all being elected by universal adult suffrage. The elected members of the States of Deliberation of Guernsey are 33 people's deputies chosen by popular franchise, 10 representatives chosen by parish authorities and two representatives of the States of Alderney (which is a dependency of Guernsey).

Elections are not held on the lines of British political parties, but in Jersey some members of the States represent the Jersey Democratic Movement.

Isle of Man

Capital: Douglas   Pop. 65,000

The Isle of Man is a dependency of the British Crown under its own laws administered by the Court of Tynwald, consisting of a governor (appointed by the Crown), an 11-member Legislative Council and the House of Keys, which is a 24-member representative Assembly elected for a five-year term by adult suffrage and which elects eight of the Legislative Council members.

In elections held on Nov. 19, 1981, to the House of Keys the Manx Labour Party obtained three seats while the remaining 21 seats went to independents.

Manx Labour Party

Leadership. Alan Clague (ch.)
History. The party commanded a majority in the House of Keys until November 1981, when its strength was reduced to three members.

Manx National Party

Leadership. Audrey Ainsworth (ch.)
Orientation. The party advocates internal independence of the UK Home Office for the Isle of Man.

Sons of Man
Mec Vannin

Address. Brottby, Peveril Road, Peel, Isle of Man, United Kingdom

Leadership. Lewis Crellin (pres.); Jack Irving (ch.); (Mrs) Hazel Hannan (sec.)
Founded. 1962
History. *Mec Vannin* was, in its beginnings, not a party in the strict sense, but now considers itself "a party of foresight", whose policies are and will be implemented gradually. It has had some success in local elections even though most Manx politicians are independents. It gained one seat (out of 24) in the Manx Parliament in 1976, but failed to retain this seat in general elections to the House of Keys held in November 1981.
Orientation. The party stands for the independence of the Isle of Man and protection of the Manx way of life.
Structure. There is a party executive, including office bearers of each of two existing branches (western and northern).

United Kingdom Dependent Territories

Anguilla

Capital: Anguilla   Pop. 6,500

Anguilla, one of the Leeward Islands, has under its 1982 Constitution the status of a British dependent territory, having at an earlier period been part of the Associated State of St Kitts-Nevis-Anguilla. In Anguilla the British monarch is represented by a Governor who presides over an Executive Council consisting of a Chief Minister, three other ministers and three ex-officio members. There is a unicameral House of Assembly of seven elected members returned for a five-year term by universal adult suffrage.

In elections to the Assembly held on March 9, 1984, the Anguilla National Alliance won four seats, the Anguilla People's Party two and an independent the remaining seat.

Anguilla National Alliance (ANA)

Leadership. Emile Gumbs (l.)
Founded. 1980
History. The ANA replaced the People's Progressive Party (PPP) which, under the leadership of Ronald Webster, had in the May 1976 elections gained six of the seven elective seats in the Legislative Assembly. In February 1977 Webster was replaced, both as leader of the PPP and as Chief Minister, by Emile Gumbs. In elections to the Legislative Assembly's seven elective seats held on May 28, 1980, the ANA obtained one seat, which rose to two in new elections in June 1981. The party was therefore in opposition until March 1984, when in further elections it obtained a majority of the elective seats in the Assembly and thereupon formed an administration with its leader as Chief Minister.

Anguilla People's Party (APP)

Leadership. Ronald Webster (l.)
Founded. 1981
History. As leader of a People's Progressive Party (PPP), then the island's only party, Ronald Webster had in 1967 declared Anguilla to be independent of the Associated State of St Kitts-Nevis-Anguilla, and in January 1969 the island was unilaterally declared an independent republic with Webster as President. However, in March 1969 he agreed with the British Government that Anguilla should be administered by a British Government representative.

Under the 1976 Constitution Webster was Chief Minister of Anguilla until February 1977, when he was defeated in a confidence vote in the Legislative Assembly. He later founded an Anguilla United Party (AUP), which in elections held in May 1980 won six of the seven elective seats in the Legislative Assembly. Following disagreements within the AUP Webster was expelled from that party and founded the Anguilla People's Party which, in new elections held on June 22, 1981, gained five seats in the Assembly (whereas the AUP retained none and subsequently became defunct). Webster thereupon was again appointed Chief Minister. However, the party lost its majority in the March 1984 elections and went into opposition to the Anguilla National Alliance.

Bermuda

Capital: Bermuda   Pop. 60,000

Bermuda is a British colony, with a representative Government and a Cabinet under a Premier (with a wide measure of internal self-government) and with a Governor appointed by the British Government. A 40-member House of Assembly is elected for a five-year term by universal adult suffrage (two members for each of 20 constituencies), voters having to be Bermudians or Commonwealth citizens with Bermudian status and above the age of 21 years. Of the 11 members of the Senate, three are appointed at the Governor's discretion, five on the recommendation of the Premier and three on that of the Leader of the Opposition.

As a result of elections held on Feb. 3, 1983, the parties represented in the House of Assembly were the United Bermuda Party with 26 seats and the Progressive Labour Party with 14 seats.

Progressive Labour Party (PLP)

Address. P.O. Box 1367, Hamilton 5, Bermuda

Leadership. (Mrs) Lois Browne-Evans (l.); E. B. Simmons (ch.)

Founded. 1963

History. The PLP, campaigning for an end to British rule and independence for Bermuda, gained only three out of 36 seats in the House of Assembly elected in 1964, but 10 out of 40 seats in 1968, and in 1976 it gained 44.4 per cent of the vote (and 14 seats—increased to 15 through a by-election later that year). In 1980 its representation in the House rose to 18 members, but in 1983 it fell back to 14.

Orientation. A mainly Black party, the PLP stands for the early independence of Bermuda; it is a left-wing party with relations with the Caribbean "new left".

United Bermuda Party (UBP)

Address. Motoblock Building, Gorham Road, Pembroke 5-32, Bermuda

Leadership. John Swan (l.); Paul A. Leseur (ch.); Altimont Roberts (sec.)

Founded. 1964

History. The multiracial UBP has held a majority in the House of Assembly and has formed the island's Government since the elections of 1968. After being traditionally identified with the White "establishment" in Bermuda, in recent years the party has, under the leadership of a Black businessman, attracted the support of an emerging Black elite.

Orientation. The party proclaims itself to be "basically conservative with liberal attitudes" and to "support the free enterprise system but with a social conscience". On the issue of possible independence for Bermuda the UBP leader has stated that he would act in accordance with "the will of the Bermudian people".

Structure. The party has a central council and an executive officer, first appointed in 1965.

Membership. 3,000

British Virgin Islands

Capital: Road Town, Tortola   Pop. 11,200

The British Virgin Islands are a British dependency with an emerging democratic party system. There is an Executive Council, consisting of a Governor, one ex-officio member and three ministers (including the Chief Minister), and a Legislative Council, which comprises one official, one nominated and nine elected members, with a Speaker elected from outside the Council. The minimum voting age is 18 years.

In elections held in November 1983 the Virgin Islands Party obtained four of the elective seats in the Legislative Council, as did the United Party (UP), with the remaining seat going to an independent who thereupon became Chief Minister in coalition with the UP.

United Party

Leadership. Willard Wheatley (l.)

History. This party held three of the then seven elective seats in the Legislative Council between Sept. 1, 1975, and November 1979, but held no seat in the 1979-83 Council. However, as a result of gaining four seats in the November 1983 elections the UP returned to power with an independent member of the Council (Cyril Romney) who became Chief Minister.

Willard Wheatley (a former Chief Minister) had resumed the party leadership in late 1982 when the then leader, Oliver Cills, had joined the Government of the Virgin Islands Party then in power.

Virgin Islands Party

Leadership. H. Lavity Stoutt (l.)

History. This party's leader was Chief Minister before 1975 and Deputy Chief Minister in 1975-79, after which he was again Chief Minister. It held three of the then seven elective seats in the Legislative Council until 1979, when it gained four of the nine elective seats. It retained these seats in the November 1983 elections but went into opposition to a coalition between an independent and the United Party.

Cayman Islands

Capital: George Town (Grand Cayman)   Pop. 17,000

The Cayman Islands are a British dependent territory with an Executive Council, of which the Governor is the chairman, and a Legislative Assembly consisting of three ex-officio members and 12 members elected by universal adult suffrage in six electoral districts for a four-year term.

   There are no political parties, and all members elected to the Legislative Assembly on Nov. 12, 1980, are independents, but there are two groups among them—(i) "Unity and Teamwork", which is led by James M. Bodden and of which four members were elected to the Executive Council on Nov. 19, 1980, and (ii) "Progress with Dignity", of whose leaders Benson Ebanks was elected to the Assembly on Nov. 12, 1980.

Falkland Islands

Capital: Port Stanley   Pop. 1,600

The Falkland Islands, a British dependent territory, are administered by a Governor advised by an Executive Council of six members (two ex-officio, two appointed and two elected by the Legislative Council). The Legislative Council has two ex-officio members and six others elected by universal adult suffrage. There are no political parties.

Gibraltar

Capital: Gibraltar   Pop. 31,000

As a British colony Gibraltar has, under its 1969 Constitution, a Governor exercising executive authority, a Gibraltar Council under a Chief Minister and a House of Assembly of two ex-officio and 15 elected members serving a four-year term. The franchise is held by British subjects and citizens of the Republic of Ireland resident in Gibraltar for at least six months prior to registration as voters. Each voter has the right to vote for up to eight Assembly members.

In elections to the House of Assembly held on Jan. 26, 1984, the Gibraltar Labour Party gained eight of the elective seats, and the Gibraltar Socialist Labour Party the remaining seven.

Democratic Party for British Gibraltar (DPBG)

Address. P.O.B. 52, Gibraltar
Leadership. Peter Isola (l.); F. Martinez (sec.)
Founded. May 1978
History. Until August 1979 the party was led by Maurice Xiberras, who had been leader of the Integration with Britain Party, which had been in power in Gibraltar in 1969-72 and from which he had resigned in September 1976, when he was elected to the House of Assembly as an independent. Xiberras became leader of the DPBG on its formation in May 1978 (and leader of the Opposition) but was replaced in both capacities by Peter Isola in 1979.

In February 1980 the party fought its first election and gained six of the 15 elective seats in the House of Assembly and over 45 per cent of the votes cast. Its campaign for the granting of British citizenship to Gibraltarians was successful when the British Government granted this right in October 1982. The party ceased to be represented in the House of Assembly after the elections of Jan. 26, 1984.

Gibraltar Labour Party—Association for the Advancement of Civil Rights (GLP—AACR)

Address. 31 Governor's Parade, Gibraltar
Leadership. Sir Joshua A. Hassan (l.); John Piris (g.s.)

Founded. 1942
History. The party's leader was elected Mayor of Gibraltar on an AACR list at Gibraltar's first post-war city council election in 1945. He was the Chief Member of the Legislative Council until 1964, and the party was in power from 1964 to 1969. It returned to office from 1972 onwards, when its leader became Chief Minister under the 1969 Constitution, with the party maintaining its majority in the House of Assembly.
Orientation. The party leader has defined the party's aim as a Gibraltar "with Britain but not under Britain".

Gibraltar Socialist Labour Party (GSLP)

Address. 1 Governor's Meadow House, Gibraltar
Leadership. Joe Bossano (l.); Joe Pilcher (ch.); Luis Sampere (g.s.)
Founded. September 1976
History. The party was formed as the Gibraltar Democratic Movement (GDM) which contested the 1976 elections (for the 15 elective seats of the Gibraltar House of Assembly) with eight candidates, of whom four were elected on a platform of "working for the decolonization of the Rock [of Gibraltar] and the creation of a new constitutional arrangement which will guarantee the future of the territory and the people". In 1977 three of these members of the GDM crossed the floor, only one remained and the GDM changed its name to GSLP.

The party contested the 1980 elections on a socialist programme with six candidates and obtained 20 per cent of the vote and one of the 15 elective seats in the House of Assembly. In January 1984, however, when it fielded eight candidates, it gained all seven opposition seats in the House.

Orientation. The party's constitution is modelled on that of the British Labour Party. Its object is "the creation of a socialist decolonized Gibraltar based on the application of self-determination".

Structure. The GSLP has a central committee of 10 lay members and up to eight members of Parliament.

Membership. 600

Hong Kong

Capital: Victoria   Pop. 5,300,000

The British colony of Hong Kong is administered by a Governor and an Executive Council of five ex-officio and nine other members. It has a Legislative Council composed of four of the ex-officio members of the Executive Council, 18 other official members and 27 unofficial members nominated by the Government.

In addition, the Governor selects (from a wide spectrum of society) unofficial members of the Executive and Legislative Councils (known under the designation UMELCO) who hold more than 300 seats outside the two councils on various committees and boards. They give advice on the formulation of government policies, participate in the enactment of legislation, consider complaints by members of the public and monitor the effectiveness of public administration. There is an UMELCO office, funded by the Government, to provide research and administrative assistance to unofficial members.

Elections to the Hong Kong Urban Council and to district boards are held on a constituency basis, with all persons above the age of 21 years and with more than seven years' residence in Hong Kong being eligible for registration as voters. Organizations which have taken part in Urban Council and district board elections are the Civic Association and the Reform Club of Hong Kong. Political parties from outside Hong Kong with organizations in the colony are the Kuomintang (based in Taiwan) and the Communist Party of China.

Following a visit to Peking, the British Foreign and Commonwealth Secretary confirmed in Hong Kong on April 20, 1984, that the UK Government would withdraw its administration from the colony in 1997, when Hong Kong would revert to China.

Montserrat

Capital: Plymouth Pop. 10,000

The British dependent territory of Montserrat is governed by a Governor and an Executive Council (with the Governor as chairman and two official and four unofficial members—a Chief Minister and three other ministers). There is a Legislative Council consisting of seven members elected by universal adult suffrage, two official members and one nominated member, and having a Speaker chosen from outside the Council.

In elections held on Feb. 25, 1983, the People's Liberation Movement obtained five of the seven elective seats in the Legislative Council, and the Progressive Democratic Party the remaining two.

People's Liberation Movement (PLM)

Leadership. John Osborne (l.)

History. In elections held in November 1978 the PLM gained all seven elective seats on the 10-member Legislative Council (and 62.09 per cent of the valid votes). Its leader thereupon became Chief Minister. In the February 1983 elections, however, its strength in the Council was reduced to five members.

Orientation. The PLM's policy is to recognize agriculture as the basis of the island's economic development; to enhance Montserrat's tourist potential; and to reduce the voting age from 21 to 18 years. The PLM also stands for free enterprise and does not favour early independence for Montserrat.

Progressive Democratic Party (PDP)

Leadership. P. Austin Bramble (l.)

History. The PDP superseded the Montserrat Labour Party (which had been led by the PDP leader's father, who had been in power since 1948). In elections held in September 1973 the PDP won five of the seven elective seats on the 10-member Legislative Council, and the PDP leader thereupon became Chief Minister.

In the 1978 election the PDP was comprehensively defeated by the People's Liberation Movement. However, it re-entered the Legislative Assembly by winning two seats in the elections of Feb. 25, 1983.

Orientation. The PDP favours continued colonial status for Montserrat because it considers the island to have no adequate economic base for independence.

Socialist United Action Front

Leadership. Dr George Irish (l.)

Founded. 1982

History. As the colony's only socialist party, this Front contested the 1983 elections but failed to gain any seat in the Legislative Council.

Pitcairn Island

Capital: Adamstown Pop. 50

Pitcairn Island (in the Pacific Ocean), with the British high commissioner in New Zealand as its Governor, has a 10-member Council, four of whose members are elected and appoint three out of five nominated members, the two others being appointed by the governor, and the island's Secretary being an ex-officio member. There are no political parties.

St Helena

Capital: Jamestown Pop. 5,300

The British colony of St Helena (with the dependencies of Ascension and Tristan da Cunha) has a Legislative Council consisting of the Governor, two ex-officio members and 12 members elected by universal adult suffrage. Its Executive Council comprises two ex-officio members and six chairmen appointed by the Governor from among members of the Legislative Council to preside over council committees. Political parties have not been active since 1976.

Turks and Caicos Islands

Capital: Cockburn Town (Grand Turk)   Pop. 7,500

The Turks and Caicos Islands, a British dependent territory, have a Governor and an Executive Council with three ex-officio members and four others—the Chief Minister and three other ministers from among the elected members of the Legislative Council. This Council consists of a Speaker, the three ex-officio members of the Executive Council, 11 members elected by universal adult suffrage (voters having to be 18 or more years old) by simple majority in single-member constituencies, and three members appointed by the Governor after consultation with the elected members.

In elections to the Legislative Council held on May 29, 1984, Nov. 4, 1980, the Progressive National Party won eight of the 11 elective seats and the People's Democratic Movement the remaining three.

People's Democratic Movement (PDM)

Address. Cockburn Town, Grand Turk, Turks and Caicos Islands
Leadership. Clement Howells (l.); Edward Taylor (ch.); Oswald Renalda Williams (sec.)
Founded. March 1976
History. The PDM had its origins in the Junknoo Club, founded in 1973 mainly to provide recreational facilities for young people, and later working for political advancement. The PDM's position as the strongest party in the Legislative Council elected in September 1976 was strengthened by two independent members joining it. Later one of its members crossed to the Opposition, reducing the PDM's majority in the Islands' Legislative Council from three to one. However, in the 1980 elections the PDM was defeated by the Progressive National Party and left with only three seats in the Council, a situation which continued to obtain after the May 1984 elections.
Orientation. The PDM intends to bring about full internal self-government and eventual independence for the Turks and Caicos Islands.

Structure. The PDM has constituency branches, action committees and a 12-member executive committee.
Membership. 600
Publications. *The Voice* (monthly newspaper), 1,000

Progressive National Party (PNP)

Leadership. Norman B. Saunders (l.)
History. The PNP was until 1978 known as the People's National Organization, which in elections held in 1976 had obtained four of the 11 elective seats in the Legislative Council and was therefore in opposition. In the 1980 elections, however, the PNP won eight seats (and 59.1 per cent of the vote), and it thereupon formed a new Executive Council. The party secured a second term in the May 1984 elections, with some 62 per cent of the vote.
Orientation. The PNP is a conservative party opposed to early independence for the islands.

United States of America

Capital: Washington, D.C.   Pop. 232,000,000

The United States of America, consisting of 50 member states with a measure of internal self-government, has an executive President elected for a four-year term (by an Electoral College elected directly in each state) and re-eligible once only; he is both head of state and head of the executive, whose other members he nominates. Legislative power is held by Congress consisting of a 100-member Senate and a 435-member House of Representatives. In each state two senators are elected by direct adult suffrage for a six-year term, with one-third of the Senate's membership being renewed every two years. Members of the House of Representatives are similarly elected for a two-year term. There is a traditional two-party system, but the constitutional separation of executive and legislative functions precludes party government in the accepted sense (as the President's party may be faced with a majority of the other party in Congress).

The minimum voting age is 18 years, and the registration of voters is controlled by the states. In elections to the House of Representatives candidates are elected by simple majority in districts of more or less the same population (over 500,000 in 1982), with the proviso that each state has at least one representative. In presidential elections voters decide, in primary elections, on a slate of delegates of the party of their choice, and the elected delegates constitute the Electoral College, in which seats are allocated to states on the basis of their population; in the final elections Electoral College delegates vote as a state bloc. Candidates for nomination as the party's choice for President receive federal grants to cover campaign expenses, provided no private funds are accepted. Candidates for Congress receive no federal funds and are free to accept private contributions.

As a result of elections held on Nov. 2, 1982, seats were distributed as follows: (i) in the Senate—Republicans 54, Democrats 46; (ii) in the House of Representatives—Democrats 269, Republicans 166. In the presidential elections held on Nov. 4, 1980, the Republican candidate, Ronald W. Reagan, was elected by 489 Electoral College votes against 49 for the Democrat, Jimmy Carter, while the percentages of their respective popular votes were 50.75 and 41.02.

American Independent Party

Address. P.O. Box 3737, Simi Valley, California 93063, USA

Leadership. Tom Goodloe (ch.)

Founded. 1968

History. The party was established to promote the candidature of George C. Wallace for the US presidency, and it later nominated as presidential candidates John Schmitz in 1972, Governor Lester Maddox in 1976, and Congressman John R. Rarick in 1980.

Orientation. The party stands inter alia for the inalienable rights of individual citizens, local (not federal) control of the school system, the election (not appointment) of judges, the right of people to keep and bear arms, the total repeal of personal income tax, improved social security, the right of trade unions to function without government interference, the free enterprise system and strong defence forces; it is strongly opposed to communism, a nuclear freeze, immigration and abortion.

490

Structure. The party functions independently in each state.

Membership. 150,000 in California; 20,000 to 30,000 elsewhere

Publications. *Statesman Newsletter* (monthly)

American Party for the United States

Address. 3600 South Market St., Salt Lake City, Utah 84119, USA

Leadership. Earl Jeppson (nat. ch.)

History. This party nominated Thomas J. Anderson as its candidate for the US presidency in 1976; he obtained 160,600 votes or 0.2 per cent of the total.

Americans for Democratic Action (ADA)

Address. 1411 K Street NW, Suite 850, Washington DC 20005, USA

Leadership. Robert F. Drinan (nat. pres.); Marvin Rich (ch. of exec. comm); Mildred Jeffrey (sec.); Leon Schull (nat. dir.)

Founded. 1947

History. ADA was founded by anti-communist Liberals (such as the late Hubert H. Humphrey and the theologian Reinhold Niebuhr) to preserve the liberal New Deal heritage. Although officially bipartisan, it is generally regarded as the liberal wing (or "conscience") of the Democratic Party. It was prominently represented in the presidential administration of John F. Kennedy; it was strongly opposed to the Vietnam war; and it endorsed Senator Eugene McCarthy against Lyndon Johnson in 1968. In 1979 ADA announced its opposition to the renomination of President Carter and its support for the presidential nomination of Senator Edward Kennedy.

Orientation. ADA is a liberal organization for grass-root political action and national lobbying with a view to obtaining economic and political justice and self-determination for all citizens. ADA has declared full employment as its long-range goal; advocated containment of inflation through control of increases in profits, dividends, rents, interest, professional fees and selected wages and prices; called for defence spending to be "guided by realistic strategies designed to prevent a nuclear war", with arms control and disarmament playing a major role; and supported the civil rights movement.

Structure. An annual convention (consisting of at large and chapter delegates) elects national officers and a national board. There are chapters in approximately 35 states and cities.

Membership. 60,000

Publications. *ADA World,* 65,000

International affiliations. Liberal International (informal membership)

Citizens Party

Address. 2000 P St. NW, Suite 200, Washington DC, USA

Leadership. Jim McClellan, Michele Prichard (co-ch.)

Founded. 1979

History. This party's presidential candidate in the 1980 elections was Barry Commoner, who gained less than 0.3 per cent of the vote. It has contested elections in 24 states and obtained seats in 11 local authorities.

Orientation. The party stands for the protection of the environment, is opposed to all nuclear power and nuclear weapons development and in favour of decentralization of economic power and greater public involvement (including co-determination) in economic policy.

Structure. The party has chapters in over 30 states.

International affiliations. The party has links with West European Green formations.

Communist Party USA (CPUSA)

Address. 239 West 23rd Street, 7th Floor, New York, NY 10011, USA

Leadership. Henry Winston (nat. ch.); Gus Hall (g.s.)

Founded. September 1919

History. Before World War II the party's leader, then William Z. Foster, unsuccessfully contested presidential elections in 1924, 1928 and 1932. The 1936 and 1940 presidential elections were similarly contested by the party's new leader, Earl Browder. In November 1940 the party decided to sever its connexions with the Communist International and other international organizations (in order to evade US legislation requiring all groups under foreign control to register with the Department of Justice). It subsequently adopted the name of Communist Political Association and, in January 1944, decided to call for the peaceful settlement of internal disputes and for the promotion of political unity to enable the decisions of the Allied leaders in World War II to be put into effect. It was also against raising the issue of socialism in the post-war period "in such form and manner as to weaken national unity". However, in July 1945 the Communist Party was reconstituted, under William Z. Foster, with a Marxist-Leninist programme. Earl Browder was expelled from the party on Feb. 13, 1946, for "gross violation of party discipline" and for "betraying the principles of Marxism-Leninism and deserting to the side of the class enemy".

Between 1947 and 1956 numerous leading party members were arrested and tried on various charges. A US House of Representatives Committee on Un-American Activities in a report of March 1947 described the party as being "in fact the agent of a foreign [i.e. the Soviet] government directing a world-wide revolutionary movement". In May 1956 the party's executive committee adopted a report criticizing "left-sectarian" errors committed in the previous 10 years and emphasizing that the party sought "constitutional and democratic solutions to current and fundamental problems". In February 1957 a party convention decided to permit some criticism of the Soviet Union and to avoid a too rigid application of traditional Marxist-Leninist principles (although this decision was rejected as "revisionist" by Foster, who subsequently died in Moscow on Sept. 1, 1961). The *Daily Worker*, which had been the party's organ for 34 years, ceased publication in December 1957.

Prosecution of party members practically ceased after the US Supreme Court had ruled in June 1964 and November 1965 respectively (i) that party membership was not sufficient ground for conviction under security legislation and (ii) that the section of the 1950 Internal Security Act requiring members of the party to register with the Department of Justice was unconstitutional. The party has nominated candidates for presidential elections since 1968, its candidate in 1980 and 1984 being Gus Hall.

Orientation. The party seeks to fulfil a "vanguard role in the struggle for advanced social legislation, for world peace and in solidarity against US imperialism, for working-class internationalism . . . and to end all forms of racist and political repression and oppression". The party's general secretary has strongly defended the theory of the dictatorship of the proletariat and the policies of the Soviet Union.

Structure. Based on the principle of democratic centralism, the CPUSA is organized in most of the 50 states in districts (subdivided by county, city or section), the basic unit being the party club. It has a 73-member central committee, which is the leading body between national conventions (held every four years) and which elects a political bureau.

Membership. 20,000

Publications. *Political Affairs* (monthly theoretical journal), over 20,000; *Daily World* (weekly Marxist newspaper), 100,000

International affiliations. The CPUSA is recognized by the Communist parties of the Soviet-bloc countries.

Conservative Caucus

Address. 7777 Leesburg Pike, Falls Church, Va. 22043, USA

Leadership. Howard Phillips (nat. dir.)

History. This organization backed Ronald W. Reagan in his successful quest for the US presidency (in 1980) and has since acted as a pressure group within the Republican Party in favour of conservative domestic policies and of a vigorous external policy to defend what are seen as US interests.

Democratic Party

Address. Democratic National Committee, 1625 Massachusetts Avenue NW, Washington DC 20036, USA

Leadership. Thomas P. O'Neill (party head and Speaker of the House of Representatives); Charles T. Manatt Jr. (California—ch. Democratic National Committee); (Mrs) Dorothy V. Bush (Florida—sec.)

Founded. 1800

History. Founded by Thomas Jefferson and originally known as the Republican Party and later the Democratic Republicans, the party shortened its name to Democratic Party under President Andrew Jackson (c. 1828). It held its first national convention in 1832 and was the dominant US party until 1860, when it was split on the issue of slavery. Between 1860 and 1912 the only Democratic President was Grover Cleveland (1885–89 and 1893–97); thereafter Democratic Presidents were Woodrow Wilson (1913–21), Franklin D. Roosevelt (1933–45), Harry S. Truman (1945–53), John F. Kennedy (1961–63), Lyndon B. Johnson (1963–69) and James Earl (Jimmy) Carter (1977–81).

Democrats have normally controlled both houses of Congress since 1932, but this has not meant that Democratic Presidents could automatically rely on congressional support, particularly in view of the strength of the conservative southern Democrats.

In the 1980 presidential election Jimmy Carter failed to secure a second term, winning some 41 per cent of the popular vote against 51 per cent for Ronald Reagan (Republican). In that year the Democrats also lost control of the Senate.

Nevertheless, the Democratic Party has in recent years remained potentially the majority national party, with strong support among industrial workers as well as among immigrant and minority groups, young voters, women and the intellectual community. Following the November 1982 gubernatorial elections the Democrats held 34 state governorships and the Republicans 16.

Orientation. While European-style political labels cannot be properly applied to the complex and changing coalitions of interests which make up both major parties, the Democratic Party can be broadly defined as occupying the centre-left of the US political spectrum. Within the context of a "regulated" free-market economy, the party has placed particular emphasis on labour and consumer rights, social equality and civil rights, and federal government funding of social security, public health and education programmes.

Structure. The Democratic Party is essentially a loose electoral alliance of many diverse local, state and regional Democratic organizations, representatives of which come together at a national convention every four years for the purpose of selecting the party's presidential candidate. Between conventions the national business of the party is carried on by the National Committee comprising proportionately-elected state party representatives. There are also state parties and committees as well as county parties.

Membership. There is no paid-up membership as such; a 1982 Gallup Poll showed that 45 per cent of the electorate considered themselves to be Democrats.

Democratic Socialists of America (DSA)

Address. 853 Broadway, Suite 801, New York, NY 10003, USA

Leadership. Michael Harrington (co-ch.); Barbara Ehrenreich (co-ch.); Gordon Haskell (pol. dir.)

Founded. April 1, 1982

History. The DSA was formed at a convention in Detroit (Michigan) by a merger of the Democratic Socialist Organizing Committee (DSOC) and the New American Movement. The DSOC had

been founded by the "coalition" caucus of the Socialist Party which subsequently changed its name to Social Democrats USA (see separate entry). At its foundation the DSOC described itself as a formation of "socialists of the democratic left" advocating "democratic socialism" as the ultimate goal, but functioning in the short run as "the explicitly socialist wing of the broader left-labour-liberal movement in the Democratic Party". The DSOC had, by 1979, a total of 40 local chapters active in Democratic Party politics and in union and labour support work and socialist education. It also had (in 1979) one member in the House of Representatives.

Orientation. The DSA announced at its foundation: "While our long-term goal is to create a majoritarian movement for democratic socialism, the immediate task of socialists is to help build a broad-based, anti-corporate left. Thus, central to our strategy is the development of a coalition of the major progressive forces in our country—trade unions, women's groups, minority organizations and others. Whether by virtue of race or sex, geography or job, the needs of the majority of Americans are fundamentally in opposition to the system of private enterprise." The DSA has also expressed opposition to any kind of inter-American military intervention in Central America or the Caribbean and support for self-determination both for Israel and for the Palestinian people, and endorsement of the nuclear freeze campaign.

Structure. The DSA has a bi-annual convention which elects a 24-member national executive committee. It is organized in 100 locals and 50 chapters and has a youth section.

Membership. 7,000

Publications. *Democratic Left*, 10,000; *Socialist Forum*, 3,000; *Days of Decision* (youth section), 2,000

International affiliations. Socialist International

Liberal Party

Leadership. Mario Cuomo (l.); James Notaro (exec. sec.)

History. This formation operates within the Democratic Party in the State of New York, where it is regarded as having political influence greatly in excess of its numerical strength. Mario Cuomo was elected Governor of New York in November 1982 (as a Democrat). He subsequently came into conflict with the Liberal Party's former leader, Raymond Harding, who alleged that Cuomo was using political patronage to extend his control of the party.

Libertarian National Committee

Address. 2300 Wisconsin Ave. N.W., Washington DC 20007. USA

Leadership. Alicia G. Clark (ch.); Eric O'Keefe (nat. dir.); Frances Eddy (sec.)

Founded. 1972

History. The Libertarian Party first took part in presidential elections in 1972 and in federal elections in 1974. Its presidential candidate in 1974 was Roger MacBride, who received 174,000 popular votes (the third highest of any party—i.e. excluding independent—candidates). It had one state representative elected in Alaska in 1978, in which year it claimed to have achieved an aggregate vote of 1,250,000. In the 1980 presidential elections its candidate obtained almost 1 per cent of the popular vote. In the 1982 congressional elections it fielded over 300 candidates for the House of Representatives and some 20 for the Senate, but none were elected.

Orientation. The party stands for "individual freedom, voluntarism, a free-market economy, civil liberties and an anti-interventionist foreign policy". It is opposed to further nuclear-weapons development.

Structure. There are structurally autonomous, affiliates in 50 states, and party activities are co-ordinated by national headquarters, which is also responsible for presidential campaigns.

Membership. 10,000–15,000

National States' Rights Party

Address. P.O.B. 1211, Marietta, Georgia 30061, USA

Leadership. J. B. Stoner (ch.); Edward R. Fields (sec.)

History. The party has unsuccessfully taken part in elections, including the congressional ones of 1982.

Orientation. This party is right-wing, racist and anti-communist.

Membership. 13,000

Publications. *The Thunderbolt* (monthly)

National Unity Party (NUP)

Leadership. John B. Anderson

Founded. 1983

History. The NUP leader, a liberal Republican member of the House of Representatives, had contested the 1980 presidential elections as an independent, having failed to secure the Republican nomination in the 1979 primaries (in which he nevertheless obtained substantial support). In the elections (won for the Republicans by Ronald Reagan) Anderson was the most successful of the 12 other candidates (i.e. apart from Reagan and Jimmy Carter), polling 5,582,482 votes (7 per cent of the total).

Orientation. The NUP subscribes to principles derived from the liberal strand of Republicanism, in opposition to what it regards as the conservative approach of the Reagan administration.

Prohibition National Committee

Address. P.O.B. 2365, Denver, Colorado 80201, USA

Leadership. Earl F. Dodge (nat. ch.); Rayford G. Feather (nat. sec.)

Founded. September 1869

History. Founded to oppose the manufacture and sale of alcoholic beverages, the Prohibition party claims to have been the first in the USA to advocate women's suffrage, laws against child labour and the direct election of US senators. Apart from the election of local, county and state legislative officials, the party has been successful only in having two congressmen and two governors elected. The party maintains that in recent years the two major parties have enacted restrictive laws which have kept Prohibition candidates off the ballot paper in most states.

Orientation. Besides opposing alcohol and other "anti-social" drugs the party "champions individual freedom, opposes abortion and euthanasia and calls for a balanced federal budget and a reduction of governmental authority". It claims to be conservative (in holding to certain traditional values), liberal (in favouring the maximum amount of personal freedom) and progressive (in advocating beneficial reforms).

Structure. Delegates to a quadrennial convention elect five office-bearers and four other members to an executive committee which acts for the national committee (the latter meeting every two years).

Publications. *The National Statesman* (monthly), 1,300

Republican Party

Address. Republican National Committee, 310 First Street SE, Washington DC 20003, USA

Leadership. Paul Laxalt (gen. ch. Republican National Committee); Frank J. Fahrenkopf Jr. (nat. ch.); Jean G. Biech (sec.)

Founded. July 1854

History. Informally known as the "Grand Old Party" (GOP), the Republican Party was founded by opponents of slavery. It first contested presidential elections in 1856 but was unsuccessful. In 1860, however, its candidate, Abraham Lincoln, was elected President with the votes of the country's 18 northern states. During the period until 1932 it won a total of 18 presidential elections. After the party had been weakened by the defection of Theodore Roosevelt and his followers (who formed a Progressive Party), the Republican Party lost the presidency and also control of Congress to the Democrats in 1912. However, the Republicans again held the presidency from 1920 to 1932, when they lost it (largely as a result of the economic depression which had begun in 1929).

They did not return to power until the election of Gen. Dwight D. Eisenhower as President in 1952. In 1960 and 1964 Republican presidential candidates were unsuccessful, but the party regained power with the election of Richard M. Nixon in 1968 (although it failed to gain control of Congress). As a result of the Watergate scandal, Nixon in August 1974 became the first US President to resign office, his successor being Vice-President Gerald Ford, who in 1976 narrowly lost the presidential elections to Jimmy Carter (Democrat).

From 1932 the Republicans were in a minority in both houses of Congress except in the immediate post-war period. Following the November 1978 gubernatorial elections, the Republicans held 18 state governorships and the Democrats 32. In 1980 the Republican presidential candidate, Ronald Reagan, was elected in a landslide victory over the Democratic incumbent, President Jimmy Carter, while the Republicans also gained a majority in the Senate for the first time since 1952 and made substantial gains in the House of Representatives.

Orientation. The Republican Party is generally more conservative than the Democratic Party, although it is pragmatic rather than orthodox conservative. It is opposed to over-centralization of government power and it favours greater freedom for incentives for the individual. It advocates lower taxes, a balanced budget and a strong defence, with the maintenance of US forces in Europe and elsewhere.

Structure. The Republican National Committee (of 162 members) has a chairman, a co-chairman (of opposite sex), eight vice-chairmen (from four geographical regions), a secretary, a treasurer, a general counsel and three members from each state and also from the district of Columbia, Guam, Puerto Rico and the US Virgin Islands.

Publications. *First Monday; County Line; Common Sense; Talking Points*

International affiliations. International Democrat Union; Pacific Democrat Union

---

Revolutionary Communist Party

Address. 14 East 18th Street, New York, NY, USA

History. In 1979 this party was one of several listed by the Californian attorney-general as left-wing groups operating in California. On April 30, 1980, two of its members poured paint over two Soviet representatives at the United Nations in New York.

Orientation. This party is a Maoist formation.

Publications. *The Revolutionary Worker*

Social Democrats USA (SDUSA)

Address. 275 Seventh Avenue, New York, NY 10001, USA

Leadership. Bayard Rustin (nat. ch.); Rita Freedman (exec. dir.)

Founded. 1901

History. The party regards itself as the successor to the Socialist Party founded in 1901 by Eugene V. Debs, Morris Hillquit and others. Until 1956 the party nominated candidates for political office and a number of Socialists were elected to Congress. Of the party's presidential candidates, Debs received 6 per cent of the vote in 1912, while Norman Thomas, who contested six presidential elections between 1928 and 1948, received 884,000 votes in 1932.

Having been a significant force in US political and trade union affairs for the first three decades of its existence, the Socialist Party declined in influence after the election of Franklin D. Roosevelt (Democrat) in 1932 and the implementation of his "New Deal" programme, since when there has been little support for socialist ideas within the US labour movement. In 1968 the party formally adopted a strategy of working within the Democratic Party to build a coalition of the trade union and civil rights movement, along with liberals and youth, to advance a social democratic programme.

In 1972 the party's then co-chairman, Michael Harrington, resigned and subsequently formed the Democratic Socialist

Organizing Committee (later the Democratic Socialists of America—see separate entry), following which the 1972 convention decided to change the name of the party to Social Democrats USA.

Orientation. The party "seeks to advance democracy in the political, economic and social life of the USA, as well as to promote democracy and human rights worldwide".

Structure. The top policy-making body of the party is the national convention, which meets every two years and elects national officers and a 40-member national committee. The latter meets every three months and elects the executive director and the editor of *New America*, as well as a national action committee of 12 members meeting monthly in New York.

Membership. 3,000

Publications. New America, 5,000

International affiliations. Socialist International

Socialist Labor Party of America

Address. P.O. Box 50218, Palo Alto, CA 94303, USA

Leadership. Robert Bills (nat. sec.)

Founded. July 1874

History. The party was founded as the Workingmen's Party, changed its name to Socialistic Labor Party in 1877 and adopted the present name in 1890. Between 1876 and 1889 the party underwent an internal struggle between Marxist and Lassallean elements; between 1890 and 1924 the party undertook the adoption of a Marxist programme, largely under the leadership of Daniel De Leon (1852–1914), who formulated "the socialist industrial union concept as the revolutionary strategy best suited to American conditions".

The party worked within the existing trade unions for several years but in 1896 it launched the Socialist Trade and Labor Alliance (ST & LA) in opposition to the American Federation of Labor (AFL). In 1905 it took part in the formation of the Industrial Workers of the World (IWW) but broke with the anarcho-syndicalist element in 1908 and pursued an independent policy until 1924; from 1925 to 1975 party activity was largely confined to electoral and educational activity.

In 1976 the party began to increase its union and non-electoral activities. From 1893 to 1976 the party (unsuccessfully) participated in every presidential election campaign, its candidate in 1976 being Jules Levin.

Orientation. The party is "Marxist-De Leonist", for the "overthrow of capitalism and the establishment of socialist government based on worker management and control of industry". The party was affiliated to the Second International prior to World War I; it supported the 1917 Bolshevik revolution but repudiated Stalinism.

Structure. Based on local sections, the party has a national executive of seven members, elected for a two-year term, and annual national conventions. All major policy decisions are subject to membership referendum.

Membership. 550–650

Publications. The People, 10,000

Socialist Workers' Party

Address. 14 Charles Lane, New York, NY 10014, USA

Leadership. Malik Miah, Barry Sheppard, Mary-Alice Waters (nat. co-ch.); Jack Barnes (nat. sec.)

Founded. 1938

History. For the 1976 presidential elections this small left-wing party nominated as its candidate Peter Camejo (who polled negligibly).

US Communist Party (Marxist-Leninist)

Address. P.O.B. 72116, Watts Station, Los Angeles, Calif. 90002, USA

Leadership. Michael Klonsky (ch.)

Founded. June 1977

Orientation. This formation is a pro-Chinese Communist party seeking to organize workers for the class struggle and the fight against "the two imperialist superpowers" (the Soviet Union and the United States).

World Socialist Party of the United States

Address. 97, Spring Street, Watertown, Mass. 02172, USA

Orientation. This party is one of the companion parties of the Socialist Party of Great Britain (see under United Kingdom).

Publications. The Western Socialist

US Dependent Territories

American Samoa

Capital: Pago Pago, Tutuila   Pop. 35,000

American Samoa, comprising the nine eastern islands of Samoa, is an "unincorporated territory" of the United States, administered by the US Department of the Interior. It has a bicameral legislature (*Fono*) consisting of a 20-member House of Representatives elected by universal adult suffrage and an 18-member Senate elected at meetings of the chiefs.

The first elected Governor of American Samoa, chosen on a second ballot on Nov. 22, 1977, assumed office for a three-year term on Jan. 3, 1978, the normal term being four years co-inciding with the US presidential term.

Republic of Belau

Capital: Koror   Pop. 13,000

This republic, consisting of the island of Palau (in the western Caroline Islands of the Pacific), has a President, a Vice-President and a National Legislature comprising a Senate and a House of Delegates. The first elections to the island's legislature were held on Nov. 4, 1980, and Palau was proclaimed the Republic of Belau on Jan. 1, 1981. A "compact of free association" with the United States was signed in Washington on Aug. 26, 1982, and was approved in a plebiscite held on Feb 10, 1983, when more than 60 per cent of the electorate voted in favour of the agreement. It provided for the Republic to obtain full control of internal and external affairs except military and security responsibilities, which were retained by the United States. There are as yet no political parties.

Guam

Capital: Agaña   Pop. 106,000

Guam, the southernmost of the Marianas Islands in the Pacific, is administered by the US Department of the Interior through a Governor. It has a unicameral legislature with powers similar to those of a US state legislature and elected every two years by universal suffrage of adults over the age of 18 years. A delegate to the US House of Representatives is also elected every two years.

Parties represented in the island's legislature are the Democratic and Republican parties of the USA, which gained respectively 10 and 11 seats in elections held in November 1980.

Marshall Islands

Capital: Majuro   Pop. 32,000

The Marshall Islands (in the western Pacific) have, under their Constitution of May 1, 1979, a parliamentary form of government with a 33-member legislature (*Nitijela*) and a Government headed by a President. In terms of a "compact of free association" signed with the United States in Honolulu on May 30, 1982, the Government of the Marshall Islands was to have full control of domestic and foreign policy, although responsibility for defence was retained by the United States. However, this agreement is still subject to approval by the US Congress and by the Marshall Islands electorate in a referendum.

Federated States of Micronesia

Capital: Kolonia, Ponape   Pop. 75,000

The Federated States of Micronesia, consisting of the Caroline Islands of Truk, Ponape, Yap and Kosrae (in the western Pacific and formerly part of the US Trust Territory of the Pacific Islands), came into being early in 1979 on the basis of a Constitution approved in a referendum held on July 12, 1978 (and rejected by the population of the Marshall Islands and of Palau). Under this Constitution the Federated States were to have full internal self-government and also authority and responsibility for foreign affairs, while for 15 years the United States would be responsible for defence and security. The Federated States' newly-elected Congress on May 11, 1979, elected the first President and Vice-President of the new state.

The four federated states each have their own governor and state legislatures elected for four-year terms: Kosrae—14 members; Ponape—24 members; Truk—28 members; and Yap—10 members (six from the Yap Islands proper and four from two outer islands).

Northern Marianas

Capital: Saipan   Pop. 17,400

The Northern Marianas—formerly, with the Caroline Islands (now Micronesia) and the Marshall Islands, part of the US Trust Territory of the Pacific Islands— were promised commonwealth status within the United States under a bill enacted on March 26, 1976, following a referendum held in June 1975 resulting in a large majority of the islands' people voting in favour of this status. In a further referendum held on March 6, 1977, the islands' voters approved a draft constitution, and in December 1977 they elected a governor and also a bicameral Congress consisting of a nine-member Senate elected for four years and a 14-member House of Representatives elected for two years. In both Houses the Territorial Party has obtained a majority over the Democratic Party.

The islands formally became a commonwealth of the United States on Jan. 9, 1978, and thus obtained the same status as the island of Puerto Rico.

Democratic Party

Leadership. Governor Pedro P. Tenorio (l.)

History. The party's leader has stated that he favours full independence for the islands but has admitted that this would be opposed by a majority of the voters.

Orientation. The party seeks to achieve economic self-sufficiency for the islands.

Territorial Party (TP)

History. As the majority party in both the Commonwealth House and in the Senate, the TP has refused to approve a number of measures taken by the Governor.

Orientation. The TP strongly supported commonwealth status for the islands.

Puerto Rico

Capital: San Juan   Pop. 3,300,000

The Commonwealth of Puerto Rico is, under its 1952 Constitution, "a free state associated with the United States", in which executive power is vested in a Governor who is elected by universal adult suffrage of resident citizens and who presides over an Executive. There is an elected bicameral legislature consisting of a 27-member Senate and a 51-member House of Representatives. The minimum voting age is 18 years. Of the 51 members of the House of Representatives, 40 are elected in 40 representative districts (one each) and the remaining 11 are elected "at large" (having no specific local constituency). If two-thirds or more of the seats are obtained by a single party, the number of seats is increased by seats reserved for minority parties. In order to be registered a new party, or one which has failed to gain 5 per cent of the votes in the previous election, must submit certified signatures from at least three-fourths of the voting districts and exceeding 5 per cent of the total votes cast for governor in the previous elections. Established parties receive subsidies for party campaigns from public funds ($75,000 per annum and $150,000 in an election year), while new parties receive such funds according to the number of votes which they gain.

In elections held on Nov. 4, 1980, 25 seats in the House of Representatives were gained by each of two parties—the New Progressive Party (PNP) and the Popular Democratic Party (PPD), with the vacant seat being filled later by a PPD member.

New Progressive Party
Partido Nuevo Progresista (PNP)

Leadership. Carlos Roméro Barceló (pres.); Rafael Rodríguez Aguayo (sec.)

Founded. August 1967

History. Taking part in elections for the first time in 1968, the PNP gained a majority in the Puerto Rican House of Representatives and its founder was elected President. The PNP was in opposition from 1972 to 1976, but after being re-organized in 1976 it won an absolute majority in both Houses of the Legislature in November 1976; moreover its candidate was elected as Puerto Rico's (non-voting) member of the US House of Representatives. However, after the November 1980 elections it lost its majority in the Puerto Rican Houses.

Orientation. The PNP's programme includes an improved distribution of wealth and the transformation of Puerto Rico into a state within the United States of America.

Structure. The party's highest authority is the general assembly, consisting of delegates directly elected by party members. Between sessions of the assembly, the supreme organ is the central board composed of leaders at municipal level, parliamentarians, mayors, etc.

Membership. 225,000

Publications. *Camino al 80* (monthly), 25,000

Popular Democratic Party
Partido Popular Demokrático (PPD)

Address. 403 Ponce de León Ave., Puerta de la Tierra, San Juan 00906, Puerto Rico

Leadership. Senator Rafael Hernández Colón (l. and pres.)

Founded. March 1939

History. In elections held in 1940 the PPD gained control of the Puerto Rican

Senate; it also obtained control of the House of Representatives before the 1944 elections and thereafter retained its control in all elections until 1968, when it was defeated owing to a split in the party. It regained control in 1972 but lost it again in the 1976 elections. After the 1980 elections, however, the PPD again held a majority of seats in both Houses.

In 1950–52 the PPD had, with the US Congress, created commonwealth status for Puerto Rico, and it had later campaigned for Puerto Rico's continued commonwealth association with the United States.

Orientation. The PPD defines itself as "a liberal party, oriented towards creating a more just society with particular emphasis on helping the poor, educating the masses and fomenting jobs through private enterprise".

Structure. The PPD has a 19-member board of governors, a general assembly, senatorial district boards and a council of founders.

Membership. 660,000

Publications. *El Yunque* (monthly newspaper), 50,000

Puerto Rican Communist Party
Partido Comunista Puertorriqueño (PCP)

Founded. September 1934

History. In the 1950s PCP party workers were prosecuted under US laws in the same way as active members of the US Communist Party. The PCP's present programme was agreed upon in 1954.

Orientation. The PCP stands inter alia for national independence involving the severance of Puerto Rico's ties with the United States.

Structure. The PCP is organized on a basis of residential areas and places of work. It has a congress which is held every five years and which elects a central committee. The latter forms a political commission.

Publications. *El Pueblo* (monthly), 3,000

International affiliations. The PCP is recognized by the Communist parties of the Soviet-bloc countries.

Puerto Rican Independence Party
Partido Independentista Puertorriqueño (PIP)

Address. Av. Roosevelt 963, Puerto Nuevo, Puerto Rico

Leadership. Rubén Berríos Martínez (pres.)

Founded. 1946

History. The party has campaigned for full independence for Puerto Rico. In July 1967, when a plebiscite was held on the island's constitutional future, less than 1 per cent of the voters called for independence; however, this vote was widely regarded as not truly representative, and a Democratic member of the US House of Representatives in 1978 called it "deformed" by the presence of agents of the Federal Bureau of Investigation who, he claimed, had harassed the PIP.

In the 1972 gubernatorial elections the PIP's leader obtained third place, and in the 1976 elections to the Puerto Rican House of Representatives the PIP gained 72,715 votes (or about 5.4 per cent of the total). In the gubernatorial elections of Nov. 4, 1980, the party's president polled 87,238 votes.

Orientation. The PIP is a moderate left-wing party calling for the establishment of an independent socialist democratic republic.

International affiliations. Socialist International (consultative member)

Puerto Rican Socialist Party
Partido Socialista Puertorriqueño

Address. 256 Padre Colón St., Rio Piedras, 00925 Puerto Rico

Leadership. Carlos Gallisá (pres.); Juan Mari Bras (s.g.)

Founded. November 1971

History. The party was founded by the conversion into a political party of its predecessor, the Pro-Independence Movement (MPI). The latter had been established in 1959, had fought for Puerto Rico's independence from the United States and had decided, in 1968, to embrace Leninism as its fundamental ideology, in the conviction "that independence will be reached together with socialism and that the social class capable of achieving this transformation is the working class".

The party first took part in elections in 1976 (when it gained less than 1 per cent of the votes). In 1974–76 it had one member in the Puerto Rican House of Representatives. It obtained the same level of support in the 1980 elections.

Orientation. The party seeks independence and the establishment of a socialist republic in Puerto Rico.

Structure. The party has a central committee, a political bureau and bureaux of political education, of democratic socialism and of organization.

Membership. 6,000

Publications. *Claridad* (weekly); *Tribuna Roja* and *Nueva Lucha* (bimonthly ideological magazines)

US Virgin Islands

Capital: St Thomas   Pop. 96,000

These islands are an "unincorporated territory" of the United States, over which the US Department of the Interior has full jurisdiction. They have a unicameral legislature with limited legislative powers, composed of 15 senators elected for two years (and representing two legislative districts) by residents over the age of 18 years who are US citizens. There is also an elected governor. The inhabitants do not participate in US presidential elections but they elect one non-voting member to the US House of Representatives.

In 1980 the Senate was composed of 12 Democrats, one member of the Independent Citizens' Movement and two independents. The (US) Republican Party is also active in the islands.

Independent Citizens' Movement (ICM)

Address. St Thomas, US Virgin Islands
Leadership. John Bernier (l.)
History. The ICM was formed by a breakaway group of the Democratic Party, and one of its members, Cyril E. King, was elected Governor in November 1974, but he died in January 1978 and was succeeded by Juan Luis, who had previously presented himself as a "no-party" candidate for the governorship. The latter was returned to power in elections held in 1982.

Upper Volta

Capital: Ouagadougou   Pop. 7,400,000

The Republic of Upper Volta is ruled by a National Revolutionary Council (*Conseil National de la Révolution*), which took power on Aug. 4, 1983. It has a Government composed of military and civilian members, but the country's only other political institutions are "committees for the defence of the revolution".

Uruguay

The "Eastern Republic of Uruguay" has, since February 1973, in effect been under military rule, with the then existing bicameral Congress being dissolved in June of that year together with the National Trade Union Confederation (*Confederación Nacional de Trabajadores*). A draft constitution designed to ensure the continued existence of the military regime was, however, rejected by some 60 per cent of the voters taking part in a referendum held on Nov. 30, 1980. On Sept. 1, 1981, the military regime thereupon promised that general elections would take place in 1984 and that power would be transferred to civilians in March 1985.

In preparation for the proposed general elections the military Government decided in January 1982 to permit three political groups—the country's two traditional parties, the Blanco (or National) Party (PN) and the Colorado Party, as well as the Civic Union (*Unión Cívica*), a small Roman Catholic conservative group—to nominate candidates for election to 500-member congresses for each group (and also to local representative bodies). The members of these congresses were to nominate candidates for the 1984 general elections. All other parties, in particular those which had in 1971 formed a Broad Front (*Frente Amplio*), remained banned, and all persons who had criticized the military regime were disqualified from standing as candidates. However, opposition to the military regime was organized within the two traditional parties in (i) an alliance of the For the Fatherland (*Por la Patria*) and *Movimiento de Rocha* groups inside the PN and (ii) the *Unidad y Reforma* group within the Colorado Party.

The preparatory elections, during the campaign for which the Broad Front had called for the casting of blank votes, were held on Nov. 28, 1982, and produced the following results: PN 46.4 per cent (of which 51 per cent were cast for the opposition alliance); Colorado Party 39.7 per cent (of which 67.5 per cent were for the opposition); and Civic Union 1.1 per cent. The remaining 12.8 per cent were blank or invalid votes and the percentage poll was 60.5.

On Aug. 2, 1983, the military Government suspended all public political activities for up to two years but confirmed that elections would be held in November 1984 and civilian rule restored in 1985.

Blanco Party
Partido Nacional (PN)

Address. 18 de Julio 2338, Montevideo, Uruguay

Founded. 1836

History. The Blanco (National) Party takes its name from the colour of the white flag of the conservative side in the 1836 civil war. Although divided into several factions in recent years, the PN won the 1958 general elections, after which it first came to power in a National Council of Government consisting of six PN members and three representatives of the Colorado Party. This position was maintained after the 1962 general elections. Following the reintroduction of the presidential system (which had been abolished in 1952) the PN was defeated in presidential and congressional elections held in November 1966 and was thereafter in opposition. In the 1971 elections it retained 40 seats in the 99-member Chamber of

Deputies, while its then leader, Wilson Ferreira Aldunate, narrowly failed to be elected President. Following the dissolution of Congress in 1973 he left the country, and with other presidential candidates he was deprived of his political rights in 1976. However, he returned from exile in June 1984.

The principal factions of the PN are (i) an alliance of the *Por la Patria* group, led by Ferreira Aldunate, and the *Movimiento de Rocha* group, led by Juan Pivel Devoto—opposed to the military Government, and (ii) a pro-Government faction led by Alberto Gallinal Héber (a former President of the Council of State set up in December 1973 to replace the Congress dissolved six months earlier).

Orientation. Although the PN is traditionally conservative, Wilson Ferreira Aldunate has advocated inter alia the nationalization of banks, land reform, the establishment of relations with Cuba and a new approach to the problem of left-wing urban terrorism.

Publications. *El País* (daily)

Christian Democratic Party—see under Civic Union

Civic Union
Unión Cívica

Leadership. Juan Vicente Chiarino (l.)
Founded. 1872
History. This Union was originally a conservative Roman Catholic party, but it gradually moved towards the left, and in 1962 it became the Christian Democratic Party (*Partido Demócrata Cristiano*), which was banned under the military regime. The Civic Union was revived as a Catholic conservative party in 1981 and it was one of the three parties authorized in January 1982 to nominate candidates for election for congresses which were to nominate candidates for the general elections proposed for November 1984.

International affiliations. The Christian Democratic Party is a member of the Christian Democratic International and of the Christian Democratic Organization of America.

Colorado Party
Partido Colorado (PC)

Address. Vázquez 1271, Montevideo, Uruguay
Founded. 1836

History. The Colorado Party takes its name from the red flag used by the liberal faction in the 1836 civil war and was in power from 1865 to 1958, during which period Uruguay became the first welfare state in Latin America. In the 1966 elections one of its two candidates was elected President and the party gained 50 of the 99 seats in the Chamber of Deputies, thereby returning to power. It continued in government until the military intervention of 1973 which led, in 1976, to the dismissal of President Juan Maria Bordaberry, who had been elected in 1971, when the PC had lost its absolute majority in the Chamber of Deputies (though remaining the strongest party with 41 seats).

During its history the PC has been divided into a number of factions which have opposed each other. These factions include three which voted against the Government's constitutional proposals in a referendum held in 1980 and which have opposed the military Government throughout—(i) the *Unidad y Reforma* group, originally led by Dr Jorge Batlle Ibáñez (barred from political activity) and currently led by Dr Julio Mario Sanguinetti, (ii) the *Libertad y Cambio* group, led by Enrique Tarigo, and (iii) the *Batllismo Radical* group, led by Manuel Flores Mora. A right-wing faction of the PC supporting the military Government is the *Unión Colorada Batllista (Pachequista)*, led by Jorge Pacheco Areco.

Orientation. As a party mainly of the urban population, the PC is liberal and progressive, standing for government participation in the economy and for inter-American co-operation.

Movement for Social Democracy
Movimiento para la Democracia Social

Leadership. President (Gen.) Gregorio Alvarez (l.)
Founded. March 1983
History. This Movement was founded by the President of the Republic in order to contest the general elections planned for November 1984.

Patriotic Union for the Salvation of Democracy
Unión Patriótica Salvadora de la Democracia

Leadership. Col. (retd.) Néstor Bolentini (l.)

Founded. September 1982

History. Col. Bolentini was a former Minister of the Interior (in 1973-74) and a member of the Council of State (established in December 1973 to replace the Congress, which had been dissolved six months earlier).

Orientation. This party is right-wing, for "strong democracy".

Vanuatu

Capital: Port Vila   Pop. 130,000

The Republic of Vanuatu (formerly the British and French condominium of the New Hebrides) is an independent state within the Commonwealth. Its President is elected for a five-year term by an electoral college consisting of Parliament and the presidents of the country's regional councils. The unicameral Parliament of 39 members is elected for a four-year term by universal adult suffrage and in multi-member constituencies with an element of proportional representation. Executive power is vested in the Prime Minister (elected by Parliament from among its members) and a Council of Ministers appointed by him.

In general elections held on Nov. 2, 1983, the Party of Our Land (*Vanuaaku Pati*) obtained 24 seats, the Union of Moderate Parties 12, and the *Na-Griamel, Frend Melanesia* and *Namake Auti* parties one seat each.

Efate Laketu Party

Founded. 1982

History. This regional party, based on the island of Efate, had links with the Natatok Efate Alliance, founded on Efate in 1977 as a mainly anglophone party. That Alliance gained five of the 38 contested seats in the November 1977 elections to the Representative Assembly, whereupon one of its members was elected Chief Minister in a coalition Government. The Alliance, however, did not take part in the coalition Government formed late in 1978 with participation by the *Vanuaaku Pati*; in April 1979 it joined the New Hebrides Federal Party, which was later superseded by the Union of Moderate Parties (see separate entry).

Frend Melanesia

Leadership. Dr Titus Path (l.)

Founded. 1983

History. This party, based on the islands of Santo and Malekula and consisting mainly of French-speaking Presbyterians, was established by Dr Path, who had been a leading member of the *Vanuaaku Pati* but sought further devolution of powers to the mainly Melanesian Santo region. In September 1983 it gained representation on the newly-established Santo (local government) Council, and on Dr Path's election to Parliament in November 1983 it joined in an informal alliance with the Union of Moderate Parties (see separate entry).

Orientation. The party seeks to represent Melanesian interests on Santo.

Na-Griamel

Founded. 1963

History. The party, based on the island of Santo, had its origins in a land reform movement seeking the return of European-owned land to Melanesians. As a political party it was opposed to the New Hebrides National Party (later the Party of Our Land, or *Vanuaaku Pati*), and it contested the island's first legislative elections in November 1975 in an alliance with a *Mouvement Autonomiste des Nouvelles Hébrides* (MANH); this alliance gained two out of 29 elective seats in the Representative Assembly (after partial fresh elections in October 1976).

The party contested elections held in November 1979 as part of a New Hebrides

Federal Party. However, on June 1, 1980, the then leader of *Na-Griamel*, Jimmy Stevens, proclaimed an "independent state of Vemerana" on the island of Santo. This attempted secession was quashed on July 24, 1980, by an Anglo-French force, and Stevens was (on Nov. 12, 1980) sentenced to 14½ years in prison; 550 other persons were also convicted in connexion with the secession attempt. The *Na-Griamel* movement was dissolved, but it was revived later and contested the 1983 general elections, in which it gained one seat in Parliament, where it joined the opposition.

Namake Auti

History. This small northern regionalist party won one seat in the November 1983 general elections resulting in the return of the Party of Our Land administration.

Party of Our Land
Vanuaaku Pati

Leadership. Fr Walter Lini (pres.); Barak Sope (s.g.)
Founded. 1972
History. The party was founded as the New Hebrides National Party, which had gained an absolute majority in the islands' first Representative Assembly elected in November 1975. In January 1977 the party adopted its vernacular name of *Vanuaaku Pati* and from February 1977 it boycotted fresh elections scheduled for November 1977 after its demands (for voting rights to be given to Melanesians only, the voting age to be lowered from 21 to 18 years, "majority rule" to be introduced after the elections, self-government to be installed and a referendum on independence to be held in 1977) had been rejected by the British and French administering powers.

The party refused to recognize the coalition Government formed after the elections and established its own "Provisional People's Government" (PPG). Following further negotiations, however, a new Government with the *Vanuaaku Pati* taking part was formed at the end of 1978, with the party's president becoming Deputy Chief Minister and Minister of Social Services. Having gained 26 of the 39 seats in the Representative Assembly elected in November 1979, the party formed a Government.

After Vanuatu's achievement of independence on July 30, 1980, Fr Lini became Prime Minister and George Kalkoa, until then Deputy Chief Minister, became the first President of Vanuatu, assuming the name of Ati George Sokomanu. The party remained in power after the November 1983 elections, though with a slightly reduced majority in Parliament.

Orientation. The party stands for "Melanesian socialism", rejects the concept of land as a saleable commodity and has maintained a non-aligned foreign policy.

Structure. The party has some 80 regional commissars to maintain contact between party leaders and their supporters.

Union of Moderate Parties (UMP)

Leadership. Vincent Boulekone (l.)
Founded. 1980
History. The UMP is a loose alliance of groups opposed to the *Vanuaaku Pati*. Having its origins in the Tan Union, the *Nakamal* and the New Hebrides Federal Party (NHFP), the Union retained 12 seats in Parliament in the November 1983 elections.

The Tan Union had been founded in 1977 and led by Fr Gérard Leymang; in elections held in November 1977 it had gained 17 of the 38 contested seats in the Representative Assembly, and it had thereupon taken part in two successive coalition Governments; in the November 1979 elections it had formed part of the NHFP. (Fr Leymang was in 1983 obliged to retire from politics because of restrictions imposed upon priests by the Roman Catholic Church.)

The *Nakamal*, of which Vincent Boulekone had been a co-founder in February 1979, had failed to obtain representation in the Representative Assembly; it sought reconciliation between the established parties and the eventual formation of a government of national reconciliation.

The NHFP had been founded in April 1979 as an alliance of groups committed to regional devolution; in the November 1979 elections it obtained 13 seats in the Representative Assembly (against 26 won by the *Vanuaaku Pati*). In 1980 numerous NHFP activists were involved in secessionist activities; some of them were exiled and others were sent to prison, but imprisoned NHFP members of Parliament took their seats upon release.

Orientation. The UMP has been backed by regional interests groups and has also been described as the party of the francophone minority.

Vanuatu Independent Alliance Party (VIAP)

Leadership. Thomas Reuben Seru, George Worek, John Tari, Morrison Tangari (founders)

Founded. 1982

History. The VIAP was established shortly after Thomas Reuben Seru and George Worek had been dismissed from their posts in the Cabinet (after allegations of misdemeanours); they had failed to gain support at a *Vanuaaku Pati* conference (which backed the Prime Minister) and had thereupon resigned from the *Vanuaaku Pati.* The VIAP presented 12 candidates for the 1983 parliamentary elections, but all of them (including, as sitting members, Reuben Seru, Worek and Morrison Tangari) were unsuccessful after the VIAP had admitted government allegations that it had accepted funds from right-wing (US) businessmen.

Orientation. The VIAP has campaigned for free enterprise, the abolition of income tax, the inalienability of land (contrary to government policy and the Constitution) and free education.

Venda

Capital: Thohoyandou   Pop. 540,000 (de iure)

The Republic of Venda, proclaimed on Sept. 13, 1979, but not internationally recognized except by South Africa, Bophuthatswana, Ciskei and Transkei, has an executive President who presides over a Cabinet and is elected by a National Assembly. The latter consists of 42 members nominated by chiefs and headmen and 42 other members elected by universal adult suffrage of Venda citizens (including those living outside the country). Of the 42 elective seats 30 were, in July 1978, won by the opposition Venda Independence People's Party (VIPP) and 12 by the ruling Venda National Party (VNP), whereas a majority of the nominated members supported the VNP.

Venda Independence People's Party (VIPP)

Address. P.O.B. 525, Meadowlands 1852, South Africa

Leadership. Gilbert M. Bakane (l.)

Founded. May 1973

History. The VIPP was established by Baldwin Mavhungu Mudau, who had since 1968 been employed by the Venda Territorial Authority as the representative of the Venda people working in urban areas in South Africa in order to "inculcate the spirit of ethnic belonging". However, he objected to the official policy of "promoting ethnic differences with other Blacks" and was dismissed by the Venda Chief Minister, and in 1973 founded the VIPP to oppose the ruling Venda National Party (VNP). In 1973 the VIPP won 15 out of 18 elective seats in the Venda legislature, and 30 out of 42 in 1978.

Following defections from the VIPP to the VNP, the VIPP had, by the end of 1983, only 23 members in the National Assembly. Mudau died in Soweto (Johannesburg) on Jan. 1, 1982.

Orientation. The VIPP advocates moving from traditional leadership to the Western democratic system.

Venda National Party (VNP)

Address. P.O. Box 204, Sibasa, Venda

Leadership. Life President and Paramount Chief Patrick R. M. Mphephu (l.); E. R. B. Nesengani (g.s.)

Founded. 1973

History. At the party's foundation its core was formed by 25 chiefs (ex-officio members of the then Legislative Assembly), 15 nominated members of local councils and six elected members of the Assembly. In the 1978 general elections the VNP gained only 12 of the elective seats in the Assembly but it obtained a majority through the support of nominated members. As a result of additional ex-officio appointments and the defection of members from the opposition Venda Independence People's Party, the VNP held at the end of 1983 a total of 62 seats in the National Assembly.

Orientation. The VNP stands for the unity of the whole nation and a democratic system constituting "a mixture of acceptable principles of Western democracies and the traditional political system of the Vhavenda people".

Structure. The party has branch committees, co-ordinating committees in local council areas, executive committees and congresses at district and regional level, a national congress and a national executive committee (with final authority).

Venezuela

Capital: Caracas   Pop. 15,400,000

The Federal Republic of Venezuela, consisting of 20 autonomous states, a federal district, two federal territories and 72 federal dependencies, has an executive President elected by universal adult suffrage for a five-year term. There is a bicameral Congress consisting of (i) a Senate to which two senators from each of the 20 states and from the federal district are elected for a five-year term by universal adult suffrage (while additional senators are selected to represent minorities and all former Presidents of the Republic are life members of the Senate) and (ii) a 199-member Chamber of Deputies similarly elected (at least two members for each state and one for each federal territory). The President is not eligible for two consecutive terms. He appoints, and presides over, a Cabinet.

Voting is compulsory for citizens between the ages of 18 and 70 years. Parliamentary seats are distributed under a system of proportional representation and an additional quotient system providing for the representation of minority parties. A Supreme Electoral Council contributes directly and indirectly to the financing of electoral campaigns in proportion to each party's percentage of the total vote obtained.

In presidential elections held on Dec. 4, 1983, the candidate of the Democratic Action (AD), Dr Jaime Lusinchi, received 56.81 per cent of the votes, against 34.58 per cent for the candidate of the ruling Christian Social Party (COPEI), Dr Rafael Caldera Rodríguez. There were 11 other candidates.

In congressional elections held on the same day parties received the following percentages of votes: AD—49.97; COPEI—28.73; Movement towards Socialism (MAS)—5.75; National Opinion Party (Opina)—1.97; People's Electoral Movement (MEP)—1.97. Some 15 other parties also contested these elections.

Christian Social Party
Partido Social Cristiano de Venezuela/ Comité de Organización Política Electoral Independiente (COPEI)

Address. Esquina San Miguel, Av. Panteón cruce con Fuerzas Armadas, San Bernardino, Caracas 1011, Venezuela

Leadership. Dr Rafael Caldera Rodríguez, Dr Godofredo González, Dr Luis Herrera Campíns, Dr Pedro Pablo Aguilar (leaders); Dr Eduardo Fernández (s.g.)

Founded. 1946

History. COPEI gained 19 (out of 160) seats in the Constituent Assembly elected in October 1946. In the presidential elections of December 1948 Dr Rafael Caldera was overwhelmingly defeated by the candidate of the Democratic Action (AD). In the 104-member Constituent Assembly elected in November 1952 COPEI gained 14 seats. It formed part of the Patriotic Junta (with the AD, the Republican Democrats and the Communists) which overthrew President Pérez Jiménez in January 1958, and also of a Civic Front (with the AD and the Republican Democrats) formed thereafter.

In the congressional elections of December 1958 COPEI won 19 (out of 133) seats in the Chamber of Deputies (and 14.4 per cent of the vote). It thereupon entered into a coalition Government with the AD, which lasted until 1963, when the COPEI leader, Dr Caldera, came second (with 20.2 per cent of the vote) in presidential elections, and the party gained 40 seats in the Chamber of Deputies. In December 1968 Dr Caldera was elected President, with 29.08 per cent of the vote, and COPEI gained 50 (out of 188) seats in the Chamber, whereupon it formed its first Government (together with independents).

In the 1973 elections COPEI's presidential candidate came second with 36.78 per cent of the vote, and the party gained 64 (out of 203) seats in the Chamber (while the AD returned to Government, having gained 102 seats in the Chamber). In 1978 COPEI returned to Government, its presidential candidate having been elected with 46.62 per cent of the vote.

In municipal elections held in June 1979 COPEI gained over 50 per cent of the votes cast. However, in the general elections of Dec. 4, 1983, COPEI was defeated, as Dr Caldera, its presidential candidate, obtained only 34.58 per cent of the vote and its congressional candidates gained 28.73 per cent of the total vote. It therefore went into opposition.

Orientation. COPEI is a Christian democratic party of the centre.

Structure. COPEI has a national convention (the party's supreme authority, meeting ordinarily every 2½ years), a national directorate (meeting at least once a year), a national committee (the party's executive organ elected for five years by the convention), a national disciplinary tribunal and two elected commissions (one presidential and the other national). The party is organized at regional, district, municipal and basic levels.

Membership. Between 400,000 and 800,000 (estimated)

International affiliations. Christian Democratic International; Christian Democratic Organization of America (ODCA)

Communist Party of Venezuela
Partido Comunista de Venezuela (PCV)

Address. Edif. Cantaclaro, esq. San Pedro, San Juan, Caracas, Venezuela

Leadership. Dr Gustavo Machado Morales (pres.); Jesús Faría (g.s.)

Founded. 1931

History. The PCV was illegal until 1945, when it was legalized by the Democratic Action (AD) Government. It gained two (out of 160) seats in the Constituent Assembly elected in October 1946, and it unsuccessfully contested the presidential elections of December 1948. It was again banned from May 1950 until the end of the dictatorship of President Pérez Jiménez in January 1958, brought about by a Patriotic Junta embracing four parties—the AD, the Christian Democrats, the Republican Democrats and the PCV.

In May 1962 the PCV was once again banned after it had engaged in guerrilla warfare against the Government. However, in 1967 the PCV's central committee decided to abandon guerilla warfare, to promote instead "a broad popular movement for progressive democratic change" and to take part in elections. The party was again legalized in 1969 and subsequently held five seats in the Chamber of Deputies until 1973 and two until 1978. In the 1978 presidential elections its candidate obtained less than 1 per cent of the vote.

In the 1983 presidential elections the PCV supported the (unsuccessful) candidature of Dr José Vicente Rangel (see entry under New Alternative). The PCV has repeatedly expelled dissidents from its ranks.

Orientation. In 1971 the PCV's congress proclaimed the party's "loyalty to Marxism-Leninism and uncompromising struggle against opportunism"; it has remained pro-Soviet.

Structure. The PCV has a congress, which elects a central committee.

Publications. *Tribuna Popular* (weekly); *Ideologia*

International affiliations. The PCV is recognized by the Communist parties of the Soviet-bloc countries.

Democratic Action
Acción Democrática (AD)

Address. Casa Nacional Acción Democrática, Calle los Cedros, La Florida, Caracas, Venezuela

Leadership. Dr Gonzalo Barrios (pres.); Manuel Peñalver (g.s.)

Founded. 1941

History. Orginally the underground *Partido Democrático Nacional*, formed in 1936, the party was founded in 1941 as a legal socialist and democratic party, which proclaimed itself to be nationalist, revolutionary, anti-feudal and anti-imperialist. It had supporters among all classes of the population but was based on the organized workers and eventually controlled the majority of trade unions. It was in power in 1945–48 when its founder, Rómulo Betancourt, headed a revolutionary junta, but its first elected President was overthrown by a military coup in 1948 and the ensuing military dictatorship was not itself overthrown until 1958. The party's candidates were elected to the presidency for 1959–64 (Rómulo Betancourt), 1964–69 (Raúl Leoni) and 1974–79 (Carlos Andrés Pérez). These years were marked by land reform, the nationalization of the country's petroleum and iron ore resources and agricultural and industrial development.

In municipal elections held in June 1979 the AD gained only about 29 per cent of the total vote. However, it was returned to power after the general elections of Dec. 4, 1983, in which its presidential candidate, Dr Jaime Lusinchi, obtained 56.81 per cent of the votes cast, and its congressional candidates 49.97 per cent.

Orientation. AD is social democratic, with the aim of political, economic and social equality for all Venezuelans and international co-operation, especially with third-world countries.

Structure. Based on internal democracy, the party has a collective leadership elected by the active party members and with statutory control of the party's parliamentary group.

Membership. 1,450,000

International affiliations. Socialist International

Democratic Republican Union
Unión Republicana Democrática (URD)

Address. Qta. Amalia, Avda. Páez, El Paraiso, Caracas, Venezuela

Leadership. Dr Jóvito Villalba (l.)

Founded. 1946

History. The URD contested the 1952 elections to a 104-member Constituent Assembly with the support of the followers of the Democratic Action (AD, which was then illegal), becoming the second strongest party with 29 seats in the Assembly. However, with other parties it was suppressed under the dictatorship until 1958, contributing to the latter's overthrow as part of the Patriotic Junta (embracing also the AD, the Christian Socials and the Communists).

The URD's representation in the Chamber of Deputies declined from 34 (out of 133) seats gained in 1958 to 29 (out of 179) in 1963, 14 (out of 188) in 1968, and five (out of 203) in 1973. Its three deputies elected in 1978 supported the Christian Social Party. The URD also unsuccessfully contested presidential elections in 1958 (when it supported Adm.Wolfgang Larrazábal, then leader of the Patriotic Junta, standing as an independent and defeated by the AD candidate), in 1964 (in alliance with the

National Democratic Front and the Popular Democratic Force) and in 1973. The party has in recent years been gravely weakened by splits.

In the 1983 presidential elections it supported the (unsuccessful) candidature of Dr José Vicente Rangel (see under entry for New Alternative).

Orientation. The URD is a left-of-centre formation.

Movement of the Revolutionary Left
Movimiento de Izquierda Revolucionaria (MIR)

Address. c/o Congreso de la República, Fracción Parlamentaria MIR, Edificio Tribunales, Esquina Pajarito, Caracas, Venezuela

Leadership. Moisés Moleiro (s.g.)

Founded. 1960

History. The MIR was formed by left-wing dissidents of the Democratic Action. Its activists were engaged in urban terrorism in 1962-64 and in guerrilla warfare from rural bases thereafter. The MIR was banned from 1962 to 1969. It supported the Movement towards Socialism (MAS) in the 1973 presidential elections and gained one seat in the Chamber of Deputies in 1973 (and four in 1978). In the 1978 presidential elections its candidate gained less than 1 per cent of the vote. In the 1983 general elections the MIR supported the Movement towards Socialism (MAS).

Orientation. The MIR is of extreme left-wing Marxist-Leninist ideology.

Movement towards Socialism
Movimiento al Socialismo (MAS)

Address. Urbanización Las Palmas, Av. Valencia, Qta. Alemas, Caracas, Venezuela

Leadership. Teodoro Petkoff (pres.)

Founded. January 1971

History. The MAS arose out of a division of the Communist Party of Venezuela over policy questions (such as the interpretation of Marxism, the form of socialism to be established, the nature of the party and an analysis of society). In the 1973 elections the MAS obtained some 275,000 votes and nine seats (out of 203) in the Chamber of Deputies and two (out of 49) in the Senate. In the presidential elections of December 1978 its candidate, José Vicente Rangel, took third place with 5.14 per cent of the vote, while in the simultaneous congressional elections it obtained some 350,000 votes; in the June 1979 municipal elections the MAS obtained 500,000 votes or 12 per cent of the total.

In the 1983 presidential elections Teodoro Petkoff obtained 4.17 per cent of the total vote, while in the congressional elections the party gained 5.75 per cent.

Orientation. The MAS has the aim of establishing socialism as appropriate to the country's experience and needs.

Structure. The party consists of cells, zonal and regional committees, a broad national leadership and a national bureau.

Membership. 180,000

Publications. Reflexiones; SDL; Punto; Boletín Nacional; Boletín Fracción Socialista

---

National Opinion
Opinión Nacional (Opina)

Address. Pájaro a Curamichate 92, 2° piso, Caracas 101, Venezuela

Leadership. Dr Pedro Luis Blanco Peñalver (pres.); Prof. Amado Corneilles (s.g.)

Founded. March 1961

History. The party has repeatedly been represented in the National Congress, and in the general elections of December 1978 it won one seat in the Chamber of Deputies. In the presidential elections held at the same time it supported the successful candidate of the Christian Social Party. However, in the 1983 presidential elections it nominated its own candidate, Jorge Olavarría, who obtained only 0.49 per cent of the votes cast, while in the congressional elections held at the same time it received 1.97 per cent.

Orientation. The party stands for the "establishment of collective integralism in Venezuela".

Structure. The party has a national congress, a supreme federal council, a central committee and a national disciplinary council. It is organized at state, district and communal level.

Membership. 22,000

Publications. Opina (monthly)

National Rally
Rescate Nacional

Leadership. Gen. (retd.) Luis Enrique Rangel Bourgoín (l.)

History. The leader of this group, who had been Minister of Defence in 1979–80, contested the 1983 presidential elections as an independent candidate but polled negligibly.

New Alternative
Nueva Alternativa

Address. Edificio "J. M. Vargas", Esquina Pajaritos, 2° piso, Caracas, 1010, Apartado Postal No. 20.193, San Martín, Caracas, Venezuela

Leadership. Dr José Vicente Rangel, Guillermo García Ponce, Américo Martín, Luis Miquelena, Estanislao González (members of national co-ordinating committee or general secretariat)

Founded. July 24, 1982

History. The New Alternative was set up as a coalition of various left-wing groups, notably the United Vanguard, a moderate faction of the Movement of the Revolutionary Left (MIR) led by Américo Martín (who had been the presidential candidate of the MIR in 1978) and the Revolutionary Popular Movement. For the 1983 presidential elections the New Alternative nominated Dr Rangel as its candidate, and he was supported by a number of other left-wing parties and groups, including *Causa Radical*, the Communist Party of Venezuela, the Democratic Republican Union, the People's Electoral Movement, the Revolutionary Action Group (*Grupo de Acción Revolucionaria*) and the Socialist Fatherland Movement (*Movimiento de Patria Socialista*, MPS) formed in May 1983 by dissidents from the Movement towards Socialism (MAS). The New Alternative has one deputy in the Chamber of Deputies and several in two state legislatures, as well as some on municipal councils.

Orientation. The coalition is in favour of fundamental reforms to end monopolistic tendencies in the economy and the accumulation of wealth by a minority.

Structure. The supreme organ of the New Alternative is its national directorate of 140 members, who elect a 21-member national political committee, which acts as the executive. A three-member co-ordinating committee deals with day-to-day political and organizational tasks.

Membership. 150,000

Publications. Decada 80 (review), 15,000; *Nueva Alternativa* (review), 15,000

New Generation
Nueva Generación

Founded. 1979

History. This right-wing group nominated Gen. (retd.) Arnaldo Castro Hurtado as its candidate for the presidential elections held on Dec. 4, 1983, but he polled only a negligible number of votes.

People's Electoral Movement
Movimiento Electoral del Pueblo (MEP)

Address. Casa Nacional del MEP, El Paraiso, Calle Bolívar, Quinta la Trinidad, Caracas, Venezuela
Leadership. Dr Luis Beltrán Prieto Figueroa (pres.); Dr Jesús Angell Paz Galarraga (s.g.)
Founded. December 1967
History. The MEP evolved from a division of the Democratic Action, partly over the latter's candidate for the 1968 presidential elections, in which the MEP's president came fourth with 19.32 per cent of the vote. In elections to Congress held at the same time, the MEP became the third strongest party with 26 (out of 188) seats in the Chamber of Deputies. In the 1973 elections, however, the MEP was reduced to eight (out of 203) seats in the Chamber. It fought the 1973 presidential elections in alliance with Venezuela's Communist Party (as the *Fuerza Nueva*, as whose candidate Dr Paz Galarraga came third with 5.1 per cent of the vote). In the 1978 presidential elections the MEP's president obtained only 1.1 per cent of the vote.

In the 1983 presidential elections it supported the candidature of Dr José Vicente Rangel (see under entry for New Alternative), and in the congressional elections held at the same time the MEP obtained 1.97 per cent of the total vote.
Membership. 100,000
International affiliations. Socialist International (consultative member)

Socialist League
Liga Socialista

Leadership. Julio Escalona (l.)
Founded. 1974
History. The League originated as part of the *Organización de Revolucionarios* (OR). In 1976 the League was suspected of involvement in a terrorist kidnapping case, and its then secretary-general was arrested and died in police custody as a result of torture (as officially reported). The League was the smallest party to gain a seat in the Chamber of Deputies in the 1978 elections, when it obtained 0.57 per cent of the vote. In March 1979 the League's leader at the time, David Nieves, was released from prison by the newly-inaugurated President Luis Herrera Campins of the Christian Social Party.

United Vanguard
Vanguardia Unitaria

Address. Apartado Postal No. 20.193, San Martín, Caracas, Venezuela
Leadership. Eduardo Machado (pres.); Guillermo García Ponce (s.g.)
Founded. November 1974
History. The party arose out of a split in the Communist Party of Venezuela (PCV), from which a number of leaders and members were expelled after they had critized that party for "excessive bureaucratization and dogmatism" and had called for a representative congress to be convened. In the 1978 presidential elections the party joined an alliance supporting the unsuccessful candidature of Dr José Vicente Rangel (of the MAS), and in municipal elections in June 1979 the party joined in an alliance with six other left-wing parties. In the 1983 presidential elections it again supported the candidature of Dr Rangel (see under entry for New Alternative, which it had joined in July 1982).
Orientation. Advocating "undogmatic Marxism" applied to the country's realities, the party seeks to set up a government of advanced democracy.

Vietnam

Capital: Hanoi   Pop. 60,000,000

The Socialist Republic of Vietnam (proclaimed after North Vietnam-backed Communist insurgents had effectively reunified the country by overthrowing the Government of South Vietnam in 1975) is, under its 1980 Constitution, "a state of proletarian dictatorship" in which the Communist Party of Vietnam is "the only force leading the state and society". It has a Council of State (the collective presidency of the Republic) elected for a five-year term by the National Assembly from among its members. The National Assembly itself is elected, also for five years, by adult suffrage. A Council of Ministers headed by a Prime Minister and also elected by the National Assembly is responsible to that Assembly. In elections to the National Assembly held on April 21, 1981, 496 candidates were elected (in a 97.96 per cent poll as officially announced on May 17, 1981) in 93 constituencies for which the Vietnam Fatherland Front (consisting of the Communist, Socialist and Democratic parties, Catholics and Buddhists, trade unions and mass organizations) had nominated 614 candidates.

The minimum voting age is 18 years. The right to vote was in 1976 withheld from officers and officials of the former regime in South Vietnam and from numerous members of "reactionary parties".

Communist Party of Vietnam
Dang Cong san Viet-Nam

Address. 10 Hoang Van Thu St., Hanoi, Vietnam

Leadership. Le Duan (s.g.); Truong Chinh, Pham Van Dong, Pham Hung, Le Duc Tho, Gen. Van Tien Dung, Vo Chi Cong, Gen. Chu Huy Man, To Huu, Vo Van Kiet, Do Muoi, Gen. Le Duc Anh, Nguyen Duc Tam (other full members of Politburo); Nguyen Co Thach, Gen. Dong Si Nguyen (alternate members of Politburo)

Founded. February 1930

History. The Communist Party of Vietnam is descended from the Communist Party of Indo-China (CPIC), founded in 1930 by Ho Chi Minh and other Communists, which in April 1931 was recognized as an autonomous section of the Third (Communist) International (or Comintern). Born in 1890 as Nguyen Tat Thanh in the Annam province of what was then French Indo-China, Ho Chi Minh (literally "Ho the seeker of enlightenment") had been a founder member of the French Communist Party in 1920 and had subsequently worked as an agent of the Comintern in Asia. Following the formation of the CPIC a peasant rebellion broke out in Indo-China with Communist backing and after its suppression Ho was sentenced to death in absentia by the French authorities. After the failure of a further Communist-led uprising in 1940, Ho joined Indo-Chinese exiles on the Chinese border and in 1941 formed the Communist-dominated Viet Minh guerrilla organization, which harried the Japanese during World War II.

Immediately after the Japanese surrender in August 1945 the Viet Minh set up a provisional government in coalition with other nationalist groups and in November 1946 the Democratic Republic of Vietnam was proclaimed in Hanoi with Ho as its President as well as Prime Minister and Foreign Minister. Various attempts to reach a compromise settlement with the re-established French authorities broke down and from early 1947 Ho's Viet Minh guerrillas engaged in bitter hostilities with the French forces which culminated in the decisive defeat of the latter at Dien Bien Phu in May 1954. Meanwhile, at its second congress in February 1951, the CPIC had divided into independent Cambodian, Laotian and Vietnamese formations, the last-named taking the name Vietnam Workers' Party (VWP).

Under the 1954 Geneva agreements Vietnam was divided at the 17th parallel and Ho Chi Minh became both President and Prime Minister of North Vietnam, relinquishing the premiership in 1955 but retaining the presidency and party chairmanship until his death in September 1969.

At its third congress in 1960 the party decided inter alia "to promote the national people's democratic revolution in South Vietnam" and "to unify the country on the basis of independence and democracy". The ensuing war against the then Government of South Vietnam, which was supported by the United States, ended in the conquest of South Vietnam in April 1975, followed by the reunification of the country as the Socialist Republic of Vietnam. At the fourth party congress held in December 1976, the party's name was changed to Communist Party of Vietnam.

Early in 1977 the three mass organizations led by the party—the National Front for the Liberation of South Vietnam (established in 1960), the Vietnamese Alliance of Democratic and Peace Forces (set up in 1968) and the (North Vietnamese) Fatherland Front (dating back to 1955)—were merged in one national Vietnamese Fatherland Front with the object of "uniting all political parties, revolutionary mass organizations, progressive classes, nationalities, religions and notables in the country and overseas Vietnamese" and of "ensuring broad unity of all forces loving the country and approving socialism under the leadership of the Communist Party of Vietnam". Other parties included in the Front were the Socialist Party and the Democratic Party (see separate entries).

Although the party until about 1972 adopted a neutral attitude towards the dispute between the Chinese and Soviet Communist parties, its links with the Soviet party became increasingly stronger after the rapprochement between China and the United States in 1972, the ending of Chinese aid to Vietnam in 1975 and Chinese support for the Pol Pot régime in Kampuchea in 1978.

Orientation. A report submitted to the fourth party congress in 1976 stated: "The party leads all activities in the conditions of proletarian dictatorship. The party leadership is the supreme guarantee of the system of collective mastery of the working people, for the existence and activity of the socialist state." The report also proclaimed respect for "the freedom of belief and the citizens' right to follow or not to follow a religion", and "full equality in all respects" among the country's nationalities. It further described the aim of foreign policy as "restoring and consolidating solidarity and promoting unified support and assistance" (among the other socialist countries and with the international communist and workers' movement) "on the basis of Marxism-Leninism and in the spirit of proletarian internationalism".

At the fifth party congress, held in Hanoi on March 27–31, 1982, Le Duan, the general secretary, declared inter alia that the party had established "the dictatorship of the proletariat in the whole country" and had waged two wars— "against the expansionism and hegemonism of the Chinese reactionary leadership" and against aggression in the South by the Kampuchean "Pol Pot clique"—and that "a militant alliance between Kampuchea, Laos and Vietnam" had also strengthened "militant solidarity with the Soviet Union". He described the task of the party during the 1980s as being to guide the people and the Army "to build socialism successfully and to defend the socialist Vietnamese fatherland". His report also emphasized the need of consolidating party unity, and he criticized members who had "damaged the prestige of the party" and who would have to be expelled from it.

Structure. The party's supreme organ is its congress. Its central committee has 116 full and 36 alternate members, and its Politburo has 13 full and two alternate members, while there is also a 10-member secretariat.

Membership. 1,800,000

Publications. *Nhan Dan* (The People, daily national official organ), 300,000; *Tap Chi Cong San* (Communist Review, monthly); *Vietnam Courier* (monthly)

Democratic Party
Dang dan chu

Address. 32 Tran Tien St., Hanoi, Vietnam

Leadership. Nghiem Xuan Yem (s.g.)

Founded. 1944

History. This party has represented sections of the middle classes and intelligentsia.

Publications. *Doc Lap* (Independence)

Socialist Party
Dang xa Hoi

Address. 53 Nguyen Du St., Hanoi, Vietnam

Leadership. Nguyen Xien (g.s.)

History. This party consists mainly of members of the intelligentsia.

Publications. *To Quoc* (Fatherland)

Western Sahara

Capital: El Aaiún Pop. n.a.

The former Spanish Western Sahara (consisting of Sakiet el Hamra and Rio de Oro) was, under an agreement concluded in Madrid on Nov. 14, 1975, partitioned between Morocco and Mauritania. However, this decision was not accepted by the territory's principal national liberation movement, the Polisario Front, which has since then been at war with Moroccan forces, while Mauritania officially renounced all claims to Western Saharan territory in August 1979. In February 1976 the Polisario Front proclaimed a Saharan Arab Democratic Republic, which has since then been recognized by some 50 foreign governments and has become a member of the Organization of African Unity.

Under this republic's Constitution of 1976 the Polisario Front's executive committee constitutes a nine-member Council for the Command of the Revolution as the republic's supreme executive organ. The Polisario Front's secretary-general is head of state; the republic's Cabinet is headed by a Prime Minister; and there is a 41-member National Council, of which 21 members are from the Polisario Front's political bureau and 20 are elected by "popular base congresses". In practice, however, all economically important areas of Western Sahara are under Moroccan control; although the Polisario Front has claimed to control about 75 per cent of the territory's area, the republic's administrative structures exist only in refugee camps in south-western Algeria.

Popular Front for the Liberation of Saguia el Hamra and Rio de Oro (Polisario Front) Frente Popular para la Liberación de Saguia el Hamra y Rio de Oro (Frente Polisario)

Address. (interior) Bir Lehlu, República Arabe Sahraui Democrática; (exterior) B.P. 10, Al Mouradia, Algiers, Algeria

Leadership. Mohamed Abdelazziz (s.g.)

Founded. May 1973

History. The Popular Front for the Liberation of Saguia el Hamra and Rio de Oro was established as a national liberation movement in the then Spanish (Western) Sahara. It entered into negotiations with Spain in June 1975, but after the tripartite Madrid agreement between Spain, Morocco and Mauritania leading to the annexation of the Western Sahara by the two last-named powers, the Front took up armed struggle against them from November 1975, and proclaimed the Saharan Arab Democratic Republic in February 1976. After the overthrow of the Mauritanian Government of President Mokhtar Ould Daddah in July 1978, Polisario declared a ceasefire in its operations against Mauritania, while those against Morocco were continued. The Front claims to have liberated 75 per cent of the territory of Western Sahara and has received substantial backing from Algeria.

Orientation. The Front seeks full national independence as the preliminary for building a socialist society.

Structure. The Front has a congress, a seven-member executive committee, a 25-member political bureau and a 41-member national council.

Publications. *Sahara Libre* (fortnightly); *20 de Mayo* (monthly)

Western Samoa

Capital: Apia (Upolu)   Pop. 158,000

Western Samoa is an independent member of the Commonwealth. Under its Constitution adopted in 1960 the head of state is elected for a five-year term by the Legislative Assembly (*Fono*). (However, the current head of state is holding this office for life.) Executive power is vested in a Prime Minister who must be supported by a majority in the *Fono* and who appoints other ministers. The 47-member *Fono* is elected under a system whereby 45 of its members are chosen through *matai* suffrage (with the right to vote restricted to the elected heads of extended family units) and the other two members through universal adult suffrage by persons (mainly naturalized citizens) registered on a separate roll.

In elections to the *Fono* held on Feb. 27, 1982, a total of 22 of those elected were members or declared supporters of the Human Rights Protection Party (HRPP), while 11 were members of a de facto political party (not formally named or constituted) of the outgoing Prime Minister, Tupuola Taisi Efi, and the remaining 14 elected members were undeclared. All members were technically independents and voted as such in electing a new Prime Minister.

Human Rights Protection Party (HRPP)

Leadership. Tofilau Eti (l.)
Founded. February 1979
History. Western Samoa's first political party was formed after the February 1979 elections by members of the Legislative Assembly (*Fono*) opposed to the premiership of Tupuola Taisi Efi. The party's leader at the time, Va'ai Kolone (a former chairman of the public accounts committee), subsequently received 23 votes when the *Fono* met to choose a new Prime Minister on March 28, 1979, as against 24 votes cast for the incumbent.

Following the 1982 elections the HRPP leader was elected Prime Minister by 24 votes to 23 on April 13, 1982, but in June of that year his Government lost its majority in the *Fono*, as one of its ministers was unseated; on Sept. 17, 1982, Va'ai Kolone was also unseated (because of irregularities in his election campaign). Tupuola Taisi Efi thereupon again became Prime Minister, but his Government fell in December 1982 when it lost its majority through by-election successes of the HRPP, with the result that Tofilau Eti was able to form a new Government on Dec. 30. After the re-election of Va'ai Kolone in a by-election in January 1983 the HRPP held 25 seats in the *Fono*.

Orientation. The party has expressed opposition to rapid advance in the rate of economic development.

Labour Party
Tautua mo Samoa

Leadership. Mapuilesua Pelenato (founder)
Founded. May 1981
History. The founder of this party had been elected to the *Fono* at a by-election held in 1980; however, he was not re-elected in 1982, and the party is thus not represented in the *Fono*.
Orientation. This party stands for private enterprise and the industrialization of the country.

One Samoa Party

Leadership. Papalii Laupepa (l.)
Founded. 1984
History. This party's leader and founder is a son of the country's head of state; he had previously been a member of the

group around former Prime Minister Tupuola Taisi Efi (see under entry for Human Rights Protection Party).

Orientation. The party seeks to serve the interests of small farmers and small businessmen.

Yemen Arab Republic

Capital: Sana'a   Pop. 9,000,000

The Yemen Arab Republic was, under a provisional Constitution of 1974, "an Arab, Islamic and independent state" in which executive and legislative power was exercised by a Command Council, whose chairman was head of state and whose general policy was carried out by a Government headed by a Prime Minister. Under a decree of the Command Council a Constituent People's Assembly was formed in February 1978 with a view to drafting an electoral law and preparing "free elections" (a previous elected Consultative Council having been dissolved in October 1975). On April 22, 1978, the Assembly voted in favour of the appointment, for a five-year term, of President (Lt.-Col.) Ahmed Hussein el Ghashmi, after which the Command Council was dissolved. The President was, however, assassinated on June 24, 1978, whereupon the Assembly formed a four-member provisional Presidential Council, and on July 17 of that year the Assembly elected, by 76 votes out of 99, a new President.

In May 1979 the membership of the Constituent Assembly was increased to 159, and a 15-member Consultative Council was set up. In May 1980 a 52-member Committee for National Consultation was established to prepare for a General People's Congress of 700 elected and 300 appointed members. This Congress first met in August–September 1982. It was to meet every two years and to be re-elected every four years. The Constituent Assembly, however, continued to meet, and on May 22, 1983, it re-elected the President for a second five-year term without opposition. The country has no political parties.

People's Democratic Republic of Yemen

Capital: Aden   Pop. 2,100,000

The People's Democratic Republic of Yemen is a one-party state in which the secretary-general of the political bureau of the Yemen Socialist Party (YSP) holds the offices of head of state, Chairman of the Presidium of the People's Supreme Council, and Prime Minister. The 111-member People's Supreme Council was elected by popular vote on Dec. 16–18, 1978, when 71 YSP members and 40 independents were elected, with voters having a choice between several candidates for each seat. The newly elected Council unanimously approved, on Dec. 27, 1978, a new Council of Ministers (Cabinet) as the country's "highest legislative body".

Yemen Socialist Party (YSP)

Leadership. Abdul Fatah Ismail (ch.); Ali Nasser Mohamed (s.g. of political bureau)

Founded. October 1978

History. The YSP was formed to supersede the National Front, which had been established in October 1975 (under the full name of the United Political Organization National Front, UPONF) and had embraced three political parties—the National Liberation Front (until then the country's leading party), the (Baathist) Popular Vanguard Party and the (Communist orientated) Popular Democratic Union.

Orientation. The YSP is Marxist-Leninist, with a programme based on "scientific socialism".

Structure. The YSP has a central committee of 47 full and 11 candidate members, a political bureau of five full and two candidate members and a five-member secretariat.

International affiliations. The YSP is recognized by the Communist parties of the Soviet-bloc countries.

Yugoslavia

Capital: Belgrade   Pop. 22,400,000

The Socialist Federal Republic of Yugoslavia, in which effective power is exercised by the League of Communists of Yugoslavia, is composed of six socialist republics (Bosnia and Herzegovina, Croatia, Macedonia, Montenegro, Serbia and Slovenia) and two autonomous provinces (Kosovo and Vojvodina). Under the 1974 Constitution there is, at federal level, a Federal Assembly or Parliament (*Skupstina SFRJ*) elected for a four-year term and consisting of (i) a Federal Chamber (*Savezno Vece*) composed of delegates of self-managing organizations and communities and of socio-political organizations and (ii) a Chamber of Republics and Provinces (*Vece Republika i Prokrajina*) consisting of delegates of the Republican and Provincial Assemblies. The Federal Assembly, with its two chambers, is defined as "the supreme organ of power within the framework of federal rights and duties". The Federal Chamber is composed of 30 delegates from each of the six constituent republics and 20 from each of the two autonomous provinces. The Chamber of Republics and Autonomous Provinces is composed of 12 delegates from each Republican Assembly and eight from each Provincial Assembly—all elected and recalled by secret ballot by all chambers of these eight assemblies sitting in joint session. Both chambers of the Federal Assembly inter alia elect the President and members of the Federal Executive Council (i.e. the Prime Minister and the Government) for a four-year term.

The nine-member Collective Presidency of the Republic is composed of the President of the League of Communists of Yugoslavia (ex officio) and one member from each of the constituent republics and autonomous provinces. Under constitutional amendments promulgated in 1981 the Collective Presidency carries out the functions of the head of state, and its President and Vice-President are elected for a one-year term, each time from a different republic or autonomous province.

The first elections under the delegate system laid down in the 1974 Constitution were held in March-May 1974, when some 1,000,000 delegates, elected by "basic organizations of associated labour" (i.e. workshops, offices, etc.) and in about 12,000 local communities, elected from among themselves delegates to about 500 communal assemblies, which in turn elected delegates to the assemblies of the republics and autonomous provinces. The communal assemblies thereupon elected delegates to the Federal Chamber, and the assemblies of the republics and autonomous provinces elected the Chamber of Republics and Provinces. All candidates are subject to screening by the Socialist Alliance of the Working People of Yugoslavia, the country's overall political organization under the leadership of the League of Communists. Such elections to the 220-member Federal Chamber and the 88-member Chamber of Republics and Autonomous Provinces were similarly completed in May 1982. The minimum voting age is 18 years.

League of Communists of Yugoslavia (LCY)
Savez Komunista Jugoslavije

Address. Bulevar Lenjina, Belgrade, Yugoslavia

Leadership. Dragoslav Markovic (pres. of the Presidency of the Central Committee), Nikola Stojanovic (sec.), Franjo Herljevic, Veljko Milatovic, Miljan Radovic, Jure Bilic, Dusan Dragosavac, Dimce Belovski, Kiro Hadzivasilev, Dobrivoje Vidic, Mitja Ribicic, Milan Kucan, Ali Sukrija, Petar Matic, Dane Cuic (members of the Presidency, two from each of the six republics and one from each of the two autonomous provinces and the Yugoslav People's Army); Hamdija Pozderac, Dobroslav Culafic, Josip Vrhovec, Krste Markovski, Andrej Marinc, Dusan Ckrebic, Ilijaz Kurtesi, Slavko Veselinov (ex-officio members representing the party committees in the republics and autonomous provinces)

Founded. April 1919

History. The LCY was founded in April 1919 as the Socialist Workers' Party of Yugoslavia (Communist) (SWPY) at a congress of unification in Belgrade; in June 1920 the party changed its name to the Communist Party of Yugoslavia (CPY). The SWPY decided at its formation to join the Third (Communist) International (Comintern) and to take part in elections if so decided in a referendum among its members. The CPY became the third strongest party in the Yugoslav Constituent Assembly elected in 1920, when it gained about 200,000 votes and 59 seats, but in 1921 the party was banned. Working underground and holding conferences abroad, the CPY eventually established, in 1937, a new leadership under Josip Broz Tito.

After the military defeat of the Kingdom of Yugoslavia in 1941 the Communists played the leading role (with emphasis on socio-political change) in the struggle for national liberation against the fascist forces and their collaborators. In 1943, at the second session of the Antifascist Council of the National Liberation of Yugoslavia (composed of democratically elected representatives of all Yugoslav nations), all claims of the Yugoslav émigré government to represent the country's people were revoked and King Peter II was debarred from returning to the country. Virtually at the same time the Tehran conference of the Allied leaders recognized Tito's partisan forces as an equal military factor in the antifascist alliance.

Having liberated most of the country by their own force of arms, the Communist Party came to power after World War II at the head of a People's Front, a republic being declared in November 1945 of which Tito became President in 1953. The new Government's successful resistance to Joseph Stalin's attempts to establish Soviet domination over Yugoslavia created a bitter dispute which culminated in the Yugoslav party's expulsion from the Communist Information Bureau (Cominform) in June 1948, although following Stalin's death in 1953 Nikita Khrushchev sought a reconciliation with Tito (the Cominform being dissolved in April 1956). Meanwhile, the Yugoslav party pursued its own road to socialism on the basis of non-alignment and was renamed the League of Communists of Yugoslavia (LCY) at its 6th congress in November 1952, when the People's Front was reconstituted as the Socialist Alliance of Working People of Yugoslavia, in which the LCY retained the predominant role.

After the establishment of workers' councils in several hundred enterprises in late 1948 and their legal promulgation in 1950, a system of socialist self-management was introduced in state-owned economic enterprises and higher economic associations by work collectives, with the ultimate aim of establishing an association of direct producers in which, as stated by Marx, material production would no longer control the people but would be controlled by them. A programme of the LCY, adopted in April 1958, defined the party's role, and in a second stage of the development of self-management, begun in 1964, the system was to be extended to the whole of "social reproduction", with the working class becoming the dominant economic and political force under the leading role of the LCY.

Following constitutional amendments in 1967, 1968 and 1971, a new Constitution was adopted in February 1974, which defined the concept of self-management founded on the associated labour delegation system and the federation as a community of equal nations and nationalities functioning by means of consultation to reach agreement among the socialist republics and socialist autonomous provinces.

Orientation. The LCY proclaims itself to be "a revolutionary organization and the leading ideological and political force of the working class and all working people of Yugoslavia". Its objective is "the further development of socialist self-management of social relations, in which the workers determine their income and decide, through a system of delegations, on all aspects of social life".

The policy of the development of socialist self-management, national equality and non-alignment, established during the life of Josip Broz Tito (who was president for

life of the LCY), was continued after his death (on May 4, 1980).

Structure. The LCY is based on local (commune) organizations, whose supreme organ is a (commune) conference which is convened every four years and itself elects a committee as its executive political organ; in each republic or province the highest League of Communists forum is a congress or conference. The LCY congress is the supreme forum and is held every four years. Between congresses the supreme organ is the central committee, which elects a 23-member presidium of which the president and secretary are elected on a rotating basis for terms of one and two years respectively; in addition, the central committee elects, from its membership, several executive secretaries. The basic principle of the LCY is that of democratic centralism.

Membership. 2,154,627 (late 1982)

Publications. *Komunist* (weekly), about 500,000; *Socijalizam* (monthly), 10,000

Zaïre

Capital: Kinshasa   Pop. 33,000,000

The Republic of Zaïre is a "united, democratic and social state" with an executive President elected for a seven-year term (and re-eligible); he is head of state, head of the National Executive Council (Cabinet) and leader of the Popular Revolutionary Movement (*Mouvement Populaire de la Révolution*, MPR), the country's sole legal political organization, whose political bureau he appoints. There is a National Legislative Council elected for a five-year term by compulsory, direct and universal adult suffrage of citizens above the age of 18 years and resident in their constituency for a year.

In elections held on Sept. 18–19, 1982, a total of 310 "people's commissioners" (one per 100,000 of the population) were elected to the National Legislative Council from 1,409 candidates selected by the MPR.

Popular Movement of the Revolution
Mouvement Populaire de la Révolution (MPR)

Address. B.P. 7171, Kinshasa 1, Zaïre

Leadership. President Mobutu Sese Seko (pres.); N'Singa Udjuu Ongwakebi Untube (exec. sec.)

Founded. May 1967

History. The party was founded by its president with the aim of overcoming tribalism and of carrying out, as the

country's sole political party, "a truly national revolution". In December 1970 the MPR officially became the country's sole party and "the supreme institution of the Republic". In December 1971 the MPR's political bureau adopted, as the party's political philosophy, the "recourse to [African] authenticity", which was endorsed at a party congress in May 1972, when it was also decided to integrate all organs of the state in the structure of the MPR and to make Zaïre a lay state, with a mixed economy under state control and with encouragement of foreign investment.

In July 1974 the MPR's political bureau decided to revise the country's Constitution so as to establish the MPR's doctrine as "Mobutism"—"the thought, teachings and actions of the President" who would preside over all organs of the MPR and of the state. In December 1977 the MPR's president was re-elected as party leader and thus, under the country's Constitution, as President of the Republic for a seven-year term. In February 1978 an executive secretariat of the MPR was set up, and in July of that year permanent MPR secretaries were appointed in all administrative units of the country (regions, sub-regions and zones).

Orientation. The MPR seeks to embrace all social strata with the object of building a nation and of finding appropriate solutions to the problems of development. The MPR's programme provides for the establishment of a democratic society in a strong and prosperous state in peace and progress.

Structure. The MPR's president is also head of state, president of the Executive Council (Cabinet) and president of the MPR's congress and of its political bureau. The congress is the MPR's supreme organ and meets in ordinary session every five years (and in extraordinary session whenever necessitated by a question of national import). There is a central committee of 114 members. Of the 38 members of the political bureau, the country's eight regions and the city of Kinshasa elect two each, and the remaining 20 are appointed by the president. All its members must be natives of Zaïre and at least 35 years old. Seven of the bureau's members constitute its permanent committee.

Membership. MPR membership is acquired by every Zaïrean at birth, and there are 13,000,000 members of its youth movement.

Publications. *Salongo* (daily), 15,000; *Elima* (daily), 18,000

Zambia

Capital: Lusaka   Pop. 5,900,000

The Republic of Zambia, an independent member of the Commonwealth, has an executive President who is head of the United National Independence Party (UNIP, the country's sole political party) and is elected (and re-eligible) for a five-year term by popular vote of citizens above the age of 18 years. The President appoints, inter alios, a Prime Minister, a secretary-general of UNIP (both of these being ex-officio members of UNIP's central committee) and also judges. The Cabinet, which is also appointed by the President, is subordinate to UNIP's central committee, which has not more than 25 members, of whom 20 are elected at the party's general conference held every five years, while three are nominated by the President. The National Assembly has 125 members elected—at the same time as the President—for five years by simple majority (also on the basis of universal suffrage of citizens above the age of 18 years) from two or more candidates approved by UNIP local committees and the party's central committee in each of the 125 single-member constituencies, while 10 additional members are nominated by the President of the Republic.

Prior to presidential elections held on Dec. 12, 1978, a UNIP general conference had agreed on new qualifications for presidential candidates (providing in particular that they must have been UNIP members for five years and must be supported by at least 20 UNIP members in each of the country's nine provinces).

In elections held on Oct. 27, 1983, (i) President Kenneth Kaunda was re-elected for a further five-year term, gaining 93 per cent of the votes cast in a 63 per cent poll, and (ii) 125 members were elected to the National Assembly from among 766 candidates approved by the central committee of UNIP (which had rejected 46 applications by other aspiring candidates).

United National Independence Party (UNIP)

Address. P.O. Box 302, Lusaka, Zambia

Leadership. President (Dr) Kenneth D. Kaunda (pres.); Humphrey Mulemba (s.g.)

Founded. October 1958

History. UNIP has its origins in the Zambia African National Congress, founded in 1958 as a breakaway group of the Northern Rhodesia African National Congress and banned by the British Governor on March 12, 1959, on the grounds that it had threatened the use of violence. From among various African nationalist groups formed to succeed the banned organization, the United National Freedom Party and the African National Independence Party merged later in 1959 to form UNIP, of which Kenneth Kaunda, after being released from detention, was elected president in January 1960. Following elections held in October 1962 under a new Constitution for the then Northern Rhodesia, UNIP formed a coalition Government with the African National Congress.

After a further election held in January 1964, following the introduction of internal self-government, UNIP formed its first one-party Government. Under the independence Constitution which came into force on October 24, 1964, Dr Kaunda became President of the Republic of Zambia, and under a constitutional amendment adopted on Dec. 8, 1972, establishing Zambia as a one-party state, UNIP became the country's sole legal party.

Orientation. In its constitution adopted in 1978 UNIP is described as the country's "revolutionary vanguard party", with its main task being "to accomplish a victorious transition from capitalism to humanism through socialism" and to "wage a relentless struggle against all domestic and international forces of reaction . . ., for the eradication of capitalism, imperialism, colonialism, neo-colonialism, fascism and racism" and of "poverty, hunger, ignorance, disease, crime and the exploitation of one man by another." The party also supports a policy of non-alignment. Its ideology has been expounded by President Kaunda in his book *Humanism in Zambia* (1974).

Structure. The highest authority of the party and its Government is the UNIP general conference, which normally meets every five years and is composed of 600 delegates, with equal representation for each province, including the members of the national council and delegates of trade unions and of organizations affiliated to the party. The conference elects the party's president, who automatically becomes the sole candidate for election of the President of the Republic, and it also elects 20 members to the central committee of 25 members as the highest executive organ of UNIP. The national council, meeting between sessions of the general conference, decides inter alia on matters of policy and also has disciplinary powers. UNIP is "supreme over all institutions of the country".

Membership. 800,000 (est.)

Publications. *Times of Zambia* (daily), 65,000

Zimbabwe

Capital: Harare (formerly Salisbury)   Pop. 8,200,000

The Republic of Zimbabwe, an independent state within the Commonwealth, has a President chosen by the Legislature and required to act on the advice of the Prime Minister and the Executive Council (Cabinet). The Legislature consists of (i) a House of Assembly of 100 members, 80 of whom are elected by universal adult suffrage on a common roll and 20 on a roll for Whites, Coloureds and Asians; and (ii) a Senate of 40 members, 10 of whom are chosen by the White members of the House of Assembly, 14 by Black members of the House, 10 by a Council of Chiefs and six by the President on the advice of the Prime Minister. While White members of the House of Assembly are elected by preference in single-member constituencies, Black members are elected from party lists presented in eight electoral districts, to each of which seats are allotted roughly in proportion to the number of voters. Parties need not nominate candidates in all districts. To qualify for seats a party must obtain more than 10 per cent of the votes in a district. The 20 White seats in the House of Assembly can, during the first seven years after the first elections, be abolished only by a unanimous vote of the House, and after seven years by 70 per cent of the members of the House, followed in each case by a two-thirds approval in the Senate. The Prime Minister must command a majority in the House of Assembly.

In elections held on Feb. 14, 1980, for the White (as well as Coloured and Asian) seats in the House, all 20 were taken by the Rhodesian Front. In elections to the 80 common roll (Black) seats held on Feb. 27–29 the result was as follows: Zimbabwe African National Union–Patriotic Front 57, Patriotic Front (Zimbabwe African People's Union) 20, United African National Council 3.

Black Parties

Patriotic Front—Zimbabwe African People's Union (PF-ZAPU)

Leadership. Joshua Nkomo (pres.); Josiah Chinamano (first vice-pres.); Joseph Msika (s.g.)

Founded. October 1976

History. Joshua Nkomo played a leading role in the early African nationalist movement of (Southern) Rhodesia. He was president of the African National Congress from 1957 to 1959, when this organization was banned; in October 1960 he was elected president of the National Democratic Party, which was banned in December 1961 and immediately replaced by ZAPU, which was in turn banned in September 1962, when Joshua Nkomo was temporarily placed under restriction.

The banned ZAPU was succeeded by a People's Caretaker Council, which was banned in August 1964. The ZAPU leadership in exile, meeting in Dar es Salaam in July 1963, was split into two factions, one of which formed the Zimbabwe African National Union (ZANU) with the Rev. Ndabaningi Sithole as president and with Robert Mugabe as a member of its executive, and the other remaining as ZAPU under Joshua Nkomo's leadership. The latter was imprisoned in 1963–64 and kept under detention or restriction from 1964 to 1974, when he became a member of the executive of the newly-created African National Council (ANC), being elected president of its internal wing in September 1975.

By early 1977, however, the ANC was divided into its internal wing, which became the United African National Congress under Bishop Abel Muzorewa, and its external wing, constituted by ZAPU and also designated as the ANC-Zimbabwe, which under Joshua Nkomo's leadership organized a Zimbabwe People's Revolutionary Army (ZIPRA) as its military wing (based in Zambia). In October 1976 the Patriotic Front was set up under an agreement between Joshua Nkomo (as ZAPU's leader) and Robert Mugabe (as leader of his wing of ZANU), but an unsuccessful constitutional conference held in Geneva in October–December 1976 was still attended by two separate delegations of these organizations.

At the London constitutional conference of September–December 1979 the Patriotic Front was represented by one delegation, but the February 1980 elections were contested separately by its two wings (these being the first elections in which they took part). In these elections PF-ZAPU gained 20 of the 80 Black seats in the House of Assembly (15 of them in Matabeleland). In municipal elections held in Bulawayo in June 1981 the party obtained all 15 seats.

However, from mid-1980 onwards sections of PF-ZAPU were involved in civil unrest, arising at first from the refusal of ZIPRA elements (mainly from Matabeleland) to agree to their incorporation in Zimbabwe's new Army. Clashes between ZIPRA dissidents and units of the Zimbabwe African National Liberation Army (ZANLA, loyal to the Prime Minister), resulted in hundreds of casualties. The Government accused Nkomo of supporting the ZIPRA dissidents (which he denied); after the discovery of large quantities of arms hidden in Matabeleland and (as officially claimed) to be used for a military coup, the Government seized, on Feb. 16, 1982, a total of 11 companies owned by Nkomo and other PF-ZAPU leaders, and on Feb. 17 Nkomo and the three other PF-ZAPU members of the Government were relieved of their responsibilities. During March 1982 large numbers of PF-ZAPU members were arrested. On Dec. 9, 1982, the Government produced two alleged PF-ZAPU supporters who were said to have admitted that they had been infiltrated into Zimbabwe from South Africa after being given sabotage training in that country.

Early in 1983 the Government sent the fifth brigade of the Army (trained by North Korean instructors) to Matabeleland to suppress the continuing unrest. During March further PF-ZAPU officials were arrested, among them two members of the House of Assembly, while hundreds of people, including PF-ZAPU office-bearers, were reported to have fled to Botswana (where they were accommodated in refugee camps). By then the fifth brigade was said

to have committed numerous atrocities and to have killed over 1,000 civilians.

On March 6, 1983, Nkomo accused Mugabe of being intent upon destroying PF-ZAPU and creating a one-party state. Fearing arrest, he left Zimbabwe for Britain on March 8. However, he returned to Zimbabwe on Aug. 16, 1983, to reclaim his seat in the House of Assembly (which he might have lost because of his prolonged absence). Earlier a number of PF-ZAPU supporters had been tried for alleged subversion, and two of them had been sentenced to death on Aug. 10, 1983, for involvement in a battle in which four persons were killed (including a policeman).

On the other hand Josiah Chinamano, who had been one of the PF-ZAPU ministers dismissed with Nkomo, had early in 1982 pledged his continued support for Mugabe and claimed that he had always worked for a merger of the two parties. On April 16, 1983, Mugabe appointed three PF-ZAPU members to his Government (two of them being promoted from their earlier status as deputy ministers). On May 13, 1983, Chinamano confirmed that the possibility of a merger of ZANU-PF and PF-ZAPU had been discussed at a preliminary meeting of two committees of the two parties during April.

Orientation. Although his party has been regarded as left of centre and in favour of a mixed economy, Nkomo has in the past maintained good relations with the Soviet Union.

Structure. The party has a central committee, the majority of whose members are Shona (from northern and central Zimbabwe), but many Shona people regard it as a predominantly Ndebele party.

United African National Council (UANC)

Address. 40 Charter Road, Harare, Zimbabwe

Leadership. Bishop Abel Tendekayi Muzorewa (pres.); Edward Mazaiwana (s.g.)

Founded. December 1971

History. The UANC was formed as the African National Council (ANC) with Bishop Muzorewa as its chairman and a 12-member executive including former office-bearers in the two banned African nationalist organizations—the Zimbabwe African People's Union (ZAPU) and the Zimbabwe African National Union (ZANU), the latter being represented by Eddison Zvobgo. The immediate object of the ANC was to campaign for the rejection of British constitutional proposals which did not provide for elections based on one man, one vote, and on which the Pearce Commission was to conduct an opinion test (which eventually found that the proposals were rejected by a majority of Rhodesia's people as a whole).

The ANC was constituted as the equivalent of a political party in March 1972, and a newly formed 23-member central committee of the ANC included Robert Mugabe (who, as former secretary-general of ZANU, was then in detention). In December 1974 the ANC was joined by ZANU and ZAPU on a basis of recognizing "the inevitability of continued armed struggle and all other forms of struggle until the total liberation of Zimbabwe".

However, in September 1975 the ANC was split into a Nkomo faction and a Muzorewa faction, and this led to the creation of an "internal" wing led by Joshua Nkomo and an "external" wing led by Bishop Muzorewa and the Rev. Ndabaningi Sithole. In May 1976 Robert Mugabe rejected the leadership of the nationalist movement by either of these two wings, and in September 1976 ZANU-Sithole withdrew from the ANC. Early in 1977 the ANC's "external" wing assumed the name of United African National Council (UANC), and as such it negotiated the "internal settlement" with the Government of Ian Smith early in 1978, together with ZANU-Sithole and the Zimbabwe United People's Organization of Chief Jeremiah Chirau, which led to the formation of a biracial "transitional" Government in April 1978.

There followed one man, one vote elections in April 1979, when the UANC won 51 seats in a House of Assembly consisting of 72 Black and 28 White members. In May 1979 Bishop Muzorewa became Prime Minister of a Cabinet which, in addition to members of the UANC, also included members of the (White) Rhodesian Front and of the United National Federal Party. Under the constitutional agreement reached in London in December 1979, this Cabinet resigned and handed over power to an interim administration under a British Governor. In the ensuing elections of February 1980 the UANC was reduced to three seats in the new House of Assembly. Independents who were aligned with the UANC unsuccessfully contested municipal elections held in Bulawayo in June 1981.

In November 1983 Bishop Muzorewa was placed in detention under emergency regulations (which had been renewed from time to time), with Prime Minister Mugabe accusing him of involvement in clandestine activities during a visit to Israel, when he was quoted as advocating the establishment of diplomatic relations between the two countries (which was contrary to government policy). The Bishop had also criticized "the new oppression" in Zimbabwe.

Orientation. The party, which was strongest among the Manyika people (in Mashonaland), has been considered moderate and non-socialist and has had extensive support from business interests.

Zimbabwe African National Union— Patriotic Front (ZANU-PF)

Address. 88 Manica Road, Harare, Zimbabwe

Leadership. Robert Mugabe (pres.)

Founded. August 1963 (as ZANU)

History. ZANU was formed in Tanzania as a breakaway group from the Zimbabwe African People's Union (ZAPU, led by Joshua Nkomo) on the initiative of Robert Mugabe and other former ZAPU committee members. ZANU being banned in 1964, most of it's leaders, among them Robert Mugabe, were in detention in Rhodesia in 1964–74. Early in 1975 Mugabe left Rhodesia for Mozambique, where he organized the Zimbabwe African National Liberation Army (ZANLA) as ZANU's military wing, which pursued guerrilla warfare by means of raids into Rhodesia which had begun in December 1972.

In October 1976 ZANU, together with Joshua Nkomo's ZAPU, formed the Patriotic Front, which sent a joint delegation to constitutional talks convened by the British Government and held in Geneva in October–December 1976 but without reaching an agreement. The PF was subsequently given full support as "the sole legitimate representatives of the people of Zimbabwe" by the Presidents of the "front-line" states (Angola, Botswana, Mozambique, Tanzania and Zambia), by the General Assembly of the United Nations and by the Organization of African Unity.

The PF did not engage in any further constitutional talks until the conference held in London in September–December 1979, which led to agreement on a new Constitution and the holding of fresh elections under British supervision in Zimbabwe. In these elections, held in February 1980, ZANU-PF gained 57 out of the 80 Black seats in the National Assembly. It thereupon formed a Government, which, however, also contained four members of Nkomo's PF-ZAPU, one member of the (White) Rhodesian Front and one independent White. (The Rhodesian Front, which changed its name to Republican Front in June 1981, left the Government in February 1982.)

Orientation. In its election manifesto published on Jan. 25, 1980, the ZANU-PF advocated inter alia far-reaching Africanization of state institutions while recognizing that "the people as a nation cannot necessarily be homogeneous in respect of their cultural and racial backgrounds, but [that] their diversity of backgrounds should become more a source of our cultural wealth than a cause of division". The manifesto stated that a ZANU-PF Government would work towards the socialist transformation of Zimbabwe's society, but that private enterprise would have to continue "until circumstances are ripe for socialist change"; that there would have to be an emergency land settlement programme; that the private sector of agriculture would be restricted to efficient farmers; and that religious freedom would be fundamental.

In January 1982 Mugabe stated that he was seeking ways to establish a one-party state, but he added in April of that year that it would not be imposed upon the people and that the proposal would be submitted to a referendum. At the same time he was quoted as saying that ZANU-PF was determined to transform itself into a truly Marxist-Leninist party.

Zimbabwe African National Union (ZANU—Sithole)

Address. 1st Floor, Century House East, Corner Baker Ave./Angwa St., P.O. Box UA 525, Harare, Zimbabwe

Leadership. The Rev. Ndabaningi Sithole (pres.); Phineas T. Sithole (nat. ch.); Joel Mandaza (s.g.)

Founded. August 1963

History. The original ZANU was banned in 1964, whereafter most of its leaders were arrested and detained for 10 years. Until 1977 it operated from Tanzania and Zambia and recruited and trained members for the armed struggle which began in 1966. Under a unity agreement concluded in Lusaka in 1974 ZANU became a member of the enlarged African National Council (ANC) led by Bishop Abel Muzorewa, but in September 1976 the ZANU wing headed by Sithole withdrew from the ANC (another ZANU wing, led by Robert Mugabe, having been set up as an independent organization in Tanzania in 1975).

ZANU—Sithole took part in the negotiations of December 1977 which led to the formation of a transitional Government and also in that Government, which functioned until May 31, 1979. It won 12 seats in the 100-member House of

Assembly elected in April 1979, but refused to take up its seats (because it believed the elections to have been "rigged") until August 1979 when two of its members were given ministerial posts. In the February 1980 elections, however, the party gained no seats.

Orientation. In its election manifesto of February 1980 the party declared its belief in non-racialism, democratic government based on free and periodic elections, free health services and education and the creation of one strong national army. It also advocated a mixed economy, equal opportunities for all and the removal of pay discrepancies between Blacks and Whites.

Zimbabwe Progressive Party (ZPP)

Leadership. Kingdom Sithole (founder)

Founded. July 28, 1981

History. Kingdom Sithole had previously been a member of the Zimbabwe United People's Organization (ZUPO), a traditionalist party which had not taken part in the 1980 elections, and of the United National Federal Party, which had advocated a federalist constitution but had gained no seats in the 1980 elections (both parties having since then ceased to exist). Kingdom Sithole has stated that the ZPP was to contest all 80 Black seats in the next elections.

Orientation. The ZPP stands for the maintenance of "freedom, peace and democracy".

White Parties

National Unifying Force (NUF)

Address. P.O. Box 8228, Harare, Zimbabwe

Leadership. (Mrs) Muriel Rosin (interim pres.)

Founded. July 1977

History. The NUF succeeded the non-racial Centre Party (led by Pat Bashford) which merged with the Rhodesia Party (led by Allan Savory) and the National Pledge Association—all being groups committed to the removal of racial discrimination. The NUF unsuccessfully contested 18 seats in the all-White constituencies in 1977, and it gained none of the 28 White seats in the House of Assembly elected in April 1979. It did not contest the February 1980 elections but its president unsuccessfully stood as an independent candidate for one of the 20 White seats. In 1983 the NUF decided to join with the National Affairs Association in a National Forum to continue as a pressure group with non-party affiliations to provide a platform for free speech.

Orientation. The NUF seeks to counter the influence of the Republican Front (led by Ian Smith) in the new non-racial Government of Zimbabwe (since 1980).

Structure. The NUF has branches in Harare, Bulawayo amd Mutare.

Membership. 600

Republican Front

Address. P.O. Box 242, Harare, Zimbabwe

Leadership. Ian Douglas Smith (pres.)

Founded. 1962

History. This party was created as the Rhodesian Front by a merger of four right-wing White parties in the then Central African Federation. It decided not to contest federal elections but to concentrate on what was then Southern Rhodesia, where in elections on Dec. 14, 1962, it gained 35 out of the 65 seats in the Legislative Assembly on a platform which included the preservation of the principles of the Land Apportionment Act (on Black and White land ownership and control) and the rejection of enforced racial integration. From Rhodesia's unilateral declaration of independence (from Britain) in 1965 until 1979 it held all 50 White seats in Rhodesia's 66-member Parliament, and it formed the Government until Black co-ministers were for the first time appointed to it in April 1978, when a transitional Government was formed, pending the introduction of (Black) majority rule. It held all 28 White seats in the House of Assembly elected in April 1979.

In the elections held on Feb. 14, 1980, the party gained all 20 seats reserved for Whites (as well as Coloureds and Asians) in the House of Assembly. In Governments formed by the Zimbabwe African National Union—Patriotic Front the party held one portfolio between March 1980 and February 1982. On June 6, 1981, it changed its name to Republican Front. As a result of defections and the loss of two by-elections in subsequent years, its representation in the House of Assembly was by the end of April 1984 reduced to seven members, the remaining 13 White seats being held by independents, some of whom have served in the Government. On Dec. 2, 1982, Ian Smith's passport was seized after he had been accused of having made critical statements about Zimbabwe's Government while travelling in Britain and the United States. On April 6, 1983, he was reported to have been granted a British passport.

Orientation. The Front is a conservative formation.

Appendix A: Democratic Socialists

Socialist International

The present-day Socialist International dates from 1951 but traces its origins back to the First International (1864-76) and more particularly to the Second International founded in Paris in 1889. Seriously weakened by the outbreak of World War I in 1914, the Second International was irrevocably split by the formation of the Third (Communist) International, or Comintern, in 1919. Four years later, in 1923, the socialist parties which rejected the Soviet revolutionary model established the Labour and Socialist International (LSI), which itself finally collapsed in 1940 when German forces occupied Brussels, the seat of its headquarters.

After World War II efforts to revive a democratic socialist world organization finally culminated in the foundation of the Socialist International (SI) at a congress held in Frankfurt (West Germany) in mid-1951. Originally consisting mainly of European parties, the SI has steadily expanded its membership in the Third World, notably since the organization was relaunched under the presidency of Willy Brandt in 1976. The supreme body of the SI is its congress held every two years; in the interim policy is determined by a bureau on which all full member parties are represented. The SI also has a permanent secretariat in London.

Address. Maritime House, Old Town, London SW4 0JW, United Kingdom

Leadership. Willy Brandt (Federal Republic of Germany, pres.); Pentti Väänänen (Finland, g.s.)

Publications. Socialist Affairs (quarterly)

Country/Territory	Member Parties
Australia	Australian Labor Party
Austria	Socialist Party of Austria
Barbados	Barbados Labour Party
Belgium	Socialist Party (PS) Socialist Party (SP)
Canada	New Democratic Party
Chile	Radical Party
Costa Rica	National Liberation Party
Denmark	Social Democratic Party
Dominican Republic	Dominican Revolutionary Party
Ecuador	Democratic Left Party
El Salvador	National Revolutionary Movement*

Country/Territory	Member Parties
Finland	Finnish Social Democratic Party
France	Socialist Party
Germany, Federal Republic of	Social Democratic Party of Germany
Grenada	New Jewel Movement
Guatemala	Democratic Socialist Party
Iceland	Social Democratic Party
Ireland	Labour Party
Israel	Israel Labour Party United Workers' Party
Italy	Democratic Socialist Party of Italy Italian Socialist Party
Jamaica	People's National Party
Japan	Democratic Socialist Party Socialist Party of Japan
Lebanon	Progressive Socialist Party
Luxembourg	Socialist Workers' Party
Malaysia	Democratic Action Party
Malta	Malta Labour Party
Mauritius	Mauritius Labour Party
Netherlands	Labour Party
New Zealand	New Zealand Labour Party
Norway	Norwegian Labour Party
Paraguay	Febrerista Revolutionary Party
Portugal	Portuguese Socialist Party
San Marino	Socialist Unity Party
Senegal	Socialist Party of Senegal
Spain	Spanish Socialist Workers' Party
Sweden	Swedish Social Democratic Labour Party
Switzerland	Swiss Social Democratic Party
Turkey	Republican People's Party*

United Kingdom
  Great Britain
  Northern Ireland
	
	Labour Party
	Northern Ireland Labour Party
	Social Democratic and Labour Party

United States	Democratic Socialists of America Social Democrats USA
Upper Volta	Progressive Front of Upper Volta*
Venezuela	Democratic Action

Consultative Parties

Cyprus	Unified Democratic Union of Cyprus (EDEK)
Danish Dependencies	
Greenland	Forward (*Siumut*)†
Guyana	Working People's Alliance
Netherlands Antilles	
Aruba	People's Electoral Movement
Curaçao	New Antilles Movement
Peru	American Revolutionary Popular Alliance
St Lucia	Progressive Labour Party
US Dependencies	
Puerto Rico	Puerto Rican Independence Party
Venezuela	People's Electoral Movement

Consultative Parties in Exile

Bulgaria	Social Democratic Party‡
Czechoslovakia	Social Democratic Party‡
Estonia	Socialist Party‡
Hungary	Social Democratic Party‡
Latvia	Social Democratic Party‡
Lithuania	Social Democratic Party‡
Poland	Socialist Party‡
Romania	Social Democratic Party‡
Yugoslavia	Socialist Party‡

*Party currently illegal or banned.

†For formal admission at next SI congress.

‡Member of Socialist Union of Central and Eastern Europe (SUCEE).

Confederation of Socialist Parties of the European Community

The Confederation was established in April 1974 as the successor to a liaison bureau set up at the first conference of the socialist parties of the European Community (then embracing six member states) held in Luxembourg in January 1957 to consolidate earlier co-operation between the participating parties dating from the creation of the European Coal and Steel Community in 1951. Following the accession of Denmark, Ireland and the United Kingdom to the European Community in January 1973, the liaison bureau was transformed into the Confederation in April 1974. Subsequently membership was expanded to include the socialist parties of the two countries seeking membership of the Community, namely Portugal and Spain, although the Pan-Hellenic Socialist Movement (PASOK) of Greece (which acceded to the Community in January 1981) has remained outside the Confederation because the party has been unwilling to join the Socialist International. PASOK representatives in the European Parliamentary Assembly nevertheless are members of the Socialist Group.

Address. 3 Boulevard de l'Empereur, B-1000 Brussels, Belgium

Leadership. Joop den Uyl (Netherlands, pres.); Mauro Giallombardo (Italy, g.s.)

Country	Member Parties
Belgium	Socialist Party (SP)
	Socialist Party (PS)
Denmark	Social Democratic Party
France	Socialist Party
Germany, Federal Republic of	Social Democratic Party of Germany
Ireland	Labour Party
Italy	Democratic Socialist Party of Italy
	Italian Socialist Party
Luxembourg	Socialist Workers' Party
Netherlands	Labour Party
Portugal	Portuguese Socialist Party
Spain	Spanish Socialist Workers' Party
United Kingdom	
Great Britain	Labour Party
Northern Ireland	Social Democratic and Labour Party
	Observer Members
Austria	Socialist Party of Austria
Israel	Israel Labour Party
Malta	Malta Labour Party
Norway	Norwegian Labour Party
Sweden	Swedish Social Democratic Labour Party
Switzerland	Swiss Democratic Party
United Kingdom	
Northern Ireland	Northern Ireland Labour Party

Asia-Pacific Socialist Organization

The Asia-Pacific Socialist Organization (APSO) was established in 1970 as a regional grouping of the Socialist International and as a successor to the Asian Socialist Conference (1953-61). In March 1979 an APSO secretariat was opened in Tokyo under the joint direction of the Socialist and Democratic Socialist parties of Japan.

Address. C.P.O. Box 2045, Tokyo, Japan

Leadership. Bill Rowling (New Zealand, ch.); Tamio Kawakami, Roo Watanabe (Japan, jt. secs.)

Country	Member Parties
Australia	Australian Labor Party
Japan	Democratic Socialist Party Socialist Party of Japan
Malaysia	Democratic Action Party
New Zealand	New Zealand Labour Party

Socialist Inter-African

This organization of African democratic socialist parties held its constituent conference in Tunis in February 1981. Asserting that democratic socialism "is the only way to develop the African countries and deliver their peoples from all forms of exploitation and oppression", the movement's charter also stated that the Socialist Inter-African would seek to promote solidarity, co-operation and co-ordination between member parties with the aim of achieving "the development of the continent and the emancipation of its peoples". The principal begettor of the Socialist Inter-African was ex-President Senghor of Senegal, one of the leading theorists of African Socialism.

Address. Boulevard 9 Avril 1938, Tunis, Tunisia

Leadership. Habib Bourguiba (Tunisia, hon. pres.); Léopold Sédar Senghor (Senegal, ch. of exec. bureau); Mongi Kooli (Tunisia, s.g.)

Countries	Member Parties
Djibouti	African Popular League for Independence*
The Gambia	People's Progressive Party
Ghana	People's National Party[†]
Mauritius	Mauritian Social Democratic Party Mauritius Labour Party
Morocco	Independence Party (*Istiqlal*) Socialist Union of Popular Forces
Senegal	Socialist Party of Senegal
Somalia	Somali Revolutionary Socialist Party
Sudan	Sudanese Socialist Union
Tunisia	Destour Socialist Party

*Dominant component of the ruling Popular Rally for Progress.

[†]Party currently banned.

Appendix B: Christian Democrats

Christian Democratic International

The Christian Democratic International was established at a conference in Quito (Ecuador) in November 1982 as the successor to the Christian Democratic World Union (founded in July 1961) with the object of expanding international co-operation between Christian Democratic parties. Its supreme organ is its political committee, which elects an executive committee. Latin American member parties are grouped in the regional Christian Democratic Organization of America (ODCA) founded in 1949.

Address. 107 via del Plebiscito, I-00186, Rome, Italy

Leadership. Andrés Zaldivar Larrain (Chile, pres.); Angelo Bernassola (Italy, s.g.)

Publications. IDC News

Country/Territory	Member Parties
Argentina	Christian Democratic Party*
Austria	Austrian People's Party
Belgium	Christian People's Party
	Christian Social Party
Chile	Christian Democratic Party*
Colombia	Christian Democratic Party*
Costa Rica	Christian Democratic Party*
Cuba	Christian Democratic Movement*†
Cyprus	Democratic Rally
Czechoslovakia	Czechoslovak People's Party†
Dominican Republic	Revolutionary Social Christian Party*
Ecuador	People's Democracy—Christian Democratic Union*
El Salvador	Christian Democratic Party*
France	Centre of Social Democrats
Germany, Federal Republic of	Christian Democratic Union
	Christian Social Union
Greece	New Democracy
Guatemala	Guatemalan Christian Democratic Party*
Honduras	Christian Democratic Party*
Hungary	People's Democratic Party†
Indonesia	Catholic Christian Party
Ireland	Fine Gael
Italy	Christian Democratic Party
Latvia	Peasants' Party†
Lithuania	Union of Christian Democrats†

Country/Territory	Member Parties
Luxembourg	Christian Social Party
Madagascar	Malagasy Christian Democratic Union
Malta	Nationalist Party
Netherlands	Christian Democratic Appeal
Netherland Antilles	National People's Party*
New Zealand	New Zealand Party
Nicaragua	Nicaraguan Social Christian Party*
Norway	Christian Democratic (or People's) Party
Panama	Christian Democratic Party*
Paraguay	Christian Democratic Party*
Peru	Christian Democratic Party*
Philippines	Christian Social Movement
Poland	Christian Labour Party[†]
Portugal	Democratic Social Centre Party
San Marino	Christian Democratic Party
Spain	Popular Democratic Party Basque Nationalist Party Democratic Union of Catalonia
Suriname	Progressive Suriname People's Party*[†]
Switzerland	Christian Democratic Party
Uruguay	Christian Democratic Party*
Venezuela	Christian Social Party*
Yugoslavia	Slovene People's Party[†]

*Member of Christian Democratic Organization of America (ODCA), a regional organization founded in Montevideo (Uruguay) in July 1949.

[†]Party in exile.

European Christian Democratic Union

The European Christian Democratic Union (ECDU) was formed in 1965 as the successor to a New International Community founded in 1947 to promote European unity on the basis of pre-war co-operation between Christian parties. It embraces Christian Democratic parties beyond the bounds of the European Community, and it is organizationally closely linked with the European People's Party (with which it has a joint general secretariat). The ECDU is one of the two regional organizations of the Christian Democratic International—the other being the Christian Democratic Organization of America (ODCA).

Address. 2 Place de l'Albertine, 2-1000 Brussels, Belgium

Leadership. Giulio Andreotti (Italy, pres.); Thomas Jansen (Federal Republic of Germany, s.g.)

Country	*Member Parties*
Austria	Austrian People's Party
Belgium	Christian People's Party
	Christian Social Party
Cyprus	Democratic Rally
France	Centre of Social Democrats
Germany, Federal Republic of	Christian Democratic Union
	Christian Social Union
Greece	New Democracy
Ireland	Fine Gael
Italy	Christian Democratic Party
Luxembourg	Christian Social Party
Malta	Nationalist Party
Netherlands	Christian Democratic Appeal
Norway	Christian Democratic (or People's) Party
Portugal	Democratic Social Centre Party
San Marino	Christian Democratic Party
Spain	Popular Democratic Party
	Basque Nationalist Party
	Democratic Union of Catalonia
Switzerland	Christian Democratic Party
	Observer
Lebanon	Lebanese Christian Democratic Union

European People's Party

The European People's Party (EPP) was founded in 1976 as a Federation of Christian Democratic Parties of the European Community in order to act as a single party in the European Parliament with the ultimate objective of "the transformation of Europe into a single European union with a view to achieving a federal union".

Address. 2 Place de l'Albertine, B-1000 Brussels, Belgium

Leadership. Léo Tindemans (Belgium, pres.); Thomas Jansen (Federal Republic of Germany, s.g.)

Country	Member Parties
Belgium	Christian People's Party
	Christian Social Party
France	Centre of Social Democrats
Germany, Federal Republic of	Christian Democratic Union
	Christian Social Union
Greece	New Democracy
Ireland	Fine Gael
Italy	Christian Democratic Party
	South Tirol People's Party
Luxembourg	Christian Social Party
Netherlands	Christian Democratic Appeal
	Observers
Portugal	Democratic Social Centre Party
Spain	Popular Democratic Party
	Basque Nationalist Party
	Democratic Union of Catalonia

Appendix C: Liberals

Liberal International

The Liberal International was established in its present form at a conference held in Oxford (England) in April 1947 but traces its origins back to pre-war international co-operation between Liberal parties. The Liberal International holds annual conferences and has an executive committee consisting of representatives of each member party.

Address. 1 Whitehall Place, London SW1A 2HE, United Kingdom

Leadership. Giovanni Malagodi (Italy, pres.); Urs Schoettli (Switzerland, exec. vice-pres.)

Publications. Liberal International Newsletter

Country	Member Parties
Austria	Liberal Party of Austria
Belgium	Freedom and Progress Party
	Liberal Reform Party
Canada	Liberal Party of Canada
Denmark	Liberal Party
	Radical-Liberal Party
Finland	Liberal People's Party
	Swedish People's Party of Finland
France	*Liberté et Démocratie**
Germany, Federal Republic of	Free Democratic Party
Iceland	Progressive Party
India	Indian Liberal Group
Israel	Independent Liberal Party
	Liberal Party of Israel
Italy	Italian Liberal Party
Luxembourg	Democratic Party
Netherlands	People's Party for Freedom and Democracy
Nicaragua	Independent Liberal Party
Norway	Liberal Party
	Liberal People's Party
Panama	Liberal Party
Spain	Democratic Reformist Party
Sri Lanka	Sri Lanka Liberal Group
Sweden	Liberal Party
Switzerland	Radical Democratic Party of Switzerland
	Swiss Liberal Party
United Kingdom	Liberal Party

Observer Members	
Finland	Centre Party of Finland
Greece	Liberal Party
Senegal	Senegalese Democratic Party

*Senate grouping including members of Radical-Socialist Party and other centre-left formations.

Federation of Liberal and Democratic
Parties of the European Community

The Federation of Liberal and Democratic Parties of the European Community, abbreviated to European Liberals and Democrats (ELD), was formally established at a congress held at The Hague in November 1976.

Address. 3 Boulevard de l'Empéreur, 1000 Brussels, Belgium

Leadership. Willy de Clercq (Belgium, pres.); Jens Nymand Christensen (Denmark, s.g.)

Country	*Member Parties*
Belgium	Freedom and Progress Party
	Liberal Reform Party
Denmark	Liberal Party
	Radical-Liberal Party
France	Radical-Socialist Party
	Republican Party
Germany, Federal Republic of	Free Democratic Party
Greece	Liberal Party
Italy	Italian Liberal Party
	Italian Republican Party
Luxembourg	Democratic Party
Netherlands	People's Party for Freedom and Democracy
United Kingdom	Liberal Party

Appendix D: Conservatives

International Democrat Union

The International Democrat Union (IDU) was established in London in June 1983 as a world-wide alliance intended to promote co-operation between conservative and centre-right parties. The governing body of the IDU is its party leaders' conference (which meets every two years), with an executive committee exercising authority in the interim

Address. 32 Smith Square, London SW1P 3HH, United Kingdom

Leadership. Dr Alois Mock (Austria, ch.); Scott Hamilton (United Kingdom, exec. sec.)

Publications. IDU Newsletter (quarterly)

Country	Member Parties
Australia	Liberal Party of Australia
Austria	Austrian People's Party
Canada	Progressive Conservative Party of Canada
Cyprus	Democratic Rally
Denmark	Conservative People's Party
Finland	National Coalition Party
France	Rally for the Republic
Germany, Federal Republic of	Christian Democratic Union Christian Social Union
Greece	New Democracy
Japan	Liberal-Democratic Party of Japan
Malta	Nationalist Party*
New Zealand	New Zealand National Party
Norway	Conservative Party
Portugal	Democratic Social Centre Party
Spain	Popular Alliance Popular Democratic Party
Sweden	Moderate Party
United Kingdom	Conservative and Unionist Party
United States	Republican Party

*Associate member.

European Democrat Union

The European Democrat Union (EDU) was established at a conference held in Salzburg in April 1978 as an organization for co-operation between a number of conservative, Christian democratic and other centre-right parties. Embracing a broader European membership than the International Democrat Union (see above), the EDU has an annual party leaders' conference as its highest authority, with a steering committee exercising authority in the interim.

Address. Tivoligasse 73, A-1120 Vienna, Austria

Leadership. Dr Alois Mock (Austria, ch.); Andreas Khol (Austria, exec. sec.)

Country	Member Parties
Austria	Austrian People's Party
Cyprus	Democratic Rally
Denmark	Conservative People's Party
Finland	National Coalition Party
France	Rally for the Republic
Germany, Federal Republic of	Christian Democratic Union Christian Social Union
Greece	New Democracy
Liechtenstein	Patriotic Union Progressive Citizens' Party
Norway	Conservative Party
Portugal	Democratic Social Centre Party
Spain	Popular Alliance Popular Democratic Party
Sweden	Moderate Party
United Kingdom	Conservative and Unionist Party
Permanent Observers	
Finland	Swedish People's Party of Finland
France	Union for French Democracy
Italy	South Tirol People's Party Trentino Tirol People's Party
Malta	Nationalist Party
Switzerland	Christian Democratic Party of Switzerland

Pacific Democrat Union

The Pacific Democrat Union (PDU) was established in Tokyo in June 1982. Providing a regional focus for the Pacific members of the International Democrat Union (see above), the PDU has an annual party leaders' conference as its highest authority, with a steering committee exercising authority in the interim.

Address. P.O. Box E13, Victoria Terrace, Canberra, ACT 2600, Australia

Leadership. Sir John Atwill (Australia, ch.); A. Eggleton (exec. sec.)

Country	Party
Australia	Liberal Party of Australia
Canada	Progressive Conservative Party of Canada
Japan	Liberal-Democratic Party of Japan
New Zealand	New Zealand National Party
United States	Republican Party

Appendix E: Ecologists

The European Greens

The European Greens organization was launched in Brussels in January 1984 on the basis of an earlier co-ordination bureau for West European ecologist parties. Having as their immediate objective the European Parliamentary Assembly elections of June 1984, the participating parties pledged that members elected by proportional representation would represent those blocked from representation by "unjust electoral systems" (this definition being applied in particular to the British system of simple majorities in single-member constituencies).

Address. c/o Dirk Janssens, Agalev, Onderrichstraat 69, B-1000 Brussels, Belgium

Country	Party
Austria	Austrian Alternative List
Belgium	Ecologist Party Live Differently (Agalev)
France	Ecologist Confederation and Ecologist Party
Germany, Federal Republic of	Green Party
Ireland	The Green Alliance
Luxembourg	The Green Alternative
Netherlands	The Greens
Sweden	Ecology Party of Sweden
United Kingdom	Ecology Party

Appendix F: Communists and Marxist-Leninists

Soviet-recognized Communist Parties

In the absence of any present-day successor to the 1919-43 Third (Communist) International—known as the Comintern—and the 1947–56 Communist Information Bureau (Cominform), there currently exists no institutionalized organization of pro-Soviet Communist parties. Nevertheless, such parties have a network of regular contacts, including periodic international conferences. The following table lists those Communist parties which participate in such activities and are thus regarded as "fraternal" organizations by the ruling Communist parties of the Soviet-bloc countries. It should be noted, however, that their degree of adherence to the "Moscow line" varies considerably and that some do not accept the leading role of the Soviet party in the world Communist movement.

Country/Territory	Party
Afghanistan	People's Democratic Party of Afghanistan*
Argentina	Communist Party of Argentina
Australia	Socialist Party of Australia
Austria	Communist Party of Austria
Bangladesh	Bangladesh Communist Party
Belgium	Communist Party of Belgium
Bolivia	Communist Party of Bolivia
Bulgaria	Bulgarian Communist Party*
Canada	Communist Party of Canada
Colombia	Communist Party of Colombia
Costa Rica	Popular Vanguard Party
Cuba	Communist Party of Cuba*
Cyprus	Progressive Party of the Working People
Turkish Republic of Northern Cyprus	Republican Turkish Party
Czechoslovakia	Communist Party of Czechoslovakia* Communist Party of Slovakia*
Denmark	Communist Party of Denmark
Dominican Republic	Dominican Communist Party
Ecuador	Communist Party of Ecuador
Finland	Communist Party of Finland
France	French Communist Party
French Overseas Departments	
Guadeloupe	Communist Party of Guadeloupe
Martinique	Communist Party of Martinique
Réunion	Communist Party of Réunion

Country/Territory	Party
German Democratic Republic	Socialist Unity Party of Germany*
Germany, Federal Republic of	German Communist Party
West Berlin	Socialist Unity Party of West Berlin
Greece	Communist Party of Greece—Exterior
Guyana	People's Progressive Party
Hungary	Hungarian Socialist Workers' Party*
India	Communist Party of India
Ireland	Communist Party of Ireland
Israel	New Communist Party (Rakah)
Italy	Italian Communist Party
Jamaica	Workers' Party of Jamaica
Japan	Japan Communist Party
Kampuchea	Kampuchean People's Revolutionary Party*
Laos	Lao People's Revolutionary Party*
Lebanon	Lebanese Communist Party
Luxembourg	Communist Party of Luxembourg
Mexico	United Socialist Party of Mexico
Mongolia	Mongolian People's Revolutionary Party*
Morocco	Party of Progress and Socialism
Netherlands	Communist Party of the Netherlands
New Zealand	New Zealand Socialist Unity Party
Nicaragua	Nicaraguan Socialist Party
Norway	Communist Party of Norway
Panama	Panamanian People's Party
Peru	Peruvian Communist Party—Unity
Poland	Polish United Workers' Party*
Portugal	Portuguese Communist Party
Romania	Romanian Communist Party*
San Marino	San Marino Communist Party
Senegal	Party of Independence and Labour
Spain	Communist Party of Spain Basque Communist Party Unified Socialist Party of Catalonia
Sri Lanka	Communist Party of Sri Lanka
Sweden	Swedish Workers' Communist Party
Switzerland	Swiss Party of Labour
Syrian	Syrian Communist Party

Country/Territory	Party
Trinidad and Tobago	People's Popular Movement
Tunisia	Tunisian Communist Party
Union of Soviet Socialist Republics	Communist Party of the Soviet Union*
United Kingdom	Communist Party of Great Britain
United States	Communist Party USA
Puerto Rico	Puerto Rican Communist Party
Venezuela	Communist Party of Venezuela
Vietnam	Communist Party of Vietnam*
Yemen, People's Democratic Republic of	Yemen Socialist Party*

*Sole ruling party.

Soviet-recognized "Vanguard Revolutionary Democratic Parties"

Country	Party
Angola	Popular Movement for the Liberation of Angola—Party of Labour*
Benin	Benin People's Revolutionary Party*
Congo	Congolese Party of Labour*
Ethiopia	Commission for Organizing the Party of the Working People of Ethiopia (COPWE)*
Mozambique	Front for the Liberation of Mozambique*

*Sole ruling party.

Soviet-recognized "Revolutionary Democratic Parties"

Country	Party
Algeria	National Liberation Front*
Guinea-Bissau	African Party for the Independence of Guinea and Cape Verde*
Madagascar	Congress Party for Malagasy Independence
São Tomé and Príncipe	Movement for the Liberation of São Tomé and Príncipe*
Seychelles	Seychelles People's Progressive Front*
Tanzania	Revolutionary Party (*Chama Cha Mapinduzi*)*

*Sole ruling party.

Index of Parties

574

Index of Names

B

C

D

G